Here are your

1993 Year Book Cross-Reference Tabs

For insertion in your WORLD BOOK set

Put these Tabs in the appropriate volumes of your **World Book Encyclopedia** now. Then, when you later look up some topics in **World Book** and find a Tab near the article, you will know that one of your **Year Books** has newer or more detailed information about that topic.

How to use these Tabs

First, remove this page from THE YEAR BOOK.

Begin with the first Tab, **ARMENIA.** Take the A volume of your World Book set. Moisten the **ARMENIA** Tab and affix it to the page with the **Armenia** article. Affix the special **U.S.S.R.** Tab to the page in the U-V volume on which the **Union of Soviet Socialist Republics** article begins. This Tab will direct you to all the new articles on the former Soviet republics.

Go on to the other Tabs. Your set may not have articles on some of the topics–**CLINTON, BILL,** for example. In that case, put the Tab in the correct volume and on the page where it would go if there were an article. The **CLINTON, BILL** Tab should go in the Ci-Cz volume on the same page as the **Clinton, De Witt** article.

New World Book Article
ARMENIA
1993 Year Book, p. 489

Special Report
ART AND THE ARTS
1993 Year Book, p. 72

Special Report
ASIMOV, ISAAC
1993 Year Book, p. 190

Special Report
CANADA
1993 Year Book, p. 354

Special Report
CITY
1993 Year Book, p. 140

New World Book Article
CLINTON, BILL
1993 Year Book, p. 483

Special Report
DIETRICH, MARLENE
1993 Year Book, p. 340

Special Report
EDUCATION
1993 Year Book, p. 206

Special Report
ENVIRONMENTAL POLLUTION
1993 Year Book, p. 220

Special Report
ESKIMO
1993 Year Book, p. 354

Special Report
HEALTH-CARE PLANS
1993 Year Book, p. 260

Special Report
NUCLEAR WEAPON
1993 Year Book, p. 56

Special Report
OLYMPIC GAMES
1993 Year Book, p. 360

Special Report
PRISON
1993 Year Book, p. 392

Special Report
PUBLIC LANDS
1993 Year Book, p. 164

New World Book Article
RUSSIA
1993 Year Book, p. 507

New World Book Article
UKRAINE
1993 Year Book, p. 541

Special Report
UNEMPLOYMENT
1993 Year Book, p. 298

New World Book Article
U.S.S.R.
1993 Year Book, p. 489

Special Report
UNITED NATIONS
1993 Year Book, p. 454

A Review of the Events of 1992

The 1993 World Book Year Book

The Annual Supplement to The World Book Encyclopedia

World Book, Inc.
a Scott Fetzer company

Chicago London Sydney Toronto

World Book, Inc.
525 W. Monroe
Chicago, IL 60661

ISBN 0-7166-0493-0
ISSN 0084-1439
Library of Congress Catalog Card Number: 62-4818

Staff

Contents

Page 322 ▾

◂ Page 24

▾ Page 40

Contributors

Contributors not listed on these pages are members of ***The World Book Year Book*** editorial staff.

Alexiou, Arthur G., B.S.E.E., M.S.E.E.; Assistant Secretary, Committee on Climatic Changes and Ocean. [**Ocean**]

Anderson, Porter, B.A., M.A., M.F.A.; Theater Critic, *Village Voice.* [**Theater**]

Andrews, Peter J., B.A., M.S.; free-lance writer; biochemist. [**Chemistry**]

Apseloff, Marilyn Fain, B.A., M.A.; Associate Professor of English, Kent State University. [**Literature for children**]

Arndt, Randolph C., Media Relations Director, National League of Cities. [**City**]

Barber, Peggy, B.A., M.L.S.; Associate Executive Director for Communications, American Library Association. [**Library**]

Berger, Jim, B.A., M.P.A.; Editor/Publisher, Trade Reports International Group. [**International trade**]

Berman, Howard A., B.A., B.H.L., M.A.H.L.; Rabbi, Chicago Sinai Congregation. [**Judaism**]

Bessman, Jim, contributor, *Billboard* magazine; Senior Editor, *Spin* magazine. [**Popular music**]

Bilocerkowycz, Jaroslaw, B.A., M.A., Ph.D.; Associate Professor of Political Science, University of Dayton. [**World Book Supplement: Belarus, Ukraine**]

Blackadar, Alfred K., A.B., Ph.D.; Professor Emeritus, Pennsylvania State University. [**Weather**]

Bourne, Eric, columnist, foreign affairs, *The Christian Science Monitor.* [**Eastern European country articles**]

Bower, Bruce, M.A.; Behavioral Sciences Editor, *Science News* magazine. [**Psychology**]

Boyd, John D., B.S.; Midwest Bureau Chief, *Journal of Commerce.* [**Economics**]

Bradsher, Henry S., A.B., B.J.; foreign affairs analyst. [**Asia and Asian country articles**]

Brett, Carlton E., B.A., M.S., Ph.D.; Professor of Geological Sciences, University of Rochester. [**Paleontology**]

Brock, Frances D., B.A., M.S.J.; free-lance writer. [**Advertising**]

Brown, Lawrence D., Ph.D.; Professor and Head, Division of Health Policy and Management, Columbia University School of Public Health. **Health issues,** Special Report: **Curing America's Health-Care Ills**]

Burke, Justin, B.A.; Moscow Correspondent, *The Christian Science Monitor.* [**Commonwealth of Independent States and former Soviet republic articles**]

Campbell, Geoffrey A., B.J.; Staff Reporter, *The Bond Buyer.* [**Civil rights; Supreme Court of the United States**]

Campbell, Linda P., B.A., M.S.L.; National Legal Affairs Correspondent, *Chicago Tribune.* [**Civil rights; Supreme Court of the United States**]

Campion, Owen F., A.B.; Associate Publisher, *Our Sunday Visitor* magazine. [**Roman Catholic Church**]

Cardinale, Diane P., B.A.; Assistant Communications Director, Toy Manufacturers of America. [**Toys and games**]

Carmody, Deirdre, Media Reporter, *The New York Times.* [**Magazine**]

Clark, Larry V., Ph.D.; Assistant Professor, Indiana University. [**World Book Supplement: Kazakhstan**]

Cormier, Frank, B.S.J., M.S.J.; former White House Correspondent, Associated Press. [**U.S. government articles**]

Cormier, Margot, B.A., M.S.J.; free-lance writer. [**U.S. government articles**]

Crenshaw, Edward, B.A., M.A., Ph.D.; Assistant Professor, Department of Sociology, Ohio State University. [**City,** Special Report: **The Ailing Cities, the Angry Poor**]

Cromie, William J., B.S., M.S.; science writer, Harvard University. [**Space exploration**]

Cummings, Milton C., Jr., B.A., M.A., Ph.D.; Professor, Department of Political Science, Johns Hopkins University. [**Art,** Special Report: **Who Should Pay for Art?**]

DeFrank, Thomas M., B.A., M.A.; White House Correspondent, *Newsweek* magazine. [**Armed forces**]

DeLancey, Mark W., B.A., M.A., Ph.D.; Professor of Government and International Studies, University of South Carolina. [**Africa and African country articles**]

Dent, Thomas H., B.S.; Executive Director, The Cat Fanciers' Association. [**Cat**]

Dienes, Leslie, B.A., M.A., Ph.D.; Professor of Geography, University of Kansas. [**World Book Supplement: Georgia**]

Dillon, David, B.A., M.A., Ph.D.; Architect Critic, *Dallas Morning News.* [**Architecture**]

Dirda, Michael, B.A., M.A., Ph.D.; writer and editor, *The Washington Post Book World.* [**Poetry**]

Dumas, Ernest C., political columnist, *The Arkansas Times,* and journalist in residence at the University of Central Arkansas. [**World Book Supplement: Clinton, Bill**]

Ellis, Gavin, Assistant Editor, *New Zealand Herald.* [**New Zealand**]

Esposito, John L., B.A., M.A., Ph.D.; Loyola Professor of Middle East Studies, College of the Holy Cross. [**Islam**]

Evans, Sandra, B.S.J.; Staff Writer, *The Washington Post.* [**Washington, D.C.**]

Farr, David M. L., M.A., D.Phil.; Professor Emeritus of History, Carleton University, Ottawa. [**Northwest Territories,** Special Report: **Creating Nunavut; Canada; Canadian provinces articles; Mulroney, Brian**]

Ferrell, Keith, Editor, *Omni* magazine. [**Deaths,** Special Report: **The Literary Legacy of Isaac Asimov**]

Fierman, William, B.A., M.A., Ph.D.; Associate Professor of Uralic and Altaic Studies and Adjunct Associate Professor of Political Science, Indiana University. [**World Book Supplement: Uzbekistan**]

Fisher, Robert W., B.A., M.A.; Senior Economist/Editor, U.S. Bureau of Labor Statistics. [**Labor,** Special Report: **What Is Happening to the U.S. Job Market?; Labor**]

Fitzgerald, Mark, B.A.; Midwest Editor, *Editor & Publisher* magazine. [**Newspaper**]

Friedman, Emily, B.A.; Contributing Editor, *Hospitals* magazine. [**Hospital**]

Garvie, Maureen, B.A., B.Ed., M.A.; Books Editor, *The* (Kingston, Ont.) *Whig-Standard.* [**Canadian literature**]

Gatty, Bob, Editor, Periodicals News Service. [**Food**]

Gillenwater, Sharon K., B.A.; Assistant Editor, *San Diego Magazine.* [**San Diego**]

Goldner, Nancy, B.A.; Dance Critic, *The Philadelphia Inquirer.* [**Dancing**]

Graham, Timothy J., City Editor, *The Houston Post.* [**Houston**]

Harakas, Stanley Samuel, B.A., B.D., Th.D.; Archbishop Iakovos Professor of Orthodox Theology, Hellenic College, Holy Cross Greek Orthodox School of Theology. [**Eastern Orthodox Churches**]

Haverstock, Nathan A., A.B.; Affiliate Scholar, Oberlin College. [**Latin America and Latin-American country articles**]

Helms, Christine, B.A., Ph.D.; free-lance writer; consultant. [**Middle East and Middle Eastern country articles; North Africa country articles**]

Higgins, James V., B.A.; Auto Industry Reporter, *The Detroit News.* [**Automobile**]

Hill, Michael, B.A.; Reporter, *Baltimore Sun.* [**Television**]

Hillgren, Sonja, B.J., M.A.; Washington Editor, *Farm Journal.* [**Farm and farming**]

Jacobi, Peter P., B.S.J., M.S.J.; Professor of Journalism, Indiana University. [**Classical music**]

Johanson, Donald C., B.S., M.A., Ph.D.; President, Institute of Human Origins. [**Anthropology**]

Keeney, Kathy, B.A.; Editor, *Modern Railroads* magazine. [**Railroad**]

Kisor, Henry, B.A., M.S.J.; Book Editor, *Chicago Sun-Times.* [**Literature; Literature, American**]

Kiste, Robert C., Ph.D.; Director and Professor, Center for Pacific Islands Studies, University of Hawaii. [**Pacific Islands**]

Knapp, Elaine S., B.A.; Editor, Council of State Governments. [**State government**]

Kolgraf, Ronald, B.A., M.A.; Publisher, *Adweek/New England* magazine. [**Manufacturing**]

Lawrence, Al, B.A., M.A., M.Ed.; Executive Director, United States Chess Federation. [**Chess**]

Lazzerini, Edward J., Ph.D.; Professor, University of New Orleans. [**World Book Supplement: Azerbaijan, Kyrgyzstan, Tajikistan, Turkmenistan**]

Lewis, David C., M.D.; Professor of Medicine and Community Health, Brown University. [**Drug abuse**]

Litsky, Frank, B.S.; Sportswriter, *The New York Times.* [**Olympic games,** Special Report: **The 1992 Olympics; Sports articles**]

Longmore, Paul K., B.A., M.A., Ph.D.; Assistant Professor of History, San Francisco State University. [**Disabled**]

Lubin, Nancy, Ph.D.; Associate Professor, Carnegie-Mellon University. [**World Book Supplement: Armenia, Commonwealth of Independent States**]

March, Robert H., A.B., S.M., Ph.D.; Professor of Physics, University of Wisconsin at Madison. [**Physics**]

Marschall, Laurence A., Ph.D.; Professor of Physics, Gettysburg College. [**Astronomy**]

Marty, Martin E., Ph.D.; Fairfax M. Cone Distinguished Service Professor, University of Chicago. [**Protestantism; Religion**]

Mather, Ian J., B.A., M.A.; Diplomatic Editor, *The European,* London. [**Great Britain; Ireland; Northern Ireland**]

Maugh, Thomas H., II, Ph.D.; Science Writer, *Los Angeles Times.* [**Biology**]

McGinley, Laurie, B.S.J.; Reporter, *The Wall Street Journal.* [**Aviation**]

Merina, Victor, A.A., B.A., M.S.; Staff Writer, *Los Angeles Times.* [**Los Angeles**]

Merline, John W., B.A.; Washington Correspondent, *Investor's Business Daily.* [**Consumerism**]

Moores, Eldridge M., B.S., Ph.D.; Professor of Geology, University of California at Davis. [**Geology**]

Moritz, Owen, B.A.; Urban Affairs Editor, *New York Daily News.* [**New York City**]

Morris, Bernadine, B.A., M.A.; Chief Fashion Writer, *The New York Times.* [**Fashion**]

Muchnic, Suzanne, B.A., M.A.; Art Writer, *Los Angeles Times.* [**Art**]

Nguyen, J. Tuyet, B.A.; United Nations Correspondent, United Press International. [**United Nations,** Special Report: **A New Era for the United Nations; United Nations**]

Nichols, Jennifer A., B.A.; Production Editor, American Correctional Association. [**Prison**]

Pennisi, Elizabeth, B.S., M.S.; Chemistry/Materials Science Editor, *Science News* magazine. [**Zoology**]

Prater, Constance C., B.S.J.; City-County Bureau Chief, *Detroit Free Press.* [**Detroit**]

Priestaf, Iris, B.A., M.A., Ph.D.; Geographer and Vice President, David Keith Todd Consulting Engineers, Incorporated. [**Water**]

Raleigh, Donald J., B.A., M.A., Ph.D.; Professor of History at the University of North Carolina at Chapel Hill. [**World Book Supplement: Russia**]

Raloff, Janet, B.S.J., M.S.J.; Policy/Technology Editor, *Science News* magazine. [**Environmental pollution**]

Reardon, Patrick T., B.A.; Urban Affairs Writer, *Chicago Tribune.* [**Chicago**]

Revzin, Philip, B.A., M.A.; Editor, *The Wall Street Journal Europe.* [**Europe and Western European country articles**]

Rose, Mark J., M.A.; Managing Editor, *Archaeology* magazine. [**Archaeology**]

Shapiro, Howard S., B.S.; Cultural Arts Editor, *The Philadelphia Inquirer.* [**Philadelphia**]

Smerk, George, B.S., M.B.A., D.B.A.; Professor of Transportation, School of Business, Indiana University. [**Transit**]

Spector, Leonard S., J.D.; Senior Associate, Carnegie Endowment for International Peace. [**Armed forces,** Special Report: **The Nuclear Threat in the New World Order**]

Stein, David Lewis, B.A., M.S.; Columnist, *The Toronto Star.* [**Toronto**]

Tanner, James C., B.S.J.; Senior Energy Correspondent, *The Wall Street Journal.* [**Petroleum and gas**]

Thomas, Paulette, B.A.; Staff Writer, *The Wall Street Journal.* [**Bank**]

Tietenberg, Tom, Ph.D.; Christian A. Johnson Distinguished Teaching Professor, Colby College. [**Environmental pollution,** Special Report: **Environmental Concern Goes Global**]

Tismaneanu, Vladimir, Ph.D.; Assistant Professor of Government and Politics, University of Maryland. [**World Book Supplement: Moldova**]

Toch, Thomas W., B.A., M.A.; Associate Editor and Education Correspondent, *U.S. News & World Report.* [**Education,** Special Report: **The Private Education Business; Education**]

Tonry, Michael, A.B., LL.B.; Sonosky Professor of Law and Public Policy, University of Minnesota Law School. [**Prison,** Special Report: **The Ballooning Prison Population**]

Tuchman, Janice Lyn, B.S., M.S.J.; Executive Editor, *Engineering News-Record.* [**Building and construction**]

Vesley, Roberta, A.B., M.S.L.; former Library Director, American Kennel Club. [**Dog**]

Vizard, Frank, B.A.; Electronics Editor, *Popular Mechanics.* [**Electronics**]

Walter, Eugene, J., Jr., free-lance writer. [**Conservation,** Special Report: **The Fight for America's Public Lands; Conservation; Zoos**]

Widder, Pat, B.A.; New York Financial Correspondent, *Chicago Tribune.* [**Stocks and bonds**]

Williams, Susan G., B.A.; journalist, Sydney, Australia. [**Australia**]

Windeyer, Kendal, President, Windeyer Associates, Montreal, Canada. [**Montreal**]

Woods, Michael, B.S.; Science Editor, *The* (Toledo, Ohio) *Blade.* [**Industry articles and health articles**]

Wuntch, Philip, B.A.; Film Critic, *Dallas Morning News.* [**Motion pictures,** Special Report: **Marlene Dietrich: A Legend Passes; Motion pictures**]

See pages 32 and 33.

1992

YEAR IN BRIEF

A pictorial review of the top news stories of 1992 is followed by a month-by-month listing of highlights of some of the year's most significant events.

The Year's Major News Stories

From the presidential election in the United States to the fighting in former republics of Yugoslavia, 1992 was a year filled with momentous events. On these two pages are the stories that ***Year Book*** editors picked as the most memorable, the most exciting, or the most important of the year, along with details on where to find information about them in ***The World Book Year Book.*** *The Editors*

The siege of Sarajevo
Civilians crouch in a doorway in April as a militia man takes aim at Serbians attacking the capital of the newly declared nation of Bosnia and Hercegovina. The fighting continued throughout the year. In the World Book Year Book Update section, see **Bosnia and Hercegovina,** page 108; **Yugoslavia,** page 475. ▶

▲
U.S. presidential elections
Democratic presidential candidate Bill Clinton and running mate Albert A. Gore, Jr., join their wives in claiming victory in the November election. See **Democratic Party,** page 193; **Elections,** page 212. In the World Book Supplement section, see **Clinton, Bill,** page 483.

◀ **Famine in Somalia**
A woman begging for food symbolizes the plight of the starving Somalis, victims of famine and civil war, that prompted the United Nations and U.S. President George Bush in December to send in troops to protect food distribution. See **Africa,** page 40; **Somalia,** page 421.

◀ **1992 Olympic Games**
The Dream Team, made up of professional American basketball stars, captured a gold medal for the United States at the Summer Olympics in Barcelona, Spain. See **Basketball,** page 101; **Olympic Games,** Special Report, page 360.

Los Angeles riots
Property in central Los Angeles burns during rioting in late April and early May triggered by the acquittal of white police officers on trial for beating a black motorist. See **City,** Special Report, page 140; **Los Angeles**, page 321.
▼

▲
Destructive hurricanes
A corridor of destruction was cut through south Florida in August by Hurricane Andrew, which then crossed the Gulf of Mexico and wreaked further havoc along the Louisiana coast. In September, Hurricane Iniki devastated Kauai, Hawaii. See **Weather,** page 471.

Earth Summit in Rio de Janeiro
Children participate in the opening ceremonies in June of the Earth Summit in Brazil, where world leaders pondered solutions to global pollution problems. See **Environmental pollution,** Special Report, page 220; **Year in Brief,** page 22. ▶

January 1992

S	M	T	W	TH	F	S
			1	2	3	4
5	6	7	8	9	10	11
12	13	14	15	16	17	18
19	20	21	22	23	24	25
26	27	28	29	30	31	

2 Russian President Boris N. Yeltsin ends price controls, resulting in prices three to five times higher than usual on some goods and services.
7 A Yugoslav Army jet downs a helicopter, killing five military observers from the European Community.
10 President George Bush ends a 10-day trip to Australia and Asia, departing from Japan with a pledge by Japanese officials to buy more American automobiles and auto parts. But Bush Administration spokesmen concede that the pledge fell short of U.S. goals.
16 The government of El Salvador and the Farabundo Martí National Liberation Front sign a peace treaty in Mexico City to end a bitter 12-year civil war that cost an estimated 75,000 lives.
18 In Nairobi, Kenya, more than 100,000 people attend the largest protest demonstration in the country's history, demanding an end to one-party rule.
19 Zhelyu Zhelev wins Bulgaria's presidency in a runoff election. Zhelev, the candidate of the Union of Democratic Forces, defeated the candidate of the Socialist (formerly the Communist) Party.
20 Despite pleas for clemency from several Latin-American presidents, a Cuban firing squad executes Eduardo Diaz Betancourt, a resident of Miami, Fla., who was found guilty of sabotage and terrorism.
21 Due to declining military spending, United Technologies Corporation of Connecticut announces plans to eliminate 13,900 jobs by 1995.
23 Federal health officials express growing concern about the spread of a drug-resistant form of tuberculosis in 13 states.
24 A judge in El Salvador sentences an army colonel and a lieutenant to 30 years in prison each for the 1989 murders of six Jesuit priests, their housekeeper, and her daughter.
China and Israel establish diplomatic relations.
26 The Washington Redskins win Super Bowl XXVI at the Metrodome in Minneapolis, Minn., defeating the Buffalo Bills, 37-24.
Security forces in Mauritania open fire on opponents of President Maaouya Ould Sid Ahmed Taya, killing at least five people.
27 R. H. Macy & Company, Incorporated, one of the nation's largest retailing chains, files for bankruptcy.
Fighting between Armenians and Azerbaijanis in the disputed territory of Nagorno-Karabakh leaves at least 60 people dead.
28 In his State of the Union address, President Bush outlines limited tax-relief measures and cuts in the defense budget amounting to $50 billion over a five-year period.
30 North Korea signs a nuclear safeguards accord with the International Atomic Energy Agency in Vienna, Austria. The accord calls for international inspection of North Korea's nuclear power plants.
31 The heads of state of the five permanent members of the United Nations Security Council and the heads of state of most of the Council's temporary members meet in New York City to help shape a new world order in the wake of the end of the Cold War.

▲ Salvadorans gather in the capital, San Salvador, to celebrate the signing of a peace treaty on January 16, ending 12 years of civil war.

Washington Redskins quarterback Mark Rypien hands ▶ off the football during his team's Super Bowl victory over Buffalo on January 26.

President George Bush becomes ill at a state dinner in Tokyo during a 10-day trip to Australia and Asia that ended on January 10.
▼

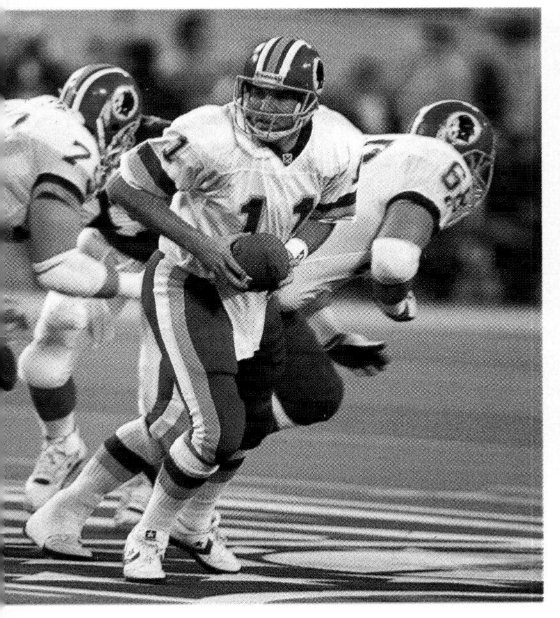

February 1992

S	M	T	W	TH	F	S
						1
2	3	4	5	6	7	8
9	10	11	12	13	14	15
16	17	18	19	20	21	22
23	24	25	26	27	28	29

1 United States President George Bush and Russian President Boris N. Yeltsin, meeting at Camp David, Md., formally declare an end to the Cold War that marked relations between the two countries since the end of World War II (1939-1945).
United States Coast Guard officials begin deporting the first of some 14,000 Haitian refugees after the Supreme Court of the United States on January 31 lifted an injunction that barred their return to Haiti.
4 Venezuelan troops loyal to President Carlos Andrés Pérez put down a coup attempt led by junior army officers in Caracas, the capital, and three other cities.
6 The U.S. Senate approves a measure calling for a faster phase-out of production of chemicals that deplete the protective ozone layer in the upper atmosphere. The phase-out had been scheduled for completion by the year 2000.
8 The 16th Winter Olympic Games open in Albertville, France.
9 The government of Algeria declares a state of emergency and suspends virtually all constitutional rights in a continuing crackdown on the fundamentalist Islamic Salvation Front.
10 Former heavyweight boxing champion Mike Tyson is found guilty of rape and criminal deviate sexual behavior by a jury in Indianapolis. On March 26, Tyson was sentenced to six years in prison.
14 Ukraine and four other nations in the Commonwealth of Independent States reject a proposal by Russian President Yeltsin to maintain a unified armed force. Ukraine, Moldova, and Azerbaijan announce that they will go ahead with plans to create armies of their own.
15 A Milwaukee jury finds serial killer Jeffrey L. Dahmer was sane at the time he murdered and dismembered 15 people. On February 17, Dahmer was sentenced to 15 consecutive life terms without the possibility of parole.
16 Israeli helicopter gunships attack a motorcade in southern Lebanon, killing Sheik Abbas al-Musawi, leader of the pro-Iranian Party of God in Lebanon, his wife, and his son. Israeli Defense Minister Moshe Arens said the assassination was in retaliation for a February 14 raid that killed three Israeli soldiers.
18 In the New Hampshire presidential primary, conservative columnist Patrick J. Buchanan makes a strong showing against President Bush with 37 per cent of the vote. Former U.S. Senator Paul E. Tsongas from Massachusetts leads a field of five Democratic candidates with 35 per cent of the vote.
23 The Winter Olympics end with the United States winning five gold, four silver, and two bronze medals, its best performance since the 1980 games in Lake Placid, N.Y.
26 The Supreme Court of the United States expands protection for students who are victims of sexual harassment, ruling that such victims can sue for monetary damages if the schools where they were victimized receive federal funds.

Former heavyweight boxing champion Mike Tyson ▶ is handcuffed following his conviction on rape charges in Indianapolis on February 10.

Opening ceremonies for the 16th Winter Olympic Games get underway on February 8 in Albertville, France.
▼

◀ A United States Coast Guard official escorts a Haitian refugee, as efforts to deport about 14,000 Haitians began on February 1.

March 1992

S	M	T	W	TH	F	S
1	2	3	4	5	6	7
8	9	10	11	12	13	14
15	16	17	18	19	20	21
22	23	24	25	26	27	28
29	30	31				

1 Senator Brock Adams (D., Wash.) ends his election campaign for a second term after a Seattle newspaper reports that eight unidentified women accused him of sexual harassment.

4 Algeria's Supreme Court bans the fundamentalist Islamic Salvation Front, which appeared likely to win control of parliament before runoff elections were canceled in January.

10 Arkansas Governor Bill Clinton emerges as the front-runner in the Democratic presidential race as he sweeps six elections in Southern states during the Super Tuesday primaries. Clinton leads former Senator Paul E. Tsongas and former California Governor Jerry Brown, the only remaining candidates. President Bush wins all eight Republican primaries on Super Tuesday, while challenger Patrick Buchanan nets about 30 per cent of the vote.

11 Manuel de Dios Unanue, former editor in chief of *El Diario-La Prensa,* New York City's largest Spanish-language daily, is slain in a restaurant in the borough of Queens after receiving death threats for his exposés of the Colombian drug cartels.

16 Russian President Boris Yeltsin announces the creation of a separate Russian army, raising doubts about whether the Commonwealth of Independent States will continue to exist.

17 South Africa's whites vote by landslide proportions in favor of negotiations to end white minority rule in a referendum on President Frederik Willem de Klerk's antiapartheid reforms.

A bomb blast levels the Israeli Embassy in Buenos Aires, Argentina, killing at least 32 people. An Islamic fundamentalist group claims responsibility for the attack, which it said was retaliation for the killing of Sheik Abbas al-Musawi in Lebanon on February 16.

19 Tsongas abandons his campaign for the Democratic presidential nomination, virtually assuring a Clinton victory.

The Dow Corning Corporation announces that it will stop producing silicone gel breast implants, becoming the third manufacturer to do so after questions were raised regarding the safety of the implants.

22 France's Socialist Party suffers a stunning defeat in regional elections, but the party's main conservative rival also lost ground. Environmental parties and the right wing National Front, led by Jean-Marie Le Pen, made gains.

The space shuttle Atlantis lifts off from Cape Canaveral, Fla., carrying an array of instruments designed to study changes in the upper atmosphere that could signal a global warming trend. The seven-member crew returned to Earth on April 2.

25 Iraq is ordered to destroy an industrial complex at Al Atheer that was being used to produce nuclear weapons. The order was issued by the International Atomic Energy Agency, an organization of the United Nations.

29 French police arrest three men believed to be leaders of a Basque terrorist group that had threatened to disrupt the Olympic Games in Barcelona, Spain.

South Africans embrace after a March 17 referendum ▶ in which whites voted overwhelmingly in support of antiapartheid reforms.

◀ Argentines inspect the damage to the Israeli Embassy in Buenos Aires, caused by a car bomb that exploded on March 17 and killed at least 32 people.

April 1992

S	M	T	W	TH	F	S
			1	2	3	4
5	6	7	8	9	10	11
12	13	14	15	16	17	18
19	20	21	22	23	24	25
26	27	28	29	30		

Mexicans sift through the rubble left by a series of sewer explosions that ripped through Guadalajara on April 22. ▶

5 An estimated 500,000 people march on Washington, D.C., in support of abortion rights, as the Supreme Court of the United States prepares to review a Pennsylvania law that would limit access to abortion.
Peruvian President Alberto K. Fujimori dissolves Congress, suspends the Constitution, imposes censorship, and has opposition politicians arrested, citing the need to take emergency measures to combat terrorism, drug trafficking, and corruption.
6 Duke University wins the National Collegiate Athletic Association men's basketball tournament, defeating the University of Michigan, 71-51, and becoming the first team to repeat as national champions since 1973.
7 Acknowledging the breakup of Yugoslavia, President George Bush recognizes the independence of Croatia, Bosnia and Hercegovina, and Slovenia. The European Community also recognizes the independence of Bosnia and Hercegovina.
Caterpillar Inc. of Peoria, Ill., begins advertising for replacement workers in an attempt to break a five-month-old strike by 12,600 members of the United Automobile Workers (UAW). On April 14, the UAW agreed to end the strike.
9 Former Panamanian dictator Manuel Antonio Noriega is convicted by a Miami, Fla., jury on eight counts of cocaine trafficking, racketeering, and money laundering—the first time a jury in the United States has ever convicted a foreign head of state of criminal charges. On July 10, Noriega was sentenced to 40 years in prison.
The ruling Conservative Party in Great Britain hangs onto power with a narrow, 21-seat majority in parliamentary elections.
16 Afghanistan President Najibullah is ousted and detained as Muslim rebels advance on Kabul, the capital. On April 26, the rebels entered Kabul, but fighting broke out among rebel factions.
22 A series of explosions in Guadalajara, Mexico, caused by a ruptured gasoline pipeline, kills at least 191 people.
23 A major finding about the universe that may explain how galaxies evolved and what the universe is made of is reported by astronomers.
25 An earthquake registering 7.1 on the magnitude scale hits several communities in northern California, injuring 53 people in the town of Scotia and causing extensive damage to roads and bridges. On April 22, an unrelated earthquake measuring 6.3 magnitude had struck a rural area in southern California, causing minor damage and injuries.
29 Los Angeles erupts in five days of rioting and looting after four white police officers accused of the videotaped beating of black motorist Rodney King in March 1991 are acquitted by a jury in Ventura County, Calif. The Los Angeles coroner's office reported that at least 50 people were killed. More than 4,000 people were injured, and more than 11,000 were arrested. About 600 fires were set, and property damage was estimated at $1 billion.

Fires burn in south-central Los Angeles as riots break out on April 29, following the acquittal of four police officers charged with beating black motorist Rodney King. ▼

716
EMBOBINADO
MOTORES
ELECTRICOS
TRACKER

POWELL
KOON
BRISINEO
WYNN
LEGALISED
THUGS
BLUE BY DAY
WHITE BY NIGHT

May 1992

S	M	T	W	TH	F	S
					1	2
3	4	5	6	7	8	9
10	11	12	13	14	15	16
17	18	19	20	21	22	23
24	25	26	27	28	29	30
31						

1 More than 100 antiabortion protesters are arrested outside an abortion clinic in the Buffalo, N.Y., area, as part of a two-week-long protest, from April 20 to May 2, organized by Operation Rescue.

7 The Michigan legislature approves a constitutional amendment, first introduced in 1789, that bars Congress from granting itself a midterm pay raise. With the approval, the amendment had been ratified by 38 states, the number needed for it to be officially adopted.

Germany's public-workers unions, representing 2.3 million members, accept a government wage offer, ending a series of ministrikes that had crippled public transportation and other services. On May 14, however, the rank and file of one of the unions rejected the pact in a ratification vote.

The space shuttle Endeavour, built to replace the shuttle Challenger, lifts off from Cape Canaveral, Fla., on its maiden flight, a mission to rescue a stranded communications satellite. On May 14, following a spacewalk the previous day by three astronauts, the satellite was sent into proper orbit.

12 The United States recalls its ambassador to Yugoslavia to protest military aggression against the former republic of Bosnia and Hercegovina.

Outgoing Los Angeles Police Chief Daryl F. Gates takes part in the arrest of four black men accused of the televised beating of a white truck driver during the Los Angeles riots.

16 A protest organized by the U.S. Conference of Mayors draws an estimated 35,000 people to Washington, D.C., demanding more aid for cities.

16, 17 A United Nations peacekeeping force withdraws from Sarajevo, capital of Bosnia and Hercegovina, as fighting escalates in the civil war there.

18, 19 Soldiers in Bangkok, Thailand, kill 15 and wound more than 350 protesters who were demanding the resignation of unelected Prime Minister Suchinda Kraprayoon. On May 19, antigovernment demonstrations spread to 13 provinces, and the official death toll was put at 52.

21 China detonates the most powerful nuclear bomb it has ever tested, and the underground blast draws a protest from the Administration of President George Bush.

24 Thailand's Prime Minister Suchinda agrees to resign in exchange for amnesty for the military officials and soldiers involved in the massacre of unarmed demonstrators.

Al Unser, Jr., wins the Indianapolis 500 in the closest finish ever and the first by the son of a former Indy 500 winner.

27 At least 16 people on a bread line in Sarajevo are killed in a mortar attack reportedly launched by Serbian irregulars. The attack also wounded up to 160 people.

30 The United Nations Security Council votes to impose economic sanctions, including an oil embargo, on the government of Yugoslavia in an effort to end its attacks on Bosnia and Hercegovina.

▲ A woman grieves at the scene of a mortar attack on a bread line in Sarajevo, Bosnia and Hercegovina, in which 16 people were killed on May 27.

Thai troops line up arrested protesters in Bangkok, the capital, following two days of antigovernment demonstrations on May 18 and 19. ▶

◀ Al Unser, Jr., celebrates his victory in the Indianapolis 500 on May 24, in the closest finish in the history of the race.

June 1992

S	M	T	W	TH	F	S
	1	2	3	4	5	6
7	8	9	10	11	12	13
14	15	16	17	18	19	20
21	22	23	24	25	26	27
28	29	30				

2 Arkansas Governor Bill Clinton clinches the Democratic presidential nomination as a result of his showing in six state primaries. Voter surveys, however, indicate a groundswell of support for the independent but unofficial candidacy of billionaire businessman Ross Perot.

Danish voters throw a monkey wrench into plans for European unity by rejecting a proposed unity treaty in a referendum. The vote greatly complicates enactment of the treaty, which was to go into effect Jan. 1, 1993, only if all 12 member nations of the European Community approved it.

3 The 12-day Earth Summit, formally called the United Nations Conference on Environment and Development, opens in Rio de Janeiro, Brazil, with delegates from 178 countries.

14 The Chicago Bulls repeat as National Basketball Association champions, defeating the Portland Trail Blazers 4 games to 2.

15 Japan's parliament approves legislation that allows a limited number of troops to take part in United Nations peacekeeping activities abroad, the first time since the end of World War II (1939-1945) that Japanese forces have been permitted such a role.

16 The most sweeping arms reduction accord ever reached, involving the elimination of about 13,000 nuclear warheads, is announced in Washington, D.C., by President George Bush and Russian President Boris N. Yeltsin.

A federal grand jury in Washington, D.C., indicts Caspar Weinberger, former secretary of defense, on five felony counts stemming from an investigation of the 1985-1986 Iran-contra affair.

17 The last of the Western hostages to be held in Lebanon—Thomas Kemptner and Heinrich Strübig, both of Germany—are released by their Shiite Muslim kidnappers.

21 Nelson Mandela, leader of the African National Congress (ANC), announces that the ANC will halt negotiations with the South African government following the June 17 massacre of more than 40 blacks in the township of Boipatong.

23 Israel's Labor Party emerges victorious in parliamentary elections, winning enough seats to form a center-left coalition and oust the right wing Likud bloc from power.

26 Navy Secretary H. Lawrence Garrett III resigns after coming under criticism for his handling of an investigation into sexual harassment.

28 Two powerful earthquakes occur within hours of each other in southern California, killing a young boy and injuring hundreds of others. The first quake—the most powerful to strike California since 1952—registers 7.6 on the Richter scale of magnitude and is centered near Landers. The second, measuring 6.7 on the Richter scale, is centered near Big Bear Lake.

29 The Supreme Court in a 5 to 4 ruling affirms the 1973 *Roe v. Wade* decision that declared abortion a constitutional right but upholds most of the provisions of a Pennsylvania law that restricts abortions.

Demonstrators gather outside the U.S. Supreme Court ▶ on June 29, as the high court upheld a Pennsylvania law that restricts abortion.

Children take part in opening ceremonies on June 3 for the Earth Summit in Rio de Janeiro, Brazil, which drew delegates from 178 countries. ▼

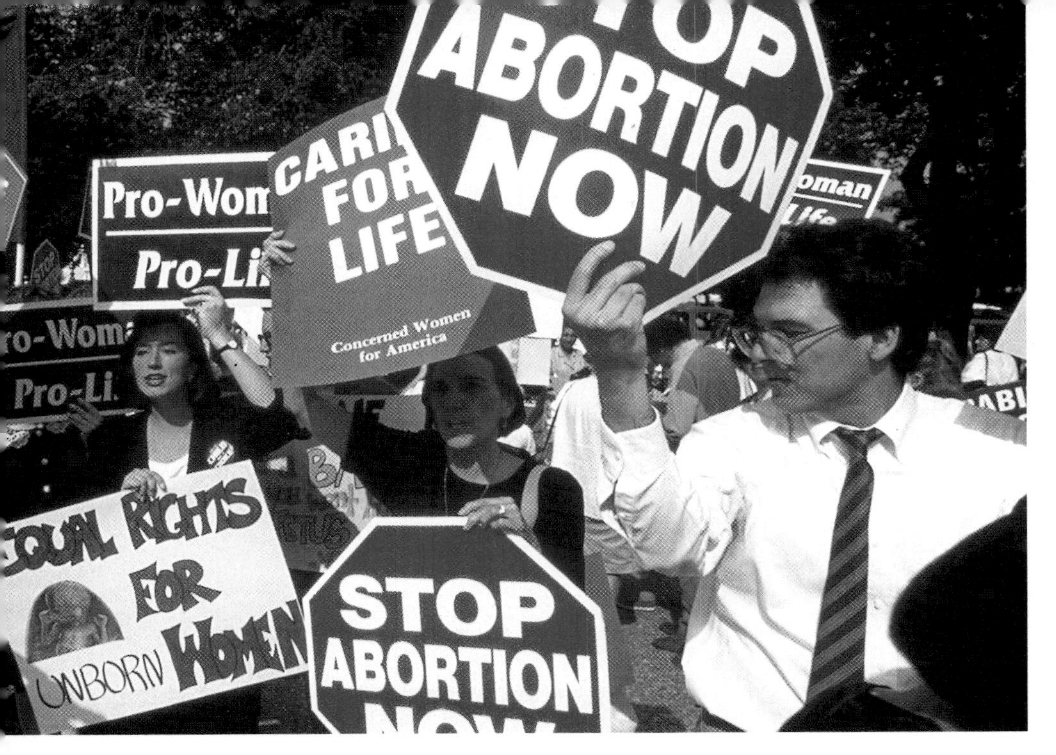

TOP
ABORTION
NOW
Pro-Wom
Pro-Li
CARI
FOR
LIFE
Concerned Women for America
oman
Life
ro-Woma
Pro-Li
QUAL RIGHTS
FOR
UNBORN WOMEN
STOP
ABORTION

July 1992

S	M	T	W	TH	F	S
			1	2	3	4
5	6	7	8	9	10	11
12	13	14	15	16	17	18
19	20	21	22	23	24	25
26	27	28	29	30	31	

Albert Gore, Jr., (left) and Bill Clinton accept the Democratic Party's ▶ nomination for Vice President and President on July 16.

4, 5 Steffi Graf of Germany wins her fourth Wimbledon title at the All-England Lawn Tennis Championship. The next day, Andre Agassi of Las Vegas, Nev., wins the men's singles title.
6-8 The leaders of the world's seven most powerful industrial nations, known as the Group of Seven, gather in Munich, Germany, for their annual summit but fail to reach any agreements on revitalizing the world economy.
8 Two major oil companies, Amoco Corporation and Unocal Corporation, announce plans to restructure by eliminating 10,000 jobs in 1992 and 1993, continuing a trend of job elimination in the oil industry. On July 7, Mobil Corporation said it would lay off 2,000 people.
9 Democratic presidential contender Bill Clinton selects United States Senator Albert Gore, Jr., of Tennessee as his vice presidential running mate.
16 Texas billionaire Ross Perot ends his unofficial bid for the presidency, saying he had concluded that it was impossible for him to win.
Arkansas Governor Bill Clinton accepts the Democratic presidential nomination on behalf of the "forgotten middle class."
17 The Slovak National Council declares the Slovak Republic a sovereign country, signaling the breakup of Czechoslovakia.
19 The cabinet of Israeli Prime Minister Yitzhak Rabin approves a freeze on new settlements in the occupied territories, a move that was expected to give new life to the Mideast peace talks and open the way for loan guarantees from the United States.
20 An airlift of food and medicine to Sarajevo, the beleaguered capital of Bosnia and Hercegovina, is suspended after 23 days due to renewed fighting.
A prototype of a controversial military aircraft, the V-22 Osprey, crashes in the Potomac River as it approached a Marine air station in Quantico, Va., killing all seven people on board.
22 President George Bush dismisses news reports that said he was planning to drop Vice President Dan Quayle as his running mate, characterizing the reports as a "lot of crazy rumors."
Convicted drug kingpin Pablo Escobar escapes from prison in Colombia, following a shootout in which at least six people were reported killed.
25 The 25th Summer Olympic Games open in Barcelona, Spain, with a record 172 nations and territories represented.
26 Iraq agrees to allow United Nations weapons inspectors to search the Agriculture Ministry building in Baghdad for records relating to Iraq's ballistic missile program, averting the threat of a bombing attack by the United States. But when UN inspectors entered the building on July 28 and 29, they found nothing and voiced their suspicion that the Iraqi records had been removed.
30 Government economic figures show that the U.S. economy grew by only 1.5 per cent in the second quarter.

A gigantic version of the Olympic flag is unfurled at opening ceremonies for the Summer Games, which drew a record number of athletes to Barcelona, Spain, on July 25. ▼

August 1992

S	M	T	W	TH	F	S
						1
2	3	4	5	6	7	8
9	10	11	12	13	14	15
16	17	18	19	20	21	22
23	24	25	26	27	28	29
30	31					

3, 4 Millions of black South Africans take part in a two-day general strike called by the African National Congress to protest the lack of progress in negotiations with the white-minority government of President Frederik Willem de Klerk. Urban business districts were reported largely deserted in one of the most massive protests ever against white rule.

5 Four Los Angeles police officers acquitted in April in the 1991 beating of black motorist Rodney King are indicted on federal civil rights charges.

6 President George Bush urges the United Nations to authorize military intervention in Bosnia and Hercegovina for the purpose of delivering food and medicine to Sarajevo, the capital.

9 The Summer Olympic Games end in Barcelona, Spain, with the Unified Team winning 112 medals, the United States 108 medals, and Germany 82 medals.

12 Canada, Mexico, and the United States formally announce a free trade agreement that is expected to make a variety of goods available at lower prices if it wins legislative approval.

13 Secretary of State James A. Baker III takes over President Bush's faltering reelection campaign, promising to focus on domestic, rather than foreign, policy issues.

17 The Republican Party opens its presidential nominating convention in Houston, as President Bush declares that he has a plan "to get this country moving again."

18 Iraqi aircraft that venture south of the 32nd parallel will be shot down, British Prime Minister John Major announces in detailing a plan supported by France and the United States to help defend Shiite Muslim dissidents fighting Iraqi President Saddam Hussein.

20 Accepting the Republican Party's nomination for the presidency, President Bush pledges a tax cut to revive the ailing economy.

24 A special Brazilian congressional commission concludes that there is sufficient evidence to begin impeachment proceedings against President Fernando Collor de Mello, finding that he had accepted millions of dollars in illegal payments and benefits from business interests.

24, 25, 26 Hurricane Andrew storms across southern Florida, then rips through southern Louisiana before dying out, leaving an estimated 250,000 people homeless and causing damage estimated at $30 billion, reportedly the costliest natural disaster in United States history.

29 Tens of thousands of German citizens demonstrate in the German port city of Rostock to protest racist attacks aimed at refugees and immigrants. The attacks by neo-Nazi youths began there on August 22.

31 White-supremacist fugitive Randall Weaver, wanted on weapons charges, surrenders to federal authorities after an 11-day stand-off outside his home near Naples, Ida. During the stand-off, a United States marshal and Weaver's wife and son were killed.

Vice President Dan Quayle, left, and President George Bush join their spouses in celebrating their Republican Party nominations on August 20 in Houston. ▶

Hurricane Andrew leaves a wide swath of destruction through Homestead, Fla., on August 24, reportedly the costliest natural disaster in U.S. history.

September 1992

S	M	T	W	TH	F	S
		1	2	3	4	5
6	7	8	9	10	11	12
13	14	15	16	17	18	19
20	21	22	23	24	25	26
27	28	29	30			

1 Chinese police in Beijing, China's capital, arrest a prominent student dissident, Shen Tong, who was among the leaders of the 1989 Tiananmen democracy movement.

3 The United States Bureau of the Census releases figures showing that the number of Americans living in poverty in 1991 reached 35.7 million, the highest figure since 1964.

7 Troops loyal to the military government in the black homeland of Ciskei in eastern South Africa open fire on demonstrators led by the African National Congress, killing at least 28 people and wounding nearly 200.

Tajikistan President Rakhman Nabiyev is forced to resign, following weeks of clan and religious warfare that left nearly 2,000 people dead.

9 Milwaukee Brewers center fielder Robin Yount rips a single into right-center field for his 3,000th career hit, becoming only the 17th player in baseball history to reach that plateau.

11 Hurricane Iniki sweeps across the Hawaiian islands of Kauai, Niihau, and Oahu, killing three people and causing an estimated $1 billion in property damage. The American Red Cross reported that on Kauai 1,439 homes were destroyed, and 14,467 homes were damaged.

12 Peruvian police seize Abimael Guzmán Reynoso, the notorious leader of the Shining Path guerrilla movement, who had eluded a 12-year manhunt while leading a terrorist campaign that had paralyzed much of Peru.

Astronaut Mae C. Jemison becomes the first black woman in space after the space shuttle Endeavour lifts off from Cape Canaveral, Fla., also carrying the first married couple to fly together on the first joint U.S.-Japan mission.

20 French voters narrowly approve the Treaty on European Union, also known as the Maastricht Treaty, with only 51 per cent in favor, raising questions about the future of European unity plans.

21 Mexico restores full diplomatic relations with the Vatican, ending a break that lasted for more than 130 years.

28 American, Colombian, and Italian law enforcement officials reveal that they have arrested more than 165 people on charges of laundering money obtained from illegal drug sales in an international crackdown on cocaine trafficking.

29 Brazil's Chamber of Deputies, the lower house of Congress, votes to impeach President Fernando Collor de Mello, the country's first freely elected leader in 29 years, on charges of corruption. Vice President Itamar Franco is named acting president.

30 The House of Representatives fails to override President George Bush's veto of a family-leave bill that would have provided workers up to 12 weeks of unpaid leave for family-related medical emergencies.

Kansas City Royals baseball star George Brett becomes the 18th player to record 3,000 career hits, with a 4-hit game against the California Angels.

▲ Telephone poles are strewn across a road on the Hawaiian island of Kauai, which was struck by Hurricane Iniki on September 11.

French supporters of the Maastricht Treaty celebrate their victory in a referendum on European unity on September 20. ▶

CENTER
LANE
ONLY
SPEED
LIMIT
35

October 1992

S	M	T	W	TH	F	S
				1	2	3
4	5	6	7	8	9	10
11	12	13	14	15	16	17
18	19	20	21	22	23	24
25	26	27	28	29	30	31

1 Texas billionaire Ross Perot reenters the presidential campaign, saying the Republican and Democratic nominees had failed "to address the problems that face the nation."
4 The government of Mozambique and leaders of a 16-year-old rebel movement sign a peace treaty in Rome, formally concluding the last of the southern African civil wars that had been spawned, in part, by the ideological divisions of the Cold War.
5 In a vote to override President George Bush's veto of a bill to reregulate the cable television industry, the United States Congress ends Bush's string of 35 successful vetoes.
7 Shining Path guerrilla leader Abimael Guzmán Reynoso is convicted by a military tribunal in Peru of treason and sentenced to life imprisonment.
10 Tens of thousands of people hold a candlelight march outside the White House, calling on the federal government to do more to end the AIDS epidemic, completing a daylong protest that included the unfolding of the AIDS Quilt, a memorial to people who have died of the disease.
11 The first of three televised debates among President Bush, Democratic presidential candidate Bill Clinton, and independent candidate Ross Perot is held as election day draws near.
12 An earthquake strikes Cairo, Egypt, and a suburb to the south, killing 543 people and injuring more than 6,500 people. Although the quake was moderate in strength, officials said the death toll was high due to poorly constructed buildings.
14 The Toronto Blue Jays become the first Canadian team to advance to baseball's World Series, winning the American League pennant by defeating the Oakland Athletics 4 games to 2. The Blue Jays won the series on October 24, defeating the Atlanta Braves and becoming the first non-U.S. team to win the series since series play began in 1903.
Japan's top political leader, Shin Kanemaru of the ruling Liberal Democratic Party, resigns from the Diet, Japan's parliament, following his conviction for receiving illegal payments.
19 China's Communist Party promotes several free market reformers to the powerful Politburo Standing Committee, signaling a defeat for hard-line ideologists.
21 Tens of thousands of coal miners march through the streets of central London to protest British Prime Minister John Major's plans to close down coal mines and reduce the number of miners.
23 Japan's Emperor Akihito begins the first Japanese imperial visit to China, telling an audience in Beijing that he felt "deep sorrow" over the "great sufferings" Japanese forces inflicted on the people of China during World War II (1939-1945).
26 Canadians vote "no" in a national referendum on constitutional reform, increasing the likelihood that the French-speaking province of Quebec will seek independence. Only 4 of Canada's 10 provinces voted "yes."

◀ Members of the Toronto Blue Jays baseball team celebrate their World Series victory in Atlanta, Ga., on October 24.

The AIDS Quilt, a memorial to people who have died of the disease, is spread out in front of the Washington Monument in the nation's capital on October 10.
▼

◀ Egyptian children step through the rubble left by an earthquake that devastated Cairo, the capital, and a suburb on October 12.

November 1992

S	M	T	W	TH	F	S
1	2	3	4	5	6	7
8	9	10	11	12	13	14
15	16	17	18	19	20	21
22	23	24	25	26	27	28
29	30					

3 Democrat Bill Clinton wins the United States presidential election with 43 per cent of the popular vote and 370 Electoral College votes, defeating Republican President George Bush with 38 per cent of the popular vote and 168 electoral votes. Independent candidate Ross Perot finished with an unexpectedly strong 19 per cent of the popular vote but did not carry a single state.
8 More than 350,000 people rally in Berlin, Germany, to protest right wing violence against immigrants but radical leftists disrupt the rally by throwing stones and eggs at Chancellor Helmut Kohl and President Richard von Weizsäcker.
11 The governing body of the Church of England approves the right of women to become priests, ending a barrier that lasted nearly 450 years.
13 The Peruvian government says it arrested a small group of army officers who allegedly planned to assassinate President Alberto Fujimori.
An unprecedented loss of ozone in the upper atmosphere over Canada, northern Europe, and Russia is reported by the World Meteorological Organization, an agency of the United Nations, which also reported dangerously low levels of ozone above southern Argentina, Chile, and the South Pole.
Riddick Bowe wins the heavyweight boxing crown, defeating Evander Holyfield in a unanimous decision.
15 Former Communists return to power in Lithuania in parliamentary elections that give a large majority of seats to the Democratic Labor Party.
16 Two Detroit police officers are charged with second-degree murder and two others are indicted on lesser charges in the beating death of black motorist Malice Green on November 5.
20 A fire scorches a section of Windsor Castle, the chief residence for Great Britain's royal family outside of London, causing extensive damage to historic St. George's banquet hall.
Over a four-day period, storms spawn an estimated 45 tornadoes that touched down in 12 states in the South and Midwest, killing at least 25 people, including 15 in Mississippi, while injuring hundreds and causing millions of dollars in damages.
23 Three Turkish residents of Möln, Germany, die in a firebomb attack attributed to a neo-Nazi group, one of more than 1,900 attacks on foreigners in Germany in 1992.
25 Voters in Ireland approve two constitutional amendments guaranteeing the right to abortion information and the right to travel abroad for an abortion. They vote down a third proposal that was opposed by forces against and in favor of abortion rights.
27 The Venezuelan government says it put down a coup attempt by a small group of rebel soldiers who bombed the presidential palace.
30 To ensure the delivery of emergency food supplies in a famine that threatens starvation for millions of Somalis, United Nations Secretary-General Boutros Boutros-Ghali urges the Security Council to approve military intervention in Somalia.

▲ President-elect Bill Clinton and Vice President-elect Al Gore, Jr., and their spouses celebrate their victory in the elections on November 3.

Fire fighters battle a blaze that heavily damaged historic Windsor Castle, the royal family's home outside London, on November 20. ▶

Carol Moseley Braun waves to supporters after becoming the first black woman elected to the United States Senate on November 3.

▼

December 1992

S	M	T	W	TH	F	S
		1	2	3	4	5
6	7	8	9	10	11	12
13	14	15	16	17	18	19
20	21	22	23	24	25	26
27	28	29	30	31		

3 A proposal to send United States troops to Somalia to protect emergency food relief for millions of people threatened with starvation is approved by the United Nations Security Council. The first unit of U.S. marines arrives in Somalia on December 9.

6 A mob of Hindu fundamentalists destroys a mosque in Ayodhya, India, triggering the worst violence between Hindus and Muslims since 1947. After a week of rioting in India, Pakistan, and Bangladesh, more than 1,200 people were killed and more than 5,000 were injured. The government outlawed five fundamentalist groups and arrested more than 4,500 members of those groups.

7 The United States wins the Davis Cup tennis tournament for the second time in three years as Jim Courier defeats Switzerland's Jakob Hiasek in the deciding match.

9 Great Britain's Prince Charles and Princess Diana have agreed to a legal separation but will not divorce, British Prime Minister John Major announces.

11, 12 The worst storm in decades batters the East Coast, bringing snow, rain, and high winds. Authorities attributed six deaths to the storm.

18 Kim Young Sam, a former dissident turned conservative, wins South Korea's presidential election, becoming the first nonmilitary president elected since 1961.

The United Nations Security Council unanimously condemns Israel's deportation of 415 Palestinians suspected of being members of Islamic fundamentalist groups opposed to the Middle East peace talks. The deportations followed the killing of five Israeli soldiers and a border guard over a 10-day period.

19 South Africa's President Frederik Willem de Klerk dismisses or suspends 23 military officers, including six generals, who were suspected of illegal or unauthorized activities aimed at disrupting negotiations with the African National Congress.

21 Serbia's President Slobodan Milošević claims victory in his race for reelection against Yugoslavia's Prime Minister Milan Panic.

24 President-elect Bill Clinton picks the last remaining members of his Cabinet, fulfilling a campaign pledge to select a Cabinet representative of America's diversity. The Cabinet includes four blacks, three women, and two Hispanics.

President George Bush grants pardons to six national security officials implicated in the Iran-contra affair, including former Secretary of Defense Caspar Weinberger, who was to go on trial in January 1993. The pardons draw fire from Democratic congressional leaders, who charge the President with "undermining the American system of justice."

27 An American warplane shoots down an Iraqi jet that violated a U.S. ban on Iraqi flights south of the 32nd parallel, the first downing since the ban was imposed in August 1992.

31 President Bush arrives in Somalia to spend New Year's Day with U.S. troops distributing food to the famine-ravaged east African country.

United States marines arrive in Somalia on December 9 as part of Operation Restore Hope, a United Nations-sponsored effort to protect food distribution to starving Somalis.

◀ Hindu fundamentalists attack a mosque in Ayodhya, India, on December 6, triggering a week of violence.

See pages 344-345

1992

WORLD BOOK YEAR BOOK UPDATE

The major events of 1992 are summarized in almost 300 alphabetically arranged articles—from "Advertising" to "Zoos." In most cases, the article titles are the same as those of the articles in ***The World Book Encyclopedia*** that they update. Included are 14 Special Reports that offer in-depth looks at particular subjects, ranging from the spread of nuclear weapons to the new role being played in the world by the United Nations. The Special Reports can be found on the following pages under their respective Update article titles.

Advertising. In the most publicized advertising dilemma of 1992, Reebok International Limited, a major advertiser on television broadcasts of the 1992 Summer Olympic Games in Barcelona, Spain, almost had to cancel its planned shoe advertising campaign when one of the featured athletes failed to qualify for the United States Olympic team. The $30-million campaign, produced by Chiat/Day/Mojo in New York City and launched in January, showed decathletes Dan O'Brien and Dave Johnson competing for the title of "the world's best athlete," with the rivalry to be settled in Barcelona. But O'Brien missed three pole vault attempts at a June qualifying meet in New Orleans and failed to make the U.S. team. Reebok quickly rebounded with a series of ads portraying O'Brien as a trainer and promoter for Johnson. The revised commercials aired during the National Broadcasting Company's (NBC's) coverage of the games from July 25 through August 9.

Controversial ads. The Federal Communications Commission in August 1992 declined to rule that political television ads showing photographs of aborted fetuses were "indecent." Commercial television stations therefore did not have the authority to restrict the ads from airing. According to FCC policy, a commercial is considered "indecent" if it depicts "sexual or excretory activities or organs" that are "patently offensive as measured by contemporary community standards." Such ads are allowed to air on commercial television only from midnight to 6 a.m.

The FCC decision concerned an advertisement paid for by Daniel Becker, an antiabortion candidate for the U.S. House of Representatives running in Georgia. The ad in question included images of dead fetuses covered in fluid. Rather than decide whether the ad was indecent, the FCC argued that restricting the hours in which the ad could be aired would block the candidate's right to "reasonable access" to television airwaves. The agency did say broadcasters can run warnings to viewers about the content of potentially upsetting political commercials before the ads air.

Fighting cigarette ads. In an unprecedented move, U.S. Surgeon General Antonia C. Novello and the American Medical Association (AMA) in March joined forces to demand that the R. J. Reynolds Tobacco Company voluntarily end its use of the cartoon character "Old Joe" Camel in its cigarette ads. Novello and the AMA also called on retailers to remove "Old Joe" Camel signs from their stores, urged publications to turn down ads featuring the character, and asked advertising agencies to stop marketing practices that they said target cigarettes to children. This event marked the first time that the surgeon general had called for an end to an ad campaign for a specific brand of cigarettes, though the surgeon general lacks the authority to enforce such a demand.

The criticism of Reynolds was sparked by three studies published in December 1991 indicating that "Old Joe" Camel ads are highly memorable and appealing to children and young adults. But the cigarette manufacturer contended that the studies were flawed and inaccurate and argued that its ads are protected by the First Amendment.

Reynolds spends about $75 million a year to promote Camel cigarettes. From 1989—the year the company adopted the "Old Joe" Camel mascot—to 1992, Camel's share of the cigarette market among smokers ages 18 to 24 almost doubled from 4.4 per cent to 7.9 per cent. And among smokers under age 18, Camel's share rose from 0.5 per cent to 33 per cent.

Another heated attack on the cigarette industry was launched in September 1992 by Minnesota's Department of Public Health. The $321,000 television and radio antismoking campaign was directed specifically toward women and played on typical female images in cigarette advertising. One ad showed a young woman dressed in leotards come alive from her billboard display and stub out her cigarette on the head of an admiring executive.

Landmark individuals. Charlotte Beers became the highest-ranking woman in the U.S. ad industry when she joined Ogilvy & Mather Worldwide, New York City, in April 1992 as chairman and chief executive. Beers in February had resigned as chief executive officer of Tatham/RSCG in Chicago, which she joined in 1979.

The advertising industry lost a leader in 1992 when Emerson Foote, cofounder in 1942 of the advertising giant Foote, Cone & Belding, died in July at age 85. Foote established his career on a campaign for Lucky Strike cigarettes but left advertising in 1964 because of his opposition to cigarette ads. He later served on the American Cancer Society's board of directors.

Awards. The 39th International Advertising Film Festival, held in June 1992 in Cannes, France, attracted entries from 44 countries, including Zimbabwe and Slovenia for the first time. A Spanish advertising firm won the festival's highest accolade, the Grand Prix, for a racy advertisement for rubber cement. Meanwhile, U.S. advertising agencies won only three gold Lions—the festival's awards for excellence in advertising. Wieden & Kennedy of Portland, Ore., took home two gold Lions, including one for an ad for Nike shoes featuring tennis star Andre Agassi inside a bouncing television set. And Goodby, Berlin & Silverstein of San Francisco won a gold Lion for their Chevys Mexican Restaurant advertising campaign.

In the United States, the Clio awards for advertising returned in 1992 after being canceled in 1991 because of financial woes and dissent among organizers. The New Clios, under the leadership of *Screen* magazine publisher Ruth Ratny, were held in September 1992 and had a respectable turnout. But because of the awards' tarnished history, industry insiders speculated it would take years for the new awards to achieve the former prestige of the old Clios.

Frances D. Brock

In ***World Book***, see **Advertising**.

Rival guerrilla groups shell Afghanistan's capital, Kabul, in April in a battle to seize control after the collapse of the Communist government.

Afghanistan. The Communist government that had come to power in a military coup in 1978 collapsed in 1992. That government had been kept in power by troops from the former Soviet Union from 1979 until 1989. The halt of economic and military aid from Russia on Jan. 1, 1992, triggered its fall. Facing the prospect of no pay and no supplies, two key divisions of militia deserted the government in early March. Then on March 18, President Najibullah announced that he was going to resign to make way for a peace plan formulated by the United Nations (UN).

Kabul falls. Militia deserters joined the Islamic guerrillas who had been fighting the Communists since 1978. Militia and moderate Islamic rebels led by Ahmed Shah Massoud began pushing toward Kabul from the north and east. Meanwhile, fundamentalist Islamic forces led by Gulbuddin Hekmatyar closed in from the south and west. The two groups of guerrillas reached Kabul in mid-April and encircled the city. On April 16, Najibullah resigned and then tried to leave the country, but he was turned back at the airport by militia forces that had switched their allegiance. He later found refuge in the Kabul office of the UN.

Under the guidance of officials from neighboring Pakistan, the leaders of various guerrilla factions on April 24 agreed to establish an interim government to rule until democratic elections could be organized. Sibghatullah Mojaddedi, a rebel leader with weak but broad backing, was named president of the caretaker government. But Hekmatyar opposed the arrangements, saying he desired a strict Islamic government. In response, Massoud, with support from the Afghan militia, drove Hekmatyar's forces from Kabul.

Mojaddedi assumed the presidency on April 28. As part of an agreed-upon plan, he then peacefully relinquished power to Burhanuddin Rabbani, the political head of Massoud's group, on June 28.

Fighting continues. Hekmatyar's forces regularly shelled Kabul for the rest of the year. In a particularly ferocious set of attacks in August, Kabul suffered its worst damage since 1978 as more than 1,800 people were killed. Numerous truces were fashioned with Hekmatyar during 1992, but they were all broken.

Chaos reigns. With the interim government unable to generate peace, rival ethnic and religious groups clashed regularly in Kabul for the remainder of the year. By contrast, most of the rest of Afghanistan was fairly quiet under the watches of local guerrilla commanders. However, millions of Afghans lacked normal government, working schools and hospitals, and even electricity and water. And an estimated 1 million Afghan refugees returned to find their villages destroyed and their farms filled with land mines.

Elected leader. On December 30, Rabbani was elected to a two-year term as president. He was the only candidate. Henry S. Bradsher

See also **Asia** (Facts in brief table). In ***World Book,*** see **Afghanistan.**

Africa

Events and trends in Africa in 1992 were a blend of movement toward, and stubborn resistance to, more democratic government; war and efforts to bring peace; and continuing economic, climatic, and health problems. World attention was drawn to the tragedy of Somalia, where armed conflict and mass starvation prompted an international intervention, and to the ongoing drama in South Africa, which achieved some progress toward resolution of differences between blacks and whites. Less notice, on the other hand, was given to the implementation of democratic reforms in several nations and the worsening economic situation over much of the continent.

Intervening in Somalia. In Somalia, a civil war that resulted in the overthrow of President Mohamed Siad Barre in January 1991 led in 1992 to chaos and anarchy as fighting continued between contending rebel factions and roving gangs of thugs. The violence disrupted food production, which had already been severely curtailed by a terrible drought. By December, an estimated 300,000 people had starved to death or been killed since the beginning of the year, and more than one-third of Somalia's population of 8.3 million was facing starvation.

On December 3, the United Nations (UN) Security Council voted unanimously to intervene to save those

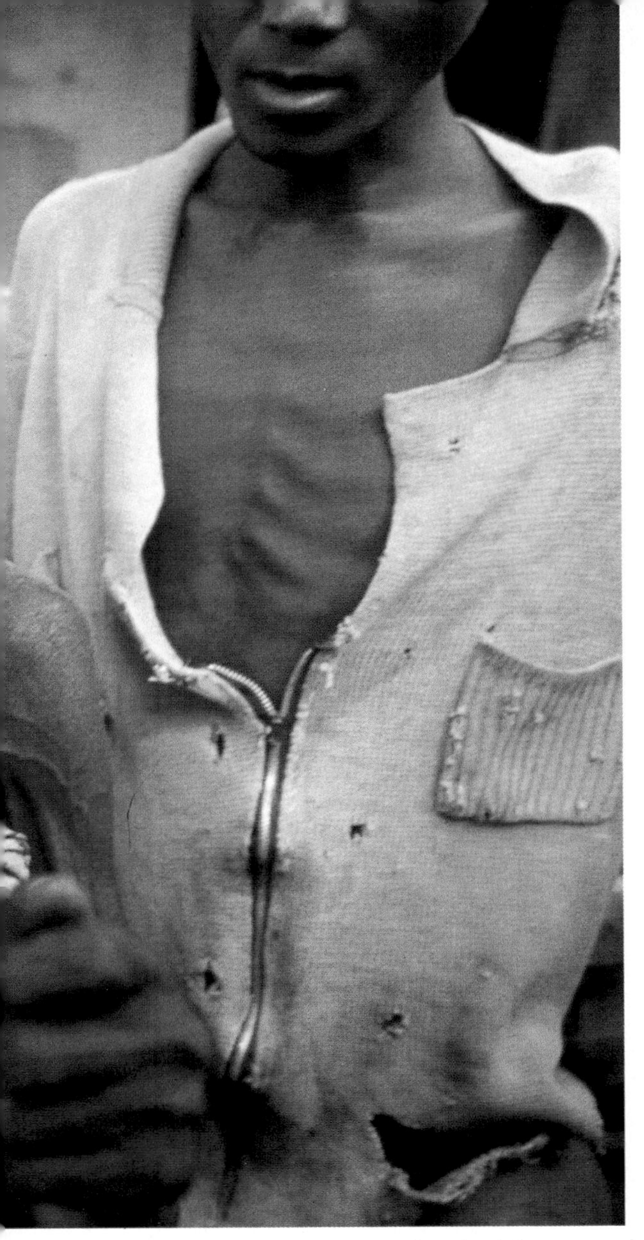

A starving woman in Baidoa, Somalia, pleads for food in July as the country, devastated by civil war and drought, is gripped by a terrible famine.

multitudes from death. The same day, United States President George Bush approved plans to send at least 28,000 U.S. troops to Somalia to protect relief workers and help oversee the distribution of food. The operation got into high gear almost immediately, with France, Italy, and several other nations also agreeing to participate. At year-end, it was unclear how long the rescue mission would last, though Bush said he hoped to have it completed by Jan. 20, 1993, when his term in office would expire. It also remained to be seen how effective the effort would be and whether it would have any lasting beneficial effect in Somalia.

Other conflicts. A number of African countries were wracked by full-scale civil war or other forms of armed violence in 1992. Efforts to end these various conflicts on the continent met with limited success during the year, and some of the "successes" toward ending conflicts in 1991 appeared to be coming undone by the end of 1992.

While the world's attention was focused on the international relief expedition in Somalia, Africa experts warned that the situation in Sudan, several hundred miles to the west of Somalia, was potentially even more grave. During the year, the Muslim government of Sudan had continued to win victories in a nine-year war with the Sudan People's Liberation Army, a Christian rebel group. The dislocation of the population resulting from the fighting and from government resettlement programs combined with drought to cause a severe famine.

In Liberia, a peacekeeping force sent in 1990 by the Economic Community of West African States (ECOWAS) to resolve the civil war there was involved in serious fighting with the forces of rebel leader Charles Taylor in 1992. In the autumn, Taylor's troops surrounded the city of Monrovia, the capital, and cut it off from resupply by either air or sea. At year-end, there was fear that the fighting in Liberia would spread and develop into a regional conflict. Taylor had already involved Sierra Leone in the conflict. His troops made raids into that country during the year to exact revenge for its support of the peacekeeping force in Liberia. Those incursions contributed to an April 29 coup that toppled Sierra Leone's President Joseph Momoh.

The peace that had come in May 1991 to Angola, which had been torn by civil war for 16 years, ended in 1992. In October, after suffering defeat in national elections the month before, Jonas Savimbi and his National Union for the Total Independence of Angola (UNITA) attacked government forces. International observers said the elections had been honest and fair, but Savimbi insisted they had been rigged, and he seemed determined to take by force what he could not win by democratic election. On December 7, however, Savimbi and his followers agreed to cease fighting and join a coalition government.

Positive developments also took place in Mozambique, where the government signed a peace treaty with representatives of the rebel Mozambique National Resistance (Renamo) on August 7. The treaty called for an end to hostilities and the scheduling of democratic elections, but it was not clear whether either the government or Renamo would be able to control their troops and put the treaty into effect.

The slow march toward democracy. The progress of democracy movements in Africa also produced mixed results in 1992. Domestic and international pressure led to multiparty elections in several nations, but authoritarian rulers in other countries stubbornly refused to give up power, resorting either to force or

Facts in brief on African political units

Country	Population	Government	Monetary unit*	Foreign trade (million U.S.$) Exports†	Imports†
Algeria	27,108,000	High State Council Chairman Ali Kafi; Prime Minister Belaid Abdesselam	dinar (21.56 = $1)	10,200	9,200
Angola	10,889,000	President José Eduardo dos Santos	new kwanza (550.00 = $1)	3,800	1,500
Benin	5,081,000	President Nicephore Soglo	CFA franc (259.88 = $1)	250	442
Botswana	1,444,000	President Quett K. J. Masire	pula (2.19 = $1)	1,800	1,700
Burkina Faso	9,799,000	Popular Front President, Head of State, & Head of Government Blaise Compaoré	CFA franc (259.88 = $1)	95	322
Burundi	5,981,000	President Pierre Buyoya	franc (212.07 = $1)	75	236
Cameroon	13,089,000	President Paul Biya	CFA franc (259.88 = $1)	2,100	1,200
Cape Verde	409,000	President Antonio Mascarenhas Monteiro; Prime Minister Carlos Alberto Wahnonde Carvalho Veiga	escudo (62.63 = $1)	7	112
Central African Republic	3,310,000	President André-Dieudonne Kolingba	CFA franc (259.88 = $1)	134	150
Chad	6,122,000	President Idriss Deby	CFA franc (259.88 = $1)	141	419
Comoros	611,000	President Said Mohamed Djohar	CFA franc (259.88 = $1)	16	41
Congo	2,503,000	President Denis Sassou-Nguesso; Prime Minister Andre Milongo	CFA franc (259.88 = $1)	976	600
Djibouti	446,000	President Hassan Gouled Aptidon; Prime Minister Barkat Gourad Hamadou	franc (177.72 = $1)	25	215
Egypt	55,881,000	President Hosni Mubarak; Prime Minister Atef Sedky	pound (3.32 = $1)	2,582	9,202
Equatorial Guinea	380,000	President Teodor Obiang Nguema Mbasogo; Prime Minister Silvestre Siale Bileka	CFA franc (259.88 = $1)	41	57
Ethiopia	53,775,000	President Meles Zenawi	birr (5.00 = $1)	294	1,076
Gabon	1,292,000	President Omar Bongo; Prime Minister Casimir Oye-Mba	CFA franc (259.88 = $1)	1,160	780
Gambia	932,000	President Sir Dawda Kairaba Jawara	dalasi (8.30 = $1)	41	200
Ghana	16,503,000	President Jerry John Rawlings	cedi (482.00 = $1)	1,024	1,275
Guinea	6,296,000	President Lansana Conté	franc (812.29 = $1)	645	551
Guinea-Bissau	1,027,000	President João Bernardo Vieira	peso (5,000 = $1)	14	69
Ivory Coast	13,433,000	President Félix Houphouët-Boigny	CFA franc (259.88 = $1)	2,931	2,185
Kenya	26,829,000	President Daniel T. arap Moi	shilling (34.75 = $1)	1,052	2,226
Lesotho	1,934,000	King Letsie III; Military Council Chairman Elias Phisoana Ramaema	loti (2.96 = $1)	66	499
Liberia	2,835,000	Interim President Amos Sawyer‡	dollar (1 = $1)	505	394
Libya	5,057,000	Leader of the Revolution Muammar Muhammad al-Qadhafi; General People's Committee Secretary (Prime Minister) Abu Zayd Umar Durda	dinar (0.28 = $1)	6,100	6,200

*Exchange rates as of Oct. 30, 1992, or latest available data.
†Latest available data.
‡Two rival rebel leaders, Charles Taylor and Prince Yormie Johnson, continued to press claims for the presidency.

Country	Population	Government	Monetary unit*	Foreign trade (million U.S.$) Exports†	Imports†
Madagascar	13,186,000	President Didier Ratsiraka; Prime Minister Guy Razanamasy	franc (1,827.37 = $1)	306	426
Malawi	9,711,000	President H. Kamuzu Banda	kwacha (4.24 = $1)	473	705
Mali	10,080,000	President Alpha Dumar Konare; Prime Minister Younoussi Toure	CFA franc (259.88 = $1)	271	500
Mauritania	2,194,000	President Maaouya Ould Sid Ahmed Taya	ouguiya (106.00 = $1)	451	351
Mauritius	1,120,000	President Cassam Uteem; Prime Minister Sir Anerood Jugnauth	rupee (15.86 = $1)	1,193	1,619
Morocco	27,051,000	King Hassan II; Prime Minister Azzedine Laraki	dirham (8.21 = $1)	4,229	6,919
Mozambique	16,934,000	President Joaquím Alberto Chissano; Prime Minister Mário da Graça Machungo	metical (2,734.94 = $1)	103	715
Namibia	1,952,000	President Sam Nujoma; Prime Minister Hage Geingob	rand (2.96 = $1)	1,021	894
Niger	8,514,000	President Ali Saibou; Prime Minister Amadou Cheiffou	CFA franc (259.88 = $1)	308	386
Nigeria	119,473,000	President Ibrahim Babangida	naira (19.37 = $1)	8,138	3,419
Rwanda	8,014,000	President Juvénal Habyarimana	franc (143.50 = $1)	101	369
São Tomé and Príncipe	129,000	President Miguel Trovoada	dobra (240 = $1)	6	27
Senegal	7,958,000	President Abdou Diouf; Prime Minister Habib Thiam	CFA franc (259.88 = $1)	801	1,000
Seychelles	71,000	President France Albert René	rupee (5.16 = $1)	48	173
Sierra Leone	4,490,000	National Provisional Ruling Council Chairman Valentine E. M. Strasser	leone (500.00 = $1)	143	164
Somalia	8,254,000	President Ali Mahdi Mohamed	shilling (2,620 = $1)	58	354
South Africa	42,823,00	State President Frederik Willem de Klerk	rand (2.96 = $1)	23,400	17,000
Sudan	27,444,000	Revolutionary Command Council for National Salvation Chairman and Prime Minister Umar Hasan Ahmad al-Bashir	pound (100.00 = $1)	465	1,000
Swaziland	872,000	King Mswati III; Prime Minister Obed Mfanyana Dlamini	lilangeni (2.96 = $1)	543	651
Tanzania	30,517,000	President Ali Hassan Mwinyi; Prime Minister John Malecela	shilling (324.69 = $1)	337	1,495
Togo	3,879,000	President Gnassingbé Eyadéma	CFA franc (259.88 = $1)	242	487
Tunisia	8,701,000	President Zine El-Abidine Ben Ali; Prime Minister Hamed Karoui	dinar (0.86 = $1)	3,595	5,550
Uganda	20,099,000	President Yoweri Museveni; Prime Minister George Cosmas Adyebo	shilling (1,181.05 = $1)	274	544
Zaire	39,138,000	President Mobutu Sese Seko	zaire (1,600,000.00 = $1)	999	886
Zambia	9,453,000	President Frederick Chiluba; Vice President Levy Mwanawasa	kwacha (220.58 = $1)	899	1,243
Zimbabwe	10,643,000	President Robert Mugabe	dollar (5.27 = $1)	1,723	1,850

trickery to put down their opponents. The greatest successes came in Zambia and Ghana, but important progress also took place in Madagascar, Seychelles, Gambia, and Burkina Faso.

In Zambia, the democratically elected government of Frederick Chiluba, which came to power in late 1991, faced a challenging year as it instituted programs to privatize government-owned enterprises and institute democratic reforms. A drought and economic difficulties caused public unrest, but Chiluba's government held on. A return to democratic rule also appeared to be on reasonably secure footing in Ghana. In the first multiparty elections in 13 years, Ghana's military leader, Jerry John Rawlings, was elected president on Nov. 4, 1992. Foreign observers said the election was conducted fairly. Elections in Mauritania in January produced a landslide victory for incumbent President Maaouya Ould Sid Ahmed Taya. That balloting, however, was marred by accusations of widespread vote fraud.

Progress toward democracy faltered badly in some nations. In Zaire, President Mobutu Sese Seko clung to power in the face of violent opposition at home and strong pressure from the United States and other members of the international community. Mobutu made no pretense of favoring democracy, and he did not hesitate to use violence to maintain his position.

The beleaguered rulers of several other countries, in contrast, employed a semblance of democratic procedures to retain power. In Kenya, President Daniel T. arap Moi was accused of using the rubber-stamp National Assembly to establish election rules that gave him a strong advantage over opposition candidates and all but assured his reelection.

In Cameroon, government officials changed the electoral laws a few weeks before an October election, used polling irregularities, and allegedly tampered with the election results to ensure the victory of President Paul Biya. Similar accusations—and ones even worse—were made about the political process in Burundi, Djibouti, Mauritania, and Sudan. Amnesty International reported that political murders and torture were common in those countries.

In Nigeria, Africa's most populous country, the detailed plans for a transfer of power from the military to a civilian democracy originally scheduled for October were further derailed in 1992. As tensions and violence increased during the year, General Ibrahim Babangida first postponed until January 1993—and then indefinitely—the transition to democracy, including presidential elections.

South Africa. The struggle in South Africa to achieve a multiracial democracy with full representation for blacks continued in 1992. Violence was rampant throughout the year, however, and its severity seemed to increase as the process moved closer to its goal. Nonetheless, there were indications by year-end that important steps had been made toward resolving the differences between the government of State President Frederik Willem de Klerk and the African National Congress, the largest of the black nationalist organizations. On November 26, de Klerk called for elections that would be open to black voters by April 1994. Some observers said such elections and the formation of a transitional government were likely in 1993.

Seeking greater self-reliance. The trend in recent years toward greater isolation of the African continent from the rest of the world continued for most of the year. Many African leaders feared the continent was becoming "marginalized" in world political and economic affairs. The end of the Cold War, the breakup of the Soviet Union, and the moves toward capitalism and democracy there and in Eastern Europe have diverted the attention of Western governments and investors away from Africa in the 1990's and lessened the strategic significance of the continent to the major powers.

In this environment, African governments have turned more and more to solving their problems with the limited resources at hand and with less reliance on foreign assistance. This was best exemplified in 1992 in the efforts of ECOWAS to resolve the civil war in Liberia. On the other hand, Somalia was left to its agony, making it necessary for Western nations to come to its rescue.

With those two examples before it, the Organization of African Unity (OAU), an association of 50 African nations, began consideration in 1992 of a comprehensive plan for managing conflict on the continent. At the OAU's 28th annual summit conference, held in July in Dakar, Senegal, Secretary-General Salim Ahmed Salim proposed establishing a bureau to monitor armed conflicts in African countries. Salim also recommended reviving a defunct agency, the OAU Defense Commission, to supervise an African peacekeeping force. Salim's proposals stimulated intense discussions among OAU representatives. Some member nations expressed concerns that the system might be too expensive for them to participate in and that it might infringe on their national sovereignty.

Economic ills and a southern drought. The economies of most African countries continued to suffer from the spreading effects of economic downturns in the United States, Western Europe, and Japan in 1992. The economic slumps in those parts of the world lessened the demand for African exports, the mainstay of most of the continent's economies. This loss of income, combined with several other factors—large foreign debts, economic mismanagement, political instability and war, and decreases in foreign aid and investment—caused much political turmoil and human misery.

For the states of southern Africa, the hardship was compounded by the worst drought of the 1900's in that region. The drought, an extension of the one affecting Somalia and other parts of northern and eastern Africa, destroyed crops and provided a serious cri-

Mozambique's President Joaquím Chissano, left, and rebel leader Afonso Dhlakama embrace on August 7 after signing a pact to end a 16-year civil war.

sis for the growing movements toward democracy in the region. There were fears that the water shortage would grow worse in 1993, making mass starvation as common in the south as in Somalia.

Population growth. In 1992, the African Development Bank, an organization that promotes economic and social development on the continent, acknowledged uncontrolled population growth as one of Africa's greatest problems. Africa's population in 1992 was about 700 million and was increasing at an annual rate of about 3 per cent—a pace at which a population doubles in 24 years. Unless something was done to check that growth, bank officials said, Africans were destined to sink deeper into poverty with each passing year.

Bank President Babacar Ndiaye announced on September 1 that the bank was adopting new policies aimed at lowering the birth rate in African countries. He said the emphasis would be on raising the educational level of women, because educated women with jobs tend to bear fewer children.

AIDS. By 1992, AIDS had become the number-one fatal disease in Africa. With just 9 per cent of the world's population, Africa by 1992 had accounted for about 60 per cent of the world's known cases of AIDS, according to estimates by the World Health Organization (WHO). That is about twice the number of cases that had been officially reported to WHO by African nations.

At an AIDS conference in late 1991 in Dakar, Senegal, WHO representatives and African health officials reported that an estimated 18 million Africans would be infected with HIV—the virus that causes the disease—by the year 2000 and that 6 million would die in the 10 years from 1992 to 2002. Recognizing the crisis, the OAU and the governments of many African countries in 1992 were coordinating an effort aimed at getting Africans to change their sexual behavior, including regular use of condoms.

The environment. Environmental degradation, long a problem in Africa, continued to increase in 1992. Deforestation and *desertification* (the spread of desert areas) were particular problems. African leaders hoped that the UN Conference on Environment and Development (commonly known as the Earth Summit), held in June in Rio de Janeiro, Brazil, might result in the adoption of agreements to preserve Africa's remaining forests and to hold back the advance of the deserts. The results of the conference were somewhat of a disappointment, however. Although the participants did agree to a plan for combating desertification, African representatives were unable to obtain passage of resolutions that might protect African forests from further destruction.

Mark DeLancey

See also the various African country articles. In ***World Book,*** see **Africa.**

Agriculture. **See Farm and farming.**

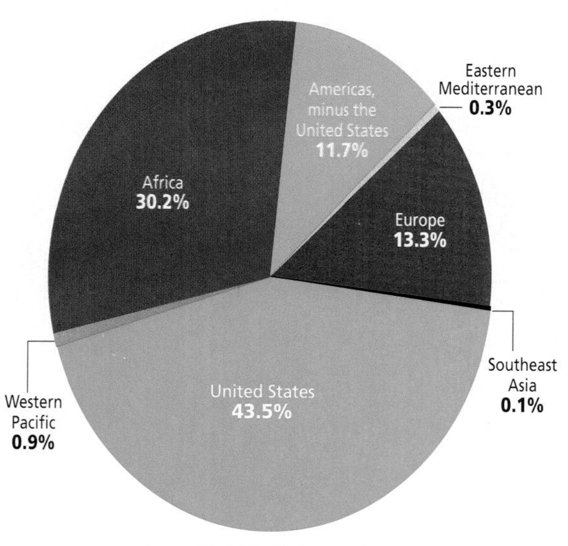

The United States had more than two-fifths of all reported AIDS cases worldwide as of June 30, 1992.

AIDS. There were reports in 1992 of an AIDS-like disease that did not show evidence of the human immunodeficiency virus (HIV), which causes AIDS. The accounts first circulated at the Eighth International Conference on AIDS, held from July 19-24 in Amsterdam, the Netherlands. Doctors reported about 30 cases of patients who tested negative for HIV but had AIDS-like symptoms, such as low white-blood-cell counts and pneumonia infections. These reports raised concerns over the possible emergence of a mutated form of HIV that might be capable of eluding blood tests.

At conferences held by the Centers for Disease Control (CDC) in August in Atlanta, Ga., and by the World Health Organization in September in Geneva, Switzerland, scientists could not explain the reports. But doctors said that there were no links among the cases, which meant a new virus would have to have arisen independently multiple times—an unlikely though not impossible scenario. Instead, doctors believed the illness might be related to cancer, tuberculosis, drug abuse, or genetic defects. To support continued study, federal health officials in August set up a national surveillance network to detect any additional cases of the AIDS-like disease.

New AIDS drug. The United States Food and Drug Administration (FDA) in June approved a new AIDS drug known as DDC. It was the third drug approved specifically for HIV infection, after AZT and DDI. It was also the first drug released under a new regulatory framework that shortens the approval path of drugs for life-threatening illnesses such as AIDS. Because DDC was released before a full series of tests was performed, the FDA said the new drug was intended for use only in conjunction with AZT, the chief AIDS fighter.

Vaccine research. Scientists in 1992 took major steps toward an AIDS vaccine. In June, researchers announced that they had found a species of monkey that becomes ill when infected with HIV. The monkey, called the pigtail macaque, is the first nonendangered species that could be used as an animal model in tests of AIDS vaccines. Also in June, scientists reported that an experimental vaccine had protected chimpanzees against HIV-infected blood in a laboratory test. The vaccine contained molecules found on the outside of HIV and HIV-infected cells, thus priming the monkeys' immune systems to recognize such cells as foreign.

U.S. statistics. The number of new AIDS cases in the United States rose by 5 per cent from 43,352 in 1990 to 45,506 in 1991, according to the CDC. As of Sept. 30, 1992, the CDC reported 242,146 cases of AIDS and 160,372 deaths caused by AIDS since June 1981, when the disease was first recognized.

Michael Woods

In *World Book*, see **AIDS**.

Air pollution. See **Environmental pollution.**
Alabama. See **State government.**
Alaska. See **State government.**

Albania underwent a political transformation in 1992. In March, the Democratic Party (DP) won a majority in national elections and emerged to form the country's first elected non-Communist government since Communist rule began in 1944. But the economic outlook in Europe's least developed nation improved little during the year. The government's first steps toward establishing a market economy benefited few Albanians, as unemployment remained high and consumer goods continued to be scarce. By winter, most of the country's citizens were still ill-fed and virtually dependent on foreign food aid.

Communist defeat. In the March 22 elections, the DP took 62 per cent of the vote. The Socialist Party—formerly the Party of Labor, or Communist Party—received about 25 per cent. A year earlier, the Communists had received a majority in the country's first multiparty elections. The nation's Communist president, Ramiz Alia, resigned his post on April 3. Three days later, the country's parliament appointed as Alia's successor DP leader Sali Berisha, a heart surgeon and former Communist who had helped found the DP in December 1990. Berisha named Aleksander Gabriel Meksi, an archaeologist, as prime minister.

Economic reforms. The new government confronted a soaring inflation rate of 150 per cent, falling agricultural and industrial production, and large-scale unemployment. As of March, an estimated 70 per cent of the country's labor force was out of work. In response, the DP announced a program of "shock therapy" designed to spur economic reform. Price controls were lifted, and on July 1, the government began phasing out a system under which some workers had continued to be paid 80 per cent of their wages after being laid off.

The impact of these moves on voters was reflected in local elections on July 26, when the Socialists won 41 per cent of the vote, compared with 43 per cent for the DP. The government was not helped by continuing disarray in the agricultural sector. In mid-1992, agricultural output for the previous 12 months was an estimated 80 per cent below that of 1989-1990.

On the positive side, about 80 per cent of Albania's farmland had been privatized by year's end. However, the rest of the government's privatization program had less success. Privatization of small local businesses made some headway. But the privatization of major state enterprises remained dependent on foreign investment, which was not yet forthcoming.

"Witch hunts" authorized. In August, the parliament passed a law authorizing state enterprises and offices to fire former Communists and denying them the right of appeal. Thousands of people lost their jobs. Critics accused the government of reverting to the authoritarian practices of its Communist predecessors. Berisha defended the law. Eric Bourne

See also **Europe** (Facts in brief table). In ***World Book,*** see **Albania**.

Alberta. Ralph Klein, a former mayor of Calgary, was chosen to lead Alberta's Progressive Conservative Party on Dec. 5, 1992, after Premier Donald R. Getty announced his resignation on September 9. Klein was sworn into office on December 14.

He had tried to diversify the economy of the oil-producing province, which was buffeted by worldwide declines in oil prices. Although Getty's Progressive Conservative administration prided itself on sound financial management, its efforts to expand the economic base led to some costly mistakes. In May, the province had to sell its money-losing cellular telephone company, NovAtel Communications Limited, costing the taxpayers up to $614 million ($493 million U.S.). And despite the premier's promise that layoffs would not occur at Alberta Government Telephones after it was privatized in 1990, the public utility announced on Sept. 24, 1992, that it needed to reduce employment by 16 per cent, or about 1,500 jobs.

The budget, released on April 13, also contained bad news for the Getty ministry. The balanced budget promised for 1991-1992 had not been achieved, and a deficit of $2.3 billion ($1.8 billion U.S.) was forecast for 1992-1993, bringing the accumulated provincial debt to $14.4 billion ($11.5 billion U.S.). For the first time since the 1930's, the debt exceeded the amount contained in the province's rainy-day fund, which was $12 billion ($9.6 billion U.S.). David M. L. Farr

In ***World Book,*** see **Alberta**.

Algeria. Political upheaval followed the unexpected resignation of President Chadli Bendjedid on Jan. 11, 1992. Three days later, military leaders established a five-member ruling council headed by Mohammed Boudiaf, a hero of Algeria's war of independence from 1954 to 1962 who had lived in exile since 1963.

Bendjedid's resignation apparently was forced by the military, which feared Islamic fundamentalists would gain control of the parliament in runoff elections scheduled for Jan. 16, 1992. In the first round of voting, held in December 1991, the fundamentalist Islamic Salvation Front (FIS) won 188 of 230 seats. In the second round of voting, the FIS was expected to win a two-thirds majority in the 430-seat parliament.

Fundamentalist crackdown. Moving quickly to crush the fundamentalists, the council set aside the results of the December 1991 vote and canceled the January 1992 elections. On January 22, the council arrested the acting leader of the FIS and outlawed all public gatherings. Other arrests followed.

Sporadic confrontations between fundamentalists and government forces escalated into widespread violence on February 7, when rioting broke out in nearly all Algeria's large cities. More than 40 people were killed and hundreds injured. On February 9, the government declared a state of emergency. An Algerian court banned the FIS and ordered the detention of 10,000 suspected Islamic activists on March 4. On April 22, the FIS called for armed resistance.

Boudiaf was shot to death on June 29 while making a public address. The government blamed the FIS, which accused the military forces of ordering the assassination to discredit the fundamentalists. Ali Kafi, another war hero, replaced Boudiaf as the head of the ruling council.

Trials and turmoil. In early May, a military court imposed the death penalty on at least 13 Islamic activists convicted of killing three soldiers in 1991. But two top leaders of the FIS, on trial for antigovernment activity and other offenses, received only 12-year sentences on July 15, 1992. Algerian newspapers suggested that the sentences were lighter than expected because the government feared renewed violence.

Violent confrontations between government forces and the fundamentalists continued throughout the rest of the year. By December, at least 300 people had been killed in the clashes.

In October, the government ordered all fundamentalists wanted by security forces to surrender within 40 days or face trial and mandatory prison sentences. On December 5, the government imposed an all-night curfew in Algiers, the capital, and in five provinces. At the same time, about 30,000 government troops began searching fundamentalist neighborhoods for fugitives. Christine Helms

See also **Africa** (Facts in brief table). In ***World Book,*** see **Algeria**.

Angola. See **Africa**.

Animal. See **Cat; Conservation; Dog; Zoology; Zoos.**

Anthropology. An ongoing debate over the origins of modern human beings remained intense in 1992. Two studies published in February strongly challenged a landmark genetic study that traced the origin of all modern people to a hypothetical woman living in Africa about 200,000 years ago. This research had served as an important foundation for the single origin theory of modern human evolution, one of two main theories explaining where and when modern human beings first appeared.

The single origin theory, popularly known as the Eve Hypothesis, contends that *Homo sapiens* evolved only in Africa and then spread out through the rest of the world, completely replacing more primitive human forms. A second major explanation for modern human evolution, known as the multiregional theory, argues that different groups of *Homo erectus,* a more primitive species that had spread out of Africa before 1 million years ago, developed into *Homo sapiens* in Africa, Europe, and Asia at roughly the same time.

A landmark study. The most important study supporting the single origin theory was research reported in 1987 by scientists led by molecular biochemist Allan C. Wilson of the University of California at Berkeley. Wilson and his co-workers examined mitochondrial DNA (deoxyribonucleic acid), a type of DNA that is inherited only from females and so is unaltered by genetic mixing from generation to generation. The researchers theorized that any *mutations* (changes) found in the DNA represent random genetic changes that have occurred over time and that the greater the number of mutations in the mitochondrial DNA in a population, the older that population is.

The scientists conducted a statistical analysis of the information on the mutation rate using a sophisticated computer program that produced a human family tree. They reported that the tree was rooted in Africa, indicating that the earliest modern human beings were African. By estimating the rate at which the mutations occurred, they determined that some populations of *Homo sapiens* began leaving Africa about 200,000 years ago.

In February 1992, however, geneticist Alan R. Templeton of Washington University in St. Louis, Mo., and another group of scientists at Pennsylvania State University in University Park independently reported finding flaws in the computer program used by Wilson and his colleagues. They contended that the order in which the data were entered into the program determined whether the tree was rooted in Africa or elsewhere—Asia, for example. As a result, the scientists argued that mitochondrial analysis was not a reliable method for dating the initial migration of modern people out of Africa.

Transitional skulls? The discovery in China of two skulls that may represent a transitional form between *Homo erectus* and *Homo sapiens* was reported in June 1992 by paleontologists Li Tianyuan of the

A 350,000-year-old human skull with modern and primitive traits found in June suggests that modern human beings evolved in Asia as well as Africa.

Hubei Institute of Archaeology in China and Dennis A. Etler from Berkeley. The scientists reported that the skulls, which they estimated are about 350,000 years old, display a combination of primitive and more modern characteristics. Specifically, the scientists pointed to the skulls' flat faces, associated with *Homo sapiens,* and their long, low, angled braincase, typical of *Homo erectus*. According to Etler and Li, the find suggests that *Homo sapiens* evolved in China as well as Africa and provides support for the multiregional theory. But some scientists argued that the skulls were too badly crushed to make definitive judgments about their characteristics.

Oldest *Homo* fossil? A 2.4-million-year-old fossilized skull fragment found in Kenya in 1967 is the oldest known evidence of the genus *Homo,* according to research published in February 1992. (The genus *Homo* includes all living people and their direct prehistoric ancestors.) Anthropologist Andrew Hill of Yale University in New Haven, Conn., and anatomist Steven Ward of Northeastern Ohio Universities College of Medicine in Rootstown, who identified the fossil, reported that the skull fragment is 500,000 years older than the oldest previously known *Homo* fossil. But other scientists argued that the fossil actually represents *Australopithecus,* an apelike creature that was an ancestor of *Homo*. Donald C. Johanson

In ***World Book,*** see **Anthropology; Prehistoric people.**

An ornate box, whose discovery near Jerusalem was reported in August, may hold the bones of Caiaphas, the Jewish high priest who presided over the trial of Jesus.

Archaeology. A bronze foot found on the floor of the Mediterranean Sea off Brindisi in southern Italy in July 1992 led archaeologists to one of the most important discoveries of ancient Greek and Roman statues ever made. At the site, archaeologists uncovered a collection of more than 1,000 bronze heads, hands, arms, and other body parts from dismembered statues. It is the most diverse collection—both in style and period—of classical bronzes known. The pieces are expected to reveal important new information about classical bronze sculpture as well as the technical aspects of bronze casting.

The Brindisi bronzes, as they are called, date from the 300's B.C. to the A.D. 200's. Archaeologists believe the ship carrying the bronzes sank sometime between the A.D. 200's and 400's. Most of the bronzes are life size, though some are up to four times larger. Among the recognizable pieces are the heads of a Roman emperor, a philosopher, and Nike, the goddess of victory.

None of the pieces fit together. For this reason and because the bronzes span different historical periods, archaeologists believe the collection represents a cargo of scrap bronze destined for recycling. Few ancient bronze sculptures have survived to the present, mainly because most were melted down and the metal was reused, especially after the rise of Christianity and the fall of the last Roman emperor in A.D. 476.

Africans' burial ground. Excavations continued in New York City in 1992 at a colonial burial ground used mostly for enslaved Africans. The cemetery, discovered in 1991, is the oldest municipal African cemetery and the only such cemetery dating from before the Revolutionary War in America (1775-1783).

The cemetery, which was used from 1712 to 1790, was established after the government of New York ordered that African slaves could no longer be buried at a cemetery that had also been used for whites. Archaeologists estimated that the Africans' cemetery may hold as many as 20,000 graves. By October 1992, 420 skeletons had been excavated. Scientists believe that a study of the skeletons will reveal important new information about the physical, social, and economic conditions of New York City's African community at a time when blacks were beginning to adapt to life in the New World.

The graves were found during construction of an office complex for the General Services Administration (GSA), an agency of the United States government. Archaeologists evaluating historical records relating to the site had reported that it was unlikely that undisturbed burials still remained. But in September 1991, construction workers discovered a number of intact graves.

At first, the archaeological excavations proceeded rapidly, with, critics charged, little input from New York City's black community and inadequate thought about the study and ultimate disposition of the remains. In addition, work also continued on the office building. After numerous protests, the House of Representatives' Subcommittee on Public Buildings and Grounds, which oversees federal construction projects, halted work at the site. On Oct. 6, 1992, President George Bush signed a law that ended all construction in the cemetery. At that time, the GSA also agreed to recommendations made by a federal advisory panel concerning the study and reburial of the remains, the creation of a memorial at the site, and the establishment of a museum of African-American history in New York City.

Ancient textiles returned. Forty-eight ancient ceremonial garments that were smuggled out of Bolivia in the 1980's were returned to Bolivia by the United States on Sept. 24, 1992. The textiles, some of which are more than 500 years old, are sacred to the Aymara people of Coroma, Bolivia. The people of Coroma had argued that the garments, valued at more than $400,000, had been taken from Bolivia in violation of a 1970 United Nations convention on the illegal trade of cultural properties.

The Aymara people, a group of Andean Indians, venerate the textiles, which they believe embody the souls of ancestors who wore the garments. Through the ancient weavings, the Aymara communicate with their ancestors and receive advice on marriages, the selection of community leaders, and the timing of planting and harvesting.

In the 1970's, some North American antiquities dealers allegedly began hiring Bolivian middlemen to bribe members of the Coroman community into selling the garments and to smuggle them out of Bolivia. In 1989, the United States, at the request of the Bolivian government, placed an emergency five-year restriction on the importation of any antique textiles from Coroma.

Bolivian anthropologists helped trace some of the textiles to an art dealer in San Francisco. The Coroman community organized a network of North American Indians, anthropologists, and lawyers who worked with the U.S. Customs Service to force the dealer to return 43 of the garments under threat of legal action. Five other garments were returned by private collectors. But in 1992, more than 150 of the textiles were still missing.

Oldest bones in the Americas. A new radiocarbon analysis of an ancient skeleton found in Midland, Tex., in 1953 has confirmed earlier findings that the bones are the oldest known human remains found in the New World. Curtis R. McKinney, director of geologic research at the Center for American Archeology in Kampsville, Ill., reported in October 1992 that the skeleton, known as the Midland Woman, is about 11,600 years old.

Earlier radiocarbon studies had concluded that the skeleton was more than 10,000 years old. But some scientists had expressed skepticism that the skeleton was really that old. Mark Rose

In *World Book,* see **Archaeology.**

Architecture. The slow economy in the United States cast an even longer shadow over architecture in 1992 than it had in 1991, and contracts for major new projects were scarce. Growing uncertainty about the economic stability of the 12-nation European Community also stalled new construction overseas. Nevertheless, 1992 did mark the completion of two mammoth international projects and the launching of a third.

The 1992 Summer Olympic Games in Barcelona, Spain, lived up to their advance publicity, with all major facilities completed in time for the opening. The Sant Jordi Sports Palace, designed by Japanese architect Arata Isozaki, and the vast Olympic Village housing complex, designed by a consortium of young Barcelona architects, received the most critical attention. But to many visitors, the city itself held the most allure.

Instead of focusing only on athletics, Barcelona used the Olympics as an opportunity to reinvent itself on a grand scale. With $8 billion in public and private funds, the city refurbished its harbor and constructed subways, freeways, museums, theaters, concert halls, and more than 100 parks and public spaces. Architecturally, it vaulted to being a first-class European city virtually overnight.

Taking note of Barcelona's transformation, officials from Atlanta, Ga., site of the 1996 Summer Olympics, continued planning their own renaissance, which included spending millions on parks and public spaces. The 71,000-seat Georgia Dome, which had been constructed for the 1996 Olympics, opened in August 1992 as the new home of the Atlanta Falcons football team. In addition, the city planned to build or renovate 26 sports facilities, an Olympic stadium, and housing for 20,000 athletes.

A Mickey Mouse project. The Euro Disneyland theme park, on the outskirts of Paris, opened in April to nearly as much hoopla as the Olympics, but with more mixed reviews. For the export of America's most popular theme park concept, the Disney company hired French architect Antoine Grumbach along with such leading American architects as Frank Gehry, Antoine Predock, Robert Stern, and Michael Graves. The designers produced an entertainment center and fanciful hotels portraying such American themes as the Wild West, New York City, Sante Fe, the redwood forests, and the New England seaboard. By the end of 1992, Euro Disneyland had not attracted as many visitors as it had hoped. Disney officials announced in December that the park had lost $138 million. With some French critics decrying it as a cultural wasteland, the park's success was in question.

Architecture for art. The Seattle Art Museum opened its new quarters in January. Robert Venturi's 155,000-square-foot (14,400-square-meter) structure cost $62 million and incorporated designs based on the art of Native Americans in the Pacific Northwest. The building that formerly housed the museum was to

The new $62-million Seattle Art Museum, designed by architect Robert Venturi, opened in January to critical acclaim.

be renovated and reopened in 1993 to house other museum collections.

Shop 'til you drop. The largest enclosed shopping mall in America opened in August in Bloomington, Minn., near Minneapolis. Designed by the Jerde Partnership of Los Angeles, the Mall of America contains 400 stores and 44 restaurants, all surrounding a 7-acre (3-hectare) amusement park with a roller coaster and a log ride. As shopping malls throughout the country were attracting declining numbers of patrons, Mall of America's opening may represent either a new beginning or a last gasp for malls.

Fish stories. The year 1992 ushered in the age of aquariums. New aquariums opened in Camden, N.J.; Chattanooga, Tenn.; Newport, Ore.; and La Jolla, Calif. A half dozen more were in various stages of planning or construction. Unlike earlier aquariums, which essentially displayed fish in glass cages, the new ones typically feature habitats, such as rain forests, river bottoms, and tidal flats, and they deliver strong conservation messages to visitors.

Prizes. The first presentation of the world's largest award for architecture was given to Japanese architect Tadao Ando. The Carlsberg Architectural Prize of $235,000 was presented to Ando by Queen Margrethe II of Denmark on June 1.

Two other top prizes went to two comparatively unheralded designers. Boston architect Benjamin Thompson in February won the American Institute of Architects' gold medal for lifetime achievement.

Thompson is best known for creating festival marketplaces that helped revive the downtown areas of such cities as Boston, New York, and Baltimore.

In May, the $100,000 Pritzker Architecture Prize for lifetime achievement went to Alvaro Siza, a Portuguese architect. Siza was commended for his warm, modern houses and churches that respect place and local architectural traditions without ceasing to be forceful presences on the landscape.

The 125th birthday of Frank Lloyd Wright was celebrated in 1992 with several events. For the first time, public tours of Taliesin, Wright's home and studio in rural Wisconsin, were conducted. And renovation was completed on Chicago's 1888 Rookery building, designed by Daniel H. Burnham and John W. Root, and later remodeled by Wright.

Baseball parks. Tiger Stadium in Detroit, the oldest major league ballpark in the United States, was saved from the wrecking ball in April when the city's residents voted down construction of a new stadium using public funds. The move increased the likelihood that the old park would be renovated.

Baltimore's Oriole Park at Camden Yards, the new home of the city's baseball team, opened in April. It received universal acclaim for the playing field itself and for the restoration of two adjoining warehouses and a railroad station. David Dillon

See also **Art; Spain; Zoos.** In ***World Book,*** see **Architecture.**

Argentina. Continuing its fight against inflation, Argentina began 1992 with a new currency, its fifth since 1971. The new currency unit, the peso, replaced the austral, which had dropped to an exchange rate of 10,000 to $1 U.S. because of hyperinflation. To make it more difficult for the government simply to print money to solve economic problems, Argentine Economic Minister Domingo Felipe Cavallo mandated that new money be backed up by reserves of gold or U.S. dollars. With its currency in order, Argentina continued selling money-losing government enterprises to private investors. By the end of 1992, such sales to private investors both in Argentina and abroad were expected to generate some $20 billion in cash and debt reduction.

Argentine conglomerates. The shift from government to private ownership spurred substantial growth in the size of Argentine conglomerates, several of which have become world class companies. By buying up previously government-operated companies, Pérez Companc, for example, has become Argentina's largest industrial group. The company's assets are presently worth more than $2.5 billion and comprise investments in oil, construction, steel, cement, and agriculture, and ownership of a resort hotel, supermarket, and shopping center chain.

Stock market. The volume of stock traded daily in Buenos Aires, the capital of Argentina, climbed from $5 million in early 1991 to more than $60 million by the last quarter of 1992. Legislation was pending at year-end to boost that volume by removing restrictions on foreign ownership of Argentine companies and allowing banks to enter the brokerage business. If the Argentine Congress permits pension funds to invest in stock, another $300 million a month could be added to Argentine capital markets, according to Martín Redrado, chairman of Argentina's National Securities Commission.

He presides over the enforcement of regulations designed to ensure the development of a healthy national stock market. Redrado, a graduate of Harvard University in Cambridge, Mass., with a master's degree in public administration, oversaw trading on a stock market whose value increased by 400 per cent during 1991, his first year on the job, only to lose about half of that gain from June through August 1992, owing to a worldwide recession.

Nazi files opened. On February 3, Argentina's President Carlos Saúl Menem ordered that secret files on Nazi war criminals who sought refuge in Argentina following World War II (1939-1945) be opened to the public. The presidential order was a much overdue victory for Jewish investigators, who have long known that the country was a favorite hiding place for Nazis.

Israeli Embassy bombing. The problems of the Middle East exploded in Buenos Aires on March 17, when a powerful car bomb demolished the five-story Israeli Embassy. The blast killed at least 32 people and wounded more than 250, many of them children attending a nearby school. An anonymous caller from a pro-Palestinian group claimed credit, relating the violence to an Israeli attack in Lebanon.

Before the week was out, some 70,000 Argentines took to the streets to condemn the bombing. Argentina has Latin America's largest immigrant Jewish population (250,000) and largest immigrant Arab concentration (more than 1.3 million). President Menem, who is himself of Arab descent, called the bombers "beasts" and "traffickers in hate."

Patagonian Express to stop? The Argentine government had planned to close the "Old Patagonian Express"—one of the world's most famous railways—on July 31. But President Menem signed a last-minute decree allowing the train to keep running through the end of 1992. The railway runs 250 miles (400 kilometers) through extremely remote but scenic territory in the southern provinces of Río Negro and Chubut. The railway was reportedly losing about $1.5 million a year, and the government said the train would cease to run unless those two provinces helped support it. American writer Paul Theroux had popularized the train and its scenic route in his 1979 book *The Old Patagonian Express.* Nathan A. Haverstock

See also **Latin America** (Facts in brief table). In ***World Book,*** see **Argentina.**

Arizona. See **State government.**

Arkansas. See **State government.**

United States armed forces come ashore in Kuwait in August during exercises to maintain military preparedness in the Persian Gulf.

Armed forces. The United States and Russia agreed on June 16 to the most massive arms cuts in the 40-year history of the nuclear age. The historic agreement seemed to confirm the end of the Cold War and the policy of massive deterrence that had dominated U.S. military strategy for decades.

United States President George Bush and Russian President Boris Yeltsin announced that both nations had agreed to reduce nuclear warheads by nearly two-thirds by the year 2003. That level is a sharp reduction below the limits of the Strategic Arms Reduction Treaty (START) signed only a year earlier and ratified by the U.S. Senate in October 1992. The two sides finalized the new agreement, called START II, on December 29. Bush and Yeltsin signed the agreement on Jan. 3, 1993, in Moscow.

The reductions would be implemented in two phases. By the end of 1999, the U.S. nuclear arsenal would be slashed to 4,250 warheads; and Russia's, to 3,800 warheads. By 2003, additional cuts would limit U.S. nuclear strength to 3,500 warheads, compared with 3,000 warheads for Russia. In 1992, Russia and the United States had 10,237 and 9,986 warheads in their respective arsenals.

The treaty required both sides to eliminate their land-based multiple-warhead missiles. The United States would give up its MX and Minuteman intercontinental ballistic missiles (ICBM's) in exchange for the elimination of Russian SS-18 and SS-24 missiles.

U.S. troops to Somalia. President George Bush announced on December 3 that the United States would send 28,000 troops to the war-torn African nation of Somalia. The move was part of a United Nations effort to deliver food and medical supplies to Somalia, where civil war and famine killed at least 300,000 people during 1992. Armed forces from the United States and several other countries took Somalia's capital and moved toward areas of heaviest famine in mid-December. The Bush Administration said it hoped the U.S. forces could return by the end of January 1993, but military leaders said the mission would probably require more time. (See **Somalia.**)

Strategic developments. The disintegration of the Soviet Union and the collapse of totalitarian regimes in Eastern Europe enabled the Bush Administration to scale back dramatically the enormous defense build-up of the 1980's. The Bush Administration said that defense spending could be reduced between $40-billion and $50 billion over six years without jeopardizing the military's basic strength or its ability to respond to regional conflicts.

Even before Bush and Yeltsin reached their arms control agreement, modernization of U.S. *strategic* (long-range) forces had been sharply curtailed. In January, U.S. Secretary of Defense Richard B. Cheney announced that the B-2 Stealth bomber program would be canceled after the production of 20 aircraft and that the single-warhead Midgetman ICBM would be terminated. Cheney announced that production of advanced cruise missiles would also be reduced from 1,000 to 640.

The Bush Administration, however, continued to give high priority to the Strategic Defense Initiative (popularly known as Star Wars). This program is designed to destroy enemy missiles in space.

In June, the U.S. Department of Defense deactivated the Strategic Air Command (SAC), the symbol of U.S. nuclear deterrence for 46 years. SAC's nuclear bombers and missiles became part of a new Strategic Command controlling all Navy and Air Force nuclear weapons.

Conventional weapons. Development proceeded on a variety of new U.S. conventional weapons in 1992. These weapons included an experimental jet fighter and the SSN-21 Seawolf-class attack submarine. Several projects were severely curtailed, however, including the Seawolf program. The Bush Administration ordered construction on the new submarine halted after the first ship was complete. The U.S. Congress subsequently approved funds for a second submarine, however.

Troubles beset various military aircraft under development in 1992. Air Force officials claimed in August that problems that had caused the B-2 Stealth bomber to fail a 1991 test of its radar-evading capabilities could be corrected. But the officials declined to discuss how much the repairs would cost. The Air Force grounded 14 B-1B bombers on March 17, 1992, after cracks were discovered in their landing gear. A test model of the controversial V-22 Osprey tilt-rotor aircraft crashed into the Potomac River near Washington, D.C., on July 20, killing seven people. The accident called into question the future of the aircraft, which takes off like a helicopter and tilts its rotors forward to fly like a regular plane. The Pentagon had sought to cancel the Osprey program in 1991, but congressional pressure forced Cheney to release $790 million in development funds three weeks before the crash. The only flying prototype of the Air Force's F-22 advanced tactical fighter crashed at Edwards Air Force Base in California in April 1992. The F-22 is expected to replace the F-15 as the Air Force's primary jet fighter by the year 2000.

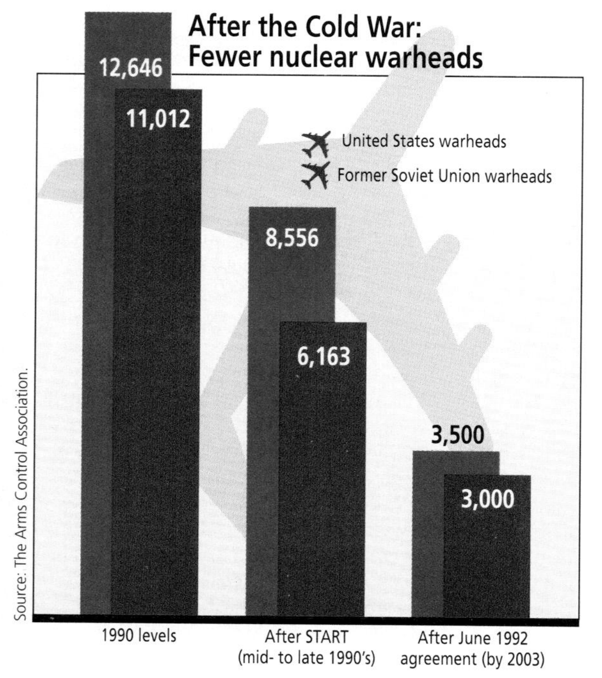

The arms reduction pact that the United States and Russia reached in June will dramatically cut each nation's nuclear warheads by the year 2003.

Other defense changes affected the Navy's fleet of warships. The Navy decommissioned its last active battleship, the U.S.S. *Missouri*, on March 31, 1992. The *Missouri*, scene of the Japanese surrender ending World War II in 1945, was recommissioned in 1986. The Navy commissioned the U.S.S. *Maryland*, the 13th Trident nuclear missile submarine, in June 1992.

Tailhook scandal. Charges of sexual harassment rocked the Navy in 1992 and forced the resignation of Secretary of the Navy H. Lawrence Garrett III in June. The Navy forced other senior officers to retire in what became known as the Tailhook scandal. Controversy arose after Lieutenant Paula Coughlin complained that several officers sexually assaulted her during a September 1991 convention of the Tailhook Association, a group of naval aviators named for the cable that stops planes landing on aircraft carriers. An investigation determined that at least 26 women had been sexually harassed during the convention in Las Vegas, Nev. Garrett resigned after Coughlin made her charges public and accused the Navy of failing to pursue vigorously its investigation of the incident.

In an unusually harsh report issued on Sept. 24, 1992, the Pentagon inspector general accused the Navy of "management failures and personal failures" that suppressed the investigation. The report suggested that some Navy officials may have deliberately restricted the scope of the investigation. Two senior officers were forced to retire, and a third was reassigned as a result of the scandal.

Cheney appointed Sean C. O'Keefe acting secretary of the Navy on July 7. O'Keefe had been comptroller of the Defense Department. He said the Tailhook incident reflected "a cultural problem which has allowed demeaning behavior and attitudes towards women to exist within the Navy," and he vowed to drive offenders from the service.

Combat role of women. The Tailhook scandal refocused attention on the debate over the role of women in combat. On November 2, a 15-member presidential commission created in 1991 to review the role of women in combat said that the military services should assign personnel to combat positions according to their qualifications, regardless of sex. It also recommended that women be allowed to volunteer for combat positions. The President and the Pentagon will formulate new guidelines in 1993.

Homosexual ban. On Nov. 11, 1992, U.S. President-elect Bill Clinton said he would lift the ban on homosexuals in the military after he takes office in January 1993. Clinton said he would study ways to proceed with lifting the ban.

A U.S. federal judge ordered the Navy on Nov. 11, 1992, to reinstate a sailor who was discharged earlier in the year after he publicly declared his homosexuality. In June, the Army removed a highly decorated Vietnam veteran from the National Guard after she admitted she was a lesbian. Colonel Margarethe Cammermeyer was discharged as chief of nursing for Washington state's Army National Guard despite an exemplary service record and the recommendation of superiors that she be retained.

Persian Gulf. Two years after U.S. forces were first deployed to the Persian Gulf in response to Iraq's 1990 invasion of Kuwait, the United States continued to maintain a sizable military presence in the region. Approximately 24,000 U.S. troops remained in the gulf, mostly offshore. About 2,000 Army and Marine Corps troops were deployed to Kuwait on August 3 and 4, 1992 for extended military maneuvers. In order to protect Iraqi Muslim minority groups under attack from the Iraqi Air Force, Bush announced a "no-fly zone" in southern Iraq in August 1992. The order said that any Iraqi aircraft entering the area south of the 32nd parallel would be shot down.

Despite the success of Operation Desert Storm, the war continued to generate considerable controversy. A U.S. General Accounting Office report in September cast doubt on the success of the Army's Patriot air defense missiles. The report suggested that only 9 per cent of Iraqi Scud missiles fired on by Patriots had been destroyed. In April, the Army downgraded its initial estimate of Patriot missile effectiveness from 80 per cent to between 40 per cent and 70 per cent.

Force reductions. United States budget realities and the diminishing threat from the former Soviet Union prompted plans in 1992 for even more substantial force reductions than those that were already underway. Congressional officials said the Pentagon had quietly begun planning for up to $80 billion in additional spending reductions over five years. Several dozen U.S. bases were already scheduled for closing by 1996, and the Pentagon announced in August that it would cease or reduce operations at 70 more overseas bases by 1995.

Defense budget. The Defense Department's budget request for the 1993 fiscal year, which began on Oct. 1, 1992, was for $253.8 billion in spending authority, a decrease of $16.3 billion from the previous year's request and a decrease of 6 per cent after adjusting for inflation. The total budget request for defense, including defense activities of the Department

United States marines lower the U.S. flag at Subic Naval Base in November, marking the end of the U.S. military presence in the Philippines.

of Energy and other government agencies, was $274-billion. The largest budget items were a $4.05-billion request for the Strategic Defense Initiative, $3.3 billion for four Burke-class destroyers, $1.81 billion for the C-17 strategic airlift plane, $2.2 billion for the F-22 Advanced Tactical Fighter, and $2.7 billion for four B-2 bombers.

Domestic deployments. The Bush Administration gave major responsibilities to U.S. military forces in domestic disaster-relief and riot control operations during 1992. More than 30,000 troops were assigned to south Florida in August after Hurricane Andrew devastated the area. The troops delivered food, water, and medical supplies, built tent cities to house the homeless, and provided security. About 4,500 Army and Marine troops were ordered to Los Angeles on May 1 during rioting that followed the acquittal of four police officers in the beating of black motorist Rodney King. They were withdrawn on May 10.

Personnel. United States military troop strength was 1,794,664 on Oct. 31, 1992, a decrease of 179,049 from 1991. Active-duty personnel were scheduled to be reduced by 99,000 in fiscal 1993. A six-year plan was intended to shrink the size of the uniformed force to 1.6 million, almost 25 per cent fewer than at the post-Vietnam War peak of 2.2 million in 1987.

Thomas M. DeFrank

In ***World Book,*** see the articles on the branches of the armed forces.

The Nuclear Threat in the New World Order

By Leonard S. Spector

As the United States and the former Soviet Union reduce their nuclear arsenals, smaller countries strive to acquire the means of nuclear destruction.

The terrifying threat of global nuclear war became dramatically less menacing in the early 1990's as the Cold War ended, the Soviet Union collapsed, and the United States and Russia planned large-scale cuts in their nuclear forces. Despite the easing of tensions between the superpowers, however, the spread of nuclear weapons to other countries continued to pose a grave danger.

Some of the countries that would like to develop nuclear arms lie in the Middle East and Asia—regions where long-standing conflicts could lead to war and the use of nuclear weapons. In addition, a number of would-be nuclear nations, such as Libya and Iran, are led by militant dictators or driven by radical ideologies and might seek nuclear arms in preparation for aggression.

The breakup of the Soviet Union, moreover, has introduced new nuclear perils. With the weakening of central authority, some observers fear that Soviet nuclear materials and expertise could find their way to other nations seeking nuclear arms. Former Soviet republics where nuclear weapons are stationed could emerge as new nuclear powers. And ethnic and political clashes among the Soviet successor nations themselves could conceivably escalate into a nuclear conflict.

Other, more hopeful signs suggest, however, that the spread of nuclear

weapons may be slowing. For example, several countries that were trying to make nuclear bombs, including North Korea and South Africa, appeared to abandon these efforts in the early 1990's.

Glossary:

Atomic bomb: A nuclear weapon that achieves its destructive power by splitting the *nuclei* (cores) of such heavy atoms as uranium and plutonium. Also known as a fission bomb because it *fissions* (splits) atoms.

Hydrogen bomb: A nuclear weapon that achieves its destructive power by *fusing* (uniting) the nuclei of hydrogen atoms. Also known as a fusion bomb or thermonuclear device.

Strategic nuclear weapon: A nuclear weapon designed primarily to launch an attack from a great distance.

Tactical nuclear weapon: A short-range or medium-range nuclear weapon designed primarily to support conventional military forces on the battlefield.

Thermonuclear device: Another name for a hydrogen bomb.

Who has nuclear weapons?

Five countries have declared that they possess nuclear arms: the United States in 1945, the Soviet Union in 1949, Great Britain in 1952, France in 1960, and China in 1964. Since 1964, no other country has acknowledged possessing nuclear weapons. Nonetheless, weapons experts agree that three other countries—India, Israel, and Pakistan—could rapidly put nuclear weapons into action if they chose. South Africa had also reached this stage but in 1991 agreed to give up its nuclear weapons program. Although a number of other countries have sought to acquire the technology necessary to develop nuclear weapons, none of them has yet reached the stage of manufacturing nuclear arms.

Each of the five declared nuclear powers has developed both atomic bombs and far more powerful hydrogen bombs and has conducted numerous nuclear tests. These countries also have built elaborate systems for delivering nuclear bombs, including long-range bomber aircraft and missiles that can be launched from the ground and the sea. The United States and the former Soviet Union have stockpiled an estimated 25,000 to 30,000 nuclear weapons in their arsenals. But under the terms of a Strategic Arms Reduction Treaty and a subsequent June 1992 agreement between the United States and Russia, these two nations will reduce their stockpiles to a few thousand nuclear weapons each by the year 2000. The smaller nuclear states—Britain, China, and France—have an estimated 300, 350, and 600 nuclear weapons, respectively. Their stockpiles are growing, however.

Intelligence analysts believe that Israel has been able to build nuclear weapons since the late 1960's, India since the early 1970's, and Pakistan since the late 1980's. Of the three, only India is known to have set off a nuclear blast, a single detonation in May 1974 that the Indian government described as a "peaceful nuclear explosion," similar to those the United States and the Soviet Union were testing at the time for large underground excavation projects. Analysts estimate that India has the essential materials to build 70 to 100 atomic bombs. They believe Israel possesses at least 100 atomic bombs and may have as many as 300. Pakistan may have the materials for 15 to 20 atomic bombs.

The author:
Leonard S. Spector is a senior associate at the Carnegie Endowment for International Peace and the author of several books on the spread of nuclear arms.

These three nations also have the means to deliver nuclear weapons throughout their respective regions. Israel reportedly has both aircraft capable of carrying nuclear weapons and missiles with a range of 400 miles (640 kilometers). Israel is also reportedly developing a long-range missile that may have a reach of 2,000 miles (3,200 kilometers). India has aircraft suitable for nuclear delivery and will soon deploy a missile with a range of 180 miles (290 kilometers). Pakistan also has nuclear-capable aircraft but is still some years away from producing a missile that can carry a nuclear weapon.

South Africa placed its nuclear program under international monitoring in 1991. Inspections revealed that South Africa had the materials to build atomic bombs, though the amount of nuclear material has not been disclosed.

What it takes to build a nuclear weapon

Much of the know-how needed to build nuclear weapons, once a secret shared by only a few, can now be obtained fairly easily. What remains difficult is producing the nuclear explosive material for the weapon.

Nuclear weapons deliver their devastating power by unleashing the tremendous energy stored in the *nuclei* (cores) of atoms. A weapon that unleashes this energy through the *fission* (splitting) of heavy atomic nuclei is generally known as an atomic bomb. A hydrogen bomb, which is also called a thermonuclear device, produces a nuclear explosion through the *fusion* (uniting) of hydrogen nuclei. But first, it uses a fission explosion to achieve the high temperatures needed for fusion.

The material for fission may be either plutonium or highly *enriched* (concentrated) uranium. Many countries mine uranium. But the extremely complex facilities needed to enrich the ore for use in weapons cannot be easily obtained. Producing plutonium calls for a different set of facilities. Only a nuclear reactor can transform uranium into plutonium, and a plutonium-extraction plant, also known as a reprocessing plant, is needed to chemically separate the plutonium from the uranium that remains. A nonindustrialized country generally requires 10 years or more to build the installations for manufacturing the explosive materials used in nuclear weapons.

In addition, a would-be nuclear power must master the design of a nuclear bomb and build and test all the nonnuclear parts needed to *detonate* (explode) the nuclear material. Weapons specialists usually do not consider a full-fledged nuclear detonation necessary to ensure that an atomic device will work. But such a test probably would be required before a country produced the more complex hydrogen bomb.

Restrictions on nuclear weapons development

A would-be nuclear country that can overcome the technical obstacles to building a bomb still faces significant political constraints. The centerpiece of efforts to limit nuclear proliferation is the 1970 Treaty on the Non-Proliferation of Nuclear Weapons.

The Non-Proliferation Treaty (NPT), as the treaty is commonly called, divides the world into two categories: countries that had detonated a nuclear device before 1967—the United States, the Soviet Union, Great Britain, France, and China—and countries that had not. Under the treaty, the five declared nuclear powers can retain their nuclear arsenals and need not submit to international inspection of their nuclear facilities. The treaty does call upon these countries to negotiate in good faith toward nuclear disarmament.

By signing the treaty, countries without nuclear weapons pledge not to manufacture or import nuclear explosives, though they may acquire the

Who has the bomb?

Five countries have declared they have nuclear weapons: the United States in 1945, the Soviet Union in 1949, Great Britain in 1952, France in 1960, and China in 1964. Since 1964, no other country has acknowledged possessing such weapons. Nonetheless, experts agree that India, Israel, and Pakistan could rapidly deploy nuclear weapons in time of war. South Africa had also reached this stage before it gave up its nuclear arms program in 1991. A number of other countries have pursued weapons development, but none of them has yet managed to manufacture nuclear arms.

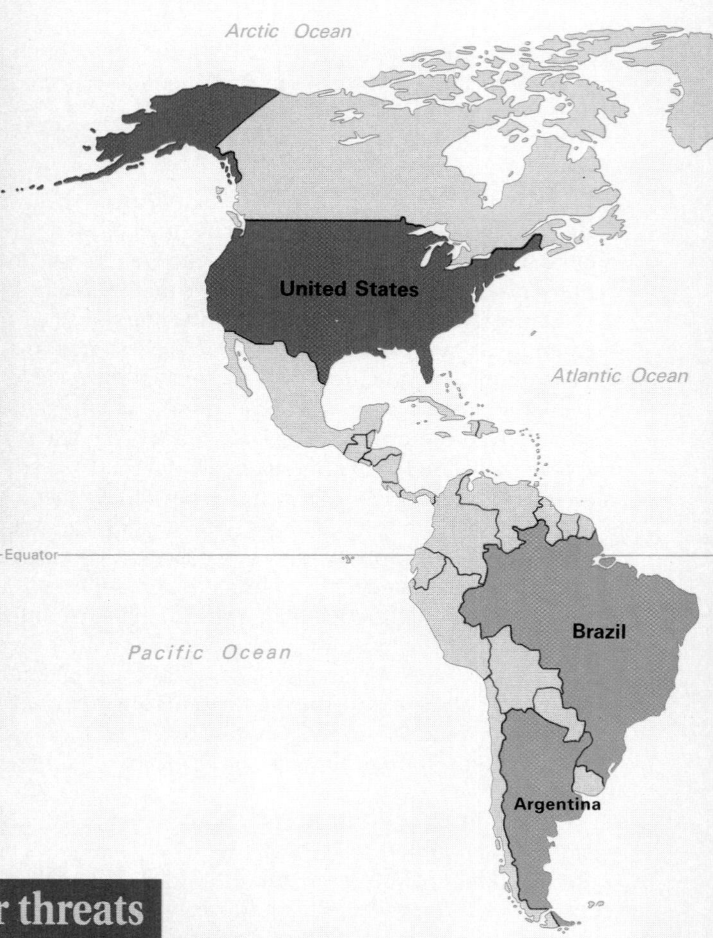

Potential nuclear threats

Middle East:
Israel and its Arab neighbors have fought four wars since 1947, and Israel was the target of Scud missile attacks by Iraq during the 1991 Persian Gulf War. In a war between Iran and Iraq from 1980 to 1988, both sides used chemical weapons and ballistic missiles.

Pakistan and India:
The two countries have fought three wars since 1948. A border dispute over the Kashmir region has repeatedly threatened to erupt into war.

North Korea and South Korea:
Agreements signed by both nations in 1992 have eased political tensions.

Former Soviet republics:
To raise much-needed foreign currency, the former republics might sell nuclear arms on their territory, or former Soviet weapons makers might sell their expertise. And ethnic and political clashes between Russia and other former republics could lead to war.

Terrorists:
Terrorists might attempt to achieve their goals by threatening to use a nuclear weapon that they had bought or stolen.

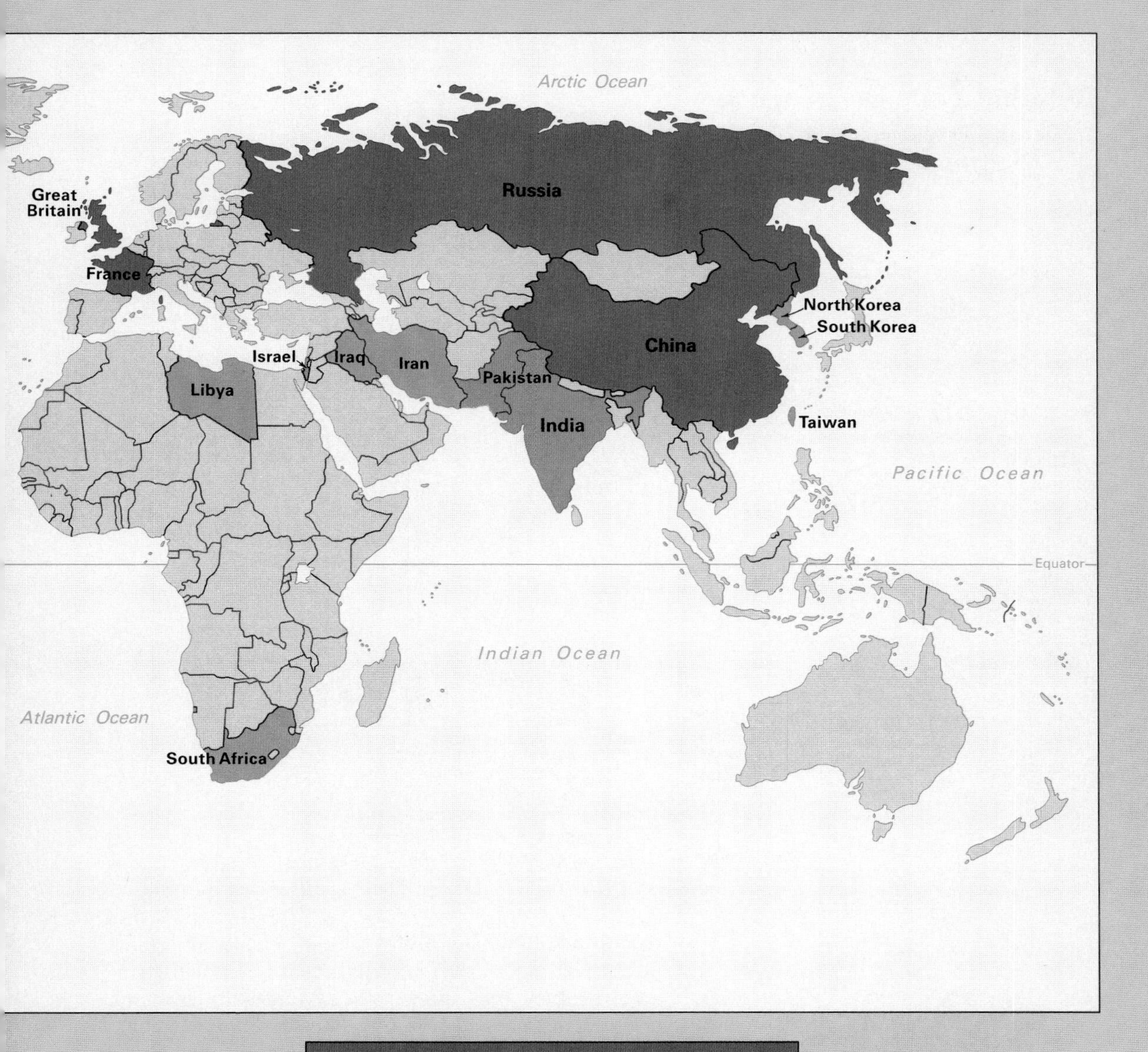

Countries that have declared they have nuclear weapons:
China, France, Great Britain, Russia, United States.

Countries that may have undeclared nuclear weapons or could quickly build them:
India, Israel, Pakistan.

Countries that have pursued nuclear weapons in the past or are doing so today:
Argentina, Brazil, Iran, Iraq, Libya, North Korea, South Africa, South Korea, Taiwan.

Building a nuclear weapon

The development of a nuclear weapon is no easy task. The assembly of the bomb and its triggering device requires nuclear explosive material, a great deal of technical know-how, and a vast array of mechanical parts.

Uranium ore provides the raw material for the explosive in a nuclear weapon. Many countries have deposits of uranium ore.

A nuclear reactor, which transforms uranium into plutonium, can be purchased for producing nuclear energy. But to do so, a country must agree to permit international inspections of the facility.

Uranium must be processed for use as a nuclear explosive. This can be done in two ways. A country can produce weapons-grade material by *enriching* (concentrating) the uranium or by transforming it into plutonium. Either way, building the necessary processing installations takes about 10 years.

A uranium-enrichment plant upgrades uranium into material for use in the core of a bomb. Its sophisticated components are difficult to purchase or manufacture.

Obtaining the materials and technology: Diversion

Some of the equipment used in nuclear power plants can also be used to make weapons. Because of agreements among the key nuclear suppliers, a country can legally purchase nuclear materials and facilities only if it places them under international inspection. Regular inspection makes it difficult to divert materials to weapons production, but a small number of diversions have occurred.

Obtaining the materials and technology: Smuggling

To avoid inspections on imported nuclear installations, some countries have built weapons facilities on their own, often relying on equipment smuggled out of more advanced nations. In 1974, the major supplier countries adopted strict regulations to control nuclear exports. Lax enforcement, however, permitted widespread nuclear smuggling during the 1980's.

technology and materials for building civilian nuclear power plants and other nonmilitary nuclear facilities. To do so, they must agree to permit inspection of all peaceful nuclear activities by the International Atomic Energy Agency (IAEA), an agency affiliated with the United Nations (UN).

By late 1992, all five declared nuclear-weapon states had become parties to the NPT, and 144 countries without nuclear weapons had signed the accord. Algeria, India, Israel, and Pakistan were the only regional powers to reject the treaty's basic rule that all nuclear facilities must come under IAEA monitoring, though Algeria hinted in January 1992 that it might sign.

Countries that export nuclear materials exercise an additional constraint on nuclear proliferation. Shortly after India tested a nuclear weapon in 1974, the advanced industrialized countries in the West and the Soviet bloc formed the Nuclear Suppliers Group. Members

A reprocessing plant, for separating plutonium from the remaining uranium, requires equipment that is strictly controlled. This means that a country seeking plutonium for weapons must engage in smuggling the equipment or else try to build the plant on its own.

Escaping detection

Nations trying to build nuclear weapons have adopted various strategies to evade detection.

- A country that has not signed the Non-Proliferation Treaty has no obligation to allow international inspection of all its nuclear facilities. Israel, India, and Pakistan fall in this category.
- A treaty signer can try to build a nuclear weapon secretly with smuggled parts and materials. Iraq chose this route, but its effort was discovered after the 1991 Persian Gulf War. This discovery led to tougher rules for inspections.
- A treaty signer may pretend to comply while secretly diverting materials from a nuclear energy program and delaying inspections. North Korea put off inspections for six years before letting the inspectors in. No country, however, has successfully diverted enough nuclear material for a nuclear bomb.

Assembling a nuclear weapon requires many mechanical parts and a blueprint. Would-be nuclear powers often manufacture and test the nonnuclear parts with smuggled equipment. They may develop the design from published sources or with secret assistance from a nuclear power.

of the group agreed to limit sales of nuclear technology and materials, which some of these countries had previously sold freely, and member governments adopted regulations on nuclear exports. By late 1992, 27 nations belonged to the Nuclear Suppliers Group. However, several new nuclear suppliers, including China and Brazil, had not joined the group.

Iraq breaks the rules

A few signers of the NPT have violated the treaty and tried to develop weapons facilities. Iraq, for example, pursued a secret program to enrich uranium during the 1980's. Iraq mined uranium within its borders and began building uranium-processing facilities with technology and equipment from Europe and the United States. The most important equipment was smuggled. But lax enforcement of nuclear export controls by a number of governments helped Iraq obtain the rest legally. In addition, Iraq purchased machinery that would enable it to manufacture the bomb-building equipment on its own. Until the 1991 Persian Gulf War, which was precipitated by Iraq's invasion of Kuwait, key parts of Iraq's nuclear weapons program escaped detection by the IAEA and intelligence analysts around the world.

After the war, UN and IAEA inspectors acted together to identify and destroy Iraq's nuclear facilities and equipment. But suspicions persist that one or two installations may have escaped discovery, and the inspectors never did succeed in obtaining a full picture of Iraq's smuggling network. UN experts estimate that Iraq was three years away from manufacturing its first nuclear weapon when the Persian Gulf War began. Resolution 687, passed by the UN in 1991 calls for long-term monitoring of Iraq's nuclear affairs, however, and prohibits all but the most harmless activities.

Steps to beef up proliferation controls followed the discovery that existing controls had failed to stop Iraq from developing a nuclear weapons program. The IAEA reactivated its long-unused authority to conduct "special inspections" of suspected, undeclared nuclear sites in nonnuclear countries that are parties to the NPT. Previously, the IAEA had confined its inspections to nuclear installations declared by the inspected country. The establishment in 1992 of a 100-person Non-Proliferation Center within the U.S. Central Intelligence Agency also sharpened a key mechanism for detecting treaty violations—U.S. intelligence resources, which include satellite surveillance. In addition, the UN Security Council has become increasingly active on non-proliferation issues. In January 1992, the Security Council issued an unusually strong reaffirmation of its commitment to stemming the spread of nuclear arms.

Furthermore, the Nuclear Suppliers Group decided in April to restrict exports of so-called dual-use industrial goods—sophisticated computers and other equipment that could have nuclear applications. The group also moved to ban major new nuclear exports to countries that operate facilities not subject to IAEA safeguards, namely Israel, India, and Pakistan. And in June, the five declared nuclear powers agreed to notify the IAEA of all transfers of nuclear technology and material they might make. This agreement marked the first step toward an international registry of all such transactions.

At the nuclear threshold

A number of countries have labored to develop nuclear weapons—and some are still doing so—without ever reaching the manufacturing stage. At the same time, several countries appear to have abandoned such efforts and accepted proliferation restraints. Argentina and Brazil, for example, built the key installations needed to produce nuclear arms during the 1980's. In 1990 and 1991, the two formally gave up their nuclear arms programs and agreed to open all their nuclear plants to inspection.

By late 1991, North Korea appeared also to have built the facilities for making nuclear weapons. Although the country signed the NPT in 1985, it thereafter refused to allow IAEA inspections. In December 1991, however, North Korea and South Korea agreed to mutual nuclear inspections and

Reducing the nuclear threat

As supervisors from the United Nations look on, workers pour concrete into equipment at a key Iraqi nuclear facility, *right*. A UN resolution passed in 1991 required Iraq to participate in the destruction of its nuclear weapons program. Under an arms reduction agreement between the United States and former Soviet Union, scrapped Soviet weapons are collected for dismantling, *below*.

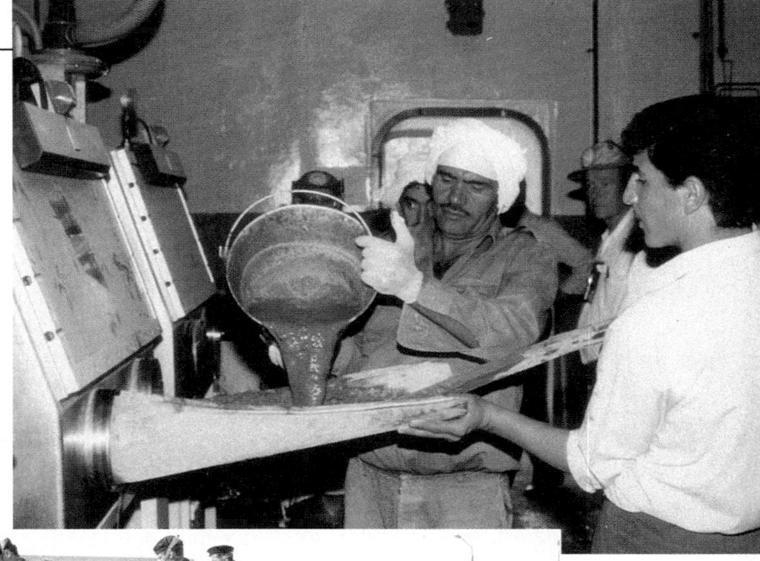

pledged not to build nuclear facilities capable of producing weapons-grade materials. And in early 1992, North Korea allowed IAEA inspections to begin. Although initial evidence indicated that the country had not yet managed to produce the key materials for nuclear weapons, suspicions lingered that it might have other, still-secret nuclear installations. Ongoing talks on implementing North-South inspections may help resolve these doubts.

Iran, although another party to the NPT, initiated a nuclear weapons program after its defeat in the Iran-Iraq War (1980-1988). Since 1990, Iran has reportedly sought the necessary hardware and technology in Western Europe and China. Nonetheless, the country possessed only limited nuclear facilities by the end of 1992, according to U.S. intelligence estimates.

To deflect suspicions about its nuclear activities, Iran agreed in early 1992 to permit IAEA inspectors to visit a number of sites it had not declared as nuclear installations. The IAEA did not observe any improper activities, though its visit was less thorough than a standard inspection.

Libya, another NPT signer, has sought unsuccessfully to purchase nuclear weapons. Despite continuing indications of Libya's interest in acquiring nuclear arms, it has made little progress toward this goal.

Algeria, which is not a party to the NPT, was secretly building a nuclear reactor with Chinese assistance that the United States discovered in early 1991. But Algeria later volunteered to place the reactor under the IAEA inspection system.

Syria was also pursuing nuclear activities with intentions described as "suspicious" by U.S. officials, though it has yet to build its first nuclear facility. Syria is a party to the NPT, and IAEA inspections will help keep its nuclear ambitions in check. Taiwan and South Korea largely suspended nuclear weapons efforts in the 1970's, when both joined the NPT.

Former Soviet nuclear arsenals

The collapse of the Soviet Union in late 1991 provoked fears that the new nations of Belarus, Kazakhstan, and Ukraine might seize the nuclear weapons stationed on their soil and emerge as nuclear powers. However, Russia has continued to exercise control of Soviet nuclear weapons, as stipulated in an agreement signed by the former Soviet republics in December 1991. By the end of May 1992, moreover, all *tactical* (short-range) nuclear weapons in Belarus, Kazakhstan, and Ukraine had been moved to Russia. In June, the three states pledged that *strategic* (long-range) nuclear weapons on their soil would be either moved to Russia or destroyed by 1999. No other former Soviet republic possessed nuclear weapons.

Russia succeeded the Soviet Union as a nuclear weapon state under the NPT, permitting it to retain its nuclear arsenal and exempting it from IAEA monitoring. But Belarus, Kazakhstan, and Ukraine agreed to join the treaty as nonnuclear weapon states "in the shortest possible time." This step requires them to place all materials in their nuclear energy programs under IAEA monitoring and to leave the nuclear weapons on their soil under Russian control. Once these arrangements are in force, the danger of new nuclear weapon nations emerging from among the former Soviet republics should be reduced.

But a far graver danger may threaten—the possible transfer to emerging nuclear weapon states of Soviet nuclear weapons, weapons-grade materials, nuclear know-how, and scientific talent. As of late 1992, however, U.S. intelligence agencies had been unable to confirm any of the numerous reports in the media of such transfers.

Regional dangers—and some bright spots

Although the danger of a full-scale nuclear holocaust arising out of a regional conflict has receded with the end of the Cold War, the possibility that a regional power might use nuclear weapons has not. Of particular concern is the Kashmir region in India. Disputes between India and Pakistan over this region have repeatedly neared the boiling point, most recently in the spring of 1990. During that crisis, Pakistan for the first time fabricated all the components for a number of nuclear weapons. Should war break out, military experts expect both sides to ready their nuclear forces, raising the all-too-real prospect of escalation to the nuclear level. The United States government terminated economic and military assistance to Pakistan in 1990, because such aid depends upon the U.S. President's ability to certify to Congress that Pakistan does not possess a nuclear explosive device. The United States is now urging both India and Pakistan to slow their nuclear programs and begin talks on regional nonproliferation arrangements.

A major conflict between Russia and another former Soviet republic is also possible. The Russian government could find itself brandishing nuclear weapons to deter the outbreak of hostilities or to prevent a military defeat. In addition, experts ponder the possibility that political instability in Russia may render the country unable to maintain long-term control over its nuclear assets.

Elsewhere, the threat of nuclear war has eased. In the Middle East, two recent events—Iraq's defeat in the Persian Gulf War and the renewal of Arab-Israeli peace talks in 1991—have significantly lessened the risk of large-scale conflict. In eastern Asia, the risk of conflict has similarly been reduced. The balance of power on the Korean peninsula has changed radically since the Korean War (1950-1953). North Korea lost a key ally when the Soviet Union dissolved in 1991 and in August 1992 saw another key ally, China, establish diplomatic relations with South Korea. In late 1991, North Korea signed a nonaggression pact with South Korea. Finally, a regional conflict involving nuclear arms in southern Africa became unlikely after South Africa and its neighbors negotiated peace settlements and joined the NPT.

Recent steps in controlling nuclear dangers have in many respects been astonishing. South Africa, Argentina, and Brazil have accepted comprehensive IAEA monitoring, after resisting it for years, and North Korea has finally permitted the inspections it agreed to in 1985. And for the first time in years, the United States and Russia can show they are negotiating in good faith toward nuclear disarmament. Yet curbing the spread of nuclear weapons will remain a prominent concern of policymakers around the world for the foreseeable future, as long as some nations continue to resist comprehensive nuclear controls.

For further reading:

Bailey, Kathleen C. *Doomsday Weapons in the Hands of Many: The Arms Control Challenge of the '90s.* University of Illinois Press, 1991.

Fischer, David. *Stopping the Spread of Nuclear Weapons: The Past & the Prospects.* Routledge, 1992.

Spector, Leonard S., and Smith, Jacqueline R. *Nuclear Threshold: The Global Spread of Nuclear Weapons 1990-1991.* Westview Press, 1993.

Armenia in 1992 continued its conflict with neighboring Azerbaijan over Nagorno-Karabakh, a region in Azerbaijan that is populated mainly by ethnic Armenians. The conflict had begun in 1988, after Armenians in Nagorno-Karabakh demanded that the Soviet Union transfer the region to Armenia. Armenia and Azerbaijan gained independence from the Soviet Union in December 1991.

In May 1992, Armenian forces took advantage of political chaos in Azerbaijan to seize control of Nagorno-Karabakh. The Armenians opened a road, known as the Lachin Corridor, linking the region with Armenia. However, Azerbaijan launched a counteroffensive in June and soon regained much of the lost territory. By mid-September, its forces controlled parts of the Lachin Corridor, threatening Armenia's access to the region.

In August, demonstrations rocked Yerevan, Armenia's capital, as protesters demanded that Armenian President Levon Ter-Petrosyan toughen his stance against Azerbaijan. In a special session of Parliament on August 17, opponents of Ter-Petrosyan failed to gain support for a referendum on his ouster.

The conflict crippled Armenia's economy in 1992. Azerbaijan blockaded railway links to Armenia during the year, causing severe fuel shortages from January through April. Justin Burke

See also **Asia** (Facts in brief table). In the World Book Supplement section, see **Armenia.**

Art. The ailing economy in the United States continued to bruise the art world in 1992. Private galleries continued to close, and public art facilities had to tighten their belts. But it was a surprisingly vigorous year for museum construction and renovation as plans laid in more prosperous times were finally realized.

On June 28, the Solomon R. Guggenheim Museum in New York City unveiled its extensively renovated, spiral-shaped building designed by American architect Frank Lloyd Wright. The building also received a new 10-story annex designed by Gwathmey Siegel & Associates. The museum's vast new exhibition space in Manhattan's SoHo district opened on the same day.

Thomas Krens, the Guggenheim's ambitious director who had pushed forward these projects, also had signed an agreement in February to build a museum branch in Bilbao, Spain. Architect Frank Gehry was commissioned to design the building. The $100-million project, to be funded by the local government and stocked from the Guggenheim's permanent collection, was expected to open in 1996.

The Seattle Art Museum in January 1992 moved into its new quarters designed by Robert Venturi. The 155,000-square-foot (14,400-square-meter) structure cost $62 million to build. And after almost three decades of planning, the University of California at Los Angeles opened its Fowler Museum of Cultural History, a $22-million showcase for the university's vast collections of ethnic art and artifacts.

Museums in Europe and Canada. Chicago financier and art collector Daniel Terra made international news in June when he opened the Musée Americain Giverny in Giverny, France, for his collection of American impressionism. The 9,000-square-foot (840-square-meter), $16-million building was designed by Paris-based architect Philippe Robert. The museum is located adjacent to French impressionist Claude Monet's house and gardens, a popular tourist attraction in Giverny.

In October 1992, Spain opened the splendidly refurbished Villahermosa, an early-1800's palace near the Prado in Madrid, to house most of the $2-billion collection of Swiss industrialist Baron Hans Heinrich von Thyssen-Bornemisza. The baron's holdings are said to be the world's second-best private collection, surpassed in quality and quantity only by those of Queen Elizabeth II of Great Britain.

Germany continued its museum boom by opening two new facilities in Bonn in June 1992. The Kunstmuseum Bonn is a city institution designed by Berlin architect Axel Schultes. And the Kunst- und Ausstellungshalle der Bundesrepublik Deutschland is a federal exhibition hall designed by Gustav Peichl of Vienna.

In Montreal, Canada, the Musée d'Art Contemporain moved into its new quarters located in Montreal's Place des Arts cultural complex. Quebec architect Gabriel Charbonneau designed the $33-million, 160,000-square-foot (15,000-square-meter) building.

Future construction and face-lifts. Several U.S. cities in 1992 revealed plans for new museum projects. In San Francisco, the California Palace of the Legion of Honor began a $25-million renovation, including the addition of underground galleries designed by Edward Larrabee Barnes.

The San Francisco Museum of Modern Art broke ground for a building designed by Swiss architect Mario Botta. Chicago's Museum of Contemporary Art unveiled a model of Berlin architect Josef Paul Kleihues' design for a 125,000-square-foot (12,000-square-meter) building to be erected near Lake Michigan. The Museum of Fine Arts in Houston chose Rafael Moneo as architect of a $40-million, 125,000-square-foot structure that will double the space of the museum's existing building.

The Barnes Foundation—a museum long known for the restrictive policies of its eccentric founder, the late Albert C. Barnes—was also slated for renovation. The museum, located in Merion, Pa., won a one-time-only court approval to tour about 80 French works from its collection as a means of raising funds to remodel its 1926 building.

The National Endowment for the Arts (NEA) remained controversial and in the news in 1992. In February, after Republican presidential candidate Patrick J. Buchanan accused President George Bush's Administration of supporting "pornographic and blasphemous" art through NEA funding, NEA Chairman John E. Frohnmayer was forced to resign. Anne-Imelda

New York City's Museum of Modern Art in 1992 included *Dance* in "Henri Matisse: A Retrospective," the largest-ever showing of Matisse's works.

Radice on May 1 took over as acting chairwoman. On May 12, Radice did not approve grants for two university art galleries for exhibitions containing sexual images. The National Council on the Arts, a 26-member advisory panel to the NEA, had recommended approval of the grants. The NEA's peer-review panels for visual arts and for solo performances protested Radice's decision by suspending reviews of grant applications. In November, Radice encountered more criticism when she refused grants for three gay and lesbian film festivals.

Threats to the NEA's survival were overcome—for the time being—when a measure to eliminate the agency's funding was killed in a 329-85 vote by the U.S. House of Representatives in July. In February, a Louis Harris poll of 1,500 people had shown that 60 per cent of Americans favored government support for the arts. Government funding for the NEA during 1992-1993 remained the same as for the previous year, $176 million.

Stolen art displayed. Art treasures—some dating back to the A.D. 700's—that were taken out of Germany during World War II (1939-1945) and worth as much as $100 million were exhibited in March 1992 at the Dallas Museum of Art. The cache had been housed in a church in Quedlinburg, Germany, and hidden in a mine shaft during the war. Joe T. Meador, a U.S. Army soldier serving overseas, came upon the art and shipped it home to Texas after the war. After Meador died in 1990, a two-year legal battle ensued between

his heirs and German attorneys, ending in a $2.75-million "finder's fee" for the family. The Dallas exhibition was then arranged, and, afterward, the artworks were returned to Quedlinburg.

Large-scale exhibitions. "Henri Matisse: A Retrospective," the largest compilation ever of the French artist's work, was displayed at the Museum of Modern Art (MOMA) in New York City from Sept. 24, 1992, through Jan. 19, 1993. Crowds poured into the museum to see the critically acclaimed show of 400 works. In addition to the museum's own extensive Matisse holdings, works came from such sources as the Hermitage Museum in St. Petersburg, Russia; the Pushkin Museum of Fine Arts in Moscow; the Statens Museum for Kunst in Copenhagen, Denmark; and the Centre Georges Pompidou in Paris. The exhibit was not scheduled to tour.

"Documenta IX," the 1992 version of an international contemporary-art extravaganza held every four or five years in Kassel, Germany, attracted a record crowd of more than 609,000 visitors. The $13.5-million display was the most expensive "Documenta" ever. Showcasing the work of about 200 artists from 40 nations, it was also the biggest. But art experts widely criticized the exhibition's curator, Jan Hoet of Belgium, because they believed the exhibit lacked standards and cohesiveness and included too much European and North American art.

"Degenerate Art: The Fate of the Avant-Garde in Nazi Germany," voted best exhibition of 1991 by the

"Documenta IX," held in 1992 in Kassel, Germany, assembled artworks from 40 nations and included Jonathan Borofsky's *Man Walking to the Sky.*

American branch of the International Art Critics Association, had an unexpected grand finale at the Altes Museum in Berlin from March through May 1992. The exhibition, which brought together modern artworks that Adolf Hitler had tried to defame, was scheduled to end in Washington, D.C., in 1991. But it stirred so much interest that the German government arranged for it to be shown in Germany.

The Summer Olympic Games in Barcelona, Spain, spurred a grand public art project. On display were such works as a 65-foot-(20-meter-) tall concrete and steel matchbook by Claes Oldenburg and Coosje van Bruggen and a 63-foot (19-meter) sculpture of a woman's head by Roy Lichtenstein.

The art market remained quiet through most of 1992. Nevertheless, a few spectacular works did switch hands. Paintings sold from the Matisse exhibition at MOMA gave the New York City auction houses of Sotheby's and Christie's a much-needed shot in the arm during the fall auctions.

The major spring auctions were disappointingly slow, with many works being left on the blocks. But in November, Christie's auction garnered the highest payment for a modern artwork since the beginning of the recession in 1990, fetching $14.5 million for Matisse's *Harmony in Yellow* (1927-1928). The price was the highest ever received for a Matisse work. *Waterlily Basin* (1919) by Claude Monet also yielded a hefty final bid of $12.1 million. Both paintings far exceeded Christie's hoped-for price of $7 million, and both purchasers remained anonymous.

Although Sotheby's November auction was less successful than Christie's, it, too, benefited from the sale of Matisse works. The artist's *Asia* (1946) was purchased for $11 million by the Kimbell Art Museum in Fort Worth, Tex.

A furor broke out among England's art lovers when Christie's auction house announced the sale on April 15 of *A Lady With a Squirrel and a Starling* (1526-1528) by Hans Holbein the Younger from the collection of the Marquess of Cholmondeley. English art lovers feared that only a wealthy foreigner could afford to pay the projected price of $25 million, and that the painting would leave the country. But the National Gallery of London bought the Holbein for $17 million in a private sale prior to the auction.

The J. Paul Getty Museum in Malibu, Calif., paid an undisclosed sum for Titian's painting *Venus and Adonis* (1555-1560). The painting had sold in 1991 for $13.47 million, a record for the artist and the highest price paid for any artwork sold at auction that year.

People. J. Carter Brown surprised the art world by resigning as director of the Smithsonian Institution's National Gallery of Art in Washington, D.C., after 22 years of service. A highly publicized search for his successor led to the appointment of Earl A. Powell III, who had left the gallery 12 years earlier to head the Los Angeles County Museum of Art. Michael Shapiro, former chief curator of the St. Louis (Mo.) Art Museum, succeeded Powell in Los Angeles.

In other high-level personnel moves, Robert P. Bergman, former director of the Walters Art Gallery in Baltimore, succeeded retiring director Evan Hopkins Turner at the Cleveland Museum of Art. Charles Moffett, former senior curator of paintings at the National Gallery of Art, became the first nonfamily member to head the Phillips Collection, a museum in Washington, D.C., when he succeeded retiring director Laughlin Phillips. Suzanne Muchnic

See also **Architecture.** In ***World Book,*** see **Art and the arts; Painting; Sculpture.**

SAM CLEME

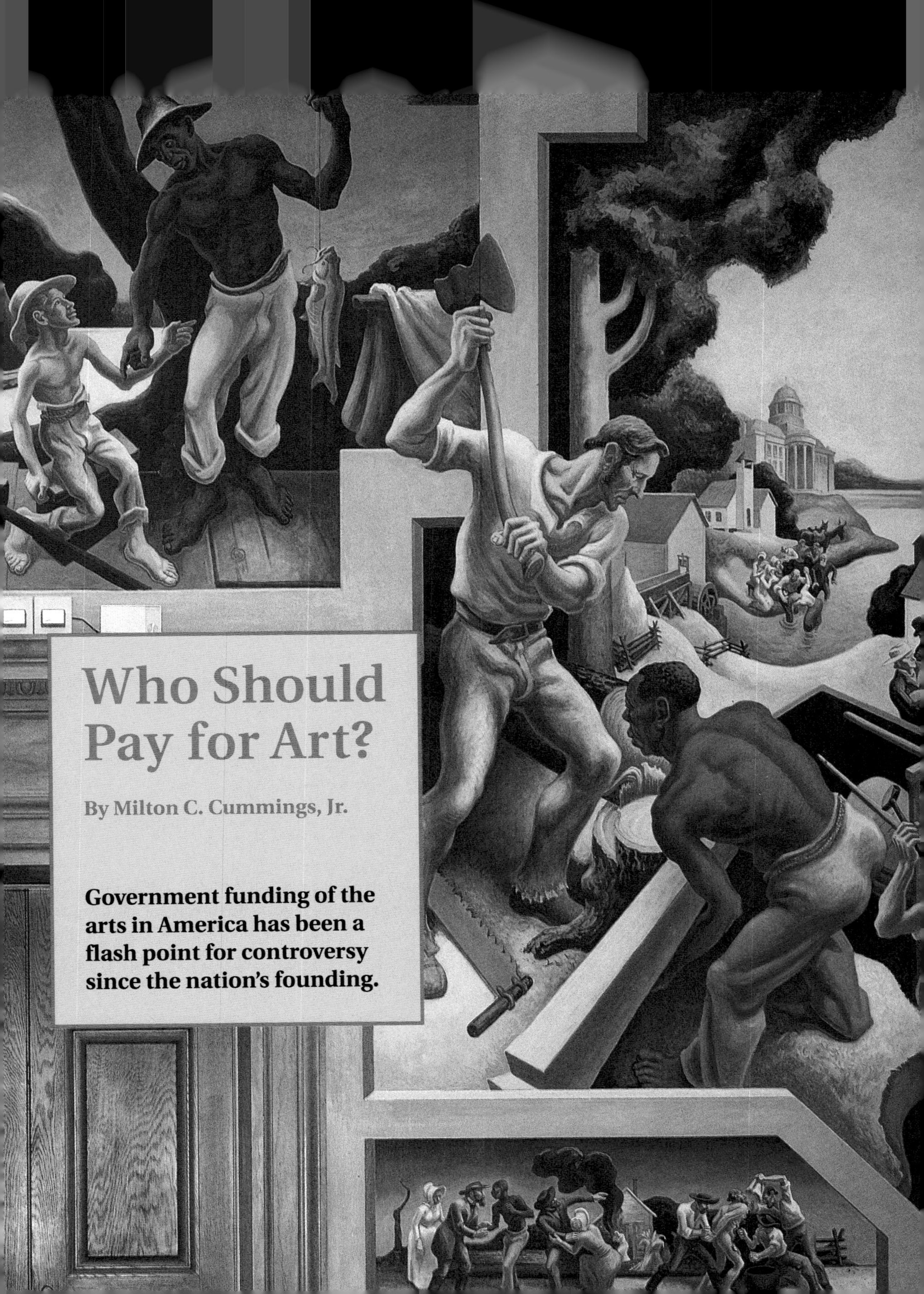

Who Should Pay for Art?

By Milton C. Cummings, Jr.

Government funding of the arts in America has been a flash point for controversy since the nation's founding.

Preceding pages: Thomas Hart Benton's images of the mistreatment of blacks and American Indians and portrayal of ordinary people in *A Social History of the State of Missouri* (1936), partly shown, provoked outcries from state legislators who had expected Benton to depict noncontroversial events and state heroes.

From 1989 to 1992, the National Endowment for the Arts (NEA), the agency that administers many of the federal programs for the arts in the United States, weathered one of its stormiest periods since its founding in 1965. The controversy culminated in the resignation on Feb. 21, 1992, of NEA Chairman John E. Frohnmayer. The attacks came from both political conservatives and liberals. Some members of the U.S. Congress and some conservative groups charged the NEA and Frohnmayer with promoting sexually explicit and sacrilegious art. At the same time, some liberal groups and members of the arts community accused the NEA of denying funds to certain artists for political reasons and of failing to provide vigorous opposition to restrictions placed on the content of federally funded art projects by Congress. For a brief time, Frohnmayer and the NEA even became an issue in the 1992 presidential campaign.

The debate focused mainly on the kind of art the agency should fund. Some people argued that the NEA, like any other government agency, was obliged to determine that the taxpayer dollars it dispensed were well spent. Specifically, they contended, the NEA should not fund projects that many people find offensive. Others argued that government restrictions on the content of publicly funded art represented censorship and, therefore, threatened freedom of expression.

Artists on their own

The very existence of this debate, however, is the result of a radical shift since the 1960's in the financial relationship between American government and the arts community. Unlike many European countries, which have subsidized their artists for centuries, America, for most of its history, has largely left artists to fend for themselves. During the 1800's and most of the 1900's, musicians, dancers, actors, playwrights, and other performing artists depended primarily on box-office revenues, while painters, sculptors, and other visual artists sold their work. Whatever additional financial support they had came mainly from private patrons.

Several factors accounted for the U.S. government's lack of involvement in the arts. In the late 1700's and early 1800's, when the nation was young, few people believed that the national government should fund the arts. Most Americans were more interested in the useful than the beautiful as they struggled to settle the frontier and build a new country. Demands on the federal treasury for new roads, canals, harbors, and other practical projects took precedence over the arts. Moreover, early American leaders, such as John Adams (who served as President from 1797 to 1801), did not put the arts high on the list of national priorities. As Adams saw it, he had to study politics and war, so that his children could study mathematics and philosophy, in order to give their children the opportunity to study painting, poetry, music, and architecture.

When government funds were allotted to the arts, it was for an official purpose—constructing government buildings, for example, and creating statues and paintings (usually of military or civilian leaders) to decorate those buildings. Even then, these modest attempts at publicly funded art had the potential to cause public scandal.

The author:

Milton C. Cummings, Jr., is a professor in the Department of Political Science at Johns Hopkins University in Baltimore.

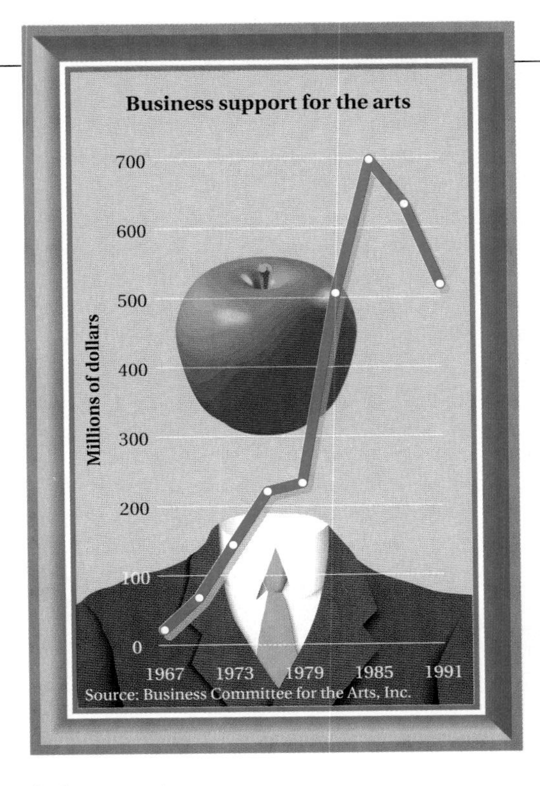

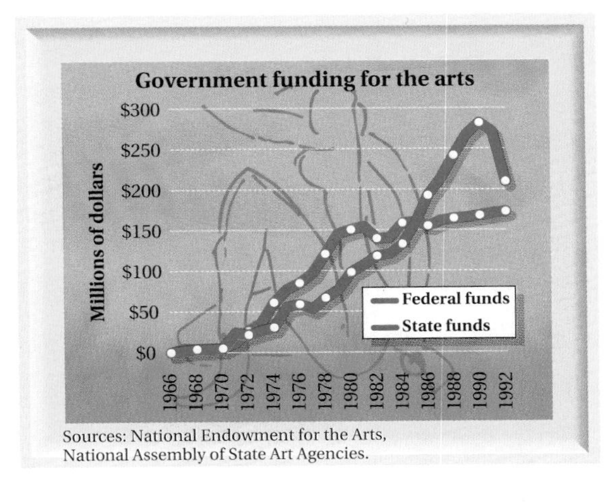

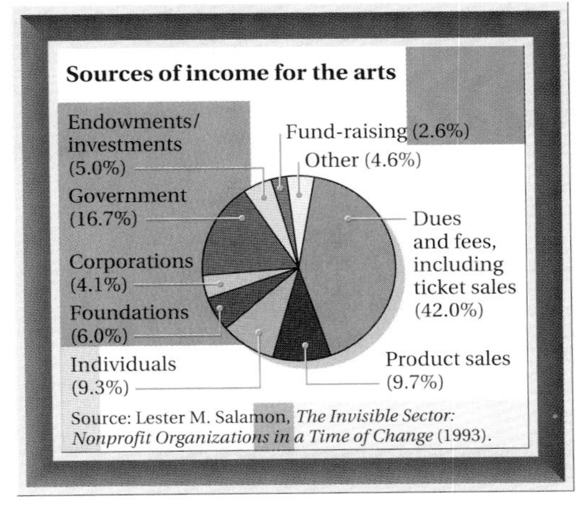

Art's new patrons

Most U.S. arts organizations obtain financial support from various sources, *right,* according to a survey of the 1989 operating income of 206 art and cultural institutions. Since the mid-1960's, corporations, *above,* and federal and state governments, *above right,* have become strong supporters of U.S. arts organizations. Although weak economic conditions have cut into state and corporate donations, federal subsidies for the National Endowment for the Arts remain steady.

In 1832, for example, Congress decided to commemorate the 100th anniversary of George Washington's birth in 1732 by commissioning a statue of the first President. Chosen to execute the project, which was unveiled in 1841, was an American sculptor named Horatio Greenough. The way in which Greenough posed Washington in the finished statue was traditional enough—seated with one arm extended and the other holding a sword. But the way in which Greenough dressed the figure was decidedly unconventional, especially for a revered Founding Father. Washington's upper body was naked; his lower body, covered only by a carved representation of a large cloth.

Outrage was the reaction of most people to the "naked statue." A New Yorker complained that the sculpture should be titled the "Venus of the Bath." According to a widely repeated joke, "Washington [was] reaching out his hand for his clothes, which were on exhibition in a case at the Patent Office." One congressman suggested saving the statue's head and throwing the body in Washington's Potomac River. Eventually, the sculpture was moved from the Capitol to the Smithsonian Institution. (It is currently on display at the National Museum of American History in Washington, D.C.)

Washington: a scandalous portrayal
A bare-chested statue of President George Washington, commissioned to commemorate the 100th anniversary of his birth, aroused shock and outrage when it was unveiled in Washington, D.C., in 1841. After sitting inside and then outside the United States Capitol, the statue ended up at the National Museum of American History, where it is now displayed.

Beginning in the mid-1800's, as the country became more settled, the arts came to occupy a more prominent position in American life. Between 1850 and 1910, the number of symphonies in the United States grew from 1—the New York Philharmonic—to about 30. The number of opera houses and concert halls rose from a handful to several dozen. One reason for this artistic expansion was the arrival of hundreds of thousands of European immigrants for whom symphonic music and opera were an integral part of their heritage. German Americans, for example, were instrumental in the establishment of symphonies in St. Louis, Mo., and Cincinnati, Ohio. Italian Americans were a driving force behind the organization of opera companies in San Francisco and other cities in the 1920's and 1930's.

Growth of private patronage

The explosion of personal wealth produced by the rapid industrialization and growth of commerce after the Civil War (1861-1865) was a major boon to the U.S. arts scene. Unlike Europe, the United States never had an aristocracy with private funds to lavish on the arts. In fact, until the mid-1800's, the United States had few truly wealthy families at all.

America's newly rich, who now had the leisure and resources to devote to culture, soon developed a passion for collecting great art and listening to great music. Also after the Civil War, wealthy individuals, either individually or in small groups, began founding art museums in major U.S. cities, such as New York City, Boston, and Chicago, in part because of their personal interest in the visual arts. But they were also motivated by a desire to improve the cultural environment of their cities and enrich the lives of the growing urban working class. Many of these philanthropists eventually donated their personal art collections to these museums. Thus, by 1900, the financial support system for artists and arts organizations in the United States rested not only on funds raised at the box office and gains from art sales but also on private donations from individuals.

During the first decades of the 1900's, a system of indirect government support gradually took shape. In essence, the government began to reward private philanthropy to the arts with tax savings. In 1916, Congress passed the first of several laws creating the modern fed-

Satire and patriotism

Intense anger greeted Grant Wood's 1932 painting, *Daughters of Revolution,* which portrayed members of a well-known patriotic organization—composed of the descendants of American rebels—as ultraconservative and smug. Wood slyly placed the women, whose organization was then anti-German, before *Washington Crossing the Delaware* (1851), a beloved American painting by German-born artist Emanuel Leutze.

eral income tax system. In the same year, it passed legislation establishing a federal estate tax. In addition to levying taxes, these laws also established tax deductions for donations made by private individuals to charitable organizations. Administrative interpretations of these laws soon established that contributions to museums, orchestras, and other arts organizations were tax deductible.

The deductions were valuable when tax rates were low. But they became even more advantageous when tax rates jumped upward, as they did during World War II (1939-1945) and thereafter. Since then, the financial benefits of contributing to arts organizations have provided an even greater incentive to private philanthropy.

In 1991, despite a weak economy and high unemployment, private donors, including individuals, foundations, and corporations, gave a record $8.81 billion to the arts, culture, and humanities in the United States, according to *Giving USA,* the yearbook of American philanthropy. And in 1989, donations from private sources accounted for about one-fifth of the total operating costs of arts organizations, according to a 1992 study by Lester M. Salamon, director of the Institute for Policy Studies at Johns Hopkins University in Baltimore.

Foundations and corporations lend support

Philanthropic foundations since the 1960's have become one of the most significant sources of private support for arts organizations. Foundations have been especially receptive to avant-garde or innovative arts organizations. Dance companies, in particular, have benefited from foundation grants. Such awards have not only provided the seed money for a number of U.S. dance companies but also continue to provide an essential source of support for many. In 1991, foundations provided more than $682.5 million for art and culture, according to the 1992 Foundation Grants Index compiled by the Foundation Center, a nonprofit clearing house for information on foundation and corporate philanthropy. In fact, the amount may be substantially higher, because that total includes grants reported

A perceived attack
California Industrial Scenes—Striking Workers (1934), partly shown, by John Langley Howard incensed people who interpreted his images of militant workers as a denunciation of the U.S. economic and political system. The prominent position Howard gave a black worker also stirred anger.

to the center by only 846 of the approximately 38,000 grant-making foundations in the United States.

Since the late 1960's, corporate America also has taken a keen interest in the arts. In 1967, the Business Committee for the Arts was established, and that year businesses allocated $22 million to the arts. In 1991, grants from businesses totaled $518 million. Business sees its support of the arts as good business. Corporations can receive financial benefits in the form of tax deductions by counting art contributions among their operating expenses. Many executives also believe that subsidizing arts organizations is a fairly inexpensive way to generate good will that may, ultimately, translate into increased sales of their products. And to some businesses, art subsidies offer an attractive way to help fulfill what they believe is a social responsibility to their community. Companies also know that a lively cultural life in their community helps them recruit top-level executives.

Government steps in

Meanwhile, the U.S. government had become involved with the arts. This involvement took the form of two major arts initiatives—the Works Progress Administration (WPA) federal arts programs in the 1930's, and the NEA, established in 1965. These federal arts programs inevitably led to controversy, which tended to center on two basic questions: Should the government be spending any public money to aid the arts? And if the government did spend money on the arts, did both government decision-makers and the general public like the art they got?

The WPA was a public jobs program enacted by Congress and President Franklin D. Roosevelt to help end the Great Depression of the 1930's. At that time, more than 13 million Americans, including many artists, found themselves out of work. The WPA's projects for artists were not only the first comprehensive U.S. arts program but also the largest public arts program in history. At their height between 1935 and 1938, the WPA arts projects employed more than 40,000 writers, painters, musicians, and other artists to produce and act in plays, hold concerts, and paint murals, among other projects.

Some WPA art projects, however, came under heavy political fire. A few of the Federal Theater Project's productions attacked America's free enterprise system. Some murals supported by the Federal Arts Project included Communist themes. And this provoked a fierce reaction.

In 1938, the House of Representatives' Committee on Un-American Activities held widely publicized hearings on some of the arts projects. Among them were skits, staged by the Federal Theater Project, that sometimes ridiculed public officials, and the play *One Third of a Nation,* a searching look at poor-

Opposite fates

Now widely honored, the Vietnam Veterans Memorial (1982), *below,* was attacked at first by some who thought it failed to convey the heroism of those who died in the Vietnam War. Public criticism of *Tilted Arc* (1982), *inset*—accused of obstructing its New York City site—grew so heated that the sculpture was dismantled in 1989.

housing and homelessness in America in the 1930's. In 1939, Congress slashed the funding for these projects. Soon after, the nation's resources were devoted to winning World War II (1939-1945) and by January 1943, the first federal arts program had come to an end.

The establishment of the NEA

After the war, some government officials and members of the arts community began campaigning for the creation of a new federal arts program. In large part, these advocates were personally interested in the arts and believed that the federal government should support art simply because art was important and worthy of public support. But advocates of new art programs also pointed out that the privately funded system then in place mainly served only New York City, Chicago, and other large cities that were major cultural centers. With public support, museum exhibits, dance companies, and musical groups could reach many more people in smaller cities and towns. In addition, the arts advocates contended that public investment in the arts would produce commercial spin-offs, such as increased restaurant revenue in theater districts.

Finally, arts advocates argued that government support for the arts would benefit the United States in its fierce postwar struggle with the Soviet Union for world leadership. They maintained that American art sent abroad would display America's creativity and culture and so attract other nations to the American political system. As a result, one of the first U.S. international arts exchange programs was launched in the early 1950's during the Administration of President Dwight D. Eisenhower.

Momentum for a federal arts policy grew during the Administration of President John F. Kennedy, who with his wife, Jacqueline, took considerable personal interest in the arts. But it was Lyndon B. Johnson, who succeeded to the presidency after Kennedy's assassination in 1963, who finally won congressional approval for a federal arts agency. In September 1965, Congress established the National Foundation on the Arts and Humanities, consisting of two grant-making endowments—the National Endowment for the Humanities and the NEA. Unlike the WPA programs, however, the NEA does not employ artists directly. Instead, it awards grants to private arts organizations, state art councils, and individual artists. Panels of experts in various art fields review grant applications submitted to the agency and make recommendations to the head of the NEA, who approves or rejects them.

During the 1960's, the NEA received only modest funds—$8 million at most. But in the early 1970's, under the Administration of President Richard M. Nixon, the agency's fortunes changed dramatically. Nixon wanted to make the arts available to a wider public and stressed this point at his first formal meeting with Nancy Hanks, whom he named to head the NEA. But Nixon reportedly also saw increased aid for the arts as a relatively inexpensive way to win political support in the arts and academic communities, groups that had generally opposed his election. By 1974, the NEA's budget topped $64 million.

For the remainder of the 1970's, the NEA budget grew steadily, reach-

Mapplethorpe protest
Demonstrators in Cincinnati protest the 1990 opening of a exhibit of photographs by Robert Mapplethorpe. The exhibit, supported in part by funds from the National Endowment for the Arts, included photographs of naked children and explicit images of men performing homosexual acts.

ing $158 million in 1981. That year, however, the NEA confronted its first major crisis. Newly elected President Ronald Reagan attempted to cut the agency's budget by 50 per cent as part of his effort to reduce government programs. Friends of the NEA both within and outside Congress quickly rallied to the agency's defense, however, and the budget was cut by only 10 per cent. Since then, the NEA's budget has risen or held steady almost every year.

The NEA is not the only government agency that provides financial support for the arts and arts organizations. Other federal patrons include the Smithsonian Institution, the National Gallery of Art, and the Institute of Museum Services, all in Washington, D.C. State legislatures in fiscal year 1992 allocated $211.9 million to state arts agencies, though this represented a sharp drop from the $273.7 million granted in fiscal 1991. In addition, city, county, and other local governments provide funds for the arts, including support for about 3,800 local arts agencies, according to the National Assembly of Local Arts Agencies, a clearing house and advocacy group for these agencies. Local expenditures for the arts in 1991 totaled at least $500 million.

But in the late 1980's and early 1990's, the NEA was certainly the most controversial government arts program. The trouble began in 1989 with protests against two arts projects that drew upon NEA funding. The first project involved an exhibit of the works of photographer Andres Serrano. Serrano had received a grant that included NEA funds through the Southeastern Center for Contemporary Art in Winston-Salem, N.C. Among the photographs in Serrano's show was the image of a crucifix submerged in urine.

The second project involved a $30,000 NEA grant to the Institute of Contemporary Art in Philadelphia, which organized a traveling exhibit of photographs by Robert Mapplethorpe. That exhibit included a number of photographs featuring naked children and explicit images of men performing homosexual acts.

Public reaction to the exhibits was intense. A fire storm also broke out in Congress when many people bombarded their legislators with objections to the use of tax money to support photographs they considered sacrilegious or obscene. In response, a number of legislators, particularly Senator Jesse A. Helms (R., N.C.) and Senator Alfonse M. D'Amato (R., N.Y.), attempted to bar NEA funds for "offensive art," which was broadly defined as "obscene or indecent materials, including but not limited to depictions of . . . homoeroticism, the exploitation of children, or individuals engaged in sex acts. . . ." The "Helms Amendment" did not pass. But in October 1989, Congress voted for the first time to impose a restriction on the content of publicly funded art. The restriction barred the use of federal funds for art defined as obscene under the standards of a 1973 decision by the Supreme Court of the United States.

As a way of implementing the law, Frohnmayer in 1990 began requiring grant recipients to sign a pledge not to use NEA funds to create obscene works of art. In June, he declined to make grants, recommended by an advisory panel, to four artists whose work dealt with nudity or sexuality. In August, however, the National Council on the Arts, a presidentially appointed group that advises the NEA, voted to eliminate the obscenity pledge for all future grants.

The battle over the NEA

During 1990, Congress faced the issue of whether to reauthorize the NEA to continue operating as a federal agency. The agency had been reauthorized in 1985 for a five-year period. Some legislators who argued for the abolition of the agency questioned whether arts funding was a productive use of tax dollars, especially considering the huge federal budget deficit. Other legislators worried whether art, a highly personal undertaking, was best left unfettered by government strings and regulations. Even some legislators who lent their support to the reauthorization bill insisted that tax dollars should not be used for art projects that citizens may find offensive or obscene.

Supporters of the NEA countered that a democratic society requires freedom of artistic expression. Such freedom, they contended, does not guarantee that every person will find every form of artistic expression to his or her liking. NEA supporters also argued that aid to arts organizations contributes to the economic vitality of the communities where arts activities are located and so provides a sound economic return. They also noted that the NEA budget is less than 2/10 of 1 per cent of the total federal budget. Eliminating the agency, they pointed out, would have scant effect on the federal budget deficit. Finally, they argued that, overall, the NEA has an excellent record. Of the more than 95,000 grants it has made in its history, only about 30 have aroused significant public controversy.

In the end, NEA critics and supporters compromised on a law to reauthorize the agency in 1990—but for only three years, rather than five. The law also called upon the NEA to reclaim any funds granted to an artist if a court later ruled that the funded art was obscene. In addition, Congress required the NEA to include on its review panels people with a wider range of artistic and cultural viewpoints and to monitor more closely how artists were using their grants. Finally, the law stated that the head of the NEA should consider "general standards of decency and respect for the diverse beliefs and values of the American public" when deciding whether to fund an arts project.

But after surviving their battles with Congress, Frohnmayer and the NEA were caught in the political cross fire of the 1992 presidential campaign. On February 18, Patrick J. Buchanan, a conservative challenger for the Republican presidential nomination, made a strong showing against incumbent President George Bush in the New Hampshire Republican primary. On February 20, Buchanan threatened to make the NEA—which he accused of "subsidizing both filthy and blasphemous art"—a campaign issue. The next day, the Bush Administration reportedly forced Frohnmayer to step down.

In May 1992, Bush named Anne-Imelda Radice acting head of the NEA. That same month, Radice declined to fund several sexually explicit art projects that had been recommended by NEA review panels. Once again, controversy flared. Her decisions drew heated criticism from many people within the arts community. But they pleased many conservatives.

Despite the controversy surrounding the NEA, America's commitment to the arts—both public and private—remains strong. Nevertheless, the relationship between government and the arts continues to be, in the phrase of writer Joan Simpson Burns, an "awkward embrace." For many in government, the goal of public funding is to make high-quality art available to the widest possible audience. Publicly supported art, they argue, should help define our national identity. At the same time, many government officials believe, taxpayers should not be forced to support art that they find obscene or offensive. For many in the arts community, however, the goal of public funding is to foster creativity in artists, though that creativity may sometimes shock the current public sensibility. Given the highly individualistic, deeply emotional nature of art, controversy about publicly funded art may be inevitable. It has been ever since the nation's founding.

For further reading:

Feld, Alan L., and others. *Patrons Despite Themselves: Taxpayers and Arts Policy.* New York University Press, 1983.

Public Money and the Muse. Ed. by Stephen Benedict. Norton, 1991.

The Patron State: Government and the Arts in Europe, North America, and Japan. Ed. by Milton C. Cummings, Jr., and Richard S. Katz. Oxford University Press, 1987.

Asia

Much of Asia in 1992 pursued economic change with varied success. Civil wars and rebel insurgencies were obstacles to progress in a few countries.

End to Afghan war. The civil war in Afghanistan came to an uncertain end in 1992 with the collapse in April of the Communist regime. *Mujaheddin*, soldiers fighting in the name of Islam, set up a temporary government in Afghanistan's capital, Kabul, on April 28. They were not able to agree, however, on how to run the country. By the end of 1992, the various mujaheddin factions were hammering out the guidelines for elections for a new government.

Cambodian truce. Asia's other big war of the 1980's—the civil war in Cambodia—subsided in 1992 as the United Nations (UN) launched a massive effort to bring peace to the country. The UN operation followed a peace plan agreed upon in 1991 by the country's four opposing factions. However, Communist rebels known as the Khmer Rouge broke numerous cease-fires, hampered UN activities, and refused to disarm their forces according to the peace plan. The UN peacekeepers faced the prospect of continuing war in the country.

Among the UN forces was a contingent of 600 soldiers from Japan. These troops were the first to be sent abroad by Japan since World War II (1939-1945). Under a law passed on June 15 by Japan's parliament, troops were permitted to be sent overseas but only for peacekeeping operations. Despite this condition, the growth of Japanese military power was the subject of much debate and concern in 1992, both within Japan and among Southeast Asian countries.

Guerrilla wars persist. In Sri Lanka, fighting continued in the 9-year-old insurgency by independence-seeking militants from the country's Tamil ethnic minority. The rebels capped off their 1992 terrorist campaign on November 16, when a Tamil assassin killed Sri Lanka's naval chief in a bomb blast.

Militants from India's Sikh religious community in 1992 also continued a terrorist campaign, this one for independence for the state of Punjab. Stepped-up police efforts led to the deaths of about two dozen militant Sikh leaders, but the rebels responded by killing more than 60 policemen or their relatives. And in the Indian state of Jammu and Kashmir, two groups of Muslim guerrillas, after years of cooperation, in 1992 began fighting with each other as well as with the government.

The 23-year-old Communist insurgency in the Philippines lost strength in 1992. The rebels staged some ambushes and terrorist attacks, but experts said their numbers had dwindled to about 13,000. A newly elected government tried to get the Communists to participate in peaceful politics, but the guerrillas were hesitant to abandon armed struggle.

Religious war in India. Riots between Hindus and Muslims erupted throughout India in December 1992. The clashes were sparked by the destruction on December 6 of a Muslim mosque by militant Hindus in the state of Uttar Pradesh. The Hindus alleged that the mosque stood on the sacred site of an ancient Hindu temple. The Muslims responded by attacking Hindus, who organized attacks in reply. Hundreds of people were killed and thousands injured in the resulting fighting. In an effort to stop the bloodshed, the Indian government gave soldiers shoot-on-sight orders in some areas and arrested a number of fundamentalist Hindu leaders. Anti-Hindu violence spread to the Muslim countries of Pakistan, Bangladesh, and Afghanistan and even to Great Britain.

Demonstrators take cover as soldiers open fire in Thailand's capital, Bangkok, during protests in May against the military-backed premier.

Nations arming. Despite poverty and the general peace among nations, the arms trade flourished in Asia in 1992. Brunei, Indonesia, Malaysia, Singapore, Taiwan, and Thailand all said they planned substantial increases in military spending over the next five years. China took advantage of the cash-starved republics of the former Soviet Union to buy warplanes and other weapons and to hire Russian military engineers. Meanwhile, India and Vietnam, both of whom had depended upon regular shipments of equipment from the Soviet military, faced the problem of keeping their armed forces in fighting condition.

China in 1992 also tried to make money by exporting arms, primarily to the Middle East. North Korea also reportedly sent weapons to the region. Efforts by Western countries to deter such trade had little effect.

Economic developments. The World Bank, an agency of the UN, in September reported that in 1991, East Asia led world economic growth with a rate of 6.8 per cent. The rate of growth in South Asia was 2.8 per cent.

Several Southeast Asian countries in 1992 raced to copy industrialization success stories in Taiwan and South Korea. The leaders of the movement were Thailand, Malaysia, and Indonesia. These three countries along with Brunei, the Philippines, and Singapore—the six nations that make up the

Facts in brief on Asian countries

Country	Population	Government	Monetary unit*	Foreign trade (million U.S.$) Exports†	Imports†
Afghanistan	652,090	Leadership Council President Burhanuddin Rabbani; Prime Minister Farid Kuhestani	afghani (1,162.50 = $1)	235	937
Armenia	3,373,000	President Levon Ter-Petrosyan	not available	no statistics available	
Australia	16,962,000	Governor General Bill Hayden; Prime Minister Paul Keating	dollar (1.44 = $1)	41,793	38,542
Azerbaijan	7,222,000	President Ebulfez Elcibey	not available	no statistics available	
Bangladesh	125,175,000	President Abdur Rahman Biswas; Prime Minister Khaleda Ziaur Rahman	taka (38.95 = $1)	1,690	3,405
Bhutan	1,621,000	King Jigme Singye Wangchuck	ngultrum (28.38 = $1)	71	138
Brunei	286,000	Sultan Sir Hassanal Bolkiah	dollar (1.62 = $1)	1.894	883
Burma (Myanmar)	44,343,000	State Law and Order Restoration Council Chairman Than Shwe	kyat (6.06 = $1)	228	540
Cambodia (Kampuchea)	8,802,000	Supreme National Council Chairman Norodom Sihanouk; Head of State of Cambodia Delegation Hun Sen	riel (2,000 = $1)	32	147
China	1,182,660,000	Communist Party General Secretary Jiang Zemin; Premier Li Peng; President Yang Shangkun	yuan (5.55 = $1)	71,910	63,791
Georgia	5,599,000	State Council Chairman Eduard Shevardnadze	not available	no statistics available	
India	907,442,000	President Shankar Dayal Sharma; Prime Minister P. V. Narasimha Rao	rupee (28.38 = $1)	17,663	23,276
Indonesia	194,529,000	President Suharto; Vice President Sudharmono	rupiah (2,044.00 = $1)	25,675	21,931
Iran	57,966,000	Leader of the Islamic Revolution Ali Hoseini Khamenei; President Ali Akbar Hashemi Rafsanjani	rial (1,437.00 = $1)	12,300	11,700
Japan	124,110,000	Emperor Akihito; Prime Minister Kiichi Miyazawa	yen (123.18 = $1)	314,525	236,744
Kazakhstan	16,992,000	President Nursultan Nazarbayev	not available	no statistics available	
Korea, North	23,051,000	President Kim Il-song; Premier Kang Song-San	won (2.15 = $1)	1,950	2,850
Korea, South	43,894,000	President Roh Tae Woo; Prime Minister Chung Won Shik	won (782.50 = $1)	71,898	81,557
Kyrgyzstan	4,409,000	President Askar Akayev	not available	no statistics available	
Laos	4,512,000	President Nouhak Phoumsavan; Prime Minister Khamtai Siphandon	kip (715.00 = $1)	81	162

Association of Southeast Asian Nations (ASEAN)—agreed on January 28 to launch an ASEAN Free Trade Area on Jan. 1, 1993, with the hopes of establishing a regional common market by 2008. Experts said such a unified trading bloc could become an important international force.

The giants of Asia—China and India—both moved toward more private enterprise in 1992. Chinese senior leader Deng Xiaoping broke a long leadership deadlock over the pace and direction of economic reform. He began the year with a January tour of booming areas in southern China where traditional Communist economic controls had been relaxed. Deng's public endorsement of the economic success in those areas set the party line for the rest of the year.

Japan, Asia's strongest economy, suffered the longest period of declining industrial production since 1975. Even Japan's long-prosperous automobile industry cut production. As a result, the Nikkei stock index dropped more than 60 per cent from a 1989 high before the government in August 1992 promised to stimulate the economy with new spending. But plummeting real estate prices left many Japanese mortgage holders owing more than their property was worth, and financial institutions tightened lending in light of depreciating real estate portfolios.

Relatively tame weather. Pakistan in September 1992 suffered the worst floods since its founding in 1947. And Sri Lanka in early 1992 experienced what was called its worst drought of the century. But for

Country	Population	Government	Monetary unit*	Foreign trade (million U.S.$) Exports†	Imports†
Malaysia	19,346,000	Paramount Ruler Azlan Muhibbuddin Shah ibni Sultan Yusof Izzudin; Prime Minister Mahathir bin Mohamad	ringgit (2.51 = $1)	34,375	36,699
Maldives	230,000	President Maumoon Abdul Gayoom	rufiyaa (11.52 = $1)	52	129
Moldova	4,460,000	President Mircea Snegur	not available	no statistics available	
Mongolia	2,375,000	President Punsalmaagiyn Ochirbat; Prime Minister Puntsagiyin Jasray	tughrik (40.00 = $1)	784	1,140
Nepal	20,519,000	King Birendra Bir Bikram Shah Dev; Prime Minister Girija Prasad Koirala	rupee (46.63 = $1)	273	790
New Zealand	3,476,000	Governor General Dame Catherine Tizard; Prime Minister James B. Bolger	dollar (1.89 = $1)	9,720	8,522
Pakistan	133,490,000	President Ghulam Ishaq Khan; Prime Minister Nawaz Sharif	rupee (25.26 = $1)	6,471	8,427
Papua New Guinea	4,144,000	Governor General Sir Wiwa Korowi; Prime Minister Rabbie Namaliu	kina (0.98 = $1)	1,283	1,403
Philippines	66,780,000	President Fidel Ramos	peso (24.64 = $1)	8,186	13,042
Russia	151,436,000	President Boris Yeltsin	not available	no statistics available	
Singapore	2,811,000	President Wee Kim Wee; Prime Minister Goh Chok Tong	dollar (1.62= $1)	59,046	66,108
Sri Lanka	17,876,000	President Ranasinghe Premadasa; Prime Minister D. B. Wijetunge	rupee (44.30 = $1)	1,965	3,083
Taiwan	21,116,000	President Li Teng-hui; Premier Hao Po-ts'un	dollar (25.36 = $1)	67,200	54,700
Tajikistan	5,252,000	Acting President Imoli Rakhmonov	not available	no statistics available	
Thailand	57,989,000	King Phumiphon Adunlayadet; Prime Minister Chuan Leekpai	baht (25.36 = $1)	23,068	33,379
Turkmenistan	3,631,000	President Saparmurad Niyazov	not available	no statistics available	
Uzbekistan	20,453,000	President Islam Karimov	not available	no statistics available	
Vietnam	70,297,000	Communist Party General Secretary Do Muoi; President Le Duc Anh; Council of Ministers Chairman Vo Van Kiet	dong (10,855.00 = $1)	2,600	2,300

*Exchange rates as of Oct. 30, 1992, or latest available data.

†Latest available data.

most of Asia, the weather in 1992 was uneventful, permitting average farm production.

Population boom. The Population Crisis Committee, an organization based in Washington, D.C., that monitors world population, said in September that China and India could add an additional 1.5 billion people before their populations level off. China, with about 1.2 billion people in 1992, was expected to stabilize at about 1.5 billion. India will probably pass China as the most populous nation some time in the next century as its population grows from about 900 million in 1992 to possibly 2 billion. The committee argued that both countries' family-planning programs should work harder to change public attitudes about population growth.

Nuclear updates. On February 7, Pakistan acknowledged for the first time that it had the means to build an atomic bomb. But the government said it had not yet built a bomb and did not plan to.

On May 21, China conducted its largest-ever underground nuclear test. The bomb was at least five times stronger than China's previous largest test in 1990.

North Korea in 1992 appeared further from nuclear weapons capability than previously believed. The country allowed independent inspection of its nuclear facilities for the first time.

After a tour of various sites, a team of experts concluded that North Korea was well short of being able to build a nuclear bomb. But U.S. and other officials were skeptical of the authenticity of the team's find-

Residents of India mourn for some of the 2,000 people killed in one week as a result of floods in northern India and Pakistan in September.

ings. (See also **Armed forces: The Nuclear Threat in the New World Order.)**

Refugees. Hong Kong in 1992 began forcibly returning to Vietnam about 55,000 refugees who had fled their country's poor living conditions over the last 10 years. Hong Kong had been the last place in Asia that had accepted the Vietnamese.

Some refugees from Afghanistan and Cambodia returned home in 1992 because of improved political situations. Their return relieved burdens on Pakistan and Thailand, which held about 3 million Afghans and about 300,000 Cambodians, respectively.

Bangladesh in 1992 had to deal with thousands of Muslims fleeing Burma. The refugees began leaving in 1989 to escape oppression by Burma's government. An agreement that would allow the refugees to return was negotiated with Burma in April, but few Muslims accepted the offer.

Hong Kong quarrel. Great Britain on April 25 selected Christopher Patten to be the new governor of Hong Kong. Britain rules Hong Kong, on the southern coast of China, until 1997 when the territory returns to Chinese hands. In his first policy speech on October 7, Patten proposed holding direct elections for local authorities and expanding the number of citizens able to vote in elections for Hong Kong's advisory council. He said his ideas did not contradict the Basic Law, China's stated plan for Hong Kong after 1997. But within hours, China denounced Patten's proposals.

Later in October, Patten made his first visit to Beijing, where he met with Chinese officials. After days of talks, the two sides could not agree on a political course for Hong Kong. China threatened to tear up agreements on Hong Kong's future if Patten carried through with his ideas for more democracy.

New Laos president. The president of Laos and head of the Laos Communist Party, Kaysone Phomvihane, died on November 21 at the age of 71. Kaysone had been the leader of the Communist party in Laos since the mid-1950's, and he had headed the country since 1975. His responsibilities were split between two people. For president, the Supreme National Assembly elected Nouhak Phoumsavan, the chairman of the assembly. For party chairman, the party chose Khamtai Siphandon.

New democracy. Mongolia, under Communist rule since 1921, in February enacted a new constitution that enshrined democracy and a free market economy. Then, in elections in June for Mongolia's single-chamber parliament, the ex-Communist People's Revolutionary Party took 57 per cent of the votes and won 70 of the 76 available seats. A badly organized coalition of opposition parties won only four seats. Mongolian voters thus restored power to their old Communist leaders, after two years of a coalition government. Henry S. Bradsher

See also the articles on the individual Asian nations. In ***World Book,*** see **Asia.**

Astronomy. The most exciting announcement of 1992 in astronomy occurred in April, when astrophysicist George Smoot of the University of California at Berkeley reported data showing variations in temperature in the microwave background radiation that permeates the universe. Most astronomers believe these variations reflect lumps of matter in the early universe that provided the gravitational seeds for the formation of galaxies and clusters of galaxies.

The data were gathered by the Cosmic Background Explorer (COBE) satellite, a spacecraft launched in 1989 to measure the intensity of faint microwave signals across the heavens. Astronomers have known since 1964 that microwave radiation permeates the universe. Most have theorized that this radiation is the afterglow of the birth of the universe in the big bang. According to the big bang theory, the universe was created about 15 billion years ago in an explosion of energy and matter. As the universe expanded, its composition progressed from a uniform sea of particles to the clusters of galaxies observed today. However, for these vast groupings to have formed, astronomers say matter must have begun lumping together gravitationally not long after the big bang. And such lumps would vary in temperature from one another and from the surrounding space, giving off more or less radiation.

The COBE satellite was launched to look for these variations in the microwave background. Most astronomers believe that the observed background radiation was produced only about 300,000 years after the big bang and has gone unchanged since, so COBE effectively views the universe in its infancy.

Pulsar planets. In January 1992, astronomer Andrew G. Lyne of the University of Manchester in England retracted his July 1991 report of a planet circling the pulsar PSR 1829-10. A pulsar is a rapidly spinning star that shoots out a beam of radio waves. Because the star spins, astronomers observe the beam from Earth as a series of pulses. Lyne announced his claim of a planet last year after finding oscillations in the arrival of radio-wave pulses from the star. But upon later examination, Lyne found that he had failed to adjust his calculations to allow for variations in Earth's orbit around the sun.

But using pulsars to find planets still holds promise. Again in January 1992, astronomers Alexander Wolszczan of Cornell University in Ithaca, N.Y., and Dale A. Frail of the National Radio Astronomy Observatory in Socorro, N. Mex., announced the existence of at least two planets orbiting another pulsar, PSR 1257+12. Like Lyne's work, Wolszczan and Frail's discovery was based on measurements of slight variations in the arrival times of radio-wave pulses from the star. The team interpreted these discrepancies as the result of gravitational tugs on the pulsar by orbiting planets. After analyzing 4,000 radio signals from the pulsar, the astronomers were even able to estimate the masses and orbits of the suspected planets. Because of the precise pattern of pulse variations, the team was able to rule out the idea that the variations were merely the result of "star quakes" in the pulsar. And other astronomers said Wolszczan and Frail's research was not subject to the errors in Lyne's work.

Hubble discoveries. The Hubble Space Telescope, orbiting Earth since April 1990, continued to provide astronomers with breathtaking pictures and amazing data. In January 1992, astronomers reported that Hubble photographs of a galaxy called NGC 1275 showed thousands of blue stars arranged in dense spherical clumps known as globular clusters.

Our Milky Way galaxy possesses globular clusters, but they contain only old, red stars formed billions of years ago. In NGC 1275, the stars are blue, indicating they are only a few hundred million years old. And astronomers in June reported that Hubble saw similar young blue star clusters in a galaxy called Arp 220. Previous studies had concluded that the raw materials and energy required for the formation of globular clusters was available only in the early universe, so astronomers were surprised to find clusters so young. Since both NGC 1275 and Arp 220 possess peculiar shapes, astronomers speculated that each is the product of a relatively recent collision of two smaller galaxies. The energetic mingling of gas and dust in such a collision might give birth to young globular clusters.

X marks the spot. The Hubble is also contributing to the hunt for *black holes* (hypothetical objects so dense that their gravity keeps even light from escaping). In June, astronomers released a photograph taken by the Hubble of a galaxy called M51. In the picture, the center of the bright galaxy appears to be crossed by a dark "X." Astronomers believe the "X" indicates a black hole at the center of M51. Astronomers interpreted the crossed arms of the "X" as possibly two flat disks of dust spinning around a black hole at the center.

Solar system findings. In August 1992, astronomers using a telescope atop Mauna Kea in Hawaii detected a small object that may be the most distant member of our solar system yet observed—about 4 billion miles (6.4 billion kilometers) from the sun. The reddish body, designated 1992 QB-1, is only about 125 miles (200 kilometers) in diameter and orbits the sun just beyond Pluto. Many astronomers believe that 1992 QB-1 is the first evidence of a swarm of small bodies at the fringe of the solar system called the Kuiper belt. The Kuiper belt is the proposed home of many comets—small bodies of frozen gas and dust that fly through the solar system. Astronomers think bodies such as 1992 QB-1 remain in the Kuiper belt until they are pulled out by the gravitational force of some passing object and shot into the orbits of the planets. As they approach the sun, the ice on their surface evaporates and streams out behind them to form the bright gaseous tails familiar of comets.

In May 1992, astronomers revealed the most detailed map yet of Pluto's surface brightness. The as-

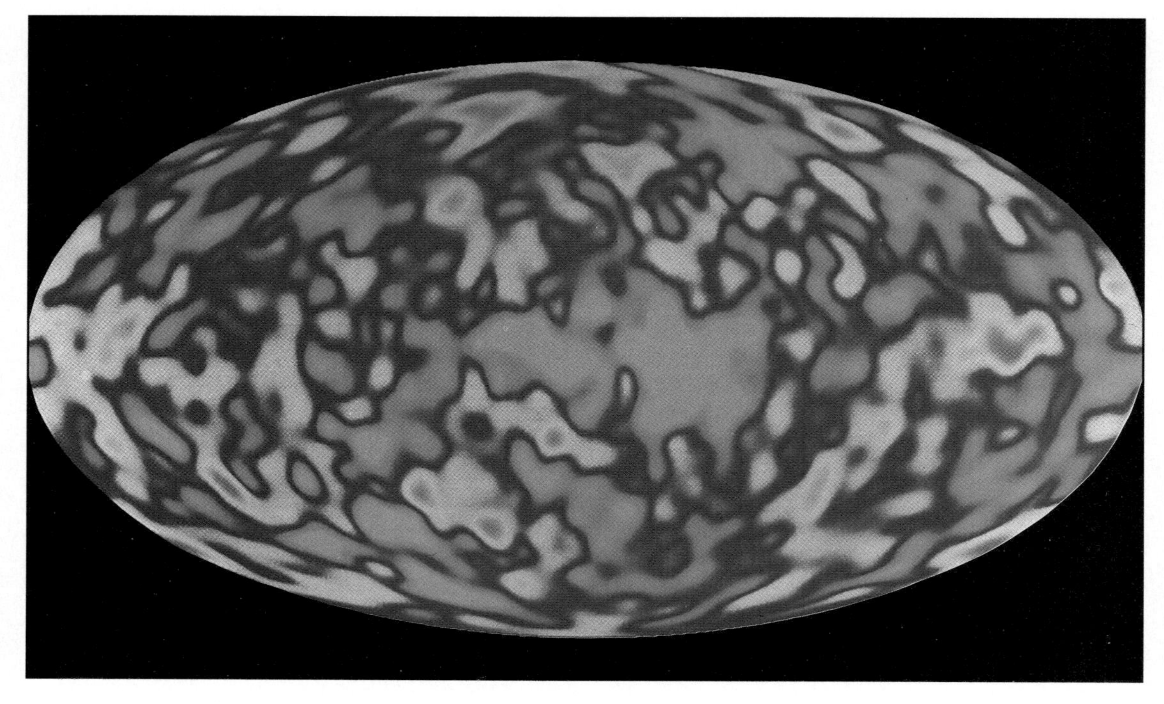

A microwave map of the sky, unveiled in April, shows cooler areas (blue) that may indicate where matter began clumping in the early universe.

tronomers took advantage of rare eclipses of Pluto by its moon, Charon, from 1985 to 1990. As Charon moved between Pluto and the sun, various areas of Pluto fell into shadow and the total brightness of the planet dropped. Using these changes in brightness, the astronomers could calculate the relative contribution of each area to Pluto's full brightness and so piece together a complete map. Among the map's prominent features were a very bright cap at Pluto's south pole and a dark band across its middle.

The spacecraft Galileo, on its way to a 1995 meeting with the planet Jupiter, in June 1992 sent back the first detailed photograph of an asteroid, one of the many small planetlike bodies that circle the sun between the orbits of Mars and Jupiter. The asteroid, known as Gaspra, appeared as a triangular fragment of rock about 10 miles (16 kilometers) long and 7 miles (11 kilometers) wide. The photograph showed more than 600 meteorite impact craters, as well as scars where astronomers believe Gaspra broke apart after a collision with a larger asteroid a few hundred million years ago. Galileo photographed Gaspra in October 1991, but because its main antenna jammed, the spacecraft was not able to transmit its best pictures until 1992, when it made a close enough pass by Earth to allow astronomers to use a slower backup antenna. Laurence A. Marschall

See also **Space exploration**. In ***World Book***, see **Astronomy**.

Australia in 1992 endured its third consecutive year of deep recession. The most fundamental economic problem was unemployment, which reached a record 11.4 per cent in November and remained well above 10 per cent for the entire year. The industries hardest hit by the recession were banking and finance, alcoholic beverages and tobacco, and building materials.

Prime Minister Paul Keating, who had taken office in December 1991, on Feb. 26, 1992, announced his Labor Party's long-term economic strategy for Australia, called "One Nation." The program centered on massive spending for infrastructure in the hopes of creating enough jobs to move the unemployment rate below 10 per cent. The program also called for deregulation of the airline industry, a one-time cash bonus for poor families, and various tax relief to spur investment. The plan was an attempt to counter a coalition of the Liberal and National parties, which had staked its bid to win national elections in 1993 on its own comprehensive economic plan called "Fightback." (See also **Keating, Paul.**)

Economy. Despite a drop in inflation to 0.75 per cent—the lowest rate since 1962—and cuts in the official interest rate to 5.7 per cent, the economy grew at a rate of only 3 per cent in 1992, not fast enough to lead to serious gains in employment.

Treasurer John Dawkins on August 18 unveiled the federal budget for the fiscal year that will end on June 30, 1993. The budget included $1.2 billion worth of spending to create 800,000 jobs by 1996. (All figures in this article are in Australian dollars.) In return, the federal deficit was expected to grow to $13.4 billion in the fiscal year ending June 30, 1993, Australia's largest deficit since the early 1950's.

The land. Eastern Australia in 1992 continued to experience a severe drought. Some 70 per cent of New South Wales, the richest and most populous state, was officially declared to be under the drought. And parts of Queensland have been drought-stricken for at least half of the years since the late 1960's.

In spite of a record area planted, Australian farmers in 1992 experienced their lowest sugar yields since 1968. The poor harvests, combined with falling world prices for sugar, caused the country's income from sugar to fall by 25 per cent. Wool production was also down about 20 per cent, with production and export earnings likely to remain low for the next five years. Although gold production was at a record high in 1992, the gold tax, the high value of the Australian dollar, increased production costs, and the recession were all expected to contribute to a drop in exploration and gold production in future years.

Wheat controversy. Relations between Australia and the United States became strained in late 1992 after U.S. President George Bush on September 2 announced his intention to subsidize U.S. wheat sales abroad, including sales to Pakistan, a traditional Australian market. Bush had previously assured Australia that the United States would not sell subsidized wheat to a market with whom Australia was already doing business. Australia is one of the world's leading wheat producers, and it does not subsidize its wheat exports. The action by the United States was expected to cost Australian farmers about $20 million in business from Pakistan. In 1991, Australia had protested similar U.S. wheat sales to Yemen, another traditional Australian market.

Tariff proposal. In September, John Hewson, leader of the Liberal-National coalition, announced that a coalition government, if elected in 1993, would cut tariffs to 5 per cent by the year 2000. The idea was greeted with derision by Australian industry. Critics claimed that such a move would increase unemployment by reducing the incentive for foreign companies to base their operations in Australia rather than exporting goods from their home nations.

State news. New South Wales (NSW) on June 20 was rocked by a report from the Independent Commission Against Corruption that found Premier Nick Greiner "technically corrupt." The case involved Greiner's appointment on April 10 of an independent member of parliament, Terry Metherell, to a post with the NSW Environmental Protection Authority. On May 2, Greiner's coalition of the Liberal and National parties won the by-election to replace Metherell, thereby giving the coalition a one-seat edge over the rival Labor Party. Critics said Greiner's motives for appointing Metherell were thus suspect. As a result of the

Australian farmers protest U.S. trade subsidies of American farm products during a January visit by U.S. President George Bush.

controversy, Greiner on June 24 resigned and was replaced as premier by John Fahey, the industrial relations minister. But on August 21, an Australian court formally cleared Greiner of corruption charges.

In the state of South Australia, Premier John Bannon resigned on September 1 to take the blame for a 1991 banking scandal involving losses by the State Bank of South Australia of more than $3 billion. Bannon was replaced by Minister for Economic Development Lynn Arnold, who became the fourth federal or state Australian leader governing in 1992 without the sanction of an election.

The state of Victoria, also in financial strife, on October 3 voted the Liberal-National coalition into power, led by new Premier Jeff Kennett. Most of Australia's manufacturing industry is based in Victoria, and the inability of Premier Joan Kirner and her Labor government to reverse the recession and the mounting financial losses led to the coalition's victory.

The most politically trouble-free state in 1992 was Queensland, which on September 19 reelected Premier Wayne Goss and his Labor government. Queensland has the lowest taxes and lowest unemployment rate in Australia.

Church and society. Roman Catholic bishops on September 16 released the results of a five-year study on the distribution of wealth in Australia. In their report, the bishops concluded that Australia had become less egalitarian than other Western nations. The report, called "Common Wealth for the Common Good," was the most comprehensive study of poverty in Australia in almost 20 years. The report argued that deregulation in the 1980's, intended to improve the efficiency and productivity of Australian industry by exposing it to international competition, had led to bankruptcies and unemployment. As a result, the middle class had suffered a drop of 20 per cent in real family income since 1975, according to the report.

The Uniting Church in NSW on September 27 became the first religious organization in Australia to officially support abortion. The policy, the product of three years of debate within the church, stated that any decision to terminate an unwanted pregnancy should be made solely by the pregnant woman.

Olympic gold. At the 1992 Summer Olympic Games held in Barcelona, Spain, Australia walked away with 27 medals and a 9th-place finish, the country's best showing since the 1956 Summer Olympics in Melbourne. The head of the Australian team, John Coates, said that for Australia to perform as well at the 1996 Olympics, funding would have to rise to $28-million from $15 million spent in 1992. Australia's success in Barcelona also buoyed the hopes of the "Sydney 2000" committee, which was bidding for the Summer Games to be held in Australia's biggest city at the turn of the century. Susan G. Williams

See also **Asia** (Facts in brief table). In ***World Book,*** see **Australia.**

Austria elected Thomas Klestil of the conservative Austrian People's Party as its president on May 24, 1992. This ended six years of diplomatic isolation for Austria under former President Kurt Waldheim, who was alleged to have been involved in Nazi war crimes during World War II (1939-1945). Many countries had refused to receive Waldheim in his role as Austria's president, and he was barred from entering the United States. Waldheim, a former secretary-general of the United Nations, denied the allegations.

In the election, Klestil, a diplomat who had served as ambassador to the United States and to the United Nations, won nearly 57 per cent of the vote in a runoff against Social Democratic Party (formerly Socialist Party) candidate Rudolf Streicher. Klestil had come in second to Streicher in the first round of the election on April 26. In the runoff, he picked up many votes that had at first gone to far right wing Freedom Party candidate Heide Schmidt.

European ties. Austria in 1992 reinforced its economic and political ties to the 12-nation European Community (EC or Common Market). In September, Austria's parliament approved the country's participation in the European Economic Area (EEA), an agreement designed to promote freer trade between the EC and the 7-nation European Free Trade Association (EFTA), to which Austria belongs. But the EEA, scheduled to take effect in early 1993, does not abolish all trade barriers or establish uniform agricultural, monetary, or financial policies between the EC and the EFTA.

Austria had applied for EC membership in 1989, making it the first EFTA country to do so. In July 1992, EC leaders said Austria met the EC's standards for new members. Talks on Austrian membership were to be put off until all EC countries had ratified the so-called Maastricht Treaty. The treaty is the EC's blueprint for European economic and political union. Progress on the ratifications was delayed in 1992 by political problems within the EC, including Denmark's rejection of the Maastricht Treaty in June. But in December, EC leaders said talks could begin in early 1993.

Full EC membership may require Austria to abandon its policy of military neutrality, especially if the EC proceeds with plans to develop a common defense policy and European army. The Austrian government said in June that it would ask the EC for concessions to accommodate its neutrality, such as those accorded to neutral Ireland.

Austria continued to be an important political and economic bridge to the former Communist countries of Eastern and central Europe in 1992. Austria's exports to Poland, Hungary, Czechoslovakia, and Bulgaria surged by 13.2 per cent in the first six months of 1992, while Austrian imports from these countries rose by 9.2 per cent. Philip Revzin

See also **Europe** (Facts in brief table). In ***World Book,*** see **Austria.**

Automobile. "Troubled" was the word that best described the global automobile industry in 1992, dragged down by an economic slump that hit all of the major industrial countries. But as usual, most automakers persevered and continued introducing attractive, technically advanced new cars and trucks.

Economic fortunes. What automakers in the United States needed in 1992 was a revival in the slumping car and truck markets, but such a turnaround did not materialize. Sales of new vehicles to American buyers grew to an estimated 12.9 million in 1992, only a slight improvement from the 12.3 million sales in 1991. And forecasts offered little hope for better fortunes in 1993, as sales were expected to rise to only 13.5 million.

As 1992 progressed, however, U.S. automakers began showing improved financial performances in spite of the small sales increases, largely as a result of gains in efficiency and rigid internal cost-cutting. For the first nine months of 1992, General Motors Corporation (GM) lost $971 million, an improvement of almost $1-billion from its $1.985-billion loss for the similar period in 1991. Chrysler Corporation showed a profit of $367 million for the nine-month period in 1992 after a loss of $892 million for the same period in 1991. And Ford Motor Company had a nine-month profit of $681 million in 1992, compared with a loss of $1.782 billion for the same period in 1991.

European and Japanese automakers suffered along

The Impact, a prototype of General Motors' first electric car, came closer to reality in 1992, as GM selected the U.S. plants that will make its key parts.

with their North American counterparts. Auto sales slumped badly in Europe, particularly in Great Britain. In response to the drop, European carmakers moved to cut production, halt expansion plans, and reduce the size of their work forces. Meanwhile, Japan suffered its sharpest decline in home market sales in decades. Nissan Corporation, Japan's No. 2 automaker, reported its first quarterly loss since 1951. And Mazda Corporation canceled plans to enter the U.S. luxury-car market after three years of work on what would have been its Amati Division.

Domestic market gains. The revived competitiveness of GM, Ford, and Chrysler against their Japanese rivals was one of the major U.S. business stories of 1992. Most consumer surveys indicated that cars built by GM, Ford, and Chrysler were approaching the quality of those designed in Japan. The Detroit firms were also aided in 1992 by a weakening American dollar, which forced many Japanese firms to raise their U.S. prices.

As a result of these developments, the U.S. firms increased their share of the home market. Through October 1992, the Big Three had captured 72.2 per cent of the U.S. new vehicle market, up from 70.2 per cent for the similar period of 1991. Asian firms held 25.2 per cent of the market in 1992, down from 26.9 per cent. And European automakers owned 2.6 per cent of the market in 1992, down from 2.8 per cent.

In response to the rising cost of doing business in America from abroad, many Japan-based automakers pushed to expand their U.S. operations. Having set up plants to assemble cars and trucks and to make major components such as engines, transmissions, and bodies, the Japanese firms now sought to increase the quantity of other materials purchased from North American companies. Each of the major Japanese carmakers invested heavily in technical centers in the United States where local parts suppliers could be taught Japanese design and supply methods. In total, Japanese automakers said they planned to increase purchases of North American parts to $19 billion by 1995, more than double the level in 1990.

Changes at the top. Each of the three domestic automakers experienced leadership shuffles during the year. At Chrysler, veteran engineer and former GM executive Robert J. Eaton was chosen on March 16, 1992, to succeed Chairman Lee A. Iacocca, who planned to retire on Jan. 1, 1993. At Ford, British native Alexander J. Trotman was named president and chief operating officer on November 12.

The changes at GM, though, were the most dramatic. Under pressure from board members impatient with the slow pace of growth in the company's fortunes, Robert C. Stempel resigned as chairman and chief executive officer on October 26. On November 2, the board selected retired Procter & Gamble Company chairman John G. Smale to take over Stempel's chairman position, and the job of chief executive was given to GM President John F. Smith. GM executives believed the company's main task was to streamline U.S. operations that had lost almost $12 billion in 1990 and 1991. To this end, the company in February and December 1992 named 23 plants to be closed by the end of 1995. GM also modified its basic manufacturing methods, copying Japanese-style production systems in order to reduce waste and boost quality. And the company reorganized its vehicle-design operations around teams of employees that concentrated on specific car lines. (See also **Labor: What Is Happening to the U.S. Job Market?**)

So eager was GM for productivity gains that for the first time in its history, it sought outside aid for its car-design operations. Fuji Technica, a major Japanese designer of car-body molds, on November 4 signed an agreement with GM giving the U.S. automaker access to its computerized die-design technology.

New models. Foremost among the new products introduced in 1993 was Toyota's T-100 pickup truck. With this vehicle, Toyota created a new market segment: the midsized pickup, positioned between the fullsized Dodge Ram, Ford F-100, and GM C/K series pickups and the compact brands. Ford planned to match Toyota by making its own midsized pickup in the mid-1990's, and experts believed that all major truck manufacturers would quickly follow. In short, the truck market moved toward segmentation into compact, midsized, and fullsized models, just like cars.

Chrysler in 1992 introduced three sedans, the Chrysler Concorde, Eagle Vision, and Dodge Intrepid. The trio broke new ground in styling and gave the No. 3 domestic automaker modern and well-equipped entries in the upscale market segment, where it had been weak. The cars, considered crucial to Chrysler's future by industry observers, were well-received by both the public and critics.

Ford boasted several important new vehicle lines in the year. The small, sporty Probe, jointly produced with Japanese automaker Mazda, underwent a major restyling, as did the Ranger compact pickup line. And Ford sought to broaden the appeal of its luxury-coupe lineup with the Lincoln Mark VIII, equipped with a new 280-horsepower, 32-valve engine.

In contrast, GM in 1992 took a breather from its redesign program. Its most significant new product was not a car but an engine—the dual overhead camshaft, 32-valve Northstar V-8 mounted in Cadillac luxury cars. The new engine gave Cadillac a drivetrain competitive with any offered by German or Japanese firms, and derivatives of the Northstar were planned for future Oldsmobile and Buick cars.

Perhaps the biggest automotive success story of 1992 was the Saturn Corporation, GM's small-car subsidiary based in Spring Hill, Tenn. Saturn dealers were regularly short of cars, and the company scrambled to devise ways of meeting consumer demand.

James V. Higgins

In ***World Book,*** see **Automobile.**

Automobile racing.

Al Unser, Jr., and Michael Andretti, 30-year-old sons of the legendary drivers Al Unser and Mario Andretti, won major honors in 1992 in American auto racing's IndyCar series. Nigel Mansell, a 39-year-old Briton, won the world drivers' championship. Then, for 1993, Mansell switched to IndyCar races, and Andretti switched to Formula One races.

Indianapolis 500. The $7,527,450 race on May 24 at the Indianapolis Motor Speedway was the world's richest. The cars were open-wheeled roadsters similar to the more powerful Formula One cars but a bit heavier.

Cold weather and numerous crashes slowed the pace of the Indianapolis 500. Crashes during the race injured four-time winner Rick Mears, Nelson Piquet of Brazil, Mario Andretti (Michael's father), and Jeff Andretti (Mario's younger son). During practice for the race on May 15, Jovy Marcelo, a 27-year-old rookie race car driver from the Philippines, crashed and was killed.

Roberto Guerrero of Colombia won the qualifying pole in a Lola-Buick in the record time of 232.482 miles per hour (mph)—374.144 kilometers per hour (kph). But on a warmup lap, Guerrero crashed into a retaining wall and made the earliest exit ever for a pole-sitter.

In the race itself, Michael Andretti, in a new Lola-Ford, was leading with 11 of the 200 laps remaining

The car driven by Al Unser, Jr., left, closes in on the finish line in May to win the closest Indianapolis 500 in the race's history.

when his fuel pressure failed. Then Unser, in a Galmer-Chevrolet, took over the lead and won by half a car length, or .043 second, over Scott Goodyear of Toronto, Canada, in the closest Indianapolis 500 finish ever.

Lyn St. James became the second woman to qualify for the race. She finished 11th.

IndyCar. The Indianapolis 500 was the showpiece of the 16-race IndyCar (formerly known as CART) series. There were 13 races in the United States, 2 in Canada, and 1 in Australia. Michael Andretti, who won 8 poles and 8 races in 1991 with a Chevrolet engine, switched to a Ford engine and did well again.

By finishing third in the final race, Bobby Rahal won the season title in a Lola-Chevrolet with 196 points to 192 for Andretti, 169 for Unser, and 151 for Emerson Fittipaldi of Brazil.

Andretti won 5 races, Rahal 4, and Fittipaldi 4. The title was the third for the 39-year-old Rahal, but his first as a car owner.

World championship. The Formula One cars competed in 16 Grand Prix races for the world drivers' championship. Mansell, in a Williams-Renault, won 9 races, breaking the one-season record of 8 by Ayrton Senna of Brazil in 1988. This time, Senna won 3 races, and his McLaren-Honda teammate, Gerhard Berger of Austria, won the Canadian Grand Prix on June 15 in Montreal, Canada. There was no Grand Prix race in the United States.

Mansell could not reach an agreement with the Williams team for 1993 and signed instead with the Paul Newman-Carl Haas IndyCar team. He replaced Michael Andretti, who moved to the McLaren Formula One team.

The Williams team replaced Mansell with Alain Prost of France. Prost, a three-time world champion, sat out the 1992 season.

Other races. The National Association for Stock Car Racing (NASCAR) ran 29 Winston Cup races for late-model sedans. By finishing third in the season's last race, Alan Kulwicki, in a Ford Thunderbird, won the series' title. Davey Allison won the $2,303,996 Daytona 500, the series' richest race, by two car lengths.

The National Hot Rod Association conducted 18 competitions over quarter-mile drag strips. On March 20 in Gainesville, Fla., 47-year-old Kenny Bernstein became the first drag racer to reach 300 mph (483 kph), clocking 301.70 mph (485.54 kph). On October 29 in Pomona, Calif., Eddie Hill turned in the fastest time ever, 4.779 seconds. Joe Amato won the season title for a record fifth time.

Petty retires. Richard Petty ended his extraordinarily successful 35-year stock car racing career on November 15 at the Hooters 500 in Atlanta. Petty won 200 races during his race-car driving career, including 7 Daytona 500's and 7 NASCAR series championships.

Frank Litsky

In ***World Book,*** see **Automobile racing**.

Aviation. The major airlines in the United States struggled through a financially disastrous year in 1992, with losses projected at almost $2 billion. That meant that losses for 1990 through 1992 totaled almost $8 billion. The red ink, which experts blamed on continued weak economic conditions and vigorous airfare wars, threatened the health—indeed, the very survival—of several U.S. airlines.

Payroll cuts. In an effort to stop the losses, carriers scrambled to slash costs. In late November, American Airlines, a unit of AMR Corporation, reduced its management ranks by 576 employees as part of a plan to cut payroll costs by 10 per cent. In June, Northwest Airlines, a unit of Wings Holdings Incorporated, announced plans to lay off 110 pilots to slash wage costs by $108 million. In another effort to save money, Northwest on December 7 canceled a $3.5-billion order for Airbus Industrie planes.

Efforts by USAir to reduce labor costs sparked a confrontation with its 8,300 members of the International Association of Machinists and Aerospace Workers. The workers went on a four-day strike in early October, seriously disrupting service at USAir, a unit of USAir Group Incorporated. About 40 per cent of the carrier's 2,600 daily departures were grounded. On October 8, the airline and its machinists reached a tentative accord that ended the strike, with union negotiators reportedly agreeing to a 4-per-cent wage cut.

International issues. USAir's money woes also produced one of the biggest aviation controversies of the year. On July 21, British Airways PLC announced plans to invest $750 million in USAir in return for 44 per cent of the airline's stock. The transaction was designed to provide USAir with needed cash and to give British Airways access to the U.S. aviation market.

Four of the nation's biggest airlines—American; Delta; UAL Corporation's United Airlines; and Federal Express Corporation, a cargo line—strenuously opposed the transaction. They charged that the plan would give British Airways illegal control of USAir, which British Air denied. Representatives of the four airlines said that the U.S. Department of Transportation should refuse to approve the deal. Then, on December 22, British Airways announced that its plan to acquire a stake in USAir had collapsed.

One way or another, analysts predicted, new linkups between U.S. and foreign airlines seemed inevitable. For one thing, financially ailing U.S. carriers were desperate for a new source of capital. In addition, the industry throughout the world was moving to bigger, globally linked carriers, which could serve greater numbers of passengers at lower costs.

For example, KLM Royal Dutch Airlines, which owned a large portion of Northwest, in September asked the Department of Transportation for permission to integrate the operations of the two carriers. The department granted tentative approval on November 16, and final approval was expected before year-end.

Flames engulf apartment buildings in Amsterdam, the Netherlands, on October 4, after an El Al cargo jet crashed into the complex.

Also in November, Continental Airlines, which was operating under the protection of Chapter 11 of the federal bankruptcy law, accepted a $450-million proposal from an investment group made up of Air Canada and Air Partners L.P. to buy a majority stake in the company. At year-end, the proposal was pending before the Department of Transportation and a federal bankruptcy judge.

To aid globalization, the U.S. government pushed for more liberal aviation agreements with foreign governments. The goal was to increase domestic and foreign carriers' service internationally. In early September, the United States and the Netherlands reached an "open skies" agreement to allow KLM and U.S. airlines to fly anywhere in the United States or the Netherlands without restriction. It was the most open aviation agreement ever negotiated by U.S. officials, who hoped it would put pressure on other countries to follow suit. But by year-end, international aviation was still tightly regulated throughout the world, and aviation was in some places coming under additional restriction.

Fares. In an effort to simplify the dizzying array of fares and to boost business, American Airlines on April 9 introduced a new streamlined fare structure called "value pricing." Under the plan, many different fares were combined into just four different categories, and prices for many tickets were lowered. But the structure collapsed after other airlines undercut American's fares and American responded by making its own fare reductions. The resulting summertime fare war contributed to the industry's heavy losses.

In another development, four major airlines in June agreed to settle charges of illegally setting ticket prices by using an electronic fare exchange. The carriers—Delta, United, American, and USAir—all denied the accusations, but nevertheless agreed to pay air travelers a total of $44 million in cash and $368.5 million in discount fare coupons.

Safety. The worst accident in the United States in 1992 occurred on March 22 at LaGuardia Airport in New York, when a USAir Fokker 28 plane crashed on take-off. Twenty-seven people died. Analysts said the accident was probably caused by ice on the wings. The plane had been sprayed with deicing compounds, but 30 minutes elapsed before take-off. Prompted by the crash, the Federal Aviation Administration (FAA) on September 25 established regulations detailing how long planes may wait before take-off after deicing.

There were several serious crashes outside the United States. On January 20, a French Air Inter jet crashed in bad weather on a ridge in eastern France. Only 9 of the 96 people on board survived. On July 31, 113 people died when a Thai Airways International plane crashed into a mountain northeast of Katmandu, Nepal. The plane was an Airbus 310-300 on its way to Bangkok. On the same day, a Soviet-built jetliner exploded in flames on take-off from the Nanjing airport in eastern China, killing 100 people and injuring 26, according to China's state-run news agency. Then, on November 24, a Boeing 737-300 crashed near Guilin in south China. All 141 people on the China Southern Airlines passenger flight were killed, making the disaster China's worst reported airplane crash.

In another major disaster, more than 60 people were believed killed when an El Al cargo plane with mechanical problems slammed into an apartment complex in Amsterdam, the Netherlands, on October 4. Most of those killed were apartment dwellers. Aviation officials investigating the crash quickly turned their attention to the pins that helped hold the Boeing 747 engines to the wings. They speculated that the pins might have broken, causing two of the plane's four engines to drop off. The FAA ordered inspections of the pins—and their replacement where necessary—on about 730 of the 747's worldwide.

In 1992, the FAA stepped up its surveillance of the commuter airline industry, which in 1991 had its worst safety record ever, with 76 passengers killed. The FAA said it planned to increase training requirements for commuter pilots, who often have less experience than pilots for major airlines. In 1992, the industry safety record improved substantially. Laurie McGinley

In *World Book,* see **Aviation**.

Azerbaijan. See **Commonwealth of Independent States.**

Bahamas. See **West Indies.**

Bahrain. See **Middle East.**

Ballet. See **Dancing.**

Bangladesh. While continuing to face the problem of providing for its own impoverished people, Bangladesh in 1992 also had to deal with refugees from neighboring Burma (also called Myanmar). Thousands of Muslims began leaving Burma in late 1989 to escape a brutal assault by Burma's military-controlled government against Muslim rebels in the southwestern province of Arakan. By April 1992, more than 200,000 Muslims had fled to Bangladesh.

Bangladesh set up camps for the refugees and received international aid through the United Nations (UN). But the government could not defuse rising hostility toward the refugees from Bangladeshis, who resented the competition for scarce resources. The foreign ministers of Bangladesh and Burma met on April 28, and a program of *repatriation* (return of the refugees) was negotiated.

However, Burma said it would recognize the citizenship of only 37,000 of the refugees. And Burma refused to allow UN officials to supervise the refugees' return. Human rights groups had said the Muslims could not return to Burma without UN protection. So the repatriation plan stalled. By the end of 1992, few Muslims had been repatriated, and new arrivals from Burma had raised the number of refugees in Bangladesh to more than 265,000, with no end to the crisis in sight.

Law and order. Prime Minister Khaleda Ziaur Rahman in 1992 faced growing criticism over the lawlessness in Bangladesh. Her Bangladesh Nationalist Party (BNP) was able to defeat a no-confidence motion on the matter that the opposition Awami League brought to Parliament on August 12. But businesspeople remained concerned about the extent to which the murders, robberies, and kidnappings were discouraging investment in Bangladesh. Gun battles also erupted on university campuses, as youths fought over political issues and for scarce dormitory space.

Border deal. On June 26, India handed over to Bangladesh a short strip of territory called Tin Bigha, ending a 45-year-old border dispute. The transfer of the strip, which measures a mere 195 yards (178 meters) in length and 3.7 acres (1.5 hectares) in area, rejoined Bangladesh to a small Muslim-populated *enclave* (an area surrounded on all sides by another country) in India.

In 1974, a leasing agreement for Tin Bigha was concluded between India and Bangladesh. But the transfer of Tin Bigha resulted in a Hindu-populated enclave in Bangladesh. The lease gave the Hindus in the new enclave the right of passage across Tin Bigha to and from India, but the agreement nonetheless stirred opposition among Hindus in India. The transfer had been continually blocked by legal challenges from Hindus until 1990, when the Indian Supreme Court ruled the lease valid, paving the way for the official transfer of the strip in 1992. Henry S. Bradsher

See also **Asia** (Facts in brief table). In *World Book,* see **Bangladesh.**

Charles H. Keating, Jr., former owner of Lincoln Savings & Loan Association, reacts to his sentence on April 10 of 10 years in prison for bank fraud.

Bank. Whereas most of the United States struggled with a sluggish economy, the nation's 12,011 banks and 2,023 savings and loans (S&L's) appeared to be headed for record profits in 1992. By the end of June 1992, banks had earned a record $15.5 billion thanks to the lowest interest rates since 1972.

Low interest rates allow banks to pay depositors far less than banks earn on loans and other investments. For much of the year, the difference between what banks earned on loans and what they paid depositors was as much as 4 percentage points. The number of banks that the government considered candidates for failure fell to 1,044 in June from 1,069 at the beginning of 1992.

Savings and loans, which only a few years before suffered such steep losses that their insurance fund required a taxpayer bailout, also profited handsomely from the interest rate plunge in 1992. They posted profits of $2.8 billion in the first half of 1992. Nearly half of the industry's former unprofitable S&L's had been closed or merged with healthier S&L's or banks by 1992. About 1,000 remained to be closed as 1992 began.

There were ominous warnings, however, amidst the welcome news for bankers. Much of the ominous news involved the Federal Deposit Insurance Corporation (FDIC), the government insurance fund meant to protect depositors' money in banks and S&L's in case those institutions fail. From 1985 through the beginning of 1992, more than 1,100 S&L and bank failures drained the FDIC of money, and it began 1992 with a $7-billion deficit. But the banks' record profitability took some of the pressure off the FDIC, and by the end of June, its deficit had narrowed to $5.55-billion.

To help relieve the deficit, the FDIC proposed that banks pay higher insurance premiums to the FDIC—28 cents per $100 of deposits. Banks had begun 1992 paying 23 cents per $100 of deposits to the FDIC. Banks resisted the change because the higher insurance premiums would cut into their profits.

The FDIC board of directors approved a more moderate increase in bank-deposit insurance premiums on September 15 to an average of 25 cents per $100. FDIC officials said that even with the higher insurance rate the agency would not be out of the red until the year 2000.

Many politicians and officials in Congress and in the Administration of President George Bush blamed banks for stifling the U.S. economy by making too few loans to businesses in 1992. Normally, when interest rates fall as they did in 1992, businesses take advantage of the lower rates to borrow money, hire new employees, and expand. But businesses were not borrowing and creating new jobs in 1992. Instead, many businesses shrank. By June 30, the amount of commercial bank loans had fallen for the sixth consecutive quarter.

Resolution Trust Corporation. The authority of the Resolution Trust Corporation (RTC) to spend money expired in April 1992. The RTC was created in 1989 to take control of failed S&L's, sell their assets, and ensure that depositors in those institutions received their money. As of November 1992, the RTC had shut down 727 S&L's. Without more funds, insolvent S&L's would continue to accumulate losses that would have to be borne by taxpayers.

Congressional Democrats said they would not pass the legislation to allow the RTC to continue unless a majority of Republicans also voted for the bill. And many Republicans, unhappy with how President Bush was handling the economy, said that they would not vote for more RTC funding unless Bush pushed harder for economic incentives, such as tax cuts. RTC officials said they expected Congress to take up the authorization in 1993 but estimated that delay could cost taxpayers as much as $2 billion as insolvent S&L's continued to fail.

More bank failures? Due to changes in U.S. banking laws scheduled to take effect on Dec. 19, 1992, banks began the year braced for another wave of government takeovers. The expected changes were a result of the Federal Deposit Insurance Corporation Improvement Act, which Congress passed in November 1991. The new law requires the government to take control of any bank or S&L whose net worth, or capital, has dwindled to less than 2 per cent of its assets. The FDIC has traditionally waited until banks have no capital remaining before taking over the institution. Government regulators warned that another 100 banks might have to be seized as a result of the new law.

International bank scandals created news in the United States in 1992. For the Bush Administration, the trouble involved Banca Nazionale del Lavoro (BNL), an Italian government-controlled bank with a branch in Atlanta, Ga. The Atlanta BNL branch allegedly made more than $4 billion in illegal loans to Iraq from 1985 to 1989.

On Oct. 7, 1992, the U.S. Central Intelligence Agency reported that it had withheld information from federal prosecutors concerning the BNL loans on orders from the U.S. Department of Justice. On October 16, U.S. Attorney General William P. Barr appointed a special prosecutor, who on December 9 reported that he found no evidence of wrongdoing. On October 11, the U.S. Federal Bureau of Investigation began its own inquiry into the affair. (See also **United States, Government of the.**)

The BCCI scandal. Clark M. Clifford, a former U.S. secretary of defense under President Lyndon B. Johnson and a prominent adviser to former President John F. Kennedy, was indicted on July 29 on several charges relating to a major international banking scandal. Clifford was indicted for allegedly taking $40-million in bribes to help a corrupt Pakistani bank gain illegal control of First American Bankshares Incorporated, the largest bank in Washington, D.C. The indictments charged that Clifford and his law partner, Robert A. Altman, helped the Bank of Credit and Commerce International (BCCI) hide BCCI's ownership of American Bankshares from U.S. banking regulators. Both men denied the charges.

Discriminatory lending. Banks finished 1992 on the defensive about the industry's record of lending to minorities. An analysis of data from the Federal Reserve System, an independent agency of the U.S. government, on lending practices in the United States was published in *The Wall Street Journal* on March 31. The study showed that mortgage loan applications from minorities are rejected more than twice as often as those from whites with similar incomes. Bankers said the credit history of applicants accounted for the difference. In October, the Federal Reserve Bank in Boston reported the results of a study showing that, in the Boston area, even when credit history and other economic factors were taken into account, minority applicants were 60 per cent more likely to be rejected than were white applicants. On September 17, the U.S. Justice Department settled its first case of mortgage discrimination, against Decatur Federal Savings & Loan in Atlanta, Ga., alleging that the S&L systematically favored whites over blacks. Decatur agreed to pay $1 million to be divided among 48 black families who were denied mortgages from January 1988 to May 1992. Paulette Thomas

In ***World Book,*** see **Bank.**

Baseball. In a traumatic 1992 season, major league club owners took control of the game from Francis (Fay) Vincent, Jr., the commissioner they elected in 1989. They forced Vincent to resign on Sept. 7, 1992, and prepared to restructure the office so that the commissioner would be responsible to the owners.

On the field, the Toronto Blue Jays won the American League championship and became the first Canadian team to reach the World Series. Then, in the series, the Blue Jays defeated the National League champions, the Atlanta Braves, 4 games to 2.

Commissioner. Many club owners felt Vincent was not responsive to them. Vincent had fought off an attempt by Richard Ravitch, the baseball owners' chief labor negotiator, to trim the commissioner's powers in labor negotiations, it was reported on June 10. Vincent would not yield, scolded the owners, and told them to stop their bickering and infighting.

Many owners did not like Vincent's attempt in July to realign teams in the National League's two divisions. National League owners were preparing for the 1993 addition of two new clubs—the Colorado Rockies in Denver and the Florida Marlins in Miami. As part of the package, 10 of the 12 National League clubs wanted Atlanta and the Cincinnati Reds to move to the Eastern Division and the St. Louis Cardinals and the Chicago Cubs to the Western Division. The Cubs vetoed the change, as was their right. Vincent then ordered the changes to be made, but the Cubs went to court and won a reprieve on July 23.

On September 3, by a vote of 18 to 9 with one abstention, the major league club owners said they lacked confidence in Vincent and asked him to resign. Vincent resisted, but on September 7 he quit for what he called "the best interests of baseball." The owners then elected Allan H. (Bud) Selig, the owner of the Milwaukee Brewers as chairman of the major league executive council, in effect making him the interim commissioner. They also rescinded the National League realignment on September 24.

Problems. Baseball was not healthy financially in 1992. Major league clubs expected to break even in 1992, lose money in 1993, and lose much more money in 1994. Eighteen of the 26 major league clubs reported lower attendance in 1992, and total attendance dropped 1.6 per cent to 55.8 million. Old, popular clubs had bad seasons. For example, the Los Angeles Dodgers finished last for the first time since 1905, and the Boston Red Sox ended up last for the first time since 1932. Meanwhile, salaries escalated, and 265 players earned at least $1 million each.

Controversy surrounded the proposed Japanese ownership of the Seattle Mariners. Hiroshi Yamauchi, a Japanese businessman, wanted to purchase the club. Major league club owners approved the sale on June 11, 1992, after Yamauchi agreed to put up $75 million of the $125 million needed to buy the Mariners but accepted less than a controlling interest in the club.

The owner of the San Francisco Giants announced

Final standings in major league baseball

American League

Eastern Division	W.	L.	Pct.	G.B.
Toronto Blue Jays	96	66	.593	
Milwaukee Brewers	92	70	.568	4
Baltimore Orioles	89	73	.549	7
Cleveland Indians	76	86	.469	20
New York Yankees	76	86	.469	20
Detroit Tigers	75	87	.463	21
Boston Red Sox	73	89	.451	23
Western Division				
Oakland Athletics	96	66	.593	
Minnesota Twins	90	72	.556	6
Chicago White Sox	86	76	.531	10
Texas Rangers	77	85	.475	19
California Angels	72	90	.444	24
Kansas City Royals	72	90	.444	24
Seattle Mariners	64	98	.395	32

American League champions— Toronto Blue Jays (defeated the Athletics, 4 games to 2)

World Series champions—Toronto Blue Jays (4 games to 2)

Offensive leaders

Batting average—Edgar Martinez, Seattle	.343
Runs scored—Tony Phillips, Detroit	114
Home runs—Juan Gonzalez, Texas	43
Runs batted in—Cecil Fielder, Detroit	124
Hits—Kirby Puckett, Minnesota	210
Stolen bases—Kenny Lofton, Cleveland	66
Slugging percentage—Mark McGwire, Oakland	.585

Leading pitchers

Games won—Jack Morris, Toronto; Kevin Brown, Texas (tie)	21
Win average (15 decisions or more)—Mike Mussina, Baltimore (18-5)	.783
Earned run average (162 or more innings)—Roger Clemens, Boston	2.41
Strikeouts—Randy Johnson, Seattle	241
Saves—Dennis Eckersley, Oakland	51
Shut-outs—Roger Clemens, Boston	5

Awards*

Most Valuable Player—Dennis Eckersley, Oakland
Cy Young—Dennis Eckersley, Oakland
Rookie of the Year—Pat Listach, Milwaukee
Manager of the Year—Tony La Russa, Oakland

National League

Eastern Division	W.	L.	Pct.	G.B.
Pittsburgh Pirates	96	66	.593	
Montreal Expos	87	75	.537	9
St. Louis Cardinals	83	79	.512	13
Chicago Cubs	78	84	.481	18
New York Mets	72	90	.444	24
Philadelphia Phillies	70	92	.432	26
Western Division				
Atlanta Braves	98	64	.605	
Cincinnati Reds	90	72	.556	8
San Diego Padres	82	80	.506	16
Houston Astros	81	81	.500	17
San Francisco Giants	72	90	.444	26
Los Angeles Dodgers	63	99	.389	35

National League champions— Atlanta Braves (defeated the Pirates, 4 games to 3)

Offensive leaders

Batting average—Gary Sheffield, San Diego	.330
Runs scored—Barry Bonds, Pittsburgh	109
Home runs—Fred McGriff, San Diego	35
Runs batted in—Darren Daulton, Philadelphia	109
Hits—Terry Pendleton, Atlanta	199
Stolen bases—Marquis Grissom, Montreal	78
Slugging percentage—Barry Bonds, Pittsburgh	.624

Leading pitchers

Games won—Tom Glavine, Atlanta; Greg Maddux, Chicago (tie)	20
Win average (15 decisions or more)—Bob Tewksbury, St. Louis (16-5)	.762
Earned run average (162 or more innings)—Bill Swift, San Francisco	2.08
Strikeouts—John Smoltz, Atlanta	215
Saves—Lee Smith, St. Louis	43
Shut-outs—David Cone, New York	5

Awards*

Most Valuable Player—Barry Bonds, Pittsburgh
Cy Young—Greg Maddux, Chicago
Rookie of the Year—Eric Karros, Los Angeles
Manager of the Year—Jim Leyland, Pittsburgh

*Selected by the Baseball Writers Association of America.

in August that he intended to sell the team to a group of Florida investors who planned to move the franchise to St. Petersburg, Fla., to begin the 1993 season. The owner, Bob Lurie, had tried unsuccessfully to get a new stadium to replace windy and soggy Candlestick Park. He then agreed on August 7 to sell the Giants for $115 million. On November 10, National League club owners rejected the sale, leaving Lurie to consider a $100-million offer from a group that promised to keep the Giants in San Francisco.

Owners discussed radical changes to reduce expenses and generate new income. Some owners wanted the players to reduce their free-agent and arbitration benefits and, if negotiations were unsuccessful, seemed willing to lock out the players from 1993 training camp. One proposal would have created an extra round of postseason play-offs to raise more money from television rights

American League. In the regular season, Toronto won the Eastern Division by four games, and the Oakland Athletics won the Western Division by six games. Toronto, with help from expensive free agents such as pitcher Jack Morris and designated hitter Dave Winfield, won its fourth division title in eight years. Playing in the spectacular SkyDome, the Blue Jays set a major league attendance record of 4,028,318.

Oakland's division title was its fourth in five years. Its key players were relief pitcher Dennis Eckersley, first baseman Mark McGwire, and outfielder Rickey Henderson.

In the pennant play-offs from October 7 to 14, Toronto defeated Oakland, 4 games to 2. Toronto's heroes were second baseman Roberto Alomar (.423 batting average and the play-offs' Most Valuable Player) and pitcher Juan Guzman (2-0 record).

National League. The division winners were Atlanta by eight games in the West and the Pittsburgh Pirates by nine games in the East. Atlanta won 13 games in a row in July en route to its second consecutive division title. It hit with power and led the league in pitching, but pitchers John Smoltz, Tom Glavine, and Steve Avery ended the season poorly.

Pittsburgh, in gaining its third straight division title, led for all but 10 days of the season. It received solid defense from left fielder Barry Bonds, center fielder Andy Van Slyke, and second baseman Jose Lind.

In the play-offs from October 6 to 14, Atlanta won in a spectacular finish, 4 games to 3. With Pittsburgh leading, 2-0, in the ninth inning of the final game, Atlanta rallied for three runs. The last two runs came on a two-out, pinch single by Francisco Cabrera, an obscure catcher/first baseman. Smoltz of Atlanta (2-0 and a 2.66 earned-run average) was voted the play-offs' Most Valuable Player.

World Series. From the start on October 17 to the finish October 24, this was a tightly fought series. Toronto defeated Atlanta in the sixth and final game, 4-3, on Winfield's two-out, two-run double in the 11th inning. Catcher Pat Borders of Toronto, with a .450 batting average, was voted the Most Valuable Player. After the series, Toronto gave Manager Cito Gaston a new two-year contract with a one-year option.

Before the second game in Atlanta, a United States Marine Corps color guard inadvertently carried the Canadian flag upside down. That prompted an uproar in Canada. Baseball officials quickly apologized, and the marines correctly displayed the Canadian flag before the third game in Toronto.

Other. On August 2, starting pitcher Tom Seaver and relief pitcher Rollie Fingers were inducted into the National Baseball Hall of Fame in Cooperstown, N.Y. Seaver was named on 98.8 per cent of the ballots, the most ever. The Hall of Fame Veterans Committee voted to add pitcher Hal Newhouser and umpire Bill McGowan.

Outfielder Robin Yount of Milwaukee and designated hitter George Brett of the Kansas City Royals became the 17th and 18th players in history to collect 3,000 hits. Yount collected his historic hit on September 9, and Brett got his on September 30. Relief pitcher Jeff Reardon of Boston broke Fingers' saves record of 341 on June 15.

Baseball hired two minority managers in 1992. The Colorado Rockies hired Don Baylor in October 1992, and the Cincinnati Reds hired Tony Perez, giving the major leagues five minority managers. Baylor is black, and Perez is Hispanic. Frank Litsky

In ***World Book,*** see **Baseball.**

Teammates mob Joe Carter (arm raised) in celebration after the Toronto Blue Jays' victory in the World Series on October 24 in Atlanta, Ga.

Basketball. The Chicago Bulls won the 1992 National Basketball Association (NBA) championship, and Duke University won the National Collegiate Athletic Association (NCAA) men's title, each for the second consecutive year. Stanford University captured the NCAA women's championship for the second time in three years. But the team that most captivated the public was the so-called Dream Team of 11 NBA professionals and one collegian that won the men's Olympic gold medal for the United States in the Summer Games.

Olympic Dream Team. In past Olympics, the United States sent collegiate all-star teams, which sometimes lost to national teams that had played together for years. When the International Olympic Committee changed the rules to allow NBA professionals in the Summer Games held in Barcelona, Spain, from July 25 to August 9, the United States sent its best players.

The guards were Earvin (Magic) Johnson, Jr., of the Los Angeles Lakers, Michael Jordan and Scottie Pippen of the Bulls, John Stockton of the Utah Jazz, and Clyde Drexler of the Portland Trail Blazers. At center were David Robinson of the San Antonio Spurs and Patrick Ewing of the New York Knicks. Larry Bird of the Boston Celtics, Charles Barkley of the Phoenix Suns, Karl Malone of the Jazz, Chris Mullin of the Golden State Warriors, and the collegian, Christian Laettner of Duke, were the forwards.

Michigan battles Duke in the National Collegiate Athletic Association's championship game on April 6. Duke won its second straight title, 71-51.

Despite health problems, the team overwhelmed its opponents. Johnson chose not to play in the 1991-1992 NBA season after he learned in November 1991 that he had HIV, the virus that causes AIDS. A bad back hampered Bird all season, and Stockton broke his leg in Olympic qualifying play. The Dream Team, nevertheless, easily won the gold medal, conquering its opponents by an average of 43.8 points in Barcelona. In the final on Aug. 8, 1992, the Dream Team defeated Croatia, 117-85.

NBA. In a tightening market for professional sports, NBA total attendance jumped from 16,876,125 to 17,367,239 during the 1991-1992 season, a 3 per cent increase. Its most visible player was Jordan, who earned $3 million in salary and as much as $20 million during the year from endorsements, commercials, and appearances. Despite disclosures that he had lost large sums of money on golf bets, his appeal remained strong.

During the 1991-1992 regular season, Jordan led Chicago to a 67-15 record, by far the best of the 27 teams. The other division winners were Portland (57-25), Utah (55-27), and Boston (51-31). For play-off purposes, Boston was crowned the Atlantic Division winner, though New York had an identical record. The tie-breaker was based on Boston's better record in head-to-head competition with the Knicks. Sixteen teams advanced to the play-offs, among them the Los Angeles Clippers for the first time since 1976.

National Basketball Association standings

Eastern Conference

Atlantic Division	W.	L.	Pct.	G.B.
Boston Celtics*	51	31	.622	
New York Knicks*	51	31	.622	
New Jersey Nets*	40	42	.488	11
Miami Heat*	38	44	.463	13
Philadelphia 76ers	35	47	.427	16
Washington Bullets	25	57	.305	26
Orlando Magic	21	61	.256	30
Central Division				
Chicago Bulls*	67	15	.817	
Cleveland Cavaliers*	57	25	.695	10
Detroit Pistons*	48	34	.585	19
Indiana Pacers*	40	42	.488	27
Atlanta Hawks	38	44	.463	29
Charlotte Hornets	31	51	.378	36
Milwaukee Bucks	31	51	.378	36

Western Conference

Midwest Division	W.	L.	Pct.	G.B.
Utah Jazz*	55	27	.671	
San Antonio Spurs*	47	35	.573	8
Houston Rockets	42	40	.512	13
Denver Nuggets	24	58	.293	31
Dallas Mavericks	22	60	.268	33
Minnesota Timberwolves	15	67	.183	40
Pacific Division				
Portland Trail Blazers*	57	25	.695	
Golden State Warriors*	55	27	.671	2
Phoenix Suns*	53	29	.646	4
Seattle SuperSonics*	47	35	.573	10
Los Angeles Clippers*	45	37	.549	12
Los Angeles Lakers*	43	39	.524	14
Sacramento Kings	29	53	.347	28

*Made play-off.

NBA champions— Chicago Bulls (defeated Portland Trail Blazers, 4 games to 2)

Individual leaders

Scoring	G.	F.G.	F.T.	Pts.	Avg.
Michael Jordan, Chicago	80	943	491	2,404	30.1
Karl Malone, Utah	81	798	673	2,272	28.0
Chris Mullin, Golden State	81	830	350	2,074	25.6
Clyde Drexler, Portland	76	694	401	1,903	25.0
Patrick Ewing, New York	82	796	377	1,970	24.0
Tim Hardaway, Golden State	81	734	298	1,893	23.4
David Robinson, San Antonio	68	592	393	1,578	23.2
Charles Barkley, Philadelphia	75	622	454	1,730	23.1

Rebounding	G.	Tot.	Avg.
Dennis Rodman, Detroit	82	1,530	18.7
Kevin Willis, Atlanta	81	1,258	15.5
Dikembe Mutombo, Denver	71	870	12.3
David Robinson, San Antonio	68	829	12.2
Hakeem Olajuwon, Houston	70	845	12.1

In 1991, Chicago, coached by Phil Jackson, had rolled through the play-offs with a 15-2 record. This time, Chicago reached the final by eliminating the Miami Heat (3 games to 0), New York (4-3), and the Cleveland Cavaliers (4-2). In the final, June 3 through 14, Chicago defeated Portland, 4 games to 2. In the last game, Chicago trailed by 15 points at the start of the fourth quarter and still won, 97-93.

Jordan unanimously won the Most Valuable Player (MVP) Award in the play-offs to become the first repeat winner of that award, and he won the regular-season MVP for the second consecutive year. During the regular season, he averaged 30.1 points per game and won his sixth consecutive scoring title.

Dennis Rodman of the Detroit Pistons led in rebounding, and his average of 18.7 per game was the

NBA's highest in two decades. Larry Johnson of the Charlotte Hornets, the first choice overall in the 1991 draft, was voted 1992 Rookie of the Year. Don Nelson was named Coach of the Year after Golden State finished with a 55-27 record, its best in 16 years. The all-star team comprised five Olympians—Jordan, Drexler, Robinson, Malone, and Mullin.

Bird retires; Magic returns, re-retires. On Aug. 18, 1992, Bird announced his retirement from professional basketball due to persistent back problems. Bird played 13 seasons with the Celtics and won the NBA's MVP Award three times, in 1984, 1985, and 1986. He led the Boston Celtics to three NBA championships (1981, 1984, 1986). Bird played in 897 games, averaging 24.3 points, 10 rebounds, and 6.3 assists per game.

Johnson, who had announced his retirement in November 1991 due to his HIV infection, officially emerged from retirement on Sept. 29, 1992. He said he would play between 50 and 60 games for the Lakers during the 1992-1993 season. On Nov. 2, 1992, however, Johnson changed his mind and said he would retire for good. Johnson said that other players' fears of contracting HIV from him led him to the decision.

College men. After the regular basketball season had ended, the final Associated Press poll ranked Duke (28-2) first, Kansas (26-4) second, Ohio State (23-5) third, the University of California at Los Angeles (UCLA) (25-4) fourth, and Indiana (23-6) fifth. All of those teams advanced to the NCAA's 64-team championship tournament.

In its early tournament games, Duke eliminated Campbell University by 82-56, Iowa by 75-62, Seton Hall by 81-69, and Kentucky by 104-103 in overtime. In the semifinals on April 4 in Minneapolis, Minn., Duke overcame a 12-point deficit and beat Indiana, 81-78, and Michigan rallied for a 76-72 victory over Cincinnati.

In the final on April 6, Duke faced Michigan, which started five freshmen. In the last 6 minutes 46 seconds, Duke turned a close game into a rout with a 23-6 scoring run and won, 71-51. Bobby Hurley, a Duke guard, was voted the MVP of the tournament. Duke, under coach Mike Krzyzewski, became the first repeat champion since UCLA in 1973. Laettner, Duke's 6-foot 11-inch (211-centimeter) senior, won the Rupp, Wooden, Naismith, and Kodak awards as the Player of the Year.

The consensus All-America team included Alonzo Mourning of Georgetown and Laettner at forward, Shaquille O'Neal of Louisiana State at center, and Jimmy Jackson of Ohio State and Harold Miner of the University of Southern California at guard. The 7-foot 1-inch (216-centimeter) O'Neal gave up his last year of college eligibility to enter the NBA draft, and the Orlando Magic made him the first choice overall.

Jerry Tarkanian, after 19 years as the highly successful coach at the University of Nevada, Las Vegas (UNLV), resigned following the season, and on April

The 1991-1992 college basketball season

College tournament champions

NCAA	(Men)	Division I: Duke
		Division II: Virginia Union
		Division III: Calvin (Mich.)
	(Women)	Division I: Stanford
		Division II: Delta State (Miss.)
		Division III: Alma (Mich.)
NAIA	(Men)	Division I: Oklahoma City
		Division II: Grace (Ind.)
	(Women)	Division I: Arkansas Tech
		Division II: Northern State (S. Dak.)
NIT	(Men)	Virginia
	(Women)	Georgia Tech
Junior College	(Men)	Division I: Three Rivers (Mo.)
		Division II: Owens Tech (Ohio)
		Division III: Sullivan County (N.Y.)
	(Women)	Division I: Louisburg (N.C.)
		Division II: Illinois Central
		Division III: Becker (Mass.)

Men's college champions

Conference	School
Atlantic Coast	Duke*
Atlantic Ten	Massachusetts*
Big East	Seton Hall—Georgetown—St. John's (tie; reg. season)
	Syracuse (tournament)
Big Eight	Kansas*
Big Sky	Montana*
Big South	Radford (reg. season)
	Campbell (tournament)
Big Ten	Ohio State (reg. season)
Big West	Nevada-Las Vegas (UNLV) (reg. season)
	New Mexico State (tournament)
Colonial A.A.	Richmond—James Madison (tie; reg. season)
	Old Dominion (tournament)
East Coast	Hofstra (reg. season)
	Towson State (tournament)
Great Midwest	Cincinnati—DePaul (tie; reg. season)
	Cincinnati (tournament)
Ivy League	Princeton (reg. season)
Metro Athletic	Tulane (reg. season)
	North Carolina-Charlotte (tournament)
Metro Atlantic	Manhattan (reg. season)
	La Salle (tournament)
Mid-American	Miami (Ohio)*
Mid-Continent	Wisconsin-Green Bay (reg. season)
	Eastern Illinois (tournament)
Mid-Eastern	North Carolina A&T—Howard (tie; reg. season)
	Howard (tournament)
Midwestern	Evansville*
Missouri Valley	Southern Illinois—Illinois State (tie; reg. season)
	Southwest Missouri State (tournament)
North Atlantic	Delaware*
Northeast	Robert Morris*
Ohio Valley	Murray State*
Pacific Ten	UCLA (reg. season)
Patriot League	Bucknell—Fordham (tie; reg. season)
	Fordham (tournament)
Southeastern	Kentucky (tournament)
Eastern Division	Kentucky (reg. season)
Western Division	Arkansas (reg. season)
Southern	East Tennessee State—Tennessee-Chattanooga (tie; reg. season)
	East Tennessee State (tournament)
Southland	Texas-San Antonio (reg. sesason)
	Northeast Louisiana (tournament)
Southwest	Houston—Texas (tie; reg. season)
	Houston (tournament)
Southwestern	Mississippi Valley State-Texas Southern (tie; reg. season)
	Mississippi Valley State (tournament)
Sun Belt	Louisiana Tech—Southwestern Louisiana (tie; reg. season)
	Southwestern Louisiana (tournament)
Trans America	Georgia Southern*
West Coast	Pepperdine*
Western	University of Texas-El Paso (UTEP)—Brigham Young (tie; reg. season)
	Brigham Young (tournament)

*Regular season and conference tournament champions.

15, he became coach of San Antonio of the NBA—only to be fired on December 18. Although UNLV won its last 23 games, it was banned from the NCAA tournament, the final punishment in the NCAA's 14-year battle with Tarkanian over recruiting violations. Rollie Massimino, Villanova's head coach, took over at UNLV.

College women. Virginia's women's team was ranked first in the nation for most of the season, and its senior guard, Dawn Staley, won the Naismith and Kodak awards as the best college player. It was favored in the NCAA's 48-team tournament. But in the April 4 semifinals in Los Angeles, Stanford eliminated Virginia, 66-65, when Staley's last-second desperation shot missed. Virginia ended the season with a 32-2 record. In the other semifinal, Western Kentucky defeated Southwest Missouri State, 84-72. In the final, Stanford whipped Western Kentucky, 78-62. Western Kentucky's shooting average of 29.6 per cent was the lowest ever in a women's championship game.

Stanford's success surprised coach Tara VanDerveer, because the team had eight freshmen and sophomores in what was expected to be a rebuilding year. Stanford's Molly Goodenbour, a junior guard, was voted the tournament MVP. Frank Litsky

See also **Olympic Games: The 1992 Olympics.** In ***World Book,*** see **Basketball; Bird, Larry; Johnson, Magic.**

Belarus. See **Commonwealth of Independent States.**

Belgium in 1992 continued on its path toward a less centralized system of government that would place most political and economic power in the hands of the country's three economic regions—Flanders, Wallonia, and Brussels. The process, known as *devolution,* was designed to ease tensions between the Dutch-speaking Flemings of Flanders and the French-speaking Walloons of Wallonia. Brussels, the third region, is the nation's capital.

Devolution gained ground with the formation of a new coalition government on March 7, 1992, nearly four months after elections in November 1991. Jean-Luc Dehaene, a Flemish Christian Democrat, became prime minister. Dehaene's center-left coalition, like its predecessor, was made up of the Flemish and Walloon Socialist and Christian Democrat parties.

The coalition in October agreed on a plan to give the regions nearly all powers of the central government, except financial, foreign, and defense policies. But the coalition still had to gain the support needed to push the plan through Parliament. Many Walloons opposed devolution, fearing Wallonia's economy would suffer if separated from that of more prosperous Flanders.

European role. Belgium continued to support rapid economic and political union within the 12-nation European Community (EC or Common Market). In November, Belgium's Senate (upper house of Parliament) ratified the so-called Maastricht Treaty, the EC's blueprint for European union. The House of Representatives (lower house) had ratified the treaty in July.

Dehaene faced the task of reducing Belgium's budget deficit and government debt in time to join in the EC's planned economic and monetary union, which was scheduled for the late 1990's. In 1992, Belgium's deficit was nearly 6 per cent of its gross domestic product (GDP—the value of all goods and services produced within a country's borders). Efforts to reduce the deficit in 1992 were hampered by Belgium's slow economic growth. This, in turn, was due in part to the high interest rates needed to keep the value of Belgium's currency, the Belgian franc, tied to that of the German mark under an EC mechanism in which Belgium participates.

Brussels failed in 1992 to cement its role as EC "capital." The city, which houses the EC's executive and legislative branches, had sought to become the home of the European Parliament, the EC's advisory branch. Work proceeded on new EC buildings in Brussels during the year, while divisions within the EC delayed a final decision. But in December, the EC decided that Strasbourg, France, would remain the Parliament's official seat. Philip Revzin

See also **Europe** (Facts in brief table). In ***World Book,*** see **Belgium.**

Belize. See **Latin America.**

Benin. See **Africa.**

Bérégovoy, Pierre (1925-), France's long-time finance minister, was appointed prime minister by President François Mitterrand on April 2, 1992. Bérégovoy succeeded Edith Cresson, who resigned after Mitterrand's Socialist Party suffered heavy losses in regional elections held in March. Bérégovoy, who had won praise for his management of the French economy in the 1980's, pledged to reduce France's high unemployment rate, a major source of public dissatisfaction with the Socialists. (See **France.**)

Pierre Eugene Bérégovoy was born in Déville-les-Rouen on Dec. 23, 1925. After dropping out of school at age 15, he worked as a machinist and railway employee. In 1950, he joined a French utility, rising to the post of executive director in 1978.

Bérégovoy became active in Socialist Party affairs in the early 1970's and held several executive positions. After managing Mitterrand's successful 1981 campaign for the presidency, he was rewarded with the post of chief of staff. In 1982, Bérégovoy was appointed minister of social affairs. Two years later, he was named minister of the economy, finance, and the budget. He held this position until 1986, when conservatives won control of the National Assembly, the more powerful of France's two houses of Parliament. Bérégovoy was reappointed to the finance ministry in 1988 after Mitterrand's reelection.

Bérégovoy and his wife, Gilberte, have a son and two daughters. Barbara A. Mayes

Berisha, Sali (1944-), a heart specialist and vocal opponent of Albania's Communist government, was elected president of Albania on April 4, 1992. He became Albania's first non-Communist president since World War II (1939-1945). Berisha, the leader of the Albanian Democratic Party, was named to the presidency by Albania's parliament after his party routed the Socialist (formerly Communist) Party in national elections in March 1992. (See **Albania.**)

Sali Berisha was born into a peasant family on July 1, 1944, in a village in northeastern Albania. In 1967, he received a medical degree from the University of Tiranë in Tiranë, the capital, and was appointed a professor at the Clinic of Cardiology at Tiranë Hospital. Formerly a member of the Communist Party, Berisha began to speak out against Albania's repressive regime in 1989 as Communist governments in Eastern Europe collapsed. In December 1990, widespread unrest forced the government to legalize opposition political parties. That month, Berisha helped found the Albanian Democratic Party, Albania's first opposition party in 45 years of Communist rule. He was elected leader of the party in September 1992.

Berisha won a seat in Albania's parliament in March 1991 in that country's first multiparty elections since the 1920's. He was reelected in March 1992.

Berisha is married and has a son and a daughter.
Barbara A. Mayes

Bhutan. See **Asia.**

Biology. The sequoia tree and the blue whale, long contenders for the title of the Earth's largest living organism, both took a back seat to the lowly fungus in 1992. In April, researchers from the University of Toronto in Mississauga, Ontario, and the Michigan Technological University in Houghton reported the discovery of a fungus covering an area of 37 acres (15 hectares) in a forest in the upper peninsula of Michigan. Like many fungi, this one consists largely of roots and shoots beneath the surface of the soil, with mushrooms occasionally growing aboveground. The researchers determined that the mushrooms in a large section of the forest were genetically identical to one another and so belonged to a single huge organism, invisibly connected underground. Scientists said the fungus might also be the oldest living organism on Earth, dating to the end of the last Ice Age about 10,000 years ago.

But Michigan's claim to the world's largest organism was short-lived. In May, scientists with the United States Forest Service Rocky Mountain Experiment Station in Ft. Collins, Colo., reported a similar fungus in Washington state measuring 1,500 acres (600 hectares). Although larger than the Michigan fungus, researchers said the Washington fungus was only about 1,000 years old.

Oldest genetic material. In September, two research teams from the University of California at Berkeley and the American Museum of Natural History in New York City announced that they had extracted pieces of deoxyribonucleic acid (DNA), the genetic material of most living creatures, from insects that died as many as 40 million years ago. The insects—a termite and a stingerless bee, both extinct—were found embedded in fossilized tree sap. When the sap hardened, it dried out the bodies of the insects trapped inside it, preventing them from decaying.

Although damaged, the ancient DNA was intact enough to be compared with modern DNA. For example, analysis showed that the DNA from the fossilized bee differed from that of modern bees by about 7 per cent—a useful clue for determining the rate of evolution for bees. This research showed that DNA can survive for tens of millions of years, longer than scientists had generally thought possible. In light of this work, scientists speculated that one day they might be able to obtain intact dinosaur DNA from blood in the stomachs of fossilized biting insects.

Killer algae. Biologists from North Carolina State University in Raleigh in July said they had located the culprit in the mysterious deaths in 1991 and 1992 of millions of fish along the East Coast of the United States. The organism is a form of algae called a *dinoflagellate*, or dino for short. Dinos are tiny organisms that move by spinning through the water.

According to the biologists, the dinos in question spend most of their lives in a dormant state inside shells on the bottom of a river or bay. When fish move

The highly destructive caterpillar of the Asian gypsy moth was the target of an intensive eradication campaign in the Pacific Northwest in 1992.

nearby, the dinos hatch from their shells and swim up to the surface of the water. There, they release a poison that kills fish and causes bits of the fishes' skin to flake off. The dinos feed on these chunks and reproduce until no live fish remain. Then the dinos fall back to the bottom, where they form new shells and again go dormant.

Poisonous bird. In October, a graduate student at the University of Chicago reported the first poisonous bird known to science. The bird—a black and orange songbird called the pitohui—lives in New Guinea. The student was alerted to the existence of the poison when he licked a scratch on his hand from a pitohui and felt his mouth go numb briefly. Formal tests later established that the bird's flesh, skin, and feathers all contain a nerve toxin. Remarkably, the same toxin has been found on the skin of tiny frogs in the Amazon. Because frogs and birds are so distantly related, each line of creatures must have evolved the poison independently as a defense against predators.

Life-span research. Scientists with the University of California at Davis in October reported the first evidence that there may not be a preset limit to how long an organism can live. The researchers raised more than 1 million fruit flies, measuring each one's life span. They learned that, contrary to conventional thinking, older flies did not necessarily have a higher risk of dying on a given day than did younger flies.

The life expectancy of flies slowly dropped until about 60 days of age, at which point it actually began to rise. In other words, a 30-day-old fly would live an average of, say, 10 more days, but a 70-day-old fly would live an average of 20 more days. Apparently, flies hardy enough to survive the first month or two did not find later life to be so perilous. This result runs counter to the traditional idea that life expectancy must decrease with each passing year. However, the scientists said more research must be done before the finding can be applied to humans and other animals.

New body temperature. A study released in September challenged the number of 98.6 °F (37.0 °C) as the normal body temperature. Researchers with the University of Maryland in Baltimore took 700 temperature readings several times a day from 148 men and women ages 18 to 40. They found the average normal body temperature to be 98.2 °F (36.8 °C). Only 8 per cent of the readings were 98.6 °F, the figure first reported by a German physician in 1878.

Noting that body temperature varies with the time of day, the researchers proposed using not one but two temperatures to determine whether a person has a fever. Around 6 a.m., when body temperature is usually lowest, a temperature above 98.9 °F (37.2 °C) should be considered a fever. And around 6 p.m., when body temperature is highest, a temperature above 99.9 °F (37.7 °C) is a fever. The researchers cautioned that these numbers may not apply to children or elderly people. Thomas H. Maugh II

See also **Medicine**. In ***World Book,*** see **Biology**.

Blair, Bonnie K. (1964-), won her second consecutive gold medal in the 500-meter speed-skating race at the 1992 Winter Olympic Games in February in Albertville, France, becoming the first female speed skater ever to win consecutive golds in that race. Blair had captured the 500-meter gold in the 1988 Winter Games in Calgary, Canada. Blair also placed first in the 1,000-meter race in Albertville, becoming the only United States athlete ever to win three gold medals overall in Winter Olympics competition.

Born on March 18, 1964, in Cornwall, N.Y., Blair was the youngest of six children. After her family moved to Champaign, Ill., Blair entered her first speed-skating competition at age 4. In 1979, Blair was introduced to Olympic-style speed skating, but she continued to compete in *pack skating* into the early 1980's. In pack skating, several skaters compete against each other on a 110-meter oval rink. In Olympic speed skating, only two skaters at a time compete on a 400-meter oval.

In 1984, only two 400-meter rinks existed in the United States. With funding from the Champaign police department, Blair trained in Europe. In 1986, she won first place in the world championships in short-track skating, a type of pack skating. At the 1988 Winter Olympics, she set a world record in the 500-meters with a time of 39.10 seconds. She competed in U.S. women's cycling in 1989 but returned full-time to speed skating in 1991. Kristine Portnoy Kelley

Boating. The most expensive campaign in the history of yachting ended in May 1992 when *America³* (pronounced *America cubed*) of the United States defeated *Il Moro di Venezia* of Italy, 4 races to 1, in the America's Cup final. The finalists were Bill Koch of Palm Beach, Fla., heir to an oil fortune, and Raul Gardini, an Italian industrialist. Koch's syndicate spent $68.5 million on its campaign and built four yachts, each with the latest technical advances. Gardini's syndicate spent $110 million and built five yachts.

New class. In most recent America's Cup races, the craft were relatively slow 65-foot (20-meter) sloops of the 12-Meter Class. For the first time, cup races employed lighter, faster sloops from the new International America's Cup Class. They were 75 feet (23 meters) long with 110-foot (34-meter) masts and 40 per cent more sail area.

The trials and finals were held over eight-leg, 20-mile (32-kilometer) courses off San Diego. From January until May 1, 1992, the potential challengers and defenders held separate trials. Most of the 28 challenging clubs, including two from Russia and one from Slovenia, dropped out before the racing began. In the challengers' best-of-nine final, *Il Moro di Venezia* defeated New Zealand, 5 races to 3.

Opposite: Bill Koch's *America³* and its crew are escorted back to port in San Diego in May after winning the America's Cup over Italy's *Il Moro di Venezia*.

The defenders' trials pitted Koch against Dennis Conner of San Diego, the cup defender and a three-time cup winner. Conner raised only $15 million to $20 million and could afford only one boat. Koch could afford superior technology, and with that advantage, *America*³ won the best-of-13 defenders' final, 7 races to 4.

*America*³ and *Il Moro* sailed the best-of-seven cup final from May 9 through May 16. *America*³ won the first race by 30 seconds, lost the second by 3 seconds (the closest race in cup history), and won the next three by 1 minute 58 seconds, 1 minute 4 seconds, and 44 seconds, respectively.

Powerboats. *Miss Budweiser* won seven of the nine races from June to October for unlimited hydroplanes. Chip Hanauer of Seattle drove the boat after a year off to race autos. *Miss Budweiser*'s victories included the Gold Cup on June 14 in Detroit. On June 11, in Gold Cup qualifying, it set a world record of 168.937 miles (271.878 kilometers) per hour over a distance of 5 miles (8 kilometers).

A power struggle between management groups marred the offshore powerboat circuit in 1992. Dissidents from the Offshore Professional Tour formed Super Boat Racing in May, but the two groups recombined in October. Still, only 9 superboats continued racing compared with as many as 16 powerboats in previous years. Frank Litsky

In *World Book,* see **Boating; Sailing.**

Bolivia. Bolivians in 1992 prepared to choose between two of the country's richest men in presidential elections scheduled for May 1993. The two candidates, Gonzalo Sánchez de Lozada, 61, of the Nationalist Revolutionary Movement and Max Fernández, 50, of the Civic and Solidarity Union Party, had vastly different backgrounds. Sánchez de Lozada's wealthy parents raised him in the United States. He returned to Bolivia at age 21 and developed the country's largest privately owned mining company. Fernández is a self-made man who triumphed over poverty to become the president of the Bolivian National Brewery.

Although the candidates concentrated their campaigning in the capital city of La Paz, there was evidence of great dissatisfaction among people elsewhere in the impoverished country, where male life expectancy is still only 50 years of age. Reports from rural areas indicated the formation of a leftist, anti-government movement patterned after the Shining Path rebels in neighboring Peru.

On Sept. 24, 1992, the U.S. government turned over to Bolivia 48 ancient textiles woven by the Aymará Indians. The objects, some up to 500 years old, are sacred to the people of the town of Coroma, from which they were looted. Nathan A. Haverstock

See also **Latin America** (Facts in brief table). In *World Book,* see **Bolivia.**

Books. See **Canadian literature; Literature; Literature, American; Literature for children.**

Boothroyd, Betty (1929-), was elected Great Britain's first female Speaker of the House of Commons, the lower house of Parliament, on April 27, 1992. By a vote of 372 to 238, Boothroyd, who is a member of the Labour Party, defeated Conservative Peter Brooke, the former British secretary of state for Northern Ireland. Boothroyd also became the first Speaker since World War II (1939-1945) to be elected from a party in opposition to the governing party. Boothroyd succeeded Bernard Weatherill, for whom she had served as deputy Speaker of the House of Commons since 1987. Weatherill did not run for re-election to the House in the April 9, 1992, general elections, but retired instead.

Boothroyd was born on Oct. 8, 1929, in Dewsbury, Yorkshire. She attended Dewsbury College of Commerce and Art. After completing secretarial training in the late 1940's, Boothroyd became a professional dancer, performing in pantomimes in the West End, a section of London. Boothroyd's political experience began in the 1950's, when she served as an assistant to various Labour ministers. During those years, she accompanied Labour Party delegates to a number of European conferences, and to conferences in the Soviet Union, China, and Vietnam. Also in the 1950's and 1960's, she won several local elections for the office of councilor. Boothroyd has been a member of Parliament from the district of West Bromwich West since 1974. Carol L. Hanson

Bosnia and Hercegovina proclaimed its independence from Yugoslavia on March 3, 1992. But the new nation, which is often called simply Bosnia, immediately became engulfed in a civil war that divided the country along ethnic lines and threatened its very survival. The war was sparked in part by the territorial ambitions of Serbia, the dominant republic of Yugoslavia. By the end of the year, the Bosnian government controlled only about 10 per cent of the country's territory. Tens of thousands of people, most of them civilians, died in the war, and more than a million were left homeless. Thousands more were expected to die from cold, disease, and hunger.

Before the war, Bosnia was a mixed society with three main nationality groups—Muslims, Serbs, and Croats. Muslims made up some 43 per cent of the population; Serbs, some 31 per cent; and Croats, about 17 per cent. In a referendum on February 29 and March 1, Bosnia's Muslims and Croats voted overwhelmingly to declare independence. Most ethnic Serbs boycotted the vote under pressure from Serb nationalists.

Civil war. On March 22, ethnic Serbs began attacking Muslim and Croat areas. The Serbs were aided by Yugoslav army troops reportedly controlled by Serbia. Serbia sought to create a link through Bosnia with Serb-held areas of Croatia, a former Yugoslav republic that had declared independence in June 1991.

Forces opposing the Serbs included Muslim and ethnic Croat militias; Croatian government forces; and

Soldiers and civilians take cover as Serbian forces attack Sarajevo, capital of Bosnia and Hercegovina, during the siege of the city that began in April.

the Bosnian territorial defense force, a multiethnic volunteer army formed by the Bosnian government. But these forces were no match for the Serbs, who by August had seized nearly 70 per cent of Bosnia's territory. In October and November, Muslim forces also came under attack from Croatian forces, who attempted to seize territory deemed vital to Croatia.

International opinion was increasingly outraged by reports of "ethnic cleansing"—expulsions of civilians, mainly Muslims, from captured areas. Witnesses also told of atrocities against Croats and Muslims in Serb-run detention camps and numerous massacres of Croat and Muslim villagers.

The United States and the European Community (EC) recognized Bosnia's independence on April 7. But for many months they made no serious attempt to stem the violence. Numerous cease-fires negotiated by the EC and United Nations (UN) failed to take hold.

On May 30, the UN Security Council imposed a trade and oil embargo on Yugoslavia, which consisted of Serbia and Montenegro. In August, the UN authorized the use of force to protect convoys bringing food and medical relief to besieged areas in Bosnia, including the capital, Sarajevo. On November 20, the United States and European nations began a naval blockade to help enforce the embargo, which had been largely ineffective. Eric Bourne

See also **Europe** (Facts in brief table); **Yugoslavia**. In ***World Book***, see **Bosnia and Hercegovina**.

Botswana. See **Africa**.

Boutros-Ghali, Boutros (1922-), saying he was "born" for the job, began his five-year term as secretary-general of the United Nations on Jan. 1, 1992. Boutros-Ghali, who campaigned vigorously for the United Nations post, had been Egypt's deputy prime minister for foreign affairs since May 1991.

Boutros-Ghali was born in Cairo, Egypt, on Nov. 14, 1922. He received a law degree from Cairo University in 1946 and a Ph.D. in international law from Paris University in 1949.

Among his professional and academic achievements, Boutros-Ghali was a Fulbright research scholar at Columbia University in New York City (1954-1955); director of the Centre of Research of The Hague Academy of International Law in the Netherlands (1963-1964); and a visiting law professor at Paris University (1967-1968). Between 1949 and 1979, Boutros-Ghali was professor of international law and international relations at Cairo University.

Boutros-Ghali has had extensive diplomatic experience. In September 1978, as a member of the Egyptian delegation, he attended the peace summit initiated by United States President Jimmy Carter at Camp David, Md., which led to a peace treaty between Egypt and Israel in 1979. In 1990, he was instrumental in helping win the release of African National Congress leader Nelson Mandela from a South African prison.

A Coptic Christian, Boutros-Ghali is married to a Jew from Alexandria, Egypt. Kristine Portnoy Kelley

Bowling. Marc McDowell of Madison, Wis., emerged in 1992 as a high achiever on and off the lanes. The 29-year-old bowling champion spent much of his time on his duties as the president of the Professional Bowlers Association (PBA) in Akron, Ohio, which conducted the men's tour.

Men's tour. McDowell led the tour in earnings with $174,215. In the event with the richest first-place pay-off, the $300,000 Firestone Tournament of Champions from April 21 to 25 in Fairlawn, Ohio, he won the $60,000 first prize by defeating Don Genalo of Perrysburg, Ohio, in the final, 223-193. The Firestone Tournament, the third triple-crown tournament, followed the $300,000 PBA national championship from March 22 to 28 in Toledo, Ohio, and the $225,000 Bowling Proprietors Association of America United States Open from April 5 to 11 in Canandaigua, N.Y. McDowell also won tournaments in Torrance, Calif., and Rochester, N.Y.

Besides McDowell, other prominent winners included Parker Bohn III of Freehold, N.J.; Eric Forkel of Chatsworth, Calif.; and Robert Lawrence of Austin, Tex. Bohn won three tournaments—in El Paso and Beaumont, Tex., and in Tokyo. Forkel won the PBA championship by routing Bob Vespi of Plantation, Fla., in the final of the five-man stepladder final, 217-133. Vespi's low score came after he failed to roll a strike or a spare in three of the first five frames. This was Forkel's first full year on the tour, and he was not even listed in the tour program. Lawrence became the U.S. Open champion with a 226-221 victory in the final over Scott Devers of Richmond, Ind.

The PBA tour encompassed 34 tournaments. One major tournament not on the tour was the American Bowling Congress Masters competition. In the May 9 final, Ken Johnson of Richland, Tex., defeated Dave D'Entremont of Parma, Ohio, 235-207.

Women's tour. The Ladies Pro Bowlers Tour conducted tournaments from January through December. Of the women's 21 tournaments, Carol Gianotti of Australia and Tish Johnson of Panorama City, Calif., won four each, and Anne Marie Duggan of La Habra, Calif., and Carol Norman of Ardmore, Okla., won two each. The year's leaders were Johnson ($96,872) and Gianoti ($85,135) in earnings and Leanne Barrette (211.36) and Johnson (211.31) in scoring. In the final of the $100,000 U.S. Open from February 24 to March 1 in Fountain Valley, Calif., Johnson beat Aleta Sill of Dearborn, Mich., 216-213.

Senior. For the second consecutive year, 51-year-old Gene Stus of Allen Park, Mich., and 54-year-old John Handegard of Las Vegas, Nev., outbowled more celebrated colleagues. In the 12 tournaments on this PBA-sponsored tour, Stus won twice and was second three times. He earned $62,725, a tour record. Handegard had the highest average (220.78) and repeated as the PBA senior champion. Frank Litsky

In ***World Book,*** see **Bowling.**

Boxing. Riddick Bowe convincingly defeated champion Evander Holyfield on Nov. 13, 1992, to capture the world heavyweight title. Both fighters entered the bout undefeated, but Bowe tallied more points on each of the three judges' scorecards to remain unbeaten in 32 professional fights. Bowe was given a good chance because he was such a hard hitter, and he dominated Holyfield nearly the entire fight. Although some boxing experts called the fight an upset, others pointed out that Holyfield, age 30, had looked unimpressive in his title defenses, notably against two 42-year-olds (Larry Holmes and George Foreman), both of whom went the full 12 rounds with him.

On December 14, the World Boxing Council (WBC) stripped Bowe of his title for allegedly reneging on a written agreement to fight British boxer Lennox Lewis. The WBC then named Lewis, the number one contender, as its heavyweight champion. The WBC action created the first split heavyweight championship since 1987.

In Holyfield's first defense of 1992, in Las Vegas, Nev., on June 19, Holyfield was a heavy favorite over Holmes, a former champion lured out of retirement. Holyfield won a unanimous decision.

Tyson convicted. Former heavyweight champion Mike Tyson was found guilty of rape and criminal deviate sexual conduct on February 10 in Indianapolis. On March 26, he was sentenced to six years in an Indiana prison. Tyson had been accused of raping an 18-

World champion boxers

World Boxing Association

Division	Champion	Country	Date won
Heavyweight	Evander Holyfield Riddick Bowe	U.S.A. U.S.A.	1990 Nov. '92
Junior heavyweight	Bobby Czyz	U.S.A.	1991
Light heavyweight	Thomas Hearns Iran Barkley	U.S.A. U.S.A	1991 March '92
Super middleweight	Victor Cordoba Michael Nunn	Panama U.S.A.	1991 Sept. '92
Middleweight	vacant Reggie Johnson	 U.S.A.	 April '92
Junior middleweight	Vinny Pazienza	U.S.A.	1991
Welterweight	Meldrick Taylor	U.S.A.	1991
Junior welterweight	Edwin Rosario Akinobu Hiranaka Morris East, Jr.	Puerto Rico Japan Philippines	1991 April '92 Sept. '92
Lightweight	vacant Joey Gamache Tony Lopez	 U.S.A. U.S.A.	 June '92 Oct. '92
Junior lightweight	Genaro Hernandez	U.S.A.	1991
Featherweight	Yong-kyun Park	South Korea	1991
Junior featherweight	Raul Perez Wilfredo Vasquez	Mexico Puerto Rico	1991 March '92
Bantamweight	Israel Contreras Eddie Cook Jorge Julio	Venezuela U.S.A. Colombia	1991 March '92 Oct. '92
Junior bantamweight	vacant Katsuya Onizuka	 Japan	 April '92
Flyweight	Yong-kang Kim Aquiles Guzman	South Korea Venezuela	1991 Sept. '92
Junior flyweight	Hiroki Ioka Yuh Myung-woo	Japan South Korea	1991 Nov. '92
Minimumweight	Hi-yong Choi	South Korea	1991

World Boxing Council

Division	Champion	Country	Date won
Heavyweight	Evander Holyfield Riddick Bowe Lennox Lewis	U.S.A. U.S.A. Great Britain	1990 Nov. '92 Dec. '92
Cruiserweight	Anaclet Wamba	Congo	1991
Light heavyweight	Jeff Harding	Australia	1991
Super middleweight	Mauro Galvano Nigel Benn	Italy Great Britain	1990 Oct. '92
Middleweight	Julian Jackson	U.S. Virgin Islands	1990
Super welterweight	Terry Norris	U.S.A.	1990
Welterweight	James McGirt	U.S.A.	1991
Super lightweight	Julio César Chávez	Mexico	1989
Lightweight	vacant Miguel Gonzalez	 Mexico	 Aug. '92
Super featherweight	Azumah Nelson	Ghana	1988
Featherweight	Marcos Villasana Paul Hodkinson	Mexico Great Britain	1990 Nov. '91
Super bantamweight	Daniel Zaragoza Thierry Jacob Tracy Patterson	Mexico France U.S.A.	1991 March '92 June '92
Bantamweight	vacant Victor Rabanales	 Mexico	 March '92
Super flyweight	Sung-kil Moon	South Korea	1990
Flyweight	Muangshai Kittikasem Yuri Arbachakov	Thailand Russia	1991 June '92
Light flyweight	Humberto Gonzalez	Mexico	1991
Strawweight	Ricardo Lopez	Mexico	1990

Riddick Bowe savors his championship belt after beating Evander Holyfield for the world heavyweight title on November 13 in Las Vegas, Nev.

year-old contestant in the Miss Black America contest in Indianapolis in 1991. When Tyson won the heavyweight title in 1987 at age 20, he was the youngest world heavyweight champion ever, but he lost his title in 1990.

Other pros. The WBC, World Boxing Association, and International Boxing Federation continued to recognize world champions in 17 weight divisions. Holyfield and Bowe, before the WBC stripped him of his title, were the only champions recognized by all three organizations.

The champions with the longest reigns were Azumah Nelson of Ghana, the WBC superfeatherweight (130-pound [59-kilogram]) titleholder since 1988, and Julio César Chávez of Mexico, the WBC superlightweight (140-pound [64-kilogram]) champion since 1989.

Olympics. Cuban boxers dominated the Summer Olympics held from July 25 through August 9 in Barcelona, Spain. Cuban fighters won seven gold medals and two silver medals in the 12 weight classes. The United States won only three boxing medals, and its only gold medalist was Oscar De La Hoya of Los Angeles at 132 pounds (60 kilograms). Eric Griffin of Broussard, La., a four-time world champion at 106 pounds (48 kilograms), lost in his second Olympic bout because the computerized scoring system failed to register many of his scoring punches. Frank Litsky

In *World Book,* see **Boxing.**

Braun, Carol Moseley (1947-), on Nov. 3, 1992, was elected the first black woman United States senator. She had won the Democratic nomination for senator from Illinois by upsetting 12-year incumbent Senator Alan Dixon in the March 17 primary. Braun had announced her candidacy on Nov. 19, 1991, following Judge Clarence Thomas' appointment to the Supreme Court of the United States. The Thomas nomination had been surrounded by controversy over charges of sexual harassment brought by law professor Anita Hill.

Braun won the Democratic nomination with a grassroots campaign. She capitalized on Dixon's support of Thomas, which alienated many women voters who believed Hill's allegations that Thomas had sexually harassed her.

Braun was born Aug. 16, 1947, in Chicago. She received a bachelor's degree in political science from the University of Illinois at Chicago in 1967 and a law degree from the University of Chicago in 1972. After receiving her law degree, Braun was a prosecutor in the United States attorney's office. In 1978, Braun was elected to the Illinois House of Representatives and became the first woman and the first black in Illinois to serve as assistant majority leader. She also acted as Chicago Mayor Harold Washington's legislative floor leader. In 1988, Braun became Cook County recorder of deeds, becoming the highest-ranking black elected official in the county. Braun is divorced and has one son. Kristine Portnoy Kelley

Brazil. Brazilians had their eyes glued to television sets on Sept. 29, 1992, as the Chamber of Deputies, the lower house of Brazil's Congress, impeached President Fernando Collor de Mello on charges of corruption. The vote was 441 to 38. Collor was formally suspended from office on October 2, while he awaited trial in the Brazilian Senate. Brazil's vice president, Itamar Augusto Franco, became acting president. Collor resigned on December 29, and Franco was sworn in as president.

Franco created controversy on October 2 by naming a man with seemingly few credentials for finance minister. The appointee was Gustavo Krause, a tax lawyer and congressional deputy from the northeast state of Pernambuco. But Krause resigned on December 16, after Franco temporarily suspended plans to sell off government-controlled industries.

The corruption allegations that led to the president's impeachment first surfaced in mid-May. Collor's younger brother, Pedro Affonso Collor de Mello, charged that Paulo César Cavalcante Farias, the president's former campaign treasurer, took kickbacks and was involved in influence peddling. The former head of Brazil's state oil company, Petrobras, alleged that Farias had repeatedly called him to discover the winners of lucrative oil contracts before they were awarded and pressured him to grant an interest-free $40-million loan to one of Farias' friends. On June 25, a retired but influential military officer, General Euclydes Figueiredo, brother of Brazil's last military chief of state, called upon Collor to resign, touching off similar appeals from many prominent Brazilians as more corruption charges surfaced.

A congressional panel formed to investigate the matter issued a 200-page report on August 24 that said Collor received "improper economic benefits" that were grounds for impeachment. The report identified Farias as the mastermind of a scheme to extort money from individuals and corporations doing business with the government. While allegedly pocketing as much as $15 million for himself, Farias reportedly presided over a kickback and extortion scheme whereby at least $23 million was said to have been diverted into private bank accounts of the president's wife, mother, ex-wife, and political cronies.

Earth Summit. From June 3 to 14, political leaders and representatives from 178 countries gathered in Rio de Janeiro for the United Nations Conference on Environment and Development, known also as the Earth Summit. The summit focused world attention on how human agricultural and industrial activities affect the global environment and on ways to encourage economic development without further destroying the environment.

The conference produced five agreements. One of the most significant achievements at the Earth Summit was the agreement among more than 150 nations on the importance of limiting *greenhouse gas* emissions. Excess greenhouse gases are produced mainly from burning coal, oil, and gasoline in industry and transportation. Excess greenhouse gas emissions have the potential to dangerously warm Earth's climate. (See **Environmental pollution: Environmental Concern Goes Global.**)

Population growth. For the first time since the 1920's, Brazil's annual population growth rate dipped below 2 per cent, according to preliminary figures from the Brazilian census. Even so, Brazil was the world's fifth most populous country after China, India, the United States, and Indonesia. The latest census figures also indicated that the movement of people to cities continued during the 1980's. Brazil now has 12 cities with more than 1 million people.

A case of rape? Environmentalists reacted in shock and dismay when Paulinho Paiakán, a Kayapó Indian chief who during the 1980's became a worldwide symbol of Brazilian Indian defense of the rain forest, was charged with rape on June 2, 1992. The alleged victim was an 18-year-old woman, a language tutor for the chief's three children.

A prison massacre. With unusual brutality, military police on October 2 put down a rebellion at São Paulo's House of Detention, Latin America's largest prison. Official figures put the number of dead at 111, but human rights investigators said that more than 200 prisoners died. Nathan A. Haverstock

See also **Latin America** (Facts in brief table). In ***World Book,*** see **Brazil**.

British Columbia. The New Democratic Party (NDP) government, led by Premier Michael Harcourt, unveiled a series of measures in 1992 to protect the Pacific coast province's spectacular environment. In January, the NDP established a commission on land use to draw up a provincewide forestry plan and to resolve disputes between loggers and conservationists. The government also imposed an 18-month suspension of logging in five contested areas on Vancouver Island, while the commission studied the cases. In announcing sites for the creation of 23 new wilderness parks by the end of 1992, the NDP upheld its election promise to double the province's park area.

On January 17, the government set standards banning all forms of chlorine in waste generated by pulp mills. In September, however, the government decided that it needed to further investigate the scientific and economic basis for the decision. It announced it would consult with industry, environmental groups, and Indian groups on the feasibility of the ban.

Former British Columbia Premier William Vander Zalm, forced to resign in April 1991 after charges that he had violated conflict-of-interest rules in selling a theme park to an Asian investor, was acquitted on June 25, 1992. The judge ruled that infringement of the Criminal Code had not been proven beyond a reasonable doubt. David M. L. Farr

In *World Book,* see **British Columbia.**

Brunei. See **Asia.**

Building and construction. The biggest surges in an otherwise lackluster construction market in 1992 came in the aftermath of disasters. Flooding in Chicago, riot damage in Los Angeles, and hurricanes in Florida and Hawaii brought work to the construction industry, but not enough to bring about an economic recovery in the industry.

The flood in Chicago on April 13 was caused by the collapse of a section of an old freight tunnel under the Chicago River. Water rushed through parts of the 60-mile (100-kilometer) tunnel system and into basements and subbasements of buildings in the Loop, the city's central business district. It took weeks for contractors to stop the flow of water, install permanent bulkheads, and pump the water out of the tunnels and basements.

The tunnel had apparently been damaged in September 1991, when a city contractor was replacing old bridge pilings in the river. Some city officials reportedly knew of the damage early in 1992, but failed to act. A city engineer said repairs would have cost $10,000 if made at that time. The flood cost the city more than $37 million in repairs, and business losses were estimated at $1 billion by the Chicagoland Chamber of Commerce. (See also **Chicago.**)

Fires set during riots that broke out in Los Angeles on April 29 after four white police officers were cleared of charges stemming from the beating of a black motorist damaged or destroyed 623 structures. The damage estimates approached $1 billion. Mayor Tom Bradley created a commission to oversee reconstruction, and the federal government promised grants and loans totaling $600 million to help finance the cost of rebuilding. (See **Los Angeles.**)

Then, in August and September, there were disastrous hurricanes. The most widespread damage—$7.3-billion in insured losses—was caused by Hurricane Andrew, which struck south Florida on August 24 and caused more destruction in Louisiana on August 25 and 26. Andrew severely damaged or destroyed 72,000 homes in Dade County, Florida.

In the aftermath, building engineers realized that they know more about how winds high above the ground affect tall buildings than they do about how ground-level winds affect single-family houses. But in some cases, investigators believed builders did not comply with the county building codes—particularly in securing the different components, such as roofs to frames. In some housing developments, roofs were made of waferboard, a material similar to cardboard, rather than plywood as the building code stipulates. Also, staples rather than nails were used to attach decking to the roof rafters.

Although the volume of disaster repair work was large enough to cause the price of plywood to shoot up 16 per cent in September, it was not a substitute for new construction markets.

Heavy construction. Passage of the Intermodal Surface Transportation Efficiency Act in December 1991 had an impact on transportation construction in 1992. The act authorized $119 billion for highway construction and $31.5 billion for mass transit over its six-year life. The act also cleared legal barriers to the joint public and private funding of transportation projects. For example, a German and Japanese consortium received a $96-million demonstration grant to build a $600-million magnetic-levitation system in the Orlando, Fla., area.

The surge in transportation as well as big gains in the power and communications markets pushed up the 1992 tally for heavy construction work. Almost $36 billion in new contracts was awarded in this sector from January to August. The total rose 7 per cent from the amount awarded during the same eight-month period in 1991.

Housing and nonresidential building. Single-family housing starts also rose to a seasonally adjusted annual rate of 1.06 million in August 1992. Multifamily construction jumped to an annual rate of 180,000 units, nearly a 22 per cent increase over July.

But markets remained poor for building new commercial and manufacturing facilities. This sector contributed just $52.5 billion in new contracts in the January to August period. This was a 6 per cent decline from the amount awarded during the same period in 1991. Contract awards for manufacturing buildings were down 32 per cent for the period, commercial buildings were down 6 per cent, and educational

The largest building in Asia, the 105-story Yu Kyong Hotel in Pyongyang, North Korea, was sagging so severely in 1992 that it may never open.

buildings were down 10 per cent. Overall, contract awards totaled $96 billion from January through August, a 3 per cent decline compared to the same period in 1991.

Major projects announced. Despite a sluggish global economy, a number of major projects were announced worldwide in 1992. In January, the World Bank, an agency of the United Nations, agreed to fund a $500-million, 3-mile (4.8-kilometer) crossing of the Jamuna River in Bangladesh. In March, officials in Sydney, Australia, awarded a contract for the nation's longest cable-stayed bridge. In a cable-stayed bridge, the cables that support the roadway are connected directly to towers, rather than to steel cables that are then anchored to towers as in a suspension bridge. The Glebe Island Bridge will span 1,130 feet (344 meters) over Blackwattle Bay in Sydney Harbour.

Swiss voters in a September national referendum approved a plan to spend more than $10 billion on two north-south rail tunnels through the Alps. A 31-mile (50-kilometer) tunnel will be built through Saint Gotthard Mountain and a 19-mile (31-kilometer) tunnel will be built through the Lötschberg Mountains.

Milestones. Three custom-designed slip-forming machines were airlifted to France in April—the largest aboard a Russian Antonov-124, the world's largest cargo plane. The machines will be used for fast-paced tunnel finishing work on the French side of the English Channel Tunnel, also known as the Chunnel, the 31-mile tunnel between Great Britain and France. In May 1992, the final cost to complete the project by September 1993 was projected to be $14.25 billion.

In September 1992, the first section of Boston's sunken-tube Third Harbor Tunnel was towed into place from a shipyard in Baltimore. The double tube, 325 feet (99 meters) in length, weighed 7,500 short tons (6,800 metric tons). Eventually, 12 sections will be floated into place, partially filled with concrete, and sunk into a gravel-lined trench prepared in Boston Harbor. The Third Harbor Tunnel is part of a $5-billion project that will replace the six-lane elevated Central Artery in Boston with the eight-lane tunnel. The project also includes the building of another tunnel under the harbor to link Logan International Airport with South Boston and the Massachusetts Turnpike.

Major projects open. A 60-story headquarters for the NCNB National Bank, completed in June, became the tallest building in Charlotte, N.C. The building is topped by a crown of aluminum spires 100 feet (30 meters) tall.

The first phase of Walt Disney Company's $4.5-billion theme park east of Paris opened in April. Contractors employed almost 12,000 workers to construct an entertainment center, a campground, a golf course, and six hotels with a total of 5,200 rooms. A second phase of the project is slated to include a film studio, a convention center, and a 2,700-room hotel.

Janice Lyn Tuchman

In *World Book,* see **Building construction.**

Bulgaria. Zhelyu Zhelev became Bulgaria's first directly elected president on Jan. 19, 1992. Zhelev, former leader of the ruling Union of Democratic Forces (UDF), had been appointed president by the country's parliament in 1990. In the election, he won 53 per cent of the vote in a runoff against Velko Valkanov, a candidate backed by the Bulgarian Socialist (formerly Communist) Party. The first round of voting, on January 12, had failed to give any candidate a majority.

The country faced political uncertainty during the year, as divisions grew among the 16 parties making up the UDF and between the UDF and other parties. On October 28, the Socialists joined forces with the small Movement for Rights and Freedom (MRF), an ethnic Turkish party, to bring down the UDF government with a no-confidence vote against Prime Minister Filip Dimitrov. Dimitrov failed in an attempt to form a new government in November. On December 30, the parliament approved MRF nominee Lyuben Berov as prime minister. Berov, who had been an economic advisor of Zhelev, was not an ethnic Turk and did not belong to any political party.

Former Communists prosecuted. In July, about 60 former officials, including three former prime ministers, were charged with abuse of office. The scale of the prosecutions disturbed many Bulgarians, who believed it had taken on the proportions of a "witch hunt" and was impeding the country's transition to democracy and a free economy.

Todor Zhivkov, the Communist head of Bulgaria from 1954 to 1989, was convicted on Sept. 4, 1992, of embezzling state funds. After an 18-month trial, a seven-judge panel sentenced Zhivkov to seven years in prison. Zhivkov, who still faced additional charges, said he would appeal the verdict. Zhivkov was the first Communist leader in the newly democratic nations of Eastern Europe to be given a public trial.

Economic reform made some headway in Bulgaria in 1992, after two years of economic stagnation. By October, inflation had fallen, and Bulgaria's currency, the lev, had become the most stable in the region. In addition, a rise in exports helped the country increase its foreign exchange reserves to about $1 billion by August. However, labor unrest during the summer, involving miners, transportation workers, and medical personnel, forced the government to agree to wage and pension increases, adding to the strains on the budget.

Privatization progressed slowly in 1992. However, a law passed on April 23 paved the way for the sale of small state-owned companies to private investors. The sale of some large enterprises was expected to begin by early 1993. Other legislation provided for the return of businesses, property, or lands seized by the Communists, including more than 1 million small farms collectivized in the 1950's. Eric Bourne

See also **Europe** (Facts in brief table). In ***World Book***, see **Bulgaria**.

Burkina Faso. See **Africa**.

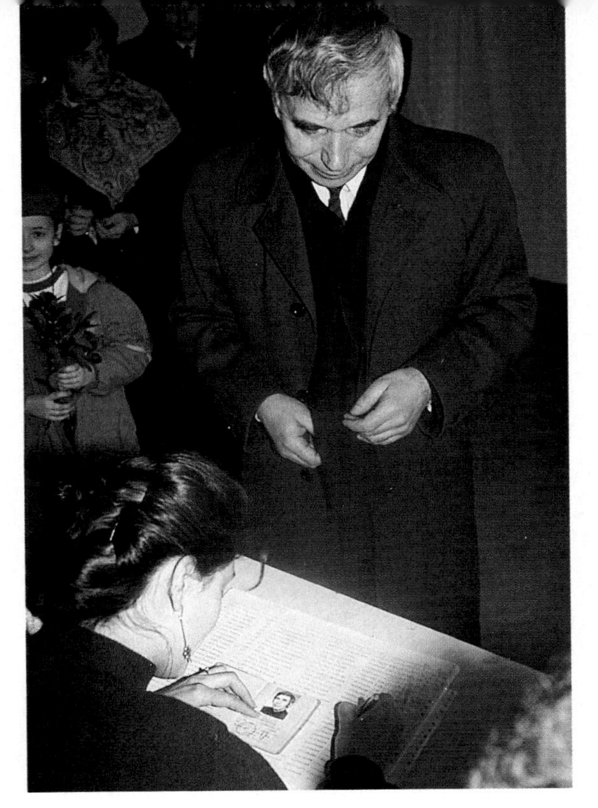

Zhelyu Zhelev, Bulgaria's first directly elected president, prepares to cast his vote in national elections on January 19.

Burma. The armed forces that have run Burma (officially called Myanmar) since 1962 changed leaders on April 23, 1992. General Saw Maung stepped down as chairman of the State Law and Order Restoration Council (SLORC). The SLORC is the ruling body created by the armed forces in 1988 to stifle popular demands for democracy. Maung was reported to have been in poor health.

Maung was succeeded by his deputy, Than Shwe, who in March had assumed Maung's role as defense minister. However, experts believed true power was held by Ne Win, the architect of the 1962 take-over, and his protégé, Khin Nyunt, chief of the secret police.

Loosening grip? Soon after Maung's resignation, the SLORC began releasing several hundred political prisoners. Some had been held since the 1988 prodemocracy demonstrations and others since a 1990 parliamentary election. In 1990, the main opposition group to the SLORC, the National League for Democracy (NLD), won a landslide victory over the SLORC, but the SLORC ignored the results and locked up the NLD winners.

Among the prisoners released was U Nu, the prime minister overthrown by Ne Win in 1962. But an estimated thousand or more opposition leaders remained in detention, including Aung San Suu Kyi, the NLD leader who won the Nobel Peace Prize in 1991 for her nonviolent campaign to restore democracy to the country. The SLORC in May 1992 allowed Suu Kyi's family to visit her for the first time since 1989, when Suu Kyi was put under house arrest.

In August 1992, the SLORC reopened the nation's colleges and universities, which were shut down in December 1991 after celebrations over Suu Kyi's Nobel Prize. And on Sept. 26, 1992, the SLORC lifted the last decrees of the martial law it had imposed in 1989. Still, the military retained tight control of the country. And there was no sign that the army planned to recognize the NLD's election victories of 1990.

Military moves. The SLORC in January 1992 launched a strong offensive against the Karens, the best armed of the country's several ethnic groups fighting for regional autonomy or independence. But the army was unable to capture the Karen headquarters in the town of Manerplaw before the start of the rainy season in May.

The army in late 1991 began an offensive that continued into 1992 against Muslims living in the western province of Arakan. The repression caused more than 200,000 Muslims to flee Burma for neighboring Bangladesh. In April 1992, Burma signed an agreement with Bangladesh to take back the refugees. But the Muslims were skeptical about their safety and few returned. (See also **Bangladesh.**) Henry S. Bradsher

See also **Asia** (Facts in brief table). In ***World Book,*** see **Burma.**

Burundi. See **Africa.**

Bus. See **Transit.**

Bush, George Herbert Walker (1924-), 41st President of the United States, lost his bid for a second term in 1992 to the Democratic challenger, Arkansas Governor Bill Clinton, in the November 3 election. Bush accepted defeat with good grace. "The people have spoken," he said in a short concession speech. "We respect the majesty of the democratic process." Bush pledged to work closely with Clinton "to assure the smooth transition [of power]."

In a final use of his presidential power, Bush in early December began sending U.S. troops to the African country of Somalia to protect shipments of food aid to starving Somalis. And on December 24, the President pardoned six people implicated in the Iran-contra affair, including former Secretary of Defense Caspar W. Weinberger. (See **Armed forces; Iran-contra affair; Somalia.**)

Asia trip. Bush began the year with a January trip to Australia and Asia. Accompanied by 21 leading U.S. business executives, the President traveled to Australia, Singapore, South Korea, and Japan in search of export opportunities that he said would create jobs for the sagging U.S. economy. In Japan, during the hardest bargaining on trade, Bush was flanked by the heads of the Big Three of American automaking.

Negotiations produced voluntary Japanese promises to increase purchases of U.S. goods by more than $10 billion a year. Makers of automobiles and auto parts would benefit most. "The visit has been a success," Bush declared. But some of the corporate leaders who accompanied him said the agreements did not win enough trade concessions from Japan. Critics contended the group had gone to Japan as beggars.

In the public mind, however, the trip was most memorable because Bush vomited and collapsed at a January 8 state dinner in Tokyo given in his honor by Japanese Prime Minister Kiichi Miyazawa. The President attributed his fainting spell to a 24-hour flu. Whatever the reason, it served as a portent of other misfortunes that lay ahead.

Popularity drops. After enjoying an approval rating of 90 per cent among the American public at the end of the 1991 Persian Gulf War, Bush was startled to see his poll ratings plummet thereafter as the U.S. economy continued to perform weakly. And, ominously, his conservative base in the Republican Party was shaky. Conservatives were mad at Bush for his 1990 decision to break a 1988 campaign pledge of "no new taxes." His concurrence in a tax hike to attack record federal budget deficits prompted conservative political commentator Patrick J. Buchanan to challenge Bush for the 1992 Republican presidential nomination.

A further sign of trouble on the right came on February 25, when Bush met in California with former President Ronald Reagan and Reagan declined to appear with him before the news media. It was not until weeks later, after Bush had declared that raising taxes was a mistake—and one he said he would not repeat—that the two men embraced publicly.

Staying the course. Throughout much of the year, as Bush's reelection looked dubious, the White House staff was said to be frustrated and in gridlock. Some top Republicans reportedly advised Bush to dump Vice President Dan Quayle in favor of a stronger running mate, and a few even suggested that Bush should consider stepping down himself after a single term. But the President declined to do either. In August, having prevailed in the primaries, he accepted his party's nomination at the Republican National Convention in Houston and once again took Quayle as his running mate.

The morale of Bush and his staff was boosted on August 13 with an announcement that James A. Baker III, his old friend and 1988 campaign aide, would resign as secretary of state and replace Samuel K. Skinner as White House chief of staff. Baker's assignment was aimed at bringing order to Bush's political and policymaking activities and coordinating an uphill battle for reelection. But in the end, it made no difference. Bush was soundly defeated in the election, winning just 168 electoral votes to Clinton's 370. (See also **Elections; Republican Party.**)

Stubborn issues. During the campaign, Bush was dogged by two persistent issues that may have contributed to his election defeat. These were his reported involvement in the Iran-contra affair and disclosures about events leading up to the Persian Gulf War.

President Bush tours a devastated section of Los Angeles in May after several days of rioting and arson left part of the city in ruins.

Bush had long said that while serving as Vice President in the Reagan Administration, he was "out of the loop" when the Iran-contra arms-for-hostages operation was being planned and carried out. Bush said he knew nothing about the scheme until late 1986. But evidence to the contrary kept surfacing in 1992. The most damaging revelation came from Iran-contra independent counsel Lawrence E. Walsh just four days before the election. Walsh made public a portion of notes kept by Weinberger in which Weinberger wrote that Bush had attended a key meeting on Jan. 7, 1986, and had expressed support for the operation.

The President was also accused in 1992 of having helped build up the military might of Iraq's President Saddam Hussein prior to the Gulf War. And a cover-up was alleged in a federal investigation of $4 billion in illegal loans to Iraq by the Atlanta, Ga., branch of an Italian bank. Hussein reportedly used the money to purchase weapons and acquire technology for building atomic bombs. Federal Judge Marvin H. Shoob, who handled part of the case, said top levels of the government had tried to interfere with the investigation of the bank's activities.

Foreign affairs. On February 1, Bush and Russian leader Boris Yeltsin met at Camp David, the President's Maryland retreat, but reached no agreement on U.S. help for Russia's fledgling market economy. On April 1, Bush and Chancellor Helmut Kohl of Germany announced a $24-billion international aid program for Russia by the Group of Seven leading industrialized nations. About one-fifth of the aid was to come from the United States. On June 16, Yeltsin and Bush agreed to an 11-year plan to scrap two-thirds of all long-range nuclear weapons. The two leaders signed the accord on Jan. 3, 1993. (See **Armed forces.**)

Iraq continued to cause problems for Bush and the United Nations (UN) in 1992. Saddam Hussein on several occasions defied UN efforts to determine whether he was developing or harboring weapons of mass destruction. Bush threatened military action if needed to gain Hussein's compliance with UN resolutions.

During the year, the Iraqis took harsh action to suppress Shiite Muslims in southern Iraq. On August 26, Bush said the United States, France, and Great Britain would patrol the area and shoot down any Iraqi aircraft flying below the 32nd parallel.

Bloodshed in the Balkans prompted the United States to impose diplomatic sanctions on Yugoslavia, which in 1992 consisted only of the republics of Serbia and Montenegro. (Four other republics had broken away.) The Yugoslav army and Serbian irregulars attacked one former Yugoslav republic, Bosnia and Hercegovina, which was claiming independence. On August 6, Bush said he would use force if need be to ensure the delivery of aid to Bosnia and Hercegovina.

Relations with Israel, rocky during early 1992, became more harmonious after the election of a new Israeli government on June 23. With Yitzhak Rabin succeeding Yitzhak Shamir as prime minister, Bush approved $10 billion in loan guarantees that had been denied Shamir. Shamir had refused to halt Israeli settlements in the occupied territories in defiance of a Bush Administration stipulation.

Earth Summit. On June 12 and 13, Bush attended the United Nations Conference on Environment and Development—known as the Earth Summit—held from June 3 to 14 in Rio de Janeiro, Brazil. Bush insisted on avoiding all binding goals and timetables in a treaty to limit the release of "greenhouse gases," which some scientists say are causing global warming. And he refused to sign a treaty aimed at protecting endangered species. The President said the pact might adversely affect the patent rights of U.S. biotechnology companies. (See **Environmental pollution: Environmental Concern Goes Global.**)

Personal matters. On March 26, physicians at the Bethesda (Md.) Naval Medical Center pronounced the President to be in "perfect" health. On April 15, the Bushes said that they had paid $211,034 in federal taxes for 1991 on an income of $1,324,456. Bush's mother, Dorothy Walker Bush, died on November 19 at her home in Greenwich, Conn., at the age of 91.

Frank Cormier and Margot Cormier

See also **Congress of the United States; United States, Government of the.** In *World Book,* see **Bush, George Herbert Walker.**

Business. See **Bank; Economics; Manufacturing.**

Cabinet, U.S. President-elect Bill Clinton in late 1992, preparing for his move into the White House in January 1993, began making appointments to his Cabinet. On December 10, he nominated Senator Lloyd M. Bentsen, Jr., (D., Tex.) as secretary of the Treasury and Representative Leon E. Panetta (D., Calif.) as head of the Office of Management and Budget.

The next day, Clinton nominated Carol Browner, secretary of the Florida Department of Environmental Regulation, to head the Environmental Protection Agency; Robert B. Reich, a political science lecturer at Harvard University, as secretary of labor; Laura D'Andrea Tyson, a professor of economics and business at the University of California at Berkeley, to chair the Council of Economic Advisers; and Donna E. Shalala, chancellor of the University of Wisconsin at Madison, as secretary of health and human services.

On December 12, Clinton nominated Ronald H. Brown, chairman of the Democratic National Committee, as secretary of commerce. He also named Thomas F. McLarty, chief executive of an Arkansas natural-gas company and one of his oldest friends, as White House chief of staff.

There were several changes in President George Bush's Cabinet during the year. (See **United States, Government of the.**) David Dreier

In *World Book,* see **Cabinet.**

California. See **Los Angeles; San Diego; State government.**

Cambodia. A United Nations (UN) force of about 16,000 troops, 3,600 police monitors, and 2,400 civilian administrators was deployed in Cambodia during 1992 in the most ambitious peacekeeping operation ever undertaken by the UN. The aim of the forces, named the United Nations Transitional Authority in Cambodia (UNTAC), was to ensure an end to civil war and establish an elected government by mid-1993.

The UNTAC, headed by Japanese diplomat Yasushi Akashi, was created under a peace treaty signed on Oct. 23, 1991, by Cambodia's four warring factions. These factions were the ruling Communist government established in the Cambodian capital, Phnom Penh, by Vietnamese invaders in 1979; the Khmer Rouge, Communist rebels who ruled Cambodia until they were ousted by the Vietnamese; and two anti-Communist groups, one led by Prince Norodom Sihanouk, a former ruler of Cambodia, and the other by former Prime Minister Son Sann. The four factions joined in a Supreme National Council (SNC) to oversee Cambodia's transition to a democratic regime.

The UNTAC job. Akashi's force, which began arriving in April 1992, had five tasks. The first was monitoring the nation's cease-fire, which was sporadically broken by the Khmer Rouge during 1992. The second task was resettling the 150,000 Cambodians who had been displaced as a result of the fighting as well as *repatriating* (returning to their home) about 350,000 Cambodians who had been living in Thailand. Most of the refugees fled Cambodia in 1979 and 1980 after the Vietnamese invasion.

The UNTAC repatriation efforts began on March 30. But the program lagged behind schedule, due in large part to time-consuming efforts to clear minefields that had been set by the Khmer Rouge. As of November 1, only about 150,000 of the refugees had returned to Cambodia.

Demobilizing fighters. The third task given to UNTAC was disarming all of the factions' forces—a total of about 200,000 soldiers—and quarantining most of them in *cantonments* (quarters for soldiers) throughout the country until the 1993 elections. In June, thousands of soldiers from the Phnom Penh regime and the two non-Communist factions began laying down their arms.

The Khmer Rouge, however, said they would participate in the disarmament program only on two conditions. One was the transfer of control of the country from the Phnom Penh regime to the SNC. The other condition was the verification of the total withdrawal of Vietnamese forces. The rebels maintained that large numbers of Vietnamese troops remained in the country.

The Khmer Rouge's demands were seen as a means to build support among Cambodians by evoking their suspicion of the Vietnamese, to maintain territorial control while plundering the country's rich natural resources, and to slow the way to elections, in which experts said they were likely to do poorly. The Khmer

Cambodian refugees begin returning from camps in Thailand in April 1992, following acceptance of a 1991 peace plan by Cambodia's rival groups.

Rouge's tactics diminished all four factions' drive to disarm. As of November 1, only about 55,000 soldiers had been disarmed.

Organizing elections. The UNTAC's remaining two tasks were to take over control of Cambodia's ministries from the Phnom Penh government until the elections and to prepare to hold those elections by May 1993. Civilian teams of Cambodians in October 1992 began registering voters from an electorate of an estimated 5 million people. But the Khmer Rouge denied the teams access to citizens in regions it controlled—about 15 per cent of all Cambodians.

On Sept. 23, 1992, UN Secretary-General Boutros Boutros-Ghali said the persistent failure of the Khmer Rouge to abide by the October 1991 treaty posed difficult problems. In particular, the 1993 elections might have to be either postponed or conducted without Khmer Rouge participation—neither action desirable.

In October, the UN gave the Khmer Rouge until November 15 to join the peace process, but the guerrillas ignored the deadline. Consequently, the UN on November 30 imposed economic sanctions on those regions of Cambodia controlled by the Khmer Rouge. In two separate incidents in December, the rebels seized 27 UN observers, but all were released unharmed within days. Henry S. Bradsher

See also **Asia** (Facts in brief table); **United Nations: A New Era for the United Nations.** In *World Book,* see **Cambodia.**

Cameroon. See **Africa.**

Canada

In a referendum held on Oct. 26, 1992, Canadians voted down proposed amendments to the nation's Constitution. In a 55 per cent to 45 per cent vote, Canadians rejected the Charlottetown Accord that had been jointly fashioned by the federal government, the 10 provinces, two territories, and four major aboriginal groups. In large part, the revisions to the Constitution had been designed in response to demands from Quebec—where sentiment for independence from Canada has been strong—for expanded powers.

The Progressive Conservative administration headed by Prime Minister Brian Mulroney had sponsored and vigorously campaigned for the constitutional revisions. The new proposals followed Mulroney's earlier constitutional reform package, the Meech Lake Accord, which had been killed by two provinces in 1990.

A long, hard fight. The Charlottetown Accord had emerged after months of painstaking negotiations. The Mulroney government had begun the process by issuing a set of constitutional proposals, the "Canada Round," in September 1991. The suggestions were referred to a parliamentary committee composed of representatives from the nation's three major political parties. They were to hold public meetings throughout the country, but they soon became embroiled in partisan debates. In January and February 1992, the federal government organized five three-

Some of the 70,000 Canadians who turned out in Ottawa to celebrate Canada's 125th anniversary on July 1 catch a glimpse of Queen Elizabeth II.

day conferences to discuss the proposed Constitution. Members from the parliamentary committee as well as provincial, territorial, and aboriginal representatives, and citizens at large attended these meetings.

The parliamentary committee on March 1 reported the outcome of the discussions, which supported many of the Mulroney-government proposals. But some of the provinces, unhappy over the federal government's domination of the constitutional process, called for federal-provincial meetings.

Quebec rejected the Mulroney-government proposals, and its governing Liberal Party issued its own report for constitutional changes that called for a loose Canadian federation with a weak central government. Quebec Premier Robert Bourassa, a federalist, was clearly uncomfortable with the report. And although he was legally obligated to hold a vote on Quebec's future by October 1992, Bourassa made it plain that he would prefer to have Quebecers vote on a revised federal system rather than on sovereignty. This looming deadline for Quebec's referendum put pressure on the federal government to wrap up its package of reforms for presentation to Quebec and the remainder of Canada.

Ottawa arranged a new round of meetings, which began on March 12. These meetings were attended by government representatives from all of the provinces except Quebec, which boycotted them. Representatives from the Northwest Territories and the Yukon, as well as the leaders of the four principal native groups, also participated. Under the chairmanship of Joe Clark, Canada's minister for constitutional affairs, the meetings sought to reach a consensus on constitutional reform. The sessions were long and arduous, but on July 7, the group reached agreement on the principal issues that had been in dispute.

The last leg. The way was now prepared for more formal discussions between Mulroney, the premiers of the 10 provinces, and the territorial and aboriginal leaders. Bourassa agreed to attend, and the first meeting in this new series was held on August 4 at Mulroney's summer residence in the Gatineau Hills north of Ottawa. The group made steady progress in hammering out a consensus. By August 22, it was ready to announce agreement on a revised Constitution for Canada. The formal text of the accord was approved on August 28 at a final meeting in Charlottetown, Prince Edward Island.

The Charlottetown Accord opened with the "Canada Clause," a preamble setting down the values Canadians share and serving to guide the courts in interpreting the document. Quebec was mentioned in the preamble as constituting a distinct society based on a French-speaking majority, a unique culture, and a civil law tradition.

The highlights of the accord included modifying the federal Senate and House of Commons to more adequately represent the Canadian population. The accord specified that the Senate, with a current membership of 104, would be reduced to 62 members, 6 from each of the 10 provinces and 1 from each of the 2 territories. Native people would also be represented in the Senate, although the accord did not spell out how this would be achieved. Ordinary bills, if defeated or amended in the Senate, would be referred to a joint sitting of the Senate and House of Commons, where a simple majority vote would prevail. Legislation affecting the French language or culture would require approval by a majority of all senators as well as by a majority of French-speaking senators.

Finally, Cabinet members could not be drawn from

Canada, provinces, and territories population data

	1991 census
Alberta	2,545,553
British Columbia	3,282,061
Manitoba	1,091,942
New Brunswick	723,900
Newfoundland	568,474
Northwest Territories	57,649
Nova Scotia	899,942
Ontario	10,084,885
Prince Edward Island	129,765
Quebec	6,895,963
Saskatchewan	988,928
Yukon Territory	27,797
Canada	**27,296,859**

City and metropolitan populations

	Metropolitan area 1991 census	City 1991 census
Toronto, Ont.	3,893,046	635,395
Montreal, Que.	3,127,242	1,017,666
Vancouver, B.C.	1,602,502	471,844
Ottawa-Hull	920,857	
Ottawa, Ont.		313,987
Hull, Que.		60,707
Edmonton, Alta.	839,924	616,741
Calgary, Alta.	754,033	710,677
Winnipeg, Man.	652,354	616,790
Quebec, Que.	645,550	167,517
Hamilton, Ont.	599,760	318,499
London, Ont.	381,522	303,165
St. Catharines-Niagara	364,552	
St. Catharines, Ont.		129,300
Niagara Falls, Ont.		75,399
Kitchener, Ont.	356,421	168,282
Halifax, N.S.	320,501	114,455
Victoria, B.C.	287,897	71,228
Windsor, Ont.	262,075	191,435
Oshawa, Ont.	240,104	129,344
Saskatoon, Sask.	210,023	186,058
Regina, Sask.	191,692	179,178
St. John's, Nfld.	171,859	95,770
Chicoutimi-Jonquière	160,928	
Chicoutimi, Que.		62,670
Jonquière, Que.		57,933
Sudbury, Ont.	157,613	92,884
Sherbrooke, Que.	139,194	76,429
Trois-Rivières, Que.	136,303	49,426
Saint John, N.B.	124,981	74,969
Thunder Bay, Ont.	124,427	113,946

Source: Statistics Canada.

the Senate. The accord also strove to adjust the House of Commons to more fairly represent the population. The Commons membership would increase to 337 from 295, with Ontario and Quebec each receiving 18 additional members, British Columbia gaining 4 members, and Alberta adding 2 seats. Quebec was guaranteed no fewer than 25 per cent of the seats in the Commons, a number corresponding to its proportion of the Canadian population.

The Charlottetown Accord also offered significant advances for aboriginal people. They were recognized as having "the inherent right of self-government within Canada," meaning that they could "safeguard and develop" their languages, cultures, institutions, and economies. However, ordinances that they passed would have to be compatible with federal laws ensuring "the preservation of peace, order, and good government" in Canada.

With the accord in place, the federal legislature on September 10 voted overwhelmingly to put the proposals before the Canadian people. A national referendum was set for October 26, and Bourassa agreed to have Quebecers vote on the constitutional changes rather than on provincial independence. The question posed to the Canadian people was short and unequivocal: "Do you agree that the Constitution of Canada should be renewed on the basis of the agreement reached on Aug. 28, 1992?"

The campaigns for and against the new Constitution began in mid-September. The federal, provincial, and territorial governments, as well as the leaders of the major native groups, all supported the revised Constitution. All the national political parties also endorsed the accord. Those opposed were a mixed group: the separatist Parti Québécois in Quebec and its counterpart the Bloc Québécois in the federal Parliament; the Reform Party in the West; some women's groups, which worried that the accord did not adequately protect the rights of women and minorities; and former Prime Minister Pierre Trudeau, who was disturbed at what he considered a weakening of the central government.

Early public opinion polls showed that those opposed to the proposals had a leading edge, particularly in Quebec, where Bourassa was criticized for giving away too much in the negotiations. Public opinion in British Columbia, where people were dissatisfied about their future representation in the House of Commons, also favored a "No" vote.

Joe Clark told Canadians that an arrangement better than the Charlottetown Accord probably could not be secured. Mulroney warned that a "No" vote would be interpreted as the next-to-last step before Quebec's secession, and that it would plunge the country into political and economic instability.

The vote. The referendum brought out more than 13 million Canadians, or 75 per cent of registered voters. The Northwest Territories and the Atlantic Provinces of Newfoundland, New Brunswick, and Prince Edward Island, which depend mainly on the federal government for financial support and employment opportunities, gave the constitutional proposals resounding approval. The Atlantic province of Nova Scotia rejected the accord by a close vote of 51 to 49 per cent.

In Quebec, a spirited debate arose between Bourassa, who defended the accord by claiming it met most of Quebec's constitutional objectives, and separatist leaders Jacques Parizeau of the Parti Québécois and Lucien Bouchard of the Bloc Québécois, who denounced the revisions as futile tinkerings with a discredited federal system. The vote in Quebec was about 42 per cent in favor and 55 per cent opposed.

In Ontario, voters were almost evenly divided, with

The "Raging Grannies" on April 8 sing songs in Montreal protesting the North American Free Trade Agreement's potential to create job losses.

a slight majority favoring acceptance. Moving west, the proposals encountered increasing hostility. The three Prairie Provinces of Alberta, Manitoba, and Saskatchewan turned them down, as did British Columbia, where the 68 per cent rejection vote was the highest in Canada. The Yukon also voted "No," and, surprisingly, Indians living on reserves rejected it as well. Observers believed that Indians feared the revisions would endanger their treaty rights and place too many restrictions on self-government.

Aftereffects. The accord's defeat did not bring the economic catastrophe some of its backers had predicted. The outcome had little effect on the Canadian dollar. In fact, immediately after the vote, the stock market advanced and short-term interest rates declined. Adverse political consequences were not immediately apparent, either. Mulroney and many provincial premiers said constitutional discussions would not resume in the immediate future. They said parts of the accord, such as those regarding aboriginal rights, might be implemented through negotiations between natives and provincial and federal governments.

To those committed to a unified Canada, the results in Quebec were somewhat reassuring. After the vote, Bourassa said: "It is the policy of my government to build Quebec within Canada and we believe we will be able to build Quebec within Canada." Subsequent polls showed that the majority of Quebecers still would not vote for sovereignty.

However, fault lines in the Canadian political terrain persisted, with competing visions of Canada being one of the deepest. The western provinces saw the country as a federation of 10 equal provinces in which there was no place for a special status for Quebec. But the Atlantic Provinces, along with Quebec and Ontario, saw Canada as a partnership of English-speaking and French-speaking Canadians, with the French having a distinct language and culture.

To many Canadians, a sovereignty vote in Quebec was regarded as the only way to end this argument. But whether Quebec remains a part of Canada will most likely be decided in a 1994 provincial election, in which voters would have the opportunity to choose leaders who favor either sovereignty or continued federalism.

Free trade agreement. After 14 months of difficult negotiations, Canada, the United States, and Mexico agreed on Aug. 12, 1992, to establish a North American Free Trade Agreement (NAFTA). NAFTA would create a free trade zone containing more than 370 million people, the largest in the world, and build on the Canada-United States free trade agreement of 1989. The treaty required ratification in the three countries. Trade unions in Canada and the United States had voiced opposition to the pact because they feared that jobs would be lost to Mexico, where wages are often lower and health and environment standards not as strictly enforced.

The Ministry of Canada*

Brian Mulroney—prime minister
Charles Joseph Clark—president of the Queen's Privy Council; minister responsible for constitutional affairs
John Carnell Crosbie—minister of fisheries and oceans; minister for the Atlantic Canada Opportunities Agency
Donald Frank Mazankowski—deputy prime minister; minister of finance
Elmer MacIntosh MacKay—minister of public works; minister for the Canada Mortgage and Housing Corporation
Arthur Jacob Epp—minister of energy, mines, and resources
Robert R. de Cotret—secretary of state of Canada
Henry Perrin Beatty—minister of communications
Michael Holcombe Wilson—minister of industry, science, and technology; minister for international trade
Harvie Andre—minister of state; leader of the government in the House of Commons; minister for Canada Post
Otto John Jelinek—minister of national revenue
Thomas Edward Siddon—minister of Indian affairs and Northern development
Charles James Mayer—minister of state (grains and oilseeds); minister of Western economic diversification
William Hunter McKnight—minister of agriculture
Benoît Bouchard—minister of national health and welfare
Marcel Masse—minister of national defense
Barbara Jean McDougall—secretary of state for external affairs
Gerald Stairs Merrithew—minister of veterans affairs
Monique Vézina—minister of state (employment and immigration); minister of state (seniors)
Frank Oberle—minister of forestry
Lowell Murray—leader of the government in the Senate
Paul Wyatt Dick—minister of supply and services
Pierre H. Cadieux—minister of state (fitness and amateur sport); minister of state (youth); deputy leader of the government in the House of Commons
Jean J. Charest—minister of the environment
Thomas Hockin—minister of state (small businesses and tourism)
Monique Landry—minister for external relations; minister of state (Indian affairs and Northern development)
Bernard Valcourt—minister of employment and immigration
Gerry Weiner—minister of multiculturalism and citizenship
Douglas Grinslade Lewis—solicitor general of Canada
Pierre Blais—minister of state (agriculture); minister of consumer and corporate affairs
John Horton McDermid—minister of state (finance and privatization
Shirley Martin—minister of state (transport)
Mary Collins—associate minister of national defence; minister responsible for the status of women
William Charles Winegard—minister for science
Kim Campbell—minister of justice and attorney general of Canada
Jean Corbeil—minister of transport
Gilles Loiselle—minister of state (finance); president of the Treasury Board
Marcel Danis—minister of labour
Pauline Browes—minister of state (environment)

*As of Dec. 31, 1992.

Premiers of Canadian Provinces

Province	Premier
Alberta	Ralph Klein
British Columbia	Michael Harcourt
Manitoba	Gary A. Filmon
New Brunswick	Frank J. McKenna
Newfoundland	Clyde K. Wells
Nova Scotia	Donald Cameron
Ontario	Robert K. Rae
Prince Edward Island	Joseph A. Ghiz
Quebec	Robert Bourassa
Saskatchewan	Roy Romanow

Government leaders of territories

Northwest Territories	Nellie Cournoyea
Yukon Territory	John Ostashek

Canada's economy performed sluggishly in 1992 with industrial output well below capacity, consumer confidence low, and unemployment rates escalating. A bright spot in the economic gloom was a growth in merchandise exports, achieved in spite of weak U.S. and European economies.

First quarter growth in the economy was estimated at 1.7 per cent, dropping to 0.7 per cent in the second quarter. The *gross domestic product* (the total value of all goods and services produced within a country) on a seasonally adjusted annual basis stood at $684.3-billion ($549 billion U.S.) at the end of June, a figure very similar to that achieved in 1991. Unemployment hit a seven-year high in February 1992, when 10.6 per cent of the work force had no job. It continued to climb into the summer, reaching 11.6 per cent in June. In October, it fell to 11.3 per cent.

Inflation was under control, with the annual rate falling to 1.1 per cent in June, the lowest level since 1962. In October, it rose to 1.6 per cent. In September, mortgage rates dropped to a 35-year low of 5.9 per cent. The prime rate fell to 6.25 per cent but climbed back up to 9.75 per cent by the end of November, causing economists to predict a stall in Canada's recovery from its recession. In September, the uncertainty about how Canadians—especially Quebec—would respond to the Charlottetown Accord caused the Canadian dollar to plunge.

The budget. Finance Minister Donald Frank Mazankowski presented his first budget on February 25, offering tax cuts and restraint in government spending. The budget called for a surtax on all personal income to be reduced in two steps, in mid-1992 and at the start of 1993. To stimulate the housing industry, the budget allowed individuals to withdraw $20,000 ($16,000 U.S.) from registered retirement savings plans to buy or build a home in the year ending March 1, 1993. The money would not be taxed but must be repaid into the savings fund over the next 15 years.

The federal budget eliminated, merged, or privatized 46 agencies and boards. Spending for the fiscal year (April 1, 1992, to March 31, 1993) was projected to be $159.6 billion ($128 billion U.S.), with revenues at $132.1 billion ($106 billion U.S.). The anticipated deficit of $27.5 billion ($22 billion U.S.) was about $4-billion ($3.2 billion U.S.) less than the previous year's. However, weaker-than-expected revenues led the government in December to predict a 25 per cent increase in the deficit.

Olympia & York Developments Limited, the Toronto-based real estate developer, filed for bankruptcy protection on May 14, 1992. The world's largest developer was also the largest company ever to declare bankruptcy in Canada. Olympia, owned by the Reichmann family, scrambled to salvage what it could of its worldwide holdings and proposed a number of reorganization plans. In November, it suggested a plan that would result in the company's retaining only 10 per cent of its Canadian properties. The bankruptcy

At the Westray Mine in Plymouth, Nova Scotia, methane gas exploded deep underground, killing 26 miners on May 9.

declaration further strained Canada's bleak economic picture as Canadian banks had loaned the company some $3 billion ($2.4 billion U.S.).

Foreign affairs. In March, 1,200 Canadian troops, which included infantry, engineers, and observers, arrived in Yugoslavia as part of a United Nations (UN) peacemaking force. In July, half of them went to Sarajevo, capital of Bosnia and Hercegovina, to open the airport for the delivery of humanitarian aid. In September, another 1,200 Canadian troops were slated to strengthen the UN presence in the strife-torn land.

Canada also offered 1,250 men and three large transport aircraft to deliver and guard food supplies in famine-stricken Somalia, and the troops began arriving in December. In September, Canada sent carpenters and building materials to help the U.S. community in south Florida rebuild after it was devastated by Hurricane Andrew in August.

A long-standing dispute between Canada and France over fishing zones was ended by an international panel on June 10. The disagreement centered on an area around the tiny French islands of Saint-Pierre and Miquelon, which lie off the southern coast of Newfoundland. The panel awarded France a zone extending 24 nautical miles (44 kilometers) out from the islands, along with a strip 200 nautical miles (370 kilometers) long and 10.5 nautical miles (19.4 kilometers) wide, leading from the islands to the open sea.

Immigration policy. Immigration Minister Bernard Valcourt on June 16 introduced an immigration

Federal spending in Canada
Estimated budget for fiscal 1992-1993*

Ministry (includes the department and all agencies for which a minister reports to Parliament):	Millions of dollars†
Agriculture	2,867
Atlantic Canada Opportunities Agency	345
Communications	
Canadian Broadcasting Corporation	1,112
Canadian Film Development Corporation	145
Other	890
Consumer and corporate affairs	203
Employment and immigration	1,988
Energy, mines, and resources	
Atomic Energy of Canada Limited	178
Other	967
Environment	1,143
External affairs	3,876
Finance	49,078
Fisheries and oceans	791
Forestry	246
Governor general	11
Indian affairs and northern development	4,300
Industry, science, and technology	
Canada Post Corporation	14
Other	2,443
Justice	718
Labour	246
Multiculturalism and citizenship	119
National defence	12,481
National health and welfare	36,974
National revenue	2,324
Parliament	296
Privy Council	178
Public works	
Canada Mortgage and Housing Corporation	2,090
Other	1,707
Secretary of state	3,246
Solicitor general	
Royal Canadian Mounted Police	1,230
Other	1,326
Supply and services	510
Transport	2,874
Treasury Board	1,330
Veterans affairs	2,041
Western economic diversification	301
Total	**140,588**

* April 1, 1992, to March 31, 1993.
† Canadian dollars; $1 = U.S. $1.2387 as of Nov. 2, 1992

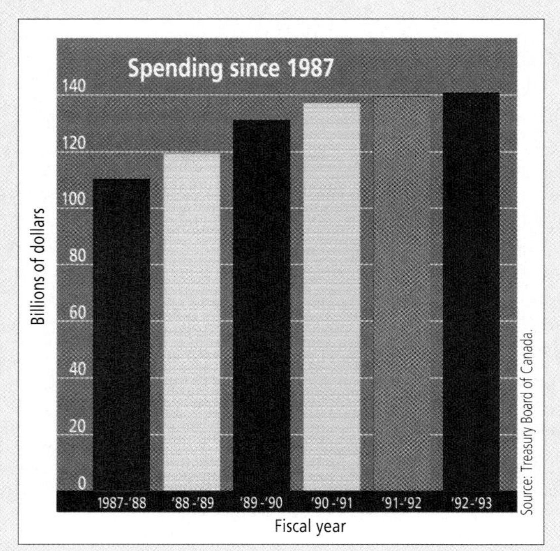

bill to the Canadian legislature that quickly caused controversy. If fully implemented, the bill could reduce immigration by about 40 per cent while streamlining the immigration process for wealthy investors. Those with skills who would agree to settle in certain areas would also be accepted into the nation more quickly. The bill also allowed the deportation of immigrants whom the government suspected of belonging to criminal or terrorist organizations.

The Canadian Civil Liberties Association criticized the bill and called for much of it to be scrapped. Other organizations representing refugees also denounced the bill, saying that it should have been subjected to full public discourse. As of December, the bill was still under discussion in Parliament.

Politics. Mulroney made no Cabinet changes in 1992, nor were there any by-elections for the federal Parliament. A Bloc Québécois member resigned from the House of Commons in August, leaving party standings in the 295-seat Commons as follows: Progressive Conservatives 158; Liberals 81; New Democratic Party 44; Bloc Québécois 8; Reform Party 1; Independent Conservatives 1; Independent 1; Vacant 1. There were no general elections in the provinces during the year.

David M. L. Farr

See **Northwest Territories: Creating Nunavut.** See also the other Canadian provinces articles; **Canadian literature; International trade; Montreal; Mulroney, Brian; Toronto.** In ***World Book,*** see **Canada.**

Canadian literature. With Canada's next federal election due in 1993 and the discussion over proposed changes to the nation's Constitution, books on Canada's history and political process were in abundance in 1992. *Canada My Canada,* a passionate history by Laurier LaPierre, described 15 turning points in Canada's history. *Tapestry of War: A Private View of Canadians in the Great War* by Sandra Gwyn plumbed the national awakening sparked by World War I (1914-1918). Novelist and essayist Mordecai Richler caused a national uproar when his *Oh Canada! Oh Quebec! Requiem for a Divided Country* criticized French-speaking nationalists for infringing on civil liberties and suppressing the rights of English-speaking citizens.

The 500th anniversary of Christopher Columbus' arrival in North America sparked a number of books examining Canada's relationship with its aboriginal people. Among the best were Ronald Wright's *Stolen Continents: The Americas Through Indian Eyes since 1942* and David Suzuki's and Peter Knudston's *Wisdom of the Elders: Honoring Sacred Native Visions of Nature.*

Michael Ondaatje in October 1992 became the first Canadian to win Great Britain's most prestigious literary award, the Booker Prize. The Sri Lankan-born poet and novelist shared the award with British writer Barry Unsworth. Ondaatje's book, *The English Patient,* told of four people taking refuge in a ruined Italian villa toward the end of World War II (1939-1945).

Author Mordecai Richler stirred controversy in 1992 with his book *Oh Canada! Oh Quebec! Requiem for a Divided Country.*

Memoirs and biographies. *My Father's Son* by Farley Mowat was a series of letters between the author as a young soldier during World War II and his parents in Canada. *Cousins,* by poet and novelist Paulette Giles, combined an oral history of the author's family in Missouri with her romance with a Texas cattleman who left his family for her.

Glenn Gould's Selected Letters, edited by John P. I. Robert and Ghislaine Guertin, compiled more than 200 letters by Canada's most famous musician. John Einarson's biography of Neil Young, *Don't Be Denied,* charted the progress of this Toronto-born rock star.

Nonfiction. Bridging business and philosophy, John Ralston Saul's *Voltaire's Bastards: The Dictatorship of Reason in the West* argued that reason and logic have been corrupted by amoral corporate managers. And in *Looking Around: A Journey through Architecture,* Witold Rybczynsky examined the meaning of our domestic surroundings.

Follow-ups. British Columbian illustrator and writer Nick Bantock followed his imaginative and popular 1991 book *Griffin & Sabine: An Extraordinary Correspondence* with *Sabine's Notebook*, which was equally well received in 1992. Douglas Coupland followed his 1991 *Generation X: Tales for an Accelerated Culture* with *Shampoo Planet,* a novel about people under age 20.

Fiction. Margaret Atwood's *Good Bones,* a collection of fairy tales and short satires, deftly skewered "politically correct" feminist rhetoric. In W. O. Mitchell's *For Art's Sake,* a white-haired professor carries out a string of art thefts for a good cause. In Carol Shields's beautifully narrated *The Republic of Love,* a talk-show host meets a scholar in a quest for someone to share a life with. Janette Turner Hospital's *The Last Magician* told the story of four people bound by the memory of a terrible trauma. Sandra Birdsell's second novel, *The Chrome Suite,* chronicled 40 years in the life of a speechwriter. John Steffler's *The Afterlife of George Cartwright: A Novel* combined fiction with the nonfiction diaries of a Victorian adventurer in Canada. And in *Deep Hollow Creek*, Sheila Watson unfolded the story of a teacher who relocates to British Columbia in the 1930's.

The novels of two immigrant writers, Neil Bissoondath's *The Innocence of Age,* and M. G. Vassanji's *Uhuru Street,* wove memories of their faraway homelands with themes of displacement, urban racism, and poverty.

Life's underbelly was given a quirky examination by younger women writers. Barbara Gowdy's *We So Seldom Look on Love,* told of freaks and fetishists. Linda Svendsen's *Marine Life* uncovered family histories marked by sibling rivalry and incest. Anne Dandurand's *Deathly Delights* told about crimes of love and passion wrought by women.

In *Murder in Montparnasse,* mystery writer Howard Engel developed a new main character who observes the literary circles occupied by writers Ernest Hemingway and F. Scott Fitzgerald in 1920's Paris. Toronto's fantasy writer Guy Gavriel Kay created a medieval epic in *A Song for Arbonne.*

Poetry. Lorna Crozier's witty and challenging *Inventing the Hawk* and Vancouver poet Evelyn Lau's sensual and streetwise *Oedipal Dreams* were among noteworthy poetry books released in 1992. *Hometown* by Laura Lush of Toronto was an impressive first collection of condensed, polished images transfiguring everyday experiences. Steve McCaffery's *Theory of Sediment* fragmented and recombined imagery of the natural world in startling new forms.

Children's books. In *The Story of Canada,* Janet Lunn and Christopher Moore filled a literary gap with a richly illustrated introduction to Canada's past. *A Coyote Columbus Story* by Thomas King used the trickster figure to provocatively and humorously retell the first encounters between whites and native peoples. A picture book, *Zoom Upstream,* by Tim Wynne-Jones brought back the little water-loving cat Zoom after a long absence. Kit Pearson's *Looking at the Moon* and Julie Johnston's *Hero of Lesser Causes* were set in the mid-1940's. In Johnston's book, a girl faces a tough challenge when her beloved brother becomes ill.

Awards. Margaret Atwood won the $12,000 Trillium Award for her 1991 collection *Wilderness Tips,* and Rohinton Mistry won the $5,000 Smith Books/Books in Canada First Novel Award for *Such a Long Journey.* The $10,000 Journey Prize, established by James A. Michener for the best short story, was won by South Africa-born writer Rozena Maart, for *No Rosa, No District Six.*

The 1992 Governor-General's Award for books in English went to Michael Ondaatje for *The English Patient* (fiction), Lorna Crozier for *Inventing the Hawk* (poetry), John Mighton for *Possible Worlds* and *A Short History of Night* (drama), Maggie Siggins for *Revenge of the Land: A Century of Greed, Tragedy and Murder on a Saskatchewan Farm* (nonfiction), Julie Johnston for *Hero of Lesser Causes* (children's literature—text), Ron Lightburn for *Waiting for the Whales* (children's literature—illustration), and Fred A. Reed for *Imagining the Middle East* (translation), the English version of Thierry Hentsch's *L'Orient imaginaire.*

The awards for French-language books went to Anne Hebert for *L'Enfant charge de songes* (fiction), Gilles Cyr for *Andromede attendra* (poetry), Louis-Dominique Lavigne for *Les Petits orteils* (drama), Pierre Turgeon for *La Radissonie, le pays de la Baie James* (nonfiction), Christiane Duchesne for *Victor* (children's literature—text), Gilles Tibo for *Simon et la ville de carton* (children's literature—illustration), and Jean Paineau for *La Memoire postmoderne, essai sur l'art Canadien* (translation), the French version of Mark Cheetham's *Remembering Postmodernism: Trends in Recent Canadian Art.* Maureen Garvie

In ***World Book,*** see **Canadian literature.**

Cape Verde. See **Africa.**

Card, Andrew H., Jr. (1947-), became the 11th secretary of the United States Department of Transportation following his nomination on Jan. 22, 1992, by President George Bush and subsequent confirmation by the U.S. Senate. Card filled the vacancy left by former Transportation Secretary Samuel Skinner, who replaced John Sununu as White House chief of staff in December 1991.

Prior to his new appointment, Card served at the White House as assistant to the president and deputy chief of staff. Card's relationship with President Bush began in 1980, when he supported Bush's first but unsuccessful campaign for the Republican presidential nomination.

Card was born in Brockton, Mass., on May 10, 1947. He graduated from the University of South Carolina in Columbia with a B.S. in engineering.

Card worked as a design engineer from 1971 to 1975. He then entered politics and, in 1979, was elected a Republican member of the Massachusetts House of Representatives, where he served until 1983. In 1982, Card launched an unsuccessful bid for governor of Massachusetts.

From 1983 to 1988, Card was an assistant to President Ronald Reagan, working primarily as a liaison to the nation's governors. In 1988, Card once again joined the Bush presidential election campaign.

Card is married to the former Kathleene Bryan. They have three children. Kristine Portnoy Kelley

Cat. Cat ownership in the United States continued to increase in 1992 as cats remained America's most popular pet. The number of cats owned was estimated to be 62.4 million, and the number of households owning at least one cat was set at 30.1 million, according to Nielsen Marketing Research. Cats reside in about 32 per cent of U.S. households.

Persians remained America's favorite purebred, with registration totals exceeding 50,000, according to the Cat Fanciers' Association, Incorporated.

A widely used test for a virus that causes abdominal inflammation in cats came into question in 1992. The test apparently detected the presence of not only the harmful virus but also of other nonthreatening microbes.

In 1992, the National Best Cat title went to Grand Champion Jadon Geoffrey Beene, a black Persian male, bred by Donna and Susan Cook of Naples, Fla., who co-owned the cat with Mark Hannon of Alexandria, Va. The National Best Kitten Award went to Grand Champion Jovan Cheers, a white-and-brown tabby, exotic shorthair female, bred and owned by Cheryl and Bob Lorditch of Cleona, Pa. A white-and-brown patched tabby, Scottish fold spay, Grand Champion and Grand Premier Kitjim's Bonny Too of Q-T Cats, won Best Alter. Kitty Angell of Bedford, Tex., bred the cat, and Marcia and Leon Samuels of Elkins Park, Pa., owned it. Thomas H. Dent

In ***World Book,*** see **Cat.**

Census. The United States Bureau of the Census in May 1992 released comprehensive statistics from its 1990 census of Americans. The statistics were compiled from detailed surveys of one-sixth of all U.S. housing units—a total of 17.7 million households.

According to the report, of the 250 million U.S. residents in 1990, some 19.7 million were of foreign birth—the largest number in the nation's history. A total of 8.6 million people entered the country during the 1980's. Almost half of those immigrants came from Latin America and the Caribbean, more than one-third came from Asia, and one-tenth came from Europe. About 14 per cent of all Americans said they spoke a language other than English in their homes in 1990.

The report also revealed that people in the United States became better educated during the 1980's. From 1980 to 1990, the fraction of Americans holding high school diplomas rose from two-thirds to three-quarters. The Southeast region made the largest gains in high school graduates, though the best-educated populations remained in the West and Midwest.

Population boom. The Census Bureau in December 1992 drastically revised its population forecasts for the coming decades. According to the report, the nation's population will jump by 50 per cent to 383 million people by the year 2050. And in the decade of the 1990's, the U.S. population will grow 7.8 per cent, the second greatest 10-year leap in population in the country's history after the 1950's.

In its previous projections in 1988, the Bureau said the number of people living in the United States in 2050 would be less than 300 million. The 1992 revisions were the result of new higher estimates of the U.S. fertility rate, immigration, and longevity.

Marriage decline. The proportion of Americans who got married in 1991 was lower than in any year since 1965, according to a report issued in July from the Census Bureau and the National Center for Health Statistics. Moreover, the median ages for first marriage in 1991 rose to 26.3 years for men and 24.1 years for women, both record high ages for the 1900's. These two statistics continued long-term trends. In 1970, only one-sixth of all Americans age 18 and older had never been married. In 1989, that fraction had risen to one-quarter.

Four-generation families. In the coming decades, an increasing number of American families will have four generations of living relatives, according to a November report by the Census Bureau. Researchers said the main implications of this rise were twofold: Children will be more likely to know their grandparents and great-grandparents, and more 50- and 60-year-old adults will find themselves arranging care for 80- and 90-year-old parents. John Burnson

See also **City; Population.** In ***World Book,*** see **Census; Population.**

Central African Republic. See **Africa.**

Chad. See **Africa.**

Chemistry. Chemists at the University of California at Irvine in August 1992 reported creating the world's smallest battery, measuring about a millionth of an inch across. It was made using a scanning tunneling microscope (STM), a device that can manipulate matter on the level of individual atoms. The chemists used the STM to place tiny pillars of copper and silver—mimicking the two ends of a battery—onto a carbon surface. When the carbon surface was immersed in a copper solution, a chemical reaction started and a current began flowing through the carbon surface from the copper pillars to the silver ones. This current ran about 45 minutes before the components of the battery were used up.

The battery was not expected to be available as a power source anytime soon because of the difficulty in working at such a small scale. Nonetheless, the battery represented a milestone in the field of *nanoelectronics* (extremely small electronic machines) and could someday power microscopic devices.

Buckyball update. *Buckminsterfullerenes,* or *buckyballs,* (hollow, soccer-ball-shaped carbon molecules) continued to surprise chemists in 1992. In January, researchers at the Very Low Temperature Research Center in France reported that subjecting buckyballs to high pressure can convert the buckyballs to diamonds, which are also made of carbon but in a very compact form. The chemists applied pressure to the buckyballs equal to 200,000 times normal air pressure. The buckyballs collapsed into a substance made up of many small diamonds. This work could lead to a new way to make industrial diamonds.

In September, chemists at the University of California in Los Angeles reported that when buckyballs are zapped with a laser, they vaporize and reassemble into far larger spheres called superballs. Using lasers, the chemists were able to create buckyballs of 400 atoms and more from 60- and 70-atom balls. Apparently, when heated, the smaller buckyballs break open slightly, then join with other opened buckyballs and reseal to create the superballs.

In June, a team of researchers at the private research firm Charles Evans and Associates in Redwood City, Calif., announced they had discovered buckyballs among debris from a meteoroid that had collided with a satellite. And in July, another team at Arizona State University in Tempe announced they had discovered buckyballs in rocks at least 600 million years old. These findings were the first proof that buckyballs occur in nature.

An uphill climb for water. In June, chemists from Dow Corning Corporation in Midland, Mich., and Harvard University in Cambridge, Mass., unveiled a way to make water run uphill using a chemical that is *hydrophobic* (water-repellant). The scientists knew that water tends to move away from areas that are hydrophobic. So they applied the hydrophobic chemical to a tilted wafer of silicon in such a way that the chemical was more concentrated at the bottom of the

Chemists in April reported progress in growing *zeolites*, crystals inside of which small molecules can combine and then become trapped (inset).

wafer than at the top. When the chemists placed a drop of water at the wafer's base, the force pushing the drop upward toward the less hydrophobic area was greater than the force of gravity pulling the drop downward, so the drop slid slowly higher.

Storing sunlight. In August, a team of chemists at Princeton University in New Jersey announced that they had succeeded in constructing a material that can convert sunlight into chemical energy and store that energy indefinitely. The material features a layer of chlorine atoms positioned near a layer of a molecule called viologen.

Sunlight is composed of subatomic particles called *photons*. When photons strike the chlorine atoms, they knock other subatomic particles called *electrons* from the chlorine into the viologen. Electricity is the flow of electrons, so in theory, the material could generate a current when the electrons flow back from the viologen to the chlorine.

Unfortunately, the viologen holds its extra electrons so well that the chemists have yet to figure out how to draw the energy out of the material. Nevertheless, the problem with earlier materials used to trap solar energy was that the electrons returned to their original atoms too quickly to be harnessed, so this work represents a vital step in the pursuit of solar-energy batteries.

Mirror-image molecules. In June, chemists at the Scripps Research Institute in La Jolla, Calif., announced the synthesis of the first mirror image of a naturally occurring *enzyme* (a molecule that promotes a specific chemical reaction). Pairs of molecules are called mirror images when they share the same composition and shape but have the opposite orientation. For example, a left hand is the mirror image of a right hand—it looks like a right hand when viewed in a mirror. Not every molecule has a mirror image, but for those that do, organisms generally create only one of the two forms. Proteins used by organisms are what is termed left-handed, or *L* in chemical notation.

The enzyme synthesized by the chemists was a protein used by the human immunodeficiency virus (HIV), which causes AIDS. In nature, the virus makes only the L form of the protein. Creating the right-handed D form allowed the chemists to investigate whether the mirror-image proteins had mirror-image properties. For example, the chemists learned that the L version of the protein attacked only other L molecules, whereas the D version attacked only D molecules. And an L inhibitor molecule was only effective against the L protein, and vice versa for a D inhibitor.

Mirror-image molecules could have a variety of uses because organisms are not familiar with them. For example, drugs made from D proteins might last longer in the human body because any biochemicals that could destroy them are prepared to face only L proteins. Peter J. Andrews

In ***World Book***, see **Chemistry**.

Chess. In 1992, the chess world was enlivened by the sudden reappearance of chess genius Bobby Fischer. Fischer returned from a self-imposed 20-year exile to battle old rival Boris Spassky for a $5-million purse. In 1972, Fischer defeated Spassky for the world chess championship and then went into seclusion.

The 1992 rematch ran from September to November in Yugoslavia, first in the coastal town of Sveti Stefan and then in the capital of Belgrade. The United States threatened Fischer, an American citizen, with a fine and a prison term for playing the match in the warring state of Yugoslavia in violation of United Nations sanctions. Fischer replied by spitting on a letter from the U.S. government at a September news conference. A federal grand jury indicted Fischer in December.

Under special rules for the rematch, the first player to win 10 games was the victor, and games could not be adjourned. As in 1972, Fischer beat Spassky, this time by a tally of 10 wins to 5 wins, with 15 draws. Fischer collected $3.35 million for his victory, and Spassky took $1.65 million.

New youngest grandmaster. In 1992, Judit Polgar of Hungary played her first match as a grandmaster. Polgar had earned the rank in late December 1991 when, at the age of 15 years and 5 months, she became the youngest grandmaster ever, beating by one month the record set by Fischer in 1958.

Championship challengers. In April 1992, Nigel Short of Great Britain and Jan Timman of the Netherlands survived elimination matches to determine who will challenge world champion Garry Kasparov of Russia for the title in 1993. The semifinal matches, held in Linares, Spain, were part of the official three-year-long world championship cycle. Short defeated former champion Anatoly Karpov of Russia, and Timman bested Artur Yusupov of the former Soviet Union. Short and Timman were to face off in January 1993, with the winner playing Kasparov in August.

Tournament results. Eric Lobron of Germany won the New York Open in New York City in April. Gregory Kaidanov of Lexington, Ky., captured both the World Open in Philadelphia in July and the U.S. Open in Dearborn, Mich., in August.

Younger players. At the U.S. Chessathon held in New York City's Central Park on July 18, more than 1,000 youngsters played simultaneously in a charity fund-raiser against 24 international stars, including Polgar. Meanwhile, in school tournament play, Dalton School of New York City won the national elementary team championship held in April in Knoxville, Tenn. Orange Grove Middle School of Tucson, Ariz., won the eighth-grade-and-under team championship, and Julia Masterman School of Philadelphia won the ninth-grade-and-under team championship, both held in May in Tallahassee, Fla. And Edward R. Murrow High School of New York City won the high school championship in May in Cherry Hill, N.J. Al Lawrence

In ***World Book,*** see **Chess.**

Chicago. A disaster that has been dubbed the Great Chicago Flood threw downtown Chicago into turmoil on April 13, 1992. The flood occurred when water from the Chicago River suddenly cascaded into an extensive network of underground freight tunnels and then into the basements of many downtown buildings, knocking out electrical service. Tens of thousands of office workers were sent home, many for a week or more, and some buildings did not reopen for a month. By some estimates, the flood resulted in business losses of at least $1 billion.

According to city officials, the leak happened because in September 1991 a private contractor driving large wooden pilings into the riverbed accidentally punctured a section of tunnel. While city officials debated the approval of a $10,000 contract to repair the damage, the rupture suddenly worsened and the river poured into the tunnel. It took engineers a week to plug the leak, and then the tunnel was drained.

Bulls triumph sparks rioting. The Chicago Bulls won their second consecutive National Basketball Association championship on June 14, defeating the Portland Trail Blazers four games to two. But there was a dark side to the victory. Immediately after the game, thousands of people poured into the streets to celebrate, and many of them became violent. During the night, looting, arson, and other violence resulted in more than 1,000 arrests. More than 200 people, including at least 95 police officers, were injured.

Bad news from census. New data from the 1990 census, released in May by the United States Bureau of the Census, showed that the income gap between Chicago and its suburbs grew by 24 per cent during the 1980's. This growing disparity in average household incomes between city and suburbs occurred even though the six-county suburban region itself experienced a modest increase in poverty.

According to the figures, 34 per cent of Chicago's children lived in poverty. For all Chicagoans, the figure was 22 per cent. In inner-city neighborhoods, the news was even bleaker. Seventy-two per cent of all the people in the Oakland community on the South Side were poor, as were 65 per cent of those in the nearby Grand Boulevard area.

Economic development. In the spring of 1992, Mayor Richard M. Daley appeared well on his way to transforming the economic and physical landscape of Chicago with two huge projects: a $10.8-billion international airport to be built near Lake Calumet on the city's southeast side, and a $2-billion casino-entertainment complex near the downtown area. But by year's end, both plans were stalled.

In February, Daley won the support of Illinois Governor Jim Edgar for the airport. But when the state legislature failed to approve the plan in July, Daley blamed the governor and, in a surprise move, declared the airport proposal dead. Then, in December, Edgar came up with a plan to build an airport near the town of Peotone, south of the city.

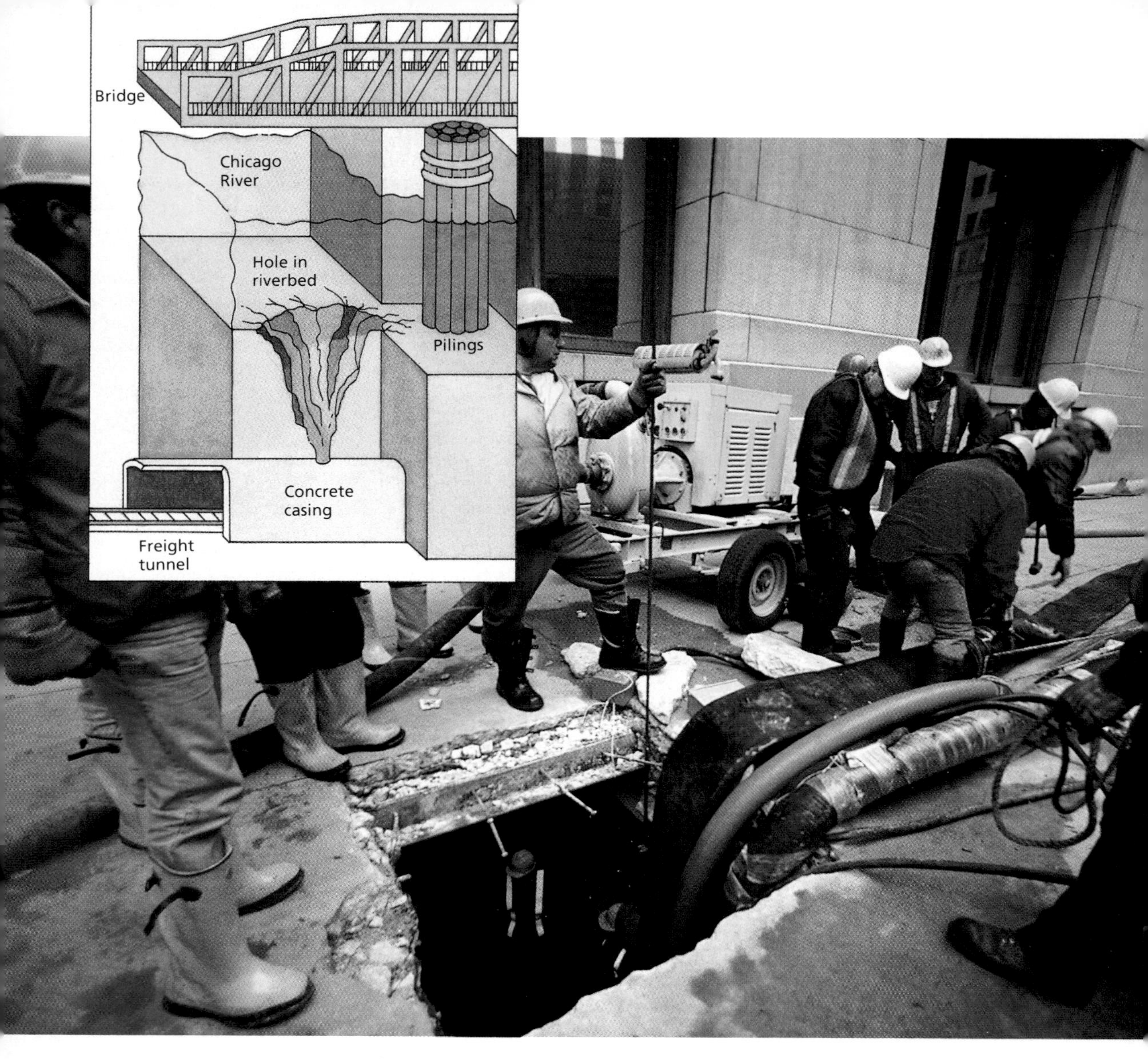

Water is pumped from Chicago's City Hall in April after a contractor sank pilings into the bed of the Chicago River, puncturing and flooding a freight tunnel (*inset*).

Meanwhile, the mayor continued to push the casino plan, which would comprise four casinos and a mammoth family-entertainment center, including a theme park. But Edgar blocked the plan in the state legislature, contending that the gambling complex would severely damage the state's horse-racing industry and increase crime in Chicago.

Schools. Daley and officials of Chicago's perennially troubled school system had to work around the clock to close a hole of $85 million in the system's $2-billion budget by the August 31 deadline. But the school system's financial crunch was still so bad that officials, looking for ways to save money, eliminated truant officers and seriously considered canceling all school sports programs. Meanwhile, a study of 43 of the largest school systems in the nation ranked Chicago as worst in drop-out rate (46 per cent) and in test scores for reading and mathematics.

Security patrols. The Chicago police and federal agents began making intensive security sweeps of the Cabrini-Green housing development in October in response to gang-related violence that was making the huge complex an increasingly dangerous place to live. The crackdown was launched after a 7-year-old boy, Dantrell Davis, was fatally shot by a sniper as he walked to school in the complex. Davis was the third student at his elementary school to be shot to death in an eight-month period. Patrick T. Reardon

See also **City**. In ***World Book,*** see **Chicago**.

Children's books. See **Literature for children**.

Chile. President Patricio Aylwin Azócar in 1992 continued to struggle against the influence of the Chilean armed forces. Significant political power remained with former Chilean military dictator General Augusto Pinochet, who can remain as head of the Chilean army until 1998 as a result of a provision in the 1980 Chilean Constitution.

Because of Pinochet's continued power, much of Chile's finances went to the armed forces in 1992. Chile spent more per capita on its armed forces than did any other nation in South America in 1992. The country spent 4 times more per capita than did Peru and 10 times more than did Brazil. Moreover, 10 per cent of the nation's copper profits, about $400 million a year, went for defense.

Municipal elections. In Chile's first municipal elections since 1973, Aylwin's Christian Democratic Party won 53 per cent of the votes on June 28, 1992. A combination of right-wing parties that supported the country's former military rulers won 30 per cent.

Arms sale scandal. In January, Chilean government officials discovered that high-ranking Chilean officers were involved in arms sales to Croatia in violation of a United Nations ban. Calling the affair a "total surprise," Chilean Defense Minister Patricio Rojas pledged an immediate investigation.

Nathan A. Haverstock

See also **Latin America** (Facts in brief table). In ***World Book,*** see **Chile**.

China. Deng Xiaoping, China's senior leader, in 1992 stepped up his drive for market-oriented economic reforms while maintaining the Communist Party's grip on political power. Deng holds no official position in the country but dominates policymaking by the influence he has achieved during his decades-long involvement in Chinese politics. Deng's conservative critics argued that his economic plans undermined China's Communist regime because they unleashed demands for greater political freedoms. But Deng maintained that his reforms, started in 1978, have been popular with the Chinese people and so have helped keep the Communist Party in power in China while Communist parties in Eastern Europe and the former Soviet Union fell in the late 1980's and early 1990's.

However, the pace of reform in China had slowed in recent years. The turning point was June 1989, when about 1 million prodemocracy demonstrators gathered in Tiananmen Square in Beijing to protest government policies. The military was called in to crush the challenge. Troops killed hundreds of demonstrators and arrested thousands. Hard-line conservatives used the massive demonstration as an example of the turmoil that Deng's economic liberalization could produce, and further reforms were halted.

Reforms backed. Deng retook the offensive in 1992, after the collapse in late 1991 of the Soviet Union, whose failed economic model China had adopted 40 years earlier. On Jan. 19, 1992, after not appearing publicly for a year, Deng began a tour of the five special economic zones in southeast China where experimental free-market reforms had led to explosive economic growth. He endorsed the results of the liberalization. "We should not be afraid of others' saying that we are practicing capitalism," he said during his trip. "Whoever is opposed to reform must leave office."

And Deng's strong personal influence was sufficient for his views to gain acceptance. On March 10, 1992, the Communist Party's leading body, the 20-member Politburo, adopted Deng's accelerated economic reform program. The National People's Congress (NPC) also threw its weight behind Deng at its 1992 session from March 20 to April 3. The NPC approved conservative Premier Li Peng's state-of-the-nation report only after making more than 150 revisions supporting Deng's market-oriented reforms.

Acceptance of Deng's reforms among the Chinese leadership was further aided by the deaths of several aging hard-line conservatives, including Communist Party official Wang Renzhong on March 16 at the age of 75; former President Li Xiannian on June 21 in his mid-80's; and Deng Yingchao, the widow of former Premier Zhou Enlai, on July 11 at the age of 88.

Communist Party congress. Deng's aggressive push for economic reform in 1992 seemed inspired by the approach of the 14th Communist Party congress in October. This meeting, the first such gathering since

Customers place orders as McDonald's opens its first restaurant in China—and its biggest outlet in the world—in Beijing, the capital, in April.

Police in the Chinese city of Shenzhen combat unruly crowds in August during a public lottery to buy new shares on the city's stock market.

1987, fixes the policies and leadership that will run the Chinese Communist Party—and thus China—until the next congress in five years. Since Deng was 88 years old and in poor health at the time of the 1992 congress, the meeting was seen as his final opportunity to ensure that his economic reforms would continue after his death.

The congress, attended by 1,989 delegates chosen from some 51 million party members, began on October 12. Communist Party chief Jiang Zemin opened the meeting by calling for economic restructuring "not to change the nature of our Socialist system but to improve and develop it." Jiang said the goal of economic reform in China was to build a "Socialist market democracy," which was "absolutely not a Western, multiparty, parliamentary system." Deng, who was hailed as "the chief architect of China's reforms," did not attend the congress, but he worked behind the scenes. After it ended on October 18, however, the frail leader slowly walked around the hall for about 20 minutes greeting delegates.

The meeting was considered a triumph for Deng. For example, the congress dismissed almost half of the members of the party's policymaking Central Committee, replacing many of them with reform-minded protégés of Deng. And three members of the seven-person Standing Committee of the Politburo—the party's highest decision-making body—were deposed and replaced, leaving only a single conservative, Premier Li Peng. The three new members were Liu Huaqing, a general who runs the Central Military Commission; Hu Jintao, who handles party organization; and Zhu Rongji, a deputy premier in charge of industry and a leading economic reformer. And even Li in the months before the congress had been lending his support to Deng's plans.

Thus, Deng's economic reforms seemed assured of being pursued by the Communist Party. But experts cautioned that conservatives had managed to overturn reformist choices of Deng's after the Communist Party congresses in 1982 and 1987, so the economic course of China was uncertain. Further complicating matters was that no clear successor to Deng had yet emerged.

Military changes. During the congress, Deng also renewed his campaign to depoliticize the armed forces. Jiang retained his position as nominal head of the Central Military Commission. But Deng cast out both President Yang Shangkun and his half-brother Yang Baibing, who were accused by reformist party members of politicizing the military.

Surging economy. Since Deng began his economic reforms in 1978, China's economy had grown at an average rate of almost 9 per cent a year, a pace that doubled the country's wealth about every eight years. But the resulting prosperity was uneven. In coastal areas, especially those close to the British territory of Hong Kong, foreign investment in new industries stimulated growth of up to 25 per cent.

On August 9 and 10, Chinese citizens eager to profit from the expansion rioted in Shenzhen, a new industrial city near Hong Kong, during a lottery for shares on the city's stock market. However, many inland regions of China continued to lag in the race to escape poverty.

Tiananmen dealings. The Chinese government in early 1992 wrapped up court actions against students held without trials since the Tiananmen Square protests in June 1989. In January and February 1992, China gave jail sentences to 27 Tiananmen Square demonstrators, including a former editor at the official *People's Daily* newspaper who had put out an extra edition leaflet supporting the demonstrators. But the sentences were generally lenient, and allowing for time already served, many of the demonstrators were soon free.

On July 21, a former aide to former Communist Party chief Zhao Ziyang was sentenced for crimes in connection with the Tiananmen demonstrations. Bao Tong, the highest-ranking official arrested after the Tiananmen crackdown, was sentenced to seven years for leaking information to protesters about the coming of martial law in May 1989. Bao was the most senior official to have been tried in China since 1981. Observers speculated that the 7-year term, less than half the maximum penalty of 15 years, was a compromise between conservatives and reformers.

In late July 1992, prodemocracy leader Shen Tong, who had fled to the United States after the 1989 Tiananmen massacre, returned to China. Shen, the first student protester known to have returned to China since the crackdown, was arrested on September 1. On the day of his arrest, he had been planning to announce a Beijing branch of the organization he had founded in the United States to promote democracy in China. International protests followed his arrest, and Shen was released on October 24. But he was expelled from China.

Nuclear bomb test. On May 21, China detonated a 1,000-kiloton atomic bomb in the country's largest underground nuclear test ever. The blast had about 70 times the explosive power of the atomic bomb dropped on Hiroshima, Japan, by the United States at the end of World War II (1939-1945). China's bomb exceeded the 150-kiloton limit for nuclear tests that had been observed informally by both the United States and the Soviet Union since 1976. (See also **Armed forces: The Nuclear Threat in the New World Order.**)

U.S. relations. On Jan. 31, 1992, Premier Li Peng met with U.S. President George Bush for the first time since the 1989 Tiananmen Square massacre. But the reception on both sides was chilly, as Li resented Bush's criticism of China's human rights record and Bush strove not to appear too friendly with the Beijing leadership.

On August 7, China and the United States signed an agreement forbidding the export to the United States of goods made by Chinese prison laborers. The U.S. Congress had been threatening to use the matter of prison labor to lower China's official trade status. China also said U.S. inspectors would be allowed to investigate Chinese facilities where the source of the labor was in dispute.

China was angered in September by President Bush's decision to sell 150 F-16 fighter jets to Taiwan. China and Taiwan have been bitter enemies since 1949, when the Communists drove the Nationalist government out of China and onto the island. China said Bush's move violated a 1982 agreement by the United States to limit the sale of weapons to Taiwan. But Bush, fighting for reelection, was more concerned about saving jobs in the U.S. defense industry than about antagonizing China. In retaliation, China in September refused to attend a meeting of the permanent members of the UN Security Council to discuss arms control in the Middle East.

Controversial dam. The NPC in April approved a huge dam on the Yangtze River. The Three Gorges Dam is to be the largest dam in the world. The government claimed the dam would supply vast amounts of hydroelectric power and help limit flooding. But critics voiced concerns about the economic and environmental costs of the project. (See **Water.**)

Henry S. Bradsher

See also **Asia** (Facts in brief table). In ***World Book,*** see **China.**

Churches. See **Eastern Orthodox Churches; Judaism; Protestantism; Religion; Roman Catholic Church.**

City. Rioting that scarred Los Angeles in April and May 1992 was widely seen as evidence of growing unrest among people living in inner cities. An increasing segment of American society reportedly felt ignored, forgotten, or abused as they struggled with poverty and discrimination. (See **City: The Ailing Cities, the Angry Poor.**)

After the Los Angeles riots ended in early May, most other cities remained calm despite widespread anger and tension. Disturbances flared up but were quickly quelled in Atlanta, Ga.; Las Vegas, Nev.; and Madison, Wis. President George Bush toured devastated sections of Los Angeles on May 7 and 8. Bush pledged that he would work to get bipartisan support from Congress on his "action agenda" to respond to the riot damage and to the problems of cities nationwide. Bush renewed a legislative proposal to create "enterprise zones" by providing tax incentives and other inducements to encourage businesses to locate in designated areas of high unemployment and poverty. The urban aid bill that finally emerged from Congress in October included authorization to create 50 urban zones and 50 rural zones. But Bush vetoed the legislation on November 4, because Congress had added tax increases and other items that he called "a blizzard of special-interest pleadings."

Detroit. A potentially explosive situation occurred in Detroit in November, when four police officers, three of them white, were charged in the beating death of a black motorist, Malice Green, during an arrest near a suspected drug house. The police chief helped to quell violent reaction by suspending the officers. All four officers were dismissed from the police force in December. A charge of involuntary manslaughter against the one black officer was dropped.

Washington march. Tens of thousands of people gathered in Washington, D.C., on May 16 for a "Save Our Cities! Save Our Children!" march. National leaders, city and state officials, teachers, labor union representatives, and community and religious leaders took part in the demonstration that began at the U.S. Capitol and ended on the grounds of the Washington Monument. Osborne Elliott, retired editor of *Newsweek* magazine, conceived the march to focus attention on the growing plight of America's cities.

Redlining. New federal data on bank lending practices added weight to claims that banks often engage in *redlining* low-income neighborhoods. Redlining is the practice of refusing to make mortgage or home-improvement loans to residents of neighborhoods that banks consider in decline. The Federal Reserve System, the nation's central bank, revealed in March that banks rejected mortgage applications by blacks more than twice as often as they rejected applications by whites. And banks used much more stringent credit criteria when reviewing applications for small loans for inner-city properties than they did when reviewing applications for much larger loans for homes in suburban areas.

Presidential action on urban ills. On January 28, President Bush announced in his State of the Union address the formation of a National Commission on America's Urban Families. The commission was to examine and report on adverse factors and conditions affecting families living in cities. He said that leading mayors of the National League of Cities had told him that the major cause of urban problems was family disintegration. By the end of the year, the new family commission was to complete its work, including recommending solutions to problems that they found.

Urban car crimes. City police departments struggled with the increasing number of *carjackings* (the armed theft of an occupied automobile). A carjacking in Howard County, Maryland, in September resulted in the death of a woman who was driving her child to preschool. The woman became entangled in the seat belt and was dragged outside her car for 2 miles (3 kilometers) as two carjackers sped off in it. The child was rescued unharmed. The Federal Bureau of Investigation said in September that the U.S. cities reporting the most carjackings were Houston; Los Angeles; Newark, N.J.; New York City; and Washington, D.C.

Newark also had the highest rate of car thefts in 1991 among cities of 50,000 or more, according to a *USA Today* newspaper report on Sept. 9, 1992. The city was also torn in 1992 by several incidents that led to the shooting deaths by police of four young people suspected of car theft. Although they tried to reduce the number of car thefts, Newark officials and prosecutors were often frustrated by their inability to obtain jail sentences for most juvenile offenders because of the lack of detention facilities.

In efforts to curb prostitution, prosecutors in Hartford, Conn., seized cars driven by prospective clients of local prostitutes. The cars were seized for allegedly being used in criminal activity. Also in Connecticut, police in Bridgeport installed a network of concrete barriers at street intersections near highway exits and other places where people were known to make drug purchases. The plan was modeled after similar, but less extensive, efforts in Los Angeles; Miami; Portland, Ore.; and Decatur, Ill.

Bleak financial news. In its annual survey of urban fiscal conditions, reported in July, the National League of Cities found that for the first time a majority of cities and towns said they were operating in the red. More than 52 per cent of the 620 cities responding to the survey said revenues fell short of expenditures in 1991. Cities were able to balance their budgets only by drawing from reserve funds.

Many city leaders reacted angrily in October 1992 when *The Wall Street Journal* reported that two major bond rating firms, Moody's Investors Service and Standard & Poors, were considering a city's "quality of life" and "social and intergovernmental patterns and pressures" in evaluating the creditworthiness of municipal bonds. Critics said less-affluent communities would be penalized and face the prospect of paying

Mayors and other national leaders, including Jesse Jackson, center, march in Washington, D.C., on May 16 to call attention to the plight of U.S. cities.

higher interest rates to borrow money because of an arbitrary rating that might have no relationship to a city's past credit history and ability to carry the debt.

Bridgeport, Conn., which jolted financial markets in 1991 with an effort to invoke bankruptcy laws, announced on Jan. 15, 1992, that it would withdraw the bankruptcy petition. The city began to regain financial stability under a plan worked out with state leaders.

Private involvement. A foundation established by the founders of *Reader's Digest* magazine announced a program in October to donate $40 million to help revitalize public library resources in 25 cities around the United States. Among the cities receiving money were Baton Rouge, La.; Cambridge, Mass.; New York City; Providence, R.I.; and Tucson, Ariz.

Baltimore began a novel test of private sector involvement in its school system when it signed an agreement in June with Education Alternatives Incorporated of Minneapolis, Minn., to run nine inner-city schools. The company claimed it could run the schools more efficiently than the public school system could. The company also had contracts with public schools in Dade County, Florida, and Duluth, Minn. (See **Education: The Private Education Business.**)

Economic pressures on many cities stemmed from job losses and plant closings by major U.S. companies, which meant an increase in unemployment among urban workers. General Motors Corporation (GM), the largest industrial company in the world, announced on February 24 that it would close 12 plants

50 largest cities in the United States

Rank	City	Population*	Per cent change in population since 1980	Unemployment rate†	Mayor‡
1.	New York City	7,322,564	+3.5	11.2%	David N. Dinkins (D, 12/93)
2.	Los Angeles	3,485,398	+17.4	11.2	Tom Bradley (NP, 6/93)
3.	Chicago	2,783,726	-7.4	7.9	Richard M. Daley (D, 4/95)
4.	Houston	1,630,553	+2.2	7.1	Bob Lanier (NP, 1/94)
5.	Philadelphia	1,585,577	-6.1	7.9	Edward G. Rendell (D, 1/96)
6.	San Diego	1,110,549	+26.8	7.3	Susan Golding (NP, 12/96)
7.	Detroit	1,027,974	-14.6	10.4	Coleman A. Young (D, 12/93)
8.	Dallas	1,006,877	+11.3	6.8	Steve Bartlett (NP, 12/95)
9.	Phoenix	983,403	+24.5	5.9	Paul Johnson (D, 12/95)
10.	San Antonio	935,933	+19.1	6.8	Nelson W. Wolff (NP, 6/93)
11.	San Jose	782,248	+24.3	6.4	Susan Hammer (NP, 12/94)
12.	Indianapolis	741,952	+4.3	4.8	Stephen Goldsmith (R, 12/95)
13.	Baltimore	736,014	-6.4	7.4	Kurt L. Schmoke (D, 12/95)
14.	San Francisco	723,959	+6.6	5.9	Frank M. Jordan (D, 1/96)
15.	Jacksonville, Fla.	672,971	+17.9	7.4	T. Ed Austin (D, 7/95)
16.	Columbus, Ohio	632,910	+12.0	5.3	Gregory S. Lashutka (R, 12/95)
17.	Milwaukee	628,088	-1.3	4.7	John O. Norquist (D, 4/96)
18.	Memphis	610,337	-5.5	5.8	W. W. Herenton (NP, 12/95)
19.	Washington, D.C.	606,900	-4.9	5.0	Sharon Pratt Kelly (D, 12/94)
20.	Boston	574,283	+2.0	7.8	Raymond L. Flynn (D, 1/96)
21.	Seattle	516,259	+4.5	5.5	Norman B. Rice (NP, 12/93)
22.	El Paso	515,342	+21.2	10.6	William S. Tilney (D, 6/93)
23.	Nashville	510,784	+6.9	5.2	Philip Bredesen (D, 9/95)
24.	Cleveland	505,616	-11.9	6.5	Michael R. White (D, 12/93)
25.	New Orleans	496,938	-10.9	7.7	Sidney J. Barthelemy (D, 5/94)
26.	Denver, Colo.	467,610	-5.1	5.9	Wellington E. Webb (D, 7/95)
27.	Austin, Tex.	465,622	+34.6	4.9	Bruce Todd (NP, 6/94)
28.	Fort Worth, Tex.	447,619	+16.2	6.7	Kay Granger (NP, 5/93)
29.	Oklahoma City, Okla.	444,719	+10.1	4.9	Ronald J. Norick (NP, 4/94)
30.	Portland, Ore.	437,319	+18.8	6.4	Vera Katz (NP, 1/97)
31.	Kansas City, Mo.	435,146	-2.9	5.2	Emanuel Cleaver (NP, 4/95)
32.	Long Beach, Calif.	429,433	+18.8	11.2	Ernie E. Kell (NP, 6/94)
33.	Tucson, Ariz.	405,390	+22.6	4.8	George Miller (D, 12/95)
34.	St. Louis, Mo.	396,685	-12.4	6.6	Vincent C. Schoemehl, Jr. (D, 4/93)
35.	Charlotte, N.C.	395,934	+25.5	6.0	Richard Vinroot (R, 12/93)
36.	Atlanta, Ga.	394,017	-7.3	6.8	Maynard H. Jackson (D, 11/93)
37.	Virginia Beach, Va.	393,069	+49.9	7.3	Meyera E. Oberndorf (NP, 6/96)
38.	Albuquerque, N. Mex.	384,736	+15.6	5.1	Louis E. Saavedra (NP, 11/93)
39.	Oakland, Calif.	372,242	+9.7	6.4	Elihu Mason Harris (D, 1/94)
40.	Pittsburgh, Pa.	369,879	-12.8	6.9	Sophie Masloff (D, 12/93)
41.	Sacramento, Calif.	369,365	+34.0	7.4	Joe Serna, Jr. (D, 11/96)
42.	Minneapolis, Minn.	368,383	-0.7	3.7	Donald M. Fraser (NP, 12/93)
43.	Tulsa, Okla.	367,302	+1.8	5.8	M. Susan Savage (D, 4/94)
44.	Honolulu, Hawaii	365,272	+0.1	3.6	Frank F. Fasi (R, 1/97)
45.	Cincinnati, Ohio	364,040	-5.5	5.6	Dwight Tillery (D, 11/93)
46.	Miami, Fla.	358,548	+3.4	10.4	Xavier L. Suarez (I, 11/93)
47.	Fresno, Calif.	354,202	+62.9	12.5	Karen Humphrey (D, 3/93)
48.	Omaha, Nebr.	335,795	+7.0	3.6	P. J. Morgan (NP, 6/93)
49.	Toledo, Ohio	332,943	-6.1	8.6	John McHugh (D, 12/93)
50.	Buffalo, N.Y.	328,123	-8.3	7.9	James D. Griffin (D, 12/93)

*1990 census (source: U.S. Bureau of the Census).
†July 1992 unemployment figures are for metropolitan areas (source: U.S. Bureau of Labor Statistics).
‡The letters in parentheses represent the mayor's party, with *D* meaning Democrat, *R* Republican, *I* Independent, and *NP* nonpartisan. The date is when the term of office ends (source: mayors' offices).

as part of the company's overall plan to close or sell 21 plants by the end of 1995. The 12 closings would affect 16,000 employees. Plant closings that affected more than 1,000 workers were in the Michigan cities of Ypsilanti and Flint and North Tarrytown, N.Y. (See **Automobile.**)

Many city economies strongly tied to major defense contractors or military installations also saw their fortunes decline. The process of converting military industries and facilities to civilian uses, which accelerated in 1992, caused serious problems to cities nationwide. They had to adjust to the changing nature of employment and business activity, and how both impacted the revenue and cost side of government. Many local government leaders appealed to Washington for help in retraining workers in new jobs and in fostering the growth of new industries. Municipal leaders also asked for assistance in rebuilding public infrastructure.

President-elect Bill Clinton, then the Democratic presidential candidate and governor of Arkansas, voiced a similar theme when he spoke to the U.S. Conference of Mayors in Washington, D.C., in January. In July, he proposed a plan to spend $200 billion on cities, infrastructure, education, and worker training.

New L.A. fault zones. Geologists studying satellite images in December identified two new fault zones in downtown Los Angeles that pose a potential threat of earthquakes. One runs almost directly beneath a portion of the Hollywood Freeway. California residents were jolted by serious earthquakes in April and June, but because their epicenters were in relatively unpopulated areas, there was relatively little damage in urban centers.

Storm damage. Hurricane Andrew pounded south Florida with winds of up to 135 miles (217 kilometers) per hour when it slammed ashore on August 24. Andrew left more than 250,000 people homeless, and 1.8 million people were without power in the area just south of Miami. The cities of Homestead and Florida City suffered the greatest damage. Total insured losses were estimated at $7.3 billion. On August 25, Andrew delivered a second onslaught of winds measuring 140 miles (225 kilometers) per hour and drenching rain on Houma and other communities in the bayou region of southern Louisiana. The storm killed 13 people in Florida and 1 in Louisiana.

On September 11, Hurricane Iniki surged across the Pacific Ocean with sustained winds of 130 miles (210 kilometers) per hour and struck the Hawaiian island of Kauai. The storm left 3 people dead and 8,000 residents homeless. Total damage was estimated at $1 billion. Kauai was cut off from outside communication and services for days.

In December, a winter storm hit the northeastern seacoast, dumping up to 4 feet (1.2 meters) of snow on inland communities. Damages were estimated in the hundreds of millions. Randolph C. Arndt

In ***World Book,*** see **City.**

50 largest cities in the world

Rank	City	Population
1.	Mexico City	10,263,275
2.	Seoul, South Korea	9,645,932
3.	Moscow	8,801,000
4.	Tokyo	8,353,674
5.	Bombay, India	8,227,332
6.	Shanghai	8,214,436
7.	Beijing	7,362,425
8.	New York City	7,322,564
9.	São Paulo, Brazil	7,033,529
10.	London	6,767,500
11.	Jakarta, Indonesia	6,761,886
12.	Cairo, Egypt	6,052,836
13.	Hong Kong	6,003,000
14.	Baghdad, Iraq	5,908,000
15.	Tianjin, China	5,855,068
16.	Teheran, Iran	5,734,199
17.	Lima, Peru	5,493,900
18.	Istanbul, Turkey	5,475,982
19.	Karachi, Pakistan	5,208,170
20.	Bangkok, Thailand	5,153,902
21.	Rio de Janeiro, Brazil	5,093,232
22.	Delhi, India	4,884,234
23.	St. Petersburg	4,468,000
24.	Santiago, Chile	4,225,299
25.	Shenyang, China	4,130,000
26.	Bogotá, Colombia	3,982,941
27.	Ho Chi Minh City, Vietnam	3,934,395
28.	Pusan, South Korea	3,516,807
29.	Los Angeles	3,485,398
30.	Wuhan, China	3,340,000
31.	Calcutta, India	3,305,006
32.	Madras, India	3,276,622
33.	Guangzhou, China	3,220,000
34.	Madrid, Spain	3,123,713
35.	Berlin, Germany	3,062,979
36.	Hanoi	3,058,855
37.	Yokohama, Japan	2,992,644
38.	Sydney, Australia	2,989,070
39.	Lahore, Pakistan	2,952,689
40.	Alexandria, Egypt	2,917,327
41.	Buenos Aires	2,908,001
42.	Rome	2,830,569
43.	Chicago	2,783,726
44.	Chongqing, China	2,730,000
45.	Melbourne, Australia	2,645,484
46.	Pyongyang, North Korea	2,639,448
47.	Taipei, Taiwan	2,637,100
48.	Osaka, Japan	2,636,260
49.	Harbin, China	2,590,000
50.	Chengdu, China	2,540,000

Sources: 1990 census figures for U.S. cities from the U.S. Bureau of the Census; censuses or government estimates for cities of other countries.

The Ailing Cities, the Angry Poor

By Edward Crenshaw

The Los Angeles riots focused attention on the unpleasant fact that many large U.S. cities are plagued with violence, poverty, and decay—problems that can no longer be safely ignored.

On April 29, 1992, the city of Los Angeles erupted in violence. For five days, thousands of people—most of them blacks and Hispanics in poor neighborhoods—took part in arson and looting that devastated large swaths of the city. When it was over, more than 50 people were dead and more than 4,000 were injured. Property damage exceeded $1 billion. It was one of the worst riots in United States history.

The immediate cause of the rampage was the acquittal on April 29 of four Los Angeles police officers who had been charged with assaulting a black motorist, Rodney King. King's beating by the policemen in 1991 had been videotaped by an onlooker, and the brutal images outraged many Americans, blacks and whites alike. The explosive response to the acquittal, however, was widely viewed as unjustified criminal behavior.

Opposite page: A gutted, graffiti-covered apartment building in New York City's Harlem is a typical example of the blight that mars many of America's large cities.

But to many, the rioting, while deplorable, was an understandable response stemming from the anger and frustration that had long been building in the inner cities of the United States as a result of years of poverty and neglect. By this view, large-scale violence could just as easily have broken out in any other major U.S. city with a sizable minority population. A number of observers thus read the upheaval as a "wake-up call" for white America. The riots, they said, were a warning that the nation had better take steps, and soon, to redeem its decaying inner cities.

It wasn't the first such warning the country had received. In the 1960's, a series of riots in poor areas of Los Angeles, Cleveland, Detroit, and other cities rocked the nation. In response, President Lyndon B. Johnson established a commission headed by Governor Otto Kerner of Illinois to investigate the causes of the unrest. In its 1968 report, the Kerner Commission placed much of the blame for the riots on white racism and noted, ominously, that the United States was becoming "two societies, one black, one white—separate and unequal." Many people would argue in 1992 that not much, or at least not enough, had changed in the intervening 25 years. Why have American cities gone so wrong over the years, and why has the nation seemingly been incapable of setting things right?

The changing nature of U.S. cities

A central tragedy of American urban history is that the industrial cities of the northern United States failed to do for black people what they had done for whites. In the 1800's and early 1900's, those cities were giant commercial engines that produced a variety of manufactured goods for national and international markets. The companies that made those goods provided blue-collar jobs for both long-time U.S. citizens and the waves of European immigrants that poured into the country.

The black migration to those cities began during World War I (1914-1918). Before that time, about 90 per cent of American blacks still lived in the South, most of them in rural areas. Eventually, some 5 million Southern blacks trekked northward—and later also westward—in search of the jobs they hoped would bring them a higher standard of living. But their high expectations turned to disappointment. In 1919, race riots and violent incidents, sparked by white resentment against the newcomers, occurred in at least 25 cities across the country. Moreover, most blacks found themselves confined to segregated neighborhoods and restricted to lower-rung service occupations. This situation persisted even after blacks won many legal inroads toward equality with whites in the civil rights movement of the 1950's and early 1960's.

At the same time that Southern blacks were moving to the cities of the North, the United States was on its way to becoming a nation of suburbanites. By the 1920's, the telephone and the automobile had begun to transform society. It was now possible for Americans—mainly of the white middle class—to live in the new suburban towns that were being built on the outskirts of many cities while maintaining close contact with the urban centers and often continuing to work there.

With suburbanization shaping up as the wave of the future, the massive urban engines began to falter. Not only large segments of the white population but also many manufacturing industries began leaving the cities at the same time that blacks were moving there in an attempt to achieve a greater share of the American economic pie. So black people now found themselves in a double bind. Besides having trouble landing the same kinds of jobs that had long served as stepping stones to the middle class for previous newcomers, blacks were faced with a situation in which those jobs were becoming ever more scarce.

The author:

Edward Crenshaw is an assistant professor of sociology at Ohio State University in Columbus.

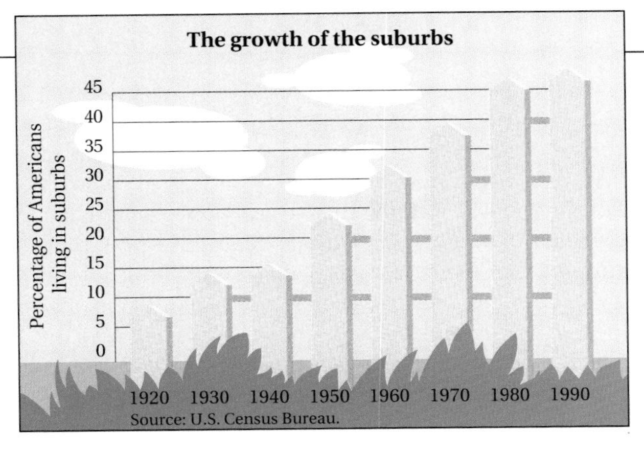

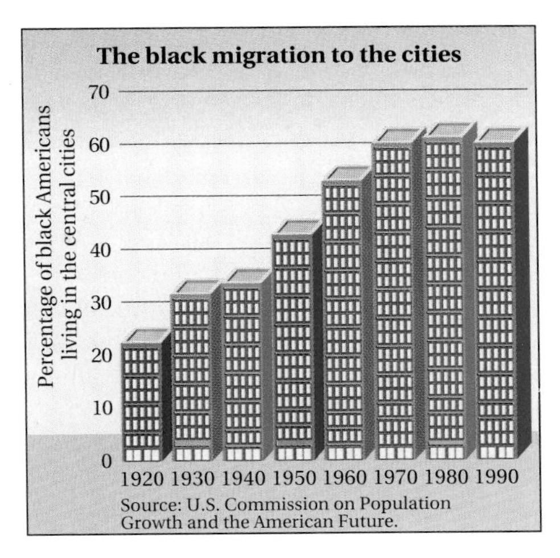

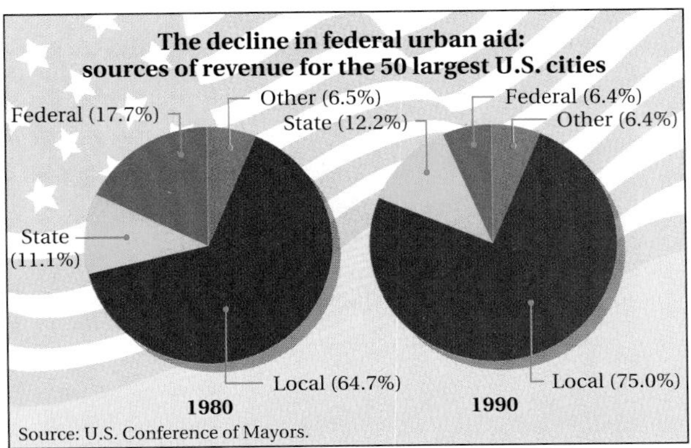

Evolution of the urban crisis

Population shifts during the 1900's were a leading cause of urban decline. At the same time that millions of poor Southern blacks were migrating to the central cities, white middle-class taxpayers were moving to the suburbs, causing the urban tax base to shrink. Federal cutbacks in the 1980's increased cities' fiscal woes.

The movement out of central cities greatly accelerated after World War II (1939-1945), spurred by intensive highway construction, subsidized home loans from the government, and the booming postwar economy. The biggest rush to the suburbs occurred in the 1950's during the height of the post-World War II baby boom and was motivated mainly by a desire for reasonably priced housing, pleasant surroundings, and good schools—amenities that the suburbs offered in abundance. By 1960, about 31 per cent of Americans lived in suburbs, up from less than 9 per cent 40 years earlier. And by 1990, the U.S. Census Bureau reported, 46.2 per cent of the nation's population was concentrated in suburban areas. What's more, federal labor statistics showed that most of the new jobs being created in the 1990's were in the suburbs. This phenomenon has given rise to so-called *edge cities*—sprawling suburban developments containing residential areas, large shopping malls, and industrial parks.

Government responses to the urban dilemma

The result of this great shift in the white population has been that many big cities have lost much of their middle-class tax base. As early as the late 1940's, government officials, alarmed at this trend, had begun taking steps aimed at turning the situation around. In the Housing Act of 1949, the U.S. Congress authorized a major program of urban renewal. Under this initiative, cities were allowed to purchase tracts of rundown housing, demolish them, and sell the cleared land to private developers at a price subsidized by the federal government.

A primary goal of urban renewal was to create attractive new housing, parks, and services for middle- and lower-income city dwellers. But that wasn't usually how things worked out. All too often, the small houses and apartment buildings that were torn down were replaced by housing projects that soon became high-rise slums. Moreover, the leveling of whole neighborhoods and the relocation of their residents destroyed all sense of community in large sections of many cities. Thus, while urban renewal was successful in revitalizing the downtowns of some cities, such as Pittsburgh, it did not do much to improve the lives of the urban poor.

Urban renewal also failed utterly to stop the hemorrhage of the white middle class to the suburbs. Some observers have concluded that more-affluent whites began leaving the cities en masse largely to escape the growing black presence. Studies have confirmed that this so-called white flight has indeed been a factor in the growth of the suburbs. However, it did not seem to be a leading impetus in suburbanization until the middle to late 1960's, when widespread rioting in the cities and rising urban crime rates made whites increasingly fearful of city life.

The next major initiatives for aiding the cities and their growing legions of low-income residents came at the same time, during the Administration of President Lyndon B. Johnson. Johnson established a number of Great Society programs aimed at helping the poor. By 1974, these initiatives had helped cut the U.S. poverty rate to half of what it had been in 1959—from about 22 per cent of the population to 11 per cent. But after 1974, the poverty rate refused to budge any lower. The percentage of Americans living under the poverty line (about $14,000 per year for a family of four in 1992) fluctuated between 11 and 14 per cent through most of the late 1970's and the 1980's. In September 1992, the U.S. Census Bureau reported that the poverty rate in 1991 had risen to 14.2 per cent. The number of people in poverty—35.7 million, nearly half of them black and Hispanic—was the highest since 1964. And an estimated 42 per cent of the poor lived in the cities.

Experts debate the failure of public policies

Opinions vary concerning the failure of public policies to lower poverty levels. Many observers think that the welfare system has been a big part of the problem. They note that the many welfare programs available to the poor in central cities—programs mandated by the federal government but administered by states and municipalities—are overlapping, confusing, badly coordinated, and often inadequate to the task. But also, they say, some policies may actually perpetuate the social ills they were meant to remedy. According to this argument, giving poor people aid without requiring anything from them in return destroys the work ethic, and funneling the lion's share of assistance to fatherless families is an incentive for men to abandon their wives and children. A growing sentiment in favor of welfare reform was in the air in 1992.

Urban experts have laid part of the blame for the persistence of urban

The failed promise of urban renewal
Dynamite demolishes a portion of the Pruitt-Igoe public housing complex in St. Louis, Mo., in 1972. High hopes had attended the construction of these and other urban renewal projects in U.S. cities in the 1950's and 1960's, but for the most part, such efforts to improve the lives of the poor were a failure. Housing projects often became high-rise slums.

poverty on the way cities have used the money they receive from the federal government. Urban analysts argue that funds such as Community Development Block Grants, intended to help the poor, have in some cases been diverted to projects that benefited only the middle class.

But federal funding to cities has also been dwindling, causing serious fiscal problems for many municipal governments. For example, federal revenue sharing with the states, a program begun in 1973, was ended in 1986 during the Administration of President Ronald Reagan. Because two-thirds of revenue-sharing money had gone to local governments, U.S. cities lost an important source of financing when the program was terminated. By 1990, the federal contribution to the budgets of the 50 largest U.S. cities had fallen to 6.4 per cent, from 17.7 per cent in 1980.

The money crunch has forced a number of cities to reduce essential services such as police protection and mass transit and to cut back on street repairs and other public works programs. As a result, low-income urban populations have found themselves living in an ever more dismal environment. This often becomes a downward spiral: The more things degrade, the more incentive there is for those middle-class people who still remain to move away. The loss of their property taxes—the main source of revenue for city governments—then makes the financial picture even grimmer, so services and upkeep must be cut back even further.

For many years, most people who abandoned the city for the suburbs at least continued to work in the central cities, commuting back and forth each day by car or train. Despite the loss of many manufacturing businesses, the cities retained a core of major service industries such as banking, real estate, and insurance. The result of this situation is what some urban experts have dubbed the *dual city,* a mismatch between the economic base of a city and the city's labor force. The best jobs available in the dual city require either specialized skills or higher education. The bulk of the positions are thus filled by middle-class workers, and the unskilled

Los Angeles in flames
A section of south-central Los Angeles is turned into a smoking ruin in 1992 as the city is rocked by widespread violence and arson. The upheaval, which began on April 29 and continued for five days, was one of the worst riots in U.S. history. Some urban experts said that such eruptions could be expected in other U.S. cities if the nation does not take action to solve the urban crisis.

city dweller is increasingly unable to find a decent job. Many sociologists blame the dual city for the formation of a seemingly permanent *underclass* in our cities, the 50 to 60 per cent of the urban poor who suffer from severe, long-term poverty.

Stuck in the worst areas of the cities but unable to find well-paying jobs there, some people have turned to the underground economy of drugs, prostitution, and gambling. These activities, and the drug trade in particular, are a root cause of the violence in inner-city neighborhoods. Much of this mayhem is committed by young people, and especially by teen-age gang members. A report released in 1992 by the Federal Bureau of Investigation shows that the arrest rate for juveniles aged 10 to 17 for violent crimes rose from fewer than 150 arrests per 100,000 youths in 1965 to nearly 450 per 100,000 in 1990. The increase occurred among all races and social classes but was especially dramatic among black youths—most of them in the central cities—who in 1990 were arrested for violent crimes at a rate of more than 1,400 per 100,000 black juveniles. A great deal of this crime is committed against other blacks, many of whom are themselves juveniles or young adults. Murder has become the leading cause of death among black males aged 18 to 24.

New prescriptions for renewal

So what is to be done about all these problems? Are America's big cities doomed, or could the right government policies revitalize the cities and elevate the urban poor into the mainstream?

Most social theorists think there is still hope for the cities, but they say the solutions will require new ways of thinking. They point out that the poor are more in touch with their own needs than are the government policymakers in Washington, D.C., so aid programs should be geared to individuals rather than groups. A recent idea that has gained support is "empowerment" of the poor, or enabling people to exert greater control over their own lives. One empowerment proposal is to let people in inner cities take over housing projects and other government-owned properties and run them as they see fit. Other suggestions include offering the poor federally financed educational and housing vouchers. The vouchers—coupons worth a set amount of money from the government—would help people send their children to good schools and buy homes in more desirable areas, perhaps in the suburbs.

Another proposal, widely touted in 1992 as a way to get inner cities back on their feet, is the creation of "enterprise zones" in run-down areas of cities. Enterprise zones are urban sectors in which businesses would be offered tax breaks and other incentives to set up operations.

Opinions vary on what chance any of these programs has of working. Critics of enterprise zones say the idea has been tried by some states without much success. With regard to empowerment proposals, some urban experts argue that unless the poor take increased responsibility for their own lives, little progress is likely. The inner cities, these observers say, are marked by widespread family breakdown and a severely eroded work ethic. They maintain that intact families and a commitment to hard work will be the key ingredients enabling the urban poor to take advantage of whatever opportunities are offered them. This viewpoint seemed to be growing more prevalent in 1992, though some national figures, such as civil rights leader Jesse L. Jackson, continued to blame inner-city poverty almost entirely on social and economic injustice.

As for the cities themselves, they will be hard-pressed to pull themselves out of the mire until they can improve their financial situation. The U.S. Conference of Mayors has been urging the federal government to come to their aid by adopting policies that would force a redistribution of wealth from the suburbs to the central cities.

A changing public attitude: Signal for hope?

So far, any urban policy that might take something away from the middle class has been a tough idea to sell. The American majority has for a long time showed little interest in riding to the rescue of the cities. But a poll conducted in July 1992 by *Newsweek* magazine and ABC News in the wake of the Los Angeles riots showed that the public's attitude toward what is unmistakably a growing crisis may be changing. Seventy-nine per cent of the respondents said that saving the cities should become a major priority of the federal government.

America's older cities will probably never again be the dominant manufacturing centers that they were at the beginning of the 1900's. But they remain home to millions of people, and they will most likely continue to fill a vital, though somewhat narrowed, role on the national stage as centers of many service industries and of culture and the arts. They will, that is, unless they are allowed to deteriorate to the point of no return. Even if a majority of people do now agree that restoring our cities to health and bringing their inner-city populations into the social mainstream is a worthwhile goal, it is still unclear how many Americans will be willing to help pay the bill.

Civil rights. Riots erupted in Los Angeles, several surrounding communities, and other United States cities on April 29, 1992, after an almost all-white jury acquitted four white Los Angeles Police Department (LAPD) officers of all charges but one in the beating of a black motorist in March 1991. A videotape of the beating of Rodney G. King, made by a bystander and widely televised, had aroused outrage throughout the United States. The videotape showed King lying on the ground being kicked and hit repeatedly by police wielding batons. The incident embodied for many blacks and other minorities the belief that the police routinely abuse minorities' civil rights, and the jury's decision fanned the flames of racial tension.

Because of widespread publicity about the case, the trial was moved from Los Angeles to Simi Valley, a predominantly white community in Ventura County. The state court jury decided that LAPD Sergeant Stacey C. Koon, Officers Laurence M. Powell and Theodore J. Briseno, and former Officer Timothy E. Wind had not used excessive force against King. The jury did not reach a verdict on one charge of assault levied against Powell.

In their defense, the police officers argued that the force used against King had been justified because King had aggressively resisted arrest after leading them on a high-speed automobile chase. They also testified that they feared King was under the influence of the hallucinogenic drug PCP. The acquittals, which were met with astonishment and outrage, triggered another round of debate about fairness and racism in the U.S. criminal justice system.

Effects of the riots. Within hours, the verdicts had also triggered widespread violence. Rioters—white, black, and Hispanic—burned and looted stores and attacked motorists who unwittingly drove into the hardest-hit areas. The drama and intensity of the anger were captured in the beating of white truck-driver Reginald O. Denny, who was dragged from his vehicle and clubbed on the street as a television crew in a helicopter filmed the incident. Four black men were charged in the attack, which left Denny with serious head injuries.

Police arrested 12,545 people in Los Angeles and Los Angeles County in connection with the rioting, which took at least 50 lives and caused an estimated $1 billion in damages. Anger at the verdicts in the King case also was blamed for looting that broke out in other cities, including San Francisco; Atlanta, Ga.; and Las Vegas, Nev.

In addition to highlighting the distrust between minorities and law enforcement officials, the riots increased the existing hostility between blacks and Korean-Americans in Los Angeles. The two groups had long been at odds, in part because some blacks resented the influx of Korean-American merchants into their neighborhoods.

The U.S. Department of Justice on Aug. 5, 1992, charged the four LAPD officers with federal civil rights violations. Some people accused federal officials of pursuing the case in response to the riots. A trial on the federal charges was expected in 1993. The remaining assault charge against Powell was also scheduled for retrial in 1993.

Civil rights complaints. The Justice Department received 9,835 civil rights complaints in 1991. The department investigated 3,583 cases and prosecuted 134 people, including 64 law officers. The cases resulted in 109 convictions, 50 of them against police.

Sexual discrimination. Students who have been the victims of sexual harassment or other forms of sexual discrimination at schools and colleges that receive federal funds may collect monetary awards from those institutions, according to a unanimous ruling by the Supreme Court of the United States on Feb. 26, 1992. The court based its ruling on a 1972 federal law that outlaws sex discrimination at schools. The ruling arose from a case involving a woman from Gwinnett County, Georgia, who alleged that her high school teacher forced her into sex and that school officials ignored her complaints about the teacher.

Jurors and race. On June 18, 1992, the Supreme Court said that the 14th Amendment to the Constitution, which guarantees all citizens equal protection under the law, prohibits criminal defendants from excluding potential jurors based on the jurors' race. The court had ruled in 1991 that prosecutors and litigants in civil trials may not discriminate against prospective jurors on the basis of race.

Haitian policy. President George Bush on May 24, 1992, ordered the U.S. Coast Guard to forcibly return to Haiti any Haitians found at sea attempting to enter the United States. The order meant that the refugees could no longer have a hearing by officials of the Immigration and Naturalization Service to determine whether they were entitled to political asylum. Administration officials said that immigration hearings were unnecessary because the refugees were fleeing poverty rather than political persecution.

Between 1991, when Haiti's military overthrew an elected government, and 1992, the Coast Guard intercepted more than 37,000 Haitians at sea. Approximately 27,000 of the Haitians were returned to Haiti after temporarily staying at the U.S. naval base at Guantánamo Bay, Cuba. The Supreme Court was expected to decide in 1993 whether the Haitians are entitled to constitutional protections, such as due process of law guaranteed by the 14th Amendment. (See **Immigration.**)

FBI settlements. The Federal Bureau of Investigation (FBI) on April 21, 1992, reached an accord with more than 300 black agents to review or modify procedures for promoting, evaluating, and disciplining agents. The FBI also promised to promote or change the assignments of 48 black agents and to train more blacks for jobs on special teams. In addition, six black agents who had been denied promotions, allegedly on the basis of race, were awarded back pay.

Korean-Americans in Los Angeles demonstrate for peace in May after looters destroyed many Korean-owned businesses during widespread rioting.

Minority preferences. On February 3, the 4th U.S. Circuit Court of Appeals in Richmond, Va., ruled that college scholarship programs reserved for minority students are unconstitutional unless university officials show that past racial discrimination continues to affect minority students. The ruling concerned a scholarship for black students awarded by the University of Maryland in College Park. A Hispanic student challenged the scholarship on the grounds that it violated the 14th Amendment to the Constitution.

The U.S. Department of Education announced on September 28 that the admissions procedure at the law school of the University of California, Berkeley, violated the Civil Rights Act of 1964 because applicants competed for entry only against members of their own racial group and not against the entire pool of applicants. The department contended that this policy amounted to racial quotas. The school denied that the policy violated the Civil Rights Act, which outlaws discrimination on the basis of race or national origin, but agreed to revise its policy.

Judicial confirmation. Edward E. Carnes, an Alabama assistant attorney general, won confirmation to the 11th U.S. Circuit Court of Appeals in the U.S. Senate on Sept. 9, 1992. The battle over Carnes's nomination had split the civil rights community. Some civil rights groups had opposed the nomination because of Carnes's support of the death penalty, which many civil rights groups and legal scholars contend is imposed in a racially biased manner. Civil rights groups considered the appointment to the 11th Circuit Court especially important because of the court's historically prominent role in desegregating the South. Two states in the 11th Circuit—Florida and Georgia—also rank near the top among all states in executions.

Activist dies. Joseph L. Rauh, Jr., a civil rights activist and one of America's foremost civil rights lawyers for almost 50 years, died on September 3. Rauh wrote the minority civil rights plank in the Democratic Party's 1948 platform that served as the foundation of many civil rights laws passed in later years.

International report. Amnesty International, a London-based human rights organization, highlighted rights violations in 142 countries in its 1992 annual report, which covered events in 1991. The report, released on July 9, 1992, indicated that tens of thousands of people were killed, tortured, or held against their will by their governments. Amnesty International singled out Iraq, Burma (officially called Myanmar), and China as major human rights abusers but noted that "gross violations increasingly take place under elected governments with explicit human rights commitments and institutions." The group, which opposes the death penalty under all circumstances, reported that there were more than 2,500 people in 34 states on death row in the United States.

Linda P. Campbell and Geoffrey A. Campbell

See also **Bank.** In ***World Book,*** see **Civil rights.**

Classical music. Worldwide festivities celebrating the 200th anniversary of the death of Austrian composer Wolfgang Amadeus Mozart in 1791 lingered into 1992. The Chicago Symphony Orchestra, for example, brought its Mozart honors to a close in February with cycles of three fully staged Mozart operas: *The Marriage of Figaro, Così Fan Tutte,* and *Don Giovanni*. In August, Lincoln Center for the Performing Arts in New York City completed an 18-month series of Mozart performances by staging, in concert form, nine infrequently heard Mozart operas, including *Mitridate, La Finta Semplice,* and *Lucio Silla*.

Rossini takes center stage. As the Mozart celebrations cooled down, events marking the 200th anniversary of the birth of Italian composer Gioacchino Antonio Rossini warmed up. The annual Rossini Festival in Pesaro, Italy—the composer's birthplace—offered an array of operas. A revival of *William Tell* highlighted a monthlong Rossini festival in San Francisco. During 1992, some Rossini operas received their first professional staging in the United States. They included *Armida* in Tulsa, Okla.; *Ermione* in Omaha, Nebr.; and *La Pietra del Paragone* in Austin, Tex. Lyric Opera of Chicago opened its season with a production of Rossini's *Otello*.

Columbus quincentennial. The 500th anniversary of Christopher Columbus' first voyage to the New World also inspired musical events. Critical reaction to the eagerly and long-awaited premiere of *The Voyage*, composer Philip Glass's opera, was lukewarm. The $2-million production was staged by the Metropolitan Opera in New York City on October 12. *The New York Times* said the opera was a "mixture of comforting cliché and aggressive pretense." *Time* magazine said the opera "takes no stand on whether the dead, white male Columbus was a genocidal maniac or the civilizing harbinger of Christianity; instead it strikes out for the noble horizon of all human striving, daring, and accomplishment. Despite the technological resources at its disposal, it never quite gets there."

The 1992 Universal Exposition world's fair in Seville, Spain, which commemorated Columbus' voyage, boasted such musical attractions as the Metropolitan Opera, the Vienna State Opera, and Milan's La Scala along with orchestras from Philadelphia; Paris; London; Berlin, Germany; and Amsterdam, the Netherlands. An opera by performance artist Laurie Anderson, *Halcyon Days/Stories from the Nerve Bible,* premiered in May in Seville. Also debuting at the fair, in July, was *Prayer for the Age of Aquarius,* a choral-orchestral-dance extravaganza by Russian composer Sofia Gubaidulina.

Alberto Franchetti's opera *Cristoforo Colombo,* which was written for the 400th anniversary of Columbus' voyage in 1892, was revived in February 1992 by the Greater Miami (Fla.) Opera. Darius Milhaud's 1928 opera, *Christophe Colomb*, appeared in New York City in October 1992, then was staged in concert form by the San Francisco Opera.

Chicago's Lyric Opera stages a new production of Giacomo Puccini's *Turandot* with vibrant sets by artist David Hockney, in January.

***McTeague* pleases.** Another much-anticipated opera premiere of 1992 was William Bolcom's *McTeague* at Chicago's Lyric Opera. *McTeague,* which is based on Frank Norris' 1899 novel about a man undone by greed, received more favorable notices than did the Glass opera. A typical reaction came from the *Chicago Tribune*, which said: "The score is a brilliant synthesis of the serious and popular Bolcom, its vocal lines carefully crafted to follow the particular cadence of American speech, yet beautiful in themselves. . . . Ragtime and blues lend flavor, gritty dissonances charge moments of emotional agitation. And yet

Bolcom never abandons the arias, duets, and ensembles that are the stuff of operatic tradition."

Other opera premieres. Another prominent operatic premiere, this one in February 1992, was Wolfgang Rihm's *The Conquest of Mexico* in Hamburg, Germany. The libretto, according to *Opera News*, consisted "of only a few actual sentences," most of which are "sung sounds, such as sighs, screams, hissing or breathing." Also in February, the Finnish National Opera performed the world premiere of Aulis Sallinen's *Kullervo* in Los Angeles. *The New Yorker* judged the new work, whose plot focuses on a Finnish folk hero, as "very well performed" but described the music as "uninspired . . . declamatory, violent, abrupt."

Also premiering on U.S. operatic stages in 1992 were *Desert of Roses*, a Beauty-and-the-Beast opera by Robert Moran (Houston Grand Opera) in February; Alfred Schnittke's *Life with an Idiot* (Netherlands Music Theater) and *The Song of Majnun*, Bright Sheng's treatment of an Islamic legend (Chicago's Lyric Opera) in April; Harry Somers' *Mario and the Magician*, based on a 1930 novella by German writer Thomas Mann (Canadian Opera Company, Toronto) in May; *Tanya*, drawn from the life of heiress Patty Hearst, by Anthony Davis (American Music Theater Festival, Philadelphia) and John Taverner's *Mary of Egypt* (Aldeburgh Festival, England) in June; and Hugo Weisgall's *The Garden of Adonis* (Opera Omaha) in September.

Other important operatic premieres included Chinese composer Jin Xiang's *Savage Land* (Washington

[D.C.] Opera) in January; *The Vanishing Bridegroom* by Scotland's Judith Weir (Opera Theatre of St. Louis) in June; and *The Sorrows of Young Werther,* based on German writer Johann Wolfgang von Goethe's 1774 novel, by Germany's Hans-Jürgen von Bose (Santa Fe [N. Mex.] Opera) in August.

Older works also made their way to the United States. Jean-Baptiste Lully's *Atys* played the Brooklyn Academy of Music in New York City in March and Alessandro Scarlatti's *La Caduta de' Decemviri* appeared at Opera Antica in Palm Beach, Fla. Two significant operatic visitors to the United States from St. Petersburg, Russia, in 1992 were the National Opera in March and the Kirov Opera in July. The Vienna Philharmonic arrived in March to help mark its 150th anniversary.

The New York Philharmonic, which celebrated its 150th birthday in 1992, began a season of special events, including a concert on December 7, the actual date in 1842 when the orchestra gave its initial concert. The anniversary program featured Kurt Masur, the current Philharmonic music director, and two former directors, Zubin Mehta and Pierre Boulez. The program presented Antonín Dvořák's *From the New World*, which the orchestra had introduced in 1893. Among the series of commissioned new works premiered by the orchestra during 1992 was *Éclairs sur l'Au-delà*, the last major work by French composer Olivier Messiaen, who died on April 27.

Grammy Award winners in 1992

Classical Album, Leonard Bernstein, *Candide;* London Symphony Orchestra, Leonard Bernstein, conductor.

Orchestral Performance, John Corigliano, Symphony No. 1; Chicago Symphony Orchestra, Daniel Barenboim, conductor.

Opera Recording, Richard Wagner, *Götterdämmerung;* Metropolitan Opera Orchestra and Chorus, James Levine, conductor.

Choral Performance, Johann Sebastian Bach, *Mass in B minor;* Chicago Symphony Chorus and Orchestra, Margaret Hillis, choral director.

Classical Performance, Instrumental Solo with Orchestra, Samuel Barber, Piano Concerto Opus 38; John Browning, pianist, with St. Louis (Mo.) Symphony Orchestra, Leonard Slatkin, conductor.

Classical Performance, Instrumental Solo Without Orchestra, Enrique Granados, Goyescas, Allegro de Concierto, Danza lenta; Alicia de Larrocha, pianist.

Chamber Music or Other Small Ensemble Performance, Johannes Brahms, Piano Quartets (Opuses 25/26); Isaac Stern and Jaime Laredo, violinists; Yo-Yo Ma, cellist; and Emanuel Ax, pianist.

Classical Vocal Performance, *The Girl with Orange Lips* (De Falla, Ravel, Kim, Stravinsky, Delage), Dawn Upshaw, soprano.

Contemporary Composition, Symphony No. 1, John Corigliano.

Orchestral events. Other important orchestral premieres by U.S. orchestras included Lowell Liebermann's Flute Concerto by the St. Louis Symphony Orchestra in November; Charles Wuorinen's *Genesis* by the Minnesota Orchestra in November; and John Harbison's Oboe Concerto by the San Francisco Symphony in December. In September, the Indianapolis Symphony Orchestra performed Franz Liszt's *Cantata for the Unveiling of the Beethoven Monument in Bonn*, a choral work written for the occasion referred to in the title in 1845 and lost for nearly 100 years.

Fiscal problems sounded the keynote in a report issued in spring 1992 by the American Symphony Orchestra League (ASOL), a service organization for U.S. orchestras. According to the report, deficits for the 19 largest U.S. orchestras averaged nearly $750,000. The ASOL attributed the shortfalls mainly to flat or declining revenues from federal, state, and local sources at a time when the expenses of most orchestras have doubled. In addition, stagnant economic conditions have led many U.S. corporations to reduce their donations to musical institutions.

The report also detailed cutbacks forced on orchestras by budget deficits. The orchestras in Philadelphia, Boston, and New York City faced cancellation of their broadcast series. The Atlanta (Ga.) Symphony Orchestra called off its annual trip to New York City's Carnegie Hall. The Los Angeles Philharmonic was forced to suspend a training program for young musicians. Musicians in the Cincinnati (Ohio) Symphony Orchestra accepted five "layoff" weeks and a delay in benefit improvements to help the orchestra's management reduce its budget deficit.

The ASOL report concluded that "the industry as a whole appears to be in the worst shape it has ever been in" and that "unless changes are made in the way orchestras do business—changes that are substantial and systemic—the future health of the orchestra industry is in serious jeopardy." The report questioned lengths of seasons, numbers of concerts, and size of orchestras and urged that creative initiatives in concert formats be instituted to encourage new support and audiences. (See **Art: Who Should Pay for Art?**)

***Fantasia* suit.** The Philadelphia Orchestra filed a suit demanding a share of profits from videotapes of Walt Disney's 1940 film *Fantasia*, which featured on its soundtrack the orchestra under conductor Leopold Stokowski. The orchestra hoped profits from the videotape would help reduce its budget problems.

Reburial. Before he died in 1941, Polish pianist Jan Paderewski asked to be buried in Arlington National Cemetery in Arlington, Va., because Poland was then occupied by the forces of Nazi Germany. But he also directed that once his homeland was free, his remains were to be buried permanently in Warsaw, the capital of Poland. In July, Paderewski's body was finally returned to Poland. Peter P. Jacobi

In ***World Book,*** see also **Classical music; Opera.**

Clothing. See **Fashion.**

Coal. The United States will increase its reliance on coal in the future, and production levels of more than 1 billion short tons (907 million metric tons) each year could become routine, according to predictions made in June 1992 by the National Coal Association (NCA). The NCA is an industry association based in Washington, D.C. American mines produced 1 billion short tons of coal for the first time in 1990, largely to meet the increasing demand by electric companies. The NCA said electric power plants consumed 8 out of every 10 tons of coal from U.S. mines in 1992, and by July, coal generated 55 per cent of the nation's electricity.

Coal production during the first half of 1992 totaled 492 million short tons (446 million metric tons). This was about a million-ton increase from the same period in 1991, the U.S. Department of Energy (DOE) reported on August 25.

Fraud in air sampling. A government investigation of possible fraud in a federal program intended to control disease-causing coal dust in mines led to guilty pleas from 13 coal mining companies on April 1. The companies admitted engaging in a conspiracy to submit falsified samples of mine air to federal mine safety officials. The samples were required under a 1969 law intended to reduce *black lung disease*, a breathing disorder caused by inhaling coal dust. But more than 500 other mining companies being investigated continued to contest the government's charges.

Mine explosions. A coal mine explosion near Plymouth, Nova Scotia, killed 26 miners on May 9, 1992. Operators of the mine blamed the disaster on highly explosive methane gas. Methane is colorless and odorless and occurs naturally in coal. Mine operators said the gas poured into the mine shafts too fast for detection by electronic monitoring devices. Canadian mine union officials, however, charged there had been repeated safety violations involving high concentrations of methane in the mine.

Another methane explosion, on March 3, killed more than 270 coal miners in the Incirharmani mine in Kozlu, Turkey. On December 7, a methane gas explosion killed 8 miners at a mine in Norton, Va. It was Virginia's worst mine disaster in 32 years.

Pollution control technology. The DOE on April 6 selected three industrial teams to develop a new coal boiler system with advanced air pollution control technology built in as part of the original design. In the past, pollution control devices usually have been add-on equipment, installed after a boiler was built. The new boiler would release two-thirds less sulfur and nitrogen air pollutants than the cleanest existing coal-fired electric power plants. The boiler will be designed by ABB Combustion Engineering of Windsor, Conn.; Babcock & Wilcox of Alliance, Ohio; and Riley Stoker Corporation of Worcester, Mass. The DOE said the project would cost up to $85 million and would be finished by the late 1990's. Michael Woods

See also **Energy supply; Mining.** In ***World Book,*** see **Coal.**

Colombia. On July 22, 1992, Pablo Escobar Gaviria, the billionaire drug kingpin who surrendered to Colombian authorities in 1991, escaped with his brother and eight other inmates from a prison in Envigado, Colombia. During his imprisonment, Escobar continued to head the infamous Medellín drug gang that exported vast amounts of cocaine to the United States and Europe and reportedly has killed hundreds of people. Escobar had surrendered on the conditions that he not be sent to the United States to stand trial for murder and drug charges and that he be allowed to serve in a prison of his own design. Escobar is wanted in the United States for the murder of a Drug Enforcement Administration informant. Colombian authorities said Escobar escaped while police were trying to transfer him to a higher security prison.

The Colombian government claimed that Escobar took two prison officials hostage at gunpoint. When troops stormed the prison to free the hostages, Escobar escaped in the confusion, according to the government. Many Colombians wondered how Escobar obtained the guns.

Escobar's escape touched off a nationwide manhunt. Military aircraft supplied by the United States joined in the search. Three leaders of Escobar's drug cartel, including his own brother, surrendered to authorities on Oct. 7, 1992, under a program that allows for reduced sentences. Authorities placed them and four other escapees who surrendered in October in a high-security prison while the hunt for their leader continued. Meanwhile, the failure to capture Escobar further eroded the popularity of Colombia's president, César Gaviria Trujillo, among Colombians already angry over his administration's actions in rationing electricity and increasing taxes.

Oil discovery. The British Petroleum Company announced in late January that it would spend about $200 million to appraise the reserves of the Cuisiana oil field, located in the remote eastern foothills of the Andes Mountains about 100 miles (160 kilometers) northeast of Bogotá. Oil experts estimate that the new oil field, discovered in July 1991, could hold nearly 3 billion barrels of crude oil. This would make it the biggest oil discovery in the Western Hemisphere since an estimated 10 billion barrels were found in Alaska's Prudhoe Bay in the late 1960's.

New salt cathedral. At the city of Zipaquirá, 35 miles (56 kilometers) north of Bogotá, people marked the 500th anniversary of Christopher Columbus' arrival in the Americas by dedicating a new underground salt cathedral in October 1992. The old cathedral, a major tourist attraction, was badly deteriorated and stood directly over an estimated 150 million short tons (136 million metric tons) of salt, a 300-year supply. Nathan A. Haverstock

See also **Latin America** (Facts in brief table). In ***World Book,*** see **Colombia.**

Colorado. See **State government.**

Common Market. See **Europe.**

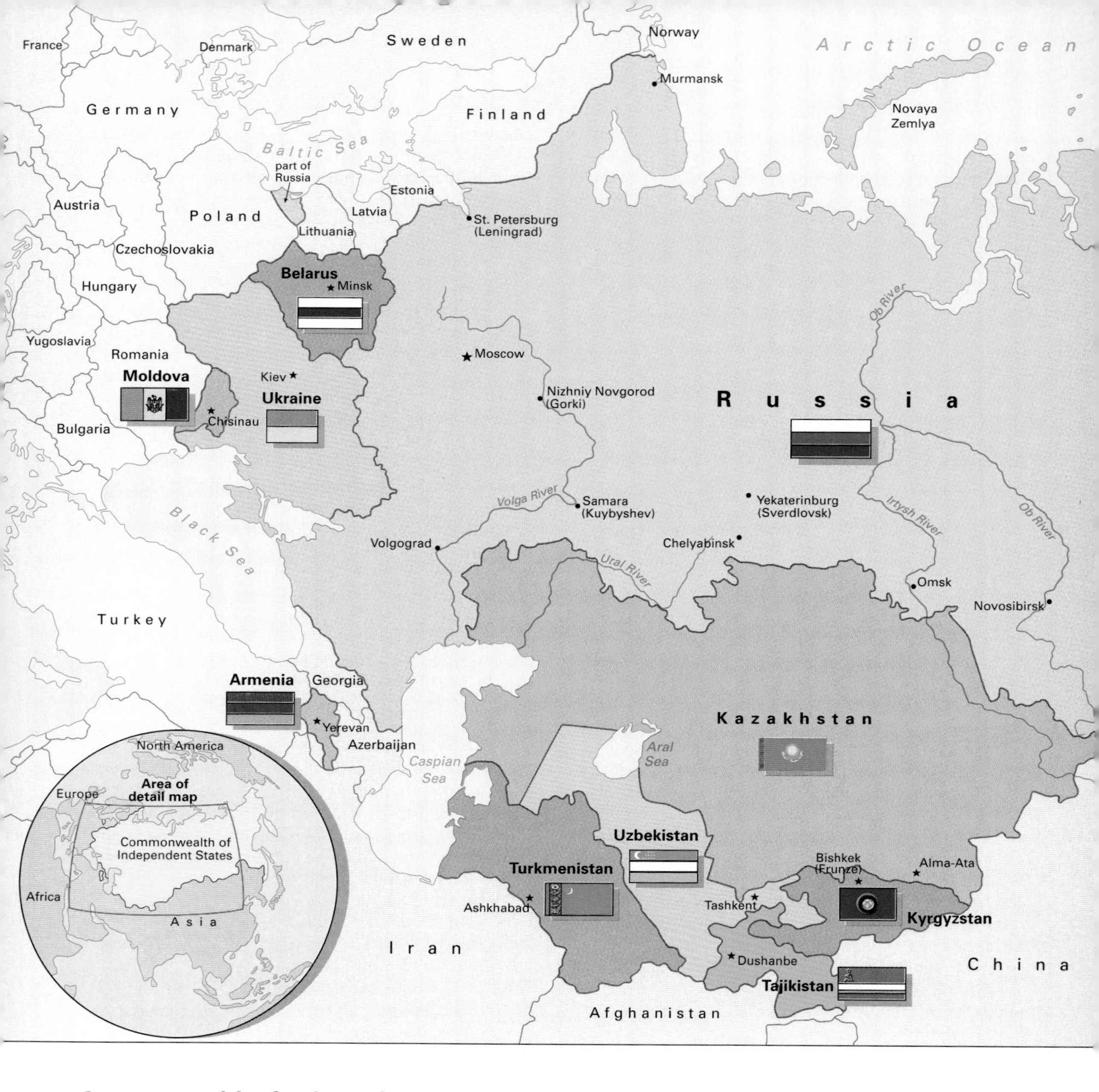

Commonwealth of Independent States (C.I.S.), a loose confederation of former Soviet republics, failed in 1992 to fill the void left when the Soviet Union broke apart in December 1991. Throughout the year, the 11 nations that originally made up the C.I.S. argued over the organization's role. Some of these states, including Russia, wanted the commonwealth to solidify military, political, and economic links among its members. Others, notably Ukraine, viewed the organization as a temporary mechanism to ease their peaceful transition to total independence.

Military role rejected. All the C.I.S. countries agreed that the Soviet nuclear arsenal should be placed under a central command. At first, most of the countries also favored creation of a unified conventional military force. However, C.I.S. members Azerbaijan, Moldova, and Ukraine had said in December 1991 that they wanted to form their own armed forces. The commonwealth failed to resolve the issue in 1992 at summits on February 14 and March 20.

On March 16, Russian President Boris Yeltsin issued a decree creating a Russian defense ministry. Russia's move essentially ended the commonwealth's chances of developing into an effective unifying structure.

The C.I.S. nearly broke apart in April over Ukraine's claims to much of the Black Sea Fleet, a naval force based on Ukrainian territory. Russia said the fleet should be under C.I.S. command. In August, Ukraine and Russia agreed to divide the fleet after controlling it jointly until 1995.

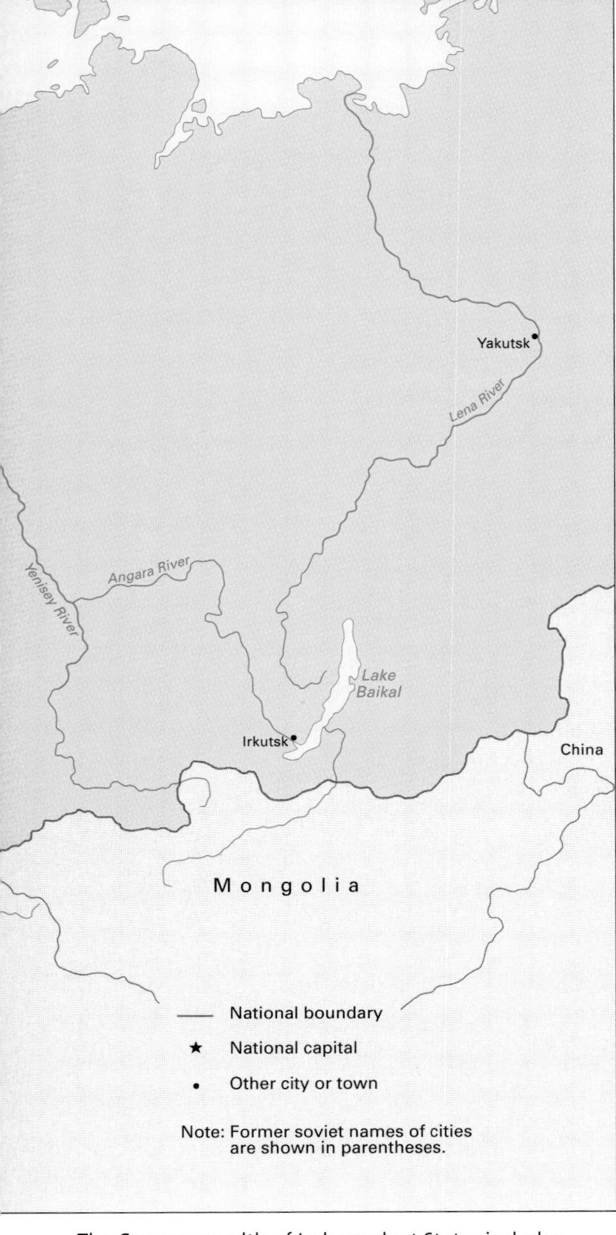

The Commonwealth of Independent States includes 10 former Soviet republics. Another member, Azerbaijan, left the confederation in October.

National conflicts. Perhaps the C.I.S.'s principal failing in 1992 was its inability to halt fighting in several former Soviet republics. These included Armenia, Azerbaijan, Moldova, and Tajikistan.

Armenia and Azerbaijan failed in 1992 to resolve their long-standing dispute over Nagorno-Karabakh, a region in Azerbaijan inhabited mainly by ethnic Armenians. Azerbaijan withdrew from the C.I.S. in October, after its parliament voted not to ratify the treaty that created the C.I.S. in December 1991. (See **Armenia.**)

In March 1992, fighting broke out in the Trans-Dnestr region of Moldova, an area inhabited mainly by ethnic Russians and Ukrainians. Russian and Ukrainian separatists in the region feared Moldova would seek unification with neighboring Romania. Moldova had been part of Romania before it became a Soviet republic in 1940. In May and June 1992, the violence threatened to expand into a war between Russia and Moldova, after witnesses said Russian army troops had aided separatists in clashes with Moldovan forces. Representatives of Moldova, Romania, Russia, and Ukraine signed a cease-fire accord on June 25, and the fighting ended in July.

In Tajikistan, the Communist Party had retained power after the Soviet Union's collapse. On May 6, a coalition of anti-Communists and Islamic fundamentalists seized most of Dushanbe, the Tajik capital, after several weeks of violent clashes. A few days later, the opposition reached a power-sharing agreement with Tajik President Rakhman Nabiyev, a Communist. Nevertheless, the civil war intensified, and on September 7, Nabiyev was forced to resign. Pro-Communist forces staged a brief coup attempt at the end of October. They again retook the capital in early December. However, at year's end the war continued to rage.

Justin Burke

See also **Armenia; Kazakhstan; Russia; Ukraine.** In the World Book Supplement section, see **Commonwealth of Independent States.**

Comoros. See **Africa.**

Computer. Price wars for personal computers heated up in 1992, as the industry leaders—International Business Machines Corporation (IBM), Apple Computer Company, and Compaq Computer—tried to regain ground lost to makers of lower-priced "clones." The three American computer manufacturers set their sights on home users, the weakest market segment.

Compaq had been the first successful producer of low-cost IBM-compatible computers. But Compaq's market share had declined as lower-cost clonemakers undercut even Compaq's prices. So Compaq in June unveiled a new computer line called Prolinea that featured models boasting the latest microprocessors but costing less than $1,000.

In September, Apple introduced a low-cost line of its Macintosh computers. The machines—the Performa 200, 400, and 600—were to sell from about $1,250 to about $2,500. The Performa models were not available through computer dealers. Rather, Apple sold the machines in 11 national retail chains across the United States.

IBM responded fiercely to both sets of moves in October, announcing new low-end models in its PS personal computer line. The PS/ValuePoint computers were to start at a suggested retail price of about $1,300. For the first time, IBM was to sell the computers over the telephone through magazine advertisements, as do Compaq and other IBM clonemakers. The strategic changes were devised by IBM's new semi-independent computer division, the IBM Personal Computer Company, created in September.

Computer virus scare. Computer users around the world were concerned in early 1992 about the threat posed by a new and highly destructive *computer virus.* A computer virus is a program that hides within the memory of computers and secretly spreads by placing copies of itself on media such as floppy disks that are then exchanged among computers.

The computer virus in question—designed by an unknown programmer—was to activate on the anniversary of the birth of Italian artist Michelangelo, March 6, leading people to refer to it as the "Michelangelo virus." When triggered, the Michelangelo virus erased the data stored on a computer's hard disk.

Some experts predicted that 1 million computers would be hit by the virus. But the virus received much publicity prior to March 6. Therefore, many computer users took extra precautions when using borrowed disks, or they purchased software designed to seek out and destroy the virus before it could do any damage. As a result, the damage was far below the virus' worst potential, with computer casualties only in the thousands worldwide.

The 1991 pact between Apple, IBM, and electronics leader Motorola Incorporated bore its first fruit in 1992 with the unveiling in October of a prototype of a next-generation microprocessor. The PowerPC microchip, created by IBM and Motorola, is smaller than existing chips and uses less electricity. The new chip was to appear first in low-end IBM workstations in late 1993, then in Apple Macintoshes in 1994.

Under the 1992 pact, IBM teamed with Motorola to develop new computer chips. At the same time, IBM paired with Apple to create software that can run on both companies' computers, which are not currently compatible.

Microchip alliances. Two international computer alliances were revealed on July 13. First, IBM announced that it was linking with Toshiba of Japan and Siemens of Germany to work on the next generation of dynamic random access memories (D-RAM), the main type of microchip used in existing computers.

Then, the U.S.-based Advanced Micro Devices Incorporated announced a joint venture with Fujitsu Limited of Japan. The two companies will pursue *flash memory*, a new type of chip that retains its random access memory when the computer is turned off.

New chip name. Intel Corporation, the world's largest producer of microprocessors, in October said that it would break with tradition and call its next microchip "Pentium." Intel's previous chips had been called the 286, the 386, and the 486, each number in the series representing an advance over the previous chip. But despite the association in the computer world of the chip names with Intel, a federal judge in 1991 ruled that the "X86" name was a generic numbering scheme and so could not be trademarked. Intel's competitors were thus free to ride on Intel's prestige and use the "X86" name for their clone microchips. So Intel decided that future chips would have protectable trademark names, beginning with Pentium.

Intel in October also said Pentium would feature technology that would send the chip into an energy-conserving "sleep" mode when the computer is on but not in use. Pentium chips were to reach the market in mid-1993.

Memory advance. Engineers at American Telephone and Telegraph (AT&T) in July said they had developed a new computer data-storage technique that could hold almost 100 times more data than a compact disc (CD) and 300 times more data than existing magnetic storage systems, such as floppy disks and hard disks. AT&T's development surpassed other experimental efforts in the United States and abroad.

The researchers achieved the advance by writing data on a storage medium using a laser that sent light beams through a fiber-optic cable. The cable allowed much finer resolution than does the current method of focusing the laser with a lens, so more information could be written in the same area. The researchers said they were able to write information on areas about 1,000 times smaller than the diameter of a human hair. Observers said the work was promising but remained experimental. John C. Burnson

See also **Electronics; Manufacturing.** In ***World Book,*** see **Computer.**

Congress of the United States.

Scandal, reelection jitters, and veto battles with President George Bush marked the 1992 session of the 102nd Congress. As a result, Congress's accomplishments in 1992 were limited.

As legislators neared their October 9 adjournment, the Democratic majority acted on two fronts to make Bush's reelection bid more difficult:

- Congress passed a series of popular bills over the President's opposition. He had to veto them or be accused of flip-flopping on the issues.
- With the President threatening to veto 7 of 13 appropriations bills for exceeding spending requests, Democrats scaled them back to deprive him of a campaign issue.

Bush and the Congress agreed on a number of other important items. The President in July signed a $100-billion five-year extension of higher education loans and grants. It was intended to make it easier for millions of students to pay for college. Another measure passed just before adjournment and signed by the President was aimed at reducing dependence on foreign oil.

Also signed into law were bills giving jobless Americans 26 extra weeks of unemployment compensation and making *carjacking* (the armed theft of an occupied automobile) a federal crime.

Several other notable actions by Congress received Bush's approval. Those included a $10-billion loan

Reprinted with special permission of King Features Syndicate.

guarantee for Israel, economic aid for the former Soviet Union, a $12-billion line of credit for the International Monetary Fund (IMF)—an agency of the United Nations—and ratification of strategic arms control and conventional forces treaties with the republics of the former Soviet Union.

Failed measures. Several major proposals fell victim to partisan bickering and election-year politics:

▪A Bush request for a constitutional amendment to require a balanced budget at the end of five years was defeated on June 11. The House of Representatives vote was 280 to 153 in favor—9 votes shy of the two-thirds majority needed for an amendment.

▪An effort by conservative Republicans to give the President line-item veto authority, enabling him to delete specific federal projects he opposed, was rejected by the Senate 54 to 44 on February 27.

▪Anticrime legislation, including a one-week waiting period to buy a handgun, was killed on October 2. The bill was blocked in the Senate by a Republican filibuster. The Republicans argued that it was not tough enough on criminals.

▪An $822-million education bill met its end on October 2. Stripped of key features sought by Bush, it died when Senate Democrats failed by one vote to cut off a Republican filibuster.

▪An Administration bill to discourage frivolous product liability suits and reduce damage awards to injured consumers was buried on September 10 when the Senate fell two votes short of cutting off a filibuster that blocked the legislation.

▪A Republican effort to restrain future spending on entitlement programs such as Medicare, Medicaid, and veterans benefits was defeated in the Senate on April 10 by a vote of 66 to 28. With entitlements making up more than half the federal budget, some members of Congress regarded restrictions on entitlement programs as essential to any serious effort to reduce huge budget deficits.

▪A Bush request for $17 billion to continue cleaning up the savings and loan mess was rejected on April 1 by a bipartisan House majority wary of voter anger at the mounting costs. The vote was 298 to 125.

High-technology projects survive. Efforts to kill or seriously crimp two massive projects on the leading edge of technology were defeated during the year. A third survived with cuts.

Congress approved funds for the continued development of a space station, expected to cost $30 billion to $40 billion to construct and another $100 billion to operate over a 30-year period. It also voted to continue funding for a proposed $8.2-billion subatomic particle accelerator called the Superconducting Super Collider (SSC) that physicists hope to build in Texas. In addition, Congress appropriated $3.8 billion for research on the Strategic Defense Initiative ballistic missile defense system, also known as "Star Wars." This was $1.6 billion less than Bush had sought.

Members of the United States Senate

The Senate of the first session of the 103rd Congress consisted of 57 Democrats and 43 Republicans when it convened on Jan. 5, 1993. Senators shown starting their term in 1993 were elected for the first time in the Nov. 3, 1992, elections. Kent Conrad of North Dakota, who was elected in a special election on December 4 to fill the seat left vacant by the death of Senator Quentin N. Burdick, first took office in the Senate in 1987. Tennessee Governor Ned Ray McWherter appointed Harlan Mathews on December 28 to fill the Senate seat left vacant when Albert A. Gore, Jr., was elected Vice President. The second date in each listing shows when the senator's term expires.

State	Term
Alabama	
Howell T. Heflin, D.	1979-1997
Richard C. Shelby, D.	1987-1999
Alaska	
Theodore F. Stevens, R.	1968-1997
Frank H. Murkowski, R.	1981-1999
Arizona	
Dennis DeConcini, D.	1977-1995
John McCain III, R.	1987-1999
Arkansas	
Dale Bumpers, D.	1975-1999
David H. Pryor, D.	1979-1997
California	
Barbara Boxer, D.	1993-1999
Dianne Feinstein, D.	1993-1995
Colorado	
Hank Brown, R.	1991-1997
Ben N. Campbell, D.	1993-1999
Connecticut	
Christopher J. Dodd, D.	1981-1999
Joseph I. Lieberman, D.	1989-1995
Delaware	
William V. Roth, Jr., R.	1971-1995
Joseph R. Biden, Jr., D.	1973-1997
Florida	
Bob Graham, D.	1987-1999
Connie Mack III, R.	1989-1995
Georgia	
Sam Nunn, D.	1972-1997
Paul Coverdell, R.	1993-1999
Hawaii	
Daniel K. Inouye, D.	1963-1999
Daniel K. Akaka, D.	1990-1995
Idaho	
Larry E. Craig, R.	1991-1997
Dirk Kempthorne, R.	1993-1999
Illinois	
Paul Simon, D.	1985-1997
Carol M. Braun, D.	1993-1999
Indiana	
Richard G. Lugar, R.	1977-1995
Dan R. Coats, R.	1989-1999
Iowa	
Charles E. Grassley, R.	1981-1999
Tom Harkin, D.	1985-1997
Kansas	
Robert J. Dole, R.	1969-1999
Nancy Landon Kassebaum, R.	1979-1997
Kentucky	
Wendell H. Ford, D.	1974-1999
Mitch McConnell, R.	1985-1997
Louisiana	
J. Bennett Johnston, Jr., D.	1972-1997
John B. Breaux, D.	1987-1999
Maine	
William S. Cohen, R.	1979-1997
George J. Mitchell, D.	1980-1995
Maryland	
Paul S. Sarbanes, D.	1977-1995
Barbara A. Mikulski, D.	1987-1999
Massachusetts	
Edward M. Kennedy, D.	1962-1995
John F. Kerry, D.	1985-1997
Michigan	
Donald W. Riegle, Jr., D.	1976-1995
Carl Levin, D.	1979-1997
Minnesota	
David F. Durenberger, R.	1978-1995
Paul D. Wellstone, D.	1991-1997
Mississippi	
Thad Cochran, R.	1978-1997
Trent Lott, R.	1989-1995
Missouri	
John C. Danforth, R.	1976-1995
Christopher S. (Kit) Bond, R.	1987-1999
Montana	
Max Baucus, D.	1978-1997
Conrad Burns, R.	1989-1995
Nebraska	
J. James Exon, D.	1979-1997
Robert Kerrey, D.	1989-1995
Nevada	
Harry M. Reid, D.	1987-1999
Richard H. Bryan, D.	1989-1995
New Hampshire	
Robert C. Smith, R.	1991-1997
Judd Gregg, R.	1993-1999
New Jersey	
Bill Bradley, D.	1979-1997
Frank R. Lautenberg, D.	1982-1995
New Mexico	
Pete V. Domenici, R.	1973-1997
Jeff Bingaman, D.	1983-1995
New York	
Daniel P. Moynihan, D.	1977-1995
Alfonse M. D'Amato, R.	1981-1999
North Carolina	
Jesse A. Helms, R.	1973-1997
Lauch Faircloth, R.	1993-1999
North Dakota	
Kent Conrad, D.	1987-1995
Byron Dorgan, D.	1993-1999
Ohio	
John H. Glenn, Jr., D.	1974-1999
Howard M. Metzenbaum, D.	1976-1995
Oklahoma	
David L. Boren, D.	1979-1997
Don Nickles, R.	1981-1999
Oregon	
Mark O. Hatfield, R.	1967-1997
Bob Packwood, R.	1969-1999
Pennsylvania	
Arlen Specter, R.	1981-1999
Harris L. Wofford, D.	1991-1995
Rhode Island	
Claiborne Pell, D.	1961-1997
John H. Chafee, R.	1976-1995
South Carolina	
Strom Thurmond, R.	1955-1997
Ernest F. Hollings, D.	1967-1999
South Dakota	
Larry Pressler, R.	1979-1997
Thomas A. Daschle, D.	1987-1999
Tennessee	
James Sasser, D.	1977-1995
Harlan Mathews, D.	1993-1995
Texas	
Lloyd M. Bentsen, Jr., D.	1971-1995
Phil Gramm, R.	1985-1997
Utah	
Orrin G. Hatch, R.	1977-1995
Robert F. Bennett, R.	1993-1999
Vermont	
Patrick J. Leahy, D.	1975-1999
James M. Jeffords, R.	1989-1995
Virginia	
John W. Warner, R.	1979-1997
Charles S. Robb, D.	1989-1995
Washington	
Slade Gorton, R.	1989-1995
Patty Murray, D.	1993-1999
West Virginia	
Robert C. Byrd, D.	1959-1995
John D. Rockefeller IV, D.	1985-1997
Wisconsin	
Herbert Kohl, D.	1989-1995
Russell D. Feingold, D.	1993-1999
Wyoming	
Malcolm Wallop, R.	1977-1995
Alan K. Simpson, R.	1979-1997

Cable TV bill. With cable television rates increasing at about three times the rate of inflation, proposals to curb rate hikes by cable operators had become politically popular in 1992. Taking note, the House on September 17 passed a bill, 280 to 128, that would require the Federal Communications Commission to set "reasonable rates" for cable TV service. The bill was also designed to promote increased competition in the industry. The Senate adopted the measure five days later, 74 to 25.

Bush vetoed the legislation on October 3, saying it represented excessive federal regulation. He also echoed the cable industry's claim that the bill would raise, not lower, cable rates.

Congress took up the veto on October 5. The Senate voted 74 to 25 to override the veto. Twenty-four Republican senators deserted the President on the issue. The House followed suit, 308 to 114. Of the 162 Republicans who voted, 77 opposed the veto. It was considered a major setback for Bush, who lost the first veto fight of his presidency after 35 successes. (See also **Television.**)

Family leave bill vetoed. During the summer, Congress debated legislation that would have required businesses with more than 50 employees to give workers up to 12 weeks of unpaid leave annually to care for a newborn child or adopted infant or to deal with family emergencies. Bush, who sought to make "family values" a major campaign issue during the year, had vetoed a similar bill in 1990.

The Senate passed the 1992 version by voice vote on August 11, and the House took final action, 241 to 161, on September 10. Thirty-four House Republicans voted for the measure.

Saying the bill would raise business costs and force layoffs, the President on September 16 proposed a voluntary program that would have provided tax credits to firms with 500 or fewer employees that granted unpaid leaves to employees. Congress ignored the suggestion, and Bush on September 22 vetoed the measure that had been sent to him.

Thirteen Senate Republicans joined Democrats in voting 68 to 31 two days later to override the veto. But the measure died on September 30 when the House upheld the veto, 258 to 169—27 votes shy of a needed two-thirds majority.

Abortion-related measures. On September 14, the Senate passed a House-approved bill to allow federally funded family planning clinics to refer women to abortion clinics. A 1988 presidential directive had barred such referrals. On October 2, the veto was overridden by the Senate, 73 to 28, but upheld in the House. On June 23, Bush successfully vetoed another abortion-related measure, to lift a 1988 ban on federally financed medical research using tissue from aborted fetuses. An attempt in the House the next day to override the veto failed.

Election reform vetoes. Two other successful vetoes dealt with voter registration and campaign financing. On April 30, the Senate, by a vote of 58 to 42, passed a bill to overhaul lax campaign finance laws affecting elections to the House and Senate. The measure, approved earlier by the House, 259 to 165, would have used public subsidies and other incentives to encourage candidates to observe voluntary campaign spending limits. Claiming the measure would give an unfair advantage to incumbents and "special interests," Bush vetoed it on May 9. The veto was upheld in the Senate on May 13.

The second veto scrapped legislation to allow people to register to vote when applying for driver's licenses, or for unemployment, welfare, or other benefits. The bill received Senate approval on May 20 and was passed by the House on June 16. Bush rejected the bill on July 2, saying it would promote fraud. The veto held again.

House bank scandal. The abuse of check-cashing privileges at the House of Representatives bank, which was shut down in late 1991, emerged as a major scandal in 1992. Although no government money was involved, the public was outraged by reports that hundreds of representatives had routinely overdrawn their accounts.

On March 5, the House Ethics Committee voted to recommend releasing the names of 19 current and 5 former representatives who had overdrawn their accounts by more than a month's salary. These were the most serious abusers among 355 current and former members who had written bad checks.The scandal's first victim was Jack Russ, the House sergeant at arms and manager of the bank, who resigned on March 12. Hoping to quiet the hubbub, the House voted 426 to 0 on March 13 for "full disclosure" of all overdrafts.

Four members of Bush's Cabinet disclosed that, while serving as representatives, they had written overdrafts. They were Secretary of Defense Richard B. Cheney, Secretary of Housing and Urban Development Jack F. Kemp, Secretary of Agriculture Edward R. Madigan, and Secretary of Labor Lynn M. Martin.

By April 16, the ethics committee had named 22 "abusers," some with more than 900 overdrafts, and 303 other representatives who had written relatively small numbers of bad checks. The list included 205 Democrats, 119 Republicans, and 1 independent.

House and Senate leaders agreed on April 3 to restrict the privileges of members of Congress. Annual dues for use of the House and Senate gyms were increased, and members were informed that they would no longer be offered free medical care and medicines from Navy facilities at the Capitol.

House post office. The House's image problems were further magnified by allegations of irregularities at the House post office. On March 19, Robert V. Rota resigned after 20 years as House postmaster. This followed guilty pleas by three employees to charges of stealing more than $35,000 in cash and stamps.

A federal grand jury investigating the House post office subpoenaed three Democratic representatives

Members of the United States House of Representatives

The House of Representatives of the first session of the 103rd Congress consisted of 258 Democrats, 176 Republicans, and 1 independent (not including representatives from American Samoa, the District of Columbia, Guam, Puerto Rico, and the Virgin Islands), when it convened on Jan. 5, 1993, compared with 268 Democrats, 166 Republicans, and 1 independent when the second session of the 102nd Congress convened. This table shows congressional district, legislator, and party affiliation. Asterisk (*) denotes those who served in the 102nd Congress; dagger (†) denotes "at large."

Alabama
1. Sonny Callahan, R.*
2. Terry Everett, R.
3. Glen Browder, D.*
4. Tom Bevill, D.*
5. Bud Cramer, D.*
6. Spencer Bachus, R.
7. Earl Hilliard, D.

Alaska
† Donald E. Young, R.*

Arizona
1. Sam Coppersmith, D.
2. Ed Pastor, D.*
3. Bob Stump, R.*
4. Jon L. Kyl, R.*
5. Jim Kolbe, R.*
6. Karan English, D.

Arkansas
1. Blanche Lambert, D.
2. Ray Thornton, D.*
3. Tim Hutchinson, R.
4. Jay Dickey, R.

California
1. Dan Hamburg, D.
2. Wally Herger, R.*
3. Vic Fazio, D.*
4. John Doolittle, R.*
5. Robert T. Matsui, D.*
6. Lynn Woolsey, D.
7. George E. Miller, D.*
8. Nancy Pelosi, D.*
9. Ronald V. Dellums, D.*
10. Bill Baker, R.
11. Richard Pombo, R.
12. Tom Lantos, D.*
13. Fortney H. (Peter) Stark, D.*
14. Anna Eshoo, D.
15. Norman Mineta, D.*
16. Don Edwards, D.*
17. Leon Panetta, D.*
18. Gary Condit, D.*
19. Richard H. Lehman, D.*
20. Calvin Dooley, D.*
21. William M. Thomas, R.*
22. Michael Huffington, R.
23. Elton Gallegly, R.*
24. Anthony Beilenson, D.*
25. Howard McKeon, R.
26. Howard L. Berman, D.*
27. Carlos J. Moorhead, R.*
28. David Dreier, R.*
29. Henry A. Waxman, D.*
30. Xavier Becerra, D.
31. Matthew Martinez, D.*
32. Julian C. Dixon, D.*
33. Lucille Roybal-Allard, D.
34. Esteban E. Torres, D.*
35. Maxine Waters, D.*
36. Jane Harman, D.
37. Walter Tucker, D.
38. Steve Horn, R.
39. Edward Royce, R.
40. Jerry Lewis, R.*
41. Jay Kim, R.
42. George E. Brown, Jr., D.*
43. Kenneth Calvert, R.
44. Al McCandless, R.*
45. Dana Rohrabacher, R.*
46. Robert K. Dornan, R.*
47. C. Christopher Cox, R.*
48. Ronald C. Packard, R.*
49. Lynn Schenk, D.
50. Bob Filner, D.
51. Randy (Duke) Cunningham, R.*
52. Duncan L. Hunter, R.*

Colorado
1. Patricia Schroeder, D.*
2. David E. Skaggs, D.*
3. Scott McInnis, R.
4. Wayne Allard, R.*
5. Joel Hefley, R.*
6. Daniel Schaefer, R.*

Connecticut
1. Barbara B. Kennelly, D.*
2. Sam Gejdenson, D.*
3. Rosa DeLauro, D.*
4. Christopher Shays, R.*
5. Gary Franks, R.*
6. Nancy L. Johnson, R.*

Delaware
†Michael Castle, R.

Florida
1. Earl Hutto, D.*
2. Pete Peterson, D.*
3. Corrine Brown, D.
4. Tillie Fowler, R.
5. Karen Thurman, D.
6. Clifford B. Stearns, R.*
7. John Mica, R.
8. Bill McCollum, R.*
9. Michael Bilirakis, R.*
10. C. W. Bill Young, R.*
11. Sam M. Gibbons, D.*
12. Charles Canady, R.
13. Dan Miller, R.
14. Porter J. Goss, R.*
15. Jim Bacchus, D.*
16. Tom Lewis, R.*
17. Carrie Meek, D.
18. Ileana Ros-Lehtinen, R.*
19. Harry A. Johnston II, D.*
20. Peter Deutsch, D.
21. Lincoln Diaz-Balart, R.
22. E. Clay Shaw, Jr., R.*
23. Alcee Hastings, D.

Georgia
1. Jack Kingston, R.
2. Sanford Bishop, D.
3. Mac Collins, R.
4. John Linder, R.
5. John Lewis, D.*
6. Newt Gingrich, R.*
7. George Darden, D.*
8. J. Roy Rowland, D.*
9. Nathan Deal, D.
10. Don Johnson, D.
11. Cynthia McKinney, D.

Hawaii
1. Neil Abercrombie, D.*
2. Patsy T. Mink, D.*

Idaho
1. Larry LaRocco, D.*
2. Michael Crapo, R.

Illinois
1. Bobby Rush, D.
2. Mel Reynolds, D.
3. William O. Lipinski, D.*
4. Luis Gutierrez, D.
5. Dan Rostenkowski, D.*
6. Henry J. Hyde, R.*
7. Cardiss Collins, D.*
8. Philip M. Crane, R.*
9. Sidney R. Yates, D.*
10. John Edward Porter, R.*
11. George Sangmeister, D.*
12. Jerry F. Costello, D.*
13. Harris W. Fawell, R.*
14. J. Dennis Hastert, R.*
15. Thomas W. Ewing, R.*
16. Donald Manzullo, R.
17. Lane A. Evans, D.*
18. Robert H. Michel, R.*
19. Glenn Poshard, D.*
20. Richard J. Durbin, D.*

Indiana
1. Peter J. Visclosky, D.*
2. Philip R. Sharp, D.*
3. Tim Roemer, D.*
4. Jill Long, D.*
5. Steve Buyer, R.
6. Danny L. Burton, R.*
7. John T. Myers, R.*
8. Frank McCloskey, D.*
9. Lee H. Hamilton, D.*
10. Andrew Jacobs, Jr., D.*

Iowa
1. Jim Leach, R.*
2. Jim Nussle, R.*
3. Jim Ross Lightfoot, R.*
4. Neal Smith, D.*
5. Fred Grandy, R.*

Kansas
1. Pat Roberts, R.*
2. James C. Slattery, D.*
3. Jan Meyers, R.*
4. Dan Glickman, D.*

Kentucky
1. Tom Barlow, D.
2. William H. Natcher, D.*
3. Romano L. Mazzoli, D.*
4. Jim Bunning, R.*
5. Harold (Hal) Rogers, R.*
6. Scotty Baesler, D.

Louisiana
1. Robert L. Livingston, Jr., R.*
2. William J. Jefferson, D.*
3. W. J. (Billy) Tauzin, D.*
4. Cleo Fields, D.
5. Jim McCrery, R.*
6. Richard Hugh Baker, R.*
7. James A. (Jimmy) Hayes, D.*

Maine
1. Thomas H. Andrews, D.*
2. Olympia J. Snowe, R.*

Maryland
1. Wayne T. Gilchrest, R.*
2. Helen Delich Bentley, R.*
3. Benjamin L. Cardin, D.*
4. Albert Wynn, D.
5. Steny H. Hoyer, D.*
6. Roscoe Bartlett, R.
7. Kweisi Mfume, D.*
8. Constance A. Morella, R.*

Massachusetts
1. John W. Olver, D.*
2. Richard E. Neal, D.*
3. Peter Blute, R.
4. Barney Frank, D.*
5. Martin Meehan, D.
6. Peter Torkildsen, R.
7. Edward J. Markey, D.*
8. Joseph P. Kennedy II, D.*
9. John Joseph Moakley, D.*
10. Gerry E. Studds, D.*

Michigan
1. Bart Stupak, D.
2. Peter Hoekstra, R.
3. Paul B. Henry, R.*
4. Dave Camp, R.*
5. James Barcia, D.
6. Frederick S. Upton, R.*
7. Nick Smith, R.
8. Bob Carr, D.
9. Dale E. Kildee, D.*
10. David E. Bonior, D.*
11. Joseph Knollenberg, R.
12. Sander M. Levin, D.*
13. William D. Ford, D.*
14. John Conyers, Jr., D.*
15. Barbara-Rose Collins, D.*
16. John D. Dingell, D.*

Minnesota
1. Timothy J. Penny, D.*
2. David Minge, D.
3. Jim Ramstad, R.*
4. Bruce F. Vento, D.*
5. Martin O. Sabo, D.*
6. Rod Grams, R.
7. Collin C. Peterson, D.*
8. James L. Oberstar, D.*

Mississippi
1. Jamie L. Whitten, D.*
2. Mike Espy, D.*
3. G. V. (Sonny) Montgomery, D.*
4. Mike Parker, D.*
5. Gene Taylor, D.*

Missouri
1. William L. (Bill) Clay, D.*
2. James Talent, R.
3. Richard A. Gephardt, D.*
4. Ike Skelton, D.*
5. Alan D. Wheat, D.*
6. Pat Danner, D.
7. Mel Hancock, R.*
8. Bill Emerson, R.*
9. Harold L. Volkmer, D.*

Montana
† Pat Williams, D.*

Nebraska
1. Doug Bereuter, R.*
2. Peter Hoagland, D.*
3. Bill Barrett, R.*

Nevada
1. James H. Bilbray, D.*
2. Barbara F. Vucanovich, R.*

New Hampshire
1. Bill Zeliff, R.*
2. Dick Swett, D.*

New Jersey
1. Robert E. Andrews, D.*
2. William J. Hughes, D.*
3. H. James Saxton, R.*
4. Christopher H. Smith, R.*
5. Marge Roukema, R.*
6. Frank Pallone, Jr., D.*
7. Bob Franks, R.
8. Herbert Klein, D.
9. Robert G. Torricelli, D.*
10. Donald M. Payne, D.*
11. Dean A. Gallo, R.*
12. Richard A. Zimmer, R.*
13. Robert Menendez, D.

New Mexico
1. Steven H. Schiff, R.*
2. Joe Skeen, R.*
3. William B. Richardson, D.*

New York
1. George J. Hochbrueckner, D.*
2. Rick Lazio, R.
3. Peter King, R.
4. David Levy, R.
5. Gary L. Ackerman, D.*
6. Floyd H. Flake, D.*
7. Thomas J. Manton, D.*
8. Jerrold Nadler, D.
9. Charles E. Schumer, D.*
10. Edolphus Towns, D.*
11. Major R. Owens, D.*
12. Nydia Velazquez, D.
13. Susan Molinari, R.*
14. Carolyn Maloney, D.
15. Charles B. Rangel, D.*
16. Jose E. Serrano, D.*
17. Eliot L. Engel, D.*
18. Nita M. Lowey, D.*
19. Hamilton Fish, Jr., R.*
20. Benjamin A. Gilman, R.*
21. Michael R. McNulty, D.*
22. Gerald B. Solomon, R.*
23. Sherwood L. Boehlert, R.*
24. John McHugh, R.
25. James Walsh, R.*
26. Maurice Hinchey, D.
27. William Paxon, R.*
28. Louise M. Slaughter, D.*
29. John J. LaFalce, D.*
30. Jack Quinn, R.
31. Amory Houghton, Jr., R.*

North Carolina
1. Eva Clayton, D.
2. Tim Valentine, D.*
3. H. Martin Lancaster, D.*
4. David E. Price, D.*
5. Stephen L. Neal, D.*
6. Howard Coble, R.*
7. Charles Rose III, D.*
8. W. G. (Bill) Hefner, D.*
9. J. Alex McMillan III, R.*
10. Cass Ballenger, R.*
11. Charles H. Taylor, R.*
12. Melvin Watt, D.

North Dakota
† Earl Pomeroy, D.

Ohio
1. David Mann, D.
2. Willis D. Gradison, Jr., R.*
3. Tony P. Hall, D.*
4. Michael G. Oxley, R.*
5. Paul E. Gillmor, R.*
6. Ted Strickland, D.
7. David L. Hobson, R.*
8. John A. Boehner, R.*
9. Marcy Kaptur, D.*
10. Martin Hoke, R.
11. Louis Stokes, D.*
12. John R. Kasich, R.*
13. Sherrod Brown, D.
14. Thomas C. Sawyer, D.*
15. Deborah Pryce, R.
16. Ralph Regula, R.*
17. James A. Traficant, Jr., D.*
18. Douglas Applegate, D.*
19. Eric Fingerhut, D.

Oklahoma
1. James M. Inhofe, R.*
2. Mike Synar, D.*
3. Bill Brewster, D.*
4. Dave McCurdy, D.*
5. Ernest Jim Istook, R.
6. Glenn English, D.*

Oregon
1. Elizabeth Furse, D.
2. Robert F. Smith, R.*
3. Ron Wyden, D.*
4. Peter A. DeFazio, D.*
5. Mike Kopetski, D.

Pennsylvania
1. Thomas M. Foglietta, D.*
2. Lucien Blackwell, D.*
3. Robert A. Borski, Jr., D.*
4. Ron Klink, D.
5. William F. Clinger, Jr., R.*
6. Tim Holden, D.
7. W. Curtis Weldon, R.*
8. Jim Greenwood, R.
9. E. G. (Bud) Shuster, R.*
10. Joseph M. McDade, R.*
11. Paul E. Kanjorski, D.*
12. John P. Murtha, D.*
13. Marjorie Mezvinsky, D.
14. William J. Coyne, D.*
15. Paul McHale, D.
16. Robert S. Walker, R.*
17. George W. Gekas, R.*
18. Rick Santorum, R.*
19. William F. Goodling, R.*
20. Austin J. Murphy, D.*
21. Thomas J. Ridge, R.*

Rhode Island
1. Ronald K. Machtley, R.*
2. John F. Reed, D.*

South Carolina
1. Arthur Ravenel, Jr., R.*
2. Floyd Spence, R.*
3. Butler Derrick, Jr., D.*
4. Bob Inglis, R.
5. John M. Spratt, Jr., D.*
6. James Clyburn, D.

South Dakota
† Tim Johnson, D.*

Tennessee
1. James H. Quillen, R.*
2. John J. Duncan, Jr., R.*
3. Marilyn Lloyd, D.*
4. James H. Cooper, D.*
5. Bob Clement, D.*
6. Bart Gordon, D.*
7. Donald K. Sundquist, R.*
8. John S. Tanner, D.*
9. Harold E. Ford, D.*

Texas
1. Jim Chapman, D.*
2. Charles Wilson, D.*
3. Sam Johnson, R.*
4. Ralph M. Hall, D.*
5. John W. Bryant, D.*
6. Joe Barton, R.*
7. Bill Archer, R.*
8. Jack Fields, Jr., R.*
9. Jack Brooks, D.*
10. J. J. (Jake) Pickle, D.*
11. Chet Edwards, D.*
12. Preston P. (Pete) Geren, D.*
13. Bill Sarpalius, D.*
14. Greg Laughlin, D.*
15. Eligio (Kika) de la Garza, D.*
16. Ronald D. Coleman, D.*
17. Charles W. Stenholm, D.*
18. Craig A. Washington, D.*
19. Larry Combest, R.*
20. Henry B. Gonzalez, D.*
21. Lamar S. Smith, R.*
22. Tom DeLay, R.*
23. Henry Bonilla, R.
24. Martin Frost, D.*
25. Michael A. Andrews, D.*
26. Richard K. Armey, R.*
27. Solomon P. Ortiz, D.*
28. Frank Tejeda, D.
29. Gene Green, D.
30. Eddie Bernice Johnson, D.

Utah
1. James V. Hansen, R.*
2. Karen Shepherd, D.
3. William Orton, D.*

Vermont
† Bernard Sanders, Ind.

Virginia
1. Herbert H. Bateman, R.*
2. Owen B. Pickett, D.*
3. Robert Scott, D.
4. Norman Sisisky, D.*
5. Lewis F. Payne, Jr., D.*
6. Robert Goodlatte, R.
7. Thomas J. (Tom) Bliley, Jr., R.*
8. James P. Moran, Jr., D.*
9. Frederick C. Boucher, D.*
10. Frank R. Wolf, R.*
11. Leslie Byrne, D.

Washington
1. Maria Cantwell, D.
2. Al Swift, D.*
3. Jolene Unsoeld, D.*
4. Jay Inslee, D.
5. Thomas S. Foley, D.*
6. Norman D. Dicks, D.*
7. Jim McDermott, D.*
8. Jennifer Dunn, R.
9. Mike Kreidler, D.

West Virginia
1. Alan B. Mollohan, D.*
2. Robert E. Wise, Jr., D.*
3. Nick J. Rahall II, D.*

Wisconsin
1. Les Aspin, D.*
2. Scott Klug, R.*
3. Steven Gunderson, R.*
4. Gerald D. Kleczka, D.*
5. Thomas Barrett, D.
6. Thomas E. Petri, R.*
7. David R. Obey, D.*
8. Toby Roth, R.*
9. F. James Sensenbrenner, Jr., R.*

Wyoming
† Craig Thomas, R.*

Nonvoting representatives

American Samoa
Eni F. H. Faleomavaega, D.*

District of Columbia
Eleanor Holmes Norton, D.*

Guam
Robert Underwood, D.

Puerto Rico
Carlos Romero-Barceló, D.

Virgin Islands
Ron de Lugo, D.*

on May 6. They were Representative Dan Rostenkowski of Illinois, chairman of the House Ways and Means Committee, and Representatives Austin J. Murphy and Joseph P. Kolter, both of Pennsylvania.

A post office supervisor reportedly told a federal grand jury, after being granted immunity from prosecution, that he improperly exchanged $18,000 to $20,000 of postage vouchers for cash at Rostenkowski's request. Rostenkowski denied the charge. He and the other subpoenaed House members refused to appear before a grand jury on July 27, asserting their right to avoid self-incrimination.

Membership changes. In the November general election, the Democrats retained control of the Senate, with 57 seats out of 100. In the House, the Republicans gained 10 seats, giving them 176 out of 435. One House member was an independent. (See also **Elections; Democratic Party; Republican Party.**)

Scandal, frustration with legislation gridlock, and redistricting after the 1990 census took the greatest toll on House and Senate memberships even before the November elections. Senator Alan J. Dixon (D., Ill.) and 20 members of the House were defeated in primaries earlier in the year. In addition, more than 50 Senate and House members decided against seeking reelection. They included two Republican luminaries, Senator Warren B. Rudman of New Hampshire and Representative Vin Weber of Minnesota. Senator Brock Adams (D., Wash.) abandoned a reelection effort after being accused of sexual harassment by eight women, charges he denied.

Senator Quentin N. Burdick (D., N. Dak.) died of heart failure on September 8. Burdick, 84, had served in the Senate for 32 years. Senator Kent Conrad (D., N. Dak.), whose own term was due to expire in 1993 and who had announced in April 1992 that he would not seek reelection, was elected on December 4 to the Senate seat vacated by Burdick.

Indictments. Joseph M. McDade (R., Pa.) was accused on May 5, 1992, of taking bribes from defense contractors. Nicholas Mavroules (D., Mass.) was indicted on August 27 on charges of racketeering, bribery, and tax evasion. McDade was reelected in November, but Mavroules was defeated.

Senators feel the heat. On August 12, the Senate Ethics Committee formally rebuked Senator Mark O. Hatfield (R., Ore.) for "improper conduct." Hatfield had failed to report receiving thousands of dollars worth of gifts.

On December 1, the Senate Ethics Committee ordered a preliminary investigation into charges of sexual harassment against Senator Bob Packwood (R., Ore.). Packwood, who won reelection in November, was accused of making unwelcome sexual advances to at least 10 women with whom he had worked.

Frank Cormier and Margot Cormier

See also **United States, Government of the.** In ***World Book,*** see **Congress of the United States.**

Connecticut. See **State Government.**

Conservation. The Endangered Species Act (ESA), scheduled for renewal in 1992, seemed endangered itself. Conservation groups advocated strengthening the act, which was designed to protect plant and animal species threatened with extinction. The Administration of United States President George Bush, however, sought to change the law and make it more favorable to commercial development. Congress deferred action after the ESA became a political issue.

In June, the Supreme Court of the United States upheld an Administration policy allowing U.S. officials to ignore the impact on endangered wildlife of federally funded projects abroad. Of the more than 1,000 animal species listed as *endangered* (close to extinction) or *threatened* (likely to become endangered), 507 live outside the United States. The court ruling, which conservationists viewed as a disaster, was only one of several controversies surrounding the law.

Controversy over the ESA. Aside from the President, Secretary of the Interior Manuel Lujan, Jr., had been the leading critic of the ESA. Lujan sided with real estate developers, farmers, ranchers, mining companies, timber interests, and other groups in protesting that the ESA blocked economic progress. "My job is to protect these species," Lujan said, "but, by the same token, I must make available to the American people these natural resources."

Conservationists disagreed. A study by the World Wide Fund for Nature, an international group based in Switzerland, found that from 1987 through 1991 the Interior Department used the ESA to block or halt only 19 out of 75,000 projects that involved a potential threat to endangered species. Similar research by the National Wildlife Federation showed that the Interior Department forced cancellation of fewer than 1 per cent of projects from 1979 through 1986. A national poll sponsored by two other private conservation groups—the National Audubon Society and the Nature Conservancy—revealed that two-thirds of the voters across the United States favored the law.

Owls and jobs. The most publicized controversy in 1992 over the ESA involved efforts to protect a threatened subspecies, the northern spotted owl, by halting logging in its only habitat, the ancient forests of the Pacific Northwest. Lujan said that enforcing the act would eliminate about 32,000 jobs, a figure that conservationists claimed was grossly exaggerated.

A provision of the ESA allows for the formation of a cabinet-level committee, nicknamed the God Squad, to weigh economic considerations in determining whether efforts should be made to save an endangered species. Lujan convened such a committee in October 1991, requesting a waiver of the ESA to permit logging in the spotted owl's habitat and save jobs. In May 1992, the committee voted 5 to 2 to waive ESA requirements and allow logging on 1,700 acres (690 hectares) of federal land in Oregon. It was only the second time the God Squad had come down against the ESA since the act went into effect in 1973.

Right after the ruling, the Bush Administration announced it would restrict logging on 5.4 million acres (2.2 million hectares) of ancient forest to protect the spotted owl in line with the law's requirements. At the same time, it proposed amending the ESA to open 2 million acres (0.8 million hectares) to logging. Conservationists charged that this loophole would cause the birds to disappear from extensive portions of their habitat, bringing them closer to extinction.

While campaigning for reelection in September, the President announced to cheering loggers in Washington state that he would seek major changes in the ESA to give "greater consideration to jobs, families, and communities," and he vowed to block the law's renewal unless it was so amended. "It's time," Bush said, "to put people ahead of owls."

In a seeming reversal of its position, the Bush Administration in December settled a lawsuit brought by environmental organizations and agreed to accelerate protection of threatened species. As a result, 400 additional plant and animal species were to receive an ESA designation over the next four years, an increase of 53 per cent. Plants accounted for nearly 90 per cent of the additional species to be safeguarded.

Earth Summit. Representatives from 178 nations gathered in Rio de Janeiro, Brazil, in June at the United Nations Conference on Environment and Development, generally referred to as the Earth Summit. During the closing days of the conference, 116 heads of state or of government were present, including President Bush, making it the largest summit ever held.

The Earth Summit enjoyed modest success in its goal of achieving global unity on environmental protection. A key treaty, designed to safeguard Earth's biological diversity by protecting millions of plant and animal species, won the support of almost all the attending nations. But the refusal of the United States to sign it lessened the treaty's effectiveness. The Bush Administration said the agreement would harm the U.S. biotechnology industry by requiring that research, profits, and technology be shared with the countries whose resources were tapped. See **Environmental pollution: Environmental Concern Goes Global.**

African elephant protection. At a March meeting in Kyoto, Japan, 112 signers of the Convention on International Trade in Endangered Species extended a ban on the trade of all African elephant products. Five countries in southern Africa had sought a relaxation of the ban so they could sell elephant meat and hides. The U.S. Fish and Wildlife Service and several conservation groups had initially supported the relaxation, because some of the countries that kill the endangered elephants for their meat also protect large elephant populations. But the ban was extended out of fear that opening trade in meat and hides would lead to poaching for ivory from elephant tusks—the cause of a sharp decline in the number of African elephants.

Whales and dolphins. Despite a six-year-old international moratorium on whaling, Norway in June announced plans to resume whale hunting. The Norwegians planned to catch minkes, the least-hunted whale species. At a meeting in Glasgow, Scotland, the International Whaling Commission in July approved a formula for calculating limits on minke catches but agreed to wait at least a year before allowing the resumption of commercial whaling. Japan said it would wait, but Norwegian officials vowed to move ahead.

The 10-nation Inter-American Tropical Tuna Commission agreed in April on a resolution that should reduce the number of dolphins killed accidentally by tuna fishing fleets. For reasons still unknown, schools of yellowfin tuna congregate under dolphin groups. When tuna nets are drawn in, they can catch and drown dolphins. The new agreement places a quota on allowable dolphin kills. An independent observer on board each tuna boat will keep track of the number of dolphins caught. A boat captain who continues fishing after reaching the quota will be subject to fines and license suspension.

Death of a condor. One of two California condors bred in captivity and released in January was found dead in autumn. An autopsy revealed the presence of antifreeze in the bird's body. Researchers speculated that the deadly antifreeze had come from a nearby recreational lake where the condors had been seen. Antifreeze attracts wildlife because it is sweet and syrupy.

Oil and water. Three years after the *Exxon Valdez* spilled about 11 million gallons (42 million liters) of oil into Alaska's Prince William Sound, a government report found the impact of the disaster to be far greater than originally suspected. The report, which was issued in April, said that damage to animal life has continued despite cleanup efforts.

Of 20,000 sea otters in the Gulf of Alaska, some 3,500 to 5,000 were killed directly by the spill, and another 2,200 have since disappeared. Harbor seal populations have shrunk significantly in areas hit by the oil. Large numbers of killer whales were missing from the social groups usually found in the sound. Moreover, the structure of the whales' society seemed to be breaking down as normally devoted whale mothers abandoned their calves. Birds killed by the spill numbered between 375,000 and 435,000. The spill also had a large negative impact on the migrations and reproductive cycles of birds, fish, mammals, and small sea creatures.

More hopeful was a 1992 study of the Persian Gulf, where 6 million barrels of oil were spilled during the 1991 Persian Gulf War. Along the shore, where the heaviest deposits of oil landed, the scientists found that animal and plant life had been devastated. But in deep water, populations of fish, sea turtles, coral, and other creatures were healthy and breeding normally. The full extent of the oil damage has yet to be evaluated, however. Eugene J. Walter, Jr.

See also **Environmental pollution.** In ***World Book,*** see **Conservation.**

The Fight for America's Public Lands

By Eugene J. Walter, Jr.

America's national forests and other federal public lands have become a bitter battleground on which private industry and conservationists are contending for very different interests.

Picture the possibility of flying in one day across the length and breadth of the United States. You take off before dawn from the coast of Maine and fly southward. With light appearing over the eastern horizon of the Atlantic Ocean, you see waves rolling in to the beach at the Cape Cod National Seashore in Massachusetts. You swoop down for a closer look at the birds scurrying about the beach. Then you head southwest and fly above a tannish ribbon of water flowing between New Jersey and Pennsylvania, the Delaware Water Gap National Recreation Area. Smallmouth bass and shad drift just below the water's surface.

Later, your flight path carries you west to North Dakota, where early morning breezes ruffle vast sweeps of tall big bluestem and other grasses in the Little Missouri National Grassland. Then it's on to Wyoming where, below, you see a mother grizzly bear and her two cubs ambling along a brook in Yellowstone National Park looking for breakfast trout.

Turning southward at midday, you head for Arizona's San Pedro River National Conservation Area, where a narrow river curves under the shade of cottonwoods and oak trees. Flying farther west into truly arid terrain, you cross California's Death Valley National Monument. Finally, you fly northward to the Pacific Northwest, where ancient stands of Douglas fir rise majestically in the Olympic National Forest of Washington State. Fol-

Preceding pages:
A hiker pauses amid a stand of Douglas fir trees in the Mount Hood National Forest in northern Oregon.

lowing the Pacific Ocean coastline, you continue north to Alaska, landing in the Arctic National Wildlife Refuge as the sun is setting.

During your odyssey across the United States, you saw places that differ greatly in their geography and ecology. But they have one important feature in common: All of them, and many other places that you had no time to visit, are part of America's public lands. These are lands owned by the public and administered by agencies of the federal government.

Federal lands comprise about 700 million acres (283 million hectares), an area more than four times the size of Texas. Although public lands are found throughout the United States, most are in 11 Western states and Alaska. The "big four" of public lands, making up 634 million acres (257 million hectares), are the national parks, national forests and grasslands, national wildlife refuges, and the extensive domains of the Bureau of Land Management (BLM), called simply public lands.

Other federal territory includes military bases, Indian reservations, and water project sites administered by the Bureau of Reclamation. In addition, more than 90 million acres (36 million hectares) of virgin forest and other undeveloped land have been set aside in the National Wilderness Preservation System, established in 1964. There are 546 wilderness areas in the system, all of them lying within national parks, forests, and wildlife refuges and BLM lands. The wilderness areas are off-limits to motorized vehicles and any form of construction or commercial activity. Almost half the land in the national parks has been designated wilderness.

Every year, millions of people visit public lands for sightseeing and recreation, and many Americans may think that such activities are the only ones allowed there. But that is not the case. Extensive tracts of public land are also used for commercial purposes. This means, for example, that a forest is preserved not only for the enjoyment of vacationers but also as a source of timber for the logging industry. Business interests contend that commercial use benefits everyone by allowing public lands to be used for activities that contribute to the national economy as well as for recreational purposes. Many conservationists, on the other hand, believe that the federal government has administered many U.S. lands more for the benefit of industry than the public. These critics charge that loggers, miners, ranchers, and other private interests are ruining the environment and making money at the expense of American taxpayers. The dispute between those who desire increased protection for federal lands and those who wish to maintain or extend their right to use them for economic gain promises to be an escalating conflict in the United States in the 1990's.

The author:
Eugene J. Walter, Jr., is a free-lance writer.

Setting aside land for the future

The battle over public lands has its roots in the late 1800's, when conservation-minded Americans sought to protect the nation's huge holdings of undeveloped land, the greatest portion of which lay in the West. In 1872, Congress established the first national park—Yellowstone—and by 1916, the year that the National Park Service was created, there were 16 parks in the system. The park service, a division of the Interior Department, was

What are the federal public lands?

The federal government owns approximately 700 million acres (283 million hectares) of land, most of it in the West. This land is divided among a number of federal agencies.

Federal agency	Type of land	Amount of land
Bureau of Land Management	BLM public lands	272 million acres (110 million hectares)
Forest Service	National forests and grasslands	191 million acres (77 million hectares)
Fish and Wildlife Service	National wildlife refuge system	91 million acres (37 million hectares)
National Park Service	National parks	80 million acres (32 million hectares)
Department of Defense	Military bases and training areas	25 million acres (10 million hectares)
Bureau of Reclamation	Water projects	6 million acres (2.4 million hectares)
Bureau of Indian Affairs	Indian reservations (held in trust)	53 million acres (21.5 million hectares)

Federal lands also include 91 million acres (37 million hectares) of wilderness areas, land that has been declared off-limits for any sort of development. The wilderness areas are included within the lands administered by the Bureau of Land Management, the Forest Service, the National Park Service, and the Fish and Wildlife Service.

A grizzly bear in Alaska heads to the edge of a lake in search of fish. A large portion of America's public lands are located in Alaska.

charged with preserving the scenery and wildlife of the parks "for the enjoyment of future generations." By 1992, the service was in charge of 50 national parks and more than 300 other federal areas, including historic sites, recreation areas, battlefields, memorials, rivers, and seashores.

After starting the national parks system, the government mounted other conservation efforts. The first of these was a measure to safeguard the nation's forests. In 1891, President Benjamin Harrison designated six forest reserves covering 13 million acres (5 million hectares), the nucleus of today's national forests. Jurisdiction over the forests was shifted from the Interior Department to the Department of Agriculture in 1905, when the U.S. Forest Service was established. The Forest Service today administers 156 national forests and 19 grasslands.

President Theodore Roosevelt in the early 1900's presided over the cre-

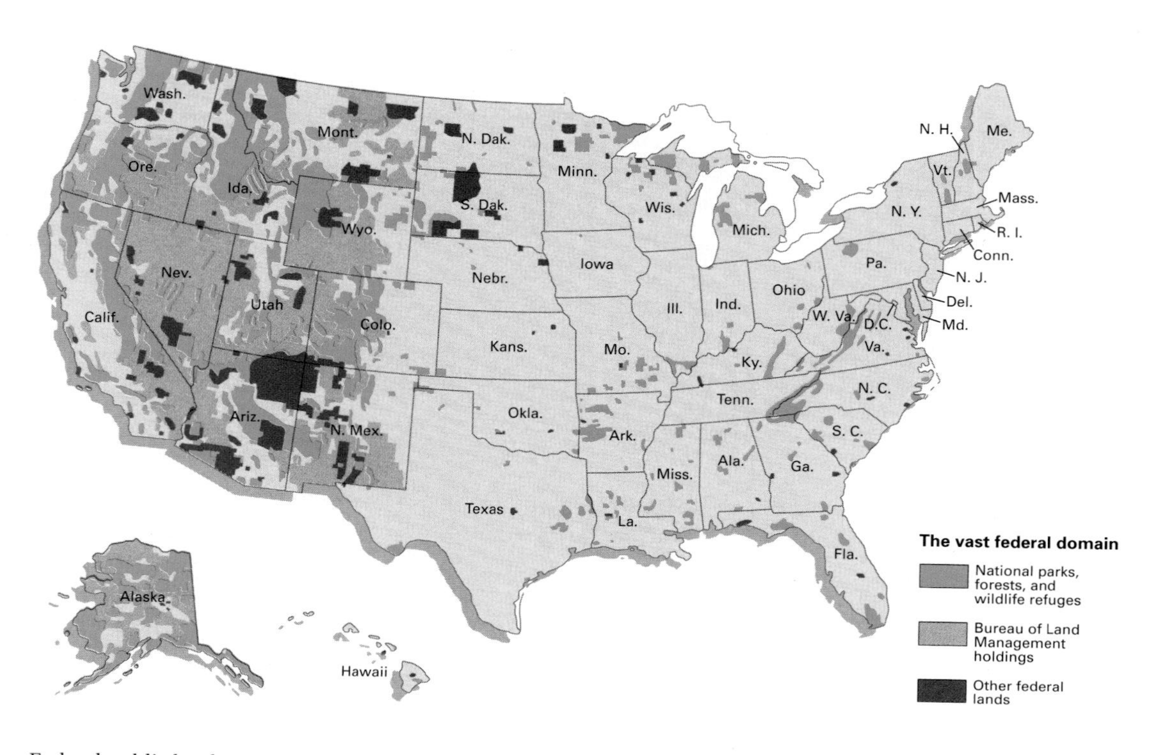

Federal public lands account for about 30 per cent of the U.S. land area. Although public lands are scattered across the entire United States, most of the acreage is in the Western states and Alaska.

ation of the first national wildlife refuges. By the time he left office in 1909, 51 of these protected habitats had been established. In 1992, the U.S. Fish and Wildlife Service (USFWS), a division of the Interior Department, was administering 477 refuges.

Even after the federal government had set aside large tracts of land for national parks, forests, and wildlife refuges, its holdings still included millions of acres of mountains, plains, deserts, and grasslands in the Western states and Alaska. Not until 1946 was the management of this diverse realm pulled together through the creation of the BLM in the Department of the Interior. The BLM is responsible for regulating the private utilization of energy resources (coal, oil, and natural gas) and mineral ores in the areas under its jurisdiction. It also oversees other uses of BLM lands, including grazing on its extensive rangelands.

The private use of federal lands predates the establishment of any of the government agencies created to administer those lands. In fact, it was the alarming rate at which the nation's forests were being cut down by settlers, and later by loggers, that led to the creation of the forest reserves. But even as the government moved to save the remaining publicly owned forests from destruction, it did so with the understanding that the forests could still be a source of timber.

For much of their history, the national forests and BLM lands were governed either by no law at all or by laws that were vague at best. In the 1960's and 1970's, Congress exercised somewhat stronger control over the Forest Service and BLM, requiring them to operate under policies that satisfied two standards. The first of those standards was *multiple use,* a balance between commercial activities, recreation, and environmental protection. The other was *sustained yield,* the idea that renewable resources such as forests or grazing land should be used in such a way that they are never used up or damaged beyond recovery.

With the growth of the environmental movement since the late 1960's, the government has come under increased fire for its management of public lands. The critics say that many agency officials give only lip service to the ideals of balanced multiple use and sustained yield. Such accusations have come not only from conservationists but also from within the government. Within the Forest Service, for example, a growing number of employees have denounced the agency for allegedly putting the long-term survival of the nation's forests in jeopardy. In the late 1980's, a Forest Service employee named Jeff DeBonis founded an organization called the Association of Forest Service Employees for Environmental Ethics (AFSEEE). AFSEEE has about 5,000 members, including 2,000 current and former employees of the Forest Service. The group is working to reform an agency that DeBonis says has "become the captive of a timber industry out of control and bent on short-term, greed-oriented profits."

The top officials of the Forest Service and the BLM deny that they are pursuing policies detrimental to the public interest or the environment. Likewise, private users of the land are outspoken in their own defense. In an effort to protect and extend their access to public lands, some 250 industry groups—loggers, ranchers, miners, real estate developers, oil companies, and others—have formed a coalition called the Wise Use Movement (WUM). WUM and the environmental movement are fierce adversaries. Ron Arnold, a leading spokesman for WUM, says its members believe in preserving the environment but are against just about all federal regulations on the private use of public lands.

On the opposing side, some conservation groups are critical of nearly any commercial endeavor on public lands. Most, however, such as the Wilderness Society in Washington, D.C., object mainly to activities that they see as serious assaults on the environment or on taxpayers' wallets. The Wilderness Society is a frequent critic of BLM and Forest Service management practices. Surveying the BLM's leasing of grazing rights on U.S. rangelands, for instance, the society calculated that the agency's policies would result in a loss to the taxpayers of $68 million in 1992.

Riding the range

In terms of acreage, rangeland is the BLM's biggest responsibility. The agency leases about 165 million acres (67 million hectares) of rangelands to about 20,000 ranchers. According to the U.S. Department of Agriculture, however, ranchers using public land account for less than 2 per cent of U.S. domestic livestock. In 1992, the BLM charged ranchers less than one-fourth as much for grazing rights as they would have had to pay on private land. By Wilderness Society estimates, if ranchers were required to pay the private rate, the U.S. Treasury would have reaped a $62-million surplus for 1992 rather than the expected $68-million loss.

How we use the land

Many public lands are managed under the concept of *multiple use,* meaning that use of the land is to be balanced evenly between commercial and recreational activities and also take into consideration the need to preserve species.

BLM public lands are used extensively for mining and ranching. Earth movers in Alaska, *left,* excavate rocky soil that will be processed to separate out small amounts of gold. On BLM rangelands in Nevada, *above,* a rancher rides herd on his cattle. Conservationists say both mining and ranching have harmed the environment in many areas, but the BLM denies most charges of environmental damage.

Trees are harvested by the lumber industry in the national forests, managed by the U.S. Forest Service. The practice of clearcutting—cutting down every tree in selected parts of forests—has been particularly controversial. A clearcut in the Olympic National Forest, *right,* in the state of Washington resembles a moonscape. But loggers say clearcutting, followed by the planting of tree seedlings, can renew a section of forest that is past its prime.

Hikers cross the Continental Divide in Montana's Glacier National Park. The national parks, mainly used by the public for recreation, are largely free of commercial activity except for private services, such as hotels and equipment rental outlets, provided for vacationers.

Cattle raisers' associations fight fee increases because, they say, low fees enable small ranchers to make a living. In response to the charge that they make a minimal contribution to the nation's beef supply, ranchers say conservationists skew the numbers by including the many dairy cows that are grazed on public land but not shipped to market. By one estimate that subtracts the dairy herds, about 40 per cent of the beef cattle in the United States graze at least part of the time on public rangelands. Cattle raisers also take issue with the conservationist argument that livestock have damaged rangelands through overgrazing. The ranchers say their cattle actually improve the land by fertilizing it with their manure and by feeding on plants that might otherwise grow out of control. But the BLM's *Annual Rangeland Report* for 1991 showed that just one-third of the range under its jurisdiction is in satisfactory condition; two-thirds is degraded.

Mining laws stir controversy

Environmentalists are even more critical of BLM's mining policies. Under an 1872 law, American citizens or corporations can prospect for gold, uranium, and other minerals on most federal lands. If they strike "pay dirt," they can file a claim for a fee of $10. To preserve a claim, they must spend at least $100 a year developing the site. Neither individual miners nor mining concerns have to pay the government any royalties on the ore—ever. Should the claim-holder wish to acquire title to both land and minerals, a deed can be obtained from the government for $2.50 to $5 an acre.

This tiny investment, say conservationists, can yield a huge return. They point to the owners of the Stillwater Mine in Montana, a large lode of platinum and palladium. The owners paid the government $10,000 for claim to the land, and, by their own estimates, the mine will eventually earn a gross profit of $36 billion. That would amount to a return of $3.6-million for each dollar invested in buying the property. The BLM points out, though, that land costs are just a portion of the expense involved in developing a mine. Mining companies must also purchase expensive

Private use of public lands: The arguments on both sides

Conservationist organizations and other citizens' groups think the time has come for the federal government to drastically rein in the use of public lands for private commercial purposes. Although the debate is far-ranging, three major industries—logging, ranching, and mining—are at the center of the controversy. The following are the main arguments for and against each of those commercial activities.

Demonstrators for and against logging in the old-growth forests of the Pacific Northwest rally in Oregon in 1992. Logging in the national forests has become a heated issue.

Logging

What advocates say:

- Maintaining the right of timber companies to log on public lands preserves thousands of much-needed jobs.
- New "low-impact" logging techniques will minimize the clearcutting of forests.
- The nation needs the wood that loggers cut on public lands.

What critics say:

- If logging isn't curtailed on public lands, the United States will lose its last remaining old-growth forests.
- Federal subsidies to logging companies are costing U.S. taxpayers millions of dollars a year.

Ranching

What advocates say:

- Livestock improve the land—their manure fertilizes the soil and their grazing keeps plants from growing out of control.
- Ranchers improve the land by installing fencing, roads, and water systems.
- Ranchers raising cattle on public lands make a valuable contribution to the nation's supply of beef.

What critics say:

- Years of overgrazing on public rangelands have polluted water, eroded soil, and caused a loss of vegetation.
- Only a small proportion of the nation's beef—2 per cent by some estimates—comes from ranching on public lands.

Mining

What advocates say:

- Miners are finding and extracting gold and other minerals that the nation needs.
- Miners are paying a fair share of their earnings in corporate taxes and are also paying to comply with federal air and water quality laws.

What critics say:

- Under the nation's antiquated mining laws, miners are able to buy parcels of public land at minimal cost and are exempted from paying royalties on minerals they extract.
- Miners are ruining the landscape, and are polluting the soil and endangering ground water with cyanide and other hazardous substances.
- Many "miners" resell their land for a large profit or use the sites for purposes having nothing to do with mining.

The threatened residents of the wild

Part of the controversy over the management of public lands centers on safeguarding the habitat of animals whose long-term survival may be in question.

The northern spotted owl, *left,* and the grizzly bear, *above,* have both been declared threatened species by the U.S. Fish and Wildlife Service. Although the grizzly bear has reportedly been making a comeback in Montana, the owl is under siege in its habitat, the forests of the Pacific Northwest. Environmentalists say that continued heavy logging of those forests could drive the bird to extinction. Loggers say that efforts to save the owl could cost them their jobs.

equipment and pay employees. The BLM says that the profit margin on hard-mineral mining is so small that royalties would drive many companies out of business. The agency also argues that it is difficult to monitor the extraction of minerals from ores.

There are other controversies surrounding mining. The GAO has found, for instance, that under the 1872 mining law, many "miners" abuse their claim rights. In a 1989 study, it reported that some people do no work to their claim sites, while others simply bulldoze the sites to make it appear that work is progressing, damaging the environment in the process. Moreover, the GAO found individuals who had obtained title to the land, then sold it for a sizable profit.

The environmental damage caused by mining has also generated criticism from conservationists. Mining not only rips up the land, they say, it also results in twice as much hazardous waste annually in the United States as all other forms of industrial activity combined. A gold-mining process known as heap leaching, for example, uses cyanide to extract gold from piles of ore, and that poisonous chemical often seeps into the ground. Even old, long-abandoned mines can continue to give off a trickle of heavy metals that end up in streams and soil.

The 1872 law does not require mining sites to be restored to their previous state once the ores are played out. Thus, conservationists say, most sites are left as is, with no effort made to clean them up. Fifty-two locations are so polluted that the Environmental Protection Agency (EPA) has designated them Superfund sites—hazardous sites requiring special attention under a Superfund program begun in 1980. The EPA, which is required by law to clean up Superfund sites, has estimated that some sites would cost $1 billion or more to restore, an expense that would be paid by the taxpayers. That still leaves thousands of other sites—many dating from the 1800's—to be reclaimed, which would cost many more billions.

A spokesperson for the BLM, however, says the agency's position is that mine sites are not an environmental problem or a burden to taxpayers. Mining companies, she says, are regulated by several laws, the primary one being the Federal Land Policy and Management Act of 1976, which specifies "no unnecessary or undue degradation of the environment." The mining industry says those laws are adequate and cost them plenty in cleanups. Conservationists, on the other hand, maintain that the nation needs a new mining law with strict requirements for site restoration.

Logging—not a clear-cut issue

Loggers have also gotten a good deal from the government, according to conservation groups. The Forest Service builds roads into national forests for the use of timber companies and allows those companies to buy the trees they fell for a fraction of their value on the open market. In 1992, the national forests contained 365,000 miles (587,000 kilometers) of roads, more than eight times the mileage of the U.S. interstate highway system. And because so many forests are in remote mountainous areas, construction costs have often been staggering.

Critics of the Forest Service contend that the costs incurred by the agency in building and maintaining logging roads are not recouped by the sale of the timber. GAO studies have also concluded that the service operates at a loss. Forest Service officials concede that many timber sales have been money-losers, but they insist that the agency produces a net surplus for the Treasury each year. The service claims that in fiscal 1990, for example, its operations returned $630 million to the Treasury. Critics say these supposed surpluses are achieved through accounting gimmicks, a charge that the Forest Service dismisses as false.

Of all the practices of the Forest Service, none arouses greater passions among environmentalists than its policy of allowing *clearcutting* in national forests. Clearcutting is the felling of every single tree within a large expanse of forest, leaving a landscape dotted with stumps. With no tree cover remaining, conservationists say, erosion and water runoff increase and soil loses its nutrients. Loggers, on the other hand, argue that clearcutting can benefit a forest by giving it a new lease on life. They claim that some kinds of replanted trees, such as the Douglas fir, will grow faster in a clearcut area, where they get plenty of light.

Much of the controversy surrounding clearcutting relates to its effects on wildlife. Biologists say clearcuts have clouded many streams with sediment, harming fish and vegetation, and have shrunk the habitats of the grizzly bear and other animals. One of those animals, which has been pushed into the national limelight, is the northern spotted owl. The owl, designated a threatened subspecies in 1990, lives mainly in areas of old-growth forest in the Pacific Northwest. After 40 years of clearcutting, less than 15 per cent of that original forest remained in 1992.

The spotted owl is protected by the Endangered Species Act of 1973. This law requires the federal government to safeguard the habitat of any animal that is found to be threatened with extinction. Efforts to protect the owl have thrust conservationists into a bitter, head-to-head conflict with timber interests. To save the bird, wildlife experts say, logging in the Pacific Northwest would have to be severely curtailed or stopped.

Loggers in the Northwest, fearing for their livelihood, have fought efforts to reduce logging in the national forests, saying that their traditional way of life is threatened. Conservationists point out that tens of thousands of jobs have already been lost in the timber industry because of dwindling forests, increased automation, and a shift of the industry to Southeastern states. They say that regardless of what laws are enacted, most loggers are sooner or later going to have to find a new line of work.

No shortage of concerns on public lands

The destruction of animal habitats is a problem that extends beyond the national forests. Conservationists contend that wildlife preservation efforts have also been lax at the BLM and that commercial activities in many national wildlife refuges pose a potential threat to animals. A 1988 GAO study of the wildlife refuges found that in more than half of them, commercial activities such as mining and the drilling of natural-gas wells posed a threat to wildlife. The Fish and Wildlife Service did its own study in 1990 and discovered that threats to animals in the refuges were even more serious and widespread than the GAO had reported.

Private enterprise in the national parks has also generated controversy. Although there is no logging or mining in the parks, the National Park Service contracts with hundreds of companies, called concessionaires, that run a wide array of service franchises in the parks, from retail stores to hotels. Conservationists have long complained that the concessionaires have overcommercialized the parks and pay too little in operating fees.

But the biggest threats to the parks often come from activities just outside their borders, including in some adjacent national forests. Clearcuts in Idaho's Targhee National Forest, for example, lie smack up against the western border of Yellowstone National Park. Environmentalists claim that water runoff from the denuded forest areas has carried large amounts of sediment into Yellowstone's streams.

The fate of America's public lands has become a hot political issue. In 1992, Congress was considering several measures relating to public lands, including bills that would raise grazing fees for ranchers, protect remaining old-growth forests, require mining companies to pay royalties and clean up mine sites, and reform concession regulations in the national parks. None of those bills had been approved at year's end. Congress also delayed taking any new action on the Endangered Species Act, which was due for renewal.

How the battle over federal lands will end is far from certain. Those who make their living from public lands will struggle to preserve their right to do so, and many lawmakers are in their corner. These prodevelopment forces charge that conservationists are unalterably negative about the profit motive. The Wilderness Society's T. H. Watkins disagrees. "We are not opposed to development as long as it is done in a manner that is sensitive to the environment," Watkins says. "We want to see federal laws implemented and public lands managed correctly in all respects."

Consumerism. The United States economy continued to linger in the doldrums in 1992. A January report from the U.S. Department of Commerce showed that retail sales in 1991 had not grown by so little since 1962. Sales continued to limp along through the year despite a low inflation rate and low mortgage interest rates. In addition, the Federal Reserve System, the nation's central bank, cut its interest rate to 3 per cent on July 2, the lowest level since 1963.

Inflation in the United States, as measured by the Consumer Price Index (CPI), was lower than it had been in 1991. The CPI was rising at an annual rate of 2.9 per cent as of September 1992, compared with 3.1 per cent in September 1991. The CPI, which is compiled by the U.S. Bureau of Labor Statistics, is the standard measure of the cost of living.

In February 1992, consumer confidence in the economy, as measured by the Consumer Confidence Index, dropped to 47.3, a 17-year low. The index measures consumers' confidence in their financial status for the next six months. An index of 100 represents the level of consumer confidence in 1985, when the U.S. economy experienced moderate growth. Consumer confidence climbed to 71.9 by May, but slid down again. In November, it was 65.5.

Food. The Administration of President George Bush announced on May 26 that most genetically altered food, such as fruits and vegetables, would not have to undergo special safety tests before being sold to the public. Fruits and vegetables can be genetically altered so that they do not spoil readily and so have a longer shelf life. Although many scientists and food technicians said that such food was safe for consumption, consumer advocates and some scientists believed the food should be tested and labeled for consumers.

On April 28, the U.S. Department of Agriculture introduced a Food Guide Pyramid, designed to replace charts depicting the "four basic food groups" as the foundation of good nutrition. The pyramid illustrates five food groups, emphasizing greater consumption of vegetables, fruits, and grains and reduced consumption of meat, dairy products, fats, and oils.

Consumers will have more information on packaged food labels in 1994, due to a December 1992 change in the food labeling law. The rules require labels to provide specific information on fat, cholesterol, sodium, and carbohydrate levels in an easy-to-understand table. Terms such as "light," "low fat," and "high fiber" will be acceptable on labels only if the food meets a strict definition of those terms.

Cable TV reregulated. The U.S. Congress on Oct. 5, 1992, overrode Bush's veto of a bill to reregulate cable television. In 1984, Congress had deregulated cable TV, allowing cable companies to determine on their own how much they would charge customers. According to studies by the General Accounting Office, an independent government agency that advises Congress, cable rates had climbed far faster than inflation had since 1984.

Critics of the new law argued that it would raise cable rates because of its other provisions affecting cable companies. Others argued that cable rates could be kept down by increased competition.

Telecommunications. The U.S. Federal Communications Commission (FCC) approved a series of measures in 1992 designed to foster competition in the telephone industry, such as the establishment of new companies providing local phone service. Consumers currently can receive local service from only one local phone company, though they can choose from several long-distance companies.

Trade. Bush in October 1992 signed the North American Free Trade Agreement, a pact among the United States, Canada, and Mexico. The treaty, according to its supporters, would benefit consumers by lowering tariffs on products imported from Mexico and sold in the United States. Congress was expected to vote on the treaty in 1993.

Energy. In October 1992, Congress passed a sweeping energy bill designed to improve domestic energy supplies and encourage energy efficiency. The bill mandates federal efficiency standards for certain lights, appliances, and electric motors, and promotes the use of cars that run on electricity. On October 24, Bush signed the bill into law. John Merline

See also **Bank; Economics; Food; International trade.** In ***World Book,*** see **Consumerism; Economics.**

Costa Rica. See **Latin America.**

Courier, Jim (1970-), was the top-seeded men's tennis player in the world through much of 1992, the first American male to capture the spot since John McEnroe in 1985. Courier attracted international attention after beating Stefan Edberg to win the Australian Open in January in four sets, 6-3, 3-6, 6-4, 6-2, and Petr Korda to win the French Open in June in three sets, 7-5, 6-2, 6-1. But he was overtaken in the rankings in September.

Courier was born on Aug. 17, 1970, and grew up in Dade City, Fla. Courier was a winning tennis player by age 11. At age 14, he joined Nick Bollettieri's tennis camp in Bradenton, Fla., where he roomed with another men's champion, Andre Agassi. Courier left the camp, however, saying he was not receiving enough personal attention. At age 16, Courier won the Orange Bowl junior tournament, but he did not win a pro-tour event until 1989. In 1991, Courier jumped from 25th to 4th in world rankings after upsetting Agassi to win the French Open. With the help of coach José Higueras, Courier continued to win championships or a spot in tournament finals during 1991.

In 1992, in addition to the French and Australian opens, Courier won the Japan Open and competitions in Hong Kong and Rome. Wearing his trademark baseball cap, Courier also competed at Wimbledon in England and at the Summer Olympics in Barcelona, Spain, but he did not reach the quarterfinals in either event.
Kristine Portnoy Kelley

Courts. In a decision hailed by advocates of children's rights, a judge in Orlando, Fla., ruled on July 9, 1992, that an 11-year-old boy had the right to sue his parents for a "divorce." Circuit Court Judge Thomas S. Kirk said the boy, Gregory Kingsley, was legally entitled under the Florida Constitution to seek to terminate his relationship with his natural parents so he could be adopted by his foster parents.

Gregory testified in court against his mother, Rachel Kingsley, on September 25. He said that during a two-year period when he was in foster care, his mother never called him or wrote to him. Gregory's father, Ralph Kingsley, had signed away his rights to his son in May, but Rachel Kingsley appeared in court in an effort to persuade Judge Kirk not to take the boy away from her. But the judge rebuffed her plea, charging that she had "abandoned and neglected" the boy. He thereby granted Gregory the legal separation he had requested and allowed the foster parents, George H. Russ and Lizabeth Russ of Leesburg, Fla., to adopt him.

This case was believed to be the first of its kind in the United States. Although U.S. courts consider thousands of cases involving abused or neglected children each year, never before had a child in such circumstances been allowed to take independent action to terminate a parental relationship.

Mobster convicted. On April 2, a jury in a federal district court in New York City convicted John Gotti, reputedly the most powerful Mafia leader in the United States, of murder and racketeering. An associate of Gotti's, Frank Locascio, was also convicted. On June 23, both men were sentenced to life in prison with no chance of parole.

Gotti's conviction capped a frustrating six-year effort by federal agents and prosecutors to put the mobster behind bars. Gotti became known as the Teflon Don because three previous prosecutions had ended in not-guilty verdicts.

This time, U.S. prosecutors presented a mountain of evidence against Gotti, including six hours of secretly taped conversations from mob hangouts. The federal case was also strengthened by testimony from a former Gotti lieutenant, Salvatore Gravano. Gravano testified that Gotti had ordered the murder of crime boss Paul Castellano in 1985.

Artistic freedom of expression. A federal judge in Los Angeles declared on June 9, 1992, that a law requiring the National Endowment for the Arts (NEA) to consider "general standards of decency" when making grants to artists was unconstitutional. Ruling in a suit brought by four performance artists who had been denied NEA grants because their work was said to be sexually explicit, Judge A. Wallace Tashima said the so-called decency standard violated the First Amendment of the U.S. Constitution because it was too vague and broadly worded.

The decency standard grew out of a congressional controversy that began in 1989. Some conservative members of Congress were upset about a pair of NEA-supported photographic exhibitions, one of which featured explicit homosexual images while the other included a photograph of a crucifix in urine. Efforts in both the House of Representatives and the Senate in 1990 to abolish the NEA ended in a compromise: The endowment's life would be extended for at least three more years if NEA officials would give grants only to artists whose works satisfied the decency requirement. (See **Art: Who Should Pay for Art?**)

Magazine liability. In another case involving First Amendment issues, a federal appeals court in Atlanta, Ga., ruled on Aug. 17, 1992, that *Soldier of Fortune* magazine was liable for a contract killing resulting from a "sinister" classified advertisement in its pages. The 2 to 1 ruling upheld a $4.3-million grant to the sons of Richard Braun, the murder victim. Braun was killed in 1985 by two business associates with the assistance of a professional mercenary, Michael Savage, whom they contacted after reading his ad in *Soldier of Fortune* offering a "gun for hire."

The case addressed the question of whether the near-absolute freedom of speech allowed in noncommercial and political speech extends to commercial expression. Ruling that commercial speech is more limited, the judges said a publication has a responsibility not to run an ad containing an offer in which "it [is] apparent that there is a substantial danger of harm to the public."

"Suicide doctor." In February 1992, murder charges were filed against retired Michigan pathologist Jack Kevorkian in the assisted-suicide death of two women in 1991. But on July 21, 1992, a circuit court judge in Pontiac, Mich., dismissed the charges, saying that no Michigan law specifically forbade participating in a suicide.

Kevorkian has been dubbed the "suicide doctor" because he advocates helping seriously ill people to end their lives if that is what the patients want. He has developed or acquired devices that a patient can trigger to receive a lethal dose of drugs or to inhale carbon monoxide. With such apparatus, Kevorkian had assisted in the suicides of four women by 1992. The two he was charged with murdering had been suffering from chronic, but not terminal, conditions.

Kevorkian's controversial actions and the legal charges brought in response to them have focused attention on the growing issue of a patient's right to die. Ethicists are debating whether in some circumstances it is acceptable for a physician to help a patient die.

Death sentence for Russian. In the Russian city of Rostov-on-Don on October 14, Andrei Chikatilo—a man described as perhaps the most brutal serial killer in the annals of crime—was convicted of murdering at least 52 boys, girls, and young women. The next day, Chikatilo was sentenced to death.

From 1978 to 1990, Chikatilo committed some of the most gruesome sex slayings ever reported. He stabbed his young victims, ripped their bodies apart, and ate pieces of their flesh. Tragically, Chikatilo was arrested in 1984 on suspicion of murder but was released when a case could not be made against him.

Other notable court actions in 1992:

▪The drug-trafficking and racketeering trial of former Panamanian dictator Manuel Antonio Noriega in Miami, Fla., ended on April 9 with a guilty verdict. On July 10, he was sentenced to 40 years in prison.

▪In Deland, Fla., Aileen Carol Wuornos was convicted on January 27 for the murder of one of seven male motorists who were found slain along Interstate Highway 75 in 1989 and 1990. Wuornos received the death sentence on Jan. 31, 1992.

▪On February 10, boxer Mike Tyson was convicted in Indianapolis of raping Desiree L. Washington, a contestant in the 1991 Miss Black America pageant. Tyson on March 26 received a six-year prison term.

▪On February 15, a jury in Milwaukee found that serial killer Jeffrey L. Dahmer was sane when he murdered and dismembered 15 men and boys over a 13-year period, a crime he had pleaded guilty to in January. On February 17, Dahmer was sentenced to 15 consecutive life terms in prison. On May 1, a 16th consecutive life term was added to Dahmer's sentence after he was found guilty in Ohio of aggravated murder.

David Dreier

See also **Crime; Supreme Court of the United States.** In ***World Book,*** see **Court.**

Crime. *Carjacking,* a combination of auto theft and armed robbery, became a growing menace to U.S. motorists in 1992. In the typical carjacking episode, a driver is approached at a stoplight or in a parking lot by a person armed with a gun or knife and ordered to hand over the keys to the vehicle, which the carjacker then drives away. In some cases, motorists have been murdered by carjackers. Carjacking came to national attention in September after two young men in Howard County, Maryland, commandeered a car being driven by a woman who was taking her 22-month-old daughter to preschool. The woman's arm became tangled in the car's seatbelt, and she was dragged to her death. The carjackers reportedly stopped only to throw the baby into the road. The child was rescued unharmed.

Just days after that incident occurred, the Federal Bureau of Investigation (FBI) reported that it was taking action to combat carjacking, which an FBI survey found was becoming an increasingly common crime in many parts of the United States. FBI Director William S. Sessions said carjacking was being added to a list of violent crimes assigned to a special 300-member arm of the agency. In addition, Congress in 1992 passed legislation that made carjacking a federal offense.

Violent crime up. Carjacking was not the only crime showing a significant increase in the United States in 1992. Other kinds of violent crime were also on the rise. Statistics released by the Department of Justice in April showed that violent crime had increased by 8 per cent from 1991. The biggest increase occurred in the crimes of rape and attempted rape, which were up by 59 per cent. Assaults also showed a sizable increase—7.5 per cent. The total number of violent crimes reported—about 35 million—was the third highest since the Justice Department began making its annual survey in 1973, but was considerably lower than the record 41.4 million reported in 1981.

New BCCI indictments. The continuing investigation of what has been called the most corrupt bank in the world led in 1992 to the indictments of two pillars of the Washington, D.C., establishment. On July 29, New York state and federal prosecutors filed criminal charges against six individuals, including Washington lawyers Clark M. Clifford and Robert A. Altman, for their involvement with the Bank of Credit and Commerce International (BCCI).

Clifford, who served as secretary of defense in the Administration of President Lyndon B. Johnson, and Altman, a partner in Clifford's law firm, were accused of accepting more than $40 million in bribes in return for helping BCCI hide its illegal ownership of First American Bankshares, Incorporated, Washington's largest bank. Both men pleaded not guilty.

BCCI, which was shut down by banking regulators in seven countries in July 1991 for allegedly engaging in fraud, was founded by a Pakistani banker and had offices in 70 countries. In December 1991, BCCI pleaded guilty in the United States to fraud and racketeering charges. Probes of the bank's operations revealed that it was involved in criminal activities that went far beyond fraud, including drug trafficking and secret arms sales. The investigation of BCCI in the United States has been led by the office of Robert M. Morgenthau, district attorney of the New York City borough of Manhattan. Morgenthau predicted in 1992 that the trials of Clifford and Altman would help disclose the extent of BCCI's criminal undertakings and the people involved in them. (See also **Bank.**)

Kidnapping ends in death. A New Jersey couple's plot to make a quick fortune by kidnapping and ransoming a business executive went terribly awry in 1992 when their victim died. On April 29, Arthur D. Seale and his wife, Irene J. Seale, abducted Sidney J. Reso, president of an Exxon Corporation subsidiary, from the driveway of his Morris Township, New Jersey, home after forcing him into their van. Inside the van, Seale and Reso scuffled, and Seale shot Reso in the arm. Four days later, after being confined without food or water, Reso died.

Nonetheless, the Seales decided to press ahead with their scheme. In a series of notes and telephone calls, they insisted that Reso was safe, and they demanded that Exxon pay an $18.5-million ransom for his return. Meanwhile, the FBI carried out its biggest nationwide kidnapping investigation since the abduction of Patricia Hearst in 1974. On June 19, 1992, the Seales were arrested at a car rental agency.

For about a week, the Seales remained silent. But then Irene Seale admitted the crime and led investigators to a corner of a state forest in southern New Jersey, where they found Reso's body buried in a shallow grave. Irene Seale was allowed to plead guilty to just two federal counts of extortion. In September, Arthur Seale pleaded guilty to both federal and state charges against him. On November 30, he was sentenced to 95 years in prison with no chance of parole.

Sting operation. Agents of the U.S. Drug Enforcement Administration (DEA) announced on September 28 that they had brought a three-year undercover operation to a conclusion with the arrest of more than 150 members of an international drug ring, 112 of them in the United States. The DEA officials said the arrests, made in cooperation with law-enforcement authorities in Italy and several other countries, disrupted the money-laundering operations of the Cali drug cartel, the most powerful cocaine-trafficking organization in Colombia. Among those arrested were 7 of Cali's alleged top money managers.

The DEA "sting" operation centered around a phony consulting firm named Trans Americas Ventures Associates. DEA informants convinced Cali leaders to work with the firm in setting up fake leather goods businesses through which drug profits were funneled to make the money look legitimate. The DEA said its investigation collected strong evidence linking Cali with the Sicilian Mafia.

Murder at a California high school. A young man armed with a 12-gauge shotgun and a .22-caliber rifle stalked the halls of Lindhurst High School in Olivehurst, Calif., on May 1 firing into classrooms, police said. Three students and a teacher were killed, and 10 other people were wounded. The gunman then held dozens of students hostage for more than eight hours before giving himself up to sheriff's deputies and FBI agents. He was identified as Eric Houston, age 20, a former student at the school. Lindhurst officials said Houston apparently bore a grudge against the school because he had failed a course and did not graduate.

Gunman kills four in New York. Terror erupted at a county office building in Watkins Glen, N.Y., on October 15 as a man armed with a 9-millimeter semiautomatic pistol killed four women whose job was to collect child-support payments. The killer, a truck driver named John T. Miller, had a history of arrests for nonpayment of child support. When confronted on the scene by sheriff's deputies, whose offices were in the same building, Miller told them that support payments had ruined his life. Then he shot himself in the head. He was taken to a nearby hospital, where he was pronounced dead.

White supremacist captured. An 11-day standoff in a mountainous area of northern Idaho, during which three people died, ended on August 31 with the surrender of Randy Weaver, a white supremacist wanted on federal weapons charges. Weaver, 44, had holed up in a cabin with several family members, defying a small army of more than 100 police officers, federal agents, and national guard troops who had come to arrest him. Exchanges of gunfire on the first two days of the siege resulted in the death of a federal marshal and of Weaver's wife and a son. A family friend, Kevin Harris, who was wounded, was charged with killing Deputy Marshal William F. Degan.

Suspect indicted in prostitute killings. On July 24, a grand jury in Riverside County, California, indicted the leading suspect in the murders of 19 local prostitutes that had occurred since 1986. The suspect, William L. Suff, a 41-year-old stock clerk, had been arrested by the Riverside, Calif., police in January after being stopped for making an illegal U-turn. Through a computer check, the traffic officers learned that Suff was wanted in Texas for a parole violation. A search of his car and later of his apartment found evidence linking him to the murders, police investigators said.

DNA test endorsed. A panel of experts at the National Research Council in Washington, D.C., in April 1992 endorsed the use of DNA fingerprinting by law enforcement authorities, saying it can provide "strong evidence for solving crimes." DNA fingerprinting is a procedure in which *DNA* (the molecule genes are made of) found in blood, hair, and other biological specimens recovered from a crime scene is compared with DNA obtained from a blood sample taken from a suspect. David Dreier

In ***World Book,*** see **Crime.**

Croatia. On March 8, 1992, the United Nations (UN) began deploying peacekeeping troops in Croatia. The move effectively ended the war launched by Serbia, the dominant republic of Yugoslavia, after Croatia declared independence from Yugoslavia in June 1991.

In December 1991, the Serb-controlled Yugoslav federal army and ethnic Serb militias occupied an area comprising about a third of Croatia's territory. The war had killed thousands, created hundreds of thousands of refugees, and paralyzed the economy. On Jan. 3, 1992, the UN negotiated a cease-fire between the Croatians and the Serb and Yugoslav forces. All parties agreed in February to permit the UN deployment pending a permanent settlement.

Recognition. On April 7, the United States officially recognized Croatia as an independent state. The European Community (EC or Common Market) had recognized Croatia on January 15. Both actions were spurred by what many observers saw as Germany's overhasty recognition of Croatia in December 1991, before the country had fully satisfied the criteria for integration with the West. These criteria included stable borders and respect for human rights.

Croatian President Franjo Tudjman, a nationalist and former Communist, faced increasing condemnation for his authoritarian rule and human rights violations. In February 1992, the U.S.-based Helsinki Watch, an organization that monitors human rights observance worldwide, accused the Croatian government of having committed atrocities during the war, including the torture and execution of ethnic Serbs. The organization had previously charged the Serbian government and Serb militias with similar acts against ethnic Croats. Witnesses also said Serbs in the occupied area of Croatia had continued to force Croats from their homes after the UN deployment.

As elections scheduled for August 2 approached, Tudjman increasingly cracked down on dissent. The government threatened to prosecute journalists and to take over newspapers critical of its policies. In the elections, Tudjman easily defeated his main challenger in Croatia's first direct presidential election. His Croatian Democratic Union took about 43 per cent of the parliamentary seats, down from 60 per cent in the previous parliament.

Bosnian role. In March 1992, war began in Bosnia and Hercegovina (commonly called Bosnia), a former Yugoslav republic with a mixed population of Muslims, Serbs, and Croats. Croatian forces at first supported the Bosnian government against Serb militias backed by Serbia. But in October and November, Croatian troops began attacking Muslim forces in an effort to seize territory for Croatia. They also expelled some Muslim civilians from their homes. The Serbs had initiated this practice, known as "ethnic cleansing," to create an ethnic partition of Bosnia. Eric Bourne

See also **Bosnia and Hercegovina; Europe** (Facts in brief table); **Yugoslavia.** In ***World Book,*** see **Croatia.**

Cuba. The Cuban economy continued to falter in 1992, the first full year without financial aid from the former Soviet Union. Increased shortages of everything from cooking oil to gasoline inspired increasing numbers of Cubans to flee the island.

On January 3, a Cuban pilot seized a helicopter in Veradero, just east of Havana, the capital, and flew 33 other Cubans to Miami, Fla., where they defected. In August and September, nearly 1,000 more Cubans reached Florida by boat.

Money woes. On September 5, President Fidel Castro blamed Cuba's plight on the breakup of the Soviet Union in late 1991. The resulting reduction in financial assistance and trade reduced Cuba's money supply. Castro acknowledged in September 1992 that Cuba's purchasing power fell from $8.1 billion in 1989 to $2.2 billion in 1992 and that imports had fallen by 70 per cent in the same period. Worse yet, the island's sugar and nickel exports were hurting from depressed world prices.

In September, work was suspended on a nuclear power plant in Juraguá, which Cubans had hoped would relieve their crushing energy shortage. A lack of hard currency was a major reason for stopping the work. The plant had been under construction since 1980 with the former Soviet Union helping pay for the $1.4-billion cost. Although the plant was 70 per cent complete, Cuba could not meet Russian demands for $200 million in hard currency to continue the work.

Troops on bicycles in a May Day armed forces parade symbolize Cuba's economic plight. There was not enough gasoline for vehicles.

Cuba increased its efforts in 1992 to find desperately needed sources of foreign currency. To raise money and help reduce fuel shortages, the government awarded contracts for offshore oil exploration to French, British, Swedish, and Brazilian companies. Despite shortages of fertilizer and pesticides, Cuba managed to boost its cigar and tobacco exports in 1992 to a value of more than $100 million.

Embargo. The United Nations (UN) General Assembly passed a resolution on November 24 that called for an end to the 30-year United States embargo of Cuba. Many UN representatives from nations that voted to end the embargo said that their vote was a protest against U.S. legislation passed in late 1992 that strengthened the embargo. The new U.S. legislation left subsidiaries of U.S. companies based abroad who trade with Cuba open to prosecution.

Dismissals. In June, Castro dismissed his own son, Fidel Castro Díaz-Balart, as head of the island's nuclear energy program, on grounds of inefficiency. In September, the government announced that Carlos Aldana Escalante, Cuba's third most powerful figure—and widely judged to be the only moderate in Cuba's top leadership—had been dismissed from his post for "serious errors of a personal character."

Nathan A. Haverstock

See also **Latin America** (Facts in brief table). In ***World Book,*** see **Cuba.**

Cyprus. See **Middle East.**

Czechoslovakia in 1992 agreed that the federation, which had united Czechs and Slovaks in one state since 1918, would cease to exist as of Jan. 1, 1993. On Nov. 25, 1992, the Federal Assembly (parliament) approved legislation under which the Czech and Slovak republics would become two nations, to be called the Czech Republic and Slovakia. Previously, public opinion polls had found that less than 40 per cent of either the Czechs or the Slovaks favored separation. Nevertheless, the split had been widely viewed as inevitable after Slovak nationalists emerged as winners in June elections.

Slovak nationalism had been on the rise since Communism fell in Czechoslovakia in 1989. The poorer, mainly agricultural Slovakia had been hurt most by the country's program of radical economic reform. By June 1992, for example, less than 5 per cent of Western investment in the country had gone to Slovakia.

In the elections on June 5 and 6, the Movement for a Democratic Slovakia (MDS) won 30 per cent of the vote for the Federal Assembly. The MDS, led by nationalist and former Communist Vladimir Mečiar, also took 37 per cent of the vote in the Slovak parliament. Mečiar remained as the republic's premier.

The conservative Civic Democratic Party (CDP) won a plurality of 33 per cent in the Federal Assembly. The CDP, a Czech party, was led by Václav Klaus, the architect of Czechoslovakia's economic reforms. The CDP also won a plurality in the Czech parliament.

Separation pact. Klaus, as CDP leader, should have become the federal premier. But Klaus refused to accept the premiership without an agreement assuring the country's future. Mečiar pressed for a loose confederation with nearly all powers transferred to the republics—a proposal Klaus rejected.

On June 20, Klaus and Mečiar announced they had agreed the republics should become independent nations. A caretaker government was formed, with Jan Strasky of the CDC eventually named as premier. Klaus became premier of the Czech Republic.

On July 3, the Federal Assembly rejected Václav Havel's bid for reelection as federal president. Havel, who had helped lead the movement that toppled Communism, opposed the country's division. He was due to leave office in October. But after Slovakia declared sovereignty on July 17, Havel resigned.

Differences resolved. The Federal Assembly narrowly rejected the separation bill twice before passing it on November 25, after opposition leaders gave up their demand for a referendum. Earlier in November, the republics agreed on a formula for dividing federal assets in proportion to population. Fixed assets such as buildings would belong to the republic in which they stood. But negotiators still had to resolve Slovak demands for compensation, since most federal buildings are in the Czech capital, Prague. Eric Bourne

See also **Europe** (Facts in brief table). In ***World Book,*** see **Czechoslovakia.**

Dancing. Although many United States dance companies were affected by the ailing U.S. economy, none was as hard hit in 1992 as was the American Ballet Theater (ABT), which is based in New York City. In May, the ABT's codirector Jane Hermann unexpectedly announced that she would resign as of September 1, in part, she said, because her artistic vision for the ABT could not be reconciled with its dwindling financial resources. Just how dwindling those resources were was soon revealed. The ABT was not able to pay its dancers all the wages they were due and was also behind in paying health insurance premiums.

Burdened by a deficit of between $4 million and $5 million, the ABT's board considered several ways to reduce its annual budget, which Hermann had already cut from $21 million to $16 million. The most radical idea—a merger with the financially ailing Joffrey Ballet—was rejected by the boards of both companies in September. Instead, the ABT trimmed its 1993 touring schedule. On October 2, the company appointed Kevin McKenzie, formerly a principal dancer with the ABT, as its artistic director and Gary Dunning, formerly the troupe's general manager, as its executive director.

The ABT's most ambitious undertaking in 1992 was a revival of Sir Frederick Ashton's *Symphonic Variations,* which he created for Great Britain's Sadler's Wells Ballet in 1946. In staging the piece on March 20, 1992, in Chicago, the ABT thus became the first American troupe to perform what is considered Ashton's

Members of AXIS, a troupe with disabled dancers, perform *Helix*, an aerial dance in which dancers move expressively while suspended in air, in April.

masterpiece. Choreographer Agnes De Mille, whose *Rodeo* (1942) and *Fall River Legend* (1948) have long been staples of the ABT, returned to the company with *The Other*, which premiered on April 3, 1992, in Washington, D.C.

Joffrey Ballet. Although the struggling Joffrey Ballet was able to fulfill most of its engagements in 1992, high production expenses forced the company to cancel its February season in New York City, which has traditionally been its primary base. The Joffrey also had to forfeit a season in its second home city, Los Angeles, because of rioting in April and May.

The company was, however, able to present the kind of ballet that has forged the Joffrey's identity as a restorer of significant but rarely performed works. On July 8 in San Francisco, the Joffrey revived Leonide Massine's *Les Présages,* created in 1933 and not performed since the 1940's. Set to Peter Ilich Tchaikovsky's Symphony No. 5, *Les Présages* is led by dancers whom Massine called Action, Temptation, Frivolity, and Passion. This so-called symphonic ballet is regarded as an important step in ballet's evolution during the 1900's from a narrative form to an abstract one.

New York City Ballet. The high point for the New York City Ballet in 1992 was the Diamond Project, a weeklong presentation of new works at the New York State Theater in New York City in May. The

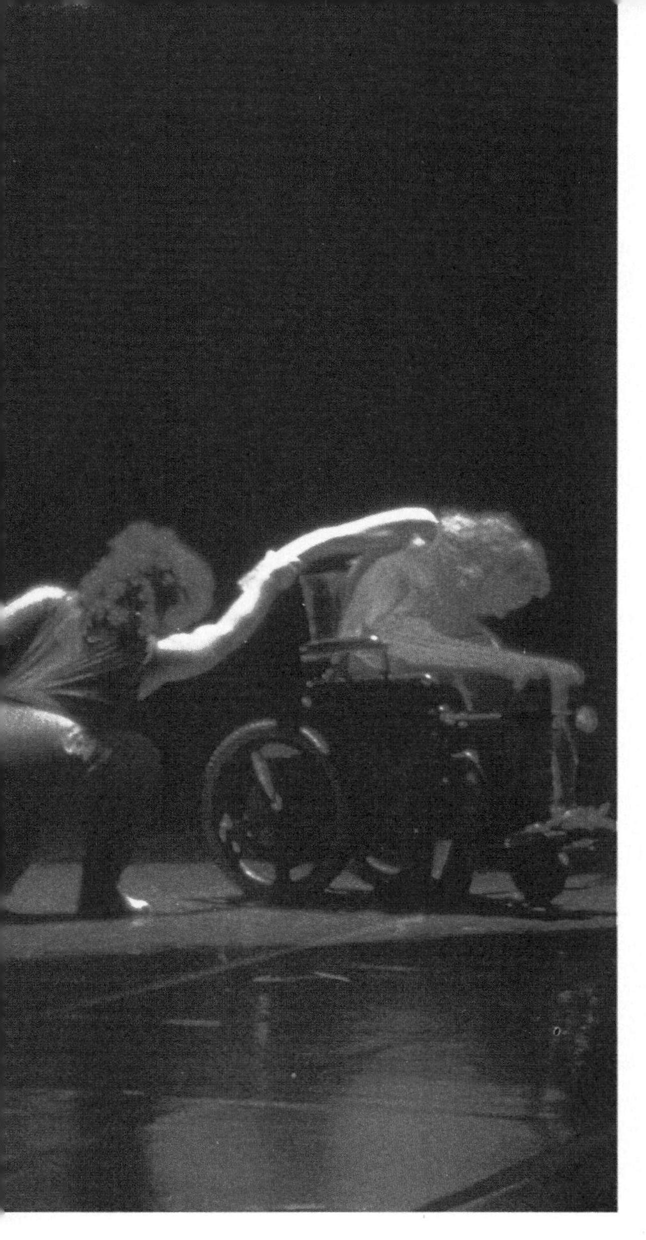

project featured 11 premieres by 11 choreographers, including Peter Martins, City Ballet's artistic director. With the exception of Martins and Frankfurt (Germany) Ballet director William Forsythe, the choreographers chosen by Martins were relatively unknown. Several were from small regional troupes.

Tharp offerings. Choreographer Twyla Tharp, who disbanded her permanent company in 1988, assembled a temporary troupe in 1992 as she had in 1991. Twyla Tharp and Dancers made its debut at the City Center Theater in New York City from Jan. 28 to Feb. 9, 1992, with a cornucopia of new works. Tharp herself was the star of *Men's Piece*, in which she both talked and danced her way through the question of how men and women could achieve equality in their romantic relationships. Although the piece did not offer a solution, it did provide Tharp with wonderful opportunities for self-parody.

Tharp's next project was to team up with dancer Mikhail Baryshnikov and an ensemble in a program of yet more new works. The Tharp and Baryshnikov group began a 2½-month nationwide tour on November 30 in Austin, Tex.

Modern dance revivals. As Tharp entered a new phase of creativity, the troupes of two other important choreographers concentrated on reviving old works. During its one-week run in October at the City Center, the Martha Graham Dance Company dug into the distant past of their late founder to present an excerpt from *Panorama*, which Graham created in 1935 but which had not been performed since, and *Salem Shore*, a solo made in 1943 and last performed in 1947. The excerpt from *Panorama*, with its striking use of a large ensemble of women, was nothing short of a sensation. It showed Graham to be a master of form as well as a keen explorer of the human psyche.

Also in October 1992, Paul Taylor's troupe presented a revival of *Epic*, a solo whose premiere in 1957 received what may be the most notorious dance review ever written—four inches of blank space in *Dance Observer* magazine. *Epic* is set to the voice of a telephone operator announcing the time of day. The movement consists of purely ordinary gesture. *Epic* had heralded in dance a revolt against traditional dance techniques, a revolt that continued into the 1970's.

European visitors. Several major European companies visited the United States in 1992. In May, the Kirov Ballet of St. Petersburg, Russia, began a six-week tour that opened in California, traveled across Canada, and ended in Mexico City. Among the full-length ballets presented was the original version of *Romeo and Juliet*, choreographed by Leonid Lavrovsky in 1940 to a score by Soviet composer Sergei Prokofiev. Not seen in the United States since 1959, *Romeo and Juliet* again impressed audiences with the grandeur of its conception and the fine opportunities it provides for acting. In presenting a mixed bill of ballets, including works by choreographers George Balanchine and Jerome Robbins, the Kirov demonstrated its ability to perform abstract Western works as well as more conventional ballets.

The Nutcracker celebrated its 100th anniversary in 1992. As groups all over the United States staged their traditional versions of this Christmas classic, choreographer Mark Morris showed a predictably offbeat interpretation of the story at the Brooklyn Academy of Music in New York City. Called *The Hard Nut*, Morris' version is set in the 1960's, is inspired by cartoons, and features an assortment of oddball characters as well as the mysterious Herr Drosselmeyer of the original version. Nancy Goldner

See also **Art: Who Should Pay for Art?** In ***World Book,*** see **Ballet; Dancing.**

José Ferrer, actor and director.

Sandy Dennis, motion-picture actress.

S. I. Hayakawa, noted semanticist.

Anthony Perkins, motion-picture actor.

Deaths in 1992 included those listed below, who were Americans unless otherwise indicated.

Acuff, Roy (1903-Nov. 23), singer and fiddler who became known as the king of country music during his stint with the Grand Ole Opry in Nashville, Tenn.

Adler, Stella (1901-Dec. 21), actress and acting teacher known as a leading exponent of Method acting and founder of the Stella Adler Conservatory in Hollywood, Calif.

Alba, Maria (?-June 24), noted flamenco dancer and teacher.

Allen, Peter (1944-June 18), Australian-born singer and songwriter.

Alzado, Lyle (1949-May 14), former football player and All-Pro defensive end who starred with the Denver Broncos and Los Angeles Raiders.

Amoros, Sandy (Edmundo Isasi Amoros) (1930-June 27), Cuban-born baseball player whose spectacular catch and throw in the seventh game of the 1955 World Series helped the Brooklyn Dodgers defeat the New York Yankees.

Anderson, Dame Judith (Frances Margaret) (1898-Jan. 3), Australian-born actress of stage and screen, best known for roles in the 1947 Broadway production of *Medea* and in the 1940 motion picture *Rebecca*.

Andrews, Dana (1912-Dec. 17), motion-picture actor best remembered for his leading roles in *Laura* (1944) and *The Best Years of Our Lives* (1946).

Arena, George (1908?-July 16), wrestler who claimed he was the original "Gorgeous George."

Arletty (Léonie Bathiat) (1898-July 23), legendary French actress known for her memorable line—"Atmosphere, atmosphere"—in the 1938 motion picture *Hôtel du Nord*.

Asimov, Isaac (1920-April 6), Russian-born American author who wrote almost 500 books, mostly nonfiction works on science and technology, though he was best known for his science fiction; former contributing editor of World Book's *Science Year*. See **Deaths: The Literary Legacy of Isaac Asimov.**

Bacon, Francis (1909-April 28), British artist known for his disturbing paintings of deformed figures.

Balfa, Dewey (1927?-June 17), fiddler and singer who helped revive interest in Cajun music.

Barber, Red (Walter Lanier Barber) (1908-Oct. 22), Hall of Fame sports broadcaster who became the voice of the Brooklyn Dodgers and altered the language of baseball.

Barnett, Marguerite Ross (1942-Feb. 26), former president of the University of Houston and the first black woman to head a major American university.

Bartholomew, Freddie (Frederick Llewellyn) (1924-Jan. 23), child actor who starred in *David Copperfield* (1935) and *Little Lord Fauntleroy* (1936).

Begin, Menachem (1913-March 9), prime minister of Israel from 1977 to 1983; shared the 1978 Nobel Peace Prize with Egyptian President Anwar el-Sadat.

Benedek, Laslo (1907?-March 11), Hungarian-born motion-picture and television director who directed *Death of a Salesman* (1951) and *The Wild One* (1953).

Bloom, Allan (1930-Oct. 7), political philosopher known for his scathing critique of American higher education in *The Closing of the American Mind* (1987).

Booth, Shirley (Thelma Booth Ford) (1907-Oct. 16), motion-picture and television actress who won an Academy Award for best actress for her performance in *Come Back, Little Sheba* (1952) and who appeared as the title character in the television series "Hazel."

Bovet, Daniel (1907-April 8), Swiss-born Italian biochemist who won the Nobel Prize for physiology and medicine in 1957 for his discovery of antihistamines. He also discovered sulfa drugs and muscle relaxants.

Brand, Neville (1921-April 16), motion-picture and television actor who played "tough-guy" roles in dozens of films and TV shows, such as *Birdman of Alcatraz* (1962) and the television series "The Untouchables."

Brandt, Willy (Herbert Ernst Karl Frahm) (1913-Oct. 8), German statesman who was awarded the Nobel Peace Prize in 1971 for his efforts to normalize relations with the Soviet Union, Poland, and East Germany.

Brooks, James (1906-March 9), abstract expressionist painter.

Brooks, Richard (1912-March 11), motion-picture director and screenwriter who directed such films as *In Cold Blood* (1967) and *Cat on a Hot Tin Roof* (1958) and who won an

Academy Award in 1960 for his screenplay of *Elmer Gantry,* based on the novel by Sinclair Lewis.
Brown, Georgia (Lillian Klot) (1933-July 5), British singer and actress best known for her role as Nancy in the 1960 musical *Oliver!*
Brown, James (1919?-April 11), actor who was best known for playing Lieutenant Rip Masters in the 1950's television series "The Adventures of Rin Tin Tin."
Buchanan, Buck (1940-July 16), professional football player known for his defensive play for the Kansas City Chiefs from 1963 to 1975; elected to the Pro Football Hall of Fame in 1990.
Buckmaster, Maurice (1902?-April 17), World War II hero who directed British spies in Nazi-occupied France.
Burdick, Quentin N. (1908-Sept. 8), United States senator from North Dakota from 1960 until his death; first elected to the U.S. Congress in 1958.
Cage, John (1912-Aug. 12), composer known for his innovations and minimalist style.
Callender, Red (George Sylvester Callender) (1918-March 8), jazz bassist who played with such jazz greats as Lester Young, Duke Ellington, and Charlie Parker.
Carnovsky, Morris (1897-Sept. 1), actor who was blacklisted in Hollywood in the 1950's and later became known for his Shakespearean stage performances.
Chabukiani, Vakhtang Mikhailovich (1910-April 5), Soviet ballet master and choreographer who starred with the Kirov Ballet in the 1930's and 1940's.
Chaliapin, Feodor, Jr. (1905?-Sept. 17), motion-picture character actor who achieved notoriety in the 1980's, after a 60-year career, for his roles in *Moonstruck* (1987) and *The Name of the Rose* (1986).
Chappell, Willa C. Brown (1906?-July 18), pioneer black woman aviator who helped break racial barriers in the military and trained hundreds of black pilots before and during World War II (1939-1945).
Cherry, Herman (1909-April 10), abstract painter.
Connors, Chuck (1924-Nov. 10), motion-picture and television actor and former professional baseball player known for his leading role in the 1950's "Rifleman" TV series.
Copley, Alfred L. (1935-Jan. 28), German-born artist and physician known for his scientific writings on physiology and for his abstract expressionist paintings.
D'Aubuisson, Roberto (1943-Feb. 20), Salvadoran political leader widely regarded as the force behind right wing death squads that murdered tens of thousands during El Salvador's civil war.
Davis, Leon (1906-Sept. 14), labor organizer who founded the largest hospital workers' union in the United States.
Deng Yingchao (1904-July 11), Chinese Communist Party leader and widow of Zhou Enlai.
Dennis, Sandy (1937-March 2), actress who won an Academy Award in 1966 for best supporting actress for her role in *Who's Afraid of Virginia Woolf?*
Devlin, Lord (Patrick Arthur Devlin) (1906?-Aug. 9), British jurist who became a prominent critic of the British judicial system and successfully campaigned for the freedom of the Guildford Four, three men and a woman wrongly imprisoned for two 1974 bombings.

Alex Haley, noted author and editor.

Robert Reed, television actor.

Joseph L. Rauh, Jr., civil rights attorney.

Grace M. Hopper, computer scientist.

Dietrich, Marlene (Maria Magdalene Dietrich) (1901?-May 6), actress whose portrayal of a seductive, husky-voiced cabaret singer in *The Blue Angel* (1930) launched a legendary motion-picture career. See **Motion pictures: Marlene Dietrich: A Legend Passes.**
Dixon, Willie (1915-Jan. 29), blues composer and producer known for his influence on a generation of rock musicians.
Drake, Alfred C. (1915-July 25), actor and singer who created the lead role in the 1943 musical *Oklahoma!*
Dubcek, Alexander (1921-Nov. 7), Czechoslovak Communist leader whose reform efforts led to the Soviet Union's 1968 invasion.
Dunne, Philip (1908-June 2), screenwriter and founder of the Screen Writers Guild who opposed the blacklisting of Hollywood actors, directors, and screenwriters in the 1950's.
Exley, Frederick (1929-June 17), author known for his autobiographical trilogy: *A Fan's Notes* (1968), *Pages from a Cold Island* (1975), and *Last Notes from Home* (1988).
Fenwick, Millicent (1910-Sept. 16), Republican congresswoman from New Jersey from 1975 to 1983, known as a strong civil rights supporter and as the model for the Lacey Davenport character in Garry Trudeau's "Doonesbury" cartoon.
Ferrer, José (José Vicente Ferrer de Otero y Cintron) (1912?-Jan. 26), actor, director, and producer who won an

Deaths

Lawrence Welk, popular bandleader.

Thomas O. Paine, oversaw moon landings.

Barbara McClintock, pathbreaking scientist.

Benny Hill, British television comedian.

Academy Award for best actor in 1950 for his role in *Cyrano de Bergerac*.

Ffrangcon-Davies, Dame Gwen (1891-Jan. 27), British actress regarded as a last link with Victorian theater and known for her Shakespearean roles.

Field, Virginia (Margaret Cynthia Field) (1918?-Jan. 2), motion-picture actress known for her appearances in the "Mr. Moto" series of detective films.

Fisher, M. F. K. (Mary Frances Kennedy Fisher) (1908-June 22), author who brought a new approach to writing about food.

Fonssagrives-Penn, Lisa (1912?-Feb. 4), prominent fashion model in the 1940's and 1950's known for her work with husband-photographer Irving Penn.

France, William (1910?-June 7), founder of the National Association for Stock Car Auto Racing and its president from 1947 to 1972; creator of the Daytona 500 automobile race in Florida.

Franjieh, Suleiman (1910-July 23), president of Lebanon from 1970 to 1976.

Freund, Paul A. (1908-Feb. 5), noted legal scholar and authority on the U.S. Constitution.

Gaines, William M. (1922?-June 3), publisher and founder of *Mad* magazine.

Gapp, Paul (1928-July 30), Pulitzer Prize-winning architecture critic for the *Chicago Tribune*.

Gardenia, Vincent (Vincent Scognamiglio) (1923-Dec. 9), character actor known for his supporting roles in *Bang the Drum Slowly* (1973) and *Moonstruck* (1987).

Garrison, Jim (1921-Oct. 21), former New Orleans district attorney known for his investigations into the assassination of President John. F. Kennedy.

Gaster, Theodor Herzl (1906-Feb. 3), comparative religion scholar known for his work on the Dead Sea Scrolls.

Gertz, Alison J. (1966?-Aug. 8), illustrator who became a prominent voice in educating people about AIDS.

Godfree, Kitty (Kathleen Godfree) (1906?-June 19), tennis star who twice won the Wimbledon singles championship in England.

Goodson, Mark (1918-Dec. 18), television producer who created the classic game shows "The Price Is Right," "To Tell the Truth," and "What's My Line?"

Habib, Philip C. (1920-May 25), career diplomat for almost three decades who won the Presidential Medal of Freedom in 1982 for fashioning a peace settlement in Lebanon.

Hair, James E. (1915?-Jan. 3), one of 13 blacks who were the first to become officers in the Navy, breaking its color barrier during World War II.

Haley, Alex (1921-Feb. 10), author known for his Pulitzer Prize-winning *Roots: The Saga of an American Family* (1976), which was later made into a television miniseries, and for editing *The Autobiography of Malcolm X* (1965).

Hayakawa, S. I. (Samuel Ichiye Hayakawa) (1906-Feb. 26), Canadian-born semanticist who achieved public notoriety during the 1960's for his tough stand against student protesters as president of San Francisco State College, now San Francisco State University. He later was elected to the United States Senate.

Hein, Mel (1909-Jan. 31), legendary center and linebacker for the New York Giants during the 1930's and 1940's and charter member of the Pro Football Hall of Fame.

Helfer, Ray E. (1929?-Jan. 27), pediatrician who specialized in researching the causes of child abuse and who helped produce two classic books on the subject, *The Battered Child* (1968) and *Helping the Battered Child and His Family* (1972).

Henreid, Paul (Paul George Julius von Hernreid) (1908-March 29), actor who gained fame for his role as the anti-Nazi Resistance leader Victor Lazlo in the classic motion picture *Casablanca* (1942).

Herman, Billy (1909-Sept. 5), baseball player elected to the National Baseball Hall of Fame in 1975; played second base, mostly for the Chicago Cubs.

Hill, Benny (1925-April 20), British comedian who starred in the popular television series "The Benny Hill Show."

Holloway, Sterling (1905-Nov. 22), motion-picture and television actor whose raspy voice was the bear Pooh in *The Many Adventures of Winnie-the-Pooh* (1983) and the snake in *The Jungle Book* (1967).

Hopper, Grace M. (1906-Jan. 1), retired rear admiral in the U.S. Navy and a mathematician who helped develop the first computer programming language and helped program the first large-scale computer.

Ichord, Richard H. (1926-Dec. 25), former representative who served in the U.S. Congress from 1961 to 1981 and was the last chairman of the House Un-American Activities Committee.

Ireland, John (1915-March 21), Canadian-born stage, film, and television actor who appeared in more than 200 motion pictures and was nominated for an Oscar in 1949 for his role in *All the King's Men.*

Jabara, Paul (1948?-Sept. 29), songwriter, singer, and actor who won an Academy Award in 1979 for his song, "Last Dance," featured in *Thank God It's Friday* (1978).

Jacobs, Lou (Jacob Ludwig) (1903-Sept. 13), clown who performed with the Ringling Brothers and Barnum & Bailey Circus for six decades.

Kang Keching (1911-April 22), Chinese Communist leader who was a veteran of the Long March and the widow of the famous military leader Zhu De.

Kendricks, Eddie (1939-Oct. 5), lead singer of the Temptations, one of the top Motown groups of the 1960's.

Kenyatta, Muhammad I. (Donald Brooks Jackson) (1944?-Jan. 3), civil rights activist and legal scholar.

King, Albert (1923-Dec. 21), rhythm-and-blues guitarist and singer known as the "godfather of the blues" for his influence on a younger generation of guitarists.

Kinison, Sam (1953?-April 10), comedian known for his shrieking, high-pitched delivery.

Kirsten, Dorothy (1910-Nov. 18), opera singer known for her roles in the operas of Italian composer Giacomo Puccini.

La Lupe (Lupe Victoria Yoli) (1938?-Feb. 28), popular singer of the 1960's known as the Queen of Latin Soul.

Lerner, Max (1902-June 5), Russian-born author and former New York City newspaper columnist who was known for his liberal commentary.

Li Xiannian (1907?-June 21), Chinese Communist leader, a veteran of the Long March and a commander of the Red Army who later became president of China from 1983 to 1988.

Little, Cleavon (1939-Oct. 22), motion-picture and stage actor known for his role as the sheriff in *Blazing Saddles* (1974).

Lopat, Eddie (Edmund Walter Lopatynski) (1918-June 15), baseball pitcher who was a member of the New York Yankees team that won five consecutive World Series from 1949 to 1953.

Louis, Victor (Vitaly Yevgenyevich Lui) (1928-July 18), Soviet journalist who reported for the Western press; known for exclusive articles because of his apparently close access to Soviet officials.

Mark, Herman F. (1895-April 6), Austrian-born chemist who became one of the world's leading authorities on *polymers* (long, chainlike molecules).

Martin, Paul (1903-Sept. 14), Liberal Party leader who served in the cabinets of four Liberal Party prime ministers and, as minister of national health and welfare from 1946 to 1957, is credited with writing much of Canada's social legislation.

McClintock, Barbara (1902-Sept. 2), geneticist credited with making a number of revolutionary discoveries in her field during more than 50 years of research; winner of the Nobel Prize for physiology or medicine in 1983.

Sam Walton, founder of retail chain.

Satyajit Ray, Indian filmmaker.

Dame Judith Anderson, Australian actress.

Menachem Begin, Israeli prime minister.

McGee, Gale W. (1915-April 9), former United States senator from Wyoming who served from 1959 to 1977.

McIntyre, Thomas J. (1915-Aug. 9), Democratic senator from New Hampshire from 1962 to 1978.

Messiaen, Olivier (1908-April 27), French composer who also taught music and became one of the most influential composers of the 1900's.

Miller, Roger (1936-Oct. 25), country music singer and songwriter best known for his 1965 hit, "King of the Road."

Mills, Wilbur D. (1909-May 2), influential congressman who served in the U.S. House of Representatives from 1939 to 1977.

Milstein, Nathan (1903-Dec. 21), Russian-born violin virtuoso.

Morgan, Barbara (1900?-Aug. 17), photographer known for her photographs of modern American dancers.

Morley, Robert (1908-June 3), memorable British character actor and author who appeared in more than 100 plays and 50 motion pictures.

Moscoso, Teodoro (1911?-June 15), U.S. ambassador to Venezuela and leader of the Alliance for Progress during the Administration of President John F. Kennedy.

Muldoon, Sir Robert (1921-Aug. 5), prime minister of New Zealand from 1975 to 1984.

Deaths

John Cage, innovative composer.

Nancy Walker, character actor.

Willy Brandt, German statesman.

Paul Henreid, actor in *Casablanca* (1942).

Murphy, George (1902-May 3), former motion-picture actor and U.S. senator from California.

Naughton, Bill (1910?-Jan. 9), British playwright who wrote the play *Alfie* (1964).

Newell, Allen (1927-July 20), computer scientist and one of the founders of the field of artificial intelligence.

Nie Rongzhen (1899-May 14), last surviving marshal of China's Communist revolution, who led the program to develop China's first atomic bomb after the Communists came to power.

Nolan, Sir Sidney (1917-Nov. 27), Australian artist known for a series of paintings that narrated the life of an Australian outlaw.

O'Meara, Edward T. (1921-Jan. 10), Roman Catholic archbishop of Indianapolis who headed Catholic Relief Services during the 1970's and 1980's.

Oort, Jan H. (1900-Nov. 5), Dutch astronomer who made major discoveries about comets, the Milky Way galaxy, and the position of our solar system within the Galaxy.

Paine, Thomas O. (1921-May 4), former head of the National Aeronautics and Space Administration who oversaw the agency during the first manned missions to the moon.

Parks, Bert (1914-Feb. 2), TV show host and emcee of the Miss America beauty pageant for 25 years.

Parnis, Mollie (1905?-July 18), fashion designer known for her dress designs for first ladies Mamie Eisenhower, Jacqueline Kennedy, Lady Bird Johnson, and Betty Ford.

Perkins, Anthony (1932-Sept. 12), actor who gained fame for his role as Norman Bates in the motion picture *Psycho* (1960).

Piazzolla, Astor (1921-July 5), Argentine composer known for his innovative contributions to tango music.

Pousette-Dart, Richard (1916-Oct. 25), artist who was a member of the first generation of abstract expressionists.

Price, Sammy (1908-April 14), jazz pianist who recorded with Lester Young and Sidney Bechet and was known as the "king of boogie-woogie."

Rauh, Joseph L., Jr. (1911-Sept. 3), attorney known as a champion of civil rights and civil liberties; founder of Americans for Democratic Action.

Ray, Satyajit (1921-April 23), Indian filmmaker who won a Western audience for his portrayals of Bengali life and received the Academy Award for lifetime achievement in cinema in 1992.

Reed, Robert (John Robert Rietz, Jr.) (1933?-May 13), actor who portrayed a model father on the television series "The Brady Bunch."

Reshevsky, Samuel (Samuel Herman Rzeszewski) (1911-April 4), Polish-born chess grandmaster who dominated American chess from 1920 until 1958.

Roach, Hal (1892-Nov. 2), motion-picture producer, director, and writer who introduced Laurel and Hardy and created the "Our Gang" comedies; winner of three Academy Awards, including an honorary award for lifetime achievement in motion pictures in 1984.

Ross, Steven J. (Steven Jay Rechnitz) (1927-Dec. 20), entrepreneur who created Time Warner Incorporated, the world's largest media and entertainment company.

Salk, Lee (1926-May 2), child psychologist who authored several popular books on child-rearing.

Schuman, William H. (1910?-Feb. 15), Pulitzer Prize-winning composer.

Segal, Vivienne (1897-Dec. 29), musical-comedy star known for her role in *Pal Joey* (1940).

Selikoff, Irving J. (1915-May 20), physician who pioneered in the field of environmental and occupational medicine and led a study of workers exposed to asbestos, which demonstrated its harmful effects.

Sergeyev, Konstantin (1910-April 1), Russian director of the Kirov ballet for 14 years and a leading star of the Soviet ballet in the 1950's.

Sevareid, Eric (Arnold Eric Sevareid) (1912-July 9), journalist known for his radio and television news reporting and commentaries from 1939 to 1977.

Shawn, William (1907-Dec. 8), magazine editor who guided *The New Yorker* from 1952 to 1987.

Sherman, Emilia (Emilia Sherman Maurer) (?-Feb. 28), choreographer and former director of the Radio City Music Hall's Rockettes.

Shines, Johnny (1916?-April 20), blues guitarist and singer, considered one of the last of the original Mississippi Delta blues musicians.

Shuster, Joseph (1914?-July 30), Canadian-born cartoonist and cocreator of Superman.
Sirica, John J. (1904-Aug. 14), federal judge who was credited with playing a pivotal role in the Watergate investigation that resulted in Richard M. Nixon's resignation from the presidency in 1974.
Stern, Philip M. (1926-June 1), author and philanthropist whose Stern Fund gave grants to groups fighting poverty and seeking social change.
Stirling, Sir James Frazer (1926-June 25), Scottish-born British architect noted for his diverse styles; winner of the 1981 Pritzker Prize.
Stotz, Carl E. (1910?-June 4), founder of Little League baseball.
Sturges, John (1911-Aug. 18), motion-picture director known for such films as *Bad Day at Black Rock* (1954), *The Magnificent Seven* (1960), and *The Great Escape* (1963).
Syms, Sylvia (1917-May 10), pop and jazz singer.
Tanenbaum, Marc H. (1925-July 3), rabbi who became a major proponent of Jewish-Christian dialogue.
Taylor, William (1939?-Aug. 21), banking regulator who briefly headed the Federal Deposit Insurance Corporation.
Tomasek, Frantisek Cardinal (1899-Aug. 4), leader of the Roman Catholic Church in Czechoslovakia since the late 1970's.
Van Fleet, James A. (1892-Sept. 23), retired four-star Army general who served in World War I (1914-1918), World War II, and the Korean War (1950-1953) and was called "the greatest general we have ever had" by President Harry S. Truman.
Varsi, Diane (1938-Nov. 19), motion-picture actress nominated for an Academy Award for best supporting actress for her role in *Peyton Place* (1957).
Ventura, Charlie (Charles Venturo) (1916-Jan. 17), jazz tenor saxophonist best known for his work with the Gene Krupa band during the 1940's.
Vieira da Silva, Maria-Helena (1908-March 6), Portuguese artist associated with the School of Paris and known for her influence on abstract expressionism.
Von Hayek, Friedrich (1899-March 23), Austrian-born British economist known as the "father of monetarism," who shared the Nobel Prize in economics in 1974.
Walker, Nancy (Anna Myrtle Swoyer) (1922-March 25), stage, motion-picture, and television actress who played Rhoda's mother in the television series of that name.
Walton, Sam (Samuel Moore Walton) (1918-April 5), founder of Wal-Mart Stores Incorporated, the largest retail chain in the United States, who amassed one of the greatest fortunes in America's history.
Wang Hongwen (1934?-Aug. 3), former Chinese Communist Party leader and a member of the "Gang of Four" that led the Cultural Revolution who was ousted from power and sentenced to life imprisonment.
Webb, James E. (1906-March 27), head of the National Aeronautics and Space Administration from 1961 to 1968, who was responsible for the Apollo moon-landing program.
Welk, Lawrence (1903-May 17), bandleader whose brand of "champagne music" captivated audiences from 1955 to

Red Barber, baseball broadcaster.

Millicent Fenwick, New Jersey congresswoman.

Shirley Booth, motion-picture and TV actress.

Francis Bacon, British artist.

1982 as "The Lawrence Welk Show" became one of the longest-running series in television history.
Wells, Mary (1943-July 26), popular-music singer whose signature song, "My Guy," was an anthem of the Motown sound.
West, Don (1906-Sept. 29), labor organizer and civil rights advocate who helped found the Highlander Folk School, one of the first schools to break racial barriers in the South in the 1930's.
Whitney, Cornelius Vanderbilt (1899-Dec. 13), founder of Pan American World Airways and a leading thoroughbred race horse owner and breeder.
Williams, Martin (1924?-April 13), jazz critic.
Williams, Tony (1928?-Aug. 14), lead singer for the 1950's rhythm-and-blues group, the Platters, who sang the hit songs "Only You" and "The Great Pretender."
Yawkey, Jean R. (Jean Remington Hollander) (1909-Feb. 26), owner of the Boston Red Sox.
Yerby, Frank (death announced Jan. 8) (1915?-Nov. 29, 1991), novelist and author of 32 historical novels, often set in the pre-Civil War South.
York, Dick (1928-Feb. 20, 1992), actor who played on the television series "Bewitched." Rod Such

Delaware. **See State government.**

The Literary Legacy of Isaac Asimov

By Keith Ferrell

In both his fiction and nonfiction, Isaac Asimov advanced the idea that reason and understanding can triumph over ignorance and prejudice.

Isaac Asimov, one of the world's most prolific writers, died on April 6, 1992, at the age of 72. In a career that spanned more than half a century, Asimov published more than 460 books, both fiction and nonfiction. His science-fiction works, which helped spawn many of the field's defining ideas, are among the most popular in the genre. But equally important are his nonfiction works, in which he explored and explained many fields of human knowledge. In particular, Asimov's science writing ranks with the finest ever published for its clarity and vividness.

Isaac Asimov was born in Petrovichi, Russia, on Jan. 2, 1920. At that time, Russia was in the midst of revolution. Sensing a bleak future, Asimov's parents, Judah and Anna, moved to the United States in 1923, settling in Brooklyn, a borough of New York City. By 1926, Judah Asimov had bought a small candy store, and two years later the Asimovs became American citizens.

While growing up, Asimov worked in the family store, starting at 6 o'clock in the morning and continuing late into the evenings after school. Asimov often said his adult character was shaped by the long hours of hard work, seven days a week, in the candy store.

When not working, Asimov read voraciously. It soon became clear to his parents and teachers that he was a genius, rarely forgetting anything he learned. Asimov graduated from high school when he was 15 years old. He moved on to Columbia University in New York City, where he eventually earned three degrees in chemistry, including his Ph.D. in 1948.

During his youth, Asimov's interest was captured by the bright science-fiction magazines on display in his father's store, and science fiction soon became his favorite reading material. He started writing stories of his own in his late teens and sold his first one when he was only 18 years old. Asimov's skill grew quickly, culminating in the short story "Nightfall" (1941). This tale of a world whose terrified people are about to experience darkness after centuries of daylight was chosen the best science-fiction short story ever written by the Science Fiction Writers of America in 1968.

In 1942, Asimov married Gertrude Blugerman. The Asimovs had two children, David and Robyn, but they divorced in 1973. Later that same year, Asimov married psychiatrist and writer Janet Jeppson.

In 1949, Asimov joined the faculty of the Boston University School of Medicine as an instructor of biochemistry. He taught at the school from 1949 to 1958, becoming renowned for his lecturing skill. He left teaching in 1958 to write full-time, but his classroom experience served him well as he became a popular and expert public speaker.

In his science fiction, Asimov created and refined many of the genre's driving concepts, especially intelligent machines and galactic empires. Over the years, his stories won five Hugo Awards (chosen by fans) and three Nebula Awards (chosen by fellow writers). He is best known for two series of stories and novels, the Foundation Series and the Robot Series, both of which took shape in the 1940's and 1950's.

The Foundation stories concern the collapse and rebirth of a galactic empire in the far future. At the heart of the rebirth is a secret group known as the Foundation, which tries to steer the galaxy out of the dark ages using *psychohistory,* a social science that can predict the actions of large groups of human beings. Logic and rationality, two cornerstones of Asimov's own philosophy, lie at the heart of the Foundation stories. Asimov even referred to his character Hari Seldon, the fictional creator of psychohistory, as his alter ego. In 1966, the trilogy of early Foundation books—*Foundation* (1951), *Foundation and Empire* (1952), and *Second Foundation* (1953)—was awarded a special Hugo as the best all-time science-fiction series.

Equally pivotal for the growth of science fiction was Asimov's Robot Series, in which he explored the consequences of machines capable of humanlike thought and action. Asimov portrayed robots not as evil but as

The author:
Keith Ferrell is the editor of *Omni* magazine.

helpful, trustworthy, and even noble. His science-fiction mysteries *The Caves of Steel* (1954), *The Naked Sun* (1957), and *The Robots of Dawn* (1983), which follow a detective team of a human and a robot, are notable for their depiction of a growing friendship between the two beings. A number of today's computer experts, including artificial-intelligence pioneer Marvin Minsky, cite Asimov's robot stories as their inspiration.

Asimov's nonfiction is as diverse as that of any writer who ever lived, and he essentially founded the field of popular science writing. Among his noteworthy nonfiction books are *Asimov's New Guide to Science* (1984), an introduction to the sciences; *Asimov's Biographical Encyclopedia of Science and Technology* (1964), an enormous collection of biographies of outstanding scientists; *The Human Body* (1963) and *The Human Brain* (1964), substantial introductions to anatomy and physiology; *Understanding Physics* (1966), a three-volume introduction to the subject; *The Collapsing Universe* (1977), an exploration of astronomy and astrophysics; and *Atom* (1991), a guide to elementary particles. Asimov also excelled at writing on a variety of nonscientific subjects, penning volumes on Shakespeare, the Bible, language, history, and even humor. And he wrote many nonfiction books for children and young adults, such as the "How Did We Find Out . . ." series on scientific discovery. In 1985, he received the Children's Book Guild Nonfiction Award for his total contribution to the quality of nonfiction for children.

Writing was virtually the complete focus of Asimov's life. He disliked vacations and rarely took even a day off from his writing. He worked a long day, sitting at his desk by 7:30 a.m. and retiring at about 9 p.m., with only occasional breaks. Asimov never used researchers or assistants, doing all of his own typing and correspondence and even indexing his books himself. And he rewrote his articles only once, largely because of his enthusiasm to move on and inform his readers of something else.

In social causes, Asimov was an outspoken liberal. He frequently expressed his fears about overpopulation, which he saw as the greatest problem facing the world. And he viewed his science writing as a weapon in the constant battle against superstition, ignorance, and prejudice.

Asimov never made great claims for his writing style. "I try only to write clearly," he once said, "and I have the very good fortune to think clearly so that the writing comes out as I think." Yet through his words, Asimov expanded the minds and fired the imaginations of millions of readers. That is a legacy few writers can claim.

For further reading:

Asimov, Isaac. *In Joy Still Felt.* Doubleday, 1980. The second volume of Asimov's autobiography, spanning 1954-78.

Asimov, Isaac. *In Memory Yet Green.* Doubleday, 1979. The first volume of Asimov's autobiography, spanning 1920-54.

Democratic presidential candidate Bill Clinton and his wife, Hillary, exult at a Chicago rally on March 17 after Illinois and Michigan primary victories.

Democratic Party. The presidential election victory of Bill Clinton, Democratic governor of Arkansas, on Nov. 3, 1992, marked only the second time in 24 years that a Democrat had captured the White House. It ended, at least for the moment, a widespread belief that Republicans had achieved a "lock" on the presidency by winning over conservative Democrats in the industrial North while also building solid support in the South and West. Clinton ran strongly in all regions and among all groups.

The Democratic Party also maintained its solid control of Congress, thwarting Republican hopes of achieving significant gains in the House of Representatives. The Republicans did, however, gain 10 seats in the House.

Sensing victory. Six men sought the 1992 Democratic presidential nomination as the year began. All but one had entered the race only after Republican President George Bush began losing the immense popularity he had achieved during the Persian Gulf War of 1991. Bush's popularity in public-opinion polls dropped from about 90 per cent in March 1991 to 51 per cent by late November 1991. Democratic optimism was further fueled by a Republican defeat in a November 1991 special Senate election in Pennsylvania. Bush's handpicked candidate, former two-term governor Richard L. Thornburgh, was trounced by an obscure Democrat, Harris L. Wofford.

The candidates. Early excitement in the campaign for the Democratic nomination was generated by the first candidate to enter the race, former Senator Paul E. Tsongas of Massachusetts. Tsongas, who had announced his candidacy in April 1991, captured the imagination of many in both parties by arguing for hard choices, including tough restraints on federal spending and a 50-cent-a-gallon hike in federal gasoline taxes, to deal with record federal budget deficits. "No more Santa Claus," he cried.

Joining Tsongas in the Democratic quest were Clinton, a five-term governor; Senator Tom Harkin of Iowa, a populist closely identified with organized labor; Senator Robert Kerrey of Nebraska, a former governor of that state and a hero of the Vietnam War (1957-1975); L. Douglas Wilder of Virginia, the nation's first elected black governor; and Edmund G. (Jerry) Brown, Jr., former governor of California.

Before the first party primary, Clinton came under attack for alleged marital infidelities in the past and for avoiding the military draft during the Vietnam War, which he had opposed. Clinton and his wife, Hillary, responded that they had experienced marital problems in the past but had surmounted them. On the draft, Clinton made a series of statements, some contradictory, over a period of months in an effort to explain his actions. Republicans and some Democratic rivals hammered away at him on both counts. In the fall campaign against Bush, Clinton's draft record and marriage problems were lumped together as "the character issue."

Primary battles. Harkin, as expected, easily won the Feb. 10, 1992, Iowa caucuses. Clinton, expected to win the February 18 New Hampshire primary, the party's first, was upset by Tsongas, who collected 35 per cent of the vote to Clinton's 26 per cent. Kerrey was third at 12 per cent, followed by Harkin and Brown. Wilder had abandoned his candidacy on January 8.

Tsongas won again at the February 23 Maine caucuses, but by a bare percentage point over Brown—30 per cent to 29 per cent. Brown, who ran 14 percentage points ahead of Clinton, preached an antiestablishment message and called for a "flat tax" to replace the graduated federal income tax. Two days later it was Kerrey's turn in the winner's circle. In the South Dakota primary, he got 40 per cent of the vote to Harkin's 25, Clinton's 19, and Tsongas' 10. As the race heated up, Clinton and Tsongas traded insults, as if it were a two-man race. On March 3, Clinton topped Tsongas in Georgia, Tsongas beat Clinton in Maryland, and Brown narrowly bested both in Colorado.

March 10 was "Super Tuesday," with primaries or caucuses in 11 states. Clinton won 8, including Florida and Texas. Tsongas carried Delaware, Massachusetts, and Rhode Island. These results narrowed the field to Clinton, Tsongas, and Brown, with the Arkansas governor claiming a commanding lead in Democratic convention delegates. On March 19, Tsongas withdrew from the race. Brown stuck it out, but Clinton could not be stopped. He clinched the nomination on June 2 with victories in California and five other states.

Democratic National Convention. The Democratic convention in New York City from July 13 to 16 was, for the normally combative party, exceptionally harmonious. Although Clinton failed to inspire unbridled enthusiasm, the party looked ahead with optimism to the November election and warmly greeted Clinton's choice for Vice President, Senator Albert A. Gore, Jr., of Tennessee. Clinton got a big lift from the convention and from a July 16 announcement by independent candidate Ross Perot that Perot was abandoning his campaign, in part because of a "revitalized" Democratic Party.

The final sprint. Clinton enjoyed double-digit leads in the polls through much of the fall campaign as he criticized the Bush record on the economy, touted his own economic recovery and health-care plans. He accused the Republicans of espousing a failed policy of "trickle down" economics.

But the presidential race tightened in the final two weeks of the campaign. Factors included the hammering Clinton took on the "character" issue, Republican claims that he would boost middle class taxes, and the return of Perot as an active candidate in October. Nonetheless, Clinton won easily, collecting 370 electoral votes to 168 for Bush and none for Perot.

Frank Cormier and Margot Cormier

See also **Elections; Republican Party.** In the World Book Supplement section, see **Clinton, Bill.** In ***World Book,*** see **Democratic Party.**

Denmark in 1992 threw a roadblock across plans of the 12-nation European Community (EC or Common Market) for rapid economic and political union. In a national referendum on June 2, Danish voters rejected the so-called Maastricht Treaty, the EC's blueprint for closer political and economic integration, including a single currency by the end of the 1990's. Opponents of the treaty outnumbered supporters by 50.7 per cent to 49.3 per cent, a margin of some 46,000 votes. Because the treaty must be ratified by all EC members to take effect, the rejection threw the EC into turmoil.

Many Danes who voted against ratification opposed relinquishing national control over defense and economic policies to a central EC government. Opponents also charged that Denmark, one of the smallest EC nations, would be overwhelmed by its stronger neighbors in the community, particularly Germany. Supporters of the treaty argued that Denmark could not afford to be left out of a united Europe, especially if neighboring Finland, Norway, and Sweden were admitted to the EC. Many proponents of ratification said after the vote that they had failed to fully explain the provisions of the complex, 400-page treaty to voters.

Danish politicians, virtually all of whom had supported ratification, were taken by surprise at the voting results. In May, the Folketing (parliament) had approved the treaty by 120 votes to 25.

A second chance. EC legal experts said that the Maastricht Treaty seemed to have no provision for excluding an EC member from the union, and that the treaty could take effect only if Denmark reversed its rejection. On September 22, Danish Prime Minister Poul Schlüter announced that Denmark would hold a second referendum in mid-1993. But Schlüter said he would press other EC nations to change the treaty to make it more acceptable to Danish voters. He proposed that the EC strengthen the separation of powers between member states and the EC government. He also demanded that Denmark be allowed to opt out of certain provisions of the pact.

Other EC leaders rejected these demands. They said Schlüter's proposals would amount to rewriting the treaty and would threaten the intricate compromises that had gone into shaping the treaty, which was approved in December 1991.

As the EC's December 1992 summit approached, EC leaders began suggesting they might legally move ahead on union without Denmark and Great Britain. (Britain had put off submitting the treaty to Parliament until after Denmark's second referendum.) But that threat faded when, at the summit on December 12 and 13, the EC agreed to exempt Denmark from any common currency and common defense system. It also adopted a declaration affirming that the EC would act only in matters that national governments were not better able to handle. Philip Revzin

See also **Europe** (Facts in brief table). In ***World Book,*** see **Denmark**.

Detroit residents on Nov. 5, 1992, were shocked by the news that a black motorist, Malice W. Green, had been beaten to death by Detroit police officers. The incident seemed almost a replay of the 1991 Los Angeles case in which four white policemen were videotaped beating a black motorist, Rodney G. King.

The day after Green's death, Police Chief Stanley Knox suspended seven officers without pay for their alleged participation in the killing. On Nov. 16, 1992, the Wayne County prosecutor's office filed charges against four of the seven. Officers Larry Nevers and Walter Budzyn were charged with second-degree murder. Sergeant Freddie Douglas was charged with involuntary manslaughter and willful neglect of duty, but the manslaughter charge was later dropped. Officer Robert Lessnau was charged with aggravated assault. Nevers, Budzyn, and Lessnau are white. Douglas is black.

The four officers pleaded not guilty. On December 16, they were all fired from the police force.

According to witnesses and investigators, Green, age 35, was stopped outside a suspected *crack house* (a house where crack cocaine is sold) by Nevers and Budzyn. The two officers allegedly began beating Green on the head with metal flashlights after he failed to comply with their order to open his hand. They had evidently suspected Green of concealing drugs in his clenched fist. While the beating was in progress, the other officers arrived on the scene.

New Detroit Tigers owner. On August 24, major league baseball owners approved the sale of the Detroit Tigers to Michael Ilitch, owner of the Little Caesar's Pizza chain, for a reported $80 million to $85-million. The former owner, Thomas Monaghan, president of Domino's Pizza, Incorporated, had said he would move the team elsewhere if the city did not agree to build a new stadium for the Tigers.

Ilitch, who also owns the Detroit Red Wings hockey team and is a major city booster, had said he would study the issue of building a new stadium but wanted to keep the franchise in Detroit. A new stadium could cost as much as $200 million. In an April referendum, voters rejected the idea of spending tax dollars for a stadium.

School strike. A bitter four-week teachers' strike, the second longest in the city's history, idled more than 168,000 public school students before it was settled on September 26. The teachers won a 4 per cent pay raise, a settlement that school-district administrators said could lead to the loss of 250 teaching jobs as the financially troubled system tries to pay for the salary increases. During the strike, a circuit court judge had ordered the teachers to return to work, but they ignored the order.

Police chief convicted. A federal court jury on May 7 convicted former Police Chief William L. Hart of embezzling $2.6 million from a taxpayer account used to fund undercover police operations. Prosecutors said that from 1982 to 1989, Hart funneled money to dummy corporations set up by a former civilian deputy police chief, Kenneth Weiner. Hart, 68, who had headed the police department from 1976 to 1991, was the longest-serving chief in Detroit history.

According to testimony at his trial, Hart lavished gifts, trips, and thousands of lottery tickets on three female friends during the years he was accused of stealing from the city. After his conviction, he filed documents in federal court claiming he was broke.

On Aug. 27, 1992, United States District Court Judge Paul Gadola sentenced Hart to the maximum sentence for his crime, 10 years in prison. The judge also ordered Hart to repay the stolen money. To help pay off the fine, federal officials seized Hart's $53,000 annual pension and nearly $200,000 in back pay and benefits he was to receive from the city.

New housing. The city's first new single-family housing development in 30 years opened in March amid cheers and controversy. Houses in the 156-unit project, costing an average of about $100,000 each, were quickly snapped up by buyers. But critics of the development claimed that it would be a losing proposition. They pointed out that Detroit spent nearly $19.4 million to clear the land, dig foundations and basements, and do other site work, though the houses will produce only $300,000 in property taxes each year for city coffers. Constance C. Prater

See also **City**. In ***World Book,*** see **Detroit**.

Dinosaur. See **Paleontology**.

Disabled. The first phase of the Americans with Disabilities Act of 1990 (ADA) went into effect on Jan. 26, 1992. As of that date, businesses open to the public, such as stores, hotels, and restaurants, and employing more than 25 people had to make reasonable efforts to remove structures on their premises that might be barriers to the disabled. On July 26, companies with 25 or fewer employees and annual revenues of $1 million had to comply with these provisions.

ADA is a federal civil rights law that applies to a wide range of disabilities. ADA covers a person with a physical or mental condition that "substantially limits one or more . . . major life activities," such as walking, seeing, and hearing. An estimated 43 million Americans meet one of these definitions of disability, according to the President's Committee on Employment of People with Disabilities.

ADA's provisions also affect private-sector employment. Under ADA provisions, a person may not be denied employment because of a disability if he or she can perform the essential functions of the job with or without *reasonable accommodation.* Reasonable accommodation is equipment or help that does not impose an undue hardship, such as excessive cost, on the employer.

A disabled person also must not be discriminated against in terms of promotion, pay, or training due to his or her disability. These provisions went into effect on July 26 for companies with 25 or more employees. Compliance for firms with 15 to 24 workers was scheduled to begin in July 1994. Firms with fewer than 15 workers are exempt.

The new law also mandates access to mass transportation, such as buses and trains, and to telecommunications. The disabled in wheelchairs must be able to use public transportation by various target dates, depending on the type of transit system. For example, new equipment for bus, train, and subway service had to be accessible by Jan. 26, 1992, and most railroads must have at least one accessible car per train by 1995. By July 1993, ADA requires that telephone companies provide relay services so that people who are hearing- or voice-impaired can use ordinary telephones to communicate.

Future legal challenges. Some small businesses voiced complaints that ADA's language was vague and would spawn endless lawsuits. For example, undue hardship could have different meanings for employers, depending upon how well a company did financially. But disability rights advocates countered that ADA's provisions were drawn largely from existing civil rights laws, which formed ample precedent for defining ADA's requirements.

Because the provisions of ADA are scheduled to take effect at varying times—up to 30 years in the future—the first lawsuits challenging specific aspects of the law or seeking clarification will probably not be brought for several years. Paul K. Longmore

In ***World Book,*** see **Disabled.**

Disasters. The worst natural disaster of 1992 was a powerful earthquake that struck eastern Indonesia on December 12. The epicenter of the quake was near the town of Maumere on Flores Island. The quake and the huge tidal waves it triggered killed at least 2,500 people.

Disasters that resulted in 25 or more deaths in 1992 include the following:

Aircraft crashes

January 20—Near Mount Sainte-Odile, France. A French Airbus A-320, en route from Lyon to Strasbourg, crashed in snow and fog. After a four-hour search by rescuers, 9 survivors were found among the 96 passengers and crew on board the aircraft.

February 9—Near Diouloulou, Senegal. The pilot of a chartered plane that was carrying tourists to a Club Med resort apparently mistook the lights in a hotel garden for a landing strip, and the resulting plane crash killed 30 of the 56 people aboard.

March 22—New York City. A USAir jetliner crashed on take-off from La Guardia Airport, bursting into flames, and landing in Flushing Bay. Of the 51 crew and passengers, 27 died, including the pilot. The incident led to the issuing of new regulations by the Federal Aviation Administration regarding procedures for deicing the wings of an aircraft.

April 26—Near Saveh, Iran. A plane chartered by Iran's national oil company crashed, killing all 39 passengers and crew aboard.

June 6—Near La Palma, Panama. A Panamanian airliner crashed in stormy weather, killing all 47 people on board.

July 20—Near Tbilisi, Georgia. A cargo plane crashed in a suburb of Tbilisi, capital of Georgia, killing 40 people, including 30 on the ground.

July 25—Near Pattimura, Indonesia. An Indonesian passenger plane crashed into a hillside while attempting to land in a fog, killing all 71 aboard.

July 31—Nanjing, China. A Chinese airliner crashed and exploded on take-off. The New China News Agency reported that 100 people died, but China's state-run television said that 106 people were killed.

July 31—Near Katmandu, Nepal. A Thai Airways jetliner crashed into a mountain in the Himalaya, killing all 113 people on board.

September 27—Lagos, Nigeria. A military transport plane crashed shortly after take-off, killing all 163 aboard.

September 28—Katmandu, Nepal. A Pakistani International Airlines plane smashed into a hillside while attempting to land. All 167 people aboard died.

October 4—Amsterdam, the Netherlands. An Israeli cargo jet lost power in two engines on take-off and crashed into an apartment complex in a suburb of Amsterdam. All three crew members and the sole passenger were killed. Initial reports placed the death toll in the residential complex, which burst into flames, in the hundreds. But Amsterdam police later revised the death toll to an estimated 63 people.

October 18—Near Bandung, Indonesia. An airliner carrying 31 people crashed into a mountain as it approached Bandung on the island of Java, killing all aboard.

A series of explosions in Guadalajara, Mexico, in April leave a deep trench where the sewer system ran. The explosions killed at least 191 people.

November 24—Near Guilin, China. A China Southern Airlines flight crashed into a mountain as it approached Guilin, China, a popular tourist stop because of its scenic mountains, killing all 141 people aboard.

December 21—Faro, Portugal. Fifty-four people were killed in a crash of a Dutch jumbo jet, which broke apart and burst into flames as it slammed into a runway. Portuguese government officials said 282 people, mostly holiday travelers, survived the crash.

December 22—Near Souk al Sabt, Libya. A domestic flight of a Libyan Boeing 727 from the city of Benghazi crashed as it approached Tripoli, the Libyan capital, killing all 157 people aboard. Authorities said they were investigating reports by witnesses who said that the airliner collided with a Libyan military aircraft.

Earthquakes

March 13, 15—Eastern Turkey. A powerful earthquake devastated the city of Erzincan, reducing much of the central part of the city to rubble and killing at least 500 people. A second quake followed on March 15 about 40 miles (64 kilometers) south of Erzincan, raising the death toll for all of eastern Turkey to at least 1,000 people.

August 19—Kyrgyzstan, near the border with China. At least 50 people were killed in a region hit by 186 tremors caused by a powerful earthquake.

September 1—Nicaragua's Pacific coast. A major undersea earthquake, measuring 7.0 on the Richter scale, created tidal waves up to 50-feet (15-meters) high that swept along a 150-mile (240-kilometer) stretch of Nicaragua's Pacific coast, killing at least 116 people and leaving thousands homeless as several villages were destroyed.

October 12—Cairo, Egypt. The strongest earthquake to hit Egypt since 1969 struck Cairo, the capital, and the suburb of Giza to the south, killing 543 people and injuring more than 6,500. Officials said that although the quake was moderate in strength, measuring 5.9 on the Richter scale, the death toll was high due to Cairo's dense population and poorly constructed buildings. More than 200 of the fatalities were schoolchildren, many of whom were trampled to death as they attempted to flee their schools.

December 12—Flores Island, Indonesia. A powerful earthquake centered near the town of Maumere on the eastern part of Flores Island killed an estimated 2,500 people. The quake triggered huge tidal waves called tsunamis, some as high as 80 feet (24 meters), that swept through coastal villages. The United States Geological Survey reported that the quake measured 7.5 on the Richter scale of magnitude.

Explosions and fires

March 24—Dakar, Senegal. A truck filled with liquid ammonia exploded at a peanut-processing factory, killing at least 60 people.

April 22—Guadalajara, Mexico. A series of explosions ripped through the city's sewer system, killing at least 191 people. The explosions were apparently caused by a leaking gasoline pipeline. On April 27, Mexican police arrested nine officials on charges of negligent homicide. Among those arrested were four officials of Pemex, the national oil company, who were responsible for maintaining the gasoline pipeline that reportedly caused the explosions.

June 17—Near Matruh, Egypt. A military bus and a fuel-oil tanker collided and caught fire, reportedly killing 42 soldiers and 6 civilians.

Landslides and avalanches

February 1-3—Southeastern Turkey. Several avalanches of snow killed at least 178 people in mountain villages, including 106 soldiers who had been sent to fight separatist Kurdish guerrillas.

March 18—Belo Horizonte, Brazil. A landslide buried part of a hillside shantytown, killing at least 30 people.

July 9—Near Loja, Ecuador. A mudslide engulfed a bus and carried it into a river, killing all 49 passengers aboard.

December 8—Llipi, Bolivia. Heavy rains caused a mudslide that covered the gold mining camp of Llipi, killing at least 153 people.

Mine disasters

March 3—Kozlu, Turkey. A methane gas explosion in a coal mine killed at least 265 miners.

May 9—Plymouth, Nova Scotia. An explosion of methane gas killed 26 coal miners at the Westray Mine.

June 9—Krasnodon, Ukraine. At least 43 coal miners were killed when an explosion sent clouds of deadly carbon monoxide gas through the mine pit.

Shipwrecks

March 8—Gulf of Thailand. At least 87 people died when a ferry crowded with Buddhist pilgrims collided with an oil tanker.

July 19—Off Source Matelas, Haiti. About 90 Haitian refugees drowned when their boat capsized shortly after launch.

September 20—Strait of Malacca, Indonesia. Forty-three crewmen were believed dead after a container ship and an oil tanker collided, and both ships burst into flames.

Storms and floods

September 11-16—Northern and eastern Pakistan and northern India. Three days of monsoon rains caused rivers to flood, including the Indus River, killing at least 2,500 people in the worst flooding in Pakistan's history. Floodgates were opened to relieve pressure on dams, devastating hundreds of towns. Most of the deaths occurred in Pakistan. About 500 people died in India. More than 1 million people in Pakistan were left homeless, and officials estimated damage to property and infrastructure at approximately $2 billion.

September 22-26—Southern France. Flash floods and flooding from swollen rivers, a result of torrential rains, caused the deaths of 41 people, including 21 people who were killed in Vaison-la-Romaine when water and mud swept through the town.

November 11-15—Southern India. Torrential rains resulting in floods and mudslides killed more than 230 people in southern India. Rod Such

Djibouti. See **Africa.**

Dog. The American Kennel Club (AKC) reported in 1992 that 1,379,544 dogs of 134 breeds were registered in 1991 alone. Cocker spaniels, which had led the number of registrations for several years, fell to second place. Labrador retrievers led the list with 105,876 registered.

The AKC and dog fanciers joined in fighting a proposed ordinance in San Mateo County, California, that sought the neutering of all cats and dogs over age 6 months. The final ruling allowed residents to keep nonneutered animals by paying a small fee.

A female wire fox terrier, Champion Registry's Lonesome Dove, won her 83rd Best-in-Show at the Westminster Kennel Club Show at New York City's Madison Square Garden in February. Marion and Samuel Lawrence of Orlando, Fla., owned the dog. Melbourne T. Downing of Timonium, Md., judged her.

Champion Pencloe Dutch Gold, a whippet, defeated 20,000 dogs of 166 breeds to win Best-in-Show at the Crufts show. The annual event was held in Birmingham, England, in January.

The AKC held a televised National Invitational Championship Show on April 7 in Baltimore. The top winner in each breed plus National Specialty winners were invited, and 325 accepted. A Lakeland terrier, Champion Black Watch Sophie Tucker, won Best-in-Show. Roberta Vesley

Dominican Republic. See **Latin America.**

Drought. See **Water; Weather.**

Drug abuse. Statistics released in May 1992 by the United States Department of Health and Human Services showed that for three straight quarters, hospitals in 21 U.S. cities reported an increase in the number of people receiving emergency room treatment for cocaine and heroin abuse. According to the statistics, 27,000 people were treated in emergency rooms for cocaine abuse from October through December 1991, a 13 per cent increase from the previous three-month period and a 46 per cent jump from the same period in 1990. The number of treated heroin abusers rose to 10,364 during the last quarter of 1991, representing a 10 per cent increase from the previous quarter and a 24 per cent increase from 1990.

The overall number of drug users remained fairly steady in 1991, according to a January 1992 report from the U.S. National Institute on Drug Abuse (NIDA). The NIDA annual household survey found that the number of people age 12 to 17 who currently (within the previous 30 days) used any type of illicit drug had decreased to 6.8 per cent in 1991 from 8.1 per cent in 1990. Young adults aged 18 to 25 currently using drugs increased to 15.4 per cent from 14.9 per cent, and adults over age 26 using drugs stayed about the same at 4.5 per cent. Based on NIDA estimates, marijuana remained the most popular illegal drug, having close to 10 million current users.

Drug use among students. The annual survey done for the NIDA by the University of Michigan

Institute for Social Research in Ann Arbor showed a continuing decline in illegal drug use among high school seniors. In the survey, reported in January 1992, 15,483 seniors were questioned on their drug use. The percentage of students who reported using illicit drugs during 1991 dropped to 29.4 per cent from 32.5 per cent in 1990. Marijuana use in 1991 decreased to 23.9 per cent from 27 per cent in 1990, and cocaine use declined to 3.5 per cent from 5.3 per cent. While these reductions appeared small, they were part of a steady downward trend.

The Michigan survey also indicated a decline in alcohol use. Seniors who in 1991 reported using alcohol during the month prior to the survey dropped to 54 per cent from 57.1 per cent in 1990. Students engaging in binge drinking (five or more drinks in a row during the previous two weeks) declined to 29.8 per cent from 32.2. But the number of daily drinkers stayed about the same at 3.6 per cent.

Seniors who reported smoking cigarettes during the month prior to the survey decreased to 28.3 per cent from 29.4 per cent in 1990. In spite of the well-publicized health risks of smoking, adolescent cigarette use had changed little since 1980.

A separate Michigan survey of college students also revealed declining drug use in most categories. But use of LSD, a powerful hallucinogen, rose to 5 per cent in 1991 from 4 per cent in 1990. David C. Lewis

In ***World Book,*** see **Drug abuse.**

Drugs. The United States Food and Drug Administration (FDA) in June 1992 approved a new drug for fighting AIDS. The drug, known as DDC, joins AZT and DDI as the only approved AIDS drugs. (See **AIDS**.)

New prostate drug. A new drug for treating enlargement of the prostate gland was approved by the FDA in June. This often painful condition, which creates pressure on the bladder and causes difficulties in urination, afflicts about one-fourth of all American men over age 50 and about 15 million men in total. Previously, surgery was the only approved treatment.

The new drug, called finasteride and marketed as Proscar by Merck and Company of Rahway, N.J., is the first medication that actually shrinks the prostate gland. The FDA said that Proscar can reduce prostate size by about 25 per cent in patients treated for 12 months. But studies also showed that not all patients benefit from the drug, and patients must often take the drug for several months before they experience any relief. In addition, patients must take Proscar daily for their entire lives to maintain the shrinkage. The FDA said there were no significant adverse effects from the drug.

Chicken pox drug. A drug capable of reducing the duration and severity of chicken pox, a viral disease that affects about 3.5 million Americans each year, was approved by the FDA in February. The drug, called acyclovir and marketed as Zovirax by Burroughs Wellcome Company of London, prevents the chicken pox virus from replicating. It is the first drug to attack the cause of the disease and not merely treat the symptoms, which include a fever and an itchy rash. The FDA said Zovirax begins to alleviate symptoms by the second day after the rash appears. But officials added that infected persons undergoing treatment with the drug can still spread the disease.

Help for cystic fibrosis. Researchers in March and May reported that a drug developed through genetic engineering appears to be effective in fighting the lung disorder known as cystic fibrosis. Cystic fibrosis is a genetic disease in which the lungs become clogged with a thick mucus, leading to breathing difficulties and bacterial infections. About 30,000 Americans suffer from the illness, according to the Cystic Fibrosis Foundation. Standard treatment for the disease consists mainly of administering antibiotic drugs to help prevent infections and pounding on the chests and backs of patients to loosen the mucus build-up.

The new drug, called DNase, is a copy of a protein that occurs naturally in humans, where its job is to cut up unwanted deoxyribonucleic acid (DNA), the hereditary material in cells. Scientists developed the drug by isolating the specific segment of human DNA that contains the genetic code for the protein, then putting the segment into the DNA of fast-growing bacteria to mass-produce the protein in a laboratory.

DNase is inhaled in a nasal spray. When the drug reaches the lungs, it chops up the DNA of white blood cells that have died while fighting infection. This DNA constitutes up to 50 per cent of the mucus in the lungs, so the activity of DNase substantially loosens the mucus. In a preliminary trial, patients who received DNase reported a 10 to 20 per cent improvement in lung function within 24 hours. DNase's manufacturer, Genentech Incorporated, located in South San Francisco, Calif., said it hoped to file for FDA approval for DNase in 1993, after further study.

New drug procedures. President George Bush in October 1992 signed a bill requiring drug companies to pay "user fees" to the FDA to help cover the costs of testing new drugs and to pay for more workers to speed the approval process. The law, the Prescription Drug User Fee Act of 1992, marked the first time that a U.S. regulatory agency was allowed to raise money from private firms to overcome budget crunches.

Under the law, drug companies will pay $100,000 for each new drug application. They will also pay a general annual fee of $50,000, plus an annual fee of $6,000 for each drug already on the market. And those figures were set to more than double by 1997. In return for the fees, which the FDA estimated will total $300 million by 1997, the agency will hire 600 new examiners. The FDA's goal was to cut in half the time for drug reviews. The FDA receives about 100 drug applications each year but expects that number to rise sharply with advances in genetic engineering.

In April 1992, the FDA adopted another set of measures to reduce the backlog of drug applications

A Russian Orthodox priest at a church in Zagorsk sanctifies water, one of many religious rituals suppressed under Communism but revived in 1992.

and to speed patients' access to new drugs. Foremost among the changes was a new "fast track" for drugs to treat life-threatening illnesses such as AIDS. The FDA will permit the marketing of such drugs while final tests are being conducted, so long as officials make a preliminary determination that the drug is safe and effective. And for the first time, the agency said it would use external, nongovernmental organizations to help review drug applications.

Blood-pressure drug warning. Women in the second and third trimesters of pregnancy should not take any of a class of blood-pressure drugs called angiotensin-converting enzyme (ACE) inhibitors, the FDA said in March. Such drugs are prescribed to control high blood pressure. The FDA and manufacturers of ACE inhibitors had previously warned that the drugs could cause harm to the fetus, including kidney failure, deformities of the face and skull, and even death. But the FDA decided that the earlier warnings were insufficient because cases of fetal difficulties linked to the drugs continued to occur. However, the agency cautioned that pregnant women who are taking an ACE inhibitor should consult their doctors before stopping treatment, because uncontrolled high blood pressure can be dangerous to both the mother and the fetus. The FDA said there does not appear to be any risk to fetuses exposed to the drugs in the first trimester. Michael Woods

See also **Medicine.** In ***World Book***, see **Drug.**

Eastern Orthodox Churches. The Serbian Orthodox Church issued an open letter on May 28, 1992, condemning Serbian government policies that it said promoted "fratricidal" fighting among Serbs, Croats, and Muslims in the former republics of Yugoslavia. The Orthodox church has traditionally had close ties to the Serbian government. The bishops also called for the resignation of Serbian President Slobodan Milošević, who was widely blamed for the fighting. Serbia is the dominant republic of a new Yugoslav federation that was proclaimed in April. The bishops cited numerous human rights violations by the Serbian government in joining a call for a boycott of parliamentary elections on May 31. The government claimed that 60 per cent of the electorate voted. On June 28, Patriarch Pavle, head of the Serbian Orthodox Church, marched with more than 100,000 protesters in Belgrade, demanding the ouster of Milošević.

The Church of the Holy Sepulcher in Jerusalem, Israel, suffered theft and violence in 1992. The church is believed to stand on the hill of Calvary, or Golgotha, where Jesus was crucified and buried.

In February, valuable ancient *icons* were stolen from the church. Icons are religious paintings considered sacred in the Eastern Orthodox religion. On May 2, a man broke into the church and smashed many holy objects, damaged the Mount Golgotha shrine, destroyed ancient oil lamps, and tried to dislodge the Holy Cross. He was eventually subdued and arrested.

In July, the Jerusalem city government razed a newly constructed Greek Orthodox church on the Mount of Olives because church officials had failed to get a building permit. There were worldwide protests, and the Greek government lodged a diplomatic protest with the Israeli government. Mayors of many cities in Greece raised funds for rebuilding the church.

Historic meeting. The heads of 13 *autocephalous* (independent) Orthodox Christian churches worldwide met together for the first time in more than a thousand years in March in Istanbul (Constantinople), Turkey. The Orthodox leaders discussed the failure of Communist ideology, the ecumenical movement, and the need to preserve Earth's environment.

In the United States, five Orthodox churches in March provisionally resumed participation in the National Council of Churches (NCC). The Orthodox churches had suspended relations with the NCC in June 1991 to protest the views of some council member denominations, such as ordaining practicing homosexuals and favoring legalized abortion.

New Ethiopian patriarch. Abuna Paulos was installed patriarch of the Ethiopian Orthodox Church on July 5 in Addis Ababa, Ethiopia. He had been a secretary to Patriarch Abuna Theophilos, who was imprisoned and killed by the Communist government of Mengistu Haile-Mariam shortly after it came to power in 1974. Stanley Samuel Harakas

In *World Book,* see **Eastern Orthodox Churches.**

Economics. The United States economy languished for much of 1992, along with the economies of many other major industrialized nations. Until late November, the economy's growth rate was so slow and unsteady that many observers described it as a continuation of the 1990-1991 recession. Public opinion polls regularly cited the nation's poor economic health as the major concern of Americans throughout 1992. And fear and impatience with the economy appeared to be the main reason why voters on November 3 ousted Republican President George Bush and chose Democratic candidate Governor Bill Clinton of Arkansas as the next President of the United States.

Voters were also concerned with such specific economic questions as the lack of affordable health care and health insurance, the huge federal debt, and the potential loss of jobs to Mexico, Japan, or other foreign countries. Billionaire businessman Ross Perot made a strong independent bid for the presidency, claiming that politics-as-usual had weakened U.S. economic strength and led to the record $290.2-billion deficit in the federal budget for the fiscal year that ended September 30.

Slow growth. The 1992 year was ushered in on a nearly stalled overall economic growth rate. The rate improved to 2.9 per cent during the first quarter but slowed again to 1.5 per cent in the second quarter. Inflation was variously measured in the low 2 per cent to 3 per cent range. In July, the Consumer Confidence

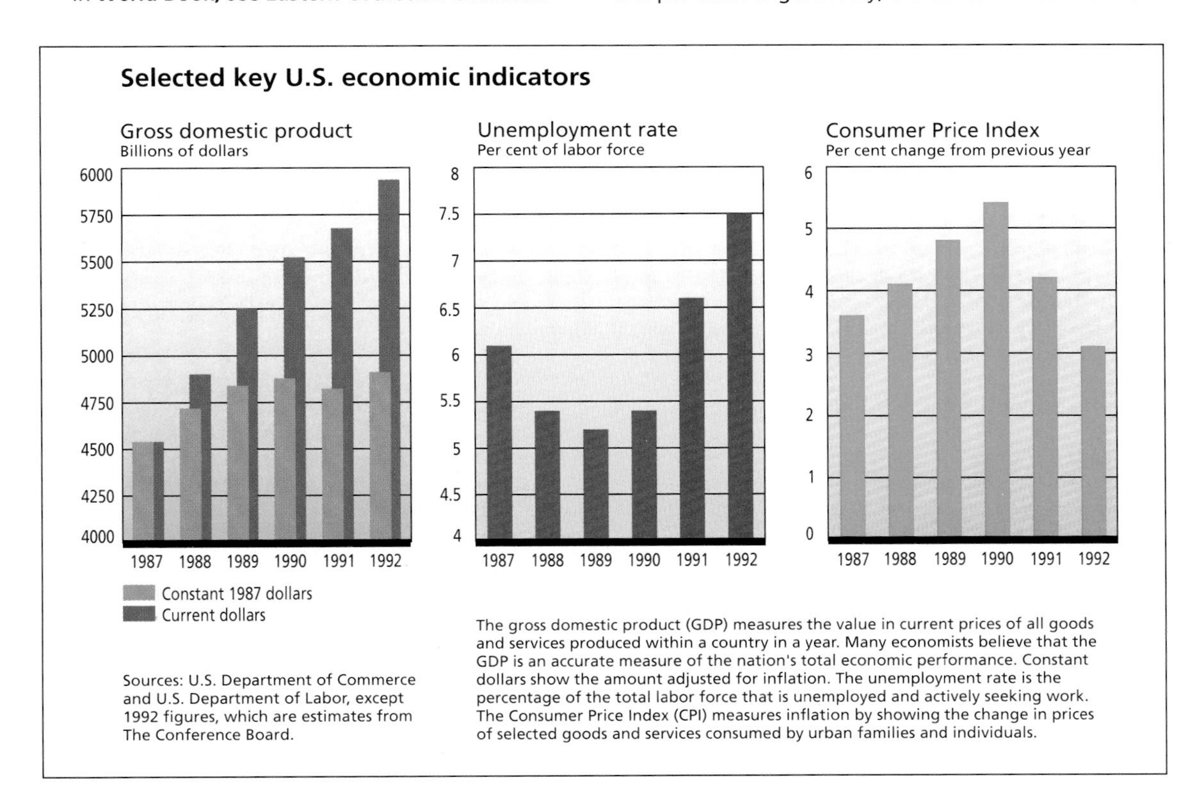

The gross domestic product (GDP) measures the value in current prices of all goods and services produced within a country in a year. Many economists believe that the GDP is an accurate measure of the nation's total economic performance. Constant dollars show the amount adjusted for inflation. The unemployment rate is the percentage of the total labor force that is unemployed and actively seeking work. The Consumer Price Index (CPI) measures inflation by showing the change in prices of selected goods and services consumed by urban families and individuals.

Leaders of the world's advanced industrialized nations gathered in Munich, Germany, in July to discuss the ailing global economy.

Index fell 11.6 points after rising since February. The index measures consumers' perceptions of how well off they will be in the next six months. An index of 100 represented the consumer confidence level in 1985, when the U.S. economy grew moderately.

Just before voters cast their ballots for a new President, preliminary statistics released on October 27 showed that the *gross domestic product* (the total value of all goods and services produced within a country) had risen by 2.7 per cent in the July through September quarter and had actually been expanding, though slowly, since spring 1991. However, various autumn economic reports suggested that the economy had weakened anew.

In November 1992, the U.S. government reported that its index of leading economic indicators fell in September for the third time in four months. Overall factory orders rose, but orders for big-ticket durable goods were decreasing. The October unemployment rate improved to 7.4 per cent from 7.5 per cent in September, but factory jobs continued to decline.

President-elect Clinton held an "economic summit" conference to study the problem before he assumed the presidency. The summit began on December 14, when Clinton met with the heads of major corporations as well as small-business owners, labor officials, and economists to get their ideas for strengthening the economy. However, by then more favorable economic reports had considerably eased fears about the short-term outlook and allowed the conference to focus on long-term needs.

By late November, polls had showed that Americans were more hopeful about the future. Claims for jobless benefits had been declining as employment picked up. Retailers had reported better profits and the overall growth rate for the third quarter was revised to 3.9 per cent.

Rock-bottom interest rates. The Federal Reserve System (the Fed), an independent federal agency that manages the U.S. money supply, continued to push interest rates downward to spur the economy. On July 2, the Fed lowered its official *discount rate* (the interest rate it charges financial institutions) to 3 per cent, the lowest rate since the early 1960's. This led banks to cut their *prime rate* (the interest rate banks charge to their best customers) to 6 per cent. The reduction helped numerous companies and homeowners refinance debts at lower interest rates. However, it also reduced the interest paid on savings accounts.

Despite the incentives that low interest rates provided, debt-laden households and businesses were reluctant to borrow, and credit remained tight as beleaguered banks rebuilt profits. In mid-October, Alan Greenspan, chairman of the Fed's Board of Governors, could not say when the sluggishness would end. A November Fed report labeled the recovery "slow and uneven," with demand falling for aircraft, primary metals, rubber, and plastics.

Production. General Motors Corporation (GM) reflected the nation's economic woes. In December 1991, GM had announced its plan to lay off 74,000 workers and to close 21 plants by 1995. The ailing giant on Oct. 29, 1992, reported a third-quarter loss of $752.9 million for a total loss of more than $7 billion since January 1990. On Oct. 26, 1992, GM Chairman Robert C. Stempel had resigned under pressure.

Major steel manufacturers continued to report losses and layoffs. The airline industry continued to weaken, prompting several airlines to seek mergers with foreign partners. The December 1991 collapse of the Soviet Union brought an end to the arms race—and sharp cutbacks in the defense industry. Freight railroads nationwide endured a June 1992 strike and worker lockout, which Congress quickly ended to limit the broad economic shock the rail problems had started to produce. Overall industrial production declined in June after four months of gains.

In August, the United States, Canada, and Mexico completed negotiations to establish the North American Free Trade Agreement, which would create the world's largest free trade zone. President-elect Clinton said he would support the pact. But U.S. labor groups generally opposed it for fear of losing jobs to Mexico, where wages are often lower. The agreement awaited ratification by the legislatures of all three countries.

Taxes. In January, Bush sent Congress a proposed economic growth plan that featured a capital-gains tax cut and tax breaks for some first-time home buyers, to be paid for with domestic spending cuts. Congress responded in March with a measure outlining a middle-class tax cut, sharper reductions in defense spending, and higher taxes on upper-income taxpayers. Bush vetoed the bill.

World economies. The United States was not alone in its economic doldrums. The International Monetary Fund, an international lending and advising agency to governments, projected in September that worldwide economic growth would be just 1.1 per cent in 1992.

The economic picture was a cloudy one for many countries in 1992. Great Britain continued to be in a recession, Canada experienced little economic growth, and economic slowdowns were felt across most of Western Europe and in Japan. Many of the new and emerging democracies of the former Soviet Union and Eastern Europe encountered economic decline as they made the hard transition to independence and attempted to institute free-market reforms.

Bright spots in the world economy included many developing Asian nations, especially China, and much of Latin America, with the exception of Brazil. Africa's economy grew overall, but weakly. Weak economies abroad further threatened the U.S. economic recovery by endangering export outlets. John Boyd

See also **Consumerism; International trade; Labor; Manufacturing; Stocks and bonds.** In ***World Book,*** see **Economics.**

Ecuador. On Aug. 10, 1992, Sixto Durán Ballén was sworn in for a four-year term as Ecuador's president. Durán, a Republican Unity Party member and former mayor of Quito, Ecuador's capital, made two unsuccessful previous bids for the presidency. He was born in Boston and graduated from Columbia University in New York City. He pledged to liberalize the nation's economy, curb inflation, and continue the war on drug trafficking.

Ecuador quits OPEC. On September 17, Ecuador announced its decision to leave the Organization of Petroleum Exporting Countries (OPEC), the first nation to do so since OPEC was founded in 1960. Durán cited OPEC's oil production limits and its annual $2-million membership fees and said that without limits, Ecuador will be able to double its oil output within a few years. Ecuador formally left OPEC on December 31.

Drug crackdown. In June, Ecuadorean authorities carried out the largest drug raid in the country's history. Police seized an estimated $100 million in assets, including ranches, mansions, bank accounts, and an air taxi service belonging to drug traffickers. They also arrested 51 people on narcotics charges. After studying documents seized in the drug raids, government investigators froze the bank accounts of 176 people, including top officials of the government and armed forces. Nathan A. Haverstock

See also **Latin America** (Facts in brief table). In ***World Book,*** see **Ecuador.**

Education. Mounting frustration with the performance of public schools in the United States led to renewed debate in 1992 over education reforms. A report published in February by the Educational Testing Service of Princeton, N.J., revealed that after a decade of costly reforms, American 9-year-olds placed 3rd among 10 industrialized countries on a test of science skills but only 9th in mathematics. Among 15 nations, American 13-year-olds placed 13th in science and 14th in math.

This and other sobering reports led education officials to ask whether the private sector should receive public money so that it could play a larger role in education. President George Bush continued his campaign for school choice programs, in which parents could use government money to send their children to the school of their choice—public, private, or parochial. In June, Bush proposed a "GI Bill for Children." The plan sought to use federal money already earmarked for education to give $1,000 scholarships, in the form of vouchers, to 500,000 middle- or low-income students.

The U.S. Congress, however, rejected Bush's legislation. Although Bush's proposals passed away with his defeat in the November presidential election, President-elect Bill Clinton said he supported school choice programs for public schools. (See **Education: The Private Education Business.**)

Baltimore plan. In June, school officials in Baltimore announced they were hiring a for-profit compa-

Filmmaker Spike Lee, center, joined a September demonstration for a new cultural center for blacks at the University of North Carolina at Chapel Hill.

ny to manage both the educational and business activities of nine of its most troubled schools—eight elementary schools and one middle school. The school system agreed to pay Education Alternatives Incorporated of Minneapolis, Minn., the same amount of money it would have spent educating the children, about $27 million per year. The five-year contract marked one of the most significant breaks with the nation's long-standing tradition of providing a public education through not-for-profit, government-run institutions.

When Baltimore schools opened in September, the new management encountered friction. Education Alternatives sought to replace and retrain a number of the schools' staff, but the Baltimore Teachers Union objected. Union members boycotted training sessions, picketed, and filed grievances. The dispute was laid to rest after teacher's aides accepted jobs elsewhere in the school system.

Edison Project. In February, Christopher Whittle, chairman of Whittle Communications, announced plans to introduce profit-making into education on a much larger scale than had been done in the past. Whittle said he had hired seven well-known educators, journalists, and businesspeople to develop a national system of 200 for-profit schools by 1996 and 1,000 schools for 2 million students by 2010. The plan, called the Edison Project, would provide elementary and secondary school education as well as day-care and preschool services. Traditionally, for-profit schools have only offered preschool programs, after-school tutoring, or vocational training.

Whittle vowed to keep his schools' tuition equal to the average spending per student in the nation's public schools, which was estimated to be $5,361 for the 1992-1993 school year. He said he would control costs by relying on new classroom technology, increased parental involvement, and administrative efficiency.

Whittle increased both the visibility and credibility of his project by hiring Benno C. Schmidt, Jr., the president of Yale University in New Haven, Conn. Schmidt's announcement in May that he was leaving Yale to head the Edison Project attracted widespread media attention.

Colleges and universities continued to struggle financially in 1992. The boom days of higher education in the 1980's—which were created by large endowments, generous federal support, and double-digit tuition hikes—had faded by 1992. Many schools, public and private alike, had to cut courses, trim enrollment, hike tuition, and cap student aid. As the number of course offerings were cut, reports surfaced on many campuses of students not graduating as scheduled because they were unable to fulfill all their course requirements in time.

Despite cuts of $8 million since 1990, Yale University reported an $8.8-million deficit at the beginning of 1992 and was expecting to be $23 million in the red by the end of the 1992-1993 term. The university's budget problems were made worse by skyrocketing insurance premiums, increasing student-aid applications, and a massive maintenance backlog. The maintenance problem resulted from decades of underinvestment in physical structures that, for example, left one of the world's best libraries without a climate control system.

Attempts by college administrators to scale back their schools' activities and academic offerings to cope with tight budgets in 1992 met with harsh opposition from professors. Such budget troubles and resulting campus tensions at institutions nationwide contributed to a record number of top college presidencies being vacant in 1992. The presidents of Columbia University in New York City, the University of Chicago, Duke University in Durham, N.C., and a number of other prestigious schools resigned or retired during 1992.

Footing the bill. Tuitions continued to rise sharply in 1992, by an average of 7 per cent at private four-year colleges and universities and by 9 per cent at public institutions, according to the College Board. On July 23, Bush signed legislation aimed at helping middle-class college students pay for rapidly rising tuition bills. After 17 months of debate, Congress in July had passed the bill, which will add at least 2.4 million college students to the nearly 6 million who already qualify for federal aid. The bill provides for direct government loans, rather than bank loans, and allows 35 per cent of those receiving the loans to repay them on the basis of their income levels following graduation. In addition, the bill established a new loan program that had no income ceiling and charged a 9 per cent interest rate. Another provision of the bill makes more students eligible for Pell Grants, the largest federal grant program for college students, by increasing the ceiling for family earnings to $42,000 from $30,000.

Attracting students. As the number of college-age students has shrunk through the years, all but a few elite colleges and universities have had to scramble to fill their classrooms. Many have resorted to using videos, telemarketing, and other high-powered selling techniques. Still others have used financial incentives to lure students to their campus, a practice that was frowned upon in the past. An increasing number of schools in 1992 offered "merit" scholarships to students who would not otherwise qualify for financial aid on the basis of need. And some schools raised their financial aid offers to students to lure applicants away from other colleges.

M.I.T. antitrust case. In a September 2 decision in Philadelphia, federal District Court Judge Louis C. Bechtle ruled that the Massachusetts Institute of Technology (M.I.T.) in Cambridge had violated a federal antitrust law by meeting with eight Ivy League schools to share information on student applicants and to determine the types of financial aid packages they would offer. The judge ruled that the schools' meetings, which had gone on for many years, reduced competition for students by fixing prices. M.I.T. vowed to appeal the decision.

The case arose after the U.S. Department of Justice filed suit against the nine schools for antitrust violations. In May, the eight Ivy League schools signed a consent decree in which they admitted no wrongdoing but promised to stop sharing information regarding student financial arrangements. M.I.T. refused to sign the decree and took the case to court. At year-end, the Justice Department was investigating other schools for similar practices.

Teaching and research. Colleges and universities struggled in 1992 to increase the quantity and quality of their professors' teaching. A strong research record, rather than a professor's classroom performance, had carried the most weight in the faculty reward system on the nation's campuses. But then schools were stung by charges that they had raised tuitions excessively while reducing the quality of undergraduate education by encouraging professors to focus on lucrative research projects instead of on teaching. In response, a small but growing number of schools sought to make teaching a higher priority in 1992.

Before retiring in October as president of the nine branches of the University of California, David Gardner instructed the chancellors of eight of the university's campuses to increase their professors' teaching duties over the next three years. In November, Syracuse University in New York adopted new guidelines for awarding tenure to its professors. The requirements placed more emphasis on teaching skills and less on research activities.

Civil rights was also a major issue in higher education in 1992. On June 22, the Supreme Court of the United States ruled against a law in St. Paul, Minn., that made the use of racist or sexist language a criminal offense. In a 9 to 0 ruling, the court decided that the law violated the First Amendment guarantee of the right to free speech. Some observers believed the ruling would affect policies introduced by about 100 colleges and universities to curb "hate speech" against minority groups and might require that many of the codes be scrapped or rewritten.

A June 26 Supreme Court decision marked the first time the court ruled specifically on the issue of desegregation within public colleges and universities. In an 8 to 1 decision in the case of *United States v. Fordice,* the court ruled that the higher education system of Mississippi still retained illegal remnants of segregation and that the state must take steps to eliminate them. The court said that simply permitting black and white students to apply to the state's colleges and universities was an insufficient response to segregation. It added that other factors, such as admissions policies that rely solely on standardized test scores and the existence of almost identical academic programs at historically black and historically white campuses located near each other, "foster segregation." The court did not specifically instruct the state on how to comply with the ruling.

Bias against girls. Girls are discriminated against in the classroom from preschool through high school, according to a February report from the American Association of University Women (AAUW) Educational Foundation in Washington, D.C. Based on research gathered by the Wellesley College Center for Research on Women in Massachusetts, the report concluded that girls receive much less attention than do boys; girls' reports of sexual harassment from boys are increasing; curricula often ignore or stereotype females; many standardized tests contain elements of sex bias; and the gender gap in math is small and declining, while the gap in science remains unchanged.

Enrollment. Nationwide, a record 14.3 million students were expected to attend the nation's colleges and universities in the fall of 1992, according to the U.S. Department of Education. Total elementary and secondary enrollment for the 1992-1993 school year was estimated in September to be 47.6 million, an increase of 600,000 students from 1991.

The nation's education bill for the 1992-1993 academic year was expected to total $445 billion, up 5 per cent from 1991 after taking inflation into account. Spending for all public schools and colleges was estimated to be $363 billion. Spending on private education was estimated to be $82 billion. Thomas Toch

In ***World Book,*** see **Education.**

The Private Education Business

By Thomas Toch

Educators, parents, and politicians are debating whether market forces such as competition can help improve America's schools.

An important debate about the future of American education took shape in the early 1990's. The debate was sparked by attempts at educational reform that blurred the lines between public and private schooling. In 1990, the city of Milwaukee introduced a program—the first of its kind in the nation—that allows some parents to use state funds to send their children to private schools. Then, in 1992, private entrepreneurs began running public schools in Baltimore, with the intent of both operating them better and making a profit.

These experiments have opened a debate about the possibility of a far larger degree of public funding of private education and private involvement in public education in the years ahead. Those who support these developments argue that the nation's system of public education has failed and must be replaced. Those who oppose them say a healthy public school system is essential to a democratic, highly diverse society.

Historically, public schools have helped ensure that all Americans, whatever their background, could fulfill their duties as informed voters in a democracy. They also have helped develop national unity among members of the country's many religious, social, and ethnic groups.

Today, however, many Americans are deeply frustrated with the performance of the nation's public schools. Too many public school stu-

MATHEMATICS

dents, they charge, graduate without the skills they need to be productive workers and informed citizens. Critics cite, for example, what appear to be generally low scores on college entrance examinations, and they point to results of the federally financed National Assessment of Educational Progress (NAEP), often called the "Nation's Report Card." In June 1991, the NAEP revealed that only half of the nation's 12th-graders had a solid grasp of fractions, decimals, and percentages—math concepts usually introduced in the 7th grade. Other studies suggest U.S. students lag behind those in much of Europe and Asia, especially in math and science.

Critics also point out that spending on U.S. public school students is higher than ever. Average spending, in 1990 dollars, increased from about $3,000 per pupil in 1970 to nearly $5,500 in 1992. However, only about 60 per cent of education funding is spent in the classroom. The rest goes toward transportation, maintenance, and other services, as well as the bureaucracies that run the schools at the district level.

Advocates of privatization say their programs could help remedy these problems. They argue that private institutions differ significantly from public schools, where, they say, efficiency and innovation are smothered by bureaucracy, union contracts, and lack of competition among schools. "The [public] schools' most fundamental problems are rooted in the [bureaucratic] institutions . . . by which they are governed," say privatization advocates John E. Chubb and Terry M. Moe, whose 1990 book *Politics, Markets, and America's Schools* helped launch the privatization debate.

Glossary

Choice: A type of educational reform that gives parents some means to choose the schools their children attend.

Privatization: The replacement of a public school system by one involving private institutions or businesses, or the private management of public schools.

Educational voucher: A government-issued certificate that would serve as cash for the purchase of education.

A matter of choice

The most popular privatization plans would give parents the means to choose their children's schools. Making public schools compete for students would, say proponents, force bad or inefficient schools to improve or risk being closed. They also say that allowing such a choice would reduce social inequalities by giving low-income students more freedom to attend private schools, a freedom already enjoyed by students from high-income families.

A choice plan would most likely work by giving government funds to parents in the form of *educational vouchers.* A voucher is simply a certificate that may be used like cash to purchase services (in this case, education), then redeemed for cash by the seller (in this case, the school). A voucher system might be open to all children in a school system, or it might include only students below a certain income level. Vouchers might be usable at any public or private school or only at nonreligious institutions. It is not clear whether a choice plan that included religious schools would violate the constitutional separation of church and state.

A student's choice of schools might also be limited by the worth of the voucher the student received. Tuition at nonreligious private schools ranges from less than $1,000 to $10,000 or more, with an average of about $3,000 for elementary schools and about $6,500 for secondary schools.

The nation's first voucher plan was launched as a pilot project in Milwaukee in 1990. There, the state of Wisconsin has given up to 1 per cent of the city's low-income students each a voucher worth $2,500 annually to

The author:

Thomas Toch is education correspondent for *U.S. News and World Report.*

Value for dollars?

One commonly cited measure of student achievement is the Scholastic Aptitude Test (SAT), a college-entrance examination. Between 1970 and 1992, average SAT scores fell from 460 to 423 on the verbal section and from 488 to 476 on the mathematics section, *below*. Each section has a minimum possible score of 200 and a maximum of 800. The decline in scores may reflect an increasing number of students taking the test who, in the past, might not have considered college a possibility. But critics say the scores are still too low.

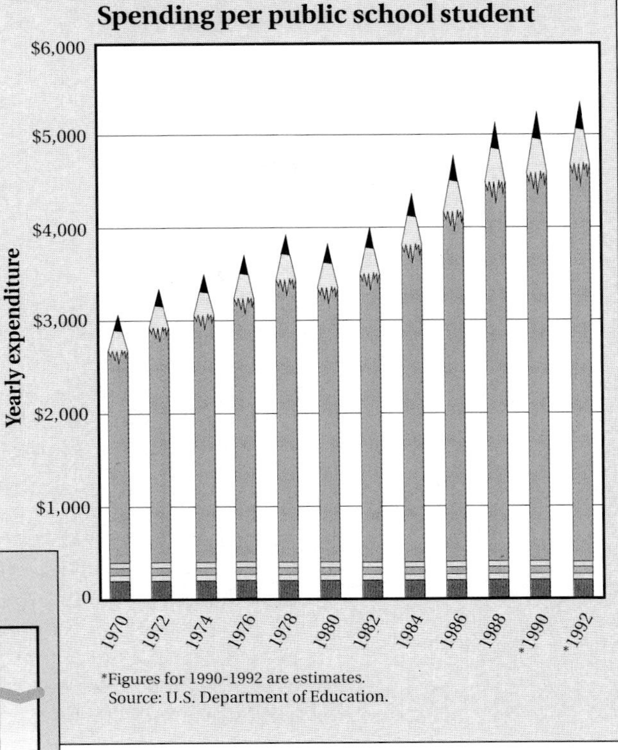

*Figures for 1990-1992 are estimates.
Source: U.S. Department of Education.

Meanwhile, spending on the nation's public school students has been increasing. Average spending, in 1990 dollars, rose from $3,071 per pupil in 1970 to $5,361 in 1992, *above*.

Average SAT scores for college-bound seniors

Score: 500, 480, 460, 440, 420, 400

Math section

Verbal section

*1970, 1972, 1974, 1976, 1978, 1980, 1982, 1984, 1986, 1988, 1990, 1992

*Figures for 1970 and 1971 are estimates.
Source: College Board.

attend nonreligious private schools in the city. After two years, the academic achievement of students in the program—as measured by standardized test scores—had not increased significantly. In addition, the number of students leaving the program was relatively high. Of the students enrolled in the program in the 1991-1992 school year, about 40 per cent chose not to continue in 1992-1993. However, parents of students who remained in the program expressed satisfaction.

During his Administration, Republican President George Bush proposed a number of voucher plans as part of his overall school reform plan, known as America 2000. Like Milwaukee's program, Bush's plans would have limited vouchers to low-income students. None of these plans was passed by Congress.

Voters in some states have considered broader voucher plans. In November 1992, Colorado voters defeated a statewide voucher plan that would have given each of the state's students a voucher worth about $2,100 a year. The vouchers would have been usable at any public or private school, including religious institutions, or for the expenses of *home schooling* (private instruction at home). A campaign to get such a measure on the California ballot fell just short of the necessary signatures.

Some public educators have sought to blunt calls for voucher programs by increasing the choice of schools within a public school system. For example, a number of school districts allow students to attend any public school within the district. As of 1992, 13 states had passed laws allowing students to cross district lines to attend school. By requiring that state aid follow students to their new districts, officials hoped the laws would spur improvements in districts faced with the loss of discontented students and their funding. But by 1992, the statewide programs all had participation rates of less than 2 per cent, in part because the programs did not meet students' transportation needs.

The profit motive—a force for change?

Another side to the privatization debate came to the fore in May 1992, when media entrepreneur Christopher Whittle announced that he had hired Yale University President Benno Schmidt to head a national network of for-profit elementary and secondary schools. Whittle's initiative, known as the Edison Project, faced daunting challenges, including the need to raise about $2.5 billion to build and staff the first schools. But Whittle said he hoped to open 200 institutions by 1996 and enroll 2 million students in 1,000 schools by 2010.

According to Whittle, tuition at Edison Project schools will be no greater than the average spent per public school pupil. The project will also offer scholarships to low-income students. Nevertheless, Whittle claims, his schools will educate students better than the public schools—and make a profit. Whittle argues that minimizing bureaucracy, having computers perform some teaching tasks, and other innovations will permit his system to spend more money in the classroom and spend it more effectively. But Whittle does not discount the possibility that some profits might come from other sources, including the sale of advertising. Whittle has already come under fire for Channel One, his controversial TV news program for schools, which carries advertising. In 1992, Channel One was shown daily to some 40 per cent of the nation's secondary students. But many educators say its use of commercial advertising is in conflict with the educational mission of the schools.

Another for-profit firm, Minnesota-based Education Alternatives, Incorporated, is hoping to prove that applying the profit motive to education can also improve the public schools. In 1991, Education Alternatives became the nation's only for-profit company to help run a public school. That year, the company signed a five-year contract with the Dade County, Florida, school system to draft a curriculum and train teachers at South Pointe Elementary School in Miami Beach.

In July 1992, Education Alternatives signed a five-year contract with the Baltimore school system to operate nine of the city's elementary and middle schools. Under the contract, the company is to manage the schools' financial as well as academic operations. It hopes to increase spending on academics and turn a profit by running the physical side of the schools—their cafeterias, buses, and maintenance—more efficiently. However, at the start of the school year in September, the company faced some protests from parents and teachers. The protesters expressed concern about some of the company's changes, including its replacement of classroom aides with lower-paid interns. The company said the interns, unlike the aides, would all be college graduates.

The grounds for debate

Would privatizing American education benefit the nation's students? Many opponents of the privatization movements charge that introducing competition and the profit motive to the schools might benefit high-achieving students at the expense of their less capable peers. A voucher or other choice plan, they argue, would result in many students being left behind in underfunded public schools, especially in the nation's beleaguered inner-city school systems. They challenge the claim that competition would spur improvement in schools with poor performance records or force them to close. On the contrary, they say, such schools would not close, but they would be unable to improve if faced with an exodus of their better students and the state and federal funding that follows student attendance. Opponents also fear that many students with disabilities or behavioral problems, who are more expensive to educate because they require special facilities and specially trained teachers, would be shunned by private and especially for-profit schools. School choice "will . . . establish two publicly funded school systems, one for the haves and one for the have-nots," says Don Cameron, executive director of the National Education Association (NEA), the nation's largest organization of educators.

Opponents also worry about the temptation of for-profit schools to cut corners, both inside the classroom and out. For-profit educators counter that they are highly accountable to parents. By cutting corners, they say, they would risk losing their clients and their profits.

The privatization movement also raises the philosophical question: Is there even a need for public education? Many argue that education is essentially a private matter. They say that government control of education limits the ability of parents to choose the education they believe is best for their children. But others argue that public education serves important public purposes—in particular, forging common bonds among one of the world's most ethnically diverse peoples. Moreover, they say, by privatizing education, the government would be abandoning its traditional role in ensuring that all citizens receive an education that is at least adequate for their functioning in the modern world.

Would an educational system that includes for-profit management of public schools and a wide range of private school alternatives serve the public interest? Or would such a system increase the fragmentation of society and the social, economic, and political segregation of its people by race and class? Ultimately, the privatization movement challenges some long-held beliefs about education and raises the question of whether common schooling is necessary for the common good.

Egypt. In early 1992, Egypt's President Hosni Mubarak tried to promote Islamic values in an unsuccessful attempt to reduce tensions between the government and Islamic fundamentalists, who believe Islamic law should be the basis of Egypt's legal system. The government's tolerant attitude toward nonviolent Islamic groups was also seen as an effort to improve Egypt's human rights record, which was strongly criticized by human rights groups. By March, however, Mubarak had adopted a harsher policy as violence by militants increased.

Violence in the south. One focus of the unrest was southern Egypt, where Islamic radicals clashed with both Coptic Christians and government forces. Leaders of the Coptic Christian community, which makes up almost 10 per cent of Egypt's population of 55.8 million, charged that violent attacks by Islamic radicals were forcing members of their community to leave the south. Those who remained claimed they were no longer able to practice their religion freely.

In the worst episode of civil violence in Egypt since 1981, Islamic radicals on May 4, 1992, ambushed and killed 12 Coptic Christian farmers in the town of Manshiet Nasser, about 130 miles (210 kilometers) south of Cairo, Egypt's capital. The radicals also murdered a doctor and a teacher. By December, at least 78 people, including security forces, Copts, and Muslims, had died in the violence.

Crackdown. In May, the government deployed thousands of security troops in southern Egypt and jailed hundreds of suspected militants. In response, Islamic radicals mounted a campaign to cripple Egypt's $3-billion tourism industry, the nation's largest source of foreign revenue, by attacking foreign tourists. In October and November, radicals killed a British tourist and wounded eight other tourists. In December, an Egyptian official said tourism had fallen by 40 per cent because of the attacks.

In mid-December, the government mounted its largest crackdown on Islamic militants in more than 10 years. About 14,000 security troops swept through a fundamentalist neighborhood in Cairo, arresting more than 600 suspected militants.

Author killed. Farag Fouda, a writer and outspoken critic of radical Islam, was gunned down on June 8 outside his office in Cairo. Police charged a member of Islamic Holy War, an outlawed fundamentalist group, with Fouda's murder.

Antiterrorism bill. A law passed by the People's Assembly, Egypt's parliament, on July 16 extended police powers and approved the death penalty for terrorism. Some human rights advocates criticized the bill because its broad definition of terrorism included less serious acts, such as disrupting the public order.

Earthquake. More than 540 people died when the strongest earthquake to rock Egypt since 1969 hit parts of Cairo and devastated a suburb on Oct. 12, 1992. The quake, which measured 5.9 on the Richter scale, also injured more than 6,500 people. Islamic fundamentalists condemned the government for responding inadequately to the crisis.

U.S. relations. Anger at the slow pace of Arab-Israeli peace talks and opposition to certain U.S. policies in the Middle East fueled the rise of anti-American feelings among Egyptians. Concerned that such sentiments were threatening Egypt's stability, Mubarak in March expressed reservations about an air and arms embargo against Libya sought by the United States and other Western nations. (See **Libya.**) In August, Mubarak also argued that the establishment of a protected zone in southern Iraq for that country's Shiite Muslims, prompted by U.S. pressure, could lead to the breakup of Iraq and greater regional turmoil.

Economic woes. Western nations remained critical of Egypt's economic policies, despite Mubarak's efforts to institute some economic reforms, including the elimination of some consumer subsidies. Egypt, which had a foreign debt of more than $29 billion in 1992, yearly spends $4 billion to import food. The trade deficit for fiscal year 1990-1991 was $7.5 billion. Unemployment was estimated at 20 per cent.

Egyptian-Israeli meeting. Israel's newly elected Prime Minister Yitzhak Rabin met Mubarak on July 21, 1992, in Cairo for the first Egyptian-Israeli summit since 1986. Mubarak accepted an invitation to visit Israel, though no date was set. Christine Helms

See also **Middle East** (Facts in brief table). In ***World Book,*** see **Egypt**.

Elections. Democrat Bill Clinton, five-term governor of Arkansas, was elected 42nd President of the United States on Nov. 3, 1992. Clinton defeated the incumbent, Republican President George Bush, by an Electoral College landslide but by only five percentage points in the popular vote. Clinton, however, received less than a majority of the popular vote. Political analysts said he would almost certainly have won a popular majority had it not been for the exceptionally strong showing of an independent candidate, Dallas billionaire Ross Perot. Clinton was the first person born after World War II (1939-1945) to be elected to the presidency.

The presidential vote. Clinton carried 32 states, received 44.9 million votes, representing 43 per cent of the popular vote, and an impressive 370 electoral votes. Bush carried 18 states, received 39.1 million votes, representing 37.5 per cent of the popular vote, and 168 electoral votes. Perot received 19.7 million votes—18.9 per cent of the popular vote—the highest proportion for an independent since former President Theodore Roosevelt ran as the "Bull Moose" candidate in 1912. But Perot did not carry a single state.

Clinton's vice presidential running mate was Senator Albert A. Gore, Jr., of Tennessee. Because Tennessee borders Arkansas, Gore's candidacy marked a departure from traditional geographical "balancing" of presidential tickets. The two men also departed from custom by often campaigning together, accompanied

Democratic presidential running mates Bill Clinton, foreground, and Albert A. Gore, Jr., shake hands with supporters in North Carolina in October.

by their wives. Their frequent bus tours were a campaign novelty.

Exit polls on election day showed that Clinton enjoyed broad support despite the narrowness of the popular vote. Among Republican voters, Bush scored highest, with 72 per cent, to 17 per cent for Perot, 10 per cent for Clinton, and 1 per cent for other candidates. Bush also held a slight edge among white voters, who gave him 41 per cent of their votes to 39 per cent for Clinton and 20 per cent for Perot.

According to the exit polls, Clinton won by the largest percentage margin over Bush among blacks, 82 per cent to 11 per cent. He also carried Democrats by 78 per cent to 10 per cent; Democrats who voted for Bush in 1988 by 54 per cent to 27 per cent; single parents by 50 per cent to 29 per cent; first-time voters, 48 per cent to 30 per cent; working women, 46 per cent to 36 per cent; and all women, 46 per cent to 37 per cent.

Perot was the "wild card" in the presidential race, posing problems for both Clinton and Bush. After the three presidential debates in October, Perot's popularity climbed, having fallen following his temporary withdrawal from the race in July. And he seemed to be taking more votes from Clinton than from Bush. But an analysis of election-day exit polls indicated that Perot's presence in the race had not changed the outcome. Either way, Clinton would have won. (See also **Perot, Ross.**)

Congressional elections. Democrats retained solid control of the Senate and House of Representatives, ending divided party control of the presidency and Congress for the first time since 1980. Partisan squabbling between Bush and congressional Democrats had led to an impasse on many key issues.

Both parties had cause for elation and disappointment over the Senate and House results. Republicans could rejoice that Democrats fell short of a hoped-for "filibuster-proof" majority—60 seats out of 100—in the Senate. The Democratic edge in the Senate stayed at 57 seats to 43. But Republicans fell short of their goal of gaining 20 or more seats in the House of Representatives. They picked up 10 seats, giving the 1993 House a makeup of 176 Republicans, 258 Democrats, and 1 independent (Representative Bernard Sanders of Vermont, who was reelected). Because there were two vacant seats in the House before the election, the results produced a net loss of 8 seats for the Democrats, their strength falling from 266.

Incumbents. Before the balloting, there was much speculation that incumbents in the House and Senate would be defeated in great numbers, because polls registered strong voter dissatisfaction with Congress. The conventional wisdom proved wrong, however, as only four incumbent senators were defeated and only 24 out of more than 340 House members seeking reelection were turned out.

In the Senate, incumbent Republican Robert W.

Ten of the 16 women running for the U.S. Senate in 1992 gather for a picture during the Democratic National Convention in New York City in July.

Kasten, Jr., of Wisconsin was defeated by Democratic state senator Russell D. Feingold, incumbent Democrat Terry Sanford of North Carolina was beaten by Republican businessman Lauch Faircloth, and Republican John F. Seymour of California fell to Democrat Dianne Feinstein, former mayor of San Francisco. Another incumbent Democrat, Wyche Fowler, Jr., of Georgia, was forced into a November 24 runoff. He was defeated by his Republican opponent, former Peace Corps director Paul Coverdell.

Republicans had hoped to score major gains in House elections because of anti-incumbency sentiments; redistricting required by population shifts recorded in the 1990 census that created new House districts in the suburbs and Sun Belt; and the House bank scandal, which saw scores of House members named for routinely writing overdrafts on their checking accounts. Fourteen of the worst offenders, as identified by the House Ethics Committee, ran for reelection. Eight were defeated and six won.

The changing face of Congress. The 103rd Congress convening in January 1993 was destined to be markedly different from its predecessors. It would include more women, more blacks, and more Hispanics. And Ben Nighthorse Campbell (D., Colo.), a Cheyenne chief, would become the first Native American member of the Senate in more than half a century.

Dubbed the "Year of the Woman" in politics, 1992 produced a significant increase in women members of Congress. Many were inspired to run because of outrage over 1991 hearings by the all-male Senate Judiciary Committee into sexual harassment charges by law professor Anita F. Hill against Supreme Court nominee Clarence Thomas.

The new Senate was to have 12 new members. Four of them were women, bringing the total number of women in the Senate to six—up from two in 1992 and the most female U.S. senators ever to serve together. The new faces were Feinstein and Barbara Boxer of California (which became the first state ever to have two female senators); Carol Moseley Braun of Illinois, the first black woman ever elected to the Senate; and Patty Murray of Washington state. All are Democrats. The two women incumbents who would be returning to the Senate in 1993 were Republican Nancy Landon Kassebaum of Kansas and Democrat Barbara A. Mikulski of Maryland. Only Mikulski faced reelection in 1992. She easily defeated her Republican challenger. (See **Braun, Carol Moseley.**)

In the House, the number of women was due to increase to 47 from 28. Of 106 women House candidates—an increase from an old record of 69 in 1990—44 per cent won. All the female winners supported abortion rights. There was also to be an increase of about 50 per cent in the number of blacks in the House, from 25 to 38. The number of Hispanic members was due to jump from 10 to 17.

Also contributing to the House's changed composition were some 50 voluntary retirements and 20 primary-election defeats, many involving representatives implicated in the House bank scandal. The new House was to have 110 fresh faces, the most since 1948.

One House newcomer, Democrat Alcee L. Hastings of Florida, set an eye-popping precedent. As a federal judge, he was impeached by the House in 1988 and convicted by the Senate in 1989 on bribery charges. He was the first person ever elected to the House after being impeached by it. Hastings' conviction, however, had been overturned on September 17 by a federal district judge in Washington, D.C.

Governors' races. Democrats scored a net gain of two governorships, increasing their advantage over the Republicans to 30 to 18. The governors of two states—Alaska and Connecticut—were independents.

In North Carolina, Democratic former Governor James B. Hunt, Jr., defeated Republican Lieutenant Governor James Gardner to reclaim a post that the GOP had held since 1985. In Delaware, Democratic Representative Thomas R. Carper defeated Republican B. Gary Scott for the governorship that was being vacated by Republican Michael N. Castle, who was elected to the U.S. House. In Missouri, Democratic Lieutenant Governor Mel Carnahan defeated Republican Attorney General William L. Webster to succeed Republican John Ashcroft. Republicans picked up a governorship in North Dakota, where businessman Edward T. Schafer defeated Democratic Attorney General Nicholas Spaeth to succeed retiring Democrat George A. Sinner.

The governorships of Indiana, Rhode Island, Vermont, Washington, and West Virginia stayed in Democratic hands, and the Republicans retained the governorships of New Hampshire, Montana, and Utah. For the first time in the 1900's, there were no Republican incumbents running in governors' races.

State legislatures. Republicans fared best in races for state legislatures. They gained control of the state senate or house in Alaska, Arizona, Idaho, Illinois, Iowa, Kansas, Montana, Nevada, and Vermont and scored a tie in the Michigan House and the Florida Senate. Democrats took over the state senates of South Dakota and Washington and evened things up in the Pennsylvania Senate.

Term limits. In all of the 14 states where the issue of term limits for the U.S. Congress was on the ballot, voters supported limiting the terms of their U.S. senators and representatives. Those states—Arizona, Arkansas, California, Florida, Michigan, Missouri, Montana, Nebraska, North Dakota, Ohio, Oregon, South Dakota, Washington, and Wyoming—joined Colorado, which previously had been the only state to adopt term limits. In every state, voters approved limiting senators to 12 years (two six-year terms) in office. For representatives, eight states adopted six-year limits (three two-year terms), four states opted for eight years (four terms), and two states decided on 12 years (six terms).

Supporters and opponents of term limits expected the issue to be tested in the courts to determine whether states have the authority to limit the tenures of federal officeholders. Some proponents of limits said they would urge Congress to approve a term-limiting amendment to the Constitution, giving that jurisdiction to the states.

In other state actions, Arizona became the 50th state to approve a holiday honoring Martin Luther King, Jr., the slain civil rights leader. Voters there also rejected by a 2-to-1 margin a proposal to eliminate state financing for abortions for women qualifying for public aid. Californians rejected a 25 per cent cut in welfare payments and refused to sanction doctor-assisted suicides for the terminally ill.

In Oregon, voters refused to amend the state constitution to declare homosexuality "unnatural and perverse." But Colorado voters approved a measure prohibiting cities and towns from adopting gay-rights ordinances. Colorado voters defeated a proposal that would have granted vouchers to parents to help pay for either public or private schooling—a plan similar to one that was advanced by Bush but stalled in Congress. Frank Cormier and Margot Cormier

See also **Congress of the United States; Democratic Party; Republican Party; State government.** In the World Book Supplement section, see **Clinton, Bill.** In ***World Book,*** see **Election; Election campaign.**

Electric power. See **Energy supply.**

Independent presidential candidate Ross Perot announces in Dallas on July 16 that he is quitting the race. But he resumed his candidacy on October 1.

Electronics. The compact disc (CD) solidified its hold as the medium of choice in the electronics industry in 1992. And computer technology made deeper forays into consumer electronics as more products used CD-ROM (read-only memory), a device typically used in computers to store data and programs.

Multimedia systems. In late autumn, the Tandy Corporation began marketing its Video Information System (VIS), which uses CD-ROM technology. The VIS player, which looks similar to a video cassette recorder, connects to a television and provides users with electronic access to reference books, instructional materials, and games stored on CDs.

Sony Corporation's PIX-100 multimedia player, which entered the market in September, is incompatible with VIS but also uses CD-ROM technology. The PIX-100 is a portable device that weighs about 2 pounds (0.9 kilogram) and is designed primarily for businesspeople on the go. The product aims to provide the user with access to vast amounts of information while remaining untethered to a computer.

A computer in your pocket. Both Apple Computer Incorporated and International Business Machines Corporation in 1992 unveiled prototypes of handheld products called personal digital assistants (PDA's). These products can store, transmit, and receive information via telephone, fax, or modem and can "read" handwritten letters. The first PDA's were expected to be on the market in 1993.

Digital compact cassette. In autumn 1992, Philips Electronics N.V. and Tandy each brought out digital compact cassette (DCC) players. DCC manufacturers say the product, which is identical in size to older analog players, offers the sound clarity of a compact disc in a tape format. DCC systems can record, are portable, and, unlike commercially unsuccessful digital audio tape systems, can play analog cassettes.

Televisions. The American debut of televisions having a screen ratio of 16 inches (41 centimeters) of width per 9 inches (23 centimeters) of height was postponed until 1993. This type of wide-screen TV is the forerunner to the expected conversion to high-definition TV, which produces clearer pictures. Meanwhile, Mitsubishi Heavy Industries Limited enlarged standard TV's with a 40-inch (102-centimeter) picture tube that provides a screen surface that is 31 per cent bigger than the next largest size.

Videophone. The American Telephone & Telegraph Company (AT&T) in August 1992 began marketing a telephone that allows callers to view one another. AT&T first introduced the concept in 1964 but left the gizmo in limbo for nearly three decades. The new product, which both caller and callee must have in order to use the video feature, carried a price of $1,499 each. MCI Communications Corporation in September 1992 announced that it would market a videophone in early 1993 for $750. Frank Vizard

See also **Computer**. In ***World Book,*** see **Computer; Electronics; Television.**

El Salvador. On Feb. 1, 1992, a cease-fire went into effect that effectively ended El Salvador's 12-year civil war, which had claimed an estimated 75,000 lives. Salvadorans formally marked the end of the civil war on December 15 after the Farabundo Martí National Liberation Front, El Salvador's main rebel group, disarmed. But carrying out the peace accords proved difficult. Military officers resisted reducing the armed forces by half, as the peace plan called for, and the country lacked money to create the new, nonpartisan police force called for in the peace accords.

Land dispute. The most difficult issue in the peace agreements involved land ownership. Former rebel leaders said their men would give up their arms only once they had been given some 600,000 acres (240,000 hectares) of land—12 per cent of El Salvador's total land area. The figure corresponded to the area that they controlled during much of the conflict.

Massacre site discovered. In late October, an investigation discovered dozens of human skeletons in El Mozote, El Salvador. Scientists said the bodies had been burned, mutilated, and shot. Human rights leaders said the discovery is evidence of a 1981 Salvadoran army massacre in which at least 800 people were reportedly murdered. Nathan A. Haverstock

See also **Latin America** (Facts in brief table). In ***World Book,*** see **El Salvador.**

Employment. See **Economics; Labor.**

Endangered species. See **Conservation.**

Energy supply. A major energy bill containing provisions affecting the production and use of virtually every form of energy was passed by the Congress of the United States on Oct. 8, 1992, after 18 months of debate. President George Bush signed the bill on October 24. James D. Watkins, secretary of the Department of Energy (DOE), said government-funded projects included in the legislation could decrease U.S. oil imports by about 5 million barrels per day by the year 2010. In 1992, the United States imported more than 8 million barrels per day, about 50 per cent of the oil consumed domestically.

The oil savings would come from tax incentives and other measures intended to encourage exploration for new sources of oil and natural gas. Other provisions intended to cut oil consumption include increasing the use of domestic natural gas and such renewable energy sources as solar, geothermal, and wind power and encouraging greater use of mass transit. The bill mandated greater energy efficiency in buildings belonging to federal agencies, provided tax deductions for cars that run on natural gas and other alternative fuels, and made it easier for electric utility companies to build new nuclear power plants.

Another bill passed on October 8 allowed the DOE to open the first permanent disposal site for radioactive wastes from nuclear weapons production in the United States. The $1-billion New Mexico Waste Isolation Pilot Plant is located near Carlsbad.

Energy production, consumption. Energy production in the United States during the first half of 1992 declined by 1.7 per cent to 33.32 quadrillion British thermal units (Btu's), the DOE reported on September 24. (A Btu is the amount of heat needed to raise the temperature of 1 pound [0.45 kilogram] of water by 1 Fahrenheit degree [0.56 Celsius degree].)

Domestic energy consumption during the first six months of 1992 increased by about 1.4 per cent. Imports of energy, which rose about 3.7 per cent, filled the gap. Coal provided about 22 per cent of all energy consumed in the United States during the first half of 1992; natural gas, 27 per cent; petroleum, 40 per cent; nuclear power, 7 per cent; and hydroelectric power, 3 per cent, according to the DOE.

Nuclear power may continue to decline as a major source of energy unless the U.S. government and nuclear power industry correct several long-standing problems, a panel of scientific experts warned on June 18. The panel was convened by the National Research Council, an agency of the National Academy of Sciences, which advises the federal government on science and technology. The panel cited a need to decrease the costs of nuclear power plants, streamline regulations for plant construction and operation, resolve uncertainties about the disposal of waste from nuclear plants, and reassure the public that nuclear plants pose "very small" health and safety risks. The panel also recommended that the government fund the development of new reactor technology.

Decommissioning decisions. Owners of the Yankee Rowe nuclear power station in Rowe, Mass., the oldest commercial reactor in the United States, announced on February 26 that they would permanently shut and dismantle the station. The 10 utility companies that own the plant decided it would be too expensive to continue operating the plant. The decision ended a nuclear power industry plan to use Yankee Rowe to demonstrate that nuclear plants can operate for up to 60 years, rather than the 40 years now considered safe. The plant, which was built in 1960, had been shut since October 1991 for safety tests.

Plant officials estimated that it would cost $247-million to decommission the plant, which cost $39 million to build. Decommissioning involves removing and disposing of a plant's radioactive material.

A 25-year battle over the operation of the Shoreham nuclear plant ended on Feb. 29, 1992, when the Long Island Lighting Company sold the $5.5-billion plant to the Long Island Power Authority, a consortium of electric power companies. On June 12, the U.S. Nuclear Regulatory Commission gave Long Island Power permission to decommission Shoreham. Although fully licensed, the plant operated for only a brief period in 1985 because opponents raised numerous questions about its safety.

Fusion research. Representatives of the United States, Japan, Russia, and several European countries agreed on July 21, 1992, to spend $1.6 billion on the design of a nuclear fusion reactor. The six-year project, called the International Thermonuclear Reactor (ITER), was to produce a full set of specifications needed to construct the facility. The actual construction of ITER would require additional funds. The goal of the project is to demonstrate the scientific and technological feasibility of nuclear fusion.

Nuclear fusion, which powers the sun and other stars, involves forcing the union of two lightweight atoms—usually forms of hydrogen—to create the *nucleus* (core) of a heavier element—usually helium. In the process, energy is released. Existing nuclear power plants produce energy by fission, the process of splitting the nuclei of atoms. Scientists believe that fusion is safer and cheaper than fission.

The development of a device that could reduce the cost of a commercial fusion reactor by $100 million was reported on September 24 by scientists at the DOE's Argonne National Laboratory near Chicago and Sandia National Laboratories in Albuquerque, N. Mex. The device is a highly sophisticated trap that removes excess helium from the inside of a fusion reactor. Scientists had thought that fusion reactors would require huge, expensive vacuum systems to remove the excess helium produced during the fusion process. The new device consists of a plate coated with nickel, which absorbs helium. As the nickel becomes saturated with helium, additional nickel is created to coat the plate and form a fresh surface for the absorption of more helium.

Electric automobiles. The Chrysler Corporation and Westinghouse Electric Corporation on March 3 announced an agreement to develop an electric automobile with double the range and speed of any electric car proposed by other auto manufacturers. Company officials said a new computerized electric motor would extend the life of the car's battery, permitting trips of about 200 miles (320 kilometers) on a single battery charge.

The United States Advanced Battery Consortium on May 20 awarded its first contract for developing a light, powerful storage battery suitable for electric cars. The consortium—a partnership of the DOE, the electric utility industry, and the major U.S. automobile manufacturers—plans to spend $260 million to develop batteries that would give electric cars a range, acceleration rate, and price competitive with those of gasoline-powered cars.

The $18.5-million contract went to the Ovonic Battery Company of Troy, Mich. Ovonic researchers will try to develop a larger version of their nickel-metal hydride battery, which was designed for use in laptop computers, mobile telephones, and power tools. The battery is twice as powerful as a conventional lead-acid storage battery of equal size.

A long-lasting light bulb that uses 75 per cent less electricity than does a conventional incandescent bulb was scheduled to go on sale in 1993, Intersource Technologies Incorporated and Diablo Research Corporation of California announced in June 1992. The E-Lamp, for electronic lamp, is a bulb that produces light with radio waves generated by a tiny computer chip and other components inside the bulb. The waves interact with a mixture of gases, producing invisible ultraviolet light. The light strikes a phosphorous coating on the inner surface of the bulb, causing the emission of visible light. Company officials said the new bulb will cost from $10 to $20 and operate for up to 14 years of average use.

Microwave dryer. The development of an energy-efficient microwave clothes dryer was announced on September 21 by the Electric Power Research Institute (EPRI) in Palo Alto, Calif. The EPRI conducts research and development for the electric utility industry. The prototype clothes dryer uses 20 per cent less electricity than conventional electric dryers, which are among the greatest electricity consumers in the typical home. The new dryer also dries at lower temperatures that are less damaging to wool and other sensitive fabrics, resulting in less shrinkage and wear.

EPRI officials said the dryer will permit home laundering of certain fabrics that now require dry cleaning. They predicted that a commercial version of the dryer would be available within three years.

Michael Woods

In *World Book,* see **Energy supply.**

Engineering. See **Building and construction.**
England. See **Great Britain.**

Environmental pollution. Representatives from 178 countries—including 116 heads of state—gathered in Rio de Janeiro, Brazil, from June 3 to 14, 1992, to discuss the future of Earth's environment at the United Nations Conference on Environment and Development, popularly known as the Earth Summit. There, world leaders adopted several new international agreements to combat pollution and protect Earth's variety of plant and animal species.

Climate change treaty. A major accord reached at the Earth Summit was an agreement to reduce the amount of *greenhouse gases* that enter Earth's atmosphere as a result of human activity. Greenhouse gases, such as carbon dioxide, methane, and water vapor, derive their name from the way they trap heat in Earth's atmosphere, much as glass in a greenhouse traps heat.

Many scientists fear that excessive amounts of greenhouse gases, especially carbon dioxide, could dangerously warm Earth's atmosphere. Excess carbon dioxide results mainly from burning *fossil fuels* (coal, oil, and gasoline) in industry and transportation. Such global warming could melt polar icecaps and flood low-lying coastal areas and islands, according to some scientists. Global warming could also give rise to more droughts, create more frequent and more forceful tropical storms, and shift prime agricultural areas northward.

The agreement reached at the Earth Summit to limit greenhouse gases was called the Convention on Climate Change. At a presummit meeting in May, most nations agreed that the proposed treaty should impose binding limits on greenhouse-gas emissions. Among major industrial nations, only the United States—which generates about one-quarter of the world's carbon dioxide emissions—opposed strict limits. Negotiators from the United States argued that America would never agree to such limits until it knew that they were necessary and what they would cost.

In the end, the two sides compromised. The resulting agreement required that ratifying governments adopt national policies to limit greenhouse gas emissions. The agreement did not specify when nations must meet those limits or how they would be enforced, however. But it said that ratifying nations should aim to reduce their greenhouse-gas emissions to 1990 levels, either individually or jointly.

Representatives of 153 nations signed the climate change agreement at the Earth Summit. The treaty was to go into effect after the national legislatures of 50 countries adopted it. Such adoptions could take several years.

Other agreements. The Earth Summit produced several other environmental agreements. These included an accord to protect Earth's plant and animal species from destruction and an accord designed to preserve Earth's forests. An agreement called Agenda 21 mapped future action on global environmental conservation strategies.

More ozone loss. Scientists reported in October 1992 that the yearly thinning of the ozone layer above Antarctica reached 8.9 million square miles (23.1 million square kilometers)—about 15 per cent larger than the 1991 hole and the widest area yet recorded. The yearly thinning of the ozone layer takes place in September and October in the *stratosphere* (upper atmosphere) above Antarctica. Chemicals called *chlorofluorocarbons* (CFC's), which are widely used in refrigeration and air conditioning systems, lead to the destruction of ozone in the stratosphere. Scientists have recorded growing ozone holes each year above Antarctica since 1986.

Ozone is a molecule made up of three oxygen atoms. Although ground-level ozone is a harmful pollutant, the ozone layer in the stratosphere is beneficial to life. This layer absorbs as much as 99.9 per cent of damaging ultraviolet radiation from the sun. Ultraviolet radiation reaching Earth can cause skin cancer, weaken the human immune system, and harm plants and marine organisms.

An Arctic ozone hole? An international team of scientists reported in February 1992 that the possibility exists for an ozone hole to develop above the Arctic. Data gathered from high-altitude aircraft and satellites flown by the National Aeronautics and Space Administration (NASA) in January showed record levels of chlorine monoxide in Arctic regions. Chlorine monoxide is a product of the breakdown of CFC's, and it destroys ozone in the presence of sunlight. Although the scientists found no Arctic ozone hole, they predicted one might occur in as little as 10 years. Recurring patches of thinned ozone also may someday begin plaguing skies over populated regions of Canada, the United States, Europe, and Asia, they warned.

NASA released a full analysis of the six-month Arctic ozone study in May. It showed a winter thinning in Arctic ozone of almost 10 per cent. Cold temperatures in the stratosphere help form ice crystals, which speed up the chemical reactions that destroy ozone. Had temperatures been lower and more typical of the season, twice as much ozone might have disappeared, the report said. Satellites showed that over the entire Northern Hemisphere, stratospheric ozone fell 10 to 15 per cent below normal—the lowest level in 13 years of observations.

Quicker CFC phase-out. Responding to the January findings of record levels of chlorine monoxide, U.S. President George Bush announced on February 11 that the United States would end its production of virtually all ozone-destroying chemicals by the end of 1995, four years earlier than had been required by the Montreal Protocol, a 1987 international treaty to protect Earth's ozone layer. In late November 1992, representatives from 74 nations and the European Community agreed in Copenhagen, Denmark, to revise the Montreal Protocol so that it too would ban CFC's by the end of 1995. The nations also agreed for the first time on a phase-out schedule for hydrofluorocarbons. These popular replacements for some CFC's also pose a slight danger to the stratospheric ozone layer.

Spanish oil spill. On Dec. 3, 1992, the Greek oil tanker *Aegean Sea* ran aground while attempting to enter the Spanish port of La Coruña on Spain's northwest coast. The tanker spilled an estimated 21.5 million gallons (81.4 million liters) into the ocean, fouling a large area and killing marine life. The spill was nearly twice as large as the disastrous 1989 *Exxon Valdez* accident, which dumped 11.5 million gallons (43.5 million liters) of oil into Alaska's Prince William Sound.

Cigarette smoke. On May 15, 1992, the U.S. Environmental Protection Agency (EPA) issued a preliminary report that characterized *environmental tobacco smoke* (room air containing smoke from cigarettes) as "a known human lung *carcinogen* (cancer-causing agent)." The report also said that smoke-filled air was a significant risk factor in many respiratory disorders—especially childhood asthma—and the development of heart disease.

In the September 16 issue of *Journal of the National Cancer Institute*, researchers from the University of South Florida in Tampa reported on the increased risk of lung cancer in women who breathe environmental tobacco smoke. The researchers observed that among nonsmoking women, those who lived with a smoking husband for at least 40 years faced 2.4 times the lung cancer risk of those who lived with nonsmokers only.

United States President George Bush and his wife, Barbara, stroll through a rain forest during the Earth Summit in Rio de Janeiro, Brazil, in June.

But when exposed to environmental tobacco smoke in childhood, it took nonsmoking women just 22 years to obtain the same 2.4-fold increase in lung-cancer risk, the researchers reported.

Asthmatics. Data reported at an American Lung Association meeting in May indicated that current U.S. limits on *particulate* levels may not protect most asthmatics. Particulates are particles of dust and other solids and liquids that are small enough to remain suspended in the air for a long period. Smog and other air pollution contains particulates that can settle deep within the lungs. United States law limits the 24-hour average, outdoor level of these microscopic particles.

Scientists with the University of Washington in Seattle and the EPA tallied hospital emergency-room admissions in Seattle, where the air is considered fairly clean. Although particulate levels never exceeded 70 per cent of the national standard, the scientists found that asthma admissions nonetheless rose and fell according to particulate concentrations the day before. "Levels of airborne particles at concentrations previously considered to be safe must now be considered a potential risk for asthmatics," noted Jane Koenig, one of the study leaders. Janet Raloff

See also **Environmental pollution: Environmental Concern Goes Global; Conservation.** In ***World Book,*** see **Environmental pollution.**

Equatorial Guinea. See **Africa.**

TAXI

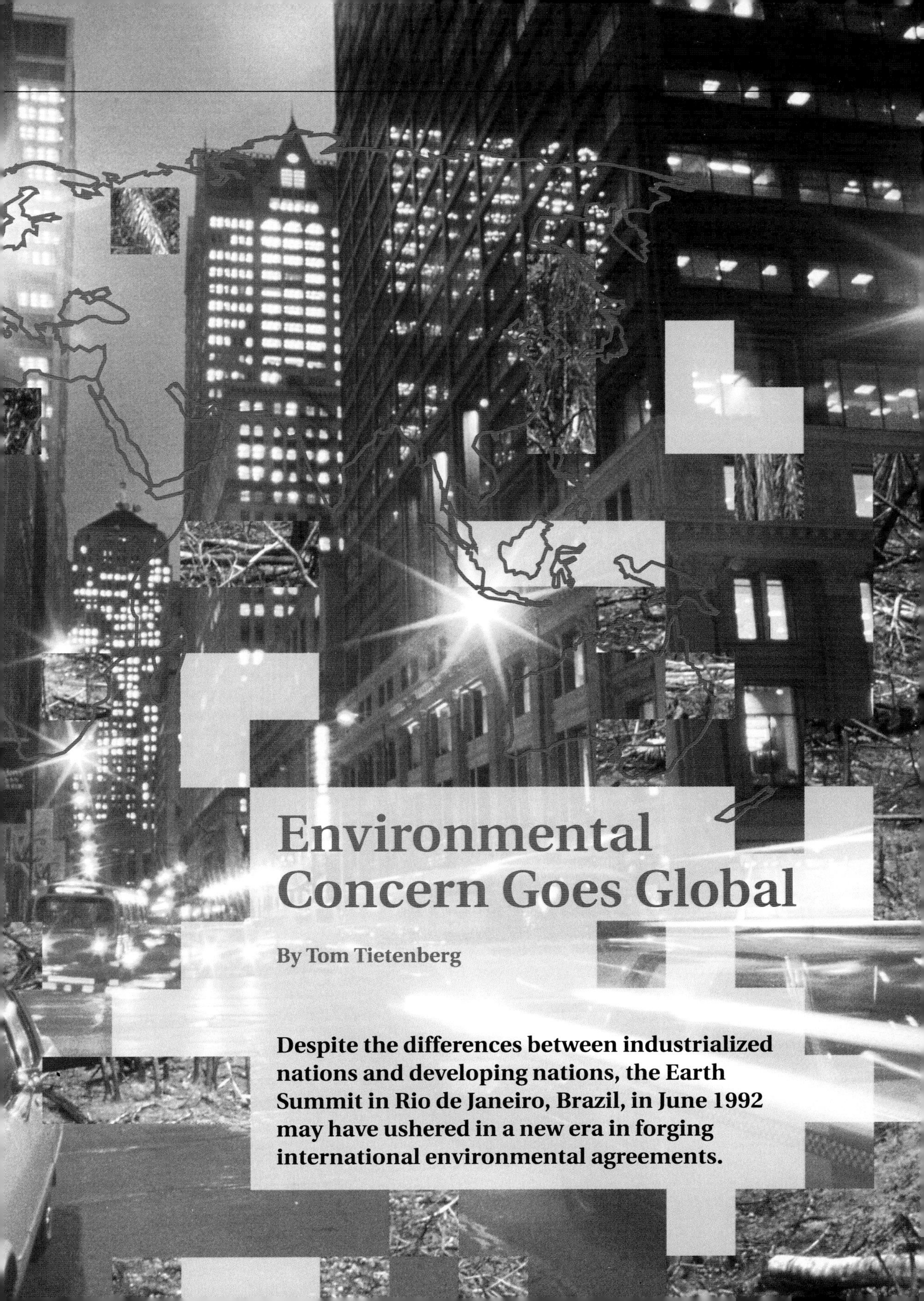

Environmental Concern Goes Global

By Tom Tietenberg

Despite the differences between industrialized nations and developing nations, the Earth Summit in Rio de Janeiro, Brazil, in June 1992 may have ushered in a new era in forging international environmental agreements.

An event of historic importance for our planet took place in Rio de Janeiro, Brazil, in June 1992. Representatives from 178 nations gathered in Rio to lay the groundwork for solving global environmental problems. As an environmental economist specializing in affordable ways to control pollution, I was among those gathered to participate in the United Nations (UN) Conference on Environment and Development, popularly known as the Earth Summit. The conference organizers called the summit the largest ever held, and the delegates' task was fittingly enormous. Nations with widely differing political, economic, and environmental concerns sought to agree on ways to save the world's forests, plants, and animals from continuing destruction, as well as ways to control pollution that could dangerously warm Earth's climate.

Almost immediately after we arrived, carrying our luggage and mindful of our lofty goals, we met the street children of Rio de Janeiro, some of them no more than 10 years old. The gleaming, air-conditioned hotel that housed the American delegation drew them like a magnet from a nearby slum, Latin America's largest. The street children taunted us, demanding money and food. Unlike other children, their eyes were cold and hard. To protect the delegates, the government soon rounded the street children up and relocated them for the duration of the conference. But behind our talk of "seeking common ground" and "solving common problems" lay the specter of the street children—a symbol of the "differing interests" that divide the developing and the developed nations.

Brazil was an appropriate choice for the Earth Summit. Its vast rain forests contain nearly half of the world's plant and animal species and are vital to the global environment. But the Brazilians—many of them so poor that they have no choice but to clear the land to grow food and gather wood for fuel—are destroying the forests at an alarming rate. And Brazil is similar to many other nations that attended the summit—those considered to be developing, or poor, by the standards of rich, industrialized nations such as the United States—but which contain the world's most extensive, untouched natural resources.

Many developing nations came to the conference to argue that environmental problems begin with economic inequality. They maintained that they cannot both develop their economies and protect the environment without aid and technical assistance from wealthier countries. But many developed nations doubted they could pay for such efforts, which the UN estimated would cost about $70 billion a year. If solutions to global pollution problems are to be found, they must be derived from international agreements based on the consent of the signatories. Given the enormous diversity among the nations of the world, forging effective agreements is no small challenge.

The author:

Tom Tietenberg is the Christian A. Johnson Distinguished Teaching Professor in economics at Colby College in Waterville, Me.

An agreement to protect the ozone layer

The industrialized and developing nations have agreed in the past, however, on ways to protect the global environment. One significant agreement set specific limits on pollutants that destroy ozone. Ozone is a molecule made up of three oxygen atoms. In the stratosphere, some 10 to 30 miles (16 to 48 kilometers) above Earth's surface, small amounts of ozone play a crucial role in protecting life. Ozone absorbs ultraviolet radiation from the sun and shields people, plants, and animals from its harmful effects. These effects can include skin cancer as well as an increase in the incidence of *cataracts* (eye disorders that can lead to blindness). Ultraviolet radiation may also weaken the human immune system and diminish the productivity of land and aquatic ecosystems.

In September 1988, representatives from 27 nations, meeting in Montreal, Canada, signed the Montreal Protocol, an agreement that called for curbing the production of chlorofluorocarbons (CFC's) to 50 per cent of 1986 levels by mid-1998. CFC's are industrial chemicals used in refrigerators and air conditioners and to make foam insulation and packaging. The Montreal Protocol was adopted largely because of overwhelming scientific evidence showing that CFC's were responsible for the depletion of stratospheric ozone. The Montreal Protocol provided an important example of international cooperation to protect the environment.

Perhaps even more significant, however, was a new ozone agreement that was adopted in June 1990 in London by many of the nations that had signed the Montreal Protocol. Soon after the Montreal Protocol had been adopted, scientific evidence showed that the ozone layer was thinning more rapidly than previously thought. In response, the London agreement called for the complete phase-out of CFC's by the year 2000. As of August 1992, 31 nations had ratified the London agreement.

The London agreement was significant for two reasons. First, it illustrated how quickly the nations of the world could act in the face of new scientific findings. Second, it addressed the issue of aiding developing countries by establishing a $240-million fund to help developing countries switch from CFC's to more expensive but less harmful chemicals.

Measurements taken in September 1992 reveal the largest area of ozone loss above Antarctica ever recorded. Ozone is a gas in Earth's upper atmosphere that absorbs harmful ultraviolet radiation from the sun. (Purple and dark purple areas represent areas of heaviest ozone loss.) Scientists discovered a "hole" in the ozone layer above Antarctica in the middle 1980's and have recorded increasing ozone loss there each year. Industrial chemicals called chlorofluorocarbons destroy ozone, which has also been depleted in the upper atmosphere above the Northern Hemisphere.

The issue of global warming

Efforts to control global warming, however, have presented a more difficult challenge. Not only is the underlying science less certain than the ozone studies, but the economic and political issues involved in taking effective action are substantially more complex. The danger of global warming stems from the build-up of greenhouse

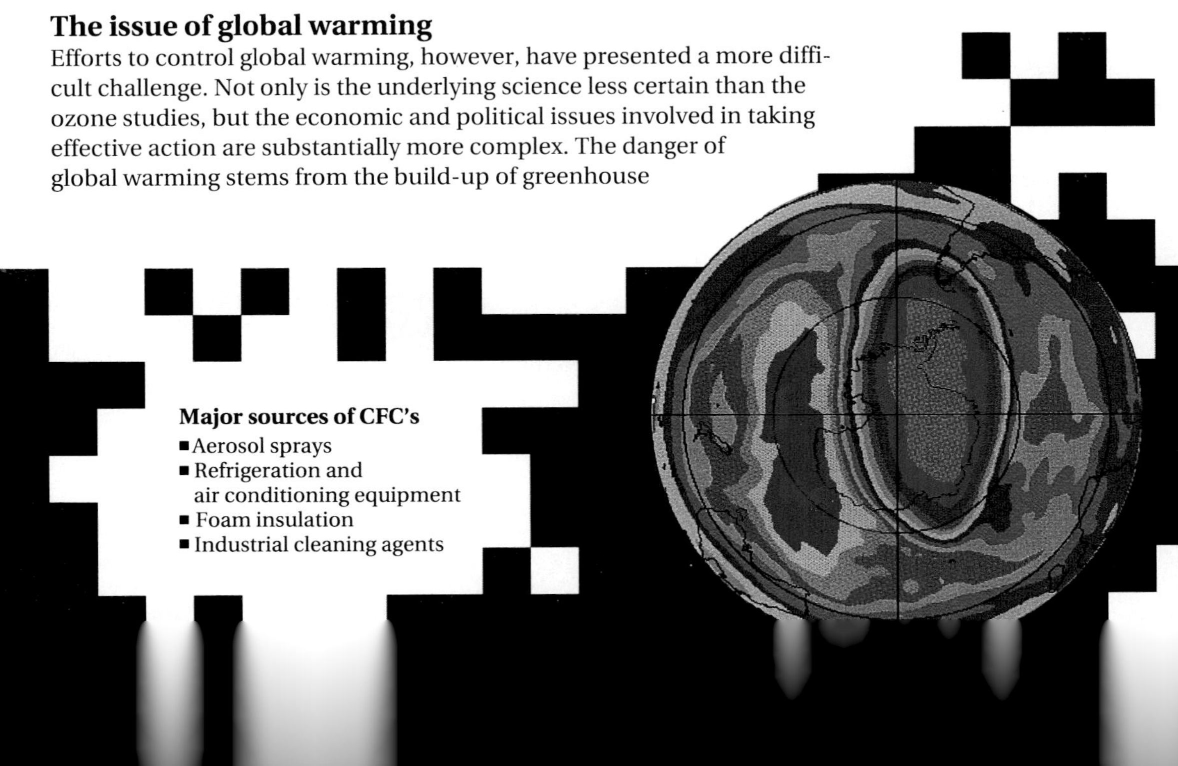

Major sources of CFC's

- Aerosol sprays
- Refrigeration and air conditioning equipment
- Foam insulation
- Industrial cleaning agents

gases, such as carbon dioxide and methane, in Earth's atmosphere. Greenhouse gases derive their name from the way they trap heat in the atmosphere, much as glass in a greenhouse traps heat. Excess greenhouse gases, especially carbon dioxide, are entering the atmosphere as a result of human activity such as burning coal, gas, and oil in industrial and home use and gasoline in automobiles. Many scientists believe that the continued accumulation of greenhouse gases in Earth's atmosphere could lead to a warming of Earth's climate.

Scientists first began warning of the likelihood of global warming in the 1950's. In the early 1970's and early 1980's, scientists from the Arctic and Antarctic Research Center in the Soviet Union, and the Laboratory of Glaciology and Environmental Geophysics in France drilled out an ice core 6,600 feet (2,000 meters) deep. The layers of ice in the core provided a record going back 160,000 years. By comparing current levels of atmospheric carbon dioxide with an analysis of air bubbles trapped in Antarctic ice samples, scientists found that the amount of carbon dioxide in the atmosphere had increased by more than 25 per cent since the mid-1700's, when industrialization began on a wide scale. In the mid-1760's, the concentration of carbon dioxide in Earth's atmosphere was 276.7 parts per million, according to the United States Department of Energy's Carbon Dioxide Information Analysis Center (CDIAC) in Oak Ridge, Tenn. (A part per million is approximately equal to a grain of salt in a glass of water.) In 1990, measurements by scientists from the Scripps Institution of Oceanography in La Jolla, Calif., taken atop Mauna Loa in Hawaii, showed that carbon dioxide concentrations were more than 350 parts per million. If carbon dioxide emissions continue to increase at their present rate, concentrations could rise to 460 to 560 parts per million by the year 2100.

Scientists use computer models to duplicate atmospheric conditions and simulate the effects of increased emissions of greenhouse gases. Because of the complexity of Earth's climate, however, many scientists realize that their computer models leave many questions unanswered. Although the scientific consensus seems to be that climate change is likely unless humanity reduces its greenhouse gas emissions, few scientists are willing to predict exactly how much climate will warm, or how fast. According to an April 1991 report by the U.S. National Research Council, however, a doubling of carbon dioxide concentrations could increase surface air temperatures between 2.7 and 8.1 Fahrenheit degrees (1.5 and 4.5 Celsius degrees).

Possible effects of global warming

Such warming would likely cause flooding of low-lying coastal areas and droughts in many regions. If Earth's climate warmed between 5.4 and 7.2 Fahrenheit degrees (between 3 and 4 Celsius degrees) by the year 2090, scientists predict that ice would melt in polar regions, raising global sea levels about 25.6 inches (65.0 centimeters). Sea-level increases of this magnitude would cause severe flooding of coastal cities and islands, significant beach erosion, and the loss of coastal wetlands.

Major crop-growing regions might shift northward, for example, from

Computer models at the National Aeronautics and Space Administration's Goddard Institute for Space Studies in New York City try to predict how much average worldwide temperatures for June, July, and August may increase in the year 2020, *top*, and the year 2050, over average temperatures that existed in 1958 if greenhouse gas emissions continue unchecked. Dark red areas represent increases of up to 9 Fahrenheit (5 Celsius) degrees.

the midwestern United States to northern Canada and Siberia. Droughts would likely ruin crops across wide areas of Earth where poverty and hunger already afflict millions of people. Developing nations, which depend heavily on agriculture and lack resources to cope with severe climate change, would probably suffer most from climate warming, according to the Intergovernmental Panel on Climate Change, a panel of scientists assembled by the UN.

Development, deforestation, and global warming

The United States and the countries that comprised the former Soviet Union are the two largest emitters of greenhouse gases. In 1989, the United States emitted about 1.4 billion short tons (1.3 billion metric tons) of carbon dioxide, followed by the former Soviet Union's 1.1 billion short tons (1 billion metric tons). When considered as a unit, the 12 nations that make up the European Community ranked third with about 880 million short tons (800 million metric tons), according to the CDIAC. Most of the emissions in these countries come from the combustion of fossil fuels in power plants and industry. Although the United States and the European Community made up just 11 per cent of the world's population in 1988, they consumed nearly 43 per cent of the world's energy, most of which was supplied by fossil fuels, according to the UN.

Deforestation also contributes heavily to carbon emissions. Trees take in carbon dioxide during *photosynthesis* (the process by which plants convert carbon dioxide and water into sugar and energy in the presence of sunlight) and give it off when they decay. Deforestation thus causes more carbon to be released and less to be removed from the atmosphere. According to the Worldwatch Institute, an environmental research organization in Washington, D.C., deforestation in Brazil alone caused about 430 million short tons (390 million metric tons) of carbon emissions in

1989, an amount 4 times greater than France's 108 million short tons (97.5 million metric tons) of carbon dioxide emissions for that year. And deforestation is occurring at an alarming rate in many areas. Each year the world loses about 65,600 square miles (170,000 square kilometers) of tropical forests—an area about the size of the state of Missouri—to make way for farming, grazing, timber cutting, or settlements, according to Worldwatch.

The most difficult issue surrounding efforts to prevent global warming is the cost that would likely be required to reduce carbon emissions. The ozone layer can be protected by substituting new, less harmful chemicals for CFC's. Although the new chemicals are more expensive, the cost is manageable. Dealing effectively with global warming, however, requires reducing the use of fossil fuel energy, and the economies of almost all countries are heavily dependent on such energy. Nearly 100 per cent of the fuels used for transportation in the United States and Europe are fossil fuels. In the United States, fossil fuels generate 71 per cent of the nation's electricity, and in Europe, that figure is 64 per cent, according to the UN.

A fire set to clear land for development burns in the Brazilian rain forest. Destruction of the world's rain forests contributes to global warming by destroying trees and other plant life that absorb carbon dioxide from the atmosphere. Common human activities that destroy rain forests include "slash-and-burn" agriculture and logging.

An agreement to limit greenhouse gas emissions

European nations and Japan pushed for an agreement at the Earth Summit that would stabilize carbon emissions at their 1990 levels by the year 2000. The United States, however, scuttled the plan, claiming that any move to limit carbon emissions would force businesses to cut workers to pay for energy improvements. As a result, the agreement signed at the Rio

Countries with the highest average yearly forest loss, 1981-1985

■ Brazil	9,700 square miles (25,000 square kilometers)
■ Colombia	3,400 square miles (8,800 square kilometers)
■ Indonesia	2,400 square miles (6,200 square kilometers)
■ Mexico	2,375 square miles (6,150 square kilometers)
■ Ivory Coast	2,000 square miles (5,200 square kilometers)

Source: World Resources Institute.

conference contains neither mandatory targets nor specific deadlines. Instead, countries agreed to take some measures to reduce the possibility of climate change and to report periodically on their progress.

Because industrialized and developing countries differ in the way in which they contribute to the build-up of greenhouse gases, the role of each type of country in reduction efforts will differ. The industrialized nations must attempt to increase energy efficiency and substitute renewable energy sources for fossil fuels. Countries such as Indonesia, China, Mexico, Brazil, and Malaysia must try to develop their economies in environmentally responsible ways. In both cases, the problem is enormously complex and revolves around the concept of *sustainable development.*

Working toward sustainable development

The main idea behind sustainable development is that economic growth with no regard for environmental consequences is self-defeating. Sustainable development recognizes that degrading natural resources undermines development. From the viewpoint of the industrialized nations, the main obstacles to sustainable development include the high rate of population growth in Africa, South America, and Asia; the inefficient manner of producing energy from fossil fuels in Eastern Europe; and the excessive deforestation in the Southern Hemisphere.

The average population growth rate in low-income countries (excluding China and India) is about 2.5 per cent per year, according to the World Bank, an agency of the UN. Although the annual growth rates in the world's two most populous countries—China and India—are moderate at 1.4 per cent and 2.1 per cent, respectively, their combined population of about 2 billion people makes even very small growth rates significant. In many parts of Africa, population growth is more than 3.0 per cent per year. In contrast, the population growth rate in high-income countries of the Northern Hemisphere is only about 0.5 per cent.

The United States and Western Europe claim that some of the most significant causes of greenhouse gas emissions are the old power plants and inefficient buildings of Eastern Europe. According to the UN, Eastern European countries use substantially more energy to produce the same amount of goods as Western industrialized nations. From 1979 through 1989, Bulgaria, Czechoslovakia, Poland, and Romania used 3.5 times more energy than did the United States to produce the same amount of goods. These countries derive most of their energy from coal, which pollutes the air heavily when it burns. More efficient technologies that use less coal or cleaner fuels such as natural gas could reduce global pollution without lowering manufacturing output or employment.

Finally, the industrialized world placed a major emphasis on curbing the high rates of deforestation in several developing countries. Although Brazil's deforestation rate slowed in the late 1980's and early 1990's, an average of about 9,700 square miles (25,000 square kilometers) of rain forest were cleared per year from 1981 to 1985, according to the World Resources Institute, an environmental research organization based in Washington, D.C.

Pollution: many causes, difficult solutions

A complex web of factors contribute to global pollution. These factors include poverty, overpopulation, energy use, deforestation, and the emission of chlorofluorocarbons.

The worst polluters

Countries with the highest estimated yearly emissions* of chlorofluorocarbons.

United States	130,000
Japan	95,000
C.I.S.†	67,000
Germany	34,000
United Kingdom	25,000
Italy	25,000
France	24,000
Spain	17,000
China	12,000
Canada	11,000
Australia	8,000

*In thousands of metric tons for 1989.
†Commonwealth of Independent States (former Soviet Union).
Source: World Resources Institute.

Countries with the highest estimated auto and industrial emissions* of carbon dioxide.

United States	1,329
C.I.S.†	1,038
China	652
Japan	284
Germany	263
India	178
United Kingdom	155
Canada	124
Poland	120
Italy	106

*In million metric tons of carbon for 1989.
†Commonwealth of Independent States (former Soviet Union).
Source: Carbon Dioxide Analysis Center.

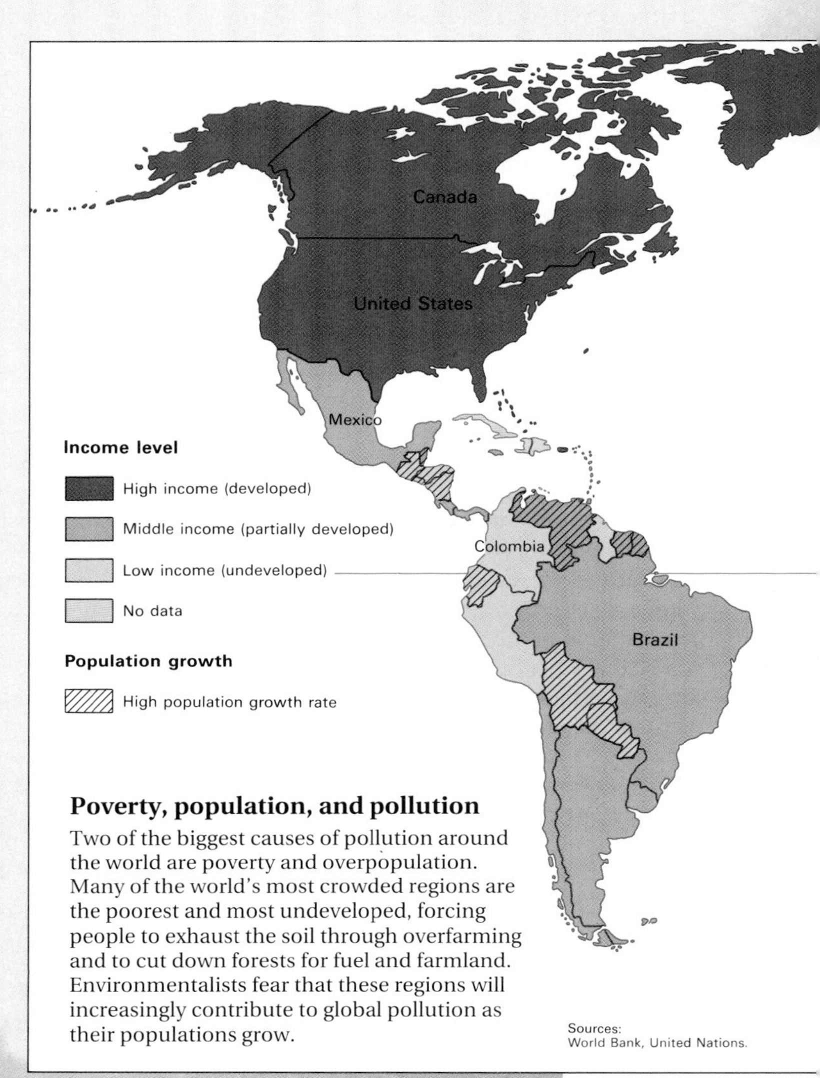

Poverty, population, and pollution

Two of the biggest causes of pollution around the world are poverty and overpopulation. Many of the world's most crowded regions are the poorest and most undeveloped, forcing people to exhaust the soil through overfarming and to cut down forests for fuel and farmland. Environmentalists fear that these regions will increasingly contribute to global pollution as their populations grow.

Sources:
World Bank, United Nations.

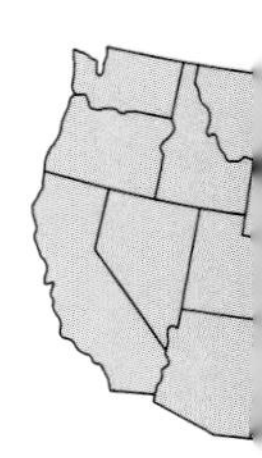

Human activities destroy 65,600 square miles (170,000 square kilometers) of tropical forests each year—an area about the size of Missouri.

Source: World Resources Institute

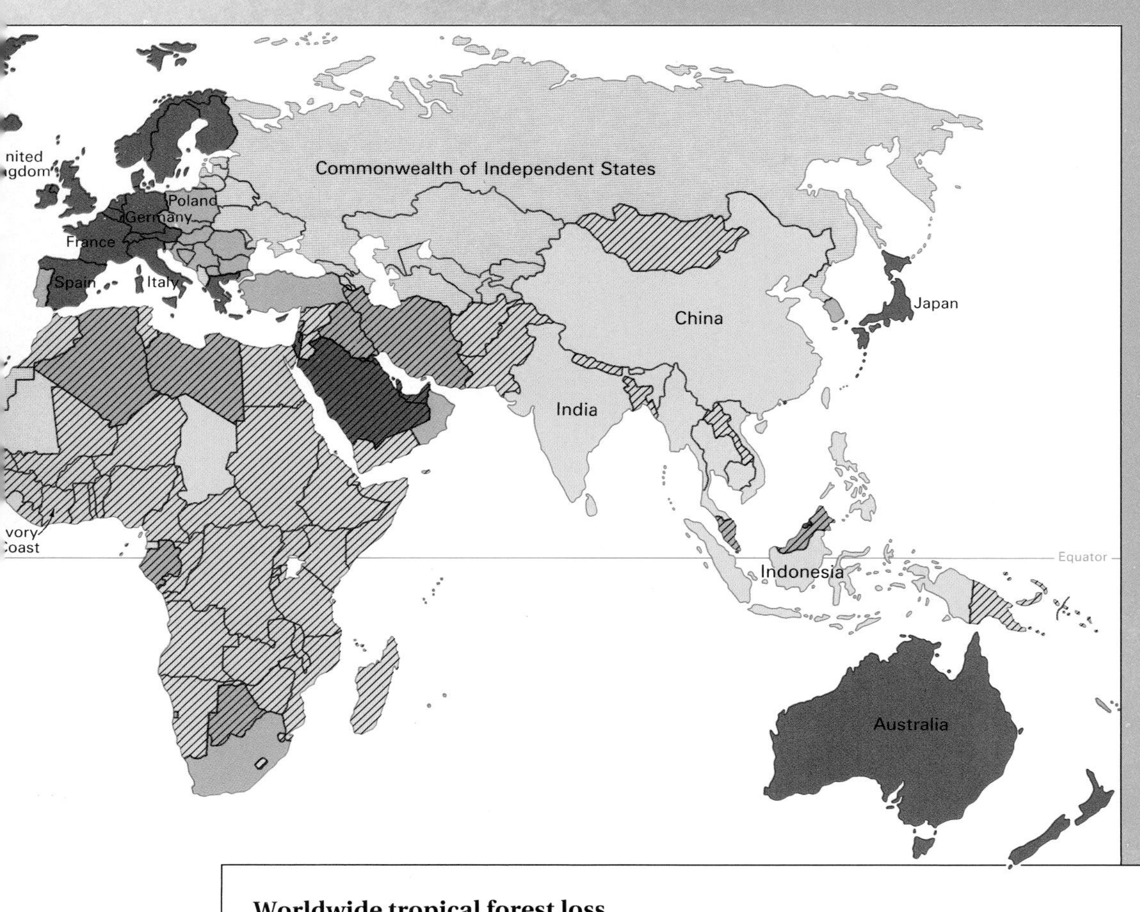

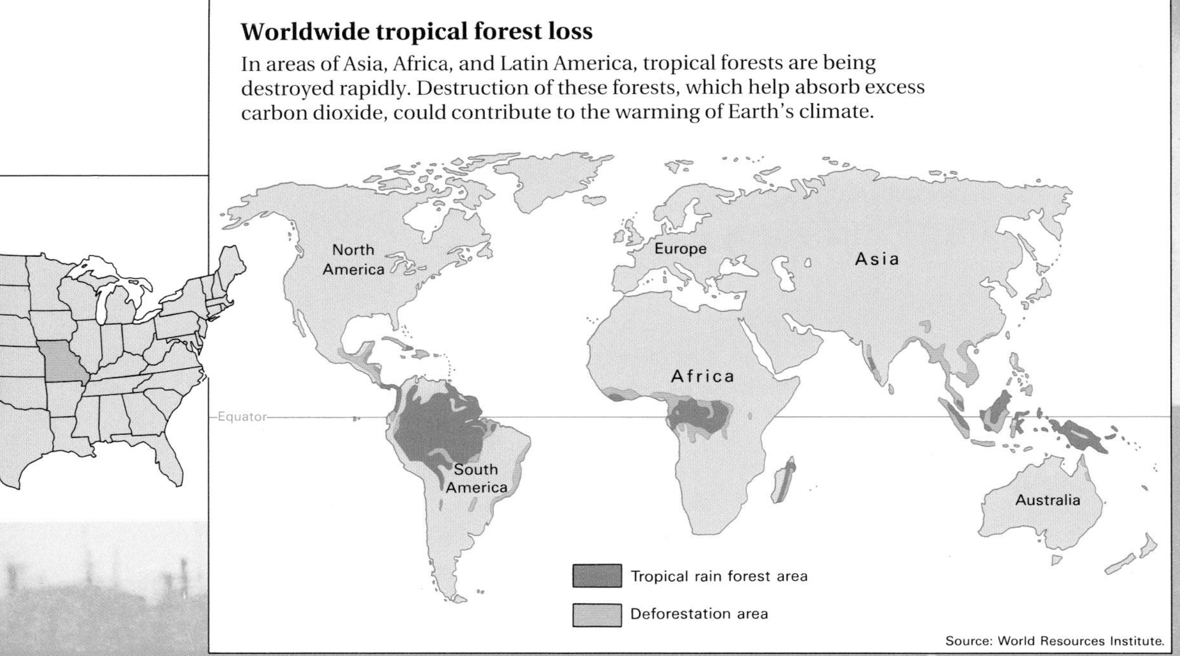

Worldwide tropical forest loss

In areas of Asia, Africa, and Latin America, tropical forests are being destroyed rapidly. Destruction of these forests, which help absorb excess carbon dioxide, could contribute to the warming of Earth's climate.

Source: World Resources Institute.

Global gathering
Representatives from 178 nations, including 106 heads of state, attended the Earth Summit. More than 17,000 people attended meetings on preserving the environment at the conference.

Results of the 1992 Earth Summit

- Agenda 21, a blueprint for sustainable development.
- The Rio Declaration, stating the rights and responsibilities of countries in the effort to attain sustainable development.
- An agreement on worldwide forest preservation.
- A climate change agreement focusing on the necessity of limiting worldwide greenhouse gas emissions.
- A broad agreement to protect the diversity of Earth's plant and animal species from destruction.
- Pledges to form a UN Sustainable Development Commission, which will monitor compliance with environmental agreements adopted at the Earth Summit.

Delegates at the United Nations-sponsored Earth Summit forged important international agreements to control global pollution and raised hopes for continued international cooperation to protect the environment.

The developing nations' perspective

Not surprisingly, the developing countries approached the negotiating table at the Earth Summit with a different viewpoint. They regard excessive consumption and waste in the industrialized nations as the major cause of rising global pollution. Developing nations point out that plentiful, cheap fossil fuel energy helped industrial nations build their wealth. As developing nations seek to raise their living standards, they are dismayed and frustrated by arguments suggesting that they cannot follow the same path to wealth for fear of creating a disastrous climate change. A group of 128 developing nations called G-77 expressed the developing nations' views and frustrations at the Earth Summit.

In a seeming contradiction, the G-77 countries argue that they must develop their economies—and produce whatever emissions are necessary to accomplish development—in order to prevent even greater levels of greenhouse gas emissions. According to this view, development creates more jobs, which provide people with the economic support that they would otherwise obtain from cutting forests down for farmland and fuel. Development also provides the wealth necessary to install pollution control equipment. This argument assumes that population growth will ease as wealth increases and families need fewer members—and resources—to support themselves.

Developing countries realize that development must be sustainable to avoid repeating the mistakes of the developed countries. Sustainable development requires new technologies—everything from road-building equipment, to more efficient power plants and alternative, cleaner forms of energy. To help reduce future greenhouse gas emissions, the G-77 nations at the Earth Summit thus appealed for large transfers of technologies and funds from the industrialized nations.

Despite the differences that divided the delegations, the Earth Summit produced five international environmental agreements. These included Agenda 21, a blueprint for future conservation efforts; the Rio de Janeiro Declaration of the Environment and Development, a set of moral principles to guide future agreements; a declaration on the need to balance forest loss with preservation; an agreement on the importance of preserving the planet's *biodiversity* (its variety of plant and animal species); and the global warming agreement.

Various nations' fears about negative economic consequences from these agreements served to weaken them, however, and they contained few specifics. The forest management agreement, for instance, contained no limits on timber cutting by developing nations and no mechanism whereby global forest loss could be monitored. And the United States refused to sign the biodiversity treaty because certain provisions in the treaty allow developing countries to claim rights to new drugs or foods derived from plants or animals found in their countries.

Although the Earth Summit took important steps toward adding broad new environmental agreements to international law, the process is not entirely complete. At the end of the conference on June 14, 153 countries had signed the global warming pact. This agreement will remain open for signatures at UN headquarters in New York City until June 19, 1993. For the agreement to enter into force, however, the legislatures of at least 50 countries must first ratify it, a process that could take two years. The biodiversity agreement was signed by 157 countries. To enact this treaty, 30 national legislatures must ratify it.

Some critics said that compromises and lack of concrete agreements weakened the outcome of the Earth Summit. But many conference participants felt that the agreements signaled the beginning of a process to bring global warming under control. These participants and many others trust that what the summit agreements lacked in specifics, they made up for in initiative and the will to view local and national environmental problems from a global perspective.

For further reading:

Preserving the Global Environment: The Challenge of Shared Leadership. Ed. by Jessica Mathews. Norton, 1991.

World Bank. *World Development Report 1992: Development and the Environment.* Oxford, 1992.

Worldwatch Institute. *State of the World.* Norton, 1992.

Estonia faced a severe fuel shortage in January 1992, after Russia, its main fuel supplier, raised its crude oil prices to world market levels. Food was also scarce, partly because of Russian cuts in wheat exports. The crisis led to the resignation of Premier Edgar Savisaar and his entire Cabinet on January 23.

On June 20, Estonia introduced its own currency, the kroon. Estonia was the first former Soviet republic to abandon the Russian ruble as its monetary unit.

Estonia adopted a new Constitution in a national referendum on June 28. But most ethnic Russians—almost 40 per cent of the population—could not vote in the referendum, under a law denying citizenship to individuals who arrived in Estonia after its annexation by the Soviet Union in 1940. The law allowed noncitizens to apply for citizenship after a year.

In elections on September 20, the nationalist Fatherland alliance emerged as Estonia's dominant political force. On October 5, the Supreme Council (parliament) elected Fatherland head Lennart Meri as the nation's president. The selection had fallen to the council after no candidate won a majority in Estonia's first direct presidential election on September 20. Russia condemned the nationalist victory and, on October 29, announced it was suspending its withdrawal of former Soviet troops from Estonia because of the treatment of ethnic Russians there. Justin Burke

See also **Europe** (Facts in brief table). In ***World Book,*** see **Estonia.**

Ethiopia. With the end of the civil war and the overthrow of the regime of President Mengistu Haile-Mariam in 1991, Ethiopians had high expectations in early 1992 that better times were at hand. They hoped that the new government would find solutions to the problems of ethnic conflict and poverty and move the nation toward democracy and economic health. Those hopes were partially satisfied in 1992.

Seeking ethnic harmony. To ease the friction among Ethiopia's various ethnic groups, the Transitional Government of Ethiopia (TGE) under President Meles Zenawi decided in 1992 to allow freedom of expression for individual ethnic identities. The country's largest ethnic group, the Oromo, represents about 40 per cent of the population. But it was the smaller Tigrean group and its political organization, the Ethiopian People's Revolutionary Democratic Front (EPRDF), that dominated the TGE. The government's attempt to seek unity through diversity did not satisfy the Oromo, who were reported to be angry about being underrepresented in the government. There were a number of skirmishes between Tigrean and Oromo troops early in the year that left hundreds dead.

The people of the province of Eritrea make up another important ethnic group in Ethiopia. The Eritreans helped overthrow Mengistu, though their goal was not so much a reformed government as complete independence. A national vote on that issue, to be supervised by the United Nations (UN), was planned for

Ethnic Russians in Estonia protest in August against strict citizenship requirements that make most ethnic Russians noncitizens.

Ethiopians in Kenya—refugees from ethnic fighting in their homeland—ride in the back of a truck in March on their way to a relief camp.

May 1993. A refusal to allow Eritrea to secede could result in renewed warfare.

Elections. The Oromo and another major ethnic group, the Amhara, boycotted regional elections on June 21, 1992. The two groups charged the EPRDF with widespread intimidation of voters and election fraud—accusations supported by international observers. In July, the TGE established a board to investigate and rectify electoral abuses. But the problem of how to create national unity while maintaining ethnic identities remained unresolved.

The economy. The government made some progress in 1992 in moving away from the Marxist economy established by Mengistu and toward a free-market economic system. It distributed land to peasants—a move aimed at increasing agricultural production—and it adopted a new investment policy to attract foreign capital. In early February, the World Bank, a UN agency, announced that it was providing $672 million in aid to Ethiopia. Aid from the United States was stalled, however, in part because of American election-year political pressures.

Emperor's remains found. In February, government officials announced that the remains of Emperor Haile Selassie, a long-time ruler of Ethiopia, had been discovered in a secret grave. Haile Selassie was overthrown in a 1974 coup, and his death was announced in 1975. Mark DeLancey

See also **Africa** (Facts in brief table). In ***World Book,*** see **Ethiopia.**

Europe

European nations continued to redefine their economic, political, and security relationships in 1992, as they adjusted to the new Europe created by the dramatic events that ended with the breakup of the Soviet Union in December 1991. The countries of Western Europe strengthened their ties with those of the former Soviet bloc. At the same time, the Western nations struggled to preserve their own vision of unity. The European Community (EC or Common Market) prepared in 1992 to become a single, customs-free market, even as it faced challenges to its broader plans for a united Europe with a federal government structure and common currency.

The process of change in Europe was limited by a global economic slowdown. Slow growth in France, Germany, and Italy, as well as a deep recession in Great Britain, cast a shadow over both Western European unity and Western Europe's ability to aid the struggling economies of Eastern Europe in their transition from Communist to free-market systems.

Europe also was preoccupied in 1992 with the civil war in what was once Yugoslavia, where ethnic tensions first erupted into war in June 1991. In March 1992, the Yugoslav republic of Bosnia and Hercegovina, with its mixed population of Muslims, Croats, and Serbs, declared independence. With the backing of Serbia, the dominant republic of Yugoslavia, ethnic Serbs launched a bloody war that soon threatened the survival of the Bosnian state and its Muslim population. The world listened in horror to stories of massacres and atrocities committed by Serbs, as well as systematic expulsions of Muslims from captured areas. European nations, along with the United States, drew criticism for their failure to take effective action against Serbia, widely regarded as responsible for the fighting. (See **Bosnia and Hercegovina; Yugoslavia.**)

Single market to open. The EC proceeded in 1992 with its plans to create one of the world's largest single markets, affecting some 340 million people, as of Jan. 1, 1993. On that date, the EC was to abolish most barriers to the movement of goods, services, and capital among member nations. The 12 EC members are Belgium, Denmark, France, Germany, Great Britain, Greece, Ireland, Italy, Luxembourg, the Netherlands, Portugal, and Spain.

However, the EC delayed plans to lift passport checks and other controls on the movement of people between EC nations. The removal of internal border controls had been scheduled to occur with the opening of the single market, according to EC legislation passed in 1987. But Britain, Ireland, and Denmark opposed the plan. They feared the EC would free travel within its borders without sufficiently strengthening external controls to keep out illegal immigrants, terrorists, and criminals.

French opponents of European union hold letters urging Parisians to vote "no" in a September referendum on the Maastricht Treaty.

In June 1990, representatives of Belgium, France, Germany, Luxembourg, and the Netherlands agreed at a meeting in Schengen, Luxembourg, to abolish border controls among themselves on Jan. 1, 1993. Greece, Italy, Portugal, and Spain later joined the agreement. The five original signers had to ratify the pact before it could take effect. But by December 1992, only France and Luxembourg had done so.

Other European nations, meanwhile, continued to seek the benefits of association with the EC. On May 2, representatives of 19 countries signed an accord, negotiated in 1991, creating an enlarged free

trade zone between the EC and the seven-member European Free Trade Association (EFTA). The zone, called the European Economic Area (EEA), was to extend most aspects of the EC's single market to the EFTA countries—Austria, Finland, Iceland, Liechtenstein, Norway, Sweden, and Switzerland. Switzerland dropped out of the agreement after Swiss voters rejected the EEA in a referendum in December 1992. The accord was expected to take effect for the remaining EFTA members in early 1993.

The EEA does not abolish all trade barriers or give the EFTA countries a voice in EC decisions that might affect the trade zone. Many EFTA nations have therefore expressed interest in joining the EC. Finland and Norway formally applied for EC membership in 1992. Austria had applied in 1989 and Sweden in 1991.

Threats to union. Even as the EC prepared to open its single market, however, tensions in Western Europe cast doubt on the organization's plans for increased political and economic integration. The plans are set forth in the Treaty on European Union, known as the Maastricht Treaty after the city in the Netherlands where it was approved in December 1991. The Maastricht Treaty actually consists of two accords. One, on political union, provides for the EC to assume certain functions now held by national governments, including the setting of foreign and security policies. The other, on economic and monetary union, calls for a European Central Bank with responsibility for a unified monetary policy. The bank would oversee the cre-

Facts in brief on European countries

Country	Population	Government	Monetary unit*	Foreign trade (million U.S.$) Exports†	Imports†
Albania	3,395,000	President Sali Berisha; Prime Minister Aleksander Gabriel Meksi	lek (110.00 = $1)	378	255
Andorra	56,000	The bishop of Urgel, Spain, and the president of France	French franc & Spanish peseta	1	531
Austria	7,594,000	President Thomas Klestil; Chancellor Franz Vranitzky	schilling (10.79 = $1)	41,086	50,740
Belarus	10,480,000	Supreme Chairman Stanislav Shushkevich	not available	no statistics available	
Belgium	9,845,000	King Baudouin I; Prime Minister Jean-Luc Dehaene	franc (31.56 = $1)	118,570 (includes Luxembourg)	121,369
Bosnia and Hercegovina	4,548,000	President Alija Izetbegovic	not available	no statistics available	
Bulgaria	9,026,000	President Zhelyu Zhelev; Prime Minister Lyuben Berov	lev (23.75 = $1)	16,000	15,000
Croatia	4,793,00	President Franjo Tudjman	not available	no statistics available	
Czechoslovakia‡	15,790,000	Premier Jan Strasky	koruna (28.07 = $1)	14,400	14,300
Denmark	5,152,000	Queen Margrethe II; Prime Minister Poul Schlüter	krone (5.89 = $1)	35,812	32,257
Estonia	1,616,000	President Lennart Meri	not available	no statistics available	
Finland	5,008,000	President Mauno Koívisto; Prime Minister Esko Aho	markka (4.83 = $1)	23,111	21,711
France	57,152,000	President François Mitterrand; Prime Minister Pierre Bérégovoy	franc (5.20 = $1)	213,299	230,786
Germany	77,425,000	President Richard von Weizsäcker; Chancellor Helmut Kohl	mark (1.53 = $1)	391,295	382,050
Great Britain	57,757,000	Queen Elizabeth II; Prime Minister John Major	pound (0.64 = $1)	185,212	210,019
Greece	10,230,000	President Constantinos Karamanlis; Prime Minister Constantinos Mitsotakis	drachma (199.00 = $1)	8,653	21,582
Hungary	10,527,000	President Arpad Goncz; Prime Minister Jozsef Antall	forint (80.17= $1)	10,200	10,100
Iceland	259,000	President Vigdis Finnbogadóttir; Prime Minister David Oddsson	krona (57.68 = $1)	1,554	1,720
Ireland	3,827,000	President Mary Robinson; Prime Minister Albert Reynolds	pound (punt) (0.58 = $1)	24,232 (includes San Marino)	20,761
Italy	57,095,000	President Oscar Scalfaro; Prime Minister Giuliano Amato	lira (1,311.50 = $1)	169,399	182,554
Latvia	2,755,000	President Anatolijs Gorbunovs	not available	no statistics available	

ation of a single EC currency, possibly as early as 1997.

Leaders of the EC signed the Maastricht Treaty on February 7, amid high expectations that all member nations would ratify the pact by the end of 1992. Ratification by all members is required for the treaty to take effect. However, the treaty became the focus of intense debate in a number of countries during the year. Supporters of the treaty argued it would help make Europe an economic and political superpower like the United States. Opponents claimed it would give too much power over national policies to unelected bureaucrats out of touch with the needs of their countries' citizens. Some opponents, notably in Britain, Denmark, and Germany, expressed concern about giving up their national currencies.

On June 2, Danish voters narrowly rejected the treaty, by 50.7 per cent to 49.3 per cent, in a national referendum. Then, on September 20, French voters approved it by a margin of only about 2 per cent. Soon after, British Prime Minister John Major said he would not submit the treaty to the British Parliament until after a second Danish referendum, to be held in mid-1993. Britain was the only country besides Denmark not to ratify the treaty by year's end.

As the year ended, officials struggled to find a way to allow Danish voters to approve the treaty in the 1993 referendum. At a summit in December 1992, EC leaders adopted a legally binding statement exempting Denmark from participation in the EC's single currency and joint defense policies. The EC also adopted

Country	Population	Government	Monetary unit*	Foreign trade (million U.S.$) Exports†	Imports†
Liechtenstein	28,000	Prince Hans Adam II; Prime Minister Hans Brunhart	Swiss franc	no statistics available	
Lithuania	3,791,000	President of the Supreme Council Algirdas Brazauskas	not available	no statistics available	
Luxembourg	375,000	Grand Duke Jean; Prime Minister Jacques Santer	franc (31.56 = $1)	118,570 (includes Belgium)	121,369
Macedonia§	2,141,000	President Kiro Gligorov	not available	no statistics available	
Malta	357,000	President Vincent Tabone; Prime Minister Eddie Fenech Adami	lira (0.33 = $1)	866	1,328
Monaco	29,000	Prince Rainier III	French franc	no statistics available	
Netherlands	15,222,000	Queen Beatrix; Prime Minister Ruud Lubbers	guilder (1.72 = $1)	133,554	125,906
Norway	4,247,000	King Harald V; Prime Minister Gro Harlem Brundtland	krone (6.25 = $1)	34,034	25,244
Poland	38,991,000	President Lech Walesa; Prime Minister Hanna Suchocka	zloty (14,867.00 = $1)	12,900	12,800
Portugal	10,372,000	President Mário Alberto Soares; Prime Minister Aníbal Cavaço Silva	escudo (136.73 = $1)	16,281	26,113
Romania	23,595,000	President Ion Iliescu; Prime Minister Nicolae Vacaroíu	leu (430.00 = $1)	9,200	10,900
Russia	151,436,000	President Boris Yeltsin	not available	no statistics available	
San Marino	24,000	2 captains regent appointed by Grand Council every 6 months	Italian lira	no statistics available	
Slovenia	1,987,000	President Milan Kucan	not available	no statistics available	
Spain	39,624,000	King Juan Carlos I; Prime Minister Felipe González Márquez	peseta (108.73 = $1)	60,182	93,314
Sweden	8,528,000	King Carl XVI Gustaf; Prime Minister Carl Bildt	krona (5.77 = $1)	55,129	49,759
Switzerland	6,653,000	President Rene Felber	franc (1.37 = $1)	61,537	66,517
Turkey	59,200,000	President Turgut Özal; Prime Minister Suleyman Demirel	lira (7,996.17 = $1)	11,800	16,000
Ukraine	53,125,000	President Leonid Kravchuk	not available	no statistics available	
Yugoslavia	10,643,000	President Dobrica Cosic; Prime Minister Milan Panic#	new dinar (200.00 = $1)	no statistics available	

*Exchange rates as of Oct. 30, 1992, or latest available data.
†Latest available data.
‡Czechoslovakia divided into two nations, called the Czech Republic and Slovakia, on Jan. 1, 1993.
§Macedonia declared independence from Yugoslavia in late 1991 but did not receive international recognition in 1992 because Greece objected to its use of the name Macedonia.
#Yugoslavia's parliament passed a vote of no-confidence in Panic on December 29, but on December 30 Panic said he would not resign.

a separate declaration affirming that it would take over national powers only in matters that could not be better handled by the individual governments.

Monetary crisis. Doubts about the advisability of monetary union increased in September after a crisis struck the European Monetary System (EMS). The EMS maintains an exchange rate mechanism that links the values of members' currencies to each other and to a standard unit of value called the European Currency Unit (ECU). The value of the ECU is based largely on that of the German mark. As of April 1992, when Portugal joined the mechanism, all EC nations except Greece participated in the system. Non-EC members Finland, Norway, and Sweden had unofficially linked their currencies to the system.

For years, the Bundesbank—Germany's central bank—had kept the mark strong to avoid inflation. But the high costs stemming from the unification of East and West Germany in late 1990 caused government spending to soar in 1992, increasing inflationary pressure on the mark. As a result, the Bundesbank on July 16 raised its base interest rate to the highest level since the 1930's. The move forced other countries in the EMS to keep their rates high also, slowing the growth of their economies.

In early September, the value of the system's weaker currencies was threatened as speculators in foreign currency markets began selling them to buy marks. Reluctantly, the Bundesbank lowered its interest rates slightly on September 14. Nevertheless, a number of

Visitors celebrate the opening in April of Euro Disney, the Walt Disney Company's first European theme park, located near Paris.

currencies, including the British pound and Italian lira, came under heavy pressure in the days that followed. The Bank of England used about a third of its foreign currency reserves to purchase pounds in an effort to defend the currency's value. But on September 16, Britain announced that it was temporarily withdrawing from the EMS. Italy pulled the lira from the system the next day. Spain remained in the EMS but was forced to devalue its currency, the peseta. Only close cooperation between the Bundesbank and the Bank of France was able to protect the value of the French franc and keep the system from collapsing.

Of the non-EC members, Finland broke its link with the EMS on September 8. Sweden on September 16 briefly raised interest rates to an astronomical 500 per cent, but in November it too left the system.

European army? The war in what had been Yugoslavia highlighted doubts about the EC's readiness to formulate a common security policy. Among other matters, the EC was divided over recognition of three former Yugoslav republics: Croatia, Slovenia, and Macedonia. Many nations criticized Germany for forcing EC recognition of Croatia and Slovenia in January, before Croatia had clearly met EC criteria for recognition. Meanwhile, Greece blocked EC recognition of Macedonia under that name, which Greece claimed solely for the Greek region of Macedonia. The EC recognized Bosnia and Hercegovina in April. (See **Croatia; Greece.**)

Despite its divisions, however, the EC took a step in 1992 toward an eventual European armed force. On May 22, France and Germany announced the formation of the Euro Corps, a French-German army corps designed to form the nucleus of a multinational European army. French and German leaders stressed that the move was not meant to undermine the North Atlantic Treaty Organization (NATO), the Western security alliance, under which the United States had traditionally played a leading role in European defense. However, many U.S. and NATO officials believed that France wanted to reduce NATO's importance. France, which withdrew its forces from NATO's command structure in 1967, had long resented U.S. influence in the alliance.

The former adversaries of the Eastern and Western blocs strengthened their links during the year through participation in common security organizations. These included the Conference on Security and Cooperation in Europe, which promotes cooperation between Eastern and Western Europe, and the North Atlantic Cooperation Council. The council was formed in November 1991 as an advisory arm of NATO.

The EC increased trade and other ties with Czechoslovakia, Hungary, Poland, and Romania in 1992. The actions were designed to prepare the Eastern European states for possible EC membership sometime in the next century. And investment by Western companies in Eastern Europe began to rise during the year as the former Soviet bloc nations instituted ambitious programs to sell state-owned industries to private investors and to write the laws and regulations necessary for a free-market economy. However, the economic slowdown in Western Europe led some companies to delay such investment, and most Eastern European economies declined in 1992.

Immigration of political and economic refugees to Western Europe remained a potent issue in 1992. Most of the refugees came from Eastern Europe, the former republics of Yugoslavia, and the former Soviet republics. The problem was most acute in Germany, whose liberal asylum laws attracted at least 368,000 asylum seekers in 1992. The refugees strained the country's welfare system and increased unemployment, even as the high cost of rebuilding the former East Germany depleted the budget and put millions of Germans out of work.

Violence erupted in Germany in August, as neo-Nazis and other right wing extremists attacked asylum seekers and set fire to hostels housing them. Foreigners who had lived legally in Germany for years also came under attack. Hundreds of thousands of Germans held rallies condemning the violence. In December, the government and opposition began drafting legislation to amend the country's asylum laws.

Trade disputes between the EC and the United States reached a tentative conclusion at the end of 1992. Since 1990, the disputes had blocked international trade negotiations held under the auspices of the General Agreement on Tariffs and Trade (GATT). At issue was the EC's controversial Common Agricultural Policy (CAP)—a system of agricultural subsidies under which EC governments pay farmers guaranteed prices for their production of grains, livestock, and dairy products. The policy has resulted in huge surpluses of cereals, butter, milk, and beef. Critics have long complained that it has distorted the prices of these goods and given EC exporters an unfair advantage over farmers in other nations.

In May, the EC reached a plan to reform the CAP. Under the accord, the EC would reduce price supports and, to satisfy farmers, supplement their income with direct subsidies. The reform must be adopted by all EC members before it can take effect.

Despite the accord, the United States demanded that the EC make additional reductions in its subsidies. A U.S.-European trade war loomed in November, as the United States threatened to impose a 200 per cent import tax on white wines and other EC goods. The crisis was defused on November 20, when the two sides reached a farm trade agreement reducing EC subsidies below the levels set in May. However, France called the agreement unacceptable and threatened to veto EC acceptance of any GATT treaty incorporating it. (See also **Farm and farming.**) Philip Revzin

See also the various European country articles. In *World Book,* see **Europe** and the country articles.

Explosion. See **Disasters.**

Farm and farming. Agricultural trade talks broke new ground in 1992. The United States and the European Community (EC) in November reached an agricultural accord that resolved an impasse of six years in global trade talks. And the United States, Mexico, and Canada in August announced a draft version of the North American Free Trade Agreement (NAFTA), much of which dealt with agriculture.

Trade dispute. On Nov. 5, 1992, U.S. Trade Representative Carla A. Hills announced that the United States on December 5 would begin levying 200 per cent tariffs on $312 million of European products unless a dispute over EC subsidies of soybeans and other oilseed crops was resolved. The tariffs would have raised the price of a $10 bottle of French, Italian, or German white wine to $30, effectively shutting down trade. The soybean controversy had thwarted completion of global talks under the General Agreement on Tariffs and Trade (GATT). The GATT talks were designed to reduce trade barriers in all sectors of the economies of 108 nations, ranging from textiles to banking to telecommunications.

The EC began subsidizing rapeseed and sunflower seed in 1966 and soybeans in 1974, raising domestic annual oilseed production in the process from 2 million short tons (2 million metric tons) in the late 1970's to 14 million short tons (13 million metric tons) by the early 1990's. As a result of the artificial boost, U.S. soybean farmers lost an estimated $1 billion in sales each year. Acting in response to a 1987 complaint by the United States, an independent GATT panel ruled in favor of the United States twice, once in late 1989 and again early in 1992.

United States and EC negotiators announced a resolution on November 20. They settled the oilseed dispute with an EC promise to reduce the acreage of land on which subsidized oilseeds are produced. The oilseed accord paved the way to larger concessions. Both sides agreed to reduce subsidized grain exports by 21 per cent and to cut crop price supports by 20 per cent over six years. Those stipulations ratified cuts the United States had begun making in 1986.

Australia, leader of the 14-nation Cairns group of food exporters, called the decision a historic step in bringing fair trade to agriculture. But in France, mobs of angry farmers protested the deal.

North American trade. Agricultural trade was also a key component of NAFTA, which was designed to combine the United States, Canada, and Mexico into the world's largest free trade zone by 2007. United States President George Bush announced preliminary agreement on Aug. 12, 1992, after 14 months of negotiations. The agreement, subject to approval by lawmakers in all three countries, effectively added Mexico to the U.S.-Canada Free Trade Agreement, which had gone into effect in 1989.

Mexico had already begun liberalizing its trade barriers for North America in the late 1980's and early 1990's. As a result, U.S. agricultural exports to Mexico

Riot police march toward farmers blockading a Paris road in May to protest a reduction of European Community subsidies for farm goods.

more than doubled from the mid-1980's to reach $3.7-billion in fiscal year 1992, making Mexico the third-largest market for U.S. farm goods behind Japan and Canada. And the pace was expected to increase. For example, NAFTA guaranteed that U.S. farmers could ship 2.8 million short tons (2.5 million metric tons) of corn into Mexico without a tariff, with that quantity to grow by 3 per cent a year for 15 years.

During the U.S. presidential campaign, Democratic candidate Bill Clinton promised to pursue export-oriented farm policies similar to those of President Bush. Clinton endorsed NAFTA but only on the condition that his concerns with the environment and labor be addressed.

Russian trade. The United States in 1992 provided credit guarantees of agricultural exports as well as direct food aid to Russia and other nations that were once part of the former Soviet Union. Two decades of trade paid in hard cash came to a halt in 1990 when the Soviet economy deteriorated so badly it could no longer secure credit.

In 1992, the United States provided $1.8 billion in credit guarantees to banks financing Russian purchases of U.S. agricultural products and an additional $180 million in credit guarantees for Ukraine. The U.S. government also paid for $296 million in direct food aid to nine former Soviet republics, the bulk of which went to Russia.

However, Russia's weakening economy made repayment uncertain. And on November 24, Russia began defaulting on its bank loans to buy U.S. food.

Clean Air regulations. President Bush on Oct. 1, 1992, announced the enaction of regulations from the Clean Air Act of 1990 designed to reduce air pollution by encouraging the use of ethanol fuel made from corn. When mixed with gasoline, ethanol helps reduce air pollution in the winter. But the implementation of the Clean Air regulations had been held up over concerns about ethanol's usefulness during the summer, when ethanol evaporation contributes to smog.

The Bush Administration estimated that the new regulations would boost U.S. ethanol production from 900 million gallons (3.4 billion liters) in 1992 to 2 billion gallons (8 billion liters) by the year 2000. The increased demand for ethanol was expected to lead to similar rises in corn production.

New laws. On Oct. 28, 1992, President Bush signed a bill to make it easier for young farmers to get loans from the Farmers Home Administration (FmHA). The FmHA is a federal agency that makes direct loans and guarantees commercial loans to farmers who do not qualify for credit from private banks. The new law provided for up to 10 years of loans to help farmers get started in the business.

And on October 30, President Bush signed a water bill that for the first time diverted California irrigation water from crops to wildlife preservation. The new law also opened the door for farmers to sell their water allotments to cities and industries. The law dealt with water from the Central Valley Project, the nation's largest federal water project. (See **Water.**)

Pesticide risk. On July 8, a U.S. Court of Appeals ruled that pesticides with even a small cancer risk cannot be used on foods if any trace of the pesticide remains on the food after processing. The decision overturned a U.S. Environmental Protection Agency (EPA) practice of allowing the use of chemicals that posed a "negligible" cancer risk—a risk of less than one additional case of cancer per million people exposed. In December, the U.S. Department of Justice refused the EPA's request to appeal the decision.

Food labels. On December 2, the Bush Administration announced that by May 1994, most containers for processed foods would feature labels of uniform specification listing the fat, cholesterol, and nutrient content of the food. The labels also would indicate how much of the U.S. Recommended Dietary Allowances of fat or cholesterol was in each serving. (See also **Food.**)

Fighting food poisoning. The U.S. Department of Agriculture (USDA) in 1992 approved two methods to rid poultry of salmonella bacteria, which can cause food poisoning. In September, the department announced the approval of the use of irradiation, which would kill salmonella and other bacteria but would not affect the poultry. Then on October 13, the USDA gave poultry processors permission to dunk poultry into water containing trisodium phosphate (TSP). One study showed that after being dunked in TSP, only 1 of 245 chickens carried salmonella bacteria, compared with 43 of 245 chickens that were not dipped in TSP.

U.S. production. A drought persisted in the West in 1992, but unseasonably cool weather—including a freeze on the first day of summer in some areas—delayed crop maturity east of the Rocky Mountains. Then heavy autumn rains slowed harvest and produced high-moisture grain. The poor weather, together with crop damage caused by Hurricane Andrew in Florida and Louisiana in August, prompted President Bush on September 1 to issue $755 million for crop disaster payments.

Despite the setbacks, U.S. farmers in 1992 produced a record corn crop of 9.3 billion bushels, up 25 per cent from 1991. Wheat farmers harvested 2.46 billion bushels, up 24 per cent. The winter wheat crop was 1.61 billion bushels, up 17 per cent. Spring-planted durum wheat for pasta was down 7 per cent to 97.2 million bushels, but other spring wheat set a record at 755 million bushels, up 50 per cent.

The cotton crop declined 8 per cent from 1991, and peanut production dropped 11 per cent. But soybeans rose 9 per cent; oats, 21 per cent; and rice, 9 per cent. And beef production rose 1 per cent; pork, 8 per cent; and poultry, 6 per cent.

World production. In 1992, world wheat production rose 2 per cent from 1991; rice, 1 per cent; corn, 7 per cent; and soybeans, 6 per cent. Cotton fell 9 per cent from the 1991 record. World beef production declined slightly, pork production rose more than 3 per cent, and poultry rose 4 per cent.

Exports and income. U.S. farm exports in fiscal year 1992, which ended on September 30, reached $42.3 billion, the second-highest amount ever after the 1981 record of $43.8 billion. And net farm income just missed the record of $51 billion set in 1990.

Science. In an intriguing development in *genetic engineering* (the transplanting of genes from one organism into another), researchers at Michigan State University in East Lansing and James Madison University in Harrisonburg, Va., reported in April 1992 that they had created a plant that made biodegradable plastic. The scientists used genes from a species of bacteria that naturally produces the plastic. The scientists were able to add the necessary bacterial genes to the genetic material of some plants. The scientists reported that those plants produced small amounts of the plastic in their leaves, stems, and roots.

If the technique could be refined, scientists could create crops such as potatoes that would make plastic instead of starch in their tubers. Growing biodegradable plastic in plants could be much cheaper than the current method of generating biodegradable plastic by fermenting starch. Sonja Hillgren

See also **Environmental pollution; International trade.** In ***World Book,*** see **Agriculture; Farm and farming.**

Fashion. Many styles of clothing in 1992 were quiet and subdued. The most popular color for the fall season, fashion's most important time of the year, was black. The major change in clothes was a lengthening hemline. Because of the sluggish economy, young designers who were hailed in 1991 did not establish themselves in business in 1992 as securely as was expected. However, there were exceptions, such as Isaac Mizrahi and Marc Jacobs, both under 30 years old, who were clearly accepted into the American fashion scene in 1992.

Designers said that they lengthened hems, after a five-year run of short skirts, in order to offer women something fresh in fashion. Of course, a second reason to lengthen hemlines was to stimulate buying. The longer hemlines did not spark any catastrophic protests among women, and short skirts were still widely available. Designers continued to offer short skirts while they introduced longer ones. Louis Dell'Olio at Anne Klein, for instance, offered many styles in three lengths, as measured from the waistband—21 inches (53 centimeters); 27 inches (69 centimeters), which covers the knee and is expected to be the most important length in 1993; and 34 inches (86 centimeters), which covers most of the calf.

For women who were undecided as to which skirt length to choose in 1992, there were pants. The pants alternative resembled the fashion choice of the early 1970's, when designers abruptly supplanted the 1960's

Fabrics that resembled animal fur or skin appeared in many 1992 fashions, such as this ensemble by Michel Klein, shown in Paris in March.

miniskirt with midi- and maxi-length hemlines. Women boycotted skirts of any length, opting for pants instead. And according to next year's spring collections, presented in the autumn of 1992, pants would still be an important option in 1993. They were featured for both day and evening wear.

In addition to new skirt lengths, other inducements to encourage women to buy new clothes included novel uses for materials such as leather. Leather was widely promoted, even in ball gowns by Gianni Versace at his showing in Milan, Italy, and by Karl Lagerfeld for Chanel in his Paris showing, both in March 1992. A mannish look for women had many supporters, including Ralph Lauren in New York City, who accented his tailored women's suits with men's ties.

Animal prints in tawny realistic tones often took the place of real fur in 1992. Many women decided not to buy new fur coats and not to wear their old ones. Animal prints and various kinds of synthetic, furlike materials took up the slack. Prints suggesting tigers, giraffes, and leopards turned up in everything from cotton T-shirts to shoes and couture dresses.

Weekend wear. Casual weekend fashions were emphasized in collections by major American designers such as Calvin Klein and Donna Karan and by Europeans such as Giorgio Armani. Weekend wear collections were usually lower priced than other categories. And the collections invariably included denim separates, long and short skirts, sweaters, and pants.

Career celebrations. Designers who have dominated fashion since the 1950's reached important milestones in 1992. In January, Yves Saint Laurent celebrated his 30th anniversary as the head of his own business with a spectacular fashion show at the Opéra de la Bastille, an opera house in Paris named after the medieval fortress torn down in 1789, the start of the French Revolution. The show featured 100 models on stage simultaneously. In January 1992, Adolfo passed his 25th milestone quietly in New York City. Valentino brought his "retrospective" fashion show that he had staged in Rome in 1991 to New York City in September 1992 and won acclaim for the exhibition of couture clothes that spanned 30 years.

Pauline Trigère held an exhibition and fashion show at the Fashion Institute of Technology in New York City in September to celebrate 50 years in the fashion business. She arrived in the United States in 1937 with her two infant sons, and in 1942, in the midst of World War II (1939-1945), she opened her own business. In addition to an exhibition of her clothes through the decades, she invited 50 of her customers to model in the fashion show. Dina Merrill, Rita Gam, Josephine Premice, and Claire Trevor were among the actresses on the stage. Social leaders and members of the fashion industry also modeled clothes. It was a tribute to a woman who had been head of her own business longer than anyone else, including Gabrielle (Coco) Chanel. Bernadine Morris

In ***World Book,*** see **Clothing; Fashion.**

Finland in 1992 remained in its worst recession since World War II (1939-1945). In October, almost 14 per cent of the Finnish work force was unemployed. But by December, the recession seemed to be nearing an end. The government estimated that Finland's *gross domestic product* (GDP—the value of all goods and services produced within a country) fell by almost 2 per cent in 1992, compared with a decline of more than 6 per cent in 1991. The GDP was expected to grow by up to 2 per cent in 1993.

European relations. Finland had turned increasingly to the West in the late 1980's, as it experienced trade losses with the Soviet Union. In 1992, Finland—like its Scandinavian neighbors Sweden and Norway—worked to cement its ties to the 12-nation European Community (EC or Common Market) as that organization moved toward political and economic union. On March 18, Finland formally applied for membership in the EC.

In October, the parliament approved Finland's participation in the European Economic Area (EEA), a free trade zone linking the EC with the seven-nation European Free Trade Association (EFTA), to which Finland belongs. The EEA was expected to take effect in early 1993 for the EFTA nations that had ratified it. Meanwhile, the EC in December 1992 said it might begin negotiations on membership for Finland, along with EFTA members Austria and Sweden, in early 1993.

Markka devalued. In June 1991, Finland had linked its currency, the markka, to the exchange rate mechanism of the European Monetary System (EMS), an EC organization that links the values of its members' currencies. The move was designed to support the markka's value on foreign exchange markets and prepare Finland for EC membership. But keeping the value of the markka tied to that of the German mark, the leading currency in the EMS, added to the strains on Finland's economy in 1992. As Germany raised its interest rates, Finland was forced to follow, slowing economic growth. The high value of the markka also kept prices for Finnish exports too high for many consumers, especially in the former Soviet republics.

In April, the government passed an emergency economic package that raised interest rates to almost 20 per cent and pledged sharp cuts in spending for 1993. The action restored stability to the shaky markka. But in mid-September, a crisis in the EMS forced Finland to break its link to the system and allow the markka to be devalued. The devaluation made Finnish exports cheaper and easier to sell, but it also increased the amount of money needed to pay off Finland's large foreign debt. In October, parliament approved an austerity plan by which government spending would be frozen at 1991 levels through 1995. Philip Revzin

See also **Europe** (Facts in brief table). In ***World Book,*** see **Finland.**

Fire. See **Disasters.**

Flood. See **Disasters.**

Florida. See **State government.**

Food. The United States Department of Agriculture (USDA) on April 28, 1992, approved the Food Guide Pyramid as the basic guide for good eating habits. The pyramid replaced the traditional food wheel that depicted four food groups, ranked in no particular order, as the basis of good nutrition. In the new design, foods are grouped into six categories and placed within the pyramid according to the recommended daily servings. Grains, represented by bread, cereal, rice, and pasta, form the base of the pyramid with a recommended 6 to 11 servings daily. Vegetables (3 to 5 servings) and fruits (2 to 4 servings) form the next level. The third level includes dairy products (2 to 3 servings) and the meat, poultry, fish, legumes, eggs, and nuts group (2 to 3 servings). Fats, oils, and sweets form the tip of the pyramid and are to be eaten sparingly.

When the pyramid was first proposed in 1991, the National Cattlemen's Association and the dairy industry objected to the placement of their products near the top of the pyramid, fearful that consumers would think their products were unhealthy. Secretary of Agriculture Edward R. Madigan then delayed implementing the new model by more than a year and spent almost $1 million in additional consumer testing of the design.

Bioengineered foods. The U.S. Food and Drug Administration (FDA) announced on May 26, 1992, that genetically engineered foods would be regulated by the same standards as all other foods. Genetically engineered foods come from plants or animals that have been genetically altered so that food products from them will have a longer shelf life or look and taste better. Although some consumer groups called for testing and labeling of bioengineered foods, the FDA did not require such measures. However, the new foods will need premarket approval if they contain substances not substantially similar to those commonly found in food. Products will also require FDA approval if an added substance is known to cause an allergic reaction, or if it raises other safety concerns.

Critics of bioengineered foods argued that these foods may pose new safety risks and should undergo the type of extensive testing the FDA requires for food additives. Critics also called for registration and labeling of all genetically engineered foods.

A number of genetically engineered foods were under development at the end of 1992. The first of them—a tomato—was expected to hit the market in 1993. The tomato contains an extra gene that delays excessive ripening and offers longer shelf life.

Labeling. The Administration of President George Bush on Dec. 2, 1992, announced sweeping new food labeling rules that had been under formal discussion for almost three years. The new labels are designed to reduce consumer confusion to help the public more accurately determine the nutritional content of their food. As of May 1994, the labels will be mandatory on all packaged food, as well as on meat and poultry.

The new FDA regulations define adjectives that

Bill Schorr, reprinted by permission of UFS, Inc.

"...'Jolly Green Giant'?...No, I'm Ed Findley and I work at the produce irradiation plant down the road."

food producers have commonly used to market their products. If food manufacturers use such terms as "light," "lean," "low-fat," and "low-calorie," the food must comply with the official definitions. The new labels must also contain complete nutritional information including the amount of total fat, saturated fat, cholesterol, calories, sodium, fiber, sugar, carbohydrates, and protein.

Irradiating food. The first food irradiation plant in the United States, Vindicator of Florida Incorporated in Mulberry, Fla., began operating in January 1992. The irradiation process exposes foods to gamma rays, which kill pests, bacteria, and other microbes that may spoil food or cause illness in human beings. The food, however, does not become radioactive.

The FDA first approved the use of irradiation in 1963 for bacon, wheat, and wheat flour. Since then, it has allowed irradiation of spices, pork, fruits, and vegetables. The FDA approved the use of irradiation for poultry in 1990, and, in September 1992, the USDA, which oversees the meat and poultry industry, issued regulations for the procedure. Irradiation of poultry kills a bacteria called salmonella, a common cause of food poisoning frequently found in poultry. Thoroughly cooking poultry also kills salmonella.

Irradiation presents no hazard to consumers and does not significantly change the nutritional value of food, according to the FDA. The process is widely supported by international health and scientific organizations, though some scientists and consumer groups have questioned its safety. Irradiated foods must be labeled with a symbol called a radura and the words "treated with radiation" or "treated by irradiation."

School lunch fat. In September 1992, Public Voice for Food and Health Policy, a consumer advocacy group in Washington, D.C., charged that school lunch programs were rife with high-fat products, such as butter, cheese, and ground beef. A Public Voice study of the commodities distributed by the USDA to school lunch programs between 1979 and 1991 found that cheese and butter made up one-third of the $10.2-billion worth of federal food supplies. Although the government had provided some reduced-fat meat products, only 15 per cent of the ground beef distributed since 1986 contained less than 24 per cent fat. More than 24 million children in 92,000 schools participated in the school lunch program in 1991, and the USDA supplied about 20 per cent of each school meal.

Total U.S. food sales were projected to be $625-billion in 1992, according to the U.S. Department of Commerce. The Food Marketing Institute in Washington, D.C., reported that weekly grocery spending per household was $78 in 1992, a slight decrease from the $79 per week in 1991. Americans spent an estimated 11.7 per cent of their disposable income (money left after taxes) on food in 1992, according to the USDA. Bob Gatty

In ***World Book,*** see **Food; Food supply.**

Football. Dramatic changes came to professional and college football in 1992. The professional game, without a collective-bargaining agreement between club owners and players since 1987, came closer to adopting a system that would eventually grant *free agency* to almost every player. Free agency is the ability of players to switch to other teams after their contracts expire. Meanwhile, the major college conferences instituted a coalition that provided post-season bowl games with match-ups designed to produce an undisputed national champion.

The year's most successful teams were the San Francisco 49ers, who ended with the best record in the National Football League's (NFL) regular season, and the University of Alabama, which captured the national college championship.

NFL and free agency. The NFL had the most restrictive free agency rules of any major sport, and during 1992 it suffered significant court defeats as the players pressed the fight for unrestricted free agency. Eight players, led by running back Freeman McNeil of the New York Jets, filed an antitrust case against the NFL. The trial ended on September 10 when a federal jury in Minneapolis, Minn., struck down the NFL's existing free agency system that provided limited movement to some players but not others. The jury awarded a total of almost $1.63 million to four of those players and nothing to the other four. But the verdict led to increased free agency gains by all players.

The NFL's free agency system allowed each team to protect 37 players, essentially preventing those players from changing teams even if their contracts expired. Unprotected players were free to sign with other teams during a two-month period. On September 24, four players who were protected under the NFL's free agency system and had not yet signed 1992 contracts were declared free agents by the federal judge who presided over the McNeil case. The judge gave the players five days to sign with any team.

The judge urged the clubs and players to settle the remaining suits by agreeing to a collective-bargaining pact. If none was reached, he said he would impose rules to govern the sport.

In late December, the two sides announced a tentative agreement that would allow players with five years of NFL experience to become unrestricted free agents. Teams would be allowed to exempt one to three players from free agency, but teams would have to pay those players liberally. The annual draft of college players would be trimmed from 12 rounds to 7 rounds, and teams that lost the most free agents would get additional draft choices. A salary cap would be instituted for rookies, and a team salary cap would be triggered if total player salaries reached 67 per cent of the combined revenues of the NFL's 28 teams.

Problems. NFL financial statements introduced in court cases showed that in 1991 the league and its teams took in $1.4 billion, including $850 million for television and radio rights and $402 million from ticket sales. However, the league predicted financial difficulties, saying television income would drop sharply after 1993 and salaries would rise because of impending free agency.

The network television contracts called for each team to receive $32.5 million in 1992 and $41 million in 1993. The networks said they were losing money on professional football because of diminished advertising income and asked the league for $238 million in rebates. If the league gave the rebates, the networks said they would sign two-year extensions at $32.5 million per year for each team. Instead, the club owners voted against those rebates, substituting a $1-million rebate by each team in 1993.

The NFL announced in September 1992 that play in the 1993 World League of American Football season would be suspended. Television ratings and revenue had fallen for the 10-team international springtime league that the NFL founded in 1991. The World League included three teams in Europe, six in the United States, and one in Canada. The NFL said the league may start up again in 1994, however.

Injuries were rampant in the NFL. One of every seven NFL players missed at least four games because of injuries during the 1992 season. Dennis Byrd, a defensive end for the Jets, was partially paralyzed on November 29 when he broke his neck in a game against Kansas City. Defensive tackle Jerome Brown of the Philadelphia Eagles and offensive guard Eric

The 1992 college football season

College conference champions

Conference	School
Atlantic Coast	Florida State
Big East	Miami (Fla.)
Big Eight	Nebraska
Big Sky	Idaho
Big Ten	Michigan
Big West	Nevada-Reno
Gateway	Northern Iowa
Ivy League	Dartmouth
Mid-American	Bowling Green
Mid-Eastern	North Carolina A&T
Ohio Valley	Middle Tennessee State
Pacific Ten	Washington
Patriot	Lafayette
Southeastern	Alabama
Southern	Citadel
Southland	Northeast Louisiana
Southwest	Texas A&M
Southwestern	Alcorn State
Western Athletic	Hawaii
Yankee	Delaware

Major bowl games

Bowl	Winner	Loser
Aloha	Kansas 23	Brigham Young 20
Amos Alonzo Stagg (Div. III)	Wisconsin-La Crosse 16	Washington & Jefferson 12
Blockbuster	Stanford 24	Penn State 3
Blue-Gray	Gray 27	Blue 17
Copper	Washington State 31	Utah 28
Cotton	Notre Dame 28	Texas A&M 3
Fiesta	Syracuse 26	Colorado 22
Florida Citrus	Georgia 21	Ohio State 14
Freedom	Fresno State 24	Southern California 7
Gator	Florida 27	North Carolina St. 10
Hall of Fame	Tennessee 38	Boston College 23
Holiday	Hawaii 27	Illinois 17
Independence	Wake Forest 39	Oregon 35
John Hancock	Baylor 20	Arizona 15
Las Vegas	Bowling Green 35	Nevada-Reno 34
Liberty	Mississippi 13	Air Force 0
Orange	Florida State 27	Nebraska 14
Peach	North Carolina 21	Mississippi State 17
Rose	Michigan 38	Washington 31
Sugar	Alabama 34	Miami 14
NCAA Div. I-AA	Marshall 31	Youngstown State 28
NCAA Div. II	Jacksonville State 17	Pittsburg St. (Kans.) 13
NAIA Div. I	Central State (Ohio) 19	Gardner-Webb (N.C.) 16
NAIA Div. II	Findlay (Ohio) 26	Linfield (Ore.) 13

All-America team (as picked by AP)

Offense

Quarterback—Gino Torretta, Miami
Running backs—Garrison Hearst, Georgia; Marshall Faulk, San Diego State
Wide receivers—Sean Dawkins, California; O. J. McDuffie, Penn State
Tight end—Chris Gedney, Syracuse
Center—Mike Compton, West Virginia
Guards—Will Shields, Nebraska; Aaron Taylor, Notre Dame
Tackles—Lincoln Kennedy, Washington; Everett Lindsay, Mississippi
All-purpose—Glyn Milburn, Stanford
Place-kicker—Joe Allison, Memphis State

Defense

Linemen—Eric Curry, Alabama; John Copeland, Alabama; Rob Waldrop, Arizona; Chris Slade, Virginia
Linebackers—Marvin Jones, Florida State; Micheal Barrow, Miami; Marcus Buckley, Texas A&M
Backs—Ryan McNeil, Miami; Carlton McDonald, Air Force; Deon Figures, Colorado; Carlton Gray, UCLA
Punter—Sean Snyder, Kansas State

Player awards

Heisman Trophy (best player)—Gino Torretta, Miami
Lombardi Award (best lineman)—Marvin Jones, Florida State
Outland Award (best interior lineman)—Will Shields, Nebraska

Quarterback Gino Torretta of the University of Miami in Florida won the 1992 Heisman Trophy in December.

Andolsek of the Detroit Lions were killed in off-season automobile accidents.

NFL season. In the National Conference, the 49ers tallied a 14-2 regular season record. They won the Western Division with Steve Young at quarterback in place of the celebrated Joe Montana, who was sidelined after elbow surgery. The Minnesota Vikings (11-5) won the Central Division. The aggressive Dallas Cowboys (13-3) won the Eastern Division, and the New Orleans Saints had a strong year, finishing the regular season at 12-4 and clinching a play-off berth. But in the first round of the play-offs, the Saints lost to Philadelphia, 36-20, and Minnesota lost to the Washington Redskins, 24-7. On Jan. 9 to 10, 1993, the 49ers beat the Redskins, 20-13, and Dallas ousted Philadelphia, 34-10, setting up a conference title game between San Francisco and Dallas.

In the American Conference, the Miami Dolphins and the Buffalo Bills finished the season with 11-5 records in the Eastern Division, but Miami was awarded the division title in accordance with a tie-breaker formula. Buffalo made the play-offs for the fifth consecutive year, but their star quarterback Jim Kelly injured a knee in the last game of the season. The Pittsburgh Steelers won the Central Division with an 11-5 record. The San Diego Chargers became the first team ever to lose its first four games and still qualify for the play-offs. The Chargers won the Western Division title with an 11-5 record. The Kansas City Chiefs (10-6) finished second in the Western Division. In the play-offs, the Chiefs lost to San Diego, 17-0, and the Bills registered the greatest comeback in NFL history, erasing a 35-3 deficit to beat Houston, 41-38, in overtime.On Jan. 9 to 10, 1993, Miami beat San Diego, 31-0, and Buffalo beat Pittsburgh, 24-3, setting up a conference showdown between Miami and Buffalo.

Other pro news. The Pro Football Hall of Fame on Aug. 1, 1992, added tight end John Mackey, fullback John Riggins, cornerback Lem Barney, and club owner/ coach Al Davis. After six years, the NFL in March ended the instant replay review of calls by officials. The Calgary Stampeders won the Grey Cup game for the Canadian Football League championship by defeating the Winnipeg Blue Bombers, 24-10, on November 29 in Toronto, Ontario.

College bowls. Until 1992, the post-season bowl games often fought one another for the best teams, and the teams ranked highest in the weekly polls seldom met. To bring order to the selections, the major bowls finalized a coalition in January 1992 whereby the bowls that had berths uncommitted to a conference would fill them according to a system that allowed the best available teams to meet each other.

The coalition used The Associated Press's final regular-season poll of sportswriters and broadcasters to match bowl contestants. That poll ranked Miami of Florida first, Alabama second, Florida State third, Texas A&M fourth, and Notre Dame fifth. Because first-ranked Miami was free to choose a bowl and second-ranked Alabama, as the Southeastern Conference champion, was committed to the Sugar Bowl on Jan. 1, 1993, in New Orleans, Miami agreed to play Alabama there. Alabama scored an impressive 34-14 victory, and the next day the Associated Press poll picked Alabama as the national champion. As the Southwest Conference champion, Texas A&M was committed to the Cotton Bowl on January 1 in Dallas. The Cotton Bowl, rather than following the rankings and choosing Florida State to play Texas A&M, selected Notre Dame. Notre Dame won the game, 28-3.

College season. Of the major colleges, only Alabama (12-0), Miami (11-0), and Texas A&M (12-0) finished the regular season unbeaten and untied. The teams with the next best records were Michigan (8-0-3), Florida State (10-1), Notre Dame (9-1-1), and Colorado (9-1-1).

Gino Torretta, Miami's senior quarterback, won the Heisman Trophy as the season's outstanding player. In 11 games in 1992, he completed 228 of 402 passes for 3,060 yards and 19 touchdowns.

In the Heisman voting, the leaders were Torretta with 1,400 points, running back Marshall Faulk of San Diego State with 1,080, running back Garrison Hearst of Georgia with 982, and linebacker Marvin Jones of Florida State with 392. Jones won the Lombardi Award as the nation's best lineman and the Butkus Award as the best linebacker. Frank Litsky

In ***World Book,*** see **Football.**

National Football League final standings

American Conference

Eastern Division	W.	L.	T.	Pct.
Miami Dolphins*	11	5	0	.688
Buffalo Bills*	11	5	0	.688
Indianapolis Colts	9	7	0	.563
New York Jets	4	12	0	.250
New England Patriots	2	14	0	.125

Central Division	W.	L.	T.	Pct.
Pittsburgh Steelers*	11	5	0	.688
Houston Oilers*	10	6	0	.625
Cleveland Browns	7	9	0	.438
Cincinnati Bengals	5	11	0	.313

Western Division	W.	L.	T.	Pct.
San Diego Chargers*	11	5	0	.688
Kansas City Chiefs*	10	6	0	.625
Denver Broncos	8	8	0	.500
Los Angeles Raiders	7	9	0	.438
Seattle Seahawks	2	14	0	.125

*Made play-off.

Individual statistics

Leading scorers, touchdowns	TD's	Rush	Rec.	Ret.	Pts.
Thurman Thomas, Buffalo	12	9	3	0	72
Barry Foster, Pittsburgh	11	11	0	0	66
Ernest Givins, Houston	10	0	10	0	60
Rodney Culver, Indianapolis	9	7	2	0	54
Haywood Jeffires, Houston	9	0	9	0	54
Derrick Fenner, Cincinnati	8	7	1	0	48
Mark Jackson, Denver	8	0	8	0	48
Anthony Miller, San Diego	8	0	7	1	48
Lorenzo White, Houston	8	7	1	0	48

Leading scorers, kicking	PAT	FG	Longest	Pts.
Pete Stoyanovich, Miami	34/36	30/37	53	124
Steve Christie, Buffalo	43/44	24/30	54	115
Gary Anderson, Pittsburgh	29/31	28/36	49	113
John Carney, San Diego	35/35	26/32	50	113
Nick Lowery, Kansas City	39/39	22/24	52	105
Al Del Greco, Houston	41/41	21/27	54	104
Matt Stover, Cleveland	29/30	21/29	51	92

Leading quarterbacks	Att.	Comp.	Yds.	TD's	Int.
Warren Moon, Houston	346	224	2,521	18	12
Dan Marino, Miami	554	330	4,116	24	16
Neil O'Donnell, Pittsburgh	313	185	2,283	13	9
Jim Kelly, Buffalo	462	269	3,457	23	19
Cody Carlson, Houston	227	149	1,710	9	11
Dave Krieg, Kansas City	413	230	3,115	15	12
Stan Humphries, San Diego	454	263	3,356	16	18
John Elway, Denver	316	174	2,242	10	17
Jay Schroeder, L.A. Raiders	253	123	1,476	11	11
Jeff George, Indianapolis	306	167	1,963	7	15

Leading receivers	Number caught	Total yards	Avg. gain	TD's
Haywood Jeffires, Houston	90	913	10.1	9
Curtis Duncan, Houston	82	954	11.6	1
Ronnie Harmon, San Diego	79	914	11.6	1
John L. Williams, Seattle	74	556	7.5	2
Anthony Miller, San Diego	72	1,060	14.7	7
Ernest Givins, Houston	67	787	11.7	10
Andre Reed, Buffalo	65	913	14.0	3
Reggie Langhorne, Indianapolis	65	811	12.5	1
Thurman Thomas, Buffalo	58	626	10.8	3
Chris Burkett, N.Y. Jets	57	724	12.7	1
Lorenzo White, Houston	57	641	11.2	1

Leading rushers	No.	Yards	Avg.	TD's
Barry Foster, Pittsburgh	390	1,690	4.3	11
Thurman Thomas, Buffalo	312	1,487	4.8	9
Lorenzo White, Houston	265	1,226	4.6	7
Harold Green, Cincinnati	265	1,170	4.4	2
Chris Warren, Seattle	223	1,017	4.6	3
Mark Higgs, Miami	256	915	3.6	7
Marion Butts, San Diego	218	809	3.7	4
Eric Dickerson, L.A. Raiders	187	729	3.9	2
Brad Baxter, N.Y. Jets	152	698	4.6	6

Leading punters	No.	Yards	Avg.	Longest
Greg Montgomery, Houston	53	2,487	46.9	66
Rohn Stark, Indianapolis	83	3,716	44.8	64
Rick Tuten, Seattle	108	4,706	44.1	65
Bryan Barker, Kansas City	75	3,245	43.3	65

National Conference

Eastern Division	W.	L.	T.	Pct.
Dallas Cowboys*	13	3	0	.813
Philadelphia Eagles*	11	5	0	.688
Washington Redskins*	9	7	0	.563
New York Giants	6	10	0	.375
Phoenix Cardinals	4	12	0	.250

Central Division	W.	L.	T.	Pct.
Minnesota Vikings*	11	5	0	.688
Green Bay Packers	9	7	0	.563
Chicago Bears	5	11	0	.313
Tampa Bay Buccaneers	5	11	0	.313
Detroit Lions	5	11	0	.313

Western Division	W.	L.	T.	Pct.
San Francisco 49ers*	14	2	0	.875
New Orleans Saints*	12	4	0	.750
Atlanta Falcons	6	10	0	.375
Los Angeles Rams	6	10	0	.375

Individual statistics

Leading scorers, touchdowns	TD's	Rush	Rec.	Ret.	Pts.
Emmitt Smith, Dallas	19	18	1	0	114
Terry Allen, Minnesota	15	13	2	0	90
Rodney Hampton, N.Y. Giants	14	14	0	0	84
Sterling Sharpe, Green Bay	13	0	13	0	78
Neal Anderson, Chicago	11	5	6	0	66
Jerry Rice, San Francisco	11	1	10	0	66
Andre Rison, Atlanta	11	0	11	0	66
Ricky Watters, San Francisco	11	9	2	0	66

Leading scorers, kicking	PAT	FG	Longest	Pts.
Morten Andersen, New Orleans	33/34	29/34	52	120
Chip Lohmiller, Washington	30/30	30/40	53	120
Lin Elliott, Dallas	47/48	24/35	53	119
Mike Cofer, San Francisco	53/54	18/27	46	107
Fuad Reveiz, Minnesota	45/45	19/25	52	102
Chris Jacke, Green Bay	30/30	22/29	53	96

Leading quarterbacks	Att.	Comp.	Yds.	TD's	Int.
Steve Young, San Francisco	402	268	3,465	25	7
Chris Miller, Atlanta	253	152	1,739	15	6
Troy Aikman, Dallas	473	302	3,445	23	14
Randall Cunningham, Philadelphia	384	233	2,775	19	11
Brett Favre, Green Bay	471	302	3,227	18	13
Bobby Hebert, New Orleans	422	249	3,287	19	16
Jim Everett, L.A. Rams	475	281	3,323	22	18
Chris Chandler, Phoenix	413	245	2,832	15	15
Jim Harbaugh, Chicago	358	202	2,486	13	12
Vinny Testaverde, Tampa Bay	358	206	2,554	14	16

Leading receivers	Number caught	Total yards	Avg. gain	TD's
Sterling Sharpe, Green Bay	108	1,461	13.5	13
Andre Rison, Atlanta	93	1,121	12.1	11
Jerry Rice, San Francisco	84	1,201	14.3	10
Michael Irvin, Dallas	78	1,396	17.9	7
Mike Pritchard, Atlanta	77	827	10.7	5
Brett Perriman, Detroit	69	810	11.7	4
Eric Martin, New Orleans	68	1,041	15.3	5
Jay Novacek, Dallas	68	630	9.3	6
Fred Barnett, Philadelphia	67	1,083	16.2	6
Gary Clark, Washington	64	912	14.3	5

Leading rushers	No.	Yards	Avg.	TD's
Emmitt Smith, Dallas	373	1,713	4.6	18
Barry Sanders, Detroit	293	1,248	4.3	9
Terry Allen, Minnesota	266	1,201	4.5	13
Reggie Cobb, Tampa Bay	310	1,171	3.8	9
Rodney Hampton, N.Y. Giants	257	1,141	4.4	14
Cleveland Gary, L.A. Rams	279	1,125	4.0	7
Herschel Walker, Philadelphia	267	1,070	4.0	8
Earnest Byner, Washington	262	998	3.8	6
Ricky Watters, San Francisco	203	998	4.9	9

Leading punters	No.	Yards	Avg.	Longest
Harry Newsome, Minnesota	72	3,243	45.0	84
Tommy Barnhardt, New Orleans	67	2,947	44.0	62
Sean Landeta, N.Y. Giants	53	2,317	43.7	71
Jim Arnold, Detroit	60	2,609	43.5	62

French truckers stage a roadblock—one of hundreds across the nation—during a 10-day protest against new licensing regulations in June and July.

France was hit by unexpected political turbulence in 1992. Much of the turmoil surrounded the country's central role in promoting closer economic and political unity within the 12-nation European Community (EC or Common Market). In the meantime, the popularity of the governing Socialist Party plummeted.

Socialist Party setbacks. Prime Minister Edith Cresson was dismissed by French President François Mitterrand in April, less than 11 months after she took office. The dismissal of the unpopular prime minister followed a disastrous showing by the Socialist Party in regional elections held in March. Shortly before the elections, Cresson's approval rating hit a record low of 19 per cent. Mitterrand named Finance Minister Pierre Bérégovoy to replace her.

Cresson's term had been marred by squabbles with Japan over trade policies; an inability to come to grips with France's economic woes, especially high unemployment; and a controversial decision in January to admit Palestinian leader George Habash into France for medical treatment. Habash heads a group that has been linked to terrorist activities.

AIDS scandal. France was rocked in June when four former government health officials went on trial for knowingly permitting transfusions of blood that had been contaminated by the virus that causes AIDS. Lawyers charged that the tainted blood had infected more than 1,200 people and killed more than 250 of those infected. Three of the defendants were convicted. The former head of the National Blood Transfusion Center received the heaviest penalty: four years in prison and a $100,000 fine. The French parliament agreed in November to appoint a special court to try three former Socialist cabinet members, including former Prime Minister Laurent Fabius, for their alleged role in the scandal.

Committed to European unity. Throughout the year, France remained firmly committed to forging closer EC unity, especially through its strong ties to Germany. Evidence of those ties appeared in autumn, in vigorous efforts by the French and German governments to defend the value of the French currency, the franc, on foreign exchange markets. Moreover, the leaders of the two countries in May announced plans to form a combined European army corps, known as the Euro Corps, made up primarily of French and German soldiers. Many observers viewed the push by Mitterrand for a greater EC role in European defense as an effort to distance France from the United States. Creation of a European army could undermine the North Atlantic Treaty Organization, a defense alliance in which the United States plays a leading role.

Mitterrand, whose presidential term expires in 1995, took a big political gamble by submitting the EC's Maastricht Treaty on European Union to French voters on Sept. 20, 1992. The treaty, which leaders of the EC nations signed in December 1991, calls for the creation of a single EC currency and a common foreign policy. Supporters of the treaty said it would enhance France's role in a thriving Europe by the end of the 1990's. Opponents claimed the treaty would force the French government to give up too much control over the country's affairs.

The treaty was narrowly approved by a vote of 51 per cent to 49 per cent. Just before the vote, Mitterrand entered a Paris hospital to have a cancerous prostate gland removed. He resumed his duties while undergoing further cancer treatment after surgery.

The closely fought Maastricht referendum fractured traditional French political alliances, particularly on the right. The leaders of the two major conservative parties—former French President Valéry Giscard d'Estaing and Paris Mayor Jacques Chirac—supported the Maastricht Treaty, despite strong misgivings within their parties. Two members of Chirac's party, Rally for the Republic, led the opposition to the treaty.

Trade negotiations between the EC and the United States succeeded in November, even though France balked at further reductions in its subsidies to farmers. The United States claimed these subsidies hurt American farmers, whereas France insisted that further cuts would drive many of its farmers out of business. Before the settlement, the United States threatened to slap a 200 per cent import tax on certain EC goods, especially white wines. France exports more white wines to the United States than does any other country. Philip Revzin

See also **Bérégovoy, Pierre; Europe** (Facts in brief table). In ***World Book,*** see **France**.

Franklin, Barbara H. (1940-), became the 29th secretary of commerce following her confirmation by the United States Senate on Feb. 27, 1992. She was well known in the business community. The American Management Association named her one of America's "50 most influential corporate directors" in 1990.

Franklin was born in Lancaster, Pa., on March 19, 1940, and graduated with distinction from Pennsylvania State University in University Park in 1962. She later became one of the first women to receive an M.B.A. from Harvard University in Boston.

Franklin has held directorships at seven companies: Aetna Life and Casualty Company; Armstrong World Industries, Inc.; Automatic Data Processing, Inc.; Black and Decker Corporation; Dow Chemical Company; Nordstrom, Inc.; and Westinghouse Electric Corporation. Franklin also was president and chief executive officer of Franklin Association, a management consulting firm that she founded in 1984. Franklin entered public service in 1971, when she was appointed by President Richard Nixon to direct a new program set up by the White House to recruit women for high-level government positions. In 1972, Franklin was named one of the first commissioners of the U.S. Consumer Product Safety Commission. In 1989, Franklin was appointed an alternate representative and public delegate to the United Nations General Assembly.

Franklin is married to Wallace Barnes, chairman of Barnes Group, Inc. Kristine Portnoy Kelley

Geology. Four large earthquakes registering at least 6.3 on the Richter scale and a number of strong aftershocks shook California in 1992. On April 25, an earthquake registering 7.1 struck northern California about 35 miles (56 kilometers) south of Eureka near Cape Mendocino. The quake occurred in a region where the Juan de Fuca Plate—also known as the Gorda Plate—one of the tectonic plates that make up Earth's outer shell, lies between the larger Pacific and North American plates. The Pacific and North American plates are grinding past each other. Two strong aftershocks, each measuring 6.6, struck the area the next day.

Mojave quakes. Three major quakes rocked the Mojave Desert in southern California in April and June. The first, which registered 6.3, struck near Joshua Tree on April 22. Two more earthquakes hit the area on June 28. The first, a magnitude 7.6 shock that occurred near Landers, was the most powerful earthquake to hit California since 1952. The second quake, which measured 6.7, struck near Big Bear Lake.

The break in the rock produced by the Landers quake was unlike any other ever observed by geologists. The Landers break involved several faults and actually jumped from one fault to another. This discovery challenges the theory that an earthquake affects only a single segment of a single fault.

The occurrence of the three earthquakes has also provided support for the theory, proposed in 1989, that a new fault is forming in the Mojave Desert east

A large crack in the Mojave Desert (arrow) formed after a powerful earthquake registering 7.6 struck near Landers, Calif., on June 28.

of Los Angeles. The scientists who proposed the theory believe the faults that ruptured in the Mojave are part of a new fault that is forming across several previously mapped faults.

Egyptian quake. The strongest earthquake to hit Egypt since 1969 struck parts of Cairo, the capital, and devastated a suburb on Oct. 12, 1992. The quake, which measured 5.9, killed 543 people and injured more than 6,500. Egyptian authorities blamed shoddy building construction for most of the casualties.

A meteorite, after all. Evidence that may solve a long-standing controversy over the origin of a geologic feature known as the Sudbury structure in Ontario, Canada, was reported in September by scientists from the Geological Survey of Canada in Ottawa. The Sudbury structure is a roughly oval formation about 37 miles (60 kilometers) long and 16 miles (26 kilometers) wide that formed about 1.85 million years ago. It holds one of Earth's largest deposits of nickel-copper ores.

Scientists have long debated whether the Sudbury structure was formed by an eruption of *magma* (molten rock) from within Earth or by a meteorite impact. Although the structure resembles an impact crater in some ways, it is oval in shape. Impact craters are generally circular.

The scientists found that the Sudbury structure originally was circular and so concluded that it had been formed by a meteorite an estimated 6 miles (10 kilometers) in diameter. Some time afterward, it was reshaped into an oval by geologic forces created by the collision of two tectonic plates.

Precambrian insights. A survey of the global record of biological and geological events leading up to the first appearance of animals on Earth about 550 million years ago was the subject of a conference convened in October 1992. The conference was the first to gather geologists, paleobiologists, and geophysicists to discuss the late Precambrian Period, the period from 1 billion to 550 million years ago.

The scientists attending the meeting agreed that about 1 billion years ago, several continents collided to form a supercontinent known as Rodinia. The chief evidence for the existence of this supercontinent consists of the presence on all modern continents of sections of an ancient mountain range, called the Grenville Belt, that apparently spanned Rodinia. Rodinia broke apart between about 750 million and 600 million years ago, and the pieces formed Laurentia (what are now North America and Greenland) and another supercontinent called Gondwanaland.

At the same time, repeated ice ages occurred, and, just before the first animals appeared, the levels of oxygen in the atmosphere increased sharply. Although the scientists agreed that the rapid increase in atmospheric oxygen was the result of a geologic event, the exact nature of that event remains unknown.

Eldridge M. Moores

In *World Book,* see **Geology.**

Georgia. When 1992 began, Georgia was in the midst of civil war, as opponents and supporters of Georgian President Zviad K. Gamsakhurdia battled each other in Tbilisi, the nation's capital. The fighting had begun on Dec. 22, 1991, three days before the Soviet Union was dissolved and Georgia became independent. Opposition leaders claimed Gamsakhurdia was trying to establish a dictatorship.

Gamsakhurdia fled Georgia on Jan. 6, 1992, and opposition forces established a provisional government. Gamsakhurdia returned to western Georgia on January 16, but Georgian troops crushed a counteroffensive by his supporters at the end of January. Gamsakhurdia later was said to be living in the autonomous republic of Chechen-Ingush in southern Russia.

Eduard A. Shevardnadze, former Soviet foreign minister and Georgian Communist Party leader, was named head of the provisional government on March 10. Shevardnadze pledged to implement democratic reforms and to begin Georgia's transition to a free-market economy. Shevardnadze also said he would not press for Georgian membership in the Commonwealth of Independent States (C.I.S.), a loose confederation of former Soviet republics that was established shortly before the Soviet Union was dissolved.

Ethnic conflicts. After taking his post as head of the government, Shevardnadze faced continuing guerrilla operations by pro-Gamsakhurdia forces, including an attempted coup on June 24. He also was confronted with two long-standing nationalist conflicts. In June, heavy fighting erupted in the northern Georgian region of South Ossetia. Since 1990, South Ossetia had sought independence or unification with North Ossetia, an autonomous region in Russia. On June 24, 1992, Shevardnadze and Russian President Boris Yeltsin agreed to establish a joint peacekeeping force in South Ossetia.

On August 18, Georgian forces moved into Abkhazia, a region in northwestern Georgia. Abkhazia's parliament had declared sovereignty on July 23, 1992. Georgia claimed that separatists in Abkhazia were sheltering Gamsakhurdia supporters. The Georgian forces captured large portions of Abkhazia in September. But by early October, Abkhazian fighers, backed by forces from Chechen-Ingush and other regions of southern Russia, had recaptured much of the lost territory.

The Georgians also charged that Russia had secretly aided the rebels. Russia denied the charge. Georgian efforts in October to convene talks with Russia on ways to achieve peace in Abkhazia failed.

In elections on October 11, Shevardnadze—who had run unopposed—was overwhelmingly elected speaker of parliament. The post is equivalent to president. Justin Burke

See also **Asia** (Facts in brief table). In the World Book Supplement section, see **Georgia.**

Georgia. See **State government.**

Rebels in the semiautonomous region of Abkhazia, in Georgia, prepare to confront Georgian soldiers after the region declared its independence in July.

A rioter hurls a firebomb at a hostel for foreigners seeking asylum in Germany, one of many such attacks during the second part of the year.

Germany. In 1992, the second year after East and West Germany became one country in October 1990, the high cost of unification remained a central issue. The country struggled to maintain its status as Europe's strongest economy. It also confronted difficult social and foreign policy issues as it worked to redefine its role in Europe and the rest of the world.

Economic effects of unification. The government estimated that spending in the former East Germany—on welfare, retraining, and other social programs; rebuilding outdated factories; and cleaning up industrial pollution—would total 180 billion Deutsche marks (about U.S. $100 billion) in 1992. These costs swelled the federal budget deficit, leading to fears that inflation also would rise. Inflation reached a peak annual rate of 4.8 per cent in March.

To fight inflation and to defend the value of the mark, Germany's central bank, the Bundesbank, kept interest rates high throughout the year. The high interest rates slowed the economy's rate of growth to less than 2 per cent in 1992. The slow growth rate, in turn, led to an increase in unemployment. By October, about 6 per cent of the total German work force was unemployed or working less than full-time. The rate was above 20 per cent in the east.

European economies also were affected by Germany's high interest rates. Most European nations link their currencies to the value of the mark through the European Monetary System (EMS), an organization set up by the 12-nation European Community (EC or Common Market). When Germany raised its interest rates, these nations had to raise theirs as well.

The EMS was thrown into crisis in early September, when currency speculators, fearing that the system's weaker currencies would be devalued, began selling these currencies in favor of the mark. In response, the Bundesbank cut its interest rate slightly. However, the cut was too small to halt the crisis, and Great Britain and Italy temporarily withdrew from the system.

The September crisis cast doubt on the future of the EC's proposed economic and monetary union, due by the end of the 1990's. In December, the German parliament ratified the so-called Maastricht Treaty establishing the union, which will include creation of a single EC currency. But many Germans expressed doubts about the wisdom of trading in the strong, well-established mark for a European currency.

Defense and security. On May 22, France and Germany announced the formation of a joint 35,000-member army corps, to be known as the Euro Corps. They said the corps, which was intended as the basis of a European army, would begin operations by 1995. But the two nations said the force would not replace the North Atlantic Treaty Organization (NATO), the Western security alliance. They also said the United States should maintain a military presence in Europe. The United States had said in 1989 it would cut by at least half the approximately 300,000 U.S. troops then stationed in Europe, mainly in Germany, by 1995.

In July 1992, a German warship and three reconnaissance planes joined an international patrol to monitor United Nations sanctions against Yugoslavia, where civil war was raging. The German parliament ruled on July 22 that the action did not violate Germany's Constitution, which bans the deployment of German troops outside NATO countries. However, the government said it would press for a constitutional amendment to permit such deployment. The Euro Corps was expected to participate in missions outside the NATO area as well as in Europe.

Violence against foreigners living in Germany flared up again beginning in August, after a period of relative calm following a wave of attacks in 1991. Much of the violence was directed against refugees seeking asylum in Germany. At least 368,000 asylum-seekers arrived in Germany in the first 10 months of 1992, many of them from the former republics of Yugoslavia, the former Soviet Union, and Eastern Europe. Hundreds of thousands of Germans took part in demonstrations condemning the violence.

As the violence increased, the German government came under increasing pressure both to stop the attacks and to halt the flow of refugees. On October 16, the ruling coalition led by German Chancellor Helmut Kohl's Christian Democratic Union (CDU) failed in a parliamentary bid to amend Germany's asylum laws, the most liberal in Europe. But in December, the CDU and the opposition Social Democratic Party (SPD) agreed to draft compromise legislation after the SPD dropped its opposition to changing the law.

On November 27, the government said it was banning the Nationalist Front, a neo-Nazi group. The ban came in response to a November 23 attack in which three members of a Turkish family died when rioters firebombed their home in Mölln, Germany. Two neo-Nazis later confessed to taking part in the attack.

In September, Germany had come under international and domestic criticism when it announced that it had reached an agreement with Romania to deport thousands of Romanian Gypsies who failed to qualify for asylum. Most Gypsies and other Romanians do not qualify for asylum under German law, which excludes refugees not fleeing political persecution. Gypsies say they are persecuted in Romania.

The trial of Erich Honecker, Communist head of East Germany from 1971 to 1989, opened on November 12, 1992. Honecker faced charges of manslaughter for allegedly ordering East German border guards to shoot anyone trying to flee from East Berlin to West Berlin. Honecker had fled to the Soviet Union in March 1991 and had taken refuge in the Chilean Embassy in Moscow in December 1991. He was extradited to Germany from Russia on July 29, 1992, after the Chilean government asked him to leave their Moscow embassy. Philip Revzin

See also **Europe** (Facts in brief table). In ***World Book,*** see **Germany.**

Ghana. See **Africa.**

Fred Couples tees off on the way to winning the Masters tournament on April 12 in Augusta, Ga.

Golf. Fred Couples, Davis Love III, and John Cook won major honors in 1992 on the men's professional tour. Lee Trevino, despite painful torn ligaments in his left thumb, dominated the senior tour. Dottie Mochrie, Betsy King, and Danielle Ammaccapane were big winners on the women's tour.

Men. The Professional Golfers' Association (PGA) tour was made up of 50 tournaments worth $50 million in prize money. Couples, Love, and Cook won three tournaments each. The leading money-winners were Couples with $1,344,188, Love with $1,191,630, and Cook with $1,165,606. In the four grand-slam tournaments, Nick Faldo of England won his fifth major title in six years, and Couples, Tom Kite, and Nick Price of England won their first.

The first grand slam was the Masters from April 9 to 12 in Augusta, Ga. Couples won with a 72-hole score of 275, beating Raymond Floyd by two strokes. Floyd spoiled his chances on the final round when his eagle putt missed by a fraction of an inch on the 15th hole, and his birdie putt slid over the edge of the hole on the 16th. By winning, Couples improved his 1992 record to three victories, two seconds, and a third in nine tournaments and passed $1 million in season earnings. He also regained the number 1 world ranking from Faldo. Faldo won it back later in the year, however.

In winds up to 35 miles (56 kilometers) per hour, Kite won the United States Open from June 18 to 21 in Pebble Beach, Calif. Kite's 285 defeated Jeff Sluman by two strokes. Gil Morgan, who led after three rounds, finished with an 81, and the wind also hurt defending champion Payne Stewart (83) and former champion Scott Simpson (88).

In the British Open from July 16 to 19 played over the Muirfield course in Gullane, Scotland, Faldo fell back with three bogeys between the 11th and 14th holes on the final round. Then he rallied with two birdies on the last four holes, and his 272 beat Cook by a stroke. Cook contributed to his downfall when he three-putted for a par on the 17th hole and bogeyed the 18th.

Price won the PGA championship from August 13 to 16 in St. Louis, Mo. His 278 total defeated Faldo, Cook, Gene Sauers, and Jim Gallagher, Jr., by three strokes. Price was steady day after day, shooting 70, 70, 68, and 70. Price preserved his lead on the final round by sinking a 30-foot (9-meter) putt on the 16th hole and a 15-foot (5-meter) putt on the 17th.

PGA senior. In its richest season ever, the circuit for 50-and-older professionals offered 42 tournaments with $22 million in prize money. Trevino, despite his injury, won five tournaments. Mike Hill, George Archer, and Gibby Gilbert won three each. Trevino also led in earnings with $847,752 and in scoring average with 69.49.

Trevino won the Tradition tournament from April 2 to 5 in Scottsdale, Ariz., beating Jack Nicklaus, the two-time defender, by a stroke. Trevino also won the PGA Seniors from April 16 to 19 in Palm Beach Gardens, Fla., beating Hill by a stroke. Dave Stockton captured the Senior Players Championship from June 11 to 14 in Dearborn, Mich., a stroke ahead of Trevino and J. C. Snead. Long-shot Larry Laoretti took the United States Seniors Open from July 9 to 12 in Bethlehem, Pa., four strokes ahead of Jim Colbert.

At age 49, on the PGA's regular tour, Floyd won the Doral Open on March 8 in Miami. On September 20, having turned 50 and playing in his second senior tournament, he won the GTE North Classic in Indianapolis and became the first player to win on the regular tour and the senior tour in the same year.

Women. The Ladies Professional Golf Association (LPGA) tour consisted of 40 tournaments worth $22-million. The 27-year-old Mochrie won four tournaments, and Ammaccapane, King, and Patty Sheehan won three. The leading money-winners were Mochrie with $693,335 and King with $551,320.

In the first major tournament, Mochrie won the Nabisco Dinah Shore from March 25 to 29 in Rancho Mirage, Calif., beating Juli Inkster in a play-off. King, with a 17-under-par 267, ran away with the Mazda LPGA championship from May 14 to 17 in Bethesda, Md., by a tournament-record 11 strokes. Sheehan won the U.S. Open from July 22 to 27 in Oakmont, Pa., beating Inkster in an 18-hole play-off after they had tied at 280. Frank Litsky

In ***World Book,*** see **Golf.**

Gore, Albert A., Jr. (1948-), Democratic senator from Tennessee, was elected Vice President of the United States on Nov. 3, 1992. He was named the Democratic vice presidential candidate at the party's national convention in New York City in July 1992. Most Democratic leaders saw his environmental record, his experience in the U.S. Congress, and his reputation as a foreign policy expert as an asset to the ticket headed by Arkansas Governor Bill Clinton.

Gore was born on March 31, 1948, the son of former U.S. Senator Albert Gore, Sr., and Pauline Gore. He received a B.A. in government with honors from Harvard University in Cambridge, Mass., in 1969. After graduation, he joined the U.S. Army and served in Vietnam. Gore also worked as an investigative reporter for the Nashville daily newspaper *The Tennessean.* In 1976, Gore won election to the U.S. House of Representatives. He was elected to the Senate in 1984. In 1988, Gore ran unsuccessfully for the Democratic nomination for President. One of the more environmentally active senators, Gore was chairman of the U.S. Senate delegation to the Earth Summit in Rio de Janeiro, Brazil, in June 1992. He also authored *Earth in the Balance: Ecology and the Human Spirit* (1992), which became a national best-seller.

Gore is married to the former Mary E. (Tipper) Aitcheson. They have four children and live on a small livestock farm near Carthage, Tenn., when Congress is not in session. Kristine Portnoy Kelley

Great Britain. Marital problems made 1992 one of the worst years for the British royal family. Speculation that the 1981 marriage of Charles, Queen Elizabeth II's eldest son and heir to the throne, and Princess Diana was in difficulties ended on Dec. 9, 1992, when Prime Minister John Major announced that the couple had agreed "amicably" to separate but not to divorce. They would fulfill separate agendas of public duties and share in the raising of their two sons, Major said.

The couple had increasingly been seen apart, and Diana undertook two lengthy foreign tours alone early in 1992. Rumors exploded in June with the publication of a controversial biography, *Diana: Her True Story,* by Andrew Morton, which apparently had Diana's tacit approval. The book described Diana as a wronged wife trapped in a desperately unhappy marriage and implied she had attempted suicide five times. Charles was depicted as a cold and uncaring product of an austere royal upbringing who put duty before love. Then, in August, two British newspapers printed extracts from an intimate telephone conversation allegedly between Princess Diana and a man named James. He allegedly declared his love for her. Prince Charles was also allegedly having an affair.

The biggest royal scandal of 1992, however, surrounded Sarah Ferguson, wife of Andrew, the Duke of York. Andrew is Queen Elizabeth's second son. Photographs published in August showed a scantily clad

Duchess of York kissing and embracing John Bryan, a Texas millionaire described as her financial adviser. The photographs were taken while the duchess was vacationing with her two daughters at a villa in the south of France. The Duke and Duchess of York had announced in March that they were legally separated.

Queen Elizabeth's daughter, Anne, was divorced from her husband, Captain Mark Phillips, on April 23 after being formally separated since 1989. On Dec. 12, 1992, she married Navy Commander Timothy Laurence in Scotland. Prince Edward, a bachelor and youngest son of the Queen, worked in the theater, after rejecting a military career, a traditional role for royal males.

The royal family's difficulties renewed debate over the millions of pounds the Queen and her family receive annually from the British treasury. In December, negotiations began among the Queen, the government, and the treasury on how the royal income could be taxed.

General elections. On March 11, 1992, Major announced a general election would be held on April 9. It was the first general election since Major became prime minister upon the resignation of Margaret Thatcher in November 1990.

Conservatives had held power since the early 1980's, but with Britain in its worst recession since World War II (1939-1945), political analysts said voters were ready for a change. Opinion polls taken before the election showed that the opposition Labour Party would win. But voters confounded the experts. Although Labour made gains, the Conservatives won their fourth election in a row, the first party to win this many successive elections since the 1840's. Conservatives captured a 21-seat majority in the House of Commons, the lower house of Parliament.

For Labour leader Neil G. Kinnock, the defeat was a stunning blow. He announced his resignation on April 13. Kinnock had transformed the Labour Party by abandoning many of its left wing policies, such as the renationalization of industries that the Conservatives had sold to private investors. Labour elected John Smith, a Scottish lawyer, as party leader on July 18. Smith was a moderate, who would have been chancellor of the exchequer had Labour won the election. The party elected Margaret Beckett its deputy leader. On April 27, 1992, the House elected Betty Boothroyd from the Labour Party as its first woman Speaker and the first Speaker to be a member of the opposition party since World War II. (See also **Boothroyd, Betty**.)

A period of optimism concerning the dismal national economy followed the election. Experts claimed they had spotted "green shoots" of economic recovery. But as 1992 progressed, Major was increasingly beset by political and economic woes. Large regions of the country suffered industrial collapse. The number of business bankruptcies climbed, and unemployment rose to more than 10 per cent of the work force by September. However, Major and Chancellor of the

Windows shattered by a terrorist bomb litter a street in London's financial district in April. The bomb killed three people and injured 91 others.

Princess Diana and Prince Charles, appearing together in June amid reports that their marriage was endangered, decided in December to separate.

Exchequer Norman S. Lamont insisted the main enemy was inflation and kept interest rates at 10 per cent.

Financial crisis. Then came "Black Wednesday," September 16, when speculators in foreign currency markets began selling the pound, causing its value to fall. On that one day, the Bank of England spent 15 billion pounds (U.S. $26.9 billion) out of its total foreign currency reserve of 44 billion pounds (U.S. $78.8-billion) to keep the pound's price up, which Britain was required to do after joining the exchange rate mechanism of the European Community (EC, or Common Market) in October 1990. The exchange rate mechanism is designed to keep the value of the members' currencies stable in relation to each other and to a central rate based on the German mark.

But the Bank of England's efforts failed to stop the pound's fall, and the government temporarily suspended membership in the exchange rate mechanism. Immediately, the pound dropped in value by 16 per cent. Then, on Sept. 22, 1992, the Bank of England announced a percentage point cut in interest rates to 9 per cent. The move signaled a change in the government's previous strategy of raising interest rates to fight inflation. The new tactic was to lower interest rates to invigorate the economy. On October 16, the Bank of England lowered the rate to 8 per cent.

Lower interest rates provided some relief for the 10 million Britons buying their homes on mortgages. One of the worst effects of the recession had been that families were unable to pay the high mortgage rate. These rates can be changed several times a year, depending on how interest rates change. Mortgage foreclosures in 1992 reached 75,000. In addition, property values by 1992 had dropped by an average of 25 per cent since 1988, a boom year. According to an August 1992 report by the Bank of England, 876,000 homeowners owed more on their mortgages than their property was worth.

The Maastricht Treaty. The currency crisis on Black Wednesday refueled the arguments in Britain about the acceptability of the Maastricht Treaty, an accord to establish closer economic and political ties among EC member nations. EC governments signed the treaty in December 1991, but it had to be ratified by each member nation. Rebel Conservative members of Parliament were opposed to the treaty. They were strongly supported by Margaret Thatcher, who was named a baroness and sworn into the House of Lords in June. Thatcher condemned the treaty as being against British interests.

Major confronted the rebel Conservatives in Parliament on November 4 with a motion that would commit Britain to a "leading role" in EC development. Parliament supported the motion, but Major put off a vote to ratify the Maastricht Treaty itself until after Denmark voted on the treaty a second time, possibly in May 1993. Danes had rejected the treaty in their first ratification vote, which was held in June 1992.

A Cabinet scandal with serious political implications erupted in July. Disclosures in the media revealed that David J. Mellor, secretary of state for national heritage, had been having an extramarital affair with a Spanish actress. Mellor's ministerial post included responsibility for sports, the arts, and a proposed national lottery, leading the news media to nickname him the Minister for Fun. Ironically, Mellor also had responsibility for possible government curbs on press intrusion into the private lives of citizens.

In September, the media alleged that Mellor had accepted a free holiday at a villa in Marbella, Spain, in 1990 and had not reported the vacation as a gift. Mellor resigned on September 24, and Peter Brooke, the former secretary of state for Northern Ireland, succeeded Mellor.

Coal mine closures. On October 13, the government announced that 31 out of Britain's 50 coal mines were to close, putting 30,000 miners out of work at a time when joblessness was growing. Secretary of Trade and Industry Michael R. Heseltine said he had no choice, because the mines' biggest customers, the electric companies, were allowed to import coal at a cheaper price than what was charged in Britain. Electric companies were also increasingly using gas to produce electricity.

Arthur Scargill, president of the National Union of Mine Workers, demanded an all-out strike. Conservative members of Parliament joined the Opposition in criticizing the government's action and asking if marketplace economics were not being carried too far. The government was forced to back down and announced on October 19 that only 10 mines would close immediately. The others would be reviewed as to their profitability before any decision on closing them would be made.

Windsor Castle was heavily damaged by fire on Nov. 20, 1992. St. George's Hall, built in the 1400's and used for state dinners, was the most severely burned section of the castle complex. Workers saved most of the priceless artworks inside the hall, but the government said it will take years to repair the damage.

Robert Maxwell's mysterious drowning on Nov. 5, 1991, near the Canary Islands developed in 1992 into one of Britain's largest financial scandals. An investigative report issued in February said the publishing magnate's death was possibly a suicide in light of company financial problems, which had surfaced after his death.

On June 18, Maxwell's sons, Kevin and Ian, and a senior company executive were arrested and charged with fraud regarding the disappearance of millions of pounds from company pension funds. On September 3, the High Court declared Kevin bankrupt. He owed creditors 406.5 million pounds ($812 million U.S.), the largest amount ever in a British personal bankruptcy case. Ian J. Mather

See also **Ireland; Northern Ireland.** In ***World Book,*** see **Great Britain.**

Greece during 1992 worked to strengthen its ailing economy in preparation for increased economic and political integration within the 12-nation European Community (EC or Common Market). Meanwhile, it maintained a stand-off with the EC and other nations over recognition of the former Yugoslav republic of Macedonia, which had declared independence in December 1991.

Greece insisted that Macedonia must change its name before it received recognition as an independent state. Greek officials said the new nation's use of the name Macedonia might stir up nationalist claims to the geographical region of Macedonia, which includes most of northern Greece as well as a small portion of Bulgaria. Macedonia is also the name of a region in Greece. Leaders of the former Yugoslav republic denied any claims to Greek territory and refused to change the nation's name. In June, Greece blocked EC recognition of Macedonia under that name. The United States also agreed to support Greece's demand.

In April, Prime Minister Constantinos Mitsotakis of the conservative New Democratic Party had fired his foreign minister, Antonis Samaras, for his hard-line stance on Macedonia. However, Mitsotakis later adopted Samaras' position that the word Macedonia should not appear in the nation's name in any form.

Economic reform progressed slowly in 1992. Government officials said in July that Greece would meet the EC's strict requirements for participation in its proposed economic and monetary union—which includes creation of a single currency—by 1997, the earliest that the system can be put in place. But as of 1992, Greece's inflation, unemployment, and, especially, its government debt remained far above the EC limits. Greece had a 1992 inflation rate of nearly 20 per cent, more than four times the EC average.

Mitsotakis had pledged to spur reform by selling many of Greece's ailing state companies to private investors, but only a handful of enterprises had been privatized by year's end. In addition, austerity measures—including a bill passed in March that froze government employees' wages—had little impact on the budget deficit.

Greece continued to receive substantial subsidies from the EC for its farms and industries in 1992. In 1993, it was due to receive even higher payments under the EC's plans to ease the transition to a single currency for member nations with weak economies.

Andreas Papandreou, prime minister from 1981 to 1989, was acquitted of corruption charges on Jan. 17, 1992. Papandreou had been charged with involvement in a scheme to embezzle money from the Bank of Crete. A 13-judge panel found the former prime minister innocent on all counts. But it convicted two of his former Cabinet members on other corruption charges. Philip Revzin

See also **Europe** (Facts in brief table). In ***World Book,*** see **Greece.**

Grenada. See **Latin America.**

Guatemala. Peace talks between the Guatemalan government and the National Revolutionary Union, the country's main armed opposition group, continued in 1992. However, they produced no formal peace agreement to end the civil war that has claimed at least 100,000 lives since 1954.

Some hope emerged on August 7 when mediators for the Roman Catholic Church announced in Mexico that the two groups had reached a partial accord to limit the activities of Guatemala's civilian defense patrols. The patrols, organized and supported by the army, have been accused of numerous assassinations.

The Nobel Peace Prize in 1992 was awarded to Rigoberta Menchú, a Mayan Indian woman of the Quiché highlands in Guatemala, on October 16. The Nobel Committee said the award was in recognition of her efforts on behalf of social justice.

Menchú's family has suffered greatly in their struggle for human rights for Indians. Her father died in a fire that ignited at the Spanish Embassy in Guatemala City in 1980 during a peaceful demonstration to protest the Guatemalan government's alleged human rights violations. Soldiers also reportedly killed her mother and brother in 1980. In 1981, Menchú fled to Mexico. Nathan A. Haverstock

See also **Latin America** (Facts in brief table); **Nobel Prizes.** In ***World Book,*** see **Guatemala.**

Guinea. See **Africa.**

Guyana. See **Latin America.**

Haiti. On June 19, Haiti's military leaders installed Marc L. Bazin, 60, as prime minister. A former World Bank official, Bazin replaced Joseph Nerette, who was installed as the country's interim president following the September 1991 military coup that overthrew Jean-Bertrand Aristide, Haiti's first democratically elected president. At his inauguration on June 20, Bazin, an aristocrat who had finished a distant second to Aristide in presidential voting in 1990, pledged to reopen talks aimed at allowing Aristide to return to Haiti.

Aristide still in exile. Since the 1991 coup, Aristide has been in exile, seeking in vain to muster sufficient international support to force his return to power as president of Haiti. On Sept. 29, 1992, speaking at the United Nations, Aristide, a former Roman Catholic priest, blasted the Vatican, which he said was the only state in the world to recognize Haiti's military government. Aristide also called for a tightening of the United States economic embargo that was imposed against Haiti.

The U.S. embargo did little to persuade Haiti's new leaders to restore Aristide to power. Many countries routinely ignored the embargo in 1992. Ships continued to deliver everything from steel and barbed wire to wine, perfume, chemicals, and cosmetics. The embargo still caused suffering among many people, however, because necessary supplies such as food and medicine became scarce.

In accord with a plan drawn up by Aristide's representatives and the Haitian government on September 11, Haiti's military rulers agreed to permit the Organization of American States to send human rights monitors to Haiti. Their presence was expected to reduce the tension and oppression on the island.

Haitian refugees. As part of an exodus that began in late 1991, thousands of Haitians continued to flee their homeland in 1992 aboard fragile and dangerously overloaded boats headed for the United States. From October 1991 to July 30, 1992, the U.S. Coast Guard intercepted about 37,000 Haitian refugees. The Coast Guard either turned them back immediately or took them to a U.S. naval base at Guantánamo Bay, Cuba, and then returned them.

Under U.S. law, refugees from a foreign country are eligible for immigration if authorities determined they are fleeing political repression, but not if they are simply fleeing economic hardships. Courts in the United States debated the legality of the refugee returns for much of 1992. On July 29, a federal court ruled that the returns were illegal, but the Supreme Court of the United States allowed the U.S. government to resume the return of refugees in August. (See also **Immigration.**) Nathan A. Haverstock

See also **Latin America** (Facts in brief table). In ***World Book***, see **Haiti**.

Harness racing. See **Horse racing.**

Hawaii. See **State government**.

Members of the U.S. Coast Guard in May hand off a Haitian child, one of thousands of Haitian refugees denied entrance to the United States in 1992.

Health issues. High levels of iron in the body may play an important role in causing heart attacks, researchers from Finland reported in September 1992. American heart disease experts praised the study, but they emphasized that much additional research was needed to verify the findings.

Iron and heart disease. The Finnish researchers monitored the health of more than 1,900 men over five years. One test measured levels of *ferritin,* a protein in the blood that binds iron and can serve as an indicator of the amount of iron in the body. The researchers found that for each 1 per cent increase in ferritin, the risk of a heart attack rose by more than 4 per cent. Men with ferritin levels above 200 micrograms per liter of blood had double the usual risk of a heart attack. Normal ferritin levels in adult men range from 100 to 150 micrograms.

The researchers said the findings may help explain why heart attacks rarely occur in younger women but increase after *menopause,* the time in a woman's life when menstruation ceases. Because of iron losses during menstruation, typical ferritin levels in women under the age of 50 range from 25 to 50 micrograms. But women's iron levels—and their risk of heart attacks—begin to rise at menopause. Experts theorize that iron may play a role in promoting the formation of *plaque*—deposits in the lining of arteries that block the flow of blood and cause most heart attacks.

What weakens bones? Researchers on July 3 announced the discovery of a fundamental cause of *osteoporosis,* a condition that makes the bones weak and vulnerable to fractures. The findings help explain why osteoporosis strikes many women after menopause, according to Stavros Manolagas, who headed the research team at the Veterans Medical Center and Indiana University School of Medicine in Indianapolis.

During menopause, production of the female hormone estrogen declines. The Indiana experiments showed that the drop in estrogen upsets the normal balance between bone-destroying cells, called *osteoclasts,* and bone-building cells, termed *osteoblasts.* Osteoclasts remove old, worn-out bone tissue, leaving pits and cracks in the bones. Before menopause, osteoblasts fill in the spaces with fresh, new bone.

The researchers found that the decline in estrogen leads to the production of interleukin-6 (IL-6), a chemical of the immune system. IL-6, in turn, stimulates the overproduction of bone-destroying osteoclasts. Manolagas said physicians long have known that estrogen supplements help prevent osteoporosis, but the reasons why remained a mystery. He predicted the discovery could lead to new drugs that prevent osteoporosis.

Drug-resistant TB. A major advance in understanding why some strains of tuberculosis (TB) become resistant to drugs was reported on August 13 by scientists in France and Great Britain. Outbreaks of TB that failed to respond to isoniazid, the standard drug therapy for the disease, have been reported since 1990. The emergence of the drug-resistant strains has become a major problem, especially among people whose immune systems have been weakened by infection with the AIDS virus. (See also **Public Health.**)

Stewart Cole, a bacteriologist at the Pasteur Institute in Paris who headed the research, reported that resistance to isoniazid involves a single gene in the TB microbe. This gene is critical for the production of two proteins that make the TB microbe vulnerable to isoniazid. Strains of TB in which the gene is missing or defective, Cole said, can survive exposure to isoniazid, even in large doses.

Researchers said the discovery could help in the development of a test to quickly identify patients with drug-resistant TB. Existing tests take months, and during that time infected patients not only get ineffective therapy but also can spread the disease.

Vitamin C and the heart. The most comprehensive analysis of the long-term health effects of vitamin C concluded in May 1992 that increased consumption of the vitamin lowers the risk of death from heart disease. The study, which monitored 11,348 adults for 10 years, was headed by James E. Enstrom, an epidemiologist at the University of California at Los Angeles.

The researchers found that men with the highest vitamin C intake had an overall mortality rate 42 per cent lower than men who consumed little vitamin C. And their mortality rate from heart disease was 45 per cent lower. The men in the high-intake group consumed at least 50 milligrams of the vitamin daily from dietary sources and also took daily vitamin C supplements. Women with the highest intakes of vitamin C had a 10 per cent lower overall mortality rate and a 25 per cent lower mortality rate from heart disease. Researchers speculated that vitamin C's protective effects result from its action as an *antioxidant,* a substance that prevents damage to cells from certain chemicals produced naturally by the body.

Chronic fatigue. A study of chronic fatigue syndrome (CFS) reported on January 15 linked the condition with abnormalities in certain nerve cells in the brain. Symptoms of CFS include exhaustion, impaired concentration, muscle aches, and memory loss, among others. Experts have disagreed over whether these symptoms constitute a newly recognized disease or result from psychological factors.

The study, conducted by researchers at Brigham and Women's Hospital in Boston, suggested that CFS involves actual physical changes in the brain. Sophisticated brain scans on 259 CFS patients revealed evidence of abnormal changes in certain nerve cells in almost 80 per cent of the cases. In some instances, the researchers found a relationship between a patient's symptoms and the region of the brain affected. CFS patients who reported disturbances in vision, for instance, had abnormalities in nerve cells in a region of the brain that controls vision. Michael Woods

See also **Medicine**. In ***World Book***, see **Disease; Health.**

Hobbies. See **Stamp collecting; Toys and games.**

MEDICAL CENTER
Fully Insured
Partially Insured

Curing America's Health-Care Ills

By Lawrence D. Brown

Dozens of proposals have been put forth to curb the cost of U.S. health care and provide coverage to millions of uninsured and underinsured Americans.

Concerns about health care held center stage in the United States during 1992. While many experts regarded the U.S. medical system as capable of delivering the highest quality care in the world, access to that care was less certain for an increasing number of Americans, who found themselves either uninsured or underinsured. And the cost of medical care in America was growing to crisis proportions, straining the resources of individuals, businesses, and governments.

Spending on health care in the United States in 1992 equaled about $3,000 for every man, woman, and child, according to the Health Care Financing Administration, an agency of the U.S. government. The agency estimated total health-care outlays for the year at $738 billion and predicted that the amount could grow to $1.6 trillion by the year 2000.

Critics contended that U.S. medical care and its financing systems had become so undisciplined and inefficient that sizable portions of the U.S. population were no longer confident of retaining affordable insurance for themselves and their families. These anxieties, along with the plight of the estimated 34 million Americans without health insurance at any given time, forced the issue onto the agendas of the presidential candidates and of many members of Congress. They responded with dozens of proposals to fix the system. The bewildering array of reform options was evidence both of the importance of the issue and of the lack of agreement on how to address it.

The causes of the crisis in health care

The two causes of the health-care crisis—inadequate insurance coverage and high cost of care—have been brought on by a number of factors. Some people without health insurance were unemployed or worked part-time. But roughly three-quarters of the uninsured in 1992 were low-income workers (or their dependents) employed in small firms—often in precarious economic straits—that could not afford expensive insurance premiums. Many more people were underinsured—that is, they were liable to incur heavy out-of-pocket costs for needed medical services because their policies carried large deductibles or copayments or because insurance companies had limited or excluded coverage for them for certain medical conditions. These limitations or exclusions were often for preexisting conditions, such as high-blood pressure or heart disease, that afflicted the person at the time he or she applied for the insurance.

Among the reasons for skyrocketing medical costs was the high quality of U.S. medical care. American medical care is rendered by highly trained professionals using advanced technology in modern facilities. It is the best care in the world for those who can pay for it.

Another factor contributing to cost is the fact that the U.S. medical system trains far more specialists than primary-care physicians and pays specialists considerably more than it does primary-care givers. American medical technology is also widely available. As a result, U.S. medicine tends to be technology-intensive, relying on expensive diagnostic procedures, such as computerized tomography and magnetic resonance imag-

The author:

Lawrence D. Brown is a professor and head of the division of health policy and management at the Columbia University School of Public Health in New York City.

ing. Added to these factors are the high costs of administration to handle the paperwork for insurance claims and the costs of repeated, excessive, or unnecessary tests ordered by doctors to protect themselves against malpractice law suits.

While medical cost control is a major issue, the current U.S. health-care crisis is primarily about the availability and affordability of health insurance. Therefore, most proposed reforms target the health insurance system directly. But experts caution that it will not be easy to reform this system. Health insurance is a patchwork of private and public programs that have grown bit by bit since the early 1900's, when medical practice became more formal, sophisticated, and expensive. At that time, companies offered insurance mainly to the upper and middle classes.

Soaring health costs

Health-care spending in the United States reached $738 billion in 1991, or about $3,000 for each American, according to the Health Care Financing Administration, an agency of the U.S. government.

Per capita health-care expenditures

$143
$346
$1,063
$1,710
$2,566
$2,948
1960 1970 1980 1985 1990 1991

Source: U.S. Health Care Financing Administration.

Total health-care expenditures

$27.1 billion
$74.4 billion
$250.1 billion
$422.6 billion
$666.2 billion
$738 billion
1960 1970 1980 1985 1990 1991

Source: U.S. Health Care Financing Administration.

Private health-care insurance

The health insurance available in the United States is of two main types: private and public. Most insured people under the age of 65 obtain private insurance coverage under a group policy provided by their employers. One common type of private insurance is the *indemnity plan,* which pays policyholders when they become ill for a portion of their insured medical costs, usually above a set amount called a deductible. Indemnity insurance is provided mainly by for-profit insurance companies or by the not-for-profit Blue Cross and Blue Shield associations, the largest medical service plans in the United States with about 70 member organizations. Indemnity plans pay providers directly for all or part of a subscriber's hospital and doctor bills. Subscribers make regular payments either into a group plan where they work or to an individual plan. Group policies are usually far less expensive than are individual policies, however, because the risk of illness is spread among the members of the group. Also, the employer generally pays a portion of the premium.

A variation of the basic indemnity plan is the *preferred provider organization* (PPO). To create a PPO, an insurer contracts with groups of doctors, hospitals, and other health-care practitioners to provide care for reduced fees.

Another type of private insurance is offered by *health maintenance organizations* (HMO's) through insurance companies, hospitals, community organizations, and other groups. HMO's operate on the principle of *managed care.* Each person and any dependents enrolled in an HMO are assigned to a primary-care physician and are not covered for specialist visits unless referred by that physician. Unlike indemnity plans, HMO's emphasize preventive care and will cover regular checkups, screenings for cancer and heart disease, and vaccinations.

Sometimes a company will choose to be self-insured. This means that the company itself devises coverage and pays for its employees' health costs rather than buying insurance.

Work-based health insurance spread steadily in the 1940's and 1950's, and by the mid-1960's, extended to most employed people. But employees receive an uneven range of insurance benefits—from extensive to just the basics—depending on their employers' plans. Worker contributions to plan premiums likewise vary according to company policy and the type of insurance provided. And there is a growing number of uninsured workers whose companies do not provide any health-care benefits, mainly because the costs have grown too great.

Public health-care insurance

Large, public insurance plans covered about 20 per cent of Americans in 1992, chiefly through Medicare and Medicaid. The legislation that created these plans was enacted by the U.S. Congress in 1965. Medicare covers nearly all citizens over the age of 65 and disabled people of all ages who meet certain requirements. Medicaid extends benefits to people with low incomes who meet the state-set criteria of eligibility for public assistance. Medicaid is financed by funds from both federal and state governments.

The advent of Medicare and Medicaid gave the federal government a major role in health-care financing for the first time. Many observers expected that a national health insurance plan to cover those left uninsured would soon be passed. Since then, however, proposals for universal coverage and their political prospects have waxed and waned, with no comprehensive program emerging.

State attempts at reform

In the absence of federal programs, a few states have tried to achieve affordable universal coverage. The most successful example of a state program to date is Hawaii, which in 1974 passed legislation requiring all employers to provide basic health coverage for anyone who works more than 20 hours a week. Employees pay either half the price of the premium or 1.5 per cent of their pay, whichever is lower. Since 1990, uninsured dependents and people who work less than 20 hours a week get limited coverage by paying a small premium and a low deductible amount for physicians' fees. The state pays the rest.

An ambitious plan put forth by Oregon in 1989 called for a system of health-care rationing. Oregon ranked 709 medical procedures on the ba-

Who pays the national health bill?

Health care in the United States is paid for by both public and private sources. Public sources accounted for more than 40 per cent of the total national health bill in 1990, up from about 25 per cent in 1965 when the Medicare and Medicaid programs began.

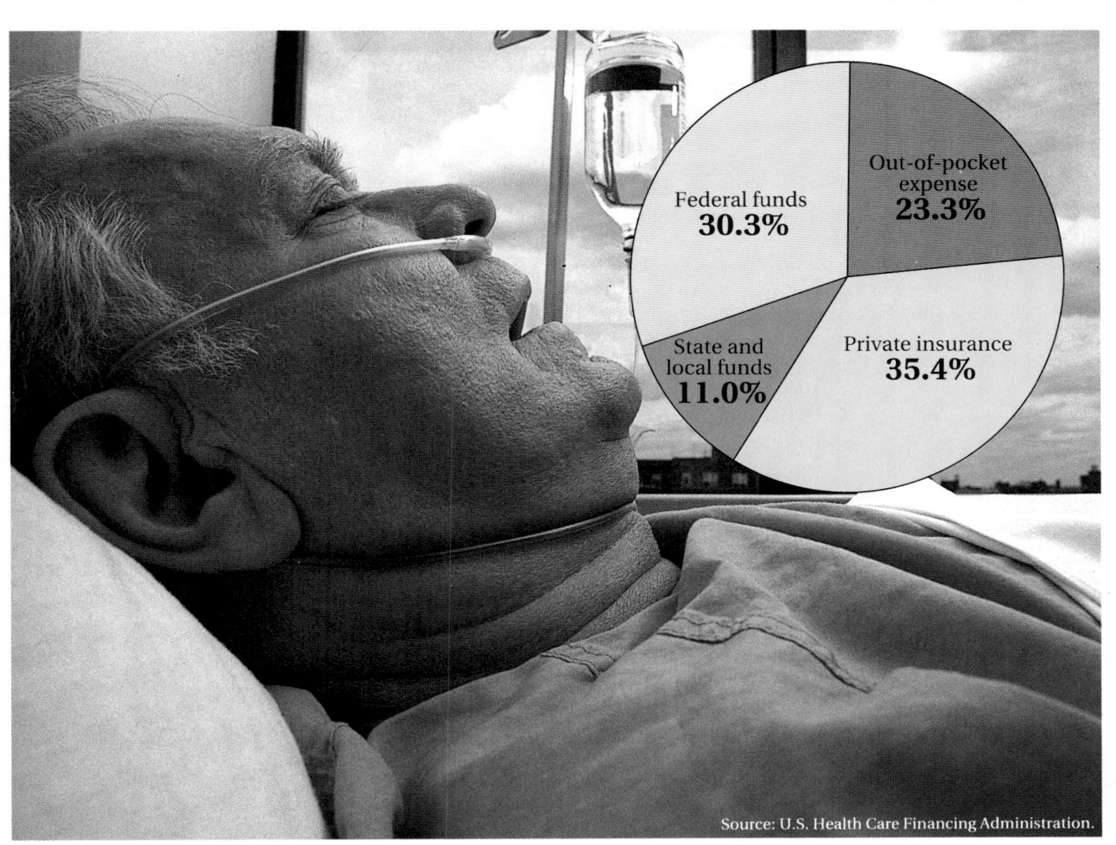

Source: U.S. Health Care Financing Administration.

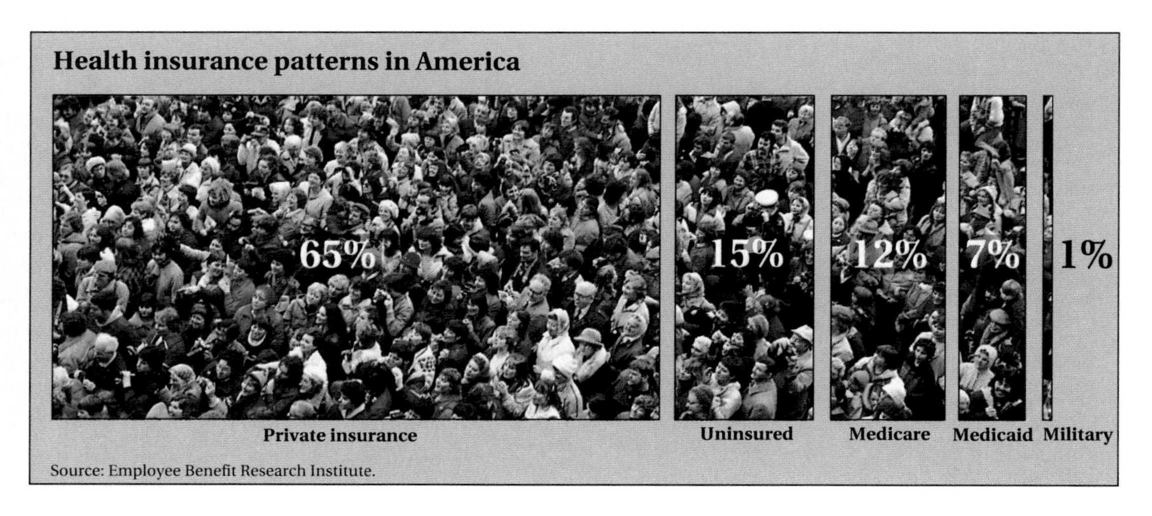

Most Americans obtain health insurance through their employers. People in the armed services and their dependents are covered by military plans. Medicare provides coverage for the elderly and some disabled. Medicaid benefits people on public assistance, but some low-income people do not qualify for this program. They, along with part-time and temporary workers, are among the 34 million who are without health insurance at any given time.

sis of their costs and benefits, with those ranked below number 587 excluded from Medicaid coverage. Oregon's proposal intended to use the resulting savings to bring at least some care under Medicaid to all citizens who meet the federal government's definition of poverty. However, the federal government, which sets general rules for Medicaid, rejected the Oregon proposal in August 1992, saying the plan discriminated against the disabled. Nevertheless, Oregon's scheme drew national attention, and the idea of health-care rationing continued to generate much controversy and debate.

Looking to other nations for model plans

Reformers also looked to other countries for ideas of how to bring universal health-care coverage to all Americans. Most nations on the European continent rely on social insurance financing to cover medical-care costs. Great Britain combines national health insurance with a National Health Service that provides doctor and hospital care. Every Briton registers with a general practitioner. Physicians and health-care workers in the system are public employees. The government owns all the health facilities in the national system and funds health services largely with tax revenues. But about 10 per cent of Britons also buy private insurance, which helps pay for treatment by private physicians or for services that the national plan does not cover.

Canada has national health insurance but no national health service to provide care. The national government pays about 40 per cent of health-care costs, and the 10 provinces pay the other 60 per cent, with most of the money coming from taxes. Most physicians are in private practice, and the hospitals are privately operated. Canadians, however, rarely see a bill, because the provinces pay for physician and hospital services according to established rates. Standardizing rates and relying on the provincial governments to handle claims has reduced administrative costs to a fraction of those in the United States. Canadians may buy private health insurance to cover other expenses, such as the cost of private hospital rooms, which the national health insurance plan does not cover.

Current U.S. reform proposals

The health-care reform proposals being debated in the United States in 1992 ranged from reforming the insurance industry to forming a national health-care system under government control. The plans usually fell into one of three main types called market-based, employer-based (play-or-pay), and national health insurance.

Market-based plans concentrate on reforming the existing insurance industry so as to discipline yet encourage free-market competition. Some of these reform plans address the problem of the uninsured by restricting insurers' rights to deny coverage to high-risk groups and individuals. They address the problems of the underinsured by preventing insurance companies from imposing limits on coverage for preexisting conditions, such as asthma or AIDS. Other market-based reforms would prohibit insurers from charging higher premiums for someone with a medical condition or a dangerous occupation—for example, someone with a heart condition or a person employed as a high-rise window washer.

While these steps might make coverage more widely available, they would, by themselves, do little to make insurance more affordable. Indeed, opponents feared that insurers might raise rates for healthier policyholders to offset actual or potential losses from groups or individuals they would be newly obliged to cover.

Other market-based plans provide for tax credits. All citizens would be encouraged or required to buy adequate health insurance, and those who could not afford it on their own or with the help of their employers would get a voucher to pay for care or credit on their income tax.

Employer-based plans would make work-based health coverage mandatory. Some analysts believe that this approach is most consistent with U.S. practices. In one version, employers would simply be obliged to provide insurance coverage, with possible public subsidies for those companies that cannot bear the financial burden. In a second version, so-called play-or-pay plans, employers who did not offer insurance would pay a payroll tax surcharge for a public insurance plan that would cover workers without private insurance.

National health insurance is favored by those who regard health care as a basic right of citizenship and opposed by those who object to a large government role in such areas. To obtain care, citizens would probably present some type of national identification card to the doctor or hospital of their choice. The government becomes either the sole payer for health services or the source of rules binding on private payers.

A national health-care system could be funded in one of two main ways. Contributions could be collected from employers and employees with some additional funding provided by taxes. Providers would be paid through insurance companies. The other approach would fund coverage with tax revenues and eliminate most of the private insurance industry.

Private health insurance today

- Indemnity plans usually pay a policyholder for a portion of covered medical expenses above a set amount, called a deductible. The insured may use any physician or hospital. The premium is usually the most expensive of any plan.
- Preferred provider organizations (PPO's) are discounted indemnity plans managed by insurance companies. The insured chooses a doctor from a list of physicians who have agreed to charge reduced fees to plan members. The insured must get approval from the plan manager before receiving expensive tests or major procedures. The premium is usually lower than for a regular indemnity plan.
- Health maintenance organizations (HMO's) cover major medical procedures as well as routine physical examinations, tests, and treatment of minor illnesses. The insured must use certain medical facilities and may not be covered for treatment from specialists unless their assigned HMO doctor approves. The premium is usually the lowest of all insurance plans.
- Self-insurance programs are set up by employers for their employees. The company pays the benefits, though it may hire an insurance company to process claims.

In the United States, notwithstanding the federal and state governments' growing role in health-care financing through Medicare and Medicaid, physicians and hospitals face few constraints on what they charge for their services. Insurers defend their immunity from federal regulation, and businesses decide whether or not to offer health coverage. Recognizing that a larger federal hand in reshaping the health-care system seems to be inevitable, these groups have begun to address the system's problems in ways that do minimal damage to their own interests. Whatever reform proposal eventually emerges from Congress will likely be shaped to a significant extent by these groups.

Influencing reform: the insurance industry

The health insurance industry has opposed government controls on insurance and has instead advocated market-based reforms that would make insurance companies curb those practices drawing the most criticism. The industry is represented mainly by the Blue Cross and Blue Shield Association, largely a trade group for the 73 not-for-profit plans nationwide, and the Health Insurance Association of America, a group representing for-profit insurance companies. These organizations fear that the rising concern over high premiums and exclusions could ultimately lead to replacing the U.S. health-care system with a Canadian-style system, which leaves little room for private insurance.

But in December 1992, the Health Insurance Association of America proposed that the federal government play a major role in changing the health insurance industry, a clear departure from the association's past position. The association called for the government to require all Americans to buy insurance. Employers would get tax incentives to provide insurance, and employees who did not buy coverage would get tax penalties. The proposal also called for the government to help define an essential benefit package, which would meet "most of the needs of Americans." And the government would help establish payments for health services so that private insurance, Medicare, and Medicaid would provide the same benefits in the same geographic area.

Critics of the insurance industry have wanted insurance companies to provide broader coverage mainly by spreading the costs of insuring riskier groups among healthier groups. But insurers reply that the system's costs depend on larger forces that they do not control, such as the health habits of the population, the use of medical technology, and society's decisions about how much to pay health-care providers.

Influencing reform: health-care providers

Health-care providers want to establish a universal health insurance system through employer-based approaches that would not invite broad new government controls on fees and charges. Providers are represented mainly by the American Hospital Association (AHA) and the American Medical Association (AMA), whose members are doctors. These groups want an end to bills left unpaid by the uninsured or the underinsured.

	Canada	Great Britain	Germany
Major Provisions	Everyone is covered. Patient chooses a physician. Primary and emergency care are covered, but not drugs. Government pays physicians and hospitals, according to established rates. Funding is mainly through taxes. The federal government pays 40 per cent of the costs, and provinces pay 60 per cent.	Everyone is covered. Patient registers with a general practitioner. Government owns all health facilities, and all doctors and health-care workers are government employees. Hospitals get an annual budget. Doctors get a fee for each registered patient. Funding is mainly through taxes.	All employed people with family incomes below about US $50,000 must join a sickness fund. Sickness funds contract for services from hospitals and doctors, paying them directly. Higher income workers join a fund or switch permanently to private insurance. Funding is through payroll taxes from employers and employees.
Strengths	Costs are controlled by government budget. Out-of-pocket costs are low. Paperwork is minimal. Patients rarely see a bill.	Costs are controlled with strict limits on medical spending. Routine medical care is free.	Retirees or those who lose their jobs keep their fund memberships. Coverage includes unlimited physician and hospital services and drugs.
Weaknesses	High-tech medical equipment is scarce. Specialists are few. Patients may wait for nonemergency surgery.	Expensive treatments, such as transplants, are restricted to those who can benefit the most. Patients may have long waits for nonemergency surgery.	Hospital stays are unnecessarily long. Physician fees are rapidly rising.

The AHA prefers the play-or-pay approach that would tax employers who cannot afford to buy insurance. These taxes would fund a public plan for the uninsured. The AMA supports a mandate on employers to provide insurance, along with government subsidies to aid small employers who cannot afford to buy insurance without such help.

Influencing reform: business and labor

The U.S. business community is sharply divided as to what approach health-care reform should take. Employers pay about 30 per cent of total spending on health insurance in the United States, and they have for years loudly denounced these costs as insupportable. Business leaders say that the high cost of health insurance reduces the international competitiveness of U.S. companies, because it adds to the cost of producing goods and thus to their price in the marketplace. Nevertheless, some large companies welcome play-or-pay plans because they believe their health insurance premiums have been inflated by the cost of treating the uninsured. Other firms—large and small—oppose play-or-pay because they resist government intervention in business on principle. And most small

Public health insurance today

- Medicare is a federal program for all people receiving benefits from Social Security, mainly after reaching age 65 or after being disabled for at least two years. Part A pays for hospital costs above a set amount.The insured must pay a monthly premium for Part B, which covers doctor's services.
- Medicaid is a state-run program to provide health care to some of the poor. The federal government sets guidelines and pays from 50 to 78 per cent of the states' costs.

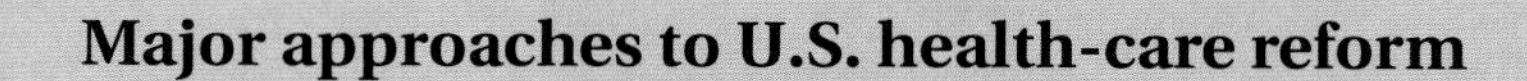

Major approaches to U.S. health-care reform

Market-based reforms

- Private companies provide insurance. Individuals purchase group coverage through employers or buy individual policies. Lower-income groups receive tax credits, tax deductions, or government vouchers to help pay for coverage.
- Premium costs are controlled through competition.
- Industry reforms such practices as excluding higher risk people.
- Medicare remains in force. Some proposals expand Medicaid to cover all the poor.

Major pros

- Increased competition among insurance companies could reduce costs and improve benefits.
- Builds on a system already in place.

Major cons

- Not all proposals mandate coverage for everyone.
- Requires the buyer to acquire detailed knowledge of insurance plans.

Employer-based (including play-or-pay) plans

- Some proposals require that employers provide private group insurance coverage for employees or pay a tax for a public plan. Others require employers to provide private coverage, with possible subsidies for employers who cannot bear the cost.
- Premiums and taxes finance at least a basic benefit package.
- Costs may be controlled by strict government budgets, payment limits to providers, and insurance industry reform.
- Some proposals keep Medicare in force. Other proposals expand Medicare.

Major pros

- Covers everyone, with no exclusions for preexisting health conditions.
- Builds on employer-based system.
- Public plan covers the unemployed.

Major cons

- Could increase employee insurance expense for small businesses.
- Increases taxes to fund a public plan or to pay subsidies to employers.

National health insurance

- Federal government provides health insurance and pays all bills for hospital and doctor services as well as for preventive care.
- Taxes, including sales, payroll, and corporate, pay for most costs.
- Costs are controlled through caps, negotiated payments, or rates set by the government for all providers and services.
- Some proposals replace Medicare, Medicaid, and all private insurance with a national health fund. Other proposals expand Medicare to include all ages, eliminating Medicaid and private insurance.

Major pros

- Covers everyone, with no exclusions for preexisting conditions.
- Coverage continues if a person loses or changes jobs.
- Greatly reduces paperwork and cuts administrative costs because a single source, the government, pays all medical bills.

Major cons

- Increases taxes.
- Places health care under government influence, possibly affecting quality or availability of care and use of new technologies.

companies strongly object to being compelled to buy health insurance for their workers—though many do so voluntarily—saying the cost would drive some of them out of business.

The controversy over play-or-pay legislation has given rise to proposals for exempting some businesses, such as very small firms and businesses with part-time and seasonal workers. Many workers would therefore remain uninsured. There also is the likelihood that some, perhaps many, employers would find it cheaper to pay the surcharge, if that option were available, than buy insurance. If universal coverage were to be attained under play-or-pay reforms, a sizable public plan would have to be in place to cover workers of exempt companies. And if the pay option were eliminated in favor of a straightforward mandate to provide health insurance, public subsidies would be needed to assist the employers most burdened by the expense.

Organized labor has not been a major player in the recent efforts to reform health insurance. Some elements of labor—notably the national leadership of the AFL-CIO and the United Automobile Workers—favor a Canadian-style, publicly funded system. But local and regional leaders of some AFL-CIO unions resist such far-reaching reforms and would be satisfied with gradual steps to change the system.

Is there an affordable solution?

Each of the various reform options could take large steps toward universal coverage. Achieving universal coverage that is also affordable is another matter, however. One reason policymakers have approached reform gingerly, despite rising public indignation, is that all of the leading proposals could send health-care spending into a sharper upward spiral.

Yet, anxiety about obtaining and keeping affordable coverage seems to be generating a coalition among middle-class citizens, advocates for the uninsured, government budgetmakers, and some businesses. With pressure for health-care reform growing, the key question is not will policymakers finally engineer change—they may have no political choice but to do so. Rather, the question now centers on whether Americans now regard health care as a right of citizenship, a belief that underpins universal coverage in other Western nations. And if health care is a right, health-care services and the money that buys them are resources of society as a whole. Government, then, bears responsibility for defining the rules for giving everyone access to care at the quality and price that society and individuals find reasonable. If these ideas have not found a home here, can some workable, distinctly American alternative be invented?

For further reading:

Callan, Mary F. *Containing the Health Care Cost Spiral.* McGraw-Hill, 1991.

McCuen, Gary E., editor. *Health Care and Social Values.* GEM McCuen Publications, 1993.

Pittsburgh Penguin defenders (in black) battle a Chicago Blackhawk in the Stanley Cup finals. Pittsburgh won its second straight Stanley Cup June 1.

Hockey. In a tumultuous 1991-1992 season marked by a first-ever players' strike and the ousting of the league president, the Pittsburgh Penguins emerged as the National Hockey League (NHL) champions. Even though they finished only third in their division during the regular season, the Penguins won the Stanley Cup play-offs for the second consecutive year.

Strike. A players' strike from April 1 to 11 delayed the last 30 games of the regular season, as well as the play-offs. In the settlement, the players received licensing rights and minimal improvement in benefits. The owners achieved a goal by limiting the contract to one year. John Ziegler, who became NHL president in 1977, helped settle the strike through his negotiating efforts. However, the NHL owners later became disenchanted with Ziegler, largely because he was not successful in his efforts to generate significant television income or exposure. After the strike, the club owners forced the 58-year-old Ziegler to resign. He was replaced on Oct. 1, 1992, by Gilbert Stein, the NHL's lawyer.

NHL season. During the regular season, the 22 teams played 80 games each. The division winners were the New York Rangers (105 points), Detroit Red Wings (98), Vancouver Canucks (96), and Montreal Canadiens (93). None reached the Stanley Cup final.

Pittsburgh and the Chicago Blackhawks raced through the early rounds of the play-offs. Chicago eliminated the St. Louis Blues, Detroit, and the Ed-

National Hockey League standings

Clarence Campbell Conference

James Norris Division	W.	L.	T.	Pts.
Detroit Red Wings*	43	25	12	98
Chicago Blackhawks*	36	29	15	87
St. Louis Blues*	36	33	11	83
Minnesota North Stars*	32	42	6	70
Toronto Maple Leafs	30	43	7	67
Conn Smythe Division				
Vancouver Canucks*	42	26	12	96
Los Angeles Kings*	35	31	14	84
Edmonton Oilers*	36	34	10	82
Winnipeg Jets*	33	32	15	81
Calgary Flames	31	37	12	74
San Jose Sharks	17	58	5	39

Prince of Wales Conference

Charles F. Adams Division	W.	L.	T.	Pts.
Montreal Canadiens*	41	28	11	93
Boston Bruins*	36	32	12	84
Buffalo Sabres*	31	37	12	74
Hartford Whalers*	26	41	13	65
Quebec Nordiques	20	48	12	52
Lester Patrick Division				
New York Rangers*	50	25	5	105
Washington Capitals*	45	27	8	98
Pittsburgh Penguins*	39	32	9	87
New Jersey Devils*	38	31	11	87
New York Islanders	34	35	11	79
Philadelphia Flyers	32	37	11	75

*Made play-off.

Stanley Cup winner—
Pittsburgh Penguins (defeated Chicago Blackhawks, 4 games to 0)

Scoring leaders	Games	Goals	Assists	Pts.
Mario Lemieux, Pittsburgh	64	44	87	131
Kevin Stevens, Pittsburgh	80	54	69	123
Wayne Gretzky, Los Angeles	74	31	90	121
Brett Hull, St. Louis	73	70	39	109
Luc Robitaille, Los Angeles	80	44	63	107
Mark Messier, N.Y. Rangers	79	35	72	107
Jeremy Roenick, Chicago	80	53	50	103
Steve Yzerman, Detroit	79	45	58	103
Brian Leetch, N.Y. Rangers	80	22	80	102
Adam Oates, St. Louis/Boston	80	20	79	99
Dale Hawerchuk, Buffalo	77	23	75	98
Mark Recchi, Philadelphia	80	43	54	97

Leading goalies (25 or more games)	Games	Goals against	Avg.
Partrick Roy, Montreal	67	155	2.36
Ed Belfour, Chicago	52	132	2.70
Kirk McLean, Vancouver	65	176	2.74
John Vanbiesbrouck, N.Y. Rangers	45	120	2.85
Bob Essensa, Winnipeg	47	126	2.88

Awards

Calder Trophy (best rookie)—Pavel Bure, Vancouver
Hart Trophy (most valuable player)—Mark Messier, New York Rangers
Lady Byng Trophy (sportsmanship)—Wayne Gretzky, Los Angeles
Masterton Trophy (perseverance, dedication to hockey)—Mark Fitzpatrick, New York Islanders
Norris Trophy (best defenseman)—Brian Leetch, New York Rangers
Ross Trophy (leading scorer)—Mario Lemieux, Pittsburgh
Selke Trophy (best defensive forward)—Guy Carbonneau, Montreal
Smythe Trophy (most valuable player in Stanley Cup)—Mario Lemieux, Pittsburgh
Vezina Trophy (most valuable goalie)—Patrick Roy, Montreal

monton Oilers and entered the finals with 11 consecutive victories, a play-off record. Pittsburgh eliminated the Washington Capitals, New York, and the Boston Bruins, winning its last seven games en route to the final. Chicago was a more physical team, but Pittsburgh swept the final in four games, tying Chicago's play-off record of 11 consecutive victories. Pittsburgh had overcome injuries and coach Bob Johnson's death.

Lemieux won the regular-season scoring title with 131 points in 63 games (he missed 17). For the second straight year, he won the Conn Smythe Trophy as the play-offs' Most Valuable Player. However, Mark Messier of New York was voted center on the NHL all-star team and received the Hart Trophy as the league's Most Valuable Player. Nineteen-year-old Eric Lindros, projected as the next superstar forward, refused to join the Quebec Nordiques, and they traded him to the Philadelphia Flyers for 5 players, first-round draft choices in 1993 and 1994, and a reported $20 million.

World. In the men's championship from April 28 to May 10 in Prague, Czechoslovakia, the favorite was Russia, basically the same team that won an Olympic gold medal as the Unified Team. But Sweden eliminated Russia, 2-0, in the quarter-finals and defeated Finland, 5-2, in the final. Canada won the women's championship in Tampere, Finland, routing the United States, 8-0, in the final. Frank Litsky

In ***World Book***, see **Hockey.**

Honduras. See **Latin America.**

Major horse races of 1992

Race	Winner	Value to winner
Arlington Million	Dear Doctor	$600,000
Belmont Stakes	A. P. Indy	$458,880
Breeders' Cup Classic	A. P. Indy	$1,560,000
Breeders' Cup Distaff	Paseana	$520,000
Breeders' Cup Juvenile	Gilded Time	$520,000
Breeders' Cup Juvenile Fillies	Eliza	$520,000
Breeders' Cup Mile	Lure	$520,000
Breeders' Cup Sprint	Thirty Slews	$520,000
Breeders' Cup Turf	Fraise	$1,040,000
Budweiser International	Zoman	$450,000
Champion Stakes (England)	Rodrigo de Triano	$403,168
Derby Stakes (England)	Dr. Devious	$662,075
Hollywood Gold Cup Handicap	Sultry Song	$550,000
Irish Derby (Ireland)	St. Jovite	$616,615
Jockey Club Gold Cup	Pleasant Tap	$510,000
Kentucky Derby	Lil E. Tee	$724,800
King George VI and Queen Elizabeth Diamond Stakes (England)	St. Jovite	$487,168
Molson Export Million Stakes	Benburb	$600,000
Pacific Classic	Missionary Ridge	$550,000
Pimlico Special Handicap	Strike the Gold	$420,000
Preakness Stakes	Pine Bluff	$484,120
Prix de l'Arc de Triomphe (France)	Subotica	$956,000
Rothmans International (Canada)	Snurge	$636,000
Santa Anita Handicap	Best Pal	$550,000
Super Derby	Senor Tomas	$450,000
Travers Stakes	Thunder Rumble	$600,000

Major U.S. harness races of 1992

Race	Winner	Value to winner
Cane Pace	Western Hanover	$182,175
Hambletonian	Alf Palema	$552,000
Little Brown Jug	Fake Left	$160,744
Meadowlands Pace	Carlsbad Cam	$500,000
Messenger Stakes	Western Hanover	$183,375
Woodrow Wilson	America's Pastime	$389,400

Sources: *The Blood-Horse* magazine and U.S. Trotting Association.

Hopkins, Anthony (1937-), won the Academy Award for best actor in March 1992 for his role as Hannibal (the Cannibal) Lecter in the motion picture *The Silence of the Lambs* (1991). Hopkins had been a motion-picture actor since 1968, when he made his debut in *The Lion in Winter.* But this was his first Oscar nomination.

Hopkins was born in Port Talbot, Wales, on Dec. 31, 1937. He received his early education at the Cowbridge boarding school in South Wales and had his first theater experience with a local drama group soon after graduation. He attended the Welsh College of Music and Drama in Cardiff, then served in the British army from 1958 to 1960. He then earned a scholarship to the Royal Academy of Dramatic Art, where he studied until 1963. Hopkins in 1967 joined the National Theatre of Great Britain (now the Royal National Theatre), then under the direction of English actor Laurence Olivier. In addition to screen and stage acting, Hopkins has had award-winning performances in made-for-television movies. He received an Emmy Award in 1976 for his performance in *The Lindbergh Kidnapping Case* and in 1981 for his role in *The Bunker.* Other awards include Variety Club Film Actor of the Year 1984 for *The Bounty,* Stage Actor of the Year 1985 for *Pravda,* and best actor at the Moscow Film Festival in 1987 for *84 Charing Cross Road.*

Hopkins married his second wife, Jennifer Lynton, in 1973. They live in London. Kristine Portnoy Kelley

Horse racing. The thoroughbreds who attracted the most attention in 1992 were the 3-year-old colts—A. P. Indy, who won the Breeders' Cup Classic, and Arazi, the would-be superstar who never lived up to expectations. The leading harness horse was Artsplace, a 4-year-old pacing colt who won big races and big money with record-breaking speed.

Arazi flops. In November 1991, Arazi, bred in the United States and trained in France, was shipped to America for the Breeders' Cup Juvenile race. He won with such force that he immediately became the favorite for the 1992 American Triple Crown races. But in the first of those races, the $974,800 Kentucky Derby on May 2 at Churchill Downs in Louisville, Ky., Arazi finished eighth. At the Breeders' Cup races on October 31 at Gulfstream Park in Hallandale, Fla., Arazi's handlers ran him in the $1-million Breeders' Cup Mile on turf rather than the $3-million Classic on dirt. Arazi, the 3-2 favorite, finished 11th in a field of 14.

Triple Crown and other winners. Lil E. Tee, a 16-to-1 shot, won the Kentucky Derby. On May 16 in the Preakness at Pimlico in Baltimore, Pine Bluff won by three-quarters of a length over Alydeed. A. P. Indy, a son of Seattle Slew and a grandson of Secretariat, both Kentucky Derby winners, won the Belmont Stakes on June 6 at Belmont Park in Elmont, N.Y. In the Breeders' Cup Classic, A. P. Indy, the 2-1 favorite, defeated Pleasant Tap and other handicap stars and finished the year with five victories in seven starts.

Lil E. Tee (with jockey Pat Day standing), though a 16-to-1 long shot, wins the 118th Kentucky Derby in Louisville, Ky., on May 2.

Pine Bluff won the most money during 1992. He won $1,970,896, including a $1-million bonus for the best overall finish in the Triple Crown races.

Injuries hampered several top horses in 1992. A. P. Indy missed the Kentucky Derby and the Preakness because of a bruised hoof. In the two weeks after the Belmont Stakes, Lil E. Tee underwent arthroscopic surgery on both front ankles and missed the rest of the season. Pine Bluff injured a leg in training and was retired from racing on July 1.

Harness. Artsplace won the 16 races in which he competed and collected purses of $932,325. On June 20 at the Meadowlands in East Rutherford, N.J., he won in 1 minute 49⅖ seconds, the fastest one-mile race in the sport's history. At season's end, he was retired with career earnings of $3,085,083, second among pacers to the retired Nihilator's $3,225,653. Peace Corps, a 6-year-old mare, won her fourth consecutive Breeders' Cup title and sent her record career earnings past $5.6 million, a record for a trotter.

In the Triple Crown series for 3-year-old pacers, Western Hanover won the Cane and the Messenger and lost the Little Brown Jug by a nose to Fake Left. In the Triple Crown races for 3-year-old trotters, McCluckey and Magic Lobell finished in a dead heat in the Yonkers' Trot, Alf Palema of Sweden won the Hambletonian, and Armbro Keepsake won the Kentucky Futurity. Frank Litsky

In *World Book,* see **Harness racing; Horse racing.**

Hospital administrators began 1992 with hopes of playing a larger role in the debate on health-care reform. They ended the year wondering about the possible consequences of President-elect Bill Clinton's stated commitment to health-care cost containment and *managed care*—organized programs that coordinate, and sometimes limit, access to health services.

Hospitals' reform plan. In February 1992, the American Hospital Association (AHA) proposed a change in the structure of health care. Under the AHA proposal, health-care providers—including doctors, clinics, nursing homes, and hospitals—would join together in "community care networks." Each network would receive a fixed payment for every patient it enrolled. The payments would come from employers or government funds.

Observers feared, however, that such collaboration might violate antitrust laws. They also expected tighter restrictions on hospital usage under Clinton's presidency. During the campaign, Clinton had endorsed greater reliance on *health maintenance organizations* (HMO's), which emphasize preventive and noninstitutional care to reduce the use of unnecessary services.

Hospital admissions for overnight stays declined by 1.1 per cent in 1991, the AHA reported in 1992. This was the largest drop in five years.

At the same time, *outpatient* visits (visits not requiring an overnight stay) increased by 5.4 per cent. Moreover, surgeries performed on an outpatient basis outnumbered surgeries that required an overnight stay for the first time since the AHA began collecting such data. Outpatient surgeries accounted for 11 million of the 22 million surgeries performed by community hospitals in 1990—the latest year for which data were available.

Emergency room visits continued to rise. An AHA survey of 808 hospitals found that in 1990 8.7 per cent reported emergency department overcrowding on a daily basis, 34.7 per cent reported experiencing the problem at least once a week, 55.1 per cent experienced it at least once a month, and 71.7 per cent said overcrowding had occurred at some point during the year. The average number of cases handled annually in emergency departments increased by 23.8 per cent from 1985 to 1990.

Hospital finances remained shaky. Revenue from patient care on average exceeded hospital costs by only 0.4 per cent in 1991, the AHA reported in 1992. When hospitals took into account revenue from all activities—including investments, charitable contributions, and other sources—profit margins averaged 5.2 per cent. In September 1992, the AHA predicted that rising costs would cause 7 out of 10 hospitals that provided services to Medicare patients—primarily patients over age 65—to lose money. Emily Friedman

See also **Health issues: Curing America's Health-Care Ills.** In ***World Book,*** see **Hospital.**

Housing. See **Building and construction.**

Houston. Bob Lanier, a millionaire real estate developer, was installed as the city's 49th mayor on Jan. 2, 1992. Lanier rode into office on a wave of discontent over the city's crime problem and a proposed $1.2-billion monorail system championed by former Mayor Kathryn J. Whitmire. Lanier moved quickly in his first few weeks in office to address both issues, installing a new police chief and a new chairman of the Metropolitan Transit Authority.

Law enforcement. Lanier made good on a campaign pledge to increase the police presence on the streets by the equivalent of 655 additional patrol officers within three months of taking office. He did so partly by making more money available for overtime pay, so that some officers could stay on patrol for longer shifts, and by reassigning some officers from desk jobs to patrol duties.

On February 17, Lanier fired Police Chief Elizabeth M. Watson, whose abrasive style had alienated many police officers and some members of the City Council. At the same time, he named a new chief, Samuel M. Nuchia, a former federal prosecutor and veteran police officer. Watson, whose 1990 appointment as Houston's first woman police chief put her into the national spotlight, was appointed chief of the Austin, Tex., police department during the summer.

Transit. Billy Burge, a real estate developer and staunch Lanier ally, was elected chairman of the Metropolitan Transit Authority (MTA) on Jan. 23, 1992. At the same meeting, the nine-member board enacted all of Lanier's campaign promises pertaining to transit. The board killed the controversial monorail plan and agreed to study a commuter railway proposal calling for MTA trains to share tracks with established freight carriers. The board also agreed to increase spending for road and street repairs and the construction of sidewalks and bike trails.

Business. The future of a leading Houston company, Continental Airlines, was in the hands of a federal bankruptcy court judge in the state of Delaware in 1992. Since 1990, the airline, with more than 12,000 employees in Houston, had been under the protection of the court as it attempted to reorganize.

During 1992, Air Canada and a financial group associated with it offered to buy a majority of Continental for $450 million. In November, the bankruptcy judge gave Continental until Jan. 15, 1993, to file a reorganization plan under which it would be acquired by Air Canada.

Sports. On October 30, the owners of the National League baseball teams approved the sale of the Houston Astros to Texas businessman Drayton McLane for $138 million. McLane took over operation of the Astros on November 9. Since 1979, the team had been controlled by an unpopular absentee owner in New Jersey, John McMullen.

Education. The Houston Independent School District, faced with rising expenses and declining state support, enacted a 32 per cent property tax increase in August 1992. Although the tax hike sparked protests from property owners, the increase was considerably less than the 47 per cent increase requested by School Superintendent Frank Petruzielo.

Efforts to concentrate on academics in the city's schools were often overshadowed by rising concerns about student drug abuse, assaults, and gang activities. In one highly publicized case in October, a seventh-grade girl was allegedly gang raped by seven teen-age boys in the restroom of a middle school.

The University of Houston (UH) mourned the death of its president, Marguerite Ross Barnett, 49, from complications of brain cancer in February. Barnett gained national prominence in September 1990 when she took the helm as the university's first black president and first woman president. In April 1992, the UH board of regents named James H. Pickering, dean of the UH College of Humanities, to serve as interim president until August 1994.

Republican National Convention. Houston rolled out the red carpet August 17 to 20 for the Republican Party's 1992 presidential nominating convention. President George Bush, who represented a suburban Houston district in the U.S. House of Representatives from 1967 to 1970, returned to his adopted hometown to accept his party's nomination for a second term. Timothy J. Graham

See also **City; Republican Party.** In ***World Book,*** see **Houston.**

Hungary. The governing coalition headed by the Hungarian Democratic Forum (HDF) began its third year in power in May 1992. The HDF faced a growing rift within its own ranks, as well as increasingly energetic political opposition and a loss of public support during the course of the year. But it also had some notable economic and political successes.

Economic gains. Hungary in 1992 further increased its trade with Western nations, a process begun in 1990. At midyear, official figures showed that the major industrialized nations accounted for 70 per cent of Hungary's trade, while trade with the former Soviet bloc had fallen to 25 per cent.

Meanwhile, the country's political stability and progress toward economic reform continued to attract foreign investment and loans. By mid-1992, more than 13,000 joint ventures by Hungarian and foreign companies had been created, up from about 5,000 the previous year. In October, the International Monetary Fund (IMF), a United Nations agency, said that Hungary had met 14 of 15 IMF criteria for loans, the highest of any country in the region.

As a sign of its growing economic relations with the West, Hungary in February signed a 10-year cooperation treaty with Germany, which already accounted for 25 per cent of Hungary's trade and for numerous joint ventures. In April, the United States granted Hungary unconditional "most favored nation" status, conferring on it advantageous terms of trade, as part of a larger economic accord.

Relations with Czechoslovakia soured in May when Hungary formally announced it would not honor a 1977 treaty for construction of twin hydroelectric dams on the Danube River, which flows between the two countries. Hungary had suspended construction on its dam for environmental reasons in 1989. The Slovak Republic—due to become independent when Czechoslovakia splits into sovereign nations in January 1993—completed its dam in October 1992, despite Hungarian protests. At the end of that month, however, the Czechoslovak and Hungarian leaders agreed to submit the issue to international arbitration.

A political rift within the HDF began to develop toward the end of 1992 with the emergence of an ultranationalist faction led by Istvan Csurka, one of the party's founders. The faction drew criticism for its anti-Semitic and anti-Western positions. Prime Minister Jozsef Antall said the HDF could accommodate a variety of opinions and should not divide into competing parties.

Censorship issue. Using a 1974 law permitting state control of the media, Antall tried in June and July to fire the chiefs of the state-run radio and television networks. President Arpad Goncz refused to approve the firings, which apparently stemmed from Antall's anger at media opposition to his policies.

Eric Bourne

See also **Europe** (Facts in brief table). In ***World Book,*** see **Hungary**.

Ice skating. Kristi Yamaguchi of Fremont, Calif., and Viktor Petrenko of Ukraine swept the figure-skating singles titles in 1992 in the Winter Olympics and the world championships. In speed skating, the year's major winners were two women—Bonnie Blair of Champaign, Ill., in the sprints and Gunda Niemann of Germany in the longer races.

Figure skating. In the United States championships and Olympic trials held from Jan. 8 to 13, 1992, in Orlando, Fla., Yamaguchi finished first, Nancy Kerrigan of Stoneham, Mass., finished second, and Tonya Harding of Portland, Ore., finished third. At the Winter Olympics in February in Albertville, France, Yamaguchi won, despite a fall in the concluding long program. Midori Ito of Japan took the silver medal. Kerrigan gained the bronze. Harding finished fourth.

In the world championships held from March 25 to 29 in Oakland, Calif., Yamaguchi won the gold medal, Kerrigan the silver, and 15-year-old Lu Chen of China the bronze. Harding dropped to sixth.

Petrenko competed for the Unified Team, representing the Commonwealth of Independent States, formerly the Soviet Union. He was a skilled artistic skater with the athletic ability to perform clean, consistent triple jumps. He won comfortably in the Olympics and in the world championships.

In the Olympics, Paul Wylie of Denver, Colo., who had never won a major title, took the silver medal in men's figure skating. Petr Barna of Czechoslovakia,

Kristi Yamaguchi performs her winning routine at the United States Figure Skating Championships in Orlando, Fla., in January.

the European champion, won the bronze medal. Christopher Bowman of Van Nuys, Calif., the U.S. champion, finished fourth. Kurt Browning of Edmonton, Canada, the world champion in 1989, 1990, and 1991, placed sixth, the victim of a bad back. Petrenko's teammates Artur Dmitriev and Natalia Mishkutienok swept the Olympic, world, and European championships in pairs. Sergei Ponomarenko and Marina Klimova, also members of the Unified Team, did the same in ice dancing.

Speed skating. Blair, who won the gold medal in the women's 500 meters in the 1988 Winter Olympics, also took the gold medal in the 500 meters and 1,000 meters. She also won the World Cup series titles in the 500 meters and 1,000 meters. Niemann became the Olympic champion in the 3,000 meters and 5,000 meters, the World Cup champion in the 1,500 meters and 3,000 meters, and the world overall champion.

Other world champions were Robert Sighel of Italy in men's overall, Igor Zhelezovski of the Unified Team in men's sprint, and Ye Qiaobo of China in women's sprint. In the men's 500 meters, Dan Jansen of West Allis, Wis., won the World Cup title and set a world record, 36.41 seconds in January. Frank Litsky

See also **Blair, Bonnie; Olympic Games: The 1992 Olympics.** In ***World Book,*** see **Ice skating.**

Iceland. See **Europe.**

Idaho. See **State government.**

Illinois. See **Chicago; State government.**

Immigration. United States President George Bush set off months of controversy in 1992 by cracking down on an influx of "boat people" from Haiti. The Haitians were seeking asylum in the United States. Haitians began making boat journeys to the mainland of the United States and to the U.S. naval base at Guantanamo Bay, Cuba, after a military coup in late 1991 ousted Haiti's first democratically elected president. The coup prompted economic embargoes by the United States and other countries.

Deportations. On Feb. 1, 1992, the Bush Administration began forcing more than 14,000 Haitian refugees to return to their homeland, after the Supreme Court of the United States on January 31 lifted a lower court's December 1991 injunction that had barred their return. The Bush Administration argued that most of the Haitians were fleeing economic hardship rather than political persecution and thus were not entitled to asylum under U.S. law.

But Haitians continued making the voyage to the United States, and by May, the refugee center at Guantanamo Bay was filled to its 12,500-person capacity. On May 24, Bush issued an executive order to the Coast Guard to intercept refugees at sea and return them to Haiti. The refugees were directed to apply for asylum at the U.S. Embassy in the Haitian capital of Port-au-Prince. Critics of the Administration policy argued that returning the Haitians without first determining whether they were political refugees was illegal. But the Administration asserted that taking claims only at the U.S. Embassy in Haiti was the best way to deter Haitians from attempting the perilous 600-mile (970-kilometer) boat trip to the United States. In July, a federal appeals court ruled that the policy was illegal under the Immigration and Naturalization Act of 1980, which says the United States must determine whether refugees face political persecution. But on Aug. 1, 1992, the U.S. Supreme Court stayed the lower court's decision pending a full review of the case.

In total, about 35,000 Haitians had attempted to reach the United States before Bush's executive order in May. About 10,500 were found to be in danger of political persecution in Haiti and were granted asylum. The rest were returned to Haiti.

Alien rights. The Immigration and Naturalization Service, in a settlement of a 1978 court case, in June 1992 agreed to inform people arrested as suspected illegal aliens of their legal rights. Such persons will be given a "notice of rights" explaining why they have been detained and offering them the opportunity to communicate with both a lawyer and an official from their native country's embassy. The suspected illegal aliens will also be informed of possible legal avenues for residency and be given the opportunity to request political asylum before an immigration judge.

Frank Cormier and Margot Cormier

In ***World Book,*** see **Immigration.**

Income tax. See **Taxation.**

India. Hindu fundamentalists on December 6 tore down a 430-year-old Muslim mosque, setting off riots throughout the country between Hindus and Muslims. The mosque had been located in the city of Ayodhya in the northern state of Uttar Pradesh. Within a week, more than 1,200 people had been killed and 5,000 injured. Prime Minister P. V. Narasimha Rao gave government security forces the authority to use live ammunition to quell the violence. He also placed the state of Uttar Pradesh under federal rule. A government Cabinet minister called the fighting the most serious threat to India since the riots between Hindus and Muslims in the late 1940's.

Members of the Hindu group Vishwa Hindu Parishad (VHP) in July began building a temple at the site of the mosque. The group alleged that the mosque had been built over an ancient Hindu temple denoting the birthplace of the god Rama. The ensuing religious dispute between Hindus and Muslims led to riots in the states of Kerala and Maharashtra. But the VHP late in July halted construction after the Indian Supreme Court refused to decide on legal questions concerning the mosque until construction had ceased.

However, on December 6, Hindus defied the court order and demolished the mosque with pickaxes and crowbars. More than 300,000 Hindus had gathered in Ayodhya to destroy the mosque and erect a new temple to Rama. The razing inflamed Muslims throughout the country, and riots ensued.

Hindus in the Indian state of Uttar Pradesh in July begin building a temple at the site of an ancient Muslim mosque, an act that led to riots in December.

Economic changes. India in 1992 stepped up plans to make its economy more market-driven. This push was prompted by the 1991 collapse of India's longtime supporter, the Soviet Union, and the state-run Soviet economic model that India had long pursued. Finance Minister Manmohan Singh on Feb. 29, 1992, unveiled a series of reforms aimed at opening up India's economy, including the reduction of import duties, the elimination of nontariff barriers to most imports, and the opening up of gas and oil fields to foreign developers. Singh also proposed selling off $1 billion of state-run operations, lowering taxes, and cutting spending to reduce the federal deficit.

Consolidation of power. Singh acted with the blessing of Rao. Rao had been elected in 1991 as the candidate of the Congress Party following the assassination of Rajiv Gandhi. A compromise choice, Rao was believed to have no mandate, but he surprised Indians by pushing hard for economic and democratic reform.

And Rao's hold on power strengthened in 1992. He faced no challenge to his leadership of the Congress Party at its annual convention in April, though the party held elections for internal posts for the first time in more than 20 years. In addition, Rao in August achieved a clear parliamentary majority for the first time when members of the opposition Janata Dal Party defected to his Congress Party.

New president. On July 13, Vice President Shankar Dayal Sharma was elected as India's president. The position is largely ceremonial, but the president's few powers expand when no party holds a majority in the parliament. As this was the case in most of 1992, the race was hotly contested. Rao's Congress Party and its allies backed Sharma, who won with about 65 per cent of the votes in an electoral college composed of members of the national and state legislatures.

Banking scandal. A $1-billion financial scandal—the worst in India's history—hit India's investment community in April. Official investigators charged that several national and foreign banks made unsecured loans to stockbrokers. A government report said that total financial losses from the scandal would amount to $1.2 billion. By June, criminal charges had been brought against 19 brokers and bank officials.

Foreign policy shifts. India in 1992 moved to deal with the waning political influence of the nonaligned movement, a group of Third World countries that had remained neutral during the Cold War between the United States and the former Soviet Union. On January 29, India announced it was establishing full diplomatic ties with Israel after more than 40 years of cool relations. India made the move in order to play a role in Middle East peace talks, a role that could give the country increased leverage in its dealings with nations of the Middle East and central Asia.

India had also long insisted that joint maneuvers of its navy with that of the United States would compromise its nonaligned status. But such exercises began in the spring of 1992 after the creation of the first U.S.-Indian military committee.

Regional trouble spots. In the state of Jammu and Kashmir, two groups of Muslim guerrillas in 1992 clashed with predominantly Hindu soldiers and police and each other. The Jammu and Kashmir Liberation Front fought for independence, whereas the Hizb-ul Mjaheddin fought for union with neighboring Pakistan. The two groups had been cooperating, but in 1992 they started competing.

In the state of Punjab, militants from the Sikh religious community continued a terrorist campaign for independence for the state. Intensified police efforts resulted in the deaths of more than 20 militant leaders in 1992. However, the Sikhs retaliated by murdering more than 60 policemen or their relatives. Since 1987, more than 12,000 people have been killed in Sikh-related clashes in Punjab.

Due to threats of violence by radical Sikhs and boycotts by Sikh groups, only 22 per cent of eligible Punjabi voters turned out on February 19 for legislative elections. This was the lowest turnout ever for any Indian state election. Many candidates, despite being given escort vehicles and armed guards by the government, still refused to campaign out of fear. The elections were the first to be held since the Indian government imposed emergency rule on Punjab in 1987.

Henry S. Bradsher

See also **Asia** (Facts in brief table). In ***World Book,*** see **India.**

Indian, American. Ben Nighthorse Campbell (D., Colo.), the only Native American serving in the Congress of the United States, on Nov. 3, 1992, became the first Native American to win a seat in the U.S. Senate since 1929. Campbell, who had served in the House of Representatives since 1986, was only the second American Indian to win election to Congress.

Inuit homeland. On May 4, 1992, voters in Canada's Northwest Territories approved a plan to create a self-governing homeland for Inuit people living in the eastern portion of the territories. The new homeland was to be established in 1996. See **Northwest Territories: Creating Nunavut.**

Hopi-Navajo settlement. The Hopi and Navajo tribal councils on Nov. 23, 1992, approved a proposed settlement to a bitter land battle that has divided the two tribes for more than 100 years. Under the terms of the agreement, which was subject to congressional approval, the U.S. government would give the Hopis nearly 400,000 acres (162,000 hectares) of public land in northern Arizona.

The conflict began in 1882, when Navajos began moving onto land claimed by both tribes. In 1974, the government divided the disputed territory, which covered 1.8 million acres (728,000 hectares), and ordered each tribe to leave the other tribe's reservation. However, some Navajos refused to move from the Hopi reservation, claiming their forced relocation would violate their religious rights.

To settle the dispute, the government offered to cede the Hopis an additional 200,000 acres (81,000 hectares) of land currently managed by the U.S. Forest Service along with another 200,000 acres consisting of state-owned land, land bought from privately owned ranches, and land currently controlled by the U.S. Bureau of Land Management. The Hopis agreed to allow the approximately 150 Navajo families still living on their reservation to remain for 75 years. Some government officials criticized the plan, arguing that public lands should not be used to settle Native American land claims.

Teen suicide rate. Native American teen-agers are four times more likely to attempt suicide than other teen-agers are. This was the conclusion of a survey of nearly 14,000 American Indian teen-agers reported in March 1992 by researchers from the University of Minnesota in Minneapolis. The researchers said that 22 per cent of the Native American girls surveyed and 12 per cent of the Native American boys reported having tried to kill themselves. Eighteen per cent of the teen-agers also reported experiencing constant feelings of sadness.

New museums. The National Museum of the American Indian opened in new quarters in New York City on November 15. The opening—at the Smithsonian Institution's George Gustav Heye Center—marked the first stage in the relocation of more than 1 million Native American artifacts and artworks collected by Heye, an oil tycoon who died in 1957. In 1989, the Museum of the American Indian, which was scheduled to close in June 1993, agreed to transfer its collection to the Smithsonian Institution.

A new Iroquois Indian Museum opened in Howes Cave, N.Y., in June 1992. The museum, whose design was based on the traditional Iroquois long house, displays both Iroquois artifacts and artwork.

Dinosaur fossil seized. The largest and best-preserved skeleton of a *Tyrannosaurus rex* ever found was seized by the Federal Bureau of Investigation on May 14 after Cheyenne River Sioux Indians charged that the skeleton had been taken illegally from tribal land in north-central South Dakota. In 1990, the Black Hills Institute of Geological Research, a commercial fossil dealer in Hill City, S.Dak., had paid a member of the Cheyenne River Sioux Indian Tribe for the right to excavate the fossil on his ranch. But the Sioux claimed that because the rancher's land was held in trust by the Bureau of Indian Affairs, the fossil actually belongs to the government. They also asserted that the tribe should have control over any fossils found on Sioux land.

On May 22, 1992, the company filed suit against the government to recover the fossil. The fossil's seizure outraged many paleontologists, who feared that moving the fossil would damage a significant scientific discovery. Barbara A. Mayes

In ***World Book,*** see **Indian, American.**

Indiana. See **State government.**

Indonesia. Repercussions from the 1991 massacre of demonstrators calling for independence for East Timor continued in 1992. The massacre by Indonesian soldiers had taken place on Nov. 12, 1991, at the funeral of an independence advocate in Dili, the capital of East Timor, a former Portuguese territory that was annexed by Indonesia in 1976. Witnesses to the massacre reported that 100 or more people were killed.

Criticism for the killings was strong worldwide but especially so in the Netherlands, Indonesia's former colonial ruler. The Dutch halted economic aid to Indonesia after the massacre but resumed aid after Indonesia in early 1992 disciplined a dozen military officers for their roles in the incident. Nevertheless, the Netherlands indicated it would link future economic aid to respect for human rights.

Indonesia refused to tolerate any use of economic aid as a lever for internal change. On March 25, it canceled all aid from the Netherlands and asked other aid givers not to work through a committee led by the Dutch. In June, a new aid group without the Netherlands voted to continue economic assistance, pledging almost $5 billion for Indonesia for 1992-1993.

Legislative elections. On June 9, the ruling Golkar political organization won a majority of the 400 contested seats in the parliament's House of People's Representatives, receiving 68 per cent of the votes. But Golkar's victory was not surprising given the rules governing the elections. For example, Golkar is the only political organization permitted to solicit votes full-time. And parties were forbidden to discuss issues deemed harmful to national unity.

The Indonesian government allowed only two other parties to field candidates. The Muslim-based United Development Party took 17 per cent of the vote, and the populist Indonesian Democracy Party earned 15 per cent. These showings were improvements over both parties' numbers in the last elections in 1987.

Rebel chief caught. Indonesian troops in November 1992 captured Xanana Gusmao, the leader of a resistance movement seeking independence for East Timor. Portugal immediately appealed for his release.

Earthquake hits. On December 12, Eastern Indonesia was rocked by an earthquake measuring 7.5 on the Richter scale. At least 2,500 people were killed, and entire coastal towns were demolished by tidal waves triggered by the quake

Bright economic future. In mid-1992, the World Bank, an agency of the United Nations, reported that Indonesia had a 20-year average economic growth rate of more than 6 per cent. The report said that if this rate can be maintained, Indonesia "can realistically expect to become a solid middle-income country with a per capita income of $1,000" by the year 2000. (The per capita income in 1990 was $570.)

Henry S. Bradsher

See also **Asia** (Facts in brief table). In ***World Book,*** see **Indonesia.**

International trade. World trade issues were prominent in the news in 1992. The United States and the 12-nation European Community (EC or Common Market) narrowly avoided a trade war in November. Conflicts over trade continued between the United States and Japan and the United States and China, but the United States, Canada, and Mexico agreed in August to form the world's largest free trade zone.

GATT talks. The United States and 107 other nations continued trade talks but were unable again in 1992 to conclude a comprehensive trade-liberalization agreement. Conflict in the trade talks—known as the Uruguay Round of the General Agreement on Tariffs and Trade (GATT)—brewed all year. The trade talks, which had been ongoing since 1986, involved loosening international rules for services, investment, and trading goods. Negotiations continued to drag until late November over a dispute between the United States and the EC over the amount of European government subsidies to farmers. The dispute over subsidies centered on payments to Europe's oilseed growers, who mainly produce soybeans. Soybean farmers in the United States insisted that the European subsidies cost them over $1 billion a year by lowering the price that European farmers were able to charge for their produce. The lower prices unfairly reserved a lucrative market for European farmers and blocked U.S. exports, the U.S. negotiators claimed.

The United States threatened in early November to impose 200 per cent tariffs on selected European agricultural products, mostly French wine, unless the EC reduced oilseed subsidies. On November 20, the two sides agreed to lower subsidies, allowing the multilateral Uruguay Round trade talks to resume.

North American free trade pact. While GATT talks faltered for most of the year, trade negotiations among the United States, Mexico, and Canada successfully concluded on August 12. After grueling negotiations during the first two weeks in August, the countries' chief trade ministers signed an agreement that would eliminate tariffs within the region by 2004 and open doors to U.S. and Canadian investment in Mexico. Mexico stuck to its constitutional ban on foreign ownership of its oil industry but opened the door to wider foreign participation in that industry. The U.S. Congress was to vote on the pact in 1993.

Concerns about two aspects of the accord sparked controversy in the United States throughout 1992. The critics, who were led by environmental, labor, and citizen groups, wanted stricter enforcement of fair labor laws and closer attention to the deteriorating environment along the U.S.-Mexican border. The critics of the pact also complained that the Administration of President George Bush had not given sufficient assurances that U.S. workers displaced by increased trade and investment in Mexico would be compensated. Newly elected U.S. President Bill Clinton pledged during the November election campaign to seek side agreements with Mexico on labor and environmental issues. He also announced a comprehensive plan to upgrade worker training programs.

Japanese trade issues. Japan's government focused all year on efforts to buy more goods from abroad in 1992. Official lending rates by the Japanese Export-Import Bank were lowered substantially for importers, but an effort to encourage Japanese consumers to buy more foreign goods apparently did not work. Japan was expected to end 1992 with a record $106-billion merchandise trade surplus. Almost half of that surplus came from trade with the United States. Japan was expected to ship more than $93-billion worth of products to the United States but take in only $48 billion in U.S. goods by the end of 1992.

Beginning in midyear, Democrats in the U.S. Congress tried to pass a trade bill designed to punish countries that engage in what are perceived as unfair trading practices with the United States. A section of the proposed legislation required that the Administration identify countries that have persistent trade imbalances with the United States and mandate resolution of the biggest trade problems within a year. Failing that, stiff import penalties would be applied. Among the legislation's more controversial aspects was a directive to the U.S. Trade Representative's Office to negotiate limits on Japanese auto imports into the United States. Automobiles represent the bulk of Japan's trade imbalance with the United States. On July 8, the House of Representatives ap-

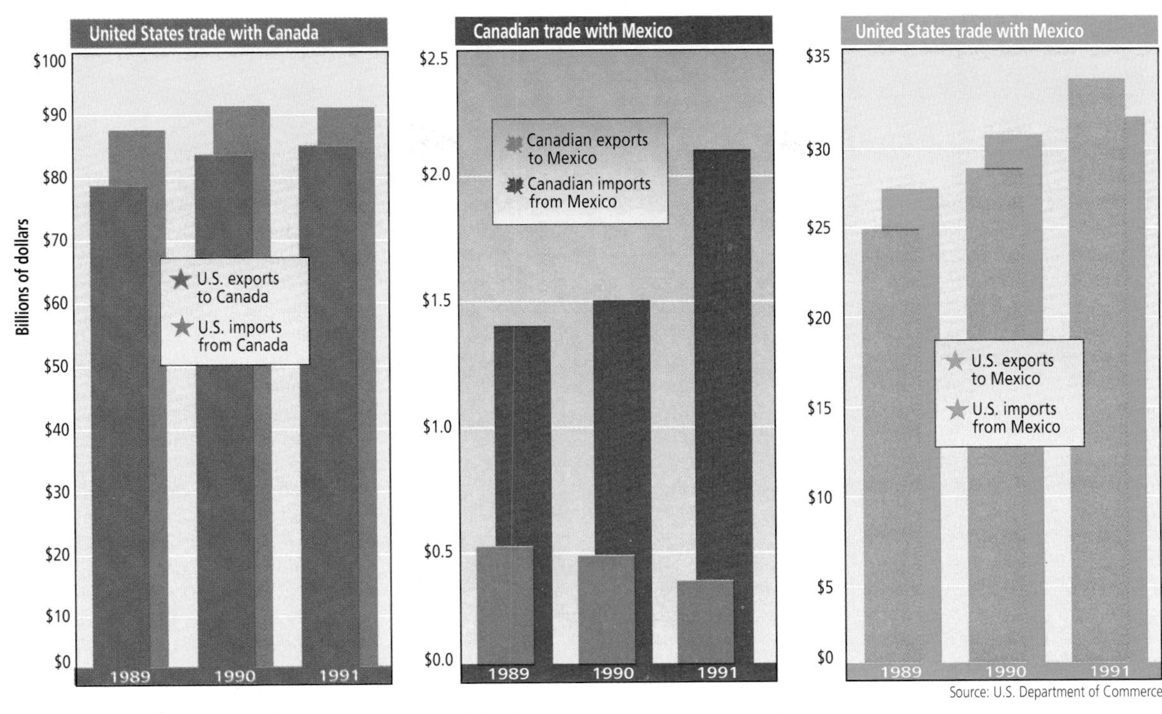

Trade among the United States, Canada, and Mexico was expected to grow after the signing of the North American Free Trade Agreement in December.

proved a slightly weaker version of the bill, but the Senate defeated the measure.

In an attempt to resolve conflicts involving trade issues between the two countries, U.S. President George Bush traveled to Japan in January. Several executives from U.S. industry, including Lee A. Iacocca, then chairman of the automaker Chrysler Corporation, accompanied Bush. Japanese automobile producers promised to import 20,000 more U.S.-made cars than they had previously planned by 1994 and to purchase $10 billion in U.S. auto parts by 1995. The Japanese also said they would allow U.S. cars to be shown in Tokyo auto showrooms.

On June 24, the U.S. International Trade Commission ruled that two Japanese automakers—Toyota Motor Corporation and Mazda Motor Corporation—were not doing any injury to U.S. car manufacturers, despite a U.S. Commerce Department ruling on May 19 that they were guilty of selling minivans in the U.S. market at below fair prices. Such selling practices, known as "dumping," are a violation of international trade laws. United States automakers had sought to impose higher tariffs on minivans from the two Japanese companies.

Trade with China. Toward the end of the year, China's monthly trade surplus with the United States was $2.3 billion. That figure was nearly double the monthly $1.4-billion trade surplus that China enjoyed with the United States in January 1991, when China surpassed Taiwan as the nation with the second largest trade surplus with the United States. Japan had the largest surplus.

The U.S. Congress failed twice in 1992 to attach political conditions to the renewal of China's most-favored-nation (MFN) trading status with the United States. Such status allows countries to pay the lowest allowable duties in trade with the United States. China gained MFN status in 1980. Congress wanted to make China adhere to higher human rights standards, restrict its arms sales abroad, and be more fair in its trading practices with the United States.

The Bush Administration opposed such conditions, insisting that they would be counterproductive. President Bush vetoed two separate bills—one in March and one in September—that put conditions on renewing China's MFN status.

The House overwhelmingly voted twice to override the vetoes, but in both cases, the Senate failed narrowly to reach the two-thirds majority needed for an override. The Bush Administration argued that imposing high duties on Chinese goods would disrupt a huge U.S. retail industry dependent on low-priced imports from China. The Administration also said such duties would threaten big U.S. exporters, such as farmers, with trade retaliation. Jim Berger

See also **Economics.** In ***World Book,*** see **International trade.**

Iowa. See **State government.**

Iran. Supporters of President Ali Akbar Hashemi Rafsanjani won a majority of the seats in Iran's 270-seat parliament in elections held in April and May 1992. Some Middle East analysts suggested that the victory of these candidates, who generally favor closer economic relations with other countries, represented a popular rejection of the anti-Western Islamic extremists who had dominated Iran's political institutions since the country's 1979 revolution.

Political analysts also pointed to Rafsanjani's call for closer cooperation with the West on May 27 and Iran's alleged involvement in the June release of the last Western hostages held in Lebanon. Other observers, however, argued that Iran's arms build-up, which may include nuclear technology, its continuing involvement in international terrorism, and its efforts to gain sole control over three islands in the Persian Gulf were evidence of Iran's desire to extend its power both regionally and in countries with large Muslim populations.

Social unrest. Riots—the worst since the 1979 revolution—rocked major Iranian cities in April and May 1992. The government formed riot squads and sentenced at least 45 protesters to long prison terms and at least 9 protesters to death.

Economic woes. Blame for the unrest was fixed chiefly on Iran's serious economic problems. Many of the rioters came from squatters' camps ringing urban areas. During 1992, a high inflation rate cut into income, which generally remained flat. Iran's population growth rate—one of the highest in the world at nearly 4 per cent in some urban areas—also eroded the impact of social programs.

Iran earned nearly $17 billion in oil-export revenues for the fiscal year ending March 1991. But oil earnings were expected to drop to $15 billion in 1992 because of weakening international oil prices. Oil provides nearly all of Iran's export earnings and about 50 per cent of its total revenues. Iran reportedly had difficulty paying its short-term debts in 1992.

Rearmament. An ambitious rearmament program accounted for a large portion of Iran's debt. Western officials estimated that between 1988 and 1991 Iran spent at least $7 billion on arms purchases from foreign suppliers. Iran was expected to spend another $2 billion in 1992. In November, Iran accepted delivery of the first of three nuclear submarines from Russia.

Foreign relations. Seven Persian Gulf nations and Syria accused Iran in early September of trying to annex the Persian Gulf islands of Abu Musa, Greater Tunb, and Lesser Tunb. Since 1971, Iran and the United Arab Emirates have jointly controlled Abu Musa, the only one of the islands that is inhabited. In response, Iran declared its sovereignty over Abu Musa on Sept. 10, 1992.

Iran continued efforts to improve relations with countries along its northern border in 1992. Early in the year, Iran tried to mediate the conflict between the former Soviet republics of Armenia and Azerbaijan over Nagorno-Karabakh, a region largely populated by Armenians that lies within Azerbaijan.

Iran also reportedly sent arms and military advisers to Sudan, where an Islamic government was battling non-Muslim rebels, and arms to Bosnia and Hercegovina, a former republic of Yugoslavia, where Bosnian Muslims were fighting Christian Croats and Serbs.

Terrorism. The United States Department of State said in May that Iran was probably involved in several terrorist incidents in 1992, include the bombing of the Israeli Embassy in Buenos Aires, Argentina, on March 17 in which at least 32 people were killed and 252 injured. Iranian officials denied the U.S. charges on May 9. Islamic Holy War, a militant pro-Iranian group, claimed responsibility for the attack.

U.S. relations. On May 6, an international tribunal at The Hague in the Netherlands ruled the United States must pay Iran compensation for nonmilitary Iranian assets impounded in 1979 when Iranian revolutionaries seized the U.S. Embassy in Teheran and held a group of American hostages until 1981.

Iraqi relations. Iranian planes on April 5, 1992, crossed into Iraq to raid a base belonging to an Iranian opposition group. In July, Iran said it would confiscate 132 military and civilian aircraft that Iraq had flown to Iran for safekeeping during the Persian Gulf War (1991). Christine Helms

See also **Middle East** (Facts in brief table). In ***World Book,*** see **Iran.**

Iran-contra affair. Lawrence E. Walsh, the independent prosecutor in the Iran-contra investigation, said on Sept. 16, 1992, that his probe of the arms-for-hostages scandal had been concluded. Walsh had decided earlier not to seek the indictments of former President Ronald Reagan or Reagan's former chief of staff, Donald T. Regan.

But Iran-contra continued to make news during the remainder of the year as revelations emerged from notes that had been kept by Caspar W. Weinberger, Reagan's former secretary of defense. Weinberger's notes allegedly revealed that President George Bush, contrary to his assertions, had apparently been informed of the operation all along and had supported it. See **Bush, George Herbert Walker.**

The Iran-contra affair involved the secret sale of arms to Iran during the Reagan Administration to obtain the release of Muslim-held American hostages in Lebanon. Money from the arms sales was used for the illegal support of *contra* rebels in Nicaragua.

Weinberger was indicted on June 16 on five felony counts, including charges that he had lied to Congress about the Iran-contra scheme and had obstructed government investigations of it. He pleaded not guilty on June 19. Weinberger was the highest official of the Reagan Administration to be charged with a crime in the investigation.

Central to the Weinberger case were some 1,700 pages of notes that Weinberger made while defense secretary and that he donated to the Library of Congress in 1988. When testifying before congressional investigators in 1987, Weinberger asserted that he kept no record of White House meetings he had attended at which Iran-contra might have been discussed.

In September, one of the charges against Weinberger—that he had deliberately concealed his notes from Congress—was dropped. In October, a new indictment was issued, reinstating the charge, but in December, a federal judge dismissed the charge.

Other developments. On January 31, Alan D. Fiers, Jr., was sentenced to one year's probation and 100 hours of community service. Fiers, the former head of the CIA's Central American Task Force, had pleaded guilty in July 1991 to a misdemeanor charge of withholding information from Congress.

On Dec. 9, 1992, Clair E. George, former head of the CIA's covert operations, was found guilty of lying to two congressional committees in 1986. He was acquitted on five other counts of lying to Congress and investigators. George was the highest-ranking CIA official to be convicted of a felony in the Iran-contra affair.

Bush's pardons. But on Dec. 24, 1992, President Bush issued pardons for Fiers, George, Weinberger, and three other top officials implicated in the Iran-contra affair. The pardons drew rebukes from Democratic congressional leaders, who accused Bush of "undermining justice." David Dreier

Iraq. Iraq's President Saddam Hussein held on to power in 1992 despite deteriorating economic conditions resulting from a 1990 United Nations (UN) trade embargo and diplomatic and military efforts by Western countries to dislodge him.

Domestic difficulties. United States intelligence agencies reported in early July 1992 that Hussein had apparently foiled an attempted military coup in late June. In July, a drop in the value of the dinar together with a continuing shortage of hard currency sharply reduced food imports and sent food prices soaring. In late July, Hussein arrested hundreds of merchants for charging excessive prices and executed at least 40. But the food shortages only grew worse, as many merchants, fearful of being accused of profiteering, shut their businesses.

"No-fly" zone. On August 27, the United States, Great Britain, and France began enforcing a ban on Iraqi military and civilian flights over Iraq south of the 32nd parallel. United States President George Bush said the no-fly zone was needed to protect Iraq's rebellious Shiite Muslims from Hussein's forces. Some analysts, however, suggested the ban was part of the West's strategy to oust Hussein. In July, U.S. officials had met with Iraqi opposition leaders to discuss ways to topple Hussein.

Some Arab officials, including representatives of Egypt, Morocco, and Syria, criticized the no-fly zone and cautioned the United States against dividing Iraq

Demonstrators in Iraq march in July to protest the search of a government building by UN inspectors seeking evidence of Iraq's weapons program.

into military zones. (In April 1991, the United States, Great Britain, and France had established a protected zone for the Kurds in northern Iraq.) Arab officials feared the breakup of Iraq would create a power vacuum that non-Arab Iran would attempt to fill. Some also feared that such a breakup would spur demands for a homeland for the Kurds, who live mainly in Turkey, Iran, Syria, and Iraq.

Kurdish affairs. In May 1992, Iraqi Kurds in the protected zone held their first free elections, to vote for representatives to a new parliament. When the vote ended in a draw, Massoud Barzani's Kurdish Democratic Party and Jalal Talabani's Patriotic Union of Kurdistan agreed to rule jointly. Economic conditions in the north deteriorated, however, as infighting among Kurdish groups increased and Hussein tightened an Iraqi blockade of the north. Turkish military incursions into northern Iraq to destroy the bases of Kurdish guerrillas fighting for a separatist state in southeastern Turkey also worsened the Iraqi Kurds' economic problems. (See **Turkey.**)

Weapons inspections. Hussein and Bush played cat-and-mouse on the issue of weapons inspections for most of 1992. Under the terms of the cease-fire agreement that ended the Persian Gulf War (1991), Iraq had agreed to allow UN inspectors to search for and destroy its facilities for producing chemical, biological, and nuclear weapons.

A major crisis arose on July 5, when Iraq refused to allow UN arms inspectors to search the Agriculture Ministry building in Baghdad, Iraq's capital, for documentary evidence of Iraq's weapons program. In response, Bush threatened military action. When the inspectors were finally admitted on July 28, they found no evidence of a weapons program. Bush claimed that incriminating documents had been removed after threats by Iraqi demonstrators forced the UN inspectors on July 22 to abandon the 24-hour guard they had been keeping on the building.

Nevertheless, the leader of a UN weapons-inspection team reported on September 3 that the team had supervised the destruction of all of Iraq's known buildings and equipment for making nuclear weapons. Inspections continued, however. (See **Armed forces: The Nuclear Threat in the New World Order.**)

War toll. About 70,000 Iraqi civilians died in 1991 after the end of the Persian Gulf War as a result of damage caused by allied bombing during the war, according to January 1992 reports by the U.S. Bureau of the Census and Greenpeace, an environmental group. The studies said most of the deaths resulted from the destruction of Iraq's electric power and transportation systems, which crippled the country's health-care and sanitary facilities. An additional 47,000 Iraqi children under age 5 died during the first half of 1991 because of war-related causes, according to a September 1992 study by the UN Children's Fund. Christine Helms

See also **Middle East** (Facts in brief table). In ***World Book,*** see **Iraq; Persian Gulf War.**

Ireland. Prime Minister Charles Haughey, tainted by financial scandals involving friends, resigned Feb. 10, 1992. He had been prime minister since January 1989, though he was first elected to the office in December 1979. Since then, his terms as prime minister totaled eight years. Haughey had been leader of the Fianna Fáil (Soldiers of Destiny) party since 1979. Former Finance Minister Albert Reynolds was elected prime minister on Feb. 11, 1992. (See **Reynolds, Albert.**)

The Progressive Democrats, the minority party in the ruling coalition, had demanded that if Haughey did not resign they would leave the government and force an early general election. Reynolds, too, was pressured by the Progressive Democrats. On November 4, the party withdrew from the ruling coalition over a dispute involving fraud in the nation's beef industry, but many observers felt the real issue was that both Fianna Fáil and the Progressive Democrats wanted new parliamentary elections. On November 5, Reynolds received a no-confidence vote in Parliament, forcing him to call for general elections. The elections, held on November 25, gave Fianna Fáil 68 seats, not enough to form a government without a coalition partner. By early December, no coalition was formed, but Reynolds was still prime minister.

Maastricht Treaty. On June 18, Ireland voted by a 69 per cent majority to ratify the Maastricht Treaty. The treaty would provide closer economic and political ties for the 12 member nations of the European Community (EC, or Common Market). Closer EC ties would provide billions in subsidies to Ireland, one of the smallest and poorest of the EC nations.

Abortion. But in the months prior to the referendum, the issue of treaty passage became tangled with the issue of Irish abortion law. The treaty had a special protocol intended to help secure its passage in Ireland, where the Roman Catholic Church is influential. The protocol said in effect that no EC treaty could alter Ireland's constitutional amendment that allows abortion only when the mother's life is at risk.

On February 17, Ireland's High Court had ruled that a 14-year-old rape victim could not travel to England for an abortion, because the life of the unborn child was guaranteed by the Irish Constitution. But the ruling clashed with the right of EC citizens to travel to member states. On February 26, Ireland's Supreme Court reversed the lower court's decision, saying that the girl's life was at risk, as she had threatened suicide. The case split Irish public opinion and forced Reynolds to hold an abortion referendum on November 25. Two amendment proposals passed. One guarantees access to abortion information, and the other allows travel outside of Ireland to get an abortion. The third proposal, which would have made abortion illegal if "self-destruction" were the risk to the mother's life, failed. Both antiabortion and proabortion forces were unhappy with the results. Ian J. Mather

See also **Northern Ireland.** In ***World Book,*** see **Ireland.**

Muslim women say evening prayers outside a mosque in Jakarta, Indonesia, in March during the Muslim holy month of Ramadan.

Islam. Political gains and losses and the emergence of the Muslim republics of the former Soviet Union dominated the Muslim world in 1992. Governments in some Muslim countries tightened their control in the face of vibrant opposition by Islamic activists.

In November, Jordan's King Hussein I warned Islamic activists not to subvert his attempts to liberalize that country's political process. In Lebanon, candidates from two Muslim parties, including Hezbollah, a pro-Iranian group widely regarded as extremist, won 30 seats in the 128-seat parliament in elections held in August and September.

Pressured by both liberal reformers and conservative religious leaders, Saudi Arabia's King Fahd bin Abd al-Aziz Al-Saud on March 1 announced the establishment of an appointed council to review national policies and advise the cabinet. Later in March, however, Fahd reaffirmed that Islam was the sole basis for Saudi society and contended that Western forms of democracy were incompatible with the traditions of the Persian Gulf countries.

In Iran, supporters of President Ali Akbar Hashemi Rafsanjani, who favors closer economic relations with other countries, defeated Islamic radicals in parliamentary elections held in April and May. But Iran also strengthened its ties with Sudan, which Western and many Arab governments increasingly regarded as a radical Islamic state. Sudan's government, backed by the militant National Islamic Front, pressed its efforts to impose Islamic law and customs throughout the country. Resistance to Islamization has fueled the ongoing civil war between predominantly Muslim northern Sudanese and southern Sudanese, who generally practice Christianity or local African religions.

Islamic crackdown. Tunisia and Algeria veered from political liberalization and democracy to move swiftly and firmly against Islamic movements denounced by those governments as extremist and terrorist. In both countries, the main Islamic parties were outlawed and their leaders tried and imprisoned. The governments charged that the parties were exploiting political reforms in order to overthrow the government and establish an Islamic state. Tunisia and Algeria also held mass trials of Islamic activists that were denounced by international human rights groups.

Muslim republics. Central Asia's six newly independent Muslim republics, formerly part of the Soviet Union, struggled in 1992 to define the role of Islam in their national identity and politics. In many of these republics, mosques and religious schools were growing at a rapid rate with financial and personnel assistance from such Muslim countries as Turkey, Iran, Saudi Arabia, and Pakistan. While emphasizing religious and cultural ties, these benefactors were also seeking trade and political influence. Islamic opposition parties were growing stronger in Tajikistan, Uzbekistan, and Azerbaijan. John L. Esposito

In ***World Book,*** see **Islam.**

Israel. Israel's Labor Party won a strong victory in national parliamentary elections held on June 23, 1992. The victory gave Labor, led by Yitzhak Rabin, control of Israel's government for the first time since 1977. Many people hailed Rabin's rise to prime minister because they believed his moderate views would lead to a formal Arab-Israeli peace. But the growing influence among Palestinians of the radical Islamic Resistance, known as Hamas, which opposes peace with Israel, led Rabin to take a harder line with the Palestinians and undermined prospects for a Middle East settlement.

Elections. The Labor Party won 44 seats in the 120-seat Knesset, Israel's parliament. In contrast, the ruling Likud bloc won only 32 seats, its worst showing since 1969. Smaller parties won the remaining seats. Many analysts attributed Likud's defeat to its opposition to self-rule by Palestinians in the occupied West Bank and Gaza Strip and its insistence on the continuing construction of Jewish settlements in the occupied territories.

Exit polls showed that the Labor Party had won 47 per cent of the vote among recent immigrants from the former Soviet Union. Between 1990 and 1992, approximately 377,700 Soviet Jewish immigrants arrived in Israel, according to the United States Department of State. Israeli Arabs, who make up slightly less than 20 per cent of Israel's population of 4.8 million, also supported the Labor Party.

Forming a government. Following his election, Rabin moved quickly to form a broad, center-left coalition in the Knesset. After the parliament confirmed Rabin as prime minister and approved his government on July 13, Rabin urged Palestinians to work toward self-rule and appealed to Arab states for peace. On August 2, he named two Arabs as deputy ministers, the highest posts held by Arabs since 1973.

Arab-Israeli conflict. In mid-February, Arab guerrillas stabbed to death three Israeli soldiers at an Israeli Army camp. Four Israeli Arabs, reportedly Islamic radicals, were sentenced to life imprisonment on April 29 for the murders. The killings of a 15-year-old Jewish girl and a rabbi by Arabs on May 24 triggered rioting by Jews. Violence worsened in mid-October, when Israeli troops killed eight Palestinians during protests on the West Bank. The death of a Jewish woman in an October 17 car bombing brought to 14 the number of Israeli Jews killed by Arabs in 1992, according to the U.S. State Department. Israeli forces killed 96 Palestinians between January and October 1, the State Department said.

B'Tselem, an Israeli human rights group, reported on April 1 that 20,000 Arabs arrested by Israeli forces since 1987 had been beaten or tortured. Amnesty International, an international human rights agency based in London, on July 9 accused Israel of the torture and the unlawful detention of 2,000 Arabs.

On July 17, a four-day siege of Al Najah University on the West Bank by the Israeli Army ended peacefully when six armed Palestinians who had sought refuge at the school agreed to accept deportation to Jordan.

Violence in the Gaza Strip grew worse after Islamic militants killed three Israeli soldiers on December 8, the largest single death toll among Israeli forces in the occupied territories since the beginning of the Palestinian uprising against Israel in 1987. In response, the government sealed off Gaza and confined hundreds of thousands of Palestinians to their homes. On Dec. 14, 1992, Islamic radicals killed a kidnapped Israeli border guard after the government did not free the jailed founder of Hamas as demanded. The kidnapping triggered a government crackdown in which more than 1,600 suspected militants were arrested. On December 17, the government deported about 400 militants without trial to Lebanon. The action provoked unanimous condemnation by the United Nations Security Council on December 18. On December 19, Israeli troops in Gaza killed six Palestinians, one of the highest daily casualty rates among Palestinians since the start of the uprising.

Violence among Arabs in the occupied territories worsened as Hamas targeted the rival Palestine Liberation Organization. About 150 Arabs accused of collaborating with Israel were killed by other Arabs in 1992, according to the U.S. State Department.

Sheik Abbas Musawi, the leader of the pro-Iranian group Hezbollah, was killed when Israeli gunships bombed his motorcade in Lebanon on February 16. On March 17, at least 32 people were killed and 252 injured when a bomb exploded outside the Israeli Embassy in Buenos Aires, Argentina. Islamic Holy War, a radical group, said that the bombing was carried out to avenge Musawi's death. Revenge for the attack on Musawi also was reportedly behind the March 7 car bombing of an Israeli Embassy guard in Turkey.

Israeli-American relations improved markedly after Labor won the Israeli elections. Before meeting United States President George Bush in August, Rabin halted the construction of at least 6,500 housing units planned for Jewish settlements in the occupied territories. But Rabin permitted the completion of another 10,500 units already under construction. The Bush Administration had criticized the settlements, which are bitterly opposed by Palestinians and Arab states, as an obstacle to an Arab-Israeli peace settlement. An estimated 245,000 Jewish settlers lived in 250 settlements in the occupied territories in 1991, according to a May 1992 report by the U.S. State Department.

Bush announced on August 11 that the United States would back Israel's request for $10 billion in loan guarantees intended mainly for the construction of housing for Soviet immigrants. In September 1991, Bush had asked the Congress of the United States to delay action on Israel's request for early payment of the loan guarantees to encourage Israeli participation in Middle East peace talks. The guarantees cleared Congress on Oct. 5, 1992. Christine Helms

See also **Middle East** (Facts in brief table). In ***World Book***, see **Israel**.

Scattered wrecks mark the scene of a Mafia-linked car bombing that killed a key government prosecutor in Palermo, Sicily, in July.

Italy encountered serious political, social, and economic problems in 1992. A new president and a new prime minister took office and began to grapple with the seemingly insoluble problems of organized crime, an economy deeply in debt, government corruption, and an immediate need for reforms to keep Italy in the front ranks of a united Europe.

Parliamentary elections in April failed to clarify Italy's muddled political situation. The country's ruling four-party coalition received only 48.8 per cent of the vote, reflecting an electorate unhappy over an economic slump, big-city crime, and well-publicized official corruption. The four parties—Christian Democrats, Socialists, Social Democrats, and Liberals—had won 53.7 per cent of the votes in the last election in 1987. Italy's largest party, the conservative Christian Democrats, racked up just under 30 per cent, its lowest total since World War II (1939-1945). The biggest gainers in the election were small regional parties, which together won 8.8 per cent of the vote, up from 0.5 per cent in 1987. Analysts explained the strong showing for the smaller parties as a protest against what voters saw as paralysis among the major parties. The Italian Social Movement, a neo-fascist party, won enough votes to give a seat in parliament to Alessandra Mussolini, granddaughter of Italy's former dictator.

Although the four-party coalition still held a tiny majority in parliament, it remained deadlocked over a successor to outgoing Prime Minister Giulio Andreotti. Italy's President Francesco Cossiga added to the confusion by announcing his resignation on April 25, 1992. It took the divided parliament until May 25 to name Cossiga's successor, veteran Christian Democrat politician Oscar Scalfaro. After another month of intricate negotiations with party leaders, Scalfaro named Socialist Giuliano Amato, a former treasury minister, to serve as prime minister in Italy's 51st government since World War II.

Austerity plan. Amato quickly announced austerity measures aimed at controlling Italy's soaring public spending and at stopping automatic increases in government wages whenever the cost of living rose. He said the country would need to make big sacrifices to meet the economic guidelines set down by the European Community (EC or Common Market). If Italy did not reduce its debt and slash its inflation rate, Amato warned, it would be unable to join other EC members as they moved toward a single currency. The austerity measures drew protests from thousands of Italians, who demonstrated in the streets against the freeze on wages and cuts in pensions.

To reduce the deficit further, Amato announced a sweeping program to sell to private investors parts of Italy's state-owned industries, which rank among the country's largest employers. He decreed all state companies—including the huge state oil company and the electric utility—eligible for privatization.

These reform programs hit a snag in September,

when intense pressure on the foreign exchange value of the Italian currency, the lira, forced Italy to withdraw temporarily from the exchange rate mechanism that links the currencies of most EC members. The pressure on the lira had the effect of lowering its value by about 10 per cent.

Crime and corruption. Giovanni Falcone, a leading investigator in the government's war against the Mafia on the island of Sicily, was assassinated in May when a bomb blew up his motorcade. Two months later, an anti-Mafia prosecutor, Paolo Borsellino, was killed in a similar car-bombing on the island.

Carlo De Benedetti, chairman of the giant Olivetti computer firm and one of Italy's best-known businesspeople, was convicted of fraud in April and sentenced to six years in jail. He had been charged with illegally selling his share in the Banco Ambrosiano while an officer of the bank, shortly before its 1982 failure. De Benedetti appealed his conviction.

As a corruption scandal engulfed top members of the Socialist Party in Milan, the entire city council and the mayor quit in May. The scandal involved bribes and kickbacks on government-funded projects. The corruption investigation soon widened to include other political parties. Philip Revzin

See also **Italy** (Facts in brief table). In ***World Book,*** see **Italy.**

Ivory Coast. See **Africa.**

Jamaica. See **West Indies.**

Japan. What was shaping up to be the biggest political scandal in Japanese history rocked the country in 1992. In February, investigators raided the offices of the country's second-largest parcel-delivery firm, Tokyo Sagawa Kyubin Company, long rumored to be a channel for money between organized crime and politicians. Japanese media reported that documents seized in the raid suggested that some 130 members of the Diet (Japan's parliament), including three former prime ministers and two cabinet ministers, took $600 million in illegal payments from the firm.

One of the politicians ensnared in the scandal was Shin Kanemaru, the most powerful man in Japanese politics. Under enormous public pressure, Kanemaru was forced to resign from his post as vice president of the Liberal Democratic Party (LDP) in August and from his seat in the Diet in October after admitting that he had improperly accepted $4 million from the company, one of the biggest payoffs in Japanese political history. Kanemaru is regarded as the true power behind many Japanese politicians, including Prime Minister Kiichi Miyazawa.

The controversy surrounding Kanemaru continued into September, when prosecutors accepted a plea bargain from Kanemaru in which he submitted a written statement of guilt in return for a fine of only $1,660 and an end to further investigation of his mob ties. The settlement prompted immediate protests among the Japanese public, though some Japanese considered it an act of courage for the prosecutors to have pursued Kanemaru at all.

Legislative elections. Miyazawa's conservative, probusiness LDP was the big winner in national elections for the Diet on July 26. The LDP took 68 of 127 contested seats in the Diet's upper house. In contrast, the Democratic Socialist Party, which had fought many of Miyazawa's moves, won only 22 seats. However, less than 50 per cent of eligible Japanese voted in the elections—the lowest turnout since the creation of Japan's democratic system in 1947. This figure suggested that the Japanese were dissatisfied with the choice of candidates.

The LDP, the dominant party in Japanese politics for almost four decades, already held a majority in the Diet's more powerful lower house, which chooses the nation's prime minister. The LDP lost control of the upper house in the last parliamentary elections in 1989 on the heels of other scandals and an unpopular new consumption tax. The 1992 election results still left the LDP short of a majority in the upper house, but the party formed coalitions with moderate members to win legislative battles.

Economic slowdown. The drive that had built Japan into one of the world's economic powers faltered in 1992. Business confidence reached a 15-year low, the Japanese stock market plunged to its lowest mark in more than 6 years, the country's dominant electronic firms slumped, and the economy's growth rate slowed to about 2 per cent. Japan's automobile industry was also hit hard, as domestic vehicle sales fell to their lowest level since 1980. (See **Automobile.**)

But there were positive signs. Unemployment remained at around 2 per cent, and the value of the yen reached a post-World War II high against the U.S. dollar. And Japan's trade surplus with the rest of the world in 1992 was expected to surpass the 1986 record of $83 billion, a fact that drew strong complaints from the United States and Western Europe.

In an effort to stimulate the economy, the Japanese government on August 18 unveiled the largest emergency spending package in its history. Officials announced a one-time spending binge of $87 billion for public works projects and for loans for small and medium-sized businesses. This amount marked a jump of 15 per cent in the government's 1992 budget. However, the package was not approved until December as the Diet debated its financing.

Troops abroad. In September 1992, Japan sent military forces abroad for the first time since World War II (1939-1945). After two years of debate, the Diet on June 15 passed a bill permitting up to 2,000 Japanese troops to take part in United Nations (UN) peacekeeping operations. Under the new law, Japanese troops can be dispatched only to regions where cease-fires have been declared and only to provide nonmilitary services such as medical care or reconstruction work. The forces may carry weapons, but they may be used only in self-defense.

The Japanese Constitution, drafted by United States advisers after World War II, requires that Japan "forever renounce . . . the use of force as a means of settling international disputes." But international calls for Japan to participate in peacekeeping operations had grown in recent years, particularly after the country's limited role in the Persian Gulf War in 1991, and Japanese officials were under pressure to soften the historically strict interpretation of the clause.

The bill's passage was seen as a victory for Miyazawa and for the LDP, which had mounted a massive public relations campaign in support of the legislation after earlier similar bills had failed. But many Southeast Asian countries protested the bill, fearing the beginning of Japanese remilitarization in the area.

The first assignment for the new forces was a UN peacekeeping mission in Cambodia. Six hundred Japanese soldiers began arriving in Cambodia in September. (See **Cambodia.**)

Legacies of war. Fueling concerns about the dispatch of Japanese troops was Japan's admission in 1992 that during World War II, its Imperial Army forced women from occupied countries in Asia to become prostitutes—so-called "comfort women"—for its soldiers. Previously, the government had not denied the existence or use of brothels, but it had maintained that they were run by private businessmen and not the government. The change of position was triggered by statements from elderly South Korean women beginning in 1991 relating their experiences in the brothels at the hands of the military and demanding compensation from Japan for their suffering. Women from other Asian countries then also began coming forward.

During a January 1992 visit to South Korea, Miyazawa apologized for the brothels for the first time. Afterward, Japanese officials acknowledged that they were searching for a way to provide financial aid to the women. Japan placed no exact figures on the number of Asian women forced into prostitution. But estimates ranged from 100,000 to 200,000.

Also in 1992, Emperor Akihito and Empress Michiko in October made a six-day visit to China. While there, Akihito said he felt "deep sorrow" over the atrocities inflicted on the Chinese by Japan during World War II. But Akihito stopped short of a formal apology, which would have angered nationalist Japanese.

Visit by U.S. delegation. President George Bush, joined by 18 American business executives, visited Tokyo in January to seek trade concessions from Japan that would boost American employment. The U.S. negotiators won several agreements from Japan to open their automobile and computer markets. But after the visit, unhappiness with the concessions was voiced by much of the Japanese press and public.

Territorial dispute. Japanese relations with Russia in 1992 were troubled by a continuing dispute

Japan's Emperor Akihito and Empress Michiko visit the Great Wall of China in October during the first-ever trip to China by a Japanese emperor.

over four of the Kuril Islands, which lie northeast of Japan. The Soviet Union seized the islands from Japan at the end of World War II and had retained them despite Japanese claims.

Japan hoped that Russia, which gained control of the territory after the collapse of the Soviet Union in 1991, would relinquish the islands in return for economic aid. But Russian President Boris Yeltsin canceled a scheduled visit to Tokyo in September under pressure from Russian nationalists opposed to any territorial concessions. Observers viewed the action as a serious setback in relations between the countries, which are the only two World War II foes to have not yet signed a peace treaty.

Plutonium controversy. On November 7, a ship bound for Japan left the French city of Cherbourg carrying 1.7 short tons (1.5 metric tons) of plutonium. The shipment was part of Japan's plans to become the world's largest stockpiler of nuclear-weapons-grade plutonium. Japanese officials said the plutonium was to be used to fuel a new generation of nuclear reactors in order for Japan to become energy independent. But environmentalists feared that the toxic chemical might be spilled or stolen by terrorists, and other Asian nations worried that Japan might someday use the plutonium as a military lever against its neighbors. Henry S. Bradsher

See also **Asia** (Facts in brief table). In ***World Book,*** see **Japan.**

Jordan. Strong pro-Iraqi and anti-American sentiments among Jordanians complicated efforts by King Hussein I in 1992 to ease Jordan's diplomatic isolation. Relations with many Western nations and some Persian Gulf states, angry over Jordan's support for Iraq during the Persian Gulf War (1991), remained cool.

Economic problems. Jordan continued to suffer severe economic problems in 1992 because of the economic embargo imposed on Iraq by the United Nations (UN) Security Council in 1990. Before the war, Iraq had been Jordan's major trading partner and source of petroleum. Jordan's food sales to Iraq, permitted under the terms of the embargo, slowed when the value of Iraq's dinar fell sharply in July 1992, leaving Iraqi importers with little buying power. Executions by Iraq in June of at least 40 Iraqi merchants accused of profiteering on food imported from Jordan also dampened trade between the two nations. In March, Jordan was able to reschedule $1.4 billion of its $7.2-billion debt to Western nations and banks.

Islamic activism. On November 10, four Islamic activists, including two members of Jordan's national legislature, received prison sentences of at least 10 years for belonging to a group that reportedly plotted to overthrow the government. The men were also convicted of possessing illegal arms, reportedly intended for transfer to an Islamic Palestinian group in the Israeli-occupied West Bank. However, Hussein granted the men an amnesty several days later. Many observers interpreted the sentences given to the men as a government warning to Jordan's Islamic activists, who oppose peace talks with Israel. In a national address on November 23, Hussein strongly warned the Islamic activists not to subvert his attempts to liberalize Jordan's political system.

U.S. relations. Hussein and United States President George Bush met on March 12 in Washington, D.C. Hussein reportedly pledged to help enforce the trade sanctions against Iraq, which the Bush Administration had accused Jordan of violating. In June, U.S. officials again accused Jordan of breaking the embargo. They claimed that 30 per cent of Jordan's trade with Iraq consisted of goods other than food and medicine, the only products officially permitted into Iraq. The United States proposed that Hussein allow the UN to inspect all Jordanian goods bound for Iraq.

But Jordanian officials protested that inspections had not been proposed for any other country bordering Iraq. They also argued that cash-strapped Jordan could not afford to pay for the inspectors. In response, the United States in early June canceled scheduled joint military exercises with Jordan and withheld $105-million in military and economic aid for Jordan.

Hussein's health. On August 20, Hussein's left kidney and ureter were surgically removed after cancerous cells were discovered. Christine Helms

See also **Middle East** (Facts in brief table). In ***World Book,*** see **Jordan.**

Judaism. The Jewish community in 1992 commemorated a major historical event of 500 years earlier—the expulsion of Jews from Spain in 1492 by a royal edict of Queen Isabella and King Ferdinand. Perhaps the most important commemoration took place in Madrid, Spain, on March 31, 1992, the day 500 years earlier that the edict was signed. King Juan Carlos I of Spain visited the synagogue of Madrid with President Chaim Herzog of Israel to pray together in a symbol of reconciliation. The king did not apologize for Spain's actions in 1492. He said, "What is important is not an accounting of our errors or successes but the willingness to think about and analyze the past in terms of our future."

The Jewish community of medieval Spain had been one of the largest and most important centers of Judaism in the world. The period from about 1000 to 1300 is often referred to as the Golden Age of Spanish Jewry because of the accomplishments of the Jews of Spain in government, science, and cultural life.

The 1492 edict declared that all Jews had until the end of July—four months—to leave Spain or face death. Three days after the deadline, on August 3, Christopher Columbus set sail from Spain on his voyage of discovery. Historians agree that some of Columbus' crew were Jews fleeing from the country. And many historians believe that Christopher Columbus himself, though a practicing Catholic, may have come from a Jewish background.

The expulsion edict implied that if Jews converted to Roman Catholicism they could stay in Spain. Some Jews chose to convert to Catholicism, but continued to practice their Jewish faith in secret. Nevertheless, about 200,000 Jews fled Spain, leaving behind their possessions and property. Exiled Spanish Jews, called *Sephardim,* settled in various Middle Eastern countries and in European cities, such as Amsterdam, Rome, and Naples, where they preserved their identity as Spanish Jews. The first Jewish colonists in North America were Dutch Sephardim, who settled in New Amsterdam, now New York City, in 1654.

The expulsion was part of King Ferdinand and Queen Isabella's efforts to conquer all of Spain. They regarded Jews as a threat to their plans. Similarly, the king and queen considered Muslim Moors in southern Spain an obstruction to national unification. The Muslim Moors living in Spain were originally from North Africa. But they had controlled southern Spain since the early 700's. And Spanish Jewry had lived under tolerant Muslim rule for centuries. Ferdinand and Isabella waged wars to recapture the region and finally were successful on Jan. 2, 1492, when their armies drove the last Moors from Granada. Following their conquest, they decreed that all of Spain would be exclusively Catholic.

The 500th anniversary of the expulsion was commemorated by Jews throughout the world in many ways. Special memorial services were held in synagogues throughout the year, and special educational conferences and museum exhibitions celebrated the continuing vitality of Sephardic Jewish culture.

A sect of ultra-Orthodox Jews, popularly known as Lubavitcher Hasidim, expected the arrival of the messiah in 1992. Hasidic Jews believe in the strict interpretation of the Bible and Jewish law, as well as the preservation of cultural traditions that originated in Eastern Europe in the 1700's. Lubavitcher Hasidim, numbering about 200,000 worldwide, follow the teachings and leadership of their chief rabbi, Menachem Mendel Schneerson, a 90-year-old scholar who is the seventh Lubavitcher leader and is descended from the founder of this particular Hasidic sect. The sect's name stems from its place of origin, Lubavitch, Russia.

Early in 1992, Rabbi Schneerson, known to his followers by the Yiddish title *Rebbe,* indicated that the recent upheavals in the world, particularly such major events as the fall of the Soviet Union and the Persian Gulf War (1991), were signs that the messiah was about to arrive. The belief in the coming of the messiah is an ancient Jewish idea, which teaches that at a time of great danger and transition, God will send a redeemer, who will deliver the Jewish people from suffering and bring about a new world of justice and peace. Two thousand years ago, when Jews were persecuted by the Romans, some followers of the rabbi Jesus of Nazareth believed that he was the messiah, and on this belief founded the Christian religion.

Many of Rabbi Schneerson's Hasidic followers have proclaimed that the rabbi is the messiah and that he would reveal his identity before the Jewish religious year ended with the High Holidays in September 1992. Most Jews, because they are neither Hasidic nor followers of Schneerson, rejected Schneerson's statements. Nevertheless, he attracted worldwide attention—particularly in New York City, where he lives, and in Israel, where many of his Hasidic followers live. His followers in Israel expected him to come to their country in 1992 to announce his divine mission. But in March 1992, Rabbi Schneerson suffered a stroke and became unable to speak. Although disappointed, many of his followers continued to believe that there would be a sign in 1992 that he is in fact their long-awaited deliverer.

The Hasidic sect is only a small part of the Orthodox Jewish community, which is itself only one denomination in the Jewish religion. More liberal Reform and Conservative Jews do not accept the beliefs of the Hasidic Jews and have very different understandings of the messianic concept. For example, Reform Judaism teaches that instead of an individual messiah, there will be a future time of justice, brotherhood, and peace on Earth, an achievement that will be brought about by people of all faiths working together. Howard A. Berman

See also **Israel.** In ***World Book,*** see **Jews; Judaism.**

Kampuchea. See **Cambodia.**

Kansas. See **State government.**

Kazakhstan enjoyed relative political and economic stability in 1992, in comparison with many of the other 11 former Soviet republics that became independent when the Soviet Union was dissolved in late December 1991. Throughout 1992, Kazakh President Nursultan Nazarbayev pressed for close economic and political links among the former Soviet republics.

Kazakhstan moved slowly on market reforms in 1992. Meanwhile, it pinned its hopes for economic development on foreign investment. On May 18, the country reached an estimated $20-billion agreement with the United States-based Chevron Corporation to develop Kazakhstan's huge Tengiz oil field.

Arms control. Kazakhstan was one of four former Soviet republics that possessed nuclear weapons. On May 23, Kazakhstan—along with Belarus, Russia, Ukraine, and the United States—signed a revision to the Strategic Arms Reduction Treaty (START), an arms control accord signed by the United States and the Soviet Union in July 1991. Under the revision, all former Soviet nuclear weapons remaining in Kazakhstan would be destroyed or sent to Russia within seven years after the treaty is ratified by all five nations. The former republics also agreed to sign the 1968 Nuclear Non-Proliferation Treaty, which bans the spread of nuclear weapons to other countries. Justin Burke

See also **Armed forces: The Nuclear Threat in the New World Order; Asia** (Facts in brief table). In the World Book Supplement section, see **Kazakhstan.**

Keating, Paul (1944-), saw his popularity plummet as prime minister of Australia during 1992 due to Australia's continuing economic woes. Keating was sworn in as prime minister on Dec. 20, 1991, after winning a party leadership challenge to Prime Minister Robert Hawke. The leader of Australia's governing party automatically becomes prime minister. Hawke's defeat was the first time an Australian prime minister was ousted by his own party. Keating had been treasurer and deputy prime minister in Hawke's government from March 1983 until his resignation in June 1991, when he failed in his first leadership challenge to Hawke. (See **Australia.**)

Keating was born on Jan. 18, 1944, in Sydney, the capital of New South Wales, one of Australia's six states. He attended De La Salle College in Bankstown, but he left school at age 14. Upon leaving school, Keating worked as a researcher for the Federated Municipal and Shire Council Employees Union of Australia.

In 1959, at age 15, Keating joined the Australian Labor Party, and in 1966, he became president of the party's youth council in New South Wales. His political career began in 1969, when he was elected to the House of Representatives as a legislator for Blaxland, a suburb of Sydney. At age 25, he was Australia's youngest legislator.

Keating and his wife, Annita, have one son and three daughters. Carol L. Hanson

Kenya. President Daniel T. arap Moi was reelected president in December 1992. But Moi's opponents charged that he had achieved victory through cynical manipulations that guaranteed his reelection despite widespread discontent with his administration.

Moi, leader of the Kenya African National Union (KANU), which since 1969 had been the country's only political party, agreed in December 1991 to let other political parties form. His decision was forced by pressure from dissident Kenyans and the world community. Moi warned, however, that multiparty democracy would not work in Kenya's multiethnic society. He predicted that new political parties would lead to increasing conflict and violence between ethnic groups.

New parties appeared quickly in 1992. First among them was the Forum for the Restoration of Democracy (FORD), which had been established in 1991 as a "discussion group." With parties flourishing, observers gave Moi little chance of political survival. Corruption, human rights violations, and a rapidly declining economy were among the many complaints leveled against him by Kenyans.

Violence erupts. In February, ethnic violence—the worst wave of violence in 30 years—broke out through much of western Kenya. An estimated 2,000 people were killed, and 50,000 were left homeless. Most of the incidents were reportedly attacks by well-armed Kalenjin, Moi's ethnic group, against Kikuyu, Luo, and Luhya peoples. There were also reports of attacks on foreign tourists. In early March, riots erupted in Nairobi, the capital, after the police broke up an encampment of people protesting the government's holding of political prisoners. In response to the rising level of violence, Moi on March 20 banned political meetings. Moi's opponents, including church leaders, accused him of organizing Kalenjin attacks to discredit multiparty democracy.

KANU versus the opposition. Whether or not Moi was behind the violence, the unrest strengthened his political position. On August 5, the National Assembly, which has long been under his control, passed a constitutional amendment requiring a presidential candidate to win a substantial portion of the vote in each section of the country, a possibility for only a well-organized party like KANU. Also in August, FORD split apart into two smaller parties. Seeing his advantage growing and the opposition splintering, Moi in October dissolved the National Assembly and set elections for December.

Other troubles included a surge of refugees from Somalia, Sudan, and Ethiopia; a drought that led to food shortages; and rising unemployment. Those problems, together with the widespread violence, had made Moi's departure seem a certainty. But most Kenyans had not counted on his resourcefulness in holding onto power. Mark DeLancey

See also **Africa** (Facts in brief table). In ***World Book,*** see **Kenya.**

North Koreans in April honor the 80th birthday of the "Great Leader," President Kim Il-song, who had ruled the Communist nation since 1946.

Korea, North. North Korea in 1992 allowed foreign inspection of its nuclear facilities for the first time. In May, a team of experts from the International Atomic Energy Agency made a six-day visit to the country. They toured three nuclear plants, an elaborate underground tunnel network, and a partially built laboratory for reprocessing nuclear-reactor fuel to obtain plutonium, a key component of nuclear arms.

The team's findings indicated that North Korea did not own enough plutonium to make an atomic bomb and that construction on the plutonium-processing plant was less than half complete. But foreign officials could not be sure whether the unfinished condition of the plant was genuine, and many experts remained uncertain of North Korea's true nuclear capabilities. (See also **Armed forces: The Nuclear Threat in the New World Order.**)

New leader. During celebrations marking his 80th birthday in April 1992, President Kim Il-song for the first time identified his son Kim Chong-il as "head of our [Communist] party, the state, and army." The father had run North Korea since 1946.

Henry S. Bradsher

See also **Asia** (Facts in brief table). In ***World Book,*** see **Korea.**

Korea, South. Voters in December 1992 elected Kim Young Sam as the new president of South Korea, succeeding Roh Tae Woo. Roh was allowed only a single five-year term under South Korea's constitution. Kim was to take office in February 1993. He beat Kim Dae Jung, South Korea's best-known dissident leader, and Chung Ju Yung, the billionaire founder of the Hyundai business conglomerate.

Legislative elections. In elections on March 24, Roh's Democratic Liberal Party (DLP) lost its majority in the 299-seat National Assembly. The DLP fell from 215 seats to 148 seats as voters blamed the party for the country's faltering economy.

The Democratic Party, led by Kim Dae Jung, won 97 seats, and minor and independent parties took 22. But observers said the biggest winner was Chung Ju Yung, whose conservative United People's Party (UPP) had been formed only two months before the election yet won 32 seats. Chung and other UPP candidates campaigned for reduced government interference in business affairs.

Presidential politicking. The poor showing of the DLP in March underscored Kim Young Sam's low standing with much of the public. Kim had been the leader of an opposition party until 1990, when he joined Roh's ruling party to create the DLP. Many DLP members objected to what they perceived as Kim's use of the DLP for his own political ambitions. At the DLP's national convention in May 1992, Kim was the only candidate for president, but he still garnered only about two-thirds of the delegates' votes. And after he was nominated, thousands of South Korean students took to the streets, upset with Kim's perceived retreat from his original democratic goals.

In the apparent hopes of bolstering his popular support, Kim began criticizing Roh's regime. He called for the firing of officials accused of buying votes in the March elections, and he demanded a voice in the selection of a new cabinet for Roh.

On October 7, Roh resigned as honorary president of the DLP. He also replaced many of his cabinet ministers with "politically neutral" people in an effort to convince South Koreans that his government would not be involved in the December election.

New ties with China. On August 24, South Korea and the People's Republic of China established diplomatic relations, ending more than four decades as Cold War enemies. China had fought against South Korea in the Korean War (1950-1953), but in recent years relations had been improving as China sought access to South Korea's booming economy. And South Korea hoped relations with China would boost its prospects for reconciliation with North Korea, one of China's closest allies.

However, South Korea was forced to break relations with the Republic of China (Taiwan), because mainland China would not deal with a country that maintained diplomatic ties with Taiwan. Taiwan retailated by ending preferential trade treatment for South Korea and suspending flights between the countries. South Korea had been the last Asian country to retain full links with Taiwan.

President Roh made South Korea's first state visit to China from September 27 to 30. Afterward, South Korean officials said China had indicated its willingness to work as an "honest broker" for the unification of South Korea and North Korea.

Obstacles to unification. South and North Korea in 1992 continued talks aimed at reconciling the two nations. But negotiators could not resolve one of the key sticking points—North Korea's refusal to permit mutual inspection of each country's nuclear facilities. North Korea did allow an independent team to examine its nuclear facilities in 1992, but South Korea called the search insufficient and demanded more stringent inspections. South Korea wants to ensure that the Korean Peninsula is free of nuclear weapons before unification occurs.

Meanwhile, the United States in October said that it would stop withdrawing troops from South Korea until the concerns about North Korea's nuclear weapons program were fully addressed. More than 37,000 U.S. troops are stationed in South Korea, though almost 7,000 others have left since 1990.

Henry S. Bradsher

See also **Armed forces: The Nuclear Threat in the New World Order; Asia** (Facts in brief table). In ***World Book,*** see **Korea.**

Kravchuk, Leonid M. (1934-), became the first popularly elected president of Ukraine following the breakup of the Soviet Union in December 1991. During 1992, Kravchuk clashed frequently with Russian President Boris N. Yeltsin over military issues, and he raised doubts about the viability of the Commonwealth of Independent States, a loose confederation of former Soviet republics to which Ukraine belonged.

Kravchuk was born in 1934 in the west Ukrainian village of Velky Zhityan. His father, a farmer, was killed in World War II (1939-1945). Kravchuk attended a vocational school and then Kiev University in the capital of Ukraine, where he studied Marxist political economy. In 1958, he began teaching political economy in the city of Chernovtsy, where he became an active Communist Party member.

As a party member, Kravchuk fought against Ukrainian nationalism, but he apparently changed his mind in the late 1980's. In September 1989, Kravchuk was the only high-ranking Communist leader to address an umbrella organization of Ukrainians seeking independence from the Soviet Union. Kravchuk became chairman of Ukraine's newly elected Parliament in July 1990, and, in September, he quit his post as an ideology secretary of the Communist Party. After the failed coup against Soviet President Mikhail S. Gorbachev in August 1991, Kravchuk quit the party.

Kravchuk is married, and he has a son and two grandsons. Kristine Portnoy Kelley

Kuwait. Political opponents of Kuwait's ruling Sabah family made a strong showing in national parliamentary elections held on Oct. 5, 1992. Opposition candidates captured 31 of 50 seats in Kuwait's National Assembly in that country's first parliamentary elections since 1985. Only men who could prove that their families had lived in Kuwait before 1921—about 14 per cent of all Kuwaiti citizens—were permitted to vote in the elections.

Kuwait's Amir Jabir al-Ahmad al-Jabir Al Sabah had dissolved the National Assembly in 1986 because of growing criticism of his policies. But in 1991, under pressure from government critics at home and Western members of the United States-led coalition that drove Iraqi forces from Kuwait, he agreed to reestablish the parliament.

During the election campaign, most opposition candidates called for a more democratic system of government and closer scrutiny of the government's financial activities. Candidates from conservative Islamic groups that favor the imposition of Islamic law in Kuwait won 19 of the opposition seats.

New Cabinet. On Oct. 12, 1992, Kuwait's amir reappointed Crown Prince Saad al-Abdallah al-Salim Al Sabah, his heir, as prime minister. Many opposition leaders had called on the amir to separate the office of crown prince from that of prime minister. On October 17, the prime minister appointed a 16-member Cabinet that included six political opponents. However, members of the Sabah family retained all the key posts, including defense and foreign policy.

Spending criticism. Many Kuwaitis were angered by what they charged was government overspending on projects to repair the damage resulting from the Iraqi occupation of Kuwait and the Persian Gulf War (1991). By early 1992, the government had reportedly allocated $65 billion, an estimated two-thirds of Kuwait's assets, to such projects. In addition, the government on May 20 agreed to buy about $20 billion in bad loans from Kuwaiti banks so that the banks could finance reconstruction projects. However, government critics alleged that many of the bad debts were held by members of the Sabah family. Kuwait's 1992 budget was the first in many years to include a deficit.

Human rights. The treatment of Asian women working as domestic servants in Kuwait came under criticism by a number of U.S. women's rights groups in spring 1992. Hundreds of Asian women, who replaced Palestinian domestics expelled after the Persian Gulf War, reportedly sought refuge in their countries' embassies. Many claimed they had been beaten by Kuwaiti employers, who refused them pay and confiscated their passports. Some said they had been raped.

Christine Helms

See also **Middle East** (Facts in brief table). In ***World Book,*** see **Kuwait.**

Kygryzstan. See **Commonwealth of Independent States.**

Changes in the United States labor force

	1991	1992
Total labor force	**126,867,000**	**128,449,000**
Armed forces	1,564,000	1,572,000
Civilian labor force	125,303,000	126,877,000
Total employment	118,440,000	119,144,000
Unemployment	8,426,000	9,419,000
Unemployment rate	6.6%	7.3%
Changes in real weekly earnings of production and nonsupervisory workers (private nonfarm sector)*	0.2%	−1.3%
Change in output per employee hour (private nonfarm sector)†	1.4%	2.8%

*Constant (1982) dollars. 1991 change from December 1990 to December 1991; 1992 change from October 1991 to October 1992 (preliminary data).

†Annual rate for 1991; for 1992, change is from third quarter 1991 to third quarter 1992 (preliminary data).

Source: U.S. Bureau of Labor Statistics.

Labor. The United States economy in 1992 continued to limp out of a recession that began in July 1990. During the first two years of the recession, the nation lost 1.5 million jobs in the manufacturing, construction, and mining sectors. There were also heavy job losses in such white-collar industries as retail trade, finance, and public utilities. The economy's continued weakness puzzled experts in government and industry and left consumers pessimistic. Workers both in and out of labor unions worried about keeping their jobs.

Nonfarm employment stood at 118.2 million in June 1990, just before the recession hit. By autumn 1992, it was still below the prerecession level, at 117.6 million workers. The economy's failure to regain the jobs lost in a recession was a new experience that frightened political, business, and labor leaders, as well as consumers. In the eight U.S. recessions since World War II (1939-1945), the economy had won back all lost jobs at a much earlier stage of the downturn.

Union membership, which peaked in 1954 at over a third of employed workers, has steadily declined since then. But it held at 16.1 per cent in 1991, the latest year for which data were available, virtually the same as in 1990. American unions had expected to lose about 500,000 members as a result of the recession that began in mid-1990.

Pay and benefit increases in 1992 generally fell below those of 1991. The wages of industrial workers rose an average of 2.7 per cent ($2.70 for each $100 of pay) between September 1991 and September 1992, according to the U.S. Bureau of Labor Statistics. In 1991, by contrast, industrial wages had gone up 4.5 per cent. The combined wage-and-benefit package increased 3.5 per cent in 1992, reflecting a steeper rise in benefits (5.2 per cent) than in wages. After taking inflation into account, real earnings for all production and nonsupervisory workers fell by 0.3 per cent, continuing a downward trend that began in the 1980's.

Some of the contract agreements reached in 1992 dealt with the issue of *family leave*—unpaid leave following the birth or adoption of a child or in the event of a family illness. Other contract negotiations struggled to reach accord on the results of restructuring, including job cuts and plant closings.

Airline settlements. On Jan. 31, 1992, Trans World Airlines Incorporated (TWA) filed for bankruptcy protection, after reaching a tentative agreement with the International Association of Machinists (IAM). This was the last of the unions TWA bargained with prior to the bankruptcy petition.

In September, a bankruptcy court approved the agreements reached between the carrier and the Air Line Pilots Association, the machinists union, and the Independent Federation of Flight Attendants. The agreements exchanged a 15 per cent reduction in wages and benefits for a 45 per cent share in the ownership of the airline. At the end of September, the three unions approved the agreement, which they

Workers picket Caterpillar's Decatur, Ill., plant during a five-month strike that ended in April, after Caterpillar threatened to hire replacements.

hoped would lift the carrier out of bankruptcy. TWA owner and chairman, Carl A. Icahn, was to turn over control of the airline to its creditors and employees.

USAir Group Incorporated and the Air Line Pilots Association tentatively agreed in May to a one-year cut in pay ranging from 10 to 12.5 per cent. The cuts were intended to provide financial help to the airline, which had lost a reported $750 million since 1990. The agreement would give pilots the option of purchasing stock in the company and joining a profit-sharing arrangement. Their wages were to go up, however, by a small percentage for the next four years.

Motor vehicle settlements. Following a bitter strike that began in November 1991, the United Automobile Workers (UAW) appeared to capitulate to Caterpillar Incorporated, the world's largest maker of heavy construction machinery and farm equipment. The union had rejected the company's "final offer" in February 1992. But in an April surprise, the union accepted the terms of the final offer, after the company threatened to hire replacement workers. No formal agreement had been reached by year's end, however.

Although contract negotiations in the auto industry were not scheduled until 1993, General Motors Corporation (GM) became involved in impromptu bargaining in 1992. At GM's Lordstown, Ohio, metal-stamping plant, 2,400 workers went on strike in August over the proposed transfer of 240 tool-and-die jobs to other plants. At its peak, the strike shut down nine other GM plants and idled more than 40,000 workers. The strike was settled on September 5, when GM agreed to postpone the job transfer, help retrain some of the tool-and-die makers, and expand the work force at Lordstown.

In an effort to reduce its hefty health-care costs of $3.4 billion, GM in 1992 required 190,000 white-collar employees and retirees to pay insurance premiums for the first time. The company also planned to increase employees' out-of-pocket expenses for health care.

Aluminum industry. The United Steelworkers of America and the Aluminum, Brick and Glass Workers ratified a one-year extension of their contracts with the Aluminum Company of America (Alcoa) and Reynolds Metals Company on May 7. The contracts provided a $1,000 bonus upon signing and an added $500 bonus if a contract is successfully negotiated in the fall of 1992. Hourly wage rates ranged from $11.90 to $15.26 under current contracts.

The steelworkers union settled a 19-month lockout at Ravenswood Aluminum Corporation in July. Under an unusual three-year agreement, the West Virginia company would recall union workers in the order of years they had served and would discharge the 1,100 workers who had replaced them. The accord put a cap on back pay of $2,000 per striker. But it provided for profit sharing through 1997 and for cost-of-living adjustments. Before the settlement, the National Labor Relations Board, a government agency, had issued a complaint against the company for locking out 1,700 union members and against the union for supporting a boycott of the cans the company produced.

Entertainment industry. The Screen Actors Guild in June agreed to a three-year pact with motion-picture and television producers. The pact raised daily and weekly pay rates for "principal performers" as well as for screen extras (who were covered under a guild contract for the first time since 1946). The agreement boosted pay by 4 per cent, raising the daily rate for principal performers to $504 and the weekly scale to $1,752. Extras would receive $65 to $75 a day, with stand-ins receiving $90 a day. The contract also guaranteed six episodes of work in television series.

In January, Disneyland employees in six labor unions approved a three-year pact, raising wages by $1 an hour for employees who do not receive tips and by 50 cents for those who do. The contract included additional wage increases by upgrading the jobs of about a fourth of the employees, including those who dress up as cowboys or cowgirls or perform as Mickey or Minnie Mouse.

Communications industry. On July 2, a stalemate ended between the American Telephone & Telegraph Company (AT&T) and two unions that together represented 125,000 employees: the Communications Workers of America and the International Brotherhood of Electrical Workers. Talks between the company and the unions had stalled because of an AT&T proposal that would peg employee retention to technical skills needed by the company rather than to seniority. Both AT&T and the unions got some of what they wanted in the three-year pact—the two unions achieved some job protection, and the company received some freedom to eliminate jobs. The contract also provided a wage increase of 4 per cent in the first year, 3.9 per cent in the next two years, and a 13 per cent boost in pensions. The company also agreed to improve benefits for family or child-care leave.

Eight regional telephone companies negotiated separate agreements with the communication workers and the electrical workers. The specific terms of the contracts varied, but they generally included some job protection, wage increases, profit-sharing, or improvements in pensions and other benefits.

One three-year agreement reflected the unions' growing concern about family leave and about protecting employees who were declared "redundant" as a result of company restructuring. The contract agreement between Illinois Bell and the International Brotherhood of Electrical Workers provided for lump-sum payments to employees who retired during a 16-month period beginning Sept. 1, 1992. It also provided for a resource and referral service for the care of dependent children and elderly parents.

Railroad industry. The nationwide rail system shut down on June 24, when 1,500 IAM members struck CSX Corporation, one of the nation's largest freight handlers. Other freight companies quickly halted operations as well. On June 25, the U.S. Congress passed a bill to restore freight traffic and to impose a 38-day waiting period covering all unresolved union-management disputes in the rail industry. The bill called for mandatory arbitration if no settlement was reached after 32 days. If negotiations reached the arbitration stage, the arbitrator could pick one of the "last, best offers" of the deadlocked parties.

Under the new legislation, President George Bush convened emergency arbitration boards to resolve three disputes between labor and management. The bargaining was made difficult by differences over pay issues, benefits—especially health-care coverage—and staff reductions.

Other settlements. The Prudential Insurance Company and the United Food and Commercial Workers in 1992 reached a two-year agreement covering 15,000 agents nationwide. The pact included some interesting provisions, in addition to wage and benefit increases. Under the contract, employees could take up to 26 weeks of unpaid leave following the birth or adoption of a child and up to 12 weeks to care for seriously ill members of their immediate family. It also provided for a discussion of company standards for insurance policy sales by new employees on probation.

On the professional sports front, a two-year contract ended a 10-day work stoppage in April, during the last days of the hockey season, and saved the National Hockey League (NHL) play-offs. The strike was the first in the league's history. The agreement between the NHL Players Association and the 24 team owners provided for salary arbitration, fewer restrictions on the movement of players age 30 years or older, and a minimum salary of $100,000.

Labor legislation. In February, President Bush signed a bill extending for an additional 13 weeks the unemployment benefits of jobless workers who had exhausted their benefits. The signing occurred without the dispute between the White House and Congress that accompanied the extension of unemployment benefits in late 1991.

On June 11, 1992, the Senate failed by five votes to stop debate on a bill that would forbid employers from hiring permanent workers to replace strikers. A second vote failed on June 16, killing the legislation, which labor unions had given top priority.

The battle between Congress and the Bush Administration over family leave legislation continued in 1992. Bush proposed giving tax credits to companies with fewer than 500 employees that voluntarily offered family leave to care for newborn babies or seriously ill family members. Congress sought to require that employers with at least 50 employees offer unpaid leave for family needs. In September, Bush vetoed the Family and Medical Leave Act. On September 30, Congress failed to muster the two-thirds vote needed to override the veto. Robert W. Fisher

See also **Economics; Manufacturing.** In ***World Book,*** see **Labor force; Labor movement.**

What Is Happening to the U.S. Job Market?

By Robert W. Fisher

Global competition, technological change, layoffs, and a sluggish economy are fueling anxiety about the loss of American jobs.

A factory stands abandoned behind a locked and chained gate. Newly constructed office buildings stand empty. Several thousand applicants line up for a few hundred jobs at a new hotel, and American business giants such as Pan American Airways go out of business, throwing thousands of people out of work. Scenes and events such as these by 1992 had become familiar symbols of a troubled job market in the United States. Many workers who were still employed lived under clouds of anxiety and uncertainty, fearing that they might be the next to lose their jobs.

With chilling regularity, U.S. business in the 1990's announced thousands of planned layoffs. Huge companies, such as General Motors Corporation and International Business Machines closed facilities and trimmed their work forces. Corporate *downsizing* (permanent staff reduc-

Preceding page. Thousands of applicants in Chicago wait in line for hours on Jan. 15, 1992, hoping to get one of the few hundred jobs advertised by a new hotel.

tions and facility closings) among insurance companies and other businesses eliminated middle managers and created smaller staffs. Failed or merged financial institutions led to the elimination of such white-collar jobs as bank tellers, bookkeepers, accountants, and loan officers.

The heaviest job losses in the 1990-1991 recession were among blue-collar workers, according to data from the U.S. Bureau of Labor Statistics (BLS). Between July 1990 and July 1992, manufacturing, construction, and mining—the goods-producing industries—lost about 1.5 million jobs. But there was also serious job loss among white-collar workers, particularly in retail trade and finance. The white-collar layoffs caused new anxiety in the labor market, because these workers had been regarded as having fairly secure jobs.

The unemployment rate rose to 7.8 per cent in June 1992, an eight-year high, then drifted down to 7.4 per cent by October, mostly because of slow growth in the number of people looking for jobs rather than job creation. The BLS reported that 9.3 million people sought work without finding it that month and that in the third quarter of 1992, 6.7 million families—1 in 10—had at least one unemployed member. These troubles in the U.S. job market stemmed both from a recession that began in 1990 and basic structural changes in the U.S. economy.

Recessions and job loss

There have been nine recessions in the United States since the end of World War II (1939-1945), varying in length from 6 months to more than 20 months. The most recent recession apparently began a slow recovery in the spring of 1991. Employment had peaked at 118.2 million civilian jobs in June 1990 before the recession began, but by October 1992 employment stood at only 117.6 million jobs. At a comparable point in past recessions, the economy had regenerated all the jobs lost in the downturn. But this time it had not. Many Americans who had been let go found other work, sometimes below their skill, experience, and previous pay level—or they found only part-time jobs. Still others were so discouraged that they stopped looking for work. The question repeatedly asked was, why hasn't the U.S. economy recouped jobs lost in the recession as it had in the past?

The reasons for this are varied and complex, and include such factors as the continuing shift from goods-producing to service-producing jobs, the tremendous burden of debt at all levels, a worldwide recession, and the increasing global competition for industrial dominance and jobs.

Recessions, such as the one that began in mid-1990, are a normal part of the business cycle. A classic recession is caused by a buildup in business inventories, such as parts for manufacturing, wholesale goods, and retail merchandise. To deal with high inventories, businesses lay off workers until the inventories are brought down. But the workers are also consumers who in turn purchase fewer goods and services which leads to new rounds of job cutbacks. When inventories are low enough and the employed work force lean enough, economic activity usually picks up as business begins to expand and consumers begin to buy.

The author:

Robert W. Fisher is a senior economist at the U.S. Bureau of Labor Statistics and has written a number of articles on labor issues and the economy. The views expressed in this article are those of the author, not those of the bureau.

Debt and consumer confidence

One of the chief factors hampering a robust economic recovery from the recession of 1990-1991 was the huge amount of debt at all levels. The debt was largely a product of the "roaring 1980's," when business, consumers, and the government took on debt at a record pace. By 1992, business debt stood at $2 trillion, consumers owed over $730 billion in installment debt, and the federal government staggered under a national debt of $4 trillion.

Consumers apparently were more concerned about paying off their debt than in buying goods and services. Data from the Federal Reserve Board showed that consumer installment debt was down from $735 billion in December 1990 to $722 billion in July 1992. Corporations tried to pay down their debt as well. They held back on new investments, trimmed work forces, and closed plants and offices.

In past recessions, the federal government was positioned to inject money into the economy to help stimulate growth. But because of its huge debt, the government was reluctant to even discuss solutions that might involve additional public spending.

Pessimism was also a factor in the 1990-1991 recession and the slow recovery. Surveys of consumers showed that they expected the economy to be in bad shape in 1992 and beyond. The unemployed and discouraged workers would be pessimistic given their situation, but people with jobs also felt threatened by the possibility of layoff, and so postponed purchases of big-ticket items such as cars and appliances. In addition, *real earnings* (the value of pay after adjusting for inflation) had failed to increase since 1982. Between October 1991 and October 1992, BLS data showed that real wages of production workers and nonsupervisory workers fell 0.3 per cent. This also contributed to weak consumer confidence.

Personal consumption makes up about two-thirds of the U.S. *gross domestic product* (GDP)—the total value of all goods and services produced within a nation's boundaries. Therefore, some economists were concerned that if consumer spending did not pick up, the economy would continue to limp along. There would be no incentive for business expansion. And continued weak demand for products might lead to new rounds of layoffs in everything from manufacturing and construction to retail trade and finance.

Every two years, the BLS surveys the number of workers who lost jobs they had held for at least three years because of plant closures, business failures, plant or business moves, elimination of shifts or positions, or in-

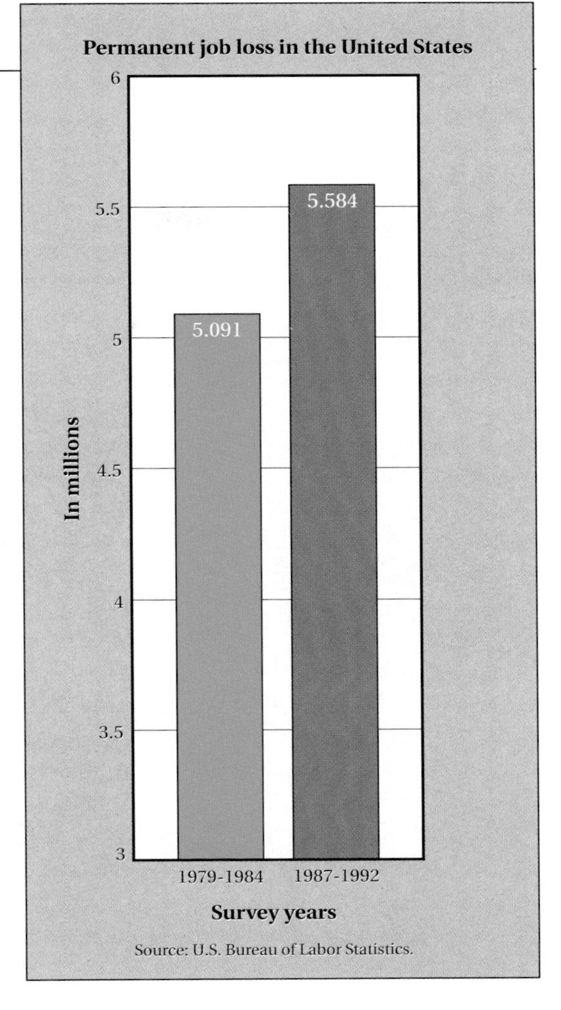

More jobs have been permanently lost in the five-year period that includes the 1990-1991 recession than in an earlier five-year period that included the recessions of 1980 and 1981-1982, according to the U.S. Bureau of Labor Statistics. The U.S. government defines a permanently lost job as one that a worker had held for at least three years until the business closed down, moved, or otherwise eliminated the position.

Losing jobs

From June 1991 to June 1992, many industries in the United States reported a loss of jobs to the U.S. Bureau of Labor Statistics. The work force in industries from construction to transportation and public utilities, *below,* fell by more than 400,000 jobs, in some cases permanently.

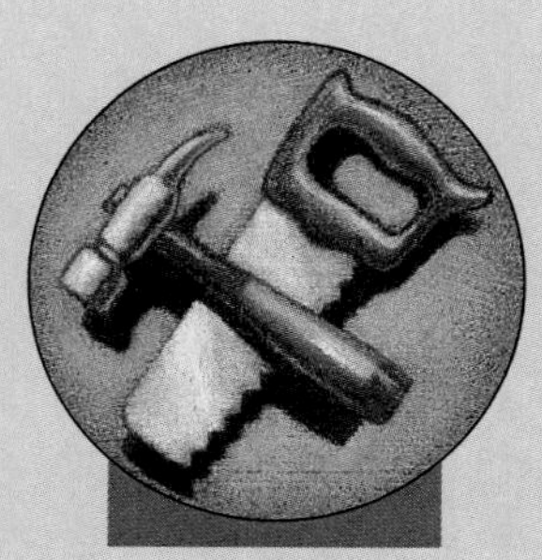

CONSTRUCTION
–97,000

INDUSTRIAL MACHINERY
–55,000

ELECTRONICS
–53,000

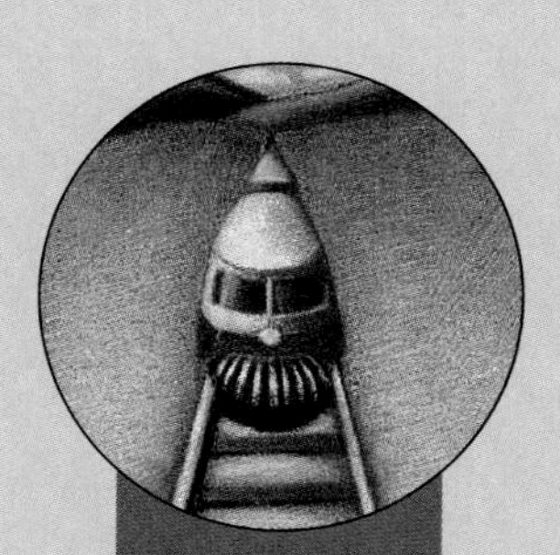

TRANSPORTATION, UTILITIES
–11,000

RETAIL
–151,000

FOOD
–9,000

INSURANCE
–25,000

sufficient work. These workers, most of whom are permanently separated, are referred to as "displaced." The most recent survey, conducted in 1992, showed that 3.1 million white-collar workers and 2.5 million blue-collar workers lost their jobs between January 1987 and January 1992. About a third of the workers had not found new jobs, and many reported taking jobs that paid less than the job they lost.

The changing nature of U.S. jobs

Taking a long perspective of the total U.S. economy, however, jobs have not been lost. Instead, they have changed as the U.S. economy has shifted from goods production to services production. In October 1992, over 117

Gaining jobs

The number of people employed in health services and by state and local governments across the United States rose from June 1991 to June 1992, according to data from the U.S. Bureau of Labor Statistics. The bureau predicts jobs in health care will continue to rise beyond the year 2000.

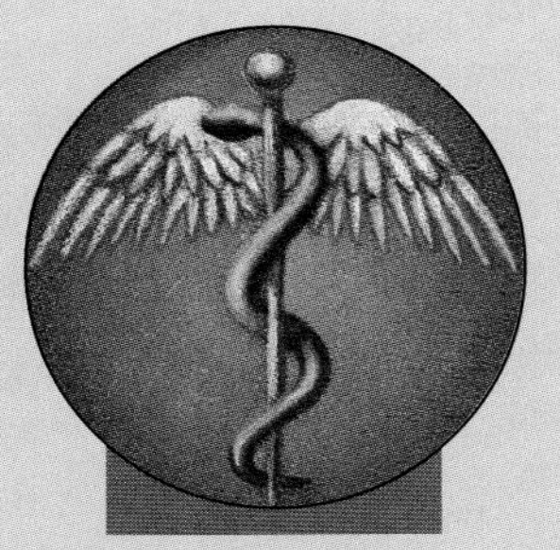

HEALTH SERVICES
+288,000

STATE AND LOCAL GOVERNMENT
+186,000

million people were employed in the United States, the vast majority of them in service jobs.

The change from an economy that produced mainly goods to one that produces mainly services has been gradual, but steady. From 1951 to 1991, the nonfarm goods-producing sector grew only slightly, from 20 million to 23.8 million jobs. In contrast, the service sector tripled, from 27.8 million to 84.5 million jobs. But the shift from making automobiles or apparel to providing health care or selling products has been devastating for some workers. Their job know-how learned in factories and shops has become obsolete in a service-oriented economy or unnecessary because increased productivity allows goods to be produced with fewer workers. Another problem is that service jobs are not as high-paying, on average, as are factory jobs. In 1991, manufacturing wages averaged $455 a week compared with $331 a week for average wages in the service industries.

Foreign competition and other causes of job loss

For some time, American workers have also worried about foreign competition taking away U.S. jobs. First, they saw American companies shift high-paying manufacturing jobs to foreign countries to take advantage of lower labor and other costs. Foreign companies also manufactured goods for export to the United States, where they successfully competed against American-made products. According to one report, in the 1960's only 7 per cent of U.S. industries faced international competition. In the 1980's, the percentage had grown to more than 70 per cent and was expected to continue rising. Among the first industries to feel strong pressure from global competition was automobile manufacturing.

In the late 1980's and in the 1990's, even the service sector of the economy felt the effects of foreign competition, in everything from insurance processing to publishing. Clerical workers in Ireland and India processed insurance claims and subscription orders for U.S. companies for less than it would cost to have the work done in the United States. Overseas operations are controlled from offices in the United States through the use of computers and communications satellites. Some economists have predicted that such global industrial and employment competition will be an important economic fact of life in the 1990's.

In addition, the fall of Communism and the end of the Cold War has had its downside in the U.S. labor market. Defense budget cuts because of the improved world situation have cost jobs across the occupational spectrum. Defense contractors and military bases are often major employers in many cities and towns across the nation.

Not surprisingly, the BLS projects a continuing relative decline in goods production jobs throughout the 1990's. Some white-collar jobs will also decline in large part because of computers. Although computer technology has extinguished some jobs, it has also created entire categories of new jobs. Microelectronic technology (of which the computer is the best-known example) will continue to cause profound changes in how the economy is structured and in how workers work.

Training workers for a technological world

The spread of computer technology in the workplace and the development of new techniques for producing goods and services means that America must have a more sophisticated work force. In May 1990, U.S. Secretary of Labor Elizabeth H. Dole created the Secretary's Commission on Achieving Necessary Skills to identify skills that American workers would need to work effectively for the rest of the 1990's and into the next century. The commission was composed of 30 members drawn from business, unions, education, and government and headed by former U.S. Labor Secretary William E. Brock. The commission found that U.S. workers of the future will need to have skills in reading, writing, and computation; be able to learn and to understand and solve problems; and have personal qualities of responsibility, sociability, and integrity.

Comparing American workers to those of some of the nation's international competitors, the commission concluded that ". . . most American workers receive very little training. Where American companies concentrate training on their college graduates—and most small firms provide no training at all—major foreign competitors concentrate on developing workplace skills at all levels of the company."

To promote the necessary workplace skills, experts say the ways in which U.S. workers are trained will have to be overhauled. In a 1991 survey, the BLS found that workers now get their training in a patchwork of ways. About 33 per cent reported that they qualified for their jobs through training in school, about 25 per cent said that they had received informal on-the-job training, about 12 per cent received formal training from their employers, and 10 per cent were trained while in the military or through correspondence or other courses. About 20 per cent did not identify a training source or their jobs did not require any particular training.

Now that the national spotlight is focused on the need for a well-educated and trained work force, many scripts have been written for achieving this. But most analysts agree that workers below the managerial or professional level will have to be trained in school and on the job to perform sophisticated tasks.

There are other incentives to being educated. BLS data show that better-educated workers typically earn more than less-educated ones. In 1990, workers with four years of college averaged $38,620 annually. In contrast, high school graduates averaged $24,308, and those with less than four years of high school averaged $19,168. Although people with college educations were not immune from layoffs in the recession, workers with the highest education had the lowest unemployment rates.

Where will jobs of the future be?

Every other year, the BLS projects the job outlook for 10 to 15 years. The most recent projections, covering 1990 to 2005, suggest that the service sector areas of health, business, education, and retail trade will be key areas for job growth. The biggest industry growth—over 5 million jobs—will be in retail trade where many jobs typically pay lower wages.

Health services will continue to be a "job machine." The BLS projects that almost 1.6 million workers will be needed in nursing specialties alone, including more than 750,000 registered nurses. Jobs in business services are projected to increase by 2.4 million, covering the spectrum from managers to janitors in such industries as advertising, equipment rental and leasing, and security services. Some of the heaviest job expansion in business will involve financial managers, accountants and auditors, receptionists and information clerks, and general secretaries.

In education, the BLS anticipates the creation of almost 1.6 million additional jobs, including over 300,000 elementary school teachers and 430,000 secondary school teachers. Expanding social work will call for about 350,000 additional child-care workers and 150,000 social workers. The continuing crime plague will spur growth of some 142,000 jobs for correction officers and 160,000 additional jobs for police officers and detectives. The spread of computers will increase jobs for systems analysts and computer scientists.

The world in terms of employment opportunities is increasingly becoming a "global village." American workers must compete for jobs with workers worldwide, and American executives and entrepreneurs must make the right decisions about what technologies to adopt and which products and services to provide. The unemployment triggered by the 1990-1991 recession has brought home the fact that workers in one part of the world can and do produce goods and services for societies in another part. To compete, the United States will need a highly educated, highly trained work force. The jobs of the future will require that all workers—blue-collar and white-collar alike—have the communication, learning, and interpersonal skills once demanded mainly of college graduates.

Latin America

Representatives of 178 nations, among them presidents, prime ministers, sultans, and kings, gathered in Rio de Janeiro, Brazil, from June 3 to 14, 1992, for the United Nations Conference on Environment and Development. The conference aimed to achieve a global consensus on ways to balance development and environmental protection.

The gathering, dubbed the Earth Summit, also attracted many other unofficial participants, from religious leaders such as Tibet's Dalai Lama to a medicine man from the Xingu region of the Amazon to motion-picture celebrities. Thousands of ordinary people from around the world converged on Rio de Janeiro, too, demanding that world leaders make the salvation of the environment a primary concern.

Their presence helped make the conference a milestone in Southern Hemisphere history. Never before had Latin Americans heard such praise for their natural resources from so many renowned scientists and internationally respected people. Chief among these resources are the rain forests, which help remove air pollution from Earth's atmosphere and whose canopies shelter diverse plant and animal species that may offer scientific benefits to human welfare.

The Earth Summit produced a comprehensive plan called Agenda 21 to guide environmental protection strategies and encourage environmentally sound development. A major accord was also reached on reducing the release into the atmosphere of so-called *greenhouse gases,* which result mainly from burning fossil fuels (coal, oil, and gasoline). Greenhouse gases, chiefly carbon dioxide, trap heat in Earth's atmosphere that would otherwise escape into space, much as glass traps heat in a greenhouse. Some scientists fear that these gases may dangerously warm Earth's climate, causing droughts across wide areas of Earth where poverty already ravishes millions of people. Such a warming may also cause polar ice caps to melt, which may cause flooding of low-lying coastal areas and some islands. (See **Environmental pollution: Environmental Concern Goes Global.**)

Shortly before the Earth Summit, the United States government nearly doubled its funding of overseas forestry development, to an annual figure of $270-million. At the conference, Germany pledged $165-million for the preservation of Brazil's rain forests. Canada joined a growing list of nations by announcing that it will forgive $145 million of Latin-American debt for investments in projects that will help preserve environmentally important areas. After the meeting, Latin-American countries were confident, given the importance of their natural resources, that they would receive a large share of some $6 billion pledged by industrialized nations for global conservation projects.

Offbeat places. Environmentalists in 1992 studied long-neglected but ecologically significant areas of Latin America in collaboration with Latin-American partners. Tourists, too, explored the region. Visitors from around the world explored Tierra del Fuego, the barren peninsula at the tip of South America. Others trekked the Pacific and Gulf coasts of Central America in their quest to glimpse rare plants and animals. Television programs throughout the world highlighted the Latin-American environment, including the marine iguanas and blue-footed boobies of Ecuador's Galapagos Islands, and the gray whales that breed in the Sea of Cortez off Mexico.

Several Latin-American nations rushed to inventory their natural resources to meet anticipated demand from environmentally aware tourists. The government of Costa Rica hired a small army of workers to collect samples of the country's plant and animal life for a museum. By mid-1992, the museum included more than 2 million specimens.

Government corruption. In Latin America's most populous country, Brazil, the Congress voted to impeach President Fernando Collor de Mello on September 29. It was the first constitutional impeachment of a president in Latin-American history. Impeachment proceeded after government officials released the results in August of a painstaking congressional examination of an estimated 40,000 canceled checks. The examination revealed that Collor de Mello's former campaign treasurer, Paulo César Farias, had diverted as much as $100 million into the private bank accounts of the president's inner circle. The money was collected during Collor de Mello's first 2½ years in office from kickbacks and influence-peddling schemes. The money reportedly included a $20,000 monthly "allowance" for Collor de Mello's wife.

On August 25, a day after the congressional report became public, massive public demonstrations broke out demanding that Congress impeach Collor de Mello. Brazilians gave further evidence of their anger by voting for candidates of the Brazilian Workers Party, a Socialist group, which scored big gains in municipal elections on October 3. Brazil's vice president, Itamar Augusto Franco, became acting president. On December 29, Collor de Mello resigned, and Franco was sworn in as president. However, Brazil's Senate voted to continue impeachment proceedings.

In Argentina, the appearance of economic progress in 1992 muffled allegations of wrongdoing by President Carlos Saúl Menem's advisers and family. But suspicion of wrongdoing in high places grew. The allegations centered on the sales of state-owned corporations, involving billions of dollars, the proceeds from which had yet to relieve the nation's foreign debt or improve the welfare of average Argentines.

Demonstrators in São Paulo march against Brazilian President Fernando Collor de Mello in September, prior to his impeachment for corruption.

FORA COLLOR
O VERDE-AMARELO
É NOSSO-PRA VOCÊS
É PRETO-BRANCO LISTRADO.
Fora Collor
do B
EM DEFESA DO ENSINO
PÚBLICO E
UNE
UBES
PMDB
Fleury
COM
ALOYSIO
PREFEITO
RETOMAMOS
NA BATALHA
EMPUNHAMOS
JÁ NÃO HÁ
NOS DETENHA
TEMPESTADE
Fora Collor

Latin America

Mexicans in several states grew increasingly uneasy in 1992 over perceived corruption under the continued rule of the Institutional Revolutionary Party, Mexico's single dominant political party since 1929. In October, demonstrators in the state of Michoacán hounded the Institutional Revolutionary Party's governor, Eduardo Villaseñor, out of office, claiming that he had attained his office through vote fraud in July. In January, the national government had persuaded Salvador Neme Castillo, the governor of the state of Tabasco, to resign over similar charges of fraud at the ballot box.

Political unrest. In Peru, the elected President Alberto K. Fujimori seized dictatorial powers on April 5 in an attempt to put down a bloody, 12-year-old uprising that had nearly created anarchy. Public approval of his action blossomed after police captured the leaders of the two terrorist organizations that had kept the country in turmoil. But many Peruvians were doubtful that this would put an end to a rebellion that has won support among some Indians and poverty-stricken slum dwellers.

On November 13, Peruvian government officials claimed that soldiers attempted a coup to overthrow Fujimori. According to the government's account, troops loyal to Fujimori put down the revolt. A government investigation into the attempted coup found the accused coup leaders innocent, however, but later, evidence surfaced that indicated some military and business leaders had plotted an attempted coup.

Venezuelan President Carlos Andrés Pérez barely escaped assassination in a February 4 coup attempt by military officers who made a second grab for power on November 27 to protest widespread corruption. Both uprisings enjoyed substantial public support from Venezuelans angry that there was so little to show from $100 billion in oil export earnings since 1982. In October 1992, Pérez escaped another assassination attempt in the city of Paraguaipoa. Polls indicated that voter disenchantment had reached a record level in Venezuela. Most Venezuelans had lost faith in both of the country's major political parties—neither one of which had proved willing or able to confront the corruption issue.

With Cuba's economy continuing its slide throughout 1992, many political observers predicted that the regime of longtime Communist President Fidel Castro would fall. Led by Jorge Mas Canosa, a group of Miami, Fla.-based Cuban exiles called the Cuban American National Foundation began to organize plans for a new government. Their plans caused controversy in the United States and Cuba, however, with some political observers claiming that Mas Canosa simply planned to set up another dictatorship on the island.

Free trade pacts. Trade representatives from Mexico, the United States, and Canada completed negotiations on the North American Free Trade Agreement on August 12. The agreement is designed to lower tariffs on goods traded among the three countries, creating the world's largest free trade zone with 360 million people. The agreement must be ratified by the national legislatures from the three countries before it takes effect. Although many economists and labor leaders in the United States felt that the agreement would cost the United States jobs, other observers thought it would create jobs by opening up traditionally closed Mexican financial markets and the country's government-controlled oil industry to participation by foreign investors.

Free trade pacts and plans for pacts involving Mexico and other Latin-American countries thrived in 1992. Mexico and Chile signed a free trade pact in September. Mexico also announced in 1992 that it planned to establish free trade agreements with El Salvador, Honduras, Costa Rica, Nicaragua, Guatemala, Venezuela, and Colombia in 1992.

Growing debts. Latin-American nations increased their borrowing from foreign nations in 1992. Successful debt renegotiations in recent years and lower interest rates in the United States spurred the increase. According to economists, Latin America's total debt was expected to increase from $435 billion to $442.7 billion by the end of 1992. By comparison, the region's debt in 1983 stood at about $275 billion. Although inflation eased dramatically in many Latin-American countries, and many of the region's national economies grew impressively, economists worried about how the increasing debt would affect the region's fragile economies. Economists worried particularly about the economies of Brazil, Chile, Mexico, and Argentina, where foreign debt has increased despite earnings of around $50 billion from the sale of state-run companies to private entrepreneurs since the beginning of 1990. Economists estimated that as much as $30 billion—3 per cent of the total Latin-American economic output—would go to debt relief in 1992.

Commodity woes. Falling prices in world markets hurt many Latin-American cocoa and coffee growers in 1992. By midyear, world prices for coffee had slipped to 17-year lows and for cocoa, to 19-year lows. A glut in world banana supplies negatively affected the economies of Costa Rica, Colombia, Ecuador, Guatemala, Honduras, Nicaragua, and Panama. Latin-American fruit producers were angered that some of their Caribbean competitors, which were still under colonial rule, enjoy preferences in tariff-protected European markets.

New billionaires. The U.S. business magazine *Forbes* reported in its July 20 issue that there were 21 Latin-American billionaires in 1992 compared with 8 in 1991. Mexico has 7 of the area's wealthiest people, led by media tycoon Emilio (El Tigre) Azcarraga Milmo, whose fortune of $2.8 billion makes him Latin America's richest person. *Forbes* estimated that Mexico's Garza-Sada family, whose fortune is in steel, petrochemicals, and glass, has a collective worth of $3.8 billion, however.

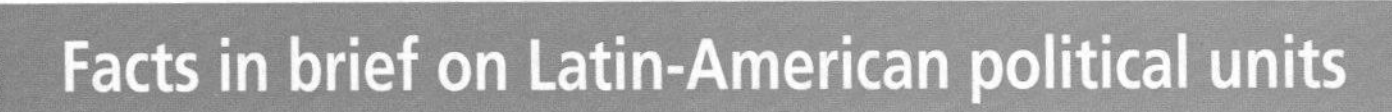

Facts in brief on Latin-American political units

Country	Population	Government	Monetary unit*	Foreign trade (million U.S.$) Exports†	Imports†
Antigua and Barbuda	77,000	Governor General Sir Wilfred Jacobs; Prime Minister Vere C. Bird, Sr.	dollar (2.7 = $1)	32	348
Argentina	33,470,000	President Carlos Saúl Menem	peso (0.99 = $1)	12,353	4,076
Bahamas	265,000	Governor General Clifford Darling; Prime Minister Hubert Ingraham	dollar (1.00 = $1)	2,786	3,001
Barbados	259,000	Governor General Dame Nita Barrow; Prime Minister Lloyd Erskine Sandiford	dollar (2.01 = $1)	209	700
Belize	199,000	Governor General Dame Minita E. Gordon; Prime Minister George Price	dollar (2 = $1)	129	211
Bolivia	7,950,000	President Jaime Paz Zamora	boliviano (4.03 = $1)	858	942
Brazil	158,962,000	President Itamar Franco	cruzeiro (7,943.80 = $1)	31,622	21,004
Chile	13,795,000	President Patricio Aylwin Azócar	peso (403.85 = $1)	8,924	7,424
Colombia	34,842,000	President César Gaviria Trujillo	peso (793.31 = $1)	6,745	5,590
Costa Rica	3,223,000	President Rafael Angel Calderón Fournier	colón (136.50 = $1)	1,543	1,853
Cuba	10,894,000	President Fidel Castro	peso (1.32 = $1)	5,400	8,100
Dominica	86,000	President Clarence Augustus Seignoret; Prime Minister Eugenia Charles	dollar (2.7 = $1)	55	118
Dominican Republic	7,604,000	President Joaquín Balaguer Ricardo	peso (12.68 = $1)	734	1,788
Ecuador	10,408,000	President Sixto Durán Ballén	sucre (1,940.00 = $1)	2,851	2,399
El Salvador	5,651,000	President Alfredo Cristiani Burkard	colón (8.82 = $1)	412	902
Grenada	84,000	Governor General Sir Paul Scoon; Prime Minister Nicholas Brathwaite	dollar (2.7 = $1)	28	116
Guatemala	10,015,000	President Jorge Serrano Elías	quetzal (5.28 = $1)	1,033	1,674
Guyana	815,000	President Cheddi Jagan	dollar (125.49 = $1)	255	512
Haiti	6,922,000	Prime Minister Marc L. Bazin‡	gourde (10.55 = $1)	103	374
Honduras	5,614,000	President Rafael Leonardo Callejas	lempira (5.92 = $1)	912	981
Jamaica	2,543,000	Governor General Howard Cooke Prime Minister P. J. Patterson	dollar (23.55 = $1)	1,116	1,864
Mexico	94,545,000	President Carlos Salinas de Gortari	peso (3,107.50 = $1)	26,524	29,993
Nicaragua	4,253,000	President Violeta Barrios de Chamorro	gold córdoba (5.53 = $1)	298	710
Panama	2,558,000	President Guillermo Endara	balboa (1 = $1)	342	1,695
Paraguay	4,577,000	President Andrés Rodríguez Pedotti	guaraní (1,553.00 = $1)	1,163	695
Peru	22,889,000	President Alberto Fujimori	new sol (1.58 = $1)	3,276	2,885
Puerto Rico	3,522,000	Governor Rafael Hernández Colón	U.S. dollar	16,400	14,000
St. Christopher and Nevis	44,000	Governor General Clement Athelston Arrindell; Prime Minister Kennedy Alphonse Simmonds	dollar (2.7 = $1)	33	90
St. Lucia	158,000	Governor General Sir Stanislaus James; Prime Minister John Compton	dollar (2.7 = $1)	112	266
St. Vincent and the Grenadines	119,000	Acting Governor General David Jack; Prime Minister James F. Mitchell	dollar (2.7 = $1)	75	128
Suriname	447,000	Acting Commander of the National Army Ivan Graanoogst; President Johan Kraag	guilder (1.79 = $1)	425	370
Trinidad and Tobago	1,336,000	President Noor Hassanali; Prime Minister Patrick Manning	dollar (4.55 = $1)	2,049	1,222
Uruguay	3,148,000	President Luis Alberto Lacalle	peso (3,343.00= $1)	1,619	1,590
Venezuela	21,165,000	President Carlos Andrés Pérez	bolívar (76.68 = $1)	17,586	6,365

*Exchange rates as of Oct. 30, 1992, or latest available data.
†Latest available data.
‡Democratically elected President Jean-Bertrand Aristide remained in exile following a military coup that installed Marc L. Bazin as prime minister.

Latin-American nations rushed to join free trade agreements in 1992 in hopes of stimulating their economies.

Columbus legacy revised. Latin America's 45 million Indians turned the 500th anniversary of the arrival of Christopher Columbus in the New World on Oct. 12, 1492, into a reassessment of his legacy. Many Indians, as well as others, took the occasion to point out that the arrival of Europeans brought disease and oppression to the New World and that much of the oppression still exists throughout Latin America.

On Oct. 6, 1992, the human rights organization Amnesty International of London released a report called *The Americas: Human Rights Violations Against Indigenous People,* which documented 500 years of Indian abuse by the governments of North, South, and Central America. Indians continue to be "more vulnerable to abuse than other sectors of society," the report charged. "Activists for indigenous rights throughout the Americas have paid for their commitment with their lives and liberty," the report concluded.

Nobel Prize winners. In recognition of the struggle of native Latin-American peoples, the Norwegian Nobel Committee awarded the Nobel Peace Prize on October 16 to Rigoberta Menchú, 33, a Mayan Indian from the Quiché highlands in Guatemala. Menchú's father died in a fire in 1980 while protesting government oppression, and government troops reportedly killed her mother and brother in 1980. Since fleeing to Mexico in 1981, Menchú has become an eloquent spokeswoman for Indian victims of oppression and the author of a 1983 book, *I, Rigoberta Menchú,* detailing her family's suffering, including her mother's rape, torture, and murder at the hands of Guatemalan soldiers. Returning to a hero's welcome in Guatemala in late 1992, Menchú vowed to use her $1.2-million prize to further Indian rights.

Derek Walcott, 62, a native of St. Lucia, won the Nobel Prize in literature on October 8. "All the races of the world" are represented in the Caribbean, providing a "tremendous possibility of an example of unity," Walcott said on hearing the news. Walcott, who teaches at Boston University, is the author of many books of poetry and several plays, which often draw on the Caribbean landscape, as well as classical and historical themes, for inspiration.

Brazilian river expedition. In February and March, a U.S.-Brazilian expedition retraced the route followed by former U.S. President Theodore Roosevelt and a band of American and Brazilian explorers down a wild river in the Brazilian Amazon region in 1914. The river, originally called the River of Doubt, has been renamed Roosevelt River. "You come away with a new respect for what they did," said Tweed Roosevelt, a member of the most recent expedition and great-grandson of Theodore Roosevelt. "The bugs were real bad," said another member of the expedition, who said that the bugs had been waiting for more than 70 years to feed on more explorers. The purpose of the 1992 trip down the 950-mile (1,500-kilometer) river was to open the area to scientific and conservation efforts in cooperation with local Indian tribes.

Art treasures. Art treasures from Colombia and Ecuador made a rare appearance in the United States from May 14 to July 12 in an exhibition organized by the Americas Society of New York City. Works on display included religious paintings, portraits, and sculpture, as well as silver and gold objects used in religious services from the mid-1600's to the late 1700's. Colombian and Ecuadoran artists had combined native artistic designs with European artistic styles to create the works, often with the patronage of the Roman Catholic Church.

The oldest shipwreck in the Americas? Archaeologists and historians determined in August 1992 that the remains of a ship discovered beneath shallow water off the Bahamian island of Grand Bahama sank in the early 1500's. According to marine archaeologists and historians, this may be the oldest known shipwreck in the Americas. Divers identified the remains of the ship in 1991, and further study revealed that it was a caravel, the sturdy class of ship that Columbus sailed to the New World. The wreck has yielded a rich harvest of artifacts, including crossbows, stone cannonballs, swords, armor, and helmets, as well as planks and ribs of the vessel and brass navigational instruments. Nathan A. Haverstock

See also **Archaeology; Literature, American; Nobel Prizes;** and articles on the individual nations. In ***World Book,*** see **Latin America** and articles on the individual nations.

Latvia enjoyed political stability during 1992, its first year of independence. Latvia had declared independence from the Soviet Union in September 1991. But the country faced hurdles in its efforts to disentangle its economy from that of the former Soviet Union.

Russian ruble replaced. On July 20, 1992, Latvia became the first former Soviet republic after Estonia to discard the Russian ruble as its currency. The Latvian ruble became the temporary monetary unit pending introduction of the permanent unit, the lat.

Relations with Russia were strained in 1992, as the Russian government accused Latvia of discriminating against Latvia's ethnic Russians, who made up more than 30 per cent of the population. A Latvian law passed in July denied citizenship rights—including the right to vote and own land—to residents who arrived after the Soviet Union annexed Latvia in 1940.

On October 29, Russia announced it would suspend its pullout of former Soviet troops from Latvia because of its concern for ethnic Russian rights there. Latvia had been unable in 1992 to reach an agreement with Russia on a timetable for the pullout. However, Russia had by the start of the suspension withdrawn some 40 per cent of the estimated 130,000 troops stationed in Latvia, Estonia, and Lithuania at the time of independence. Justin Burke

See also **Europe** (Facts in brief table). In ***World Book,*** see **Latvia.**

Law. See **Courts; Supreme Court of the U.S.**

Lebanon. Deteriorating economic conditions and election turmoil in 1992 threatened the fragile political stability that had prevailed in Lebanon since the end of that country's 16-year civil war in 1991.

Karami resigns. Prime Minister Omar Karami resigned on May 6, 1992, after strikes and riots rocked Beirut, Lebanon's capital, and other Lebanese cities. Protesters accused Karami's government of corruption and mismanagement in failing to control the country's skyrocketing inflation rate and plunging currency. Public ire with Karami had risen in early 1992 with the disclosure that the government had boosted the salaries of members of parliament and the Cabinet by 400 per cent while increasing the price of bread and other essential products. On May 13, President Ilyas Harawi appointed Rashid al-Sulh, a former prime minister, as Lebanon's new prime minister. Harawi named Rafik Hariri, Lebanon's most prominent business leader, to the post on October 22.

Economic problems. In February, Lebanon's Central Bank abandoned its attempts to prop up the country's shaky pound. Within days, the Lebanese pound fell in value from 880 per United States dollar to 1,200. In 1992, Arab states failed to follow up on promises of aid made to Lebanon after the Persian Gulf War (1991). But on Oct. 4, 1992, the World Bank, an agency of the United Nations, announced it would lend Lebanon $300 million to rebuild basic services damaged by the civil war.

A woman runs between burning tires in Beirut, Lebanon, in early May, during nationwide rioting to protest the country's severe economic problems.

Elections for a new 128-seat National Assembly, the first since 1972, were surrounded by controversy. The major Christian political parties as well as some Muslims protested the government's decision to hold the elections in late August and early September 1992, before Syria was scheduled to withdraw an estimated 40,000 of its troops from the outskirts of Beirut to eastern Lebanon. The protesters contended that the presence of the troops would intimidate voters and lead to the election of a government even more strongly dominated by Syria.

When the government refused to postpone the vote, many Christians boycotted the election, causing one Christian candidate to win with as few as 41 votes. Muslim fundamentalist parties captured at least 30 seats, stunning Christians and more moderate Muslims. Amal, a pro-Syrian party, won 18 seats. The pro-Iranian party Hezbollah won 12 seats.

Assassination. Sheik Abbas Musawi, Hezbollah's leader, was killed in southern Lebanon on February 16 when a motorcade in which he was riding was attacked by Israeli helicopter gunships.

Civil war casualties. In March, the Lebanese government released its first official casualty figures for the 16-year civil war. It reported that 144,240 people were killed and another 197,506 people were wounded. An estimated 17,415 people remained missing and were presumed dead. Christine Helms

See also **Middle East** (Facts in brief table). ***In World Book***, see **Lebanon.**

Liberia. The promise of peace in Liberia seemed real at the beginning of 1992 but proved to be illusory. Fighting resumed despite the presence of troops from a five-nation west African peacekeeping force. The resumption of hostilities was due largely to Charles Taylor, leader of the National Patriotic Front of Liberia (NPFL), the largest of the two rebel groups that overthrew Liberia's President Samuel K. Doe in 1990.

Blocking the peace process. Throughout 1992, Taylor refused to implement the provisions of a 1991 peace agreement. Attacks on his troops by a new rebel group called the United Liberation Movement of Democracy for Liberia (Ulimo) provided Taylor with an excuse to keep his troops armed. Taylor also authorized raids by his soldiers into Sierra Leone to retaliate for its government's support of the west African force in Liberia. Taylor's raids contributed to the overthrow of Sierra Leone's President Joseph Momoh on April 29 by mutinous government troops.

During the year, Taylor also established his own government at the rural village of Gbarnga as an alternative to the interim government established by the peacekeeping force in Monrovia, Liberia's capital. He exported gold, rubber, timber, and other Liberian resources and established his own currency and banking system.

Fighting resumes. At a July summit meeting, officials of the Economic Community of West African States (ECOWAS)—the organization that sent the peacekeeping force to Liberia—ordered Taylor to comply with the peace agreement by August 29. The group threatened Taylor with a naval blockade, and the commander of ECOWAS forces in Liberia was given permission to take the military offensive.

Rather than giving in to the ECOWAS demand, Taylor in October launched his own offensive against Monrovia. By early November, his troops had the city surrounded and under siege. As the fighting continued, Monrovia was cut off from sea and air supply routes, and the death toll mounted. Among those killed were five Roman Catholic nuns from the United States, who were shot to death near their convent on the outskirts of the city.

Fear of a regional conflict. There was growing fear in late 1992 that the hostilities would spread to nearby countries. Ulimo's leaders accused Ivory Coast of allowing weapons to be transmitted across its territory to Taylor, and they threatened to invade. Taylor accused Sierra Leone of allowing Ulimo to train on its territory, and he, too, threatened retaliation. On November 5, the United States recalled its ambassador to Burkina Faso, claiming that country was covertly supplying arms to Taylor. As deaths and costs mounted, there were indications that the united front of west African leaders was crumbling and that some nations might withdraw from the peacekeeping force.

Mark DeLancey

See also **Africa** (Facts in brief table). In ***World Book,*** see **Liberia.**

Library. Disasters—caused by both natural forces and human activity—hit libraries in the United States in 1992. Hurricane Andrew assaulted southern Florida on August 24, causing about $20 million in damages to the Miami-Dade County Public Library system. Four of the library system's 31 branches were severely damaged and remained closed at year-end.

Earthquakes in southern California on June 28 damaged four academic libraries and one county public library system. The library at the University of Redlands in Redlands was the hardest hit. About 42,000 volumes spilled from the library shelves during the earthquakes.

Los Angeles riots. One branch library of the Los Angeles Public Library system was looted and two branches burned in late April during riots triggered by the acquittal of four white police officers charged with the videotaped beating of black motorist Rodney King. (See **Los Angeles.**) Efforts to restore library services and rebuild the damaged libraries began immediately. Librarians quickly dispatched bookmobiles to the communities served by the destroyed libraries. Choreographer-director Debbie Allen kicked off a campaign to rebuild the branch libraries by donating $10,000. By September, the campaign had raised $100,000. But a budget crunch forced Los Angeles in August to cut $2.78 million from the library's personnel budget and $500,000 from its book budget.

Sarajevo library destroyed. The National and University Library of Bosnia and Hercegovina, located in Sarajevo, the capital of Bosnia and Hercegovina, was destroyed in late August during the ongoing civil war between Serbs, Croats, and Bosnian Muslims. The library burned after it was repeatedly shelled. An estimated 3 million volumes, including rare Islamic texts, were destroyed.

Financial problems. A weak national economy and local and state funding problems continued to devastate U.S. libraries in 1992. Friends of the Enoch Pratt Free Library in Baltimore barely raised enough money to rescue five branches that were scheduled for closing in March. The Newark (N.J.) Public Library closed branches and reduced staff, hours, and services because of a $1.2-million budget cut. The refusal by voters in Dracut, Mass., to increase property taxes resulted in the suspension of all library services there. Sacramento, Calif., opened its new public library but for only 35 hours a week. Josephine County, Oregon, an area hard hit by depressed conditions in the lumber industry, closed its public libraries.

School library gift. The DeWitt Wallace-Reader's Digest Fund, one of the largest U.S. philanthropic foundations, announced in October that it would give $40 million to libraries in 25 U.S. cities. The libraries would otherwise be forced to close because of financial problems.

New York City boost. New York City's beleaguered library system received good news in 1992—a $13-million budget increase. As a result, all branch li-

braries were able to be open at least five days a week. In 1991, funding problems had prevented some of the branches from opening more than twice weekly.

ALA campaign. To increase public awareness of the financial problems facing U.S. libraries, the American Library Association (ALA) continued its "Rally for America's Libraries" campaign, which was launched in 1991. During the campaign, then-ALA President Patricia G. Schuman and other ALA members took part in more than 150 interviews on national and local radio programs to promote the campaign.

On March 16, 1992—Freedom of Information Day—the ALA launched a petition drive in support of increased government funding for school, public, and college libraries. People could either sign petitions or call a special toll-free number to register their support. On June 17, ALA leaders presented the names of 306,465 supporters to legislators in Washington, D.C.

Censorship. The ALA's Office for Intellectual Freedom recorded more than 500 cases of censorship or attempted censorship in 1992. Among the books challenged or banned were *Sweet Sixteen and Never* by Jeanne Betancourt, *Holding Me Here* by Pam Conrad, and *The Learning Tree* by Gordon Parks. The school board in Jacksonville, Fla., put the fairy tale "Snow-White" on the restricted list in elementary school libraries in that city because some parents objected to violence in the story. Peggy Barber

In ***World Book,*** see **Library.**

Libya. A five-month stand-off between Libya and three Western countries over international terrorism led the United Nations (UN) Security Council on March 31, 1992, to approve a resolution imposing limited economic sanctions against Libya. The action followed Libya's refusal to surrender for trial six men accused of involvement in the bombing of two civilian aircraft. The sanctions went into effect on April 15, when Libya failed to meet a UN deadline to surrender the men. The sanctions included an air traffic ban and a ban on sales of military equipment to Libya.

In October 1991, a French judge had issued arrest warrants for four Libyans linked to the 1989 bombing of a French airliner over Niger in which 171 people died. In November 1991, the United States and Great Britain charged two Libyan intelligence agents with planting the bomb that exploded aboard a Pan American World Airways jetliner over Lockerbie, Scotland, in 1988, killing 270 people.

Sanction threat. In January 1992, the Security Council threatened to impose economic sanctions against Libya unless Libya's leader Muammar Muhammad al-Qadhafi allowed the two men accused in the Pan Am bombing to stand trial in the United States or Scotland. Apparently worried about the effect of such sanctions, Qadhafi in February called on the United States to open direct talks on the issue and to reopen its embassy in Libya, closed since 1979.

On March 3, 1992, however, Qadhafi asked the

International Court of Justice, the UN's highest judicial agency, to rule that the United States and Great Britain were violating international law by threatening sanctions against Libya. The court rejected Libya's request on April 14. On March 27, the United States froze the American assets of 46 companies and financial institutions said to be controlled by Libya.

Compromise efforts. Many Arab leaders opposed the UN sanctions, fearing that they would create a backlash of anti-Western sentiment and fuel Islamic and Arab radicalism in their countries. Egypt, which had an estimated 1 million citizens working in Libya, unsuccessfully attempted to persuade Qadhafi to compromise on the issue of the investigation into the bombing. A similar effort by the Arab League in March also failed.

Sanctions protest. On April 2, following the UN vote to impose sanctions, Libyan protesters burned the Venezuelan Embassy in Tripoli, Libya's capital. Venezuela's representative to the UN headed the Security Council at the time of the vote. Libyans also staged violent demonstrations outside the embassies of other countries that had supported the resolution. Libya on April 16 expelled diplomats from countries that had voted for the resolution. Christine Helms

See also **Africa** (Facts in brief table); **United Nations: A New Era for the United Nations.** In ***World Book,*** see **Libya.**

Liechtenstein. See **Europe.**

Literature. A wide range of literature in English was published outside the United States and Canada in 1992. In addition, large numbers of works were translated from other languages.

Original fiction. England produced many excellent novels in 1992. Highlights among them were Pat Barker's *Regeneration;* Anita Brookner's *A Closed Eye;* Fay Weldon's *Life Force;* Margaret Drabble's *The Gates of Ivory;* Peter Ackroyd's *English Music;* and Louis de Bernieres' *The War of Don Emmanuel's Nether Parts.*

From Australia came Peter Carey's wittily inventive *The Tax Inspector.* South Africa contributed André Brink's *An Act of Terror,* about a white South African's opposition to apartheid, the country's system of rigid racial separation that was legally abolished in 1990 and 1991. The Nigerian Ben Okri wrote the stunningly lyrical *The Famished Road.* Shashi Tharoor's *Show Business* was a rich novel of life in India's film industry.

Translations. Two Israeli novels appeared in translation in 1992: *Mr. Mani,* by A. B. Yehoshua, and *Katerina,* by Aharon Appelfeld. Translations from Europe included *Fields of Glory,* by French writer Jean Rouaud, and *The Call of the Toad,* by prominent German author Günter Grass.

From Russia came Anatoly Rybakov's *Fear,* the second volume of Rybakov's projected Arbat Trilogy.

Henry Kisor

See also **Canadian literature; Literature, American; Literature for children.**

Literature, American. Works by black American writers were at the forefront of American literature in 1992. These books included a range of fiction as well as criticism, essays, and other works.

Toni Morrison provided two major examples of black American writing in 1992. Her novel *Jazz* was an arresting celebration of New York City's black neighborhood, Harlem, in the 1920's. *Playing in the Dark: Whiteness and the Literary Imagination,* an important critical work, challenged scholars to reexamine the African-American presence in all American literature.

Alice Walker's powerful novel *Possessing the Secret of Joy* dealt with ritual female mutilation in Africa. Caryl Phillips, a novelist born in the West Indies, wrote *Cambridge,* about a proud slave on a West Indian plantation in the 1800's. Closer to home, *Bailey's Cafe,* by Gloria Naylor, was a splendid tale of survival set in a Brooklyn cafe. Terry McMillan's *Waiting to Exhale* was a best-selling novel about the love relationships of four African-American women.

Darryl Pinckney's *High Cotton* was a splendid first novel about a young black intellectual's coming to terms with his heritage. Other fine first novels by black Americans included *I Been in Sorrow's Kitchen and Licked Out All the Pots,* by Susan Straight; and *Your Blues Ain't Like Mine,* by Bebe Moore Campbell.

Short stories by black authors published during the year included *The Stories of John Edgar Wideman.* In this collection, Wideman explores urban dead-end streets through a rich, evocative language.

Two semiautobiographical works by black Americans were influential in 1992. Gayle Pemberton's *The Hottest Water in Chicago,* a series of essays on literature and art, serves as a forum for Pemberton's memories of growing up in a black middle-class family. Marian Wright Edelman's *The Measure of Our Success* took the form of a moving letter to her sons. Edelman argues that self-sufficiency and service to others were important components of the struggle for black civil rights in the 1960's.

Other fiction. Two distinguished writers produced historical novels in 1992, the first work of fiction for both. The essayist and poet Annie Dillard showed herself to be a fine novelist with *The Living,* set in Washington Territory in the 1800's. The critic Susan Sontag delivered *The Volcano Lover,* a beguiling romance based on an affair between British Admiral Horatio Nelson and the Lady Emma Hamilton in Naples in the late 1700's.

Robert Stone's *Outerbridge Reach* told the dazzling story of a solo round-the-world sea voyage. Maureen Howard's *Natural History* was a highly imaginative work that explores a variety of narrative techniques. Joyce Carol Oates wrote *Black Water,* a thoughtful novella based on the real story of a young woman who drowned when her companion, a United States senator, drove his car off a bridge.

The little-known novelist Cormac McCarthy broke into the publishing mainstream with *All the Pretty*

Poet Derek Walcott won the 1992 Nobel Prize for literature. Walcott divides his time between the United States and his native West Indies.

Horses, a charming novel of boyhood with echoes of Mark Twain. William Kennedy continued to mine his native Albany, N.Y., for distinguished fiction in his sixth novel about that city, *Very Old Bones.*

Other important novels were Richard Bausch's *Violence;* Mona Simpson's *The Lost Father;* Nicholson Baker's *Vox;* Jonathan Franzen's *Strong Motion;* E. Annie Proulx's *Postcards;* Alice McDermott's *At Weddings and Wakes;* Alice Hoffman's *Turtle Moon;* John L'Heureux's *The Shrine at Altamira;* Reynolds Price's *Blue Calhoun;* Jay McInerney's *Brightness Falls;* Richard Price's *Clockers;* Thomas Berger's *Meeting Evil;* Barry Unsworth's *Sacred Hunger;* Rosellen Brown's *Before and After;* Ken Kesey's *Sailor Song;* Tama Janowitz' *The Male Cross-Dresser Support Group;* Thomas McGuane's *Nothing But Blue Skies;* Paul Auster's *Leviathan;* Susan Minot's *Folly;* and John Updike's *Memories of the Ford Administration.*

Excellent first novels came from Allen Kurzweil, *A Case of Curiosities*; Dorothy Allison, *Bastard Out of Carolina*; and Cristina Garcia, *Dreaming in Cuban*.

Short stories. Major collections of short stories included *Cowboys Are My Weakness,* by Pam Houston; *Billie Dyer and Other Stories,* by William Maxwell; *Stardust, 7-Eleven, Route 57, A&W, and So Forth,* by Patricia Lear; and *Up in the Old Hotel,* by Joseph Mitchell.

Biographies. Among the best literary biographies of 1992 was David Marr's *Patrick White,* which explored the character of the Australian novelist. Jay Tolson's *Pilgrim in the Ruins: A Life of Walker Percy* was the first biography of this distinguished American novelist to appear since his death in 1990. Martin Stannard's *Evelyn Waugh: The Later Years 1939-1966* explored the adulthood of the English satirist.

The year's historical biographies included *Eleanor Roosevelt 1884-1933,* the first volume of Blanche Wiesen Cook's feminist reinterpretation of the activist first lady's life. *Woman of Valor,* by Ellen Chesler, examined the life of Margaret Sanger, founder of the American birth control movement.

Three biographies of American political figures gained attention. David McCullough's *Truman,* a warm yet rigorous account of the life of former President Harry S. Truman, reached the best-seller list. Walter Isaacson's *Kissinger* was an exhaustive profile of former Secretary of State Henry Kissinger. Nigel Hamilton was the author of *Reckless Youth,* the first volume in a projected three-volume life of former President John F. Kennedy.

Other important historical biographies were Jack Beatty's *The Rascal King,* about legendary Boston politician James Michael Curley; William C. Davis' *Jefferson Davis: The Man and His Hour*; Kai Bird's *The Chairman,* a life of diplomat John J. McCloy; and Alan Bullock's *Hitler and Stalin*.

Among the year's performing-arts biographies, Joseph McBride's *Frank Capra* argued that the film director, far from being a champion of the common man, was a political reactionary. Steven Bach's *Marlene Dietrich,* an encyclopedic look at the actress' career, was published six months after her death. David Thomas wrote the prodigiously researched *Showman: The Life of David O. Selznick,* about the ill-starred producer of the classic film *Gone with the Wind.*

Genius, James Gleick's life of Richard Feynman, topped the list of science biographies in 1992. Feynman, a Nobel Prize-winning physicist, was renowned for his antic humor as well as his brilliance.

Autobiographical works. In *Intellectual Memoirs,* the novelist and critic Mary McCarthy took a look back at her Bohemian life in New York City during the 1930's. The journalist Gay Talese mined the exuberant immigrant history of his Italian-American forebears in *Unto the Sons.*

Other autobiographies included *Screening History,* novelist Gore Vidal's account of his early years; *Prodigal Son,* by ballet star Edward Villella; *"I've Seen the Best of It,"* by journalist Joseph W. Alsop; and *Down from Troy,* by surgeon-essayist Richard Selzer.

Outstanding volumes of correspondence included *The Letters of Evelyn Waugh and Diana Cooper,* edited by Artemis Cooper; and *Vita and Harold: The Letters of Vita Sackville-West and Harold Nicolson,* edited by Nigel Nicolson.

Criticism. Robert Hughes's *Barcelona* was a scholarly yet readable look at the cultural history of the capital of Catalonia, a province of Spain. Garry Wills's *Lincoln at Gettysburg* was a magisterial study of the enduring power of Abraham Lincoln's Gettysburg Address.

Contemporary nonfiction. Books on social issues published in 1992 included three works dealing with the persistence of racial inequality in the United States. Two of these were Andrew Hacker's *Two Nations: Black and White, Separate, Hostile, Unequal;* and *Race*, an oral history by Studs Terkel. The third, Derrick Bell's *Faces at the Bottom of the Well,* presented a disturbing argument that racism is a permanent feature of American life.

Two politically opposed books explored a national trend toward linking welfare payments with work. These were the liberal Christopher Jencks' *Rethinking Social Policy* and the conservative Lawrence M. Mead's *The New Politics of Poverty.* Another influential work on American society was Juliet B. Schor's *The Overworked American*. Schor's book deals with the decline in U.S. workers' leisure time since the 1950's.

In *Molehunt*, David Wise provided an absorbing analysis of the Central Intelligence Agency's search for traitors in its midst in the 1960's and 1970's. William J. Broad's *Teller's War* explored the influence of nuclear scientist Edward Teller on the Strategic Defense Initiative, popularly called "Star Wars," a project begun in the 1980's to create a defensive system that would shoot down incoming missiles.

Four books brought the biological nature of women to the social forefront. Germaine Greer's controversial *The Change: Women, Ageing and the Menopause;* Gail Sheehy's best-selling *The Silent Passage;* and Lois W. Banner's *In Full Flower* explored the point in women's lives when they reach the end of their childbearing years and the changes this entails. In contrast, Jessica Mitford's *The American Way of Birth* provided a scathing look at childbirth as handled by the U.S. medical establishment.

Travel. *Crossing Antarctica,* by Will Steger and Jon Bowermaster, told of a voyage across the unknown continent by dog sled in 1990. *The Happy Isles of Oceania* was a striking departure for Paul Theroux, who left behind his beloved trains to paddle around the South Pacific in a kayak.

History. In one of the year's important historical works, *The Radicalism of the American Revolution,* Gordon S. Wood offered an argument against the generally accepted view that the Revolutionary War in America (1775-1783) did not lead to significant social change.

Two other books dealt with U.S. military history. *The Civil War in the American West,* by Alvin M. Josephy, Jr., revealed the role of American Indians in the military events of 1861-1865. *We Were Soldiers Once . . . and Young,* by Harold G. Moore and Joseph L. Galloway, revisited the battle of Ia Drang in November 1965, a pivotal clash that foreshadowed the outcome of the Vietnam War (1957-1975).

Several books on the Holocaust of World War II (1939-1945) appeared during the year. They included *Benevolence and Betrayal: Five Italian Jewish Families Under Fascism,* by Alexander Stille; and *Ordinary Men,* by Christopher R. Browning, an exploration of the behavior of German policemen during roundups and murders of Jews in Poland.

Other works of history included *Soldiers of the Sun*, about the Imperial Japanese Army, by Meirion Harries and Susie Harries; *The Last Tsar,* a look at the death of Russian Czar Nicholas II during the October Revolution of 1917, by Edvard Radzinsky; and *Olympia: Paris in the Age of Manet,* a view of Paris in the 1800's, by Otto Friedrich.

Science. Timothy Ferris' *The Mind's Sky* explored the relationship between the universe and the human mind. Edward O. Wilson's *The Diversity of Life* examined the disturbing effect of human civilization on the world's plant and animal species.

Social science. *The Pursuit of Pleasure* was Lionel Tiger's amiable anthropological study of the importance of pleasure in human culture.

Best sellers. *The Pelican Brief,* by John Grisham, joined Grisham's courtroom thriller *The Firm* on the best-seller list. *America: What Went Wrong?,* by Donald L. Barlett and James B. Steele, explored what the authors see as the decline of the American middle class since the early 1980's. Henry Kisor

See also **Canadian literature; Literature; Literature for children; Poetry.** In ***World Book,*** see **American Literature.**

Illustrations from *Tuesday* by David Wiesner won him the 1992 Caldecott Medal for most distinguished picture book for children.

Literature for children published in 1992 featured a large number of books about Christopher Columbus, in observance of the 500th anniversary of his first landing in the Americas. Picture books continued to be plentiful, as did books on multicultural and environmental subjects for all ages.

Outstanding books of 1992 included the following:

Picture books. *Noah's Cats and the Devil's Fire* by Arielle North Olson, illustrated by Barry Moser (Orchard Bks.). Cats foil the devil when he tries to cause trouble on Noah's ark. Wonderful paintings help tell the story. Ages 4 to 7.

Dreamcatcher by Audrey Osofsky, illustrated by Ed Young (Orchard Bks.). In this Ojibwa Indian tale, a dream net protects a baby from bad dreams. Haunting pictures accompany the text. Ages 4 to 7.

Encounter by Jane Yolen, illustrated by David Shannon (Harcourt Brace Jovanovich). Columbus' arrival is viewed through the eyes of a Taino Indian boy who tries to warn his people not to welcome the strangers. Dramatic paintings. Ages 6 to 12.

Seven Blind Mice by Ed Young (Philomel). In this version of an old fable, fine collage illustrations help teach colors and days of the week. Ages 4 and up.

Bravo, Tanya by Patricia Lee Gauch, illustrated by Satomi Ichikawa (Philomel). Tanya loves to dance, but at dancing school she has problems. Ages 4 to 8.

The Jade Stone, retold by Caryn Yacowitz and illustrated by Ju-Hong Chen (Holiday House). When Chan Lo cannot carve a jade dragon as ordered, he must be punished. Ages 4 to 8.

Journey of the Red-Eyed Tree Frog by Tanis Jordan, illustrated by Martin Jordan (Green Tiger Pr.). Humans are destroying the Central American forest, and Hops-a-Bit makes a dangerous journey to get help. Ages 5 and up.

Duckat by Gaelyn Gordon, illustrated by Chris Gaskin (Scholastic). A duck that acts like a cat appears at Mabel's back door. Ages 2 to 6.

The Field Beyond the Outfield by Mark Teague (Scholastic). Ludlow's parents have him play baseball to restrain his imagination, with astonishing results. Ages 6 to 9.

Sukey and the Mermaid by Robert D. San Souci, illustrated by Brian Pinkney (Four Winds). Sukey has a hard life until a mermaid befriends her, but then she is forced to make a choice. Ages 5 to 9.

ANTics! by Cathi Hepworth (Putnam). Wonderful illustrations accompany alphabet words, all with ANT in them. InstANT fun! All ages.

Bently & Egg by William Joyce (HarperCollins). Bently agrees to guard a friend's egg, but then he must rescue it. Ages 4 to 8.

The Widow's Broom by Chris Van Allsburg (Hough-

ton Mifflin). When the witch's broom no longer flies, it takes on a new role. Ages 5 to 8.

Drylongso by Virginia Hamilton, illustrated by Jerry Pinkney (Harcourt Brace Jovanovich). A young boy appears on a farm during a drought, bringing hope for the future. Ages 8 to 12.

Sheep Out to Eat by Nancy Shaw, illustrated by Margot Apple (Houghton Mifflin). Shaw's latest hilarious tale of sheep mishaps is set in a tea shop. Ages 3 to 7.

Old Black Fly by Jim Aylesworth, illustrated by Stephen Gammell (Henry Holt). A fly wreaks havoc in this rollicking alphabet book with wildly comical illustrations. All ages.

Jack's Fantastic Voyage by Michael Foreman (Harcourt Brace Jovanovich). When Jack doubts that his Grandpa was ever a sailor, the two make an unusual trip. Ages 4 to 8.

Puss in Boots, retold by Lincoln Kirstein and illustrated by Alain Vaes (Little, Brown). Richly detailed paintings make this classic tale a visual feast. All ages.

Gilgamesh the King, retold by Ludmila Zeman (Tundra Bks.). The first part of the epic tale of the half-god, half-man tells how his friendship with Enkidu began. Compelling illustrations. All ages.

The Lost Sailor by Pam Conrad, illustrated by Richard Egielski (HarperCollins). When a famous sailor is marooned on an island, it seems as if his luck has run out. Fine paintings. Ages 5 to 9.

Fiction. *Morning Girl* by Michael Dorris (Hyperion). The story of Morning Girl and her brother, set in the Bahamas in 1492, has a startling ending. Ages 7 to 10.

Life's a Funny Proposition, Horatio by Barbara Garland Polikoff (Henry Holt). Horatio's dad has died, and life at home changes as his grandfather moves in and his mom starts dating. Ages 10 to 12.

Letters from Rifka by Karen Hesse (Henry Holt). Rifka and her family flee Russia and persecution but encounter many difficulties getting to Ellis Island, where Rifka is detained once more. Ages 11 and up.

The Coming of the Bear by Lensey Namioka (HarperCollins). A ravaging bear on a Japanese island brings a Japanese and a native Ainu settlement closer to war. Ages 12 and up.

Brothers Like Friends by Klaus Kordon (Philomel). Frank and his half-brother, Burkie, dislike their mother's new husband. But when Frank makes Burkie a promise, everything changes. Ages 10 and up.

Somewhere in the Darkness by Walter Dean Myers (Scholastic). Jimmy's father suddenly appears and takes Jimmy with him so he can explain himself to his son while there is still time. Ages 12 and up.

Missing May by Cynthia Rylant (Orchard Bks.). May is dead, and her husband, Ob, misses her terribly. Summer and Cletus seek a way to help. Ages 11 and up.

Yaxley's Cat by Robert Westall (Scholastic). When Rose and her two children rent a mysterious cottage, they place their lives in danger. Ages 12 and up.

The Leaving by Budge Wilson (Philomel). This Canadian Young Adult Book Award winner contains nine memorable stories about young women. Ages 12 and up.

Attaboy, Sam! by Lois Lowry, illustrated by Diane de Groat (Houghton Mifflin). Anastasia's younger brother decides to make perfume for his mom for Mother's Day, with humorous results. Ages 7 to 12.

When the Road Ends by Jean Thesman (Houghton Mifflin). Mary Jack, one of three foster children, wants their stay with the Percy family to work out, but the unexpected happens. Ages 10 to 14.

The Cellar by Ellen Howard, illustrated by Patricia Rose Mulvihill (Atheneum). Faith wants to help out like her siblings, but something always happens. Ages 7 to 9.

Song of the Buffalo Boy by Sherry Garland (Harcourt Brace Jovanovich). Loi, an Amerasian in Vietnam, fakes her death to escape a forced marriage, but many hardships lie in wait for her. Ages 12 and up.

Underrunners, by Margaret Mahy (Viking). When Tris helps Winola run away from the Children's Home, he puts them in terrible danger. Ages 10 to 14.

Ajeemah and His Son by James Berry (HarperCollins). Ajeemah and Atu are captured in Africa and taken to Jamaica, where they are sold into slavery. Ages 10 and up.

The Fire Raiser by Maurice Gee (Houghton Mifflin). Someone is setting fires in a New Zealand town. Four children try to catch him. Ages 11 and up.

Poetry. *Talking Like the Rain,* selected by X. J. Kennedy and Dorothy M. Kennedy and illustrated by Jane Dyer (Little, Brown). A delightful illustrated collection of "first poems" by a wide variety of poets. Ages 3 to 8.

Red Dragonfly on My Shoulder, translated by Sylvia Cassedy and Kunihiro Suetake and illustrated by Molly Bang (HarperCollins). An unusual format makes this haiku book unique. All ages.

And the Green Grass Grew All Around, selected by Alvin Schwartz and illustrated by Sue Truesdell (HarperCollins). This superb collection of folk poetry shows its variety. Humorous illustrations. All ages.

Who Shrank My Grandmother's House? by Barbara Esbensen, illustrated by Eric Beddows (HarperCollins). In these "poems of discovery," everyday sights and events are viewed with fresh insight. Ages 8 to 11.

I Never Told and Other Poems by Myra Cohn Livingston (McElderry Bks.). The varied selection of subjects and moods in these poems has strong appeal. Ages 8 to 12.

Just Beyond Reach and Other Riddle Poems by Bonnie Larkin Nims, illustrated by George Ancona (Scholastic). Clever riddles are presented on one page, followed by the solution with its photograph on the next. All ages.

Neighborhood Odes by Gary Soto, illustrated by David Diaz (Harcourt Brace Jovanovich). The subjects of these poems range from tennis shoes to tortillas. Unusual black and white illustrations. Ages 8 to 12.

Animals, people, places, and things. *Otters Under Water* by Jim Arnosky (Putnam). A simple text and luminous paintings show how otters swim and what they see and do. Ages 3 to 6.

The Life and Times of the Apple by Charles Micucci (Orchard Bks.). Aided by detailed color illustrations, Micucci reveals fascinating information about apples, including where they come from and how they are grown. Ages 5 to 8.

The Invisible Thread by Yoshiko Uchida (Julian Messner). The author describes her childhood as a Japanese-American and tells how her family coped when they were placed in internment camps during World War II (1939-1945). Ages 8 to 12.

Talking with Artists by Pat Cummings (Bradbury Pr.). Fourteen popular illustrators respond to questions children often ask. Samples of their artwork and autobiographical sketches are included. All ages.

A River Ran Wild by Lynne Cherry (Harcourt Brace Jovanovich). The Nashua River, winding and free, becomes polluted by paper mills and other industries until a woman does something about it. Ages 6 to 10.

Buried in Ice: The Mystery of a Lost Arctic Expedition by Owen Beattie & John Geiger, illustrated by Janet Wilson (Scholastic). An anthropologist tries to discover what killed the men on a well-equipped 1845 expedition. Ages 8 to 12.

Wings Along the Waterway by Mary Barrett Brown (Orchard Bks.). Brown describes some of the birds who depend on waterways so the reader can see how technology is endangering them. Ages 8 to 11.

E. B. White: Some Writer! by Beverly Gherman (Atheneum). A fascinating look at the life of the author of children's classic *Charlotte's Web.* Ages 8 to 12.

Eskimo Boy by Russell Kendall (Scholastic). Readers learn about life in an Eskimo village. Ages 5 to 8.

The Magic School Bus on the Ocean Floor by Joanna Cole, illustrated by Bruce Degen (Scholastic). An unusual bus ride reveals the strange world of the ocean floor. Ages 8 to 11.

Hummingbirds: Jewels in the Sky by Esther Quesada Tyrrell, illustrated by Robert A. Tyrrell (Crown). Superb color photographs capture some of the more than 300 kinds of these tiny birds, while the text describes some of their special features. All ages.

The Amazing Potato by Milton Meltzer (HarperCollins). Meltzer reveals fascinating information about the popular tuber and its importance in our diet. Ages 8 to 12.

Into the Mummy's Tomb by Nicholas Reeves (Scholastic). The discovery of King Tutankhamen's tomb and its treasures unfolds in text and photographs. Ages 12 and up.

Fantasy. *Mariel of Redwall* by Brian Jacques (Philomel). Once more Redwall is in danger, and though all will end well, plenty of action keeps the reader entranced. Ages 10 to 14.

River Rats by Caroline Stevermer (Harcourt Brace

Jovanovich). Orphans who survived a nuclear holocaust run a paddlewheeler. When they rescue a stranger, their troubles begin. Ages 12 and up.

The Promise by Monica Hughes (Simon & Schuster). Princess Rania is apprenticed to the mystical Sandwriter. As time passes, she must learn the meaning of a promise and make difficult choices. Ages 12 and up.

Dragon War by Laurence Yep (HarperCollins). In this continuation of the Dragon saga, three friends try to save the world from the Boneless King and rescue a magecaller. Ages 12 and up.

Untold Tales by William Brooke (HarperCollins). Traditional tales go beyond their original conclusions in witty twists and turns. Ages 11 and up.

The Dark-Thirty: Southern Tales of the Supernatural by Patricia C. McKissack, illustrated by Brian Pinkney (Knopf). McKissack presents 10 African-American tales to tingle the spine—perfect for reading aloud. Ages 8 and up.

Awards. Phyllis Reynolds Naylor won the 1992 Newbery Medal for her novel *Shiloh.* The medal is given by the American Library Association (ALA) for outstanding children's literature published the previous year. The ALA's Caldecott Medal for "the most distinguished American picture book for children" went to David Wiesner, the illustrator and creator of *Tuesday.*

Marilyn Fain Apseloff

In ***World Book,*** see **Caldecott Medal; Newbery Medal; Literature for children.**

Lithuania returned former Communists to power in elections held on Oct. 25, 1992. The Democratic Labor Party (DLP), formerly the Communist Party, defeated the governing Sajudis, the Lithuanian nationalist movement. The DLP gained an absolute parliamentary majority in runoff elections on November 15.

DLP leader Algirdas Brazauskas was named president of parliament, a post equivalent to national president, replacing Sajudis head Vytautas Landsbergis. Brazauskas, a former Communist Party head, had broken with the Communist Party of the Soviet Union in 1989, helping pave the way for Lithuanian independence in September 1991.

Voters on October 25 also accepted a new constitution, which provides for a directly elected president with some expanded powers. Both Brazauskas and Landsbergis were expected to run in direct presidential elections scheduled for 1993.

Disenchantment with the cost of economic reform aided the Sajudis defeat. Another factor was strained relations with Russia, mainly over its slow pullout of former Soviet troops from Lithuania. On September 8, Russia agreed to complete the pullout by August 1993. The pullout issue, along with price disputes between the two nations, led Russia to cut oil shipments to Lithuania from August to October, causing severe shortages.

Justin Burke

See also **Europe** (Facts in brief table). In ***World Book,*** see **Lithuania.**

Los Angeles. The worst riot in the United States in the 1900's erupted in Los Angeles on April 29, 1992. In five days of violence, looting, and arson, more than 50 people died and hundreds more were injured. The rioting was ignited by the verdict in the case of Rodney G. King, a black motorist who was beaten in March 1991 by four white Los Angeles Police Department (LAPD) officers after a high-speed pursuit. A bystander videotaped the beating, and the incident, shown widely on television, attracted national attention.

The trial of the four officers was held in the nearby town of Simi Valley. A jury acquitted the officers of all charges except for a single assault charge against one officer. Within hours, riots had broken out in many parts of Los Angeles and in several surrounding communities. On April 30, the National Guard was called in, and order was restored by May 4, when a four-day curfew was lifted. The riots caused more than $1 billion in damages. (See also **City: The Ailing Cities, the Angry Poor.**)

On August 5, a federal grand jury indicted the four officers involved in the King beating and charged them with violating his civil rights. That trial was scheduled for 1993. The remaining assault charge against one officer was also scheduled to be retried.

New police chief. Willie L. Williams, former police commissioner of Philadelphia, was sworn in on June 26 as the first black chief in the history of the LAPD. During his inaugural address, Williams unveiled a new police recruitment drive designed to increase the number of minorities in the department. He said racism, sexism, or brutality among LAPD officers would not be tolerated.

Williams, 48, replaced former Police Chief Daryl F. Gates. Gates, who retired after 43 years with the department, had been widely criticized for the LAPD's handling of the 1992 riots and for allegedly condoning racism and brutality among members of the police force.

On October 21, a special panel, which prepared a report for the Los Angeles Police Commission on the LAPD response to the riots, sharply criticized Gates for failing "to provide a real plan...to control the disorder." The panel called on the LAPD to redeploy police officers away from elite special-assignment units and back to basic patrol duties. The panel also said the department should move quickly to prepare for future emergencies.

Report on sheriff's department. The Los Angeles County Sheriff's Department also came in for criticism during 1992. The results of an official probe of the department by an independent panel of investigators, released on July 20, concluded that there was a "deeply disturbing" pattern of excessive force and brutality by deputies. In a formal written response on October 28, Sheriff Sherman Block defended his department and criticized a number of the report's conclusions. Block said that some reforms had already been implemented in the department.

Political changes. Mayor Tom Bradley announced on September 24 that he would not seek reelection for a sixth term. The 74-year-old Bradley, the city's first black mayor, said he would step down in June 1993, exactly 20 years after he was first sworn in.

On Nov. 3, 1992, Yvonne Brathwaite Burke, a former United States representative, became the first black elected to the Los Angeles County Board of Supervisors. Burke had to wait until November 16 to declare victory because of a prolonged ballot count and challenges by her opponent.

Rail system. A new era of rapid mass transit in the Los Angeles area began on October 26 when a network of double-deck trains began carrying passengers between downtown Los Angeles and suburban stations. Officials of the Southern California Regional Rail Authority, which operates the network, predicted that the trains may ultimately take as many as 45,000 cars off the road each day.

Budgets. The Los Angeles City Council approved a $3.8-billion budget on May 22 that averted heavy cuts in police and fire services. In Los Angeles County, the Board of Supervisors adopted a $13-billion budget on September 29. Facing the worst fiscal crisis in the county's history, the board pared about $250 million from a variety of programs. Victor Merina

In ***World Book,*** see **Los Angeles.**
Louisiana. See **State government.**
Luxembourg. See **Europe.**

Magazine. The biggest news in magazines in 1992 came in June when *The New Yorker* announced that Tina Brown, editor in chief of *Vanity Fair*, would become *The New Yorker*'s new editor in chief. The 38-year-old Brown made her mark at *Vanity Fair* with celebrity profiles and eye-catching covers, including a 1991 cover showing pregnant actress Demi Moore in the nude. As a result of Brown's handiwork, *Vanity Fair*, with its mix of flashy and serious journalism, was considered the "hot" title of the late 1980's and early 1990's.

Redesign for *New Yorker*. Throughout the summer, observers wondered how Brown could revitalize the stately, old *New Yorker* without losing the loyal readers devoted to its distinct editorial style and look. Brown's first issue of *The New Yorker* in October included a detailed table of contents, color illustrations, and a scented perfume ad—small but telling indications of Brown's gentle push of *The New Yorker* into the 1990's.

Another British publishing superstar shifted to the American scene in 1992. Elizabeth Tilberis, editor of *British Vogue*, was lured by Hearst Corporation in January to become editor in chief of the 125-year-old fashion magazine *Harper's Bazaar*, which had been

An arson fire rages in Los Angeles on April 29 as riots break out after the acquittal of four police officers charged with beating a black motorist.

losing ground to competitors. The elegant look of Tilberis' first issues generated enormous publicity.

Time, the newsweekly published by Time Warner Incorporated, in April unveiled a reorganization that placed short, snappy news items in the front, in-depth articles in the middle, and reviews and criticism in the back. The redesign addressed the growing problem faced by weekly news magazines about how to present news in a fresh way to readers who are already familiar with it from television or daily newspapers. *Time's* solution was to devote only one-third of the magazine to hard news coverage and the rest to original commentary. The science magazine *Discover*, published by Walt Disney Company, also underwent a bold, bright revamp beginning in March.

Start-ups. Lingering economic problems in 1992 led to only a modest burst in major new magazines. In March, Lang Communications Incorporated, creator of the brash *Sassy* for teen-age girls, unveiled its counterpart for teen-age boys, *Dirt*. Jann S. Wenner, the founder of *Rolling Stone*, in April launched *Men's Journal*, which showcased male-oriented articles on travel and outdoor adventure. And in September, Time Warner and the musician Quincy Jones published a test issue of *Vibe*, a magazine devoted to a black cultural phenomenon called *hip-hop*, which includes rap music. Other new entries included two magazines for investment-minded readers: *Worth*, by the mutual fund company Fidelity Investments, and *Smart Money*, a joint venture between Hearst and Dow Jones & Company, publisher of *The Wall Street Journal*.

Shut-downs. Most prominent among 1992's victims was *Connoisseur*, which folded in February after a last-ditch effort in 1991 to turn the 91-year-old fine arts magazine into a more celebrity-oriented title. In November, Fairchild Publications shut down *M*, its 9-year-old men's fashion magazine, because it could not attract enough fashion advertising. And overseas, the venerable British humor magazine *Punch* ceased publication in April after 150 years.

Magazine liability. A federal appeals court in August upheld a ruling that *Soldier of Fortune*, a magazine for mercenaries, was liable in the 1985 murder of an Atlanta, Ga., man whose killers were aided by a mercenary hired through one of the magazine's advertisements. The ad in question began "Gun for hire" and ended "All jobs considered."

The judges said the publishers were liable for printing an ad whose text "makes it apparent that there is a substantial danger of harm to the public." Some legal experts feared that the ruling would threaten a free press by making publishers responsible for harmful happenings linked to their ads. But others believed that the ruling simply required magazines to examine the language of their ads to determine whether they suggest a threat to the public. Deirdre Carmody

In ***World Book,*** see **Magazine.**

Maine. See **State government.**

Malawi. See **Africa.**

Malaysia. The United Malays National Organization (UMNO), Malaysia's ruling party, in 1992 moved to curb the power of the hereditary rulers who head 9 of Malaysia's 13 state governments. Although they are not part of the elected governments, the nine sultans have considerable influence within their states as the guardians of Islam, Malaysia's official religion, as well as the protectors of Malaysian political dominance over the nation's Chinese and Indian minorities.

The UMNO effort, led by Prime Minister Mahathir bin Mohamad, arose from a dispute in April over whether sultan Ismail Petra of the state of Kelantan had to pay a duty on an imported car. Mahathir alleged that Petra broke a rule allowing each sultan to import only seven cars without paying import duty. The sultan maintained that he was bound only by the teachings of Islam and not by earthly rules. Mahathir used the dispute to revive a 1990 UMNO plan for a written code of conduct for the sultans.

After negotiations, the sultans on July 4 accepted a code, though it lacked constitutional authority. The sultans agreed to stay out of politics and abide by the decisions of their state legislatures. They also agreed to pursue business ventures only through trustees.

Political manuevering within the UMNO intensified in 1992 in anticipation of elections scheduled for late 1993. After 12 years as prime minister, Mahathir avoided designating an apparent successor, and he warned against those "restless for power."

On May 14, the leader of the opposition Democratic Action Party, Lim Kit Siang, was suspended from Parliament after accusing a member of the governing coalition of impropriety. Lim charged that his suspension indicated an "increasing antidemocratic trend" by Mahathir's government. Other officials complained that Parliament was being increasingly ignored by Mahathir and his cabinet.

Economic policy turmoil. The official Foreign Investment Committee in January issued guidelines to ensure that new enterprises complied with government aims to shift economic power from the ethnic Chinese minority to the Malay majority. However, the guidelines were withdrawn on March 25 after protests that they would slow investment. Finance Minister Anwar Ibrahim, a leading contender to succeed Mahathir, was criticized for the reversal.

Dignitaries visit. Leaders from two nearby countries made trips to Malaysia in 1992. The president of China, Yang Shangkun, and the premier of Vietnam, Vo Van Kiet, visited Malaysia separately in January. It was the first visit by a Vietnamese premier since 1978 and the first visit ever by a Chinese head of state. Both sets of talks were aimed at promoting bilateral trade and investment. Henry S. Bradsher

See also **Asia** (Facts in brief table). In ***World Book,*** see **Malaysia.**

Maldives. See **Asia.**

Mali. See **Africa.**

Malta. See **Europe.**

Manitoba. The federal House of Commons on March 10, 1992, passed a resolution honoring Louis Riel, the *métis* (people of mixed Indian and white ancestry) leader hanged as a traitor in 1885. The resolution recognized Riel's "unique and historic role" as a founder of Manitoba. It also expressed support for the efforts of the *métis* to achieve constitutional rights.

Riel, born in 1844, was the leader of the Red River Settlement, which became the province of Manitoba in 1870. He was hanged after leading a *métis* and Indian revolt to secure lands in Saskatchewan.

Elections. The Progressive Conservative (PC) government of Premier Gary A. Filmon held on to its slim majority in the legislature after by-elections on Sept. 15, 1992, to fill two vacancies. The PC's captured one seat and the Liberal Party took the other, leaving party standings unchanged.

Money matters. The budget, delivered by Finance Minister Clayton Manness on March 11, confined public spending increases to 3.3 per cent in fiscal 1992-1993 (April 1, 1992, to March 31, 1993). A transfer of $200 million ($160 million U.S.) from the province's "rainy-day" stabilization fund kept the projected deficit down to $330 million ($265 million U.S.). The government expected $5.1 billion ($4 billion U.S.) in revenues but planned to spend $5.45 billion ($4.4-billion U.S.), including $1.8 billion ($1.4 billion U.S.) on health care. David M. L. Farr

In ***World Book,*** see **Manitoba; Riel, Louis.**

Manufacturing. The manufacturing sector, which slumped badly in the last quarter of 1991, continued to sputter throughout 1992. According to a regional summary of United States business activity by the Federal Reserve System (the Fed), which sets the country's monetary policy, the economy continued to grow "at a slow and uneven pace," and "the manufacturing sector lost some momentum in much of the nation."

There were a number of reasons for this weak performance. Layoffs by businesses attempting to cut costs continued to shake consumer confidence, and consumers reacted by cutting their spending. With fewer orders from consumers, businesses cut orders to factories and postponed buying new equipment and building new plants.

Due to the breakup of the Soviet Union in December 1991, there was less need to produce military equipment and supplies. By 1992, the U.S. defense industry had lost 16.5 per cent of its output compared with 1990 levels. Defense contractors had accounted for two-thirds of U.S. factory jobs lost since 1990, and their backlog of unfilled orders had fallen by 12.4 per cent since mid-1991. Nearly 1.2 million defense-related jobs were expected to be cut between 1992 and 1994. (See **Armed forces.**)

Industrial production was soft for most of 1992. It fell 0.8 per cent in January, led by a large 8.2 per cent drop in auto production as car sales stalled. Production rose moderately thereafter, with a 0.5 per cent increase in February, the first increase since October 1991; a 0.3 per cent increase in March; and a 0.4 per cent increase in April, according to the Fed. Increases in production of furniture, paper, and business equipment, especially computers, led the growth. And as housing starts picked up, orders for building materials such as glass, wood, and plumbing surged between February and April 1992.

Production began to slide again in the second half of 1992, with a 0.3 per cent drop in August, and a 0.2 per cent dip in September, due largely to a strike against General Motors Corporation and slowing exports, which were still up 6.2 per cent through the first nine months of 1992 compared with the first nine months of 1991. Output rebounded 0.3 per cent in October, according to the Fed.

Factory orders. Factory orders totaled $2.84 trillion for 1991, down 2.7 per cent from 1990. This was the first annual decline since 1986. The situation improved modestly in 1992. In April 1992, orders were up 1.0 per cent from March levels, to $243.85 billion. After a small drop in May, June orders rose a substantial 2.4 per cent, to $244.2 billion. But in July, they fell again, down 1.1 per cent, to $241.76 billion, including a 25.8 per cent drop in defense orders. Orders slipped further in August but increased 1.3 per cent in September, to $239.44 billion. October saw a 1.7 per cent rise in orders—the second monthly rise in a row. The backlog of unfilled manufacturing orders declined for the 14th consecutive month, indicating that new orders would be filled by existing staff, not additional new workers.

Durable goods orders. *Durable goods* are those expected to last three years or more, such as home appliances. Orders for durable goods were up 1.5 per cent in January, including a 9.1 per cent jump in orders for nondefense capital goods, such as computers. Orders jumped 2.1 per cent in March to $122.59-billion. But after a 1.9 per cent gain in April, orders for durable goods fell an alarming 2.4 per cent in May, to $119.53 billion. May's decline was due partly to a 27.7 per cent plunge in defense orders, especially for aircraft. Orders tumbled another 3.4 per cent in July, 0.1 per cent in August, and 0.4 per cent in September, to $118.88 billion. But they jumped 4.1 per cent in October, the biggest increase in 15 months, to $124.66 billion.

Machine tools, used to bend, shape, and form metal, are used in the production of goods such as cars, airplanes, and appliances. This industry is looked upon as an indicator of the strength of industrial production and plans by manufacturers to invest in new equipment. Orders for machine tools dropped 36.7 per cent in January, but recovered 6.4 per cent in February to $231.4 million, according to the Association for Manufacturing Technology in McLean, Va. Gains came in large part from overseas orders.

Machine tool orders rose 9.3 per cent in March but fell back 9.4 per cent in April before plunging 28 per cent in May, to $159.12 million. Manufacturers were buying just enough equipment to continue running at current levels, but they were not expanding for the future. Orders leaped 31.1 per cent in June to $208.6 million, but export orders dropped. Drops in July and August were offset by a 77.1 per cent increase in September orders to $283.8 million, the largest month-to-month increase in 20 years. But orders slipped 24.9 per cent in October.

Capital spending. The U.S. Department of Commerce's quarterly surveys indicated that *capital spending* (investment in new equipment and plants) was expected to increase 4.6 per cent in 1992. There were significant cuts and increases in capital spending in 1992. In April, Cathay Pacific Airlines Limited of Hong Kong ordered 11 Boeing 777's, made by the Boeing Company of Seattle and worth $1.7 billion. United Airlines Incorporated of Elk Grove Village, Ill., in February postponed accepting the delivery of airplanes worth $3.6 billion from Boeing. The Mobil Corporation of Fairfax, Va., announced an $800-million cut in its capital expenditures budget, and in May, the Amoco Corporation of Chicago slashed its capital spending budget by 12 per cent, or $430 million, to $3.3 billion.

Not all of the capital expenditure news was bad. In June, German luxury carmaker Bayerische Motoren Werke AG (BMW) announced plans to build an assembly plant in Spartanburg, S.C. And the Intel Corporation, a semiconductor chip manufacturer, announced it would expand its Santa Clara, Calif., manufacturing plant and spend $1.2 billion on capital goods.

NAPM survey. Each month, the National Association of Purchasing Management surveys 300 industrial companies on orders, exports, and employment and confidence levels. Many view the survey results as an indication of the health of the manufacturing sector. Manufacturing accounts for 25 per cent of the U.S. *gross domestic product*—the value of all goods and services produced within a country in a given period. Generally, a reading above 50 per cent indicates the manufacturing sector is growing. At the end of 1991 and in January 1992, the index stood at 47.4 per cent, reflecting a declining manufacturing base.

The index had peaked at 54.3 per cent in September 1991, when it began to decline. But in February 1992, the index rose to 52.4 per cent, showing signs of expansion. In March, with strength in apparel, glass, paper, wood, and furniture, the index rose again, to 54.1 per cent. The index surged to 56.3 per cent in May, but it slipped to 50.6 per cent by October. In November, it rose again to 55 per cent.

Factory capacity. In December 1991, manufacturers used only 79 per cent of plant operating capacity. That level slipped to just 78 per cent in January 1992, according to the Fed, the lowest production capacity since August 1983, when the level of use was 76 per cent. In 1992, levels remained flat, with a 78.2 per cent reading in February followed by moderate monthly downturns and slight gains to 78.4 per cent in September and 78.5 per cent in October.

Employment. The manufacturing sector employs about 20 per cent of the U.S. work force. Manufacturers added 14,000 workers in February 1992, the first payroll increase since August 1991. By April 1992, the national unemployment rate stood at 7.2 per cent, having fallen for the first time since July 1991. Factories in April hired 8,000 more workers.

But in May, growth in overseas as well as domestic orders began to slow. Manufacturers cut 10,000 jobs in May and increased the factory work week to 41.3 hours.

With orders scarce and factories running at low capacity, manufacturers continued to reduce their payrolls to stay profitable and competitive. From May 1991 to May 1992, manufacturing lost more than 300,000 jobs. Defense cuts accounted for almost 40 per cent of these jobs. The jobless rate rose to 7.8 per cent in June, the highest rate since 1984. All told, manufacturers laid off 225,000 workers from May through October. Even the successful computer industry shed 50,000 jobs in 1992. Ronald Kolgraf

See also **Labor: What Is Happening to the U.S. Job Market?** In ***World Book,*** see **Manufacturing.**

Maryland. See **State government.**
Massachusetts. See **State government.**
Mauritania. See **Africa.**
Mauritius. See **Africa.**

Medicine. The world's first transplant of a baboon liver into a human being was carried out by surgeons at the University of Pittsburgh (Pa.) Medical Center on June 28, 1992. The patient was a 35-year-old man whose own liver was being destroyed by hepatitis B, a disease caused by a virus. A human liver transplant would not have worked because the virus remaining in the man's body also would have infected the new organ. But doctors hoped that the virus would not be able to attack the baboon liver. The man eventually died 71 days after the transplant, but his death was due to other causes.

Following the 11-hour transplant operation, the patient appeared to be recovering well. Doctors put him on a drug regimen to help prevent his body's immune system from rejecting the new organ.

By early August, the man's condition had improved markedly. But in late August, he developed a severe infection in his skull when doctors injected him with dye to provide contrast in an X ray. And on September 7, he died as a result of bleeding in his skull. Doctors later reported that the man had also been infected with the virus that causes AIDS, but they did not believe it played a part in his death.

The researchers said they would continue with their transplant program. Doctors are looking at animal-to-human transplants as a way to overcome the severe shortage of human donor organs. Researchers think baboons could become an important new source

Reports of silicone-gel breast implants that leak, left, led the U.S. Food and Drug Administration in April to allow their use only in health-risk studies.

of organs because they resemble humans anatomically, are not an endangered species, and breed easily in captivity. Another possibility is pigs, millions of whose organs go to waste when they are killed for food.

Using genes as a drug. The world's first therapy involving the direct injection of genetic material into a patient was performed in June at the University of Michigan Medical Center in Ann Arbor. The procedure was performed on a 67-year-old woman suffering from advanced melanoma, a skin cancer that is usually fatal. The genetic material consisted of many copies of a fragment of deoxyribonucleic acid (DNA) known as a *gene*. In previous gene-therapy experiments, researchers first removed cells from the patient's body, then added new genetic material in a lab and returned the modified cells to the patient. But the Michigan doctors did not extract any of the woman's cells. Instead, they packaged the genes inside microscopic spheres that can slip into cells and deliver the genes to the cell nucleus, where genetic instructions are carried out. The researchers then injected the spheres directly into the woman's tumor.

The gene in this procedure, when added to human cells, directs the cells to make a molecule called HLA-B7 that stimulates the immune system. The doctors wanted to force the woman's cancer cells to produce HLA-B7 so her immune system would destroy them. The doctors planned to monitor the woman to see if the gene injection helped her defeat the cancer.

Breast implant decision. After a long debate during 1991 and 1992 over the safety of silicone-gel breast implants, the United States Food and Drug Administration (FDA) in April 1992 announced that the implants would remain available to women. But the FDA restricted the implants almost solely to women participating in studies to measure the safety and effectiveness of the implants. These studies would be open mainly to women desiring silicone-gel implants for breast reconstruction following cancer surgery and not to women seeking the implants for cosmetic reasons. Breast implants are performed on about 150,000 women each year, according to the FDA.

The FDA's move was based on recommendations of an advisory panel that met in February 1992. The panel found it impossible to determine from existing data whether silicone-gel implants truly cause serious health problems. Some reports linked the implants to cancer or *autoimmune diseases*, in which the body attacks its own tissue. These reports had led some physicians, breast-implant recipients, and consumer groups to urge that the FDA ban the devices. But the advisory panel decided that the implants served an important psychological role in the treatment of breast-cancer patients and should remain on the market while studies are conducted to obtain conclusive safety data.

Michael Woods

See also **AIDS; Health issues.** In ***World Book,*** see **Cell; Medicine.**

Mental health. Psychiatric facilities for people with mental illness are so scarce in the United States that jails have begun to serve as the nation's largest mental institution, a study concluded in September 1992. The study, which tabulated data from 1,391 local jails around the country, was conducted by the Alliance for the Mentally Ill, a mental health support organization, and the Public Citizen Health Research Group, a health advocacy organization based in Washington, D.C. The study found that 29 per cent of the jails hold mentally ill people without any criminal charges because of the shortage of treatment centers. An additional 23 per cent of jails hold mentally ill people on minor charges such as vagrancy or disorderly conduct.

The study estimated that about 30,000 people with serious mental illnesses serve time in jails each day—7 per cent of the total jail population. These figures mark a return to levels of the criminalization of the mentally ill comparable to those that existed in U.S. jails during the early 1800's, according to psychiatrist E. Fuller Torrey, a principal author of the study.

Among the report's recommendations to remedy the situation were national legislation to make it illegal to hold the mentally ill in jail without charges and increased funding of community-based treatment programs for the mentally ill.

Depression finding. In an advance expected to improve the diagnosis and treatment of severe depression, researchers at the Washington University School of Medicine in St. Louis, Mo., in September reported the first direct identification of specific areas of the brain involved in clinical depression. Clinical depression, which affects about 12 million Americans, creates a profound sense of sadness, hopelessness, and loss of interest in life for long periods.

The researchers used a technique called positron emission tomography (PET), which produces images of the brain's chemical activity. The researchers studied 23 depressed individuals with a family history of the illness and 33 people who did not suffer clinical despression. In the depressed patients, the PET scans revealed increased activity in two areas of the brain, one near the front of the left side of the brain and the other in a nerve pathway in a structure in the center of the brain called the amygdala. In fact, the amygdala showed heightened activity even in individuals whose depression was in remission, suggesting that the structure may be a biological marker for a risk of clinical depression.

Supreme Court ruling. The Supreme Court of the United States in May limited the ability of states to force mentally ill defendants to take antipsychotic medication during trials for criminal offenses. The court ruled that states can force a defendant to take such medication only if they can prove that the treatment is both medically appropriate and essential for the safety of the defendant or those in contact with the defendant.

The case involved a Nevada man who was convicted of murder and sentenced to death in 1988. During the trial, he was forced to take large doses of a drug to control a severe form of mental illness called paranoid schizophrenia. Attorneys argued that the medication had made the man appear sane to the jury, thus interfering with his insanity defense.

Happy birthday? Researchers at the University of California in San Diego in September reported that birthdays influence when men and women die. The researchers studied 2,750,000 deaths from natural causes. They found that women were more likely to die in the week after their birthdays, but men were more likely to die right before their birthdays. The researchers suggested that, in general, women make an effort to live until their birthdays because they look forward to seeing loved ones, whereas men dread their birthdays because they are often the occasion for taking stock of their lives.

New Australian policy. Australia in May announced a new national policy for treating mentally ill people. The new policy emphasized *deinstitutionalization*—treating mentally ill people in general hospitals rather than in isolated mental institutions—and called for greater availability of mental health services in community facilities. Also, all states will be required to amend their laws to eliminate discrimination against people with mental illnesses. Michael Woods

See also **Psychology.** In ***World Book,*** see **Mental illness.**

Mexico. The North American Free Trade Agreement between the United States, Mexico, and Canada was signed by Mexico on Aug. 12, 1992. Trade representatives from the United States and Canada signed the agreement on the same day. To many Mexicans, the successful negotiation of the free trade pact represented a giant stride forward, evidence that Mexico had joined the world's developed nations. The free trade agreement was designed to reduce tariffs on goods traded among the three countries, but the legislatures of all three countries must ratify it before the agreement takes effect. There was little doubt that Mexico's Senate, where members of the president's party hold 61 of 64 seats, would ratify the pact.

U.S. lobbying. The Mexican government immediately began a lobbying campaign in the United States to persuade Americans that the agreement will help their economy. The Mexican Embassy in Washington, D.C., provided free studies showing anticipated U.S. business and job gains that would result from the agreement in each state and congressional district.

Seeking to ease fears of job losses in the United States, Mexican President Carlos Salinas de Gortari struck a deal with U.S. President George Bush in San Diego on July 14, whereby Mexico would open up its banking, insurance, and securities industries—sectors long closed to foreigners—to American and Canadian companies by the year 2000. Mexican trade representatives the next day announced that Mexico would pay

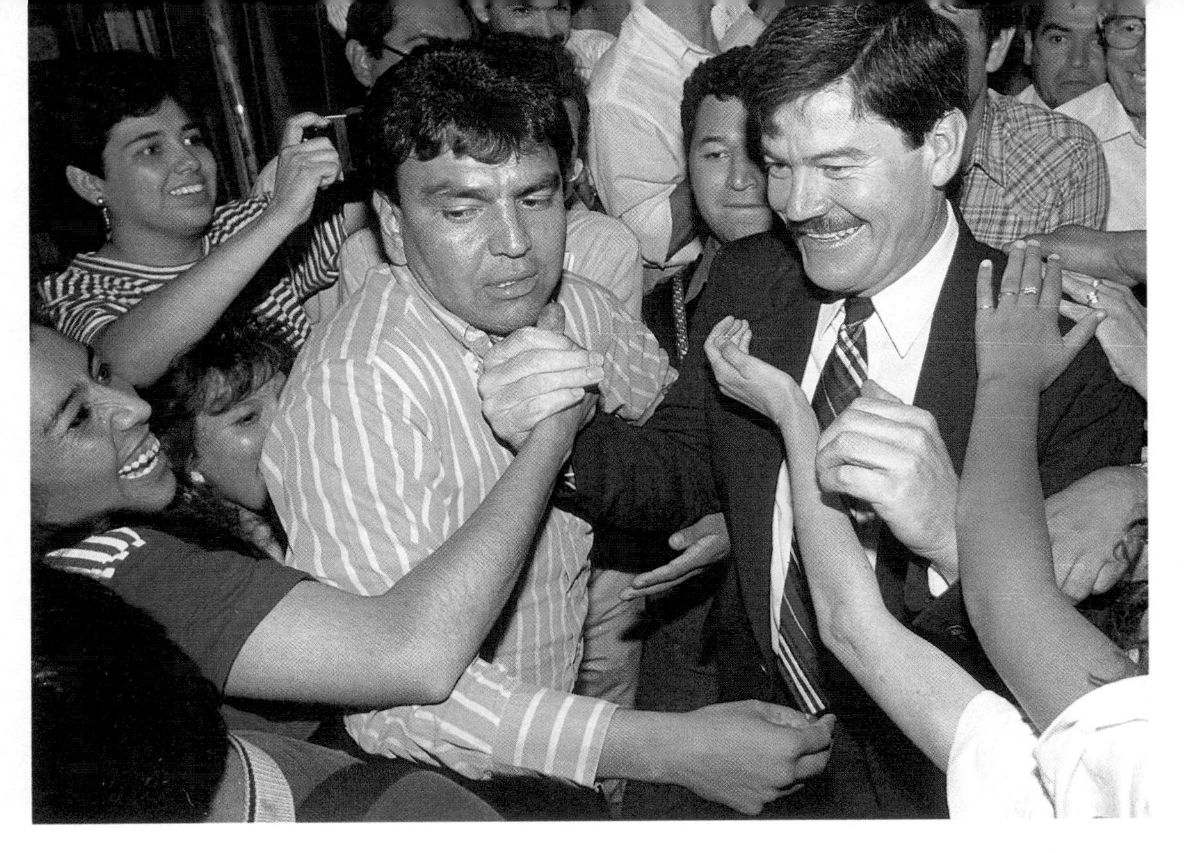

Supporters mob opposition candidate Francisco Barrio Terrazas, right, after he won the governorship of the Mexican state of Chihuahua in July.

bonuses to U.S. and Canadian oil drillers for work on Mexican oil contracts. This step seemed to widen the opening for foreign participation in the oil industry, which had been nationalized in 1936.

Gas explosion. On April 22, 1992, a series of explosions rocked a working-class neighborhood of Guadalajara, Mexico's second most populous city. At least 191 people were killed and hundreds more injured. Officials said a pipeline leaked gasoline into the sewers from a local refinery. In the wake of the disaster, nine city and national oil and gas company officials were indicted for negligence, and the governor of the state of Jalisco, in which Guadalajara is located, was forced to resign.

U.S. kidnapping. Mexicans were angry at a June 15 U.S. Supreme Court decision that gave U.S. authorities approval to kidnap persons wanted for trial in U.S. federal courts from foreign countries without following procedures set out in extradition treaties. The case at issue involved a Mexican doctor, Humberto Álvarez Machaín, whom U.S. agents abducted from Mexico in 1990 to stand trial on murder charges in the death of a U.S. narcotics agent in 1985.

On July 24, in response to popular anger over what Mexicans viewed as a clear violation of their sovereignty, Attorney General Ignacio Morales Lechuga announced that his country would no longer accept U.S. assistance in the fight against narcotics trafficking. On December 14, a U.S. judge dismissed the charges against the doctor for insufficient evidence.

Opposition wins. Other political parties began to break the monopoly in 1992 that Mexico's ruling Institutional Revolutionary Party (PRI) has traditionally enjoyed. On July 12, the opposition National Action Party's candidate, Francisco Barrio Terrazas, won the governorship of the northern border state of Chihuahua. It marked only the second time that an opposition candidate had won a governor's seat since the dominant PRI was organized in 1929.

In January, the national government, apparently motivated by a desire to clean up its own house, pressured Salvador Neme Castillo, the governor of the state of Tabasco, to resign in reaction to persistent public demonstrations alleging fraud at the ballot box. On October 6, the governor of the state of Michoacán, Eduardo Villaseñor, voluntarily stepped aside after popular demonstrations in which he was accused of winning the July election by fraud.

Vatican ties. On September 21, Mexico and the Vatican reestablished full diplomatic relations after a break of more than 130 years. The Mexican government in July had formally restored the Roman Catholic Church's right to own property and conduct religious education, though the church unofficially enjoyed these benefits for decades.

Nathan A. Haverstock

See also **Latin America** (Facts in brief table). In ***World Book,*** see **Mexico.**

Middle East

Israeli soldiers walk among tanks deployed at the Israel-Lebanon border in late October after rocket attacks on northern Israel by radical Muslims.

The United States-led coalition that ousted Iraqi forces from Kuwait in the Persian Gulf War (1991) felt less certain of its victory in 1992. Despite Iraq's military defeat and the punishing consequences of economic sanctions imposed by the United Nations (UN), Iraq's President Saddam Hussein clung to power. The war and its aftereffects continued to exact a toll on the economies of the Arab countries. In addition, a surge of Islamic fundamentalism and militant Kurdish nationalism, attributed in part to the war, produced civil violence and government crackdowns.

Although the Arab-Israeli peace talks showed some progress, Arab wariness about U.S. goals in the Mideast grew. Iran began to reassert itself as a regional power, much to the fear of its Arab neighbors. And despite calls by the United States and other major powers for a reduction in arms shipments to the Middle East, the flow of weapons into the region rose dramatically in 1992.

War losses. The Iraqi invasion of Kuwait and the Persian Gulf War seriously damaged the economies of many Arab countries, according to the Arab Economic Report. The report, released in September, is an annual study of Middle Eastern economic conditions based on information provided by leading Arab organizations. The study attributed much of the decline to the disruption in oil exports from Kuwait and Iraq and economic losses to other countries that depended on trade with Iraq and Kuwait. In addition, many countries lost tourist income and money sent home by citizens working in Iraq and Kuwait.

The study reported that the invasion and war cost Arab states an estimated $620 billion. Saudi Arabia, Kuwait, and other gulf states paid $84 billion to the United States, Great Britain, and France for military expenses and spent an additional $51 billion on logistical support for coalition troops. The report estimated that damage to oil fields, factories, roads, and other public works totaled about $160 billion in Kuwait and $190 billion in Iraq.

U.S. relations. During 1992, public opinion in the Middle East grew increasingly resentful of American involvement in the region's affairs. Ahmed Esmat Abdel-Maguid, secretary general of the Arab League, said on May 25 that many Arabs wanted the UN to ease its economic embargo against Iraq, imposed in 1990 after Iraq's invasion of Kuwait. The Arab League is an organization of 20 Middle Eastern and African countries and the Palestine Liberation Organization (PLO). Many Arabs also opposed UN sanctions imposed on Libya in March 1992 in an attempt to force Libya to turn over suspects in the terrorist bombings of U.S. and French aircraft. (See **Libya.**)

In 1992, many Arabs were also angered by what they charged was U.S. foot-dragging in diplomatic efforts to protect Bosnian Muslims from attacks by Christian Serbs and Croats in Bosnia and Hercegovina, a former republic of Yugoslavia. A number of Arab and Muslim states reportedly sent aid and weapons to the Bosnian Muslims. (See **Bosnia and Hercegovina.**)

Fragmenting Iraq. In August, Turkey, Syria, and Egypt—all members of the U.S.-led coalition against Iraq—criticized the United States, Great Britain, and France for issuing a "no-fly" order for southern Iraq. The order, which went into effect on August 27, prohibited Iraqi civilian and military aircraft from flying

south of the 32nd parallel. United States President George Bush contended that the order was necessary because of repeated attacks by Iraqi forces on Shiite Muslims in southern Iraq. The Shiites had rebelled against Hussein at the end of the Persian Gulf War.

Middle Eastern countries with large Kurdish populations also criticized Western support for efforts by Kurds to establish a self-governing homeland in northern Iraq. In April 1991, the United States, Great Britain, and France had established a protected zone for the Kurds in northern Iraq. In May 1992, Kurds in the protected zone held their first free elections, for a Kurdish parliament.

Egyptian and Syrian officials warned that dividing Iraq into military zones could lead to Iraq's breakup. Such fragmentation, they contended, would create a power vacuum on the eastern flank of the Arab world that Iran's revolutionary government would attempt to fill. On November 14, the foreign ministers of Iran, Syria, and Turkey, which have large Kurdish populations, publicly warned that the formation of an autonomous Kurdish zone threatened the stability of states neighboring Iraq.

Rearming. Middle Eastern countries purchased about $46 billion in arms between the end of the Persian Gulf War and October 1992, according to a report by the Congressional Research Service (CRS), an agency of the Library of Congress. The report also said that the United States had accounted for about half those sales.

Iraqi Kurds celebrate in May after holding their first free election to choose a leader and a legislature for a self-governing region in northeastern Iraq.

Representatives from the United States, Great Britain, France, China, and Russia—the world's top arms suppliers—failed at a meeting in May to reach agreement on limiting sales of conventional weapons to Mideast countries. Although China refused to approve a U.S. plan to provide advance notice of all such sales, the five nations agreed to cooperate in halting the spread of technology that could be used to produce biological, chemical, or nuclear weapons.

In September, however, Iran announced that China had agreed to provide it with a nuclear power plant. China's foreign ministry said the plant would be subject to UN inspections in compliance with the Nuclear Non-Proliferation Treaty. But after intense U.S. lobbying against the sale, Chinese officials indicated they might not follow through with the deal.

Over U.S. objections, cash-strapped Russia reportedly sold three nuclear submarines to Iran, the first of which was delivered in November. Russia, which could earn $750 million from the deal, contended that the sale would not affect Mideast stability or upset the region's balance of power.

On September 11, President Bush announced the sale of 72 F-15 fighter planes worth approximately $10 billion to Saudi Arabia. In 1992, nearly 40 per cent of all U.S. arms sales—$5.6 billion—went to Saudi Arabia, according to the CRS. The Bush Administration also reported in September that the United States would give Israel an additional $1 billion in military aid, which would include $650 million in Harpoon missiles as well as Apache and Black Hawk helicopters.

Arab-Israeli peace talks. The victory of Israel's Labor Party over the conservative Likud bloc in national parliamentary elections held on June 23 changed the tone if not the results of the ongoing peace talks between Israel and its Arab neighbors. In contrast to Likud, the Labor Party, headed by Yitzhak Rabin, had stated its willingness to exchange occupied land for a Middle East peace settlement.

For much of 1992, the peace talks remained stalemated, largely over the issue of Palestinian self-rule in the Israeli-occupied Gaza Strip and West Bank. But the sixth round of *bilateral* (one-on-one) talks—the first talks held since Rabin's confirmation as prime minister on July 13—produced a more substantive dialogue.

On August 25, one day after the sixth round began, Israel agreed for the first time that a 1967 UN resolution calling on Israel to withdraw from the occupied territories in exchange for a regional peace settlement applied to all territories captured by Israel in the 1967 Six-Day War. Among these territories was the Golan Heights, taken from Syria and later annexed. Previously, Israeli politicians had maintained that the resolution applied only to the Sinai Peninsula—returned to Egypt in 1982. On Aug. 31, 1992, Syria indicated a willingness to approve a peace settlement before the return of any land in the Golan Heights if Israel assured a future withdrawal.

Facts in brief on Middle Eastern countries

Country	Population	Government	Monetary unit*	Foreign trade (million U.S.$) Exports†	Imports†
Bahrain	565,000	Amir Isa bin Salman Al-Khalifa; Prime Minister Khalifa bin Salman Al-Khalifa	dinar (0.38 = $1)	3,758	3,711
Cyprus	720,000	President George Vassiliou (Turkish Republic of Northern Cyprus: Acting President Rauf R. Denktas)	pound (0.46 = $1)	960	2,621
Egypt	55,881,000	President Hosni Mubarak; Prime Minister Atef Sedky	pound (3.32 = $1)	3,800	11,400
Iran	57,966,000	Leader of the Islamic Revolution Ali Hoseini Khamenei; President Ali Akbar Hashemi Rafsanjani	rial (1,437 = $1)	12,300	11,600
Iraq	20,910,000	President Saddam Hussein	dinar (0.31 = $1)	392	4,834
Israel	4,810,000	President Chaim Herzog; Prime Minister Yitzhak Rabin	shekel (2.55 = $1)	11,889	16,906
Jordan	3,362,000	King Hussein I; Prime Minister Sharif Zeid bin Shaker	dinar (0.69 = $1)	902	2,512
Kuwait	2,216,000	Amir Jabir al-Ahmad al-Jabir al-Sabah; Prime Minister & Crown Prince Sad al-Abdallah al-Salim al-Sabah	dinar (0.30 = $1)	11,476	6,303
Lebanon	2,883,000	Prime Minister Rafik Hariri; President Ilyas Harawi	pound (1,975.00 = $1)	1,000	1,900
Oman	1,677,000	Sultan Qaboos bin Said Al-Said	rial (0.39 = $1)	5,215	2,681
Qatar	407,000	Amir and Prime Minister Khalifa bin Hamad Al-Thani	riyal (3.64 = $1)	2,600	1,400
Saudi Arabia	15,826,000	King & Prime Minister Fahd bin Abd al-Aziz Al-Saud	riyal (3.75 = $1)	44,417	24,069
Sudan	27,444,000	Revolutionary Command Council for National Salvation Chairman and Prime Minister Umar Hasan Ahmad al-Bashir	pound (100.00 = $1)	465	1,000
Syria	13,608,000	President Hafez al-Assad; Prime Minister Mahmud Zubi	pound (21 = $1)	3,143	3,151
Turkey	59,200,000	President Turgut Özal; Prime Minister Suleyman Demirel	lira (7,996.17 = $1)	13,603	20,019
United Arab Emirates	1,698,000	President Zayid bin Sultan Al-Nuhayyan; Prime Minister Maktum bin Rashid Al-Maktum	dirham (3.67 = $1)	15,000	9,000
Yemen	13,013,000	President Ali Abdallah Salih; Prime Minister Haydar Abu Bakr al-Attas	rial (18.00 = $1)	720	1,854

*Exchange rates as of Oct. 30,1992, or latest available data.
†Latest available data.

Palestinian issues. The sixth round of the talks also produced what may have been the first real progress toward resolving the conflict between Israelis and Palestinians. In August, Israel for the first time issued a proposal for holding elections in the Gaza Strip and the West Bank. Under the plan, elections would be held in spring 1993 to fill positions on a new administrative body to be called the Palestinian Administrative Council. The 13- to 15-member Palestinian council would control social, agricultural, educational, judicial, tax, environmental, and police affairs as the first step toward Palestinian self-rule. Palestinian representatives countered with a demand for the establishment of a 180-member legislature.

The seventh round of talks began on Oct. 21, 1992. Israel and Jordan showed the most progress by agreeing on a future agenda for peace talks. Talks between Israel and Lebanon broke down because of renewed fighting along the Israel-Lebanon border in October. Despite hard-line statements, Syria and Israel made some progress on mutual security arrangements and pledged to continue negotiations.

Multilateral talks—regional talks by all parties to the Mideast peace talks—were held in May. Conferences were devoted to arms control, water resources, refugees, the environment, and economic development. Syria and Lebanon boycotted the talks because in the bilateral negotiations Israel had refused to discuss surrendering some of its occupied territory in return for a peace settlement. Israel boycotted the con-

The last Western hostages held in Lebanon—German relief workers Heinrich Strübig, left, and Thomas Kemptner—are freed in Beirut in June.

ferences on refugees and economic development because the United States had agreed to allow Palestinians from outside the occupied territories to attend. On October 8, however, Israel announced it would attend future conferences on refugees and economic development, which were held in late October and early November, even though such Palestinians were present.

Border disputes. In 1992, Saudi Arabia began a campaign to claim an oil-rich territory controlled by neighboring Yemen, which supported Iraq in the Persian Gulf War. Saudi Arabia in June threatened possible military action against Western companies that were exploring for oil in the territory, which covers several thousand square miles.

On September 30, Saudi troops attacked a Qatari outpost on a disputed border area between Saudi Arabia and Qatar. Two soldiers died in the fighting. Saudi Arabia seized the outpost on October 1.

Iranian-Arab relations deteriorated as Iran attempted to gain sole control over three islands in the Persian Gulf. Iran and the United Arab Emirates (UAE) had jointly governed the islands since 1971, when Iranian troops occupied Abu Musa, the only one of the islands that is inhabited. After the UAE and seven other Arab countries complained to Iran about its "virtual annexation" of Abu Musa in early September, Iran declared its sovereignty over the three islands. Diplomatic efforts to resolve the dispute broke down on September 28 when Iran withdrew from the talks.

Arafat's crash. Yasir Arafat, the leader of the PLO, was injured in an airplane crash in the Sahara in southeastern Libya on April 7. On June 1, Arafat underwent brain surgery in Jordan to treat complications resulting from the crash. The accident renewed concerns about Arafat's domination of the PLO and fears that his death would leave the PLO in disarray.

Assassinations and terrorism. Atef Bseiso, the PLO's director of security and Arafat's intelligence chief, was assassinated by unknown gunmen in Paris on June 8. Walid Khalid, spokesman for a rival Palestinian group headed by terrorist Abu Nidal, was killed by unknown assailants in Beirut, Lebanon, on July 23.

Iraq, Iran, Libya, and Syria were accused of supporting terrorism in the U.S. Department of State's annual report on global terrorism, issued on April 30. The report linked Iraq, its allies in the Persian Gulf War, and groups sympathetic to Iraq to a 22 per cent rise in terrorist incidents in early 1991 compared with 1990 levels. International incidents by Palestinians, however, dropped by 50 per cent in 1991, according to the report.

BCCI scandal. A U.S. federal judge seized $104-million in U.S. assets of the ruling Al Nahyan family of the UAE in July 1992 to cover losses by four U.S. banks illegally controlled by the Bank of Credit and Commerce International (BCCI), a worldwide banking company. The Nahyans owned 77 per cent of the BCCI on

July 5, 1991, when banking regulators in seven countries closed bank offices, amid wide-ranging charges of fraud.

The U.S. government in July 1992 also fined two prominent Saudis involved in the BCCI scandal. Sheik Kamal Adham, former chief of Saudi Arabia's intelligence agency, agreed to pay $105 million in fines after admitting his participation in a BCCI conspiracy to buy a U.S. bank. Sheik Khalid Bin Mahfouz, a leading Saudi banker, was fined $170 million.

Environment. Environmental experts warned that severe pollution in the Mediterranean Sea off the coast of North Africa was affecting public health as well as fishing and other local industries. In September, the World Bank, a UN agency, reported that 606 short tons (550 metric tons) of pesticides and 717,000 short tons (650,000 metric tons) of petroleum products were dumped yearly into the Mediterranean Sea. In addition, nearly all sewage released into the Mediterranean from North Africa is untreated. Rampant population growth in North Africa was expected to intensify the problems.

Hostages released. The last Western hostages held in Lebanon—two German relief workers—were released on June 17. The two men had been seized in 1989. Christine Helms

See also articles on the various Middle Eastern countries. In ***World Book,*** see **Middle East** and individual Middle Eastern country articles.

Mining. The Newmont Gold Company of Denver, Colo., the largest gold producer in the United States, and the American Barrick Resources Corporation of Toronto, Canada, announced an agreement on Jan. 29, 1992, to jointly develop one of the world's largest gold deposits. The gold is in an area called the Carlin Trend, which is located near Elko, Nev. Ore deposits in the Carlin Trend contain an estimated 9 million troy ounces (280 million grams) of gold. Newmont owns about 5 million troy ounces (155 million grams) and American Barrick about 4 million troy ounces (124 million grams). But their properties and land claims overlap, making joint mining operations the most efficient way of exploiting the deposits, the companies said.

In February, Newmont officials also announced an agreement on a joint gold mining project with Uzbekistan, a former republic of the former Soviet Union. The mine is located about 250 miles (400 kilometers) northwest of Tashkent, the capital city. Uzbekistan, now an independent nation, has rich gold deposits and produced about 30 per cent of the estimated 400 short tons (360 metric tons) of gold mined each year in the former Soviet Union.

Chile's national parliament in May passed a law that permits foreign companies to invest in Codelco, the state-owned copper mining company. Codelco produces about half of Chile's copper and controls about one-third of the country's mineral resources. But the company lacked sufficient cash to modernize its operations. Other new joint ventures could follow.

The U.S. Bureau of Mines estimated in February 1992 that the nation's mines produced about $30.8-billion worth of metals and minerals during 1991, a decline of about 5.8 per cent from 1990. The figures included 21 nonfuel minerals, ranging from aluminum to zinc, that account for 95 per cent of total U.S. mine production. The bureau said that much of the decline was due to reduced demand for minerals used in the construction industry, which was affected by a slow recovery from the 1990-1991 economic recession.

The bureau said that 1992 production figures could show a slight improvement due to the Intermodal Surface Transportation Efficiency Act signed into law in December 1991. The act authorized $119 billion for the construction of highways and designated $31.5-billion for mass transit systems, which could boost demand for crushed stone, sand, and gravel for road construction and iron ore used to make steel for mass transit rail systems. Michael Woods

See also **Coal; Petroleum and gas.** In ***World Book,*** see **Mining.**

Minnesota. See **State government.**
Mississippi. See **State government.**
Missouri. See **State government.**
Moldova. See **Commonwealth of Independent States.**
Mongolia. See **Asia.**
Montana. See **State government.**

Montreal in 1992 celebrated the 350th anniversary of its founding while it faced one of the toughest economic years in its history. Overall unemployment dipped to 10 per cent over the summer but climbed to 12.5 per cent by November, as some of the largest core industries in the city went into bankruptcy or imposed massive layoffs. In the downtown area alone, about 25,000 white-collar workers lost their jobs during the year. The recession also dragged down small retailers, with some 400 stores and restaurants going out of business in the central shopping area around St. Catherine Street.

In the service industry, Air Canada, the national airline based in Montreal, announced on July 1 that it would eliminate 1,809 positions by November 1. The national railway, Canadian National, also based in Montreal, announced cutbacks to its work force in late summer and fall. Les Cooperants, a long-established insurance company and one of Quebec's financial mainstays, suddenly declared bankruptcy in May. The shut-down put about 1,000 people out of work and left vacant eight floors of a recently opened downtown office building.

In the retail industry, Steinberg Incorporated, owners of one of the largest grocery chains in the Montreal metropolitan area, sold off 107 of its stores to competitors and closed the remaining 16. Pascal's, a large hardware chain, simply closed its doors.

The festivities surrounding the city's 350th anniversary provided a little help to business by creating the first rise in tourism since 1988. The 6 per cent increase in tourist visits, however, was not enough to boost the hotel occupancy rate above the profit level.

Belt-tightening. The Montreal government responded to the city's economic difficulties with a series of major cutbacks in both essential services and in some of the large, costly projects it had previously planned. Police were told to spend less time in court for petty offenses, a decision predicted to save a little more than $1 million ($802,000 U.S.) a year. The number of accountants, attorneys, and consultants hired by the city also were reduced, saving $2.3 million ($1.8 million U.S.).

Money slated in the 1992 budget for industrial parks and recreational areas was reduced to $165 million ($132 million U.S.) from $184 million ($147 million U.S.). The city reduced funds for the construction of a courthouse to $30 million ($24 million U.S.) from $50-million ($40 million U.S.). Spending for new libraries dried up, and a plan for a new $55-million ($44-million U.S.) city library was abandoned.

Police problems. More than 2,500 Montreal police officers on February 13 staged a demonstration against their police chief, Alain Saint-Germain. They were protesting the chief's criticism of officers involved in the 1991 shooting death of an unarmed black man. However, the coroner's report on the killing, released May 7, 1992, criticized not only the officers involved in the slaying but the entire police force. It said that the killing was unjustified and represented a failure of the entire police department, where a "totally unacceptable" level of racism required "changes of attitude and behavior." On May 15, Quebec Public Security Minister Claude Ryan announced that the operations and conduct of the Montreal police department would be thoroughly investigated.

Campus killings. A man armed with three handguns went on a shooting spree on August 24 at Concordia University in downtown Montreal and killed four of the school's faculty members. The alleged gunman, Valery Fabrikant, an associate professor of mechanical engineering, had been denied tenure and had been quarreling with his colleagues about his research work. The incident reopened debate in Montreal about the need for stricter handgun laws.

Happy birthday, Montreal. Despite the problems the city faced in 1992, a joyous atmosphere prevailed at the public parties held from spring through fall. Beer and wine festivals, art exhibits, film fests, gourmet foods, ethnic dancing, comedy presentations, fireworks, and a circus helped the city celebrate its 350th birthday. Many events were free of charge and none were expensive.

Kendal Windeyer

See also **Canada; Quebec.** In ***World Book,*** see **Montreal.**

Morocco. Pressured by economic woes and demands for political reforms, the government of King Hassan II held a referendum on a new Constitution on Sept. 3, 1992. Voters overwhelmingly approved the Constitution, which expands parliament's powers. Government opponents, however, complained that under the new Constitution, Hassan retained the authority to preside over parliament and to appoint the prime minister. In addition, Hassan has the right to appoint five of the nine members of a new council responsible for proposing legislation.

Western Sahara. A referendum on the status of Western Sahara, originally scheduled for January and then postponed until September, failed to take place at all. The referendum was to decide whether Western Sahara, claimed by Morocco since the early 1970's, would gain its independence or become a province of Morocco. The United Nations (UN), which was to have supervised the referendum, said it could not guarantee a free vote.

Foreign policy. Concerned about anti-Western sentiment in the Arab world, Morocco in March cast one of five abstentions in a vote by the UN Security Council to impose sanctions against Libya for refusing to surrender for trial six men accused of involvement in the bombing of two civilian aircraft. (See **Libya.**)

Christine Helms

See also **Africa** (Facts in brief table); **Middle East.** In ***World Book,*** see **Morocco.**

Motion pictures. Three promising directors made their debuts in 1992: Carl Franklin, Quentin Tarantino, and Allison Anders. Franklin directed *One False Move,* a superbly detailed film about a robbery that goes awry. Tarantino was responsible for *Reservoir Dogs,* in which a failed jewelry heist leads to torture, murder, and betrayal. Anders' film, *Gas Food Lodging,* told of a middle-class single mother's attempts to cope with her two teen-age daughters. All three features enjoyed solid runs at cinemas devoted to art films.

"Yuppies in peril" was a prevalent theme in American movies throughout the year. These movies dealt with ambitious professionals who were terrorized by the worst nightmares of the upwardly mobile class. In *The Hand That Rocks the Cradle,* the villain was a psychopathic nanny; in *Unlawful Entry,* it was a crazed law officer; in *Single White Female,* a mad roommate; in *Consenting Adults,* over-the-edge neighbors. Audiences of all demographic groups seemed to enjoy seeing affluent people scared out of their wits.

Biographies and historical epics represented another film trend in 1992. Spike Lee's *Malcolm X* opened in November and was the most hotly discussed film of the year. The film traced the black leader's many incarnations, from petty thief to political activist to spiritual icon. Denzel Washington's portrayal of the title character was particularly impressive, as was Lee's direction, which sustained interest throughout the film's 3-hour, 21-minute running time. The film's highly sympathetic look at Malcolm X caused discussion, but few could deny the film's power.

Michael Mann, who created the trend-setting television series "Miami Vice," brought his hard-hitting style to a new version of the James Fenimore Cooper novel *The Last of the Mohicans.* Daniel Day-Lewis played the main character, Hawkeye, as a bold yet sensitive romantic, and Madeleine Stowe portrayed his love interest, Cora, as a sort of feminist frontier woman.

In *Hoffa,* Jack Nicholson won praise for his portrayal of the famous union leader Jimmy Hoffa. And John Goodman filled out the role of Babe Ruth in a movie for baseball lovers, *The Babe.*

The 500th anniversary of Christopher Columbus' landing in the New World inspired two film biographies of the explorer. Both sank without notice. *Christopher Columbus: The Discovery,* with Marlon Brando and Tom Selleck, returned to the cardboard-costume pictures of an earlier era. *1492: Conquest of Paradise* was a more dignified, if dull, epic featuring Gérard Depardieu, Armand Assante, and Sigourney Weaver.

Animation. In time for the holidays, the Walt Disney Company released *Aladdin.* The film's stylish, frantic animation departed from the classic form of Disney's 1991 success *Beauty and the Beast,* but the result was just as enjoyable. Robin Williams provided the voice of the talkative genie, who was capable of assuming disguises ranging from actors Arnold Schwarzenegger to Robert De Niro. The film was an instant critical and commercial smash, setting a new box-office record for an animated feature with an opening four-day gross of $21.5 million.

Other animated features did not fare as well. *FernGully . . . The Last Rainforest,* with Robin Williams doing the voice of a bat, was a disappointment. Ralph Bakshi's ambitious, occasionally lurid *Cool World,* which combined animation with live action, was a flop with both critics and audiences. The British animated feature *Freddie As F.R.O.7.* was at best a modest success, while *Bebe's Kids, Little Nemo,* and *Rover Dangerfield* all failed to draw sizeable audiences.

Year-end entertainment. As with many previous years, some of the best films were reserved for the final months of the year. Francis Ford Coppola's elaborate version of *Bram Stoker's Dracula* met varying critical response. Some critics dismissed it for its "commercial" aspects, while others jeered its mixture of comedy, horror, and Gothic gloom. But all were impressed with the look of the film and with its surging romanticism.

The crowd-pleasing *Home Alone 2: Lost in New York* brought the expressive Macaulay Culkin back to the business of outwitting bumbling bad guys Daniel Stern and Joe Pesci. The sequel collected $74.2 million at the box office in its first 12 days.

A Few Good Men won critical and popular endorsement with its story of murder on a military base.

Jodie Foster and Anthony Hopkins won the Academy Awards for Best Actress and Actor for *The Silence of the Lambs* in March.

Critics praised the performances of Tom Cruise as a Navy lawyer and Jack Nicholson as a tradition-bound Marine colonel.

Robert Downey, Jr., received praise for his portrayal of legendary comic Charlie Chaplin in Sir Richard Attenborough's biography *Chaplin.* Other critically praised performances at the end of 1992 were those of Al Pacino as a blind man espousing the joys of life in *Scent of a Woman* and Robin Williams as the heir to a toy firm who attempts to thwart his evil uncle in *Toys.* The popular Mel Gibson had the most romantic part of his career in the heartwarming fantasy *Forever Young,* which sought to rekindle the simple joys of movies of the 1940's.

Exploring the dark side. Director Robert Altman won some of the best reviews of his distinguished, unorthodox career with *The Player.* The director of such previous critical favorites as *M*A*S*H* (1970) and *Nashville* (1975), this time held a mirror to Hollywood's hypocrisy and deceit. The story tells of a young studio executive, played by Tim Robbins, who does everything possible to hold his own among Hollywood sharks. Robbins also directed, wrote, and starred in his own exposé of corruption in *Bob Roberts,* a hilarious, if broadsided, story of a right-wing folk singer who runs for President.

Two Hollywood icons of the 1970's made impressive features as directors of 1992 films. Robert Redford, directing only his second film since winning an

The Best Intentions, written by Swedish director Ingmar Bergman, won the Cannes Film Festival's top award in May.

Academy Award in 1981 for *Ordinary People*, made a critically acclaimed version of Norman Maclean's haunting story *A River Runs Through It.* Tom Skerritt, portraying a stoic minister in a small Montana town, Craig Sheffer as his dutiful son, and Brad Pitt as his rebellious son, all won solid reviews.

Clint Eastwood had one of his biggest successes, as both actor and director, with *Unforgiven.* Eastwood played a poor farmer, once a notorious gunfighter, who reluctantly returns to violence to earn a bounty for avenging the disfiguring of a prostitute.

Other films that stood out from the Hollywood norm included Paul Schrader's *Light Sleeper,* with Willem Dafoe as a drug delivery man vacillating in his desire for a better life. And James Foley's adaptation of David Mamet's searing, if talky, play, *Glengarry Glen Ross,* dramatized the unethical behavior of real estate salesmen, played by Al Pacino, Jack Lemmon, Ed Harris, Kevin Spacey, Alec Baldwin, and Alan Arkin.

Blockbusters. As expected, *Batman Returns* was the biggest hit of 1992. Nevertheless, the film was something of a commercial disappointment. Grossing about $160 million in the United States, the spectacular Tim Burton fantasy, released in June, ran almost $100 million behind the box-office tally of its 1989 predecessor *Batman.* Moreover, sales of *Batman Returns* toys and posters fell far short of the $500 million earned by merchandise inspired by the first film. Critics hailed the film's visual style and psychologically dark undercurrents. But some audiences found the movie too disturbing and violent. Michelle Pfeiffer, in the role of Catwoman, won major critical endorsement, leaving Danny DeVito's ill-mannered, vindictive Penguin and Michael Keaton's wan Batman far behind, in the critics' views.

The summer's other high-voltage blockbuster was *Lethal Weapon 3,* in which Mel Gibson and Danny Glover reteamed as a manic young cop and responsible older cop. Like *Batman Returns,* this action comedy opened to enormous business, then fell off rapidly. As a result, the summer films of strongest endurance turned out to be two pictures about two very different groups of women.

In *Sister Act,* Whoopi Goldberg portrayed a Reno lounge singer who disguised herself as a nun after witnessing a gangland murder. In *A League of Their Own,* Geena Davis and Madonna were players with the All American Girls Professional Baseball League, which had flourished during World War II (1939-1945) when many male players were off at war.

Sex arouses ire. One of the year's most publicized movies was the steamy psychological thriller *Basic Instinct,* in which Michael Douglas played a gritty detective attracted to a possible killer, portrayed by Sharon Stone. The film was controversial not only because of its erotic content but also for its depiction of lesbians and bisexuals. Homosexuals called for a boycott of the movie.

Unflattering portraits of gay characters could also be found in such films as *Swoon, The Living End,* and *Edward II.* However, the stereotype of the kind, gay confidante resurfaced in *Single White Female.*

Other films also aroused debate over their sexual content. *The Lover* was about a 1929 romance in Vietnam between an impoverished French teen-ager and a Chinese playboy almost twice her age. *Bad Lieutenant* depicted a ruthless policeman pursuing a nun's rapist. *Damage,* directed by Louis Malle and starring Jeremy Irons, dealt with an affair between a sophisticated man and his son's fiancee. *Bad Lieutenant* received the rarely used NC-17 rating for its explicit sexual content.

International winners. Foremost among the year's art-film triumphs was *Howards End,* an elegant adaptation of E. M. Forster's novel about the social classes in early 1900's England. The performances of Emma Thompson, Anthony Hopkins, Vanessa Redgrave, and Helena Bonham Carter contributed to the film's success.

Other quiet successes included *Mississippi Masala,* a romance between a black man, played by Denzel Washington, and a woman of East Indian ancestry, played by Sarita Choudhury, who lived in a small town in the American South. *Indochine* gave Catherine Deneuve one of her best roles as a woman who discovers that she and her daughter love the same man. *The Hairdresser's Husband* was a lyrical examination of obsessive love. *Tous les matins du monde* presented Gérard Depardieu as a failed musician in the court of Louis XIV. *Enchanted April* told a cozy tale of four British women liberated by a trip to Italy. *The Best Intentions,* from a screenplay by Ingmar Bergman, relayed the courtship and marriage of the famous Swedish director's tragically mismatched parents.

Down the drain. The year had its share of unexpected flops. Woody Allen's *Husbands and Wives,* about a pair of couples experiencing drastic changes in their relationships, earned the wryly comic Allen his best reviews in years. Judy Davis' performance as a high-strung career woman was singled out for particular praise. However, the comedy-drama was released at the peak of unsavory publicity for Allen, who was involved in a heated child-custody case with his former companion and co-star Mia Farrow. The public, perhaps feeling an excess of publicity surrounding the couple, stayed away.

Hero, a somewhat cynical update of old-time populist comedy, starred Dustin Hoffman, Andy Garcia, and Geena Davis and was the year's most unexpected box-office flop. Garcia portrayed a flawed hero, while Hoffman played a heroic bum. Praise for actress Meryl Streep's comic skills could not turn *Death Becomes Her* into a hit, while Robert De Niro's energetic turn as a street hustler did not lure audiences to *Night and the City.* Philip Wuntch

See also **Hopkins, Anthony.** In ***World Book,*** see **Motion picture.**

Academy Award winners in 1992

Best Picture, *The Silence of the Lambs.*
Best Actor, Anthony Hopkins, *The Silence of the Lambs.*
Best Actress, Jodie Foster, *The Silence of the Lambs.*
Best Supporting Actor, Jack Palance, *City Slickers.*
Best Supporting Actress, Mercedes Ruehl, *The Fisher King.*
Best Director, Jonathan Demme, *The Silence of the Lambs.*
Best Original Screenplay, Callie Khouri, *Thelma and Louise.*
Best Screenplay Adaptation, Ted Tally, *The Silence of the Lambs.*
Best Cinematography, Robert Richardson, *JFK.*
Best Film Editing, Joe Hutshing and Pietro Scalia, *JFK.*
Best Original Score, Alan Menken, *Beauty and the Beast.*
Best Original Song, Howard Ashman and Alan Menken, "Beauty and the Beast" from *Beauty and the Beast.*
Best Foreign-Language Film, *Mediterraneo* (Italy).
Best Art Direction, Dennis Gassner and Nancy Haigh, *Bugsy.*
Best Costume Design, Albert Wolsky, *Bugsy.*
Best Sound, Tom Johnson, Lee Orloff, Gary Rydstrom, and Gary Summers, *Terminator 2: Judgment Day.*
Best Sound Effects Editing, Gary Rydstrom and Gloria S. Borders, *Terminator 2: Judgment Day.*
Best Makeup, Stan Winston and Jeff Dawn, *Terminator 2: Judgment Day.*
Best Animated Short Film, *Manipulation.*
Best Live-Action Short Film, *Session Man.*
Best Feature Documentary, *In the Shadow of the Stars.*
Best Short Subject Documentary, *Deadly Deception: General Electric, Nuclear Weapons and Our Environment.*

Mozambique. See **Africa.**

Marlene Dietrich: A Legend Passes

By Philip Wuntch

Marlene Dietrich, the glamorous motion-picture actress and cabaret singer whose smoky voice and seductive manner made her an international legend, died on May 6, 1992. One of Hollywood's biggest stars in the 1930's and 1940's, she had, in fact, rather limited acting abilities. But for more than 50 years, she captivated fans with an image that combined a provocative sexuality with studied nonchalance.

To the end, her timing was perfect. A sensuous photograph of Dietrich taken from her 1932 film *Shanghai Express* had been chosen to publicize the 1992 international film festival in Cannes, France, which opened on the day after her death. When news of her demise reached the public, her face adorned billboards across France.

The author:

Philip Wuntch is the film critic for the *Dallas Morning News.*

Dietrich was born to a police lieutenant and his wife in Berlin, Germany, probably on Dec. 27, 1901. (She was reluctant to answer questions about the important dates in her life—especially the year of her birth.) When a hand injury frustrated her plans for a career as a concert violinist, she turned to drama. She adopted the name Marlene—a contraction of her given names, Maria Magdalene—to disguise her identity because her middle-class family frowned on her entry into the theater.

In the 1920's, Dietrich won some notice in Europe playing small parts in German films and stage productions. Then, in 1930, she was "discovered" by American movie director Josef Von Sternberg, who cast her as the female lead in the German-made film *The Blue Angel,* released later that year. Dietrich's performance as Lola Lola, a cabaret singer who entrances a naive professor, created an international sensation.

Von Sternberg brought Dietrich to the United States and devoted his next six films to establishing her as a star. He found Dietrich's beautiful but impassive face to be the perfect centerpiece for the exotic sets and costumes he loved. Never the vamp, Dietrich managed to convey a charged sexuality with only subtle facial movements.

Dietrich and Von Sternberg's second collaboration was *Morocco* (1930), in which Dietrich portrayed a cabaret singer who spurns and then discovers her love for a soldier in the Foreign Legion. It was the only film for which she received an Academy Award nomination. She and Von Sternberg went on to create *Dishonored* (1931), about a spy who turns traitor for love; *Shanghai Express,* in which she played a prostitute who sacrifices herself for a former lover; *Blonde Venus* (1932), about a romantic triangle involving a cafe singer; *The Scarlet Empress* (1934), a lavish, fantasized depiction of the life of Russia's Catherine the Great; and *The Devil Is a Woman* (1935), the story of a temptress who corrupts a soldier.

Initially, Paramount Pictures promoted Dietrich as competition for Greta Garbo, another alluring European-born actress who worked for Metro-Goldwyn-Mayer. But the differences between them soon became clear. Dietrich was more scornful of men than Garbo was. Yet she often was willing—at least on screen—to sacrifice everything for a man. Insinuating and glamorous, she also colored many of her roles with a hint of mannishness. Her movie wardrobes, for example, frequently included mannish clothes, a style she continued offscreen by wearing trousers before it was socially acceptable for women to do so.

Ironically, Dietrich's star appeal outpaced her box-office success. She had remarkably few big hits. Several of her movies, including *The Scarlet Empress* and *The Devil Is a Woman,* were appreciated by film scholars only in retrospect—and then only for their cinematic adventurousness, such as the use of outlandish camera angles.

By the mid-1930's, audiences had wearied of seeing Dietrich portray jaded sophisticates, and her box-office popularity declined. Her response was to redefine her image by turning to comedy. In *Desire* (1936), she played a chic jewel thief who falls for an unsophisticated automobile engineer. In the smash hit *Destry Rides Again* (1939), she played a glamorous saloon keeper opposite James Stewart's bashful sheriff.

Alfred Hitchcock, who directed Dietrich in *Stage Fright* (1950), was astounded by her knowledge of lighting, costume, and set design. But her perfectionism about the technical aspects of moviemaking contributed to a reputation she had for being demanding.

Dietrich was an outspoken critic of the tyrannies of Nazi Germany beginning in the 1930's and refused to return to Germany after filming *Knight Without Armor* (1937) in Great Britain. She became a United States citizen in 1939. During World War II (1939-1945), Dietrich made few movies. Instead, beginning in March 1943, she risked her life entertaining Allied soldiers at the front. After the war, she received the Medal of Freedom, the highest civilian honor bestowed by the U.S. government.

In the 1950's, with movie roles becoming scarce, she again altered her image by turning to the cabaret stage with remarkable success. As part of her act, she often downplayed her screen career, claiming her movies were trivial. Yet many of the songs she spotlighted in her nightclub act were those she had sung onscreen. Among them were "Falling in Love Again" from *The Blue Angel* and "The Boys in the Back Room" from *Destry Rides Again.*

For 20 years, Dietrich's name alone assured record audiences at nightclubs in the United States and Europe. When she finally returned—somewhat apprehensively—to Berlin in 1960 for a concert performance, she was warmly received.

She was rarely seen off-stage, however, avoided fans, and almost never granted press interviews. In the mid-1970's, she left the nightclub circuit. Her final screen appearance—a cameo role—came in *Just a Gigolo* (1978), which flopped.

Dietrich's performance as the enticing cabaret singer Lola Lola in the 1930 motion picture *The Blue Angel* created an international sensation.

During the last 10 years of her life, Dietrich rarely left her apartment in Paris or saw others, though she regularly telephoned her family and friends. Such was her vanity and insistence on privacy that when actor-director Maximilian Schell filmed *Marlene,* his biographical study of her in 1984, she refused to be photographed. She consented only to have her unmistakable voice used for the candid, unsentimental narration.

Dietrich was married only once, to casting director Rudolf Sieber, who eventually retired from the film industry and took up chicken farming in California. Their marriage, which was largely a long-distance union, produced one daughter, Maria. By all reports, Dietrich was a devoted mother and, later, grandmother, who often wheeled her grandsons' baby carriages through New York City's Central Park.

Generous, intelligent, and witty, she had an array of famous admirers during her lifetime. American author Ernest Hemingway, a longtime friend, said of her, "If she had only her voice, she would break your heart." Italian director Franco Zeffirelli remarked on "her severity, her toughness, her warrior ways."

In 1959, the Museum of Modern Art in New York City honored Dietrich with a film tribute. On that occasion, Dietrich, who was always pragmatic about her career and her legend, said, "I don't ask whom you are applauding—the legend, the performer, or me. I personally liked the legend, not that it was easy to live with. But I felt privileged to witness its creation at such close quarters. And it served me well."

Mulroney, Brian (1939-). Brian Mulroney pondered his future in the closing months of 1992. Despite his major accomplishments during eight years in office, the public-approval rating of Mulroney's Progressive Conservative Party, at historically low levels during much of his term and at 12 per cent in 1991, climbed to only a weak 15 per cent by October 1992.

A poll released on October 9 showed that Mulroney was the least trusted among the nation's major political leaders. More than 50 per cent of people polled said they had no trust at all in the prime minister. Another poll, reported on October 17, found that 60 per cent of Canadians thought Mulroney should either resign or call a national election if the constitutional revisions he had ardently campaigned for were rejected. Canada did vote down the revisions on October 26, but Mulroney's Cabinet and his supporters in Parliament stood behind him as he announced that he intended to lead his government in the next federal election in 1993. He said he would focus on the economy and implementation of the recently signed North American Free Trade Agreement. David M. L. Farr

See also **Canada.** In ***World Book,*** see **Mulroney, Brian.**

Music. See **Classical music; Popular music.**

Myanmar. See **Burma.**

Namibia. See **Africa.**

Nebraska. See **State government.**

Nepal. See **Asia.**

Netherlands. The year 1992 was marked in the Netherlands by difficult economic times and by concern for the future of the Maastricht Treaty, a blueprint for European economic and political union named for the Dutch city where it was approved in December 1991. The Netherlands had played a major role in drawing up the treaty (officially called the Treaty on European Union), which would affect the 12 nations of the European Community (EC or Common Market).

European union threatened. In February 1992, EC leaders met at a gala ceremony in Maastricht to sign the treaty, which calls for a united Europe with a single currency and a federal government structure by the end of the decade. But after the signing, unity began to unravel. The treaty, which must be ratified by all 12 EC countries before it takes effect, was rejected by Danish voters in June and only narrowly approved in a French referendum in late September. Doubts about its future increased after a financial crisis in mid-September caused the temporary unraveling of the European Monetary System, an organization that links the values of its members' currencies. The Netherlands, which stayed in the system during the crisis, continued to support rapid European integration.

Economic issues. The Netherlands had a 1992 budget deficit of more than 4 per cent of the country's gross domestic product (GDP), the value of all goods and services produced. In September, the government announced a tough 1993 budget that cuts government spending, especially on the generous social security and disability benefits that nearly one in seven Dutch workers receive. The budget aims for a 1993 deficit of about 3.4 per cent of GDP. Guidelines under the Maastricht Treaty call for EC members to have budget deficits of 3 per cent of GDP or less.

The future of the partly state-owned aircraft maker NV Fokker created a political storm in 1992. The company sought to merge with an international consortium led by Deutsche Aerospace AG, in a deal that would give the German company control of the firm. The Dutch government, which owns about 32 per cent of Fokker, blocked the deal for months until it received concessions from the Germans in November. The Dutch had worried that the Germans would cut airplane production and jobs in the Netherlands to move them to countries with lower costs.

Popular Prime Minister Ruud Lubbers said in May that he would step down in 1994. He said he favored Elco Brinkman, a member of parliament from Lubbers' party, the Christian Democratic Appeal, as his successor. Observers thought Lubbers might seek the job of president of the European Commission, the EC's executive branch. Jacques Delors of France was reappointed to that post in 1992, but he was expected to leave when his term ends in 1994. Philip Revzin

See also **Europe** (Facts in brief table). In ***World Book,*** see **Netherlands.**

Nevada. See **State government.**

New Brunswick. Premier Frank J. McKenna's government in 1992 faced official opposition for the first time in four years. The Liberal Party, which once held all 58 seats in the legislature, had lost 12 seats to three other parties in the September 1991 elections.

The provincial budget, announced on March 31, 1992, forecast a deficit of $135 million ($108 million U.S.) on expenditures of $4 billion ($3.2 billion U.S.). In an effort to save money, the plan called for the abolition of 750 public service jobs, but it lifted the wage freeze of the previous year and replaced it with limited increases. The budget suspended public service contracts for two more years and allowed a wage increase for public-sector workers of no more than 3 per cent. In response, half of the province's 40,000 public sector workers engaged in a series of illegal strikes.

A report on New Brunswick's schools, released on May 7, advocated a longer school year, increased testing, a stronger core curriculum for the first nine years of schooling and more mathematics and science during high school. The government positioned itself to implement the suggestions by merging English- and French-language school boards, reducing the number of boards from 42 to 18, and transferring the resulting savings to the school budget. David M. L. Farr

New Hampshire. See **State government.**

New Jersey. See **State government.**

New Mexico. See **State government.**

New York. See **State government.**

New York City. Mayor David N. Dinkins and the City Council agreed on Oct. 29, 1992, to establish an independent 13-member civilian review board to investigate complaints against police officers. The new board replaced a 12-member board on which half the members were appointed by the police commissioner. The action was one of several developments in 1992 involving the police department.

In the year's most publicized incident, a police officer on July 3 fatally shot José Garcia, a suspected drug dealer from the Dominican Republic, in the Washington Heights section of the borough of Manhattan. Residents of the predominantly Dominican neighborhood marched on a local police station on July 6 to protest the shooting and were met by police in riot gear. The confrontation led to three nights of rioting. City officials feared the protests would jeopardize the Democratic National Convention, due to be held at New York City's Madison Square Garden July 13 to 16.

Community leaders and a strong police presence defused the protest while Mayor Dinkins walked the streets and, in the face of police union criticism, expressed sympathy to Garcia's widow. A Manhattan grand jury in September exonerated the officer who shot Garcia, saying he had acted in self-defense.

About 10,000 police officers staged an anti-Dinkins rally on September 16 in response to the mayor's frequent criticism of the department and to his proposal to establish a civilian review board to oversee the police. The officers stormed City Hall and blocked traffic on the Brooklyn Bridge.

New police commissioner. On August 3, Police Commissioner Lee P. Brown resigned, saying he wanted to be able to spend more time with his ailing wife. On October 16, Dinkins appointed Raymond W. Kelly, 51, a Harvard-educated veteran of the New York City force, to succeed Brown. Kelly agreed to work with the civilian review board.

Trump project. Developer Donald Trump's proposal for Riverside South, a $3-billion "city-within-the-city" to be built on a vacant rail yard on Manhattan's West Side, won the unanimous approval of the City Planning Commission on October 26. The project will include a 21-acre (8.5-hectare) waterfront park, Manhattan's largest after Central Park; housing for 15,000 residents; and subway improvements.

The courts. John Gotti, reputed head of the Gambino crime family, the most powerful of New York's five Mafia families, was convicted in federal court on April 2 on 13 charges of murder and racketeering. On June 23, Gotti was sentenced to life in prison without parole. (See **Courts.**)

On January 3, four of seven young men convicted in December 1991 of attacking and killing Brian Watkins, a tourist from Utah, on a subway platform in

A replica of Christopher Columbus' ship the *Niña* sails into New York Harbor on June 26 to take part in a celebration of Columbus' arrival in America.

1990, were each sentenced to 25 years to life in prison. In April 1992, the three remaining defendants were convicted of robbery and murder, and in May they were also sentenced to 25 years to life in prison.

On October 30, a jury in the borough of Brooklyn acquitted Lemrick Nelson, 17, of murder and manslaughter in the August 1991 stabbing death of Yankel Rosenbaum. Rosenbaum, a Jewish scholar from Australia, was attacked by a crowd of black youths during disturbances in Brooklyn that erupted after a Jewish driver accidentally struck and killed a 7-year-old black child, Gavin Cato. Police officers had testified that Nelson was found with the murder weapon and confessed to the stabbing, and that he was identified by the dying Rosenbaum as the assailant. But the jury found that the police testimony contained discrepancies. The verdict created outrage in the city's Jewish community.

On November 7, Federal Bureau of Investigation agents in New York City arrested Sol Wachtler, chief judge of the New York state Court of Appeals, the state's highest court. Wachtler was charged with trying to blackmail his former girlfriend, Joy Silverman, and threatening her teen-age daughter. Wachtler, 62, had been mentioned as a possible candidate for the New York governorship in 1994. He was confined to a psychiatric ward and on November 10 announced his resignation from the bench. Owen Moritz

See also **City.** In ***World Book,*** see **New York City.**

New Zealand. Economic and social reforms begun in New Zealand in the mid-1980's appeared to be finally taking hold in 1992. In August, Prime Minister James B. Bolger announced that the economy had its first surplus in the *balance of payments* since 1973. The balance of payments is a record of the value of all economic transactions that one nation has with other nations during a certain period.

New Zealand exports reached a record $NZ 17.2-billion (about $9.1 billion U.S.) for the fiscal year ending June 30. This was $NZ 2 billion (about $1.1 billion U.S.) more than in the previous fiscal year. Although more than three-quarters of the increase came from New Zealand's traditional exports—meat, wool, and dairy products—exports of manufactured goods rose about 20 per cent over the previous year.

New Zealand's *gross domestic product* (the total value of all goods and services produced within a nation's boundaries) was expected to rise by more than 2 per cent in 1992. And with inflation at 1 per cent, New Zealand had the lowest rate of price increases among Western industrialized nations.

Unemployment afflicted more than 10 per cent of the work force throughout 1992. In September, the government projected that unemployment would go even higher because it will take time for the growth in exports to boost investment and create new jobs.

Weather woes. Drought in crucial catchment areas reduced hydroelectric dam reservoirs to their lowest levels in more than 60 years. In June 1992, normally a dry winter month in New Zealand, consumers were asked to cut power use by 10 per cent to avoid blackouts. Rains late in the season restored lake levels, but the government instituted an inquiry to find out why emergency measures were not taken sooner.

In September, the worst snowstorms in decades blanketed South Island. The government estimated that more than a million sheep and lambs died in drifts up to 10 feet (3 meters) deep. Farmers said the losses would cost them about $NZ 40 million ($21-million U.S.).

Murders. Two mass killings stunned New Zealand, where such crimes are a rarity. In May, a 64-year-old farmer in a small settlement near Auckland, New Zealand's largest city, killed six members of his family, then took his own life. In June, in Masterton, a town northeast of Wellington, the nation's capital, a 25-year-old man killed seven people, including his three sons, and wounded another man. He was found guilty of murder and sentenced to life imprisonment.

United Nations Security Council seat. Prime Minister Bolger successfully promoted New Zealand's bid for one of two nonpermanent seats on the United Nations (UN) Security Council. The UN vote in October gave New Zealand the seat over Sweden. The other seat went to Spain. Gavin Ellis

See also **Asia** (Facts in brief table). In ***World Book,*** see **New Zealand.**

Newfoundland. The largest single layoff in Canadian history hit Newfoundland in July 1992 when federal Fisheries Minister John Crosbie announced a two-year shut-down of the inshore cod fishery located on the province's east coast. The fishery supported about 20,000 fishermen and plant workers living in 400 communities. Severely declining stocks of cod and capelin prompted the government decision, which came on the heels of a February ruling that had slashed cod quotas at the offshore fishery by 35 per cent.

Fleets from Spain, Portugal, and other countries were blamed for diminishing the cod stocks by overfishing the waters of the Grand Banks, which are just beyond Canada's 200-mile (322-kilometer) controlled fishing zone. Newfoundlanders also criticized conservationists for forcing an end to seal hunting, which allowed the cod-eating seal population to increase. After talks with the Canadian government, the European Community agreed to suspend its fishing temporarily near the 200-mile zone and to respect the international fishing quotas for the North Atlantic.

Newfoundland suffered another blow in February when Gulf Canada Resources pulled its 25 per cent stake out of the partnership developing the $5.2-billion ($4.1-billion U.S.) Hibernia oil project off the province's east coast. The move delayed the project's completion until at least 1997. David M. L. Farr

See also **Canada; Petroleum and gas.** In ***World Book,*** see **Newfoundland.**

Newsmakers of 1992 included the following:

Woody and Mia. Filmmaker Woody Allen and actress Mia Farrow, the toast of New York City's cultural scene and one of the town's most celebrated couples, were caught in the glare of a less glamorous limelight in 1992. In August, Allen filed suit against Farrow, requesting custody of their three children. Although Allen and Farrow have never been married, they have two adopted children and a biological son. Farrow also has eight other children.

Allen's suit was just the opening shot in a domestic war that was devoured by the tabloids and news magazines. Allen declared that he was in love with one of Farrow's other children, 21-year-old Soon-Yi Farrow Previn, and had been conducting an affair with her since late 1991. The wounded Farrow claimed that Allen had sexually molested two of the couple's children. Allen denied the accusation, and no charges had been brought against him as of year-end.

Meanwhile, Allen released his latest movie, *Husbands and Wives,* about a college professor, played by Allen, who has an affair with a young female student. Farrow plays the professor's wife.

Profile in courage. John Thompson has quite a story to tell his grandchildren, and he should be able to hold them in his arms when he tells it. On the morning of January 11, Thompson, 18, was working alone at his family's farm outside Hurdsfield, N.Dak., operating an *auger*, a machine that moves grain into feeding bins. Suddenly, he slipped on a patch of ice and fell onto a rotating shaft powering the auger. Within moments, the shaft ripped off both of his arms just below the shoulder and threw him to the ground.

Suppressing panic, Thompson got to his feet and dashed to the house. After kicking open the front door, he went to the push-button phone and, with a pen held in his teeth, punched the digits of his uncle's telephone number to summon help.

Thompson was flown to Minneapolis, Minn., where surgeons reattached his arms. He returned home in late February and began physical therapy. Thompson's doctors said he might regain sensation in his hands within two years, and they predicted that he would eventually be able to do most things for himself.

Traces of Amelia Earhart? The fate of the pioneering female aviator Amelia Earhart has been one of the enduring mysteries of this century. Earhart and her navigator, Fred Noonan, disappeared over the central Pacific Ocean on July 2, 1937, during one leg of a flight around the world. Theories have been offered about where their plane went down, but there has been no evidence to support any of them.

In March 1992, Richard Gillespie, head of a nonprofit organization called the International Group for Historic Aircraft Recovery, announced that he had solved the puzzle. Gillespie said he found a remnant of Earhart's plane, a Lockheed 10-E Electra, on the island of Nikumaroro, about halfway between New

Astronaut Mae C. Jemison, the first black woman to go into space, works in the science module of the space shuttle Endeavour in September.

Senator Edward M. Kennedy (D., Mass.) and Victoria Anne Reggie cut their wedding cake on July 3 after being wed at Kennedy's McLean, Va., home.

Guinea and Hawaii. He also discovered several personal effects, including a size-9 woman's shoe—the size Earhart wore. Gillespie's case seemed fairly strong, but at least one aviation buff was not convinced. Said Lockheed expert Frank Schelling, "The fragment did not come from an Electra."

Making their own luck. It's probably a common fantasy among state lottery players: to buy lotto tickets with every possible combination of numbers in the game, so that no matter what numbers are drawn, you win. It would cost you millions, but if the jackpot was big enough, you'd still make a pile.

Well, that's just what an investment syndicate from Australia set out to do in the Virginia lottery in February. With the pot at $27 million, representatives of the group frantically bought tickets at a number of outlets, managing to amass about 5 million before the drawing. Although that was some 2 million short of the total needed to cover all possible combinations of the six numbers to be drawn (from 1 to 44), it was enough—the Australians had the winning ticket. Lottery officials balked at paying the group, saying that it had broken the rules. In March, however, they said the jackpot would be paid out. Each of the 2,500 investors is due to receive $410 a year after taxes for 20 years, for a total of $8,200.

An ancient riddle solved? Since its discovery in the late 1500's, an ancient Roman glass vessel known as the Portland vase has intrigued classical scholars. The vase depicts two scenes, containing various human figures, that seem to hold a hidden meaning. Many interpretations of the puzzle—none widely accepted—have been advanced over the years.

In May, *Arion,* an art journal devoted to the classics and humanities, published a new theory of the vase that some experts think may be correct. Its author, Randall L. Skalsky, 43, a graduate student at the University of Massachusetts in Amherst, noted that two architectural motifs on the vase were shaped like the Greek letters P and I. He speculated that some major elements of the artwork might begin with those letters. Further investigation led Skalsky to conclude that one scene depicts "The Marriage of Peleus and Thetis," a poem by the Roman poet Catallus. The other scene, he theorized, is set on Mount Ida in Greece. He said the figures in that scene must then be the mythical Greek lovers Paris and Helen, who were betrothed on Mount Ida. Skalsky said the vase also bears the coded command "Drink!"

Two years before the mast. Cheered by more than 1,000 well-wishers who lined the pier of Boston Harbor on June 9, William Pinckney docked his sailboat at the Charlestown Navy Yard, thus completing a 22-month solo voyage around the world. Pinckney, a 56-year-old public relations executive from Chicago, became the first black mariner to sail around the globe alone by the longest and most dangerous route, around the southern tips of Africa and South America. Speaking to a greeting party of schoolchildren, Pinckney, who was raised in a single-parent household on welfare, said, "No matter who you are . . . your dreams are important and doable."

Coming soon in paperback. Vitaly Klimakhin's groundbreaking novel, a prodigious achievement by anyone's standards, earned him a place in the Guinness Book of World Records, Russian edition, in 1992. The 17-year-old Moscow boy had dropped out of high school in 1991 to work on the book, and at Christmas of that year, after 107 grueling days of labor, he penned the final word—Ford. Ford was also the first word on page 1. In fact, every one of the 400,000 words in Klimakhin's epic novel—nearly as many as Leo Tolstoy used in *War and Peace*—is Ford. The Guinness editors were so impressed that they created a new category for Klimakhin: the most times a single word has been written in one place. But why Ford? "Well, I like Ford cars," said Klimakhin. "Maybe Ford will give me some money or something."

New life for a legend of the seas. The S.S. *United States*, one of the great luxury ocean liners of this century, was saved from the scrap heap in April by a businessman with fond memories of the famous ship. Frederick A. Mayer of New York City paid $2.6-million for the *United States* at an auction in Newport News, Va., where the ship had been docked in rusting grandeur for years. The *United States* was once one of the fastest vessels afloat. On its maiden voyage in July 1952, it set a speed record for a transatlantic crossing—3 days, 10 hours, and 40 minutes—that stood until 1990. The ship was taken out of service in 1969. Mayer, who immigrated to this country aboard the *United States* in 1964, said he planned to spend about $145 million to refurbish the liner as a cruise ship.

Hounds 187, foxes 175. The sport of fox hunting—galloping behind a pack of dogs in hot pursuit of a fox—is much loved by the English gentry. But there is a growing sentiment in Great Britain that it's time for "riding to the hounds" to ride into the sunset. Opponents of the sport say there is no place in modern Britain for a pastime that results in the violent death of an estimated 12,000 to 13,000 foxes each year. In February, the House of Commons voted on a bill to ban fox hunting. It was defeated, but the closeness of the vote—187 to 175—gave little cheer to proponents of the hunt. "This is the first battle in what will undoubtedly be a prolonged war," said one Conservative member of Parliament.

No exoneration for Doctor Mudd. For 75 years, the descendants of Samuel A. Mudd have been trying to clear their ancestor's name. Mudd, the physician who in 1865 set the broken leg of Abraham Lincoln's assassin, John Wilkes Booth, was convicted by a military court of being a co-conspirator in the assassination and sentenced to life in prison. Although he was freed in 1869, the conviction stood. In January 1992, a panel of the Army Board for Correction of Military Records (ABCMR) recommended that Mudd's conviction be reversed. But in July, Assistant Secretary of the Army William D. Clark rejected the recommendation, commenting that "it is not the role of the ABCMR to settle historical disputes."

Reaching for the stars. As a young girl growing up in Chicago, Mae C. Jemison wanted more than anything to be an astronaut. She never gave up on that dream, and to prepare herself she earned an engineering degree at Stanford University in California and a medical degree at Cornell University Medical College in New York City. She was accepted for the astronaut program in 1987. On Sept. 12, 1992, Jemison, then age 35, rocketed into orbit with six other astronauts aboard the space shuttle Endeavour, becoming the first black woman to go into space.

Time stands still—for one second. On June 30, scientists at the U.S. Naval Observatory in Washington, D.C., stopped the observatory's atomic clock to insert a "leap second." The second was added to keep the extremely accurate clock—actually 24 such clocks linked together and averaged—in synchronization with time measurement based on the Earth's rotation. Since 1972, the Naval Observatory has inserted 16 leap seconds into the atomic clock to compensate for a tiny slowing in the Earth's rate of rotation.

Angel of Death confirmed dead. Genetic tests performed in Berlin, Germany, in April confirmed that skeletal remains buried in Embu, Brazil, are those of the infamous Nazi physician Josef Mengele. Mengele, known as the "Angel of Death," was a brutal doctor at the Auschwitz concentration camp in Poland during World War II (1939-1945). After the war, he fled into hiding in South America.

In 1985, authorities in Brazil were told that Mengele had died in a swimming accident in 1979 and was buried in an Embu cemetery. Forensic experts who examined the remains identified them as Mengele's, but not with absolute certainty. The 1992 tests settled the issue. *DNA* (deoxyribonucleic acid, the molecule genes are made of) from the remains was compared with DNA from blood samples donated by Mengele's first wife and their son Rolf. DNA analysis proved that the man buried in Embu was Rolf's father.

Balloonists lose race but set record. Richard Abruzzo, 29, and Troy Bradley, 28, landed their balloon in Morocco on September 22, seven days after taking off from Bangor, Me. Competing in a field of five identical helium and hot-air balloons in a race across the Atlantic Ocean, Abruzzo and Bradley got blown off course and came in third. A Belgian team won the race. Two teams ditched at sea.

Despite losing the race, Abruzzo and Bradley were happy. Their flight, in addition to being the first successful balloon flight from the United States to Africa, set a new record for time aloft in a balloon—146 hours. The previous record of 137 hours had been set in 1978 by Abruzzo's late father, Ben Abruzzo.

Magic Johnson cancels return. Basketball star Earvin (Magic) Johnson, Jr., who announced in September that he would return as a player to the Los Angeles Lakers, changed his mind on November 2 and said he was calling it quits for good. Johnson first resigned from the Lakers in November 1991 after being diagnosed with HIV, the virus that causes AIDS.

Johnson had been serving on President George Bush's National Commission on AIDS in 1992 as a high-profile spokesman, but he left the group in September. Explaining that resignation, Johnson said he felt the government was not doing enough to fight AIDS.

Lucky for him he wasn't speeding. They don't take kindly to drunk driving in Warren County, Kentucky, and District Court Judge JoAnn Coleman meant to teach James Jaggers a lesson. One night in March as he was returning home from a bar, Jaggers had been stopped by a police officer and ticketed for driving under the influence of alcohol. There was, however, a mitigating circumstance: Jaggers, a double amputee, was driving a motorized wheelchair. No matter, Judge Coleman ruled in June that a motorized vehicle is a motorized vehicle, and Jaggers had been driving on the road. She said the charge against Jaggers would be dropped after a year if he refrained from operating his wheelchair when he has been drinking.

"Twin Peaks" invades Japan. American entertainment is one U.S. export that sells well in Japan, and in 1992 the television series "Twin Peaks" took the Land of the Rising Sun by storm. The bizarre drama had been defunct in the United States since early 1991, though an American motion picture based on

U.S.-born sumo wrestler Konishiki, background, failed in May to become a sumo "grand champion" after losing four straight matches in a Tokyo tournament.

the program was released in 1992. "Twin Peaks"—series and movie—became such a mania in Japan that thousands of fans attended mock funerals for Laura Palmer, the slain teen-ager (murdered by her father) around whom the plot centers. Several hundred of the most devout even made tours to Snoqualmie, Wash., to visit locations where the show was filmed.

No crown for Konishiki. Salevaa Atisanoe, a 576-pound (261-kilogram) Hawaiian-born hulk who competes as a sumo wrestler in Japan under the name Konishiki, had a disappointing year in 1992. Konishiki had hoped to become the first non-Japanese to be named a *yokozuna,* or grand champion sumo wrestler. It was widely agreed that if he won a major Tokyo tournament in May, the sumo authorities would be forced, however reluctantly, to confer the coveted title on a foreigner. But Konishiki performed badly at the competition, losing four consecutive matches.

Gorby buries Cold War. Speaking on May 6 at Westminster College in Fulton, Mo., former Soviet leader Mikhail S. Gorbachev pronounced the Cold War over. Gorbachev said the long stand-off between the Western nations and the Soviet Union could have been avoided. It began, he asserted, when the United States and its allies launched "a monstrous arms race." The site of Gorbachev's talk was significant. It was at Westminster College in 1946 that Winston Churchill, Great Britain's former prime minister, warned that the Soviet Union had lowered an Iron Curtain across Europe. David Dreier

Newspaper publishers did not have to look far for bad news in 1992. The newspaper industry suffered through its third year of poor advertising sales and flat circulation numbers. In addition, several newspapers were affected by natural disasters, rioting, and strikes. Hurricane Andrew, arriving in southern Florida on August 24, badly damaged the premises of the *South Dade News Leader* in Homestead and left many employees without homes. Just two weeks later, Hurricane Iniki shut down *The Garden Island* for several days when it hit the Hawaiian island of Kauai.

In rioting in Los Angeles following the April 29 acquittal of four policemen in the Rodney King beating case, a mob caused $500,000 damage to the *Los Angeles Times* building. Reporters and newspaper photographers were shot at, beaten, and robbed. (See also **Los Angeles.**)

No news is bad news in Pittsburgh. Residents of Pittsburgh, Pa., through most of 1992 had to function without a city newspaper. A strike by delivery drivers that began on May 17 and continued into December, shut down *The Pittsburgh Press* and the *Pittsburgh Post-Gazette.* On October 2, *Pittsburgh Press* owner, E. W. Scripps Company, announced that it would try to sell the publication. In November, the *Post-Gazette* arranged to buy the rival paper, and, at year's end, the papers were waiting for the United States Department of Justice to approve the sale.

More papers bite the dust. On January 3, the 213-year-old *Elizabeth Daily Journal,* the oldest newspaper in New Jersey, became the first paper to fold in 1992. On July 31, the *Spokane* (Wash.) *Chronicle* folded after 111 years. *The Tulsa* (Okla.) *Tribune,* founded in 1919, closed on September 30 despite having a 51-year joint operating agreement with the larger *Tulsa World* that allowed them to share profits or losses while still competing on news stories. The *Daily News* of Duluth, Ga., closed on September 6 despite ownership transfers, major infusions of capital, and a doubling of its circulation since 1987.

In Texas, the Hearst Corporation, publishers of the *San Antonio Light,* decided to end a vigorous newspaper war on Oct. 6, 1992, by buying the rival *San Antonio Express-News* from News Corporation Limited. Hearst planned to close the *Light* if, as was expected, no one was willing to buy it.

Purchases. In October, a federal judge approved the sale of the financially strapped New York *Daily News*, which once had the largest circulation in the United States, to Morton Zuckerman, owner of *U.S. News & World Report*, for $38 million. At year's end, Zuckerman was trying to reach an agreement with the labor unions so that the sale could be finalized. Troubled United Press International Incorporated also won a new lease on life when Middle East Broadcasting Centre Limited, a Saudi Arabian company, bought the 85-year-old wire service at auction for $3.95 million.

Mark Fitzgerald

In ***World Book,*** see **Newspaper.**

Nicaragua. Nicaraguan President Violeta Barrios de Chamorro drew criticism at home and abroad in 1992 for her failure to remove the leaders of the army and the police, who had been supporters of the previous Marxist Sandinista regime. Among her critics were the Administration of United States President George Bush and Republican members of the U.S. Senate Foreign Relations Committee. In June, the U.S. Congress halted a payment of $104 million, the last remaining from a total U.S. aid package of $731 million. The U.S. Congress had approved the package shortly after Chamorro took office in April 1990.

In an apparent effort to satisfy critics, Chamorro replaced 12 high-level police officers on Sept. 5, 1992. Among them was René Vivas, the controversial Sandinista national police chief. She replaced him with Fernando Caldera Azmitiá, a more moderate Sandinista. But conservatives in the U.S. Congress continued to berate Chamorro for tolerating General Humberto Ortega Saavedra, brother of the former Sandinista President Daniel Ortega, as army commander.

On September 1, an earthquake off the Pacific coast sent waves up to 50 feet (15 meters) crashing ashore along a 150-mile (240-kilometer) stretch of coast. At least 116 people were killed and some 16,000 people left homeless.

Nathan A. Haverstock

See also **Latin America** (Facts in brief table). In ***World Book,*** see **Nicaragua.**

Niger. See **Africa.**

Nigeria. The military government of President Ibrahim Babangida proceeded throughout most of 1992 with its plan to return Nigeria to civilian rule. But by November, that plan had been derailed by rising tension and violence and continuing problems with the economy. At year-end, it was unclear when the transition to civilian government, originally scheduled for October 1992, would be accomplished.

Elections. On July 4, elections were held for the National Assembly. Although the voting was marred by charges of bribery and fraud, the election was concluded successfully. When the results were in, the left-of-center Social Democratic Party had won a narrow victory over the more conservative National Republican Convention in both the upper and lower houses of the assembly. In October, primary elections were held for the presidential elections, the last step in the transition. But the military voided the results of the primaries and suspended all political activity because of alleged widespread fraud at the polls.

Census. On March 19, the government released results of a national census. The official figure of 88.5 million people surprised many Nigerians. By most estimates, the country has between 110 million and 120 million people. Moreover, the official finding that the predominantly Muslim north had more than 50 per cent of the population scared inhabitants of the mostly Christian south. Census results were to be used as a basis for distributing federal funds to Nigeria's states.

Violence. Ethnic and religious conflicts and disappointment with the economy led to several outbreaks of violence during the year. In Taraba state, fighting between two ethnic groups, which began in October 1991, had resulted in more than 5,000 deaths by February 1992. On May 13, gasoline shortages caused rioting in Lagos, the capital. A few days later, Christians and Muslims began fighting in the cities of Zaria and Kaduna and the town of Zango, outbreaks that left an estimated 500 to 800 people dead.

The economy. The ailing economy was a constant source of complaint for Nigerians in 1992. Unemployment in Lagos was reported to be 40 per cent, and the price of food and other commodities rose significantly. In January, the Babangida regime reduced the number of government ministries to help cut its huge budget deficit. During the year, the government also began negotiations with the International Monetary Fund, an agency of the United Nations, to reschedule Nigeria's large foreign debt. Nonetheless, expenses—along with corruption by many government officials—continued to drain vast amounts of money from the national treasury.

As troubles mounted, some Nigerians called for the military to remain in power. Other Nigerians, however, demanded a speed-up in the transition to civilian government. Mark DeLancey

See also **Africa** (Facts in brief table). In ***World Book,*** see **Nigeria.**

Nobel Prizes in literature, peace, economics, and the sciences were awarded in October 1992 by the Norwegian Storting (parliament) in Oslo and by the Royal Swedish Academy of Sciences, the Karolinska Institute, and the Swedish Academy of Literature in Stockholm, Sweden. The value of each prize was $1.2-million in United States currency. Two of the prizes seemed linked to the 500th anniversary of Christopher Columbus' arrival in the Americas.

The literature prize was given to Derek Walcott, a West India-born poet and playwright who teaches literature and creative writing at Boston University. The 62-year-old Walcott became the first native Caribbean writer to receive the award. The Nobel Committee praised Walcott for his work's "great luminosity, sustained by a historical vision, the outcome of a multicultural commitment." Walcott—a product of African, Dutch, and English ancestry—draws on his experiences shuttling between the United States and the Caribbean to portray people struggling with questions of identity and home.

Walcott writes in English but he spices his work with African and Caribbean slang and rhythms. His books include the poetry collection *In a Green Night* (1962), the autobiographical poem *Another Life* (1973), and the epic poem *Omeros* (1990).

The peace prize went to Rigoberta Menchú, who has campaigned for human rights for *indigenous* (native) people throughout the world, especially in her Central American homeland of Guatemala. The Nobel Committee said the 33-year-old Menchú "stands out as a symbol of peace and reconciliation across ethnic, cultural, and social dividing lines."

Menchú, a Maya Indian of the Quiché group, fled Guatemala in 1981 after her father, mother, and a brother were killed. In 1980, Menchú's father was among a group of protesters who staged a sit-in at the Spanish Embassy. When government security forces stormed the embassy, a protester reportedly threw a gasoline bomb, and Menchú's father died in the resulting blaze. In *I, Rigoberta Menchú* (1983), her autobiography, she accused the military of torturing and killing her brother and her mother around the time of her father's death. Since then, she has spoken around the world on the persecution of Guatemalan Indians by the government. (See also **Guatemala.**)

The economics prize went to Gary S. Becker, a professor at the University of Chicago. It was the third straight year in which the economics prize had been awarded to a faculty member from that university. The Nobel Committee praised the 61-year-old Becker for having "extended the sphere of economic analysis to new areas of human behavior and relations." In his work, Becker applies the economic language of costs, rewards, and incentives to personal decisions relating to such matters as crime, education, and drug abuse. One of Becker's most well-known and controversial ideas is to treat families as businesses whose members make rational judgments about marriage, work, and children based on considerations of time and money. Becker writes a regular column for *Business Week* magazine.

The chemistry prize was awarded to Rudolph A. Marcus, a Canadian-born scientist at the California Institute of Technology in Pasadena. The Nobel Committee honored the 69-year-old chemist for his mathematical analyses during the 1950's and 1960's of how subatomic particles called *electrons* move among molecules during chemical reactions. Marcus' research has shed light on such chemical reactions as *photosynthesis* (the use of solar energy to drive chemical reactions), rust, and electrical conduction. Marcus' theoretical predictions were not always accepted by other chemists at the time of their reporting. The Nobel Commitee noted that the scientific community had to wait until the late 1980's before some of Marcus' predictions could be experimentally verified.

The physics prize went to George Charpak, a Polish-born French scientist who has worked since 1959 at the European Organization for Nuclear Research (CERN), a laboratory near Geneva, Switzerland, where studies of subatomic particles are conducted. The 68-year-old Charpak won the Nobel Prize for his work on detectors for *particle accelerators*, devices that hurl subatomic particles together at extremely high speeds. The resulting collisions break apart the particles and so give scientists a glimpse of other, smaller particles that do not exist isolated in nature.

In the mid-1900's, scientists could record the smaller particles only by taking photographs of the trails the particles left as they streaked through a gas or liquid. But in 1968, Charpak built an electronic detector that could record the paths of millions of particles each second. This advance greatly increased the rate at which physicists could make discoveries about the subatomic world.

The physiology or medicine prize was shared by Edmond H. Fischer and Edwin G. Krebs, two American scientists with the University of Washington in Seattle. The 72-year-old Fischer and 74-year-old Krebs won the prize for their discovery of a regulatory pathway in cells whereby proteins are modified in order to alter their function. The Nobel Committee said this finding "initiated a research area which today is one of the most active and wide ranging."

In the 1950's, the two scientists were studying how muscle cells get a burst of energy when adrenalin is released into the blood. They happened to discover a network of molecules responsible for activating and deactivating *enzymes* (molecules that speed up chemical reactions). These changes are now known to underlie the functioning of all cells. And imbalances in this pathway have been linked to cancer, organ-transplant rejection, and allergies. John Burnson

In ***World Book***, see **Nobel Prizes.**

North Carolina. See **State government.**

North Dakota. See **State government.**

Northern Ireland. Negotiations to restore self-government to Northern Ireland and end years of violence between the nation's Protestants and Roman Catholics made some progress in 1992. The British government wanted a new regional government for Northern Ireland based on some form of power-sharing between the two warring factions. Such an agreement would end Great Britain's largely direct rule of Northern Ireland, which had begun in 1972. There also was hope that the Republic of Ireland and Northern Ireland would discuss a new political relationship that would deprive the outlawed Irish Republican Army (IRA) of support for its ongoing campaign of terror to force the British out of Northern Ireland.

A new spirit of compromise during preliminary talks in July 1992 in London led to an agreement that negotiations should begin between the Protestant Unionists of Northern Ireland, who want to remain a part of the United Kingdom, and the Republic of Ireland, which in its Constitution claims Northern Ireland as part of the republic. Such negotiations began on September 21, when James Molyneaux, leader of the Ulster Unionist Party, traveled to Dublin, the republic's capital, for talks with Deputy Prime Minister John Wilson and Foreign Minister David Andrews. Molyneaux became the first Protestant Unionist to meet in the predominantly Roman Catholic Irish republic since 1920, when Ireland was divided.

Also attending the talks were British ministers and officials of other political parties of Northern Ireland—the Social Democratic and Labor Party, which wants reunification with Ireland and is supported by most Catholics, and the Alliance Party, a small Unionist party supported by both Protestants and Catholics. Democratic Unionists, the other major Protestant party, refused to attend, signaling its objection to the republic's constitutional claim to Northern Ireland. Sinn Fein, the political wing of the IRA, was excluded.

However, in early November 1992, negotiations broke down. Officials, hopeful that talks would resume, gave no date for the next meeting.

Violence continues. Hardly a month passed in 1992 without the IRA claiming responsibility for a bombing on the British mainland. On April 10, the day after the British national elections, the IRA exploded its most powerful bomb ever, killing three people and injuring 91 in London's financial district.

Terrorism conviction overturned. Judith Ward was released from a British prison in May after serving 18 years of a life sentence imposed in 1974. She had confessed to being involved with the IRA and to a bombing, which killed 12 people near Leeds, England. Her appeal noted that many police interviews with her had not been revealed to the defense. Prosecutors said she had a vivid imagination and may have fantasized her story. Ian J. Mather

See also **Ireland**. In ***World Book,*** see **Northern Ireland.**

Northwest Territories. In a November 1992 referendum, 69 per cent of the *Inuit* (Eskimo) people voting approved a land-claim settlement that will split the Northwest Territories and create a primarily Inuit territory called Nunavut.

A bitter labor dispute and strike by 240 workers at the Giant gold mine in Yellowknife, the territorial capital, allegedly led to the deaths of nine miners on September 18. A criminal investigation conducted by the Royal Canadian Mounted Police (RCMP) concluded that an explosion, which killed three replacement workers and six union members who had crossed the picket line, had been deliberately set. Explosives had been left in a tunnel about 755 feet (230 meters) underground. They went off as the miners passed beside them in a rail car, according to the RCMP report.

The strike had begun on May 23 when Royal Oak Mines Incorporated, the mine's owners, demanded that its workers accept wage and benefit cuts and a new contract that based salary levels on the price of gold. The workers demanded salary increases and better benefits and safety standards. During the resulting strike, violent clashes frequently occurred.

The Northwest Territories' budget for the fiscal year (April 1, 1992, to March 31, 1993), announced on September 10, totaled $1.14 billion ($914 million U.S.) in spending and forecast a deficit of $25 million ($20 million U.S.). David M. L. Farr

In ***World Book,*** see **Northwest Territories.**

Creating Nunavut

By David M. L. Farr

Canada has agreed to carve out a large section of the Northwest Territories as a homeland for its native Inuit people.

Canada's Eskimo people realized a long-held hope in 1992 when they secured for themselves the promise of a homeland. The area to be created for the Eskimos, who prefer to be called Inuit, will be carved out of Canada's Arctic land in the Northwest Territories. The new territory is called Nunavut, *NUHN uh vuht,* meaning our land, and will consist of 770,000 square miles (1.9 million square kilometers), an expanse one-fifth the size of Canada and larger than Alaska and California combined. Nunavut's creation represents the first change in Canada's boundaries since 1949.

Nunavut is to be treated as a new Canadian territory with the same governmental powers as Canada's other territories—the Yukon and what will remain of the Northwest Territories. Because a new government must be set up and the Inuit must prepare themselves to take over its management, Nunavut was not expected to separate from the Northwest Territories until 1999. At that time, the 17,500 Inuit who account for 80 per cent of the population of Nunavut, will become masters of the region. However, "outsiders," or nonnatives, may continue to reside there and take part in the new territory's affairs.

The Inuit and the Canadian government had reached a nonbinding agreement on Dec. 16, 1991, to settle the Inuit's land claim and to establish Nunavut. And on May 4, 1992, the people of the Northwest Territories approved the boundaries for Nunavut. The agreement between Canada, the Inuit, and the Northwest Territories was formally ratified in November 1992.

Of the 770,000 square miles of Nunavut, the Canadian government retained ownership of 635,000 square miles (1.6 million square kilometers), and the Inuit gained absolute title, or exclusive ownership, to 135,000 square miles (350,000 square kilometers). In the area the Inuit own, they will be able to hunt, trap, and fish without any restriction. On about 10 per cent of this area, they will also own exclusive rights to any oil, gas, or minerals the land might contain. Zinc and lead have been mined in the Nunavut area, and experts say that reserves of oil and gas may exist but probably are not extensive.

The Inuit will also share in the royalties from all resources obtained from the Canadian-owned section of Nunavut. This arrangement gives the Inuit 50 per cent of the first $2 million ($1.6 million U.S.) worth of royalties, and 5 per cent of the remainder. In addition, Canada will pay the Inuit a land-claims settlement of $1.15 billion ($922 million U.S.), to be paid over 14 years.

The Inuit's history

For thousands of years the Inuit have lived on the inhospitable northern margin of the North American continent. Their ice-locked coasts and snow-covered terrain have constituted a forbidding environment, and their survival has represented a triumph of adaptation.

The forebears of the Inuit were from northeast Asia. Most anthropologists believe that these people came to North America across a narrow land bridge that, until 10,000 years ago, connected the areas now known as Siberia and Alaska. To survive the harsh and isolated conditions of the Arctic, the Inuit developed a unique way of life. They used dog sleds to travel and built igloos from blocks of snow to use as housing during the winter months. They hunted polar bear, caribou, whale, seal, and walrus for meat and used animal skins to create shelters and boats. The furs of other wildlife served as clothing.

Until the 1500's, when European explorers came to the Arctic, the Inuit were isolated from the remainder of the world. By the 1800's, the Inuit were working and bartering with European whalers and fur traders. In 1870, when Canada gained control of the Northwest Territories, Royal Canadian Mounted Police detachments and missionaries from the south began to make their presence felt in the Inuit's homeland. By the 1930's, bush pilots and mineral prospectors also began to appear in the isolated north. During and after World War II (1939-1945), Canada and the United States used the Arctic as a first line of defense against a potential air at-

The author:

David M. L. Farr is Professor Emeritus at Carleton University in Ottawa, Canada.

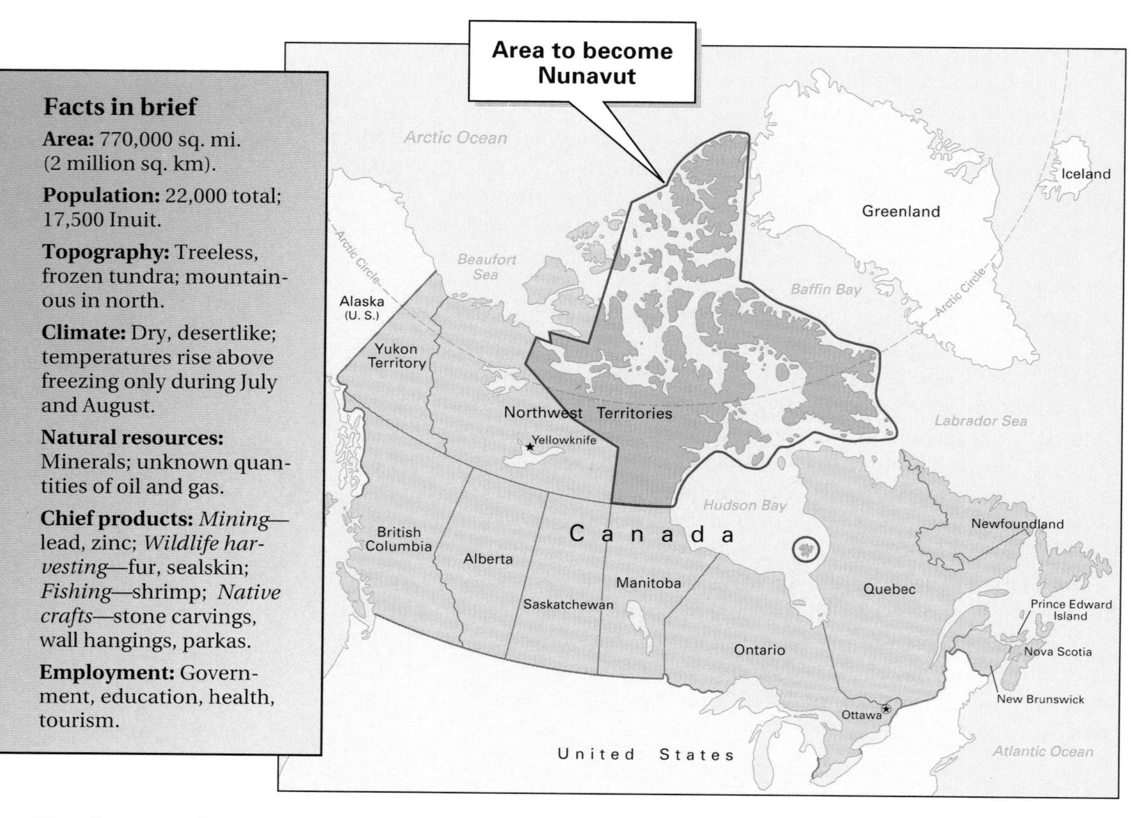

Facts in brief

Area: 770,000 sq. mi. (2 million sq. km).

Population: 22,000 total; 17,500 Inuit.

Topography: Treeless, frozen tundra; mountainous in north.

Climate: Dry, desertlike; temperatures rise above freezing only during July and August.

Natural resources: Minerals; unknown quantities of oil and gas.

Chief products: *Mining*—lead, zinc; *Wildlife harvesting*—fur, sealskin; *Fishing*—shrimp; *Native crafts*—stone carvings, wall hangings, parkas.

Employment: Government, education, health, tourism.

Carving out a home

The land to be turned over to the Inuit people splits the Northwest Territories and comprises one-fifth of Canada's total area. The land agreement marks the first change in Canada's boundaries since 1949.

tack. Air fields, highways,and government offices sprang up, and the white population increased dramatically. At the same time, the animals the Inuit used were dwindling in number from overhunting, and the people began to give up their traditional life in exchange for prefabricated houses built near white settlements. But with skills not suited to the modern world, many Inuit could not secure employment.

In the 1950's, with government help, the Inuit began to set up small commercial fisheries and handicraft businesses. Many Inuit had a talent for sculpture and printmaking. Using the local soapstone and drawing inspiration from traditional designs, they established a healthy trade in native art. Other Inuit founded cooperatives and began to serve the growing flow of tourists who came north to experience their wild and beautiful land. But unemployment and welfare dependency also persisted.

In the 1970's, the Inuit began to work formally toward establishing a territory where they could manage their own affairs. The government of the Northwest Territories was too remote from the Inuit. Yellowknife, the capital of the Northwest Territories, lay 1,500 miles (2,400 kilometers) to the west, and political affairs were dominated by those who lived nearer that town—whites and the Dene Indians and *métis* (people of Indian and European ancestry) of the Mackenzie River Valley.

A *plebiscite* (a public vote on an issue) in 1982 showed a strong desire among the Inuit to partition the Northwest Territories. In 1990, a boundary line was drawn. From the southern edge of the territory, the boundary ran in a northwesterly direction along the tree line that divided the tundra of the east from the sparse woodlands occupied by the Dene Indians and métis. At the Arctic Ocean, the line continued north through the Arctic islands, separating the Inuit living in the eastern Arctic from a smaller group occupying the Mackenzie River Delta. Nunavut would comprise all the land of the Northwest Territories lying east of this boundary.

An accord initialed in April 1992 by representatives of Canada, the Northwest Territories, and the Inuit detailed the political structure of Nunavut. It provided for a fully elected legislative assembly, an executive council chosen from the assembly, and a judiciary. Local governments in the Inuit's scattered settlements are to bring territorial regulations directly to the people. The new territorial government will manage education, social services, and housing. Like Canada's other territories, Nunavut is required to abide by Canada's federal laws. But the Inuit will have equal representation with government officials on a wildlife management board and will be involved in agencies responsible for environmental protection. Revenues will come partly from local taxation and resource royalties, but the federal government will provide most of Nunavut's funding, as it does for its other territories.

Compromises and challenges

Nunavut is truly a form of native self-government, not a state within a state. This is because the settlement the Inuit accepted is based on the principle of "extinguishment," in which the federal government agrees to certain political and land-claim arrangements in exchange for the surrender of all other native claims to land, water, and resources in the region. The Inuit viewed their acceptance of extinguishment as a pragmatic decision, since a demand for a more comprehensive settlement could have resulted in the Canadian government rejecting the claim outright. However, the Assembly of First Nations, the organization representing Indians living on reservations across Canada, said that by accepting extinguishment, the Inuit had weakened the case for about 50 comprehensive land claims being advanced by other native groups.

The Inuit's soapstone carvings, which are usually based on traditional designs, are popular with tourists and have helped the Inuit earn a living in the modern world through an age-old practice.

Nunavut has been launched with brave words from Inuit leaders. But the new territory faces grave economic and social problems. Unemployment and its frequent companions—welfare dependency, alcoholism, family violence, and suicide—remain high, and economic opportunities are bleak. Traditional Inuit values and skills are disappearing, and young Inuit can no longer cope well with their environment nor fit easily into the modern world.

Within the last 50 years, the Inuit life style has been pulled from the Stone Age and confronted with the computer age. But for thousands of years, the Inuit have demonstrated a remarkable ability to adapt and survive. Now, with greater control over their destiny, perhaps the Inuit will both master modern ways and preserve their unique culture as they strike out on their own in their vast new homeland of Nunavut.

Norway in 1992 continued to move on a measured timetable toward membership in the European Community (EC or Common Market), despite political problems at home and in the EC. The country formally applied for EC membership on November 25. The move represented a political risk for the government of Prime Minister Gro Harlem Brundtland, who heads the ruling Labor Party. Opinion polls in 1992 showed that most Norwegians opposed EC membership. Norway planned to hold a national referendum on the issue after settling the terms of membership with the EC, but observers noted this might not occur for years.

European ties. In October, Norway's parliament approved Norway's participation in the European Economic Area (EEA). This agreement, designed to promote freer trade between the 7-member European Free Trade Association (to which Norway belongs) and the 12-member EC, was scheduled to take effect in early 1993. However, the EEA will not remove all trade barriers or give non-EC members decision-making powers within the EC.

Norwegian opponents of EC membership feared it would prove costly to Norway, which might have to channel some of its income from petroleum and natural gas to poorer EC countries, possibly including future EC members in Eastern Europe. But Brundtland and others argued that the country could not afford to stay out of the EC, especially if Sweden and Finland—both of which have applied for membership—join the organization. (Neighboring Denmark had joined in 1973.) Norway's trade with the EC, which had grown steadily for years, comprised more than half the country's import and export trade in 1992.

Brundtland's stance on the EC helped weaken the Labor Party and strengthen the opposition Center and Conservative parties. Center Party leader Anne Enger Lahnstein continued to keep Brundtland's minority government in power, but Lahnstein in 1992 made clear her opposition to Norway's joining either the EEA or the EC. The Conservative Party favored EEA and EC membership. New parliamentary elections were scheduled for the spring of 1993, with the EC issue certain to play a big role.

Norway's economy survived Europe's general economic slowdown better than did most of its neighbors. The government estimated that the economy, buoyed by oil and gas revenues, grew by more than 2 per cent in 1992. Both unemployment and inflation remained relatively low, though the government's budget deficit rose. Norway's economic health allowed it to keep its currency, the krone, within the EC's European Monetary System—an organization linking the values of its members' currencies—despite turbulence in September that led some nations to withdraw from the system. Norway raised its interest rates to the highest levels in four years to defend the value of the currency during the crisis. Philip Revzin

See also **Europe** (Facts in brief table). In ***World Book,*** see **Norway.**

Nova Scotia. An explosion of methane gas deep underground at the Westray Mine in Plymouth killed 26 miners on May 9, 1992. The mine, located in Pictou County along the Foord Seam, holds the world's largest depository of bituminous coal—as well as high levels of methane gas. Since the mid-1800's, more than 240 miners have died in Pictou's mines. The miners' union claimed that safety measures at the mine were lacking. On Oct. 5, 1992, the provincial government charged the mining company and four of its managers with 52 violations of the Occupational Health and Safety Act.

Premier Donald Cameron in January announced plans to privatize the province-owned Nova Scotia Power Corporation. The premier stated that the corporation's $2.4-billion ($1.9-billion U.S.) debt had hurt the province's credit rating, and that private investors would be offered shares amounting to a 57 per cent stake in the company.

Canada's first commercial production of offshore crude oil began on June 5, when an oil rig located 159 miles (256 kilometers) southeast of Halifax, N.S., began pumping oil. The project, owned by Lasmo Nova Scotia Limited, was expected to produce 14,000 barrels of oil per day. The reserves were estimated to contain 50 million barrels of crude oil. David M. L. Farr

In ***World Book,*** see **Nova Scotia.**

Nuclear energy. See **Energy supply.**

Nutrition. See **Food.**

Ocean. The most advanced space mission ever designed to study ocean currents was launched in 1992. The Topex-Poseidon mission is a joint project undertaken by the United States and France. The European Ariane rocket, launched from Kourou, French Guiana, on August 10, sent the ocean-exploring spacecraft into an orbit 820 miles (1,320 kilometers) above Earth.

The spacecraft carried two high-precision radar altimeters and three precision location systems. This equipment can measure the general *topography* (shape) of the ocean surface to an unprecedented accuracy of about 1.5 inches (3.8 centimeters). Because wind-driven currents affect the shape of the ocean surface, oceanographers can determine the speed and direction of the currents by measuring the topographical changes. Studies of such ocean variations are crucial to understanding long-term climate change.

Past ocean temperatures. Using a new method for determining the temperature of ancient tropical seas, scientists from France and the United States in July 1992 reported that 10,000 years ago the water temperature of an area in the southwestern Pacific Ocean was about 10 Fahrenheit degrees (6 Celsius degrees) colder than it is now. Scientists study ocean temperatures to determine long-term changes in weather patterns and in the atmosphere.

The new technique involves drilling into coral to measure its ratio of strontium (a metallic element) to calcium. This ratio depends on the relative concentra-

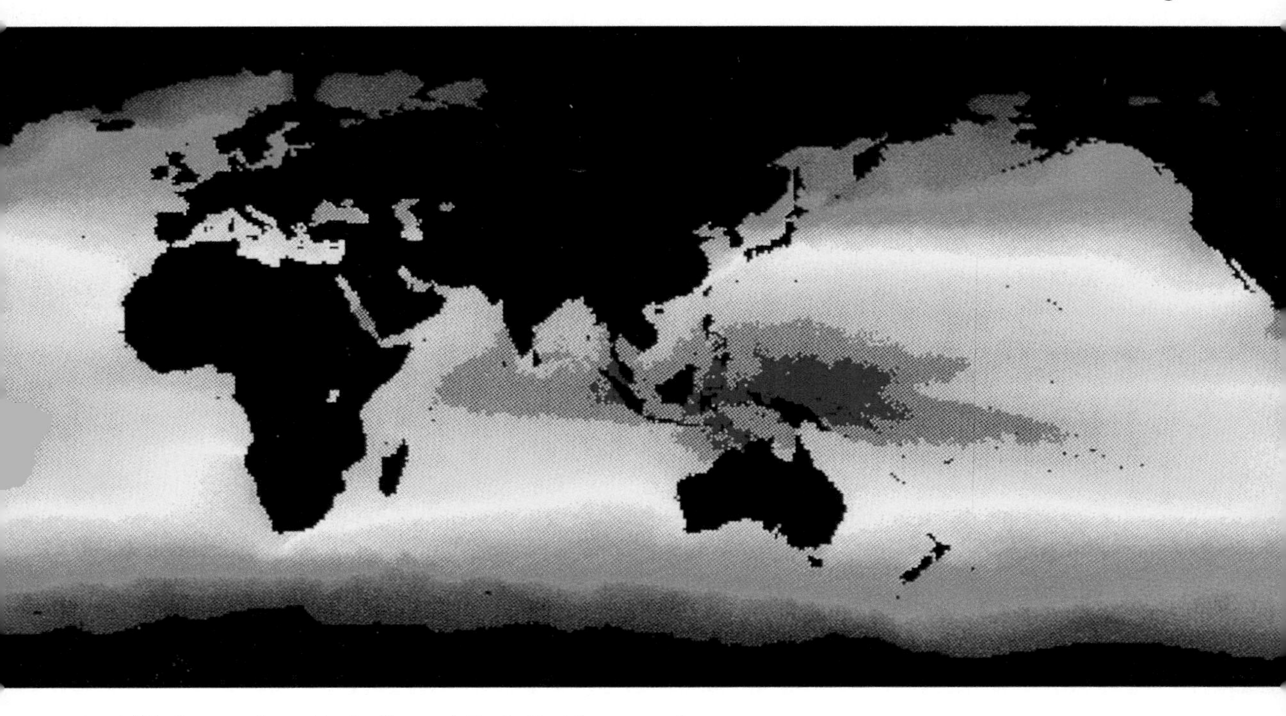

A satellite image released in April reveals the hottest known surface area of the Pacific Ocean (red area) where temperatures reached 86 °F (30 °C).

tions of these elements in seawater, as well as water temperature, at the time the coral formed.

Darwin knew atolls. Oceanographers from the Ocean Drilling Program, which is operated by Texas A&M University in College Station, announced in July 1992 that their study of *atolls* (ring-shaped coral reefs surrounding a lagoon) in the western Pacific Ocean supported British naturalist Charles Darwin's 1842 theory of the origin of the ancient reefs. Although Darwin's analysis does not apply to all the details of atoll formation the scientists investigated, the main premise of the 150-year-old theory seems to have stood the test of time, the researchers said.

Darwin postulated that when a young volcanic island emerges above sea level, a reef constructed by corals grows along its sides. Over time, the volcano erodes and its top is submerged, but the reef continues to grow. Sometimes the reef is submerged, other times not, depending on sea levels. The end product is a ring-shaped reef with a central lagoon. The cycles of submergence and uplift affect the coral growth rate and chemical composition in ways that provide a permanent record of sea level fluctuations and climate changes.

Old charts endanger ships. Passengers had to evacuate the luxury liner *Queen Elizabeth II* on August 7 after the ship ran into an unchartered rocky ledge off the coast of Massachusetts and the ship's hull was severely damaged. An investigative hearing revealed that charts of the area were based on a 1939 survey. According to an official from the National Oceanic and Atmospheric Administration, more than half of the charts used by commercial vessels and pleasure ships in U.S. waters are based on ocean-bottom information that is at least 50 years old.

Radioactive waste. Russian officials in May 1992 acknowledged that the former Soviet Union had dumped large amounts of radioactive waste into the Arctic Ocean for more than 20 years. Russian authorities agreed to cooperate with an international scientific research expedition to locate, test, and clean up the disposal sites, which are in the Barents and Kara seas. The dumping violated international laws on the disposal of radioactive materials. The waste, from both civil and military sources, included nuclear reactors, a nuclear submarine, and leaking barrels of solid waste. Although other nations are known to have unloaded radioactive waste at sea, none have been cited for the high levels of radiation that the Soviets are thought to have discarded. Officials in Russia and Norway expressed concern over the possibility that the waste has fouled or will contaminate the waters and fish of the Arctic. Fishing industries of both nations rely on Arctic waters. Arthur G. Alexiou

In ***World Book,*** see **Ocean.**

Ohio. See **State government.**
Oklahoma. See **State government.**
Old age. See **Social security.**

The 1992 Olympics

By Frank Litsky

National borders may have changed, but the Olympic spirit endured as the world's best athletes performed in France and Spain.

Preceding pages:
An archer's burning arrow ignites the Olympic flame to start the 1992 Summer Games in Barcelona, Spain, in July.

The Summer and Winter Olympic Games of 1992 marked the end of one chapter of international sport and the start of another. Since the last Olympic Games, the formerly Communist nations of Eastern Europe had become democratic and the Soviet Union had dissolved. Entering the 1992 Olympics, the teams of new nations competed as did the team of a newly unified nation—Germany. The Summer Games in Barcelona, Spain, from July 25 through August 9, drew more athletes from more countries than had any previous Olympic Games and represented a milestone in international cooperation. The games were the first since the Summer Olympics of 1972 in which no country staged a boycott.

The 1992 Olympics were also the last Winter and Summer Games to be held in the same year. The Winter Olympics will start a new four-year cycle in 1994 in Lillehammer, Norway, and the next Summer Olympics will be held in Atlanta, Ga., in 1996. From then on, the Summer and Winter Olympics will alternate every two years.

New teams from new nations

The Baltic republics of Latvia, Lithuania, and Estonia, part of the old Soviet Union, had become independent again and competed separately, as they did before World War II (1939-1945). Many athletes from republics that were once part of the Soviet Union also wanted to compete independently. In the Winter Olympics, athletes from five former Soviet republics (Russia, Ukraine, Belarus, Kazakhstan, and Uzbekistan) competed as the Unified Team and used the Olympic flag and Olympic hymn in the medals ceremonies. In the Summer Games, formally called the Games of the XXV Olympiad, the Unified Team included athletes from 12 former Soviet republics marching behind 12 different flags at the opening ceremonies. The International Olympic Committee (IOC) decreed that after 1992 the Unified Team will no longer exist. Former Soviet republics will compete independently as separate IOC members.

Croatia and Slovenia, which had declared independence from Yugoslavia in 1991, fielded independent teams. Athletes from the former Yugoslav republic of Bosnia and Hercegovina, where civil war raged, left the city of Sarajevo under sniper fire and arrived in Barcelona on an IOC-chartered plane three hours before the opening ceremonies. The IOC allowed the remaining Yugoslav athletes to compete at Barcelona in individual sports under the name of Independent Olympic Participants, but they were not permitted to compete in team sports. Czechoslovakia competed in the Winter Olympics under its own name and in the Summer Olympics as the Czech and Slovak Federative Republic after leaders from the Czech and Slovak republics within Czechoslovakia agreed in June 1992 to form two separate countries.

The author:
Frank Litsky is a sportswriter for *The New York Times*.

South Africa, which had been banned from the Olympics because of its restrictive racial policies, returned to the Olympics for the first time since 1960, competing in the Summer Games. Ten members of South Africa's 96-member team were black. Namibia, once part of South Africa, competed as a new nation. Cuba and North Korea sent full teams to Barcelona after boycotting the 1984 Summer Games in Los Angeles and the 1988 Summer Games in Seoul, South Korea. Not all countries represented at Barcelona competed, however. Afghanistan sent an observer but no athletes to the 1992 Summer Games.

The Winter Olympics

The Winter Olympics, from February 8 through 23 in Albertville, France, and surrounding sites in the French Alps, were the first major international multisport competition since the breakup of the Soviet Union in late 1991 and the merger of West Germany and East Germany in October 1990. Despite the political changes, athletes from the former Soviet Union and the former East Germany continued their domination of the Winter Olympics. Former East German athletes won 20 of Germany's 26 total medals in Albertville, more than any country at the Winter Games. The Unified Team's 23 medals were the second highest total.

Organizers conducted the Albertville games over terrain that covered 650 square miles (1,680 square kilometers) in the Savoy mountain area of the French Alps, near Italy and Switzerland. The games were costly. France spent $1.2 billion in permanent improvements to the area, and the organizers, with a budget of $836-million, reported a loss of $57 million.

By other than strictly financial measures, however, the games were highly successful. Organizers reported that crowds were 20 per cent larger than expected, but there were no major security problems. The events attracted a Winter Games record of 2,174 athletes from 63 nations. The German team led the medal count by winning 10 gold, 10 silver, and 6 bronze medals for a total of 26. The Unified Team followed with 23 total medals (9 gold, 6 silver, and 8 bronze). Austria won 21 medals (6, 7, 8); Norway, 20 medals (9, 6, 5); Italy, 14 medals (4, 6, 4); and the United States, 11 medals (5, 4, 2).

Women monopolize winter gold

Women won all five U.S. gold medals at Albertville. Bonnie Blair of Champaign, Ill., took the gold in 500-meter and 1,000-meter speed skating; Cathy Turner of Rochester, N.Y., in 500-meter short-track speed skating; Kristi Yamaguchi of Fremont, Calif., in figure skating; and Donna Weinbrecht of West Milford, N.J., in moguls freestyle skiing. These were the first Olympics in which the IOC recognized short-track speed skating and freestyle skiing as medal sports.

Medals standings, Winter Olympics

Nation	Gold	Silver	Bronze	Total
Germany	10	10	6	26
Unified Team*	9	6	8	23
Austria	6	7	8	21
Norway	9	6	5	20
Italy	4	6	4	14
United States	5	4	2	11
France	3	5	1	9
Finland	3	1	3	7
Canada	2	3	2	7
Japan	1	2	4	7

*Athletes from five former republics of the Soviet Union.

Ice dancing
Marina Klimova and Sergei Ponomarenko of the Unified Team won the gold medal in ice dancing during the Winter Olympic Games.

Women champions
Bonnie Blair of Champaign, Ill., *right,* earns one of her two speed skating gold medals in the Winter Games. Blair won the 500 meters and 1,000 meters. Kerrin Lee-Gartner of Canada races to a gold medal in women's downhill skiing, *above.*

Official results of the 1992 Olympic Games

Winners of the Winter Olympics

Event	Winner	Country	Mark
■ Men's skiing			
Downhill	Patrick Ortlieb	Austria	1:50.37
Combined	Josef Polig	Italy	14.58 pts.
Super giant slalom	Kjetil-Andre Aamodt	Norway	1:13.04
Giant slalom	Alberto Tomba	Italy	2:06.98
Slalom	Finn Christian Jagge	Norway	1:44.39
Cross-country:			
10 kilometers	Vegard Ulvang	Norway	27:36.0
15 kilometers	Bjorn Dahlie	Norway	38:01.9
30 kilometers	Vegard Ulvang	Norway	1:22:27.8
50 kilometers	Bjorn Dahlie	Norway	2:03:41.5
40-kilometer relay	Langli, Ulvang, Skjeldal, Dahlie	Norway	1:39:26.0
■ Ski jumping			
90-meter jump	Ernst Vettori	Austria	222.8 pts.
120-meter jump	Toni Nieminen	Finland	239.5 pts.
Team	Nikkola, Laitinen, Laakkonen, Nieminen	Finland	644.4 pts.
■ Nordic combined skiing			
Men's individual	Fabrice Guy	France	426.47 pts.
Men's team	Mikata, Kono, Ogiwara	Japan	1,247.18 pts.
■ Women's skiing			
Downhill	Kerrin Lee-Gartner	Canada	1:52.55
Combined	Petra Kronberger	Austria	2.55 pts.
Super giant slalom	Deborah Compagnoni	Italy	1:21.22
Giant slalom	Pernilla Wiberg	Sweden	2:12.74
Slalom	Petra Kronberger	Austria	1:32.68
Cross-country			
5 kilometers	Marjut Lukkarinen	Finland	14:13.8
10 kilometers	Lyubov Yegorova	Unified Team	25:53.7
15 kilometers	Lyubov Yegorova	Unified Team	42:20.8
30 kilometers	Stefania Belmondo	Italy	1:22:30.1
20-kilometer relay	Valbe, Smetanina, Lasutina, Yegorova	Unified Team	59:34.8
■ Freestyle skiing			
Men's moguls	Edgar Grospiron	France	25.81 pts.
Women's moguls	Donna Weinbrecht	U.S.A.	23.69 pts.
■ Figure skating			
Men's singles	Viktor Petrenko	Unified Team	1.5
Women's singles	Kristi Yamaguchi	U.S.A.	1.5
Pairs	Artur Dmitriev, Natalya Mishkutienok	Unified Team	1.5
Ice dancing	Sergei Ponomarenko, Marina Klimova	Unified Team	2.0
■ Men's speed skating			
Long track			
500 meters	Uwe-Jens Mey	Germany	:37.14
1,000 meters	Olaf Zinke	Germany	1:14.85
1,500 meters	Johann Koss	Norway	1:54.81
5,000 meters	Geir Karlstad	Norway	6:59.97
10,000 meters	Bart Veldkamp	Netherlands	14:12.12
Short track			
1,000 meters	Kim Ki Hoon	S. Korea	1:30.76*
5,000-meter relay	Kim, Lee, Jmo, Song	S. Korea	7:14.02*
■ Women's speed skating			
Long track			
500 meters	Bonnie Blair	U.S.A.	:40.33
1,000 meters	Bonnie Blair	U.S.A.	1:21.90
1,500 meters	Jacqueline Boerner	Germany	2:05.87
3,000 meters	Gunda Niemann	Germany	4:19.90
5,000 meters	Gunda Niemann	Germany	7:31.57
Short track			
500 meters	Cathy Turner	U.S.A.	:47.04
3,000-meter relay	Cutrone, Daigle, Lambert, Perreault	Canada	4:36.62
■ Men's biathlon			
10-kilometer event	Mark Kirchner	Germany	26:02.3
20-kilometer event	Yevgeni Redkine	Unified Team	57:34.4
30-kilometer relay	Gross, Steinigen Kirchner, Fischer	Germany	1:24:43.5
■ Women's biathlon			
7.5-kilometer event	Anfissa Restsova	Unified Team	24:29.2
15-kilometer event	Antje Misersky	Germany	51:47.2
22.5-kilometer relay	Niogret, Claudel, Briand	France	1:15:55.6
■ Bobsledding			
Two-man	Gustav Weder, Donat Acklin	Switzerland	4:03.26
Four-man	Appelt, Winkler, Haidacher, Schroll	Austria	3:53.90
■ Men's luge			
Singles	Georg Hackl	Germany	3:02.363
Doubles	Stefan Krausse Jan Behrendt	Germany	1:32.053
■ Women's luge			
Singles	Doris Neuner	Austria	3:06.696
■ Ice hockey	Unified Team		7 wins, 1 loss

*New world record.

Overall, however, Americans achieved limited success in traditional sports in Albertville. Blair was the only American medalist in speed skating, a sport in which the United States usually performs well. No American man won a medal in Alpine skiing, and Paul Wylie of Denver, Colo., was the only American male medalist in figure skating. Dan Jansen of West Allis, Wis., finished fourth in 500-meter speed skating, and the U.S. hockey team took fourth place. As usual, however, Americans finished far out of medal contention in cross-country skiing, luge, and biathlon competition.

Stars came in all ages. Sixteen-year-old Toni Nieminen of Finland, using the new V method of soaring through the air, won two gold medals and one silver medal in ski jumping and became the youngest Winter Olympic gold medalist ever. Raisa Smetanina of the Unified Team, almost 40 years old, set a record with her 10th career medal in Olympic cross-country skiing.

Medals standings, Summer Olympics

Nation	Gold	Silver	Bronze	Total
Unified Team*	45	38	29	112
United States	37	34	37	108
Germany	33	21	28	82
China	16	22	16	54
Cuba	14	6	11	31
Hungary	11	12	7	30
South Korea	12	5	12	29
France	8	5	16	29
Australia	7	9	11	27
Spain	13	7	2	22
Japan	3	8	11	22

*Athletes from 12 former republics of the Soviet Union.

Heptathlon

Jackie Joyner-Kersee of Conoga Park, Calif., leaps 23 feet 3½ inches to win the long jump during heptathlon competition on August 2 in Barcelona. Joyner-Kersee won the heptathlon for the second time and took the bronze in the individual long jump competition.

Summer Olympics

At Barcelona, 10,563 athletes from 171 nations participated in the Summer Games. Security was a concern because Barcelona is the capital of Catalonia, a province with its own customs and language and a strong movement for independence from Spain. Perhaps because of the presence of 45,000 police and militia, there were few disturbances, however. Spain's King Juan Carlos I pleased the Catalonians at the opening ceremonies when he declared the games open with words spoken not in Spanish but in Catalan, the local language. After the king spoke, an archer fired a flaming arrow over a huge gas-fed titanium dish, igniting the gas and the Olympic flame, and the Summer Games began.

These, too, were high-cost Olympics. The national, provincial, and local governments spent $8 billion to give Barcelona a face-lift. The Olympic budget was $1.4-billion. The National Broadcasting Company (NBC) spent $401 million to buy U.S. television rights and showed 161 hours of the Olympics.

The "Dream Team"

The most successful athletes included American sprinters, Cuban boxers and baseball players, Chinese divers, and Unified Team gymnasts. But none received more attention than the U.S. men's basketball team, dubbed the "Dream Team," certainly the best basketball team ever assembled. It was the first time that the United States sent professional players from the National Basketball Association (NBA). The team included Earvin (Magic) Johnson, Jr., of the Los Angeles Lakers, Michael Jordan of the Chicago Bulls, and Larry Bird of the Boston Celtics. They overwhelmed every opponent to capture the gold medal. The dynamic Johnson, who chose not to play the NBA's 1991-1992 season because he had tested positive for the HIV virus, which causes AIDS, came out of retirement for the Olympics.

Summer stars

In the Summer Olympics, Unified Team athletes from the former Soviet Union, who traditionally won the most medals, led again. They won 45 gold medals, 38 silver medals, and 29 bronze medals for a total of 112. The United States followed with 108 total medals (37 gold, 34 silver, 37 bronze), and Germany, with 82 total medals (33 gold, 21 silver, 28 bronze), was third.

The United States won 57 medals in track and field

Teamwork

Larry Bird, Michael Jordan, Scottie Pippen, and Earvin (Magic) Johnson, Jr., (left to right) of the U.S. men's basketball "Dream Team" crash the boards, *left,* during the team's 117-85 gold medal win over Croatia on August 8 during the Summer Games. Many called the team—made up for the first time of professionals from the National Basketball Association—the best ever assembled. Carl Lewis, *below,* finishes the anchor leg for the U.S. 400-meter relay team that set a world record in Barcelona.

Up in the air

Fu Mingxia of China, *right,* just 13 years old, spins Earthward on the way to winning the platform diving gold medal on July 27 during the Summer Games. She became the second-youngest person to win an individual Olympic gold medal. Tatiana Goutsou of the Unified Team, *below,* takes the all-around gold medal in gymnastics on July 30.

More U.S. medals

Mike Barrowman of Potomac, Md., *above,* wins the gold in the 200-meter breaststroke during the Summer Games. He set a world record in the event. Gail Devers of Palmdale, Calif., *left* (far right), wins the gold medal in the 100 meters. The United States won 57 medals in swimming and track and field—more than half of its total medals in the Summer Games.

Official results of the 1992 Olympic Games

Winners of the Summer Olympics

■ Archery

Event	Winner	Country	Mark
Men	Sebastien Flute	France	110 pts.
Women	Cho Youn Jeong	S. Korea	112 pts.
Team (men)	Spain	Spain	238 pts.
Team (women)	S. Korea	S. Korea	236 pts.

■ Badminton

Event	Winner	Country	Mark
Singles (men)	Alan Budi Kushuma	Indonesia	
Singles (women)	Susi Susante	Indonesia	
Doubles (men)	Kim Moon So, Park Joo Bong	S. Korea	
Doubles (women)	Hwang Hae Young, Chung So Young	S. Korea	

■ Boxing

Event	Winner	Country	Mark
Light flyweight	Rogelio Marcelo	Cuba	
Flyweight	Su Choi Choi	N. Korea	
Bantamweight	Joel Casamayor	Cuba	
Featherweight	Andreas Tews	Germany	
Lightweight	Oscar De La Hoya	U.S.A.	
Light welterweight	Hector Vinent	Cuba	
Welterweight	Michael Carruth	Ireland	
Light middleweight	Juan Lemus	Cuba	
Middleweight	Ariel Hernandez	Cuba	
Light heavyweight	Torsten May	Germany	
Heavyweight	Felix Savon	Cuba	
Super heavyweight	Roberto Balado	Cuba	

■ Canoeing, men

Event	Winner	Country	Mark
Single kayak slalom	Pierpaolo Ferrazzi	Italy	1:46.89
Kayak 500-meter singles	Mikko Kolehmainen	Finland	1:40.34
Kayak 500-meter doubles	Bluhm, Gutsche	Germany	1:29.84
Kayak 1,000-meter singles	Clint Robinson	Australia	3:37.26
Kayak 1,000-meter doubles	Bluhm, Gutsche	Germany	3:16.10
Kayak 1,000-meter fours	Von Appen, Kegel, Reineck, Wohllebe	Germany	2:54.18
Double canoe slalom	Jacobi, Strausbaugh	U.S.A.	2:02.41
Canoe slalom	Lukas Pollert	Czechoslovakia	1:53.69
Canoe 500-meter singles	Nikolai Boukhalov	Bulgaria	1:51.15
Canoe 500-meter doubles	Masseikov, Dovgalenok	Unified Team	1:41.54
Canoe 1,000-meter singles	Nikolai Boukhalov	Bulgaria	4:05.92
Canoe 1,000-meter doubles	Papke, Spelly	Germany	3:37.42

■ Canoeing, women

Event	Winner	Country	Mark
Kayak slalom	Elisabeth Micheler	Germany	2:06.41
Kayak 500-meter singles	Birgit Schmidt	Germany	1:51.60
Kayak 500-meter doubles	Portwich, Von Seck	Germany	1:40.29
Kayak 500-meter fours	Donusz, Czigany, Meszaros, Koban	Hungary	1:38.32

■ Cycling, men

Event	Winner	Country	Mark
Individual road race	Fabio Casartelli	Italy	4:35.21
Sprint	Jens Fiedler	Germany	
1,000-meter time trial	Jose Moreno	Spain	1:03.34
4,000-meter individual pursuit	Chris Boardman	Great Britain	3:21.65
4,000-meter team pursuit	Gloeckner, Lehmann, Steinweg, Walzer	Germany	4:08.79
100-kilometer team time trial	Dittert, Meyer, Peschel, Rich	Germany	2:01.39
50-kilometer points race	Giovanni Lombardi	Italy	44 pts.

■ Cycling, women

Event	Winner	Country	Mark
79-kilometer road race	Kathryn Watt	Australia	2:04.42
Sprint	Erika Salumae	Estonia	
Pursuit	Petra Rossner	Germany	3:41.75

■ Equestrian

Event	Winner	Country	Mark
Three-day, team	Green, Rolton, Hoy	Australia	
Three-day, individual	Matthew Ryan	Australia	
Dressage, team	Uphoff, Theodorescu, Werth	Germany	
Dressage, individual	Nicole Uphoff	Germany	
Show jumping, individual	Ludger Beerbaum	Germany	
Show jumping, team	Lansink, Raymakers, Romp	Netherlands	

■ Fencing, men

Event	Winner	Country	Mark
Individual foil	Philippe Omnes	France	
Team foil	Wagner, Schreck, Weidner, Koch, Weissenborn	Germany	
Individual epee	Eric Srecki	France	
Team epee	Borrmann, Felisiak, Schmitt, Proske, Reznitchenko	Germany	
Individual sabre	Bence Szabo	Hungary	
Team sabre	Kirienko, Chirchov, Pogossov, Gouttsait, Pozdniakov	Unified Team	

■ Fencing, women

Event	Winner	Country	Mark
Individual foil	Giovanna Trillini	Italy	
Team foil	Bortolozzi, Bianchedi, Vaccaroni	Italy	

■ Gymnastics, men

Event	Winner	Country	Mark
All-around	Vitali Scherbo	Unified Team	59.025 pts.
Long horse vault	Vitali Scherbo	Unified Team	9.856 pts.
Pommel horse	(tie) Vitali Scherbo, Pae Gil Su	Unified Team, N. Korea	9.925 pts.
Horizontal bar	Trent Dimas	U.S.A.	9.875 pts.
Parallel bars	Vitali Scherbo	Unified Team	9.90 pts.
Rings	Vitali Scherbo	Unified Team	9.937 pts.
Floor exercise	Li Xiaosahuang	China	9.925 pts.
Team		Unified Team	585.450 pts.

■ Gymnastics, women

Event	Winner	Country	Mark
All-around	Tatiana Goutsou	Unified Team	39.737 pts.
Balance beam	Tatiana Lyssenko	Unified Team	9.975 pts.
Uneven parallel bars	Lu Li	China	10.00 pts.
Side horse vault	(tie) Henrietta Onodi, Lavinia Milosovici	Hungary, Romania	9.925 pts., 9.925 pts.
Floor exercise	Lavinia Milosovici	Romania	10.00 pts.
Team		Unified Team	198.159 pts.
Rhythmic	Alexandra Timoshenko	Unified Team	59.037 pts.

■ Judo, men

Event	Winner	Country	Mark
132 pounds (60 kg)	Nazim Gousseinov	Unified Team	
143 pounds (65 kg)	Rogerio Sampaio	Brazil	
157 pounds (71 kg)	Toshihiko Koga	Japan	
172 pounds (78 kg)	Hidehiko Yoshida	Japan	
190 pounds (86 kg)	Waldemar Legien	Poland	
209 pounds (95 kg)	Antal Kovacs	Hungary	
over 209 pounds	David Khakhaleichvili	Unified Team	

■ Judo, women

Event	Winner	Country	Mark
106 pounds (48 kg)	Cecile Nowak	France	
115 pounds (52 kg)	Almudena Munoz Martinez	Spain	
123 pounds (56 kg)	Miriam Blasco Soto	Spain	
134 pounds (61 kg)	Catherine Fluery	France	
146 pounds (66 kg)	Odalis Reve	Cuba	
159 pounds (72 kg)	Kim Mi Jung	S. Korea	
over 159 pounds	Zhuang Xiaoyan	China	

■ Modern pentathlon

Event	Winner	Country	Mark
Individual	Arkadiusz Skrzypaszek	Poland	
Team	Skrzypaszek, Czyzwicz, Gozdziak	Poland	

■ Rowing, men (all races 2,000 meters)

Event	Winner	Country	Mark
Single sculls	Thomas Lange	Germany	6:51.40
Double sculls	Hawkins, Antonie	Australia	6:17.32
Four sculls	Willms, Hajek, Volkert, Steinbach	Germany	5:45.17
Pairs without coxswain	Redgrave, Pinsent	Great Britain	6:27.72
Pairs with coxswain	Searle, Searle, Herbert	Great Britain	6:49.83
Fours without coxswain	Cooper, McKay, Green, Tomkins	Australia	5:55.04

Event	Winner	Country	Mark
Fours with coxswain	Talapan, Ruican, Popescu, Taga, Raducanu	Romania	5:59.37
Eights with coxswain	Wallace, Robertson, Forgeron, Barber, Marland, Rascher, Crosby, Porter, Paul	Canada	5:29.53

■ Rowing, women (all races 2,000 meters)

Event	Winner	Country	Mark
Single sculls	Elisabeta Lipa	Romania	7:25.54
Double sculls	Koeppen, Boron	Germany	6:49.00
Pairs without coxswain	McBean, Heddle	Canada	7:06.22
Four sculls	Mueller, Schmidt, Peter, Mundt	Germany	6:20.18
Fours without coxswain	Barnes, Taylor, Monroe, Worthington	Canada	6:30.85
Eights with coxswain	Barnes, Taylor, Delehanty, Crawford, McBean, Worthington, Monroe, Heddle, Thompson	Canada	6:02.62

■ Shooting, men

Event	Winner	Country	Mark
Free pistol	Konstantine Loukachik	Unified Team	658 pts.
Rapid-fire pistol	Ralf Schumann	Germany	885 pts.
Small bore rifle—prone position	Lee Eun Chul	S. Korea	702.5 pts.
Small bore rifle—three positions	Gracha Petikian	Unified Team	1,267.4 pts.
Running game target	Michael Jakosits	Germany	673 pts.
Air rifle	Iouri Fedkine	Unified Team	695.3 pts.
Air pistol	Wang Yifu	China	684.8 pts.

■ Shooting, women

Event	Winner	Country	Mark
Air rifle	Yeo Kab Soon	S. Korea	498.2 pts.
Small bore rifle—three positions	Launi Meili	U.S.A.	684.3 pts.
Sport pistol	Marina Logvinenko	Unified Team	684 pts.
Air pistol	Marina Logvinenko	Unified Team	486.4 pts.

■ Shooting, open

Event	Winner	Country	Mark
Skeet	Zhang Shan	China	223 pts.
Trapshooting	Petr Hrdlicka	Czechoslovakia	219 pts.

■ Swimming and diving, men

Event	Winner	Country	Mark
50-meter freestyle	Alexander Popov	Unified Team	:21.91*
100-meter freestyle	Alexander Popov	Unified Team	:49.02
200-meter freestyle	Evgueni Sadovyi	Unified Team	1:46.70*
400-meter freestyle	Evgueni Sadovyi	Unified Team	3:45.00†
1,500-meter freestyle	Kieren Perkins	Australia	14:43.48†
100-meter backstroke	Mark Tewksbury	Canada	:53.98*
200-meter backstroke	Martin Lopez-Zubero	Spain	1:58.47*
100-meter breaststroke	Nelson Diebel	U.S.A.	1:01.50*
200-meter breaststroke	Mike Barrowman	U.S.A.	2:10.16†
100-meter butterfly	Pablo Morales	U.S.A.	:53.32
200-meter butterfly	Melvin Stewart	U.S.A.	1:56.26*
200-meter medley	Tamas Darnyi	Hungary	2:00.76
400-meter medley	Tamas Darnyi	Hungary	4:14.23*
400-meter medley relay	Rouse, Diebel, Morales, Olsen	U.S.A.	3:36.93‡
400-meter freestyle relay	Hudepohl, Biondi, Jager, Olsen	U.S.A.	3:16.74
800-meter freestyle relay	Lepikov, Pychnenko, Taianovitch, Sadovyi	Unified Team	7:11.95†
Platform diving	Sun Shuwei	China	677.31 pts.
Springboard diving	Mark Lenzi	U.S.A.	676.53 pts.

■ Swimming and diving, women

Event	Winner	Country	Mark
50-meter freestyle	Yang Wenyi	China	:24.79†
100-meter freestyle	Zhuang Yong	China	:54.65*
200-meter freestyle	Nicole Haislett	U.S.A.	1:57.90
400-meter freestyle	Dagmar Hase	Germany	4:07.18
800-meter freestyle	Janet Evans	U.S.A.	8:25.52
100-meter backstroke	Krisztina Egerszegi	Hungary	1:00.68*
200-meter backstroke	Krisztina Egerszegi	Hungary	2:07.06*
100-meter breaststroke	Elena Roudkovskaia	Unified Team	1:08.00
200-meter breaststroke	Kyoko Iwasaki	Japan	2:26.65*
100-meter butterfly	Quian Hong	China	:58.62*
200-meter butterfly	Summer Sanders	U.S.A.	2:08.67
200-meter medley	Lin Li	China	2:11.65†
400-meter medley	Krisztina Egerszegi	Hungary	4:36.54
400-meter freestyle relay	Haislett, Torres, Martino, Thompson	U.S.A.	3:39.46†
400-meter medley relay	Loveless, Nall, Ahmann-Leighton, Thompson	U.S.A.	4:02.54†
Synchronized swimming (solo)	Kristen Babb-Sprague	U.S.A.	191.85 pts.
Synchronized swimming (duet)	Josephson, Josephson	U.S.A.	192.18 pts.
Platform diving	Fu Mingxia	China	461.43 pts.
Springboard diving	Gao Min	China	572.40 pts.

■ Table tennis, men

Event	Winner	Country	Mark
Singles	Jan Ove Waldner	Sweden	
Doubles	Lin, Tao	China	

■ Table tennis, women

Event	Winner	Country	Mark
Singles	Deng Yaping	China	
Doubles	Yaping, Hong	China	

■ Tennis, men

Event	Winner	Country	Mark
Singles	Marc Rosset	Switzerland	
Doubles	Becker, Stich	Germany	

■ Tennis, women

Event	Winner	Country	Mark
Singles	Jennifer Capriati	U.S.A.	
Doubles	Fernandez, Fernandez	U.S.A.	

■ Track and field, men

Event	Winner	Country	Mark
100 meters	Linford Christie	Great Britain	:9.96
200 meters	Mike Marsh	U.S.A.	:20.01
400 meters	Quincy Watts	U.S.A.	:43.50*
800 meters	William Tanui	Kenya	1:43.66
1,500 meters	Fermin Cacho	Spain	3:40.12
5,000 meters	Dieter Baumann	Germany	13:12.52
10,000 meters	Khalid Skah	Morocco	27:46.70
110-meter hurdles	Mark McKoy	Canada	:13.12
400-meter hurdles	Kevin Young	U.S.A.	:46.78†
3,000-meter steeplechase	Matthew Birer	Kenya	8:08.84
Marathon	Hwang Young Cho	S. Korea	2:13:23
400-meter relay	Marsh, Burrell, Mitchell, C. Lewis	U.S.A.	:37.40†
1,600-meter relay	Valmon, Watts, Johnson, S. Lewis	U.S.A.	2:55.74†
20-kilometer walk	Daniel Plaza Montero	Spain	1:21:45
50-kilometer walk	Andrei Perlov	Unified Team	3:50.13
High jump	Javier Sotomayor	Cuba	7 ft. 8 in. (2.34 m)
Long jump	Carl Lewis	U.S.A.	28 ft. 5½ in. (8.67 m)
Triple jump	Mike Conley	U.S.A.	57 ft. 10¼ in. (17.63 m)*
Pole vault	Maksim Tarasov	Unified Team	19 ft. ¼ in. (5.80 m)
Discus	Romas Ubartas	Lithuania	213 ft. 8 in. (65.13 m)
Javelin	Jan Zelezny	Czechoslovakia	294 ft. 2 in. (89.66 m)*
Shot-put	Michael Stulce	U.S.A.	71 ft. 2½ in. (21.70 m)
Hammer	Andrei Abduvaliyev	Unified Team	270 ft. 9 in. (85.52 m)
Decathlon	Robert Zmelik	Czechoslovakia	8,611 pts.

■ Track and field, women

Event	Winner	Country	Mark
100 meters	Gail Devers	U.S.A.	:10.82
200 meters	Gwen Torrence	U.S.A.	:21.81
400 meters	Marie-Jose Perec	France	:48.83
800 meters	Ellen Van Langen	Netherlands	1:55.54
1,500 meters	Hassiba Boulmerka	Algeria	3:55.30
3,000 meters	Elena Romanova	Unified Team	8:46.04
10,000 meters	Derartu Tulu	Ethiopia	31:06.02
100-meter hurdles	Paraskevi Patoulidou	Greece	:12.64
400-meter hurdles	Sally Gunnell	Great Britain	:53.23
400-meter relay	Ashford, Jones, Guidry-White, Torrence	U.S.A.	:42.11

*Olympic record. †World record. ‡Tied world record.

Event	Winner	Country	Mark
1,600-meter relay	Ruzina, Dzhigalova, Nazarova, Bryzgina	Unified Team	3:20.20
10-kilometer walk	Chen Yueling	China	44:32*
High jump	Heike Henkel	Germany	6 ft. 7½ in. (2.02 m)
Long jump	Heike Drechsler	Germany	23 ft. 5¼ in. (7.14 m)
Discus	Maritza Marten	Cuba	229 ft. 10 in. (70.06 m)
Javelin	Silke Renk	Germany	224 ft. 2 in. (68.33 m)
Shot-put	Svetlana Krivaleva	Unified Team	69 ft. 1¼ in. (21.06 m)
Marathon	Valentina Yegorova	Unified Team	2:32:41
Heptathlon	Jackie Joyner-Kersee	U.S.A.	7,044 pts.
■ Weightlifting			
115 pounds or less	Ivan Ivanov	Bulgaria	584 lbs. (265 kg)
123 pounds or less	Chun Byung Kwan	S. Korea	634 lbs. (287.5 kg)
132 pounds or less	Naim Suleymanoglu	Turkey	705 lbs. (320 kg)
149 pounds or less	Israel Militossian	Unified Team	744 lbs. (337.5 kg)
165 pounds or less	Fedor Kassapu	Unified Team	788 lbs. (357.5 kg)
182 pounds or less	Pyrros Dimas	Greece	816 lbs. (370 kg)
198 pounds or less	Kakhi Kakhiachvili	Unified Team	909 lbs. (412.5 kg)**
220 pounds or less	Victor Tregoubov	Unified Team	904 lbs. (410 kg)
242 pounds or less	Ronny Weller	Germany	953 lbs. (432.5 kg)
Over 242 pounds	Alexander Kourlovitch	Unified Team	992 lbs. (450 kg)
■ Wrestling (freestyle)			
106 pounds or less	Kim Il	N. Korea	
115 pounds or less	Li Hak Son	S. Korea	
126 pounds or less	Alejandro Puerto	Cuba	
137 pounds or less	John Smith	U.S.A.	
149 pounds or less	Arsen Fadzaev	Unified Team	
163 pounds or less	Park Jang Soon	S. Korea	
181 pounds or less	Kevin Jackson	U.S.A.	
198 pounds or less	Makharbek Khadartsev	Unified Team	
220 pounds or less	Leri Khabelov	Unified Team	
Over 220 pounds	Bruce Baumgartner	U.S.A.	
■ Wrestling (Greco-Roman)			
106 pounds or less	Oleg Koutcherenko	Unified Team	
114 pounds or less	Jon Ronningen	Norway	
125 pounds or less	Ahn Han Bong	S. Korea	
136 pounds or less	Akif Pirim	Turkey	
150 pounds or less	Attila Repka	Hungary	
163 pounds or less	Mnatsakan Iskandarian	Unified Team	
180 pounds or less	Peter Farkas	Hungary	
198 pounds or less	Maik Bullmann	Germany	
220 pounds or less	Hector Milian	Cuba	
286 pounds or less	Alexander Kareline	Unified Team	
■ Yachting, men			
Finn	Jose van der Ploeg	Spain	33.4 pts.
Flying Dutchman	Doreste, Manrique	Spain	29.7 pts.
Soling match racing	Bank, Secher, Seier	Denmark	2 pts.
Star	Reynolds, Haenel	U.S.A.	31.4 pts.
Tornado	Loday, Henard	France	40.4 pts.
Sailboard	Franck David	France	70.7 pts.
470	Calafat, Sanchez	Spain	50 pts.
■ Yachting, women			
Europe	Linda Andersen	Norway	48.7 pts.
Sailboard	Barbara Kendall	New Zealand	47.8 pts.
470	Zabell, Guerra	Spain	29.7 pts.
■ Team sports			
Baseball	Cuba		
Basketball (men)	U.S.A.		
Basketball (women)	Unified Team		
Field hockey (men)	Germany		
Field hockey (women)	Spain		
Handball (men)	Unified Team		
Handball (women)	S. Korea		
Soccer (men)	Spain		
Volleyball (men)	Brazil		
Volleyball (women)	Cuba		
Water polo (men)	Italy		

**Ties Olympic record. Weight is total of two lifts, snatch and clean and jerk.

and swimming—more than half of its total medals. In track and field, U.S. athletes won 30 medals, including 12 gold medals, 8 silver, and 10 bronze. American winners included such favorites as Jackie Joyner-Kersee and Mike Conley along with Carl Lewis, Kevin Young, and Gail Devers. Lewis won his only individual event, the men's long jump, for the third consecutive Olympics and added a gold medal in the 400-meter relay, giving him eight gold medals for his career. Young won the men's 400-meter hurdles in 46.78 seconds, breaking Edwin Moses' nine-year-old world record. Devers won the women's 100-meter dash and led in the 100-meter hurdles until she crashed into the last hurdle and crawled across the finish line in fifth place. Eighteen months earlier, doctors had almost amputated her feet because of burns she suffered as a result of radiation treatment for a severe thyroid ailment.

In swimming, U.S. athletes won 27 medals, including 11 gold medals, 9 silver medals, and 7 bronze medals. Mike Barrowman set a world record in the 200-meter breaststroke with a time of 2 minutes 10.16 seconds. Pablo Morales, 27, a standout on the 1984 U.S. Olympic team who retired in 1988, tried again, made the team, and won the men's 100-meter butterfly. Summer Sanders, the most versatile American swimmer, won four women's medals. Hungary provided a women's triple winner in 18-year-old Krisztina Egerszegi and a men's double winner in Tamas Darnyi.

In gymnastics, Vitali Scherbo of Belarus, competing with the Unified Team, won six gold medals. Fifteen-year-old Shannon Miller, a 4-foot 7-inch (140-centimeter), 71-pound (32-kilogram) American who performed with a tiny screw holding her dislocated left elbow in place, captured two silver medals and three bronze medals.

Surprise performances

There were some surprise gold-medal winners among the Americans, such as 16-year-old Jennifer Capriati in tennis, Quincy Watts in the 400 meters, Mark Lenzi in springboard diving, Trent Dimas on the horizontal bar in gymnastics, and Nelson Diebel in the 100-meter breaststroke.

There were some surprise setbacks, too. Michael Johnson of the United States, favored to win the 200 meters, contracted food poisoning and did not reach the final. Dave Johnson, also of the United States but unrelated to Michael, took the bronze medal in the decathlon, but many observers had regarded him as the favorite after Dan O'Brien, the heavy favorite, failed to make the U.S. team. Kim Zmeskal, the American who held the world women's all-around championship in gymnastics, won no individual medal. Sergei Bubka, the Ukrainian world recordholder and favorite to take the gold medal, failed to clear any height in the pole vault.

Controversy and emotion

There were controversial moments. In track and field, the IOC stripped Khalid Skah of Morocco of the gold medal in the men's 10,000 meters because Skah's teammate seemed to impede Richard Chelimo, a Kenyan fighting for first place. A day later, the IOC reinstated Skah after officials decided that his teammate had not really impeded Chelimo. In boxing, a computer system designed to make scoring more accurate made it more confusing and controversial and led to the early elimination of Eric Griffin, an American gold-medal favorite.

Several performances under hardship produced emotional moments. Ron Karnaugh, an American swimmer, finished sixth in the 200-meter individual medley six days after his father died of a heart attack while watching the opening ceremonies. When Derek Redmond of Great Britain tore his right hamstring muscle during the 400-meter semifinals and courageously hopped on his left leg toward the finish line, determined to finish, his father ran out of the stands and helped him.

One moment reflected the marriage in Barcelona of the old Olympic powers and the struggling new nations. Three teams stood on the medal stand for men's basketball. The U.S. gold-medal team wore fancy dress uniforms. The silver medalists from the new nation of Croatia wore bland outdated warm-up suits that suggested styles of the 1950's. But the bronze medalists from the recently independent nation of Lithuania wore tie-dyed shirts and shorts donated by the American rock band, the Grateful Dead.

Ontario. Hit hard by the economic recession, Canada's leading manufacturing province tightened spending for public services in 1992. Premier Robert K. Rae, head of the New Democratic Party (NDP) government, went on television on January 21 to announce stiff restraints on government spending. Increases in provincial allowances for hospitals, schools, and municipalities were to be limited to 1 per cent for fiscal 1992-1993 and to 2 per cent for each of the next two years.

The budget, introduced by Treasurer Floyd Laughren on April 30, relied mainly on personal income taxes to reduce the province's ballooning deficit. The budget adjusted the tax rate to 54.5 per cent of federal taxes—up from 53 per cent—beginning in July 1992. In 1993, taxes would jump to 55 per cent of the federal rate. A 14 per cent surtax, previously applied to incomes in excess of $84,000 ($67,000 U.S.), would now cut in at $53,000 ($42,500 U.S.). For many Ontario taxpayers, the surtax equaled the reduction in income taxes provided in the federal budget released in February. To spur economic recovery, the plan slightly reduced tax rates for corporations and small businesses.

Even with the new taxes, the provincial deficit for the current fiscal year was projected to be $9.9 billion ($7.9 billion U.S.). Government spending would total $54.8 billion ($43.9 billion U.S.) and revenues would come to $44.9 billion ($36 billion U.S.). Ontarians were promised casinos, sports lotteries, and off-track betting as revenue producers in the near future.

Rescuing jobs. Continued plant closings drove Ontario's unemployment rate up to 11.3 per cent in August 1992, the highest level since 1983. In February 1992, General Motors of Canada announced it would close a foundry and engine line in St. Catharines, leaving 2,300 people out of work.

To prevent other job losses, the provincial government moved to rescue two companies in danger of closing. On January 22, Ontario purchased a 49 per cent equity interest in de Havilland, an aircraft manufacturer and subsidiary of Boeing Company of Seattle, for $49 million ($39.9 million U.S.) and pledged another $300 million ($240 million U.S.) in subsidies. Bombardier Incorporated of Quebec purchased a controlling interest in the company. On February 28, Ontario provided loan guarantees and support for employee training programs to allow the 5,100 workers of Algoma Steel Corporation Limited to gain a controlling ownership in their company. The workers agreed to wage cuts and a reduction of the work force.

In a surprising policy reversal, the NDP government announced on June 3 that all retail stores could remain open on Sundays. It had previously allowed Sunday shopping only in designated tourist areas and for small convenience stores. The move was designed to improve retail sales and to cut down on cross-border shopping. David M. L. Farr

In *World Book,* see **Ontario.**

Opera. See **Classical music.**

Oregon. See **State government.**

Pacific Islands. American Samoa and Western Samoa, hit hard by Typhoon Val early in December 1991, recovered in 1992 from the storm's devastation. Lasting for five days, Val was the worst typhoon to hit the region in 30 years, leaving thousands homeless and destroying most food crops.

Fiji. In late May 1992, after delays of more than a year, Fiji held parliamentary elections for the first time since 1987, when the government was overthrown twice by military coups. The coups reflected long-standing tensions between the indigenous Fijians and Fiji-Indians, descendants of indentured laborers brought from India around 1900 who now control much of Fiji's economy.

In the elections, no political party gained enough seats to select a prime minister. Under the Fiji Constitution adopted in 1990, Fijians are guaranteed 37 of the 70 seats in the House of Representatives. Fiji-Indians have 27 seats, other ethnic groups have 5 seats, and the outlying island of Rotuma has 1 seat.

The Fijian Political Party, the largest of the three Fijian political parties, won only 30 seats in the elections. The party is headed by the leader of the 1987 coups, Major General Sitiveni Rabuka. Ironically, he was able to form a coalition by gaining the support of one of the two major Fiji-Indian parties that he had ousted in 1987. To forge the coalition, he promised to review the new Constitution and address other grievances. On June 2, 1992, Rabuka became prime minister, but observers predicted that the fragile coalition would be unstable.

Observers believed that Ratu Sir Kamisese Mara, who had been prime minister for most of the years since Great Britain granted Fiji independence in 1970, would probably continue to play a pivotal role in the nation's political life. Mara did not admire Rabuka. Mara could succeed Fiji's ailing President Ratu Sir Penaia Ganilau and so have the power to remove a sitting government.

Papua New Guinea held parliamentary elections in June 1992 for the fourth time since granted independence by Australia in 1975. The hotly contested election reflected a tumultuous political process in a nation of nearly 4 million people of various cultures who speak more than 700 languages. Political parties are numerous, and party loyalties are in constant flux. More than 1,000 candidates ran for 109 seats. The result was a turnover of 54 seats to new members.

Incumbent since 1987, Prime Minister Rabbie Namaliu faced a challenge by three former prime ministers: Sir Michael Somare (1975-1980 and 1982-1985), Sir Julius Chan (1980-1982), and Paias Wingti (1985-1987). After Parliament voted on July 17, Wingti and Namaliu were tied with 54 votes each. Then, for the first time ever, the Speaker of the Parliament used his vote to break the tie, casting his vote for Wingti. Within days, Wingti rallied the support of 5 more members to form a working majority of 60. The question remained if the coalition could hold up, but un-

Facts in brief on Pacific Island countries

Country	Population	Government	Monetary unit*	Foreign trade (million U.S.$) Exports†	Imports†
Australia	16,962,000	Governor General Bill Hayden; Prime Minister Paul Keating	dollar (1.27 = $1)	41,793	38,542
Fiji	799,000	President Ratu Sir Penaia Ganilau; Prime Minister Sitiveni Rabuka	dollar (1.47 = $1)	451	652
Kiribati	73,000	President Teatao Teannaki	Australian dollar	6	27
Nauru	9,000	President Bernard Dowiyogo	Australian dollar	93	73
New Zealand	3,476,000	Governor General Dame Catherine Tizard; Prime Minister James B. Bolger	dollar (1.78 = $1)	9,720	8,522
Papua New Guinea	462,840	Governor General Sir Wiwa Korowi; Prime Minister Paias Wingti	kina (0.95 = $1)	1,283	1,403
Solomon Islands	372,000	Governor General Sir George Lepping; Prime Minister Solomon Mamaloni	dollar (2.75 = $1)	70	92
Tonga	94,000	King Taufa'ahau Tupou IV; Prime Minister Baron Vaea	pa'anga (1.27 = $1)	13	65
Tuvalu	9,000	Governor General Tupua Leupena; Prime Minister Bikenibeu Paeniu	Australian dollar	1	3
Vanuatu	160,000	President Fred Timakata; Prime Minister Maxime Carlot	vatu (109.60 = $1)	19	97
Western Samoa	170,000	Head of State Malietoa Tanumafili II; Prime Minister Tofilau Eti Alesana	tala (2.41 = $1)	9	87

*Exchange rates as of Oct. 30, 1992, or latest available data.
†Latest available data.

der constitutional amendments made during Namaliu's rule, a no-confidence motion cannot be launched against a new government for 18 months. Sir Julius Chan was selected as deputy prime minister.

Rebellion on Bougainville against Papua New Guinea continued throughout 1992. Bougainvilleans sought refuge and support from relatives and neighbors in the Solomon Islands. In September 1992, border incursions in the Solomon Islands by military forces from Papua New Guinea resulted in the killing of two Solomon Islanders. This incident and other killings have severely strained relations between the Solomon Islands government and the government of Papua New Guinea and were of great concern to the other island nations of the Pacific.

Culturally and linguistically, Bougainville's 160,000 residents are linked with the Solomon Islands to the east. But in granting independence to Papua New Guinea, Australia included Bougainville in the national boundaries for economic reasons—the island produced huge revenues from its Panguna copper mine. In 1988, an armed rebellion closed the mine. Bougainville landowners demanded local autonomy, a larger share of the mine's revenue, and compensation for environmental damage. Negotiations, government suspension of all basic supplies and services, and military action have all failed. At least 150 deaths have occurred, and atrocities and human rights abuses were reported by both sides.

Small states. In January 1992, the leaders of five of the region's smallest states, the Cook Islands, Kiribati, Nauru, Niue, and Tuvalu, held a summit meeting on Rarotonga and formed Small Island States (SIS), a new regional organization. Leaders of the five states, which have a combined population of about 100,000, believe that their interests are often neglected in other regional forums. Sir Geoffrey Henry, prime minister of the Cook Islands, initiated the formation of SIS, designed to focus on economic developments.

Nuclear testing stopped. In April, France suspended its nuclear testing program in French Polynesia for the remainder of 1992. France's Prime Minister Pierre Bérégovoy said that the policy would be reviewed in 1993. France began nuclear testing in the Pacific in 1960. Eight national governments in the region signed a treaty in 1985 declaring the South Pacific a nuclear-free zone.

Milestones. Hammer DeRoburt, the first president of Nauru, died on July 15, 1992. He was a major figure in helping Nauru gain independence in 1968. After World War II (1939-1945), Nauru had been a trust territory of the United Nations under control of Australia, New Zealand, and Great Britain. In 1971, DeRoburt helped found the South Pacific Forum, an organization that promotes regional cooperation in trade and other matters. Robert C. Kiste

In *World Book,* see **Pacific Islands.**

Painting. See **Art.**

Pakistan in 1992 suffered the worst floods in its history. Heavy rains in the Himalaya in early September swelled rivers in northern Pakistan. To relieve pressure on dams, floodgates were opened, devastating hundreds of villages and farms. At least 2,000 people were killed and more than 1 million left homeless. Officials estimated the infrastructure damage at some $2 billion. There was widespread anger over the government's lack of preparedness for the disaster.

Nuclear bomb capabilities. Foreign Minister Shahryar Khan in February acknowledged that Pakistan has the means to build an atomic bomb. The admission was the government's first public confirmation of its nuclear program. But Khan claimed the country had not yet built a bomb and did not intend to. The statements came as the minister was visiting the United States in an effort to assure officials that Pakistan had no nuclear weapon ambitions. In 1990, the U.S. Congress had suspended about $570 million in aid to Pakistan because of fears of the country's growing nuclear capabilities. (See also **Armed forces: The Nuclear Threat in the New World Order.**)

The role of Islam. Pakistanis in 1992 worked to decide the place of Islamic law in the country's government. When Pakistan was created out of India in 1947, it was given a British legal system. But Islamic scholars soon demanded that religious law be given precedence. In 1980, a court chaired by Muslim scholars was established. Since then, the court had gradually expanded its authority. In 1992, the court passed new laws requiring television actresses to wear veils over their heads and mandating the death penalty for individuals found guilty of blasphemy. And it debated banning the charging of interest on loans.

Bhutto leads protests. Former Prime Minister Benazir Bhutto in 1992 continued charging that Prime Minister Nawaz Sharif had rigged the 1990 elections that unseated her and was trying to crush her Pakistan People's Party (PPP). In response, Sharif called Bhutto "an enemy of Pakistan."

On November 18, Bhutto led marches in Pakistan's capital, Islamabad, against Sharif. Government forces fiercely attacked her supporters, then detained more than 1,000 of them and sent Bhutto to the city of Karachi. Clashes between Bhutto supporters and government forces lasted for the rest of the year.

Provincial trouble. In May, Sharif decided to move the army into the southern province of Sind to help restore order. For years, conditions in the area had deteriorated as various ethnic and political groups struggled for power, and tactics such as assassination, kidnapping, and torture became common. Within weeks of the army's arrival in June, dozens of people had been killed and hundreds arrested. Critics of Sharif's move argued that the crackdown was aimed not at the crime syndicates but at supporters of the PPP, which is based in Sind. Henry S. Bradsher

See also **Asia** (Facts in brief table). In ***World Book,*** see **Pakistan.**

Paleontology. The discovery of six transitional species of dinosaurs in Montana, reported in July 1992, has helped paleontologists determine that dinosaurs living in that area about 75 million years ago were the descendants of earlier inhabitants and not migrants from elsewhere. Paleontologists led by John R. Horner of the Museum of the Rockies at Montana State University in Bozeman also reported that the new species evolved at a surprisingly rapid rate.

During the late Cretaceous Period, from 70 million to 75 million years ago, large numbers of dinosaurs lived on coastal plains in what is now western Montana. These plains lined the western shore of a shallow sea that ran through North America between the Arctic Circle and the Gulf of Mexico.

Horner and his colleagues studied the fossilized remains of four groups of dinosaurs that lived in this area. The fossils were found in two sections of rock, each of which contained different species within these groups. Previously, scientists were unable to determine whether the species found in the upper, younger section of rock were descended directly from dinosaurs found in the lower, older section of rock or were newcomers to the area.

According to the scientists, the new species represent transitional forms that link the older dinosaurs with the younger dinosaurs. They calculated that the new species evolved in less than 500,000 years, a short time by paleontological standards. By comparison, the species found in rock above and below the new species were stable for up to 5 million years.

These findings provide support for the theory of *punctuated equilibrium*. This theory states that most evolutionary change occurs in short bursts after long periods of stability.

The scientists also determined that the accelerated evolution took place at a time when water levels in the sea rose, flooding the coastal plains and reducing and breaking up the dinosaurs' habitat. They concluded that this change in the environment triggered the dinosaurs' rapid evolution.

Fossil seized. The largest, best-preserved skeleton of *Tyrannosaurus rex* was seized by federal officials in May after Cheyenne River Sioux Indians charged that the fossil had been removed illegally from tribal lands in South Dakota. (See **Indian, American.**)

Oldest algae. The first organisms with complex cells may have existed 2.1 billion years ago, rather than 1.5 billion years ago as scientists had believed, according to research published in July. Scientists reported finding hundreds of fossilized spiral filaments that they identified as the oldest known examples of *eucaryotes*—organisms having cells in which the genetic material is contained within a nucleus. Eucaryotes include all multicellular plants and animals.

The fossils, which were found in northern Michigan, are the remains of spiral organisms that measured about 0.03 inch (1 millimeter) wide and up to 3.5 inches (90 millimeters) long. The filaments themselves

A *Tyrannosaurus rex* skull found in South Dakota was seized by federal officials in May after Sioux Indians charged it had been excavated illegally.

contain no fossilized eucaryotic cells. But the scientists believe the filaments represent a eucaryotic algae similar to a later form called *Grypania*.

The discovery of the fossils has challenged widely held theories about the evolution of Earth's atmosphere. Previously, most scientists believed that the atmosphere contained little oxygen until about 2 billion years ago. But algae such as *Grypania* require oxygen for respiration. Thus, the presence of algae 2.1 billion years ago raises questions about how quickly oxygen levels in the atmosphere increased.

Youngest therapsids. Therapsids, mammallike reptiles regarded as the evolutionary link between reptiles and mammals, may have become extinct about 100 million years later than scientists had previously believed. In July, a team of paleontologists reported finding a fossilized section of a therapsid jaw in Alberta, Canada, in rock about 60 million years old. Previously, fossil evidence had suggested that the therapsids, which were about the size of a dog, died out about 160 million years ago. The scientists speculated that so few therapsid fossils from this later period have been found because the animals were small and paleontologists have failed to recognize their remains. In addition, later therapsids may have lived only in northern areas that are inhospitable today.

Carlton E. Brett

In ***World Book,*** see **Dinosaur; Mammal; Paleontology; Prehistoric animal.**

Panama. Former Panamanian dictator General Manuel Antonio Noriega was sentenced on July 10, 1992, by a United States federal judge to 40 years in prison for his April 9 conviction on eight counts of drug trafficking, money laundering, and racketeering. Before being sentenced, a defiant Noriega delivered a two-hour speech in which he berated U.S. President George Bush for what Noriega called his illegal apprehension by a U.S. military invasion of Panama in 1989 and the conduct of his trial, the first of a foreign head of state by a U.S. court.

Noriega was not the only one left unsatisfied by his trial. Several U.S. representatives also faulted government prosecutors for giving other convicted felons reduced sentences in order to obtain their testimony, which was needed to convict Noriega.

Two U.S. grand juries had indicted Noriega in Miami and Tampa, Fla., in February 1988. During Noriega's trial, testimony revealed that U.S. agencies had paid Noriega as an informer in an attempt to curtail drug trafficking through Panama. Testimony revealed that Noriega had instead allowed Colombian cocaine dealers to ship cocaine through Panama for delivery to the United States in exchange for millions of dollars in bribes. Evidence mounted of Noriega's corruption, and when he became increasingly hostile to the United States, the United States invaded Panama with 25,000 troops and seized him in 1989. The invasion cost the lives of 23 American soldiers and several hundred Panamanians, not to mention more than $1 billion in property damage.

Bush tear-gassed. On June 11, 1992, President Bush, intending to benefit in a political year from a show of Panamanian gratitude for the 1989 ouster of Noriega, made a brief appearance in Panama while traveling to Brazil. But protesters disrupted the visit, and Panamanian police fired tear gas into the crowd. The gas irritated Bush's eyes and forced him to deliver his speech from the safety of a nearby U.S. Air Force base. Following the tear gas incident, many Panamanians criticized the police force. They said that it had been a mistake to incorporate large numbers of Noriega's old officers into the new police force created after the U.S. invasion in 1989. Critics said that the new police force was as incompetent and brutal as Noriega's had been.

Constitution. Panamanians defeated a package of proposed changes to Panama's constitution on Nov. 15, 1992. One proposed amendment would have prohibited Panama from having an army. Panama had not had an army since 1989. Other proposed changes included raising minimum education levels and increasing welfare benefits. Nathan A. Haverstock

See also **Latin America** (Facts in brief table). In *World Book*, see **Panama**.

Papua New Guinea. See **Asia; Pacific Islands.**
Paraguay. See **Latin America.**
Pennsylvania. See **Philadelphia; State government.**

United States President George Bush winces from the effect of tear gas fired by Panamanian police to disperse demonstrators in June.

Perot, Ross (1930-), ran unsuccessfully for president of the United States, coming in third in the November 1992 elections. He had taken himself out of contention on July 16, saying he could not win, but then reentered the race in October. The billionaire executive attracted support from people dissatisfied with "politics as usual," according to pollsters.

Perot was born in Texarkana, Tex., on June 27, 1930. He graduated from the U.S. Naval Academy in Annapolis, Md., in 1953. Perot left the Navy in 1957 to sell computers for International Business Machines Corporation. In 1962, he set up a computer company called Electronic Data Systems, Inc. (EDS). With the help of numerous government health-care contracts, EDS made Perot a billionaire. In 1984, Perot sold the company for about $2.5 billion to General Motors Corporation. In 1988, he founded a second computer firm, Perot Systems Corporation.

During and after the Vietnam War (1957-1975), Perot became actively involved, as a private citizen, in issues relating to American prisoners of war and servicemen missing in action. In 1979, Perot attempted to free two EDS employees jailed in Teheran, Iran. Perot organized a paramilitary team with the aim of staging a jailbreak, but the two men were freed along with all the jail's prisoners as a rebellion led by the Ayatollah Ruhollah Khomeini swept Teheran.

Perot and his wife, the former Margot Birmingham, have five children. Kristine Portnoy Kelley

Peru. On Sept. 22, 1992, President Alberto Fujimori predicted victory in an armed struggle that had cost Peru an estimated 25,000 lives, $22 billion in damages, and 12 years of civil strife. His assessment followed the September 12 capture of Abimael Guzmán Reynoso, the 57-year-old mastermind of the Maoist Shining Path guerrilla group, which had attempted to overthrow the Peruvian government since 1980. Guzmán was convicted of treason, and on October 7 a military tribunal sentenced him to life imprisonment.

Peruvian police apprehended Guzmán with several of his top lieutenants at a home in the middle-class Lima suburb of Surco. His capture followed eight months of violence, during which an estimated 1,500 people, mostly innocent bystanders, were killed in some 800 bombings and other attacks. Although the Shining Path claimed responsibility for most of the attacks, some of it was attributed to another group, the pro-Cuban Tupac Amaru Revolutionary Movement, whose leader, Victor Polay, was captured in June.

Suspension of democracy. On April 5, Fujimori had decided to suspend the Peruvian Constitution, dissolve Congress, and impose censorship. These steps, he told surprised Peruvians via a national television address, were necessary to win the fight against "terrorism, drug trafficking, and corruption."

Fujimori's stern action was popular with Peruvians who have borne the brunt of civil strife, and particularly with members of the armed forces and police.

Guerrilla leader Abimael Guzmán Reynoso stares from his jail cell in Lima, Peru, in September. Peruvian police captured him on September 12.

Army units quickly surrounded the Government Palace in Lima, the building where Congress meets, and began patrols of Lima's streets in what was widely characterized as a "necessary" coup d'etat. But abroad, and especially in Washington, D.C., many saw Fujimori's actions as a setback for democracy.

The Administration of U.S. President George Bush immediately branded Fujimori's take-over unjustified and unconstitutional. The United States suspended all economic and military aid to Peru, even though the latter move undermined U.S. support for Peru's war on drug trafficking. As the year unfolded, legal rights experts were aghast at the repressive trials of alleged terrorists and drug traffickers that followed Fujimori's seizure of dictatorial powers. Judges and prosecutors concealed their faces behind one-way glass. Their voices were altered electronically, and they signed their decisions with code names to prevent reprisals.

An attempted coup? Peruvian government officials claimed that a small group of soldiers tried to kill President Fujimori on November 13. Loyal troops prevented the alleged coup, according to the government. Although many accused Fujimori of making up the story to gain votes in an upcoming election, evidence surfaced that many military officers and influential business leaders had orchestrated an attempted overthrow. Nathan A. Haverstock

See also **Latin America** (Facts in brief table). In ***World Book***, see **Peru.**

Pet. See **Cat; Dog.**

Petroleum and gas. In 1992, for the first time since 1989, few major crises disrupted the world oil industry. Oil production in Russia and the other republics of the former Soviet Union continued to decline because of political and economic problems, and border disputes flared between Saudi Arabia and two of its neighbors. But in 1992, no single event, such as the Persian Gulf War (1991), disrupted supplies or sent petroleum prices sharply higher.

Ample supplies, flat prices. Iraq remained sidelined from the world oil market in 1992 by a continuing economic embargo, imposed by the United Nations (UN) Security Council after Iraq's 1990 invasion of Kuwait. The absence of Iraqi oil was offset to some extent by oil from Kuwait, whose petroleum industry made a rapid recovery from damages inflicted by Iraqi forces. By late 1992, Kuwait's oil output had reached the country's prewar level of 1.5 million barrels per day (bpd).

In addition, other member nations of the Organization of Petroleum Exporting Countries (OPEC), the international oil cartel, continued to pump near capacity. This kept the international oil market well supplied. As a result, the price of fuel remained relatively flat. For much of 1992, the price of the main United States crude oil, known as West Texas Intermediate, ranged from $20 to $22 per barrel, slightly lower than the 1991 average.

Natural gas. Early in 1992, natural gas prices fell below $1 per thousand cubic feet, the lowest level in 20 years. Because of the low prices and expectations that a gas surplus would continue for another year, many natural gas producers stopped drilling. But Hurricane Andrew, which hit Florida and Louisiana in late August, quickly changed the picture.

In addition to battering those two states, the hurricane swept across the Gulf of Mexico, where much of the United States' natural gas is produced. The storm destroyed some offshore production platforms and damaged pipelines.

The resulting disruptions in gas supplies sent prices surging. Within weeks of the storm, gas prices had climbed beyond $2 per thousand cubic feet, more than double their February level. By October, gas was selling for $2.50 per thousand cubic feet. The increase promised higher-than-expected fuel bills for the winter of 1992-1993.

Increased consumption. Even if Hurricane Andrew had not affected gas supplies, however, prices probably would have increased from the depressed levels of recent years. That was partly because a cold snap in February and March 1992 boosted U.S. gas consumption. In addition, the national economy improved somewhat.

For July, for example, U.S. consumption of gas totaled 1.3 trillion cubic feet (376.8 billion cubic meters), a 1 per cent increase over July 1991 levels. For the first half of 1992, deliveries of gas to residential customers rose 2 per cent over the same period in 1991, according to the U.S. Department of Energy. Deliveries to industrial users were up 8 per cent.

Domestic gas production totaled 10.38 trillion cubic feet (293.9 billion cubic meters) during the first seven months of 1992. However, that amount was only slightly above 1991 levels and well below the 11.54 trillion cubic feet (326.8 billion cubic meters) consumed during the first seven months of 1991. Imported oil and withdrawals from storage made up the difference.

Priming the pumps. Still, rising gas prices helped to trigger a turnaround in U.S. drilling for oil and natural gas. The number of active drilling rigs had fallen from a high of 4,500 in late 1981 to fewer than 800 in 1991. The rig count continued to slip through much of 1992, reaching 610, the lowest level ever recorded. By November, the rig count was up to 838. But the higher drilling rates failed to halt the continuing slide in U.S. crude oil production.

Domestic oil production, consumption. By October, U.S. crude oil production averaged less than 7 million bpd, according to the American Petroleum Institute, an oil-industry group. This figure was about 400,000 bpd less than U.S. output for the same period in 1991.

Petroleum use in the United States in 1992 stayed steady at about 17 million bpd. That figure was slightly higher than the 1991 level, which was held down by the national recession. But imports increased, accounting for some 50 per cent of all oil used by the United States. Saudi Arabia remained the chief foreign supplier for the United States.

World petroleum consumption rose slightly in 1992, but not by as much as had been expected. Sluggish economies in many nations continued to act as a drag on consumption. For 1992, world oil consumption was generally estimated at 67 million bpd, up 300,000 bpd from 1991. Oil output by countries outside OPEC, except for the United States and Russia, remained flat.

OPEC production. In late 1992, total output by nations within OPEC climbed to more than 25 million bpd, up from the 23 million to 24 million bpd they produced in 1991. The production increase came despite Iraq's failure to win UN permission to resume oil exports. In 1990, before the Persian Gulf crisis, Iraq had been producing 3.2 million bpd.

With Iraq out of the world oil picture, those OPEC members with spare capacity pushed their production levels even higher in 1992. Although OPEC maintained a theoretical production ceiling, most members ignored it. Still, even though individual country quotas were scrapped—at least temporarily—nearly all oil-producing nations except Saudi Arabia and Iran had reached their full capacity by midyear.

By late 1992, Saudi Arabia had increased its production slightly to more than 8.5 million bpd. And for one week in October, Iran produced 4 million bpd. Then, Iranian production fell somewhat, averaging about 3.8 million bpd. This amount, however, was sharply higher than Iran's previous OPEC quota of 3.2 million bpd.

Because of the increases, OPEC was able to produce enough oil to stir new worries of a possible petroleum glut, causing an October price drop. But some oil economists suggested that oil supplies could grow tight if the winter of 1992-1993 turned very cold.

Ecuadorian withdrawal. In the fall of 1992, OPEC ran into problems of another sort. In September, Ecuador, OPEC's smallest producer, announced it would become the first member to pull out of the cartel, as of December 1992. Ecuador said, however, that it would like to continue as an associate member of OPEC. Unlike full members, associate members cannot vote on organization policies. Ecuador said the main reason for the withdrawal was that the country could no longer afford the $2-million annual fee for a full membership in OPEC. Ecuador also questioned whether it was getting its money's worth, because OPEC had failed to keep oil prices high.

OPEC officials noted that Ecuador was delinquent in paying its dues. Still, Ecuador's announcement focused attention on OPEC's uniform rate for dues. It requires small oil exporters, such as Ecuador and Gabon, which produce about 300,000 bpd each, to pay the same annual assessment as does Saudi Arabia, the world's largest oil producer.

The Iraq factor. Many petroleum industry analysts expected Iraq would resume its role as an active player in the world oil market sometime during 1993. The November 1992 electoral defeat of U.S. President George Bush, who was the driving force behind international action against Iraq in 1990 and 1991, along with the worsening economic conditions inside Iraq, were expected to produce a move toward softening the UN embargo.

Iraq's enormous oil reserves—an estimated 100 million barrels—exceed those of any other country except Saudi Arabia. But Iraq's oil facilities were severely damaged in the two wars it had fought since 1980—the Iran-Iraq War (1980-1988) and the Persian Gulf War. Despite a lack of spare parts, the Iraqis have repaired much of the damage and report they are ready to resume some oil exports as soon as the UN embargo is lifted.

Just how much oil Iraq would be able to produce should the ban end was debatable. While experts doubted that export volumes could rise as fast as Iraqi oil officials maintain, they thought Iraq could reach 1 million or 1.5 million bpd quickly. And whenever Iraq resumes oil exports, other OPEC members may have to reduce their production to prevent a crash in petroleum prices. However, some oil experts doubt whether OPEC could or would act to fully offset Iraqi oil exports. As a result, the return of Iraq to the market could put downward pressure on world oil prices for some time. James Tanner

In ***World Book,*** see **Gas; Gasoline; Petroleum.**

Philadelphia. Edward G. Rendell took the oath of office on Jan. 6, 1992, to become Philadelphia's 127th mayor. The 49-year-old Rendell, a Democrat, told Philadelphians that the city had "put off difficult choices for far too long" in dealing with its severe budget crisis, and he warned of "sacrifices and pain" to come. He made clear that much of that sacrifice and pain would have to be borne by the city's public-school teachers, transit workers, and other municipal employees, whose contracts were due for renewal in 1992.

The new mayor succeeded W. Wilson Goode, also a Democrat, who had served two four-year terms and was barred by law from running for a third. Rendell was first elected to office in 1977 as the city's district attorney. In 1981, he was reelected to that post, then unsuccessfully ran for governor of Pennsylvania in 1986 and for mayor of Philadelphia in 1987. He won a landslide victory for mayor in the November 1991 general election.

Financial plan. On Feb. 20, 1992, Rendell announced a five-year financial plan aimed at changing the way the city conducts its business. The plan called for city employees to accept a four-year wage freeze and cutbacks in health benefits, sick time, and holidays—measures that would save an estimated $1.1 billion through 1996. Rendell said he and the city officials he appointed would make the first move by taking immediate 5 per cent pay cuts.

In June 1992, the Pennsylvania Intergovernmental Cooperation Authority—a board created by the state legislature to oversee Philadelphia's finances—sold $474.5 million in bonds to erase city deficits dating from 1988. The money was also used to purchase new and more efficient equipment for city departments and to repair some public facilities.

Union negotiations. City workers resisted the provisions of Rendell's financial plan, and the mayor backed off a bit. The city's 5,150 transit workers were offered a contract calling for a 10.5 per cent wage increase over three years, which they accepted on March 27, 1992. Midyear negotiations for other new union contracts became deadlocked, however.

At the July 1 deadline, the 15,000 blue-collar and white-collar city employees voted to keep on working while contract talks continued. The negotiations remained deadlocked through the summer, and on September 23 Rendell announced that he was imposing the terms of what he called his "last, best offer" on the employees. The contract, which called for a two-year wage freeze, prompted a strike on October 6. After 16 hours, the workers ended the strike, agreeing to a wage freeze for the first two years of a four-year contract.

Earlier in the month, on September 7, the city's 10,000 teachers approved a two-year contract. That agreement called for a 3 per cent wage hike in January 1994 but no increase until then.

New police, fire chiefs. On September 8, Richard Neal, who rose through the ranks of the Philadelphia

Edward G. Rendell, right, a former prosecutor, is sworn in as the new mayor of Philadelphia on January 6.

Police Department, became the 24th police commissioner in the department's 120-year history. He replaced Willie L. Williams, who in April was named police commissioner of Los Angeles.

Also sworn in on September 8 was new Fire Commissioner Harold Hairston, the first black leader of the city's fire department. He had been a member of the department for 28 years.

Feds seize Philadelphia Housing Authority. On May 20, the U.S. Department of Housing and Urban Development (HUD) took control of the Philadelphia Housing Authority (PHA), charging that it was riddled with corruption. HUD officials said they had appointed an outside director to run the PHA, which had gained a reputation as one of the nation's most poorly managed public-housing agencies.

Stadium demolished. JFK Stadium, long the site for the annual Army-Navy football game, was demolished in 1992 to make way for a new 22,000-seat arena that will house the city's basketball and hockey teams. The arena was scheduled to open in 1994.

Conductor departs. After 20 years at the podium of the Philadelphia Orchestra, conductor Riccardo Muti stepped down as music director on May 30 in Jerusalem, Israel, where the orchestra was on tour. Wolfgang Sawallisch, music director of the Bavarian State Opera in Munich, Germany, was slated to fill Muti's post in September 1993. Howard S. Shapiro

See also **City**. In ***World Book***, see **Philadelphia**.

Philippines. Fidel V. Ramos, a 64-year-old retired general and former defense secretary, on June 30, 1992, was inaugurated as the new president of the Philippines. Ramos garnered about 24 per cent of the votes in May 1992 elections, beating six other contenders. The election determined the successor to outgoing President Corazon C. Aquino. Ramos became the first former military officer and the first Protestant to head the largely Roman Catholic country. (See **Ramos, Fidel V.**)

About 70 per cent of the 32 million eligible Filipinos voted in the elections, which also featured more than 17,000 races for the national legislature and local offices. Observers characterized the elections as the most peaceful in decades, though about 100 people lost their lives in election-related clashes.

Aquino had endorsed Ramos, as had Philippine businessmen, who feared a return to the system of government-run monopolies that had existed under former President Ferdinand Marcos. Ramos also benefited from popular disgust with the traditional politicians who had controlled the Philippine Congress.

Joseph Estrada, a senator and former motion-picture star, was elected Ramos' vice president, even though he had run on a different ticket. And a third party won most of the congressional and local posts.

Peace with guerrillas? One of Ramos' priorities upon assuming office was to bring a halt to the 23-year-long battle between the government and Communist rebels. On September 22, he signed a bill that legalized the Communist Party, ending a 35-year-old ban. The symbolic move was designed to encourage the Communists to abandon their armed insurgency and enter the electoral arena. Ramos also ordered the release of some guerrillas, including Satur Ocampo, a resistance leader who had been held in jail since 1989 on kidnapping and arms charges. But rebel leaders hesitated to accept Ramos' overtures, saying they doubted the sincerity of the former defense secretary who had previously opposed a peaceful resolution of their differences.

U.S. base closure. The largest U.S. overseas base, the naval station at Subic Bay in the Philippines, closed in 1992. In 1991, the Philippine Senate had voted not to renew the lease for the base, and the U.S. Navy was given until December 1992 to leave. The United States handed over the base on Sept. 30, 1992, and the last Americans left on November 24.

However, earlier in November, the Philippine government agreed to allow the United States to periodically use Philippine military facilities for American ships and planes in Asia. The decision drew criticism from Filipinos opposed to the presence of U.S. forces in the country.

Some 40,000 Filipino workers lost their jobs because of the closing. But even before the base had been relinquished, the Philippine government had begun seeking private firms to take over the shipyard and other facilities. To encourage the conversion from military to commercial use, the Philippine Senate in January had approved the creation of special economic zones at the Subic Bay base.

Volcanic damage. Pinatubo, the volcano that had destroyed more than 100,000 homes and led to the deaths of more than 700 people in 1991, erupted again in August 1992, killing 72 people. But most of the damage this time was caused not by the ashfall but by the subsequent storms. Weeks of monsoon rains caused tremendous avalanches of volcanic ash and debris to flow into the Philippine countryside, leveling towns, clogging rivers, and burying farmland. Ramos in October ordered the evacuation of tens of thousands of families from low-lying areas near the volcano to temporary tent cities. The avalanches were expected to recur each rainy season for the next 5 to 10 years.

Economic problems also confronted the new administration. Electrical power outages have hampered Philippine industry for years, but money for investment in new power plants was scarce. However, on July 23, 1992, the government signed a financing package with commercial banks to reduce the share of export earnings slated to pay off foreign debts, thereby freeing money for domestic investment.

Henry S. Bradsher

See also **Asia** (Facts in brief table). In ***World Book,*** see **Philippines.**

Fidel Ramos (in yellow shirt) and his supporters celebrate his election in May as the new president of the Philippines.

Physics. Scientists in April 1992 announced the discovery of the long-sought "cosmic seeds" needed to start the formation of stars and galaxies in the early universe after the big bang. The team studied data from the Cosmic Background Explorer (COBE) satellite, which measures the faint glow of microwave radiation that fills all of space. (See **Astronomy**.)

Neutrinos. In June 1992, physicists obtained an important new clue in the mystery of the missing *solar neutrinos*—subatomic particles created by nuclear reactions in the sun. The sun generates most of its energy in reactions in which the nuclei of four hydrogen atoms fuse to form a helium nucleus. Each hydrogen nucleus is a single proton, whereas a helium nucleus is two protons and two neutrons. Therefore, for each helium nucleus produced, two protons from the hydrogen nuclei must change into neutrons. In the process of this conversion, a proton releases a particle called an electron neutrino. Scientists can calculate the rate at which the sun generates energy by hydrogen fusion, so they can estimate how many electron neutrinos should be created by the sun and detected on Earth.

Four neutrino detectors currently exist. One operates in a gold mine in South Dakota, another in a lead mine in Japan, and a third, called SAGE, in a cave in Russia. GALLEX, which began collecting data in 1991, lies beneath Italy's Gran Sasso Mountain.

All four of these detectors indicate a discrepancy between observations and the current theory of what nuclear reactions occur in the sun. The South Dakota detector sees only about 30 per cent of the number of solar neutrinos predicted by the theory; the Japanese detector, about 40 per cent; and SAGE, about 15 per cent. In June, researchers announced that GALLEX also reports a shortfall but it sees about 60 per cent of the expected number. That relatively high figure lent credibility to the current theory but also suggested that the theory is not complete.

Several explanations have been offered to account for the missing neutrinos. One idea holds that the core of the sun is about 10 per cent cooler than the current estimate of 27,000,000 °F (15,000,000 °C). The lower temperature would suppress the production of high-energy neutrinos, which the U.S. and Japanese sites detect, while not affecting lower-energy neutrinos, which the GALLEX and SAGE sites detect. Another explanation is that some electron neutrinos are transformed into another type of neutrino before they reach Earth. There are two other types of neutrinos—the muon and tau neutrinos—but current detectors can only record electron neutrinos. Researchers plan to test this idea using a detector currently under construction in Canada that will be sensitive to all three types of neutrinos.

Antimatter charge. One of the fundamental ideas of physics is that electrical charge comes in specific units. Scientists have been able to show to a very high precision that the charges of the electron and the proton are equal in strength (though the signs of the charges are opposite, with the electron having a negative charge and the proton a positive charge). But scientists had never investigated whether this relationship also held true for matter and its *antimatter* counterpart. Antimatter is matter made up of elementary particles that are the opposite of ordinary particles. The antiparticle of the electron is called the *positron*, and the antiparticle of the proton is called the *antiproton*. Since the electron has a charge of -1, scientists believe that the positron must have a charge of +1. And the proton's charge of +1 should mean that an antiproton has a charge of -1. But these notions had never been formally checked.

In July 1992, two researchers from the Los Alamos National Laboratory in New Mexico and the University of Århus in Denmark reported that they had verified these ideas. The pair devised a way to calculate the relative strengths of the charges of the positron and the antiproton from existing data. Their results indicated that the strengths of those charges do match those for the electron and proton.

However, because of the difficulty in working with antimatter, the researchers' measurements were at a much lower precision than were corresponding measurements for the electron and the proton. The researchers planned to refine their charge measurements using antihydrogen. Robert H. March

In ***World Book***, see **Antimatter**; **Neutrino**; **Physics.**

Poetry in 1992 offered works for every taste. David Ferry's *Gilgamesh,* for example, transforms the ancient Mesopotamian epic into a superb and moving poem for contemporary readers. In unrhymed couplets, it relates the adventures of Gilgamesh, one who "knew the way things were before the Flood," and who ultimately "went/ to the end of the earth, and over" in a fruitless quest for eternal life. Smaller in scope but equally concerned with mortality, Tess Gallagher's *Moon Crossing Bridge* gathers this poet's heartbreaking and fragile meditations on the last days of her husband, writer Raymond Carver. One poem asks: "Do you want me to mourn?/ Do you want me to wear black?/ Or like moonlight on whitest sand/ to use your dark, to gleam, to shimmer?/ I gleam. I mourn."

John Ashbery's *Hotel Lautréamont* offers lyrics as beautiful and slippery as mercury, and as hard to grasp. The Lautréamont of the title was a French writer of surreal prose poems in the late 1860's. In this jazzy, colloquial, yet highly literary work, Ashbery plays with language, confidently juggling words and images. In the poem "Revisionist Horn Concerto," he says, "Buttons, strings, bits of fluff/ it's all there, the vocabulary of displaced images,/ so that if its message doesn't add up to much, whose/ fault is it?"

Alexander Theroux's playful collection *The Lollipop Trollops* puts puns, wordplay, and arcane vocabulary into strict poetic forms. More down-to-earth is C. K. Williams' *A Dream of Mind,* whose proselike verses examine contemporary life. A number of poems in a section called "Some of the Forms of Jealousy" tell stories. "A Cautionary Tale" opens: "A man who's married an attractive, somewhat younger woman conceives a painful jealousy of her." It goes on to depict the husband's destruction of the marriage.

As he has in past collections, William Bronk offers in *Some Words* Zenlike observations of only a few lines' length. The poem "Forget It" reads, from start to finish: "Don't remember; all this will go away:/ the good, the bad, will go. We'll go away./ And something already is that still will be."

A poet rediscovered. One of the best "new" books of American poetry in 1992 was *First Awakenings: The Early Poems of Laura Riding.* Most of these never-before-published poems were written in the 1920's, when Riding was in her early 20's. They make clear why many famous poets—among them John Crowe Ransom, W. H. Auden, and Robert Graves—deeply admired Riding's musical, assured, and varied work. Echoes of Irish poet William Butler Yeats appear in these lines from "How Can I Die": "How can I die/ When I have kept my beauty bare/ For sorrow and for merriment/ And worn a flower in my hair/ To be a fair acknowledgement/ What things may die?"

Other notable collections of 1992 included Judith Hall's *To Put the Mouth To,* with its sensual, provocatively lush and tangled language. Louise Gluck's more exalted *The Wild Iris* offers a series of philosophical poems that examine such themes as the nature of speech and the question of God's existence. A similar seriousness can be found in Gjertrud Schnackenberg's *A Gilded Lapse of Time,* which reflects upon God and history. To her somber themes Schnackenberg brings an exact and evocative language, as in these lines from "A Monument in Utopia": "Particles of twilight's mauve, pushing past/ The momentarily lustrous glass panes/ Of eternity where you had laid/ The humid whorls of childhood's breath."

Collections of past work. Several major poets brought out retrospective volumes in 1992. Chief among these was James Merrill, whose *Selected Poems, 1946-1985* was accompanied by a reissue of his masterwork trilogy, *The Changing Light at Sandover.* Gary Snyder's *No Nature: New and Selected Poems;* Al Young's *Heaven: Collected Poems, 1956-1990;* and James Dickey's *The Whole Motion: Collected Poems, 1948-1992* gathered the work of these three important poets. William Carlos Williams' epic of ordinary American life, *Paterson,* was reissued in a scholarly, annotated text expected to be the standard edition of this work for years to come.

Anthologies and criticism. The 1992 edition of *The Best American Poetry,* edited by Charles Simic in consultation with David Lehman, includes some 75 poems by as many writers. This annual series, under the general direction of Lehman, provides an ongoing register of the best work from both emerging and established poets.

Mona Van Duyn was named the sixth poet laureate of the United States in June 1992. She was the first woman to hold the title.

Outstanding critical works of 1992 included David Lehman's *The Line Forms Here* and Dana Gioia's *Can Poetry Matter?,* whose title essay caused controversy when it was first published in 1991. Donald Hall's *Their Ancient Glittering Eyes* provides an account of the author's encounters with such figures as T. S. Eliot, Ezra Pound, Marianne Moore, and Yvor Winters.

Awards and honors. West Indian poet Derek Walcott was awarded the 1992 Nobel Prize for literature. Walcott is known for his sonorous, evocative verses, which—as in his 1990 epic *Omeros*—weave together the traditions of classical and English poetry and the rich culture of the Caribbean. (See also **Nobel Prizes.**)

The Pulitzer Prize for poetry in 1992 went to James Tate for his *Selected Poems* (1991). The poems in the volume exemplify Tate's highly comic and individual voice.

Mona Van Duyn, who won the 1991 Pulitzer Prize, was named sixth poet laureate of the United States on June 14, 1992. Van Duyn, the first woman to fill the post, succeeds Soviet-born poet Joseph Brodsky. Brodsky caused a stir during his tenure by denouncing the Library of Congress—creator of the poet laureate position—for failing to support poetry in general and, in particular, Brodsky's own efforts to make American poetry more widely known. Michael Dirda

See also **Van Duyn, Mona.** In ***World Book,*** see **Poetry.**

Poland. Political infighting and a weak government clouded progress toward economic and political reform in Poland in the first half of 1992. But a hopeful turn came with the formation in July of a new government and the resolution of conflicts between Poland's President Lech Walesa and parliament. Meanwhile, the country's recession seemed to be at last ending.

Political consensus. Since late 1991, Walesa had demanded that the Sejm (lower house of parliament) give him wider executive powers, but to no avail. Walesa threatened to form his own party if conflict between the Sejm's many factions was not ended. In June 1992, the parliament dismissed Poland's prime minister, but his successor failed to form a government. Finally, seven centrist and church-based parties nominated Hanna Suchocka, a lawyer, as prime minister. Walesa endorsed the choice, and the Sejm confirmed the nomination on July 10.

On August 1, the Sejm adopted a series of constitutional amendments establishing a mixed presidential-parliamentary system of government. The amendments permitted the cabinet to enact economic laws by decree, a power long sought by Walesa.

Labor unrest. Thousands of workers marched through Warsaw, the capital, in April, demonstrating discontent with the country's continuing recession. From January to July, the government disclosed, workers staged 38 strikes and 47 other stoppages. Miners and farmers, among the hardest hit by Poland's move toward a market economy, led much of the unrest. Meanwhile, a strike at an automobile plant in Tychy, in southern Poland, jeopardized a deal for a partnership with Italy's Fiat company. Suchocka's government refused to yield to the strikers, and in September, workers at the plant reduced their demands, allowing the deal to go through.

Privatization. In September, the government announced an "enterprise pact" designed in part to speed Poland's privatization program. Under the pact, state enterprises were given three months to produce plans for privatization or face possible liquidation. Official estimates showed that the share of private firms in Poland's *gross domestic product* (GDP—the value of all goods and services produced within a nation's borders) had reached about 50 per cent by mid-1992. But the government still owned about 8,000 firms, many of them on the verge of bankruptcy.

On the positive side, the economy showed signs of recovery in midyear. The government estimated that a surge in exports had given Poland a trade surplus of nearly $1 billion. To speed the recovery, the Sejm on October 9 approved Suchocka's guidelines for economic austerity in 1993. The guidelines included strict wage controls, reductions in welfare spending, and sharp increases in income tax rates. Eric Bourne

See also **Europe** (Facts in brief table). In ***World Book,*** see **Poland.**

Pollution. See **Environmental pollution.**

Polish President Lech Walesa prays at a ceremony in May in Katyn, Russia, honoring thousands of Polish officers killed by Soviet secret police in 1940.

Popular music. Even the popular music industry was not immune from the 1992 presidential election campaign in the United States. In June, Democratic candidate Governor Bill Clinton of Arkansas criticized rap artist Sister Souljah for allegedly racist remarks she made in *The Washington Post* on May 13 in reference to the Los Angeles riots in April. Souljah said that she was giving the rioter's point of view in the offending quote—". . . if black people kill black people every day, why not have a week and kill white people?" She said she was not issuing a call to action for blacks.

When Clinton named Senator Albert A. Gore, Jr., of Tennessee as his vice presidential running mate in July, a controversy seemed to be in the making concerning the recording industry. In 1985, Gore's wife, Mary (Tipper) Gore, spearheaded the crusade for record companies to put parental warning stickers on albums containing explicit lyrics, such as those that deal with sex, drug use, or violence. The music industry opposed these proposals, but in July 1990, an advisory sticker policy went into effect. By 1992, however, the animosity felt by the music industry against Tipper Gore seemed to have faded.

Politicians criticized the song "Cop Killer" from Ice-T's hard-core rock album *Body Count.* The album was released in March, but it did not generate controversy until June. The lyrics included the lines, "I'm 'bout to dust some cops off. . . . Die, pig, die." President George Bush referred to the song indirectly in speaking against records that approve the killing of law enforcement officers. Vice President Dan Quayle, citing the song directly, criticized Time Warner Incorporated for selling the album. Ice-T said that the lyrics were meant to explain the causes of violence.

Nevertheless, protests by police groups and members of the U.S. Congress mounted, and more than 1,500 record stores nationwide refused to carry *Body Count.* Citing free artistic expression, Time Warner refused to pull the album, though police picketed the company's annual shareholders meeting. Then, on July 28, Ice-T requested that "Cop Killer" be removed from future issues of the album, claiming law enforcement officers had made bomb and death threats against Time Warner employees. And Time Warner said that record store owners had been asked to return unsold copies of the original album.

Making headlines. Madonna grabbed headlines with a new album, *Erotica,* released in October along with *Sex,* a book of controversial photographs of her. Sinead O'Connor caused a furor by tearing up a picture of Pope John Paul II during an October performance on the television show "Saturday Night Live." Publicity about her behavior overshadowed attention for her new album *Am I Not Your Girl?*

Million-dollar deals. Huge recording contracts were again negotiated in 1992. Prince's joint venture with Warner Brothers Records and Warner/Chappell Music reportedly brought him more than $100 million for six albums, expansion of his Paisley Park recording

Grammy Award winners in 1992

Record of the Year, "Unforgettable," Natalie Cole (with Nat King Cole).

Album of the Year, *Unforgettable,* Natalie Cole.

Song of the Year, "Unforgettable," Irving Gordon, songwriter.

New Artist, Marc Cohn.

Pop Vocal Performance, Female, "Something to Talk About," Bonnie Raitt.

Pop Vocal Performance, Male, "When a Man Loves a Woman," Michael Bolton.

Pop Performance by a Duo or Group with Vocal, "Losing My Religion," R.E.M.

Pop Instrumental Performance, *Robin Hood: Prince of Thieves,* Michael Kamen, conductor, and the Greater Los Angeles Orchestra.

Rock Vocal Performance, Solo, *Luck of the Draw,* Bonnie Raitt.

Rock Performance by a Duo or Group with Vocal, "Good Man, Good Woman," Bonnie Raitt and Delbert McClinton.

Hard Rock Performance with Vocal, *For Unlawful Carnal Knowledge,* Van Halen.

Metal Performance with Vocal, *Metallica,* Metallica.

Rock Instrumental Performance, "Cliffs of Dover," Eric Johnson.

Rock Song, "Soul Cages," Sting, songwriter.

Alternative Music Album, *Out of Time,* R.E.M.

Rhythm-and-Blues Vocal Performance, Female (tie), *Burnin',* Patti LaBelle, and "How Can I Ease the Pain," Lisa Fischer.

Rhythm-and-Blues Vocal Performance, Male, *Power of Love,* Luther Vandross.

Rhythm-and-Blues Performance by a Duo or Group with Vocal, *Cooleyhighharmony,* Boyz II Men.

Rhythm-and-Blues Song, "Power of Love/Love Power," Luther Vandross, Marcus Miller, and Teddy Vann, songwriters.

Rap Solo Performance, "Mama Said Knock You Out," L. L. Cool J.

Rap Performance by a Duo or Group, "Summertime," D. J. Jazzy Jeff and the Fresh Prince.

New-Age Album, *Fresh Aire 7,* Mannheim Steamroller.

Contemporary Jazz Performance, "Sassy," The Manhattan Transfer.

Jazz Vocal Performance, *He Is Christmas,* Take 6.

Jazz Instrumental Performance, Soloist, "I Remember You," Stan Getz.

Jazz Instrumental Performance, Group, *Saturday Night at the Blue Note,* Oscar Peterson Trio.

Large Jazz Ensemble Performance, *Live at the Royal Festival Hall,* Dizzy Gillespie and the United Nations Orchestra.

Country Vocal Performance, Female, "Down at the Twist and Shout," Mary-Chapin Carpenter.

Country Vocal Performance, Male, "Ropin' the Wind," Garth Brooks.

Country Performance by a Duo or Group with Vocal, "Love Can Build a Bridge," The Judds.

Country Vocal Collaboration, "Restless," Steve Wariner, Ricky Skaggs, and Vince Gill.

Country Instrumental Performance, *The New Nashville Cats,* Mark O'Connor.

Bluegrass Album, *Spring Training,* Carl Jackson, John Starling, and the Nash Ramblers.

Country Song, "Love Can Build a Bridge," Naomi Judd, John Jarvis, and Paul Overstreet, songwriters.

Music Video, Short Form, "Losing My Religion," R.E.M.

Music Video, Long Form, "Madonna: Blonde Ambition World Tour Live," Madonna.

Natalie Cole holds some of the six Grammys her album *Unforgettable* won at the 34th annual awards presentation in New York City on February 25.

operation, and his appointment as an executive talent scout at Warner Brothers. Madonna's joint venture with Time Warner was valued at $60 million and included the launch of her own multimedia entertainment company, Maverick, which consists of a record company and a music publishing company. ZZ Top signed a contract reportedly worth $30 million for a six-album deal with RCA Records.

Compact disc prices hit a new high—$16.98—when Garth Brooks's album *The Chase* and Michael Bolton's *Timeless* were released in September. They became the highest priced standard-length compact discs by a single artist.

Copy compensation. On October 7, the U.S. Senate passed the Audio Home Recording Act of 1992. The U.S. House of Representatives had passed a similar bill in September. The act authorized a tax on blank digital tapes and recording equipment that would be used to finance royalty payments to musicians, recording companies, and music publishers. The music industry anticipated lost sales and royalties because digital audio tape recorders and blank digital tapes make it possible to copy music on home recorders with near-perfect reproduction.

Legal issues. In May, a federal circuit court of appeals in Atlanta, Ga., reversed a 1990 federal district court ruling that 2 Live Crew's album *As Nasty As They Wanna Be* was obscene. The appeals court said that the judge in the lower court had relied on his own, rather than community, standards in his decision. In Louisiana, Democratic Governor Edwin W. Edwards vetoed in July 1992 legislation making it illegal for minors to purchase records carrying the parental advisory sticker.

Concerts with a cause. On April 20, the "Freddie Mercury Tribute: Concert for AIDS Awareness" was televised in 70 countries and raised $35 million for AIDS organizations worldwide. The concert, held at London's Wembley Stadium, was a tribute to Freddie Mercury, the lead singer of Queen, who died of AIDS on Nov. 24, 1991. Among the 100 stars participating were David Bowie, U2, Guns N' Roses, and Elton John, as well as members of Mercury's band.

On Sept. 26, 1992, at Joe Robbie Stadium near Miami, Fla., "Hurricane Relief" raised $1.3 million for victims of Hurricane Andrew, which struck Florida and Louisiana in August 1992, and Hurricane Iniki, which hit Hawaii in September. The concert featured Gloria Estefan, Jimmy Buffett, and Paul Simon.

Rock. After a long absence from recording and touring, Bruce Springsteen released two new albums simultaneously—*Human Touch* and *Better Days.* Both were hailed by critics. Eric Clapton, Paul McCartney, and Mariah Carey released material recorded from the "Unplugged" performance series by the cable television channel MTV.

Other rock artists returning to prominence in 1992 included R.E.M., Def Leppard, Peter Gabriel, Roger Waters, Patty Smyth, the Black Crowes, Megadeth, Red Hot Chili Peppers, Faith No More, and Queen, whose classic 1976 hit single "Bohemian Rhapsody" was once again a success, this time in the soundtrack for the motion picture *Wayne's World.*

New rock bands arose out of Seattle's "grunge rock," the newest subcategory of rock music. Led by Nirvana, these included Soundgarden and Pearl Jam, who starred in the second Lollapalooza touring festival of alternative rock bands, a name the music industry has given to music influenced by another subcategory, punk rock.

Country music newcomer Billy Ray Cyrus enjoyed the longest running chart-topping debut album of the rock era when *Some Gave All* stayed number one for 17 weeks on the top 200 albums chart of *Billboard,* a major recording industry magazine. His debut single "Achy Breaky Heart" and its accompanying music video caused a country dance craze and became the first platinum country single since 1983.

Garth Brooks increased his superstar stature with a network TV special and two hit albums, *The Chase* and *Beyond the Season,* a Christmas album released in August. Wynonna Judd dropped her surname for her first solo album and repeated the success she previously enjoyed with her mother in The Judds duo. Brooks & Dunn emerged as the major country music duo of 1992. Solo female vocal standouts included Mary-Chapin Carpenter and Trisha Yearwood. Solo male vocalists with hits during the year were Vince Gill and

Alan Jackson. Tammy Wynette crossed over to pop when she was a guest with the British dance group, The KLF, on "Justified & Ancient."

Rap evolves. Alternative rap acts, such as Arrested Development, Disposable Heroes of Hiphopracy, Me Phi Me, Basehead, and Divine Styler were influenced by hard rock and heavy metal, blues and bluegrass, and even jazz. Kriss Kross, the young rap duo of Chris Kelly and Chris Smith, wore their clothes backwards and topped the pop charts with the smash hit single "Jump," as well as a first album, *Totally Krossed Out.* Sir Mix-A-Lot's "Baby Got Back" single also hit number one on the pop chart.

Rhythm and blues. *Cooleyhighharmony* by Boyz II Men was the best-selling album ever by a rhythm and blues group. Vanessa Williams' "Save the Best for Last" topped the pop, rhythm and blues, and adult-contemporary singles charts. Bobby Brown and En Vogue had strong albums, and Mary J. Blige and Trey Lorenz proved important newcomers. Whitney Houston's "I Will Always Love You" was a top single.

Jazz. Saxophonist Branford Marsalis took over as bandleader on the "Tonight" TV show when Jay Leno became the new host in May. Veteran jazz artists with noteworthy releases in 1992 included vocalists Abbey Lincoln and Shirley Horn. Harry Connick, Jr., released two albums at once in November. Jim Bessman

In ***World Book,*** see **Country music; Jazz; Popular music.**

Population. Ecologists and population experts in 1992 warned that the world's burgeoning birth rate was an environmental issue in need of immediate attention. Speakers at the United Nations (UN) Conference on Environment and Development, held in Rio de Janeiro, Brazil, in June predicted that the current rate of population growth would lead to irreversible depletion or destruction of natural resources, more widespread poverty and famine, and increasing migration from poor nations to wealthy ones.

The UN Fund for Population Activities, which predicted in 1991 that the world's population would increase from 5.48 billion in 1992 to 10 billion by 2050, called on the United States and other nations to help curb population growth by supporting family-planning programs in developing countries. About 95 per cent of population growth is in Third World nations, where many women have no access to family-planning services.

Population control programs in China and India have not successfully curbed the birth rates of the two most populous nations, according to September 1992 reports from the Population Crisis Committee, a nonprofit group in Washington, D.C. India and China have made strides in lowering birth rates, but shortcomings in family planning present major obstacles to stabilizing their populations, the reports said. Lori Fagan

See also **Environmental pollution: Environmental Concern Goes Global.** In ***World Book,*** see **Population.**

Portugal in 1992 felt both the benefits and complications of its membership in the European Community (EC or Common Market). In April, Portugal linked the value of its currency, the escudo, to that of the German mark and other currencies in the European Monetary System. In so doing, Portugal pledged to follow economic policies—such as cutting government spending—that would help strengthen its economy in preparation for the EC's planned economic and monetary union, expected to be in place by the late 1990's.

The EC's plans for economic and political integration also provided for increased economic aid to poorer EC nations, including Portugal, Greece, Ireland, and Spain. But these nations maintained they would need even more financial help from richer countries, such as Germany and France, to adapt to the new, more integrated Europe.

Portugal held the presidency of the Council of Ministers, the EC's policymaking body, for the first half of 1992. The presidency rotates among member nations every six months. During its tenure, Portugal proposed the creation of a special fund that would direct more EC money to poorer regions. EC leaders adopted the idea at a summit in Lisbon, Portugal's capital, in late June, and officials said a $13.8-billion fund could be created early in 1993. But an economic slowdown in Western Europe, continued pressure for aid to Eastern European countries, and political difficulties within the EC made quick implementation of the fund unlikely.

Modernization. Center-right Prime Minister Aníbal Cavaço Silva continued Portugal's course toward economic modernization, begun when the country joined the EC in 1986. Attractive terms for setting up new factories—along with the relatively low wages of Portuguese workers—continued to attract foreign investors. The government estimated that foreign investment in Portugal would total nearly $6 billion in 1992. Meanwhile, the government moved forward in its ambitious program to sell state-owned companies to private investors. In July, it said it would sell 70 per cent of the country's biggest insurance company, Imperio S.A., to Portuguese and foreign investors.

Diplomatic role. During its EC presidency, Portugal engaged in diplomacy to help resolve a number of political problems, including helping to organize the EC's efforts to halt the war that followed the breakup of Yugoslavia in 1991. Meanwhile, the EC's plans for economic and political union—set forth in the so-called Maastricht Treaty, or Treaty on European Union—were threatened as member countries expressed concern over the transfer of power from national governments to a central EC government based in Brussels, Belgium. Cavaço Silva tried to help resolve those concerns at the June 26-27 summit, but at year-end the fate of the treaty was uncertain.

Philip Revzin

See also **Europe** (Facts in brief table). In ***World Book,*** see **Portugal.**

Postal Service, United States. On February 28, 1992, Anthony M. Frank resigned as postmaster general, a position he had held since 1988. During his tenure, Frank often clashed with postal unions, but he was credited with persuading the unions to accept automation and a reduction in the work force.

Marvin T. Runyon, Jr., 67, chairman of the Tennessee Valley Authority (TVA) and a longtime auto industry executive, was named on May 5 to succeed Frank. "The post office," Runyon said, "faces many of the same challenges that TVA and many other employers face today: increased competition, costs growing faster than revenue . . . rapid changes in technology. . .[and] a need for improved employee relations."

That Runyon planned to make sweeping changes in the Postal Service became evident on July 8, when he announced that the agency would no longer pay to be an official sponsor of the Olympic Games, a project budgeted at about $122 million in 1992. Runyon said, however, that the Postal Service might be willing to offer the Olympics free mailing privileges in exchange for the right to market mementos bearing the Olympic four-ring symbol.

Management cuts and restructuring. On August 7, Runyon said he would slash the Postal Service's management ranks by more than 20 per cent—a reduction of 30,000 out of about 130,000 management-level employees. Runyon said the cuts would be made by offering older managers early-retirement incentives. The staffing cutback was necessary, he said, to reduce a projected $2-billion Postal Service deficit in 1993 and to make it possible to delay raising mailing rates until at least 1995. The retirement program far exceeded its goal, with 46,000 senior postal employees opting to retire. Meanwhile, Runyon announced plans to cut the payroll further by paring the staff at the Postal Service's Washington, D.C., headquarters.

Runyon also decreed a complete overhaul of the Postal Service's military-style hierarchy. He said the 42 highest management positions would be pared to 24, with most of those positions carrying the title of vice president instead of general.

The moves were expected to save about $700 million in the first year and $1.4 billion in the second year. In addition, Runyon said the agency would save $2 million by canceling a plan to purchase robots to clean bathrooms in Postal Service facilities.

Elvis stamp. On January 9, Frank announced plans to print 320 million stamps in 1993 honoring singer Elvis Presley, who died in 1977. The public was invited to choose between two competing designs. By a vote of 851,200 to 277,723, a design featuring a young Elvis was chosen over one depicting Presley later in his life. Frank Cormier and Margot Cormier

In *World Book,* see **Post office; Postal Service, United States.**

President of the United States. See **Bush, George H. W.; United States, Government of the.**

Elvis Presley fans at Presley's Memphis, Tenn., estate on June 4 admire a blow-up of the "Young Elvis" stamp—the winning design for the 1993 issue.

Prince Edward Island. Islanders were stunned on Oct. 30, 1992, when Premier Joseph Ghiz announced he was resigning his post for personal reasons. Ghiz had been a strong supporter of Canada's failed constitutional reform package and the controversial free trade agreement between Canada, the United States, and Mexico.

Faced with difficult economic conditions, Canada's smallest province sought to diversify its economy in 1992. On March 23, Ghiz told the legislature that the recession had hurt the island's traditional economic mainstays of agriculture and fishing, and that the province needed to encourage new enterprises. Ghiz mentioned communications and aerospace as possible areas for development and said that the recently closed air force base at Summerside would be turned into an industrial park.

The provincial budget, announced on April 7 further reflected a desire to attract investment. Corporate income tax rates were slashed—in some instances by 50 per cent—while property taxes were eased. The budget forecast an operating deficit of $26.8 million ($21.5 million U.S.), half the actual 1991-1992 deficit of $51.8 million ($41.5 million).

In 1992, provincial officials decided to place an image of Anne of Green Gables (a character from a fictional story set on Prince Edward Island) on automobile license plates for 1993. David M. L. Farr

In ***World Book,*** see **Prince Edward Island.**

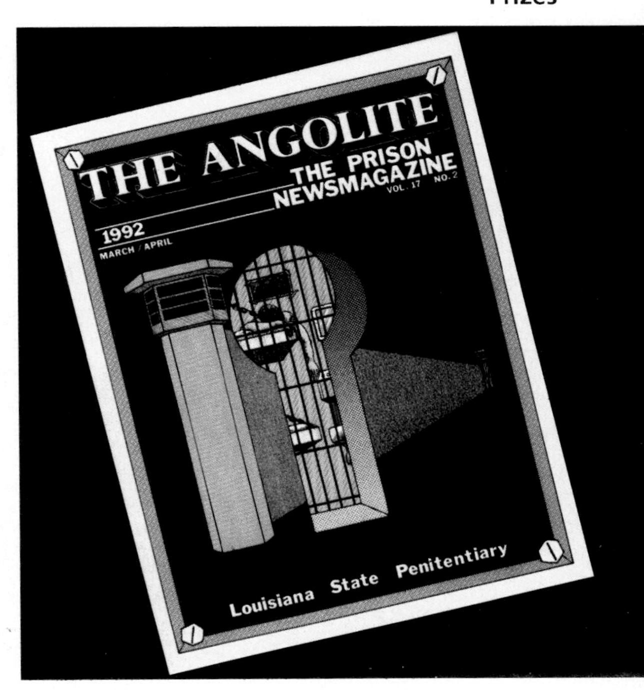

The Angolite, an award-winning magazine, lost one of its two founders and editors when Ron Wikberg was released from prison in August.

Prison. The largest number of executions in the United States since 1962 took place in 1992. On October 21, the number reached 26 with the execution of Ricky Lee Grubbs in Missouri. In 1987, the death penalty was enforced 25 times, and in 1962, it was used 47 times.

During 1992, several states conducted their first execution in decades. In Wyoming, the death penalty was used for the first time since 1965 as the state on Jan. 22, 1992, put to death Mark Hopkinson for ordering the killing of a witness testifying against him at a trial in which he was convicted of three murders.

For the first time since 1946, Delaware implemented the death penalty by killing Steven Brian Pennell with a lethal injection on March 14, 1992. Pennell had tortured and killed four women. On April 6, Arizona used capital punishment for the first time since 1963, executing Donald Eugene Harding for the murders of two businessmen. And on April 21, 1992, California executed Robert Alton Harris for the 1978 murders of two teen-age boys. California had not used the death penalty since 1967.

By Dec. 15, 1992, a total of 31 men had been executed during the year. A woman had not been put to death since 1984.

Incarceration rate. The number of people held in U.S. federal and state prisons reached 855,958 as of June 30, 1992, according to the U.S. Department of Justice's Bureau of Justice Statistics (BJS). The number represented a 6.4 per cent increase over the number of people in prisons during the same period in 1991. From January 1992 to June 1992, the number of women held in state and federal prisons grew by 3.8 per cent, with women prisoners accounting for 5.8 per cent of the total prison population.

Drug offenders. A 1990 survey released in August 1992 by the National Institute of Justice, a branch of the U.S. Department of Justice, found that 86 per cent of prison wardens and jail administrators reported that increased arrests of drug dealers had a major impact on the crowding of their institutions. More than two-thirds of jail supervisors said that their facilities were operating at more than 100 per cent of their capacity. According to the BJS, the incarceration rate among state prisons was 16 per cent to 31 per cent above capacity, and federal prisons were operating at 46 per cent over their limit.

The United States leads the world in the rate of incarceration, according to a February report from The Sentencing Project, a private research and advocacy group in Washington, D.C. The number of prisoners held in U.S. prisons and jails in 1990 was 455 per 100,000 citizens. South Africa had the second highest rate with 311 incarcerations per 100,000 people.

Jennifer A. Nichols

See also **Crime; Supreme Court of the United States.** In ***World Book,*** see **Prison.**

Prizes. See **Nobel Prizes; Pulitzer Prizes.**

The Ballooning Prison Population

By Michael Tonry

The "war on drugs" has led to rampant prison overcrowding, forcing officials to explore alternative punishments.

An increasing number of Americans are witnessing life through the bars of prison cells. More than 450 of every 100,000 United States residents were confined in jails and prisons on any given day in 1990, according to the U.S. Department of Justice's Bureau of Justice Statistics (BJS). That is the highest rate of *incarceration* (imprisonment) in American history and more than double the 1980 rate of 206 per 100,000 U.S. residents.

The U.S. incarceration rate is more than four times that of most other developed countries. For example, in 1989, the rates for Great Britain, France, Spain, Australia, Italy, and Japan were all below 100 per 100,000, according to the Sentencing Project, a group that compiles international incarceration figures. The only developed countries with incarceration rates approaching America's in 1989 were South Africa (333 prisoners per 100,000) and the former Soviet Union (268 per 100,000).

The chief reason for the rise in U.S. prison numbers is the federal government's "war on drugs," launched in the 1980's. To combat illegal drug use, the government

pushed for more arrests and stiffer sentences. But many states now find themselves grappling with the problem of prison overcrowding, and legislators across the country are being forced to consider the merits of less costly alternatives to imprisonment.

The flood of prisoners

About 70 per cent of the $10 billion spent by the federal government in 1991 in the war on drugs went to law enforcement and prosecution. As a result, the total number of people arrested and prosecuted for drug crimes rose greatly. According to the Federal Bureau of Investigation (FBI), arrests in the United States for all crimes rose 28 per cent from 1980 through 1989, but arrests for drug crimes shot up 126 per cent.

Harsher sentencing procedures also contributed to the leap in prison populations. In 1989, judges sentenced 87,859 people to prison for drug crimes, almost a 700 per cent increase from the 11,487 people sentenced in 1981. Much of the increased severity resulted from laws requiring that every person convicted of a particular crime—especially a drug-related one—receive a mandatory sentence. In Florida, for example, one-third of the state's 34,000 new inmates in 1991 were imprisoned under mandatory sentences. One problem that prison experts see with mandatory-sentence laws is that many of the people caught in their nets are first-time offenders. Before mandatory sentences, such offenders often received probation. With mandatory-sentence laws, judges and prosecutors are less able to adjust the punishment to suit the criminal.

Even rising parole violations have added to the prison population. For example, in California in 1978, only 1,011 ex-convicts were sent back to prison because they had violated their parole. By 1988, this number had grown to 34,014 parole violators, representing almost half the people sent to California prisons that year—by far the largest category of new prisoners. Most of this rise in people imprisoned for parole violations stemmed, again, from the antidrug campaign. The development of low-cost drug tests allowed officials to test most parolees, and many failed.

Not enough cells

The rising prison populations have created serious overcrowding in both state and federal prisons. Prison administrators often measure prison crowding by comparing a prison's population with its rated capacity. A prison's rated capacity is the number of people the prison is designed to house, taking into account the needs for sleeping space, recreation, shops and schools, cafeterias, and administrative offices. Most prison administrators believe that a prison's population should never be more than 95 per cent of its rated capacity, to allow for population turnover, maintenance and repairs, and response to short-term crises.

But most U.S. prisons have been operating in excess of 100 per cent of capacity throughout the 1980's and early 1990's. In 1991, for example, state prisons operated at 131 per cent of total capacity and federal prisons at 146 per cent. As a result, many inmates slept crammed two or three to a

The author:

Michael Tonry is a professor of law at the University of Minnesota Law School.

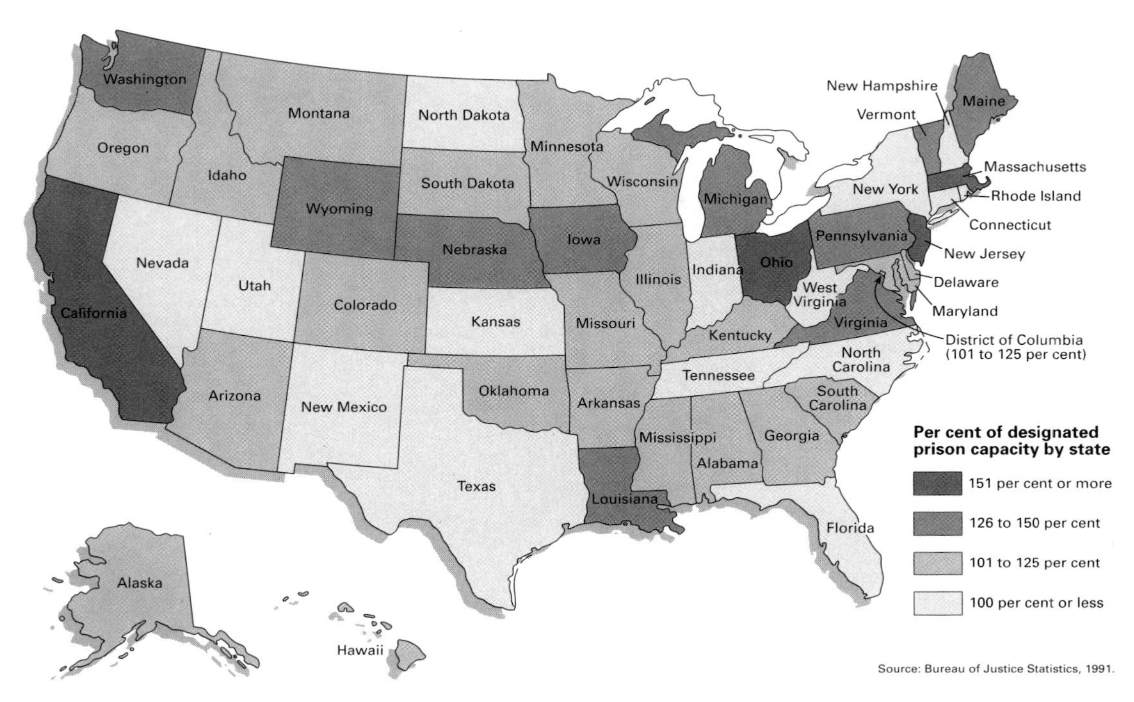

The prison crunch

Prison overcrowding is a problem across the United States. Of the 50 states and the District of Columbia, only 15 states in 1991 operated at or below their designated capacity. And 14 states operated at 126 per cent of their capacity or higher.

cell, or in large, makeshift dormitories. Forcing people to live in congested circumstances makes them more difficult to manage and results in idleness, increased tension, and violence. Overcrowding also means that the resources to provide prisoners with medical care, educational or vocational training, or drug or alcohol treatment are stretched thin. For these reasons, the majority of states are under court orders to reduce prison overcrowding.

The price tag for prisons

Many states have responded to the growing number of prisoners by building new prisons, but this approach has proven costly. Construction costs for prisons range from about $30,000 per prisoner for minimum-security facilities to about $75,000 per prisoner for maximum-security facilities. These figures bring the average total construction cost to about $28-million per prison, according to the Criminal Justice Institute (CJI), a private research organization. The annual cost to operate prisons ranges from $15,000 to $50,000 per prisoner per year, depending on the state. Total operating costs in fiscal year 1991 ranged from $7 million for North Dakota to about $3 billion for California. And the amount of federal and state money spent to operate prisons is rapidly increasing. In 1980, about $4 billion was spent to operate 556 federal and state prisons, according to the CJI. By 1991, spending had leaped to $18 billion to operate 1,315 prisons. In light of strained budgets and voter resistance to tax hikes, state governments simply cannot keep pace with the record incarceration rates

Convictions outpace construction

Because of budget constraints, prison officials have been unable to build facilities fast enough to meet the surge in convicted offenders.

The U.S. incarceration rate more than tripled from 1974 to 1991, *below*, surpassing the availability of cells. As a result, many jail and prison administrators had to grapple with overcrowding. For example, in the Broward County Jail in Fort Lauderdale, Fla., *right*, overflow inmates had to sleep in a renovated recreation room.

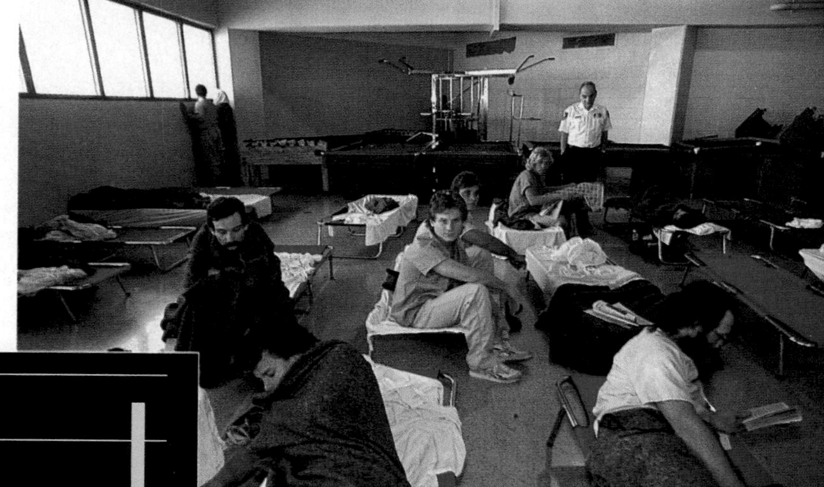

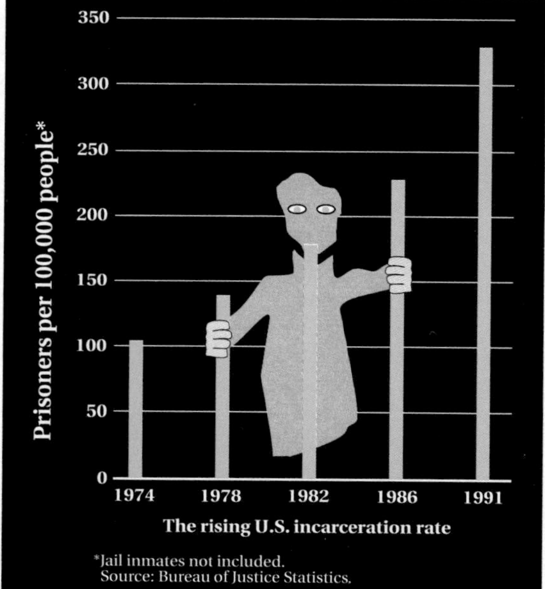

The rising U.S. incarceration rate

*Jail inmates not included.
Source: Bureau of Justice Statistics.

by building and operating more prisons.

Instead of sinking money into new prisons, a few states, notably Minnesota and Washington, decided to treat their existing prisons as expensive, scarce resources. According to this view, prison use should be determined not by the uncoordinated decisions of prosecutors, judges, and lawmakers but by consensus policy decisions about how best to use prison resources.

These states established agencies called *sentencing commissions*, which devise sentencing guidelines for judges to consider in deciding whom to imprison and for how long. In setting those guidelines, the sentencing commissions took account of prison capacity and made trade-offs among sentences for serious and less serious crimes in order to avoid putting excessive pressure on their prison resources. For example, Minnesota's sentencing commission in the mid-1980's decided to increase penalties for sex crimes and to reduce penalties for persons convicted of minor property crimes. Because of such trade-offs, Minnesota and Washington were among a handful of states whose prison populations did not grow rapidly in the late 1980's.

Sentencing commissions have been tried in other states and in the

In the drive to keep costs down, new prisons have begun taking unfamiliar shapes. To avoid paying for expensive real estate, the New York Department of Corrections built a prison barge, *above*, which is moored to a dock in New York City's East River. And the Texas Department of Corrections moved away from the idea of a walled prison entirely, setting up a "tent city," *left*, at the New River Correctional Institution in Raiford, though the tents were to be replaced by dormitories.

federal system. But many officials do not support the idea of trade-offs, arguing that the severity of criminal punishments should not hinge on prison capacities.

A spectrum of alternatives

Concern for prison crowding and the increasing costs of correctional budgets has led many states to develop intermediate punishments that do not require prison terms. These include such programs as intensively supervised probation (ISP), house arrest, community service, restitution, day fines, and boot camps.

One of the most widespread intermediate punishments is ISP, which was designed in the late 1970's to provide intensive supervision of convicts. The advantage of ISP is that it monitors criminals without increasing the burden on prisons. In ISP, a probation officer may have as few as 12 offenders to supervise, unlike an ordinary probation officer's caseload of 150 to 300 offenders, which is so large that little supervision can be provided. In Georgia's ISP program, for example, 2 officers are assigned to 25 offenders and are in contact with those offenders 15 to 20 times a month. The offenders must work, participate in drug treatment programs if needed, and satisfy other program conditions. ISP programs take different forms. In Georgia, judges have the discretion to sentence offenders otherwise bound for prison directly to ISP. In New Jersey, offenders are released early from prison to take part in ISP.

Another common intermediate punishment is *house arrest,* in which offenders remain in their own homes rather than in prison for the terms

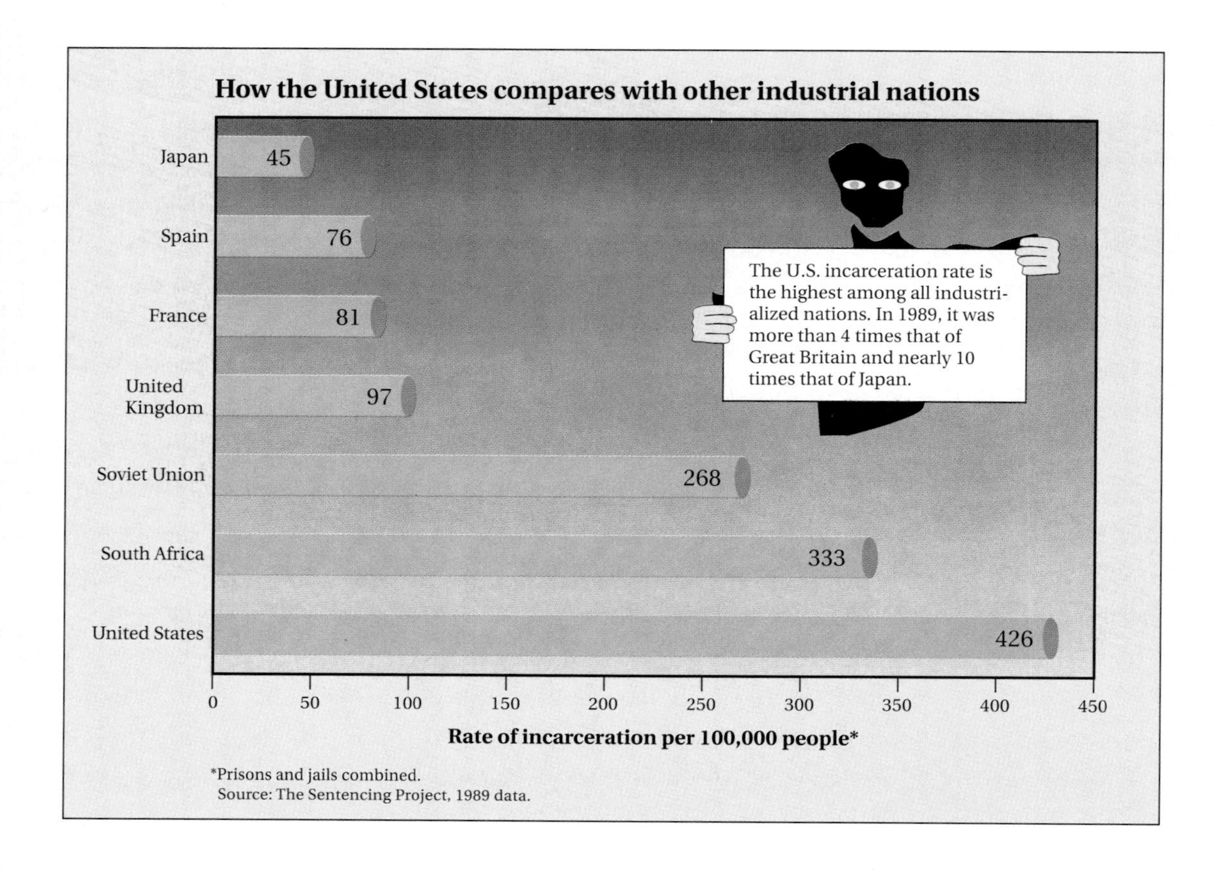

of their sentences. Offenders are usually confined to their homes for 24 hours a day, but some are allowed to go to a job. House arrestees are often supervised using electronic monitoring equipment. In a typical case, the offender wears an irremovable bracelet that can be plugged into an electronic device attached to a telephone. When a probation officer phones the house, the offender verifies his or her presence by plugging the bracelet into the device. The use of electronic monitoring has grown rapidly from a few hundred units in use nationally in the mid-1980's to tens of thousands in the 1990's. The largest program is in Florida, where more than 50,000 offenders have been sentenced to house arrest. As with ISP programs, house arrest programs take different forms. In some states, such as Florida, offenders are sentenced directly to house arrest by judges. In others, such as Oklahoma, offenders are released early from prison into house arrest. Both approaches reduce the load on prisons.

Community service is an intermediate punishment in which offenders provide unpaid work for a nonprofit or government agency instead of serving a prison sentence. Although a few celebrated community service programs exist, most notably a program in New York City for people who repeatedly commit property offenses such as theft and vandalism, few states have well-organized programs. Consequently, community service in the United States tends to be used either as a condition of probation or as a penalty for business crimes.

Financial penalties are another form of intermediate punishment. The use of *restitution* (orders to repay the victim the amount lost as a result of the crime) is increasing in the United States, but it is generally ordered only as an add-on to probation or a prison sentence and not as a punishment in its own right. However, a few cities have changed their laws to replace prison terms for selected crimes with the *day fine.* Day fines are financial penalties scaled to the severity of the crime and the offender's ability to pay. Day fines are based on an offender's income and wealth at the time of the offense. Thus, the day fine for a well-to-do offender may be 50 or 100 times higher than that of a poor offender. The offender either pays the amount immediately or continues at his or her regular job and applies a portion of future paychecks toward the fine. Experiments with day fines are underway in New York City, Phoenix, and Madison, Wis. In those places, judges have accepted fines as punishment for serious crimes. But in general, day fines are not yet widely used in the United States.

Boot camps, another intermediate punishment, are patterned after military boot camps. These special prison programs are for younger offenders—those in their late teens and 20's—and usually last three to six months. Discipline is rigid, and physical work and daily drills are part of everyday schedules. Some boot camps, such as those in New York State, also include vocational and educational training and drug treatment.

Boot camps have become very popular with elected officials and the public. There is appeal to the idea that the discipline of boot camp will help offenders learn good work habits, self-control, and self-respect. However, research by Abt Associates, a private firm in Cambridge, Mass., has found no solid evidence that boot camps rehabilitate offenders better than prisons do. There is some evidence that boot camps do enhance the self-esteem and self-discipline of offenders while they take part in the program. However, once offenders return to the environments in which they first got into trouble, the effects of boot camp usually wear off.

The outlook for America

U.S. experience with intermediate punishments is mixed. For one thing, intermediate punishments have been used largely in place of ordinary, inexpensive probation rather than costly prison sentences. Thus, the

Who is in U.S. prisons?

The average U.S. prisoner is male, white, and in his late 20's or early 30's. However, of particular concern to many prison experts is that, relative to the general population, a disproportionate number of prisoners are black.

Sex

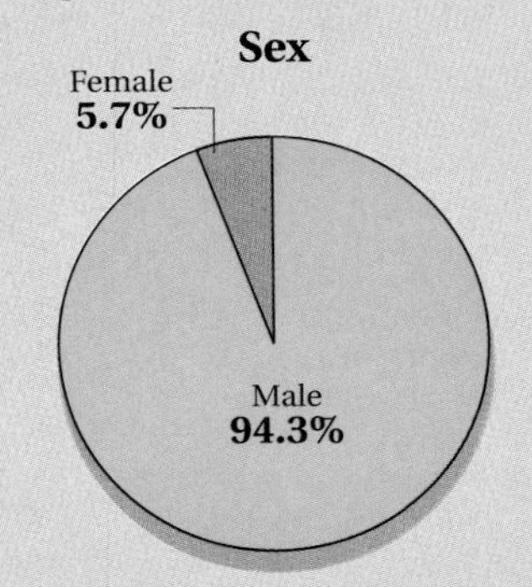

Source: Bureau of Justice Statistics, 1990 data.

Race*

Asian/Pacific Islander 0.4%

Other 3.7%

White 47.7%

Black 47.4%

Native American 0.8%

*Hispanics do not constitute a separate group. Depending on the state, they may be classified as white, black, or other.
Source: Bureau of Justice Statistics, 1990 data.

Age

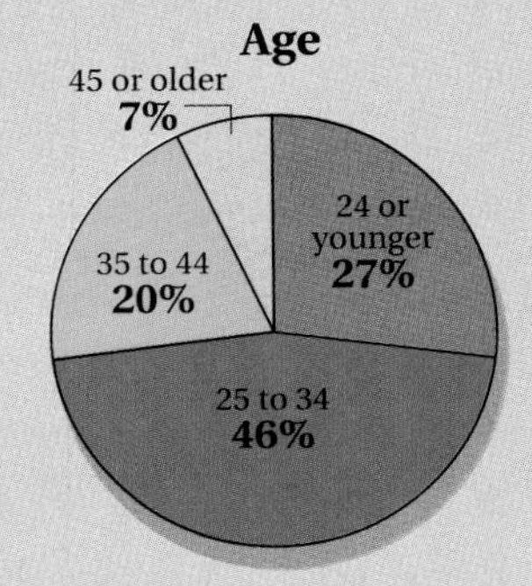

Source: Bureau of Justice Statistics, 1986 data.

Prison alternatives

Given the high costs of building and maintaining prisons, officials have begun to experiment with less expensive alternatives to incarceration.

One popular alternative is the boot camp. At Camp Monterey in Beaver Dams, N.Y., *right,* inmates go through six months of rigorous drills and calisthenics.

A radio transmitter attached to an offender's ankle, *left,* helps monitor a person's compliance with a sentence of home confinement, another alternative to incarceration.

In some prison systems, inmates can reduce the terms of their sentences by performing tasks such as litter cleanup, *below,* for government agencies or nonprofit firms.

punishments often cost more than would probation. Second, the close surveillance to which U.S. offenders in intermediate punishments are generally subject results in the discovery of many more program violations, which often lead to incarceration. Given these drawbacks, many researchers are skeptical about the current use of intermediate punishments in the United States. By contrast, intermediate punishments have been successful at reducing prison populations in Europe and elsewhere because they are applied to more serious crimes, such as robbery, and offenders sentenced to intermediate punishments are not as strictly monitored for minor infractions.

No one argues that prison is unnecessary for persons convicted of violent offenses. But the emphasis on incarceration in the United States as a punishment for less serious crimes has given prison administrators little incentive to create more cost-effective alternatives. As a result, the development of intermediate punishments is much more limited in the United States than elsewhere. In 1991, only about 40,000 of the more than 800,000 offenders in U.S. prison systems were sentenced to intermediate punishments, according to the CJI. Yet data indicated that at least one-third of inmates were sentenced to prison for nonviolent crimes, and many of those inmates were first-time offenders. These people would be prime candidates for intermediate punishments, say prison experts.

Experts say the know-how exists to effectively implement intermediate punishments in the United States. First, states would have to analyze their prison populations and determine who could be placed in less expensive intermediate punishments without increasing the risk to the public. Next, they would have to reverse many of the mandatory-sentence laws enacted during the 1980's. Last, they would have to educate their citizens about intermediate punishments to generate public acceptance.

At the 1992 meeting in Princeton, N.J., of the National Governors Association, a shift from incarceration to intermediate punishments was the subject of much discussion. "What we have been doing [with the prison system] is not right," said Governor L. Douglas Wilder of Virginia, "but it's very difficult for politicians to say we have been wrong and that we've got to revisit, revise, and restructure the whole system." The task for U.S. politicians, many prison experts believe, is to create a correctional system that reduces its reliance on prisons while maintaining adequate safeguards to protect the public against criminals and upholding public notions of just and proper punishment.

For further reading:

America's Prisons: Opposing Viewpoints. Ed. by Bonnie Szumski. Greenhaven, 1985.

Byrne, James M., and others. *Smart Sentencing: The Emergence of Intermediate Sanctions.* Sage Publications, 1992.

Morris, Norval, and Tonry, Michael. *Between Prison and Probation: Intermediate Punishments in a Rational Sentencing System.* Oxford University Press, 1990.

Protestantism. Although Protestant religious groups did not openly endorse a candidate in the 1992 presidential campaign, they were a factor in the elections. The Republican and Democratic candidates for President and Vice President were all members of Protestant churches. President George Bush, an Episcopalian, and Vice President Dan Quayle, who attends a conservative evangelical church, focused on "family values" and other issues that consolidated support among conservative religious groups.

At a largely evangelical gathering in Dallas after the Republican convention in August, the President noted that the Democratic Party platform did not mention God. Council members of the National Council of Churches, including President Syngman Rhee and General Secretary Joan Brown Campbell, sent a letter in August to President Bush indicating their opposition to the President's implication that God favored the Republican Party.

Religious leaders also appealed to the Democratic Party to refrain from making religion a campaign issue. The Democratic presidential candidate, Governor Bill Clinton of Arkansas, and the vice presidential candidate, Senator Albert A. Gore, Jr., of Tennessee, are members of the Southern Baptist Convention, the largest Protestant denomination in the United States. Both Clinton and Gore reportedly identify with the convention's moderate element.

Moderate Baptists have opposed the control of the denomination in recent years by conservatives who interpret the Bible as literally true. The convention's conservative Christian Life Commission issued voting guides that some observers believed implicitly discouraged members from voting for Clinton and Gore. The guides did not openly endorse the Republican Party's candidates but sided with the Republicans' platform positions on almost all issues, including opposition to abortion. The National Association of Evangelicals issued similar voter advisories, seeming to imply support for the Republicans. (See also **Elections.**)

The Southern Baptist Convention in February elected archconservative Morris H. Chapman to the presidency of its executive committee, the denomination's top administrative post. Chapman, who had served two terms as president of the convention, succeeded Harold C. Bennett, who retired. Chapman's election made virtually complete a 13-year effort by fundamentalists to win control of the 15.2-million-member body.

Homosexuality issue. The United Methodist Church at its general conference in Louisville, Ky., in May voted to maintain its policy that homosexuality is "incompatible with Christian teaching." The conference, which meets every four years to set policy, rejected the majority view of a committee authorized in 1988 to study homosexuality. The committee wanted the church to withdraw its condemnation of homosexual activity in recognition that church members did not agree on the subject.

Two Southern Baptist congregations in North Carolina were expelled from the Southern Baptist Convention in June 1992 because they condoned homosexuality. One church had blessed the union of two homosexual men, and the other had licensed a homosexual divinity student to preach.

The Evangelical Lutheran Church in America decided in March to extend from 1993 to 1995 the period for preparing a church document on human sexuality. Many groups are studying the church's guide, "Human Sexuality and the Christian Faith," in preparation for a statement that will cover homosexuality, sexual relationships outside of marriage, and sexual abuse.

In November 1992, the highest court of the Presbyterian Church (U.S.A.) effectively nullified the *calling* (hiring) of Jane Adams Spahr as co-pastor of the Downtown Presbyterian Church in Rochester, N.Y. Spahr was the first openly lesbian Presbyterian minister called to be a pastor when the Rochester church hired her in 1991. Conservative churches immediately challenged her calling. The Presbyterian court ruled "that a self-affirmed practicing homosexual may not be invited to serve in a Presbyterian Church position which presumes ordination." The church's ruling said that a call might be approved if the person were no longer an active homosexual.

Abortion issue. The general assembly of the Presbyterian Church (U.S.A.) at its policymaking meeting in Milwaukee in June moderated its previously strong support for abortion rights. The new policy acknowledges that there could be "legitimate" government interest in regulating abortion practices and rejects abortions that are performed solely as a means of birth control.

Tyson supported. Theodore J. Jemison, the president of the National Baptist Convention, U.S.A., Inc., and other leaders came under criticism for their support of former heavyweight boxing champion Mike Tyson, who was convicted in February of raping a black woman and sentenced to six years in prison. Many members of the black denomination accused Jemison of supporting Tyson in the hope of receiving a $5-million pledge from the boxer to help pay for the Baptist World Center, the denomination's new $10-million headquarters in Nashville. Jemison denied the charges, and he expressed surprise that so many black women were hurt by his support of Tyson. With 5.5 million members, the convention claims to be the largest organization of blacks in the world.

First female Lutheran bishops. A German Lutheran synod in April elected Maria Jepsen the first Lutheran female bishop in the world. She became bishop of Hamburg. In June, the Evangelical Lutheran Church in America elected its first female bishop, April Ulring Larson. She became head of the La Crosse (Wis.) Area Synod. Martin E. Marty

See also **Eastern Orthodox Churches; Islam; Judaism; Religion; Roman Catholic Church.** In ***World Book,*** see **Protestantism.**

Psychology. People experience more nightmares in the weeks following a natural disaster, such as an earthquake, than they usually experience. But those nightmares pack a surprisingly modest emotional punch, psychologists reported in May 1992.

Psychologist James M. Wood of the University of Arizona in Tucson and his colleagues studied the dreams of college students following the October 1989 earthquake that killed 62 people and caused an estimated $7 billion in property damage in the San Francisco Bay Area. A total of 91 students attending two Bay Area universities kept a diary of their dreams every morning for three weeks, starting about one week after the quake hit. A second group of 97 students attending an Arizona university that was not affected by the earthquake also filled out diaries for the same time period.

More than two-thirds of the California students, but only one-half of the Arizona students, had at least one nightmare during the study period. The researchers defined a nightmare as a frightening dream that uses visual images to tell a story. Of the students having nightmares, the California group reported an average of three nightmares per student during the study, twice the average number cited by the Arizona students. The nightmares of the California volunteers often involved an earthquake, whereas those of the Arizona students rarely included an earthquake. Yet students in both states typically described nightmares of only slight to moderate intensity.

Researchers know little about the nature of dreams following natural disasters or other stressful events, Wood said. His research was reportedly the first controlled study of nightmares occurring in people who have experienced a natural disaster.

Infantile arithmetic. Infants who are as young as 5 months old can add and subtract small numbers of items, according to research published in August 1992. Research psychologist Karen Wynn of the University of Arizona said that her work suggests that human beings may possess an inborn ability for arithmetic that can be observed even in infants.

Wynn relied on the tendency of babies to look longer at new or unexpected objects than at recently observed or familiar objects. This behavior is the basis for most studies of how babies think. Wynn tested 48 boys and girls, all about 5 months old, dividing them into two groups. She showed the infants in one group a doll on a table, and then she hid the doll behind a screen. Wynn put a second doll behind the screen while the infants watched to simulate the arithmetical equivalent of $1 + 1 = 2$. For the other group, she placed two dolls on a table, hid them with a screen, and then removed one doll to simulate $2 - 1 = 1$.

The babies viewed the addition or subtraction procedures six times. In half the cases, the screen was removed to show that the number of dolls behind the screen was not the same number that the infants had observed being placed there, corresponding either to $1 + 1 = 1$ or $2 - 1 = 2$. In the remaining cases, the correct number of dolls appeared. The infants looked considerably longer at the incorrect results than at the correct results. Also, they showed no preference for looking at one or two dolls in the procedures with the correct number of dolls displayed.

Benefits of presurgical anxiety. Evidence reported in June suggested that worrying about an upcoming surgical operation proves more healthful than trying to relax and forget about the surgery. Psychologist Anne Manyande of University College in London and her co-workers found that relaxation training reduces tension before and after minor operations, but it also sparks a potentially harmful surge of two stress hormones—adrenaline and cortisol—during and after surgery. In contrast, surgical patients who received no relaxation training reported that they had plenty of anxiety, but their stress hormones remained stable or dipped slightly.

The body increases adrenaline and cortisol in response to stress and danger. But previous research suggested that high levels of these hormones following surgery contribute to weight loss, fatigue, and a weakened immune system, which hinders recovery, Manyande said. The new findings support a theory, proposed more than 30 years ago, that worrying acts as a type of mental preparation for surgery, thus reducing surgery's stress on the body. Bruce Bower

In *World Book,* see **Psychology.**

Public health. Citing increased concern about the effects of exposure to lead, United States health officials in September 1992 ordered that millions of children covered by the Medicaid program be tested for lead poisoning. Lead poisoning can cause mental retardation, learning disabilities, stunted growth, and other disorders. Medicaid is a joint federal-state program that provides health care for people receiving public assistance, including about 6 million children under the age of 6.

Evidence that even very low levels of lead can be harmful prompted the Health Care Financing Administration (HCFA), which manages Medicaid, to call for the testing. In instructions issued to physicians, the HCFA said that all children aged 6 months to 6 years should be considered at risk for lead poisoning and screened for exposure to the metal. Although lead poisoning can affect anyone, the greatest risk is for children who live in houses built before 1960 that contain peeling lead-based paint. The children may ingest lead by eating bits of the paint.

Eliminating polio. The Pan American Health Organization (PAHO) on September 10 announced a milestone in efforts to eradicate polio from the Americas: Not a single new case of polio had been reported in North, Central, or South America for a full year.

Carlyle Guerra de Macedo, director of PAHO, attributed the polio decline to a major vaccination program begun in 1985. The World Health Organization

The unexpected rise of tuberculosis in the United States

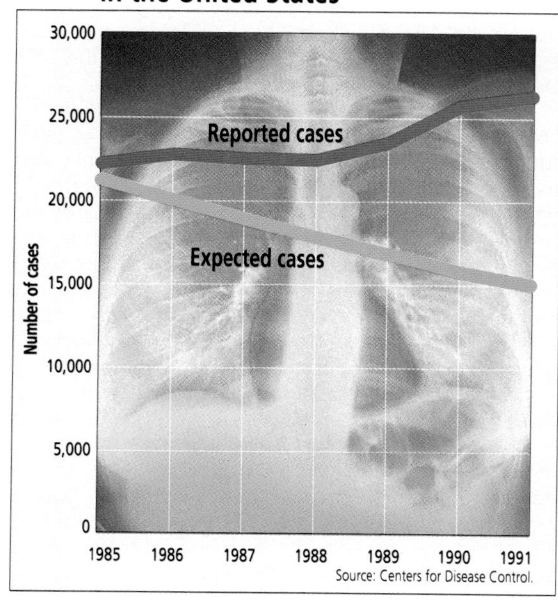

The number of cases of tuberculosis in the United States unexpectedly began to increase in the late 1980's. The upswing continued through 1991.

(WHO), an agency of the United Nations, emphasized the need to continue vaccination programs, since polio still can be brought into the region by travelers. PAHO officials said a special international commission would monitor infectious diseases in the Americas until 1995 to determine whether polio has indeed been eliminated from the Western Hemisphere.

Public health workers reported progress in battling polio in other regions as well. WHO reported in January 1992 that the number of cases of polio worldwide declined by 72 per cent between 1981 and 1990.

Tuberculosis comeback. WHO on June 17 warned that tuberculosis (TB)—once almost eradicated in industrialized nations—was making a comeback in the United States and Western Europe. The agency said that an estimated 400,000 new cases of TB and 40,000 TB-related deaths had occurred in industrialized countries in 1991.

Until the mid-1980's, TB was on the decline in those nations. According to WHO, AIDS (acquired immune deficiency syndrome) was the major cause of the increase. Infection with the virus that causes AIDS weakens the immune system, increasing vulnerability to TB as well as other diseases. Another factor, WHO said, was the emergence of new TB strains resistant to standard drug treatments.

The U.S. Centers for Disease Control (CDC) in Atlanta, Ga., on June 19 announced a national action plan to combat drug-resistant TB. The CDC said that the drug-resistance problem was growing worse, with about 15 per cent of the 1992 cases caused by microbes resistant to at least one anti-TB drug. The action plan included measures to quickly identify and treat drug-resistant cases.

Cholera. The CDC on September 10 reported that 96 cases of cholera had been reported in the United States in 1992, the most since the agency began monitoring the disease in 1961. Most of the cases occurred among travelers returning from Latin America, where a cholera epidemic was raging. According to the CDC, 5,000 people throughout the Americas had died during the epidemic, which began in 1991 in Peru.

Low birth weight. More and more abnormally small babies are being born each year, the U.S. Public Health Service (PHS) reported on April 21. Low-birth-weight infants—those weighing less than 5.5 pounds (2,500) grams—have higher than normal risks of mental and physical defects and of death soon after birth. The PHS said that about 7 per cent of the 4 million babies delivered in 1989 were of low birth weight. The figure was the highest since 1978. Public health experts said that maternal cigarette smoking during pregnancy and the lack of proper prenatal care accounted for many of the low-weight births. Children with low birth weight remain in poorer health when they begin school, researchers at Harvard University reported on April 21. Michael Woods

See also **AIDS.** In ***World Book***, see **Public Health.**

Puerto Rico. Pedro Rosselló of the New Progressive Party was elected governor of Puerto Rico in November 1992. Rosselló, a pediatric surgeon with no previous political experience, was to take office in January 1993. He pledged an early plebiscite on whether Puerto Rico should become a state, an independent nation, or remain a commonwealth. And he promised to achieve reforms that would establish a new health-care system for the island. Rosselló also said he would make English the official government language, reversing the policy of his predecessor, Governor Rafael Hernández Colón of the Popular Democratic Party, who established Spanish as the official language.

The arrival of a stately procession of Tall Ships in late June 1992 gave a boost to Puerto Rico's flagging tourism industry. The square-rigged sailing vessels made a stopover in San Juan, Puerto Rico's capital, as part of the 500th anniversary observances of Christopher Columbus' voyage to the New World. For five days, hotels on the island were booked to capacity, and the streets of the old port were filled to bursting with 8,000 crew members of the historical armada and crowds estimated at from 100,000 to 250,000 daily.

Puerto Ricans mourned the death on Jan. 26, 1992, of José Ferrer. The star of stage and screen was born José Vicente Ferrer de Otero y Cintrón in Santurce, Puerto Rico. Nathan A. Haverstock

See also **Latin America** (Facts in brief table). In ***World Book,*** see **Puerto Rico.**

Pulitzer Prizes in letters, drama, music, and journalism were awarded for the 76th year in April 1992 by Columbia University in New York City, acting on the recommendations of the Pulitzer Prize Board.

Awards for letters and the arts. The Pulitzer Prize for fiction went to Jane Smiley for *A Thousand Acres*. The prize for poetry was given to James Tate for *Selected Poems*. The drama prize was won by Robert Schenkkan for *The Kentucky Cycle*. Lewis B. Puller, Jr., captured the biography prize for *Fortunate Son: The Healing of a Vietnam Vet*. The prize for general nonfiction went to Daniel Yergin for *The Prize: The Epic Quest for Oil, Money and Power*. The history prize was won by Mark E. Neely, Jr., for *The Fate of Liberty: Abraham Lincoln and Civil Liberties*. Wayne Peterson won the music prize for "The Face of the Night, the Heart of the Dark." A special Pulitzer was given to Art Spiegelman for *Maus I* and *Maus II*, the tale of a Holocaust survivor in comic-book form.

Journalism awards. Three newspapers—*Newsday*, *The New York Times*, and *The Sacramento* (Calif.) *Bee*—each won two prizes. *Newsday* won for international reporting by Patrick J. Sloyan on the Persian Gulf War after the military's restrictions on journalists ended, and for spot news reporting by its *New York Newsday* staff for its coverage of a subway derailment. *The New York Times* won for feature writing by Howell Raines, who is white, for his memoir of his friendship with his family's black housekeeper, and for commentary by Anna Quindlen for her opinion column. *The Sacramento Bee* won for public service for a series by Tom Knudson on the ecological plight of California's Sierra Nevada, and for beat reporting by Deborah Blum for articles on the ethical issues surrounding scientific experiments on primates.

Other journalism awards: Editorial writing, Maria Henson, the *Lexington* (Ky.) *Herald-Leader*, for editorials on the legal problems facing battered women in Kentucky. Investigative reporting, Lorraine Adams and Dan Malone of *The Dallas Morning News* for a series documenting police misconduct in Texas. National reporting, Jeff Taylor and Mike McGraw, *The Kansas City* (Mo.) *Star*, for critical articles on the United States Department of Agriculture. Explanatory journalism, Robert S. Capers and Eric Lipton, *The Hartford* (Conn.) *Courant*, for a series on problems in the American space program.

Editorial cartooning, Signe Wilkinson, *The Philadelphia Daily News*, the first woman to win in this category. Feature photography, John Kaplan, *The* (Monterey, Calif.) *Herald* and the *Pittsburgh* (Pa.) *Post-Gazette*, for seven photo essays of the lives of 21-year-olds across the United States. Spot news photography, the staff of the Associated Press news service, for photos of the 1991 coup attempt in Russia and the collapse of the Communist leadership. For the first time, there was no prize for criticism. John Burnson

In ***World Book,*** see **Pulitzer Prizes.**

An image of the toppled statue of a Soviet leader in Moscow was among the photographs that helped the Associated Press win a 1992 Pulitzer Prize.

Demonstrators in Montreal in May call for Quebec's premier to hold a popular vote on whether the province should separate from Canada.

Quayle, Dan (1947-), 44th Vice President of the United States, fought hard in a losing effort to win reelection for himself and President George Bush in 1992. Prior to the Republican National Convention in August, Quayle survived an effort by some Republicans to replace him on the 1992 ticket. Bush termed such talk "absurd," though he reportedly weighed the option.

The Vice President defended Bush's record and emphasized the issue of "family values." In an October 13 televised debate among the vice presidential candidates, Quayle was seen as more aggressive than his Democratic counterpart, Senator Albert A. Gore, Jr., of Tennessee. Quayle repeatedly attacked Gore's running mate, Arkansas Governor Bill Clinton, as having "trouble telling the truth."

Quayle's role as chairman of the Bush Administration's Council on Competitiveness was controversial in 1992. He and the council, which was formed to find ways of increasing the global competitiveness of U.S. industry, battled the Environmental Protection Agency (EPA) over regulations to implement the Clean Air Act. And critics accused the council of trying to turn over protected wetlands to real estate developers.

Quayle visited the Baltic nations in February and Japan in May. In April, the Quayles reported paying $45,271 in federal taxes on a 1991 adjusted income of $181,652. Frank Cormier and Margot Cormier

In ***World Book,*** see **Quayle, Dan.**

Quebec. More than 5,000 Quebecers marched in Montreal on Oct. 24, 1992, demonstrating opposition to proposed revisions to Canada's Constitution and foreshadowing the "No" vote Quebec delivered two days later. All but four of Canada's provinces voted against the revisions, which were created in large part to appease Quebec's desire for greater autonomy.

Although the separatists—those who want Quebec to secede from Canada—rallied behind the "No" vote, a poll conducted just prior to the referendum by *The* (Toronto) *Globe and Mail* found that 33 per cent of Quebecers opposing the new Constitution were also against secession. In all, 57 per cent of those voting in Quebec turned down the constitutional changes. Forty-three per cent supported the revisions, which proposed Quebec's continued unity with Canada. Jacques Parizeau, leader of the separatist party, Parti Québécois, said he would challenge Premier Robert Bourassa in the next election and would base his campaign on the sovereignty question.

Hydroelectric project snags. Plans to construct the huge Great Whale hydroelectric project in northern Quebec suffered a blow when New York state on March 27 canceled plans to purchase $17-billion ($13.6-billion U.S.) worth of electric power from Quebec. The Canadian and Quebec governments had supported the project, which was managed by Hydro-Québec, the provincial utility. But Quebec's native *Inuit* (Eskimo) and Cree Indians, as well as a number of environmental groups, had strongly opposed the plan, which would divert five rivers and flood 1,700 square miles (4,400 square kilometers) of land in the James Bay area. Although authorities from Hydro-Québec said New York's decision would not delay completion of the project, some analysts predicted that the pull-out could cause the plan to be shelved permanently.

A spy in their midst? Radio-Canada in May 1992 revealed that Claude Morin, a former cabinet minister in the Parti Québécois government of René Lévesque, had been a paid informer for the federal police force, the Royal Canadian Mounted Police (RCMP). The report said that the RCMP had asked Morin to provide information on supporters of the separatist movement in Quebec. Morin admitted to attending meetings with the RCMP in the mid-1970's, but he claimed to have acted in Quebec's best interest by obtaining more information than he had revealed.

New budget. Finance Minister Gérard-D. Levesque presented the budget for the fiscal year (April 1, 1992, to March 31, 1993) on May 14 and announced that the provincial sales tax would be extended to cover services as well as goods. Beginning July 1, a 4 per cent tax was levied on services. Expenditures for the fiscal year were set at $40.7 billion ($32.6 billion U.S.), and revenues at $36.9 billion ($29.6 billion U.S.), leaving a deficit of about $3.8 billion ($3 billion U.S.).

David M. L. Farr

See also **Canada.** In ***World Book,*** see **Quebec.**

Rabin, Yitzhak (1922-   ), the leader of Israel's Labor Party, recaptured the office of prime minister on July 13, 1992, after guiding the party to its first decisive parliamentary victory since 1974. Rabin had served as prime minister from 1974 to 1977, when he stepped down because of a financial scandal. Rabin, who agreed to curb new Jewish settlements in the occupied territories, was expected to advance the Middle East peace process. (See **Israel; Middle East.**)

Rabin was born on March 1, 1922, in Jerusalem, which was then part of Palestine. After graduating from the Kedoorie Agricultural College in 1940, he joined the Palmach, a unit of the Jewish underground army in Palestine. He served as a brigade commander during the first Arab-Israeli war in 1948. After the war, he continued to rise in Israel's defense forces, becoming chief of staff in 1964. In 1967, Rabin devised the strategy that led to Israel's victory against Arab forces in the Six-Day War.

In 1968, Rabin retired from the armed forces and became Israel's ambassador to the United States. In 1973, he returned to Israel and was elected to parliament. He served in the Cabinet as minister of labor from April to June 1974, when he became prime minister. After resigning that office, Rabin remained in parliament. He returned to the Cabinet in 1984 as minister of defense, a post he held until 1990.

Rabin married the former Lea Schlossberg in 1948. They have a daughter and a son. Barbara A. Mayes

Railroad. Despite a sluggish economy in the United States in 1992, most major U.S. railroads improved their profits by taking advantage of flexible labor agreements and aggressively cutting costs. Railroads operated more efficiently as the federal transportation agencies began eliminating unnecessary rules and regulations that did not compromise railroad safety. Railroad stock prices rose in 1992, reflecting investor confidence in the industry's efforts to cut expenses and improve productivity.

Continental trade benefits. United States and Canadian railroads anticipated benefits under the proposed North American Free Trade Agreement, which was negotiated by the United States, Canada, and Mexico in August, and was due to go into effect in 1994. Currently, trucks transport most of the freight in Mexico—more than 60 per cent—and only about 10 per cent moves by rail. Thus, U.S. and Canadian railroads formed partnerships with Mexican transportation companies, and several railroads invested in terminals and other facilities within Mexico.

Freight hauling. Intermodal freight loadings continued to be a shining star for rail carriers in 1992. Intermodal freight loadings are truck trailers or containers from ships that are loaded directly onto railcars. As of October 1992, intermodal loadings were reportedly up about 7.5 per cent over October 1991.

Railroads also moved toward more precise scheduling to meet demands of manufacturers who intentionally limit their inventories. These manufacturers produce enough goods "just in time" to meet customer requirements, thus reducing the need for expensive warehousing facilities. Just-in-time manufacturing operations match railroad timetables with the scheduling requirements of their customers.

Labor strike. On June 24, the International Association of Machinists called a strike over wages and work rules against CSX Corporation, a rail carrier in the East. Although the strike technically targeted only one railroad, all major U.S. railroads shut down operations and locked out their employees. The strike ended on June 26, when President George Bush signed legislation passed by Congress that provided for a 38-day cooling-off period and final binding arbitration if no agreement was reached. Railroad officials estimated that the shutdown cost the nation's major railroads about $80 million a day in lost business. The strike also prompted calls to change the Railway Labor Act of 1926, which has governed disputes between labor and management in the railroad industry since enactment.

Kansas City Southern Industries, parent company of the 2,500-mile (4,000-kilometer) Kansas City Southern Railroad, announced on Sept. 21, 1992, its agreement to purchase MidSouth Corporation for about $220 million. MidSouth is a holding company for four small railroads that operate over 1,200 miles (1,900 kilometers) of track in Louisiana, Mississippi, Alabama, and Tennessee. Kathy Keeney

In ***World Book,*** see **Railroad.**

Religious groups with 150,000 or more members in the United States*

Religious group	Members
African Methodist Episcopal Church	2,210,000
African Methodist Episcopal Zion Church	1,200,000
American Baptist Association	250,000
American Baptist Churches in the U.S.A.	1,535,971
Antiochian Orthodox Christian Archdiocese of North America	350,000
Armenian Apostolic Church of America	150,000
Armenian Church of America, Diocese of the	450,000
Assemblies of God	2,181,502
Baptist Bible Fellowship, International	1,405,900
Baptist Missionary Association of America	229,166
Christian and Missionary Alliance	279,207
Christian Church (Disciples of Christ)	1,039,692
Christian Churches and Churches of Christ	1,070,616
Christian Methodist Episcopal Church	718,922
Christian Reformed Church in North America	226,163
Church of God (Anderson, Ind.)	205,884
Church of God (Cleveland, Tenn.)	620,393
Church of God in Christ	3,709,661
Church of God in Christ, International	200,000
Church of Jesus Christ of Latter-day Saints	4,267,000
Church of the Nazarene	573,834
Churches of Christ	1,683,346
Conservative Baptist Association of America	210,000
Coptic Orthodox Church	165,000
Episcopal Church	2,446,050
Evangelical Free Church of America	165,000
Evangelical Lutheran Church in America	5,240,739
Free Will Baptists	197,206
General Association of Regular Baptist Churches	168,068
Greek Orthodox Archdiocese of North and South America	1,950,000
International Church of the Foursquare Gospel	199,385
International Council of Community Churches	250,000
Jehovah's Witnesses	858,367
Judaism	5,981,000
Liberty Baptist Fellowship	180,000
Lutheran Church--Missouri Synod	2,602,849
National Baptist Convention of America	2,668,799
National Baptist Convention, U.S.A., Inc.	5,500,000
National Primitive Baptist Convention	250,000
Orthodox Church in America	1,000,000
Polish National Catholic Church	282,411
Presbyterian Church in America	223,935
Presbyterian Church (U.S.A.)	3,788,009
Progressive National Baptist Convention, Inc.	521,692
Reformed Church in America	326,850
Reorganized Church of Jesus Christ of Latter Day Saints	189,524
Roman Catholic Church	58,568,015
Salvation Army	445,566
Seventh-day Adventist Church	717,446
Southern Baptist Convention	15,038,409
Unitarian Universalist Association	191,543
United Church of Christ	1,599,212
United Methodist Church	8,904,824
United Pentecostal Church, International	500,000
Wisconsin Evangelical Lutheran Synod	420,039

*A majority of the figures are for the years 1990 and 1991. Includes only groups with at least 150,000 members within the United States itself.

.National Council of the Churches of Christ in the U.S.A., *Yearbook of American and Canadian Churches* for 1992.

Ramos, Fidel V. (1928-), became the president of the Republic of the Philippines on June 30, 1992. He was endorsed by outgoing President Corazon Aquino and won a seven-way race. His stated goals for his six-year term included lowering trade barriers, resolving the country's energy crisis, and negotiating an amnesty for both the right wing military rebels who staged several coup attempts against Aquino and the left wing rebels who have been waging a guerrilla war. (See also **Philippines**.)

Fidel "Eddie" Valdez Ramos was born on March 18, 1928, in the Philippine city of Lingayen. He graduated from the United States Military Academy at West Point, N.Y., in 1950, then fought against the Communist forces in the Korean War (1950-1953) and the Vietnam War (1957-1975) as a member of the Philippine military. He became the chief of the Philippine constabulary (the national police force) in 1972 for President Ferdinand Marcos and held that position during the period of martial law from 1972 to 1981.

In 1981, Ramos became the deputy armed forces chief of staff for Marcos. But in 1986, he abandoned Marcos and helped lead the "People Power" revolution that toppled Marcos' dictatorship and put Aquino in power.

Ramos was the armed forces chief of staff under Aquino until 1988, when he became her secretary of defense. From 1986 to 1991, he helped Aquino survive six coup attempts. John Burnson

Religion. Religious differences were at the root of a number of conflicts in the world in 1992. The main new trouble spot was Yugoslavia. Under a Communist government, Yugoslavia had suppressed ancient ethnic and religious rivalries. When freedom came with the fall of Communism in 1991, four of the six Yugoslav republics declared their independence. The result was a fight over boundaries that became interwoven with religious differences.

An announced policy of "ethnic cleansing" by the president of the Serbian republic, Slobodan Milošević, was directed chiefly against Muslims in the new state of Bosnia and Hercegovina (often simply called Bosnia). Serbs are mainly Eastern Orthodox, and Croats, who also live in Bosnia, are mainly Roman Catholic. As Serbia attempted to extend its borders, it began wholesale expulsions of Muslims, who were also reportedly victims of massacres and executions. Serbian Orthodox bishops, who traditionally have had close ties with the government, broke with Milošević's government in an open letter on May 28. The letter condemned Serbian policy in the former republics of Yugoslavia and called for Milošević's resignation. Jews, Muslims, and Christians also united to protest the Serbian policy. (See **Bosnia and Hercegovina.**)

Islamic politics. The Islamic Salvation Front (FIS), a fundamentalist Islamic political party in Algeria, probably would have won enough support in parliamentary elections in January to take over the government. But the interim government of secular and military leaders canceled the elections and banned nonreligious activities at mosques, where FIS supporters frequently met. And in Sudan, the fundamentalist National Islamic Front of Hassan al-Turabi inspired the military government of General Omar Hassan Ahmed al-Bashir to consolidate its hold on all but three southern provinces, where most people are Christian. In July, the government seemed to be winning the fight.

Hindu and Muslim riots in India. More than 1,200 people died in riots that erupted in towns all across India after Hindu fundamentalists on December 6 tore down the Babri mosque in Ayodhya, a city in the province of Uttar Pradesh. More than 5,000 people were injured in violence that lasted for a week. The Indian government banned three Hindu fundamentalist groups and two Islamic fundamentalist groups and arrested more than 4,500 of their members in an effort to halt the violence.

Ownership of the Babri mosque has been disputed between Muslims and Hindus in Indian courts nearly every year since India won independence from Great Britain in 1947. In 1990, Hindus had attempted to tear down the mosque, resulting in riots that left more than 1,000 dead. Muslim invaders built the Babri mosque in the 1500's. Many Hindus believe that the mosque was built over the ruins of a Hindu temple, but no archaeological evidence to support their claim has been found.

In the Americas, particularly in the United States, religious issues surfaced over how to observe the 500th anniversary of Christopher Columbus' arrival in the Western Hemisphere in 1492. During the 400th commemoration in 1892, Columbus was regarded as a Christian hero because his discovery of America extended Christendom to the New World.

The image suffered greatly in 1992. In Latin America and North America alike, Columbus was often portrayed as a villain. He and his fellow explorers were depicted as having deliberately killed off the natives. They were also portrayed as Catholic imperialists from a country—Spain—that also conquered the Muslims and in 1492 expelled the Jews.

Many Native American groups claimed that the people Columbus met were already religious and not in need of being converted to Christianity. In their view, the Indians lived in peace with nature, which was sacred to them, and with each other. They portrayed the Indians' life as a pastoral utopia that the Catholic conquerors ruined.

Some scholars and Christian Native Americans expressed more moderate views. They pointed out that Aztec, Mayan, and other native peoples had engaged in human sacrifice and warfare among each other long before the arrival of Columbus.

Religious influence. According to a Gallup survey taken throughout 1991 and reported in May 1992, 55 per cent of Americans said religion was losing its influence and only 36 per cent said its influence was increasing. This was the first time since 1975 that a majority thought religion's influence was declining. Another Gallup survey found that almost 15 per cent of American adults had changed denominational affiliation at least once. People reported turning to Protestantism 9 times more frequently than they reported turning to Catholicism. Gallup also found that 32 per cent of Americans in 1992 believed that the Bible was literally true. In 1963, 65 per cent of Americans reported that they believed in the Bible's literal truth.

School prayer. On June 24, 1992, the Supreme Court of the United States ruled 5 to 4 in a Rhode Island case, *Lee v. Weisman,* that prayers by a rabbi at a high school baccalaureate service violated constitutional principles separating church and state. The decision, unpopular among those who advocated religious practices in public life, was surprising to those who anticipated that a conservative court would favor such religious expression.

Templeton Prize. The 1992 John M. Templeton Prize for Progress in Religion was awarded to Kyung-Chik Han, founder of the Young Nak (Everlasting Joy) Presbyterian Church in Seoul, South Korea. The award, worth $986,000 in 1992, was created in 1972 as a way to honor progress in religion similar to Nobel Prize awards in other disciplines. Martin E. Marty

See also **Eastern Orthodox Churches; Islam; Judaism; Protestantism; Roman Catholic Church.** In ***World Book,*** see **Religion.**

Republican Party. President George Bush was defeated in the election of Nov. 3, 1992, marking the end of a 12-year grip on the United States presidency by the Republican Party (GOP). The balloting also ended GOP hopes of scoring big gains in Congress. Although the Republicans did gain 10 seats in the House of Representatives, voters again gave the Democrats solid control of both the House and Senate.

Before the 1992 party primaries began, the Republican National Committee (RNC) had a change at the top. Bush on January 31 tapped 41-year-old Richard N. Bond, a veteran of his 1980 and 1988 campaigns, to be RNC chairman. Bond succeeded Clayton K. Yeutter, who joined the White House staff.

The primaries. As the year began, Bush faced two challengers for the Presidential nomination. They were David Duke, a former Ku Klux Klan leader who failed in a 1991 bid for the Louisiana governorship, and Patrick J. Buchanan, a conservative commentator who had been an aide to Presidents Richard M. Nixon and Ronald Reagan.

Republican officials, embarrassed by Duke's identification with the GOP, tried with limited success to keep him off the ballot in some states, arguing that he was not a real Republican. South Carolina's March 7 primary was Duke's first test, and he won a paltry 7 per cent of the Republican vote. Three days later, in the "Super Tuesday" primaries, he won 11 per cent in Mississippi and was limited to single digits in Louis-

Balloons and confetti cascade upon President George Bush and his wife, Barbara, at the Republican National Convention in Houston in August.

iana, Massachusetts, Oklahoma, Rhode Island, Tennessee, and Texas. Faring even worse later, Duke abandoned his campaign on April 22.

Buchanan was a tougher adversary. He vowed to "send a message" of discontent over Bush's economic policy and to "take our party back." Buchanan was particularly scornful of Bush for agreeing with congressional Democrats on a 1990 tax hike, aimed at lowering the deficit, that violated Bush's 1988 campaign pledge of "no new taxes."

In the year's first primary, in New Hampshire on Feb. 18, 1992, voters stunned the President by giving Buchanan 37 per cent of their votes to 53 per cent for Bush. "I understand the message of dissatisfaction," President Bush said after the results were in. Buchanan claimed to be leading "a full-fledged middle-American revolution."

Voter dissatisfaction also was evident a week later in South Dakota. Buchanan was not on the ballot there, but an uncommitted slate drew 31 per cent of the Republican vote. Although Bush went on to win every Republican primary and caucus, Buchanan often claimed at least 20 per cent of the vote. Ignoring pleas from Chairman Bond and others to abandon a losing cause, Buchanan persisted even while acknowledging that only "celestial intervention" could deny Bush renomination.

Republican National Convention. Conservatives and the "religious right" were the dominant forces at the party's national convention in Houston. Before the four-day gathering began on August 17, the GOP platform committee urged adoption of a conservative statement of policy positions. Included was a call for a constitutional amendment to bar abortion under any circumstances, even to save a mother's life. The committee voted 84 to 16 against a motion to drop mention of abortion from the platform. Although a *Washington Post*-ABC News survey of Republican delegates found that 55 per cent opposed a constitutional ban on abortion, to only 28 per cent in favor, the platform was adopted without debate.

In what some saw as a calculated effort to placate "prochoice" Republicans, first lady Barbara Bush said she did not think abortion belonged in the platform. Both the President and Vice President Dan Quayle, who publicly favored the antiabortion cause, said that they would support a child or grandchild of their own who decided to have a legal abortion.

Controversy also was fanned by convention speakers, notably Buchanan, evangelist Pat Robertson, and Quayle's wife, Marilyn. All emphasized "family values" in a way that, to some listeners, seemed to suggest that Democrats opposed such values.

In accepting renomination, Bush emphasized his wartime service and foreign policy experience and suggested these would help him mount a new "crusade" for peace and prosperity. Bush said that if reelected he would propose an across-the-board tax cut, but he gave no specifics.

The campaign. During the fall campaign, Bush emphasized "trust" and "character" issues, contending that his Democratic opponent, Arkansas Governor Bill Clinton, lacked the integrity to be President. He criticized Clinton's explanations of how he avoided the military draft in the 1960's, and he said Clinton should "level" about a visit to Moscow as a college student in 1968, leaving the impression that there was something sinister about the trip. Bush also repeatedly claimed Clinton would tax the middle class heavily to pay for increased federal spending.

Bush initially rejected plans for three televised debates with Clinton, then proposed four himself. The two camps arranged for three presidential debates in October and included Dallas billionaire Ross Perot, who was running as an independent. They also agreed to one debate among the vice presidential candidates, including Perot's running mate, retired Navy Vice Admiral James B. Stockdale.

Entering the final weekend of the presidential campaign, one poll had Bush and Clinton in a statistical dead heat, heartening the President. But some voters were disturbed by Bush's 11th-hour rhetoric. He referred to his Democratic opponents as "these two bozos" and called the Democratic vice presidential nominee, Albert A. Gore, Jr., "Ozone Man" because of his interest in the environment.

Frank Cormier and Margot Cormier

See also **Elections; Democratic Party.** In ***World Book,*** see **Republican Party.**

Reynolds, Albert (1932-), was elected prime minister of the Republic of Ireland on Feb. 11, 1992. He succeeded Charles J. Haughey, who had resigned the previous day. (See **Ireland.**)

Reynolds was elected leader of the Fianna Fáil party on Feb. 6, 1992, as a required preliminary step before his election as prime minister. He had been minister for finance under Haughey from November 1988 until November 1991, when Haughey dismissed him for backing a factional revolt within the Fianna Fáil.

Reynolds was born on Nov. 3, 1932, in Rooskey, a village in county Roscommon of Connacht province. In the 1950's, he attended Summerhill College in Sligo, also in Connacht, but he broke his leg and was unable to take the final examinations.

In the 1960's, Reynolds and two brothers built a ballroom, the first of a successful chain. Reynolds also founded C and D Foods Limited, a pet food company that earned him a fortune, and he bought a newspaper in county Longford of Leinster province.

Reynolds was first elected to the House of Representatives of the Irish parliament in July 1977. Beginning in 1979, he held six cabinet posts, including minister for posts and telegraph, minister for transport, minister for industry and energy, and minister for industry and commerce.

Reynolds and his wife, Kathleen, have two sons and five daughters. Carol L. Hanson

Rhode Island. See **State government.**

Roman Catholic Church. Pope John Paul II underwent surgery in Rome on July 15, 1992, to remove his gall bladder and a tumor from his colon. Some cells in the tumor were in the process of becoming malignant, but physicians said these cells had not yet invaded intestinal tissue.

Under his doctors' advice, the pope curtailed plans to observe in October the 500th anniversary of Christopher Columbus' introduction of Christianity to the New World. Instead of visiting Jamaica, Mexico, and Nicaragua, the pope limited his travel to the Dominican Republic, where he opened a meeting of Latin-American bishops in Santo Domingo, the nation's capital. The meeting, which took two years to arrange, focused on a proposed document that addressed the role of the Catholic Church in the culture of Latin America. The document described that culture as a unique blend of European Christian, native, and African-American cultures. The document also cited growing poverty and social injustice as the paramount problems the church must address in Latin America.

A new universal catechism was issued on November 16 in Paris, the first one that the Roman Catholic Church has issued since the Tridentine Catechism of 1566. The new catechism is an updated compendium of Catholic doctrine, including teachings that were expressed in recent papal encyclicals and Vatican policy statements. The catechism also states moral positions on issues confronting modern society, such as

Crowds fill St. Peter's Square in Rome on May 17 for the beatification of Josemaría Escrivá de Balaguer, the controversial founder of Opus Dei.

drug abuse, artificial insemination, genetic engineering, and environmental abuse. The new document will not replace diocesan catechisms or those prepared by national conferences. Rather, Catholic educators and bishops will use it to prepare other religious materials.

Controversial beatification. On May 17, Pope John Paul II beatified Monsignor Josemaría Escrivá de Balaguer of Spain in a celebration that attracted more than 200,000 people from 60 countries to St. Peter's Square in Rome. Critics within the church said that the beatification of Escrivá had progressed too fast. He had died in 1975. Critics also said that Escrivá was quick to anger, intolerant, and vain. His followers countered that Escrivá was among the first to be investigated for sainthood under the pope's 1983 reforms, which halved the time period for the process.

Beatification is a pope's official declaration that a person is blessed. It follows a long investigative process. If additional investigation proves that the person was associated with two miracles, a pope may canonize the person. According to Roman Catholic doctrine, canonization is a declaration that a person was very holy during his or her lifetime and is in heaven with God. The Vatican ruled in July 1991 that Escrivá was responsible for one miracle.

Escrivá founded a conservative Roman Catholic organization called Opus Dei (Work of God) in 1928. Members, numbering about 77,000 in 42 countries including 1,500 priests, are guided by Escrivá's teachings that Christians should aspire to saintliness in the routine of work and family life. But for years, church liberals have criticized Opus Dei members, saying they are secretive and elitist and were trying to build a personality cult around Escrivá. Pope John Paul II, however, has praised Escrivá and gave Opus Dei responsibility for bringing Roman Catholicism to former Communist countries.

Recognition of Croatia and Slovenia. On Jan. 13, 1992, the Vatican recognized the independence of Croatia and Slovenia, two former republics of Yugoslavia. Both Croatia and Slovenia are predominantly Roman Catholic. The Vatican also sent a message to officials in Belgrade, the capital of Yugoslavia, saying the pope's representative there would remain accredited to the Yugoslav federation and that the recognition of Croatia and Slovenia was not "a hostile act."

Throughout 1992, Pope John Paul II appealed for an end to fighting in the region. As violence escalated in Bosnia and Hercegovina, another republic that broke away from Yugoslavia and became an independent nation, the pope pleaded for all parties to cease their fighting.

Earth Summit message. Archbishop Renato R. Martino, the Vatican's observer at the United Nations (UN), attended the UN Conference on Environment and Development, known as the Earth Summit, in Rio de Janeiro, Brazil, in June. Martino said that if it is the developed countries' wish to protect the environment and relieve chronic, severe poverty in developing areas, industrialized nations must assume a "new and austere manner of living." He called on the developed, industrialized nations to show more solidarity with developing nations. (See also, **Environmental Pollution: Environmental Concern Goes Global.)**

Abortion issue. On March 4, 1992, Helen Alvare, an attorney and director of pro-life planning and information for the U.S. National Conference of Bishops, appeared before a U.S. House of Representatives subcommittee hearing on the proposed Freedom of Choice Act. The act would ban states from restricting abortions. In urging the bill's defeat, Alvare said that the legislation would "trivialize" human rights and trespass on the views of millions of Americans.

A pastoral letter on the role of women in the church and society was not approved by the National Conference of Catholic Bishops, meeting in Washington, D.C., in November 1992. Work on the letter began in 1983. Many bishops at the meeting indicated their concern that the letter would alienate many women. The final draft reportedly emphasized Pope John Paul II's position that equality among men and women could not be based on minimizing the differences between them. The bishops authorized that the letter be published as the text of a report, which does not give it teaching authority. Owen F. Campion

See also **Religion.** In ***World Book,*** see **Roman Catholic Church.**

Romania. Elections on Sept. 27 and Oct. 11, 1992, returned former Communist Party official Ion Iliescu to a second term as Romania's president. But in parliamentary elections, none of the 80 competing parties received enough votes to form a government.

Iliescu named Nicolae Vacaroiu, an economist without a party affiliation, as prime minister on November 4. But his government failed to win opposition support because four cabinet posts went to members of the planning committee under Romania's former Communist government.

Elections. In the first round of voting, Iliescu, who ran as the candidate of the Democratic National Salvation Front (DNSF), fell just short of the 50 per cent of votes needed for election. His nearest rival, Emil Constantinescu, dean of Bucharest University, trailed with 30.5 per cent. But in an October 11 runoff between the top two contenders, Iliescu won comfortably, receiving just over 61 per cent of the votes.

The margin between the parties of the two presidential contenders was considerably narrower in September elections for the two-chamber parliament. Iliescu's DNSF, which is dominated by former Communists and Romanian nationalists, took 27.5 per cent of the vote. Constantinescu's centrist Democratic Convention (DC) polled 23 per cent.

Economic reform. A number of former Communist officials retained relatively widespread public support, especially in the DNSF, and they pledged to slow the pace of economic reform. The opposition Democratic Convention, on the other hand, urged more radical steps toward privatization. In September, the United States House of Representatives voted against granting Romania most-favored-nation trade status, reflecting Western misgivings about the country's commitment to economic reform.

The International Monetary Fund (IMF) and the World Bank, both agencies of the United Nations, supported the policies of Theodor Stolojan, Romania's prime minister until the autumn elections. In June, the World Bank approved a $400-million loan, and in August, an IMF director said Romania had achieved all the reform targets listed in a 12-month agreement.

A cloudy future? Also in August, Stolojan spoke optimistically of the prospects for economic upturn in 1993. But official figures cast a cloud over his optimism. For most Romanians, living conditions had improved little since the December 1989 overthrow of the country's Communist dictatorship. Government statistics indicated that more than half the population still lived below the official poverty line. They also showed a continuing decline in the output of Romania's petroleum industry. By July 1992, overall industrial production had fallen 11 per cent from earlier in the year. Eric Bourne

See also **Europe** (Facts in brief table). In ***World Book,*** see **Romania.**

Rowing. See **Sports.**

Russia remained in a state of political, economic, and social transition through 1992. The country, formerly the dominant republic of the Soviet Union, had become independent when the Soviet Union was dissolved in December 1991. The newly sovereign state faced formidable tasks, including reshaping the institutions of government it had inherited from the Soviet Union and transforming its economy from a centrally planned system into a free-market one.

As the year progressed, political reform took second stage to economic issues, as Russian President Boris Yeltsin sought to prevent former Communists and other opponents from derailing his program for radical economic reform. Despite his efforts, industrial production fell by more than 20 per cent in the first 10 months of 1992, and inflation rose to an annual rate of about 2,000 per cent in December. And at year's end, the future of radical reform was thrown into doubt as Yeltsin lost much of his control over economic policy to conservatives.

The reform program began on January 2, when the government—led by Yeltsin and Yegor T. Gaidar, the chief architect of the reforms—lifted price controls on most consumer goods. The government also began to pursue a "tight-money" policy, restricting loans to state-owned industries and limiting the amount of money in circulation. The policies were designed to prevent inflation and set the stage for making Russia's currency, the ruble, internationally convertible.

By the end of July, however, the government was losing its grip on its tight money policies. To stem the growing budget deficit, it had put more money into circulation, allowing inflation to rise. In addition, industrial production had plummeted, and the Russian Central Bank—whose chairman opposed radical reform—began in August to make large-scale credits available to ailing state-owned firms.

On the positive side, Russia on June 1 became a full member of the International Monetary Fund (IMF), a United Nations agency. The move paved the way for Russia to receive significant amounts of foreign aid.

A new phase of reform opened in October, as the government prepared to sell major state-owned enterprises to private investors. On October 1, officials began distributing *vouchers* (certificates) worth 10,000 rubles (about U.S. $25)—the amount, on average, that a worker earns in six weeks—to each of Russia's more than 150 million citizens. The vouchers were to be used to buy shares in state-owned companies. The first sale of a large state-owned firm began in December.

The battle over reform was accompanied by political power struggles. On April 6, the Congress of People's Deputies—Russia's highest legislative body—began a 9-day session, its first since November 1991. Yeltsin wanted the congress to concentrate on drafting a new constitution that would define the roles of the various government branches and protect such free-market principles as private property. However, all moves to draft a constitution were postponed amid the struggle over economic reform. On April 11, the congress passed a resolution stripping Yeltsin of the emergency powers, granted him by the congress in 1991, that enabled him to govern by decree. In response, the government threatened to resign. Yeltsin defused the crisis with a compromise allowing him to retain his emergency powers until December 1.

On October 24, nationalists and former Communists joined forces to form a bloc called the National Salvation Front (NSF). The NSF vowed to topple the government and roll back reform. In response, Yeltsin on October 27 issued a decree banning the NSF. The next day, he ordered the transfer of a 5,000-member parliamentary security force commanded by conservative parliament Speaker Ruslan Khasbulatov. The force was later restored to parliament. Russia's Constitutional Court, its highest judicial body, began hearings on the legality of the NSF ban in November.

On December 1, the Congress of People's Deputies opened a new session. The congress pitted Yeltsin against the Civic Union, a centrist movement formed in June. The organization, led by industrialist Arkady Volsky and Russian Vice President Aleksandr Rutskoy, wanted reforms scaled back to stop the rapid decline in industrial production.

On December 5, the congress narrowly rejected constitutional amendments that would have required legislative approval of top government officials. Such approval was then required only for prime minister, a post formally held by Yeltsin. But on December 9, the congress rejected Gaidar, whom Yeltsin had named acting prime minister in June, as prime minister.

Yeltsin, in response, called for a popular referendum to decide who should control economic reform. But the strength of the opposition forced Yeltsin to retract his call. In a compromise, he and the congress agreed to hold a referendum on a new constitution in April 1993. On Dec. 14, 1992, Yeltsin nominated a conservative, Viktor S. Chernomyrdin, as prime minister.

Communist ban upheld. The Constitutional Court on November 30 upheld Yeltsin's ban of the country's Communist Party. Yeltsin had banned both the Russian and Soviet Communist parties on Nov. 6, 1991, in the aftermath of the failed August 1991 coup. However, the court ruled that Communist Party *cells*—the lowest party units—could legally operate.

In its decision, the court did not rule on the central issue of whether the Communist Party was illegal regardless of Yeltsin's ban. The failure to rule disappointed supporters of the government, who had charged that the party was not a political body but a criminal organization whose rule by dictatorship had violated the Soviet Union's constitution.

Earlier, the hearings had sparked a confrontation between Yeltsin and former Soviet President Mikhail S. Gorbachev, the Soviet Union's leader from 1985 until its collapse in 1991. On Sept. 28, 1992, Gorbachev said he would ignore a summons to testify before the court. In response, Russian authorities on October 2 revoked Gorbachev's right to travel abroad. On October 7, Yeltsin confiscated the headquarters and other property of the Gorbachev Foundation, a research institute established by Gorbachev in January 1992. Gorbachev later was able to lease part of the headquarters. Gorbachev was permitted to travel to Germany to attend the October 16 funeral of former West German Chancellor Willy Brandt. The travel ban was lifted completely in November.

Ethnic tensions. The Soviet Union's collapse in 1991 stemmed in part from a rise in nationalist feeling among the country's numerous ethnic and national groups. In 1992, Yeltsin worked to stem the rise of nationalism in Russia, whose citizens comprise more than 100 such groups. Separatist factions had already arisen within some of the country's approximately 30 ethnic homelands—autonomous territories that had limited self-rule under the Soviet government.

On March 31, leaders of Russia and most of the country's administrative regions signed a Federation Treaty. The signers included 18 autonomous republics, the most important of the ethnic homelands. The pact granted greater authority to the regions, which in turn pledged continued allegiance to Moscow. Two autonomous republics, both primarily Muslim, did not sign the treaty: the Tatar republic, in western Russia, and Chechen-Ingush, located in the southern Transcaucasian region of southwestern Russia. On March 21, Tatar voters had approved a referendum proclaim-

Tens of thousands of Communist Party supporters rally in Moscow's Red Square in May against the government of Russian President Boris Yeltsin.

ing the Tatar republic a sovereign state. Chechen-Ingush had declared independence in November 1991.

The southern Transcaucasus soon emerged as a potentially dangerous flashpoint of ethnic unrest. In August, separatists from a number of Transcaucasian groups joined Muslim rebels fighting in the Abkhazia region of Georgia, a former Soviet republic on Russia's southern border. In June, Russia and Georgia had established a joint peacekeeping force in South Ossetia, another region in Georgia, which was seeking unification with the Russian region of North Ossetia.

At the end of October, violence erupted between Ossetians and ethnic Ingush living in North Ossetia. More than 100 people, most of them Ingush, were killed, and thousands of others were left homeless. Russian troops halted the fighting in early November.

In foreign policy, Russia worked toward integration with the West after years of Cold War confrontation. As part of its overtures to the West, Russia made public long-held Soviet secrets. On October 14, Russian officials gave Polish President Lech Walesa documents confirming top-level Soviet responsibility for the 1940 execution of more than 20,000 Polish officers and other Poles in Katyn, Russia, during World War II (1939-1945). The Soviet Union, which had long claimed that German Nazis carried out the massacre, had first admitted responsibility in April 1990.

Arms control. After the Soviet Union's collapse, four former republics—Russia, Belarus, Kazakhstan, and Ukraine—possessed nuclear weapons. On May 23,

Russian nationalists in September protest against the possible return to Japan of four of the Kuril Islands, seized by the Soviet Union in 1945.

the four signed a revision to the Strategic Arms Reduction Treaty (START), an arms control accord signed by the United States and the Soviet Union in July 1991. Under the revision, all *strategic* (long-range) nuclear weapons in Belarus, Kazakhstan, and Ukraine would be transferred to Russia, which would assume the Soviet Union's obligations under START. The Russian parliament ratified START on Nov. 4, 1992.

The former republics also agreed to sign the 1968 Nuclear Non-Proliferation Treaty. The treaty bans the spread of nuclear weapons to other countries.

During the year, some delays occurred in the weapons transfers. In November 1992, Ukraine threatened to halt its transfer of strategic arms, in part because of concerns that Russia would deploy the weapons. However, all the republics' *tactical* (short range) nuclear arms had been shipped to Russia by early May. The arms issue was one of several disputes between Russia and Ukraine in 1992. (See **Ukraine.**)

On June 16, Yeltsin and U.S. President George Bush announced a new arms control accord. Under the pact, which became known as START II, both nations would reduce the number of nuclear warheads in their arsenals to significantly less than that permitted by START. In December, negotiators resolved a number of differences that had threatened the pact, allowing Yeltsin and Bush to sign it on Jan. 3, 1993.

Continuing issues. On Nov. 19, 1992, Yeltsin gave South Korean President Roh Tae Woo flight recorders from Korean Air Lines flight 007, a South Korean passenger airliner shot down by a Soviet fighter plane in 1983. However, the tapes had been removed from the recorders, and at the end of the year, their location and contents remained unclear. At the time of the incident, Soviet officials said the jet had flown into Soviet airspace on an apparent spy mission and that they could not identify it as a civilian aircraft.

On October 29, Russia announced it was suspending its withdrawal of former Soviet troops from Latvia and Estonia because of concern over the treatment of ethnic Russians there. These countries had denied citizenship rights to ethnic Russians.

In a major setback, Russia failed in 1992 to normalize relations with Japan. Japan and the Soviet Union had never signed a peace treaty after World War II. The main obstacle to improved relations was four islands in the Kuril chain occupied by the Soviets in 1945, at the close of the war. Japan insisted Russia return the islands, which it calls the Northern Territories, before it would normalize relations or give Russia large amounts of aid. In March 1992, Russia began withdrawing troops from the islands. But pressure from hard-line nationalists forced Yeltsin on September 9 to cancel a scheduled visit to Japan. Relations between the nations then cooled. Justin Burke

See also **Armed forces: The Nuclear Threat in the New World Order; Europe** (Facts in brief table). In the World Book Supplement section, see **Russia.**

Rwanda. See **Africa.**

Safety. Some types of soft cheeses may not be safe for pregnant women, the elderly, and people suffering from certain medical conditions that weaken the immune system. Such people are at risk of developing a rare but potentially fatal form of food poisoning called *listeriosis,* the United States Centers for Disease Control (CDC) in Atlanta, Ga., cautioned in April 1992. The CDC warned that feta cheese, Brie, Camembert, blue-veined cheeses, and Mexican-style cheeses such as queso blanco and queso freso could cause listeriosis. The CDC noted that Mexican cheeses generally are not sold in major U.S. supermarkets but are available at smaller Hispanic grocery stores and through street vendors. Undercooked chicken and certain delicatessen foods, such as cold cuts, may also cause listeriosis for those at risk of developing the illness, according to the report.

Infant sleep positions. Concern about the safety of the traditional stomach-down sleeping position for infants led the American Academy of Pediatrics (AAP) in April to recommend that most healthy infants be put to bed on their back rather than their stomach. The recommendation came after studies suggested that infants put to bed stomach-down had a slightly higher risk of sudden infant death syndrome (SIDS), also known as "crib death." SIDS is the leading cause of death for infants between the ages of 1 month and 1 year and kills about 7,000 infants annually in the United States. Many factors have been implicated in SIDS, but its cause remains unknown.

The AAP said that parents tend to put infants in a stomach-down position in the belief that it reduces an infant's risk of inhaling and choking on vomited milk. But the AAP said there was no evidence that otherwise healthy infants were at increased risk for choking when lying on their back. The AAP recommended that parents consult their pediatrician about the proper sleep position for infants with respiratory disorders, a tendency to vomit, or other health problems.

Dangerous infant bedding. Certain types of bedding material carry a risk of suffocating infants sleeping face-down, according to an April report from pediatric researchers at the Washington University School of Medicine in St. Louis, Mo. The materials were foam couch cushions, foam pads covered with a comforter, sheepskin infant bedding, and soft bassinet cushions covered with a blanket. The report, which was based on an animal study, said that such bedding might cause suffocation by trapping exhaled carbon dioxide near the infant's face, so that the infant is unable to inhale enough oxygen. The researchers said that possibly 25 per cent of SIDS cases could be attributed to reduced oxygen from such bedding materials. Beanbag cushions for babies had previously been linked to suffocation and recalled from the market.

Cloth and paper towels exposed to large quantities of cooking oil may pose a home fire hazard, according to a January report from the U.S. Consumer Product Safety Commission, the U.S. Fire Administration, and the International Association of Fire Chiefs. Normal laundering may not remove all oil from cloth towels, the report said, and the towel may ignite spontaneously if dried in a clothes drier, left in a pile while still warm, or stored in a warm area. Paper towels soaked with cooking oil or furniture-refinishing oils may also spontaneously combust if not disposed of properly. Safety officials advised consumers to dispose of oil-soaked cloth and paper towels in ventilated, fireproof trash containers away from direct sunlight or other sources of heat.

Motorboat propeller accidents could be greatly reduced if the U.S. Coast Guard required propeller guards on recreational motorboats, according to a September report from researchers at Johns Hopkins University in Baltimore. Propeller guards surround the spinning blades of a propeller and prevent contact with people. The researchers said that the Coast Guard, which establishes safety standards for recreational boats, greatly underestimates the frequency of propeller accidents. The study estimated that 2,000 to 3,000 such accidents occur each year in the United States, rather than the average 100 per year reported by the Coast Guard. Propeller guards have been available for more than 35 years, but no major manufacturer uses them, the report said. Michael Woods

See also **Consumerism; Food.** In ***World Book,*** see **Safety; Sudden infant death syndrome.**

Sailing. See **Boating.**

San Diego. Figures from the 1990 census released in 1992 revealed that San Diego residents, on the average, make more money, are better educated, and are more likely to be employed than they were in 1980. But despite that seemingly rosy picture, San Diego's economic outlook remained grim throughout 1992. The effects of the weak national economy, coupled with further cutbacks in the local defense industry, pushed San Diego County's unemployment rate to 7.9 per cent in August, the second-highest monthly rate in almost a decade.

The bad economic news was compounded in July, when federal regulators seized San Diego-based HomeFed Bank. HomeFed, the nation's eighth-largest savings and loan, became insolvent after losing $1 billion as a result of bad loans and real estate foreclosures. Financial experts predicted that the loss of HomeFed, a major source of construction financing in the region, would hamper the city's growth.

There was more bad economic news on the horizon. Local defense-industry companies, including the General Dynamics Corporation and the Hughes Aircraft Company, said they expected to be making thousands of additional layoffs within the next two years.

A new mayor. On Nov. 3, 1992, Susan Golding, San Diego County supervisor, was elected mayor of San Diego, succeeding Maureen O'Connor, the mayor since 1986. Golding defeated Peter Navarro, a professor at the University of California at Irvine.

Population shift. Figures released in June by the state of California showed a dramatic shift in San Diego County population trends, indicating that net migration into the county from other parts of the United States had all but stopped. State population experts blamed the 1990-1991 recession for the halt of domestic migration to the San Diego area. The experts attributed 97.8 per cent of the county's population growth in 1991 to international immigration, most of it from Asia. Because of heavy foreign immigration, the population of San Diego County grew by more than 55,000 in 1991. That raised the county's population to more than 2.6 million.

Killer executed. After numerous last-ditch appeals, convicted killer Robert Alton Harris, 39, was put to death on April 21 in the gas chamber at the California State Prison in San Quentin. Harris had been convicted of brutally murdering two San Diego teenagers in 1978 after stealing their car for use in a bank robbery. He was the first person to be executed in California since 1967.

America's Cup victory. Bill Koch's *America*^{3} beat out Italy's *Il Moro di Venezia* on May 16, 1992, to keep the America's Cup trophy in the United States. Koch's team won a 4-to-1 victory over the Italian racers in the best-of-7 final series of runs. The victory marked the San Diego Yacht Club's second consecutive defense of the America's Cup. San Diego was scheduled to host the race again in 1995. (See **Boating.**)

All-Star summit. President George Bush and Mexican President Carlos Salinas de Gortari were among the 60,000 baseball fans on hand at Jack Murphy Stadium on July 14, 1992, as San Diego hosted the All-Star Game. Bush and Salinas were in San Diego to discuss the North American Free Trade Agreement, which would unite the United States, Mexico, and Canada into the world's largest free trade zone. As for the results of the game, the American League beat the National League 13 to 6.

Budgetary turmoil at state university. On June 29, the faculty senate of San Diego State University (SDSU) handed down an unprecedented "no confidence" vote against SDSU President Thomas Day in response to budget-cutting measures. Day had sent layoff notices to 145 tenured professors and proposed eliminating nine academic departments in an effort to trim $11.5 million from the university's budget. His actions were part of a statewide effort to bring a fiscal crisis in California under control.

After the no-confidence vote, Day promised to postpone as many as half of the planned layoffs by using money earmarked for equipment purchases and library operations to pay for faculty salaries. But he offered little hope for those university students whose academic majors would be eliminated when such departments as anthropology, aerospace engineering, Russian, and German were phased out.

Sharon K. Gillenwater

See also **City.** In ***World Book,*** see **San Diego.**

Saskatchewan. After a decade of drought, the central prairie province experienced a disastrously wet and cold summer in 1992, resulting in a projected $1-billion ($802-million U.S.) loss in the grain crop. By mid-September, only 23 per cent of the crop had been harvested, compared with 74 per cent in 1991.

The first budget of the New Democratic Party (NDP) government under Premier Roy Romanow reflected the province's difficult economic situation. The budget, introduced on May 7, 1992, imposed a broad range of spending cuts and income tax increases for Saskatchewan residents, who already were shouldering the heaviest taxes in Canada. The $5-billion ($4-billion U.S.) budget showed a $517-million ($415-million U.S.) deficit for the fiscal year (April 1, 1992, to March 31, 1993). This brought the total provincial debt to $13.8 billion ($11 billion U.S.), the highest in the nation on a per capita basis.

A radical redesign of the health-care system in Saskatchewan was announced by the NDP government in August. In an effort to promote more healthy life styles and to provide a more efficient health service, the plan aimed to place health-budgeting responsibilities into the hands of 20 to 30 new regional health boards. Community-based "wellness" programs were to be established at local facilities, and nurses were to be given a more prominent role in health-care delivery. David M. L. Farr

In ***World Book,*** see **Saskatchewan.**

Saudi Arabia. Increasingly vocal Islamic activists in Saudi Arabia in 1992 criticized the pro-Western policies of the government and its attempts to modernize Saudi society. The country's Islamic religious establishment, which has traditionally supported the government, also came under fire from the activists.

The main focus of the activists' criticism was government support for the Arab-Israeli peace talks. But the activists also criticized the presence of women in the work force, Saudi business ventures with Western countries, economic advantages for members of the royal family, a lack of political freedom, and the high unemployment rate that existed among young, educated Saudis.

Activists challenged. In January, King Fahd bin Abd al-Aziz Al-Saud threatened Saudi Arabia's Islamic activists with serious consequences if they continued to attack the government's social and foreign policies. Saudi authorities also reportedly tried to halt the distribution of antigovernment cassette tapes, detained Muslim clergy for questioning, and curtailed public demonstrations. But in March, Fahd said that Western forms of democracy were incompatible with Islam and Middle East societies.

Throughout the year, the government also urged wealthy Saudis to reconsider making donations to Islamic activist groups in other countries. In the 1980's, the Saudi government and Saudi citizens had channeled millions of dollars to such groups. Fearful that the aid had encouraged Islamic militancy, the government noted that many of the activist groups that had received Saudi funds had supported Iraq during the Persian Gulf War (1991).

New Constitution. In an attempt to deflect his political critics, Fahd on March 1, 1992, issued a new Constitution intended to liberalize the country's political system. In addition to establishing Saudi Arabia's first bill of rights, the Constitution specified the creation of a 60-member Consultative Council that would review national policies and advise the cabinet. But critics noted that all members of the council would be appointed by the king. In addition, the council reportedly could not propose legislation, and its recommendations would be nonbinding. On September 17, Fahd appointed his minister of justice as speaker of the council.

The new Constitution also altered the method for choosing Saudi Arabia's next king. It decreed that in addition to the sons of the founder of Saudi Arabia, Abd al-Aziz ibn Saud, his grandsons could also assume the throne. This change increased the number of candidates from approximately 40 to about 500 Saudi princes.

Saudi-U.S. relations weathered uncertainty during 1992. United States President George Bush indicated his gratitude to Saudi Arabia for its support of his anti-Iraq policies and of the Arab-Israeli peace talks. On September 11, Bush announced the United States would sell Saudi Arabia 72 F-15 fighter planes worth $10 billion. But rising anti-Americanism among Saudis fueled the government's reluctance to sign a joint defense agreement similar to the pacts the United States had signed with Kuwait and Bahrain at the end of the Persian Gulf War.

Iraqi refugees in the Saudi desert camp of Artawiyah have been tortured and more than 1,000 of them were forcibly returned to Iraq, according to a report issued in spring 1992 by the Lawyers Committee for Human Rights, an advocacy group based in New York City. Most of the refugees apparently were Iraqi soldiers who had refused to return to Iraq at the end of the Persian Gulf War. Some 30,000 Iraqi refugees reportedly remained in the camp at the end of 1992.

Friction with Yemen. Saudi Arabia's uneasy relations with neighboring Yemen, which had made pro-Iraqi statements during the Persian Gulf War, worsened in 1992 as Saudi Arabia began asserting claims to an oil-rich territory controlled by Yemen. In June, the Saudis threatened possible military action against Western oil companies exploring in the territory in Yemen. Christine Helms

See also **Middle East** (Facts in brief table). In ***World Book,*** see **Saudi Arabia.**
School. See **Education.**
Senegal. See **Africa.**
Sierra Leone. See **Africa.**
Singapore. See **Asia.**
Skating. See **Hockey; Ice skating.**

Italy's Alberto Tomba competes in the giant slalom in February during the Winter Olympics in Albertville, France. Tomba won the gold medal.

Skiing. Petra Kronberger of Austria became 1992's most successful Alpine skier, winning two Olympic gold medals and her third straight World Cup overall championship. Although Paul Accola of Switzerland took the World Cup overall title for men, Alberto Tomba of Italy, the flamboyant runner-up, gained more attention. In the Winter Olympics in the Savoy region of the French Alps, Austria won 3 of the 10 gold medals, Italy won 3, and Norway won 2.

Women. The World Cup season ran from November 1991 to March 1992, with time out for the Olympics. Kronberger totaled 1,262 points in the World Cup, followed by Carole Merle of France with 1,211 points, and Katja Seizinger of Germany with 937 points. In individual disciplines, Merle won the giant slalom and super giant slalom, and Seizinger won the downhill. Vreni Schneider of Switzerland won the slalom.

In the Winter Olympics, Kronberger won gold medals in the slalom and the combined (a special slalom combined with a special downhill). Kerrin Lee-Gartner of Canada won the downhill, and Deborah Compagnoni of Italy won the super giant slalom.

The American women did well in the World Cup overall standings. Diann Roffe of Potsdam, N.Y., finished 10th with 607 points; Julie Parisien of Auburn, Me., was 15th with 472 points; and Eva Twardokens of Santa Cruz, Calif., was 16th with 465 points.

Roffe won a silver medal in the Olympics in the giant slalom, and Hilary Lindh of Juneau, Alaska, won a silver medal in the downhill. Parisien finished fourth in the slalom and fifth in the giant slalom.

Men. Accola won the World Cup overall championship with 1,699 points, followed by Tomba with 1,362 points. A. J. Kitt of Rochester, N.Y., tied for 10th with 594 points and won a World Cup men's downhill in Val d'Isère, France. Tomba won the season championship in the slalom and giant slalom, Accola in the super giant slalom, and Franz Heinzer of Switzerland in the downhill.

In the Winter Olympics, Tomba took the gold medal in the giant slalom and the silver in the slalom. He won nine World Cup races and in an unsuccessful quest for the overall title even took part in super giant slaloms, which he had avoided since 1989.

Nordic. In Olympic cross-country competition, two Russian women on the Unified Team (Lyubov Yegorova and Yelena Valbe) won five medals each and two Norwegian men (Vegard Ulvang and Bjorn Dahlie) gained four medals each. In the World Cup, Valbe won the women's title, and Dahlie barely beat Ulvang for the men's title. The other World Cup champions were 16-year-old Toni Nieminen of Finland in jumping and Fabrice Guy of France in Nordic combined. Both also won Olympic gold medals. Frank Litsky

See also **Olympic Games: The 1992 Olympics.** In *World Book,* see **Skiing.**

Slovenia. See **Europe.**

Soccer. The United States National Team, looking forward to the 1994 World Cup on home soil, made progress in 1992. But the collapse in July 1992 of the Major Soccer League (MSL), the only nationwide professional league, set American soccer back.

The National Team won the first U.S. Cup on July 6 in Chicago. The Americans defeated Ireland and Portugal. Then they tied Italy, 1-1. New U.S. citizens such as Roy Wegerle, formerly of South Africa; Thomas Dooley, formerly of Germany; and Ernie Stewart, formerly of the Netherlands, helped the U.S. team.

U.S. league folds. American soccer flourished at the high school and college level, but the professional game fell to its lowest point since the early 1960's. From October 1991 to May 1992, the MSL played its 14th season. The San Diego Sockers won the regular-season title and then their fifth consecutive play-off championship. The league's season average attendance reached 7,851, a 20 per cent increase. But when franchises in St. Louis, Mo., and Tacoma, Wash., could not raise money for the 1992-1993 season, only five teams remained and the league folded.

Olympic soccer during the Summer Olympic Games in Barcelona, Spain, was limited to players under 23 years of age. Spain took the gold medal on August 8. The United States, with one victory, one loss, and one tie, barely missed qualifying for what would have been its first appearance in the Olympic quarterfinals.

World Cup. National teams from 134 nations began eliminations in 1992 to qualify 22 teams for the 1994 World Cup competition. There will be two automatic qualifiers—the United States as the host and Germany as the defending champion. In March 1992, the International Federation of Association Football (FIFA), the international governing body for soccer, selected nine American stadiums to stage 1994 World Cup games. They were Soldier Field in Chicago; the Cotton Bowl in Dallas; Giants Stadium in East Rutherford, N.J.; Foxboro Stadium in Foxboro, Mass.; the Citrus Bowl in Orlando, Fla.; Stanford Stadium in Palo Alto, Calif.; the Rose Bowl in Pasadena, Calif.; the Silverdome in Pontiac, Mich.; and RFK Stadium in Washington, D.C. The Silverdome will be the first indoor facility in the 62-year history of the cup.

European soccer. When the FIFA barred war-torn Yugoslavia from international competition 11 days before the start of the European championship, Denmark was invited as a replacement. In the final on June 26 in Göteborg, Sweden, Denmark surprisingly defeated Germany, 1-0.

The European club champions were Barcelona in the Champions Cup, Werder Bremen of Germany in the Cup Winners' Cup, and Ajax of the Netherlands in the UEFA Cup. Leeds United won England's new Premier League, and Liverpool won the English Football Association Cup. Frank Litsky

In *World Book,* see **Soccer.**

Social security. Monthly social security benefits were set to increase by 3 per cent on Jan. 1, 1993, boosting the average monthly check by $19, to $653 from $634. At the same time, the maximum wage subject to the 6.2 per cent social security payroll tax was to rise to $57,600 from $55,500.

The amount of money that social security beneficiaries from age 65 to 69 could earn without sacrificing benefits was to climb to $10,500 from $10,200. For every $3 earned above this amount, a retiree loses $1 of benefits. People age 70 and older are not subject to an earnings limit.

The Social Security Administration informed a Senate Finance subcommittee on April 27, 1992, that the social security disability insurance fund would run out of money in 1997 unless Congress acted to replenish it. The fund provides monthly benefits for 3 million workers who are physically unable to work. The report said that the sagging economy and an increase in the number of disabled workers depleted the fund.

Bias with disability benefits? A study released in May by the General Accounting Office, a branch of the U.S. Congress, reported that blacks were less likely than whites to be approved for disability benefits. The study noted that, in 1988, 29 per cent of blacks and 36 per cent of whites who applied for benefits under the regular social security disability program were granted them. Frank Cormier and Margot Cormier

In *World Book,* see **Social security.**

Somalia. Mass starvation, brought on by civil war and drought, claimed at least 300,000 lives in Somalia in 1992. Responding to this mounting tragedy, the United Nations (UN) Security Council on December 3 authorized military intervention in Somalia to protect relief workers and shipments of food aid from the rebel soldiers and roughnecks who had plunged the east African nation into anarchy. United States President George Bush then authorized sending at least 28,000 U.S. troops to Somalia.

There had been constant warfare in Somalia, most of it between rival branches of the United Somali Congress. The fighting broke out in late 1991 between factions led by President Ali Mahdi Mohamed and General Mohamed Farah Aideed. They were vying for control of the government following the January 1991 ouster of Somalia's President Mohamed Siad Barre.

Disrupted aid, a UN resolution. UN peace efforts led in February 1992 to a cease-fire agreement, but it had little effect in lessening the hostilities. Food aid from the Red Cross started entering the country in late April, and an airlift of food from the United States began in August. By most accounts, however, less than half of the food being sent to Somalia was reaching famine victims because of looting and the harassment of relief workers. In September, 500 UN peacekeeping troops arrived in Somalia to protect food shipments and relief workers, but the UN forces proved too small for the task.

In November, the Bush Administration proposed sending up to 30,000 U.S. and allied troops to Somalia to guard food convoys, and the UN Security Council considered a resolution authorizing such an action. The unanimous December 3 vote marked the first time that the 15-member council had asserted the right to intervene in a country's internal affairs to protect the lives of its citizens. Several nations, including France, Italy, Nigeria, and Saudi Arabia, said they would participate.

The operation. About 1,800 U.S. Marines went ashore at Mogadishu, the capital, on December 9. They secured the airport, making it safe for planes carrying 16,000 more Marines and 10,000 Army troops to land. Bush had expressed hope that the mission would be completed by Jan. 20, 1993, when his term in office ends, but some U.S. military experts doubted it would be over by then. A longer timetable seemed especially likely if, as some in the military expected, the operation involved efforts to bring a degree of stability to Somalia so as to avoid a recurrence of anarchy and starvation once the troops withdraw.

In other developments in 1992, the independent Somaliland Republic that had been declared in the north in May 1991 by one of the rebel groups apparently split apart due to ethnic rivalries. In the south, the forces of Barre battled against troops led by Aideed. Mark DeLancey

See also **Africa** (Facts in brief table). In ***World Book,*** see **Somalia.**

South Africa. The many political factions in South Africa made progress in 1992 in their quest to resolve their differences and establish a new democratic political system in which all of the nation's racial groups are fairly represented. Outbreaks of violence were common, however, and their increasing severity threatened to bring the process to a halt.

National convention. On January 20, delegates from 19 political groups reconvened the Convention for a Democratic South Africa (Codesa), a national conference that first met in late 1991. Codesa was organized to establish the rules for writing a new constitution and making the transition to full-fledged democracy. The two main black political organizations—the African National Congress (ANC) and the Inkatha Freedom Party, a group made up of members of the Zulu ethnic group—took part in the talks. The white National Party of South Africa's State President Frederik Willem de Klerk was also represented. But the white Conservative Party, which supports the continuation of South Africa's system of *apartheid* (racial separation), declined to participate.

A vote of confidence. On Feb. 19, 1992, the National Party was defeated in a special election to fill a vacant seat in the white chamber of Parliament. The defeat caused many South Africans to believe that de Klerk's efforts to reform the government had lost the support of the white population.

To settle the question, de Klerk on February 20 called a special whites-only referendum for March 17 on the issue of sharing power with the nation's black majority. De Klerk said he would resign if a majority voted against him, but he did not have to make good on that pledge. The voters supported him by more than a 2 to 1 margin.

Despite the mandate for democratization, important questions remained unanswered for the rest of the year. Neither de Klerk nor any other South African leader—white or black—could come up with a universally acceptable plan for the organization of a constitutional convention or the form of a transitional government. The most serious negotiations on those issues were not at Codesa but between de Klerk and ANC President Nelson Mandela.

A violent year. The incidence of violence increased throughout the year, and the estimated death toll had risen to more than 12,000 by year-end. Several large-scale slaughters brought political negotiations on the future of South Africa to a temporary standstill. The worst incident occurred on June 17 in the black township of Boipatong, which was attacked by an armed mob—reportedly members of Inkatha. At least 39 people were killed. Witnesses claimed that white South African police assisted in the attack, an accusation that the police denied.

A government commission and United Nations observers tried to determine who was behind all the violence. They found blame everywhere. The evidence pointed alike to right wing white groups, ANC and

Militants opposing the government of Ciskei, a South Africa-created black homeland, are fired on by troops in Ciskei's capital, Bisho, in September.

Inkatha militants, and a mysterious "third force" of government soldiers and police officers.

Brighter prospects? The warring factions in South Africa threatened to doom de Klerk's reforms. A particular thorn in de Klerk's side was Inkatha's leader, Chief Mangosuthu Gatsha Buthelezi, who was widely accused of trying to subvert progress toward democratization in order to preserve his own power. By November, however, Buthelezi appeared to be losing support among his Zulu followers, and de Klerk turned more toward Mandela.

On November 26, de Klerk called for universal elections to be held in April 1994. Mandela insisted that elections should be held before the end of 1993. Compromise on that point seemed imminent at year-end, and it looked as though de Klerk and Mandela realized that by working together they might be able to bring democracy and peace to South Africa.

Buthelezi, left out of the approaching compromise and facing opposition in his Zulu homeland, moved more closely to the far-right white groups. He threatened to join with them in breaking South Africa apart into small ethnically and racially based independent nations. But few observers saw that as a likely outcome to the situation. Mark DeLancey

See also **Africa** (Facts in brief table). In ***World Book,*** see **South Africa.**

South America. See **Latin America.**

South Carolina. See **State government.**

South Dakota. See **State government.**

Space exploration. The world celebrated "International Space Year" during 1992, as nations sought to promote global cooperation in space exploration. Many of the missions launched in 1992 by the National Aeronautics and Space Administration (NASA) in the United States reflected this international spirit.

Low-gravity work. The U.S. space shuttle Discovery lifted off on January 22 with a Canadian neurologist and a German physicist among the crew. (All shuttle flights take off from the Kennedy Space Center [KSC] in Cape Canaveral, Fla.) The Canadian, Roberta L. Bondar, was a member of the Canadian Space Agency. The German, Ulf D. Merbold, represented the European Space Agency (ESA).

Bondar, Merbold, and the five other astronauts worked in the International Microgravity Laboratory, a research module in the shuttle's cargo bay. The lab's 54 experiments, designed by researchers from 16 nations, dealt with the effects of near-zero gravity on the growth of crystals as well as on the behavior of fruit flies, frog eggs, and the astronauts themselves. The findings were to be utilized in long-duration stays aboard NASA's planned space station, Freedom. Discovery landed at Edwards Air Force Base (EAFB) in California on January 30.

Atmospheric mission. Two physicists, Dirk D. Frimout of Belgium—the first Belgian to fly in space—and Michael Foale of Great Britain, were part of the seven-person crew that rode the shuttle Atlantis into space on March 24. Scientists from the United States, Belgium, France, Germany, Japan, the Netherlands, and Switzerland contributed instruments to the Atmospheric Laboratory for Applications and Science (ATLAS), a lab in the shuttle's cargo bay for studying the sun's effects on Earth's atmosphere. The experiments included the creation of artificial *auroras* (light displays) in the atmosphere. ATLAS will be reflown aboard a shuttle each year until 2003 to record a full 11-year cycle of solar energy changes. Atlantis returned to KSC on April 2.

Space salvage. Endeavour, built to replace the shuttle Challenger, which was destroyed in a 1986 explosion, began its maiden flight on May 7. The chief goal of the mission was to salvage the Intelsat-6, an international communications satellite stranded in a useless orbit since 1990.

On May 10 and 11, Endeavour crew member Pierre J. Thout tried to snag the satellite with a specially designed "capture bar," but he was thwarted by the sensitivity of the satellite to the slightest motion. On May 13, Richard J. Hieb and Thomas D. Akers joined Thout on the first U.S. three-person spacewalk. The trio steadied the satellite with their gloved hands, then used the capture bar and the shuttle's robot arm to bring it into the cargo bay. The operation took 8½ hours. Once the Intelsat-6 was in the cargo bay, the astronauts attached a new rocket to it, then released it. The rocket sent the satellite into its proper orbit.

On May 14, Akers and Kathryn Thornton took a spacewalk to practice construction techniques for use on Freedom. The four spacewalks in one mission set a shuttle record. Endeavour landed at EAFB on May 16.

Longest shuttle flight. On June 25, Columbia left KSC on the longest shuttle mission to date—13 days 19 hours. The mission was the first in a series of "extended duration orbiter" flights planned by NASA to prepare astronauts for long stays aboard Freedom. The crew of seven worked around the clock on the U.S. Microgravity Laboratory, whose aim was similar to that of the microgravity lab aboard the January Discovery flight. Columbia landed at KSC on July 19.

Satellite on a wire. Atlantis rocketed into orbit again on July 31, carrying an Italian-built satellite attached to 12.5 miles (20 kilometers) of wire. The crew included telecommunications expert Franco Malerba, the first Italian astronaut, and astrophysicist Claude Nicollier, the first astronaut from Switzerland.

The plan was to release the satellite from the cargo bay and fly it like a kite. Movement of the wire through the *ionosphere* (a layer of charged particles in Earth's upper atmosphere) would generate electricity in the wire. However, when the astronauts tried to deploy the satellite on August 4, the reel mechanism jammed after only 850 feet (260 meters) of wire had been played out, and the project had to be scrapped.

The Atlantis crew had better luck deploying an ESA research satellite, the European Retrievable Carrier (Eureca), on August 2. Eureca carried 15 automated experiments that were to be conducted before the satellite was retrieved in 1993. Atlantis ended its mission with an August 8 landing at KSC.

A crew of firsts. Endeavour soared into space again on September 12 carrying the first married couple, Mark C. Lee and N. Jan Davis; the first black woman, Mae C. Jemison, a physician and chemical engineer; and the first Japanese on a U.S. space mission, chemist Mamoru Mohri. The flight was the first joint mission of the United States and Japan. Japan provided 34 of the 43 experiments carried in a microgravity laboratory called Spacelab-J. The seven-person crew examined the effects of weightlessness on fish, frogs, flies, and hornets. The astronauts and their space zoo landed at KSC on September 20, completing the 50th shuttle flight.

Italian satellite deployed. Columbia returned to space on October 22 with a crew of six. The shuttle's cargo included the Laser Geodynamics Satellite 2 (LAGEOS-2), built by the Italian Space Agency. On October 23, the crew deployed the satellite, which joined LAGEOS-1, in orbit since 1976. The satellites have reflective surfaces so scientists can bounce lasers off them from Earth in order to measure movements of the planet's crust. Columbia touched down at KSC on November 1.

Military mission. The final shuttle voyage of 1992 was a mission for the U.S. Defense Department. Discovery lifted off on December 2. While in orbit, the five-man crew deployed a secret satellite and received

Three American astronauts haul an errant communications satellite into the cargo bay of the space shuttle Endeavour in May.

laser signals beamed up from a military base in Florida. However, a dead battery forced the astronauts to scrap a project involving the release of metal balls into space in order to test radar tracking from the ground.

The return trip also had its difficulties. Discovery landed on December 9 at EAFB rather than KSC because of cloud cover over Cape Canaveral. And the astronauts had to remain in the shuttle for an hour after landing while ground crews sealed a jet thruster that leaked poisonous fumes during the descent.

New flight to Mars. On September 25, NASA launched the first U.S. mission to Mars since 1975. A Titan 3 rocket blasted off from Cape Canaveral, then released the Mars Observer into space 15 minutes later. The $1-billion Observer was to make the 450-million-mile (720-million-kilometer) trip to Mars in 11 months, arriving in August 1993. The spacecraft will map the planet's surface while circling the planet for at least a Martian year, or 687 Earth days.

New NASA chief. On April 1, Daniel S. Goldin became the new administrator of NASA. He replaced Richard H. Truly, a former astronaut who had run the agency since 1989. Goldin had been a vice president at TRW Incorporated, a U.S. aerospace contractor, where he had presided over the construction of 13 spacecraft still in orbit in 1992. William J. Cromie

See also **Astronomy**. In ***World Book,*** see **Space travel.**

Spain. Two events focused the world's attention on Spain in 1992. They were the 25th Summer Olympic Games, which opened in the city of Barcelona on July 25, and Expo '92, which took place in Seville from April 20 to October 12.

The Olympics. A number of building projects in and around Barcelona were hurried to completion in time for the Olympics, at a total cost of about $8 billion. The projects included new roads and buildings intended for permanent use. The inflow of money gave a big boost to Spain's northern region of Catalonia, of which Barcelona is the capital. But tensions surfaced over who should get credit for the benefits brought by the games—the national government based in Madrid or the regional government of Catalonia, which favors greater independence from Madrid.

The Seville world's fair commemorated the 500th anniversary of Christopher Columbus' 1492 voyage to the New World, a trip he prepared for in Seville. The total bill for facilities related to the fair—including a new airport and a high-speed rail link between Madrid and Seville—topped $12 billion. Financing the building costs of the Seville Expo and the Barcelona Olympics set back government efforts to cut a large budget deficit.

The economy. Another much-anticipated event—the tighter economic integration of 12 Western European nations within the European Community (EC or Common Market)—proved a mixed blessing for Spain. In December 1991, EC leaders signed the Treaty on European Union, or the Maastricht Treaty, which could lead to the creation of a single European currency by the end of the 1990's. Participating countries, however, must meet strict EC standards on such economic indicators as inflation and unemployment. To help Spain meet the targets, Prime Minister Felipe González Márquez in September 1992 announced sharp spending cuts in the government's 1993 budget.

Spain's inflation rate, expected to reach 6.4 per cent in 1992, remained well above the Maastricht goal, as did Spain's unemployment rate of about 15 per cent. Moreover, the economic slowdown experienced by Germany, France, and other European countries spread to Spain in 1992. The country's *gross national product* (GNP—the total value of all goods and services produced) was expected to increase by only about 1.5 per cent, after a 2.5 per cent rise in 1991 and growth rates of almost 5 per cent in the late 1980's. Spain's budget deficit totaled about 4.4 per cent of its GNP in 1992, while the Maastricht Treaty set a limit of less than 3 per cent.

The foreign-exchange value of the peseta, the Spanish currency, came under intense pressure in early autumn. In September and again in November, the Spanish government lowered the peseta's value, making Spanish exports less expensive but raising the price of imported goods in Spain. Philip Revzin

See also **Europe** (Facts in brief table); **Olympics: The 1992 Olympics.** In ***World Book,*** see **Spain.**

Sports. Because of the rapidly changing political map in Eastern Europe, new nations competed in international sport in 1992 and some old nations did not. Of the republics that made up the former Soviet Union before it collapsed in December 1991, Latvia, Lithuania, and Estonia competed individually, as they did before World War II (1939-1945). The other former Soviet republics combined to compete as the Unified Team representing the Commonwealth of Independent States.

The United Nations imposed economic and diplomatic sanctions against Yugoslavia in May because of its continued warlike actions against the breakaway republic of Bosnia and Hercegovina. These sanctions also applied to Yugoslav sporting teams. The International Olympic Committee barred Yugoslavia from team (but not individual) events in the Summer Olympic Games in Barcelona, Spain, from July 25 to August 9. (See **Olympic Games: The 1992 Olympics.**) Meanwhile, South Africa, having repealed its system of *apartheid* (strict racial separation), returned to international sports competition for the first time since 1960 at the 1992 Summer Olympics.

Drug troubles. Suspicions of illegal drug use resulted in the suspension of several star athletes in 1992. In February, the German Track and Field Federation banned Katrin Krabbe, the women's 1991 world 100- and 200-meter champion, for allegedly tampering with urine samples taken from her in January. The International Amateur Athletic Federation (IAAF), track and field's governing body, later banned Krabbe and the others for four years for the same incident but reversed the decision in June.

The IAAF expelled several athletes from the Summer Olympics because of suspected illegal drug use. They included Jud Logan, the best U.S. male hammer thrower, and U.S. shot-putter Bonnie Dasse.

Magic retires again. Earvin (Magic) Johnson, Jr., the fabulous playmaker for the Los Angeles Lakers, canceled his return to the National Basketball Association in November 1992. Johnson had retired from basketball in November 1991 after learning he was infected with the virus that causes AIDS. He ended his brief retirement by helping the United States win the Olympic gold medal as part of the Dream Team on Aug. 8, 1992. Johnson announced on September 29 that he would return to the Lakers to play between 50 and 60 games during the NBA's 1992-1993 season.

On Nov. 2, 1992, however, Johnson changed his mind and said he would retire for good. He said that other players feared contracting the virus from him and that he did not want to create controversy or lessen his competitors' enjoyment of the game.

Little League controversy. The Zamboanga team from the Philippines won the Little League World Series in August. But Philippine newspapers reported that all of the Philippine players were either overage or lived out of the team's area. Little League

Spain's Miguel Indurain, foreground, heads toward the finish line in Paris in the last stage of the Tour de France, which he won in July.

international officials confirmed that, took the title away, and on September 17 gave it to the beaten finalists from Long Beach, Calif.

Awards. On March 2, Mike Powell, who set a world long-jump record of 29 feet 4½ inches (8.95 meters) in August 1991, was voted the Amateur Athletic Union's James E. Sullivan Memorial Award as America's outstanding amateur athlete for 1991. In January 1992, the United States Olympic Committee named sprinter and long jumper Carl Lewis and gymnast Kim Zmeskal the 1991 Sportsman and Sportswoman of the Year.

Among the winners in 1992 were:

Cycling. In June and July, Miguel Indurain of Spain won the Tour de France and the Tour of Italy, the world's two most important stage races, both by wide margins. In the world championships, Gianni Bugno of Italy won his second consecutive professional road-racing title, and Mike McCarthy of New York City, normally a road racer, won the professional pursuit title on the track.

Diving. Mark Lenzi of Fredericksburg, Va., in addition to winning an Olympic gold medal for his performance off the men's 3-meter springboard at Barcelona, won the United States 1-meter and 3-meter titles indoors and outdoors. Julie Farrell-Ovenhouse of Howell, Mich., like Lenzi coached by Dick Kimball, swept the two springboard titles for women in the indoor nationals.

Gymnastics. Sixteen-year-old Kim Zmeskal of Houston, the world all-around champion in 1991, took gold medals in the 1992 world championships from April 15 to 19 in Paris in floor exercise and balance beam. Vitali Scherbo of the Unified Team won men's gold medals in rings and pommel horse.

Rowing. Denmark won world lightweight championships in men's eights, men's single sculls (Jens Mohr Ernst), and women's single sculls (Mette Bloch Jensen). The University of London captured the Grand Challenge Cup in the Henley Royal Regatta in England, and the Harvard men and the Boston University women won the American collegiate rowing titles.

Triathlon. Mark Allen of Cardiff, Calif., won his fourth consecutive men's title, and Paula Newby-Fraser of Encinitas, Calif., won her fifth women's title in the Ironman championships on October 10 in Kailua-Kona, Hawaii. Simon Lessing of Great Britain won the world men's championship, and Michellie Jones of Australia won the women's.

Wrestling. Tricia Saunders of Phoenix won the world women's championship in the 110-pound (50-kilogram) class and the outstanding-wrestler award in the United States championships. The national superheavyweight champions were Bruce Baumgartner of Cambridge Springs, Pa., for the 10th consecutive time in freestyle and Matt Ghaffari of Chandler, Ariz., for the 2nd time in Greco-Roman.

Other champions

Archery, world freestyle field champions: men, Jay Barrs, Mesa, Ariz.; women, Carole Ferriou, France.

Biathlon, U.S. champions: men's 10-kilometer and 20-kilometer, Josh Thompson, Gunnison, Colo.; women's 7.5-kilometer, Joan Guetschow, Minnetonka, Minn.; women's 15-kilometer, Angie Stevenson, Bend, Ore.

Bobsledding, World Cup champions: two-man, Gunther Huber, Italy; four-man, Wolfgang Hoppe, Germany.

Canoeing, U.S. champions: men's 500-meter canoe, Jim Terrell, Milford, Ohio; men's 500-meter kayak, Norman Bellingham, Washington, D.C.; women's 500-meter kayak, Sheila Conover, Newport Beach, Calif.; men's slalom canoe, Jon Lugbill, Bethesda, Md.

Cross-country, world champions: men, John Ngugi, Kenya; women, Lynn Jennings, Newmarket, N.H.

Equestrian, World Cup champions: jumping, Thomas Fruhmann, Austria; women, Isabell Werth, Germany.

Fencing, world women's epee champion: Marianna Horvath, Hungary.

Field hockey, Intercontinental Cup men's champion: Cuba.

Handball, U.S. four-wall champions: men, Octavio Silveyra, Commerce, Calif.; women, Lisa Fraser, Winnipeg, Canada.

Judo, U.S. heavyweight champions: men, Damon Keeve, San Francisco; women, Carole Scheid, Nevada, Iowa.

Lacrosse, U.S. college champions: men, Princeton; women, Maryland.

Luge, World Cup champions: men, Markus Prock, Austria; women, Suzy Erdmann, Germany.

Modern pentathlon, U.S. champions: men, Mike Gostigan, Newtown Square, Pa.; women, Terry Lewis, San Antonio.

Motorcycle racing, world 500-meter champion: Wayne Rainey, Downey, Calif.

Racquetball, world amateur champions: men, Chris Cole, Flint, Mich.; women, Michelle Gilman, Ontario, Ore.

Racquets, world champion: James Male, England.

Rhythmic gymnastics, world all-around champion: Oksana Skaldina, Ukraine.

Rodeo, world all-around champion: Ty Murray, Stephenville, Tex.

Shooting, U.S. International three-position champions: men's free rifle, Bob Foth, Colorado Springs, Colo.; women's standard rifle, Launi Meili, Cheney, Wash.

Softball, U.S. fast-pitch champions: men, National Health Care, Sioux City, Iowa; women, Raybestos Brakettes, Stratford, Conn.

Squash racquets, world open champion: Jansher Khan, Pakistan.

Surfing, world amateur champions: men, Grant Frost, Australia; women, Lyn MacKenzie, Australia.

Synchronized swimming, U.S. solo champion: Kristen Babb-Sprague, Pleasanton, Calif.

Table tennis, U.S. open champions: men, Johnny Huang, Toronto, Canada; women, Csilla Batorfi, Hungary.

Volleyball, U.S. college champions: men, Pepperdine; women, UCLA.

Water polo, U.S. outdoor champions: men, San Francisco Olympic Club; women, Beach women's water polo, Long Beach, Calif.

Water skiing, U.S. open overall champions: men, Patrice Martin, France; women, Julie Shull-Petrus, Hartsville, Mo.

Weightlifting, U.S. superheavyweight champion: Mario Martinez, South San Francisco, Calif. Frank Litsky

See also articles on the various sports. In ***World Book,*** see articles on the sports.

Sri Lanka. The decadelong civil war between the Sri Lankan government and separatist rebels continued undiminished in 1992. Since 1983, the government has been battling a guerrilla group called the Liberation Tigers of Tamil Eelam, which seeks to carve a separate state out of the northeast section of the country for Sri Lanka's Tamil ethnic minority.

President Ranasinghe Premadasa repeatedly proposed peace talks with the rebels in 1992, and several delegations of Buddhist and Roman Catholic priests made peace missions to Tiger strongholds. But these efforts led to nothing, and many officials endorsed an all-out military campaign against the Tigers. These officials pointed to a similar decision by India on May 20, 1992, to officially outlaw the Tigers, who had been operating out of Tamil areas of southern India.

Tamil refugees return. In January, Sri Lanka reached an agreement with India to *repatriate* (bring back home) tens of thousands of Tamil refugees living in India. Most of the refugees had fled Sri Lanka in 1990 and 1991 to escape renewed violence among rival Tamil factions after India withdrew its peacekeeping forces from Sri Lanka in 1990. The Indian government had desired the repatriation agreement because of its mounting trouble keeping order among the refugees.

Rebel attacks. On April 12, 1992, 20 soldiers were killed in ambushes and 40 civilians were killed in two bomb attacks, one on a bus in eastern Sri Lanka and another at a bazaar near Sri Lanka's capital, Colombo. The government blamed the Tigers for the incidents.

On April 28 and again on October 15, the Tigers, who are Hindus, attacked Muslim-populated villages in eastern Sri Lanka. The October attack took the lives of 146 Muslim civilians and 20 security personnel, making it the deadliest Tiger attack on Muslims since August 1990. Muslim gunmen killed Tamil villagers in retaliation after both attacks.

Military mission. The government on June 27 launched an offensive to seal off the Jaffna peninsula at the northern tip of Sri Lanka, which serves as the base of Tiger operations. But like a similar mission in 1991, this one failed. The army claimed they killed 500 rebels, but the Tigers said they lost only 17 people.

Then on August 8, a land mine planted by the Tigers killed 10 senior military officers near the peninsula. Among the dead was the leader of government operations against the Tigers. At his funeral, an angry crowd attacked government officials for their failure to defeat the Tigers.

Suicide bomber. On November 16, a member of a Tiger suicide squad killed both himself and Sri Lanka's naval chief, Clancy Fernando, in a bomb blast in Colombo. The attack was similar to the assassination in 1991 of Indian Prime Minister Rajiv Gandhi, a killing believed to have been the work of the Tigers.

Henry S. Bradsher

See also **Asia** (Facts in brief table). In ***World Book,*** see **Sri Lanka.**

State government. The major concern for state governments in 1992 was avoiding big budget cuts or tax hikes that would upset voters in an election year. The resulting tight budgets meant that states lacked the funds to launch new programs—with the exceptions of ground-breaking health-care and welfare reforms in a few states.

Taxes and finance. Despite the continuing economic downturn in the United States, individual states in 1992 benefited from the massive sales-tax and income-tax increases passed in 1991. California, Florida, and Maryland in 1992 adopted a variety of higher fees and taxes to cover budget shortages. Florida lawmakers, refusing to adopt Governor Lawton Chiles's proposals to broaden the sales tax and adopt a value-added tax, instead enacted a more limited set of revenue-raising measures. Most states also instituted across- the-board spending cuts.

The largest source of new tax revenues for fiscal year 1993 were health-related taxes totaling some $1.8 billion, according to the National Conference of State Legislatures, an organization based in Denver, Colo. States enacted these levies on hospitals, nursing homes, and other health-care providers. Typically, the taxes were earmarked for Medicaid, the joint federal-state health-care program for people receiving public assistance.

The most dramatic budget standoff of 1992 was between California Governor Pete Wilson and the California legislature. For 63 days after the end of the fiscal year, California was without a budget, and the state had to issue I.O.U.'s to meet payrolls and buy goods. The officials ended their impasse on September 2, agreeing to a $57.4-billion budget in part financed by $700 million in new fees and charges.

Despite the tough economic times, some states followed through on promises to cut taxes. New Jersey Republicans—who had won the statehouse majority by pledging to roll back state income tax increases enacted by Democrats in 1990—kept their promise in March 1992. The state's Democratic administration warned that massive state government layoffs would result. In Massachusetts and Pennsylvania, state leaders allowed income tax surcharges to expire. In Connecticut, legislative opponents failed to repeal that state's income tax, which had been adopted in 1991. Connecticut concluded fiscal year 1992 with a slight surplus, in contrast to its 1991 $1-billion deficit.

States continued to turn to gambling as a new source of revenue. Texas launched a lottery in May 1992. On June 11, Louisiana became the third state, after Nevada and New Jersey, to legalize high-stakes gambling in land-based casinos. The measure, pushed through by Governor Edwin W. Edwards, called for the state to choose a private developer to open a casino in New Orleans in 1993. Mississippi joined the states that allowed riverboat casinos in August 1992.

Health care. A handful of states took major steps toward providing health care for people too poor to

Demonstrators in California protest the impending execution of Robert A. Harris. The April 21 execution was the state's first in 25 years.

buy insurance but not poor enough to qualify for Medicaid. Minnesota began phasing in health subsidies for low-income families as provided by a 1992 law. To pay for the subsidies, the state raised the tax on cigarettes and began taxing health-care providers. In addition, Minnesota created a new agency charged with finding ways to hold down health-care costs.

Florida and Vermont established similar cost-control agencies as part of their own health-care reforms. Vermont's new commission was to devise a plan for providing health care to all the state's residents. Florida set a December 1994 deadline for employers to provide basic health care to employees or to pay into a fund to cover the uninsured.

New York in July 1992 became the fourth state to require health insurers and health maintenance organizations to accept all customers without regard to age or health status. The requirement was to take effect on April 1, 1993.

The Administration of President George Bush in August 1992 denied approval to Oregon to set priorities on the types of medical procedures paid by Medicaid. The Administration's objection was based on fears that the scheme might deny benefits to people with disabilities. Leaders in other states had been considering Oregon's approach as a way to hold down exploding health-care costs.

Frustration with states' ever-increasing tab for the Medicaid program reached the boiling point in Colorado, where the legislature voted to withdraw from

Selected statistics on state governments

State	Resident population*	Governor†	Legislature†				State tax revenue‡	Tax revenue per capita‡	Public school expenditures per pupil§
			House		Senate				
			(D)	(R)	(D)	(R)			
Alabama	4,062,608	Guy Hunt (R)	82	23	28	7	$ 3,943,000,000	$ 960	$3,680
Alaska	551,947	Walter J. Hickel (I)	20	18#	9	10**	1,806,000,000	3,170	8,190
Arizona	3,677,985	J. Fife Symington (R)	25	35	12	18	4,711,000,000	1,260	4,490
Arkansas	2,362,239	Jim Guy Tucker (D)	89	10**	30	5	2,366,000,000	1,000	3,680
California	29,839,250	Pete Wilson (R)	49	31	23	14††	44,874,000,000	1,480	4,870
Colorado	3,307,912	Roy Romer (D)	31	34	16	19	3,214,000,000	950	5,260
Connecticut	3,295,699	Lowell P. Weicker, Jr. (I)	87	64	20	16	4,983,000,000	1,510	8,310
Delaware	688,696	Tom Carper (D)	18	23	15	6	1,165,000,000	1,710	6,080
Florida	13,003,362	Lawton Chiles (D)	71	49	20	20	13,764,000,000	1,040	5,240
Georgia	6.508.419	Zell Miller (D)	128	52	41	15	7,154,000,000	1,080	4,750
Hawaii	1,115,274	John Waihee (D)	47	4	22	3	2,639,000,000	2,330	5,450
Idaho	1,011,986	Cecil D. Andrus (D)	20	50	12	23	1,205,000,000	1,160	3,280
Illinois	11,466,682	Jim Edgar (R)	66	52	27	32	13,292,000,000	1,150	5,250
Indiana	5,564,228	Evan Bayh (D)	55	45	22	28	6,182,000,000	1,100	5,850
Iowa	2,787,424	Terry E. Branstad (R)	49	51	27	23	3,447,000,000	1,230	5,030
Kansas	2,485,600	Joan Finney (D)	59	66	14	26	2,796,000,000	1,020	5,110
Kentucky	3,698,969	Brereton C. Jones (D)	72	28	25	12‡‡	5,043,000,000	1,360	4,620
Louisiana	4,238,216	Edwin W. Edwards (D)	88	16#	33	6	4,309,000,000	1,010	4,300
Maine	1,233,223	John R. McKernan, Jr. (R)	90	61	20	15	1,558,000,000	1,260	5,970
Maryland	4,798,622	William Donald Schaefer (D)	116	25	38	9	6,401,000,000	1,320	6,310
Massachusetts	6,029,051	William F. Weld (R)	124	35**	31	9	9,684,000,000	1,620	6,690
Michigan	9,328,784	John Engler (R)	55	55	18	20	11,103,000,000	1,190	5,670
Minnesota	4,387,029	Arne H. Carlson (R)	87	47	45	22	7,051,000,000	1,590	5,500
Mississippi	2,586,443	Kirk Fordice (R)	93	27#	39	13	2,461,000,000	950	3,340
Missouri	5,137,804	Mel Carnahan (D)	99	64	20	13‡‡	4,996,000,000	970	4,340
Montana	803,655	Marc Racicot (R)	47	53	30	20	818,000,000	1,010	5,270
Nebraska	1,584,617	E. Benjamin Nelson (D)	unicameral (49 nonpartisan)				1,767,000,000	1,100	4,570
Nevada	1,206,152	Bob Miller (D)	29	13	10	11	1,683,000,000	1,310	4,890
New Hampshire	1,113,915	Steve Merrill (R)	136	257§§	11	13	625,000,000	570	5,950
New Jersey	7,748,634	James J. Florio (D)	22	58	13	27	11,645,000,000	1,500	9,940
New Mexico	1,521,779	Bruce King (D)	52	18	27	15	2,086,000,000	1,350	4,520
New York	18,044,505	Mario M. Cuomo (D)	101	49	26	35	28,300,000,000	1,570	8,610
North Carolina	6,657,630	James B. Hunt, Jr. (D)	78	42	39	11	7,850,000,000	1,170	5,080
North Dakota	641,364	Edward T. Schafer (R)	33	65	25	24	755,000,000	1,090	3,760
Ohio	10,887,325	George V. Voinovich (R)	53	46	13	20	11,556,000,000	1,060	5,450
Oklahoma	3,157,604	David Walters (D)	69	32	37	11	3,862,000,000	1,220	3,900
Oregon	2,853,733	Barbara Roberts (D)	28	32	16	24	3,030,000,000	1,040	5,470
Pennsylvania	11,924,710	Robert P. Casey (D)	105	98	25	25	13,021,000,000	1,090	6,980
Rhode Island	1,005,984	Bruce Sundlun (D)	85	15	39	11	1,257,000,000	1,250	6,830
South Carolina	3,505,707	Carroll A. Campbell, Jr. (R)	73	50**	30	16	3,933,000,000	1,100	4,310
South Dakota	699,999	George S. Mickelson (R)	29	41	20	15	528,000,000	750	4,260
Tennessee	4,896,641	Ned Ray McWherter (D)	63	36	19	14	4,311,000,000	870	3,740
Texas	17,059,805	Ann W. Richards (D)	91	58‡‡	18	13	16,017,000,000	920	4,600
Utah	1,727,784	Michael O. Leavitt (R)	26	49	11	18	1,861,000,000	1,050	3,090
Vermont	564,964	Howard Dean (D)	87	57##	14	16	685,000,000	1,210	6,050
Virginia	6,216,568	L. Douglas Wilder (D)	58	41**	22	18	6,852,000,000	1,090	5,490
Washington	4,887,941	Mike Lowry (D)	67	31	28	21	7,990,000,000	1,590	5,320
West Virginia	1,801,625	Gaston Caperton (D)	79	21	32	2	2,328,000,000	1,290	5,400
Wisconsin	4,906,745	Tommy G. Thompson (R)	52	47	16	15***	7,017,000,000	1,420	5,970
Wyoming	455,975	Mike Sullivan (D)	19	41	10	20	637,000,000	1,390	5,360

*1990 Census (source: U.S. Bureau of the Census).
†As of January 1993 (source: state government officials).
‡1991 figures (source: U.S. Bureau of the Census).
§1991-1992 figures for elementary and secondary students in average daily attendance (source: National Education Association).
#Two independents.
**One independent.
††Two independents, one vacancy at time of publication.
‡‡One vacancy at time of publication.
§§One independent; four libertarians; two vacancies at time of publication.
##Four independents; two progressives.
***Two vacancies at time of publication.

the program. Governor Roy Romer vetoed the withdrawal in June, however, saying the state had no alternative plan.

Abortion. Most state legislatures avoided new legislation regarding abortion. Kansas and Wisconsin, among the few that did act, required one parent's consent for a minor's abortion. On June 29, the Supreme Court of the United States upheld Pennsylvania's restrictive abortion law in a 5 to 4 ruling. But the high court reaffirmed a woman's constitutional right to an abortion, saying that such restrictions cannot place an "undue burden" on a woman's ability to obtain an abortion. A federal court of appeals in September struck down Louisiana's 1991 ban on abortion. (See **Supreme Court of the United States.**)

Welfare came under increasing fire from state legislators and governors looking for places to cut spending and enact reforms. Reforms in New Jersey and Wisconsin centered on encouraging welfare recipients to work, marry, and delay childbearing. Both states moved to cut off additional aid for children born to women already receiving welfare. Maryland received federal approval to reduce welfare grants and give additional aid only to families that could show that the children attended school and received health care. California cut welfare grants by almost 6 per cent and held new residents to grant levels they were getting in the state where they previously lived.

Education. Nationwide, 23 states in 1992 were facing court suits over spending gaps between rich and poor schools. For example, Texas lawmakers' efforts at school finance reform were struck down by the state's high court for the third time since 1989. The Texas Supreme Court in January 1992 gave the legislature until June 1993 to devise a constitutional plan to correct funding inequities among districts.

Kansas succeeded where Texas failed by adopting a plan that equalized property tax rates among districts, set a statewide spending level per pupil, and required schools to be evaluated on how well they educate students. Increased state funding for education and related property tax relief came from a hike in state sales and income taxes. Kansas' action caused poor districts to drop court suits over unequal spending, but some wealthy districts sued over the cap on student spending and the uniform property tax levy.

In Maryland, a controversial new state requirement mandated that middle- and high-school students perform up to 75 hours of community service. Maryland was the first state to require that students perform public works in addition to meeting academic requirements for graduation.

Indiana, Texas, and Washington in 1992 adopted education reforms similar to a plan that Oregon had adopted in 1991, which called for high-school students to earn certificates of mastery. The reforms were designed to ensure that students were academically qualified and that non-college-bound students were trained in a technical or vocational skill. Tennessee also replaced the general curriculum in high school with a program that favored stronger vocational education and academic competency.

Crime. Maryland's new child-accident prevention law called for a fine of up to $1,000 on adults who leave a loaded firearm in reach of an unsupervised minor. Seven other states had firearm-storage laws, but those laws applied only in cases of injury or death caused by a minor using a gun.

More states made *stalking* (following and harassing someone with the threat to do harm) a felony following a landmark 1990 California stalking law. Delaware, Florida, Illinois, and Kentucky were among the states in 1992 that made stalking a crime.

Minnesota enacted a package of antiviolence laws. The measures included tougher sentences for violent crimes and sex crimes and increased funds for Head Start programs and for school programs aimed at teaching ways to avoid violence.

Michigan lawmakers in late November and early December passed a bill making it a felony to assist a person in committing suicide. The legislation was prompted by the deaths of gravely ill people who committed suicide in Michigan using devices created by physician Jack Kevorkian. The Michigan law banned assisted suicide while a state commission studied the issue. Elaine S. Knapp

See also **Elections.** In ***World Book,*** see **State government** and the articles on the individual states.

Stocks and bonds. In 1992, financial markets in the United States and around the world struggled with faltering economies and the worst job market in years. In the United States, the markets were also skittish for much of the year from uncertainty over the outcome of the three-way presidential race.

Looking only at numbers, 1992 was a good year for U.S. stocks. Most market averages reached record highs, consumer and mortgage interest rates continued to drop to levels not seen in 30 years, and inflation remained at around 3 per cent. But for most of the year, American financial markets meandered listlessly, and they were easily spooked by news of rising unemployment or earnings disappointments. During 1992, constant layoffs, even by healthy companies cutting their work forces to be more competitive in the global economy, hurt consumer confidence and led even those with jobs to worry about the future. The financial markets reflected those concerns.

However, in October, the markets leaped out of their doldrums, fostered by improving employment reports, rising consumer confidence, and optimism about 1993 earnings. All of the U.S. markets enjoyed a significant rally in the last quarter of the year.

New highs. The Dow Jones Industrial Average (the Dow), a composite of the stock values of 30 large industrial firms, began 1992 at 3,168.83. The index moved past 3,400 for the first time on June 1, setting a record high of 3,413.21. It closed on December 15 at

3,284.36, a gain for the year of 3.6 per cent. Perhaps the biggest Dow story for 1992 was that of International Business Machines Corporation (IBM). IBM's stock plunged to an 11-year low in December after the company presented a bleak earnings forecast.

The Standard & Poor's 500-Stock Index, a broader measure of the market than the Dow, began 1992 at 417.09. On December 8, the index closed at a new record high of 436.99. By December 15, the index had slipped to 432.57, a 3.7 per cent gain for the year.

And in the over-the-counter market, the National Association of Securities Dealers Automatic Quotations (NASDAQ) composite index began the year at 586.34. The index, a measure of the performance of smaller stocks, reached a record high of 667.12 on December 8. The index closed on December 15 at 650.75, a jump of almost 11 per cent for 1992. The NASDAQ was buoyed by the belief of many experts that smaller stocks would perform better than larger stocks under the Administration of President Bill Clinton. The NASDAQ was also helped by an early appearance in late 1992 of the so-called January Effect, a historical trend in which small stocks outpace large stocks near the turn of the year.

International stock markets. In Japan, the Nikkei Index of 225 large Japanese companies continued a decline that began in 1990. At the beginning of 1992, the Nikkei 225 stood at 22,983.77. By December 15, it had lost about 25 per cent of its value to close at 17,480.74. Japanese markets were rocked throughout the year by news of government scandals and the effects of the global recession.

In Canada, the Toronto Stock Exchange's 300-Stock Index began the year at 3,512.36. It closed on December 15 down 7 per cent, at 3,264.61.

The Australia All-Ordinaries Index began 1992 at 1,651.4. It fell in value 8.5 per cent during the year to reach 1,509.6 on December 15.

In Great Britain, the London Financial Times-Stock Exchange Index of 100 stocks (FT-SE 100) opened the year at 2,418.7. Contrary to other major foreign markets, the FT-SE 100 reached 2,717.9 on December 15, a gain of more than 12 per cent. British stocks were helped in late 1992 by the withdrawal of the pound from the European Monetary System in September. The devaluation of the pound boosted the foreign earnings of British firms when the earnings were translated back into the pound.

Hong Kong's stock market also performed well for most of the year. But its Hang Seng Index plunged in December on news of escalating tensions between the Chinese government and Hong Kong's new governor.

The U.S. bond market. The 30-year U.S. Treasury bond yielded 7.6 per cent at the beginning of the year. The yield dropped below 7.5 per cent in late summer as the threat of inflation became increasingly minimal. On December 15, the yield stood at 7.44 per cent. Pat Widder

In *World Book,* see **Bond**; **Investment**; **Stock.**

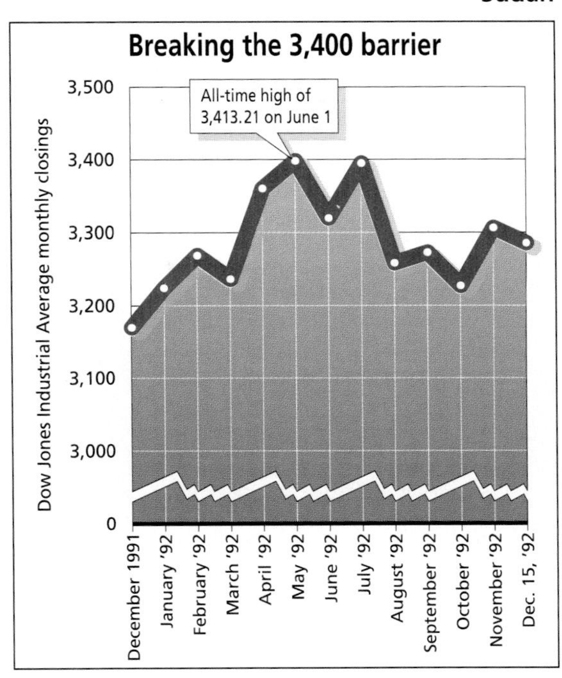

The Dow Jones Industrial Average in 1992 went above 3,400 for the first time, reaching a high of 3,413.21 on June 1 before falling later in the year.

Sudan. Hasan al-Turabi, leader of the National Islamic Front party, in 1992 intensified the government's drive to impose Islam and Islamic law and culture on Sudan. Although former General Umar Hasan Ahmad al-Bashir serves as prime minister, Al-Turabi is regarded as the real power in Sudan. Attempts by Muslim northern Sudanese, who control Sudan's government, to establish Islamic law in southern Sudan, where most people practice Christianity or local religions, has fueled a 10-year civil war. About one-third of Sudan's 27 million people practice religions other than Islam. An estimated 500,000 Sudanese have died and 3 million have become refugees since the war began in 1983.

Government forces, strengthened by new recruits, Iranian advisers, and new weapons—reportedly from China, Iran, and Libya—launched a major military offensive against the rebel Sudan People's Liberation Army in March. By July, the Sudanese Army had captured most of the rebels' strongholds.

Famine. The government's campaign halted efforts by international relief agencies to distribute food in Sudan, which is wracked by drought and famine as well as war. On April 9, Sudan's leaders agreed not to hinder humanitarian relief efforts in the south. But on April 13, the United Nations temporarily suspended aid operations out of concern for the safety of relief workers. UN relief efforts were halted again in September after three UN aid workers and a journalist were killed by Sudanese rebels.

Refugees. Some 500,000 squatters living outside Khartoum, Sudan's capital, were forcibly relocated to desert camps after their makeshift shelters and few possessions were bulldozed by government troops in early 1992. Most of the squatters were southerners who had sought refuge from famine or the civil war. The squatters were reportedly offered aid if they converted to Islam.

The government denied relief agencies access to the new camps, which allegedly lacked water, food, or housing. About 50,000 Nuba, a group of non-Arab people living in northern Sudan, were also forcibly evicted from their homes.

Religious censorship. In January, the Sudan Catholic Bishops' Conference issued a letter protesting the imposition of Islamic law in Sudan. Bishops who signed the letter were interrogated by government officials. In April, the Sudanese government banned radio broadcasts by Catholic religious leaders and banned the printing of Catholic religious publications.

Radical state. In 1992, many Western and Arab governments expressed growing concern that Sudan was becoming a haven for Islamic terrorists. Members of radical Palestinian groups as well as such pro-Iranian groups as Hezbollah and Islamic Jihad reportedly were using Sudan as a base of operations.

Christine Helms

See also **Middle East** (Facts in brief table). In ***World Book,*** see **Sudan.**

Conservative activist Phyllis Schlafly leads a prolife rally outside the Supreme Court building in June after the court affirmed but limited abortion rights.

Supreme Court of the United States. The Supreme Court of the United States ended its 1991-1992 term on June 29 with a key abortion decision, affirming that the U.S. Constitution protects a woman's right to have an abortion but broadening the restrictions states can impose on the procedure.

The abortion case was the hottest dispute before the court all year because activists on both sides of the debate expected the court to overturn the landmark 1973 Supreme Court abortion ruling of *Roe v. Wade.* That case first recognized a constitutional right to abortion and legalized the procedure nationwide. Although the *Roe v. Wade* ruling said states could restrict abortions during the final three months of pregnancy, the court had until 1989 struck down most limits that state legislatures passed.

In the 1992 decision, the court ruled 5 to 4 that abortion restrictions are constitutional if they do not put an "undue burden" on a woman's right to terminate a pregnancy. The court said an abortion law passed by the state of Pennsylvania satisfied that standard. Regulations in the Pennsylvania law included a 24-hour waiting period for women seeking abortions and a requirement that an unmarried woman younger than age 18 obtain the consent of one of her parents or a court order before being allowed to have an abortion. The court, however, struck down a provision requiring a married woman to notify her husband before getting an abortion.

Free speech. States and communities cannot make certain kinds of "hate speech" illegal, the court said on June 22 in a 9 to 0 ruling that struck down a St. Paul, Minn., ordinance. Five of the justices said the ordinance was directed at limited categories of offensive speech and violated First Amendment guarantees of free expression. The remaining justices ruled against the law on other grounds, but they disagreed with the majority opinion, saying it jeopardized other hate-crime laws that did not infringe on free speech. The case involved a St. Paul youth charged with burning a cross on the lawn of a black family.

In a Georgia case decided on June 19, the court ruled that the First Amendment bars cities and states from charging higher parade permit fees for controversial groups that require extra police patrols to maintain order. The 5 to 4 decision struck down a Forsyth County, Georgia, law that was challenged by a white supremacist group demonstrating against the federal holiday honoring the birthday of slain civil rights leader Martin Luther King, Jr.

On June 26, the court ruled 6 to 3 that airport authorities may prohibit groups from soliciting for money at terminals. But in a separate 5 to 4 vote, the court ruled that authorities cannot prevent organizations from distributing literature at airports. The justices said limitations on handing out literature violate the First Amendment. The ruling came in a case brought by the International Society for Krishna Consciousness (commonly called the Hare Krishna movement), whose members solicit money and distribute books in public places. The group challenged regulations adopted by the Port Authority of New York and New Jersey, which operates three airports in the New York City metropolitan area.

Religion. On June 24, the court ruled 5 to 4 that it violates the constitutional separation of church and state to include prayers in public school graduation ceremonies. The court said such prayers, even if they are nondenominational, essentially coerce students into participating in a government-sponsored religious exercise. The First Amendment prohibits the government from sponsoring religious activities or forcing religious participation. The graduation prayers were challenged by a Providence, R.I., high school student and her parents.

Civil rights. In an important victory for women's rights, the court ruled 9 to 0 on February 26 that students at schools and colleges receiving federal funds can collect monetary awards for sexual harassment and other forms of sexual discrimination. The court said a federal law, Title IX of the Education Amendments Act of 1972, not only gives the government the authority to cut off funding to institutions that permit sexual offenses but also allows individual victims of such behavior to seek compensation in federal court. The ruling allowed a high school student in Gwinnett County, Georgia, to sue the school for not acting on her complaint that a teacher had forced her into a sexual relationship.

On March 31, the court made it slightly easier for some public school districts to end federal court supervision over certain aspects of their desegregation efforts. Ruling 8 to 0 in a case from DeKalb County, Georgia, the court said school districts can regain local control bit by bit when a federal judge has concluded that school officials have shown good faith in complying with desegregation plans. The court also said student populations at individual schools can be predominantly black or white, rather than racially balanced, as long as the imbalance is caused by parents' choices about where to live and not by official segregation.

In its first ruling on desegregation in higher education, the court on June 26 said officials in Mississippi had not done enough to desegregate the state's public colleges and universities. Voting 8 to 1, the court said Mississippi must do more than adopt race-neutral admissions policies.

Criminal law. On June 15, the court ruled 6 to 3 that U.S. agents are entitled to have a criminal suspect in a foreign country kidnapped and brought to the United States for trial. The ruling involved a Mexican physician, Humberto Álvarez Machaín, who was seized by bounty hunters in Mexico in 1990 and flown to El Paso, Tex. The doctor was charged with participating in the murder of a U.S. drug agent. (See **Mexico.**)

Hazardous waste. On June 19, the court by a 6 to 3 vote struck down a key provision of a federal law that required states to assume responsibility for disposing of radioactive waste within their borders. The court said the provision violated the Constitution's 10th Amendment, which deals with powers retained by the states, because the provision required states to take specified actions. But the court unanimously found that other portions of the waste law, providing incentives for states to dispose of radioactive waste safely, were constitutional.

At a January rally in Philadelphia, six months prior to the Supreme Court's abortion ruling, prochoice advocates demand a continued right to abortion.

In a pair of rulings on June 1, the court ruled that states may not bar garbage and hazardous waste from being brought in from other states, even if their goal is to protect their residents' health and safety. In an 8 to 1 decision, the justices said an Alabama tax imposed on garbage brought into the state for disposal placed an unconstitutional barrier on interstate commerce. And, splitting 7 to 2, the court overruled a Michigan law prohibiting private landfill operators from accepting solid waste from another county. The court said the Michigan law had the effect of limiting the free flow of interstate trade.

Cigarette liability. Parties on both sides of the issue claimed victory on June 24, when the court issued a decision on whether cigarette companies can be held liable for smoking-related illnesses. The court ruled 7 to 2 that a federal law mandating warning labels on cigarette packages does not protect manufacturers from suits based on state personal injury laws. This decision opened the door for lawsuits based on accusations that tobacco companies have lied or withheld information about the hazards associated with cigarette smoking. But the justices were unanimous in holding that smokers may not sue cigarette makers for failing to post even more urgent warnings on their packages than have been required by federal law.

Property rights. The court on June 29 said states must compensate landowners when state land-use regulations make property economically valueless. The 6 to 3 decision came in a case brought by a South Carolina man who had been prevented, under a state environmental-protection law, from building on two pieces of beachfront property. But the justices left room for states to regulate land use by stipulating that property owners need to be compensated for their land only if it is rendered completely valueless.

State taxation. The court on May 26 dealt a blow to state coffers when it ruled 8 to 1 that states cannot require out-of-state mail order firms to collect and remit state sales taxes on merchandise. But the court said Congress, which has the power to regulate interstate trade, could pass legislation allowing states to force the collection of sales taxes on mail orders.

Linda P. Campbell and Geoffrey A. Campbell

See also **Courts.** In ***World Book,*** see **Supreme Court of the United States.**

Surgery. See **Medicine.**
Suriname. See **Latin America.**
Swaziland. See **Africa.**

Sweden moved ahead in 1992 with plans to reduce generous government benefits and heavy government involvement in the economy. But it encountered some serious problems along the way. A currency crisis in September forced the coalition government of Prime Minister Carl Bildt to make quicker and larger spending cuts than it had planned.

Currency crisis. Sweden had applied for membership in the 12-nation European Community (EC or Common Market) in 1991 and had linked the value of its currency, the krona, to that of currencies in the EC's foreign exchange system. In September 1992, the krona came under pressure from currency traders, who thought it overvalued in relation to Sweden's economic performance. Expecting the government to devalue the krona, speculators borrowed krona from Swedish banks and then sold the currency. They hoped to repurchase devalued krona later at a profit and repay the loans. To halt speculation, Sweden temporarily raised its interest rates to unheard-of levels—first to 75 per cent, then to 500 per cent. In November, however, Sweden cut the krona loose from the EC system, resulting in a devaluation of about 7 per cent.

To ease pressure on the krona and reduce high interest and inflation rates, Bildt and opposition leader Ingvar Carlsson of the Social Democratic Party agreed in September on a plan to slash government spending. The plan would freeze subsidies paid to people with children, raise the official retirement age from 65 to 66 years, reduce state pension payouts, and shift some of the cost of Sweden's generous government health insurance to employers and union members. Bildt also delayed for a year a plan to repeal Sweden's wealth tax, a tax on a person's total assets.

Privatization program. A month after taking office in October 1991, Bildt had unveiled a sweeping program to sell large government-owned companies to private investors. Through these sales, he hoped to raise as much as $50 billion for the Swedish treasury. In March 1992, the government announced the first candidate for privatization, the steelmaking firm Svensk Stal AB. But the currency crisis in September forced the government to put the program on hold.

The program suffered another blow in early 1992, when the automobile manufacturer AB Volvo, one of Sweden's largest private companies, objected to a government plan to sell the state's 40 per cent stake in Procordia AB, a big pharmaceutical company. Volvo, which owned 45 per cent of Procordia, feared that if the state's share of Procordia fell into private hands, Procordia and Volvo itself could become targets for take-over. In a move that stunned Sweden, Volvo tried to have itself taken over by Procordia, which would make it impossible for the government to sell its Procordia stake. Although the government vetoed this plan, it did not sell its stake. Philip Revzin

See also **Europe** (Facts in brief table). In ***World Book,*** see **Sweden.**

Swimming. The United States remained the world's strongest nation in swimming in 1992. American men and women swimmers ranked first in Olympic medals with a total of 27, 11 of them gold medals. Americans also broke six world records and tied one during the year. But other nations also demonstrated their gold-medal and world-record strengths.

Olympics. At the Summer Olympic Games in Barcelona, Spain, from July 26 to 31, Germany followed the United States in total medal winnings for swimming with 11 (1 gold, 3 silver, 7 bronze). The Unified Team, made up of swimmers from the former Soviet Union, won 10 medals (6, 3, 1).

Before the Olympics, the most heralded swimmers were Kieren Perkins of Australia; Jenny Thompson of Dover, N.H.; and Summer Sanders of Roseville, Calif. All won gold medals, but all suffered disappointments as well. Perkins, who set world records earlier in the year in the 400-meter, 800-meter, and 1,500-meter freestyles, was favored in the Olympic 400 and 1,500. After losing the 400 by 1 foot (30 centimeters), he easily won the 1,500 and set another world record of 14 minutes 43.48 seconds.

In the United States Olympic trials, held in Indianapolis from March 1 to 6, Thompson became the first U.S. woman in 61 years to break the world record in the 100-meter freestyle. Her time was 54.48 seconds. Although she had a chance for five Olympic gold medals, her only gold came in relays. Sanders,

Summer Sanders of the United States reacts to winning a gold medal in the 200-meter butterfly at the Summer Olympic Games on July 31.

who also had an opportunity for five gold medals, won two gold and four total medals.

Krisztina Egerszegi, an 18-year-old Hungarian, won three individual gold medals, taking both the 100-meter and 200-meter backstrokes and the 400-meter individual medley. Three men won two individual gold medals each: Tamas Darnyi of Hungary in the 200-meter and 400-meter individual medleys; Alexander Popov of the Unified Team in the 50-meter and 100-meter freestyles; and Evgueni Sadovyi of the Unified Team in the 200-meter and 400-meter freestyles.

U.S. swimmers. Four U.S. men won individual gold medals in Barcelona. Mike Barrowman of Potomac, Md., won the 200-meter breaststroke in 2 minutes 10.16 seconds, breaking his previous world record. Pablo Morales of Santa Clara, Calif., back from a 3½-year retirement, won the 100-meter butterfly in 53.32 seconds. Nelson Diebel of Hightstown, N.J., won the 100-meter breaststroke in 1 minute 1.50 seconds, and Melvin Stewart of Charlotte, N.C., won the 200-meter butterfly in 1 minute 56.26 seconds, both Olympic records. The women's gold medal winners included Janet Evans of Placentia, Calif., in the 800-meter freestyle (8 minutes 25.52 seconds); Nicole Haislett of St. Petersburg, Fla., in the 200-meter freestyle (1 minute 57.90 seconds); and Sanders in the 200-meter butterfly (2 minutes 8.67 seconds). Frank Litsky

See also **Olympic Games: The 1992 Olympics.** In ***World Book,*** see **Swimming.**

Switzerland in 1992 ended decades of strict political neutrality that had kept the country out of nearly all international organizations, including the United Nations (UN). In a referendum on May 17, Swiss voters approved by a margin of 56 per cent to 44 per cent their country's application to become the 164th member of two organizations affiliated with the UN—the International Monetary Fund and the World Bank.

The next day, the Swiss government announced plans to join the 12-nation European Community (EC or Common Market). The decision also requires approval in a public referendum, expected to take place in 1993. On Dec. 6, 1992, however, Swiss citizens voted against participation in a free trade zone that would link the EC with the seven-member European Free Trade Association, to which Switzerland belongs. The vote was interpreted as a rejection of EC membership.

Officials in Zurich ended a closely followed experiment in drug treatment when they closed the Platzspitz, better known as Needle Park, in January 1992. For several years, officials had allowed heroin addicts to use the park freely in an effort to isolate the addicts and provide them with clean needles and medical treatment. The city closed the park, however, after Zurich residents complained about the unruly behavior of some park users. The city planned instead to house homeless addicts in shelters. Philip Revzin

See also **Europe** (Facts in brief table). In **World Book,** see **Switzerland.**

Syria. President Hafez al-Assad's image, which had improved somewhat in 1991 because of Syrian participation in the Middle East peace talks, suffered in 1992 from allegations of arms purchases, human rights abuses, interference in Lebanon, and drug trafficking.

Peace talks. A Syrian proposal concerning the Golan Heights buoyed Arab-Israeli peace negotiations on August 31. Israel captured the Golan Heights from Syria in 1967 and annexed it in 1981. Syria indicated its willingness to sign a peace settlement with Israel before any Israeli withdrawal from the Golan Heights if Israel would provide assurances about a future withdrawal. In addition, Syria said it would be willing to sign an accord with Israel before the Israelis and Palestinians reached an agreement. But talks stalled over issues of territorial security.

Arms purchases. The German Navy on Jan. 29, 1992, halted a German-owned freighter in the Mediterranean Sea after learning that the ship was taking an illegal cargo of 16 Soviet T-72 tanks to Syria. The tanks were believed to be among 300 bought by Syria from Czechoslovakia in 1991.

A North Korean vessel reportedly delivering Scud surface-to-surface missiles to Syria by way of Iran evaded a U.S. naval search and docked in Iran on March 9, 1992. Israel accused Syria in mid-August of test-launching two of the North Korean missiles earlier that month.

Human rights. The United States claimed in January that Syrian jails held 7,500 political prisoners, many of whom allegedly were tortured and denied legal rights. Despite Syrian claims that it had released some 3,400 prisoners, Amnesty International, a human rights group based in London, reported in May that Syria still held several thousand political prisoners.

In March, a special government court sentenced 14 people, apparently members of Syrian human rights groups, to prison terms of 3 to 10 years. Those convicted had reportedly questioned the legitimacy of a 1991 referendum in which 99.98 per cent of Syrian voters had approved Assad's election to a fourth term.

Lebanon. About 40,000 Syrian troops remained in Lebanon in 1992 despite a 1989 pledge to withdraw to the eastern Bekaa Valley in September 1992. Many Western officials continued to express concerns that Syrian troops and officials in Lebanon were engaged in drug smuggling.

Syrian Jewry. Assad lifted travel restrictions on Syrian Jews on April 27. About 20 per cent of Syria's 4,500 Jews had emigrated by August. Assad also ordered in late July that Syrian citizenship cards should no longer identify Jews.

The economy. Syria's economy reportedly improved in 1992 thanks to aid from oil-rich Arab states and economic reforms that boosted foreign investment and sales of government-owned concerns to private business. Christine Helms

See also **Middle East** (Facts in brief table). In ***World Book,*** see **Syria.**

Taiwan in 1992 took new steps in its cautious transition from authoritarian control by an entrenched political party to democratic government. Elections for the Legislative Yuan, Taiwan's lawmaking body, were held on December 19. For the first time, all 161 seats were filled by popular vote. Before 1992, the ruling Kuomintang (KMT) party had kept 80 seats filled with permanent members.

In an outcome that was hailed as "the dawn of a new era," the opposition Democratic Progressive Party (DPP) won almost one-third of the seats, far more than was expected. The KMT retained 96 seats but received a record-low 53 per cent of the vote. Analysts predicted that the surprisingly strong support for the DPP would speed political change in the country.

Domestic changes. In May, President Li Teng-hui approved a more lenient version of Taiwan's law concerning *sedition* (speech or action leading to discontent with the government). Under the new law, public support of Communism was no longer a criminal offense. In June, the Legislative Yuan passed a bill abolishing the "thought police," officials who monitored the loyalty of government workers to the KMT. And on July 31, the Taiwan Garrison Command, which had controlled Taiwan for 38 years until martial law was ended in 1987, was formally abolished.

American warplanes. United States President George Bush on Sept. 2, 1992, announced that his country would sell 150 F-16 jet fighters to Taiwan. The United States had long rejected Taiwan's requests for the planes because of a 1982 promise to China to limit arms sales to Taiwan. But Bush said that the F-16 sale would "help maintain peace and stability" in the region in the wake of China's fighter purchases from other countries in 1992. (See also **China.**)

Foreign relations. Ties with Communist China, long the enemy of the Nationalist Chinese government on Taiwan, improved in 1992. In January, a policy took effect allowing 240 Taiwanese to emigrate yearly from China to rejoin their spouses, from whom some had been separated since the end of the Chinese civil war in 1949. In June, visiting Chinese scientists agreed on academic and technological cooperation.

The African country of Niger in June 1992 broke relations with China and established them with Taiwan. The move reportedly was brought about in part by Taiwan's promise of a $50-million loan to Niger.

South Korea on August 24 established formal ties with China. Taiwan responded by breaking relations with South Korea. The move left Taiwan with diplomatic ties to only 29 countries. Prominent among those was South Africa, which reaffirmed its friendship during a March visit to Taiwan by South African Foreign Minister R. F. Botha. Henry S. Bradsher

See also **Asia** (Facts in brief table). In ***World Book,*** see **Taiwan.**

Tajikistan. See **Commonwealth of Independent States.**

Tanzania. See **Africa.**

Taxation. President George Bush and Congress wrestled with amending United States tax policy during most of 1992. Election-year politics ultimately blocked decisive action, however.

On October 8, the Senate, by a vote of 67 to 23, passed a $27-billion tax and urban aid bill. The measure had barely passed the House of Representatives two days earlier by a vote of 208 to 202. Although the bill contained many features sought by Bush, it also included revenue-raising provisions to keep it from boosting the record federal deficit. Because those sections of the bill could be considered tax hikes, Bush—who had made a 1992 campaign pledge to "never . . . ever" again raise taxes—declined to sign the measure, thereby killing it.

In rejecting the legislation, Bush killed its urban aid provisions, passed in response to the Los Angeles riots. These included the creation of 50 enterprise zones, urban sectors where businesses would be offered special incentives to establish operations. The zones had been an Administration objective.

Bush had also backed a number of tax-relief provisions in the bill. These "economic growth incentives" would have restored income tax deductions for individual retirement accounts for nearly all Americans; repealed a luxury tax on yachts, private airplanes, jewelry, and furs; and restored tax deductions sought by the real estate industry.

Bush's tax package. The President, facing intense pressure to stimulate the economy, outlined a proposed tax package in his January 28 State of the Union address. He asked Congress to enact nearly 50 tax measures by March 20, including the following:

- A $500 increase in the personal income tax exemption for children under 18, to be phased out for families with annual incomes of more than $157,000.
- A tax credit for first-time home buyers of 10 per cent of the price of a house purchased in 1992, up to a maximum credit of $5,000.
- A cut in the capital gains tax from 28 per cent to 15.4 per cent for assets held for at least three years.

On February 7, the Administration unveiled a "streamlined" tax package limited to seven items, mostly affecting business and the well-to-do. Missing from that package was the biggest middle-class tax break—the $500 increase in exemptions for children. Critics charged that the earlier proposals had simply been campaign gestures.

Democrats' plan. Rejecting the Bush initiative, Democrats put forth an alternative package featuring an income tax credit of up to $300 for couples making up to $70,000 annually. The Democrats also proposed hiking the top income tax rate from 31 to 36 per cent and imposing a 10 per cent surcharge on million-dollar incomes. Both houses of Congress passed the bill on March 20. Bush vetoed the bill the same day, and the House sustained the veto on March 25.

Frank Cormier and Margot Cormier

In ***World Book,*** see **Taxation.**

Television, which had long been involved in the political process, had an even more pronounced role during the 1992 presidential election year. Much of that was due to the decision by Vice President Dan Quayle to criticize the popular CBS comedy series "Murphy Brown." The program had ended its season in the spring with its title character, an unmarried television news-magazine reporter played by Candice Bergen, giving birth to a baby. Quayle, as part of the election-year strategy to emphasize family values, said that the "Murphy Brown" plot glamorized single motherhood, devalued the role of the father, and demonstrated Hollywood's lack of respect for traditional values. Controversy ensued as Quayle was accused of attacking the worth of single parents.

Bergen on August 30 won the Emmy Award for best lead actress in a comedy, an honor for which she thanked Quayle. Then, on September 21, the show's season premiere was lengthened to one hour and used footage of Quayle's remarks as if they were part of the program. Murphy Brown responded directly to Quayle on her television show, explaining the struggles of unconventional families and defending their capacity for "commitment, caring, and love."

Televised debates again played a role in the presidential campaign. After extensive discussions about the format, President George Bush, Democratic nominee Governor Bill Clinton of Arkansas, and independent businessman Ross Perot met in an unprece-

The cast of "Beverly Hills, 90210" enjoyed fame in 1992 when their show about high school students became hugely popular with young viewers.

Saxophonist Branford Marsalis took charge of the music, and Jay Leno replaced Johnny Carson on "The Tonight Show" in May.

Top-rated U.S. television series

The following were the most-watched television series for the 31-week regular season—Sept. 16, 1991, through April 12, 1992—as determined by Nielsen Media Research.

1. "60 Minutes" (CBS)
2. "Roseanne" (ABC)
3. "Murphy Brown" (CBS)
4. "Cheers" (NBC)
5. "Home Improvement" (ABC)
6. "Designing Women" (CBS)
7. "Coach" (ABC)
8. "Full House" (ABC)
9. (tie) "Murder, She Wrote" (CBS)
   "Unsolved Mysteries" (NBC)
11. (tie) "Major Dad" (CBS)
   "NFL Monday Night Football" (ABC)
13. "Room for Two" (ABC)
14. "CBS Sunday Night Movie" (CBS)
15. "Evening Shade" (CBS)
16. "Northern Exposure" (CBS)
17. "A Different World" (NBC)
18. "The Cosby Show" (NBC)
19. "Wings" (NBC)
20. (tie) "America's Funniest Home Videos" (ABC)
   "Fresh Prince of Bel-Air" (NBC)
22. "20/20" (ABC)
23. "Empty Nest" (NBC)
24. "NBC Monday Night Movies" (NBC)
25. (tie) "ABC Monday Night Movie" (ABC)
   "America's Funniest People" (ABC)

dented series of three 90-minute debates over eight days in October. In the first debate, a panel of reporters posed questions to the candidates. In the second debate, the candidates took questions from an audience of undecided voters. In the third, there was a single moderator for the first half and a panel for the second.

A single-moderator debate among the three vice-presidential candidates—Quayle, Democrat Al Gore, Jr., and independent James Stockdale—took place between the first and second presidential encounters. The debates were carried on all four national broadcast networks—CBS Inc., the American Broadcasting Companies (ABC), the National Broadcasting Company (NBC), and the Fox network—as well as the Public Broadcasting System, Cable News Network, and C-SPAN. The debates attracted near-record audiences, with almost half of the nation's households tuned in.

Perot bypassed personal appearances to campaign almost exclusively on television, buying both traditional 30-second commercials and a series of 30-minute "infomercials" on network television. His 30-minute television slots attracted surprisingly high ratings. The candidates also seemed to break new ground by appearing on a variety of television talk shows, one of which featured Clinton playing the saxophone.

Cable regulation. For the first time during Bush's term, Congress overrode the President's veto when it voted on October 5 to support a bill designed to regulate cable television. The new law, the Cable Television Consumer Protection and Competition Act, allowed broadcast channels to charge cable companies for carrying their signals. It also called for the Federal Communications Commission to establish guidelines for the cost of basic cable packages offered by local cable operators. However, the law also allowed operators to redefine their basic package, a decision that raised concern about the possibility that cable companies would begin to charge for shows that previously had been included in their basic package.

The growth of cable audiences appeared to halt during the year as the broadcast networks' share of television viewers stabilized at about 60 per cent during the evening prime-time hours. And for the first time since the mid-1980's, broadcast networks saw an increase in their audience during the 1991-1992 season. As more cable shows became available—such as Turner Broadcasting's 24-hour cartoon channel and a science-fiction channel—it appeared that cable stations were competing more with each other than with the networks. The average household received 37 channels in 1992. Nevertheless, in this crowded television environment, the networks found it increasingly difficult to launch successful new programs.

Attracting an audience. CBS went from third place to first in the 1991-1992 prime-time Nielsen ratings race, but the final number of viewers for CBS, NBC, and ABC was quite low and without much disparity. The yardstick for success began to shift during the year from overall ratings to a show's ability to attract the type of viewers advertisers wanted.

Fox, which planned to expand to seven nights of programming in the spring of 1993, led the way with two more shows cast from the same mold as its successful "Beverly Hills, 90210." "The Heights," designed to appeal to the "twentysomething" generation, premiered to high ratings in the summer and took over the Thursday night time slot of "90210." But by midautumn, its audience had declined considerably. "Melrose Place" also premiered and did well in the summer but skidded downward in the autumn. "The Round Table," a youth-oriented offering from CBS, suffered a similar fate.

In its search for younger audiences, NBC jettisoned two shows that ended up on CBS. "In the Heat of the Night" was shown on CBS on Wednesday nights, and "The Golden Palace," a revamped version of "The Golden Girls," appeared on Fridays, joining a new comedy lineup that included "Major Dad," "Designing Women," and the return of comedian Bob Newhart in "Bob."

The end of an era. On May 22, 1992, Johnny Carson made his last appearance as host of "The Tonight Show" to record ratings for the show. Jay Leno took over as host but found the competition intense, as the late-night talk show arena added comedian Whoopi Goldberg and conservative radio personality Rush Limbaugh to its ranks.

Emmy Award winners in 1992

Comedy

Best Series: "Murphy Brown"
Lead Actress: Candice Bergen, "Murphy Brown"
Lead Actor: Craig T. Nelson, "Coach"
Supporting Actress: Laurie Metcalf, "Roseanne"
Supporting Actor: Michael Jeter, "Evening Shade"

Drama

Best Series: "Northern Exposure"
Lead Actress: Dana Delany, "China Beach"
Lead Actor: Christopher Lloyd, "Avonlea"
Supporting Actress: Valerie Mahaffey, "Northern Exposure"
Supporting Actor: Richard Dysart, "L.A. Law"

Other awards

Drama or Comedy Miniseries or Special: *A Woman Named Jackie*
Variety, Music, or Comedy Program: "The Tonight Show Starring Johnny Carson"
Made for Television Movie: *Hallmark Hall of Fame: Miss Rose White*
Lead Actress in a Miniseries or Special: Gena Rowlands, *Face of a Stranger*
Lead Actor in a Miniseries or Special: Beau Bridges, *Without Warning: The James Brady Story*
Supporting Actress in a Miniseries or Special: Amanda Plummer, *Hallmark Hall of Fame: Miss Rose White*
Supporting Actor in a Miniseries or Special: Hume Cronyn, *Neil Simon's "Broadway Bound"*

In the fall, NBC started its first season without "The Cosby Show." Bill Cosby instead starred in a remake of "You Bet Your Life," the comedy game show once hosted by Groucho Marx. Although the nonnetwork program quickly sold to stations across the country, its initial ratings were disappointing.

Thumbs up. ABC's "Home Improvement," the only show that had emerged from the 1991-1992 season as a hit, moved to Wednesday nights where it continued to flourish and easily bested NBC's critically acclaimed "Seinfeld" in the early ratings. A number of other shows survived into their second season, but for many, such as CBS's "Brooklyn Bridge" and NBC's "I'll Fly Away," that decision was based on their quality, not their popularity.

CBS's "Love and War," a show written by Diane English that followed her "Murphy Brown" on Mondays, was considered among the best new shows of the new season. Indeed, CBS's Monday night was widely touted as the best night of television programming, beginning with "Evening Shade" and the new "Hearts Afire" and ending with "Northern Exposure."

Cable programs. With the popularity of videotape rentals taking away the appeal of cable's uncut movies, cable channels began to emphasize their individual series and original programming. Home Box Office (HBO) received critical acclaim for "The Larry Sanders Show," starring Garry Shandling in a half-hour comedy about a late-night talk show. HBO also received high ratings for airing a Michael Jackson concert taped in Romania, and was noted for airing original movies on attorney Roy Cohn and Joseph Stalin.

Other cable channels also increased their original movies and series. Nickelodeon, for example, offered a Saturday night lineup aimed at teen-agers and anchored by its inventive, animated "The Ren & Stimpy Show."

The pay-per-view industry took a hit when NBC's "Triplecast" coverage of the Summer Olympics in Barcelona, Spain, failed to get many people to pay an average of $125 for three channels of commercial-free coverage. It was the first time the Olympics were offered with a pay-per-view option.

Other events, such as a tennis match between Martina Navratilova and Jimmy Connors, had similarly disappointing returns. But boxing and special concerts, such as an all-star tribute to musician Bob Dylan in October, continued to attract audiences.

In news, NBC's "Today" show, which celebrated its 40th anniversary in January, rode the popularity of co-host Katie Couric back to the top of the morning ratings, although ABC's "Good Morning America" still challenged. "Today" also expanded to Saturday mornings, displacing the traditional cartoon lineup. "ABC World News Tonight" with Peter Jennings remained the top-ranked nightly news program. Michael Hill

In ***World Book,*** see **Television.**

Tennessee. See **State government.**

Andre Agassi of the United States returns a shot on the way to winning his first Wimbledon singles title on July 5 in Wimbledon, England.

Tennis. For the second consecutive year, the world's leading tennis player was 18-year-old Monica Seles, born in Yugoslavia and trained in Florida. As in 1991, she won three of the four grand-slam tournaments, and in the fourth, at Wimbledon, she lost in the final to Steffi Graf of Germany.

In the men's four grand slams, Jim Courier of the United States won the first two, Andre Agassi of the United States won the third, and Stefan Edberg of Sweden won the fourth. In the computer rankings, Seles was the top-ranked woman all year, while Edberg and Courier alternated as the leading man.

Women. Seles, a left-hander, won the first two grand-slam titles. She beat Mary Joe Fernandez of Miami, 6-2, 6-3, in the Australian Open final on January 25 in Melbourne and Graf, 6-2, 3-6, 10-8, in a close French Open final on June 6 in Paris. The French title was her third straight.

Seles' streak of grand-slam wins ended on July 4 in Wimbledon, England, when Graf routed her, 6-2, 6-1, in a 58-minute final. Graf's title was her fourth in five years at Wimbledon. In the U.S. Open in Flushing Meadow, N.Y., Arantxa Sánchez Vicario of Spain eliminated Graf in the quarterfinals, and Seles whipped Sánchez Vicario, 6-3, 6-3, in the September 12 final. In her seven U.S. Open matches, Seles lost no sets and only 20 games.

Seles again earned more than $2 million in prize money, but she had bad moments, too. Opponents complained that she grunted on every point, and in trying to control the grunting she lost three consecutive finals in July and August.

On February 16, in the Virginia Slims of Chicago, Martina Navratilova won her 158th professional tennis tournament with a victory over Jana Novotna of Czechoslovakia. The win broke the record she shared with Chris Evert for the most professional tournament titles by a man or a woman. At the Summer Olympics in Barcelona, Spain, Jennifer Capriati, a 16-year-old American, won the Olympic gold medal on August 7 in the women's singles event.

Men. Courier won the Australian Open final on January 26 from Edberg, 6-3, 3-6, 6-4, 6-2. Courier also won the French Open by beating Petr Korda of Czechoslovakia, 7-5, 6-2, 6-1, on June 7. But at Wimbledon, Andrei Olhovsky of Russia, ranked 193rd in the world, eliminated Courier in the third round.

In the Wimbledon final, the 12th-seeded Agassi, wearing uncharacteristically conservative tennis clothing, outfought Goran Ivanisevic of Croatia, 6-7, 6-4, 6-4, 1-6, 6-4. In his seven Wimbledon matches, the left-handed Ivanisevic served 206 aces, including 37 in beating Pete Sampras in the semifinals. In the longest Wimbledon doubles final ever in games (83) and in time (5 hours 1 minute), Michael Stich of Germany and John McEnroe of the United States defeated Jim Grabb and Richey Reneberg, 5-7, 7-6, 3-6, 7-6, 19-17.

In the U.S. Open, Courier eliminated Agassi in the quarterfinals, and Sampras beat Courier in the semifinals. Edberg reached the final by overcoming fifth-set deficits against three seeded opponents. In the final on September 13, Edberg, the defender, defeated Sampras, 3-6, 6-4, 7-6, 6-2. Earlier in the year, Sampras won the U.S. Pro Indoor title and the Association of Tennis Professionals title. At the Summer Olympics, Marc Rosset of Switzerland won the Olympic gold medal in men's singles.

Davis Cup. In the early rounds of the Davis Cup competition for men, the United States eliminated Argentina (5-0), Czechoslovakia (3-2), and Sweden (4-1). The Americans used Courier, Agassi, and Sampras in singles and McEnroe teaming with Rick Leach and then Sampras in doubles. In the final, held from December 4 to 6 in Fort Worth, Tex., the United States defeated Switzerland, (3-1), with Courier winning the deciding match against Jakob Hlasek.

Germany won the Federation Cup for women, defeating Spain 2-1 in the July 19 final in Frankfurt, Germany. Graf and Anke Huber clinched the cup with singles victories.

AIDS revelation. Arthur Ashe, the former tennis champion and the first black man to win the Wimbledon singles title (1975), announced on April 8 that he had AIDS. Ashe said he apparently was infected with HIV, the virus that causes AIDS, in 1983 from a blood transfusion during heart surgery. Frank Litsky

See also **Courier, Jim.** In ***World Book,*** see **Tennis.**

Texas. See **Houston; State government.**

Thailand in 1992 experienced its worst civil unrest since 1973. The National Peacekeeping Council (NPC), set up by the military after its February 1991 coup, held its first parliamentary elections on March 22, 1992. A coalition of five promilitary parties captured a narrow majority of seats.

On March 26, the coalition chose as prime minister Narong Wongwan, whose party had won the most seats. But within hours, the United States government reported that Narong had been refused a U.S. visa in 1991 because of suspected links to drug traffickers. In light of this, Narong on April 7, 1992, withdrew himself from consideration. In his place, the NPC named General Suchinda Kraprayoon, the leader of the coup.

Demonstrations crushed. The selection of the nonelected Suchinda led more than 100,000 protesters on May 7 to gather in the capital of Bangkok to demand his resignation. Chamlong Srimuang, a former mayor of Bangkok, became the rallying point for public anger by engaging in a hunger strike from May 4 to 8. On May 11, the protesters peacefully disbanded after the government agreed to pass constitutional amendments curtailing the military's powers and requiring the prime minister to be popularly elected.

But on May 17, some 200,000 protesters staged another rally in Bangkok to keep the pressure on Suchinda. Security forces used water cannons on the protesters, who responded with rocks and gasoline bombs. Thai troops then attacked the crowds. On May 18, the

A well-wisher presents flowers to Chuan Leekpai, who became the prime minister of Thailand in September following antigovernment protests.

government declared a state of emergency in Bangkok. By May 19, the turmoil had ended.

An official report later said 52 people had been killed. But 217 people were still missing in September. The army was believed to have destroyed the bodies.

King intervenes. King Phumiphon Adunlayadet (also called Bhumibol Adulyadej) had originally approved the nomination of Suchinda. But on May 20, he summoned Chamlong and Suchinda to his palace and urged them to compromise. Under pressure from the king, Suchinda resigned on May 24.

Then on June 10, the king blocked an effort by the NPC to name another military man as prime minister. The king arranged instead for former Prime Minister Anan Panyarachun to take the job until fall elections.

Reining in the generals. During his brief term, Anan sought to curb the power of the military. On August 1, he fired the four top military commanders for their roles in the attacks on demonstrators.

New parliamentary elections were held on September 13. Four prodemocracy parties, dubbed "angels" by opponents of military rule, won a slim majority. Of these, the Democratic Party received the most votes, so the party's head, Chuan Leekpai, was chosen prime minister on September 23. Chuan is the first modern Thai leader without ties to either the military or the aristocracy. Henry S. Bradsher

See also **Asia** (Facts in brief table). In ***World Book,*** see **Thailand.**

Theater. Live theater in the United States—which has never enjoyed the popularity it has in Europe—looked increasingly threatened in 1992 by both economic forces and changing tastes. Of particular concern was the threat faced by professional nonprofit regional theater, which has long been considered the most important laboratory for new American dramatic literature.

Financial pressures. The Theater Communications Group (TCG), the national organization of regional theaters, reported that 92 key American theaters—fully half of its listing of 184 theaters—entered 1992 with deficits. Operating budgets for those 184 theaters ranged from $52,600 to $10.3 million.

In fiscal year 1991, box-office income covered less than half of the theaters' expenses. Contributed income—donations from individuals, corporations, foundations, and government sources—failed to make up the difference. With the closing of eight theaters in 1991, including the pivotal Los Angeles Theatre Center, the five-year total of lost companies reached 25 in 1992.

National attendance at regional theaters in the 1990-1991 season stood at 16.9 million people, down 3.6 per cent from the 1989-1990 season. This drop marked the first decline in attendance since the TCG began its surveys in 1973. In order to attract more ticket buyers, many artistic directors backed away from developing new, untested works.

Funding controversy. A major source of funding for regional theaters, the National Endowment for the Arts (NEA), continued to face criticism from political conservatives. Republican presidential challenger Patrick J. Buchanan led attacks against the NEA's use of taxpayer money to subsidize sexually explicit art. As a result of the controversy, NEA Chairman John E. Frohnmayer on Feb. 21, 1992, reportedly was forced to resign by the Administration of President George Bush.

Shortly afterward, Anne-Imelda Radice, who was appointed acting chairwoman, pledged to curtail funds for controversial exhibits. On May 12, she vetoed two $10,000 grants earmarked for sexually explicit art shows at two college galleries. Playwright Jon Robin Baitz on June 1 protested the move by awarding the two galleries grants of $7,500 each from a $15,000 grant he received from the NEA. (See also **Art: Who Should Pay for Art?**)

Competition from other media. As usual, the box-office take of theatrical performances in 1992 paled in comparison to that of motion pictures. For example, on a single weekend in June, the Whoopi Goldberg film *Sister Act* sold more than $9 million in tickets across the country. That amount could have run the Arena Stage in Washington, D.C., for a year; the Arizona Theatre Company in Tucson for three years; or Théâtre de la Jeune Lune in Minneapolis, Minn., for a decade.

To combat Hollywood's entertainment machine, regional theaters typically resorted to lighter fare. The most-produced regional-theater show of the 1991-1992 season was the annual money-maker *A Christmas Carol*, with 19 stagings nationwide of the Charles Dickens story. That play was followed by Terrence McNally's AIDS-era comedy *Lips Together, Teeth Apart* and Ken Ludwig's farce *Lend Me a Tenor* (8 stagings each) and Willy Russell's one-woman comedy *Shirley Valentine* (6 stagings).

Regional companies produced several significant dramatic events in 1992. These included the staging at the Intiman Theatre in Seattle of the nine-play *The Kentucky Cycle,* for which Robert Schenkkan won the 1992 Pulitzer Prize for drama; the La Jolla (Calif.) Playhouse's presentation of an opulent new interpretation of The Who's rock opera *Tommy*; and the premiere at the Mark Taper Forum in Los Angeles of the second part of Tony Kushner's *Angels in America*.

Personnel changes. Carey Perloff took over the artistic direction of San Francisco's huge American Conservatory Theatre. David Esbjornson replaced Perloff at the helm of New York City's comparatively tiny but influential Classic Stage Company. Richard Hamburger, formerly head of Maine's Portland Stage, was named artistic director of the Dallas Theater Center, which had lost his predecessor, Ken Bryant, in a fatal 1990 accident. And William T. Gardner, the producing director of the Pittsburgh (Pa.) Public Theatre, in April 1992 died of a heart attack at age 57.

Gregory Hines, front right, performs as jazz composer Jelly Roll Morton in the musical biography *Jelly's Last Jam,* a Broadway hit in 1992.

Broadway. The financial woes weakening the nation's regional theaters in 1992 bypassed Broadway, which brought in $292 million in ticket sales for the 1991-1992 season, which ended May 31. This amount represented a leap of 9 per cent from the 1990-1991 season and Broadway's biggest take ever. Much of the record was due to higher ticket prices, as attendance increased only slightly over 1991. Several shows raised their top ticket price to $65, including *The Phantom of the Opera, Miss Saigon,* and *The Will Rogers Follies.*

Musicals dominated the 1991-1992 season, but even "new" shows were unusually dependent on existing material. Leading the pack was an especially energetic revival of Frank Loesser's *Guys and Dolls* (1950) that seemed to spark Broadway. Other musicals that opened included *Jelly's Last Jam*, George C. Wolfe's dark biography of jazz composer Jelly Roll Morton; *Crazy for You,* Ken Ludwig's retooling of George and Ira Gershwin songs; a revival of Loesser's *The Most Happy Fella* (1956); the London import *Five Guys Named Moe,* a revue of the music of singer-saxophonist Louis Jordan (1908-1975); and *Falsettos,* a composite of two one-act off-Broadway musicals from 1981 and 1990. All told, 37 shows were produced in the 1991-1992 Broadway season, more than in any of the previous five years.

Another interesting aspect of Broadway's 1991-1992 season was the wealth of screen stars making appearances on the stage. The names included Glenn Close, Gene Hackman, and Richard Dreyfuss in Ariel Dorfman's *Death and the Maiden;* Alan Alda in Neil Simon's *Jake's Women;* Larry Fishburne in August Wilson's *Two Trains Running;* Alec Baldwin and Jessica Lange in Tennessee Williams' *A Streetcar Named Desire* (1947); Rob Lowe, Tony Randall, and Lynn Redgrave in Georges Feydeau's *A Little Hotel on the Side* (1957); and Tyne Daly, Ethan Hawke, and Jon Voight in Anton Chekhov's *The Sea Gull* (1896).

Touring theater. The most profitable sector of the theater industry in 1992 involved touring shows. Touring plays earned a record-breaking take of $503-million, up from $450 million in 1991. Once considered a poor relation of the New York City commercial theater, "the road" has become such an obvious path to big payoffs that Broadway producers such as Roger Horchow (*Crazy for You*) opened their 1992 shows in New York City with plans already on the drawing boards for the productions' touring counterparts.

With rare exceptions, such as playwright John Guare's *Six Degrees of Separation*, most of the 34 touring productions that crisscrossed the country in 1992 were lightweight comedies and musicals rather than dramas. Many shows were revivals of past hits such as *Brigadoon*, *The Wiz,* and *Sophisticated Ladies.* In addition to the continued touring success of London-based producer Cameron Mackintosh's *The Phantom of the Opera* and *Les Misérables*, the touring season featured new road-show productions of *The Will*

Tony Award winners in 1992

Best Play, *Dancing at Lughnasa,* Brian Friel.
Best Musical, *Crazy for You.*
Best Revival, *Guys and Dolls.*
Leading Actor in a Play, Judd Hirsch, *Conversations with My Father.*
Leading Actress in a Play, Glenn Close, *Death and the Maiden.*
Leading Actor in a Musical, Gregory Hines, *Jelly's Last Jam.*
Leading Actress in a Musical, Faith Prince, *Guys and Dolls.*
Featured Actor in a Play, Larry Fishburne, *Two Trains Running.*
Featured Actress in a Play, Brid Brennan, *Dancing at Lughnasa.*
Featured Actor in a Musical, Scott Waara, *The Most Happy Fella.*
Featured Actress in a Musical, Tonya Pinkins, *Jelly's Last Jam.*
Direction of a Play, Patrick Mason, *Dancing at Lughnasa.*
Direction of a Musical, Jerry Zaks, *Guys and Dolls.*
Book of a Musical, William Finn and James Lapine, *Falsettos.*
Original Musical Score, William Finn, *Falsettos.*
Scenic Design, Tony Walton, *Guys and Dolls.*
Costume Design, William Ivey Long, *Crazy for You.*
Lighting, Jules Fisher, *Jelly's Last Jam.*
Choreography, Susan Stroman, *Crazy for You.*
Regional Theater, The Goodman Theatre in Chicago.

Rogers Follies with original Broadway star Keith Carradine, the 1991 Broadway hit *The Secret Garden,* and *The World Goes 'Round*, a revue of musicals including *Cabaret* and *Chicago*.

Off-Broadway. Some of off-Broadway's most dedicated groups—particularly the Joseph Papp Public Theatre and Ellen Stewart's La Mama ETC—experienced financial difficulty in 1992. Yet both Stewart and JoAnne Akalaitis, who succeeded Papp in 1991 at the helm of the Public, strove to help other companies weather the bad economic times by turning their theaters into shelters for smaller companies that had lost their own performance spaces.

Scott McPherson's *Marvin's Room* was named the best off-Broadway play of 1992 by New York's Drama Desk, shortly before the playwright died in November of AIDS-related illnesses. And the autumn off-Broadway season was full of promise, with a slate including 1989 Pulitzer Prize winner Wendy Wasserstein's comedy *The Sisters Rosensweig,* Larry Kramer's rambling semiautobiographical *The Destiny of Me,* and David Mamet's controversial antifeminist *Oleanna*. Also noteworthy was the Brooklyn Academy of Music's presentation in October of Ariane Mnouchkine's majestic *Les Atrides,* a four-play cycle of ancient Greek tragedies that featured the New York City debut of Paris' acclaimed Théâtre du Soleil. Porter Anderson

In *World Book,* see **Theater.**

Togo. See **Africa.**

Toronto. The Toronto Blue Jays on Oct. 14, 1992, became the first Canadian baseball team to enter the World Series. On October 24, the team won the World Series against the Atlanta Braves in Atlanta, Ga., with a 4 to 3 victory in the 11th inning of the sixth game. Within minutes of the win, residents of Metropolitan Toronto poured into the city's downtown to celebrate. Police closed the main streets to traffic, and people paraded up and down throughout the night. Police estimated that almost half a million people took part in the festivities but there was no violence and few arrests. The extraordinary outpouring of emotion was partly an expression of hope that times will get better for Toronto, which once called itself "the city that works," but which went through one of its most difficult economic years in 1992.

Unemployment. In the spring, an 11 per cent unemployment rate swelled the number of welfare recipients in Metro Toronto to 97,000, an increase of almost 80 per cent from 1991. (Metro Toronto consists of the local municipalities of Etobicoke, Scarborough, Toronto, York, and North York, and the borough of East York.)

To cope with the costs of the welfare expansion, the Metropolitan Council ordered cutbacks in public transportation, closed six publicly funded day-care centers, and froze the police budget. Even with these constraints, the Council had to either increase across-the-board property taxes by 14.75 per cent or reduce the welfare benefits. In April 1992, it approved the tax increase. The welfare system was further strained as the year went on and the unemployment rate rose to 12.5 per cent—the highest in Canada—in October.

Toronto's first race riot occurred on May 4, after riots had erupted in Los Angeles and a white Toronto police officer on May 2 had shot and killed Raymond Lawrence, a black man. Lawrence, whom police suspected was a drug dealer, allegedly had threatened the officer with a knife.

The Black Action Defense Committee held a rally to protest the killings, but it grew into a rampage of black and white youths. Rioters smashed windows and looted stores on Yonge Street, Toronto's main thoroughfare. The police brought the mob under control within a couple of hours, but the event shocked Toronto residents who had believed their city was immune to such acts of violence.

New digs for Metro officials. In September, the Metropolitan Council and Metro government workers who had operated out of the Toronto City Hall moved into a new $211-million building of their own on Ring Street, just west of the city's financial center. The new Metro Hall had no sooner opened when it became the scene of angry demonstrations by people protesting property tax increases.

Property taxes. The Metropolitan Council in September proposed taxing all property in Metro Toronto on the basis of its 1988 market value. For 56.6 per cent of Metro Toronto property owners, the new

Striking workers at the *Toronto Star* protest the newspaper's decision to lay off 1,600 drivers and use independent contractors instead.

market-value assessment would actually result in a tax decrease. However, a few older commercial streets had not been assessed since 1953, and for some store owners in these areas, the new assessment would increase taxes by 300 to 400 per cent. In October 1992, business owners demonstrated their anger against the new property-tax scheme by blockading Yonge Street and Danforth Avenue.

On October 30, after two days of debate, the Metro Council voted on a gradual phase-in of the new property taxes. For homeowners whose taxes would increase, the plan called for a 10 per cent increase spread out over two years. Commercial properties were to incur a 25 per cent increase, spread out over three years. Those entitled to tax decreases would have their payments reduced by only 50 per cent. In December, however, after nine weeks of public hearings, the provincial government refused to approve the tax scheme. Instead, the province sent it back to the city for reconsideration.

Subway extension. In May, the provincial government approved extending the Spadina subway one mile north. The expansion is the first for Toronto's subway system since completion of the Scarborough line in 1985. Further extensions of the Spadina line—either going west toward York University or east along Sheppard Avenue—were still under consideration at the end of the year. David Lewis Stein

In ***World Book,*** see **Toronto.**

Toys and games. Retail toy sales in the United States in 1992 grew nearly 5 per cent over 1991 sales, the first healthy gain since 1987. Industry observers attributed the growth to signs of a recovery in the U.S. economy, which resulted in increased spending.

Baby boomerabilia. Several items that were first popular when today's baby boomers (born between 1946 and 1964) were youngsters hit the comeback trail in 1992. The Magic Maker Creepy Crawler Workshop, last produced in the mid-1960's, was reintroduced in 1992 by Toymax, Incorporated of Westbury, N.Y. With the workshop, children can produce rubbery creatures by filling insect-shaped molds with one of a variety of colorful, nontoxic liquids, called Plasti Goop, and then baking the molds in a special oven.

Trolls, popular dolls first introduced in the United States in 1960, also enjoyed a rebirth in 1992. The original trolls were based on a woodcarving made in 1958 by Danish artist Thomas Dam, who patterned his creation after the characters popular in Scandinavian folklore. Small and gnomelike, the toy trolls have hard plastic bodies, wrinkled faces, and bright round eyes. The figures were available with long, wispy hair in a variety of colors. Several manufacturers jumped on the troll bandwagon, including Ace Novelty Company of Bellevue, Wash.; Applause Incorporated of Woodland Hills, Calif.; Russ Berrie & Company of Oakland, N.J.; and Uneeda Doll Company of Brooklyn, N.Y.

G.I. Joe was called up for active duty in 1992 in a

After a Super Soaker water gun fight led to real gunfire in Boston in May, the city's mayor asked stores not to sell the high-powered toy.

numbered, collectors' edition of the original doll from Hasbro Inc. of Pawtucket, R.I., the largest toy manufacturer in the United States. The 12-inch (30-centimeter) toy soldier was first introduced in 1964. The collector dolls wore official dog tags and authentically styled battle-dress uniforms of the U.S. service branch that they represented. Each doll came with a combat manual. G.I. Joe was also available in the 4-inch (10-centimeter) size first introduced in 1982.

Dinomania. Children's interest in the prehistoric era continued to inspire the toy industry in 1992. The children's series "Barney & Friends" on public television stations helped to spur an increase in the sales of dinosaur-related products. Barney, the show's purple-and-green reptile host, had his own boutique in J. C. Penney stores. The boutiques offered Barney videotapes and Barney stuffed toys, introduced in 1992 by Dakin Incorporated of San Francisco, Calif.

Hasbro in 1992 introduced Talking Baby Sinclair, which was a toy inspired by a character on the ABC-TV network series "Dinosaurs." The stuffed dinosaur had a pull-string voice mechanism that produced favorite expressions used on the show, such as "Feed my mouth!" and "Not the Mama!"

And for children age 2 and up there was Dino-Roars from Fisher-Price, Incorporated of East Aurora, N.Y. These soft, cuddly dinosaurs, with names such as Stego the Stegosaurus and Terry the Pterodactyl, "roared" when squeezed.

Realism in toyland. Tyco Toys, Incorporated of Mt. Laurel, N.J., brought out the Incredible Crash Dummies, characters based on the mannequins used by the U.S. Department of Transportation to simulate human beings in automobile crash tests. The controversial Incredible Crash Dummies toy figures survive an "accident" when wearing safety belts. However, when their seat belts are not buckled, their heads, arms, and legs fly off on impact.

Baby Rollerblade from Mattel Toys of El Segundo, Calif., was a battery-operated, fully jointed doll that wears Rollerblade in-line skates. She also wears protective elbow and knee pads and wrist guards. Her head bobs, arms sway, and legs move as she skates.

The Judith Corporation of Lake Forest, Ill., premiered the Mommy-to-Be Doll, an 11½-inch (29-centimeter) "pregnant" doll. Inside the doll's abdomen is an anatomically correct male or female newborn. Remove the newborn doll and the Mommy doll's abdomen becomes flat. Tyco Toys introduced the Magic Potty Baby in 1992. When this doll is placed on her potty-chair, the see-through canister "fills up." The potty-chair can be flushed by a working handle, which produces a realistic flushing sound as the potty "empties." The potty chair's contents are self-contained, and the toy is battery-operated. The doll also comes with a potty training manual and reward stickers.

The next level of video. Advances in CD-ROM (compact disc read-only memory) technology enabled the video game industry to expand in 1992. Sega of America, Incorporated, of Redwood City, Calif., introduced Mega CD, a multimedia system for use with its Genesis home video game system. Mega CD enhances game play through full-motion graphics, rather than the limited motion of cartridge video games. Mega CD also features computer graphics, footage with live actors, and the audio quality of a CD. Mega CD can also function as an audio CD player. In October, Nintendo of America, Incorporated of Redmond, Wash., and the Sony Corporation of America of Park Ridge, N.J., announced that they will introduce CD-ROM technology into the Super Nintendo home video game system in 1993.

Talking Barbie. "Math class is tough," said some Teen Talk Barbie dolls, a new line of the successful dolls from Mattel. The sentence was one out of a pool of 270 expressions, from which four were randomly selected in the manufacture of each doll. Mattel's source for Teen Talk Barbie was interviews with teenagers nationwide. But the math phrase troubled many teachers and the American Association of University Women. The group thought that the phrase might undermine the confidence of young girls to learn math and so asked Mattel to remove the phrase from Teen Talk Barbie's vocabulary. The controversy caught media attention nationwide, and subsequently, the company removed the controversial phrase from the pool of expressions. Diane P. Cardinale

In ***World Book,*** see **Doll; Game; Toy.**

Track and field. Among track and field athletes, none seemed surer to win gold medals in the Summer Olympic Games in Barcelona, Spain, from July 25 to Aug. 9, 1992, than decathlete Dan O'Brien of Moscow, Ida., and pole vaulter Sergei Bubka of the Unified Team. Both were reigning world champions, but neither won a medal.

O'Brien's downfall was the pole vault in the 10-event decathlon. In the United States Summer Olympic trials from June 19 to 28 in New Orleans, O'Brien could have started pole vaulting at 14 feet 5¼ inches (4.40 meters). Instead, he chose 15 feet 9 inches (4.80 meters), a height he cleared comfortably in practice every day. He missed his three attempts, received no points for the pole vault, and finished 11th. Failure to make the U.S. Olympic team did not stop O'Brien, however. On Sept. 5, 1992, in Talence, France, he set a world record of 8,891 points in the decathlon.

Dave Johnson of Pomona, Calif., won the U.S. trials in the decathlon with 8,649 points. Johnson became the Olympic favorite, but he finished third. Robert Zmelik of Czechoslovakia won with 8,611 points.

A strained Achilles' tendon contributed to Bubka's demise in the Summer Olympics. He missed twice at 18 feet 8½ inches (5.70 meters) and once at 18 feet 10¼ inches (5.75 meters) in Barcelona. Bubka's teammate, Maksim Tarasov, won the pole vault at 19 feet ¼ inch (5.80 meters).

Before and after the Olympics, Bubka broke his world records—once indoors and three times outdoors. On Sept. 19, 1992, he raised the outdoor record to 20 feet 1¼ inches (6.13 meters). That gave him 16 world records outdoors and 16 indoors.

Olympics. In the 24 events for men and 19 for women, the United States won 12 gold medals, 8 silver, and 10 bronze. The 12 gold and 30 total medals were the most by any nation, and the U.S. women, with 10 medals, made their best performance in any nonboycotted Olympics.

The U.S. men who won gold medals were Mike Marsh (200 meters); Quincy Watts (400 meters); Kevin Young (400-meter hurdles in 46.78 seconds, a world record); Carl Lewis (long jump); Mike Conley (triple jump); and Michael Stulce (shot-put). The 400-meter relay team anchored by Lewis, and the 1,600-meter relay team that included Watts also won gold medals. The 400-meter relay team's time of 37.40 seconds was a world record, as was the 1,600-meter relay team's time of 2:55.74. The U.S. women's winners were Gail Devers (100 meters); Gwen Torrence (200 meters); Jackie Joyner-Kersee (heptathlon); and the 400-meter relay team anchored by Torrence.

Devers would have also won the women's 100-meter hurdles had she not crashed into the last hurdle and fallen just short of the finish line on August 6. Eighteen months earlier, doctors almost amputated her feet because of radiation burns from treatment for a thyroid ailment.

World outdoor track and field records* established in 1992

Event	Holder	Country	Where set	Date	Record
4 x 100 meters	Mike Marsh Leroy Burrell Dennis Mitchell Carl Lewis	U.S.A.	Barcelona, Spain	Aug. 8	0:37.40
4 x 400 meters	Andrew Valmon Quincy Watts Michael Johnson Steve Lewis	U.S.A.	Barcelona, Spain	Aug. 8	2:55.74
4 x 200 meters	Mike Marsh Leroy Burrell Floyd Heard Carl Lewis	U.S.A.	Philadelphia	April 25	1:19.11
400-meter hurdles	Kevin Young	U.S.A.	Barcelona, Spain	Aug. 5	0:46.78
Pole vault	Sergei Bubka	Ukraine	Tokyo	Sept. 19	20 ft. 1¼ inch (6.13 m)
1,500 meters	Noureddine Morceli	Algeria	Rieti, Italy	Sept. 6	3:28.82
3,000 meters	Moses Kiptanui	Kenya	Cologne, Germany	Aug. 16	7:28.96
3,000-meter steeplechase	Moses Kiptanui	Kenya	Zurich, Switzerland	Aug. 19	8:02.08
20 km walk	Stefan Johanssen	Sweden	Fana, Norway	May 15	1:18:35.2
30 km walk	Maurizio Damilano	Italy	Cuneo, Italy	Oct. 3	2:01:44
Javelin throw	Steve Backley	Great Britain	Auckland, New Zealand	Jan. 25	300 ft. 1 inch (91.46 meters)
Decathlon	Dan O'Brien	U.S.A.	Talence, France	Sept. 5	8,891 points

*There were no women's world records set in 1992, according to the Athletics Congress in Indianapolis.

Moses Kiptanui of Kenya leaps a hurdle in breaking the world record in the 3,000-meter steeplechase on August 19 in Zurich, Switzerland.

Lewis' two gold medals gave him a total of eight gold medals and a silver won in three Olympics. The long jump was his only individual event in Barcelona because he finished sixth in the 100 meters in the U.S. trials, an unexpected turn for the two-time, 100-meter Olympic champion and world record holder in the event.

Other athletes. Michael Johnson, the American who held the world championship at 200 meters, suffered food poisoning before the Olympic Games and was eliminated in the semifinals. Moses Kiptanui, even though he failed to qualify for the Kenyan Olympic team, set world records on August 16 and 19, respectively, in the 3,000-meter run (7:28.96) and the 3,000-meter steeplechase (8:02.08).

Noureddine Morceli of Algeria, the world champion at 1,500 meters, finished seventh in the Olympics, but he lowered the world record to 3:28.82 on September 6. Mark McKoy of Canada, in the men's 110-meter hurdles, was Canada's only track and field gold medalist.

The United States Olympic Trials were so competitive that five 1991 world champions failed to make the team in their title events. They were O'Brien (decathlon), Lewis (100 meters), Antonio Pettigrew (400 meters), Greg Foster (110-meter hurdles), and Kenny Harrison (triple jump). Frank Litsky

See also **Olympic Games: The 1992 Olympics.** In ***World Book,*** see **Track and field.**

Transit. The Intermodal Surface Transportation Efficiency Act, passed by the Congress of the United States in 1991, allocated $5.8 billion in federal funds for transit in 1992. However, the recession and a desire to bring the federal deficit under control led Congress to appropriate only $3.8 billion. This money went for training, equipment, and operations. Meanwhile, total U.S. ridership in 1992 remained at about the 1991 level of 9 billion trips.

Purchases of new buses by transit agencies were slack. The Federal Transit Administration, the federal agency responsible for overseeing the nation's mass transit systems, eased rules on bus purchases to stimulate sales. But bus manufacturers reported operating at only 25 per cent of capacity during 1992.

Transit agencies and bus and engine manufacturers continued to work on cleaner engines to comply with the Clean Air Act of 1990. In response to concerns about air quality, the Southern California Rapid Transit District made plans to convert 10 of the most heavily used bus lines in Los Angeles County to electric trolley buses by 1997.

Rapid transit. In Baltimore, work continued on the 1.5-mile (2.4-kilometer) subway extension to Johns Hopkins Hospital, which was scheduled to open in 1994. In San Francisco, the Bay Area Rapid Transit system celebrated its 20th anniversary and continued work on the 8-mile (13-kilometer) extension from Concord, Calif., to Pittsburg, Calif.

Chicago in 1992 celebrated the 100th anniversary of its elevated rapid transit service. Construction proceeded on the city's rapid transit line from the downtown Loop to Midway Airport, with a planned 1993 opening. Philadelphia continued its structural renewal on the Frankford Elevated. In Miami, Fla., expansion proceeded on the automated Metromover system, with an expected opening in 1994.

Streetcar boom. The San Francisco Municipal Railway in 1992 began reconstruction of streetcar tracks on Market Street and ordered 36 new streetcars. Construction continued in San Diego on the 3-mile (5-kilometer) extension of the San Diego Trolley's East Line to Santee, Calif. In Portland, Ore., work proceeded on the Westside Light Rail Line, which was to include a station located a record 270 feet (80 meters) underground. Memphis in 1992 was busy constructing a 4-mile (6-kilometer) trolley loop in the Mid-America Mall downtown, to be served by rehabilitated vintage trolleys.

Baltimore completed the first phase of the Central Light Rail Line between Lutherville-Timonium, Md., on the north and Camden Yards in the center of the city. The first service was offered in conjunction with the opening of the Baltimore Orioles' new major league baseball stadium at Camden Yards on April 6.

Commuter rail service expanded in many areas in 1992. The Virginia Railway Express (VRE) in June began rush-hour service on a 30-mile (48-kilometer) line between Manassas, Va., and Union Station in Washington, D.C. In July, the VRE opened a 62-mile (100-kilometer) line between Fredericksburg, Va., and Union Station.

On October 26, Los Angeles' first commuter rail network, called Metrolink, went into operation. A total of 112 miles (180 kilometers) of Metrolink track were opened for 12 diesel-powered trains. The cost of this phase of the project was more than $1 billion. Eventually, a total of 450 miles (720 kilometers) of track will serve commuters in the five counties that make up the Southern California Regional Rail Authority—Los Angeles, Orange, Riverside, San Bernardino, and Ventura.

In the San Francisco Bay area, a new multiple-county Public Benefit Agency in April took over the operation of the commuter service between San Francisco and San Jose and immediately extended the service 30 miles south to Gilroy, Calif. Metra, Chicago's commuter rail service, ordered 173 new bilevel cars and began to rehabilitate older cars and upgrade stations and parking. The Northern Indiana Commuter Transportation District extended its service between Chicago and South Bend, Ind., into the Michiana Regional Airport in South Bend, making it one of the few U.S. rail operations to serve an airport directly.

George M. Smerk

See also **Automobile; Railroad.** In ***World Book,*** see **Bus; Electric railroad; Subway; Transportation.**

Trinidad and Tobago. See **Latin America.**

Tunisia. President Zine El-Abidine Ben Ali on Jan. 4, 1992, openly called for the suppression of Islamic fundamentalists seeking to make Tunisia an Islamic state. His remarks, addressed to a group of Arab interior ministers from 16 nations, outlined his view that Islamic fundamentalism was a growing threat to political stability in the Middle East. The Tunisian government's fears of Islamic activists reportedly intensified when the militant Islamic Salvation Front in neighboring Algeria appeared poised in January to win a majority of seats in that country's parliament

Human rights. In March, Amnesty International, a human rights group based in London, charged that the Tunisian government had illegally jailed thousands of Islamic activists and that it routinely tortured political prisoners. About 300 Islamic activists went on trial in August on charges of planning to overthrow the government in 1990 and kill Ben Ali.

The Tunisian League for the Defense of Human Rights disbanded on June 15, 1992. Although only 15 years old, it was one of the Arab world's oldest human rights groups. The league's leaders opposed a new law forcing private organizations to accept all applicants as members. Critics of the law charged that it permits the government to flood the ranks of such opposition groups and thus control their activities.

Christine Helms

See also **Africa** (Facts in brief table); **Algeria.** In ***World Book,*** see **Tunisia.**

Turkey. Turkey's domestic and foreign affairs in 1992 were buffeted by a deadly escalation in the continuing battle between government forces and Kurds fighting for a separate state in southeastern Turkey. Clashes between the government and the Kurds escalated in March. But by November, a large-scale government offensive against the separatists had severely weakened the Kurds' military capabilities.

The uprising. Kurdish attacks on government officials and troops surged in the week of March 20 after the Marxist Kurdish Workers' Party (PKK), the main separatist group, called for a general uprising. More than 100 people were killed. Through the spring and summer, PKK attacks intensified against government troops and buildings as well as against Kurds accused of collaborating with the government. By September, about 1,300 people had died in the violence, almost one-third of the overall death toll of 4,500 killed since 1984, when the PKK began its campaign.

Many PKK fighters took refuge in a protected Kurdish zone in Iraq established by the United States, Great Britain, and France in 1991. Turkey responded to their attacks by massing about 130,000 troops along its border with Iraq and by staging land and aerial attacks on the PKK camps in northern Iraq.

Kurd against Kurd. But in July 1992, self-interest led Iraq's Kurds to turn against the PKK, which was reportedly receiving military supplies from Iran. Because Turkey controlled the only protected overland supply route into northern Iraq, the Iraqi Kurds ordered the PKK to cease its raids on Turkish forces from Iraqi territory. The PKK responded by attacking trucks carrying supplies to the Iraqi Kurds. In October, the Kurdish parliament in the protected zone voted to expel the PKK. Iraqi Kurds attacked PKK forces, helping Turkey kill many separatists and drive others into Turkey.

U.S. relations. Relations between Turkey and the United States were strained by U.S. support for Iraqi Kurds. In September, Prime Minister Suleyman Demirel warned that the formation of a Kurdish state in Iraq would inflame the Kurdish separatist movement within Turkey. On November 14, the foreign ministers of Turkey, Syria, and Iran—all of which have large Kurdish populations—publicly warned that the formation of an autonomous Kurdish zone threatened the stability of states neighboring Iraq.

Turkey also reacted with outrage to an accidental U.S. missile attack on the Turkish destroyer *Muavenet* on October 2 during naval exercises in the Aegean Sea. Two missiles mistakenly fired from the U.S. aircraft carrier *Saratoga* slammed into the *Muavenet,* killing five of the crew, including the captain.

Relations with Germany, Turkey's largest trading partner, deteriorated in late March after revelations that Turkey had used German-made weapons to attack PKK positions in southeastern Turkey. Using the weapons against the Kurds violated the terms of sale. On March 26, the German government halted all weapons shipments to Turkey. The next day, German officials admitted that 15 tanks had been delivered to Turkey despite a 1991 arms embargo imposed by the German parliament. In response to the new arms ban, Turkey withdrew its ambassador to Germany and canceled visits by Turkish officials. By June 1992, German arms shipments reportedly had resumed.

During 1992, Turkey also protested what it said was inadequate government action to combat violence against Turkish immigrants in Germany by neo-Nazi groups. On November 23, three members of a Turkish family died when rioters firebombed their home in Mölln, Germany. (See **Germany.**)

Terrorism. A car bomb killed an Israeli diplomat in Ankara, the capital, on March 7. Two militant Islamic groups claimed responsibility. The bombing followed a grenade attack on March 1 at Istanbul's Neve Shalom Synagogue. The assaults were reportedly linked to the February killing of the leader of the pro-Iranian group Hezbollah by Israeli forces in Lebanon.

The worst earthquake to strike Turkey since 1983 rocked the eastern part of the country on March 13, 1992. About 1,000 people died and thousands more were injured in the quake and another that followed on March 15. Christine Helms

See also **Middle East** (Facts in brief table). In ***World Book,*** see **Turkey.**

Turkmenistan. See **Commonwealth of Independent States.**

Uganda. See **Africa.**

Ukraine in 1992 made little headway in transforming its economy from a Communist system to a free-market one. Political struggles, as well as a number of disputes with neighboring Russia, slowed progress toward economic reform during the country's first year as an independent state. Ukraine had gained independence when the Soviet Union broke apart in December 1991. However, a new government formed in October 1992 took steps to speed reform. Also, most of the disputes with Russia were resolved, at least temporarily, by the end of the year.

Reform delayed. On January 10, the government began to circulate coupons as a temporary currency alongside the Russian ruble. The coupons, which had been created as ration cards in late 1991, were to be used until a permanent Ukrainian currency, the hryvnia, could be introduced. However, the introduction of the coupons increased the money supply, causing inflation to soar.

As the year progressed, the government failed to institute a cohesive economic policy or to relinquish control of failing state industries. As a result, industrial production declined by 20 per cent in the first 10 months of 1992. In the same period, prices rose by up to 22 times, while salaries increased only fourfold.

The slow pace of reform led opposition leaders increasingly to withdraw their support from the government of Prime Minister Vitold Fokin, which was dominated by former Communists. But the opposition failed in efforts in June and again in July to oust the government.

At the start of parliament's fall session on September 15, the government failed to present an economic reform program. Fokin presented a plan to parliament on September 25. Nevertheless, the opposition, led by the nationalist movement Rukh, passed a no-confidence vote on October 1.

On October 13, parliament confirmed President Leonid Kravchuk's nomination of Leonid Kuchma as prime minister. In November, Kuchma ended the nation's use of the ruble. The same month, parliament gave Kuchma expanded authority to make economic laws, and it approved a program to sell state-owned enterprises to private investors.

Relations with Russia were tense through much of 1992. One conflict involved control of military assets of the former Soviet Union—in particular, the 350-vessel Black Sea Fleet. The fleet was based at Sevastopol, on Ukraine's Crimean Peninsula. Ukraine sought most of the fleet as the basis for its planned navy. But the fleet had been the core of Russia's navy before the formation of the Soviet Union and so was an important symbol for Russian nationalists.

Russia claimed the flotilla should remain under the command of the Commonwealth of Independent States (C.I.S.), a loose association of former Soviet republics. It said the fleet, which had nuclear capabilities, should be considered a strategic force. C.I.S. members had agreed to place such forces under C.I.S.

control. Ukraine denied the fleet had much strategic value. On June 23, Kravchuk and Russian President Boris Yeltsin agreed to keep the fleet under C.I.S. control until the two nations determined on a formula for dividing it. But this settlement fell apart in July after a vessel from the fleet defected to the fledgling Ukrainian navy. Kravchuk and Yeltsin announced on August 3 that they had agreed to postpone a division of the fleet until 1995. Until then, Russia and Ukraine would jointly control the flotilla.

The Crimea. The Black Sea Fleet question was complicated by a dispute over the Crimean Peninsula, a region of Ukraine inhabited mainly by ethnic Russians. The peninsula, also called simply the Crimea, had belonged to Russia until 1954, when the Soviet Union transferred it to Ukraine. On May 5, 1992, the Crimean parliament voted to declare sovereignty. It scheduled a regional referendum for August to confirm the declaration. The parliament repealed the declaration on May 20, under pressure from the Ukrainian government. But Crimean officials said they still intended to hold the August referendum.

On May 21, the Russian parliament declared the 1954 Crimean transfer invalid. The action angered Ukrainians, who feared that Russia would bow to the demands of Russian nationalists and seek to reclaim the peninsula. However, Russia did not pursue the issue. In June, Ukraine granted the Crimea political and economic autonomy. In return, Crimean leaders agreed to cancel the referendum and abandon their drive for independence.

Arms control. Ukraine was one of four former Soviet republics to possess nuclear weapons. In January 1992, Ukraine, along with Belarus and Kazakhstan, pledged to transfer all their nuclear weapons to Russia and to become nuclear-free nations.

On March 12, Ukraine said it was suspending its transfer of *tactical* (short-range) nuclear arms to Russia because of concerns that the weapons were being stockpiled rather than destroyed. Ukraine resumed the transfer on April 16, after Russia agreed to allow Ukrainian observers to monitor the weapons' destruction. The tactical arms tranfer was completed by May.

On May 23, the former republics signed a revision to the Strategic Arms Reduction Treaty (START), an arms control accord reached by the United States and the Soviet Union in July 1991. Under the revision, all *strategic* (long-range) nuclear weapons in Ukraine would be destroyed or transferred to Russia by the end of the 1990's. Ukraine said it would transfer all its strategic nuclear weapons to Russia by 1994. But in November 1992, Ukraine threatened to halt the transfer if it did not receive additional security guarantees and financial assistance. Justin Burke

See also **Armed forces: The Nuclear Threat in the New World Order; Europe** (Facts in brief table); **Kravchuk, Leonid M.** In the World Book Supplement section, see **Ukraine.**

Unemployment. See **Economics; Labor.**

Soldiers in Ukraine load nuclear warheads—part of the Soviet arsenal based there—in preparation for their removal to Russia beginning in January.

United Nations. The United Nations (UN) Security Council on Jan. 31, 1992, held its first-ever summit meeting with the leaders of each of its 15 member nations. The summit addressed the role of the UN in the post-Cold War period and noted that the meeting was being held "at a time of momentous change." The end of the Cold War "raised hopes for a safer, more equitable, and more humane world," a summit declaration said. See **United Nations: A New Era for the United Nations.**

At the summit, the Security Council asked Boutros Boutros-Ghali, who had become UN secretary-general on January 1, to draw up a blueprint for future UN activities to promote peace and social development throughout the world. In June, Boutros-Ghali presented his 53-page plan, called "Agenda for Peace," in which he emphasized the need for preventive diplomacy and other measures designed to halt the escalation of conflict.

Boutros-Ghali warned that civil wars, fired by nationalist demands, present tough, new challenges for the international community. He then asked the member nations to provide troops for a military force that could be deployed rapidly to monitor a cease-fire agreement or to intervene in disputes that threatened to explode into war. The UN Charter (the world organization's constitution) allows for the creation of such a military force. Under Boutros-Ghali's proposal, however, the secretary-general could deploy the force

A United Nations inspector videotapes Iraqi demonstrators blocking arms inspectors from entering Iraq's Ministry of Agriculture in July.

only with the approval of the Security Council. Many UN members voiced their support for this sort of "standing army," but the Council was not scheduled to discuss the plan in detail until the spring of 1993.

Despite optimism over the UN's potential to help bring about a "new world order," the organization in 1992 was often called upon to solve problems beyond its practical abilities and economic resources. The number of conflicts and their complexity stretched the UN to the breaking point.

Yugoslavia. The Security Council decided on February 21 to establish the United Nations Protection Force in the breakaway republics of the former Yugoslavia—the first-ever deployment of a UN peacekeeping force in continental Europe. About 14,000 peacekeepers were slated to supervise a cease-fire and protect areas occupied by Serb minorities in Croatia, a former republic of Yugoslavia that declared its independence in June 1991. The independence declaration had angered the large community of Serbs living in Croatia, who remained loyal to the Yugoslav republic.

Despite a UN-negotiated truce in January 1992, fighting continued and spread to Bosnia and Hercegovina (often called Bosnia), another republic that had declared independence from Yugoslavia in March. Heavily armed Serb forces laid siege to Sarajevo, the capital of Bosnia, with a daily pounding of artillery. Serb forces gained control of Sarajevo's airport, blocking a UN-led airlift of food and supplies to the capital's starving residents. On May 13, Boutros-Ghali called the situation in Bosnia "tragic, dangerous, violent, and confused" and ordered most of the 300 peacekeepers in Sarajevo, the headquarters for the UN Protection Force, to pull out temporarily.

On May 30, the Security Council voted 13 to 0, with China and Zimbabwe abstaining, to impose a worldwide trade embargo on Serbia and Montenegro—the two remnant republics of Yugoslavia that had created a new Yugoslav republic. The embargo cut off air and sea links and banned the new Yugoslavia from participating in international sporting events.

Serb forces continued their daily attacks on Sarajevo. On June 29, Serb troops relinquished control of the airport to a small group of UN peacekeepers. On the same day, the Security Council decided to send in 850 troops to secure and reopen the airport to flights delivering humanitarian aid.

On August 13, the Security Council authorized the use of military force to ensure the delivery of badly needed food, medicine, and essential supplies to Bosnia. It also strongly condemned the practice of "ethnic cleansing" in which Serb forces forcibly expelled Muslim and Croat villagers in territories under Serb control, and the Council called on UN members to gather information on atrocities reportedly committed by Serb forces.

Continued attacks on UN food convoys prompted the Security Council on September 14 to authorize Boutros-Ghali to request up to 6,000 additional troops to protect the convoys. Then, on September 22, the General Assembly voted to expel Yugoslavia from UN membership. The Security Council further demanded that Serbs give international organizations immediate access to prisons and detention camps to investigate reports of Serb atrocities.

On October 6, the Security Council ordered the formation of a commission of experts to examine and analyze reports of human rights violations committed by all sides in the Yugoslav conflict. The commission was patterned after the Allied War Crimes Commission, which had investigated Nazi war crimes during World War II (1939-1945). Members of the Security Council said the next step would be to prosecute all of those charged with war crimes.

UN officials reported on December 10 that a total of 316 peacekeepers had been wounded and 20 others killed during the conflict in Croatia and Bosnia in 1992. As the fighting continued, and various countries violated the UN sanctions, the Security Council on November 16 approved a naval blockade against Yugoslavia. As of December 10, there were 23,023 UN peacemakers stationed in Croatia and Bosnia.

Cambodia. The UN in 1992 undertook a comprehensive peacekeeping mission in Cambodia, the second largest and costliest peace effort the organization had ever mounted. The mission was expected to cost almost $2 billion for 15 months, with 15,600 military personnel and a civilian contingent of more than 5,000, temporarily responsible for administering vital government operations. The UN staff would also undertake the repatriation and resettlement of some 370,000 Cambodian refugees along the border between Thailand and Cambodia.

The peace plan called for the mission to be accomplished by mid-1993, after UN-organized general elections were held in May of that year. However, the project stalled. One of the four warring factions in Cambodia, the Communist Khmer Rouge, refused to disarm and cooperate with an October 1991 peace treaty provision calling for troops to be contained in UN-supervised camps. The Khmer Rouge also objected to administrative powers granted to the pro-Vietnam government in Phnom Penh under the peace treaty, and the Khmer Rouge claimed that Vietnamese troops were still in Cambodia.

The Khmer Rouge's refusal to abide by the peace timetable harmed the UN operation. On Oct. 13, 1992, the Security Council decided that the organization of general elections should move forward with or without the Khmer Rouge, which was still considered the best-armed faction in Cambodia. On November 30, in an effort to force cooperation from the Khmer Rouge, the Security Council voted to ask Cambodia's neighbors to begin an oil embargo to any areas occupied by the Khmer Rouge. Few observers expected the embargo to work, however.

Somalia. On July 23, Boutros-Ghali criticized the Security Council for ignoring the crisis in Somalia, where hundreds of thousands of people were starving to death. Although UN food relief shipments had been sent to Somalia, warring factions or bandits there had intercepted them. In September, 655 UN troops from Pakistan entered Somalia to guard food shipments. Then, on December 3, the Council authorized an international military operation, led by the United States. The troops began arriving in Mogadishu, the seaport capital, on December 9 to secure the port and airport and ensure food deliveries. The UN was to begin a program for "national reconciliation and reconstruction" in Somalia in 1993.

Iraq. In enforcing the terms of the Persian Gulf War (1991) peace plan, UN arms inspectors in July 1992 tried to search Iraq's Ministry of Agriculture. But Iraqi officials barred the inspectors from entering the building, and a crowd of Iraqi citizens harassed the UN team. After 17 days, the inspectors were allowed to enter the building.

Mozambique's 16-year civil war came to an end under an agreement signed in October. On December 16, the Security Council approved a peacekeeping mission to Mozambique consisting of 7,500 troops and other personnel.

Refugees. One of the most challenging tasks the UN encountered in 1992 was the need to service an unprecedented number of refugees, most of whom were buffeted by war or natural disasters. The UN High Commissioner for Refugees, Sadako Ogata of Japan, said in October that 1.5 million refugees returned home voluntarily in 1992, but a staggering 18 million refugees existed worldwide.

Environment. The UN organized its first international conference on the environment in Rio de Janeiro, Brazil, from June 3 to 14. Representatives from 178 nations attended the "Earth Summit," which set forth plans to protect the Earth and to promote environmentally safe development. See **Environmental pollution: Environmental Concern Goes Global.**

General Assembly. On March 2, the General Assembly admitted eight former Soviet republics: Armenia, Azerbaijan, Kazakhstan, Kyrgyzstan, Moldova, Tajikistan, Turkmenistan, and Uzbekistan. San Marino, a tiny European country, was also admitted. On May 22, the General Assembly admitted Croatia, Bosnia, and Slovenia, another breakaway republic of Yugoslavia. On July 31, it admitted Georgia, the last of the 15 republics of the former Soviet Union to join the UN.

The General Assembly opened its 47th session on September 21. On October 27, it elected Pakistan, Brazil, Djibouti, Spain, and New Zealand as nonpermanent members of the Security Council for the 1993-1994 term. These countries will replace India, Ecuador, Zimbabwe, Austria, and Belgium, whose two-year term expired on Dec. 31, 1992. J. Tuyet Nguyen

See also **Bosnia and Hercegovina; Cambodia; Croatia; Environment; Somalia.** In ***World Book,*** see **United Nations.**

A New Era for the United Nations

By J. Tuyet Nguyen

With the end of the Cold War, a new consensus at the United Nations may help the world organization play a more active and prominent role in international affairs.

"Never before has the United Nations seemed to be so popular with its members. Never before have its services been requested with such frequency, not only in its traditional role of peacekeeping and peacemaking, but in new roles (as well)." So said Boutros Boutros-Ghali in May 1992 after becoming secretary-general of the United Nations (UN) in January.

The 1990's have brought an unexpected reversal of fortune to the UN. Throughout most of its existence, the international organization has been hobbled by ideological differences and fierce competition for leadership as a result of the conflict between the former Soviet Union and its Communist allies and the United States and its democratic allies. By the mid-1980's, many countries had, for all practical purposes, shunned the UN as an ineffective bureaucracy. Conservative voices within the United States called for the removal of UN headquarters from New York City, and in response to what it perceived as political hostility, the United States began withholding its dues to the world body. But as Communism disintegrated in the Soviet Union and in Eastern Europe in the late 1980's and early 1990's, the Cold War thawed and finger-pointing within the UN increasingly gave way to handshakes.

As a result, the UN has begun to play an increasingly active and prominent role in world affairs. Its traditional roles of peacekeeping and hu-

Power struggles shaped UN history

A quest for power and leadership among the UN's members—particularly the United States, the Soviet Union, and some developing countries—have affected UN activities since the organization's founding in 1945.

General Douglas MacArthur led U.S. troops in the Korean War (1950-1953), the first military action backed by the UN and a symbol of U.S. influence within the world body.

Former Soviet premier Nikita Khrushchev shouted and banged his fist on his desk at the UN in 1960—behaviors that seemed to typify the UN as a forum for Cold War hostilities.

manitarian assistance have been expanded to include such areas as international environmental agreements. What lies behind this reversal of fortune, and what does the future hold for the UN?

A turbulent past

Successes and defeats have marked the UN's history since representatives from 50 nations met in San Francisco on June 26, 1945, to sign the Charter of the United Nations, which established the organization. The nations that had created the charter had been allies against Germany, Italy, and Japan during World War II (1939-1945), and they believed that an international peace agency could help prevent another world war.

The charter set forth the goals of the organization, which were broadly defined as procuring and maintaining peace, ensuring human rights, and promoting better standards of living throughout the world. The charter also established the Security Council, which has the main responsibility for ensuring peace. The Security Council consists of 15 members, including the five permanent members of the United States, Russia (formerly the Soviet Union), France, China, and Great Britain. These five members each have the power to veto any proposal brought before the council.

Many of the smaller nations that attended the San Francisco conference opposed the veto power of the Security Council's permanent members. It was approved at the insistence of the delegations from Great Britain, the United States, and the Soviet Union, who believed that they could guarantee the peace only if they continued to operate as they had during World War II. But soon after the charter was signed, the alliance and good relations that had existed between the Soviet Union and the

The author:

J. Tuyet Nguyen is the United Nations correspondent for United Press International.

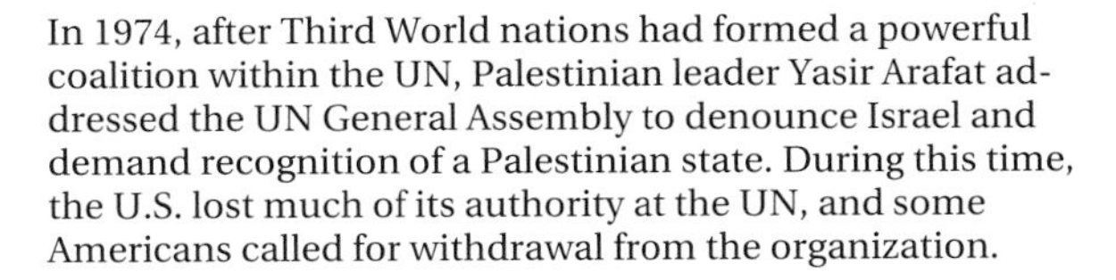

In 1974, after Third World nations had formed a powerful coalition within the UN, Palestinian leader Yasir Arafat addressed the UN General Assembly to denounce Israel and demand recognition of a Palestinian state. During this time, the U.S. lost much of its authority at the UN, and some Americans called for withdrawal from the organization.

In 1990, with Communism dying in the Soviet Union and Eastern Europe, the U.S. received UN approval for military action against Iraq—a move some hailed as a step toward a "new world order."

United States during World War II gave way to a Cold War. As early as 1946, the Soviet Union exercised its veto power, rejecting a U.S. proposal to establish an international agency to control nuclear energy production.

Despite such stand-offs, the United States had great influence at the UN. In 1950, for example, most UN members quickly supported a U.S. proposal to send military forces to South Korea to repel an invasion by Communist North Korea. The Soviet Union could not veto the proposal because it had temporarily abandoned its Security Council seat in protest against another matter.

Although some U.S.-Soviet cooperation dots UN history, the two superpowers were primarily antagonists. Soviet Premier Nikita Khrushchev dramatized this antagonism in 1960 when he attended a session of the UN General Assembly and interrupted the speeches of other delegates by shouting and banging his shoe on his desk. Khrushchev was venting frustration at the UN's refusal to fire Secretary-General Dag Hammarskjöld, whom he called a "willing tool" of the United States and its Western allies.

In the 1960's and 1970's, U.S. leadership at the UN began to slip when developing nations in Asia, Africa, and Latin America formed coalitions to promote specific agendas. These Third World countries made up the majority of votes in the UN General Assembly. This development led to further rifts. In 1971, Third World countries were the principal force behind the admission of Communist China to the UN and the UN Security Council, resulting in the ouster of Nationalist China (Taiwan). In 1974, Yasir Arafat, chairman of the Palestine Liberation Organization (PLO), addressed the UN General Assembly for the first time to request statehood for Palestinian Arabs. The proposal was opposed by the United States and its ally Israel. But led by Arab nations, and with the support of most Third

World countries, the General Assembly voted not only to recognize the Palestinians' right to nationhood but also to allow the PLO to attend General Assembly sessions as a nonvoting member. Then, in 1975, the General Assembly passed a resolution declaring that Zionism (the movement to create the Jewish state of Israel) "is a form of racism." This act infuriated Israel, most Western nations, and many Jewish people. Some Jews in the United States called for U.S. withdrawal from the UN.

Unhappy with the actions of Arab and Communist delegates, the United States in 1977 withdrew from the UN's International Labor Organization (ILO) to protest the politicization of labor issues. The United States returned to the ILO in 1980, but in 1984 withdrew its support of another UN agency, the UN Educational, Scientific and Cultural Organization (UNESCO), charging it with an anti-Western bias and mismanagement.

Installed in January 1992 as the UN's first secretary-general from Africa, Boutros Boutros-Ghali (left) met with such heads of state as Akbar Rafsanjani of Iran and quickly established himself as an advocate for international cooperation and "preventive diplomacy."

Pulling together

With the end of Communist rule in Eastern Europe and the break-up of the Soviet Union, a new consensus began to characterize the UN. Since the UN's founding, the five permanent Security Council members had used their individual veto powers 279 times. However, between June 1990 and November 1992, no veto was cast. Although the People's Republic of China, still a Communist country, has opposed particular Security Council resolutions, it has simply abstained from voting on such matters rather than be the lone dissenting voice.

A significant example of the UN's new collective voice came in August 1990 when the Security Council condemned Iraq's invasion of Kuwait and voted 13 to 0—with Yemen and Cuba abstaining—to impose sweeping economic sanctions on the country. This was only the third time in history that the UN had approved sanctions. Then, in November 1990, the Security Council approved military action for only the second time in its history, voting 12 to 2 to authorize the use of force to expel Iraq from Kuwait. China abstained, and Yemen and Cuba voted against the resolution. A total of 32 member countries contributed military forces or combat support in the 1991 Persian Gulf War. The endeavor demonstrated a renewed position of leadership and authority for the United States, which led the campaign.

As the UN entered the post-Cold War era, world leaders hoped the agency would be better able to fulfill its goals. And indeed, the UN has greatly expanded its peacekeeping missions, made new efforts in the areas of election monitoring and humanitarian aid, and passed an unprecedented number of human rights resolutions. In June 1992, the UN also drew world leaders together in Rio de Janeiro, Brazil, to address environmental problems at the United Nations Conference on Environment and Development, popularly known as the Earth Summit. See **Environmental pollution: Environmental Concern Goes Global.**

Peacekeeping around the world

The UN in 1988 won the Nobel Peace Prize for its peacekeeping missions. At the end of 1992, the UN was involved in 12 peacekeeping operations—half the total number of peace missions mounted in the 47 years of its existence—and had committed more than $3 billion and about 50,000 military and civilian personnel to peacekeeping activities.

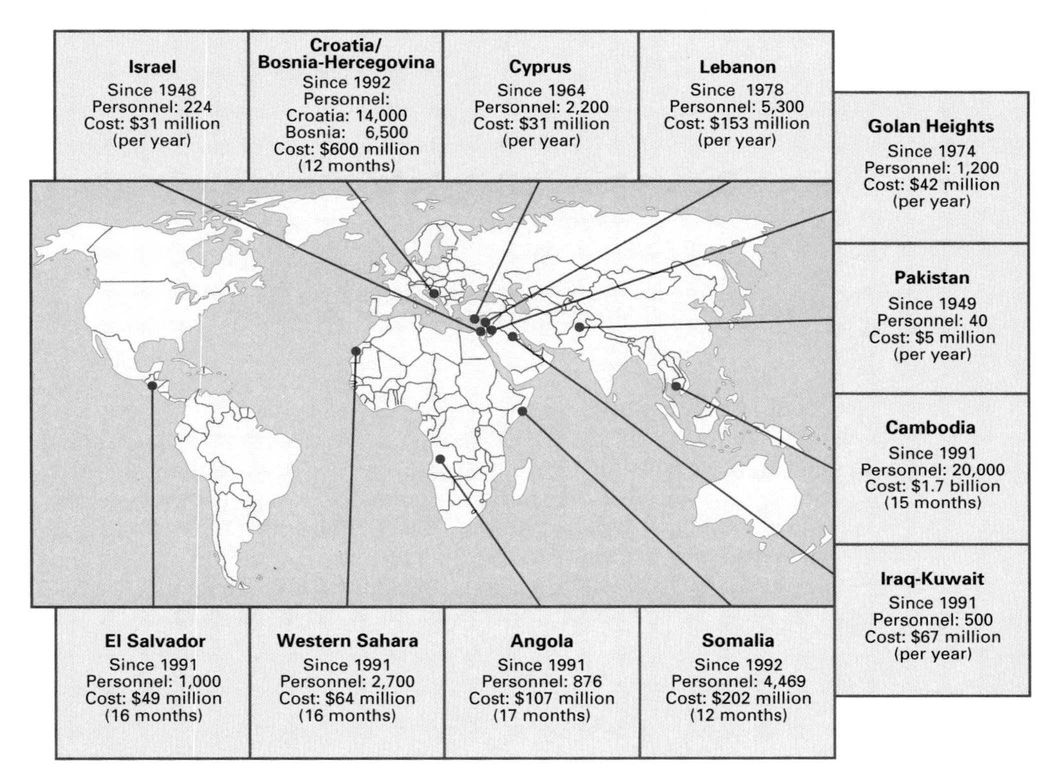

UN peacekeeping troops in April 1992 monitor a cease-fire in Croatia, which had declared its independence from Yugoslavia and subsequently came under attack from Serbian rebels and the Yugoslav federal army.

Weapons belonging to Namibian guerrillas lie waiting to be destroyed as part of a UN-negotiated settlement between Namibia and South Africa that paved the way for democratic elections in 1989.

UN intervention

- **Elections**
The UN in 1992 organized elections to be held in Cambodia, Angola, and Western Sahara.
- **Human rights**
The UN in 1991 condemned a record number of countries for human rights abuses.
- **Humanitarian aid**
Civil war, political oppression, natural disasters, hunger, and poverty in 1991 and 1992 produced 20 million refugees, many of whom were helped with UN funds.
- **Sanctions**
As of mid-1992, the UN was enforcing sweeping sanctions against Yugoslavia and Iraq for their aggressive actions against neighboring countries. The UN also imposed an embargo on Libya for sheltering suspects in the bombings of two airplanes in 1988 and 1989.

Keeping the peace

Between 1988 and 1992, the UN mounted 13 operations—as many as it had undertaken in the previous 42 years. Twelve peacekeeping operations, involving more than 50,000 personnel, were still underway at the end of 1992. Two missions, one in Croatia, a former republic of Yugoslavia, and another in Cambodia, represented the organization's largest and costliest peace campaigns to date. The price tag for maintaining all 12 peacekeeping operations in 1992 was an estimated $3 billion.

Although the UN has worked hard to promote peace, not all its peacekeeping operations have been successful. Some have dragged on for decades, such as those in Israel, Cyprus, and Pakistan. In addition, recent UN-negotiated peace settlements have brought warring factions together to agree on a plan only to see them hedge on it later. In El Salvador, for example, rebel forces in 1992 balked at the UN's 1991 demobilization plan and refused to disarm until the government complied with the peace agreement by disbanding the National Guard and Treasury Police. Both sides fell far behind in carrying out the timetable of the peace accords, which ended a 12-year civil war.

The comprehensive peace plan arranged for Cambodia also encountered snags. That plan included monitoring the cease-fire, disarming and removing troops, repatriating refugees, organizing elections, and providing humanitarian relief. The UN also went beyond these customary undertakings to manage Cambodia's government and infrastructure, which more than 20 years of warfare had left in ruin. The first 12 months of this endeavor cost about $2 billion. However, in mid-1992, the Khmer Rouge, one of the four warring factions in Cambodia, refused to disarm. This problem threatened the UN's investment in the region and, perhaps, foreshadowed the need for an even costlier, long-term mission.

Conflict in Bosnia and Hercegovina, a former republic of Yugoslavia that declared independence in 1991 and then came under attack by Yu-

Using materials supplied by the UN in 1992, Cambodian refugees construct new homes to replace temporary shelters. In a huge undertaking, the UN sought to help 370,000 Cambodian refugees return to their country.

goslav forces and Serbian irregulars, further revealed the UN's limited ability to keep the peace. UN peacekeeping troops there were completely ineffective and had to beat a hasty retreat from the country. Those that remained as observers risked their lives. The Security Council subsequently voted to impose stiff sanctions on Yugoslavia, similar to those it had imposed on Iraq in 1990. But the violence continued.

Sanctions and humanitarian efforts

Like peacekeeping missions, sanctions do not always work. The UN imposes sanctions to punish governments for breaching international peace and security. Sanctions may ban trade, diplomatic relations, air travel, cultural and scientific contact, military aid—even participation in the Olympic Games. But the UN cannot enforce sanctions absolutely. It depends on the cooperation of its member governments as well as private citizens and corporations, who might pursue business opportunities in a sanctioned country. Even when most of the world cooperates with sanctions, the punished nation can be intractable. For example, the UN imposed economic sanctions on Rhodesia (now Zimbabwe) in 1966 to end the white minority's control of the government, but Rhodesia weathered the embargoes until 1980, when democratic elections were finally held.

Just since 1990, the UN has leveled sanctions on Iraq for its invasion of Kuwait, on Libya for its refusal to surrender suspected terrorists in two airline bombings, and on Yugoslavia. As of the end of 1992, all these countries were still under sanctions with no resolution in sight.

Although aimed at governments, sanctions often fall hardest on civilians. Embargoes can raise the cost of living enormously and lead to unemployment and shortages of food, medicine, and other commodities. Populations feeling the hardship of sanctions often direct their anger at the UN rather than at their political leaders. For example, Libya's leader,

The UN Security Council in 1990 votes to impose sweeping sanctions against Iraq for its invasion of Kuwait. The 13-0 vote, with Cuba and Yemen abstaining, represented an unusually strong consensus among Council members.

Muammar Muhammad al-Qadhafi, called the UN's 1992 imposition of sanctions on his nation a "crusader war against Arabs and Muslims," and Libyans supported him by attacking the embassies of two UN members.

Even the politically impartial, traditionally respected humanitarian efforts cannot be certain of success. In Bosnia and Hercegovina, for example, nearly all sides in the civil war have blocked supplies of food and medicine and have attacked relief workers. In Somalia, bandits routinely carried off UN shipments of food meant for the starving.

Paying the bills

Economic strains have further challenged the UN. A cash shortage has plagued the UN for years, but at the end of July 1992 inadequate funds threatened to shut down the UN by year's end, the organization reported. To help contain costs, which for the two-year period ending in 1991 had risen to over $15 billion, the UN instituted a hiring freeze and shifted personnel from headquarters to the field. But it wasn't nearly enough.

Charges of mismanagement, patronage, negligence, and corruption were reported as being among the long-standing causes of the financial crises. But delinquent payments from UN members contributed to the problem as well. As of September 1992, the UN was owed more than $1.5-billion in dues. Peacekeeping arrears totaled $839 million, while regular dues were short by $911 million. Although UN members are legally bound to pay their dues, the agency can do little more than exert moral pressure on those with dues in arrears.

Regular dues are levied based on a nation's ability to pay, but, in accordance with the charter, no nation should or may pay more than 25 per cent of the UN's budget. The United States, which is assessed the maximum 25 per cent of the regular budget and 30 per cent of peacekeeping costs, was the largest debtor until October 1992. At that time, it brought its $524 million in outstanding dues down to $390 million, just slightly lower than Russia's debt of $402 million.

The reluctance of many governments to pay their dues has stemmed in part from prolonged economic recessions. But compared with worldwide military expenditures during the Cold War—$1 trillion per year or $2 million per minute—the price for UN peacekeeping can be seen as a bargain.

A new world order?

Struggles among UN members also challenge the progress of the organization. Although the end of the Cold War brought greater consensus to the Security Council, members of the General Assembly have voiced concern over the future direction of the UN. Boutros-Ghali and other world leaders have envisioned a "new world order." But just what this meant, or how it would be accomplished, remained elusive. Some nations, particularly Arab states and others in the developing world, voiced more than a little skepticism about whose interests this new "order" would represent. These groups criticized Western nations for focusing on peacekeeping missions at the expense of economic programs for poor nations. And they expressed fears that, with the Cold War over, the United States would again dominate the UN, and the needs of developing countries would be ignored. Experts note that if the world views the UN as being controlled by the United States, this could aggravate hostilities and lead to deadlocks.

To expand the power of other nations, UN members have proposed revising the charter to change or expand the permanent Security Council members. For example, Japan, Germany, Brazil, India, Nigeria, and Egypt have all been suggested as potential candidates for permanent council seats. Japan and Germany are seen as the most likely winners of seats because of their economic strength. If the UN decides to replace rather than increase permanent Security Council members, France and Great Britain are seen as likely losers of their seats.

Other revisions of the charter are expected as well, with some nations targeting the UN's 50th anniversary

Who pays the UN's bills?

Members of the UN must contribute to the organization based on their ability to pay. However, no nation is allowed to pay more than 25 per cent of the regular budget, *below*. No such limitation applies to peacekeeping costs, *bottom*, which are charged separately .

Dues for regular budget

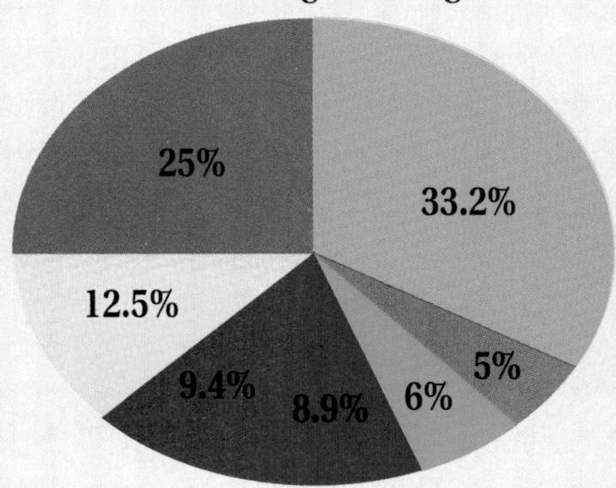

Source: United Nations.

Dues for peacekeeping

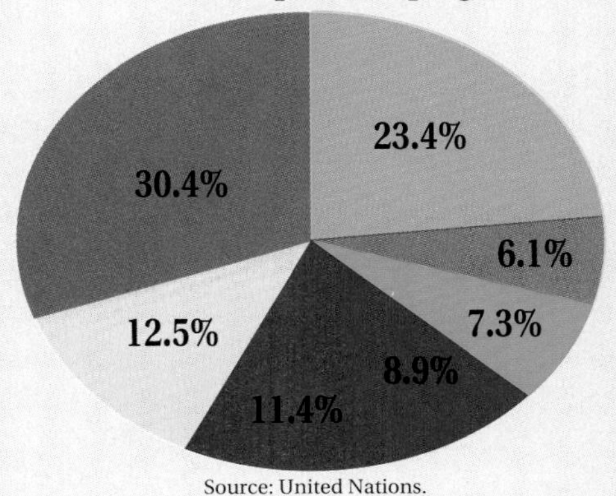

Source: United Nations.

Color key to countries

Debts

As of October 1992, the UN was owed more than $1.5 billion in regular and peacekeeping dues. The nations with the largest debts (in millions of dollars) are:

Russia	$402
United States	$390
South Africa	$49
Brazil	$33
Ukraine	$17

in 1995 as the deadline for such reforms. An updated charter might help the UN become more forceful in world events. Revisions could, for example, lift the charter's prohibitions on UN interference in the internal affairs of its members. Such a change would allow the agency to act more aggressively in ending civil wars. It could also put muscle into UN resolutions against countries that violate human rights.

As the Security Council in 1992 sought "new ideas and a new impetus" for the UN, it called on Boutros-Ghali, an expert on international law and the first secretary-general from Africa and the Arab world, to draft a blueprint for policies and activities that would revitalize the UN. Boutros-Ghali immediately took up the challenge to reform the world body. He immersed himself in plans for an active yet streamlined organization, and he was outspoken on the need for greater cooperation between industrialized nations and the developing world.

Agenda for peace

After six months in office, Boutros-Ghali introduced "An Agenda for Peace," a plan that emphasized preventive diplomacy and peacemaking. Part of this plan called for the creation of standing armed forces. Citing Article 43 of the UN charter, which allows the secretary-general to request forces to maintain peace and security, Boutros-Ghali asked that each nation agree to contribute up to 1,000 troops who could mobilize with a 24-hour notice. Such a standing force would enable the secretary-general, with the Security Council's approval, to rapidly dispatch troops to enforce a cease-fire or to intercede in any country where conflict was poised to explode. Because the stand-by military would be financed through the defense budgets of the contributing nations, Boutros-Ghali hoped the arrangement would also help resolve some of the UN's chronic cash shortage. On October 29, the Security Council approved the creation of a rapid-deployment peace force and asked the members of the General Assembly to state their position on contributing troops to such a force.

Boutros-Ghali's agenda also called for establishment of a worldwide intelligence service that would assist the UN in spotting and settling arguments before they erupted into warfare. Such an early warning system could also help the UN counter a range of problems, such as the spread of disease, by organizing humanitarian aid in a more timely manner.

The Agenda for Peace further proposed that all nations recognize the jurisdiction of the International Court of Justice, which is headquartered at The Hague, the Netherlands. In the past, verdicts by the World Court, an arm of the UN, had been largely disregarded by many nations.

The General Assembly opened its 47th session in September 1992 with discussion of Boutros-Ghali's agenda for peace. While the UN was a long way from establishing a new world order, it had recognized the opportunity to shake off old rivalries. Now, as the UN finds ways to handle struggles for power and position fairly, the demands placed on it may be an encouraging sign. Such demands seem to indicate renewed respect, authority, and hope for an organization born of war but bred for peace.

United States, Government of the. For yet another year, the United States government had to contend with a sagging economy and a record budget deficit. Those persistent problems and election-year politics overshadowed most other concerns of the federal government in 1992.

The deficit in 1992, though a record, turned out to be much smaller than expected. But it was a case of bad news postponed rather than avoided. In January, President George Bush predicted a deficit of $399.7 billion for the 1992 fiscal year. The actual deficit for the fiscal year, which ended on September 30, was $290.2 billion, up from the previous record of $269.5 billion one year earlier. Robert D. Reischauer, director of the Congressional Budget Office (CBO), said the smaller deficit was only "superficially good news," because the government in fiscal 1992 spent tens of billions less than planned to bail out failed savings and loan institutions (S&L's). He said that more money would still have to be spent on S&L's, adding to future deficits.

The deficit was much on voters' minds during the 1992 election season, with Bush and his Democratic opponent, Governor Bill Clinton of Arkansas, promising to do something about it. Only independent presidential candidate Ross Perot outlined a detailed proposal for eliminating the deficit, however. Perot's plan called for balancing the budget within five years.

The international community viewed the continuing U.S. deficits with alarm. The directors of the Federal Reserve System (the Fed), the nation's central bank, repeatedly pushed down interest rates in 1992 in an effort to revive the economy. As a result, the dollar plunged in August to its lowest value against the German mark since World War II (1939-1945). In September, the International Monetary Fund (IMF), an agency of the United Nations (UN), was unusually critical of U.S. government fiscal policies—a stance generally reserved for developing countries with shaky economies. The IMF's annual report said long-term economic growth in the United States would be hampered if the U.S. deficit was not reduced.

On September 30, a bipartisan congressional commission proposed balancing the budget in 10 years. The group proposed stiff budget cuts, changes in the income tax system, caps on entitlement programs other than social security, and $376 billion in tax hikes.

The economy. A variety of government actions aimed at stimulating the economy in 1992 seemed to result in only marginal improvements. In January, Bush tried to spur consumer spending by issuing an executive order reducing income tax withholding. On February 18, the Fed reduced by more than $7 billion the amount banks must set aside as a reserve, or margin of safety, hoping to boost bank profits and encourage lending. And several times during the year, the Fed cut interest rates. None of these measures produced much of a stimulative effect on the economy, however. (See also **Bank; Economics.**)

President-elect Bill Clinton, who centered his presidential campaign on the economy, hosted an economic conference in Little Rock, Ark., on December 14 and 15. The more than 300 economists, business leaders, and others in attendance had been invited to take part in "intensive discussions" on the economy. But Clinton's aides said an overriding purpose of the meeting was to generate widespread support for Clinton's proposed economic agenda.

Personnel changes. Many government personnel changes in 1992 were dictated by presidential politics. In January, Bush named Andrew H. Card, Jr., deputy White House chief of staff, to succeed Samuel K. Skinner as secretary of transportation. Skinner had replaced John H. Sununu, judged a political liability, as Bush's chief of staff in December 1991. Robert A. Mosbacher resigned as secretary of commerce in February 1992 to become general chairman of the Bush campaign. He was succeeded by Barbara H. Franklin, a Republican activist. Edward J. Derwinski resigned on September 26 as secretary of veterans affairs. His ouster had reportedly been sought by veterans groups, notably the Veterans of Foreign Wars (VFW).

On February 21, John E. Frohnmayer was forced to resign as chairman of the National Endowment for the Arts (NEA). The NEA's funding of arts institutions that exhibited sexually explicit art had been attacked by Patrick J. Buchanan, Bush's major Republican primary challenger. (See **Art: Who Should Pay for Art?**)

On April 1, Richard H. Truly resigned as head of the National Aeronautics and Space Administration (NASA). He was forced out after feuding with the advisory National Space Council, chaired by Vice President Dan Quayle. Truly was succeeded by Daniel S. Goldin, an aerospace executive.

The biggest personnel change came on August 13, when James A. Baker III resigned as secretary of state to take over as White House chief of staff from Skinner. Baker was recruited to bring order to the White House and Bush's presidential campaign, both of which were said to be in disarray. Deputy Secretary of State Lawrence S. Eagleburger took over Baker's duties at the State Department on an acting basis, and on December 8 he was sworn in as Baker's successor.

On Eagleburger's recommendation, Bush on November 10 fired Elizabeth M. Tamposi, assistant secretary of state for consular affairs. Her office had searched the passport files of Clinton, Clinton's mother, and Perot in search of information that might have proved politically damaging to the candidates.

Navy scandal. The U.S. Navy underwent an upheaval in its top ranks in 1992, the result of sexual harassment charges against a group of Navy and Marine pilots and attempts at a cover-up. The pilots reportedly sexually assaulted or harassed at least 26 women during a 1991 convention of the Tailhook Association, a pilots' organization, at a Las Vegas, Nev., hotel. Secretary of the Navy H. Lawrence Garrett III, accused of failing to vigorously investigate the scandal, resigned

Selected agencies and bureaus of the U.S. government*

Executive Office of the President
President, George Bush
Vice President, Dan Quayle
White House Chief of Staff, James A. Baker III
Presidential Press Secretary, Marlin Fitzwater
Assistant to the President for National Security Affairs, Brent Scowcroft
Assistant to the President for Science and Technology, D. Allan Bromley
Council of Economic Advisers—Michael J. Boskin, Chairman
Counselor to the President for Domestic Policy—Clayton Yeutter
Office of Management and Budget—Richard G. Darman, Director
Office of National Drug Control Policy—Bob Martinez, Director
U.S. Trade Representative, Carla A. Hills

Department of Agriculture
Secretary of Agriculture, Edward R. Madigan

Department of Commerce
Secretary of Commerce, Barbara H. Franklin
Bureau of Economic Analysis—Carol S. Carson, Director
Bureau of the Census—Barbara E. Bryant, Director

Department of Defense
Secretary of Defense, Richard B. Cheney
Secretary of the Air Force, Donald B. Rice
Secretary of the Army, Michael P. W. Stone
Acting Secretary of the Navy, Sean C. O'Keefe
Joint Chiefs of Staff—
General Colin L. Powell, Chairman
General Merrill A. McPeak, Chief of Staff, Air Force
General Gordon R. Sullivan, Chief of Staff, Army
Admiral Frank B. Kelso II, Chief of Naval Operations
General Carl E. Mundy, Commandant, Marine Corps

Department of Education
Secretary of Education, Lamar Alexander, Jr.

Department of Energy
Secretary of Energy, James D. Watkins

Department of Health and Human Services
Secretary of Health and Human Services, Louis W. Sullivan
Public Health Service—James O. Mason, Assistant Secretary
Centers for Disease Control—William L. Roper, Director
Food and Drug Administration—David A. Kessler, Commissioner
National Institutes of Health—Bernadine P. Healy, Director
Surgeon General of the United States, Antonia C. Novello
Social Security Administration—Louis D. Enoff, Acting Commissioner

Department of Housing and Urban Development
Secretary of Housing and Urban Development, Jack F. Kemp

Department of the Interior
Secretary of the Interior, Manuel Lujan, Jr.

Department of Justice
Attorney General, William P. Barr
Bureau of Prisons—J. Michael Quinlan, Director
Drug Enforcement Administration—Robert C. Bonner, Administrator
Federal Bureau of Investigation—William S. Sessions, Director
Immigration and Naturalization Service—Gene McNary, Commissioner
Solicitor General, Kenneth W. Starr

Department of Labor
Secretary of Labor, Lynn M. Martin

Department of State
Secretary of State, Lawrence S. Eagleburger
U.S. Representative to the United Nations, Edward J. Perkins

Department of Transportation
Secretary of Transportation, Andrew H. Card, Jr.
Federal Aviation Administration—Thomas C. Richards, Administrator
U.S. Coast Guard—J. William Kime, Commandant

*As of Dec. 31, 1992.

Department of the Treasury
Secretary of the Treasury, Nicholas F. Brady
Internal Revenue Service—Shirley D. Peterson, Commissioner
Treasurer of the United States, Catalina Vasquez Villalpando
U.S. Secret Service—John W. Magaw, Director
Office of Thrift Supervision—T. Timothy Ryan, Jr., Director

Department of Veterans Affairs
Acting Secretary of Veterans Affairs, Anthony J. Principi

Supreme Court of the United States
Chief Justice of the United States, William H. Rehnquist
Associate Justices—
Byron R. White
Harry A. Blackmun
John Paul Stevens
Sandra Day O'Connor
Antonin Scalia
Anthony M. Kennedy
David H. Souter
Clarence Thomas

Congressional officials
President of the Senate pro tempore, Robert C. Byrd
Senate Majority Leader, George J. Mitchell
Senate Minority Leader, Robert J. Dole
Speaker of the House, Thomas S. Foley
House Majority Leader, Richard A. Gephardt
House Minority Leader, Robert H. Michel
Congressional Budget Office—Robert D. Reischauer, Director
General Accounting Office—Charles A. Bowsher, Comptroller General of the United States
Library of Congress—James H. Billington, Librarian of Congress
Office of Technology Assessment—John H. Gibbons, Director

Independent agencies
ACTION—Jane A. Kenny, Director
Agency for International Development—Ronald W. Roskens, Administrator
Central Intelligence Agency—Robert M. Gates, Director
Commission on Civil Rights—Arthur A. Fletcher, Chairman
Commission of Fine Arts—J. Carter Brown, Chairman
Consumer Product Safety Commission—Jacqueline Jones-Smith, Chairman
Environmental Protection Agency—William K. Reilly, Administrator
Equal Employment Opportunity Commission—Evan J. Kemp, Jr., Chairman
Federal Communications Commission—Alfred C. Sikes, Chairman
Federal Deposit Insurance Corporation—Andrew C. Hove, Jr., Acting Chairman
Federal Election Commission—Joan D. Aikens, Chairman
Federal Emergency Management Agency—Wallace E. Stickney, Director
Federal Reserve System Board of Governors—Alan Greenspan, Chairman
Federal Trade Commission—Janet D. Steiger, Chairman
General Services Administration—Richard G. Austin, Administrator
Interstate Commerce Commission—Edward J. Philbin, Chairman
National Aeronautics and Space Administration—Daniel S. Goldin, Administrator
National Endowment for the Arts—Anne-Imelda Radice, Acting Chairman
National Endowment for the Humanities—Lynne V. Cheney, Chairman
National Labor Relations Board—James M. Stephens, Chairman
National Railroad Passenger Corporation (Amtrak)—W. Graham Claytor, Jr., Chairman
National Science Foundation—Walter E. Massey, Director
National Transportation Safety Board—Carl W. Vogt, Chairman
Nuclear Regulatory Commission—Ivan Selin, Chairman
Peace Corps—Elaine L. Chao, Director
Securities and Exchange Commission—Richard C. Breeden, Chairman
Selective Service System—Robert William Gambino, Director
Small Business Administration—Patricia F. Saiki, Administrator
Smithsonian Institution—Robert McC. Adams, Secretary
U.S. Arms Control and Disarmament Agency—Ronald F. Lehman II, Director
U.S. Information Agency—Henry E. Catto, Director
U.S. Postal Service—Marvin T. Runyon, Jr., Postmaster General

under fire in June 1992. His acting successor, Sean C. O'Keefe, later fired or reprimanded three admirals and the Navy's civilian undersecretary for their failure to investigate the allegations against the pilots. (See also **Armed forces.)**

New amendment. Nearly everything in 1992 seemed to be politically sensitive, even a 203-year-old proposed amendment to the Constitution that finally was adopted in May. The 27th Amendment had been proposed in 1789 by James Madison, one of the framers of the Constitution and the nation's fourth President. It bars Congress from voting itself midterm pay raises, an issue that angered many voters in the 1992 elections. Ratification by legislators in Michigan on May 7 gave the amendment the required support of three-fourths of the states.

Presidential handouts. Many executive branch actions had political overtones in 1992. When hurricanes hit Florida and Hawaii in late summer, Bush said the government would pay eligible damage claims in full, instead of the customary 75 per cent. During his campaign travels, the President announced $1 billion in new subsidies for grain farmers and reversed past policy stands against selling modern jet fighters to Saudi Arabia and Taiwan. Orders for the planes promised continuing employment for thousands of aerospace workers in key electoral states.

Relations with Iraq probed. The events leading up to the 1991 Persian Gulf War came under close scrutiny in 1992. Some Democrats claimed that Bush had coddled Iraq's President Saddam Hussein almost until the day Hussein invaded Kuwait in August 1990, the event that led to the war. The Democrats also alleged that the Administration was taking part in a cover-up to hide the facts about its relations with Iraq.

During 1992, the Department of Justice accused the Atlanta, Ga., branch manager of an Italian bank, Banca Nazionale del Lavoro (BNL), of illegally loaning Iraq $4 billion for food and arms without the knowledge of the bank's Rome headquarters. But the Central Intelligence Agency (CIA) later said that many of the loans had been approved by the Rome bank. A federal judge, Marvin H. Shoob, said, "It is apparent that decisions were made at the top levels" of the U.S. Justice, State, and Agriculture departments and within the intelligence community "to shape this case."

Unseemly bickering among federal agencies followed. On October 8, CIA officials told congressional investigators that it had sent misleading information to prosecutors on orders from the Justice Department. The Federal Bureau of Investigation (FBI) began its own inquiry into CIA and Justice Department actions. Democrats in Congress said an independent counsel should investigate the Administration's relations with Iraq. Rejecting the request, Attorney General William P. Barr on October 16 named a retired federal judge, Frederick B. Lacey, to investigate on his behalf. On December 9, Lacey reported that the government's

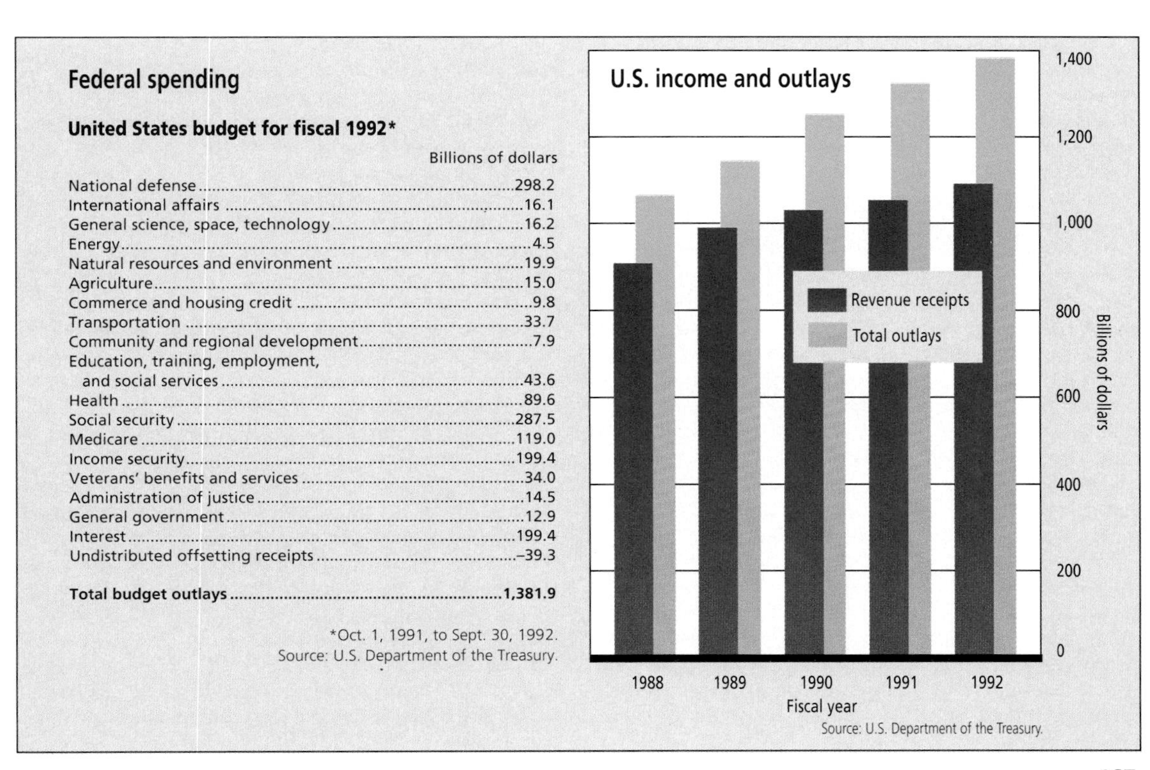

Federal spending

United States budget for fiscal 1992*

	Billions of dollars
National defense	298.2
International affairs	16.1
General science, space, technology	16.2
Energy	4.5
Natural resources and environment	19.9
Agriculture	15.0
Commerce and housing credit	9.8
Transportation	33.7
Community and regional development	7.9
Education, training, employment, and social services	43.6
Health	89.6
Social security	287.5
Medicare	119.0
Income security	199.4
Veterans' benefits and services	34.0
Administration of justice	14.5
General government	12.9
Interest	199.4
Undistributed offsetting receipts	–39.3
Total budget outlays	**1,381.9**

*Oct. 1, 1991, to Sept. 30, 1992.
Source: U.S. Department of the Treasury.

investigation had been a "fiasco" but that he had found no evidence of wrongdoing by any federal officials. But Democrats in Congress expressed dissatisfaction with Lacey's conclusions. (See also **Bank.**)

Iran-contra revelations. Another nettlesome problem for Bush in 1992 was the Iran-contra affair, a 1985-1986 arms-for-hostages operation carried out when Bush was President Ronald Reagan's Vice President. Bush had long claimed that he knew nothing about the operation until December 1986. But former Secretary of State George P. Shultz said in 1986 that Bush had attended a key White House meeting on the subject on Jan. 7, 1986. Notes taken by former Secretary of Defense Caspar W. Weinberger, and made public in 1992, supported Shultz. The notes indicated that Bush had favored a proposed shipment of U.S. arms to Iran in exchange for American hostages being held by pro-Iranian terrorists in Lebanon. (The operation also included military support for *contra* rebels fighting the Marxist government of Nicaragua.)

On September 16, independent counsel Lawrence E. Walsh announced that he was winding up his six-year, $32-million inquiry into the Iran-contra affair. Walsh said he did not expect more indictments.

Walsh's most controversial move in 1992 came on June 16 with the indictment of Weinberger, who was charged with obstructing investigators and lying about his knowledge of the operation. Trial was set for Jan. 5, 1993. But on Dec. 24, 1992, Bush pardoned Weinberger and five other officials involved in Iran-contra.

On May 25, former CIA officer Thomas G. Clines became the first Iran-contra figure to enter a federal prison. He began serving a 16-month term for failing to disclose to the Internal Revenue Service $260,000 in profits made from arms dealings with the contras. Clair E. George, former chief of CIA covert operations, was tried in August on charges of perjury and obstruction of justice but the jury was unable to agree on a verdict. A new trial began on October 19, and on December 9 George was found guilty of lying to congressional investigators in 1986. George received a pardon but Clines did not. (See also **Iran-contra affair.**)

Other court actions. A continuing influence-peddling inquiry involving appointees of Samuel R. Pierce, Jr., secretary of housing and urban development in the Reagan Administration, brought three guilty pleas and eight other indictments in 1992. Among those indicted was Deborah Gore Dean, Pierce's executive assistant, who was accused of bribery and lying to Congress. Pierce was not charged with any crime.

Also continuing in 1992 was the "Ill Wind" Pentagon weapons-procurement scandal. A former deputy assistant Navy secretary, James E. Gaines, was convicted on March 6 of accepting gifts in exchange for providing classified documents to agents of defense contractors. United Technologies Corporation pleaded guilty to four felonies in August and agreed to pay $6-million in fines.

In a more celebrated case, federal prosecutors won a conviction of former Panamanian leader Manuel Antonio Noriega. Noriega was found guilty on April 9 in Miami, Fla., of racketeering, drug trafficking, and money laundering. On July 10, he was sentenced to 40 years in federal prison.

Treasury appointee investigated. On October 29, U.S. Treasurer Catalina V. Villalpando was placed on administrative leave while reportedly being investigated by the FBI for possible criminal violations of federal ethics laws. She was suspected of having accepted payments from a former employer while at the Treasury Department.

Aircraft crashes. Two major military aircraft development programs suffered setbacks in 1992. The only flying prototype of the F-22 advanced tactical fighter crashed and burned at Edwards Air Force Base in California on April 25, but with only minor injuries to the pilot. A crash in Virginia on July 20 destroyed the prototype of a controversial tilt-rotor aircraft sought by the Marines. Seven people were killed.

Frank Cormier and Margot Cormier

See also **Bush, George H. W.; Congress of the United States.** In *World Book,* see **United States, Government of the.**

Uruguay. See **Latin America.**

Utah. See **State government.**

Uzbekistan. See **Commonwealth of Independent States.**

Van Duyn, Mona (1921-), the winner of the 1991 Pulitzer Prize for poetry, was named the first woman poet laureate of the United States on June 14, 1992. In her poems, Van Duyn has often used everyday images to explore the ways in which love and art serve as strongholds of meaning for life.

Van Duyn was born on May 9, 1921, in Waterloo, Iowa. She graduated from what is now the University of Northern Iowa in Cedar Falls in 1942. In 1943, she received her master's degree from the University of Iowa in Iowa City and began working there as an instructor. From 1950 to 1967, she lectured at University College, the night school of Washington University in St. Louis, Mo. From 1947 to 1967, she was also poetry editor and copublisher of *Perspective: A Quarterly of Literature*, which she and her husband, Jarvis A. Thurston, founded. Since then, she has worked as a visiting professor or poet-in-residence at a number of universities and writers' workshops.

In addition to the Pulitzer Prize, Van Duyn has collected numerous other awards for her work. She won the Bollingen Prize in 1970 and in 1971 received the National Book Award for Poetry for *To See, To Take* (1970). Van Duyn's first collection of poetry, *Valentines to the Wide World*, appeared in 1959. Her other volumes include *A Time of Bees* (1964), *Bedtime Stories* (1972), *Merciful Disguises* (1973), *Letters from a Father and Other Poems* (1983), and the Pulitzer Prize-winning *Near Changes* (1990).

Barbara A. Mayes

Venezuelan troops loyal to President Carlos Andrés Pérez guard the capital city of Caracas after a failed coup attempt in February.

Venezuela. President Carlos Andrés Pérez weathered two attempted coups in 1992. Rebellious officers led both uprisings, the first on February 4 and the second on November 27.

The leader of the February coup attempt was 37-year-old Lieutenant Colonel Hugo Chavez Frías, whose paratroopers attempted to seize key locations in Caracas, the capital, and Valencia, 100 miles (160 kilometers) west of the capital. The fighting killed an estimated 78 people. The president escaped from the presidential palace through a secret tunnel.

In the November coup attempt, officers of Venezuela's air force, army, navy, and national guard tried to take control of the government. Leftist antigovernment groups also reportedly took part in the uprising. At least 230 people died in the fighting.

A large factor in the uprisings was the resentment many Venezuelans felt at perceived government corruption. Despite the nation's record earnings of $117-billion from oil exports since 1982, Venezuelan workers found it more difficult to afford cars and homes and to educate their children in 1992. In a late January poll, 81 per cent of Venezuelans said they had "little or no trust" in the government.

Nathan A. Haverstock

See also **Latin America** (Facts in brief table). In ***World Book,*** see **Venezuela.**

Vermont. See **State government.**

Vice President of the U.S. See **Quayle, Dan.**

Vietnam. The National Assembly, Vietnam's law-making body, adopted a new Constitution on April 15, 1992. The document recast the country's executive branch and fortified the market-oriented economic reforms undertaken in the mid-1980's. The Constitution said the Communist Party of Vietnam (CPV) was still "the leading force of the state and society." The new Constitution also allowed citizens to engage in private business and replaced the ruling Council of State with a president, who was given executive powers and became the commander in chief of the armed forces.

New executives. On September 23, the assembly elected as president General Le Duc Anh, a former defense minister and political conservative. Anh, the only candidate for the position, was expected to keep a tight rein on economic change. On September 24, the assembly reelected Vo Van Kiet, an economic reformer, as Council of Ministers chairman (prime minister). Both men were senior leaders of the CPV, which continued to be headed by Do Muoi.

Fighting corruption. In an unusual broadcast news conference after his reelection, Vo Van Kiet said the government was trying to fight the "very painful problem of corruption, smuggling, debauchery, and lavish spending." Vietnamese citizens were reportedly becoming very concerned about the need for bribes in order to get services from government workers.

Releasing detainees. Vietnam on April 30 freed the last South Vietnamese held in its reeducation camps. An estimated 100,000 military and civilian officials of South Vietnam had passed through the camps after the Vietnam War (1957-1975), when North Vietnam united the country under Communism. About 25 people were reportedly still in the camps in 1992.

Release of these prisoners had been demanded by the United States as a condition for dropping its economic embargo against Vietnam, in effect since 1975. In support of the move, the United States on April 29 announced a partial lifting of the embargo.

American MIA's. Vietnam in October 1992 revealed that during the summer it had handed over to the United States some 5,000 photographs of Americans killed during the Vietnam War. The pictures were expected to aid in the U.S. effort to resolve the fates of American soldiers reported as missing in action (MIA) in the war. Vietnam also said it would open all of its archives to U.S. investigators. For years, Vietnam had maintained that it had given the United States all the information it had concerning U.S. soldiers.

As thanks for the documents, U.S. President George Bush in October said the United States would increase its humanitarian aid to Vietnam. And in December, the Bush Administration further relaxed the U.S. economic embargo. Henry S. Bradsher

See also **Asia** (Facts in brief table). In ***World Book,*** see **Vietnam.**

Virginia. See **State government.**

Vital statistics. See **Census; Population.**

Washington, D.C. Former Mayor Marion S. Barry, Jr., who was convicted of cocaine possession in 1990, completed his six-month sentence in federal prison on April 23, 1992. After his release, Barry returned to Washington, D.C., accompanied by a caravan of about 300 supporters on six tour buses. He moved into an apartment in Ward 8, the poorest area of the city, and announced his candidacy for the City Council.

In the Washington, D.C., Democratic primary on September 15, Barry defeated long-time City Council member Wilhelmina J. Rolark for a place on the November 3 ballot. In November, Barry was elected with 90 per cent of the vote to serve a four-year term on the council.

Among other winners in the November balloting was Eleanor Holmes Norton, a Democrat, who was reelected as Washington, D.C.'s, delegate to the United States House of Representatives. Norton collected 85 per cent of the vote in holding on to her House seat.

Washington voters by a 2 to 1 margin also approved one of the strictest campaign finance laws in the country. The initiative limits campaign contributions for local races to $100 per person.

Death penalty. Despite a continuing high crime rate in the city and public concern about gun violence, Washington residents on November 3 overwhelmingly voted against reinstating the death penalty, outlawed in the District in 1981. The 1992 initiative would have created one of the broadest death penalty measures in the country, making most convicted murderers, including juveniles and mentally retarded people, eligible for the death sentence. The measure was ordered onto the ballot by Congress at the request of Senator Richard C. Shelby (D., Ala.) after one of his aides was killed outside his Washington home.

The order for the capital-punishment initiative was included in the fiscal 1993 appropriations bill for the District, which gets about one-fifth of its revenue from the federal government. In that bill, Congress also prevented the District from implementing a city-approved law allowing unmarried city workers to put their "domestic partners" on their health insurance, a measure backed primarily by the gay community.

Crime. In 1992, for the first time in five years, the number of murders committed in the District declined. By December 1, a total of 416 homicides had been reported, down from 449 at that time in 1991.

Despite the drop in the number of killings, crime was rampant in the District in 1992. *Carjackings* (holdups in which thieves force drivers to give up their vehicles, sometimes at gunpoint) became increasingly common throughout the area. Citing his frustration at being unable to stem the city's violence, Washington Police Chief Isaac Fulwood, Jr., announced his resignation on September 8.

In an effort to get tough on criminals, the City Council on February 4 unanimously approved a new bail law. The law allows anyone accused of committing a crime with a firearm to be held without bond until trial for up to 120 days, even if the person has no criminal record.

City furloughs. To help balance the city's $3.3-billion fiscal 1993 budget, Mayor Sharon Pratt Kelly in 1992 ordered one-day-a-month unpaid furloughs for most city workers. The first furlough, on October 23, kept children and teachers out of school and closed down city offices. Some analysts questioned the savings, pointing out that trash pickup had to be done the next day by employees who were paid overtime.

Football stadium. Jack Kent Cooke, owner of the Washington Redskins professional football team, reached agreement with the District government on December 7 to build a new 78,600-seat stadium for the team next to the old RFK Stadium. Cooke agreed to pay for and be the owner of the new stadium, which will be named for him. The city was to issue $46 million in bonds to pay for road and sewer construction. Earlier in the year, negotiations between Cooke and the city had broken down, and Cooke had announced that he would build a stadium across the Potomac River in Alexandria, Va. But intense opposition from Virginians caused him to abandon that plan.

Power outage. A massive power failure shut off electricity to most of downtown and Georgetown and to parts of the city's southeastern area for about two hours on January 6. The blackout snarled rush-hour traffic and silenced telephones. Sandra Evans

See also **City.** In ***World Book,*** see **Washington, D.C.**

Water. Southern Africa in 1992 experienced its worst drought of the 1900's. Meteorologists attributed the absence of rains to *El Niño,* a periodic warm ocean current in the Pacific Ocean that disrupts weather patterns worldwide. The drought worsened food-supply problems in the east African country of Somalia. (See also **Africa; Somalia.**)

U.S. water legislation. On Oct. 31, 1992, United States President George Bush signed a $2.4-billion water bill meant to make federal water policy more responsive to the needs of urban residents and the environment. The bill was also to finance projects in the West and Midwest, including dams, reservoirs, and pipelines for providing water to farms and cities.

The focus of the water bill was California's Central Valley Project (CVP), a network of 20 dams and 500 miles (800 kilometers) of waterways constituting the largest federally managed water system in the United States. The CVP, which opened in 1951, was built to bring inexpensive, taxpayer-subsidized water to the dry farmland of the Central Valley of California. However, during the state's ongoing 6-year-old drought, the CVP had come under increasing criticism for directing vast amounts of water to farmers while city dwellers endured water rationing. Moreover, the farmers' heavy use of water during the drought had resulted in environmental damage such as the decline of fish populations and the draining of wetlands.

The CVP reforms in the water bill included raising the prices on water to encourage conservation by farmers and diverting more than 10 per cent of the project's yearly water delivery back to rivers and wetlands. More important for California's urban areas, the legislation allowed farmers for the first time to sell their water allotments to cities at a profit in a newly created water market.

Environmental groups praised the legislation. But agricultural interests said farm output would suffer.

Water cutoff averted. On Feb. 14, 1992, the U.S. government announced that because of California's drought, the CVP did not have enough water to supply the 25,000 farms in the system. Consequently, some 7,000 farmers had their water supplies cut off entirely, and the remaining 18,000 lost from one-quarter to one-half of their normal allotment. The action marked the first time in the CVP's history that the government had completely cut off farmers.

However, as a result of heavy rains in February, the government on March 5 changed the orders. Officials said farms that had been cut off would instead receive 15 per cent of their normal water supply, and the other farms would receive additional water as well.

British drought. The worst drought in Western Europe in more than 200 years had a serious impact on the environment of Great Britain, as countless of the country's wetlands, ponds, and small streams dried up. In the past, the British landscape was dotted with small ponds, which served as a source of water for villagers and their livestock. But in the last 100 years, many such ponds have been filled in as a result of suburban development or neglect. The few remaining ponds were threatened by the drought.

New Chinese dam. China's parliament, the National People's Congress, in April approved the controversial Three Gorges Dam on the Yangtze River. The structure would be the largest of its kind in the world, with a planned height of more than 600 feet (180 meters). It would create a reservoir 350 miles (560 kilometers) long that would submerge the Three Gorges, an area of beautiful cliffs treasured by the Chinese. The dam would also threaten the habitat of a rare freshwater porpoise and force the relocation of 1.1 million Chinese. And opponents noted that the cost of the project was high, estimated in 1992 at about $11 billion and likely to be far higher by the project's end.

But proponents maintained that the dam, to be the world's largest source of hydroelectric power, would promote industry in China. Furthermore, the huge reservoir would allow the passage of heavy barges into central China.

Supporters also pointed out that the dam would save lives by helping provide flood control. The middle and lower reaches of the Yangtze River are devastated regularly by floods, such as those in July 1991 that resulted in the deaths of more than 2,000 people.

Iris Priestaf

In *World Book,* see **Water.**

Weather. The year 1992 began with the warmest winter on record in the contiguous United States, surpassing by nearly 1 Fahrenheit degree (0.5 Celsius degree) the previous record set in the winter of 1953-1954. Above-normal temperatures prevailed in every major region of the nation, and five Midwestern states recorded their warmest winter since observations began. Only in northern Maine did winter temperatures average below normal.

Farther east, below-normal temperatures were the rule. Gander, Canada, experienced its coldest February on record. One of the worst winter storms in decades occurred in Canada's Atlantic Provinces from Jan. 31 to Feb. 3, 1992. Pressure in the offshore storm center dropped to 962 millibars (28.41 inches) of mercury. Wind gusts reached 96 miles per hour (mph) (155 kilometers per hour [kph]), and snowfall at Moncton, Canada, totaled 63 inches (160 centimeters).

In some areas of the northwestern United States, the winter was one of the driest on record, but northern Mexico and the southern fringe of the United States experienced heavy rainfall. Texas and New Mexico had their wettest recorded winter. On January 17 and 18, a vigorous storm along the northern Gulf of Mexico brought one of the 10 heaviest snowfalls of the 1900's—up to 8 inches (20 centimeters)—to northern Texas and eastward to northern Georgia.

Heavy precipitation continued into much of the spring. In mid-May, a series of storms caused extensive

A jumble of crushed boats demonstrates the power with which Hurricane Andrew hit south Florida in late August.

flooding of the San Antonio and Guadalupe rivers. By the end of May, the city of San Antonio had accumulated more than 33 inches (84 centimeters) of rain, exceeding the city's normal yearly total.

Cool, wet summer. In contrast to the warm winter, the three midsummer months were the coolest since 1915 in the contiguous United States as a whole, and the third-coldest summer since recordkeeping began. The lowest temperatures were concentrated mainly in the east, however, with above-average temperatures prevailing in Nevada and the West Coast states. In the north-central states, the temperature for the season averaged up to 7 Fahrenheit degrees (4 Celsius degrees) below normal.

For the contiguous United States as a whole, it was also the wettest summer since 1941. Precipitation was more than 50 per cent greater than normal in the Southwest, Central Plains, and the Southeast.

Hurricane Andrew. The 1992 Atlantic hurricane season was slow to start. But on August 23, the year's first tropical storm, Andrew, suddenly intensified as it moved over the island of Eleuthera in the Bahamas with a 23-foot-high (7-meter-high) storm surge. Early the next morning, Andrew, now a hurricane, moved inland through a densely populated area south of downtown Miami. During the hurricane's four-hour trek across southern Florida, steady winds of an estimated 140 mph (225 kph) prevailed, with some gusts measured at 164 mph (264 kph). An estimated 72,000 homes, including mobile homes, were damaged or destroyed, and 200,000 people were left homeless. The estimated damage total of up to $20 billion made Andrew the costliest disaster in U.S. history.

After leaving Florida, the storm moved northwest across the Gulf of Mexico and made a second landfall in southwestern Louisiana during the late evening of August 25. Moving more slowly, the storm weakened quickly as it continued northward. After sending heavy rain and several tornadoes along its path, it finally died out in Pennsylvania.

Florida's well-executed evacuation plan helped keep the official death toll relatively low. Thirteen people were killed in Florida, and one person was killed in Louisiana. Perhaps as many as 39 people died either as a direct or indirect result of the storm.

Altogether, the Atlantic hurricane season produced only five storms. One of these, Danielle, lashed coastal areas with gales from Cape Hatteras, N.C., to eastern Pennsylvania on September 25 and 26.

Hurricane Iniki. Hawaiians on the island of Kauai had to cope with Hurricane Iniki, which roared across the Pacific on September 11 with 130-mph (209-kph) sustained winds. The storm left an estimated 8,000 of the island's 52,000 inhabitants homeless.

Typhoons. In 1992, the western third of the tropical Pacific Ocean had a record number of typhoons. Guam weathered six in three months. The first one, named Omar, struck on August 28, with winds up to 150 mph (240 kph), causing major damage to more than 75 per cent of the island's buildings. From October 9 to November 23, five more typhoons struck the island, but damage was less severe.

Hailstorms and tornadoes. On March 6, 1992, portions of Seminole County in central Florida were buried more than ankle deep in golfball-sized hailstones. Buildings and crops suffered $25 million in damage. On March 25, hail caused $60 million in damages to the nursery industry in the Orlando, Fla., area.

By December, there had been more confirmed tornado occurrences across the United States than in any previous year. In June, 399 tornadoes were sighted, a record for that month. From June 15 through 18, large hailstones, strong winds, and more than 200 tornadoes hit the area from the central and northern Plains eastward into the Appalachian Mountains.

November, usually a quiet month for tornado activity, brought 173 reports. Most of these occurred from November 20 to 24 in 12 states, including Mississippi, Georgia, North and South Carolina, Kentucky, and Tennessee. At least 25 people were killed.

Drought and floods. As 1992 began, California was experiencing its sixth winter in a row with below-normal rainfall. The snowpack in the Sierra Nevada, which feeds California's reservoirs as it melts throughout the year, was only 45 per cent of its normal size.

Then, from February 5 to 21, a series of heavy rains caused flooding and mud slides in several communities northwest of Los Angeles. Above-normal levels of precipitation continued through most of March. Nevertheless, for the 1991-1992 water season—which began on Oct. 1, 1991, and ended on Sept. 30, 1992—the total precipitation was only 90 per cent of normal, not enough to end the water shortage that had persisted since 1986. (See also **Water.**)

In Oregon, Washington, Idaho, and Nevada—where much smaller amounts of precipitation fell—the drought became extreme. Hawaii experienced drought conditions as well.

Every country in southern Africa was affected by the worst growing-season drought of the 1900's. Crop production was estimated to be only 60 per cent of the amount in 1991. In Zimbabwe, the hardest-hit area, rainfall was less than 20 per cent of normal. Thousands of cattle deaths were reported.

In mid-September 1992, heavy flooding reportedly killed 2,000 people in northern Pakistan and 500 people in India. About 1,800 villages in the Indian state of Punjab were reportedly washed away by tidal surges that rushed down rivers. Every river bridge and half the crops in the state of Jammu and Kashmir were reported to have been destroyed.

Record-breaking December storm. The worst east-coast winter storm in decades, and probably the worst ever in December, developed and stalled over northeastern Virginia on December 11. High winds and heavy snow caused 640,000 power outages in Pennsylvania. The snow accumulated to more than 36 inches (91 centimeters) in western Pennsylvania and the mountains of southern New England. Coastal areas in New Jersey and the New York metropolitan area were extensively flooded.

Trying to explain the weather. The warm winter of 1991-1992 in the United States fueled the ongoing debate about global warming, the theory that increasing levels of carbon dioxide in the atmosphere are causing Earth's average surface temperature to rise. As cold weather became entrenched in the eastern half of the United States, however, meteorologists focused their interest on the June 1991 eruption of Mount Pinatubo in the Philippines. The eruption had sent dust and gases high into the atmosphere, forming a cloud that circled the globe. Scientists believed that the cloud may have caused a temporary lowering of Earth's average temperature of about 1.8 Fahrenheit degrees (1 Celsius degree). This would not be enough to account for the low summer temperatures of 1992 in the United States and Canada, however.

The most likely cause of 1992's unusual weather patterns was the reappearance of El Niño, a vast area of warm water in the tropical Pacific Ocean that appears at irregular intervals of 2 to 12 years. Meteorologists believed that the droughts in Hawaii and southern Africa and the heavy precipitation along the southern fringe of the United States were by-products of an El Niño that appeared in November 1991.

Alfred K. Blackadar

See also **Disasters.** In *World Book*, see **Weather.**

Weightlifting. See **Sports.**

Welfare. The number of Americans living in poverty increased for the second straight year in 1991, the United States Bureau of the Census reported in September 1992. The tally showed 35.7 million impoverished Americans, up from 33.6 million in 1990. The 1991 figure was the highest since 1964, when the federal government under President Lyndon B. Johnson declared war on poverty. Poor Americans accounted for 14.2 per cent of the population in 1992, compared with 13.5 per cent in 1991.

A single individual was defined as poor in 1991 if he or she had an annual income of less than $6,932. For a family of four, the poverty line was $13,924.

Blacks had the highest poverty rate among ethnic groups—32.7 per cent. Meanwhile, the rate for Hispanics was 28.7 per cent; for Asians and Pacific islanders, 13.8 per cent; and for whites, 11.3 per cent.

Federal assistance. Of all impoverished Americans, 73 per cent received public assistance, according to a separate April 1992 report by the Census Bureau. The agency said the federal government spent $17 billion on the food stamp program in 1991 and $15 billion on welfare for the aged, blind, and disabled. An additional $53 billion in aid went to states and localities to help provide Medicaid for the poor, and $23 billion went to families with dependent children and to various social programs for children and the poor.

Welfare reform appraisal. A study released in April 1992 said federal legislation designed to move people off welfare and into jobs was showing promise. The legislation, the Family Support Act of 1988, requires every state to run a work, education, or training program for people on welfare.

The Manpower Demonstration Research Corporation, a nonprofit research group based in New York City, said that participants in a California welfare-to-work program called Greater Avenues for Independence (GAIN), which adopted the new federal guidelines in 1989, experienced a rise in earnings and a decline in welfare payments. The study found that one year after enrolling in GAIN, people on average earned 17 per cent more and received 5 per cent less in public aid than did people who had not joined.

However, federal officials in June 1992 said another aspect of the Family Support Act of 1988 was failing. The legislation guarantees child-care assistance to families for one year after parents leave welfare to go to work. The Congressional Budget Office had predicted that the law would help 280,000 children a month. But the U.S. Department of Health and Human Services said the aid had reached only 56,000 children a month by May 1992.

Frank Cormier and Margot Cormier

In *World Book,* see **Welfare.**

West Indies. See **Latin America.**
West Virginia. See **State government.**
Wisconsin. See **State government.**
Wyoming. See **State government.**

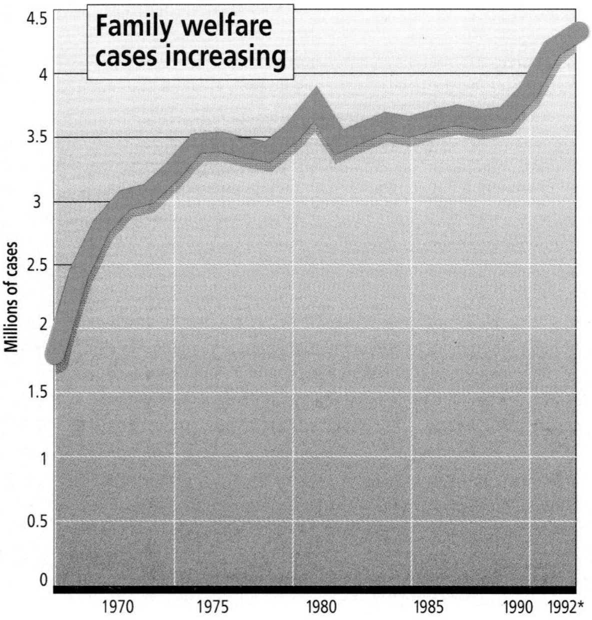

Family welfare cases increasing

Millions of cases: 0, 0.5, 1, 1.5, 2, 2.5, 3, 3.5, 4, 4.5

1970 1975 1980 1985 1990 1992*

*Projected.
Source: *1991 Green Book,* U.S. House Ways and Means Committee.

After showing little movement in the 1980's, the number of families receiving Aid to Families with Dependent Children rose to a record level in 1992.

Yamaguchi, Kristi (1971-), won the gold medal in women's figure skating at the 1992 Winter Olympics in February in Albertville, France. In doing so, Yamaguchi became the first American woman to win the Olympic gold in women's figure skating since Dorothy Hamill in 1976.

Yamaguchi was born on July 12, 1971, in Hayward, Calif. She began skating at the age of 5. A year after participating in her first competition at age 8, Yamaguchi began a rigorous training program, waking at 4 a.m. each day to practice with her singles coach.

In 1983, Yamaguchi added pairs skating to her regime, joining skater Rudi Galindo. In 1985, they finished fifth in the National Junior Championships. Yamaguchi and Galindo won first place in that championship in 1986. In 1988, she won gold medals at the World Junior Championships in both the singles and the pairs events.

Yamaguchi continued her medal-winning performances in 1989. She took first place in the pairs competition in the United States Championships and second place in the singles category.

Then, in 1990, Yamaguchi decided to concentrate solely on singles skating. In 1991, she won the singles title at the World Championships in Munich, Germany. In March 1992, she won her second consecutive world championship title, the first American woman to do so since Peggy Fleming in 1967 and 1968.

Kristine Portnoy Kelley

Serb protesters in June demand that President Slobodan Milošević resign. Many hold pictures of Prince Alexander, son of Yugoslavia's last king.

Yugoslavia. War continued to rage in what was once Yugoslavia as the country in 1992 completed its breakup into five separate states. The process had begun in June 1991, when the Yugoslav republics of Croatia and Slovenia declared their independence. Macedonia began to seek its independence in September 1991, and the republic of Bosnia and Hercegovina (commonly called simply Bosnia) declared independence in March 1992.

In January and February, the United Nations (UN) established a cease-fire in Croatia, where Yugoslav and Croatian forces had been fighting since July 1991. However, war erupted in Bosnia in March 1992, as ethnic Serbs in the new nation sought to establish a Serb state there. The Bosnian Serbs were supported by Serbia, the dominant republic of the two that remained in Yugoslavia. (The other was Montenegro.) Serbian President Slobodan Milošević, Yugoslavia's most powerful leader, was widely regarded as responsible for the war.

By year's end, Serb forces held 70 per cent of Bosnia's land. Croatian forces, formally allied to the Bosnian government, controlled some 20 per cent. Tens of thousands of people had died, and about 2 million—most belonging to Bosnia's Muslim ethnic group—had been forced from their homes. Most of the refugees were the victims of "ethnic cleansing"—mass expulsions designed to promote an ethnic partition of Bosnia. Witnesses also charged the Serbs with torturing ethnic Croats and Muslims held in detention camps and massacring Croat and Muslim villagers.

Serbia and Montenegro on April 27 proclaimed the establishment of a "new" country under the name Yugoslavia. The government said it had withdrawn from Bosnia all Yugoslav military forces who were citizens of Serbia or Montenegro as of May 30. But large numbers of federal troops remained in Bosnia.

Also on May 30, the UN Security Council imposed a trade and oil embargo on the new Yugoslavia. In August, analysts said the embargo, along with soaring inflation, was bringing the economy near collapse. But oil shipments and other goods continued to enter the country. On November 16, the Council authorized a naval blockade to help enforce the embargo.

On September 22, the UN General Assembly voted to expel the new Yugoslavia, which had assumed the seat of its predecessor.

On October 9, the UN banned Serbian flights over Bosnia. But at year's end, the UN and Western nations continued to debate authorizing the use of force to enforce the ban. The UN had in August authorized using force to protect convoys bringing food and medicine to beseiged areas of Bosnia, where it was feared thousands would die from cold, hunger, and disease.

Internal politics. Milošević came under increasing domestic criticism as the war and embargo continued. In May and June, thousands of Serbs demonstrated in Belgrade, Yugoslavia's capital, calling for his removal. Meanwhile, opposition parties boycotted parliamentary elections on May 31. The boycott helped Milošević's Socialist Party of Serbia (SPS) win a majority in both the Serbian and Yugoslav parliaments.

On July 14, the Yugoslav parliament confirmed Milan Panic, a Serb-born businessman and United States citizen, as prime minister. Panic had been nominated by Yugoslav President Dobrica Cosic, initially an ally of Milošević, who had taken office in June. Panic soon emerged as Milošević's chief rival. In August, he angered the SPS by supporting calls to end the partition of Bosnia and by vowing to close Serb-run detention camps there. Panic also favored restoring some self-government to Kosovo, a province in Serbia inhabited mainly by ethnic Albanians. In defiance of Serbian authorities, the province had on May 24 held underground parliamentary elections, in which an Albanian nationalist movement won a large majority.

On September 2, the SPS narrowly gave up an effort to oust Panic in a no-confidence vote. On November 3, Panic survived an attempted ouster by one vote.

On December 1, Panic announced he would oppose Milošević in December 20 elections for Serbia's presidency. Opinion polls had shown Panic to be Serbia's most popular politician. But a number of opposition candidates helped split the anti-Milošević vote, and Milošević was reelected. On December 29, Panic lost a no-confidence vote in parliament.

Eric Bourne

See also **Bosnia and Hercegovina; Croatia; Europe** (Facts in brief table). In ***World Book,*** see **Yugoslavia.**

Yukon Territory held a general election on Oct. 19, 1992, in which the New Democratic Party (NDP) government, led by Tony Penikett, was narrowly defeated for a third term in office. The Yukon Party, a new party drawn from the Progressive Conservatives, won 7 of the legislature's 17 seats. Six seats went to the NDP's, 1 to the Liberal Party, and 3 to independents. The new government was sworn in on November 7. The Yukon Party was led by a 56-year-old former outfitter, John Ostashek, who said he would call himself by the traditional title of "government leader" rather than "premier" as Penikett had done. In Canada, the title of premier is reserved for heads of provinces, not territories.

The Yukon Party benefited from an antigovernment mood among voters, a slow economy, and the impression that the former NDP government was not listening to the people. Penikett was also criticized for spending too much time out of the Yukon.

Celebrations were held during the year to mark the 50th anniversary of construction of the 1,500-mile (2,400-kilometer) Alaska Highway, built to ensure the defense of Alaska in World War II (1939-1945). Starting in British Columbia, running through the Yukon, and terminating in Delta Junction, Alaska, the road was finished in about eight months in 1942 and represented one of the greatest engineering feats of the day. David M. L. Farr

In ***World Book,*** see **Yukon Territory.**

Zaire. A political crisis that began in 1990 when opposition leaders demanded that Zaire's President Mobutu Sese Seko allow multiparty democracy persisted through 1992. But during the year, opposition leaders formed a transitional government.

Zaire had been disrupted by antigovernment violence in late 1991, and 1992 brought more of the same. On Jan. 22, 1992, a group of rebel soldiers attempted a coup but were defeated the next day by loyal troops. And on February 16, government troops fired on a group of Christian youths who were demonstrating against Mobutu, killing at least 13.

Partly as a result of the political instability, the nation's ailing economy continued its decline. Mineral production, the mainstay of the economy, decreased by 50 per cent in 1992. Inflation had risen to an estimated 23,000 per cent by April.

Under pressure from the United States, Belgium, and France—Mobutu's strongest allies—the president on April 14 reconvened a conference that had met briefly before to plan for multiparty democracy. In August, the conferees elected Etienne Tshisekedi, Mobutu's most prominent opponent, as prime minister of a transitional government. That government's powers were yet to be tested in late 1992. The other government—Mobutu's—still controlled the army, the bureaucracy, and the treasury. Mark DeLancey

See also **Africa** (Facts in brief table). In ***World Book,*** see **Zaire.**

Zambia. President Frederick Chiluba, who was elected in October 1991 on a promise to reintroduce a free-market economy in Zambia, took strong action in 1992 to make good on that pledge. Chiluba fired corrupt government officials, took steps to privatize government-owned enterprises, and encouraged foreign investment in Zambia. The World Bank, a United Nations agency, and a number of major industrial nations were impressed with Chiluba's actions. Foreign aid and investments flowed into the country.

But the government measures to reorganize the economy produced hardships for many Zambians. Many jobs were lost, and the price of food and other commodities rose. To make matters worse, the most severe drought on the continent in this century struck southern Africa in 1992. The drought destroyed much of Zambia's corn crop and made it necessary for the government to import food. Funds that had been earmarked for restructuring the economy had to be used instead to pay for those imports.

As troubles mounted, so did Zambians' discontent with the Chiluba administration. Sensing the nation's angry mood, former President Kenneth Kaunda began agitating against Chiluba. At year-end, it was not clear whether Zambia's democracy would be able to survive the rising tensions. Mark DeLancey

See also **Africa** (Facts in brief table). In ***World Book,*** see **Zambia.**

Zimbabwe. See **Africa.**

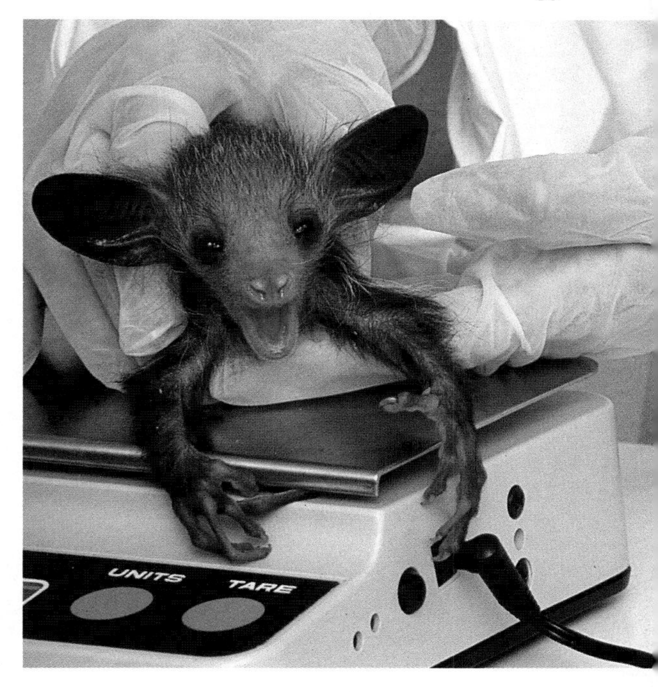

A 5-ounce (142-gram) aye-aye, the first to be born in the Western Hemisphere, weighed in on April 5 at Duke University Primate Center in Durham, N.C.

Zoology. An octopus can learn by imitating another octopus, according to an April 1992 report by Italian biologists at the Zoological Station of Naples. The biologists trained one group of octopuses to attack a red ball and a second group to attack a white ball. Then, each group performed the task four times in front of an untrained group. When the scientists threw a ball to an untrained octopus, it attacked the same color ball as was attacked by the octopuses it had been observing. Biologists have thought that only social vertebrates, such as dolphins or human beings, were capable of learning by observation. Octopuses are solitary animals, whose parents usually die after the young hatch. Some scientists suggest that, because the octopus cannot rely on parents to teach it survival skills, it developed observation skills to learn how to avoid predators.

Squealing stallions. A wild stallion can determine if a rival stallion is more dominant, not by fighting, but by listening to the rival's shrill squeals, reported *ethologists* (scientists who study animal behavior) from Princeton University in Princeton, N.J., in May. They studied wild horses living on an island off the coast of North Carolina and observed that the call of a dominant stallion lasted about 20 per cent longer than the call of a subordinate stallion. Apparently, the researchers said, a long call indicates large lung capacity and strong neck muscles, which translate into a lot of stamina for fighting a rival.

The ethologists also found that a stallion sniffed the dung of a newcomer twice as long as that of a familiar male. This behavior seemed to convey information about the newcomer's territory. If the dung of a new and dominant stallion is prevalent in an area, he will probably fight to keep this territory.

Thirsty spiders. Even though making a web is hard work, some spiders eat and then rebuild their webs every day. The reason for this is that they are thirsty, British biologists at the University of Oxford in England reported in May. They studied the chemical makeup of webs of the garden-cross spider and discovered these webs take up water from air. The silk is coated with molecules that soak up moisture and provide the spider with 10 per cent of its daily water intake, which it needs to keep its lungs damp. Water also helps make the web stickier for entangling prey.

Hazardous homes. A bird called a lapwing builds its nest in the middle of a farm field even though nests are routinely destroyed when farmers plow. But wildlife ecologist Ake Berg and his colleagues from the University of Agricultural Sciences in Uppsala, Sweden, reported in August that when lapwings nest on the ground near trees, crows and other birds were likely to eat lapwing eggs. Berg found that the birds in the farm fields have time to build a second nest after the plowing, and most are then successful at raising young. Elizabeth Pennisi

In ***World Book,*** see **Zoology.**

Zoos and aquariums in the United States opened an array of facilities in 1992 that simulated the wild habitats of the animals in the exhibits. And four new aquariums featured water life found in the geographic region in which the aquarium was located.

The New Jersey State Aquarium in Camden opened on February 29 with a centerpiece exhibit called Open Ocean, a 760,000-gallon (2.9-million-liter) exhibit that is the second-largest indoor tank in America. Open Ocean holds 400 fish of 40 species, including several types of shark, striped bass, and cownose rays, a species related to sharks. The giant tank provides visitors with several different viewpoints, largest of which is the Edge of the Abyss, a replica of the Hudson Canyon, an underwater region of the continental shelf off the New Jersey coast. Periodically, human divers appear within the exhibit and answer visitors' questions via an underwater microphone system.

Other habitats represented include a barrier beach, a pine barrens pond and stream, and pilings beneath a boardwalk. Outdoors, visitors can see a shoreline habitat where gray and harbor seals swim in machine-made waves. Altogether, the aquarium's 47 exhibits of nearly 2,600 animals feature 175 species.

The Tennessee Aquarium opened on May 1 in Chattanooga, featuring wildlife and habitats found along the Tennessee River. It is the world's first major aquarium devoted to freshwater environments. The aquarium's first gallery, Appalachian Cove Forest, is a habitat that simulates the Tennessee River's mountain source surrounded by a living hardwood forest, home to 20 species of birds, all allowed to fly freely. Here also are a series of shallow streams and deep sinks, filled with a variety of fish usually found in such water, and a pool for river otters.

Another gallery presents displays of the Tennessee River before and after it was dammed for flood control. The Mississippi Delta gallery reproduces a cypress swamp with alligators, snapping turtles, and fish. The Gulf of Mexico gallery, the aquarium's only saltwater display, contains more than 40 fish species found in that body of water.

The Oregon Coast Aquarium opened on May 25 in Newport. Large outdoor exhibits simulated coastal habitats, such as rocky pools and beaches, that are inhabited by harbor seals, sea lions, and sea otters. An undersea coastal cave is home to a giant octopus of the Pacific Ocean, the largest species of octopus in the world. And tufted puffins, rhinoceros auklets, pigeon guillemots, common murres, and sea ducks populate the tall, weathered "cliffs" and ocean "shore" in America's largest walk-through seabird aviary. Galleries display coastal habitats: a salt marsh; a rocky shoreline with a sandy beach washed by machine-made waves; and a deepwater environment, featuring a forest of giant seaweed called kelp.

The Scripps Institution of Oceanography, a division of the University of California, San Diego, opened its new aquarium-museum in September. The aquarium focuses on ocean life off southern California and in the Sea of Cortéz (the Gulf of California) along Mexico's Baja Peninsula. The centerpiece of the 34 exhibits is a 70,000-gallon (265,000-liter) tank containing a kelp forest that sways with the surges of an underwater wave machine. A video display operated by visitors provides close-up views of the fish and *invertebrates* (animals without backbones) that live there. Other displays depict life on coral reefs and islands and in deep ocean canyons and undersea caves.

Carnivores galore. On April 24, the Philadelphia Zoo opened Carnivore Kingdom, an exhibit of *carnivores* (animals that eat flesh) in a variety of naturalistic environments. North American river otters, for example, are at home in a marshy setting where visitors can observe their playful behavior both above and below the surface of a pool. Other carnivores in the exhibit include jaguars; snow leopards; *coatimundis* (members of the raccoon family); *jaguarundis* (small wildcats); and giant monitor lizards.

Marine World Africa USA in Vallejo, Calif., held a premiere on May 23 for its new exhibit complex called Shark Experience. The focal point of the exhibit is a 300,000-gallon (1.1-million-liter) tank called Deep Reef Habitat. The habitat captures the look of a coral reef found at the edge of a continental shelf. Visitors explore underwater depths from a moving walkway that carries them through a clear acrylic tunnel 60 feet (18 meters) in length. From the tunnel, visitors see 60 sharks representing 13 tropical and cold-water species, including some monster-sized sharks, and two species of rays, which are related to the shark.

Rain forests now thrive in the Henry Doorly Zoo in Omaha, Nebr. The zoo opened Lied Jungle, the world's largest indoor exhibit on rain forests, on April 4. Giant fig trees, palms, and bamboo grow in a structure eight stories tall that is divided into three areas representing rain forests found in Asia, Africa, and South America. Visitors follow an elevated walkway through the tree canopy to see primates, such as gibbons and several monkey species. Below are small-clawed otters, pygmy hippos, crocodilians called false gavials, and other aquatic animals in streams and ponds. At the end of the South American exhibit, visitors descend to the jungle floor, where, surrounded by giant trees, cliffs, and eight roaring waterfalls, they can view the aquatic animals underwater.

The National Zoological Park in Washington, D.C., opened the Amazonia exhibit in November. More than 1,700 tropical plants of 358 species flourish as a natural habitat for some 100 animal species, 60 per cent of them aquatic. After passing a waterfall at the entrance, visitors go "underwater" to see a sample of the diversity of life found in the Amazon River itself. In addition to piranhas, electric eels, and freshwater stingrays, there are frogs, turtles, and lizards, such as iguanas. Monkeys, toucans, and parrots move freely throughout the trees. Eugene J. Walter, Jr.

In *World Book,* see **Zoo.**

DICTIONARY SUPPLEMENT

spe·cies·cape
twin·kie
de·tox
na·no·tech·nol·o·gy
closed·loop
fragile X syndrome
Roll·er·blade
buck·y·ball
hy·per·me·di·a
bi·o·di·ver·si·ty
he·li·o·seis·mol·o·gy
vid·e·og·ra·pher

A list of new words added to the 1993 edition of **The World Book Dictionary** because they have been used enough to become a permanent part of our ever-changing language.

A a

a|ble|ism (ā′bəl iz′əm), *n.* discrimination favoring those who are physically or mentally fit: *The trustees are committed to diversity . . . [and] talked about ableism* (Bryn Mawr Now).

acid fog, fog containing a high concentration of acidity, resulting from pollutants emitted into the atmosphere: *The United Nations environment programme listed five growing threats: blooms of algae . . . acid fog (100 times more acidic than acid rain)* (The Economist).

action plan, a plan to alleviate an undesirable environmental, occupational, or social condition: *Students develop action plans and responses that individuals and groups can choose to enact* (Joyce Miller).

an|ti|lock brakes (an′tē lok′) a system of brakes on a motor vehicle that prevents loss of traction while braking, especially on an icy or wet road surface. A computer adjusts brake pressure on the wheels to keep them from locking into one position, causing the vehicle to skid. *Although antilock brakes are of most benefit on slick roads, they can also provide an advantage in normal driving conditions* (Don Schroeder).

anxiety attack, **1** = panic attack. **2** intense concern: *The pennant-race parts are in place now and anxiety attacks are breaking out in Boston* (Toronto Star).

B b

bi|o|di|ver|si|ty (bī′ō də vėr′sə tē, -dī-), *n.* variety that exists among different types of animals and plants, including the differences in species and gene pools within a species, especially as they affect the preservation of plant and animal types: *Man cannot manage nature through a series of ad hoc rescue attempts, ignoring the underlying causes for the loss of biodiversity* (Time).

birth mother, a woman who gives birth to her own genetically related child, as opposed to a surrogate gestational mother who gives birth to a child from an implanted fertilized egg: *The pregnant woman (the "birth mother") . . . and her sexual partner choose the prospective adopters (the "adoptive parents")* (New Yorker).

brain bleed, a hemorrhage in the brain: *His son . . . born at 28 weeks gestation weighing 2½ pounds, had a major brain bleed* (New York Times).

buck|y|ball (buk′ē bôl′), *n. Chemistry.* a highly stable molecule consisting of sixty carbon atoms arranged as interlocking pentagons and hexagons: *The molecular structure of buckyballs is so radically different that researchers hope this third form of carbon will lead to a whole new class of materials with multiple uses* (Time). [American English < *Buck(minster)* Fuller, 1895-1983, an American designer who developed the geodesic dome, which this molecule resembles in structure + *ball*]

C c

closed-loop (klōzd′lüp′), *adj.* **1** *Electronics.* of or having to do with a feedback loop. **2** of or having to do with something that can be processed and used again for the same purpose or in the same way as it was originally used: *In the future one plastic will not necessarily have an advantage over another as a result of "closed-loop" recyclability* (Chemical Marketing Reporter).

D d

de|fin|ing moment (di fīn′ing), a particular time when some issue, policy, action, or the like, becomes clear or is made specific: *"It's a defining moment politically . . . he's going to be talking to 50 million plus Americans, and I think he has to define what he's about* (New York Times Magazine).

des|ig|nat|ed driver (dez′ig nā′tid), a person who agrees not to drink alcoholic beverages at a social gathering in order to be fit to drive for others: *There will be temptations to grab a beer every now and then, he says, "but it's out of the question . . . Now I can be the designated driver"* (San Francisco Chronicle).

de|tox (*n.* dē′toks; *v.* di toks′), *n., v.*
—*n.* treatment to remove toxins, especially drugs, from the body; detoxification: *"Detox" from drugs—whether in a hospital or other drug treatment facility—is only the beginning of recovery* (Dianne Hales).
—*v.t., v.i.* = detoxify.

E e

energy belt or **Energy Belt**, *U.S.* a region where there is a plentiful, and usually inexpensive, supply of fuel, such as oil, natural gas, or coal, to produce energy: *The energy belt states are becoming saturated with malls* (Fortune).

engineered wood, a light, strong, structural building material usually made from laminated wood products similar to plywood, and used in construction to replace conventional lumber: *Some of these [building] details are unlikely to be called for on every project, but they show the versatility of engineered wood* (Fine Home Building).

environmental terrorism, **1** the act or practice of engaging in sabotage of polluters of the environment or in civil disobedience to further an environmental cause: *[The corporation] a major Oregon lumberer, labeled the spiking tactics [of live trees] "environmental terrorism"* (Maclean's). **2** the act or practice of engaging in sabotage that damages the environment in order to gain a political objective.

F f

family leave, a leave of absence given to an employee because of illness or some other problem in the family: *Three states, Connecticut, Wisconsin, and Maine, allow family leave as well as extended medical leave for employees* (New York Times).

fragile X syndrome, a common form of inherited mental retardation, believed to be related to a defective gene on the X chromosome: *A clue to the unusual inheritance pattern of fragile X syndrome was provided by researchers . . . [who] found that the DNA fragment that is prone to breaking away from the X chromosome is longer in people with the syndrome than those without it* (J.D. McInerney).

G g

global warming, the gradual warming of the earth's atmosphere caused by concentration of gases, especially carbon dioxide, that absorb heat from the sun: *Scientists were warning that continued release of carbon dioxide from burning large amounts of fossil fuels could cause a global warming* (Rod Such).

H h

HDTV (no periods), high-definition television (a system of television transmission that displays a very sharp image using a high density of picture elements that are converted from digital form by a television set equipped with a microprocessor): *An American company announced it had developed a system that can send HDTV signals over a standard television channel in digital form* (Donald Cunningham).

heat island, an area of higher temperature averages than the surrounding area: *Cities form heat islands, a phenomenon reported as long ago as 1833* (Joseph Wallace).

he|li|o|seis|mol|o|gy (hē′lē ō sīz mol′ə jē, -sīs-), *n.* the study of the waves in the sun's atmosphere: *The study of the waves, known as helioseismology, has revealed variations in temperature, density, and chemical composition in the sun's interior* (Robert W. Noyes). —**he′li|o|seis|mol′o|gist**, *n.*

hy|per|me|di|a (hī′pər mē′dē ə), *n.* a system of information storage in a computer memory that includes different forms of data, such as a text, video images, sound recordings, and graphics: *[It] gave rise to a rapidly growing field of software called hypermedia, which makes use of a number of media to present data* (Keith Ferrell).

J j

juice box, a paper container that holds a single portion of juice: *Mother Goose in one hand and a leaky juice box in the other, I begin the sad, infuriating task shared by all modern mothers* (Time).

K k

key|board|ist (kē′bôr′dist, -bōr-), *n.* a person who plays an electronic or acoustic keyboard instrument: *"Touring is second nature to us, kind of automatic," explains Andrew Farriss, 30, the keyboardist and songwriter of the band* (Time).

Pronunciation Key: hat, āge, cãre, fär; let, ēqual, tėrm; it, īce; hot, ōpen, ôrder; **oi**l, **ou**t; cup, pu̇t, rüle; **ch**ild; lo**ng**; **th**in; **ᴛʜ**en; **zh**, measure; **ə** represents **a** in about, **e** in taken, **i** in pencil, **o** in lemon, **u** in circus.

L l

lam|i|nat|ed-ve|neer lumber (lam′ə nā′tid və nir′), lumber made from thin layers of wood held together with very strong, waterproof glue: *In laminated-veneer lumber, the grain of each layer of veneer runs in the same direction* (Fine Home Building). *Abbr:* LVL

lap pool, a shallow pool designed for swimming laps, sometimes with the water flowing in a current to swim against: *The two decided to build an indoor pool—not a big showcase pool, but a serious lap pool* (Washington Post).

M m

mi|cro|ac|tu|a|tor (mī′krō ak′chü ā tər), *n.* an extremely small device that sets a mechanical process in motion: *A microactuator . . . is one of many micromachines that release an automobile's airbag* (Doug Stewart).

mi|cro|ma|chine (mi′krō mə shēn′), *n.* a device made of extremely small parts: *Another possibility is to build somewhat bigger micromachines, ones that are perhaps 20 times the width of a human hair* (World Book Science Year).

mind map, a chart or diagram made to organize plans, ideas, or the like: *Mind maps can be used for almost anything—from planning the day, to taking notes, to organizing a presentation or simply exploring one's own thoughts* (PC Week).

mood swing, a change, often occurring suddenly, in a person's state of mind, especially as a symptom of a nervous disorder or as a reaction to a drug or medication: *Psychic derangements may appear when corticosteroids are used, ranging from euphoria, insomnia, mood swings, personality changes, and severe depression* (Upjohn Drug Extract).

N n

na|no|tech|nol|o|gy (nā′nō tek nol′ə jē), *n.* the techniques, machines, tools, and processes needed to manipulate matter the size of atoms and molecules: *Their* [*researchers'*] *territory is the realm of individual atoms and molecules . . . This infant discipline is known as nanotechnology* (Ivan Amato).

ne|o-com|mu|nism or **ne|o-Com|mu|nism** (nē′o kom′ye niz əm), *n.* a form of communism that advocates less centralized government and accepts the political role of opposition parties, developed in response to the economic and political failure of traditional communism: *Neo-communism may turn out to be a healthy development as long as the party continues to shed its pretensions of monopoly power* (Stephen Handelman).

O o

oil shock or **oil|shock** (oil′shok′), *n.* the economic effects of an acute shortage in the supply of oil: *"The economy is now on a weaker growth path . . . partly, but not exclusively, because of the oil shock," said . . .* [*the*] *chairman of the President's Council of Economic Advisors* (New York Times).

P p

palliative care, medical treatment that emphasizes a patient's comfort through relief of symptoms and pain, rather than concentration on a cure: *Physicians historically haven't been well trained in palliative care and symptom management* (Paul Galloway).

palm|top (päm′top′, pälm′-), *n.* a portable computer small enough to fit the hand: *If the palmtops come with a Japanese name on the box, they could also mark the end of an era for this region* [*Silicon Valley*] (New York Times).

R r

respite care, temporary care of someone who needs constant attention because of grave illness or physical incapacity, in order to give the usual attendants time off: *Another especially important job is respite care—sitting for a few hours at a dying patient's bedside to give family members a break from an emotionally draining vigil* (World Book Health and Medical Annual).

ri|bo|zyme (rī′bə zīm, -zim), *n.* a segment of RNA that acts as an enzyme by causing chemical reactions in a cell without being changed or consumed in the process: [*Sidney Altman*] *was able to establish certain catalytic RNA segments that became known as ribozymes* (G.A. Cheney). [< *ribo*(nucleic) acid + (en)*zyme*]

road kill or **road|kill** (rōd′kil′), *n.* **1** an animal accidentally killed on a road or highway: *When Harris' students study animals, they dissect and skin road kills* (M.C. Franklin). **2** something left over or discarded; waste: *But what if the borrowed stuff* [*writing*] *is a flat, lifeless mess—the road kill of passing ideas?* (Time).

Roll|er|blade (rō′lər blād′), *n., v.,* **-blad|ed, -blad|ing.** *Trademark.* **—*n.*** a roller skate with wheels arranged in a line; blade: *Last Christmas my son, Josh, asked for a pair of Rollerblades, those skates . . . built to go fast and look cool* (Esquire).
—*v.i.* to skate on Rollerblades: *Mercer Street brims with life—an artist sketching . . . children Rollerblading curbside* (New York Times). **—Roll|er|blad′er**, *n.*

S s

spe|cies|cape (spē′shēz skāp′), *n.* **1** a chart in which the size an animal is drawn reflects known population or number of kinds of a species: *In . . . a speciescape . . . the giant beetle represents insects, the largest group . . . The tiny elephant stands for the 4,000 mammals, including people* (New York Times). **2** the known population of a species in a given area.

sub|men|u or **sub-men|u** (sub men′yü, -mā′nyü), *n.* a list of options in a computer program that are available under a larger category of functions: *Now, the menu has a single Helvetica listing—a type family . . . and an arrow that indicates a submenu* (New York Times).

suicide machine, an apparatus consisting of hypodermic syringes, one of which contains a self-administered lethal dose of a drug, taken by a patient who is terminally ill: *His homemade suicide machine . . . Kervorkian's spooky Rube Goldberg contraption, rigged up in the back of his VW van, that enabled* [*the patient*] *to dispatch herself* (Tina Brown).

T t

tax|ol (tak′sôl), *n.* a drug extracted from the bark of the Pacific yew tree, used to treat certain kinds of cancer: *Taxol has drawn great interest because of its success as an experimental treatment for ovarian tumors and, more recently, lung and breast cancers* (Science News).

twin|kie (twing′kē), *adj.* giving only immediate satisfaction; not long lasting: [*The candidate*] *would offer more help for business in order to rejuvenate the nation's industrial base. He rejects a middle-class tax cut as "Twinkie economics"* (New Yorker). [from the brand name for a mass-produced cupcake]

U u

un|de|lete or **un-de|lete** (un′di lēt′), *v.,* **-let|ed, -let|ing,** *adj.* **—*v.t., v.i.*** to restore data previously taken out of a computer field or file; reinsert: *To move a block of text, you actually have to delete the block and then "undelete" it in the new location* (M.S. Zachmann).
—*adj.* restored or able to be restored: *A good editor* [*program*] *will have some sort of "undelete" operation* (Byte).

urban forest, the trees in an urban environment, including trees along streets and in parks: *The likelihood of creating a healthy urban forest is enhanced when a city has a formal plan for planting and maintenance* (World Book Science Year).

V v

vid|e|og|ra|pher (vid′ē og′rə fər), *n.* a person who uses a video camera to record images and sound on videotape: *Sharp showed a tiny color monitor . . . that attaches to a video camera, allowing amateur videographers to watch their work* (Newsweek).

W w

white-knuck|le (hwīt′nuk′əl), *adj.* filled with tension or fear as if to make one clench one's fists; trying; frightening: *And for those in the area who have been told they will be laid off, or fear they will be, it is white-knuckle time* (New York Times).

wobble motor, a device with rotors designed to wobble as they spin in order to reduce the effects of friction and increase rotational force: *Wobble motors would be better suited than other kinds of micromotors for controlling the movements of the tiny robotic machines* (Ivan Amato).

1992

WORLD BOOK SUPPLEMENT

See page 550

To help **World Book** owners keep their encyclopedias up to date, the following articles are reprinted from the 1993 edition of the encyclopedia.

© Robert Kusel, Sipa Press

© Michael Evans, Sygma

Clinton, Bill (1946-), was elected President of the United States in 1992. Clinton, a Democrat, won the presidential election while serving his fifth term as governor of Arkansas. In the election, he defeated President George Bush, his Republican opponent, and Ross Perot, a Texas businessman who ran as an independent.

Clinton took office at a time when the nation's attention had shifted sharply from foreign affairs to domestic issues. The years before his election had seen a series of turbulent world events, including the end of the Cold War struggle between the United States and the Soviet Union, and—in 1991—the breakup of the Soviet Union itself. By 1992, Americans were troubled chiefly by fears about their country's economic health. The unemployment rate had climbed to the highest level since 1984. Many people were concerned about what they saw as a decline in U.S. productivity compared with that of other nations. Another concern involved the federal government's policy of *deficit spending,* or borrowing to finance expenditures, which over the years had resulted in a large national debt. In addition, Americans had become increasingly frustrated over signs of growing racial conflict, crime, and poverty, especially in the nation's cities.

During his campaign, Clinton argued that he was the best candidate to solve the country's economic and social problems. He promised to reduce the need for deficit spending and to expand the educational and economic opportunities of poor and middle-class Americans. Clinton's positions included both traditionally liberal and traditionally conservative ideas. He once declared, "The change I seek . . . isn't liberal or conservative. It's different and it's both."

Clinton, who was 46 when he took office, was the third youngest person ever to serve as President, after Theodore Roosevelt and John F. Kennedy. In 1978, Clinton had become one of the youngest Americans ever elected as a governor, when he won that office in Arkansas at the age of 32. Clinton was a skillful public speaker known for his ability to seize the attention of a wide variety of audiences. His hobbies included reading, solving crossword puzzles, and playing the tenor saxophone. Clinton also enjoyed jogging and playing golf.

Ernest C. Dumas, the contributor of this article, is a political columnist for The Arkansas Times *and Journalist in Residence at the University of Central Arkansas.*

Early life

Boyhood. Clinton was born on Aug. 19, 1946, in Hope, Ark. His given and family name was William Jefferson Blythe IV. Clinton's parents were Virginia Cassidy Blythe (1923-) and William Jefferson Blythe III (1918-

Important dates in Clinton's life

1946 (Aug. 19) Born in Hope, Ark.

1968 Graduated from Georgetown University.

1968-1970 Attended Oxford University as Rhodes Scholar.

1973 Graduated from Yale Law School.

1975 (Oct. 11) Married Hillary Rodham.

1977-1978 Served as attorney general of Arkansas.

1979-1980 Served first term as governor of Arkansas.

1982 Again elected governor of Arkansas, and later reelected three more times. Held office until 1992.

1992 Elected President of the United States.

1946). His father, a traveling heavy-equipment salesman and former automobile dealer, was killed as a result of a car accident three months before Bill was born. Later, relatives and friends often told the boy how much he resembled his father, who was known for his good looks and lively personality.

During the first years of his life, young Bill—called Billy—lived with his mother and her parents in Hope. When the boy was about 2, his mother left him in the care of his grandparents for a year while she studied in New Orleans to become a nurse-anesthetist. When Billy was 4, his mother married Roger Clinton (1909-1967), a car dealer. The family lived for a time in Hope, then moved to Hot Springs, Ark., in 1953. There, Virginia and Roger Clinton had another son, Roger, Jr. (1956-). Billy began using his stepfather's last name while in elementary school. He formally changed his name to William Jefferson Clinton when he was 15.

Virginia Clinton had a strong influence on her older son. She cared deeply about the problems of people she met in her hospital work, and she and Bill often had long conversations about situations one or the other considered unfair. But Clinton's life at home was not easy. Roger Clinton, Sr., was an alcoholic who sometimes verbally or even physically abused his wife. At least once, Bill stood up to his stepfather to protect his mother. Clinton later said that his troubled family life made him skilled at solving disagreements and avoiding conflicts. Clinton grew close to his stepfather shortly before the older man died of cancer in 1967.

School life. In Hot Springs, Clinton attended a Roman Catholic school for two years before enrolling in public school. The Clintons, who were Baptists, sent their son to the smaller Catholic school to ease his move to the large public school system of Hot Springs. Young Bill enjoyed his schoolwork and earned good grades. In high school, he was active in a variety of clubs and held many offices. He also played tenor saxophone in the high school band, serving as band major during his senior year.

Clinton early showed an interest in—and a gift for—politics. As a schoolmate later recalled, Bill was always "running for something." Clinton became convinced he

Clinton Campaign Headquarters

Young Bill, shown at about the age of 5, spent his early childhood in the town of Hope, Ark. The boy resembled his father, who was killed in a car accident before Bill was born.

WORLD BOOK photo by Brian Dickerson

The Clinton home in Hope, Ark., became young Bill's home after his mother's second marriage when the boy was 4. The family moved to Hot Springs, Ark., a few years later.

Clinton Campaign Headquarters

Seventeen-year-old Clinton shakes hands with President John F. Kennedy, *above.* Clinton's meeting with Kennedy helped persuade the youth to pursue a political career.

would pursue a political career in 1963, when, at the age of 17, he met President John F. Kennedy. Clinton met Kennedy while visiting Washington, D.C., as a delegate to the American Legion Boys Nation, a citizenship training program in which young people form a model of national government.

College education. After graduating from high school in 1964, Clinton attended Georgetown University in Washington, D.C. In college, Clinton majored in international affairs. He studied hard and remained active in school life, serving as class president during his freshman and sophomore years. Between 1966 and 1968, Clinton helped pay his college expenses through a job with the Senate Foreign Relations Committee, then headed by Senator J. William Fulbright, an Arkansas Democrat.

Clinton had been strongly influenced by black Americans' fight for social justice during the civil rights movement of the 1950's and 1960's. In April 1968, the assassination of civil rights leader Martin Luther King, Jr., led to widespread rioting in Washington. Clinton and a friend worked as Red Cross volunteers during the rioting, bringing food and clothing to people whose homes had been burned. Clinton graduated from college a few months later.

Following his graduation, Clinton entered Oxford University in Oxford, England, as a Rhodes Scholar. He had won the scholarship during his senior year at Georgetown. Clinton remained at Oxford for two years.

Law school. Clinton entered Yale Law School in 1970, after leaving Oxford. He helped pay his expenses through a scholarship and by holding part-time jobs, sometimes three at a time.

From August to November 1972, Clinton worked in Texas as a state coordinator for the presidential campaign of Democratic nominee George S. McGovern. Clinton showed skill in managing the campaign, though McGovern failed to win the state's electoral votes in the election.

Clinton's family. At Yale, Clinton met fellow law student Hillary Rodham (Oct. 26, 1947-) of Park Ridge, Ill. Hillary and Bill began to date in 1971 and were married on Oct. 11, 1975. The couple had one child—a daughter, Chelsea (1980-). After the marriage, Hillary continued to pursue her own career as an attorney, eventually becoming one of the nation's most prominent lawyers. She also played an active role in public affairs. She remained known as Hillary Rodham until 1982, when she adopted her husband's last name.

Entry into politics

After receiving his law degree in 1973, Clinton returned to Arkansas. There, he took a position on the faculty of the University of Arkansas Law School in Fayetteville. Soon afterward, Clinton announced his intention to run for a seat in the U.S. House of Representatives. In 1974, Clinton became the Democratic nominee to represent Arkansas's Third Congressional District, which includes Fayetteville. Representative John Paul Hammerschmidt, a popular Republican, narrowly defeated Clinton in the general election.

In 1976, Clinton won the Democratic primary for attorney general of Arkansas. He ran unopposed in the general election and took office in January 1977. As attorney general, Clinton became known as a supporter of consumers' interests. For example, he opposed the construction by an Arkansas utility company of two large coal-burning power plants, demanding that the company promote efficiency and conservation instead. The plants were eventually built. Clinton also unsuccessfully fought several increases in utility rates.

Clinton became a candidate for governor of Arkansas

Allan Tannenbaum, Sygma

Clinton's family includes his wife, Hillary Rodham Clinton, and their daughter, Chelsea. *Above,* the Clintons wave to supporters at the Democratic National Convention in 1992.

Clinton Campaign Headquarters

Clinton entered politics in 1974, campaigning for a seat in the U.S. House of Representatives. Clinton won the Democratic primary, but he was narrowly defeated in the general election.

in early 1978, midway through his two-year term as attorney general. In his campaign, Clinton focused on a number of issues important to Arkansans, including the need for economic development and improvements in the state's educational system. He also promised to upgrade the state's road and highway network.

Clinton overwhelmed his four Democratic opponents in the primary, winning 60 per cent of the vote. He went on to easily defeat Republican Lynn Lowe in the general election. Clinton's impressive showing in the election, combined with his liberal policies and his youth, brought him his first national attention.

Governor of Arkansas, 1979-1980

Early difficulties. Clinton was inaugurated governor in January 1979. Once in office, he began efforts to establish a wide range of programs and policies. But he failed to gather broad support for these efforts, and most of them met with little success. To pay for a road improvement program, Clinton pushed through the legislature a measure increasing various fees and taxes, including motor vehicle license fees. Clinton had been elected partly on the basis of his campaign promise to upgrade the highways. But the increase in license fees was extremely unpopular, especially among poor, rural Arkansans. Clinton also came under attack by local leaders, who accused him of failing to attract industries to the state. In addition, the powerful wood-products industry—one of the state's largest employers—began working against Clinton because his administration had condemned the industry's timber-management practices, called *clearcutting.*

Reelection defeat. Clinton ran for reelection in 1980 against conservative Republican Frank D. White, a savings and loan executive. Despite the troubled nature of Clinton's first term, few political experts expected White to win. But White's campaign stressed Clinton's unpopular license fee increase. White also profited from a federal government decision to hold about 18,000 Cuban refugees temporarily at Fort Chaffee, then a military reserve training facility, near Fort Smith, Ark. In May and June 1980, discontent among the Cubans led to breakouts and rioting at the facility. White claimed that Clinton had not done enough to persuade President Jimmy Carter to hold the Cubans elsewhere. In the election, White gained 52 per cent of the vote to Clinton's 48 per cent.

Clinton was deeply affected by his defeat. He returned to private life, joining the law firm of Wright, Lindsey and Jennings in Little Rock, Ark. For the next year, he reviewed his actions as governor, trying to understand what personal and political weaknesses had caused him to lose the election. He also began planning to challenge White in the election of 1982.

Governor of Arkansas, 1983-1992

Return to office. In his 1982 campaign, Clinton worked to convince voters that he understood his mistakes, had matured, and had learned the importance of listening. He failed to win a majority of votes in the Democratic primary, but he won the nomination in a runoff against former Lieutenant Governor Joe Purcell. In the general election, Clinton defeated White by 55 per cent to 45 per cent of the vote.

© *Arkansas Democrat-Gazette* from Sipa Press

Clinton's inauguration as governor of Arkansas in 1983 marked his return to office after two years in private life. Clinton had been elected governor in 1978 but lost a reelection bid in 1980. He was elected to a total of five terms as governor.

Clinton returned to office in January 1983. During his second term, he worked to build a broad base of support for his policies. He abandoned some of the strongly liberal positions of his first term. In addition, Clinton decided to concentrate on two main problems—education and the economy—instead of a wide range of issues, as he had in his first term.

Clinton's opponents argued that his 1980 defeat had taught him to avoid taking stands or raising issues that might be unpopular. Nevertheless, Clinton was reelected in 1984 and again in 1986, each time by a wide margin. In 1984, Arkansas passed a constitutional amendment changing the governor's term of office from two years to four, beginning with the 1986 election. Clinton was elected to a fifth term in 1990.

Reforms in education. Beginning in 1983, Clinton set as his main goal the improvement of the Arkansas public school system. Arkansas had long ranked near the bottom of the states in many measures of educational achievement. For example, a smaller percentage of the state's adults had a college education than in nearly any other state. During his first term, Clinton had taken preliminary steps toward improving education in Arkansas. In one such move, he proposed a measure—passed into law in 1979—that required new teachers to pass a certifying examination before being allowed to teach.

In 1983, at Clinton's urging, the legislature passed a series of educational reforms. These reforms included a measure—the first of its kind in the nation—requiring

Clinton Campaign Headquarters

As governor, Clinton worked to improve education in Arkansas, which lagged behind other states in many measures of achievement. *Above,* Clinton studies a computer with a student.

that teachers pass a basic skills test to keep their jobs. The legislature passed the measure despite strong opposition from the Arkansas Education Association, an organization of Arkansas teachers. Other reforms increased the number of courses offered by Arkansas schools, reduced class sizes, and imposed a test for entry into high school. To pay for the 1983 reforms—and to raise teachers' salaries—the legislature approved an increase in the state sales tax.

Clinton continued to promote educational reform in the years following 1983. For example, under his leadership, Arkansas became the second state to establish a policy of open enrollment, allowing children to attend public schools outside their district. To raise college enrollment rates, the state offered scholarships to poor and middle-class students who demonstrated academic achievement in high school.

Economic developments. Arkansas has traditionally been a state with few major resources and an underdeveloped economy. It has relied heavily on low-skill, low-paying manufacturing jobs to employ its workers. Since the 1940's, the movement of industries to the Southern States has helped the Arkansas economy grow. But the state has had to struggle to compete for jobs with its more prosperous neighbors.

During his first term, Clinton had sought unsuccessfully to reduce the state's dependence on manufacturing jobs. After his reelection, he worked instead to broaden its industrial base. In 1985, at his urging, the legislature passed an economic package designed to attract businesses and capital to Arkansas. Clinton made special efforts to bring high-technology companies such as computer and electronics firms to the state. His actions helped Arkansas reduce unemployment and increase production in the late 1980's and early 1990's.

Steps to the presidency. Throughout his years as governor, Clinton played an active role in Democratic Party politics and in regional and national political life. For example, in 1985 and 1986, he served as chairman of the Southern Growth Policies Board. This organization, which then included 12 Southern states and Puerto Rico, works to help its members plan for rapid economic and population growth. Also in 1985, he was elected vice chairman of the National Governors' Association (NGA), made up of the governors of the 50 states and 5 U.S. territories. Clinton served as chairman of the NGA in 1986 and 1987. In 1990 and 1991, he headed the Democratic Leadership Council, an organization of moderate Democratic officeholders from all levels of government, as well as business and community members.

In 1987 and 1988, Clinton worked to obtain the support of Congress and President Ronald Reagan for the NGA's proposals on welfare reform. The proposals led to passage of the Family Support Act of 1988 (see **Welfare** [Recent developments in welfare programs]).

At the Democratic National Convention in 1988, Clinton gave the speech nominating Michael S. Dukakis as the party's candidate for President. Dukakis lost the election to Bush, then Vice President.

Election as President

The Democratic nomination. In October 1991, Clinton formally announced his candidacy for the Democratic nomination for President. His chief challengers for the nomination were former Massachusetts Senator Paul E. Tsongas and former California Governor Edmund G. Brown, Jr., known as Jerry. Clinton also faced opposition from Texas businessman Ross Perot. Perot, running as an independent, began a presidential campaign without formally declaring his candidacy.

For a time, Clinton's campaign faltered over charges of marital infidelity. The Clintons acknowledged that they had encountered some difficulties in their relationship, but they said their marriage was strong. Clinton also came under attack for his actions during the early 1970's, which, his opponents charged, showed that he had sought to evade military service during the Vietnam War (1957-1975). Clinton denied that he had acted improperly, and his campaign rapidly regained ground. Tsongas, an early front-runner, suspended his campaign for lack of funds in March 1992. Clinton had already seized a commanding lead over Brown, and he soon had enough delegates to ensure the nomination.

During the spring and early summer, opinion polls showed strong voter support for Perot. Voters liked Perot largely because of his status as an "outsider,"

Clinton's election

Place of nominating convention	New York City
Ballot on which nominated	1st
Opponents in general election	George H. W. Bush (Republican) Ross Perot (Independent)
Age at inauguration	46

The *table* in the article on **Electoral College** gives the electoral vote by states.

Running mates Clinton and Senator Al Gore of Tennessee, *left,* accepted the Democratic nomination for President and Vice President at the party's national convention in New York City in July 1992.

© Ira Wyman, Sygma

someone unconnected to the political life of Washington, D.C. Americans mistrusted Washington politicians because of their links to powerful interest groups. In addition, the capital had recently emerged from a series of scandals, including several involving misuse of official privileges. Clinton chose not to mount an active campaign against Perot. Instead, he worked to convince voters that, as a governor who had never served in Washington, he, too, was an "outsider." He also suggested that his Democratic Party ties would enable him—unlike Perot—to work with Congress and so achieve his goals as President.

At the Democratic National Convention in New York City in July 1992, Clinton was named the Democratic presidential nominee. At his request, Senator Al Gore of Tennessee was nominated for Vice President. The Republicans nominated President Bush and Vice President Dan Quayle to oppose Clinton and Gore.

The 1992 election. During the presidential campaign, Clinton took advantage of many Americans' perception of Bush as unconcerned about domestic issues. He also seized upon the widespread belief that the gap between rich and poor had grown under Bush and his predecessor, Ronald Reagan. Clinton promised to stimulate economic growth by encouraging business expansion in various ways, including tax breaks for new plants, new technology, and new small businesses. He also called for rebuilding the nation's transportation and communication networks and improving education. He proposed to raise the taxes of wealthy Americans to help reduce the federal budget *deficit* (shortage).

Bush, for his part, charged that Clinton lacked experience in foreign affairs. He also argued that the only effective way to stimulate the economy and reduce the deficit was to cut spending and lower taxes. Bush defended his record on the economy and other domestic issues, claiming that Congress—which was made up largely of Democrats—had refused to enact most of his proposals.

Perot had dropped his undeclared candidacy in mid-July, explaining that he had determined he could not win. However, at the beginning of October, Perot reentered the race, formally announcing his candidacy. He chose as his running mate Vice Admiral James B. Stockdale, a retired Navy officer.

Perot proposed to eliminate the federal budget deficit through, in part, a wide range of measures to lessen government spending and increase tax revenues. He also called for reducing certain taxes to encourage investment. In the election, Clinton defeated Bush and Perot. Ernest C. Dumas

See also **Democratic Party; Gore, Al; President of the United States.**

Outline

I. **Early life**
   A. Boyhood
   B. School life
   C. College education
   D. Law school
   E. Clinton's family

II. **Entry into politics**

III. **Governor of Arkansas, 1979-1980**
   A. Early difficulties
   B. Reelection defeat

IV. **Governor of Arkansas, 1983-1992**
   A. Return to office
   B. Reforms in education
   C. Economic developments
   D. Steps to the presidency

V. **Election as President**
   A. The Democratic nomination
   B. The 1992 election

Questions

What was Clinton's original name? How did he get the name Clinton?
What difficulties did Clinton encounter in his first term as governor? What issues were most important in his reelection defeat?
What were Americans' main concerns when Clinton became President?
How did Clinton work to improve education in Arkansas?
Why did young Clinton become skilled at avoiding conflicts?
When did Clinton become convinced he would pursue a political career?
How did Clinton build support for his policies after he won election for a second term as governor in 1982?
What factors have traditionally affected the Arkansas economy?
How did Clinton campaign against President George Bush in the 1992 presidential race?
How did Clinton first gain national attention?

Armenia is a country that lies in the Caucasus Mountain region. It became independent in 1991, after nearly 70 years as a part of the Soviet Union. Armenia is a member of the Commonwealth of Independent States, a loose association of former Soviet republics.

Armenia covers about 11,500 square miles (29,800 square kilometers) on the rugged, mountainous Armenian Plateau. Most of its 3,373,000 people live in cities. Yerevan is the capital and largest city.

Present-day Armenia and much of what is now eastern Turkey make up historic Armenia, the original homeland of the Armenian people. This land was conquered many times in its long history. By 1915, the Turks had driven most Armenians out of western Armenia, which became eastern Turkey. In 1920, Russian Communists took control of eastern Armenia. This area became part of the Transcaucasian Republic of the Soviet Union in 1922. In 1936, it became a separate Soviet republic called the Armenian Soviet Socialist Republic. The Soviet central government held tight control over Armenia. But in September 1991, as political upheaval swept through the Soviet Union, the people of Soviet Armenia voted to become an independent nation. The Soviet Union ceased to exist three months later.

Armenia

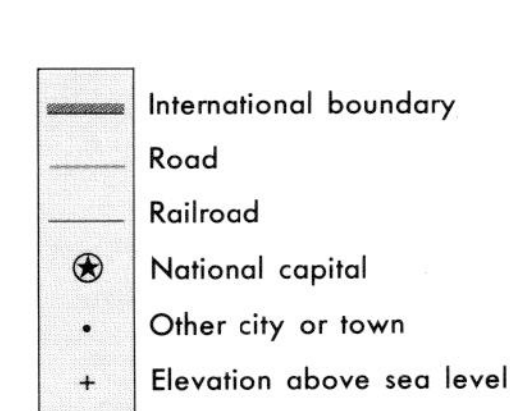

WORLD BOOK map

Only about half of the world's approximately 6 million Armenians live in Armenia. The strong national identity of Armenians worldwide helped keep the Armenian culture alive during the years of Soviet control.

Government. The most powerful government official in Armenia's national government is the president, who is elected by the people to a five-year term. The president appoints a vice-president, who also serves as prime minister. This official heads a cabinet called the Council of Ministers, which helps carry out government functions. Council members are appointed by the president. A one-house Parliament makes Armenia's laws. Its 259 members are elected by the people. Members of Parliament serve five-year terms.

Armenia's main units of local government are regions, cities, and *city regions* (regions within cities). Each of these political units has a governing council, whose members are elected by the people. All Armenians 18 years old or older may vote.

Armenia's highest court is the Supreme Court. There are also regional courts. Yerevan has a city court.

People. About 90 per cent of Armenia's people are Armenians. Kurds and Russians make up the country's largest minority groups. Until the late 1980's, Azerbaijanis formed the largest minority group. But most of them fled to Azerbaijan after violence broke out between Azerbaijanis and Armenians. For details, see the *History* section in this article.

Before the beginning of Soviet rule in the 1920's, most Armenians lived in rural areas and worked as farmers or herders. Also, the region lies on ancient trade routes, and many Armenians became merchants or traders. Under Soviet rule, Armenia became industrialized. The Soviet government built many factories and modern apartment buildings in Armenia's cities. Large numbers of people moved from farms and villages to the cities. Today, about 70 per cent of the people live in urban areas, and about 30 per cent live in rural areas.

Most Armenians live in apartment buildings. But

Facts in brief

Capital: Yerevan.
Official language: Armenian.
Official name: Haikakan Hanrapetoutioun (Republic of Armenia).
Area: 11,500 sq. mi. (29,800 km²). *Greatest distances*—north-south, 170 mi. (275 km); east-west, 130 mi. (210 km).
Elevation: *Highest*—Mount Aragats, 13,419 ft. (4,090 m) above sea level. *Lowest*—Aras River at the southeastern border, 1,475 ft. (450 m) above sea level.
Population: *Estimated 1993 population*—3,373,000; density, 293 persons per sq. mi. (113 per km²); distribution, 68 per cent urban, 32 per cent rural. *1989 census*—3,283,000. *Estimated 1998 population*—3,485,000.
Chief products: *Agriculture*—apricots, barley, cattle, peaches, quinces, sheep, walnuts, wheat, wine grapes. *Manufacturing*—chemicals, electronic products, machinery, processed food, synthetic rubber, textiles. *Mining*—copper, gold, lead, zinc.
Flag: Armenia's flag has three horizontal stripes. From top to bottom, the stripes are red, blue, and orange. See **Flag** (picture: Flags of Asia and the Pacific).

Robert Harding Picture Library

Armenia's rugged land includes mountains and gorges. The country lies on the Armenian Plateau and has an average altitude of 5,000 feet (1,500 meters) above sea level.

many people in smaller cities and villages live in single family houses. Yerevan is an attractive city. It has broad boulevards and many colorful buildings constructed of yellow, pink, and other volcanic stones.

Armenians place great importance on hospitality and on close family ties. Often, more than two generations of a family live together. Many city women hold jobs outside the home, but they still do most of the housework and shopping.

Most people in Armenia speak the Armenian language. Armenian is unlike any other language, though scholars classify it in the same language family as most European languages. The language has its own alphabet.

Armenia was the first country in the world to make Christianity its official religion. It did so in the early 300's. Today, most Armenians belong to the Armenian Church, an Eastern Orthodox Church.

Armenians enjoy such foods as barbecued shish kebab, bean salads, a thin bread called *lavash,* and *dolma* (cabbage or grape leaves stuffed with rice and meat). Fruit juices, wine and cognac, and *tan* (a mixture of water, yogurt, and salt) are popular beverages.

Chess and backgammon are popular forms of recreation in Armenia. Yerevan has many theaters for motion pictures, concerts, and drama. It also has an opera house and a symphony hall. Armenians enjoy such sports as basketball, tennis, and soccer. During the summer, many Armenians vacation at Lake Sevan—a popular resort area—or at summer homes in the countryside.

Armenia has a rich artistic tradition. Its people have excelled at such crafts as rug weaving and metalwork. The making of decorative carved stone monuments called *khatchkars* is a purely Armenian art form. Armenian architecture through the ages has produced beautiful stone churches, many with domed roofs. Armenia also has a highly developed tradition of religious music dating to the Middle Ages. Many Armenian craftsworkers and artists carry on old traditions today.

Nearly all adults in Armenia can read and write. The government requires children to attend school between the ages of 6 and 16. A student may then attend a technical school or go on to higher education at a university or specialized institute. Armenia has 14 schools of higher education.

Land and climate. Armenia lies on the Armenian Plateau, a rugged highland that extends from the Little Caucasus Mountains southwest into Turkey. The land is broken by mountains and deep gorges. Armenia has an average altitude of 5,000 feet (1,500 meters) above sea level. The highest mountain ranges stand in central Armenia. The country's highest point, Mount Aragats, rises 13,419 feet (4,090 meters). The lowest altitudes are in the northeast and southeast.

Much of the Armenian Plateau was formed millions of years ago by volcanic activity. For this reason, most of Armenia is covered with volcanic stones. *Faults*—fractures in the earth's rocky outer shell—crisscross the plateau, and earthquakes sometimes occur in Armenia.

Armenia has about 100 mountain lakes. Lake Sevan, in the east, is the largest. It covers about 5 per cent of Armenia. The country also has a number of small, fast-flowing rivers and streams. The longest river, the Aras, separates Armenia from Turkey and Iran. The streams and rivers serve as a source for irrigation and energy. A chain of hydroelectric power stations stands along the Razdan River, between Lake Sevan and Yerevan.

Most of Armenia's vegetation consists of grasses and shrubs. Some forests of beech, hornbeam, juniper, and oak are found in the northeast and southeast.

Armenia's climate is dry, with long cold winters and short hot summers. January temperatures usually range from 10 °F to 23 °F (−12 °C to −5 °C) and can fall below −22 °F (−30 °C). July temperatures average about 50 °F (10 °C) in the mountains and about 77 °F (25 °C) elsewhere. Armenia receives a yearly rainfall of about 8 to 31 inches (20 to 80 centimeters), rising with elevation. The highest peaks are snow-covered all year.

Economy. Manufacturing and mining account for about two-thirds of the value of Armenia's economic production. The chief industries make chemicals, electronic products, machinery, processed food, synthetic rubber, and textiles. Armenia is a leading distiller of cognac. Alaverdi, Kafan, Kirovakan, Kumayri, and Yerevan are the main industrial centers. Copper is Armenia's most important mineral.

Service industries account for about a fourth of Armenia's economic production. These industries include education, health care, and government activities.

Agriculture accounts for about 10 per cent of the production. Farm products include apricots, barley, peaches, potatoes, quinces, walnuts, wheat, and wine grapes. Crop production benefits from Armenia's many areas of fertile black topsoils called *chernozem* soils. The Aras River Valley is the chief farming region. Herders raise cattle and sheep on mountain slopes.

During the period of Soviet control, the government owned most of Armenia's businesses, factories, and farmland. But in January 1991, it began a program to introduce more elements of a free-enterprise system. By the time the Soviet Union broke up in December 1991, the government had sold about three-fourths of Armenia's farmland to private owners. It also had begun to sell many state-owned businesses and industries.

Armenia has several railways and an extensive road and highway system. However, relatively few people own cars. Buses and trolleys serve as the main forms of transportation in most cities and towns. Yerevan has a subway system. An international airport also operates at Yerevan.

Armenia's radio and television studios are in Yerevan. About 90 newspapers are published in Armenia.

History. People lived in historic Armenia by 6000 B.C. The earliest societies in the region were probably tribal groups that lived by farming or raising cattle. In the 800's B.C., a coalition of several tribes formed the kingdom of Urartu. The Urartians introduced irrigation and built fortresses, palaces, and temples. The kingdom was conquered by the Medes, a people from what is now Iran, in the 500's B.C.

In the 600's B.C., ancestors of the Armenians migrated—probably from the west—to the Armenian Plateau. They settled with the native population.

Soon after Urartu fell to the Medes, the Medes were conquered by the Persians. Armenia was under Persian and then Greek rule for hundreds of years. But it maintained a degree of independence. King Tigran II, who came to power in 95 B.C., built an independent Armenian empire that reached from the Caspian Sea to the Mediterranean Sea. The Romans defeated Tigran in 55 B.C., and as a result Armenia became part of the Roman Empire.

In the early A.D. 300's, Armenia became the first nation to adopt Christianity as its state religion. The Armenian alphabet was developed in the early 400's by an Armenian cleric. In 451, Armenians under Vartan Mamikonian defended their religion against the Persians in the Battle of Avarair.

Arabs conquered Armenia in the 600's. In 884, an independent Armenian kingdom was established in the northern part of the region. Seljuk Turks conquered Armenia in the mid-1000's, but Armenians established a new state in Cilicia on the Mediterranean coast. This last Armenian kingdom fell to Mameluke invaders in 1375.

By 1514, the Ottoman Turks had gained control of Armenia. They ruled western Armenia until their defeat in World War I in 1918. Persians gained control of eastern Armenia in 1639. They ruled it until 1828, when it was annexed by Russia. During the 1800's, the growth of nationalism among Turks, Armenians, and other peoples caused conflicts.

During the late 1800's, Armenians under Turkish rule suffered increasingly from discrimination, heavy taxation, and armed attacks. From 1894 through 1896, the Turks and Kurds, under Sultan Abdul-Hamid II, carried out a campaign to wipe out Armenians. Hundreds of thousands of Armenians were killed.

Armenia became a battleground between Turkey and Russia during World War I. Turkey feared the Armenians would aid the Russians. In 1915, the Turkish government deported Armenians living in Turkish Armenia into the deserts of what is now Syria. About 1 million Armenians died from lack of water and starvation or were killed by Turkish soldiers or Arabs and Kurds. Many survivors fled to Russian Armenia, where, in 1918, an independent Armenian republic was established.

Conflicts resurfaced between the Armenian republic and Turkey. Armenia's leaders reluctantly turned to Communist Russia for protection. In December 1920, eastern Armenia became a Communist republic. Turkey kept the rest of Armenia. In early 1922, Armenia joined Azerbaijan and Georgia to form the Transcaucasian Republic. This republic was one of the four republics that joined to form the Soviet Union in late 1922. In 1936, Armenia, Azerbaijan, and Georgia became separate republics of the Soviet Union.

Joseph Stalin became dictator of the Soviet Union in 1929. He ruled by terror, allowed little expression by nationalist groups within the Soviet Union, and had many political and cultural leaders in Armenia and elsewhere killed. After Stalin's death in 1953, the Soviet Union became more tolerant of national differences. Armenia developed into a more modern, European-style society while preserving its ethnic culture.

Nagorno-Karabakh, an area in the neighboring Muslim republic of Azerbaijan, has long been a source of dispute between Armenia and Azerbaijan. In 1923, the Soviet government had given Nagorno-Karabakh to Azerbaijan. Until the late 1980's, a large majority of the people of Nagorno-Karabakh were Armenians, while a minority were Azerbaijanis. In 1988, large numbers of Armenians demonstrated in Yerevan and other cities, demanding that Nagorno-Karabakh be made part of Armenia. The protests soon led to fighting between Armenians and Azerbaijanis, and violence reached a high level by the early 1990's. After the violence began, about 250,000 Armenians fled to Armenia from Azerbaijan. About 200,000 Azerbaijanis—almost all those who lived in Armenia—fled to Azerbaijan.

On Dec. 7, 1988, a severe earthquake struck Armenia. It killed about 25,000 people and destroyed much property. About 500,000 people were left homeless. The destruction caused by the earthquake, along with the large number of refugees from Azerbaijan, led to a severe shortage of housing and jobs in Armenia.

Mikhail S. Gorbachev became the leader of the Soviet Union in 1985. He introduced a series of measures to promote reform of the government. In 1990, non-Communists won control of Armenia's government. The republic's Parliament then declared that Armenia's laws took precedence over those of the Soviet Union. In September 1991, the Armenian people voted in favor of independence from the Soviet Union in a referendum. In October, the people elected Levon Ter-Petrosyan president. In December, the Soviet Union broke apart, after Armenia and other republics withdrew from it.

Nancy Lubin

Azerbaijan, *AH zuhr by JAHN,* is a country in the Caucasus Mountain region on the western shore of the Caspian Sea. It became independent in 1991, after nearly 70 years as a part of the Soviet Union. The country's full name in Azerbaijani, the official language, is Azerbaijan Respublikasi (Azerbaijani Republic).

Facts in brief

Capital: Baku.
Official language: Azerbaijani.
Area: 33,436 sq. mi. (86,600 km²). Greatest distances—north-south, 240 mi. (385 km); east-west, 295 mi. (475 km).
Elevation: *Highest*—Bazar Dyuzi, 14,652 ft. (4,466 m) above sea level. *Lowest*—Coast of Caspian Sea, 92 ft. (28 m) below sea level.
Population: *Estimated 1993 population*—7,222,000; density, 216 persons per sq. mi. (83 per km²); distribution, 54 per cent urban, 46 per cent rural. *1989 census*—7,029,000. *Estimated 1998 population*—7,462,000.
Chief products: *Agriculture*—cotton, fruit, grain, livestock, tea, tobacco, vegetables. *Manufacturing*—machine building, petroleum refining, textile production, processing of chemicals. *Mining*—aluminum, copper, iron, natural gas, petroleum, salt.
Flag: The flag's three horizontal stripes are light blue, red, and green. In the flag's center is a white crescent and star.
Money: *Basic unit*—manat (ruble is also used).

Azerbaijan covers about 33,436 square miles (86,600 square kilometers) and has a population of about 7,222,000. It lies mostly in Asia, but part of northern Azerbaijan is in Europe. A part of Azerbaijan called the Nakhichevan Autonomous Republic is separated from the rest of the country by Armenian territory. Baku is Azerbaijan's capital and largest city.

Government. A president is Azerbaijan's most powerful government official. The people elect the president to a 5-year term. A Cabinet of Ministers, headed by a prime minister, helps carry out the operations of government. Cabinet members are appointed by the president. A 50-member parliament called the *Milli Mejlis* (National Assembly) makes Azerbaijan's laws.

Azerbaijan's main units of local government include the Nakhichevan Autonomous Republic and districts, cities, and villages. Each unit has a governing council to manage local affairs. All Azerbaijanis 18 years old or older may vote.

Azerbaijan's highest court is the Supreme Court. There are also regional courts.

People. About 83 per cent of the country's people are Azerbaijanis. Armenians and Russians each make up about 5 per cent of the population.

About 54 per cent of Azerbaijan's people live in urban areas, and about 46 per cent live in rural areas. Most city dwellers live in multistory apartment buildings. In rural areas, most of the people live in one- or two-story houses.

Most Azerbaijanis are Muslims. Most Armenians are Christians, and many belong to the Armenian Church, an Eastern Orthodox Church. Some Russians are Russian Orthodox Christians.

Until the 1980's, the Communists tried to discourage the practice of religion. They closed down almost all mosques and religious schools. The government relaxed its restrictions on religion in the late 1980's and ended them in 1990.

Most people in Azerbaijan wear Western-style clothing. On holidays, some men wear a traditional costume consisting of pants, a long shirt, boots, and a long jacket. Some rural women wear wide skirts and blouses with long, wide sleeves. Muslim women in rural areas often wear a black shawl that covers the head and shoulders and may be drawn over the face. The wearing of the shawl is based on a Muslim custom. Some city women wear shawls with brightly colored designs on a black background.

The Azerbaijani language developed from the languages of Persians and Turkic people who once inhabited the region. Today, Azerbaijani closely resembles the modern Turkish language.

Azerbaijanis enjoy *pilaf* (a rice dish) and a variety of grilled and boiled meats, including beef, goat, and lamb. Traditional dishes include *bozartma* (mutton stew) and *dovga* (soup made of yogurt, meat, and herbs). Tea and wine are popular drinks.

Soccer is a popular sport in Azerbaijan. Many people walk or swim for recreation. Men spend much of their leisure time visiting one another in teahouses.

Azerbaijanis are known for their greatly admired handwoven rugs. In addition, their brightly patterned shawls are highly admired.

Nearly all adults in Azerbaijan can read and write. The literacy rate is high because the government requires

Azerbaijan

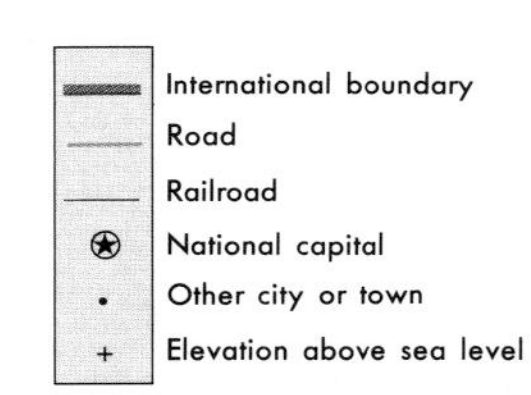

WORLD BOOK map

children to attend school from the age of 6 to 17. The country has 17 schools of higher education.

Land and climate. The Caucasus Mountains extend from northwestern to northeastern Azerbaijan, and the Little Caucasus Mountains stretch from the Southwest to the Southeast. The area north of the Caucasus Mountains is considered part of Europe. The area south of the range is considered part of Asia. The country's highest mountain, Bazar Dyuzi, rises 14,652 feet (4,466 meters) above sea level in the Caucasus Mountains.

The rugged Armenian Plateau, a land broken by deep gorges, covers part of southwestern Azerbaijan. The Kura, Azerbaijan's main river, flows through the central valley between the mountain ranges and across a broad, dry plain called the Kura-Aras Lowland. From the lowland, the Kura drains into the salty Caspian Sea. The Kura's main tributary, the Aras, flows along part of Azerbaijan's southern border. Other important rivers in Azerbaijan include the Terter and the Akera. The rivers serve as a source of irrigation water and energy. For example, the Mingechaur dam on the Kura River provides hydroelectric power for Baku and the Gyandzha industrial region.

Summers in the lowlands of Azerbaijan are long and hot. Winters are cool. The lowlands have an average temperature of 79 °F (26 °C) in August and 39 °F (4 °C) in January. Parts of the Caucasus Mountains have average temperatures of 56 °F (13 °C) in August and 21 °F (6 °C) in January. Annual precipitation ranges from about 5 to 15 inches (13 to 38 centimeters) in most of the country's lowland areas. The highlands and a region in southeastern Azerbaijan on the Caspian Sea receive approximately 40 to 55 inches (100 to 140 centimeters) of precipitation every year.

Economy. Industries account for about half of the value of Azerbaijan's economic production. They include machine building, mining, petroleum refining, textile production, and the processing of chemicals. Chief industrial centers are Baku, Gyandzha, Sheki, Stepanakert, and Nakhichevan.

Petroleum ranks as Azerbaijan's most important mining product by far. It is the country's chief source of wealth. The largest producing oil fields lie in the Baku region, on the western shore of the Caspian Sea and in the sea. Other minerals produced in Azerbaijan include aluminum, copper, iron, natural gas, and salt.

Agriculture accounts for about a third of the value of Azerbaijan's economic production. About 70 per cent of the country's farmland is irrigated. Farmers in the lowlands grow such crops as cotton, fruit, grain, tea, tobacco, and vegetables. Some farmers raise silkworms for the raw silk industry. Herders raise cattle, goats, and sheep on mountain slopes. Fish are caught in the Caspian Sea.

During the period of Soviet control, the government owned most of Azerbaijan's farms, factories, and other businesses. In 1991, the Soviet government began to allow some free enterprise. In 1992, the Azerbaijani government slowly began to pass laws that encouraged a free enterprise economy.

Azerbaijan has a limited road and railway system. A port at Baku handles most of the country's trade on the Caspian Sea. The country's main airport is located at Baku.

Azerbaijan's main radio and television stations broadcast from Baku. The country publishes newspapers and magazines in Azerbaijani and Russian.

History. People have lived in the region that is now Azerbaijan since prehistoric times. Medes invaded the region in the 700's B.C. Later invaders were Persians of the Achaemenid Empire in the 500's B.C. and Alexander the Great in the 300's B.C. Persians of the Sassanid dynasty controlled much of the region from the A.D. 200's until the 600's, when the Arabs conquered the area. The Arabs then introduced Islam, which is the Muslim religion.

From the 1000's to the 1200's, Turkic tribes migrated into the Azerbaijani region in large numbers and mixed with the Persians who lived there. These people became the ancestors of the Azerbaijanis. In the early 1500's, Azerbaijan fell to the Safavid Empire, which ruled Iran. The Ottoman Turks took control of Azerbaijan from the Safavids in the late 1500's but lost it to them again in the early 1600's.

Russia gained control of Azerbaijan in the early 1800's. Under Russia, industry, especially petroleum production, developed in Azerbaijan. By the late 1800's, Baku had become the world's leading producer of refined petroleum.

Communists seized control of the Russian government in 1917. In 1918, Azerbaijani nationalists set up an independent state in western Azerbaijan. But the Russian Communists regained the area in 1920.

In early 1922, Azerbaijan, Georgia, and Armenia combined to form the Transcaucasian Republic under Russia's leadership. Later that year, the Transcaucasian Republic joined Byelorussia (now Belarus), Russia, and Ukraine to form the Soviet Union. In 1936, the three parts of the Transcaucasian Republic became separate republics of the Soviet Union. Azerbaijan was called the Azerbaijan Soviet Socialist Republic.

The Soviet Union made many changes in Azerbaijan. The Soviet government took over strict control on all aspects of Azerbaijani life. It established a powerful Communist government and took control of all industry and land in Azerbaijan. It *collectivized* agriculture—that is, it ended private farming and transferred control of farms to the government. The Soviet rulers destroyed many Azerbaijani traditions and tried to reduce the influence of Islam in the republic. However, the Soviets also built roads, schools, modern housing, hospitals, and communication systems in Azerbaijan.

In the late 1980's, the Soviet government made reforms toward giving people more freedom. In 1989, Azerbaijan declared that its laws overruled Soviet laws. The Soviet Union broke up in late 1991, and Azerbaijan became an independent nation.

An area known as Nagorno-Karabakh in southern Azerbaijan has been a source of dispute between Azerbaijan and neighboring Armenia. Most of Nagorno-Karabakh's people are Armenians, and Armenia claims the area. Since the late 1980's, much fighting has taken place between Azerbaijanis and Armenians over the issue of control of Nagorno-Karabakh. After the violence began, about 200,000 Azerbaijanis—almost all those who lived in Armenia—fled to Azerbaijan. About 250,000 Armenians fled Azerbaijan for Armenia.

Edward J. Lazzerini

Belarus, *BEHL uh ROOS,* or *BYEHL uh ROOS,* also spelled *Byelarus,* is a country in eastern Europe. From 1922 to 1991, it was part of the Soviet Union. It was called the Byelorussian Soviet Socialist Republic, or, simply, Byelorussia. Minsk is the capital and largest city.

The Belarusians trace their history to Kievan Rus, a state founded by East Slavs in the 800's. Belarus became part of Lithuania in the 1300's. It passed to Poland in the 1500's and to Russia in the late 1700's. The Russian Revolution overthrew the czar of Russia in 1917 and established Communist rule there. In 1918, the Russian Communists invaded Belarus. They renamed the country Byelorussia, a name derived from the Russian words *Belaya Rus* (White Russia), and established a Communist government there in 1919. Byelorussia became a republic of the Soviet Union in 1922. It gained independence in 1991, when the Soviet Union broke up.

Government

Belarus has a parliamentary government. Voters elect the 360 members of the parliament, called the Supreme Soviet, to five-year terms. These members make laws and select a chairman, the country's head of state and top leader. People in other countries often refer to the chairman as the "president" of Belarus. The chairman directs domestic and foreign policy. The Supreme Soviet also selects a prime minister, who picks a cabinet known as the Council of Ministers. The Council helps run the government.

The major political organization in Belarus is the Belarusian Popular Front. The Popular Front unites political parties and groups that support democratic reform. Belarus has about 10 political parties, most of which are small. They include the National Democratic Party, the Social Democratic Party, and the Christian Democratic Union. The Soviet Communist Party—Belarus' only party before independence—was outlawed in August 1991. In December of that year, a new Communist group called the Belarus Party of Communists was formed.

Belarus is divided into six provinces, each named for its provincial capital city: (1) Brest, (2) Gomel, (3) Grodno, (4) Minsk, (5) Mogilev, and (6) Vitebsk. A council elected by the voters governs each province.

The Supreme Court is the highest court of Belarus. The Supreme Soviet appoints judges to five-year terms on the court. The judicial system also includes provincial, city, and district courts. Belarus began to create its own armed forces in 1992.

Facts in brief

Capital: Minsk.
Official language: Belarusian.
Official name: Respublika Byelarus (Republic of Belarus).
Area: 80,155 sq. mi. (207,600 km²). *Greatest distances*—north-south, 340 mi. (545 km); east-west, 385 mi. (620 km).
Elevation: *Highest*—Dzerzhinskaya Gora, 1,135 ft. (346 m) above sea level. *Lowest*—Neman River at northwestern border, 295 ft. (90 m) above sea level.
Population: *Estimated 1993 population*—10,480,000; density, 131 persons per sq. mi. (50 per km²); distribution, 66 per cent urban, 34 per cent rural. *1989 census*—10,200,000. *Estimated 1998 population*—10,828,000.
Chief products: *Agriculture*—barley, cattle, flax, hogs, potatoes, rye, sugar beets. *Manufacturing*—bicycles, clocks, computers, engineering equipment, furniture, metal-cutting tools, motorcycles, plywood and paper, potassium fertilizer, refrigerators, television sets, textiles, trucks and tractors.
Flag: The flag has three horizontal stripes, two white above and below one red. See **Flag** (picture: Flags of Europe).
Money: *Basic unit*—ruble.

Bill Swersey, Gamma/Liaison

Minsk, Belarus' capital, lies on the Svisloch River. Minsk was almost entirely destroyed during World War II (1939-1945). It was rebuilt afterward as a modern city.

People

Population and ethnic groups. Belarus has about $10\frac{1}{2}$ million people. With an average of 131 persons per square mile (50 persons per square kilometer), it is one of the most densely populated of the former Soviet republics. Minsk is the country's largest city by far, with a population of more than $1\frac{1}{2}$ million.

Ethnic Belarusians, a Slavic people, account for 79 per cent of the population. Russians make up 12 per cent. Smaller groups include Poles and Ukrainians.

Language. In 1990, Belarusian became the official language of Belarus. It replaced Russian, the official language under Soviet rule. The Soviet government had discouraged use of Belarusian and promoted use of Russian. As a result, more people speak Russian than Belarusian, especially in the large cities.

Belarusian is a Slavic language that resembles Russian and Ukrainian. It is written in the Cyrillic alphabet, the same system of writing used for Russian.

Way of life. About two-thirds of Belarus' people live in cities. Most Belarusian families are small, with one or two children. Most city people live in apartments.

About a third of the people live in rural areas. Many of them work on large collective or state farms, run by the government. Many rural people live in small wooden houses or community housing blocks.

Most people in Belarus wear Western-style clothing. Traditional Belarusian costumes, which are white with colorful embroidery, are worn on special occasions.

Potato and mushroom dishes are particularly popular in Belarus. Belarusians also like thick stews, hearty vegetable soups such as turnip borsch, and rye and oat bread. Tea and coffee are the most popular beverages.

Belarusians enjoy a number of recreational activities. These include soccer, volleyball, track and field, swimming, camping, and chess.

Religion. Most Belarusians follow either the Belarusian Catholic religion or an Eastern Orthodox faith. Belarusian Catholics are also called "Greek" Catholics or Uniates. They follow Eastern Orthodox rituals. But they accept the authority of the Roman Catholic pope, whereas the Orthodox faiths do not. Orthodox Christians belong to either the Russian Orthodox Church or the Belarusian *Autocephalous* (self-governing) Orthodox Church. The Belarusian Autocephalous church long promoted Belarusian independence from the Soviet Union. As a result, it was banned from the 1920's until 1990, except for a brief period in the 1940's.

Other religious groups in Belarus include Roman Catholics, Protestants, and Jews. Before World War II (1939-1945), Jews made up about 8 per cent of the population. But the Nazis killed almost all the Jewish people during the war.

Education. Most Belarusians finish high school, and many receive higher education. Belarus has three universities, the Belarusian State University in Minsk, Gomel State University in Gomel and Grodno State University in Grodno. The country also has about 30 technical colleges or institutes.

The arts. The Belarusians are known for their weaving, straw-inlaid boxes, and other traditional handicrafts, and for such performing arts as dancing and puppetry. The village of Neglyubka is especially famous for textiles woven in elaborate patterns. In the early 1900's, two Belarusian poets, Ianka Kupala and Iakub Kolas, helped promote the use of the Belarusian language in literature. Formerly, most literary works were written in Russian or Polish.

Land and climate

Belarus covers 80,155 square miles (207,600 square kilometers). Most of the country consists of flat lowlands. Forests cover the northern part. A ridge of higher ground runs from northeast to southwest in central Belarus. It includes the country's highest point, a hill called Dzerzhinskaya Gora that rises only 1,135 feet (346 meters) above sea level. Southern Belarus is made up of marshes, swamps, and forests. This region includes a vast, forested swamp called the Pripyat Marshes.

The chief rivers in Belarus are the Bug, the Dnepr, the Neman, and the Western Dvina. The country has more than 10,000 lakes, most of which are small.

The forests of Belarus teem with deer, foxes, hares, minks, and squirrels. Belarus and Poland jointly administer the Belovezha Forest (Białowieza in Polish), a nature preserve along the border between the two nations. This area is a remnant of the virgin forest that covered much of Europe in prehistoric times. It has majestic old spruces and other trees. Its rare animals include a herd of European bison, also called wisent.

Belarus has cold winters and warm summers. The temperature averages about 22 °F (−6 °C) in January, the coldest month, and about 65 °F (18 °C) in July, the hottest. Annual precipitation, including rain and melted snow, ranges from 20 to 26 inches (50 to 66 centimeters).

Economy

Belarus has a well-developed economy. But it suffers from a shortage of modern technology. For nearly 70 years, the Communist government of the Soviet Union

Belarus

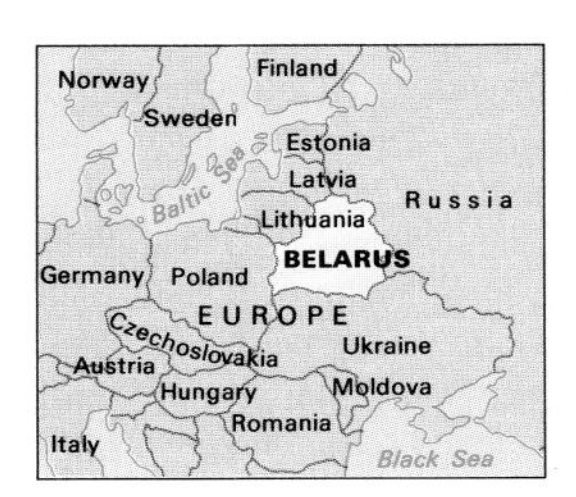

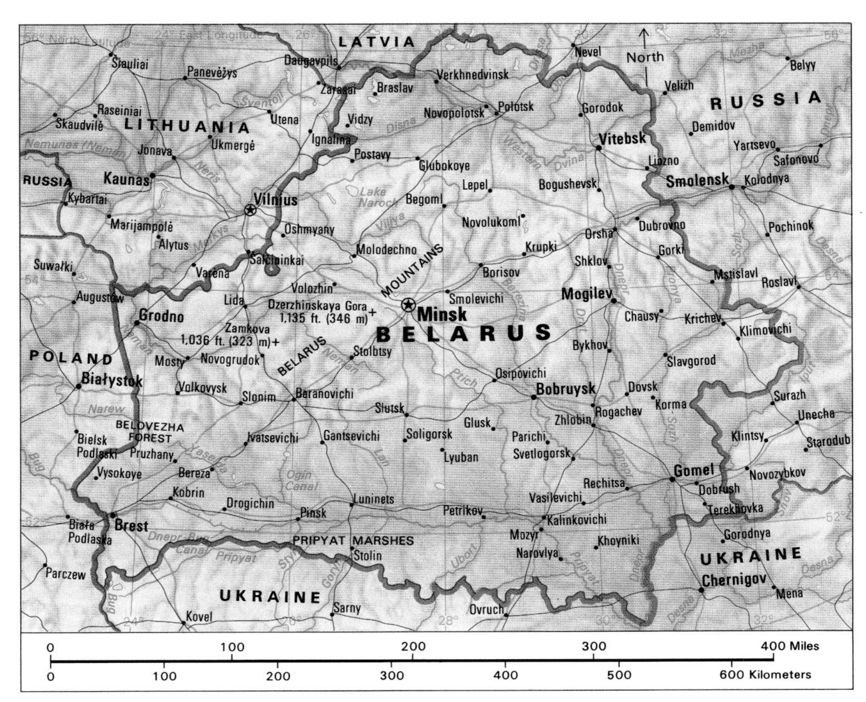

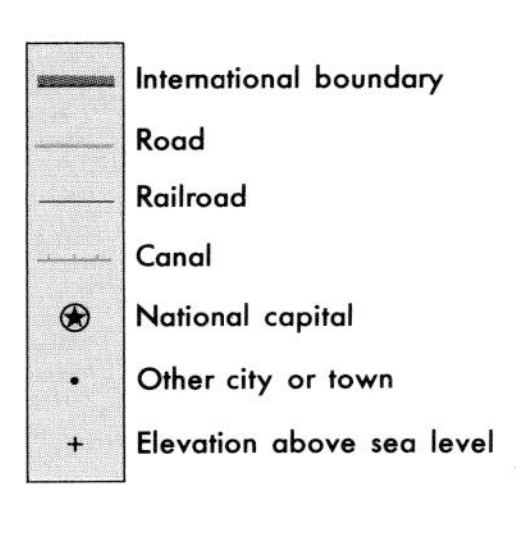

WORLD BOOK maps

European bison, or *wisent,* graze in the Belovezha Forest, a nature preserve in western Belarus and eastern Poland. The area is a remnant of ancient forest that once covered much of Europe.

Novosti

controlled the entire economy, resulting in much waste and inefficiency. Like other former Soviet republics, Belarus plans to reduce government control of economic activities. The plans call for many inefficient state-owned factories, farms, and other businesses to close, and for the number of private businesses to grow. The change to a free-market system is expected to take years.

Manufacturing produces more than half of the economic output of Belarus. The country is known for its heavy-duty trucks and tractors. Belarus also manufactures computers, engineering equipment, metal-cutting tools, and such consumer goods as bicycles, clocks and watches, motorcycles, refrigerators, and television sets. The chief chemical product is potassium fertilizer. Belarusian forests yield many wood products, including furniture, matches, plywood, and paper goods.

Agriculture accounts for about a fourth of Belarus' economic output. The country's major crops include barley, flax, potatoes, rye, and sugar beets.

Mining. Belarus has only a few mineral resources. It is rich in peat, which is used for fuel, and potassium and rock salts. Southern Belarus has coal and petroleum.

Trade. The major Belarusian exports include tractors to Australia, Canada, New Zealand, and the United States. Belarus' chief trading partners are Russia and Ukraine. Significant trade also occurs with Austria, Germany, Great Britain, Poland, and Switzerland.

Transportation and communication. Belarus has an adequate transportation system, including railroad and highway networks connecting its cities with other major European cities. Trains are Belarus' most important means of long-distance travel. The country's chief airport is in Minsk. Buses provide most of the transportation within cities. The Dnepr-Bug Canal and other canals improve water transportation by linking many of the rivers with ports on the Baltic and Black seas.

History

Early days. The area that is now Belarus was inhabited by various groups of people beginning in prehistoric times. Slavic tribes moved in by the A.D. 500's.

The Belarusians, along with the Ukrainians and Russians, trace their history to the first East Slavic state. The state, called Kievan Rus, was formed in the 800's. Belarus made up the northwestern part of Kievan Rus. During the 900's and 1000's, Kievan Rus was a major European political, economic, and military power.

Lithuanian, Polish, and Russian rule. In the 1200's, Mongol invaders overran the eastern part of Kievan Rus, while Germanic tribes threatened from the west. To protect themselves from invaders, the Belarusians formed a military alliance with neighboring Lithuania. The alliance led to Belarus becoming part of Lithuania, which grew into a large and powerful state.

In 1386, the grand duke of Lithuania married the queen of Poland and began to rule both Lithuania and Poland as king. Lithuanian-Polish kings ruled the two states for nearly 200 years until Lithuania—including Belarus—merged with Poland in 1569.

Between 1772 and 1795, Russia, Prussia, and Austria divided Poland. Russia received much of eastern Poland, including Belarus. In the 1800's, Russian officials began a policy called *Russification.* This policy promoted the Russian culture and language at the expense of other cultures and languages, including Belarusian. Nevertheless, the Belarusian people's sense of national distinctiveness grew during the 1800's and 1900's, as did their resentment of Russian control.

Soviet rule. The Russian Revolution of 1917 overthrew the czar of Russia and established a Communist government there. In March 1918, the Belarusians established an independent, non-Communist state called the Belarusian National Republic. However, Russian Communists invaded the republic later that year. In January 1919, they proclaimed a Communist-ruled state called the Byelorussian Soviet Socialist Republic. Poland gained control of western Belarus in 1919, at the start of the Polish-Russian War. In 1922, Byelorussia became one of the founding republics of the Soviet Union.

In the 1930's, Joseph Stalin, the dictator of the Soviet Union, pushed the policy of Russification in Byelorussia and other non-Russian republics. The Soviet government also seized land from private farmers to form larger, state-run farms, causing much suffering.

In 1939, the Soviets occupied western Belarus, which Poland had controlled since 1919, and reunited it with Byelorussia. Nazi Germany occupied Byelorussia and other Soviet territory from 1941 to 1944, during World War II. The area suffered great damage during the war. Minsk was almost entirely destroyed. After the Nazis lost the war, the Soviets regained Byelorussia, including western Belarus.

An explosion and fire at the Chernobyl nuclear power plant in Ukraine in 1986 had a major impact on Byelorussia. The winds caused about 70 per cent of the radioactive fallout from Chernobyl to fall on Byelorussia. The radiation contaminated the republic's food and water supplies and caused many health problems, including increased cancer deaths.

Independence. In 1990, the Byelorussian parliament declared that the republic's laws took precedence over those of the Soviet Union. In August 1991, Byelorussia declared its independence. In September, the republic changed its name from the Russian form *Byelorussia* to the Belarusian form *Belarus.* In December, the Soviet Union broke apart and Belarus became an independent nation. It joined with 10 other former Soviet republics to form the Commonwealth of Independent States (C.I.S.) to deal with their common economic, political, and military problems.

The Soviet Union had put part of its arsenal of nuclear weapons in Belarus. In 1992, Belarus transferred its short-range nuclear weapons to Russia to be destroyed. Belarus also pledged to remove its longer-range nuclear weapons by the late 1990's. Jaroslaw Bilocerkowycz

Commonwealth of Independent States is a loose association of independent nations that were formerly republics of the Soviet Union. These member nations are Armenia, Belarus, Kazakhstan, Kyrgyzstan, Moldova, Russia, Tajikistan, Turkmenistan, Ukraine, and Uzbekistan. The headquarters of the commonwealth is Minsk, in Belarus.

The Soviet Union was made up of 15 republics. In the early 1990's, two of the republics, Georgia and Lithuania, declared their independence. In August 1991, the Soviet Union began to break apart after an attempted coup. All the other republics except Russia declared their independence during the coup or soon after. Russia proclaimed itself the successor to the Soviet Union. Eleven republics formed the Commonwealth of Independent States (C.I.S.) in December 1991, shortly before the Soviet Union ceased to exist. In October 1992, Azerbaijan, one of the 11, announced that it was no longer a member. The four former republics that did not join the C.I.S. were Georgia, Estonia, Latvia, and Lithuania.

The C.I.S. was created for several reasons. Many of the members wanted to keep some of the economic ties they had with one another as Soviet republics. Each of the members also wanted to guarantee its own territory and sovereignty. The C.I.S. members also sought to reassure the rest of the world that the nuclear weapons of the former Soviet Union were under reliable control.

Despite the goals of the C.I.S., members soon began to dispute various matters. The C.I.S. originally aimed to have a single military for all its members. But most of the member countries have announced their intention of creating their own armed forces. Russia and Ukraine have disputed the ownership of the Crimea, a strategically important peninsula in the Black Sea. Many of the C.I.S. countries rejected the idea of a common economic market in which the ruble—the former Soviet monetary unit—would continue to be used. Some of them have already created their own currencies.

Experts believe many of the commonwealth's problems result from a lack of clear purpose or structure. Russia, for example, seemed to see the C.I.S. as permanent. But other members expressed fears that Russia—with its great size and power—might dominate the C.I.S. Some of the members, such as Ukraine, viewed the C.I.S. as just a temporary association to help the former republics become truly independent countries. The C.I.S. does not have a charter that sets forth its duties and powers. It also lacks a governing body to enforce decisions or settle conflicts. Nancy Lubin

Members of the Commonwealth of Independent States

Name	Area		Population	Capital	Official language
	In sq. mi.	In km²			
Armenia	11,506	29,800	3,373,000	Yerevan	Armenian
Azerbaijan*	33,436	86,600	7,222,000	Baku	Azerbaijani
Belarus	80,155	207,600	10,480,000	Minsk	Belorussian
Kazakhstan	1,049,156	2,717,300	16,992,000	Alma-Ata	Kazakh
Kyrgyzstan	76,641	198,500	4,409,000	Bishkek	Kyrgyz
Moldova	13,012	33,700	4,460,000	Chisinau	Romanian
Russia	6,592,850	17,075,400	151,436,000	Moscow	Russian
Tajikistan	55,251	143,100	5,252,000	Dushanbe	Tajik
Turkmenistan	188,456	488,100	3,631,000	Ashkhabad	Turkmen
Ukraine	233,090	603,700	53,125,000	Kiev	Ukrainian
Uzbekistan	172,742	447,400	20,453,000	Tashkent	Uzbek

*A founding member; in October 1992, announced that it was no longer a member.

Georgia is a nation in the Caucasus Mountains that became independent in 1991 after nearly 200 years of Russian and Soviet rule. Georgia lies mostly in Asia, but part of northern Georgia is located in Europe. Georgia has a population of about 5,599,000 and an area of 26,911 square miles (69,700 square kilometers). Tbilisi, which is located in eastern Georgia, is the capital and largest city.

Government. At the time Georgia became independent, it had a parliamentary system of government. Georgia's one-house parliament is called the Supreme Council. It has about 250 members, who are elected by the people. A president, also elected by the people, serves a five-year term. The president appoints a cabinet called the Council of Ministers, whose members head government departments.

In 1992, opponents of Georgia's president forced him out of office and suspended the parliament. Opposition leaders formed a small State Council to rule Georgia until new parliamentary elections could be held.

People. About 70 per cent of the people of Georgia are ethnic Georgians. About 8 per cent of the population are Armenians. Russians and Azerbaijans each make up about 6 per cent. About 3 per cent of the people of Georgia are Ossetians, and about $1\frac{1}{2}$ per cent are Abkhazians.

Most of the people of Georgia are Christians who belong to the Georgian Orthodox Church. Some of the people are Muslims. The country's primary language is Georgian. The Georgian language is not related to any other languages in the region. It is written in its own alphabet.

More than half the people of Georgia live in urban areas. Many city houses are closely grouped, one- or two-story structures. Large public buildings erected while Georgia was under Soviet control also stand in some of the cities. In the villages and small towns, many people build large, spacious, two-story homes. They often keep gardens or orchards.

The Georgian people are known for their strong family ties. Family gatherings and celebrations are important occasions. A wide variety of food is often served at these gatherings. Popular Georgian foods include *shashlik,* a type of shish kebab; and *chicken tabaka,* which is pressed fried chicken. Georgia is also famous for its wines.

Almost all the people of Georgia can read and write. Children must attend school through the 10th grade. Tbilisi University is Georgia's most important university. The Georgian Academy of Sciences has its headquarters in Tbilisi.

Georgia has a rich literary tradition. Music and poetry are especially popular among the Georgian people. Shota Rustaveli, one of the country's greatest poets, wrote around A.D. 1200.

Land and climate. Much of Georgia has a rugged landscape. The Caucasus Mountains cover the northern part of Georgia, and the Little Caucasus Mountains extend over much of the south. The lower mountain slopes close to and facing the Black Sea have a mild, wet climate. Mountains farther inland and slopes facing away from the sea have colder, drier climates. The highest areas are permanently snow covered. Forests cover many of the mountains and hills. Evergreen, beech, and oak trees are common. Mount Shkhara, in the Caucasus Mountains, is Georgia's highest peak. It rises 17,163 feet (5,201 meters) above sea level.

Western Georgia includes the Rioni valley and other lowlands near the Black Sea. This region has a warm, humid climate. Rainfall is heavy, and temperatures rarely

Facts in brief

Capital: Tbilisi.
Official language: Georgian.
Area: 26,911 sq. mi. (69,700 km²). *Greatest distances*—north-south, 175 mi. (280 km); east-west, 350 mi. (565 km).
Elevation: *Highest*—Mount Shkhara, 17,163 ft. (5,201 m) above sea level. *Lowest*—sea level along the coast.
Population: *Estimated 1993 population*—5,599,000; density, 208 persons per sq. mi. (80 per km²); distribution, 56 per cent urban, 44 per cent rural. *1989 census*—5,449,000. *Estimated 1998 population*—5,785,000.
Chief products: *Agriculture*—citrus fruit, corn, grapes, silk, tea, tobacco, tung oil, wheat. *Manufacturing and processing*—food products. *Mining*—barite, coal, copper, manganese.
Flag: The flag has a red field. A cantor in the upper left corner is divided into two horizontal stripes of black and white. See **Flag** (picture: Flags of Europe).
Money: *Basic unit*—ruble.

Georgia

International boundary
Road
Railroad
National capital
Other city or town
Elevation above sea level

WORLD BOOK map

SCR Photo Library

Tbilisi, Georgia's capital, lies on the banks of the Kura River. Part of the city is modern, but the older section has buildings that date from hundreds of years ago.

drop below freezing. Much of western Georgia is productive farmland.

Eastern Georgia includes part of the upper Kura valley, which extends into Azerbaijan. This region has a much drier climate than does western Georgia. The lack of rainfall requires farmers to irrigate some crops. Eastern Georgia has cold winters and warm summers.

Economy. Georgia's greatest natural resources are its fertile soil and mild climate, which make farming a major economic activity. In western Georgia, farmers produce citrus fruit, tea, and tung oil. Farther inland, tobacco and wheat; and grapes, corn, and a variety of other fruits and vegetables are grown. Georgia also produces silk. Farmers in the mountainous regions raise sheep and cattle.

Food processing is Georgia's chief industry, and food products are its main export. Mining is another important industry in Georgia. Mines in Georgia yield *barite* (barium ore), coal, copper, and manganese. Tourism ranks as an important economic activity in some parts of the country. Health resorts that lie along the coast of the Black Sea attract thousands of vacationers every year. Georgia's swift rivers and rugged terrain provide many good sites for hydroelectric power plants.

Russia and Ukraine are Georgia's most important trading partners. Transportation between Georgia and Russia, across the Caucasus Mountains, is limited. The major highway crossing the mountains is often closed in winter. Railroads skirt the mountains along the Black and Caspian seas.

History. People have lived in what is now Georgia for thousands of years. The first Georgian state was established in the 500's B.C. In the 200's B.C., most of what is now Georgia was united as one kingdom. But for most of its history, Georgia was divided, and powerful empires fought over it. From the 60's B.C. until the A.D. 1000's, Georgia was invaded by Romans, Persians, Byzantines, Arabs, and Seljuk Turks. The first Christian state appeared in Georgia in the A.D. 300's.

During the 1000's and 1100's, a series of Georgian rulers gradually freed Georgia of foreign control and centralized its government. These efforts eventually produced Georgia's "Golden Age" during the reign of Queen Tamara (1184-1212), when Georgians made great advances in culture, science, and art.

Beginning in the early 1200's, however, Georgia again suffered attacks from other nations. Mongol armies, including those of Asian conquerors Genghis Khan and Tamerlane, raided Georgian lands from the 1220's to the early 1400's. These attacks sent Georgia into a period of decline. From the 1500's to the 1700's, the Ottoman Empire and Iran fought over Georgian territory.

In the late 1700's, the ruler of one of the kingdoms in east Georgia accepted partial Russian rule in exchange for military protection. By the early 1800's, all of Georgia became part of the Russian Empire.

A socialist republic was established in Georgia after World War I (1914-1918). But Russian Communist forces invaded Georgia in 1921 and proclaimed it a Communist republic. In early 1922, Georgia, Armenia, and Azerbaijan joined to make up the Transcaucasian republic. This republic was one of the four original republics that combined to form the Soviet Union in late 1922. Joseph Stalin, who ruled the Soviet Union as a dictator from 1929 to 1953, was a Georgian. In 1936, Georgia, Armenia, and Azerbaijan became separate Soviet republics.

Georgia has sometimes suffered from tension between Georgians and other ethnic groups. During the early 1990's, this tension erupted into violence. In 1990, South Ossetia, an *autonomous* (self-governing) region of Georgia inhabited by Ossetians, declared itself independent. The Georgian government ruled the declaration invalid, and fighting broke out between Ossetians and Georgians. The autonomous region of Abkhazia has also threatened to secede from Georgia. Ethnic violence occurred in this region also in the 1990's.

In the late 1980's, a strong independence movement emerged in Georgia. Until 1990, Georgia's Communist Party controlled the republic's government. Elections were held in October and November 1990, and non-Communist candidates won a majority of seats in Georgia's parliament. The parliament elected Zviad K. Gamsakhurdia, leader of the non-Communist majority, as president.

In April 1991, the parliament declared Georgia independent. The people elected Gamsakhurdia president the next month. Opposition leaders soon accused Gamsakhurdia of moving toward dictatorship. He jailed political opponents and censored the press. In December 1991, the Soviet Union broke apart. Eleven former Soviet republics agreed to form a Commonwealth of Independent States, but Georgia did not join.

Opposition to Gamsakhurdia continued to grow after the Soviet Union dissolved. In January 1992, opposition forces formed an alternate government, and Gamsakhurdia fled the country. In March, Eduard A. Shevardnadze became head of the State Council that would rule Georgia until new elections, which were planned for late 1992. Leslie Dienes

Kazakhstan, *KAH zahk STAHN,* is a country in west-central Asia. It became an independent country in 1991, after about 70 years as a part of the Soviet Union. Kazakhstan joined the Commonwealth of Independent States (C.I.S.), a loose association of former Soviet republics. The country's name in Kazakh, which is the country's official language, is Qazaqstan Respublikasy (Republic of Kazakhstan).

Kazakhstan covers 1,049,156 square miles (2,717,300 square kilometers). A small part of the country lies west of the Ural River on the European continent. Kazakhstan has a population of 16,992,000. Most of the people are Kazakhs or Russians. Alma-Ata is the country's capital and largest city.

For hundreds of years, the Kazakh people were wandering herders who raised their livestock on the region's plains. They relied on their herds of sheep, camels, cattle, and horses for food, clothing, and transportation. This traditional life style changed in the 1800's, when the Russian Empire conquered the Kazakh region and many Russians settled in the area. Also, industry grew rapidly in Kazakhstan during most of the 1900's, while the country was under Soviet rule. Under these influences, most of the Kazakh people ended their nomadic ways and settled in rural villages or cities.

Government. Kazakhstan has a parliamentary system of government. The parliament, a 360-member body called the Supreme Soviet, is the country's highest governing body. It enacts legislation and supervises government administration. A president serves as head of state. The people elect both the president and the members of the Supreme Soviet to five-year terms. All citizens 18 years old or older may vote.

Kazakhstan is divided into 19 *oblasts* (provinces) for purposes of local government. The president appoints a governor to administer each oblast.

Under Soviet rule, the Communist Party was Kazakhstan's only political party until 1990. It strictly controlled the government. Since 1990, other political parties have been allowed to form and have gained influence in the country. In 1991, the Communist Party was renamed the Socialist Party of Kazakhstan. In addition to the Socialists, important parties now include the Alash, the Azat, the Zheltoksan, the National-Democratic, and the People's Congress Party.

Kazakhstan's highest court is the Supreme Court. There are also regional courts and local courts. All judges are elected to five-year terms.

Kazakhstan has three types of military units. The largest unit is the Kazakh armed forces. The second largest unit is the C.I.S. armed forces, under the joint command of Kazakhstan and the C.I.S. There is also a small Kazakhstan border patrol unit.

Kazakhstan maintains control of the nuclear weapons in the country. Before Kazakhstan became independent, these weapons belonged to the Soviet nuclear arsenal. According to a treaty signed in May 1992 by Kazakhstan

Facts in brief

Capital: Alma-Ata.
Official language: Kazakh.
Area: 1,049,156 sq. mi. (2,717,300 km²). *Greatest distances*—north-south, 1,000 mi. (1,600 km); east-west, 1,800 mi. (2,900 km).
Elevation: *Highest*—Mt. Tengri, 20,991 ft. (6,398 m) above sea level. *Lowest*—Karagiye Depression, 433 ft. (132 m) below sea level.
Population: *Estimated 1993 population*—16,992,000; density, 16 persons per sq. mi. (6 per km²); distribution, 58 per cent urban, 42 per cent rural. *1989 census*—16,538,000. *Estimated 1998 population*—17,557,000.
Chief products: *Agriculture*—grain, meat, wool. *Manufacturing*—chemicals, food products, heavy machinery. *Mining*—Coal, copper, lead, natural gas, petroleum.
Flag: The flag is blue, with a yellow sun and eagle in the center and a yellow stripe of national ornamentation at the left. See **Flag** (picture: Flags of Asia and the Pacific).
Money: *Basic unit*—ruble.

Kazakhstan

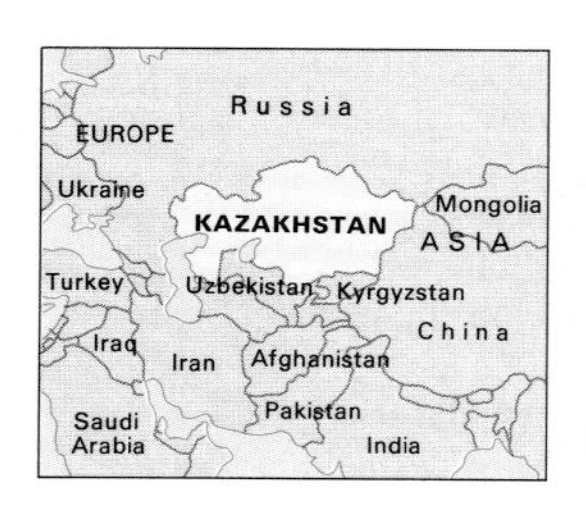

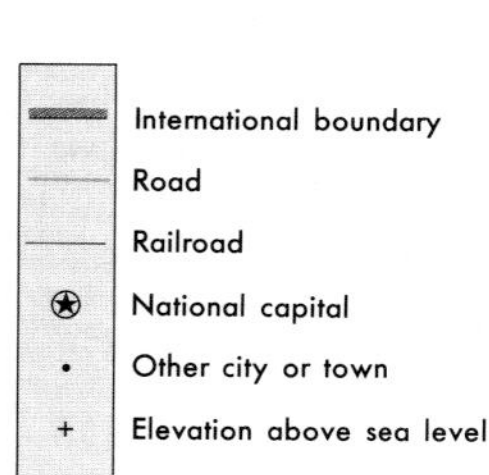

WORLD BOOK maps

and the former Soviet republics of Belarus, Russia, and Ukraine, all nuclear weapons under the former republics' control are to be transferred to Russian control or destroyed within seven years.

People. Kazakhs make up about 42 per cent of Kazakhstan's population and Russians account for about 37 per cent. Germans and Ukrainians each make up about 5 per cent of the population. Other ethnic groups include Belarusians, Tatars, Uygurs, and Uzbeks. A majority of Kazakhstan's people, including the Kazakhs, Tatars, Uygurs, and Uzbeks, are Muslims. Most Russians and Belarusians are Orthodox Christians.

About 58 per cent of Kazakhstan's people live in urban areas and about 42 per cent live in rural areas. Most of the urban people dwell in modern apartments or houses. In the rural villages, most people live in houses. However, some Kazakh villagers still live in the traditional tentlike dwellings of their nomadic past. Called *yurts,* these portable homes are constructed of a circular wooden frame covered with felt. Most of Kazakhstan's rural villages do not have electricity or running water.

The social life of the country's Kazakh people is centered around the family. Kazakh men and their children generally remain a part of their parents' households. Married women become part of the household of their husband's family. The women of Kazakhstan rarely work outside the home.

Kazakh weddings are festive celebrations that include many traditional customs. Before the wedding, the groom's family must offer a *kalym* (bride price) to the family of the bride. The two families argue over the amount of the kalym, which can amount to as much as several years' salary. The families usually hold the wedding during the summer after the kalym has been paid.

The Kazakh people wear both Western-style and traditional clothing. Women generally wear colorful handmade dresses. Most Kazakh men wear Western-style clothing and a felt skullcap.

Common Kazakh foods include meat dishes and milk products, such as cheese and curds. *Besh barmak,* thinly sliced meat and noodles boiled in broth, is a popular dish. *Kumiss,* made from fermented mare's milk, is a traditional drink. Tea is also popular.

The country's Kazakh people enjoy folk songs and legends, and they recite them for many different occasions. At some events, Kazakhs participate in a singing competition called an *aitys.* The recitation of *epics* (poems about heroic events) is another important part of Kazakh culture.

Most of Kazakhstan's Russian people live in cities. They wear Western-style clothing and follow Russian customs. The Russian population has maintained its own culture in Kazakhstan. Performances of Russian ballet, theater, and music are put on in all the major cities.

Popular sports in Kazakhstan include volleyball, skating, and wrestling. *Kopkar* is a traditional Kazakh game in which dozens of skilled horsemen try to carry the carcass of a goat or sheep across a goal.

Russian was Kazakhstan's official language under Soviet rule. The Kazakh language replaced it in 1989. However, many Kazakhs, especially urban people, continue to speak Russian.

Nearly all of Kazakhstan's people can read and write.

© Keith Gunnar, FPG

Alma-Ata is the capital of Kazakhstan. It lies in a fertile valley at the foot of a mountain range called the Tian Shan. Broad, tree-lined streets run through the city.

The government requires children to attend school between the ages of 6 and 17. Kazakhstan has 55 schools of higher learning, including Kazakh State University and Karaganda State University. The Kazakh Academy of Sciences is an institution that includes more than 30 separate research institutes.

Land and climate. Kazakhstan's landscape varies greatly from west to east. In the west, the dry plains of the Caspian lowland border the Caspian Sea. The Karagiye Depression, the country's lowest point, lies near the Caspian Sea at 433 feet (132 meters) below sea level. Dry lowlands extend over much of western Kazakhstan and around the Aral Sea on the country's southwest border.

High, grassy plains called *steppes* cover large areas of northern Kazakhstan. Sandy deserts cover much of the south. Northeastern Kazakhstan consists of flat, highly elevated lands that are suitable for farming.

A series of mountain ranges, including the Tian Shan and the Altai Mountains, forms Kazakhstan's eastern and southeastern borders. Mount Tengri, the country's highest point, rises 20,991 feet (6,398 meters) in the southeast. Several mountain rivers in the east feed into Lake Balkhash, the largest lake entirely within Kazakhstan. Major rivers in Kazakhstan include the Ili, the Irtysh, the Syr Darya, and the Ural.

Kazakhstan has extremely cold winters and long, hot summers. It receives little rainfall. January temperatures average about 0 °F (−18 °C) in the north and about 23 °F (−5 °C) in the south. July temperatures average about 68 °F (20 °C) in the north and about 81 °F (27 °C) in the south. Average annual rainfall totals only about 4 to 16 inches (10 to 40 centimeters). Mountainous regions are colder, and receive more rainfall, than the rest of the country.

Animal life in Kazakhstan varies between the steppes and the desert. Larks, eagles, marmots, tortoises, and squirrels live in the steppes. Gazelles and a variety of rodents and reptiles inhabit the desert.

SCR Library

Northern Kazakhstan includes grassy plains called *steppes.* A herd of sheep grazes on the steppes, *above.* Livestock farming is a major economic activity in Kazakhstan.

Economy. Agriculture accounts for about two-fifths of the value of Kazakhstan's economic production. Farmers raise sheep and cattle throughout Kazakhstan. Chief livestock products are dairy goods, meat, leather, and wool. The country's major crops include barley, cotton, rice, and wheat. Since the 1950's, Kazakhstan's crop production has increased sharply due to expansion of agricultural lands and the irrigation of dry lands.

Kazakhstan's industries, which include food processing, mining, and chemical, textile, and heavy machinery manufacturing, account for about one-third of the value of the country's economic production. Alma-Ata, Chimkent, Pavlodar, and Karaganda rank among the country's chief industrial centers. Russia and Ukraine are Kazakhstan's most important trading partners.

The mines of the region yield many valuable minerals, including bauxite, borax, chromium, gold, iron, lead, nickel, phosphate, silver, tin, tungsten, uranium, and zinc. Coal is mined in central, eastern, and northeastern Kazakhstan. Petroleum and natural gas come from fields near the Caspian Sea. Copper mines operate in central, northern, and eastern Kazakhstan.

Several rail lines connect Kazakhstan's cities to urban areas in Russia, China, and other neighboring countries. Kazakhstan has a limited system of roads. Buses and trains are the country's most common forms of transportation. An airport at Alma-Ata handles all international flights to Kazakhstan.

Newspapers in Kazakhstan are published in several languages, including Kazakh and Russian. A radio and a television station in Alma-Ata broadcast in Kazakh, Russian, and several other local languages.

History. Nomadic people lived in what is now Kazakhstan before the birth of Christ. Turkish tribes began to settle in the region in the A.D. 500's. During the 1200's, Mongols from the east invaded the area and defeated the Turkish people. Many of the country's people are descended from the Turkish and Mongol tribes.

During the early 1700's, Russians began migrating to the Kazakh region. In 1731, after suffering attacks from neighboring peoples, the Kazakhs accepted Russian rule for protection. By the mid-1800's, the Russians had set up forts throughout the Kazakh area. The Russian government took control of vast areas of land and encouraged Russian and Ukrainian peasants to settle in the region. Such efforts, however, greatly reduced Kazakh grazing lands.

A nationalist movement to gain independence from Russia emerged in Kazakhstan following the Russian Revolution of 1917. Kazakh nationalists set up a central government and sent troops to fight against the *Bolsheviks,* Communists who had seized power in Russia during the Russian Revolution. By late 1919, however, the Kazakh nationalists had decided to side with the Bolsheviks.

In 1920, the Communists set up Kazakhstan as an *autonomous* (self-governing) republic called the Kyrgyz Autonomous Soviet Socialist Republic. Kazakhstan was renamed the Kazakh Autonomous Soviet Socialist Republic in 1925. The Soviet Union had been formed in 1922 under Russia's leadership. Kazakhstan became a union republic of the Soviet Union in 1936. It was called the Kazakh Soviet Socialist Republic.

Soviet rule changed many aspects of life in Kazakhstan. The Soviet Union established a powerful Communist central government in Moscow and took control of all industry and land in Kazakhstan and the other republics. The Communist Party became the only legal political party. Soviet law forbade certain traditional cultural practices, such as religious instruction. However, the Soviet government helped develop agriculture and industry in Kazakhstan. School and health-care systems were improved.

During World War II (1939-1945), the Soviet government forced many people from the western part of the Soviet Union to move to Kazakhstan. These people included Chechens, Germans, Tatars, and Ukrainians.

During the 1950's, the Soviet government launched a program to expand the use of Kazakhstan's vast steppes for agriculture. Much of the land was planted with grain. This program, called the *Virgin Lands* project, brought thousands of people from other parts of the Soviet Union to Kazakhstan.

During the 1980's, the Soviet government, under Mikhail S. Gorbachev, made reforms toward giving people more freedom. In 1990, Kazakhstan declared that its laws took precedence over those of the Soviet Union. In December 1991, Nursultan Nazarbayev became the first democratically elected president in the history of the Kazakh people. On December 16, Kazakhstan declared its independence, just nine days before the Soviet Union broke apart. As an independent country, Kazakhstan has sought to replace its government-controlled economy with a free enterprise system. It has replaced its Communist government and has begun a transition to a more democratic system. Larry V. Clark

Kyrgyzstan, *kihr GEEZ stan,* formerly known as *Kirghiz,* is a mountainous country in central Asia. It became an independent country in 1991, after about 70 years as a part of the Soviet Union.

Kyrgyzstan covers 76,641 square miles (198,500 square kilometers) and has a population of about 4,409,000. Bishkek is the country's capital and largest city. The official language is Kyrgyz.

Government. A president serves as head of state and is Kyrgyzstan's most powerful governmental official. The people elect the president to a five-year term. A Cabinet of Ministers, headed by a prime minister, carries out the operations of the government. The president appoints the prime minister and other ministers of the cabinet. A one-house parliament called the Supreme Council makes Kyrgyzstan's laws. Its 350 members serve five-year terms. Kyrgyzstan's main units of local government are regions and districts.

Kyrgyzstan's highest court is the Supreme Court. There are also regional and local courts. All judges are elected to five-year terms.

People. About 52 per cent of Kyrgyzstan's people belong to the Kyrgyz ethnic group. They speak Kyrgyz, a Turkic language. Most of the ethnic Kyrgyz live in rural areas and live by herding and farming. Ethnic Russians make up about 22 per cent of the population. They speak Russian, live mainly in urban areas, and hold most of the country's industrial and technical jobs. Other ethnic groups include Uzbeks, Ukrainians, and Germans. All Kyrgyz people and Uzbeks are Muslims. Most of the other people are Christians.

Among the ethnic Kyrgyz, tribal organizations and large kinship units called *clans* play important roles in social customs. Each tribe consists of a number of clans. A Kyrgyz clan includes all people who are descended from a common ancestor through their father's side of the family. Senior clan members function as community leaders. Traditionally, tribal leaders have been the most respected members of Kyrgyz society. When the Soviets took over, Kyrgyz tribal leaders were given high governmental positions. Today, tribal leaders hold most of the regional and national government offices in Kyrgyzstan.

Kyrgyz social life is centered around the family. Members of an extended family live together in one household. Such a household might include parents, children, married sons and their children, and other relatives. Kyrgyz tend to marry only people in their own clan.

About 60 per cent of Kyrgyzstan's people live in rural areas, and about 40 per cent live in urban areas. Most urban dwellers live in cement apartment buildings or stucco houses. For hundreds of years, large numbers of rural Kyrgyz were nomadic (wandering) herders who raised livestock in mountain valleys in the summer and moved them to the foothills in the winter. In the 1930s, the Soviet Union set up government farms and forced herders to live on them. Today, most of the rural people live in mud-brick houses in villages. But some rural people still raise livestock in the nomadic life style at least part of the year. These people live in portable, tentlike *yurts,* constructed of a round wooden frame covered with felt.

The Kyrgyz people wear both Western-style and traditional clothing. Traditional clothing for men includes a padded or a sheepskin coat, boots, and a white felt hat with black flaps. Married women often wear a white turban made of a long scarf.

Traditional Kyrgyz foods include *shurpa* (mutton and vegetable soup), and *besh barmak* (lamb and noodles

Facts in brief

Capital: Bishkek.
Official language: Kyrgyz.
Area: 76,641 sq. mi. (198,500 km²). *Greatest distances*—east-west, 580 mi. (935 km); north-south, 270 mi. (435 km).
Elevation: *Highest*—Peak Pobedy, 24,406 ft. (7,439 m) above sea level. *Lowest*—Naryn river at the western border, 1,640 ft. (500 m) above sea level.
Population: *Estimated 1993 population*—4,409,000; density, 58 persons per sq. mi. (22 per km²); distribution, 40 per cent urban, 60 per cent rural. *1989 census*—4,291,000. *Estimated 1998 population*—4,555,000.
Chief products: *Agriculture*—cattle, cotton, eggs, fruit, goats, grain, milk, pigs, vegetables, wool. *Manufacturing*—construction materials, food products, machinery, metals, textiles. *Mining*—antimony, mercury.
Flag: The flag has a red field with a yellow sun in its center. The sun bears a yellow disk with two intersecting sets of three curved red bands. See **Flag** (picture: Flags of Asia and the Pacific).
Money: *Basic unit*—ruble.

Kyrgyzstan

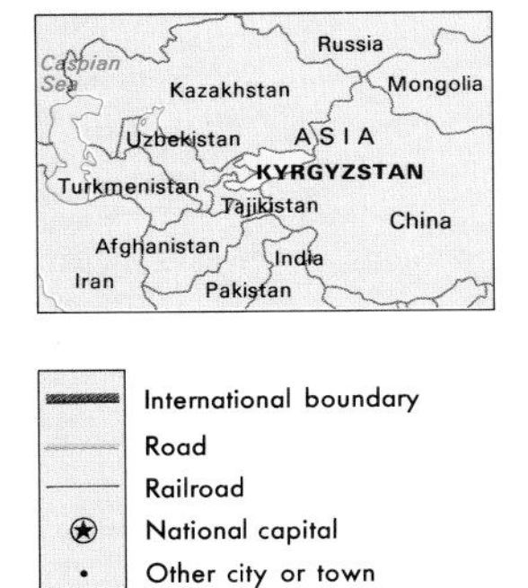

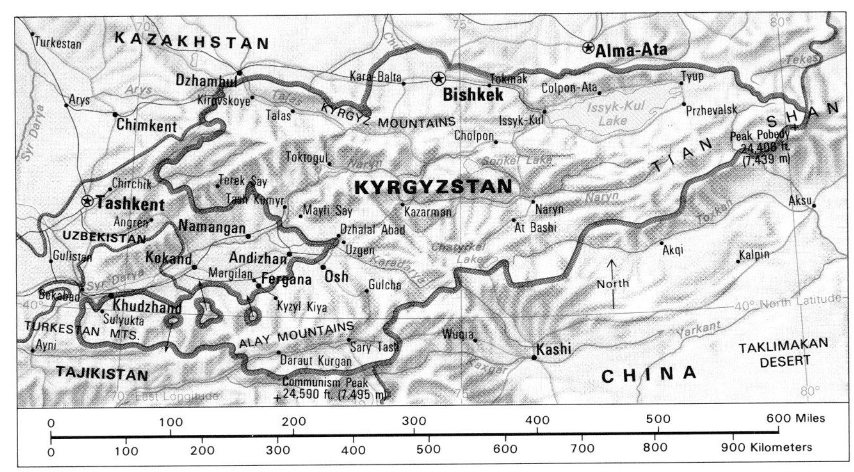

WORLD BOOK map

© Frans Lanting, Minden Pictures

Kyrgyz shepherds guide sheep across a grassy hillside. Livestock raising is Kyrgyzstan's chief agricultural activity, with sheep being the nation's most important kind of livestock.

with broth). Popular milk products include cheese, *ayran* (a yogurtlike drink), and *kumiss* (fermented mare's milk).

The Kyrgyz people enjoy folk songs and dancing. The recitation of *epics* (poems about heroic events) is a traditional Kyrgyz event.

The government requires children to attend school between the ages of 7 and 17. The country has 10 schools of higher education.

Land and climate. The Tian Shan and Alay mountains cover most of Kyrgyzstan. About three-quarters of the country lies at an altitude of more than 4,950 feet (1,500 meters) above sea level. Peak Pobedy, the country's highest mountain, rises 24,406 feet (7,439 meters) in the Tian Shan along the border with China. Only about 15 per cent of Kyrgyzstan is below 3,000 feet (915 meters) above sea level.

Temperatures in Kyrgyzstan vary with altitude. Summers are very warm and dry in the valleys and plains, and cool in the mountains. July temperatures average 60 to 75 °F (16 to 24 °C) in the valleys and plains and about 41 °F (5 °C) in the mountains. Winters are chilly in the lowlands, but extremely cold in the mountains. January temperatures average 7 to 23 °F (−5 to −14 °C) in the lowlands and −18 °F (−28 °C) in the mountains.

Economy. Agriculture accounts for about two-fifths of the value of Kyrgyzstan's economic production. Livestock raising is the chief agricultural activity. Sheep are the most important kind of livestock. People also raise cattle, goats, and pigs. They graze yaks in the high mountains. Less than 10 per cent of the land is suitable for raising crops.

Manufacturing makes up about a third of the value of production in Kyrgyzstan. Chief manufactured products include construction materials, food products, machinery, metals, and textiles. The country's major industrial center is Bishkek.

History. Nomads who raised livestock were the first people to live in what is now Kyrgyzstan. They settled into the region from various parts of northern Asia. During the 500's and 600's, Turkic tribes began to invade the region. Waves of Turkic invasions continued into the 1100's. Mongols conquered the area in the early 1200's. The Mongols established regions called *khanates,* which were ruled by chieftains. Some of the country's people probably descended from the Turkic and Mongol tribes. In the 1600's, Islamic missionaries called *sufis* brought Islam to the region.

Kyrgyzstan remained primarily under the domination of Mongol peoples until 1758, when China gained control. The Chinese maintained loose rule over the Kyrgyz until the 1830's, when the oppressive Khanate of Kokand conquered the Kyrgyz people.

The Russian Empire began to expand into central Asia in the mid-1800's. It defeated the Khanate of Kokand in 1876 and made the region a Russian province. The Russian government took control of vast areas of land and encouraged Russian, Ukrainian, and other Slavic peasants to settle there. Tens of thousands of foreign agricultural workers settled in Kyrgyzstan. The settlement restricted grazing land and lowered the Kyrgyz standard of living. In 1916, the Kyrgyz staged an unsuccessful rebellion against the Russians. Thousands were killed on both sides, and as many as 150,000 Kyrgyz people fled to China.

In 1917, Communists overthrew Russia's czar and took control of that country. The Soviet Union was formed in 1922 under Russian Communist leadership. In 1924, the Soviets made Kyrgyzstan an *autonomous oblast* (self-governing region) of the Soviet Union called the Kara-Kyrgyz Autonomous Oblast. In 1936, the region became a Soviet republic and was called the Kyrgyz Soviet Socialist Republic.

Soviet rule changed many aspects of life in Kyrgyzstan. The Soviet Union established a powerful Communist government and took control of all industry and land in Kyrgyzstan. It forced nomadic herders to settle on government farms. The Communist Party also became the only legal political party. In addition, Soviet law forbade certain traditional cultural practices, such as religious instruction. However, the Soviet government helped develop agriculture and industry in Kyrgyzstan. School and health-care systems were also improved.

In the late 1980's, the Soviet government began giving people more freedom. In 1990, Kyrgyzstan declared that its laws overruled those of the Soviet Union. In mid-1991, the Communist Party was dissolved, and Kyrgyzstan began moving toward creating a free-enterprise economy. The government began selling off farmland and businesses to private owners. The Soviet Union broke apart in December 1991, and Kyrgyzstan became an independent country. The country joined the Commonwealth of Independent States, a loose association of former Soviet republics.

The new nation's problems include tensions between ethnic groups. Conflicts exist between the Kyrgyz and the Uzbeks over territorial claims and other disputes. In 1990, violence broke out between the two groups, resulting in hundreds of deaths. Edward J. Lazzerini

Moldova, *mawl DOH vuh,* is a country in south-central Europe bordered by Romania on the west and by Ukraine on the other three sides. From 1940 to 1991, Moldova was a republic of the Soviet Union. It was called the Moldavian Soviet Socialist Republic, or simply Moldavia. With the collapse of the Soviet Union in 1991, the republic declared its independence.

Moldova belonged to Romania before it became part of the Soviet Union, and it shares Romania's language, history, and culture. Moldova has especially close ties with a region in eastern Romania that is still called Moldavia. For much of their history, Moldova and the Romanian region of Moldavia were united.

Moldova covers 13,012 square miles (33,700 square kilometers) and has a population of 4,460,000. Chisinau, called Kishinev under the Soviets, is the capital.

Government and politics

Political power in Moldova is divided between the president, Parliament, and the Council of Ministers. Voters elect the president to a five-year term. The Parliament has 365 members, who are also elected to five-year terms. The president appoints the Council of Ministers.

The country's largest political party is the Moldovan Popular Front, which supports reunification of Moldova with Romania. The National Alliance for Independence supports independent statehood. It is made up of about 10 political, cultural, and professional organizations. The Joint Council of Work Cooperatives is the major political force in an industrial region on the east bank of the Dnestr (also spelled Nistru) River in eastern Moldova. Many of the people in this region, called Trans-Dnestr, are of Russian or Ukrainian descent and oppose union with Romania. The activities of the Communist Party—which had been the only party under Soviet rule—were outlawed in 1991.

People

Ethnic groups and language. Moldova is the most densely populated of all the former Soviet republics. About two-thirds of the people are ethnic Moldovans. Most of the rest of the population is made up of Russians; Ukrainians; Gagauz, a Turkic people; and Bulgarians. More than half of the people of Moldova live in rural areas, clustered in villages. Most of these people work as farmers.

Facts in brief

Capital: Chisinau.
Official language: Romanian.
Official name: Republica Moldova (Republic of Moldova).
Area: 13,012 sq. mi. (33,700 km²). *Greatest distances*—north-south, 210 mi. (340 km); east-west, 165 mi. (265 km).
Elevation: *Highest*—Mount Balaneshty, 1,407 ft. (429 m). *Lowest:* Dnestr River at southeastern border, 80 ft. (25 m).
Population: *Estimated 1993 population*—4,460,000; density, 343 persons per sq. mi. (132 per km²); distribution, 53 per cent rural, 47 per cent urban. *1989 census*—4,341,000. *Estimated 1998 population*—4,608,000.
Chief products: *Agriculture*—eggs, grain, grapes, milk, sugar beets. *Manufacturing*—construction materials, refrigerators, tractors, washing machines.
National anthem: *"Deşteapta-te, Române"* ("Romanian, Arise").
Money: *Basic unit*—ruble.

The country's official language is Romanian. The Moldovans used the Roman alphabet in writing their language. Under Soviet rule, they were forced to adopt the Cyrillic alphabet, which is used to write the Russian language. But in 1989, the republic's parliament ordered a return to the Roman alphabet.

Religion. Most Moldovans are Eastern Orthodox Christians. From 1940 until the late 1980's, the Soviet Union forbade religious instruction in Moldova and discouraged church attendance. In 1990, the Soviet Union restored religious freedom.

Education. Moldovan children are required to attend school from the ages of 6 to 18. Almost every Moldovan 15 years of age or older can read and write. The Moldovan State University is in Chisinau. The Academy of Sciences in that city oversees the workings of about 30 academic institutes.

Land and climate

Most of Moldova consists of hills broken by river valleys. The highest elevations are in the scenic forests of the central region. The country's tallest peak is Mount Balaneshty, which rises 1,407 feet (429 meters) in the Kodry Hills in west-central Moldova. Lush uplands and *steppes* (grassy plains) cover much of northern and eastern Moldova. A large plain stretches across the south.

Moldova has more than 3,000 rivers, but only 8 are

Moldova

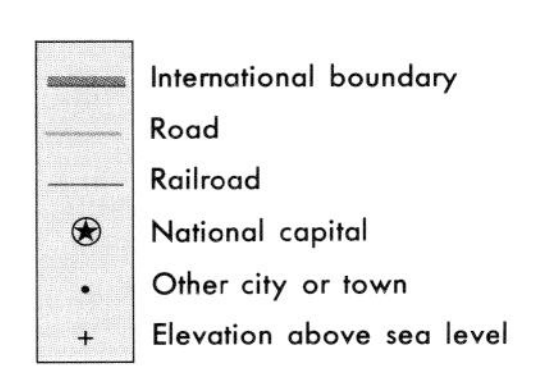

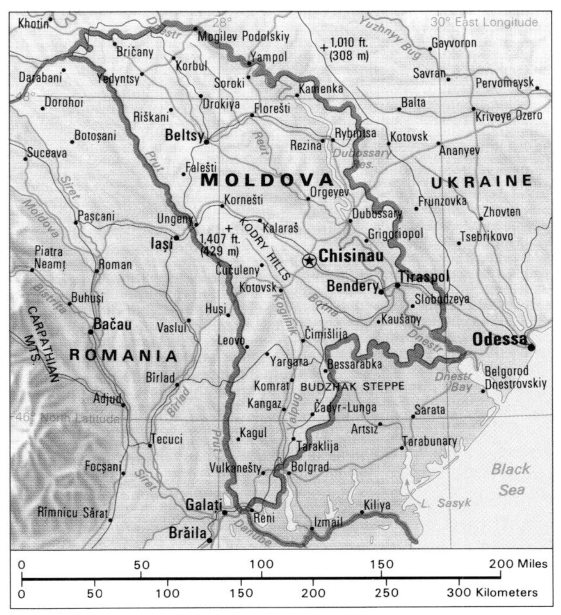

WORLD BOOK map

A. Boulat, Sipa Press

Rich farmland covers three-fourths of Moldova, and the country's economy is based largely on agriculture. Farmers load bales of hay, which will be used as feed for cattle.

longer than 60 miles (95 kilometers). The country's main waterway is the Dnestr River, which flows through eastern Moldova.

Rich, black soil that is good for farming covers three-fourths of the country. In the north and along the Dnestr, where the most fertile soils are, farmers grow fruits, sugar beets, and some grain. Less rich soils in the south are used for corn, wheat, and sunflowers.

The animals found in Moldova include wolves, badgers, wild boars, and Siberian stags. The rivers hold carp, pike, and perch.

Temperatures average about 25 °F (−4 °C) in January and about 70 °F (21 °C) in July. The average annual precipitation provides about 20 inches (50 centimeters) of rain, snow, and other forms of moisture.

Economy

Moldova has a developing economy supported mainly by agriculture. The central and southern regions produce grapes for wine. Farms in the south also grow corn and winter wheat. The northern and central regions have fruit orchards and fields of grain. Moldova's other crops include sugar beets, sunflowers, and tobacco. Dairy farming, hog farming, and cattle raising are also important.

Moldova's chief industries process food and other agricultural products and manufacture construction materials, refrigerators, television sets, tractors and other agricultural machinery, and washing machines. The country has plants for canning fruits and vegetables, refining sugar from sugar beets, and making wine. Other plants process furs and make footwear and silk and woolen garments.

Moldova's chief trading partners are former Soviet republics, especially Russia and Ukraine; and other countries of Eastern Europe. Its major exports include wine, leather and fur, and clothing. Its main imports include fuel, automobiles, and electronic items.

History

Early days. From about 700 B.C. until about A.D. 200, the region that is now Moldova was under the control of Iranian peoples from central Asia—first the Scythians and later the Sarmatians. From about A.D. 200 until the A.D. 1200's, various other peoples from the west and east invaded and ruled the area. These invaders included the Goths, Huns, Avars, and finally the Mongols (also called the Tatars). The people of Moldova gradually united and by the mid-1300's, they formed an independent state under a single ruler, a prince. The state was called the principality of Moldavia. It included present-day Moldova, then called Bessarabia, and an area between the Moldavian Carpathian Mountains and the Prut River in modern Romania.

Ottoman and Russian rule. The Ottoman Empire, based in present-day Turkey, gained control of the principality of Moldavia by the early 1500's. The Ottomans ruled the region until 1812, when Russia took control of Bessarabia. The Treaty of Paris that ended the Crimean War in 1856 gave southern Bessarabia to the principality of Moldavia, following Russia's defeat in that war. In 1861, the principality of Moldavia united with the principality of Walachia, now a region in present-day Romania, to form the new nation of Romania.

Romanian and Soviet rule. After World War I (1914-1918), all of Bessarabia became part of Romania. The Soviet Union, which had been formed as a Communist state under Russia's leadership in 1922, refused to recognize Bessarabia's unification with Romania. In 1924, the Soviets established the Moldavian Autonomous Soviet Socialist Republic (A.S.S.R.) in the Trans-Dnestr region. In 1940, during World War II, the Soviet Union seized Bessarabia and merged most of it with part of the Moldavian A.S.S.R. to form the Moldavian Soviet Socialist Republic.

Breakup of the Soviet Union. The Moldavian Supreme Soviet, as the republic's legislature was then called, declared in 1990 that its laws took precedence over those of the Soviet Union. Moldavia also changed its name to Moldova.

In August 1991, conservative Communist officials failed in an attempt to overthrow Soviet President Mikhail S. Gorbachev. During the upheaval that followed, Moldova and several other republics declared their independence. Moldova and 10 other former republics of the Soviet Union formed a loose association called the Commonwealth of Independent States in December, after which the Soviet Union dissolved.

Moldova's leaders restored many of the country's ties to Romania. They reintroduced Romanian history as a basic subject in the school curriculum and sent thousands of Moldovans to study in Romanian schools.

Threats to Moldovan unity. In 1990—before Moldova became independent—both the Gagauz people in southern Moldova and Russians and Ukrainians in the Trans-Dnestr region had announced that they were forming independent states. In March 1992, fighting between ethnic Moldovans and separatists in the Trans-Dnestr broke out. In July, a peacekeeping force entered the region, and fighting ceased.

Vladimir Tismaneanu

Superstock

Red Square is the center of activity in Moscow, Russia's capital and largest city. Famous landmarks in Red Square include St. Basil's Cathedral, *left,* and the Kremlin, *right.*

Russia

Russia is the world's largest country in area. It is almost twice as big as Canada, the second largest country. From 1922 until 1991, Russia was the biggest republic in the Soviet Union, the most powerful Communist country in the world. The Soviet Union broke apart in 1991, and Russia began to set up a new political, legal, and economic system.

Russia extends from the Arctic Ocean south to the Black Sea and from the Baltic Sea east to the Pacific Ocean. It covers much of the continents of Europe and Asia. Moscow, the capital and largest city of Russia, is the world's third largest city in population. Only Mexico City and Seoul, South Korea, have more people. St. Petersburg, on the coast of the Baltic Sea, is Russia's chief seaport.

Most of Russia's people are ethnic *Russians*—that is, descendants of an early Slavic people called the Russians. More than 100 minority nationalities also live in Russia. Approximately three-fourths of the people make their homes in urban areas. Russian cities have better schools and health-care facilities than the rural areas do. However, the cities suffer from overcrowding and from frequent shortages of many consumer goods, including food and clothing.

Russia has abundant natural resources, including vast deposits of petroleum, natural gas, coal, and iron ore. However, many of these reserves lie far from settled areas. Russia's harsh, cold climate makes it difficult to take advantage of many of the country's valuable resources.

Russia traces its history back to a state that emerged in Europe among the East Slavs during the 800's. Over time, large amounts of territory and many different peoples came under Russian rule. For hundreds of years, *czars* (emperors) and empresses ruled Russia. They had almost complete control over most aspects of Russian life. Under these rulers, the country's economic development lagged far behind the rapid industrial progress that began in Western Europe in the 1700's. Most of

Donald J. Raleigh, the contributor of this article, is Professor of History at the University of North Carolina at Chapel Hill.

ITAR-Tass from Sovfoto

Fields of wheat spread over vast areas of Russian farmland. Russia ranks as one of the world's major producers of wheat and other grains.

Scene from a Kirov Ballet production of *Don Quixote* (ITAR-Tass from Sovfoto)

Russian ballet troupes perform throughout the world. They are famous for their skill and beauty.

© Ken Proctor, Superstock

Snow covers more than half of Russia for six months of the year. This village is near the city of Irkutsk in Siberia.

the people were poor, uneducated peasants.

Russia made many great contributions to the arts during the 1800's. Such authors as Anton Chekhov, Fyodor Dostoevsky, and Leo Tolstoy wrote masterpieces of literature. Russian composers, including Modest Mussorgsky, Nikolai Rimsky-Korsakov, and Peter Ilich Tchaikovsky, created music of lasting greatness. Russians also made valuable artistic contributions in the fields of architecture, ballet, and painting.

Opposition to the czars' absolute power increased during the late 1800's and the early 1900's. Revolutionaries overthrew the Russian government in 1917. The next year, Russia became the Russian Soviet Federative Socialist Republic (R.S.F.S.R.). In 1922, the R.S.F.S.R. and three other republics established a new nation called the Union of Soviet Socialist Republics (U.S.S.R.), also known as the Soviet Union. The R.S.F.S.R. became the largest and most influential republic of the Soviet Union, which grew to 15 republics by 1956. In 1991, Communist rule in the Soviet Union collapsed, and the country broke apart. Russia and 10 other republics formed a new, loose federation called the Commonwealth of Independent States.

After the breakup of the Soviet Union, Russia entered a transitional period. The Communist leaders of the Soviet Union had controlled all aspects of the country's economy and government. Russia's new national government worked to move the country from a state-controlled economy to one based on private enterprise. The government also began to establish new political and legal systems in Russia.

This article deals with Russia from its early history to the present. For more detailed information about the history of Russia between 1922 and 1991—when it was part of the Soviet Union—see **Union of Soviet Socialist Republics.**

Russia in brief

General information

Capital: Moscow.
Official language: Russian.
Official names: *Rossiya* (Russia) or *Rossiyskaya Federatsiya* (Russian Federation).

Largest cities (1990 official estimates)
Moscow 8,769,000
St. Petersburg 4,295,000

The Russian flag was adopted in 1991. It had been the unofficial ethnic flag of the Russian people since 1988. The Russian empire used the flag from 1699 to 1918.

Land and climate

Land: Russia is the world's largest country in area. It covers a large part of both Europe and Asia. It has coastlines on the Arctic Ocean, Baltic Sea, Black Sea, Caspian Sea, and Pacific Ocean. Russia borders eight European countries, three Asian countries, and three countries with lands in both Europe and Asia. Much of the west is a large plain. The Ural Mountains separate Europe and Asia. Siberia, east of the Urals, has low western plains, a central plateau, and a mountainous wilderness in the east. Major Russian rivers include the Lena in Asia and the Volga in Europe. Lake Baikal in Siberia is the world's deepest lake.
Area: 6,592,850 sq. mi. (17,075,400 km²). *Greatest distances*—east-west, 6,000 mi. (9,650 km); north-south, 2,800 mi. (4,500 km).
Elevation: *Highest*—Mount Elbrus, 18,510 ft. (5,642 m). *Lowest*—Coast of Caspian Sea, 92 ft. (28 m) below sea level.
Climate: Most of Russia has long, bitterly cold winters and mild to warm—but short—summers. In northeastern Siberia, the country's coldest area, January temperatures average below −50 °F (−46 °C). Rainfall is moderate in most of Russia. Snow covers more than half of the country during six months of the year.

WORLD BOOK map

Government

Form of government: Transitional.
Head of state: President.
Head of government: Prime minister.
Legislature: The Congress of People's Deputies is the highest parliamentary body. The Supreme Soviet also passes laws. It consists of two houses—the Council of the Federation and the Council of Nationalities—whose members are chosen from the Congress of People's Deputies.
Political subdivisions: 49 *oblasts* (regions), 6 *krais* (territories), 20 *autonomous* (self-governing) republics, 10 autonomous areas, 1 autonomous region. All of these are divided into *raions* (districts).

People

Population: *1993 estimate*—151,436,000. *1989 census*—147,400,537. *1998 estimate*—156,489,000.
Population density: 23 persons per sq. mi. (9 per km²).
Distribution: 74 per cent urban, 26 per cent rural.
Major ethnic/national groups: About 83 per cent Russian. Smaller groups include Tatars (or Tartars), Ukrainians, Chuvash, Bashkirs, Belarusians, Mordvins, Chechen, Germans, Udmurts, Mari, Kazakhs, Avars, Jews, and Armenians.
Major religions: The Russian Orthodox Church is the largest religious group. Other religious groups include Muslims, Protestants, Roman Catholics, and Jews.

Population trend

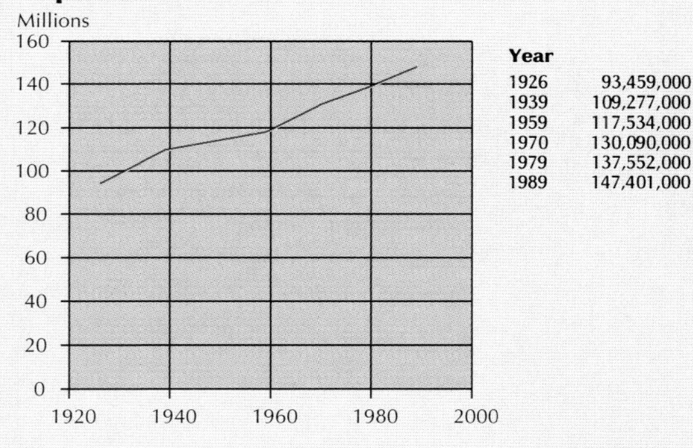

Year	
1926	93,459,000
1939	109,277,000
1959	117,534,000
1970	130,090,000
1979	137,552,000
1989	147,401,000

Economy

Chief products: *Agriculture*—barley, cattle, flax, fruits, hogs, oats, potatoes, rye, sheep, sugar beets, sunflowers, wheat. *Fishing*—cod, haddock, herring, salmon. *Manufacturing*—chemicals, construction materials, electrical equipment, iron and steel, lumber, machinery, paper. *Mining*—coal, iron ore, manganese, natural gas, nickel, petroleum, platinum-group metals.
Money: *Basic unit*—ruble. For value in U.S. dollars, see **Money** (table: Exchange rates).
Foreign trade: *Major exports*—chemicals, machinery, minerals, paper products, petroleum, wood products. *Major imports*—consumer goods, food and beverages, industrial equipment, machinery. *Major trading partners*—former Soviet republics, Bulgaria, Czechoslovakia, Cuba, Finland, Germany, Hungary, Japan, Poland, Romania.

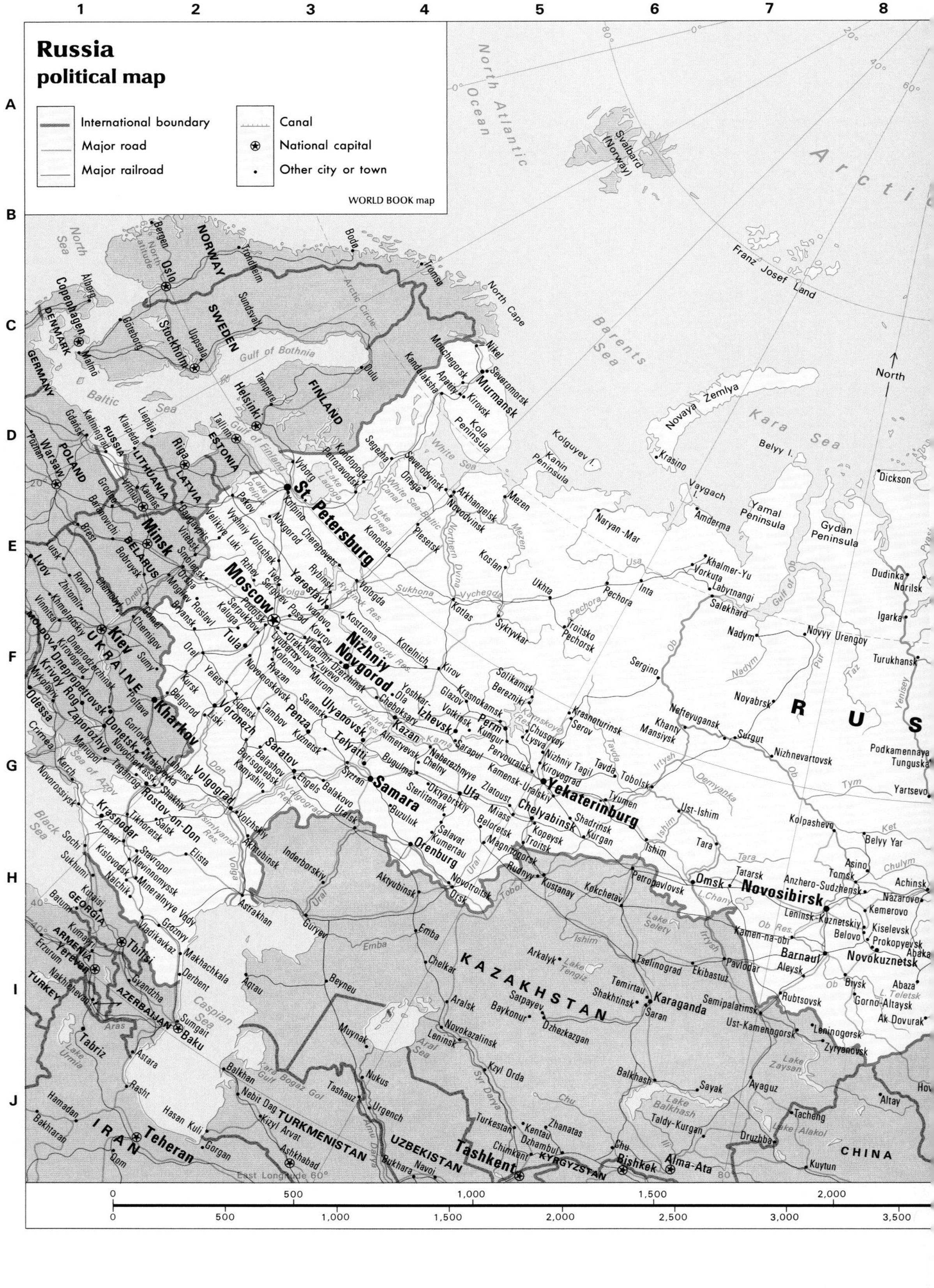

1
2
3
4
5
6
7
8
A
B
C
D
E
F
G
H
I
J
Russia
political map
International boundary
Major road
Major railroad
Canal
National capital
Other city or town
WORLD BOOK map
North Atlantic Ocean
Svalbard (Norway)
Arctic
Franz Josef Land
North Cape
Barents Sea
North
Novaya Zemlya
Kara Sea
Belyy I.
Dickson
Krasino
Kolguyev I.
Kanin Peninsula
Vaygach I.
Amderma
Yamal Peninsula
Gydan Peninsula
Gulf of Ob
North Sea
Bergen
Oslo
NORWAY
Trondheim
Bodø
Tromsø
Ålborg
Copenhagen
DENMARK
Göteborg
Stockholm
Uppsala
SWEDEN
Sundsvall
Arctic Circle
Malmö
Gulf of Bothnia
Oulu
Tampere
Helsinki
FINLAND
Nikel
Severomorsk
Murmansk
Monchegorsk
Kandalaksha
Apatity
Kirovsk
Kola Peninsula
GERMANY
Baltic Sea
Liepāja
Tallinn
ESTONIA
Gulf of Finland
Gdańsk
Kaliningrad
RUSSIA
Klaipėda
LITHUANIA
Riga
LATVIA
Poznań
Warsaw
POLAND
Vilnius
Kaunas
Daugavpils
Lake Peipus
Pskov
Vyborg
St. Petersburg
Lake Ladoga
Kondopoga
Petrozavodsk
Segezha
Lake Onega
White Sea
White Sea-Baltic Canal
Severodvinsk
Onega
Arkhangelsk
Novodvinsk
Mezen
Plesetsk
Northern Dvina
Naryan-Mar
Grodno
Baranovichi
Brest
Minsk
BELARUS
Vitebsk
Smolensk
Bobruysk
Velikiye Luki
Vyshniy Volochek
Novgorod
Cherepovets
Konosha
Kotlas
Koslan
Ukhta
Pechora
Inta
Usa
Vorkuta
Khalmer-Yu
Labytnangi
Salekhard
Lutsk
Lvov
Rovno
Zhitomir
Chernobyl
Gomel
Mogilev
Orsha
Dnepr
Roslavl
Bryansk
Rzhev
Tver
Rybinsk
Yaroslavl
Vologda
Sukhona
Vychegda
Syktyvkar
Pechora
Troitsko-Pechorsk
Nadym
Novyy Urengoy
Igarka
Dudinka
Norilsk
Vinnitsa
Khmelnitskiy
MOLDOVA
Kiev
UKRAINE
Chernigov
Sumy
Kaluga
Serpukhov
Moscow
Sergiyev Posad
Ivanovo
Rybinsk Res.
Kostroma
Kovrov
Podolsk
Tula
Orel
Lyubertsy
Orekhovo-Zuyevo
Vladimir
Dzerzhinsk
Nizhniy Novgorod
Gorki Res.
Kotelnich
Kirov
Solikamsk
Berezniki
Sergino
Ob
Noyabrsk
Turukhansk
Kirovograd
Dneprodzerzhinsk
Dnepropetrovsk
Krivoy Rog
Mykolayiv
Odessa
Poltava
Kharkov
Kursk
Belgorod
Yelets
Lipetsk
Voronezh
Liski
Ryazan
Kolomna
Novomoskovsk
Murom
Tambov
Saransk
Cheboksary
Yoshkar-Ola
Glazov
Krasnokamsk
Votkinsk
Izhevsk
Perm
Kungur
Chusovoy
Lysva
Kamskoye Res.
Krasnoturinsk
Serov
Nefteyugansk
Khanty-Mansiysk
Surgut
Nizhnevartovsk
RUS
Podkamennaya Tunguska
Zaporozhye
Donetsk
Gorlovka
Makeyevka
Novocherkassk
Taganrog
Mariupol
Crimea
Kerch
Sea of Azov
Novorossiysk
Penza
Ulyanovsk
Kuybyshev Res.
Kazan
Kama
Almetyevsk
Naberezhnyye Chelny
Sarapul
Pervouralsk
Nizhniy Tagil
Kirovgrad
Tavda
Tobolsk
Irtysh
Demyanka
Yartsevo
Luhansk
Shakhty
Rostov-on-Don
Volgograd
Don
Saratov
Balashov
Borisoglebsk
Kamyshin
Engels
Balakovo
Syzran
Tolyatti
Samara
Bugulma
Oktyabrskiy
Sterlitamak
Ufa
Zlatoust
Kamensk-Uralskiy
Yekaterinburg
Tyumen
Ust-Ishim
Tym
Kolpashevo
Ket
Black Sea
Krasnodar
Tikhoretsk
Salsk
Armavir
Sochi
Tsimlyansk Res.
Volga
Volzhskiy
Uralsk
Buzuluk
Salavat
Kumertau
Orenburg
Miass
Beloretsk
Chelyabinsk
Kopeysk
Magnitogorsk
Shadrinsk
Kurgan
Troitsk
Ishim
Tara
Belyy Yar
Sukhumi
Kislovodsk
Stavropol
Nevinnomyssk
Mineralnyye Vody
Nalchik
Elista
Aktubinsk
Inderborskiy
Ural
Novotroitsk
Orsk
Rudnyy
Tobol
Kustanay
Kokchetav
Petropavlovsk
Omsk
Tatarsk
Novosibirsk
Asino
Tomsk
Chulym
Anzhero-Sudzhensk
Achinsk
Nazarovo
Kemerovo
Kutaisi
GEORGIA
Batumi
Kumayri
ARMENIA
Yerevan
Erzurum
TURKEY
Nakhichevan
Tbilisi
Vladikavkaz
Groznyy
Makhachkala
Derbent
Gyandzha
AZERBAIJAN
Sumgait
Baku
Aras
Astrakhan
Guryev
Emba
Aktyubinsk
Lake Selety
Lake Chany
Leninsk-Kuznetskiy
Belovo
Kiselevsk
Prokopyevsk
Kamen-na-obi
Ob Res.
Barnaul
Novokuznetsk
Abakan
Caspian Sea
Aqtau
Beyneu
Chelkar
KAZAKHSTAN
Arkalyk
Lake Tengiz
Ishim
Tselinograd
Ekibastuz
Pavlodar
Aleysk
Biysk
Abaza
Lake Teletsk
Gorno-Altaysk
Ak Dovurak
Temirtau
Shakhtinsk
Karaganda
Saran
Satpayev
Baykonur
Dzhezkazgan
Aralsk
Novokazalinsk
Leninsk
Aral Sea
Semipalatinsk
Rubtsovsk
Ust-Kamenogorsk
Leninogorsk
Zyryanovsk
Lake Zaysan
Tabriz
Lake Urmia
Astara
Rasht
Balkhan
Kara Bogaz Gol
Muynak
Nukus
Kzyl Orda
Syr Darya
Balkhash
Sayak
Ayaguz
Lake Balkhash
Hamadan
Bakhtaran
IRAN
Teheran
Hasan Kuli
Nebit Dag
TURKMENISTAN
Kizyl Arvat
Gorgan
Qom
Ashkhabad
Tashauz
Urgench
Amu Darya
UZBEKISTAN
Bukhara
Navoi
Turkestan
Kentau
Dzhambul
Chimkent
Tashkent
KYRGYZSTAN
Zhanatas
Chu
Bishkek
Alma-Ata
Taldy-Kurgan
Lake Alakol
Druzhba
Tacheng
Altay
CHINA
Kuytun
East Longitude 60°
0
500
1,000
1,500
2,000
2,500
3,000
3,500

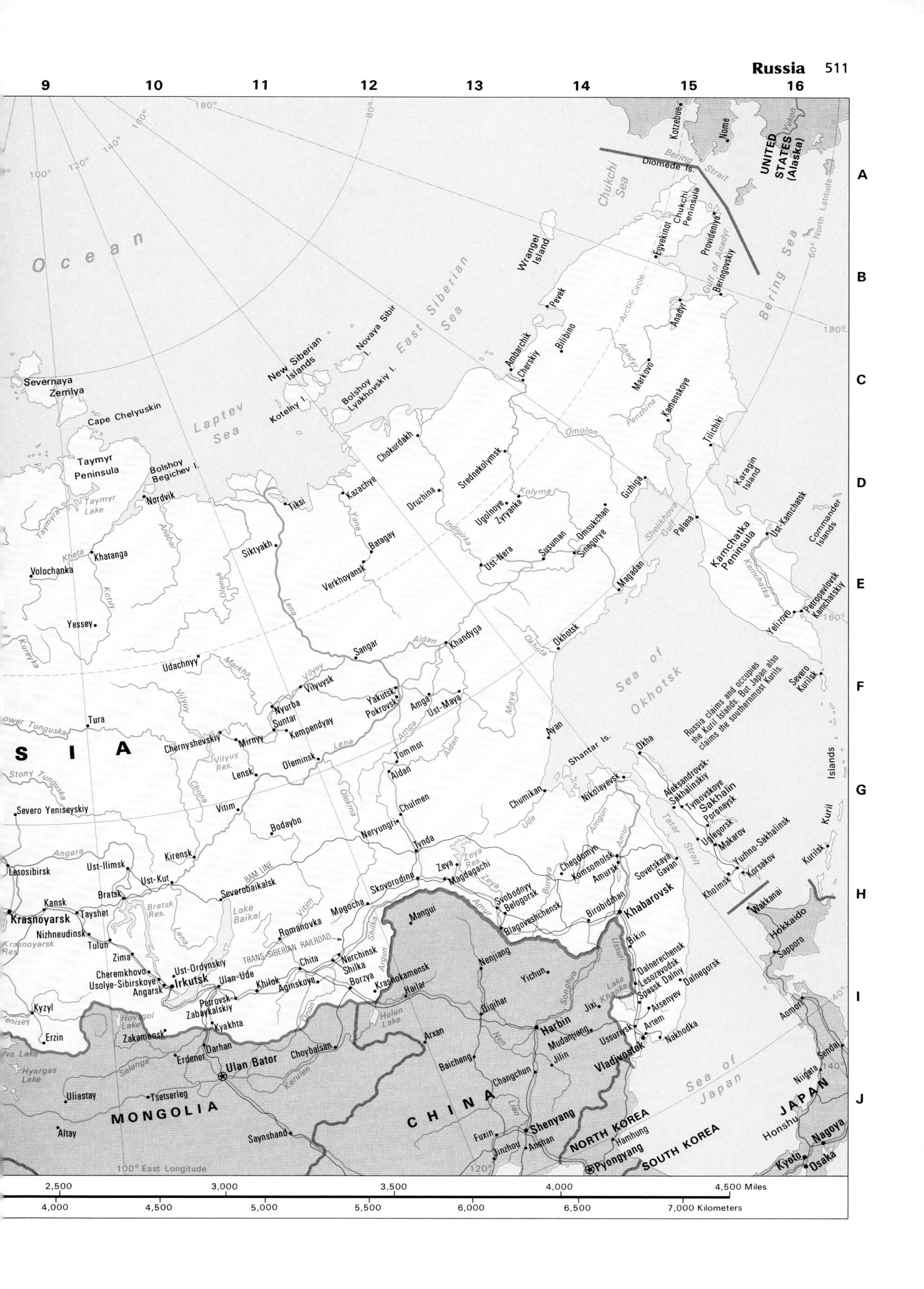
Ocean
Severnaya Zemlya
Cape Chelyuskin
Laptev Sea
Taymyr Peninsula
Bolshoy Begichev I.
Nordvik
New Siberian Islands
Novaya Sibir I.
Kotelny I.
Bolshoy Lyakhovskiy I.
East Siberian Sea
Wrangel Island
Chukchi Sea
Bering Strait
Diomede Is.
Kotzebue
Nome
UNITED STATES (Alaska)
Chukchi Peninsula
Egvekinot
Provideniya
Gulf of Anadyr
Beringovskiy
Bering Sea
Pevek
Bilibino
Ambarchik
Cherskiy
Anadyr
Markovo
Kamenskoye
Tilichiki
Karagin Island
Chokurdakh
Srednekolymsk
Kazachye
Tiksi
Druzhina
Ugolnoye
Zyryanka
Kolyma
Gizhiga
Omsukchan
Palana
Ust-Kamchatsk
Commander Islands
Kamchatka Peninsula
Khatanga
Volochanka
Siktyakh
Batagay
Verkhoyansk
Ust-Nera
Susuman
Sinegorye
Magadan
Petropavlovsk Kamchatskiy
Yelizovo
Yessey
Okhotsk
Khandyga
Sangar
Udachnyy
Sea of Okhotsk
Vilyuysk
Nyurba
Yakutsk
Pokrovsk
Amga
Ust-Maya
Severo Kurilsk
Tura
Suntar
Kempendyay
Chernyshevskiy
Mirnyy
Ayan
Russia claims and occupies the Kuril Islands. But Japan also claims the southernmost Kurils.
Okha
Shantar Is.
Oleminsk
Lensk
Tommot
Aldan
Severo Yeniseyskiy
Vitim
Chulmen
Chumikan
Nikolayevsk
Aleksandrovsk-Sakhalinskiy
Tymovskoye
Sakhalin
Poronaysk
Kuril Islands
Bodaybo
Neryungri
Uglegorsk
Makarov
Tatar Strait
Tynda
Kirensk
Lesosibirsk
Ust-Ilimsk
Ust-Kut
Zeya
Magdagachi
Chegdomyn
Komsomolsk
Amursk
Sovetskaya Gavan
Yuzhno-Sakhalinsk
Kholmsk
Korsakov
Kurilsk
BAM LINE
Severobaikalsk
Skovorodino
Svobodnyy
Belogorsk
Blagoveshchensk
Birobidzhan
Khabarovsk
Wakkanai
Hokkaido
Sapporo
Bratsk
Kansk
Krasnoyarsk
Tayshet
Nizhneudinsk
Tulun
Lake Baikal
Mogocha
Mangui
Romanovka
TRANS-SIBERIAN RAILROAD
Bikin
Dalnerechensk
Lesozavodsk
Spassk Dalniy
Dalnegorsk
Arsenyev
Zima
Ust-Ordynskiy
Cheremkhovo
Usolye-Sibirskoye
Angarsk
Irkutsk
Ulan-Ude
Khilok
Chita
Nerchinsk
Shilka
Aginskoye
Borzya
Krasnokamensk
Hailar
Nenjiang
Yichun
Qiqihar
Harbin
Jixi
Lake Khanka
Artem
Nakhodka
Aomori
Kyzyl
Petrovsk-Zabaykalskiy
Kyakhta
Zakamensk
Erzin
Darhan
Erdenet
Ulan Bator
Choybalsan
Arxan
Mudanjiang
Ussuriysk
Vladivostok
Jilin
Baicheng
Changchun
Sea of Japan
Sendai
Niigata
Uliastay
Tsetserleg
MONGOLIA
CHINA
Shenyang
NORTH KOREA
Hamhung
SOUTH KOREA
JAPAN
Honshu
Nagoya
Altay
Saynshand
Fuxin
Jinzhou
Anshan
Pyongyang
Kyoto
Osaka
100° East Longitude
2,500 3,000 3,500 4,000 4,500 Miles
4,000 4,500 5,000 5,500 6,000 6,500 7,000 Kilometers

Russia map index

Cities and towns

City or town	Population	Map key
Abakan	157,000	I 8
Abaza		I 8
Achinsk	122,000	H 8
Aginskoye		I 11
Ak Dovurak		I 8
Aldan		G 12
Aleksandrovsk Sakhalinskiy		G 15
Aleksin*	70,000	F 2
Aleysk		I 7
Almetyevsk	130,000	G 4
Ambarchik		C 13
Amderma		E 6
Amga		F 13
Amursk		H 15
Anadyr		B 15
Andropov, see Rybinsk		
Angarsk	267,000	I 10
Anzhero-Sudzhensk	108,000	H 8
Apatity	74,000	D 4
Arkhangelsk	419,000	D 4
Armavir	162,000	H 1
Arsenyev		I 15
Artem	71,000	I 15
Arzamas*	111,000	F 3
Asbest*	81,000	G 5
Asino		H 8
Astrakhan	510,000	H 2
Ayan		F 14
Azov*	79,000	G 1
Balakovo	200,000	G 3
Balashikha*	137,000	F 3
Balashov	97,000	G 3
Barnaul	603,000	I 7
Batagay		E 12
Bataysk*	95,000	G 2
Belgorod	306,000	F 2
Beloretsk	74,000	G 5
Belovo	116,000	I 8
Belyy Yar		H 8
Berdsk*	74,000	H 7
Berezniki	201,000	F 5
Beringovskiy		B 15
Bikin		I 15
Bilibino		C 14
Birobidzhan	77,000	H 14
Biysk	234,000	I 8
Blagoveshchensk	208,000	H 13
Bodaybo		G 11
Borisoglebsk		G 2
Borzya		I 12
Bratsk	258,000	H 10
Brezhnev, see Naberezhnyye Chelny		
Bryansk	456,000	F 2
Bugulma	85,000	G 4
Buzuluk	79,000	G 4
Chapayevsk*	86,000	G 4
Chaykovskiy*	76,000	G 4
Cheboksary	429,000	F 4
Chegdomyn		H 14
Chelyabinsk	1,148,000	G 5
Cheremkhovo	73,000	I 10
Cherepovets	313,000	E 3
Cherkessk*	115,000	H 1
Chernogorsk*	77,000	I 9
Cherskiy		C 13
Chita	372,000	I 11
Chokurdakh		D 12
Chulmen		G 12
Chumikan		G 14
Chusovoy		G 5
Daknerechensk		I 15
Dalnegorsk		I 15
Derbent	78,000	I 2
Dickson		D 8
Dimitrovgrad*	133,000	G 4
Druzhina		D 13
Dudinka		E 8
Dzerzhinsk	286,000	F 3
Egvekinot		B 15
Elektrostal*	153,000	F 3
Elista	80,000	H 2
Engels	183,000	G 3
Erzin		I 9
Gatchina*	78,000	D 3
Gizhiga		D 15
Glazov	105,000	F 4
Gorki, see Nizhniy Novgorod		
Gorno-Altaysk		I 8
Groznyy	401,000	H 2
Gubkin*	70,000	F 2
Gus-Khrustalnyy*	74,000	F 3
Igarka		F 8
Inta		E 6
Irkutsk	635,000	I 10
Ishim		H 6
Ivanovo	482,000	F 3
Izhevsk (Ustinov)	642,000	G 4
Kabytnangi		E 6
Kalinin, see Tver		
Kaliningrad (Konigsberg)	406,000	D 1
Kaliningrad	161,000	F 3
Kaluga	314,000	F 2
Kamen-na-Obi		I 7
Kamenskoye		C 15
Kamensk Shakhtinskiy*	75,000	G 2
Kamensk-Uralskiy	208,000	G 5
Kamyshin	123,000	G 3
Kandalaksha		D 4
Kansk	110,000	H 9
Kazachya		D 12
Kazan	1,103,000	G 4
Kemerovo	521,000	H 8
Kempendyay		F 11
Khabarovsk	608,000	H 14
Khalmer-Yu		E 6
Khandyga		F 13
Khanty		G 6
Khasavyurt*	72,000	I 2
Khatanga		E 9
Khilok		I 11
Khimki*	135,000	F 3
Kholmsk		H 15
Kineshma*	105,000	F 3
Kirensk		H 10
Kirov	487,000	F 4
Kirovo-Chepetsk*	83,000	F 4
Kirovograd		G 5
Kirovsk		D 4
Kiselevsk	128,000	H 8
Kislovodsk	116,000	H 1
Klin*	94,000	E 3
Klintsy*	71,000	F 2
Kolomna	163,000	F 3
Kolpashevo		H 8
Kolpino	143,000	E 3
Komsomolsk	318,000	H 14
Kondopoga		D 3
Konigsberg, see Kaliningrad		
Konosha		E 4
Kopeysk	134,000	G 5
Korsakov		H 15
Koslan		E 5
Kostroma	280,000	F 3
Kotelnich		F 4
Kotlas		F 4
Kovrov	161,000	F 3
Krasino		D 6
Krasnodar	627,000	G 1
Krasnogorsk*	86,000	H 15
Krasnokamensk		I 12
Krasnokamsk		F 5
Krasnoturinsk		F 5
Krasnoyarsk	922,000	H 9
Kropotkin*	73,000	G 2
Kumertau		H 4
Kungur	82,000	G 5
Kur	430,000	F 2
Kurgan	360,000	H 5
Kuybyshev, see Samara		
Kuznetsk	97,000	G 3
Kyakhta		I 10
Kyzyl	73,000	I 9
Leningrad, see St. Petersburg		
Leninsk-Kuznetskiy	134,000	H 8
Lensk		G 11
Lesosibirsk		H 9
Lesozavodsk		I 15
Lipetsk	455,000	F 2
Liski		G 2
Lysva	76,000	G 5
Lyubertsy	165,000	F 3
Magadan	154,000	E 14
Magdagachi		H 13
Magnitogorsk	443,000	H 5
Makarov		H 15
Makhachkala	327,000	I 2
Mansiysk		G 5
Markovo		C 15
Maykop*	151,000	G 1
Mezen		E 5
Mezhdurechensk*	107,000	F 5
Miass	169,000	G 5
Michurinsk*	109,000	F 3
Mineralnyye Vody	72,000	H 2
Mirnyy		F 11
Mogocha		H 12
Monchegorsk		C 4
Moscow	8,801,000 †8,967,000	F 3
Murmansk	472,000	D 4
Murom	125,000	F 3
Mytishchi*	153,000	F 3
Naberezhnyye Chelny (Brezhnev)	507,000	G 4
Nadym		F 7
Nakhodka	163,000	I 15
Nalchik	237,000	H 1
Naryan-Mar		E 5
Navyy Urengoy		F 7
Neftekamsk*	109,000	G 4
Nefteyugansk	72,000	G 7
Nerchinsk		I 12
Neryungvi		G 12
Nevinnomyssk	122,000	H 1
Nikel		C 4
Nikolayevsk		G 14
Nizhnekamsk*	193,000	G 4
Nizhneudinsk		H 9
Nizhnevartovsk	246,000	G 7
Nizhniy Novgorod (Gorki)	1,443,000	F 3
Nizhniy Tagil	440,000	G 5
Noginsk*	123,000	F 3
Nordrik		D 10
Norilsk	173,000	E 8
Novgorod	232,000	E 3
Novocheboksarsk*	117,000	G 3
Novocherkassk	188,000	G 2
Novokuybyshevsk*	114,000	G 3
Novokuznetsk	601,000	I 8
Novomoskovsk		F 2
Novorossiysk	188,000	G 1
Novoshakhtinsk*	108,000	G 1
Novosibirsk	1,443,000	H 7
Novotroitsk	107,000	H 4
Nyurba		F 11
Obinsk*	102,000	F 3
Odintsovo*	127,000	F 2
Okha		G 15
Okhotsk		F 14
Oktyabrskiy	106,000	G 4
Oleminsk		G 12
Omsk	1,159,000	H 6
Omsukchan		D 14
Onega		D 14
Ordzhonikidze, see Vladikavkaz		
Orekhovo-Zuevo	137,000	F 3
Orel	342,000	F 2
Orenburg	552,000	H 4
Orsk	271,000	G 4
Palana		D 15
Pavlovo*	70,000	F 3
Pavlovskiy Posad*	71,000	F 3
Pechora		E 6
Penza	548,000	G 3
Perm	1,094,000	G 5
Pervomaysk*	76,000	F 3
Pervouralsk	143,000	G 5
Petrodvorets*	77,000	D 3
Petropavlovsk-Kamchatskiy	271,000	E 16
Petrovsk Zabaykalskiy		I 11
Petrozavodsk	274,000	D 3
Pevek		B 14
Plesetsk		E 4
Podkamennaya Tunguska		G 8
Podolsk	209,000	F 3
Pokrovsk		F 12
Poronaysk		G 15
Prokopyevsk	274,000	I 8
Provideniya		A 15
Pskov	206,000	E 2
Pushkin*	91,000	D 3
Pushkino*	74,000	F 3
Pyatigorsk*	130,000	H 1
Ramenskoye*	84,000	F 3
Romanovka		H 11
Roslavl		E 2
Rostov-on-Don	1,025,000	G 2
Rubtsovsk	172,000	I 7
Ryazan	522,000	F 3
Rybinsk (Andropov)	252,000	E 5
Rzhev	70,000	E 2
St. Petersburg (Leningrad)	4,468,000 †5,020,000	D 3
Salavat	151,000	H 4
Salekhard		E 6
Salsk		G 2
Samara (Kuybyshev)	1,258,000	G 4
Sangar		F 12
Saransk	316,000	F 3
Sarapul	111,000	G 4
Saratov	909,000	G 3
Segezha		D 4
Sergino		F 6
Sergiyev Posad (Zagorsk)	115,000	E 3
Serov	104,000	G 5
Serpukhov	144,000	F 3
Severobaikalsk		H 11
Severodvinsk	250,000	D 4
Severo Kurilsk		F 16
Severomorsk		D 4
Severo Yeniseyskiy		G 9
Shadrinsk	86,000	G 5
Shakhtersk*	71,000	G 15
Shakhty	227,000	G 2
Shchekino*	70,000	F 2
Shchelkovo*	109,000	F 3
Shilka		I 12
Shostka*	84,000	E 2
Shuya*	72,000	D 4
Siktyakh		E 11
Sinegorye		E 14
Skvorodino		H 11
Smolensk	346,000	E 2
Sochi	339,000	H 1
Solikamsk	110,000	F 5
Sovetskaya Gavan		H 15
Spassk Dalniy		I 15
Srednekolymsk		D 13
Stalingrad, see Volgograd		
Staryy Oskol*	178,000	F 2
Stavropol	324,000	H 1
Sterlitamak	250,000	G 4
Stupino*	72,000	F 3
Suntar		F 11
Surgut	256,000	G 7
Susuman		E 14
Sverdlovsk, see Yekaterinburg		
Svobodnyy Belogorsk		H 13
Syktyvkar	235,000	F 5
Syzran	174,000	G 3
Taganrog	293,000	G 1
Tambov	307,000	F 3
Tara		H 7
Tatarsk		H 7
Tavda		G 6
Tayshet		H 9
Tikhoretsk		G 1
Tiksi		D 11
Tilichiki		D 15
Tobolsk	72,000	G 6
Tolyatti	642,000	G 3
Tommot		G 12
Tomsk	506,000	H 8
Torey*	87,000	I 10
Troitsk	90,000	H 5
Troitska Pechorsk		F 5
Tula	543,000	F 2
Tulun		H 10
Tura		F 9
Turukhansk		F 8
Tver (Kalinin)	454,000	E 5
Tymovskoya		G 15
Tynda		H 12
Tyumen	487,000	G 6
Udachnyy		F 10
Ufa	1,094,000	G 4
Uglegorsk		G 15
Ugolnoye		D 13
Ukhta	111,000	E 5
Ulan-Ude	359,000	I 11
Ulyanovsk	638,000	G 3
Usolye-Sibirskoye	107,000	I 10
Ussuriys	159,000	I 14
Ust-Ilimsk	93,000	H 10
Ustinov, see Izhevsk		
Ust-Ishim		G 6
Ust-Kamchatsk		E 16
Ust-Kut		H 10
Ust-Maya		F 13
Ust-Nera		E 13
Ust-Ordynskiy		I 10
Velikiye Luki	115,000	E 2
Verkhoyansk		E 12
Vilyuysk		F 11
Vitim		G 11
Vladikavkaz (Ordzhonikidze)	303,000	H 2
Vladimir	353,000	F 3
Vladivostok	643,000	J 15
Volgodonsk*	178,000	G 2
Volgograd (Stalingrad)	1,005,000	G 2
Volochanka		E 9
Vologda	286,000	E 3
Volzhskiy	275,000	G 2
Vorkuta	117,000	E 7
Voronezh	895,000	F 2
Voskresensk*	79,000	F 3
Votkinsk	104,000	G 4
Vyborg	79,000	D 3
Vyshniy Volochek	71,000	E 3
Yakutsk	191,000	F 12
Yaroslavl	636,000	E 3
Yartsevo		G 8
Yegoryevsk*	73,000	F 3
Yekaterinburg (Sverdlovsk)	1,372,000	G 5
Yelets	115,000	F 2
Yelizovo		E 16
Yessentuki*	82,000	H 1
Yessey		E 9
Yeysk*	75,000	G 1
Yoshkar-Ola	246,000	F 4
Yurga*	87,000	H 7
Yuzhno-Sakhalinsk	162,000	H 15
Zagorsk, see Sergiyev Posad		
Zakamansk		I 10
Zelenodolsk*	88,000	G 4
Zelenograd*	160,000	F 3
Zeya		H 13
Zheleznodorozhnyy*	84,000	F 3
Zheleznogorsk*	74,000	F 2
Zhukovskiy*	101,000	F 3
Zima		I 10
Zlatoust	208,000	G 5
Zyryanka		D 13

*Does not appear on map; key shows general location.

†Population of metropolitan area, including suburbs.

Sources: 1990 official estimates for places over 100,000; 1989 census for metropolitan areas; 1984 official estimates for other places.

National government. In 1992, Russia had a *transitional* (temporary) government headed by Boris N. Yeltsin. Yeltsin had been elected president of the R.S.F.S.R. in 1991. After the breakup of the Soviet Union, Yeltsin continued to serve as president of Russia. However, the political situation remained unstable. Many former Soviet leaders and Communist Party members opposed economic and governmental reform.

The president of Russia is the head of state. A prime minister acts as the head of government. The government has a cabinet called the Council of Ministers.

Russia has an elected parliament called the Congress of People's Deputies, with more than 1,000 members. This body is Russia's highest legislative authority. Another body called the Supreme Soviet also passes laws in Russia. *Soviet* is a Russian word meaning *council.* The Supreme Soviet has two houses—the Council of the Federation and the Council of Nationalities. The members of the Supreme Soviet are elected from among the members of the Congress of People's Deputies.

Local government. Russia contains 49 administrative units called *oblasts* (regions) and 6 large, sparsely settled *krais* (territories). Russia also has about 30 other territories, each of which has a dominant nationality group. These territories are known as autonomous republics and autonomous areas. There is also one autonomous region. *Autonomous* means *self-governing,* but these units actually had little control over their own affairs in the Soviet Union. The future of the autonomous units is unclear, because some of their populations are pressing for increased self-rule. All the divisions may contain smaller units called *raions* (districts). Councils called soviets manage local affairs in both urban and rural areas.

In 1991, the Congress of People's Deputies granted Yeltsin broad powers to stabilize the political situation. He removed many local officials and appointed new agents to carry out his reforms. The national government postponed local elections to avoid interfering with economic reform. Meanwhile, local soviets removed some unpopular leaders from office.

Politics. The Communist Party was the only legal political party in the U.S.S.R. until March 1990. At that time, Article 6 of the Soviet Constitution—which gave the Communist Party its broad powers—was amended. A loose coalition of political parties with a democratic platform, known as the Democratic Russia Movement, began to play a key role in the reform movement. The Democratic Russia Movement secured Yeltsin's victory in free presidential elections in June 1991. The collapse of the Communist Party and the former Soviet Union caused the Democratic Russia Movement to break apart. A number of the groups that had opposed the Communist Party developed into separate political parties.

The Russian Christian Democratic Party backs a parliamentary democracy with a monarchy, based on law and principles of Christian morality. The Social Democratic Party calls for a political, social, and economic democracy in which each ethnic group can maintain its identity. It seeks to achieve its goals through social and legal revolution. The Democratic Party of Russia, which has attracted many intellectuals, wants to base the new Russian government on individual freedom and on private ownership of property. The Republican Party of the Russian Federation seeks political and economic freedom through rapid change to private ownership and a less centralized government. The People's Party of Free Russia formed in 1991 as a democratic party of Communists within the Communist Party of the Soviet Union. It later declared itself the sole successor to the Communist Party. A number of extremist groups, such as the Liberal Democratic Party, have also emerged.

New political parties continue to form in Russia to promote the interests of specific groups. All adults who are at least 21 years old may vote.

Courts. The former Soviet government had a political police system called the Committee on State Security, known as the KGB. The KGB could interfere with and influence the legal system, and major violations of human rights took place. The KGB no longer exists in Russia. Today, Russia has two security agencies. The Russian

RIA-Novosti from Sovfoto

The Congress of People's Deputies is the highest legislative authority in Russia. It has more than 1,000 members, who are elected by the Russian people.

Security Services handles internal security, and the Foreign Intelligence Service collects information from other countries. In addition, new laws are being passed to protect the rights of all Russian citizens. The *procurator-general,* the chief legal officer of Russia, is nominated by the president and approved by the Congress of People's Deputies.

Russia's highest court is the Constitutional Court. This court, established in 1992, rules on the constitutionality of the country's laws. The local courts are called *people's courts.* Their judges are elected by the people to five-year terms. The functions of these courts may change as the Constitutional Court works to restructure Russia's legal and judicial system. A commission for judicial reform has been established to recommend changes in the judicial system.

Armed forces. The Soviet Union had the largest armed forces in the world. About 4 million people served in its army, navy, and air force. Required military service for young men began at age 18 and lasted at least two years.

When the Soviet Union collapsed, command of the Soviet armed forces passed to the Commonwealth of Independent States. But several former republics—including Russia—also announced intentions to create their own armed forces. In 1992, Russia began to form its own armed forces and absorbed some of the former Soviet forces. In 1992, Russia and the three other former republics with Soviet nuclear weapons on their lands—Belarus, Kazakhstan, and Ukraine—agreed that all the weapons would either be destroyed or turned over to Russia within seven years.

People

Russia has a population of about 151,436,000. The people are distributed unevenly throughout the country. The vast majority of the population lives in the western—or European—part of Russia. The more rugged and remote areas to the east are sparsely inhabited.

Population. About 83 per cent of Russia's people are of Russian ancestry. These ethnic Russians make up the largest group of Slavic peoples. Members of more than 100 other nationality groups also live in Russia. The largest groups include Tatars (or Tartars), Ukrainians, Chuvash, Bashkirs, Belarusians, Mordvins, Chechen, Germans, Udmurts, Mari, Kazakhs, Avars, Armenians, and Jews, who are considered a nationality group in Russia. Many of them live in Russia's autonomous territories. Remote parts of the Far North are sparsely inhabited by small Siberian groups, including Aleuts, Chukchi, Eskimos, and Koryaks. These northern peoples differ from one another in ancestry and language, but they share a common way of life shaped by the harsh, cold climate.

The government of the Soviet Union had granted Russians special privileges. It repressed the distinctive cultures of other nationalities and did not always uphold their rights. This policy sharpened resentment among some peoples. Today, pride in their culture and the desire for greater independence are growing among the members of many nationalities, including Russians.

Ancestry. Ethnic Russians are descended from Slavs who lived in eastern Europe several thousand years ago. Over time, migration split the Slavs into three subgroups—the East Slavs, the West Slavs, and the South Slavs. The Russians trace their heritage to the first East Slav state, Kievan Rus, which emerged in the 800's.

Kievan Rus suffered repeated invasions by Asian tribes, including the Pechenegs, Polovtsians, and Mongols. The Mongol invasions forced some people to migrate to safer, forested regions near present-day Moscow. Moscow became an important Russian state in the 1300's. This area has remained at the heart of Russia ever since. But people of many ethnic groups have lived in Russia, especially since the 1500's, when extensive expansion and colonization began.

Language. Russian is the official language of Russia. Spoken Russian sounds fairly uniform from one end of the country to the other. Nevertheless, the language has three major regional accents—northern, southern, and central. The small differences rarely interfere with understanding. Russian is written in the Cyrillic alphabet (see **Alphabet** [The Cyrillic alphabet]). Many minority nationality groups in Russia have their own language and speak Russian as a second language.

Way of life

The government of the Soviet Union controlled many aspects of life in the country. It exerted great influence over religion, education, and the arts. The independence of Russia following the breakup of the Soviet Union brought greater freedom and triggered many other changes in the lives of the people.

City life. About three-fourths of Russia's people live in urban areas. Approximately 35 cities in Russia have populations over 500,000. Two cities—Moscow and St. Petersburg—each have more than 4 million inhabitants.

Russian cities are crowded. Beginning in the 1930's, large numbers of people migrated from the countryside to urban areas. During World War II (1939-1945), bombs destroyed many houses and other buildings. These circumstances combined to create a housing shortage in Russian cities that continues to this day. Millions of city dwellers live in small apartments in high-rise buildings. The scarcity of housing forces some families to share kitchen and toilet facilities. Single-family houses are common in small towns and on the outskirts of large cities. But some of these houses lack indoor plumbing and other modern conveniences.

Shortages of food, services, and manufactured goods are common features of city life in Russia. The shortages became even more widespread in 1992, when the government lifted price controls. Shoppers often must wait in long lines and visit many stores to get what they need, if it is available at all. In addition, Russian cities face such urban problems as increased crime and environmental pollution.

Population density

The map at the right shows the population density throughout Russia. Most of Russia's people live in the western part of the country. Central and eastern Russia are sparsely inhabited.

Major cities

- More than 2 million inhabitants
- Less than 2 million inhabitants

Persons per sq. mi.	Persons per km²
More than 125	More than 50
60 to 125	25 to 50
25 to 60	10 to 25
5 to 25	2 to 10
Less than 5	Less than 2

WORLD BOOK map

Arctic Ocean
Baltic Sea
KARELIANS
St. Petersburg
RUSSIANS
Moscow
KOMI
Nizhniy Novgorod
UDMURTS
MARI
CHUVASH
Kazan
MANSI
Perm
Rostov-on-Don
TATARS
Saratov
Samara
BASHKIRS
Yekaterinburg
Volgograd
MORDVINS
Ufa
Chelyabinsk
Omsk
NENTSY
KHANTY
NGANASANY
EVENKI
RUSSIANS
Krasnoyarsk
Novosibirsk
TUVINIANS
BURYATS
YAKUTS
YAKUTS
EVENKI
RUSSIANS
CHUKCHI
Bering Sea
Sea of Okhotsk
Sea of Japan
Caspian Sea

Rural life. About one-fourth of the Russian population lives in rural areas. Single-family housing is common in these areas, but the Soviet government built many city-style apartment buildings. In the most remote areas of Russia, some homes lack gas, plumbing, running water, and electricity. In addition, the quality of education, health care, and cultural life is lower than in the cities. Rural stores are poorly stocked, offering even less selection than city stores. But food is more plentiful in rural areas than in the cities.

During the existence of the Soviet Union, most rural people worked on huge farms run by the government. After the Soviet Union collapsed, Russia began to break up these farms. New laws allow people to withdraw from the government farms and set up private farms.

Clothing. Most people in the Soviet Union wore plain, simple clothes. Stores offered little variety in clothing styles, and most people had only a few different outfits. In the 1970's, consumers began to demand greater variety in apparel. People preferred to buy imported Western clothing whenever it was available. As a result, clothing manufacturers began to pay more attention to style and quality. But scarcity, high cost, and Russia's cold climate continue to affect Russian clothing styles. When possible, rural dwellers buy their clothes in cities, where they find a wider selection.

Traditional Russian clothing consists of colorfully embroidered shirts and blouses, embroidered headwear, and shoes woven from *bast,* a tough fiber from the bark of certain trees. Rural dwellers wore these costumes on

A Moscow family gathers for dinner at home. Most people in Russia eat their main meal at midday.

ITAR-Tass from Sovfoto

High-rise apartment buildings, such as those shown in the photograph above, house millions of people in Russia's cities. Nevertheless, a housing shortage persists in urban areas.

special occasions, such as weddings and holidays. However, the traditional costume is rarely worn today.

Food and drink. The Russian diet is hearty. Russians eat bread at virtually every meal. Beef, chicken, pork, and fish are popular main dishes. The most commonly eaten vegetables include beets, cabbage, carrots, cucumbers, onions, potatoes, radishes, and tomatoes. Russians are fond of soups and dairy products, and they consume large quantities of sugar. Frying remains a widespread method of preparing food.

Many Russian dishes are popular around the world. They include *blinis* (thin pancakes served with smoked salmon or other fillings and sour cream) and *beef Stroganoff* (beef strips cooked with onions and mushrooms in a sour cream sauce). Other favorite dishes include *borscht* (beet soup) and *piroshki* (baked or fried dumplings filled with meat and cabbage).

Typical breakfast foods in Russia include eggs, porridge, sausages, cheese, bread, butter, and jam. Most of the people eat their main meal at midday. It consists of a salad or appetizer; soup; meat or fish with potatoes or *kasha* (cooked buckwheat); and dessert, such as stewed fruit or pastries. In the evening, most Russians eat a light supper.

Russians drink large quantities of tea. Many people enjoy coffee, but it is expensive and often unavailable. *Kvass,* a beerlike beverage made from fermented black bread, is especially popular in summer. Russians also enjoy soft drinks and mineral water.

Vodka is Russia's trademark alcoholic beverage. Russians also drink wine, champagne, cognac, beer, and other alcoholic beverages. Alcohol abuse has been and remains a major social problem in Russia.

Health care in the Soviet Union was free, and the Russian government remains committed to providing free care to all its people. The country has large numbers of doctors, nurses, hospitals, and other facilities. However, a lack of medicines and equipment, poor training of health-care workers, low wages, and bureaucracy create serious problems. Many people bribe health-care workers to guarantee careful, competent work. A private health-care sector is emerging in Russia. As in many countries, rural areas have fewer facilities and doctors than cities have.

Recreation. Russians enjoy watching television, reading, playing chess, seeing motion pictures and plays, visiting museums, walking, and taking part in sports. The government actively promotes athletic activities, especially team sports. Soccer is the most popular participant and spectator sport in Russia. Other popular

© Andy Hernandez, Sipa Press

Shoppers wait in line to buy food. Such lines are a common sight in Russia's cities, which lack sufficient amounts of food and other consumer goods.

At outdoor markets, farmers sell produce that is fresher than that found in stores, but more expensive. This market is in Krasnodar, a city in southwestern Russia.

ITAR-Tass from Sovfoto

sports include gymnastics, basketball, and such winter sports as hockey, ice skating, and skiing. Tennis is growing in popularity.

Russia has many athletic clubs, stadiums, recreational centers, and other sporting facilities. Schools provide physical education at all levels. There are also special sports camps and clubs for children and adults.

The people of Russia are avid nature lovers, and they enjoy spending time in the countryside. Many wealthy Russians have country cottages called *dachas.* There, they garden, hike, bicycle, swim, fish, gather mushrooms, and take part in other outdoor activities.

The majority of Russia's people vacation in the summer. Popular destinations include resort areas along the Black Sea, the Baltic Sea, and the Volga River, and in Siberia. However, price increases and ethnic unrest have made vacationing away from home less appealing.

Religion. The Soviet Union was hostile to religion. But religion played an important role in the lives of many of the country's people. In the late 1980's, religious toleration began to increase dramatically. Churches recovered property seized by the Soviet government. Thousands of new parishes opened. Church attendance shot up. Sunday schools opened across the country, and churches took part in charity work. Publication of religious literature resumed, and new seminaries opened. The celebration of Russian Orthodox Christmas on January 7 was made a national holiday.

The Russian Orthodox Church is the largest religious denomination in Russia. Other important religious groups in the country include Muslims; Baptists, Pentecostalists, and other Protestant denominations; Roman Catholics; and Jews.

Education. The Soviet government controlled education and considered it a major vehicle of social advancement. As a result, almost all Russians can read and write. Today, public education in Russia remains free for all citizens. New private schools are also opening. The Soviet government had banned such schools.

Russian educators are changing the school curriculum to better prepare students for the new economy. They are working to remove the emphasis on Communist Party ideology. Educators are also trying to better satisfy the interests of Russia's nationality groups.

All children attend school for 11 years, from age 6 to 17. Elementary education includes nine primary and intermediate grades. When pupils finish ninth grade, they may choose to complete their schooling by enrolling in a secondary school or vocational school. The secondary schools emphasize science and mathematics. They also teach language, literature, history, social sciences, and physical education. English is the most widely taught foreign language. The vocational schools prepare young people for careers as technicians or in various branches of industry and agriculture.

Starting with the intermediate grades, pupils must pass annual exams to advance to the next grade. Students who pass a national examination upon the completion of secondary school receive a certificate, and those who score well also receive a gold or silver medal. Schools use a number grading scale of 1 to 5, with 5 being the highest.

Many children with special talents attend special schools. These schools stress individual subjects such as mathematics or physics, languages, or the arts. Russia also has schools for children with physical or learning disabilities.

Students must pass an entrance exam to be admitted to a university or institute of higher education. Russia has 500 institutions of higher education equivalent to colleges and universities, with about 3 million students. Moscow State University, the largest university in Russia, has 28,000 students.

Museums and libraries. The people of Russia spend more time in museums than do the people of the United States or most European countries. Russia has more than 660 museums. The State Historical Museum in Moscow is the country's chief historical museum. Sev-

© Chris Waddle, Gamma/Liaison

Soccer is the most popular sport in Russia, among both participants and spectators. Russia has many sports camps and clubs, recreational centers, and other athletic facilities for children and adults.

eral museums dealing with the history of the Russian Revolution are also in Moscow. They include the Central Museum of the Revolution and the Central Lenin Museum. The Hermitage Museum in St. Petersburg has one of the world's largest art collections.

Russia has about 62,000 libraries. Most towns and large villages have a public library. There are also libraries specializing in particular subjects and libraries run by factories, schools, labor unions, and professional and civic organizations. The Russian State Library in Moscow is the largest library in Russia. Other major libraries in Moscow include the All-Russian State Library of Foreign Literature, INION (Institute of Scholarly Information for the Social Sciences of the Academy of Sciences), the State Historical Library, and the Gorki Library at Moscow State University. St. Petersburg is home to the Saltykov-Shchedrin State Library and the Library of the Russian Academy of Sciences.

The arts

The arts in Russia date back to the earliest days of the country. But Russian artists did not produce internationally recognized works in many fields until the early 1800's. Throughout much of the 1800's and the early 1900's, Russia became an international leader in classical music, ballet, drama, and literature. Several Russian painters and sculptors also gained worldwide fame.

This section discusses Russian architecture, music, ballet, painting, and sculpture. For information on Russian drama and literature, see **Russian literature** with its list of *Related articles.*

Architecture in Russia has been shaped by religious and Western influences combined with local traditions. In 988, Grand Prince Vladimir I, ruler of the state of Kievan Rus, was converted to the Byzantine (Eastern Orthodox Christian) faith. For hundreds of years, Russian architecture reflected the influence of the Byzantine style. The most important structures were churches, which had distinctive onion-shaped domes. The best-known Byzantine church is St. Basil's Cathedral in Moscow, built by the first czar, Ivan IV (also called Ivan the Terrible), from 1555 to 1560. See **Byzantine art.**

In 1682, Peter I, also known as Peter the Great, became czar. Peter introduced Western European artistic styles into Russia. He founded the city of St. Petersburg in 1703 and brought Western European architects and artists to help design it. Many of the buildings dating from his reign and through the mid-1700's were designed in the Western European baroque style by Italian and French architects. A famous example is the Great Palace, begun in the early 1700's at Peterhof (now Petrodvorets), near St. Petersburg.

Among the most widely recognized architectural works in Russia are the buildings within the enclosed fortress in Moscow called the Kremlin. The Kremlin includes churches, palaces, and other buildings erected from the late 1400's to the mid-1900's. Some Kremlin buildings house Russia's government, and others serve as museums. See **Kremlin.**

Music. Until the mid-1700's, Russian music consisted almost entirely of vocal music sung in church worship services and of folk music, which was also mainly vocal. Nonreligious music began to flower during the reign of Elizabeth, the empress of Russia from 1741 to 1762. She established the Academy of Arts in 1757, which taught music. Italian opera became popular during her reign. The popularity of music in Russia expanded further during the reign of Catherine II, known as Catherine the Great, who ruled from 1762 to 1796. The earliest written collection of Russian folk songs appeared in four vol-

Kurt Scholz, Shostal

St. Basil's Cathedral in Moscow has colorful onion-shaped domes that have made it one of the most widely recognized buildings in Russia. It was built by Ivan the Terrible from 1555 to 1560. The Byzantine-style cathedral is now a historical museum.

umes published between 1776 and 1795.

Mikhail Glinka is credited with founding a distinctively Russian school of classical music in the early and middle 1800's. He blended folk songs and religious music into his works and also introduced subjects from Russian history. His most influential work is probably his second opera, *Ruslan and Lyudmila* (1842), based on a fairy tale written by the Russian poet Alexander Pushkin.

By the late 1800's, Russian music flourished. Such composers as Modest Mussorgsky, Nikolai Rimsky-Korsakov, Peter Ilich Tchaikovsky, and Alexander Borodin wrote operas and instrumental music. Much of their work was based on Russian history and folklore. In the early 1900's, Sergei Rachmaninoff and Igor Stravinsky gained international fame for their musical compositions. Stravinsky wrote several influential ballet scores, including *The Firebird* (1910), *Petrouchka* (1911), and *The Rite of Spring* (1913). See the list of Russian composers in the *Related articles* section of **Classical music.**

Ballet. Russian ballet became internationally famous starting in the mid-1800's. The leading ballet companies, which continue to perform today, are the Kirov Ballet (formerly the Russian Imperial Ballet) of St. Petersburg and the Bolshoi Theater Ballet of Moscow. See **Ballet** (Russian ballet); **Bolshoi Theater Ballet.**

The Trinity by Andrei Rublev; Tretyakov Gallery, Moscow

Religious paintings called *icons* dominated Russian art from the late 900's to the late 1600's. Icons were created for Russian Orthodox worship services and were considered sacred.

Painting and sculpture. Until the early 1900's, the most important Russian paintings were created for religious purposes. Russian artists decorated the interiors of churches with wallpaintings and mosaics. Stylized paintings called *icons* were produced for many centuries. An icon is a religious painting considered sacred in Eastern Orthodox Christianity. Icons were produced according to strict rules established by the church, and their style changed little over the years. See **Icon.**

By the mid-1800's, Moscow and St. Petersburg had busy art schools. Russian artists also began to create paintings and sculptures on more varied subjects.

A burst of creativity in Russian art exploded during the years before the start of World War I in 1914. Russian artists were strongly influenced by the modern art movements emerging in Western Europe. The painters Marc Chagall, Alexei von Jawlensky, and Wassily Kandinsky eventually settled in Western Europe.

Artists who remained in Russia developed two important modern art movements, *suprematism* and *constructivism.* Both movements produced paintings that were *abstract*—that is, they had no recognizable subject matter. The leading suprematist was Kasimir Malevich. The major constructivists included Naum Gabo, Antoine Pevsner, and Vladimir Tatlin. See **Chagall, Marc; Gabo, Naum; Kandinsky, Wassily; Pevsner, Antoine.**

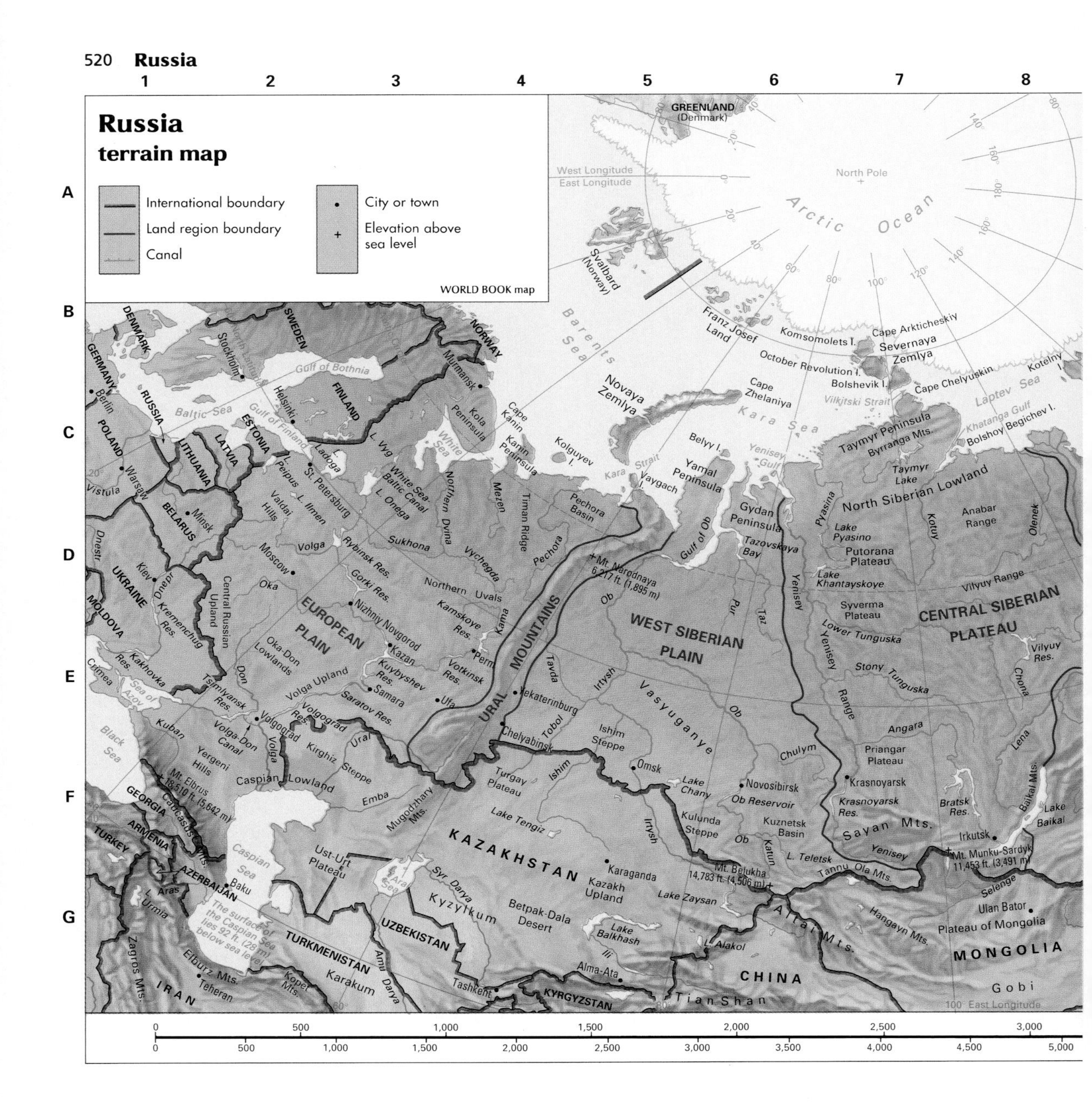

Physical features

Aldan Mountains ....E 10
Aldan River ....E 10
Amga River ....E 9
Amgun River ....E 11
Amur River ....F 10
Anabar Range (mountains) ....D 8
Anadyr Range ....B 10
Anadyr River ....B 11
Angara River ....E 7
Argun River ....F 9
Ayon Island ....B 10
Baikal Mountains ....F 8
Barents Sea ....B 5
Bear Island ....B 10
Belyy Island ....C 5
Bering Strait ....A 11
Black Sea ....F 1
Bolshoy Begichev Island ....C 8
Bratsk Reservoir ....F 7
Bureya River ....F 10
Byrranga Mountains .....C 7
Caspian Lowland ....F 2
Caspian Sea ....G 2
Caucasus Mountains .....F 1
Central Russian Upland ..D 2
Cherskiy Range (mountains) ....D 10
Chona River ....E 8
Chukchi Sea ....A 10
Chukotsk Mountains .....B 10
Chulym River ....F 6
Commander Islands .....C 12
Don River ....E 2
Dzugdzhur Range (mountains) ....E 10
East Siberian Sea ....B 10
Franz Josef Land (islands) ....B 6
Gorki Reservoir ....D 3
Gulf of Anadyr ....A 11
Gulf of Ob ....D 5
Gydan Peninsula ....D 6
Indigirka River ....C 10
Irtysh River ....E 5
Ishim River ....F 4
Ishim Steppe ....F 5
Kama River ....E 4
Kamchatka Peninsula ....D 12
Kamskoye Reservoir .....D 3
Kanin Peninsula ....C 4
Kara Sea ....G 6
Kara Strait ....C 5
Khatanga Gulf ....C 8
Klyuchevskaya (volcano) ....C 10
Kola Peninsula ....C 4
Kolguyev Island ....C 4
Kolyma Lowland ....C 10
Kolyma Mountains ....C 11
Kolyma River ....C 10
Komsomolets Island .....B 6
Koryak Mountains ....B 11
Kotelny Island ....B 8
Kotuy River ....D 7
Krasnoyarsk Reservoir ...F 7
Kulunda Steppe ....F 5
Kuril Islands ....E 12
Kuybyshev Reservoir ....E 3
Kuznetsk Basin ....F 6
Lake Baikal ....F 8
Lake Chany ....F 5
Lake Ilmen ....D 2
Lake Ladoga ....C 2
Lake Onega ....D 3
Lake Peipus ....C 2
Lake Teletsk ....G 6
Laptev Sea ....C 8
Laptev Strait ....B 9
Lena Plateau ....F 9
Lena River ....E 9
Longa Strait ....A 10
Lower Tunguska River ...E 7
Maya River ....D 10
Mezen River ....D 4
Mount Belukha ....C 12
Mount Elbrus ....F 1
Mount Munku-Sardyk ...G 8
Mount Narodnaya ....D 5
Mount Pobeda ....C 10
New Siberian Islands ....B 9
North Siberian Lowland ....D 7
Northern Dvina River ....D 3
Northern Uvals (hills) .....D 3
Novaya Sibir Island ......B 9
Novaya Zemlya (island) ..C 5
Ob Reservoir ....F 6
Ob River ....E 6
October Revolution Island ....B 6
Oka River ....D 2
Oka-Don Lowlands ......E 2
Okhota River ....D 10
Olenek River ....D 8
Oloyskiy Mountains ......B 11
Omolon River ....C 10
Onon River ....F 9
Pechora Basin ....D 5
Pechora River ....D 4
Prianger Plateau ....F 7
Putorana Plateau ....D 7
Pyasina River ....D 5
Rybinsk Reservoir ....D 3
Sakhalin Island ....E 11
Sayan Mountains ....F 7
Sea of Azov ....E 1
Sea of Japan ....G 11
Sea of Okhotsk ....D 11
Severnaya Zemlya (islands) ....B 7
Shantar Island ....E 11
Shelikhova Gulf ....C 11
Shilka River ....F 9

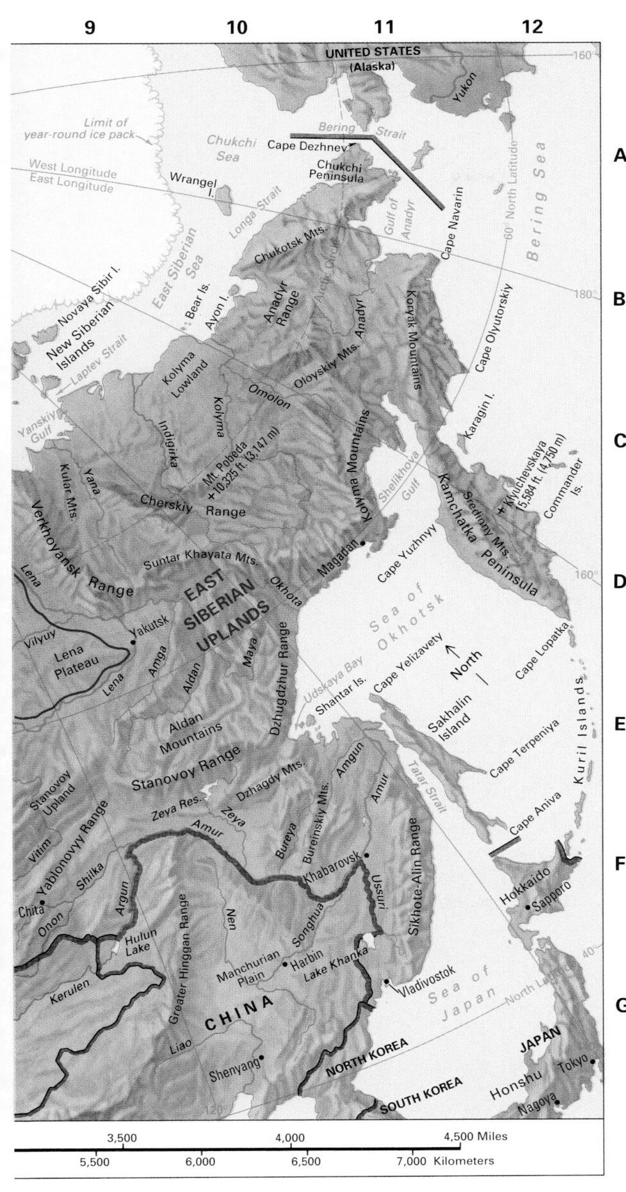

Sikhote-Alin Range (mountains) . . . F 11
Stanovoy Range (mountains) . . . E 10
Stanovoy Upland . . . F 9
Stony Tunguska River . . . E 7
Sukhona River . . . D 3
Suntar Khayata Mountains . . . D 10
Syverma Plateau . . . D 7
Tatar Strait . . . E 11
Tavda River . . . E 4
Taymyr Lake . . . C 7
Taymyr Peninsula . . . C 7
Taz River . . . E 6
Tazovskaya Bay . . . D 6
Tobol River . . . E 4
Tsimlyansk Reservoir . . . E 2
Udskaya Bay . . . E 11
Ural River . . . F 3
Ussuri River . . . F 11
Valdai Hills . . . D 2
Vasyuganye (marshes) . . . E 5
Verkhoyansk Range (mountains) . . . D 9
Vilkitski Strait . . . C 7
Vilyuy Range (mountains) . . . D 8
Vilyuy Reservoir . . . E 8
Vilyuy River . . . D 9
Vitim River . . . F 9
Volga River . . . F 2
Volga Upland . . . F 2
Volga-Don Canal . . . F 2
Volgograd Reservoir . . . E 2
White Sea . . . C 3
White Sea-Baltic Canal . . . C 3
Wrangel Island . . . A 10
Yablonovyy Range (mountains) . . . F 9
Yamal Peninsula . . . C 5
Yana River . . . C 9
Yanskiy Gulf . . . C 9
Yenisey Gulf . . . C 6
Yenisey Range (mountains) . . . E 6
Yenisey River . . . D 6
Zeya Reservoir . . . F 10
Zeya River . . . F 10

Russia is the largest country in the world. It has an area of 6,592,850 square miles (17,075,400 square kilometers), almost twice that of Canada, the second largest country. A train trip between Moscow in the west and Vladivostok in the east takes seven days and passes through eight time zones, including that of Moscow.

Land regions

Many scientists divide Russia into four zones according to soil conditions and plant life, which are based mainly on climate. The zones form broad belts across Russia, and no sharp transitions separate them. From north to south, the zones are (1) the tundra, (2) the forest zone, (3) the steppes, and (4) the semidesert and mountainous zone.

The tundra lies in the northernmost part of Russia. It is largely a treeless plain. The tundra has short summers and long, severe winters. About half the region has permanently frozen soil called *permafrost.* Few people live in this bleak area. Plant life consists chiefly of low shrubs, dwarf trees, and moss. Animals of the tundra include reindeer, arctic foxes, ermines, hares, and lemmings. Waterfowl live near the Arctic Sea in summer.

The forest belt lies south of the tundra. The northern part of this belt is called the *taiga.* It consists of *coniferous* (cone-bearing) trees, such as cedar, fir, pine, and spruce. This area has poor, ashy soil, known as *podzol,* that makes it largely unfit for agriculture. Farther south, the coniferous forests give way to mixed forests of conifers, aspen, birch, elm, maple, oak, and other species. The soils in this zone support agriculture in some areas, and the area has a mild, moist climate. Brown bears, deer, elk, lynx, reindeer, and smaller animals such as beavers, rabbits, and squirrels roam the forests.

Grassy plains called *steppes* stretch across Russia south of the forests. The northern part of the steppe zone consists of wooded plains and meadows. The massive southern part is largely a treeless prairie. The best soils in Russia—brown soil and black, rich soil called *chernozem*—are found there. Most of the steppe zone is farmland. Birds, squirrels, and mouselike mammals called *jerboas* live in the steppes. Antelope live in the eastern steppes.

The semidesert and mountainous zone, the southernmost zone in Russia, has diverse soils and climate due to variations in elevation. It includes the dry, semidesert lowlands near the Caspian Sea, as well as the lush vegetation and mild climate of the Caucasus Mountains.

Geologists also divide Russia into five land regions that differ from the soil and vegetation zones. From west to east, the regions are (1) the European Plain, (2) the Ural Mountains, (3) the West Siberian Plain, (4) the Central Siberian Plateau, and (5) the East Siberian Uplands.

The European Plain makes up most of the European part of Russia. It is the most densely populated region in the country. The European Plain is predominantly flat to gently rolling, averaging about 600 feet (180 meters) above sea level. Most of the nation's industries are there, but the plain is poor in natural resources. Forest covers much of it. The region is home to a variety of animal life. The Caucasus Mountains rise at the southern edge of the plain, between the Black and the Caspian seas. The mountains include 18,510-foot (5,642-meter) Mount Elbrus, the highest point in Europe.

© Patrick David, Sipa Press

The East Siberian Uplands are mainly a wilderness of mountains and plateaus. The region has valuable mineral resources, but its harsh climate makes it difficult to use them. Small towns, such as the one shown above, are sparsely scattered throughout the East Siberian Uplands.

The Ural Mountains form the traditional boundary between the European and Asian parts of Russia. These mountains, worn down by streams, reach an average height of only about 2,000 feet (610 meters). The middle and southern Ural Mountains are rich in deposits of iron, copper, and other metals. The middle section is the region's most heavily populated and highly industrialized area. Major cities in the region include Yekaterinburg and Chelyabinsk.

The West Siberian Plain is the largest level region in the world. This enormous plain covers more than 1 million square miles (2.6 million square kilometers) and

© Laski, Sipa Press

A belt of rich farmland stretches across Russia from east to west. In the photograph at the left, farmworkers harvest wheat on the European Plain. This mainly flat landform makes up most of the European part of Russia.

rises no more than 500 feet (150 meters) above sea level. It is drained by the Ob River system, which flows northward into the Arctic Ocean. But drainage is poor, and the plain is marshy. Rich in oil and natural gas deposits, the West Siberian Plain is being developed rapidly. The cities of Novosibirsk and Omsk lie in the region.

The Central Siberian Plateau slopes upward toward the south from coastal plains along the Arctic Ocean. It has an average height of about 2,000 feet (610 meters). Streams cut deeply through the region. The Sayan and Baikal mountains rise more than 11,000 feet (3,350 meters) along the plateau's southern edge. Thick pine forests cover much of the Central Siberian Plateau, and its climate reaches extremes of heat and cold. The region has a wide variety of rich mineral deposits. Krasnoyarsk and Irkutsk are its largest cities.

The East Siberian Uplands are mainly a wilderness of mountains and plateaus. The mountains rise to 10,000 feet (3,000 meters) and form part of a series of ranges along the eastern coast of Asia and some offshore islands. About 25 active volcanoes are found on the Kamchatka Peninsula. The tallest volcano, snow-capped Klyuchevskaya, rises 15,584 feet (4,750 meters). The region has valuable mineral resources, but its harsh climate makes it difficult to tap them. Vladivostok on the Pacific Ocean and Khabarovsk on the Amur River are the region's most important cities.

Rivers and lakes

Russia's many large rivers have served as important means of communication and commerce. The construction of canals further improved these activities.

The Lena River in Siberia, 2,734 miles (4,400 kilometers) long, is the longest river in Russia. It empties into the Arctic Ocean. Other major rivers in Siberia include the Amur, Ob, and Yenisey rivers, all frozen seven to nine months a year. The Volga River is the longest river in European Russia. The river originates in the Valdai Hills northwest of Moscow and flows 2,194 miles (3,531 kilometers) to the Caspian Sea. The Volga freezes for about three months each year. The Don and Northern Dvina rivers are also in European Russia.

Russia has about 200,000 lakes. The Caspian Sea, a saltwater lake 92 feet (28 meters) below sea level, is the world's largest inland body of water. It touches the southern part of European Russia. Lake Ladoga, near St. Petersburg, covers 6,835 square miles (17,703 square kilometers). It is the largest lake entirely in Europe. Lake Baikal, near the Baikal Mountains, is the deepest lake in the world. It plunges 5,315 feet (1,620 meters) deep.

A thick forest blankets the northern part of Russia from Europe to the Pacific Ocean. It covers much of Siberia. Few people live in this vast area.

ITAR-Tass from Sovfoto

Lake Baikal, the deepest lake in the world, lies in Siberia. It has a depth of 5,315 feet (1,620 meters). A small community, *right,* is nestled between Lake Baikal and the surrounding mountains.

© Paolo Koch, Photo Researchers

Climate

Russia is known for its long and bitter winters. The country's hostile climate helped stop various invaders during its history, including the large armies of Napoleon in 1812 and of Adolf Hitler in 1941 and 1942. In the Moscow region, snow covers the ground for about five months each year. In the northernmost part of Russia, snow abounds for eight to nine months a year. The small percentage of Russia's land that is fit for agriculture has a short growing season and insufficient rainfall. Half the land has permafrost beneath the surface. Most of the coastal waters, lakes, and rivers freeze for much of the year.

Russia's weather varies from extremely cold to extremely hot. Northeastern Siberia is one of the coldest regions in the world. January temperatures there average below −50 °F (−46 °C). Temperatures as low as −90 °F (−68 °C) have been recorded. The average July temperature in this region is 60 °F (16 °C), but it can climb to nearly 100 °F (38 °C). No other part of the world registers such a wide range of temperatures.

Precipitation (rain, melted snow, and other forms of moisture) is light to moderate. The European Plain and parts of the East Siberian Uplands receive the most rain. Vast inland areas get little rain. The heaviest snowfalls—up to 4 feet (120 centimeters) of snow a year—occur in western and central Siberia.

ITAR-Tass from Sovfoto

Winters are long and cold in most parts of Russia. Snow covers the ground in the Moscow region for about five months each year. This photograph shows a Moscow street in winter.

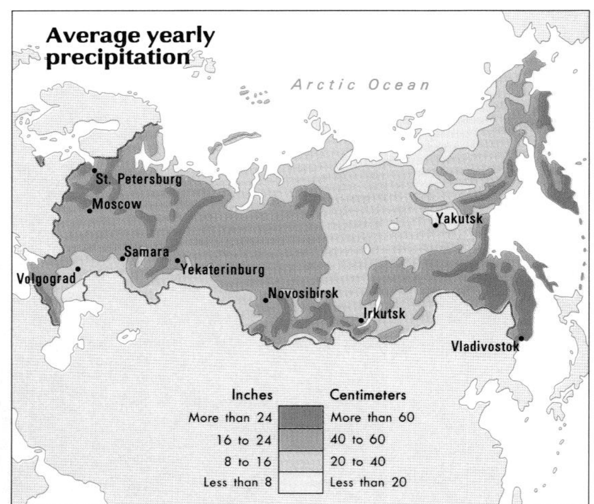

WORLD BOOK map

Rainfall in Russia is heaviest on the European Plain, in parts of the East Siberian Uplands, and in mountainous regions along the southern border. Vast areas of the interior get little rain.

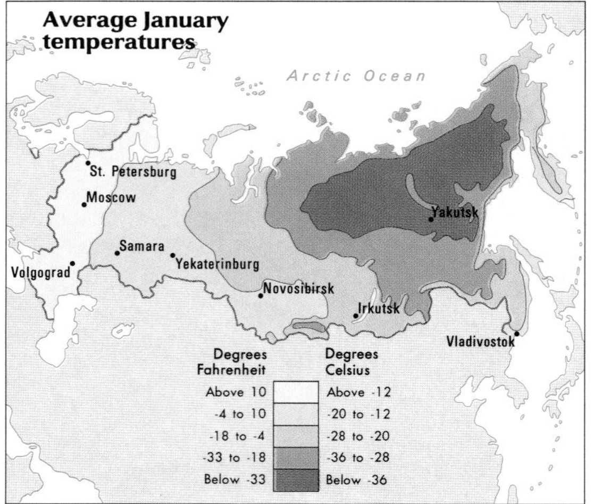

WORLD BOOK map

January temperatures in eastern Siberia are among the coldest in the world, dropping as low as −90 °F (−68 °C). January temperatures in Russia average above 10 °F (−12 °C) only in the westernmost part of the country.

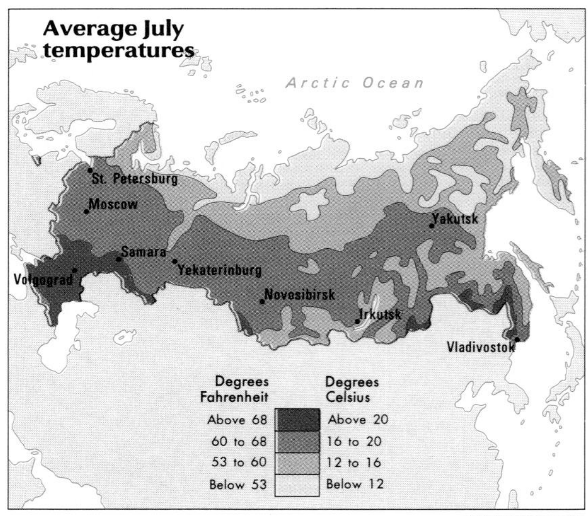

WORLD BOOK map

July temperatures in Russia vary widely. Most of the country has an average July temperature above 60 °F (16 °C), but temperatures can hit almost 100 °F (38 °C) in northeastern Siberia and drop below 32 °F (0 °C) on islands in the Arctic Ocean.

In the Soviet Union, central government agencies planned almost all aspects of the economy. The government owned and controlled all factories and farms, and private businesses were illegal. Soviet leaders changed Russia from a farming country into an industrial giant. Heavy industry—such as chemicals, construction, machine tools, and steel—developed rapidly. Government ministries supplied factories with materials, set production quotas, and told managers what to produce and to whom to sell their goods. This planning led to rapid industrial development and impressive economic gains. But once the economy developed, central control began to suppress new ideas and discourage quality.

Russia has inherited the successes and problems of the former Soviet Union's industrial policy. The Russian government is working to convert state-owned property, including large factories and farms, to private ownership. Many small businesses and joint ventures with foreign partners have started. Russia is turning to Western countries and Japan for assistance in modernizing and restructuring its manufacturing sector.

When the Soviet Union collapsed, the economy was in a state of disarray. To stabilize the Russian economy, reduce inflation, and attract foreign investment, the government plans to allow the conversion of the ruble into other forms of currency. This will enable it to be exchanged for other currencies at international rates. The Russian government has also begun to set up a modern banking system. The government lifted price controls on most items in 1992, and prices soared. But most people's incomes remained near previous levels, putting many items out of their reach.

The Russian government's bold break from past Soviet economic policies caused great instability in the early 1990's. Industrial output fell, and inflation rose dramatically. The links between economy and government that existed in the Soviet Union had been breaking down, but new institutions had not yet replaced them.

On the positive side, Russia has a skilled labor force and an abundance of natural resources. There are signs of robust private undertakings, including many new businesses, throughout the country.

Natural resources. Russia is one of the richest countries in the world in terms of natural resources. It has the world's largest forest reserves, enormous energy supplies, vast stretches of farmland, extensive mineral deposits, and many potential sources of hydroelectric power. The country also has a wide variety of plant and animal life.

Manufacturing. Heavy industry is the most highly developed sector of the Russian economy. The machine-building industry is concentrated in Moscow and St. Petersburg, along the Volga River, and in the Ural Mountains. It makes various types of tractors and other heavy machinery and electrical equipment. The chemical industry produces chemical fibers, mineral fertilizers, petrochemicals, plastics, soda ash, and synthetic resins. The construction materials industry is also important.

The Moscow area is Russia's leading manufacturing center. Its factories produce chemicals, electrical equipment, electronics, motor vehicles, processed foods, steel, and textiles. Ships and industrial equipment are manufactured in St. Petersburg. Metal processing and machinery production are important in the Urals. Most oil refining takes place in the Volga-Urals region. New industries are being developed in Siberia to make use of the region's mineral and hydroelectric resources. Light industry, particularly textile production, is centered in the region around Moscow and along the Volga River. The paper industry operates along the southern edge of the forest belt.

Agriculture. Russia has a large amount of farmland. But a short growing season, insufficient rainfall, and a lack of fertile soil make farming difficult. The Soviet Union's wasteful and inefficient system of state-run farms added to Russia's agricultural problems.

There are about 25,000 large, state-controlled farms in Russia. About half are state farms operated like government factories, called *sovkhozy.* Workers on sovkhozy receive wages. The rest are collective farms called *kolkhozy,* which are government-controlled but managed in part by farmers.

By the beginning of 1992, about 50,000 private farms had been established. But these farms included only a tiny percentage of Russia's farmland. New laws called for the breakup of unprofitable government farms and for more aid to farmers who wished to strike out on their own. Nevertheless, the transition to private farms proved to be slow and difficult.

Approximately 13 per cent of Russia's land is cropland. One of the main agricultural regions is the Black Earth Belt, a portion of the steppes stretching from the

© Laski, Sipa Press

Collective farms called *kolkhozy* are controlled by the Russian government but managed in part by farmers. This photograph shows a potato harvest at one such farm.

RIA-Novosti from Sovfoto

Manufacturing is an important economic activity in Russia. Many of the country's metal-processing and machine-building plants, such as the steel mill at the left, are in the Ural Mountains region.

Economy of Russia

This map shows the major uses of land in Russia. The map also shows where the leading farm, fishing, mineral, and forest products are produced, and it locates the chief manufacturing centers.

WORLD BOOK map

ITAR-Tass from Sovfoto

Long pipelines, such as the one shown above, transport natural gas from fields in Siberia to European Russia. The gas is burned to provide energy for industry and heat for homes. It is also a natural resource for the production of certain chemicals.

Ukrainian border to southwestern Siberia that is famous for its dark chernozem soil. Other important farming regions are the Volga area, the northern Caucasus Mountains, and western Siberia. Russia is one of the world's major grain producers. However, the country still must import grain for food. Major crops grown in Russia include barley, flax, fruits, oats, potatoes, rye, sugar beets, sunflowers, vegetables, and wheat. Russian farmers also grow many *fodder crops*—that is, food crops for animals. Grasses and corn are the most important fodder crops.

Livestock breeding is another main component of Russian agriculture. Cattle, hogs, and sheep are the most important livestock raised in the country.

Mining. Russia has vast amounts of most of the minerals used in modern industrial production. The country has abundant coal deposits and huge reserves of petroleum and natural gas. Other resources include calcium phosphate minerals and phosphorites, used in fertilizers, and diamonds.

Russia is a major producer of iron ore, manganese, nickel, and the platinum-group metals, a group of rare metals including platinum and iridium. Nickel is mined in the Kola Peninsula, eastern Siberia, and the southern Urals. Platinum is mined in the Urals and in northern Siberia. The country ranks as a leading producer of gold, lead, salt, tin, tungsten, and zinc. It is also an important source of copper and silver. Bauxite, a mineral used in making aluminum, is mined in western Siberia.

Fishing industry. In the northern Barents Sea and the White Sea, Russian fishing crews catch cod, had-

Cary Wolinsky, Stock, Boston

A fishing crew brings in sturgeon from the mouth of the Volga River. Sturgeon eggs are used to make a salty delicacy called *caviar.* Russia is famous for its flavorful caviar.

ITAR-Tass from Sovfoto

Railroads transport freight and passengers between Russia's major cities, many of which are separated by vast distances. The photograph at the left shows a train on the Trans-Siberian Railroad, which runs between Vladivostok in the southeast and Moscow in the west.

dock, herring, salmon, and other fishes. Sturgeon are caught in the Caspian Sea. *Caviar,* the salted eggs of sturgeon, is a famous Russian delicacy. Crews also fish in inland waterways, the Atlantic and Pacific oceans, and the Baltic and Black seas.

Service industries are industries that produce services, not goods. In the former Soviet Union, these industries were underdeveloped. Most service-industry workers were poorly trained and underpaid. They had little incentive to satisfy their customers, who competed for services that were in short supply.

Today, private economic activity in the service sector is flourishing. Many individuals and families are starting small businesses such as restaurants, barbershops, dry cleaners, and taxi services.

Energy sources. Russia has enormous natural energy reserves, especially petroleum and natural gas. The country is the world's largest producer of crude oil. Oil fields in western Siberia supply more than half of Russia's petroleum. The Volga-Ural Oil-Gas Region, the Northern Caucasus, and the Timan-Pechora Oil-Gas Basin are also important. Russia also produces large amounts of coal and natural gas. Pipelines carry oil and natural gas from western Siberia to European Russia. The country's largest coal mines lie in the Kuznetsk and Pechora basins. Peat bogs also furnish some of the fuel used in Russia.

Most of Russia's electric power plants are steam-turbine plants. Huge hydroelectric plants also generate electricity. Russia also ranks as a major producer of nuclear power.

Trade. The Soviet Union traded mainly with the Eastern European countries of Bulgaria, Czechoslovakia, Hungary, and Poland. Since the overthrow of the Communist regimes of Eastern Europe and the breakup of the Soviet Union, Russia's trading activity with those countries has declined but remains important. Russia also trades heavily with the other former Soviet republics. Trade with some developing nonsocialist countries, such as Syria and Turkey, has increased. In addition, Russia exchanges goods with Cuba, Finland, France, Germany, Italy, and Japan.

Russia exports mostly petroleum, minerals, machinery, chemicals, and wood and paper products. Its major imports include consumer goods, industrial equipment, foods and beverages, and machinery.

Transportation and communication. Because of Russia's vast size and harsh climate, transportation facilities and communications systems are unevenly distributed throughout the country. They are less efficient than the transportation and communications networks of Western Europe, the United States, and Japan.

Railroads handle most freight transportation in Russia. But the system is heavily loaded and in urgent need of modernization. Russia's poorly developed highway network, combined with the country's vast size, make truck transport ineffective and costly. It makes up only about 5 per cent of total freight movement. River transportation carries only a small percentage of Russia's freight traffic, because most rivers are frozen for much of the year. Canals such as the Volga-Don Canal and the Moscow Canal, which connects Moscow with the Volga River, make an important contribution to river traffic.

Aeroflot is Russia's national airline. It had been the national airline of the Soviet Union. Aeroflot carries freight and passengers between all major Russian cities and between Russia and many other countries. Fuel shortages and rising ticket costs have reduced air traffic.

Russia's most important seaports—Arkhangelsk, Kaliningrad, Murmansk, Nakhodka, St. Petersburg, and Vladivostok—handle a large portion of the country's foreign trade. However, the water at many Russian ports is frozen for many months of the year.

Automobile production is increasing, but it remains small in comparison with other developed nations. Only about 56 of every 1,000 Russians own cars. It is difficult for car owners to obtain servicing and spare parts.

Public transportation is modern and inexpensive, but crowded. Several large cities, including Moscow, have clean, efficient subway systems. Buses, trams, and trolleys also operate in the cities. Bicycles are seldom seen in large cities, but they are common in rural and vacation areas. Horses and buggies can also be found in rural parts of Russia.

Russia has an underdeveloped telecommunications system. It takes years to install telephones in new apartment complexes.

During most of the history of the Soviet Union, the government controlled all communications media, including broadcasting, motion-picture production, and publishing. The government required all broadcasts and publications to follow Communist Party policies. Such censorship began to ease in the late 1980's, and it no longer exists in Russia. As a result, the number of independent newspapers and publishing houses has increased dramatically. Most families own radios and television sets. Videocassette recorders are in great demand, but they are expensive and hard to find.

History

Russia's unique geographic location astride both Europe and Asia has influenced its history and shaped its destiny. Russia never has been entirely an Eastern or a Western country. As a result, Russian intellectuals have long debated the country's development and contribution to world history.

This section traces the major developments of Russian history. In 1917, revolutionaries overthrew the Russian czarist government. They changed Russia's name to the Russian Soviet Federative Socialist Republic (R.S.F.S.R.). In 1922, the R.S.F.S.R. and three other republics formed a new nation called the Union of Soviet Socialist Republics (U.S.S.R.), also known as the Soviet Union. The U.S.S.R. broke apart in 1991, and Belarus, Russia, and Ukraine invited the other republics to join a federation called the Commonwealth of Independent States. For more detailed information about this period, see **Union of Soviet Socialist Republics** (History).

Early days. Beginning about 1200 B.C., the Cimmerians, a Balkan people, lived north of the Black Sea in what is now southern Ukraine. They were defeated about 700 B.C. by the Scythians, an Iranian people from central Asia. The Scythians controlled the region until about 200 B.C. They fell to the Sarmatians, another Iranian group. The Scythians and the Sarmatians lived in close contact with Greek colonies—later controlled by the Romans—along the northern coast of the Black Sea. They absorbed many Greek and Roman ways of life through trade, marriage, and other contacts. See **Cimmerians.**

Germanic tribes from the West, called the Goths, conquered the region about A.D. 200. The Goths ruled until about 370, when they were defeated by the Huns, a warlike Asian people. The Huns' empire broke up after their leader, Attila, died in 453. The Avars, a tribe related to the Huns, began to rule the region in the mid-500's. The Khazars, another Asian people, won the southern Volga and northern Caucasus regions in the mid-600's. They became Jews and established a busy trade with other peoples. See **Goths; Hun.**

By the 800's, Slavic groups had built many towns in eastern Europe, including what became the European part of Russia. They had also developed an active trade. No one knows where the Slavs came from. Some historians believe they came in the 400's from what is now Poland. Others think the Slavs were farmers in the Black Sea region under Scythian rule or earlier. Slavs of what are now Belarus, Russia, and Ukraine became known as East Slavs. See **Slavs.**

The earliest written Russian history of the 800's is the *Primary Chronicle,* written in Kiev, probably in 1111. It says that quarreling Slavic groups in the town of Novgorod asked a Viking tribe to rule them and bring order to the land. The Vikings were called the *Varangian Russes.* Historians who accept the *Primary Chronicle* as true believe that Russia took its name from this tribe. According to the *Primary Chronicle,* a group of related Varangian families headed by Rurik arrived in 862. Rurik settled in Novgorod, and the area became known as the "land of the Rus."

Many historians doubt that the Slavs of Novgorod invited the Vikings to rule them. They believe the Vikings invaded the region. Some historians claim the word *Rus,* from which Russia took its name, was the name of an early Slavic tribe in the Black Sea region. It is known,

Important dates in Russia

A.D. 800's East Slavs established the state of Kievan Rus.
1237-1240 The Mongols conquered Russia.
c. 1318 The Mongols appointed Prince Yuri of Moscow as the Russian grand prince.
1480 Ivan III broke Mongol control over Russia.
1547 Ivan IV became the first Russian czar.
1604-1613 Russia was torn by civil war, invasion, and political confusion during the Time of Troubles.
1613 Michael Romanov became czar. He started the Romanov line of czars, which ruled until 1917.
1703 Peter I founded St. Petersburg and began building his capital there.
1812 Napoleon invaded Russia, but he was forced to retreat.
1861 Alexander II freed the serfs.
1905 Japan defeated Russia in the Russo-Japanese War. A revolution forced Nicholas II to establish a parliament.
1914-1917 Russia fought Germany and Austria-Hungary in World War I.
1917 A revolution overthrew Nicholas II in March. The Bolsheviks (later called Communists) seized power in November. V. I. Lenin became head of government. Russia withdrew from World War I.
1918-1920 The Communists defeated their anti-Communist opponents in a civil war.
1922 The U.S.S.R. was established.
1991 Communist rule ended, and the republics declared their independence. The Soviet Union was dissolved on December 25.

however, that the first state founded by East Slavs—called Kievan Rus—was established at present-day Kiev in the 800's. Kiev, now the capital of Ukraine, was an important trading center on the Dnepr River. Whether it had been developed by the Vikings is unclear.

The state of Kievan Rus. The *Primary Chronicle* states that Oleg, a Varangian, captured Kiev in 882 and ruled as its prince. During the 900's, the other *principalities* (regions ruled by a prince) of Kievan Rus recognized Kiev's major importance. Kiev lay on the main trade route connecting the Baltic Sea with the Black Sea and the Byzantine Empire. In addition, Kiev's forces defended Kievan Rus against invading tribes from the south and east. The ruler of Kiev came to be called *grand prince* and ranked above the other princes of Kievan Rus.

In 988, Grand Prince Vladimir I (*Volodymyr* in Ukrainian) became a Christian. At that time, the East Slavs worshiped the forces of nature. Vladimir made Christianity the state religion, and most people under his rule turned Christian. Vladimir later became a saint of the Russian Orthodox Church.

Several grand princes were strong rulers, but Kiev's power began to decrease after the mid-1000's. The rulers of other Kievan Rus principalities grew in power, and they fought many destructive wars. In Novgorod and a few other towns with strong local governments, the princes were driven out. Badly weakened by civil wars and without strong central control, Kievan Rus fell to huge armies of Mongols called *Tatars,* or *Tartars,* who swept across Russia from the east during the 1200's.

Mongol rule. In 1237, Batu, a grandson of the conqueror Genghis Khan, led between 150,000 and 200,000 Mongol troops into Russia. The Mongols destroyed one Russian town after another. In 1240, they destroyed Kiev, and Russia became part of the Mongol Empire. It was included in a section called the Golden Horde. The capital of the Golden Horde was at Sarai, near what is now Volgograd.

Illustration from a Russian manuscript of the 1500's; Russian State Library, Moscow (Historical Pictures Service)

The Battle of Kulikovo in 1380 was the first Russian victory over the Mongol forces. It took place near the Don River.

Batu forced the surviving Russian princes to pledge allegiance to the Golden Horde and to pay heavy taxes. From time to time, the Mongols left their capital and wiped out the people of various areas because of their disloyalty. The Mongols also appointed the Russian grand prince and forced many Russians to serve in their armies. But they interfered little with Russian life in general. The Mongols were chiefly interested in maintaining their power and collecting taxes.

During the period of Mongol rule, which ended in the late 1400's, the new ideas and reforming spirit of the Renaissance were dramatically changing many aspects of life in Western Europe. But under Mongol control, Russia was cut off from these important Western influences.

The rise of Moscow. In the early 1300's, Prince Yuri of Moscow married the sister of the Golden Horde's *khan* (ruler). Yuri was appointed the Russian grand prince about 1318. Mongol troops helped him put down threats to his leadership from other principalities. The Mongols also began letting the grand prince of Moscow collect taxes for them. This practice started with Ivan I (called the Moneybag) about 1330. Ivan kept some of the tax money. He bought much land and expanded his territory greatly. Other princes and *boyars* (high-ranking landowners) began to serve in Moscow's army and government. In addition, Ivan persuaded the chief bishop of the Russian Orthodox Church to remain in Moscow. Until then, Kiev had been the spiritual center of Russia.

Moscow grew stronger and richer. But the Golden Horde grew weaker, chiefly because of struggles for leadership. In 1380, Grand Prince Dmitri defeated a Mongol force in the Battle of Kulikovo, near the Don River. The victory briefly freed Moscow of Mongol control. The Mongols recaptured Moscow in 1382, but they no longer believed they could not be beaten.

During the late 1400's, Moscow became the most powerful Russian city. Ivan III (called Ivan the Great) won control of Moscow's main rivals, Novgorod and Tver, and great numbers of boyars entered his service. In 1480, Ivan made the final break from Mongol control by refusing to pay taxes to the Golden Horde. Mongol troops moved toward Moscow but turned back to defend their capital from Russian attack.

Ivan the Terrible. After the rise of Moscow, its grand prince came to be called *czar.* In 1547, Ivan IV, also known as Ivan the Terrible, became the first ruler to be crowned czar. Ivan made the power of the czar over all Russia complete.

Ivan was brutal, extremely suspicious, and perhaps, at times, insane. He formed a special police force and began a reign of terror in which he ordered the arrest and murder of hundreds of aristocrats. Ivan gave his victims' estates as payment to the *service gentry* (landowners serving in the army and government). He also established strict rules concerning the number of warriors and horses each landowner had to supply to the army. Ivan burned many towns and villages, and he killed church leaders who opposed him. In a fit of rage, Ivan even struck and killed his oldest son.

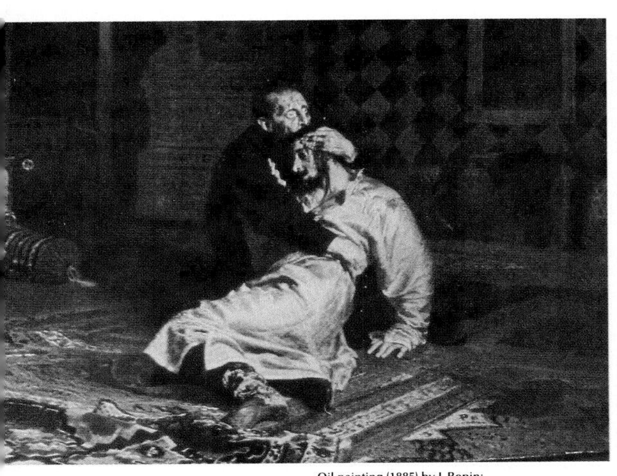

Oil painting (1885) by I. Repin; Tretyakov Gallery, Moscow (ITAR-Tass from Sovfoto)

Ivan the Terrible became Russia's first czar in 1547. He expanded Russia's territory and made Moscow his capital. This painting shows Ivan after he killed his son in a fit of rage.

The number of service gentry increased rapidly. But their estates had no value unless the peasants remained on the land and farmed it. Ivan and later czars passed a series of laws that bound the peasants to the land as *serfs.* Serfdom became the economic basis of Russian power. The development of Russian serfdom differed sharply from changes occurring in Western Europe at the time. There, during the Renaissance, the growth of trade led to the use of money as royal payment. It also led to the disappearance of serfdom in Western Europe.

Ivan fought Tatars at Astrakhan and Kazan to the southeast, and he won their lands. Russian forces then crossed the Ural Mountains and conquered western Siberia. Ivan also tried to win lands northwest to the Baltic Sea, but he was defeated by Lithuanian, Polish, and Swedish armies.

The Time of Troubles developed because of a breakdown of the czar's power after Ivan's death. Theodore I, Ivan's second son, was a weak czar. His wife's brother, Boris Godunov, became the real ruler of Russia. Theodore's younger brother, Dmitri, was found dead in 1591, and Theodore died in 1598 without leaving a male heir.

The *Zemskii Sobor* (Land Council), a kind of parliament with little power, elected Boris czar. But a man believed to be Gregory Otrepiev, a former monk, posed as Dmitri. This *False Dmitri* claimed Dmitri had not died, and he fled to Lithuania to avoid arrest. In 1604, False Dmitri invaded Russia with Polish troops. The invaders were joined by many discontented Russians. This invasion marked the beginning of the Time of Troubles. Russia was torn by civil war, invasion, and political confusion until 1613.

False Dmitri became czar in 1605, but a group of boyars killed him the next year. Prince Basil Shuisky then became czar. In 1610, Polish invaders occupied Moscow. They ruled through a powerless council of boyars until 1612. Meanwhile, a new False Dmitri and a number of other pretenders to the throne won many followers. Peasant revolts swept through Russia. Landowners and frontier people called *Cossacks* fought each other, and sometimes joined together to fight powerful aristocrats. The Polish control of Moscow led the Russians to unite their forces and drive out the invaders. They recaptured the capital in 1612.

The early Romanovs. After the Poles were defeated, there was no one of royal birth to take the throne. In 1613, the Zemskii Sobor elected Michael Romanov czar. The Romanov czars ruled Russia for the next 300 years, until the February Revolution of 1917 ended czarist rule.

During the 1600's, Russia annexed much of Ukraine and extended its control of Siberia eastward to the Pacific Ocean. During this same period, the Russian Orthodox Church made changes in religious texts and ceremonies. People called *Old Believers* objected to these changes and broke away from the church. This group still follows the old practices today.

Peter the Great. In 1682, a struggle for power resulted in the crowning of two half brothers—Peter I (later known as Peter the Great) and Ivan V—as co-czars. Both were children, and Ivan's sister Sophia ruled as *regent* (temporary ruler) until Peter's followers forced her to retire in 1689. Peter made close contact with the many Western Europeans living in Moscow and absorbed much new information from them. He came into full power in 1696, when Ivan died.

Peter was greatly influenced by ideas of commerce and government then popular in Western Europe. A powerful ruler, he improved Russia's military and made many important conquests. During Peter's reign, Russia

RIA-Novosti from Sovfoto

Peter the Great ruled Russia from 1682 until his death in 1725. Peter was a powerful ruler whose many conquests expanded Russia's empire. He also reorganized the government.

Czars and empresses of Russia

Ruler	Reign	Ruler	Reign
* **Ivan IV**	1547-1584	**Peter II**	1727-1730
Theodore I	1584-1598	**Anne**	1730-1740
Boris Godunov	1598-1605	**Ivan VI**	1740-1741
Theodore II	1605	**Elizabeth**	1741-1762
False Dmitri	1605-1606	**Peter III**	1762
Basil Shuisky	1606-1610	* **Catherine II**	1762-1796
Michael Romanov	1613-1645	**Paul**	1796-1801
Alexis	1645-1676	* **Alexander I**	1801-1825
Theodore III	1676-1682	* **Nicholas I**	1825-1855
Ivan V	1682-1696	* **Alexander II**	1855-1881
* **Peter I**	1682-1725	* **Alexander III**	1881-1894
* **Catherine I**	1725-1727	* **Nicholas II**	1894-1917

*Has a separate article in *World Book*.

expanded its territory to the Baltic Sea in the Great Northern War with Sweden. In 1703, Peter founded St. Petersburg on the Baltic, and he moved the capital there in 1712. After traveling throughout Europe, he introduced Western-type clothing, factories, and schools in Russia, and reorganized Russia's government to make it run more efficiently.

Peter forced Russia's nobility to adopt many Western customs. He also increased the czar's power over the aristocrats, church officials, and serfs. He dealt harshly with those who opposed these changes. Under Peter, the legal status of serfs further deteriorated.

Catherine the Great. After Peter's death in 1725, a series of struggles for the throne took place. The service gentry and the leading nobles were on opposite sides. Candidates for the throne who were supported by the service gentry won most of these struggles and rewarded their followers. The rulers increased the gentry's power over the serfs and local affairs. The gentry's enforced service to the state was gradually reduced. It was ended altogether in 1762.

RIA-Novosti from Sovfoto

Catherine the Great became empress of Russia in 1762. She expanded the country's territory and encouraged the development of the arts. But she preserved and extended serfdom.

Magnificent royal parties and other festivities, all in the latest Western fashion, took place during the 1700's. The arts were promoted, and many new schools were started, mainly for the upper classes. The Russian Imperial School of Ballet was founded, and Italian opera and chamber music were brought to Russia. It also became fashionable in Russia to repeat the newest Western ideas on freedom and social reform, especially during the rule of Empress Catherine II, known as Catherine the Great. In 1767, Catherine called a large legislative assembly to reform Russian laws. However, the assembly achieved nothing.

The great majority of Russians remained in extreme poverty and ignorance during this period. In 1773 and 1774, the peasants' discontent boiled over in a revolt led by Emelian Pugachev, a Cossack. The revolt swept through Russia from the Ural Mountains to the Volga River. It spread almost to Moscow before being crushed by government troops. In 1775, Catherine further tightened the landowners' control over the serfs.

Under Catherine the Great, Russia rose to new importance as a major world power. In the late 1700's, Austria, Prussia, and Russia gradually divided Poland among themselves. Russia gained nearly all of Belarus, Lithuania, and Ukraine from Poland. In wars against the Ottoman Empire (based in present-day Turkey), Russia gained the Crimea and other Ottoman lands. Catherine died in 1796. She was succeeded by her son, Paul, who became czar.

Alexander I. Paul's five-year rule ended with his murder in 1801. Alexander I, Paul's son, became czar and talked about freeing the serfs, building schools for all young Russians, and even giving up the throne and making Russia a republic. He introduced several reforms, such as freeing many political prisoners and spreading Western ways and ideas. But he did nothing to lessen the czar's total power or to end serfdom. Alexander knew that Russia's military strength and its position as a major world power depended on income provided by serfdom. Under Alexander's rule, Russia continued to win territory from Persia, Sweden, and the Ottoman Empire.

In June 1812, Napoleon led the Grand Army of France into Russia. He wanted to stop Russian trade with Great Britain, France's chief enemy, and to halt Russian expansion in the Balkan region. The French swept forward and reached Moscow in September 1812. Most of the people had left the city, and Napoleon and his army entered easily.

Soon afterward, fire destroyed most of Moscow. Historians believe the Russians themselves set the fire. After 35 days, the French left the city because they feared they might not survive the approaching bitter Russian winter. They began a disastrous retreat with little food and under continual attack by the Russians. Of the estimated 600,000 French troops in Russia, about 500,000 died, deserted, or were captured. Russia then became a major force in the campaign by several European countries that defeated Napoleon.

Although Alexander had begun some reforms, harsh rule continued in Russia. Beginning in 1816, many young aristocrats became revolutionaries. They formed secret groups, wrote constitutions for Russia, and prepared to revolt. Alexander died in 1825, and Nicholas I became czar. In December of 1825, a group of revolutionaries, later called the *Decembrists,* took action. At the urging of the Decembrists, about 3,000 soldiers and officers gathered in Senate Square in St. Petersburg, and government troops arrived to face them. After several hours, the Decembrists fired a few shots. Government cannons ended the revolt.

Nicholas I. The Decembrist revolt deeply impressed and frightened Nicholas. He removed aristocrats, whom he now distrusted, from government office and replaced them with professional military officers. He tightened his control over the press and education, reduced travel outside Russia, and prohibited organizations that might have political influence. He established six special government departments. These departments, which included a secret police system, handled important economic and political matters. Through the special departments, Nicholas avoided the regular processes of Russian government and increased his control over Russian life.

In spite of Nicholas' harsh rule, the period was one of outstanding achievement in Russian literature. Nikolai Gogol, Mikhail Lermontov, Alexander Pushkin, and others wrote their finest works. Fyodor Dostoevsky, Leo Tolstoy, and Ivan Turgenev began their careers. Many educated Russians began to debate the values of Westernized Russian life against those of old Russian life. The pro-Western group argued that Russia must learn from and catch up with the West economically and politically. The other group argued for the old Russian ways, including the czarist system, a strong church, and the quiet life of the Russian countryside.

Nicholas became known as the "policeman of Europe" because he sent troops to put down revolutions in Poland and Hungary. Nicholas also declared himself the defender of the Eastern Orthodox Churches and fought two wars with the Muslim Ottoman Empire. In the war of 1828 and 1829, Russia gained much territory around the Black Sea. Russia also won the right to move merchant ships through the straits connecting the Black Sea with the Mediterranean Sea. The Ottoman Empire controlled these straits.

In 1853, the Crimean War broke out between Russia and the Ottoman Empire. Great Britain and France aided the Ottomans. These countries objected to Russian expansion in the Black Sea region. Russia was defeated and signed the Treaty of Paris in 1856. This treaty forced Russia to give up some of the territory it had taken earlier from the Ottoman Empire, and the pact forbade warships on and fortifications around the Black Sea.

Expansion in Asia. After its defeat in the Crimean War, Russia began to expand in Asia. In the Far East, Russia won disputed territories from China. In 1858 and 1860, the Chinese signed treaties giving Russia lands north of the Amur River and east of the Ussuri River. By 1864, Russian forces defeated rebel tribes in the Caucasus. Central Asia was won during a series of military campaigns from 1865 to 1876. In 1867, Russia sold its Alaskan territory to the United States for $7,200,000.

Alexander II. Nicholas I died in 1855, during the Crimean War. His son, Alexander II, became czar. Russia's defeat in the Crimean War taught Alexander a lesson. He realized that Russia had to catch up with the West to remain a major power. Alexander began a series of reforms to strengthen the economy and Russian life in general. In 1861, he freed the serfs and distributed land among them. He began developing railroads and organizing a banking system. Alexander promoted reforms in education, reduced controls on the press, and introduced a jury system and other reforms in the courts. He also established forms of self-government in the towns and villages.

But many young Russians believed that Alexander's reforms did not go far enough. Some revolutionary groups wanted to establish socialism in Russia. Others wanted a constitution and a republic. These groups formed a number of public and secret organizations. After a revolutionary tried to kill Alexander in 1866, the czar began to weaken many of his reforms. The revolutionaries then argued that Alexander had never been a sincere reformer at all. During the mid-1870's, a group of revolutionaries tried to get the peasants to revolt. They wanted to achieve either socialism or *anarchism* (absence of government) for Russia (see **Anarchism**). After this effort failed, a terrorist group called the People's Will tried several times to kill the czar. Alexander then decided to set up a new reform program. But in 1881, he was killed by a terrorist's bomb in St. Petersburg.

Alexander III, Alexander's son, became czar and soon began a program of harsh rule. Alexander III limited the freedom of the press and of the universities, and he sharply reduced the powers of Russia's local self-governments. He set up a special bank to help the aristocrats increase their property. He also appointed officials called *land captains* from among the aristocrats and gave them much political power over the peasants. Alexander started some programs to help the peasants and industrial workers. But their living and working conditions improved very little during his reign.

Nicholas II became Russia's next, and last, czar in 1894. The revolutionary movement had been kept in check until the 1890's, when a series of bad harvests caused starvation among the peasants. In addition, as industrialization increased, discontent grew among the rising middle class and workers in the cities. Discontented Russians formed various political organizations, of which three became important. (1) The *liberal constitutionalists* wanted to replace czarist rule with a Western type of parliamentary government. (2) The *social revolutionaries* tried to promote a revolution among peasants and workers in the cities. (3) The *Marxists* wanted to promote revolution among the city workers. The Marxists followed the socialist teachings of Karl Marx, a German social philosopher (see **Marx, Karl**). In 1898, the Marxists established the Russian Social Democratic Labor Party.

Between 1899 and 1904, the discontent of the Russian people increased. Worker strikes and other forms of protest took place. In 1903, the Russian Social Democratic Labor Party split into two groups—the *Bolsheviks* (members of the majority) and the *Mensheviks* (members of the minority). V. I. Lenin was the leader of the Bolsheviks, later called Communists.

Sovfoto

V. I. Lenin, *with raised arm,* led the Bolshevik take-over of the Russian government in the October Revolution of 1917. He became the first leader of the Soviet Union.

The Revolution of 1905. On Jan. 22, 1905, thousands of unarmed workers marched to the czar's Winter Palace in St. Petersburg. The workers were on strike, and they planned to ask Nicholas II for reforms. Government troops fired on the crowd and killed or wounded hundreds of marchers. After this *Bloody Sunday* slaughter, the revolutionary movement, led mainly by the liberal constitutionalists, gained much strength. In February, Nicholas agreed to establish an elected Duma (parliament) to advise him. However, more strikes broke out during the summer, and peasant and military groups revolted. In part, the growing unrest was linked to the increasingly unpopular Russo-Japanese War. This war had broken out in February 1904 after a Japanese attack on Russian ships. The war ended with Russia's defeat in September 1905.

In October 1905, a general strike paralyzed the country. Revolutionaries in St. Petersburg formed a *soviet* (council) called the Soviet of Workers' Deputies. Nicholas then granted the Duma the power to pass or reject all proposed laws. Many Russians were satisfied, but many others were not. The revolution continued, especially in Moscow, where the army crushed a serious uprising in December.

Each of the first two Dumas, which met in 1906 and 1907, was dissolved after a few months. The Dumas could not work with Nicholas and his high-ranking officials, who refused to give up much power. Nicholas illegally changed the election law and made the selection of Duma candidates less democratic. The peasants and workers were allowed far fewer representatives in the Duma than the upper classes. The third Duma served from 1907 to 1912, and the fourth Duma met from 1912 to 1917. During this period, Russia made important advances in the arts and education and in farming, and industry.

World War I. By the time World War I began in 1914, Europe was divided into two tense armed camps. On one side was the Triple Entente (Triple Agreement), consisting of Russia, France, and Great Britain. Russia and France had agreed in 1894 to defend each other against attack. France and Britain had signed the Entente Cordiale (Friendly Understanding) in 1904, and Russia had signed a similar agreement with Britain in 1907. The Triple Entente developed from these treaties. Opposing the Triple Entente was the Triple Alliance, formed in 1882 by Austria-Hungary, Germany, and Italy.

On Aug. 1, 1914, Germany declared war on Russia. Soon afterward, Russia changed the German-sounding name of St. Petersburg to Petrograd. German troops crushed the Russian army at Tannenberg, in East Prussia. However, the Russians defeated an Austrian army in the Battles of Lemberg in the Galicia region of Austria-Hungary.

In 1915, Austrian and German forces drove back the Russians. The next year, the Russians attacked along a 70-mile (113-kilometer) front in Galicia. They advanced about 50 miles (80 kilometers). Russian troops moved into the Carpathian Mountains in 1917, but the Germans pushed them back.

The February Revolution. During World War I, the Russian economy could not meet the needs of the soldiers and also those of the people at home. The railroads carried military supplies and could not serve the cities. The people suffered severe shortages of food, fuel, and housing. Russian troops at the front were loyal, but the untrained soldiers behind the fighting lines began to question the war. They knew they would probably be sent to the front and be killed. The soldiers and civilians behind the lines consequently grew increasingly dissatisfied.

By the end of 1916, almost all educated Russians opposed the czar. Nicholas had removed many capable executives from high government offices and replaced them with weak, unpopular officials. He was accused of crippling the war effort by such acts. Many Russians blamed his action on the influence of Grigori Rasputin, adviser to the czar and the czarina. The royal couple believed that Rasputin was a holy man who was saving their sick son's life. In December 1916, a group of nobles murdered Rasputin. But the officials who supposedly had been appointed through his influence remained.

In March 1917, the people of Russia revolted. (The month was February in the old Russian calendar, which was replaced in 1918.) Violent riots and strikes over shortages of bread and coal accompanied the uprising in Petrograd, the capital of Russia. (Petrograd was known as St. Petersburg until 1914, was renamed Leningrad in 1924, and again became St. Petersburg in 1991.) Nicholas ordered the Duma to dissolve itself, but it ignored his command and set up a *provisional* (temporary) government. Nicholas had lost all political support, and he gave up the throne on March 15. Nicholas and his family were then imprisoned. Bolshevik revolutionaries almost certainly shot them to death in July 1918.

Many soviets were established in Russia at the same time as the provisional government was formed. The soviets rivaled the provisional government. Workers and soldiers tried to seize power in Petrograd in July, but the attempt failed.

The October Revolution. In August 1917, General Lavr Kornilov tried to curb the growing power of the soviets. But the attempt failed, and the Russian masses became increasingly radical. On November 7 (October 25 in the old Russian calendar), workers, soldiers, and sailors led by the Bolsheviks took over the Winter Palace, a former royal residence that had become the headquarters of the provisional government. They overthrew the provisional government and formed a new government headed by Lenin. Lenin immediately withdrew Russia from World War I. The new government soon took over Russia's industries and also seized most of the peasants' farm products.

In 1918, the Bolsheviks made Moscow the capital of Russia. They also changed the name of the Russian Social Democratic Labor Party to the Russian Communist Party. This name was later changed to the Communist Party of the Soviet Union.

Civil war and the formation of the U.S.S.R. From 1918 to 1920, civil war raged between the Communists and the anti-Communists over control of Russia. The anti-Communists received support from several other countries, including France, Great Britain, Japan, and the United States. Nevertheless, the Communists defeated their opponents. They also established Communist rule in Georgia, Ukraine, eastern Armenia, Belarus, and Central Asia. The civil war contributed to the increasing discontent among the Russian people.

In 1921, more peasant uprisings and workers' strikes broke out. That same year, Lenin established a New Economic Policy (NEP) to strengthen Russia. Under this policy, the government controlled the most important aspects of the economy, including banking, foreign trade, heavy industry, and transportation. But small businesses could control their own operations, and peasants could keep their farm products.

In December 1922, the Communist government created a new nation called the Union of Soviet Socialist Republics (U.S.S.R.). It consisted of four republics—the Russian Soviet Federative Socialist Republic, Byelorussia (as Belarus was renamed), Transcaucasia, and Ukraine. By late 1940, Transcaucasia had been divided into Azerbaijan, Armenia, and Georgia, and 10 more republics had been established, for a total of 16 republics. The new republics included what are now Estonia, Kazakhstan, Kyrgyzstan, Latvia, Lithuania, Moldova (then Moldavia), Tajikistan, Turkmenistan, and Uzbekistan. The Karelo-Finnish Soviet Socialist Republic, established in 1940, was changed to an autonomous republic in 1956.

Stalin. Lenin died in 1924. Joseph Stalin, who had been general secretary of the Communist Party since 1922, rapidly gained power. He defeated his rivals one by one. By 1929, Stalin had become dictator of the Soviet Union.

In the late 1920's, Stalin began a socialist economic program. It emphasized the development of heavy industry and the combining of privately owned farms into large, government-run farms. Many citizens of the Soviet Union opposed Stalin's policies. In the mid-1930's, Stalin started a program of terror called the Great Purge. His secret police arrested millions of people. Most of the prisoners were shot or sent to prison labor camps. Many of those arrested had helped Stalin rise to power. Stalin thus eliminated all possible threats to his power and tightened his hold over the Soviet Union.

World War II. By the late 1930's, German dictator Adolf Hitler was ready to conquer Europe. In August 1939, the U.S.S.R. and Germany signed a *nonaggression pact,* a treaty agreeing that neither nation would attack the other. In September, German forces invaded Poland from the west. The Soviet Union's forces quickly occupied the eastern part of Poland.

In June 1941, Germany invaded the Soviet Union and began to advance into the country. The turning point of the war in the Soviet Union was the Soviet defeat of the Germans in the Battle of Stalingrad (now Volgograd) in 1943. Soviet troops then drove the Germans back out of the country and across eastern Europe. They attacked Berlin in April 1945. Berlin fell to the Soviets on May 2,

Expansion of Russia

This map shows the increase in territory that took place in Russia between 1462 and 1914. Russia gained these lands through wars, conquests, and annexations. The boundary of present-day Russia appears as a solid red line on the map.

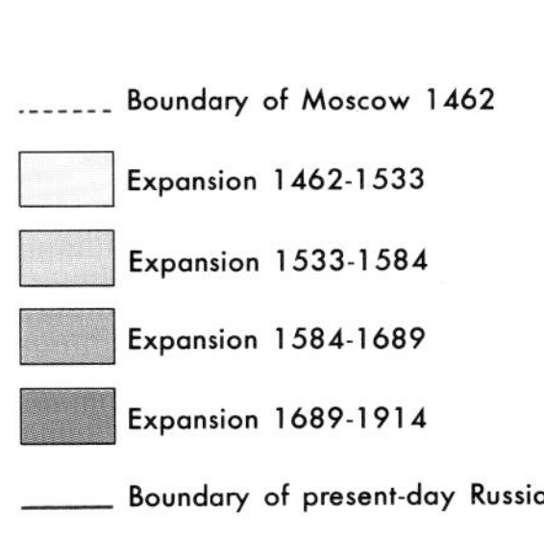

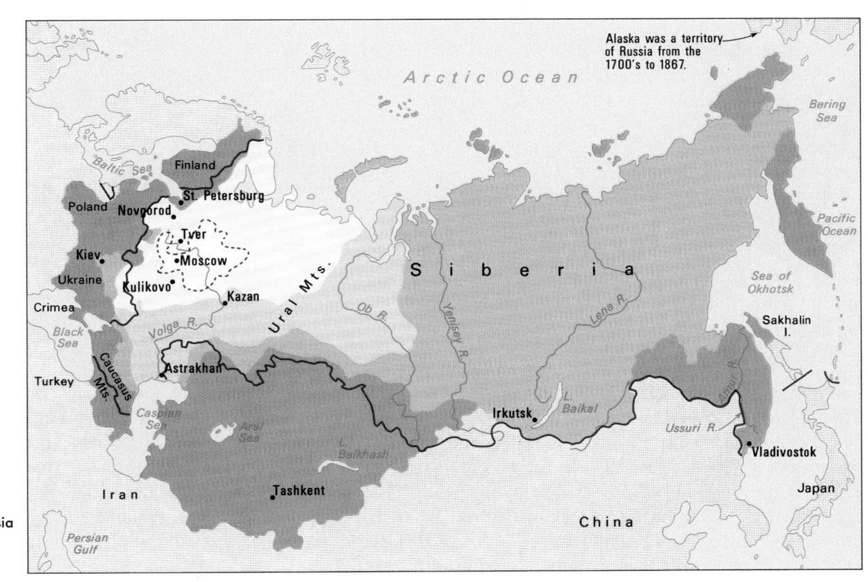

WORLD BOOK map

and German troops surrendered to the Allies five days later. In August 1945, the U.S.S.R. declared war on Japan. Japan surrendered to the Allies on Sept. 2, 1945, ending World War II.

The Cold War. After World War II ended, the Soviet Union extended the influence of Communism into Eastern Europe. By early 1948, several countries had become *Soviet satellites* (countries controlled by the Soviet Union). The satellites were Bulgaria, Czechoslovakia, Hungary, Poland, Romania, and—later—East Germany. The U.S.S.R. also influenced Communist regimes in Albania and Yugoslavia. It cut off nearly all contact between its satellites and the West. Mutual distrust and suspicion between East and West developed into a rivalry that became known as the Cold War. The Cold War shaped the foreign policy of the Soviet Union and of many Western countries until the late 1980's.

Stalin died on March 5, 1953. In September of that year, Nikita S. Khrushchev became the head of the Communist Party. In 1958, he also became premier of the Soviet Union. Khrushchev eased the terrorism that had characterized Stalin's dictatorship and relaxed some of the restrictions on communication, trade, and travel between East and West. However, the U.S.S.R. continued working to expand its influence in non-Communist countries. Khrushchev improved Soviet relations with the West, but many of his other policies failed.

In 1964, the highest-ranking Communists overthrew Khrushchev. Leonid I. Brezhnev became Communist Party head, and Aleksei N. Kosygin became premier. Brezhnev and Kosygin increased the production of consumer goods and the construction of housing, and they expanded Soviet influence in Africa.

By the mid-1970's, Brezhnev was the most powerful Soviet leader. He sought to ease tensions between East and West, a policy that became known as *détente.* However, détente began to collapse in the late 1970's. Relations between the Soviet Union and the United States worsened over such issues as Soviet violations of human rights, the Soviet invasion of Afghanistan, and an increase in the number of nuclear weapons by both nations.

The rise of Gorbachev. In 1985, Mikhail S. Gorbachev became head of the Communist Party. Gorbachev instituted many changes in the U.S.S.R., including increased freedom of expression in politics, literature, and the arts. He worked to improve relations between the Soviet Union and the West and to reduce government control over the Soviet economy. In 1989, the U.S.S.R. held its first contested elections for the newly created Congress of People's Deputies. The following year, the government voted to allow non-Communist political parties in the Soviet Union. Many Communist Party members and other Soviet officials opposed Gorbachev's reforms. But in March 1990, Gorbachev was elected by the Congress of People's Deputies to the newly created office of president.

The breakup of the U.S.S.R. During the late 1980's, people in many parts of the Soviet Union increased their demands for greater freedom from the central government. In June 1990, the Russian republic declared that laws passed by its legislature took precedence over laws passed by the central government. By the end of the year, all 15 Soviet republics had done the same.

In July 1991, Gorbachev and the leaders of 10 republics agreed to sign a treaty giving the republics a large amount of self-government. Five of the republics were scheduled to sign the treaty on August 20. But on August 19, conservative Communist Party leaders staged a coup against Gorbachev's government. They imprisoned Gorbachev and his family in their vacation home. The president of the Russian republic, Boris N. Yeltsin, led popular opposition to the coup, which collapsed on August 21. After the coup, Gorbachev regained his office of president. But he resigned as the leader of the Soviet Communist Party.

The collapse of the coup renewed the republics' demands for more control over their own affairs. In September 1991, the Congress of People's Deputies established an interim government to rule until a new union treaty and constitution could be written and approved. This government included a State Council, made up of Gorbachev and the leaders of the republics.

On December 8, 1991, Yeltsin and the presidents of Belarus and Ukraine announced the formation of the Commonwealth of Independent States (C.I.S.). They declared that the Soviet Union had ceased to exist and invited the remaining republics to join the commonwealth. The members would be independent countries tied by economic and defense links. Eleven republics—all except Georgia and the Baltic states of Estonia, Latvia, and Lithuania—joined the C.I.S. Yeltsin took control of what remained of the central government of the Soviet Union, including the Kremlin. On December 25, 1991, Gorbachev resigned as Soviet president, and the Soviet Union ceased to exist.

A nation in transition. Russia faced the challenges of setting up new governmental and economic systems. The lifting of price controls caused prices to soar and resulted in a lower standard of living for the Russian people. In October 1992, the government began issuing certificates that citizens could use to buy shares in state-owned firms.

Russia also had to establish new relationships with the members of the C.I.S. Some Russian leaders wanted the country to take a leading role. However, the smaller states feared domination by Russia because of its great size and power.

In March 1992, all but two regions of Russia signed a treaty that formed the basis of the new Russian nation. Those two regions—Tatar and Chechen-Ingush—declared a desire for greater independence.

In May 1992, the Supreme Soviet voted to declare the Soviet government's 1954 grant of Crimea to Ukraine null and void. It called for negotiations between Russia and Ukraine on the issue.

The breakup of the Soviet Union helped eliminate much of the friction that still remained between the East and the West. The Russian government slashed military spending in 1992 and made significant cutbacks in the number of people in the armed forces. This, in turn, forced large numbers of former military personnel to find homes and jobs as civilians. In 1992, the four former republics with Soviet nuclear weapons on their lands—Belarus, Kazakhstan, Russia, and Ukraine—agreed that all the weapons would either be destroyed or turned over to Russian control within seven years.

Donald J. Raleigh

Tajikistan, *tuh JIHK uh STAN,* also spelled *Tadzhikistan,* is a mountainous country in central Asia. It became independent in 1991, after more than 60 years as a republic of the Soviet Union. The country's name in Tajik, the official language, is Jumhurii Tojikiston (Republic of Tajikistan).

Tajikistan covers 55,251 square miles (143,100 square kilometers) and has a population of 5,112,000. Tajikistan's capital and largest city is Dushanbe.

Government. Tajikistan is a republic. The head of state is the president, who is elected by the voters. The president appoints a prime minister, who heads a cabinet called the Council of Ministers. The cabinet helps carry out the functions of the government. The president also appoints council members. A legislature elected by the people makes Tajikistan's laws. The main units of local government are regions and cities.

Tajikistan's highest court is the Supreme Court. There are also regional courts and local courts. All judges are elected to five-year terms.

People. About 62 per cent of Tajikistan's people are ethnic Tajiks. Uzbeks make up about 23 per cent of the population, and Russians account for about 9 per cent. Other ethnic groups include Tatars, Kyrgyzs, Kazakhs, and Turkmens.

Most Tajiks are Sunni Muslims. Groups of Shiite Muslims live in remote mountain areas. In addition, small communities of a sect called the Ismaili Khoja Muslims live in the Pamirs, a mountain range.

Under Soviet rule, religious activity was severely restricted. The government closed many mosques, prohibited religious services outside officially recognized places of worship, and tried to discourage religion through propaganda and education. But religious feeling remained strong among Tajiks. Islamic leaders held secret prayer meetings, gave sermons, and practiced religious rituals despite Soviet restrictions.

About two-thirds of Tajikistan's people live in rural areas. The most heavily settled regions of the country are along rivers and oases. Most people live in rural villages made up of sun-dried earthen houses surrounded by earthen walls. City dwellers live in single-story houses and multistory apartment buildings.

Most families in Tajikistan are large. Many members of an extended family may live together in one household. Such a household might include parents, married children and their offspring, and other relatives. Because of marriage patterns, it is common for all people in a village to be related. Some Tajiks follow a Muslim custom that permits a man to have as many as four wives.

Tajiks wear both Western-style and traditional clothing. Traditional garments include loose cotton trousers and a dark or multicolored robe for men and colorful, embroidered silk dresses for women. Both men and women wear embroidered skullcaps.

Traditional Tajik foods include a rice dish called *pilaf* and *shashlik* (lamb or beef broiled on skewers). Green tea is the most popular drink.

Tajik is an Iranian language. It is much like Farsi, the chief language of Iran.

The government requires children to attend school between the ages of 6 and 17. Tajikistan has one university and several other schools of higher education.

Land and climate. Over 90 per cent of Tajikistan is mountainous, and over half lies above 10,000 feet (3,050 meters). The highest peaks are snow-covered all year. The towering Pamirs rise in the southeast. The Alay and Tian Shan mountain ranges stretch across much of the rest of the country. Fedchenko Glacier, one of the world's longest glaciers, extends 48 miles (77 kilometers) in the Pamirs. Two major rivers, the Amu Darya and the

Facts in brief

Capital: Dushanbe.
Official language: Tajik.
Area: 55,251 sq. mi. (143,100 km²). Greatest distances—north-south, 300 mi. (485 km); east-west, 425 mi. (685 km).
Elevation: *Highest*—Communism Peak, 24,590 ft. (7,495 m). *Lowest*—Syr Darya river at northwestern border, 980 ft. (300 m).
Population: *Estimated 1993 population*—5,252,000; density, 95 persons per sq. mi. (37 per km²); distribution, 67 per cent rural, 33 per cent urban. *1989 census*—5,112,000. *Estimated 1998 population*—5,427,000.
Chief products: *Agriculture*—cotton, fruit, grain, livestock, vegetables. *Manufacturing*—food processing, textiles, wine. *Mining*—antimony, coal, fluorite, lead, molybdenum, natural gas, petroleum, salt, tungsten, uranium, zinc.
Flag: The flag has horizontal stripes of reddish orange, white, green, and reddish orange. A yellow star with a reddish-orange center over a yellow hammer and sickle sit on the left of the top reddish-orange stripe. See **Flag** (picture: Flags of Asia and the Pacific).
Money: *Basic unit*—ruble.

Tajikistan

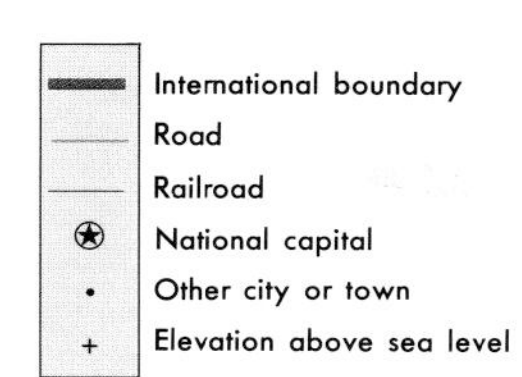

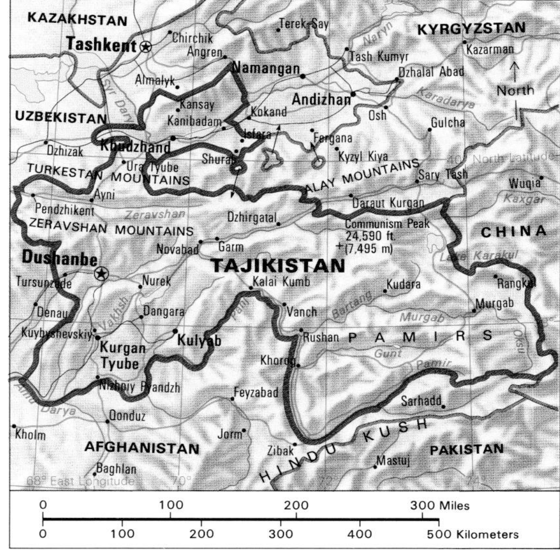

WORLD BOOK map

© Naomi Duguid, Asia Access

A mountain village in Tajikistan lies nestled in a narrow valley. Mountains cover more than 90 per cent of Tajikistan. Many Tajiks live in valleys near rivers or oases.

Syr Darya, cross Tajikistan. Other rivers include the Vakhsh, Kafirnigan, and Zeravshan. Earthquakes often occur throughout the region.

Summers in the valleys are typically long, hot, and dry. Winters in the highlands are long and cold. Temperatures in the valleys average 36 °F (2 °C) in January and 86 °F (30 °C) in July. Temperatures in the highlands average −4 °F (−20 °C) in January and 72 °F (22 °C) in July. In parts of the eastern Pamirs, temperatures can drop to −58 °F (−50 °C). Tajikistan receives annual rainfall of less than 8 inches (20 centimeters).

Economy. Agriculture accounts for about two-fifths of the value of Tajikistan's economic production. Cotton is Tajikistan's chief agricultural product. Other crops include various fruits, grains, and vegetables. Farmers also raise a variety of livestock, including cattle, chickens, horses, Karakul sheep, and yaks. Chief agricultural areas lie in the country's southwest and north.

Tajikistan's industries, which include food processing, hydroelectric power generation, mining, and textile manufacturing, account for about a third of the value of the country's economic production. Chief industrial centers are the cities of Dushanbe and Khudzhand. The mines of the region yield a variety of minerals, including antimony, coal, fluorite, lead, molybdenum, salt, tungsten, uranium, and zinc. The huge Nurek Dam on the Vakhsh River provides hydroelectric power for a large aluminum plant and other industries, as well as water for irrigation projects.

Tajikistan has a limited highway and railroad system. Heavy snows close roads in the Pamirs at least six months of the year.

A radio and a television station broadcast from Dushanbe in several languages. The country also publishes newspapers and magazines in several languages.

History. People have inhabited the area that is now Tajikistan for thousands of years. Persians of the Achaemenid Empire settled in the region as early as the 500's B.C. These Persians became the ancestors of the Tajiks. They ruled the region until Alexander the Great gained control of their empire in 331 B.C. After Alexander's death in 323 B.C., the region split into a number of independent states. Part of Tajikistan was absorbed by the Seleucids, who ruled until about 250 B.C. Another part came under the control of the Bactrian State, which ruled until about 130 B.C. At that time, nomadic tribes from western China invaded the region. They were overthrown by the Kushans by the A.D. 100's. Sassanians from Persia and White Huns from Central Asia defeated the Kushans by the 400's.

Turkic tribes began moving into Central Asia in about the 500's. Arab armies swept into the region in the mid-600's and introduced Islam. Various Turkic peoples from eastern Persia and central Asia ruled what is now Tajikistan from about 900 to 1200. Mongols led by Genghis Khan conquered the region in the 1200's. Turkic tribes called Uzbeks ruled the region from the 1500's to the 1800's.

In the late 1800's, czarist Russian forces conquered part of the region. In 1917, Communists took control of Russia. By 1921, Russians controlled all of what is now Tajikistan. In 1922, the Soviet Union was formed under Russia's leadership. A rebel group of nationalist Muslim Tajiks known as the *Basmachis* resisted Soviet control into the mid-1920's. In 1924, the Tajik Autonomous Soviet Socialist Republic was formed within the Uzbek Soviet Socialist Republic. In 1929, it acquired additional territory inhabited mostly by Uzbeks and became the Tajik Soviet Socialist Republic.

The Soviets made many changes in Tajikistan. The Soviet government built roads, railroads, schools, and modern housing. It also developed industries, especially agriculture and mining. In addition, the Soviets *collectivized* agriculture—that is, they transferred control of farms and livestock to the government. They also tried to reduce the influence of Islam and prohibited the Tajiks from practicing many of their traditions. The government maintained strict control of all aspects of Tajik life until the late 1980's. At that time, the government made reforms that gave people more freedom.

In the 1980's, opposition groups began to demonstrate against the Communist-controlled government, demanding better housing and more control over their own affairs. In 1989, Tajik replaced Russian as the official language of the republic. Then, in 1990, Tajikistan declared that its laws overruled Soviet laws. In 1991, the government introduced a free-enterprise system and began to sell off businesses to private owners. In September 1991, Tajikistan declared its independence. After the collapse of the Soviet Union in December, the country joined a loose association of former Soviet republics called the Commonwealth of Independent States, which is headquartered in Minsk, Belarus.

In September 1992, anti-Communist and Islamic opposition groups forced the resignation of President Rakhman Nabiyev, a former Soviet Communist Party chief. Unrest in Tajikistan has continued.

Edward J. Lazzerini

See also **Commonwealth of Independent States.**

Turkmenistan is a mostly desert country in west-central Asia. For nearly 70 years, it had been one of the republics of the Soviet Union. It was called the Turkmen Soviet Socialist Republic, or Turkmenia. In 1991, Turkmenistan became independent.

Turkmenistan lies in a broad, dry lowland extending east from the Caspian Sea. It covers 188,456 square miles (488,100 square kilometers). Most of the country is desert. Turkmenistan has more than $3\frac{1}{2}$ million people. The country's capital and largest city is Ashkhabad. The official language is Turkmen, a Turkic language.

Government. Turkmenistan is a republic. It has a president as head of state and head of government, and a Cabinet of Ministers to help carry out government operations. The voters elect the president to a five-year term. The president appoints the Cabinet members. The country also has a 50-member legislature called the Majlis, whose members are elected by the voters to five-year terms. Turkmenistan is divided into five regions for the purpose of local government.

Turkmenistan's highest court is the Supreme Court. There are also regional courts and local courts.

People. About 70 per cent of Turkmenistan's people are ethnic Turkmens, also called Turkomans, and about 10 per cent are Russians. Other ethnic groups include Uzbeks, Kazakhs, Tatars, Ukrainians, and Armenians. Most people live along rivers or in oases.

The Turkmens are Sunni Muslims. Other religious groups in Turkmenistan include Shiite Muslims and Russian Orthodox Christians. Although most Muslims worship in mosques, Turkmens follow a special Muslim practice of worshiping primarily at tombs of holy men.

About 48 per cent of the people of Turkmenistan live in cities, and about 52 per cent live in rural areas. Most city dwellers live in red brick or limestone apartment buildings. Some rural dwellers live in tentlike *yurts,* constructed of a wooden frame covered with felt.

Tribal organizations play an important role in Turkmen social customs. Turkmen social life is centered around the family. In the countryside, many members of an extended family live together in one household. Such a household might include parents, married children and their offspring, and other relatives. Some Turkmens practice a Muslim style of marriage that permits a man to have as many as four wives. Many Turkmens marry only within their own tribe.

People in Turkmenistan wear both Western-style and traditional clothing. Traditional dress for men includes a white shirt, dark trousers, and a red robe. Some men also wear a shaggy sheepskin hat. Women typically wear a long, loose dress trimmed with embroidery.

Turkmen dishes include *chorba* (a peppery meat soup); *chishlik* (meat roasted on a skewer); and *palov,* a rice dish. Milk products form an important part of the Turkmen diet. Turkmens drink green tea after meals.

Turkmens are known for weaving beautiful woolen carpets displaying geometric patterns in reds, yellows, and blues. Other crafts include embroidery, handmade fabrics, leathercraft, and jewelry.

Nearly all adults can read and write. The government requires children to attend school between the ages of

Facts in brief

Capital: Ashkhabad.
Official language: Turkmen.
Area: 188,456 sq. mi. (488,100 km²). *Greatest distances*—east-west, 750 mi. (1,205 km); north-south, 525 mi. (845 km).
Elevation: *Highest*—Kugitangtau (mountain range), 10,292 ft. (3,137 m) above sea level. *Lowest*—Kara Bogaz Gol Gulf, 102 ft. (31 m) below sea level.
Population: *Estimated 1993 population*—3,631,000; density, 19 persons per sq. mi. (7 per km²); distribution, 52 per cent rural, 48 per cent urban. *1989 census*—3,534,000. *Estimated 1998 population*—3,752,000.
Chief products: *Agriculture*—camels, cotton, grains, grapes, horses, pigs, potatoes, sheep. *Manufacturing*—cement, chemicals, glass, textiles. *Mining*—bromine, copper, gold, iodine, lead, mercury, natural gas, petroleum, salt, sodium sulfate, zinc.
Flag: The flag has three unequal vertical stripes of green, maroon, and green. On the maroon stripe are five different carpet patterns in black, white, maroon, and orange. To the upper right of the maroon stripe are five white stars and a white crescent. See **Flag** (picture: Flags of Asia and the Pacific).
Money: *Basic unit*—ruble.

Turkmenistan

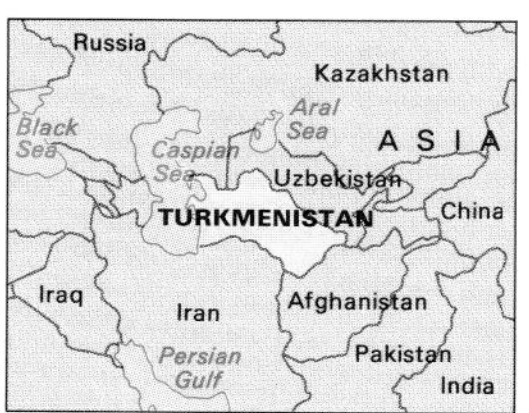

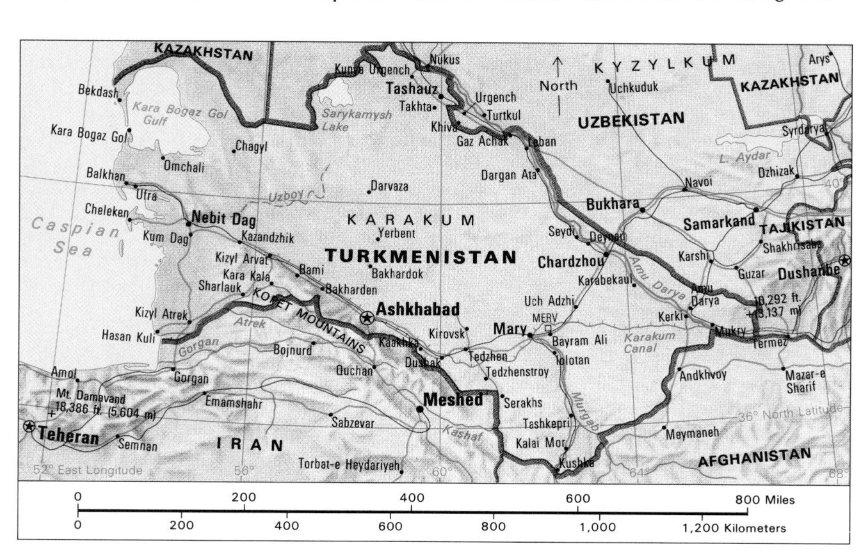

International boundary
Road
Railroad
National capital
Other city or town
Elevation above sea level

WORLD BOOK maps

© Shepard Sherbell, SABA

Turkmen carpet vendors, *above,* peddle their wares at a market in Ashkhabad, Turkmenistan's capital. Turkmen carpets are known for their beautiful geometric patterns in reds and blues.

6 and 17. The country has one university.

Land and climate. The Karakum desert covers more than 80 per cent of Turkmenistan. This vast desert is largely uninhabited. The Kopet-Dag mountains stretch along the south and southwest of the country. The Amu Darya river flows from mountains southeast of Turkmenistan into Uzbekistan, where it drains into the Aral Sea.

Summers in Turkmenistan are long, hot, and dry. Winters are cold. Desert temperatures range from about 95 °F to 122 °F (35 °C to 50 °C) in summer. Winter temperatures in the desert can drop below 32 °F (0 °C). Turkmenistan receives about 3 to 12 inches (8 to 30 centimeters) of rainfall annually.

Economy. Agriculture accounts for almost half the value of Turkmenistan's economic production. Cotton, the chief crop, occupies more than 50 per cent of the farmland. Other farm products include grains, grapes, potatoes, wool, and *Persian lamb* (a fur taken from young lambs).

Crops in Turkmenistan can only be grown by irrigation. An extensive system of canals moves water from the major rivers of the region to dry areas. The 750-mile (1200-kilometer) long Karakum Canal transports water across the desert from the Amu Darya, past Ashkhabad, to Kizyl-Arvat. Most of the farming regions in Turkmenistan lie along the Amu Darya and the Karakum Canal.

Manufacturing makes up about a fifth of the value of production in Turkmenistan. Chief manufacturing industries produce petrochemicals, cement, glass, and textiles of cotton, wool, and silk.

Turkmenistan's chief natural resources are natural gas and petroleum. Other resources include bromine, copper, gold, iodine, lead, mercury, salt, sodium sulfate, zinc, and such building materials as sand and limestone.

Under Soviet control, the government owned most of Turkmenistan's businesses, factories, and farmland. In the late 1980's, the Soviets began to allow free enterprise. However, the economy of independent Turkmenistan is still largely controlled by government.

Turkmenistan has a limited highway and railroad system, linking only major urban areas. An airport at Ashkhabad handles all flights to and from Turkmenistan.

A radio station and a television station broadcast out of Ashkhabad in Turkmen and Russian. Newspapers and magazines are published in the same two languages.

History. People have lived in the area now known as Turkmenistan for thousands of years. The earliest inhabitants were probably nomads who lived by raising livestock in the desert areas and farmers who lived along rivers and oases. Persians of the Achaemenid Empire ruled the area from about 500 to 331 B.C., when Alexander the Great gained control of much of their empire. The kingdom of Parthia controlled the region between about 250 B.C. and A.D. 224, followed by Persians of the Sassanid dynasty. In the mid-600's, Muslim Arabs invaded the area.

Turkic tribes began moving into Central Asia in about the 500's. By the 900's, some had settled in the area of Turkmenistan. The term *Turkmen* dates from this period. These tribes ruled until the Mongols, led by Genghis Khan, invaded the region in the early 1200's. By the 1300's, Islamic missionaries called *Sufis* had established Islam, the Muslim religion, in the region.

In the late 1300's, the Turkic conqueror Tamerlane made the area part of his vast empire. Between the 1400's and 1600's, the Safavids, a Turkish tribe, controlled the southern part of what is now Turkmenistan. Uzbek tribes spread through the region in the 1400's and briefly set up an empire in the 1500's. In the 1800's, an alliance of Turkic tribes called the Tekke Confederation gained control of the area.

Russia began a conquest of the region in the mid-1870's. By 1885, all Turkmen lands were under Russian control. Communists gained control of Russia in 1917. In 1922, the Soviet Union was formed under Russia's leadership. In 1924, after much resistance from local tribes, Turkmenistan became a republic of the Soviet Union called the Turkmen Soviet Socialist Republic.

The Soviets made many changes in Turkmenistan. They built roads, schools, housing, hospitals, and communications systems. The Soviets *collectivized* agriculture—that is, they ended private farming and transferred control of farms and livestock to the government. They also tried to discourage religious worship and suppress much of traditional Turkmen culture.

In the 1980's, the Soviet government instituted reforms that gave people more freedom. Opposition groups began criticizing oppressive government policies and poor economic conditions in the late 1980's. In 1990, Turkmenistan declared that its laws overruled those of the Soviet Union. In October 1991, the republic declared its independence. In December, following the collapse of the Soviet Union, Turkmenistan joined a loose association of former Soviet republics called the Commonwealth of Independent States. In June 1992, Saparmurad A. Niyazov, the president of the former Turkmen Soviet Socialist Republic, was elected president.

Edward J. Lazzerini

© Havlicek, ZEFA

Kiev, Ukraine's capital and largest city, lies along the Dnepr River, *foreground,* in north-central Ukraine. The city has many attractive parks and high-rise apartment and office buildings, and is a major transportation and manufacturing center.

Ukraine

Ukraine, *yoo KRAYN,* is the second largest country in area in Europe. Only Russia, its neighbor to the east, is bigger. Until 1991, both Ukraine and Russia were part of an even larger country—the Soviet Union. Ukraine lies in southeastern Europe and borders the Black Sea. Kiev is Ukraine's capital and largest city.

Ukraine has about 53 million people. About three-fourths of the people are ethnic Ukrainians, a Slavic nationality group that has its own customs and language. Russians are the second largest group and make up about a fifth of Ukraine's population.

Ukraine is famous for its vast plains called *steppes.* The plains are covered with fertile black soil, which has made Ukraine one of the world's leading farming regions. Ukraine is also rich in minerals and has large deposits of coal, manganese, and natural gas.

Ukraine is a major producer of iron and steel, machines, ships, chemical fertilizers, grain, sugar beets, dairy products, meat, and wine. In the early 1990's, Ukraine began changing its economy from one owned and controlled by the government to an economy based on free enterprise, in which individual owners and managers run their own businesses.

During the A.D. 800's, Kiev became the center of a Slavic state called Kievan Rus. In the 1300's, most of Ukraine came under Polish and Lithuanian control. Ukrainian soldiers called Cossacks freed Ukraine from Polish rule in 1648. In the late 1700's, nearly all of Ukraine came under Russian control.

A revolt by Russian Bolsheviks in 1917 led to the es-

Jaroslaw Bilocerkowycz, the contributor of this article, is Associate Professor of Political Science at the University of Dayton.

Facts in brief

Capital: Kiev.
Official language: Ukrainian.
Official name: Ukrayina (Ukraine).
Area: 233,090 sq. mi. (603,700 km²). *Greatest distances*—north-south, 550 mi. (885 km); east-west, 830 mi. (1,335 km). *Coastline*—1,800 mi. (2,900 km).
Elevation: *Highest*—Mount Goverla, 6,762 ft. (2,061 m) above sea level. *Lowest*—sea level along the coast of the Black Sea.
Population: *Estimated 1993 population*—53,125,000; density, 228 persons per sq. mi. (88 per km²); distribution, 67 per cent urban, 33 per cent rural. *1989 census*—51,706,742. *Estimated 1998 population*—54,891,000.
Chief products: *Agriculture*—barley, beef and dairy cattle, corn, hogs, potatoes, sugar beets, sunflowers, tobacco, wheat. *Manufacturing*—chemical fertilizers, clothing, iron and steel, machinery, military equipment, processed foods, shoes, refrigerators, television sets, transportation equipment, washing machines. *Mining*—coal, iron ore, manganese, natural gas, salt.
National anthem: "Shche ne vmerla Ukraina" ("Ukraine has not yet perished").
Money: *Basic unit*—hryvnia.

tablishment of a Communist government in Russia. The next year, Ukraine became an independent country but soon came under the rule of Communist Russia. It later became part of the Soviet Union and was called the Ukrainian Soviet Socialist Republic. In 1932 and 1933, millions of Ukrainians died of famine. For many decades, a Soviet policy called *Russification* forced Ukrainians to use the Russian language and favored the Russian culture over the Ukrainian one. Ukrainians began protesting these restrictions in the 1960's.

In 1991, following an upheaval in the Soviet government, Ukraine declared its political independence. Late that year, it became recognized as an independent country after the breakup of the Soviet Union. It also joined the Commonwealth of Independent States, a loose association of former Soviet republics.

Government

National government. Ukraine has a democratic political system. The government features an executive branch headed by a president with strong powers and a legislative branch consisting of a national parliament.

The president is commander in chief of the military and can issue orders called *edicts* without the approval of parliament in some matters. The people of Ukraine elect the president to a five-year term. Ukrainians 18 years old or older may vote.

The president is assisted by a Cabinet, which the president appoints. A prime minister heads the Cabinet. Other ministers have responsibility for such areas as foreign affairs and the economy. A council called the State Duma advises the president regarding science and technology, law, humanitarian matters, and the economy.

Ukraine's parliament, called the Supreme Council, is the nation's lawmaking body. It has 450 members, who are elected by the voters to five-year terms.

Local government. Ukraine—excluding the Crimea—is divided into 24 regions called *oblasts.* The Crimea, a peninsula in southern Ukraine that separates the Black Sea and the Sea of Azov, has special status as an *autonomous* (self-governing) republic. The Crimea has greater control over its internal affairs than do the oblasts.

Politics. The most important political organization in Ukraine is a broad movement known as Rukh. It was established in 1989 and includes various political parties, groups, and individual citizens. It has strongly supported democracy and national independence for Ukraine. In 1990, Rukh had more than 633,000 members. By 1992, however, divisions appeared within Rukh over its structure and approach to democratic reforms.

Ukraine has about 10 registered political parties. They include the Green Party, which promotes environmental issues, and the Ukrainian Republican Party, which favors free enterprise and anti-Communist policies. The Democratic Party of Ukraine supports democratic political development. The Christian Democratic Party promotes religious issues, and the Peasant-Democratic Party represents agricultural concerns. The Socialist Party consists of former members of the Communist Party and opposes many changes.

Courts. In 1992, Ukraine began creating a legal system based on the rule of law—that is, a set of rules that apply equally to everyone. Under Soviet rule, political considerations affected how the laws were enforced. People who criticized the Communist Party or Soviet government had limited legal rights.

Armed forces. Ukraine began establishing its own army, navy, and air force in 1992. It planned to have about 200,000 troops in its armed forces.

People

Population. Ukraine has about 53 million people. The Ukrainian ethnic group makes up 73 per cent of the population. The second largest ethnic group is the Russians, who make up 21 per cent of the population. Other groups include Jews, Belarusians, Moldovans, Bulgarians, and Poles. Rukh and Ukrainian government leaders have encouraged cooperation among ethnic groups. Independent Ukraine has tried to accommodate the cultural concerns of its ethnic minorities.

Ancestry. Most Ukrainians are of East Slavic ancestry. In the A.D. 800's, the East Slavs included the ancestors of the Ukrainians, Belarusians, and Russians. The three groups became separate states in the centuries that followed. Ukrainians are proud of having a nationality separate from the Russians and dislike being mislabeled as "Russians."

Language. Ukrainian became the official language of Ukraine in 1990. From the 1930's to the 1980's, the Soviet policy of Russification forced Ukrainians to use the Rus-

Symbols of Ukraine. The Ukrainian flag was adopted in 1992. The flag's blue stripe symbolizes the sky, and its yellow stripe represents the wheat fields of Ukraine. The coat of arms features a design that dates from the late 900's.

WORLD BOOK map

Ukraine is a large country in southeastern Europe. It borders seven other countries and the Black Sea.

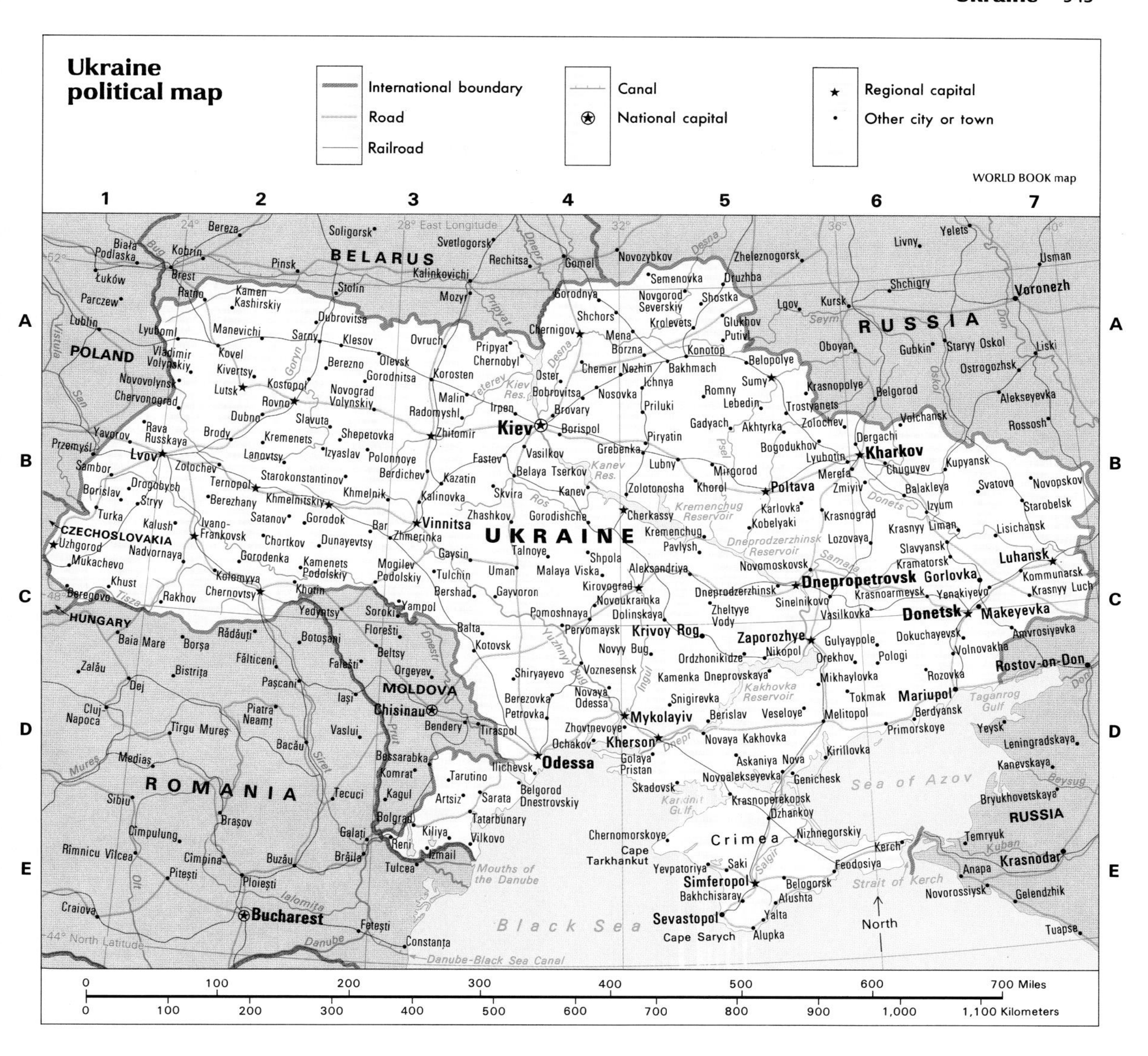

Ukraine map index

Regions*

Region	Key	
Cherkassy	B	4
Chernigov	A	4
Chernovtsy	C	2
Crimea (special status)	E	5
Dnepropetrovsk	C	5
Donetsk	C	7
Ivano-Frankovsk	C	2
Kharkov	B	6
Kherson	D	5
Khmelnitskiy	B	2
Kiev	B	4
Kirovograd	C	4
Luhansk	C	7
Lvov	B	1
Mykolayiv	D	4
Odessa	D	4
Poltava	B	5
Rovno	B	2
Sumy	A	5
Ternopol	B	2
Vinnitsa	B	3
Volyn	A	2
Zakarpatye	C	1
Zaporozhye	C	5
Zhitomir	B	3

Cities and towns

City	Population	Key	
Aleksandriya	104,000	C	5
Alupka		E	5
Alushta		E	5
Amvrosiyevka		C	7
Askaniya Nova		D	5
Bakhchisaray		E	5
Bakhmach		A	5
Balakleya		B	6
Belaya Tserkov		B	4
Belogorsk		E	5
Berdyansk	134,000	D	6
Berislav		D	5
Bobrovitsa		B	4
Bogodukhov		B	6
Borispol		B	4
Brovary		B	4
Cherkassy	297,000	B	4
Chernigov	301,000	A	4
Chernobyl	44,000	A	4
Chernomorskoye		E	5
Chernovtsy	257,000	C	2
Chuguyev		B	6
Dergachi		B	6
Dneprodzerzhinsk	284,000	C	5
Dnepropetrovsk	1,187,000	C	5
Dokuchayevsk		C	6
Dolinskaya		C	5
Donetsk	1,117,000	C	7
Dubrovitsa		A	2
Dzhankoy		E	5
Fastov		B	4
Feodosiya		E	6
Genichesk		D	5
Golaya Pristan		D	5
Gorlovka	338,000	C	7
Grebenka		B	4
Gulyaypole		C	6
Irpen		B	4
Ivano-Frankovsk	220,000	C	2
Izyum		B	6
Karlovka		B	5
Kerch	176,000	E	6
Kharkov	1,618,000	B	6
Kherson	361,000	D	5
Khmelnitskiy	241,000	B	2
Kiev	2,616,000	B	4
Kirovograd	274,000	C	4
Kommunarsk	126,000	C	7
Korosten		A	3
Kostopol		A	2
Kovel		A	2
Kramatorsk	199,000	C	6
Krasnoarmeysk		C	6
Krasnograd		B	6
Krasnoperekopsk		E	5
Krasnyy Luch	114,000	C	7
Kremenchug	238,000	C	5
Kremenets		B	2
Krivoy Rog	717,000	D	5
Kufyansk		B	7
Lozovaya		C	6
Lisichansk	127,000	B	7
Lubny		B	5
Luhansk	501,000	C	7
Lutsk	204,000	A	2
Lvov	798,000	B	1
Lyubotin		B	6
Makeyevka	427,000	C	7
Malin		B	3
Mariupol	520,000	D	6
Melitopol	176,000	D	6
Mikhaylovka		D	6
Mykolayiv	508,000	D	4
Nikopol	158,000	C	5
Nizhnegorskiy		E	5
Nosovka		B	4
Novoalekseyevka		D	5
Novomoskovsk	146,000	C	5
Novopskov		B	7
Novyy Bug		C	5
Ochakov		D	4
Odessa	1,106,000	D	4
Orekhov		C	6
Oster		A	4
Pologi		C	6
Poltava	317,000	B	5
Pripyat		A	4
Radomyshl		B	3
Rovno	233,000	B	2
Saki		E	5
Sevastopol	361,000	E	5
Simferopol	349,000	E	5
Sinelnikovo		C	6
Skadovsk		D	5
Slavyansk	136,000	C	6
Snigirevka		D	5
Sumy	296,000	A	5
Ternopol	212,000	B	2
Tomkak		D	6
Uzhgorod	120,000	C	1
Vasilkov		B	4
Vinnitsa	379,000	B	3
Volnovakha		C	7
Yalta	89,000	E	5
Yevpatoriya		E	5
Zaporozhye	891,000	C	5
Zhitomir	296,000	B	3
Zolochev		B	2

*Not on map, key shows general location.
Source: 1990 official estimates, except Chernobyl, which is a 1984 official estimate.

sian language in government, schools, and newspapers and television. Many Ukrainians resented this policy. But decades of Russification caused many Ukrainians to know the Russian language better than Ukrainian. In the late 1980's and early 1990's, a growing number of ethnic Ukrainians and non-Ukrainians began studying the Ukrainian language. The government allows ethnic minorities to use their own languages in schools and other local affairs.

Ukrainian has several regional dialects, which vary according to a region's history and the influence of other cultures on the region. Ukrainian dialects spoken by west Ukrainians, for example, show some Polish influence, while eastern dialects reflect more Russian traits.

Way of life

City life. About two-thirds of Ukraine's people live in cities. Ukraine's capital and largest city, Kiev, has about 2.6 million people. It is an attractive city known for its treelined boulevards. Other Ukrainian cities with more than 1 million people are Kharkov (also spelled Kharkiv), Dnepropetrovsk (also spelled Dnipropetrovsk), Odessa, and Donetsk.

High-rise apartments built during Soviet rule are common in Ukrainian cities. Many of the buildings, however, were poorly constructed, and the apartments are small and overcrowded.

Pollution is a major problem in Ukraine, especially in its cities. The quality of air and water have been damaged by factory smoke and other wastes, particularly in the heavily industrialized Donbas region of eastern Ukraine. An environmental movement led by a group called Green World has worked to protect the environment and public health in Ukraine.

Ukraine faces growing unemployment as it moves toward an economy based on free enterprise. Poor economic conditions have contributed to a growing crime rate.

Rural life. About a third of Ukraine's population lives in rural areas. Western Ukraine is heavily rural. In six of its seven regions, more than half of the people live in the countryside. Small homes are common in rural villages. Most rural Ukrainians work on farms or in the timber industry, or make small handicrafts.

The standard of living in the countryside is generally lower than that in the cities. Rural Ukrainians have strong ties to their families and farms. In recent decades, however, many young people have left the countryside to live and work in the cities.

Clothing. Ukrainians generally wear Western-style clothing. But on special occasions, they may wear traditional peasant costumes. These costumes feature white blouses and shirts decorated with colorful embroidery.

Food and drink. The Ukrainian diet includes chicken, fish, and such pork products as ham, sausage, and bacon. Ukrainians also eat large amounts of potatoes, cooked buckwheat mush called *kasha,* sour rye bread, and sweetened breads. Popular drinks include tea, coffee, cocoa, a special soured milk drink, honey liqueur, and vodka with pepper.

Traditional Ukrainian dishes include *varenyky, borsch,* and *holubtsi.* Varenyky consists of boiled dumplings filled with potatoes, sauerkraut, cheese, plums, or blueberries. The dumplings may be eaten with sour cream, fried onions, or bacon bits. Borsch is a soup made of beets, cabbage, and meat. It is served with sour rye bread and sour cream. Holubtsi are stuffed cabbage rolls filled with rice, buckwheat, and meat.

Recreation. Ukrainians enjoy many sports, including soccer, volleyball, track and field, basketball, ice hockey, skating, and swimming. Soccer is by far the most popular team sport in Ukraine. Kiev Dynamo has ranked as one of Europe's top soccer teams for decades.

Ukrainians also enjoy music, and many of them perform in choruses and folk dance groups. Chess is a popular game. Many Ukrainians vacation by camping in the Carpathian Mountains. Ukrainians also travel to the Black Sea coast for its warm weather and mineral springs and for swimming.

Religion. Ukrainians have remained a strongly religious people in spite of decades of religious restrictions under Soviet rule. About 80 per cent of Ukrainians are Orthodox Christians. Other groups include Ukrainian Catholics, Protestants, and Jews.

Most Orthodox Christians live in eastern and central Ukraine and belong to the Ukrainian Orthodox Church or the Ukrainian *Autocephalous* (independent) Orthodox Church. The Orthodox Church was a branch of the Russian Orthodox Church until the early 1990's and opposed Ukrainian independence. The Autocephalous Church, however, strongly supported independence. In 1930, Soviet dictator Joseph Stalin banned the Autocephalous Church. But in 1990, it regained legal status.

Ukraine has about 5 million Ukrainian Catholics, also

© Peter Turnley, Black Star

Central marketplaces in Ukrainian cities offer shoppers a wide variety of fruits, vegetables, and other foods. Workers in white coats, *above,* serve customers at Kiev's central market.

Natalie Sluzar

Ukrainian Easter eggs, known as *pysanky,* feature colorful, intricate designs. The woman above draws a design in wax on an egg before dipping the egg in a deep-colored dye.

© Shone, Gamma/Liaison

Worshipers crowd a Ukrainian Catholic Church, *above.* Ukrainian Catholics use Eastern Orthodox forms of worship. But they recognize the authority of the Roman Catholic pope.

known as Uniates or "Greek" Catholics. The Ukrainian Catholics practice Eastern Orthodox forms of worship but recognize the authority of the Roman Catholic pope. The church is strongest in western Ukraine.

Education. Since 1989, Ukraine has tried to broaden the use of the Ukrainian language in its schools. In the 1990-1991 school year, however, only 48 per cent of Ukraine's students were taught in Ukrainian. Some areas of eastern Ukraine, such as Odessa and the Donbas region, had no schools that used Ukrainian. In 1992, a few schools that teach in Ukrainian opened in eastern Ukraine. In a growing number of schools, Ukrainian is becoming the primary language of instruction.

Ukrainian law requires children to attend school for 11 years, from about 7 to 18 years of age. After the ninth grade, students may continue a general academic program or may enroll in technical or trade schools to complete their education. Ukraine's schools have more than 7 million students, and about 800,000 students attend technical and trade schools.

Natalie Sluzar

Ukraine has rich farmland, most of which belongs to large, government-controlled farms. But many farmers have small, private plots, where they can raise livestock like the cattle above.

Ukraine has about 150 schools of higher education, including 9 universities. About 880,000 students attend these schools. The largest and best-known universities are Kiev State University, Lvov (also spelled Lviv) State University, and Kharkov (or Kharkiv) State University.

The arts. Ukrainians are well known for their folk arts and crafts. *Pysanky*—Ukrainian Easter eggs decorated with colorful designs—are world famous. Craftworkers in the Hutsul region of the Carpathian Mountains make woodcarvings with striking inlaid designs.

Ukrainian music often features a stringed instrument called the *bandura.* In a popular Ukrainian folk dance called the *hopak,* male dancers compete against each other in performing acrobatic leaps.

The poet Taras Shevchenko, who wrote during the mid-1800's, is the country's most famous cultural and national figure. He urged Ukrainians to struggle for freedom and social equality against the Russians. His *Kobzar* (1840), a collection of poems, dealt with Ukrainian historical themes and made Ukrainian a popular language for poetry and books. Other notable Ukrainian writers include Ivan Franko and Lesia Ukrainka.

The land

Ukraine lies in southeastern Europe, north of the Black Sea and the Sea of Azov. It covers 233,090 square miles (603,700 square kilometers). Ukraine consists mainly of a flat, fertile plain. About a third of the land is suitable for growing crops. Ukraine can be divided into six main land regions: (1) the Dnepr-Pripyat Lowland, (2) the Northern Ukrainian Upland, (3) the Central Plateau, (4) the Eastern Carpathian Mountains, (5) the Coastal Plain, and (6) the Crimean Mountains.

The Dnepr-Pripyat Lowland lies in northern Ukraine. Forests once blanketed all of the lowland but now cover only about a fourth of its area. Farmers use much of the region's land as pasture for dairy cattle. The eastern lowland includes the Dnepr River basin and the city of Kiev. The Pripyat River drains the western lowland, which has many marshes and forests of pine and oak.

The Northern Ukrainian Upland consists of a low plateau in northeastern Ukraine. Farmers in the region grow wheat and sugar beets and raise livestock. Large deposits of natural gas lie south of Kharkov.

The Central Plateau extends from eastern to western Ukraine and is part of the Great European Plain. Rich, black soils called *chernozem* and sufficient rain make the region Ukraine's most productive farmland.

The Donets Basin, often called the Donbas, lies in the eastern part of the plateau. This area is Ukraine's leading industrial region and includes the cities of Donetsk, Gorlovka (also spelled Horlivka), and Luhansk, and has large deposits of coal.

The Eastern Carpathian Mountains rise in western Ukraine. Ukraine's highest peak, Mount Goverla (also spelled Hoverla), soars 6,762 feet (2,061 meters). Farming in the river valleys, raising livestock, and logging are major economic activities in the region. The mountains have deposits of oil and natural gas.

The Coastal Plain extends along the coasts of the Black Sea and the Sea of Azov and includes most of the Crimean Peninsula. Its coastline has cliffs and many shallow lagoons. The region receives less rain than other parts of Ukraine and sometimes suffers from droughts. The Dnepr River flows through the central plain. Farmers use its water to irrigate crops.

The Crimean Mountains rise in the southern part of the Crimean Peninsula. The mountains climb gradually from the north but slope steeply to the Black Sea in the south. The highest point in the Crimean Mountains, a peak called Roman-Kosh, stands 5,069 feet (1,545 meters) above sea level.

Rivers and lakes. The Dnepr River (Dnipro in Ukrainian), Ukraine's longest river, flows through Ukraine from the north to the Black Sea. It measures 1,400 miles (2,200 kilometers) long and ranks as Europe's third longest waterway. Only the Volga and Danube rivers are longer. Ships travel along most of the Dnepr's length. Ukraine's second longest river, the Dnestr (Dnister in Ukrainian), measures 875 miles (1,408 kilometers). It flows through western Ukraine from the Carpathian Mountains to the Black Sea. Other important waterways include the Yuzhnyy Bug, Desna, Pripyat, and Donets rivers. Ukraine has about 3,000 lakes.

Climate

Most of Ukraine has cold winters and warm summers, which favor growing crops. Eastern Ukraine is

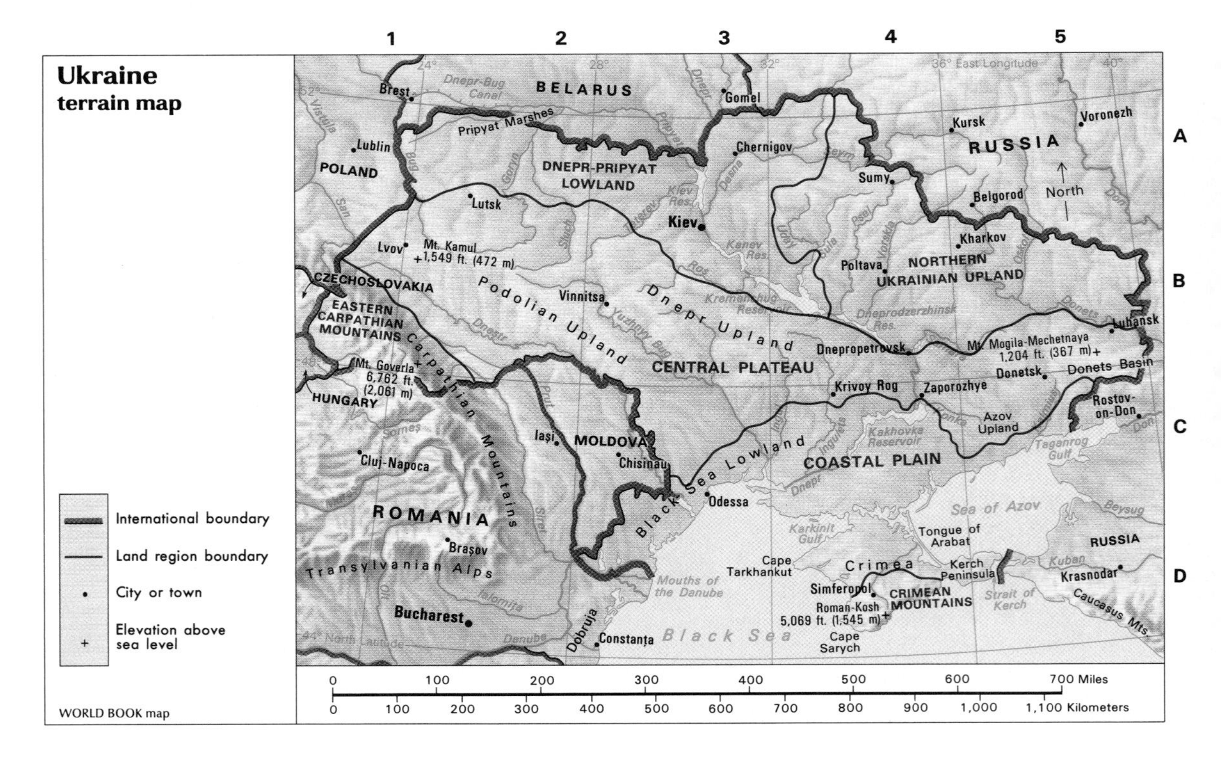

Physical features

- Azov Upland ... C 5
- Black Sea ... D 3
- Black Sea Lowland ... C 3
- Bug River ... A 1
- Cape Sarych ... D 4
- Cape Tarkhankut ... D 3
- Carpathian Mountains ... C 1
- Danube River ... D 2
- Desna River ... A 3
- Dnepr Upland ... B 3
- Dnepr River ... C 4
- Dneprodzerzhinsk Reservoir ... B 4
- Dnestr River ... B 2
- Donets Basin (Donbas) ... C 5
- Donets River ... B 5
- Goryn River ... A 2
- Ingul River ... C 3
- Ingulets River ... C 4
- Kakhovka Reservoir ... C 4
- Kalmius River ... C 5
- Kanev Reservoir ... B 3
- Karkinit Gulf ... D 4
- Kerch Peninsula ... D 4
- Kiev Reservoir ... A 3
- Konka River ... C 4
- Kremenchug Reservoir ... B 3
- Mount Goverla ... C 1
- Mount Kamul ... B 1
- Mount Mogila-Mechetnaya ... B 5
- Podolian Upland ... B 2
- Pripyat Marshes ... A 2
- Pripyat River ... A 3
- Psel River ... B 4
- Roman-Kosh (mountain) ... D 4
- Ros River ... B 3
- Samara River ... B 4
- Sea of Azov ... D 5
- Seym River ... A 4
- Sluch River ... B 2
- Strait of Kerch ... D 5
- Sula River ... B 4
- Taganrog Gulf ... C 5
- Teterev River ... B 2
- Tongue of Arabat ... D 4
- Vorskla River ... B 4
- Yuzhnyy Bug River ... B 2

ITAR-Tass from Sovfoto

Sandy beaches and warm weather make Yalta a favorite vacation spot for Ukrainians. The city lies on the southern coast of the Crimean Peninsula along the Black Sea.

slightly colder in winter and warmer in summer than western Ukraine. Temperatures in Kharkov in eastern Ukraine average about 19 °F (−7 °C) in January and 68 °F (20 °C) in July. But temperatures in Lvov in the west average about 25 °F (−4 °C) in January and 64 °F (18 °C) in July. *Precipitation* (rain, snow, and other measurable forms of moisture) ranges from about 30 inches (76 centimeters) a year in the north to about 9 inches (23 centimeters) in the south. Rainfall is highest in June and July. In the Carpathian and Crimean mountains, weather is colder and wetter at higher elevations.

Economy

During Soviet rule, the government owned most factories, farms, and businesses. By the 1980's, many farms and factories operated inefficiently and wasted resources. The economy slumped, and the government struggled to meet demands for consumer goods. In the late 1980's, the Soviet government took steps to increase private ownership of economic activities. After Ukraine gained its independence in 1991, it started to change its economy to one based on free enterprise. Ukraine planned to introduce a new currency called the *hryvnia* to replace the Soviet ruble in 1993.

Ukraine has a developed economy with strong industry and agriculture. However, the nation lacks modern technology and equipment in its factories and on its farms. About two-fifths of Ukraine's people work in industry, and about a fifth work in agriculture. Most other Ukrainians have jobs in such service industries as education and health care.

Manufacturing. Ukraine's heavy industries produce iron and steel and such machines as tractors, machine tools, and mining equipment. The machine industry accounts for a third of Ukraine's industrial output and employs about a fourth of Ukraine's workers. Ukraine also produces automobiles, trucks, buses, locomotives and railway cars, airplanes, and ships. Many of Ukraine's heavy industries are in the Donbas region of eastern Ukraine, near mines that supply raw materials. Ukraine also manufactures chemical fertilizers; such processed foods as refined sugar, meat, canned foods, and wine; and consumer goods, including television sets, washing machines, refrigerators, clothes, and shoes.

Ukraine has a strong defense industry. During Soviet rule, defense factories accounted for about a fourth of Ukraine's industrial output. But independent Ukraine plans to cut its military spending and convert many defense factories to manufacture other products.

Agriculture. Ukraine is famous for its agricultural production and is known as the *breadbasket of Europe.* Its moderate climate and rich black soils, called *chernozem,* have made the country one of the world's most productive farming regions.

Most farms in Ukraine are owned and controlled by the government. They include *state farms* and *collective farms.* State farms are managed entirely by the government, which pays wages to farmworkers. Collective farms are owned and managed in part by the workers, who receive wages as well as a share in the farm's profits. Ukraine has about 8,500 collective farms and 2,600 state farms. Collective farms have an average area of about 8,300 acres (3,360 hectares) and employ about $3\frac{1}{2}$ million Ukrainians. Each farm supports about 600 households. State farms are larger and have more mechanical farm equipment than collective farms. During Soviet rule, farmers were allowed to have small plots and sell their products for a profit. These private plots became the most productive farming areas in Ukraine.

Ukraine leads the world in sugar beet production and ranks as a leading wheat-growing country. Other important crops include barley, corn, potatoes, sunflowers, and tobacco. Ukrainian farmers also raise beef and dairy cattle and hogs. Near cities, farmers often grow fruits and vegetables to sell at markets.

Service industries employ more than a fourth of Ukraine's workers. The country's chief service industries include education, scientific research and engineering, health care, transportation, and trade.

Mining. Ukraine is a leading producer of manganese, which is used in making steel. The country also produces nickel and titanium. Huge coal deposits lie in the Donbas, the center of Ukraine's heavy industry. Ukraine also mines iron ore, natural gas, and salt.

ITAR-Tass from Sovfoto

A combine harvests wheat on a farm in the Khmelnitskiy region of Ukraine. The region lies in the Central Plateau, which has the country's most productive farmland.

ITAR-Tass from Sovfoto

A natural gas pipeline links Ukraine with gas fields in Siberia in northern Russia. Ukraine uses natural gas to generate electricity for homes and industry.

Fishing. Ukrainian fishing fleets operate mainly in the Antarctic and Indian oceans, and in the Black Sea and Sea of Azov. Ukrainians also fish in Ukraine's rivers and lakes. Ocean fleets catch mackerel and tuna. River fishing is most important on the Dnepr and lower Danube rivers. The chief commercial fish from seas and rivers include bream, carp, perch, pike, and trout.

Energy sources. Coal, natural gas, and petroleum have long been important sources of electric power in Ukraine. The country also has hydroelectric plants located mainly on the Dnepr River. During the 1980's, nuclear power plants began providing an important new source of energy. Today, these plants produce about a fourth of Ukraine's electricity. Many Ukrainians, however, oppose the use of nuclear energy because of an accident at the Chernobyl nuclear power plant in north-central Ukraine in 1986.

Ukraine imports much oil and natural gas from Russia and Tajikistan. In 1992, Ukraine signed an agreement with Iran to build a pipeline through Azerbaijan to bring Iranian oil and gas to Ukraine.

Trade. Ukraine's chief exports are wheat, sugar beets, coal, construction equipment, and manufactured goods. Ukraine imports oil, natural gas, wood products, rubber, and consumer goods. Ukraine's major trading partners include Canada, Germany, Hungary, Iran, Poland, Russia, and Tajikistan.

Transportation and communication. Ukraine has a well-developed transportation system. Most of the system is owned by the government. Ukraine's highways include about 91,000 miles (147,000 kilometers) of paved roads. About a third of Ukraine's people own automobiles or motorcycles. Buses and taxis are common in larger cities. Kiev and Kharkov have subway systems. A large railroad network connects major cities and industrial centers. Ukraine's chief airports are at Borispol, near Kiev, and at Kharkov and Odessa. Major ports include Illichevsk, Kerch, Kherson, Mariupol, Mykolayiv, Odessa, Sevastopol, and Yalta.

Ukrainian newspapers are privately owned. Leading daily papers include *Pravda Ukrainy, Rabochaya Gazeta, Radyanska Ukraina, Silski Visti,* and *Vilna Ukraina.* The country has an average of one radio for every four people. Almost all Ukrainian families own a TV set.

History

Early days. Human beings have lived in the Ukraine region for about 300,000 years. One of the earliest cultures was that of the Trypillians, who lived in southwestern Ukraine from about 4000 to 2000 B.C. The Trypillians raised crops for a living, decorated pottery, and made drills for boring holes in wood and stone.

By about 1500 B.C., nomadic herders occupied the region. They included a warlike, horse-riding people called the Cimmerians. The Scythians, a people from central Asia, conquered the Cimmerians about 700 B.C. Between 700 and 600 B.C., Greeks started colonies on the northern coast of the Black Sea. But the Scythians controlled most of the region until about 200 B.C., when they fell to a group called the Sarmatians. The region was invaded by Germanic tribes from the west in A.D. 270 and by the Huns, an Asian people, in 375.

Kievan Rus. During the A.D. 800's, a Slavic civilization called Rus grew up at Kiev and at other points along river routes between the Baltic Sea and the Black Sea. Kiev became the first of the East Slavic states and was known as Kievan Rus. Scandinavian merchant-warriors called Varangians (also known as Vikings) played a part in organizing the East Slavic tribes into Kievan Rus. Oleg, a Varangian, became its first ruler in 882. During the 900's, other states recognized Kiev's leadership.

Vladimir I (Volodymyr in Ukrainian), the ruler of the Russian city of Novgorod, conquered Kievan Rus in 980. Under his rule, the state became a political, economic, and cultural power in Europe. In 988, Vladimir became a Christian and made Christianity the state religion. Before the East Slavs became Christians, they had worshiped idols and nature spirits. In 1240, Mongol tribes known as Tatars swept across the Ukrainian plains from the east and conquered the region.

Robert Harbison, © 1992 *The Christian Science Monitor*

Textile manufacturing is an important light industry in Ukraine. Mills such as the one in Kherson, *above,* provide fabrics for making clothing and other consumer goods.

Lithuanian and Polish rule. After the fall of Kievan Rus, several *principalities* (regions ruled by princes) developed in the Ukraine region. The state of Galicia-Volhynia grew in importance in what is now western Ukraine. In the 1300's, however, Poland took control of Galicia. Lithuania seized Volhynia and later, Kiev. Under Polish and Lithuanian rule, Ukrainian peasants were bound to the land as *serfs,* farmworkers who were not free to leave the land they worked. By 1569, Poland ruled all of the region.

Many discontented peasants joined bands of independent soldiers that became known as Cossacks. They occupied the territory that lay between the Poles and the Tatars. In 1648, a Cossack named Bohdan Khmelnitsky led an uprising that freed Ukraine from Polish control. In 1654, Khmelnitsky formed an alliance with the *czar* (emperor) of Russia against Poland.

Russian rule. Ukraine was divided between Poland and Russia in 1667. Poland gained control of lands west of the Dnepr River, while Ukrainian lands east of the Dnepr had self-rule but came under Russian protection. By 1764, Russia abolished Ukrainian self-rule. In the 1790's, Russia gained control of all of Ukraine except Galicia, which Austria ruled from 1772 until 1918.

Russia favored its language and culture over those of the Ukrainians and other peoples. From 1863 to 1905, it banned publications in Ukrainian. The Austrians, however, allowed the Ukrainians greater freedom than did the Russians. As a result, Galicia became a major center of Ukrainian culture during the 1800's.

Soviet rule. Russian Bolsheviks established a Communist government in Russia after the October Revolution of 1917. In 1918, the Ukrainians formed an independent, non-Communist country called the Ukrainian People's Republic. Communist Russia, however, had superior military power and seized eastern and central Ukraine by 1920. The rest of Ukraine came under Polish, Czechoslovak, and Romanian control.

Ukraine became one of the four original republics of the Soviet Union in 1922. During the 1920's, the Soviet government encouraged Ukrainian culture and the use of the Ukrainian language to weaken opposition to the Communist system. By the 1930's, however, Soviet dictator Joseph Stalin began his policy of Russification, which imposed the Russian language and culture on the Ukrainian people.

In the late 1920's and early 1930's, the Communist government took over privately owned farms in Ukraine and combined them into larger, state-run farms. This program, called *collectivization,* brought great hardship to Ukraine's people. Several hundred thousand Ukrainian farmers resisted the seizure of their land and were sent to prison labor camps in Siberia or Soviet Central Asia. In 1932 and 1933, the Soviet government seized grain and food from people's homes, causing a major famine. Between 5 million and $7\frac{1}{2}$ million Ukrainians died of starvation.

World War II. Nazi Germany occupied Ukraine from mid-1941 to mid-1944, during World War II. About 5 million Ukrainian civilians, including 600,000 Ukrainian Jews, were killed during the war. The Ukrainian Insurgent Army, a force of about 40,000 soldiers, fought both Germany and the Soviet Union for Ukrainian independence. It continued fighting the Soviets until the early 1950's.

By the end of World War II in 1945, the Soviet Union had taken control of many parts of Ukraine that had belonged to Poland, Czechoslovakia, and Romania. That year, Soviet Ukraine became one of the original mem-

Important dates in Ukraine

A.D. 800's East Slavs established the state of Kievan Rus.
988 Vladimir I made Christianity the state religion of Ukraine.
1240 The Mongols destroyed Kiev and conquered Ukraine.
1569 Ukraine came under Polish control.
1648 A Ukrainian Cossack revolt freed Ukraine from Polish rule.
1790's Russia gained control of most of Ukraine.
1918 Ukraine became an independent country after a revolution in Russia in 1917. But Communist Russia regained control of most of Ukraine by 1920.
1922 Ukraine became one of the four original republics of the Soviet Union.
1932-1933 Millions of Ukrainians died from a famine after Soviet authorities took food from their homes.
1941-1945 The Ukrainian Insurgent Army fought for Ukrainian independence against German and Soviet forces during World War II. It continued fighting the Soviets until the early 1950's.
1960's Ukrainians began a protest movement against Soviet rule. Soviet authorities imprisoned thousands of protesters.
1991 The Ukrainian parliament declared Ukraine an independent country. The Soviet Union was dissolved.

AP/Wide World

Ukrainians in Kiev protested Soviet rule in October 1990. Ukraine declared its independence in 1991, after conservative Communists failed to overthrow the Soviet government.

bers of the United Nations. In 1954, Russia transferred control of the Crimea to Ukraine.

Protest movements. Many Ukrainians opposed Soviet Russian control and the limits on Ukrainian culture. In the 1960's, a protest movement developed to advance human rights and the rights of the Ukrainian people. Although thousands of protesters were arrested, the movement continued during the 1970's and 1980's.

The Chernobyl disaster. In 1986, an explosion and fire at the nuclear power plant in Chernobyl, near Kiev, released large amounts of radioactive material into the atmosphere. Nuclear fallout from the accident caused many health and environmental problems.

Soviet officials claimed only 31 people died from the accident and about 200 were seriously injured. But in the early 1990's, Ukrainian officials estimated that 6,000 to 8,000 people died as a result of the explosion and its aftermath. The disaster has caused high rates of cancer and other illnesses in Ukraine, Belarus, and Russia.

Independence. A Ukrainian nationalist movement began to gain strength during the late 1980's. Ukrainians demanded more control over Ukraine's government, economy, and culture. In 1990, Ukraine's parliament passed a declaration of *state sovereignty.* This declaration stated that Ukraine would follow its own laws if they came in conflict with those of the Soviet Union.

In August 1991, conservative Communists failed in an attempt to overthrow a reform-minded Soviet government. The failed coup renewed demands for self-rule among the Soviet republics, including Ukraine. Soon afterward, Ukraine's parliament declared Ukraine independent. Several other republics made similar declarations. On December 1, more than 90 per cent of Ukrainians voted in favor of independence. Leonid M. Kravchuk, a former Communist official who became a Ukrainian nationalist and a democrat, was elected president.

On Dec. 25, 1991, the Soviet Union was dissolved. Russia, Ukraine, and nine other former Soviet republics created a loose association called the Commonwealth of Independent States (C.I.S.). Many Ukrainians viewed the C.I.S. as a temporary association to deal with economic and military problems caused by the breakup of the Soviet Union. They feared that a commonwealth led by Russia would limit Ukrainian independence. Ukraine and Russia have argued over many issues. These disputes include how much of the Soviet Union's national debt each country should assume, the division of the Soviet Navy's Black Sea fleet, and which country should control the Crimea. Jaroslaw Bilocerkowycz

Related articles in *World Book* include:

Azov, Sea of
Bessarabia
Black Sea
Cimmerians
Commonwealth of Independent States
Cossacks
Crimea
Dnepr River
Dnepropetrovsk
Dnestr River
Donetsk
Galicia
Kharkov
Kiev
Lvov
Odessa
Ruthenia
Sevastopol
Shevchenko, Taras
Union of Soviet Socialist Republics
Vladimir I
Yalta

Outline

I. **Government**
A. National government
B. Local government
C. Politics
D. Courts
E. Armed forces

II. **People**
A. Population
B. Ancestry
C. Language

III. **Way of life**
A. City life
B. Rural life
C. Clothing
D. Food and drink
E. Recreation
F. Religion
G. Education
H. The arts

IV. **The land**
A. The Dnepr-Pripyat Lowland
B. The Northern Ukrainian Upland
C. The Central Plateau
D. The Eastern Carpathian Mountains
E. The Coastal Plain
F. The Crimean Mountains
G. Rivers and lakes

V. **Climate**

VI. **Economy**
A. Manufacturing
B. Agriculture
C. Service industries
D. Mining
E. Fishing
F. Energy sources
G. Trade
H. Transportation and communication

VII. **History**

Questions

Why is Ukraine called the *breadbasket of Europe*?
Who led a Cossack rebellion against Polish rule in 1648?
What is the Donbas? Why is it important to Ukraine?
Which ethnic groups in Ukraine are descended from the East Slavs?
What is the largest religious group in Ukraine?
What caused the deaths of millions of Ukrainians during the early 1930's?
What is Rukh?
Who is Ukraine's most famous cultural and national figure?
Why do many Ukrainians know the Russian language better than the Ukrainian language?
When did Ukraine gain its independence?

Additional resources

Encyclopedia of Ukraine. Ed. by Volodymyr Kubijovyč. Univ. of Toronto Pr., 1984- . Multivolume work, publication in progress.
Magocsi, Paul R. *Ukraine: A Historical Atlas.* Univ. of Toronto Pr., 1985.
Oparenko, Christina. *The Ukraine.* Chelsea Hse., 1988. For younger readers.
Subtelny, Orest. *Ukraine: A History.* Univ. of Toronto Pr., 1988.

Uzbekistan, *OOZ behk ih STAN,* is a country in central Asia. It became independent in 1991, after nearly 70 years as a republic of the Soviet Union. Uzbekistan is a member of the Commonwealth of Independent States, a loose association of former Soviet republics.

Uzbekistan extends from the foothills of the Tian Shan and Pamir mountains to the land just west of the Aral Sea. The country covers 172,742 square miles (447,400 square kilometers) and has about 20 million people. Tashkent is Uzbekistan's capital and largest city.

Government. Uzbekistan has a president, a prime minister, and a Cabinet of Ministers. The people elect the president, the most powerful government official, to a five-year term. The president appoints the prime minister and Cabinet members, as well as governors of the country's provinces. The prime minister and Cabinet carry out government operations. Members of the country's legislature are elected to five-year terms.

When Uzbekistan was a Soviet republic, its only legal political party was the Communist Party. The party was disbanded in 1991, the year Uzbekistan became independent. A new party, called the People's Democratic Party of Uzbekistan, was founded. This party, which kept much of the Communist Party's membership and policies, became the new dominant party. The first presidential elections following independence were held in December 1991. Only one other party was allowed to nominate a candidate. Former Communist Party leader Islam A. Karimov won the election.

People. Many different ethnic groups live in Uzbekistan. The largest is the Uzbeks, who make up more than 70 per cent of the population. The Uzbeks are descended from Turkic tribes, Mongols, Persians, and other peoples. They live mainly in rural areas. Uzbek, the official language, is related to Turkish. Russians, the second largest group, make up less than 10 per cent of the population. They speak Russian and live mainly in cities. Other groups include Tatars, Kazakhs, Tajiks, and Karakalpaks. Many non-Russians also speak Russian because the Soviet government encouraged people to learn the language when Uzbekistan was a Soviet republic. Most people in Uzbekistan are Muslims. Islam (the Muslim religion) is an important force in Uzbek society.

About 60 per cent of Uzbekistan's people live in rural areas. Most of them are farmers. In rural areas, most homes are made of sun-dried earthen bricks. Many of these buildings have no indoor plumbing or central heating. City dwellers live in single-story homes and multi-story apartment buildings.

Throughout Uzbekistan, people wear both traditional and Western-style clothing. Traditional dress for men includes long robes and black boots. Women sometimes wear bright cotton or silk dresses and silk scarves. People often wear traditional embroidered skullcaps, both with traditional and Western-style clothing.

Most families in Uzbekistan are large, and many include six or more children. In rural areas, many members of an extended family may live together in one household. Such a household might include parents,

Facts in brief

Capital: Tashkent.
Official language: Uzbek.
Official name: *Uzbekiston Respublikasi* (Republic of Uzbekistan).
Area: 172,742 sq. mi. (447,400 km²). *Greatest distances*—north-south, 575 mi. (925 km); east-west, 900 mi. (1,450 km).
Elevation: *Highest*—peak in the Gissar mountain range, 15,233 ft. (4,643 m). *Lowest*—Sarykamysh Lake (seasonal salt lake bed), 65 ft. (20 m) below sea level.
Population: *Estimated 1993 population*—20,453,000; *density,* 118 persons per sq. mi. (46 per km²); *distribution,* 59 per cent rural, 41 per cent urban. *1989 census*—19,906,000. *Estimated 1998 population*—21,133,000.
Chief products: *Agriculture*—cotton, eggs, grapes, livestock, milk, potatoes, rice. *Manufacturing*—agricultural machinery, chemicals, food products, paper, textiles. *Mining*—coal, copper, gold, natural gas, petroleum.
Flag: The flag has three broad horizontal bands—light blue, white, and light green (top to bottom)—separated by thin red lines. The blue band shows a white crescent and stars. See **Flag** (picture: Flags of Asia and the Pacific).
Money: *Basic unit*—ruble.

Uzbekistan

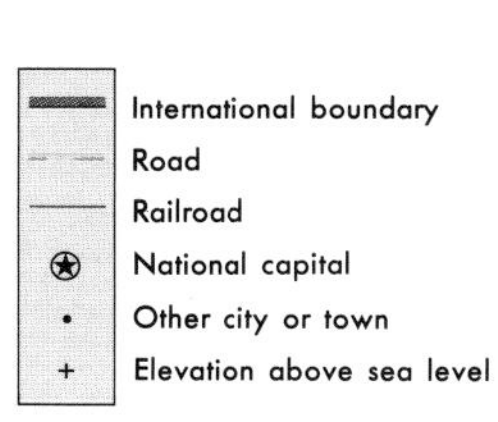

WORLD BOOK map

© Charles Lenars, The Stock Market

Farmworkers in Uzbekistan pick cotton in a large field. About 60 per cent of the country's people live in rural areas and most of them have farm jobs. Cotton is Uzbekistan's chief crop.

married children and their offspring, and other relatives. Because of marriage patterns, it is common for all the people in a village to be related to one another. Many marriages are arranged by the families of the bride and groom. People in Uzbekistan spend much time entertaining guests, and they have elaborate customs related to hospitality.

Foods commonly eaten in Uzbekistan include rice, vegetables, fruit, mutton, and a flat, round bread called *nan. Palav,* also called *pilaf,* is a well-known Uzbek dish of mutton and rice. Tea is the most popular drink.

Soccer is widely enjoyed in Uzbekistan. Traditional Uzbek recreational activities include wrestling and tightrope walking. Another favorite sport is *ulaq,* a game played on horseback in which riders try to grab a dead sheep and carry it across a goal.

Uzbeks are known for their crafts. These include carpet making, embroidery, glazed pottery, jewelry making, metalwork, and woodcarving.

Children in Uzbekistan attend elementary and general secondary schools, and many young people continue their education in trade schools, institutes, or universities. The country has numerous universities and other institutes of higher education.

Land and climate. About 80 per cent of Uzbekistan's land consists of plains and deserts. The vast Kyzylkum desert lies in central Uzbekistan. It is largely uninhabited except for mining towns. Plains south and east of the desert are used mostly for growing cotton. Livestock are raised in the plains and in irrigated desert areas. Uzbekistan's most densely populated region is the Fergana Valley, in the east. The valley receives its water from mountains of the Tian Shan range that surround it. Central Asia's two most important rivers, the Syr Darya and the Amu Darya, flow to the Aral Sea from the Tian Shan and Pamir mountains.

Summers in Uzbekistan are long, dry, and hot. Winters are cold. Summer temperatures in southern Uzbekistan may reach 113 °F (45 °C). In the north, winter temperatures may drop to −35 °F (−37 °C). Over 70 per cent of Uzbekistan's precipitation falls in the winter.

Economy. Most of Uzbekistan's economy is controlled by the government, and most businesses are state owned. But in 1990, the government began to allow some free enterprise. Before 1991, most of Uzbekistan's trade was with other Soviet republics. Since then, the country has worked to increase its number of trading partners.

Cotton is Uzbekistan's chief agricultural product. Other important products include grapes, melons, and other fruits; milk; rice; and vegetables. Wool from the *karakul,* a breed of sheep raised in Uzbekistan, is highly prized for coats. The country's mines produce coal, copper, gold, natural gas, and petroleum. Uzbekistan's important manufactured products include agricultural machinery, chemicals, food products, and textiles.

An airport in Tashkent handles international flights. Studios in that city broadcast radio and television programs in both Uzbek and Russian. The country publishes newspapers and magazines in several languages.

History. People have lived in what is now Uzbekistan for thousands of years. Alexander the Great conquered the region in the 300's B.C. From this time through the 1400's, the area was important because of its location along the Silk Road. The Silk Road was a major trade route for caravans carrying silk and other luxury goods from China to the Middle East. Turkic tribes began to arrive in the region in the 500's.

In the 600's, Arabs invaded what is now Uzbekistan and introduced Islam to the area. Mongols, led by Genghis Khan, conquered the region in the early 1200's. In the late 1300's, the Mongol conqueror Tamerlane founded the capital of his vast Asian empire in Samarkand, now Uzbekistan's second largest city.

A group of Turkic tribes known as the Uzbeks invaded what is now Uzbekistan in the 1500's. Over time, political states called *khanates* were established in the region. In the 1800's, the khanates were conquered by Russia or came under Russian influence. Communists won control of Russia in 1917. In 1924, Uzbekistan became a republic of the Soviet Union, which had been formed under Russia's leadership in 1922.

The Soviets made many changes in Uzbekistan. The Soviet government built roads, schools, and modern housing, and it expanded industry. The Soviets also *collectivized* agriculture—that is, they ended private farming and transferred control of farms to the government. The Soviets strongly emphasized cotton production, which caused serious environmental problems. For example, overplanting of cotton harmed the soil, and overuse of fertilizers polluted drinking water.

The Soviet government maintained strict control of all aspects of life in Uzbekistan until the late 1980's. In 1990, the Uzbek government declared that its laws overruled those of the Soviet Union. With the collapse of the Soviet Union in 1991, Uzbekistan became an independent country. The rapid changes in Uzbekistan brought some unrest. Changes in economic policy increased both prices and unemployment. Economic hardship, in turn, worsened the already strained relations between ethnic groups. William Fierman

Index

How to use the index

This index covers the contents of the 1991, 1992, and 1993 editions of *The World Book Year Book.*

Each index entry gives the edition year and the page number or numbers—for example, **Reich, Robert B., 93:** 118. This means that information on Reich may be found on page 118 of the 1993 *Year Book.*

When there are many references to a topic, they are grouped alphabetically by clue words under the main topic. For example, the clue words under **Riots** group the references to that topic under six subtopics.

When a topic such as **ROMANIA** appears in all capital letters, this means that there is a *Year Book* Update article entitled Romania in at least one of the three volumes covered by this index. References to the topic in other articles may also appear after the topic name.

When only the first letter of a topic such as **Romanow, Roy,** is capitalized, this means that there is no article entitled Romanow, Roy, but that information on this topic may be found in the edition and on the pages listed.

An index entry followed by *WBE* refers to a new or revised *World Book Encyclopedia* article in the supplement section, as: **RUSSIA, 93:** 507. This means that a *World Book Encyclopedia* article on Russia begins on page 507 of the 1993 *Year Book.*

The "see" and "see also" cross references are to other entries in the index—for example, **Sailing,** see **Boating.**

The indication (il.) means that the reference is to an illustration only, as in the **St. Louis** picture on page 145 of the 1993 edition.

Index

A

B

C

F

H

K

L

N

O

Q

R

U

V

W

X

Y

Z

Acknowledgments

The publishers acknowledge the following sources for illustrations. Credits read from top to bottom, left to right, on their respective pages. An asterisk (*) denotes illustrations and photographs that are the exclusive property of *The Year Book*. All maps, charts, and diagrams were prepared by *The Year Book* staff unless otherwise noted.

4 Catherine LeRoy, Sipa Press; Gangne, Agence France-Presse
5 Mark Peters, Sipa Press
8 Ira Wyman, Sygma
10 Ira Wyman, Sygma; Mark Peters, Sipa Press; Agence France-Presse; Campbell, Sygma
11 John W. McDonough, *Sports Illustrated* © Time Inc.; © Husack, *Palm Beach Post* from Sygma; Antonio Ribeiro, Gamma/Liaison
12 Agence France-Presse; Focus on Sports
13 Charles Steiner, JB Pictures
14 Gary Mook, Sygma; Gamma/Liaison
15 Chris Brown, Sipa Press
16 Derek Hudson, Sygma; Victor Grubicy, Sipa Press
18 Sergio Dorantes, Sygma; Campbell, Sygma
20 Peter Marshall, Black Star; Dominic Faulder, Sygma
21 Focus on Sports
22 © Diane Walker, *Time* Magazine; Antonio Ribeiro, Gamma/Liaison
24 Gangne, Agence France-Presse
25 Ira Wyman, Sygma
26 © Husack, *Palm Beach Post* from Sygma
27 Ralf-Finn Hestoft, SABA
28 Bruce Asato, *The Honolulu Advertiser*
29 Reuters/Bettmann
30 Thomas Hartwell, Sygma
31 AP/Wide World; Jeff Tinsley, Smithsonian Institution
32 Ira Wyman, Sigma; Tim Graham, Sygma
33 Bob Black, *Chicago Sun Times* from Sipa Press
34 Ettore Malamca, Sipa Press
35 Rama, Sipa Press
36 Reuters/Bettmann
39 Michel Porro, Agence France-Presse
40 Mark Peters, Sipa Press
45 Reuters/Bettmann
48 Li Tianyuan, Hubei Institute of Archeology, Hubei, China
49 Garo Nalbandian
51 Susan Dirk
53 Gustavo Ferrari, Sipa Press
55 Reuters/Bettmann
56 U.S. Department of Energy
62 Don Wilson*
65 Vadim Mouchkin, IAEA from Sipa Press; Novosti from Sipa Press
69 *Dance* by Henri Matisse, 1909. Oil on canvas. Museum of Modern Art, New York City. Gift of Nelson A. Rockefeller
70 Dirk Bleicker
72 "Pioneer Days and Early Settlers," a wall mural detail from *A Social History of the State of Missouri* by Thomas Hart Benton, 1936. Missouri State Capitol, Jefferson City (Missouri Department of Natural Resources)
75 Edward Schweitzer*
76 *George Washington* by Horatio Greenough, 1841. Marble. Museum of American History, Smithsonian Institution, Washington, D.C.
77 *Daughters of Revolution* by Grant Wood, 1932. Oil on Canvas. Cincinnati Art Museum, The Edwin and Virginia Erwin Memorial
78 "Striking Workers," a wall mural detail from *California Industrial Scenes* by John Langley Howard, 1934. Coit Tower, San Francisco, California (San Francisco Art Commission)
79 *Vietnam Veterans Memorial* by Maya Ying Lin, 1982. Polished black granite. Washington, D.C. (Art on File); *Tilted Arc* by Richard Serra, 1982. Steel wall. The plaza of the Jacob K. Javits Federal Building, New York City. Now removed. (Art on File)
81 © Mike Williams
84 V. Miladinovic, Sipa Press
88 Reuters/Bettmann
90 NASA
91 Lorrie Graham, Wildlight
93 General Motors Corporation
94 AP/Wide World
96 *De Telegraaf*/RBP from Gamma/Liaison
98-101 AP/Wide World
102 John McDonough, *Sports Illustrated* © Time Inc.
105 Laurie Smith, USDA/APHIS
107 Bill Eppridge, *Sports Illustrated* © Time Inc.
109 Agence France-Presse
111 AP/Wide World
114 Ron MacMillan, Gamma/Liaison
115 Sichov, Sipa Press
117 Diana Walker, Gamma/Liaison
119 Peter Charlesworth, JB Pictures
120 Peter Bregg, *Maclean's Magazine*
123 Christopher Morris, SABA
125 Canapress
127 Scott MacDonald, Canapress
130 Walter G. Klemperer, Todd A. Marquart, Carlos Suchicital and Hee K. Chae, Beckman Institute, University of Illinois
131 Paul Merideth, Sygma; Carol Brozman*
133 Mike Fiala, Agence France-Presse
134 Reuters/Bettmann
137 Agence France-Presse
141 Robert Maass, Sipa Press
143 Edward Schweitzer*
145 UPI/Bettmann
146 Reuters/Bettmann
149 Allan Tannenbaum, Sygma
150 Dan Rest, Lyric Opera of Chicago
157 Jim Borgman © 1992 *Cincinnati Enquirer*. Reprinted with special permission of King Features Syndicate
164 George Wuerthner
167 Michio Hoshino, Allstock
170 Paul Chesley; Steve McCutcheon; Calvin Larsen, Photo Researchers
171 Paul Chesley
172 Trygve Steen
173 Michael Townsend, Allstock; Johnny Johnson, Allstock
180 Rafael Perez, Agence France-Presse
182 R. Norman Matheny, *The Christian Science Monitor*
184 UPI/Bettmann; Archive Photos; UPI/Bettmann; Joyce Ravid, Sipa Press
185 UPI/Bettmann; UPI/Bettmann; Archive Photos; UPI/Bettmann
186 Springer/Bettmann; UPI/Bettmann; UPI/Bettmann; AP/Wide World
187 AP/Wide World; Bettmann; Bartholomew, Gamma/Liaison; UPI/Bettmann
188 Bettmann; AP/Wide World; UPI/Bettmann; UPI/Bettmann
189 Bettmann; AP/Wide World; Mark Sherman, Archive Photos; Camera Press from Archive Photos
190 P. F. Bentley, Black Star
193 Ira Wyman, Sygma
197 AP/Wide World
200 Klaus Reisinger, Black Star
202 Regis Bossu, Sygma
204 Karen Tam
206 Jan Sonnenmair
213 Steve Liss, SABA
214 Mark Reinstein, Photoreporters
215 Weaver, Sipa Press
219 AP/Wide World
220 Hans-Jurgen Burkhard, Bilderberg from SABA; Paul Fusco, Magnum
223 Goddard Space Flight Center
225 Goddard Institute, New York
226 H. C. Irardet, The Environmental Picture Library
228 AP/Wide World
230 Antonio Ribeiro, Gamma/Liaison
232 Albert Truuvaart, NYT Pictures
233 Betty Press
234 Reuters/Bettmann
238 Agence France-Presse
240 Reuters/Bettmann
242 Darthelemy, Sipa Press
244 Bill Schorr reprinted by permission of UFS, Inc.
246 Steven Murphy, Sports Picture Network
248 Pascal Crapet, Gamma/Liaison
250 I. K. Curtis Services, Inc.
251 Cinar-Milliyet, Sipa Press
252 DPA from Photoreporters
253 Focus on Sports
255 AP/Wide World
256 Tim Graham, Sygma
258 U.S. Coast Guard
260-263 Kate Brennan Hall*
265 Al Francekevich, The Stock Market
266 Robert Semeniuk, The Stock Market
269-270 Kate Brennan Hall*
272 Reuters/Bettmann
274 Patrick Murphy, Allsport
276 Tim Defrisco, Allsport
278 Agence France-Presse
283 Maher Attar, Sygma
285 Agence France-Presse
287 Marinelli, Prisma from Photoreporters
289 Agence France-Presse
292 Jeffrey Aaronson, Network Aspen
296 Chris Young, Black Star
298 Ralf-Finn Hestoft, SABA
307 Angular, Sipa Press
312 Ramzi Haydar, Agence France-Presse

314 Jeff Danziger, *The Christian Science Monitor*, reprinted with the permission of the Los Angeles Times Syndicate
316 Brooks Kraft, Sygma
318 Illustration copyright © 1991 by David Wiesner from *Tuesday*, Clarion Books
322 Catherine LeRoy, Sipa Press
327 Bruce Strong
329-330 AP/Wide World
332 Agence France-Presse
334 AP/Wide World
337 Gamma/Liaison
338 © SVT 1992, All Rights Reserved (The Samuel Goldwyn Company)
340 Bettmann
344 Reuters/Bettmann
347 NASA
348 AP/Wide World
350 Chris Cole, Allsport
354 © Davie Atchealak (Government of the Northwest Territories); © Mike Beedel (Canadian Consulate, Chicago)
355 © Davie Atchealak (Government of the Northwest Territories)
357 © Kiawak Ashoona (Government of the Northwest Territories)
359 Xiao-Hai and Chung-Ru Ho, Center for Remote Sensing, College of Marine Studies, University of Delaware
360 David Burnett, Contact Press
363 Reuters/Bettmann
364 Zoom/Vandystadt from Allsport; Al Teilemans, Duomo
366 Mike Powell, Allsport
367 John McDonough, *Sports Illustrated* © Time Inc.; Bill Frakes, *Sports Illustrated* © Time Inc.
368 Focus on Sports; Tony Duffy, Allsport; Duomo
369 Duomo
377 © Ed Gerken, Black Hills Institute of Geological Research, Inc.
378 Reuters/Bettmann
379 Canal Cuatro, Agence France-Presse
382 Richard McMullin, Office of the City Representative
383 Malcolm Linton, Sipa Press
385 Library of Congress
386 Grochowiak, Sygma
388 AP/Wide World
390 Wilkins, Agence France-Presse
391 *World Book* photo
392 © William Campbell, *Time* Magazine
396 James Kamp, Black Star
397 Ron Bell, Picture Group; Andrew Popper, Picture Group
400 J. Chiasson, Gamma/Liaison; J. Chiasson, Gamma/Liaison; E. Kashi, Gamma/Liaison
404 Chris Bjornberg, Photo Researchers
405 AP/Wide World
406 Ryan Remiorz, Canapress
410 © James Keyser, *Time* Magazine
412 Zizola/Dossier from Sipa Press
415 Shone, Gamma/Liaison
416 AP/Wide World
419 Bob Martin, Allsport
422 Greg Marinovich, Sygma
424 NASA
425 Reuters/Bettmann
428 Gropp, Sipa Press
432-433 AP/Wide World
435 Richard Mackson, *Sports Illustrated* © Time Inc.
437 Mark Sennet, Onyx
438 © NBC, Inc. All rights reserved.
440 Bob Martin, Allsport
441 AP/Wide World
443 © Martha Swope
445 Canada Wide
446 Ira Wyman, Sygma
448 Mike Hewitt, Allsport
451 © Epix from Sygma
452 Maher Attar, Sygma
454 Comstock
455 © Telegraph Colour Library from FPG
456 UPI/Bettmann; AP/Wide World; UPI/Bettmann
457 AP/Wide World
458 Eslami Radirn, Gamma/Liaison
459 Christopher Morris, Black Star
460 P. Magubane, Gamma/Liaison
461 Kim Garnick, Gamma/Liaison
462 AP/Wide World
469 Wesley Bosxe, Sipa Press
472 © John Lopinot, *Palm Beach Post* from Sygma
475 Reuters/Bettmann
477 Jim Wallace, Duke University
482 AP/Wide World

Family Milestones of 1992

In the preceding pages, *The World Book Year Book* reported the major events and trends of 1992. Use these two pages to record the developments that made the year memorable for *your* family.

Family members (names)	Ages	Family pets

Births (name)	Date	Where born	Weight	Height

Weddings (names)	Date	Where held

Religious events

Graduations

Anniversaries

In memoriam

Awards, honors, and prizes

Sports and club achievements

Vacations and trips

Most enjoyable books

Most-played recordings and tapes

Most unforgettable motion pictures

Most-watched television programs

Paste a favorite family photograph or snapshot here.

Date

Location

Occasion